McDougal Littell

MODERN WORLD HISTORY

PATTERNS OF INTERACTION

Napoleon,
Portrait, 1810

Queen Victoria,
Portrait, 1861

Bolivar,
Portrait, 1820

Aung San,
Portrait, 2001

MODERN
WORLD
HISTORY

PATTERNS OF INTERACTION

Roger B. Beck

Linda Black

Larry S. Krieger

Phillip C. Naylor

Dahia Ibo Shabaka

Ghandi,
Portrait, 1948

McDougal Littell
A DIVISION OF HOUGHTON MIFFLIN COMPANY

Senior Consultants

Roger B. Beck, Ph.D.

Roger B. Beck is a professor of African History, World History, History of the Third World, and Social Studies Methods at Eastern Illinois University. He is also a social studies student teacher supervisor at that university. Dr. Beck recently served as associate dean of the Graduate School and International Programs at Eastern Illinois University. In addition to his distinguished teaching career at high school, college, and graduate school levels, Dr. Beck is a contributing author to several books and has written numerous articles, reviews, and papers. He is also an active member of the National Council for the Social Studies, the World History Association, and the African Studies Association. Dr. Beck was a key contributor to the National Standards for World History.

Linda Black, B.A., M.Ed.

Linda Black teaches World History at Cypress Falls High School in Houston, Texas, and has had a distinguished career in education as a teacher of world history, American history, and Texas history. In 1993–1994, Mrs. Black was named an Outstanding Secondary Social Studies Teacher in the United States by the National Council for the Social Studies. In 1996, she was elected to the Board of Directors of the National Council for the Social Studies. She is an active member of that council, the Texas Council for the Social Studies, and the World History Association. She served on the College Board Test Development for Advanced Placement World History from 1995 to 2003.

Larry S. Krieger, B.A., M.A., M.A.T.

Larry S. Krieger is the social studies supervisor for grades K-12 in Montgomery Township Public Schools in New Jersey. For 26 years he has taught world history in public schools. He has also introduced many innovative in-service programs, such as "Putting the Story Back in History," and has co-authored several successful history textbooks. Mr. Krieger earned his B.A. and M.A.T. from the University of North Carolina and his M.A. from Wake Forest University.

Phillip C. Naylor, Ph.D.

Phillip C. Naylor is an associate professor of history at Marquette University and teaches European, North African, and West Asian undergraduate and graduate courses. He was the director of the Western Civilization program for nine years where he inaugurated a "transcultural approach" to the teaching of the traditional survey. He has authored *France and Algeria: A History of Decolonization and Transformation*, coauthored *The Historical Dictionary of Algeria*, and coedited *State and Society in Algeria*. He has published numerous articles, papers, and reviews, and produced CD-ROM projects. In 1996, Dr. Naylor received the Reverend John P. Raynor, S.J., Faculty Award for Teaching Excellence at Marquette University. In 1992, he received the Edward G. Roddy Teaching Award at Merrimack College.

Dahia Ibo Shabaka, B.A., M.A., Ed.S.

Dahia Ibo Shabaka is the director of Social Studies and African-Centered Education in the Detroit Public Schools system. She has an extensive educational and scholarly background in the disciplines of history, political science, economics, law, and reading, and in secondary education, curriculum development, and school administration and supervision. Ms. Shabaka has been a teacher, a curriculum coordinator, and a supervisor of social studies in the Detroit Secondary Schools. In 1991 she was named Social Studies Educator of the Year by the Michigan Council for the Social Studies. Ms. Shabaka is the recipient of a Fulbright Fellowship at the Hebrew University in Israel and has served as an executive board member of the National Social Studies Supervisors Association.

Copyright © 2007 by McDougal Littell, a division of Houghton Mifflin Company. All rights reserved.

Maps on pages A2–A47 © Rand McNally & Company. All rights reserved.

Warning: No part of this work may be reproduced or transmitted in any form or by any means, electronic or mechanical, including photocopying and recording, or by any information storage or retrieval system without the prior written permission of McDougal Littell unless such copying is expressly permitted by federal copyright law. With the exception of not-for-profit transcription in Braille, McDougal Littell is not authorized to grant permission for further uses of copyrighted selections reprinted in this text without the permission of their owners. Permission must be obtained from the individual copyright owners as identified herein. Address inquiries to Supervisor, Rights and Permissions, McDougal Littell, P.O. Box 1667, Evanston, IL 60204.

Acknowledgments begin on page R117.

ISBN-13: 978-0-618-69012-1   ISBN-10: 0-618-69012-3

Printed in the United States of America.

8 9—0868—15 14 13 12 11
4500327104

This text contains material that appeared originally in *World History: Perspectives on the Past* (D.C. Heath and Company) by Larry S. Krieger, Kenneth Neill, and Dr. Edward Reynolds.

Consultants and Reviewers

Content Consultants

The content consultants reviewed the content for historical depth and accuracy and for clarity of presentation.

Jerry Bentley
Department of History
University of Hawaii
Honolulu, Hawaii

Marc Brettler
Department of
  Near Eastern and
  Judaic Studies
Brandeis University
Waltham, Massachusetts

Steve Gosch
Department of History
University of Wisconsin
  at Eau Claire
Eau Claire, Wisconsin

Don Holsinger
Department of History
Seattle Pacific University
Seattle, Washington

Patrick Manning
World History Center
Department of History
Northeastern University
Boston, Massachusetts

Richard Saller
Department of History
University of Chicago
Chicago, Illinois

Wolfgang Schlauch
Department of History
Eastern Illinois
  University
Charleston, Illinois

Susan Schroeder
Department of History
Loyola University
  of Chicago
Chicago, Illinois

Scott Waugh
Department of History
University of California,
  Los Angeles
Los Angeles, California

Multicultural Advisory Board Consultants

The multicultural advisers reviewed the manuscript for appropriate historical content.

Pat A. Brown
Director of the Indianapolis
  Public Schools
  Office of African Centered
  Multicultural Education
Indianapolis Public Schools
Indianapolis, Indiana

Ogle B. Duff
Associate Professor of English
University of Pittsburgh
Pittsburgh, Pennsylvania

Mary Ellen Maddox
Black Education
  Commission Director
Los Angeles Unified
  School District
Los Angeles, California

Jon Reyhner
Associate Professor and
  Coordinator of the
  Bilingual Multicultural
  Education Program
Northern Arizona University
Flagstaff, Arizona

Ysidro Valenzuela
Fresno High School
Fresno, California

Teacher Review Panels

The following educators provided ongoing review during the development of prototypes,
the table of contents, and key components of the program.

Patrick Adams
Pasadena High School
Pasadena, Texas

Bruce Bekemeyer
Marquette High School
Chesterfield, Missouri

Ellen Bell
Bellaire High School
Bellaire, Texas

Margaret Campbell
Central High School
St. Louis, Missouri

Nancy Coates
Belleville East High School
Belleville, Illinois

Kim Coil
Francis Howell North
  High School
St. Charles, Missouri

Craig T. Grace
Lanier High School
West Austin, Texas

Katie Ivey
Dimmitt High School
Dimmitt, Texas

Gary Kasprovich
Granite City High School
Granite City, Illinois

Pat Knapp
Burgess High School
El Paso, Texas

Eric R. Larson
Clark High School
Plano, Texas

Linda Marrs
Naaman Forest High School
Garland, Texas

Harry McCown
Hazelwood West High School
Hazelwood, Missouri

Terry McRae
Robert E. Lee High School
Tyler, Texas

Joseph Naumann (retired)
McCluer North High School
Florissant, Missouri

Sherrie Prahl
The Woodlands High School
The Woodlands, Texas

Dorothy Schulze
Health Careers High School
San Antonio, Texas

Liz Silva
Townview Magnet Center
Dallas, Texas

Linda Stevens
Central High School
San Angelo, Texas

Leonard Sullivan
Pattonville High School
Maryland Hts., Missouri

Carole Weeden
Fort Zumwalt South
  High School
St. Peters, Missouri

Rita Wylie
Parkway West Sr. High School
Ballwin, Missouri

Reviewers (continued)

Teacher Consultants

Glenn Bird
Springville High School
Springville, Utah

Michael Cady
North High School
Phoenix, Arizona

William Canter
Guilford High School
Rockford, Illinois

Nancy Coates
Belleville East High School
Belleville, Illinois

Paul Fitzgerald
Estancia High School
Costa Mesa, California

Craig T. Grace
Lanier High School
West Austin, Texas

Tom McDonald
Phoenix Union HSD
Phoenix, Arizona

Joy McKee
Lamar High School
Arlington, Texas

Terry McRae
Robert E. Lee High School
Tyler, Texas

Myra Osman
Homewood Flossmoor
  High School
Flossmoor, Illinois

Dorothy Schulze
Health Careers High School
Dallas, Texas

Linda Stevens
Central High School
San Angelo, Texas

The following educators wrote activities for the program.

Charlotte Albaugh
Grand Prairie High School
Grand Prairie, Texas

Mark Aguirre
Scripps Ranch High School
San Diego, California

Sharon Ballard
L.D. Bell High School
Hurst, Texas

Bryon Borgelt
St. John's Jesuit High School
Toledo, Ohio

William Brown (retired)
Northeast High School
Philadelphia, Pennsylvania

Haley Brice Clark
DeBakey Health Prof. High School
Houston, Texas

John Devine
Elgin High School
Elgin, Illinois

Karen Dingeldein
Cudahy High School
Cudahy, Wisconsin

Joanne Dodd
Scarborough High School
Houston, Texas

Jan Ellersieck
Ft. Zummalt South High School
St. Peters, Missouri

Craig T. Grace
Lanier High School
West Austin, Texas

Korri Kinney
Meridian High School
Meridian, Idaho

Jerome Love
Beaumont High School
St. Louis, Missouri

Melissa Mack
St. Margaret's High School
San Juan Capistrano, California

Harry McCown
Hazelwood West High School
Hazelwood, Missouri

Terry McRae
Robert E. Lee High School
Tyler, Texas

Joseph Naumann (retired)
McCluer North High School
Florissant, Missouri

Theresa C. Noonan
West Irondequoit High School
Rochester, New York

Robert Parker
St. Margaret's High School
San Juan Capistrano, California

Janet Rogolsky
Sylvania Southview High School
Sylvania, Ohio

Dorothy Schulze
Health Careers High School
San Antonio, Texas

Evelyn Sims
Skyline Center High School
Dallas, Texas

Brenda Smith
Colorado Springs School District 11
Colorado Springs, Colorado

Linda Stevens
Central High School
San Angelo, Texas

Leonard Sullivan
Pattonville High School
Maryland Heights, Missouri

Linda Tillis
South Oak Cliff High School
Dallas, Texas

Andrew White
Morrow High School
Clayton, Georgia

Reviewers (continued)

Student Board

The following students reviewed prototype materials for the textbook.

LaShaunda Allen
Weston High School
Greenville, MS

Brandy Andreas
Rayburn High School
Pasadena, TX

Adam Bishop
Jordan High School
Sandy, UT

Jennifer Bragg
Midlothian High School
Midlothian, VA

Nicole Fevry
Midwood High School
Brooklyn, NY

Phillip Gallegos
Hilltop High School
Chula Vista, CA

Matt Gave
Stevenson Senior High School
Sterling Heights, MI

Blair Hogan
Leesville Road High School
Raleigh, NC

Ngoc Hong
Watkins Mill Senior High School
Gaithersburg, MD

Iman Jalali
Glenbrook North High School
Northbrook, IL

Vivek Makhijani
Durfee High School
Fall River, MA

Todd McDavitt
Derby High School
Derby, KS

Teniqua Mitchell
Linden-McKinley High School
Columbus, OH

Cicely Nash
Edmond Memorial High School
Edmond, OK

Brian Nebrensky
Hillsboro High School
Hillsboro, OR

Jesse Neumyer
Cumberland Valley High School
Mechanicsburg, PA

Nora Patronas
Alba High School
Bayou La Batre, LA

Lindsey Petersen
Stoughton High School
Stoughton, WI

Nicholas Price
Central Lafourche Senior
 High School
Mathews, LA

Ben Richey
Fort Vancouver High School
Vancouver, WA

Karen Ryan
Silver Creek High School
San Jose, CA

Matt Shaver
Weatherford High School
Weatherford, TX

Richie Spitler
Atlantic High School
Port Orange, FL

Jessie Stoneberg
Burnsville High School
Burnsville, MN

Kelly Swick
Ocean Township High School
Oakhurst, NJ

Jason Utzig
Kenmore East High School
Tonawanda, NY

Justin Woodly
North Cobb High School
Kennesaw, GA

Introduction

Juries in Athens
(page 9)

The Qur'an (page 15)

Constitutional
Convention, 1787
(page 26)

UNIT 1
1300–1800
Beginnings of the Modern World

Elizabeth I of England
(page 59)

Safavid shah (page 72)

Early globe (page 95)

1500–1900
Absolutism to Revolution

Louis XIV of France
(page 154)

Early telescope
(page 192)

Riots in Paris
(page 256)

1700–1914
Industrialism and the Race for Empire

Singer sewing machine
(page 286)

Marie Curie (page 331)

England as an octopus in an
American political cartoon
(page 351)

1900–1945
The World at War

Machine gun (page 414)

Mohandas K. Gandhi
(page 432)

Japanese attack on
Pearl Harbor (page 498)

UNIT
5

1945–Present

Perspectives on the Present

Winston Churchill, Franklin D. Roosevelt, and Joseph Stalin (page 531)

Nelson Mandela (page 610)

ISS satellite (page 638)

Human Transporter
(page 676)

Families of the missing in Chile
march for justice (page 695)

REFERENCE

Skillbuilder Handbook

Skillbuilder Handbook — R1

Primary Source Handbook

Primary Source Handbook — R39

Patterns of Interaction Video Series

VIDEO

Each video in the series *Patterns of Interaction* relates to a *Global Impact* feature in the text. These eight exciting videos show how cultural interactions have shaped our world and how patterns in history continue to the present day.

The video icon in the *Global Impact* feature provides you with a link to the *Patterns of Interaction* video series.

Features

Features

Science & Technology

Panama Canal Cross-section

History *in* Depth

History *in* Depth

Ethnic Groups in the Former Yugoslavia

Many ethnic and religious groups lived within Yugoslavia, which was a federation of six republics. The map shows how the ethnic groups were distributed. Some of those groups held ancient grudges against one another. The chart summarizes some of the cultural differences among the groups.

Ethnic Groups in the Former Yugoslavia, 1992

Differences Among the Ethnic Groups

Group	Language (slavic unless noted)	Religion
Albanians	Albanian (not Slavic)	mostly Muslim
Croats	dialect of Serbo-Croatian*	mostly Roman Catholic
Hungarians	Magyar (not Slavic)	many types of Christians
Macedonians	Macedonian	mostly Eastern Orthodox
Montenegrins	dialect of Serbo-Croatian*	mostly Eastern Orthodox
Muslims	dialect of Serbo-Croatian*	Muslim (converted under Ottoman rule)
Serbs	dialect of Serbo-Croatian*	mostly Eastern Orthodox
Slovenes	Slovenian	mostly Roman Catholic

* Since Yugoslavia broke apart, many residents of the former republics have started to refer to their dialects as separate languages: Croatian for Croats, Bosnian for Muslims, Serbian for Serbs and Montenegrins.

SKILLBUILDER: Interpreting Visuals
1. **Analyzing Issues** Use the chart to find out information about the various groups that lived in Bosnia and Herzegovina (as shown on the map). What were some of the differences among those groups?
2. **Contrasting** Kosovo was a province within Serbia. What group was in the majority there, and how did it differ from Serbs?

Struggles for Democracy **623**

History *in* Depth

Building the Taj Mahal

Some 20,000 workers labored for 22 years to build the famous tomb. It is made of white marble brought from 250 miles away. The minaret towers are about 130 feet high. The building itself is 186 feet square.

The design of the building is a blend of Hindu and Muslim styles. The pointed arches are of Muslim design, and the perforated marble windows and doors are typical of a style found in Hindu temples.

The inside of the building is a glittering garden of thousands of carved marble flowers inlaid with tiny precious stones. One tiny flower, one inch square, had 60 different inlays.

INTEGRATED TECHNOLOGY

INTERNET ACTIVITY Use the Internet to take a virtual trip to the Taj Mahal. Create a brochure about the building. Go to **classzone.com** for your research.

History *through* Art

Connect *to* Today

Global Impact

Global Patterns

Features (continued)

History Makers

Comparing & Contrasting

Historical and Political Maps

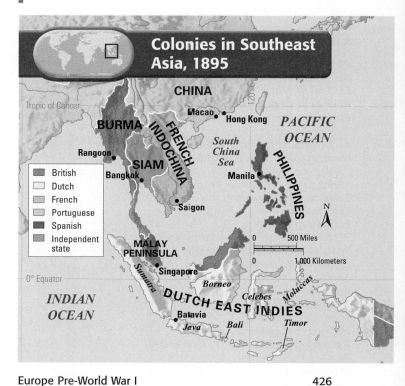

Colonies in Southeast Asia, 1895

Charts and Graphs

Charts

Graphs

Time Lines, Infographics, and Political Cartoons

Time Lines

Infographics

Political Cartoons

Primary and Secondary Sources

PRIMARY SOURCE

Soldiers! I am pleased with you. On the day of Austerlitz, you justified everything that I was expecting of [you]… In less than four hours, an army of 100,000 men, commanded by the emperors of Russia and Austria, was cut up and dispersed… 120 pieces of artillery, 20 generals, and more than 30,000 men taken prisoner—such are the results of this day which will forever be famous… And it will be enough for you to say, "I was at Austerlitz," to hear the reply: "There is a brave man!"

NAPOLEON, quoted in *Napoleon* by André Castelot

Primary and Secondary Sources (continued)

World History Themes

While historical events are unique, they often are driven by similar, repeated forces. In telling the history of our world, this book pays special attention to eight significant and recurring themes. These themes are presented to show that from America, to Africa, to Asia, people are more alike than they realize. Throughout history humans have confronted similar obstacles, have struggled to achieve similar goals, and continually have strived to better themselves and the world around them.

Power and Authority

History is often made by the people and institutions in power. As you read about the world's powerful people and governments, try to answer several key questions.

- Who holds the power?
- How did that person or group get power?
- What system of government provides order in this society?
- How does the group or person in power keep or lose power?

Religious and Ethical Systems

Throughout history, humans around the world have been guided by, as much as anything else, their religious and ethical beliefs. As you examine the world's religious and ethical systems, pay attention to several important issues.

- What beliefs are held by a majority of people in a region?
- How do these major religious beliefs differ from one another?
- How do the various religious groups interact with one another?
- How do religious groups react toward nonmembers?

Revolution

Often in history, great change has been achieved only through force. As you read about the continuous overthrow of governments, institutions, and even ideas throughout history, examine several key questions.

- What long-term ideas or institutions are being overthrown?
- What caused people to make this radical change?
- What are the results of the change?

Interaction with Environment

Since the earliest of times, humans have had to deal with their surroundings in order to survive. As you read about our continuous interaction with the environment, keep in mind several important issues.

- How do humans adjust to the climate and terrain where they live?
- How have changes in the natural world forced people to change?
- What positive and negative changes have people made to their environment?

Economics

Economics has proven to be a powerful force in human history. From early times to the present, human cultures have been concerned with how to use their scarce resources to satisfy their needs. As you read about different groups, note several key issues regarding the role of economics in world history.

• What goods and services does a society produce?
• Who controls the wealth and resources of a society?
• How does a society obtain more goods and services?

Cultural Interaction

Today, people around the world share many things, from music, to food, to ideas. Human cultures actually have interacted with each other since ancient times. As you read about how different cultures have interacted, note several significant issues.

• How have cultures interacted (trade, migration, or conquest)?
• What items have cultures passed on to each other?
• What political, economic, and religious ideas have cultures shared?
• What positive and negative effects have resulted from cultural interaction?

Empire Building

Since the beginning of time, human cultures have shared a similar desire to grow more powerful—often by dominating other groups. As you read about empire building through the ages, keep in mind several key issues.

• What motivates groups to conquer other lands and people?
• How does one society gain control of others?
• How does a dominating society control and rule its subjects?

Science and Technology

All humans share an endless desire to know more about their world and to solve whatever problems they encounter. The development of science and technology has played a key role in these quests. As you read about the role of science and technology in world history, try to answer several key questions.

• What tools and methods do people use to solve the various problems they face?
• How do people gain knowledge about their world? How do they use that knowledge?
• How do new discoveries and inventions change the way people live?

Geography Themes

Geography is the study of the earth and its features. It is also an important part of human history. Since the beginning of time, all civilizations have had to control their surroundings in order to survive. In addition, geography has played a vital role in many historical events. Like history itself, geography reflects several key themes. These themes help us to understand the different ways in which geography has helped shape the story of world history.

Location

Location tells us where in the world a certain area is. Geographers describe location in two ways: absolute location and relative location. An area's absolute location is its point of latitude and longitude. Latitude is the distance in degrees north or south of the equator. Longitude is the degree distance east or west of an imaginary vertical line that runs through Greenwich, England, called the prime meridian. An area's relative location describes where it is in terms of other areas.

In absolute terms, the middle of Singapore lies at 1°20' north latitude and 103°50' east longitude. This information allows you to pinpoint Singapore on a map. In relative terms, Singapore is an island country on the southern tip of the Malay Peninsula near where the South China Sea and the Indian Ocean meet. How might Singapore's location on the sea have helped it develop into an economic power?

Human/Environment Interaction

Throughout history, humans have changed and have been changed by their environment. Because they live on an island, the people of Singapore have built a bridge in order to travel more easily to mainland Malaysia. In addition, Singapore residents have carved an inviting harbor out of parts of its coastline in order to accommodate the island's busy ocean traffic.

Singapore is one of the most densely populated countries in the world. Many of its over four million citizens live in the capital city, Singapore. The country's population density is almost 18,000 persons per square mile. In contrast, the United States has a population density of 82 persons per square mile. What environmental challenges does this situation pose?

Region

A region is any area that has common characteristics. These characteristics may include physical factors, such as landforms or climate. They also may include cultural aspects, such as language or religion. Singapore is part of a region known as Southeast Asia. The countries of this region share such characteristics as rich, fertile soil, as well as a strong influence of Buddhism and Islam.

Because regions share similar characteristics, they often share similar concerns. In 1967, Singapore joined with the other countries of Southeast Asia to form the Association of Southeast Asian Nations. This body was created to address the region's concerns. What concerns might Singapore have that are unique?

Place

Place, in geography, indicates what an area looks like in both physical and human terms. The physical setting of an area—its landforms, soil, climate, and resources—are aspects of place. So are the different cultures which inhabit an area.

The physical characteristics of Singapore include a hot, moist climate with numerous rain forests. In human terms, Singapore's population is mostly Chinese. How does Singapore's human characteristic tie it to other countries?

Movement

In geography, movement is the transfer of people, goods, and ideas from one place to another. In many ways, history is the story of movement. Since early times, people have migrated in search of better places to live. They have traded with distant peoples to obtain new goods. And they have spread a wealth of ideas from culture to culture.

Singapore, which is a prosperous center of trade and finance, attracts numerous people in search of greater wealth and new goods. What about Singapore's geography makes it the ideal place for the trading of goods?

Time

While history is the story of people, it is also the examination of when events occurred. Keeping track of the order of historical events will help you to better retain and understand the material. To help you remember the order and dates of important events in history, this book contains numerous time lines. Below is some instruction on how to read a time line, as well as a look at some terms associated with tracking time in history.

How to Read a Time Line

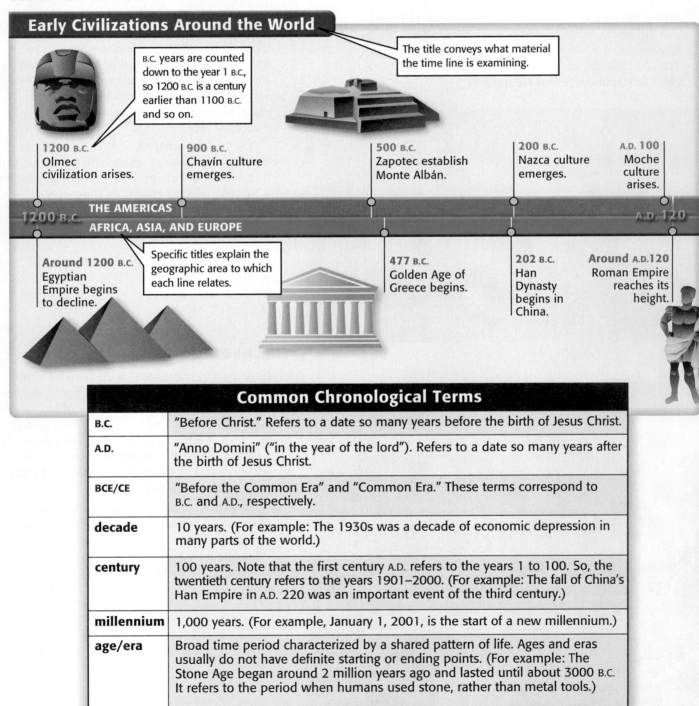

Early Civilizations Around the World

The title conveys what material the time line is examining.

B.C. years are counted down to the year 1 B.C., so 1200 B.C. is a century earlier than 1100 B.C. and so on.

1200 B.C.
Olmec civilization arises.

900 B.C.
Chavín culture emerges.

500 B.C.
Zapotec establish Monte Albán.

200 B.C.
Nazca culture emerges.

A.D. 100
Moche culture arises.

THE AMERICAS
1200 B.C.

AFRICA, ASIA, AND EUROPE

A.D. 120

Around 1200 B.C.
Egyptian Empire begins to decline.

Specific titles explain the geographic area to which each line relates.

477 B.C.
Golden Age of Greece begins.

202 B.C.
Han Dynasty begins in China.

Around A.D. 120
Roman Empire reaches its height.

Common Chronological Terms	
B.C.	"Before Christ." Refers to a date so many years before the birth of Jesus Christ.
A.D.	"Anno Domini" ("in the year of the lord"). Refers to a date so many years after the birth of Jesus Christ.
BCE/CE	"Before the Common Era" and "Common Era." These terms correspond to B.C. and A.D., respectively.
decade	10 years. (For example: The 1930s was a decade of economic depression in many parts of the world.)
century	100 years. Note that the first century A.D. refers to the years 1 to 100. So, the twentieth century refers to the years 1901–2000. (For example: The fall of China's Han Empire in A.D. 220 was an important event of the third century.)
millennium	1,000 years. (For example, January 1, 2001, is the start of a new millennium.)
age/era	Broad time period characterized by a shared pattern of life. Ages and eras usually do not have definite starting or ending points. (For example: The Stone Age began around 2 million years ago and lasted until about 3000 B.C. It refers to the period when humans used stone, rather than metal tools.)

Place

You are about to examine not only thousands of years of history, but nearly every region of the globe. To help you visualize the faraway places you read about, this book contains numerous maps. Many of these maps contain several layers of information that provide a better understanding of how and why events in history occurred. Below is a look at how to read a map in order to obtain all of the rich information it offers.

How to Read a Map

Western-Held Territories in Asia, 1910

The title explains what area and events the map covers.

The locator globe shows where in the world the map area is.

White lines denote national boundaries.

Latitude line

The legend or key explains the symbols, lines, and special colors on the map.

Legend:
- France
- Germany
- Great Britain
- The Netherlands
- United States

The compass rose indicates the direction of the map.

A scale tells the map's proportion relative to the area's actual size. It is used to measure the approximate distance between two points on the map.

0 — 1,000 Miles
0 — 2,000 Kilometers

Based on an estimation from the map, Manila is located at about 12° north latitude and 120° east longitude.

Longitude line

Equator

Common Geographic Terms	
equator	the line of latitude midway between the North and South poles
latitude	imaginary lines that circle the globe from east to west, measuring an area's distance north and south of the equator
longitude	imaginary lines that circle the globe from north to south, measuring an area's distance east or west of the prime meridian
prime meridian	the line of longitude at 0° that runs through Greenwich, England
hemisphere	half the globe. The globe can be divided into Northern and Southern hemispheres (separated by the equator) or into Eastern and Western hemispheres (separated by the prime meridian).

How Do We Know?

Do you like puzzles? If so, you are in luck. You are about to encounter the greatest puzzle there is: history. The study of history is much more than the recollection of dates and names. It is an attempt to answer a continuous and puzzling question: what really happened?

In their effort to solve this puzzle, historians and researchers use a variety of methods. From digging up artifacts, to uncovering eyewitness accounts, experts collect and analyze mountains of data in numerous ways. As a result, the history books you read more accurately depict what life was like in a culture 5,000 years ago, or what caused the outbreak of a devastating war. The following two pages examine some of the pieces used to solve the puzzle of history.

Clues from an Ancient Girl

In 1995, an anthropologist discovered the mummified and frozen remains of a teenage girl in the Andes Mountains of South America. Scientists believe that she is about 500 years old and was a member of the Inca Empire. Because much of her remains are well preserved, scientists hope she will provide them with new information about one of the Americas' most powerful ancient cultures.

An analysis of her stomach content may provide information about the Inca diet.

Some of her DNA remains intact, which will help scientists determine whether she has any living descendants.

Her clothing, believed to belong to the upper class, should shed new light on how noble Inca women dressed.

Modern Science

The ever-improving field of science has lent its hand in the search to learn more about the past. Using everything from microscopes to computers, researchers have shed new light on many historical mysteries. Here, a researcher uses computer technology to determine what the owner of a prehistoric human skull may have looked like.

Written Sources

Historians often look to written documents for insight into the past. There are various types of written sources. Documents written during the same time period as an event are known as *primary* sources. They include such things as diaries and newspapers. They also include drawings, such as the one shown here by Italian painter and inventor, Leonardo da Vinci. His rough sketch of a helicopter-type machine tells us that as early as the late 1400s, humans considered mechanical flight. Material written about an event later, such as books, are known as *secondary* sources. Some written sources began as oral tradition—legends, myths, and beliefs passed on by spoken word from generation to generation.

Digging Up History

Researchers have learned much about the past by discovering the remains of ancient societies. Spearheads like these, which date back to around 9,500 B.C., were found throughout North America. They tell us among other things that the early Americans were hunters. These spearheads were once considered to be the earliest evidence of humankind in the Americas. However, as an example of how history continues to change, scientists recently found evidence of human life in South America as early as 10,500 B.C.

RAND McNALLY
World Atlas

Contents

Complete Legend for Physical and Political Maps

Symbols

Lake

Salt Lake

Seasonal Lake

River

Waterfall

Canal

△ Mountain Peak

▲ Highest Mountain
Peak

Cities

■ Los Angeles — City over
1,000,000 population

▣ Calgary — City of 250,000 to
1,000,000 population

• Haifa — City under
250,000 population

✵ Paris — National Capital

★ Vancouver — Secondary Capital
(State, Province,
or Territory)

Type Styles Used to Name Features

CHINA — Country

ONTARIO — State, Province,
or Territory

PUERTO
RICO (U.S.) — Possession

ATLANTIC
OCEAN — Ocean or Sea

Alps — Physical Feature

Borneo — Island

Boundaries

International
Boundary

Secondary
Boundary

Land Elevation and Water Depths

Land Elevation

Meters	Feet
3,000 and over	9,840 and over
2,000 - 3,000	6,560 - 9,840
500 - 2,000	1,640 - 6,560
200 - 500	656 - 1,640
0 - 200	0 - 656

Water Depth

Less than 200	Less than 656
200 - 2,000	656 - 6,560
Over 2,000	Over 6,560

ARCTIC OCEAN

GREENLAND
(Den.)

Arctic Circle

Baffin
Bay

ICELAND
FAROE IS.
(Den.)

RUSSIA   ALASKA
Yukon (U.S.)   UN
KIN
Anchorage   IRELAND
Aleutian Islands   C A N A D A   Lor.

Hudson
Bay   FR.

Vancouver
Missouri   Newfoundland

Montréal
Ottawa

Chicago   Ma
Azores   PORTUGAL
UNITED STATES   New York   (Port.)
Washington D.C.   Casablanca
Colorado
Los Angeles   Canary   MOROC
Islands
Houston   ATLANTIC   (Sp.)
Gulf of Mexico   MAURITANIA
MEXICO   BAHAMAS   CAPE
VERDE
Tropic of Cancer
Hawaiian   CUBA   SENEGAL
Islands   Mexico City   HAITI   DOM. REP.   GAMBIA
(U.S)   BELIZE JAMAICA   PUERTO RICO (U.S.) GUINEA-BISSAU   GUINEA
GUAT. HOND. Caribbean   C
D'IV
PACIFIC   EL. SAL. NIC.   Sea   SIERRA LEONE
COSTA   Caracas   TRINIDAD AND TOBAGO   LIBERIA
RICA PANAMA VENEZUELA   GUYANA
SURINAME
COLOMBIA   FRENCH GUIANA
Galapagos Islands   ECUADOR
(Ecuador)   Amazon   OCEAN
Equator   BRAZIL
KIRIBATI   PERU
Lima
OCEAN
SAMOA   BOLIVIA
AMERICAN   ST. HELENA
SAMOA   (U.K.)
COOK   PARAGUAY
ISLANDS (N.Z.)
TONGA   Rio de Janeiro
Tropic of Capricorn   FRENCH POLYNESIA

Easter Island
(Chile)   ARGENTINA

URUGUAY
Santiago
Buenos
Aires   N

0   1000   2000 Miles

0   1000   2000   3000 Kilometers   FALKLAND IS.   South
Copyright by Rand McNally & Co.   (U.K.)   Georgia
Robinson Projection   (U.K.)

South
Orkney Is.
(U.K.)

Antarctic Circle
South
Shetland Is.
(U.K.)   W e d d e l l
S e a

ARCTIC OCEAN

75°

Franz Josef
Land

sbergen
(Nor.)

Novaya
Zemlya

R   U   S   S   I   A

60°

Bering
Sea

NORWAY

FINLAND

Yenisey

Sea of Okhotsk

SWEDEN

EST.
LAT.
LITH.

Ob'

Lena

DEN

Volga

BELARUS

Moscow

Novosibirsk

45°

GERMANY

POLAND

UKRAINE

KAZAKHSTAN

MONGOLIA

CZ

SLVK

AUS HUNG.

MOLD.

UZBEKISTAN

Beijing

NORTH
KOREA

SWITZ CRO.

ROM.

Black Sea

GEO.
ARM. AZER.

KYRG.

Caspian

30°

ITALY BOS.

BUL.

TURKMENISTAN

TAJIK.

CHINA

SOUTH
KOREA

JAPAN

Sea of Japan

Rome

ALB.

GREECE

TURKEY

SYRIA

IRAQ

IRAN

AFGHANISTAN

Tokyo

Mediterranean Sea

CYPRUS LEB.
ISRAEL

JORDAN

KUWAIT

PAKISTAN

NEPAL

Chang Jiang
(Yangtze)

Shanghai

TUNISIA

Crete

SAUDI

QATAR

Ganges

BHU.

Guangzhou

PACIFIC

Tropic of Cancer

ERIA

Cairo

LIBYA

EGYPT

ARABIA

U.A.E.

Kolkata
(Calcutta)

BNGL.

TAIWAN

30°

NIGER

CHAD

SUDAN

Nile

Red Sea

YEMEN

OMAN

Mumbai
(Bombay)

INDIA

MYANMAR

LAOS

NORTHERN
MARIANA ISLANDS
(U.S.)

WAKE ISLAND
(U.S.)

Arabian
Sea

Bay of
Bengal

THAILAND

South China

Bangkok

VIETNAM

15°

IGERIA

agos

CENTRAL
AFRICAN
REPUBLIC

Addis
Ababa

DJIBOUTI

ETHIOPIA

SRI LANKA

CAMBODIA

Sea

PHILIPPINES

GUAM (U.S.)

OCEAN

CAMEROON

SOMALIA

MALDIVES

BRUNEI

PALAU

FED. STATES OF
MICRONESIA

EQUATORIAL
GUINEA

Congo

UGANDA

KENYA

MALAYSIA

MARSHALL
ISLANDS

GABON

RWANDA

SINGAPORE

Borneo

New Guinea

Equator

0°

P. OF
ONGO

DEM. REP.
OF CONGO

BURUNDI

SEYCHELLES

INDIAN

Sumatra

Jakarta

INDONESIA

PAPUA
NEW GUINEA

SOLOMON
ISLANDS

TANZANIA

Java

EAST TIMOR

ANGOLA

ZAMBIA

COMOROS

OCEAN

Darwin

Coral Sea

VANUATU

15°

NAMIBIA

ZIMBABWE

MADAGASCAR

MAURITIUS

NEW CALEDONIA
(Fr.)

FIJI

MOZAMBIQUE

REUNION
(Fr.)

Tropic of Capricorn

BOTSWANA

MALAWI

AUSTRALIA

SWAZILAND

Perth

Darling

Sydney

30°

SOUTH
AFRICA

LESOTHO

Melbourne

Cape Town

Kerguelen
Islands
(Fr.)

OCEAN

Tasmania

NEW ZEALAND

Wellington

45°

60°

SOUTHERN OCEAN

Antarctic Circle

A   N   T   A   R   C   T   I   C   A

75°

15° 30° 45° 60° 75° 90° 105° 120° 135° 150° 165° 180°

ARCTIC OCEAN

Greenland

Baffin
Bay

Baffin
Island

Jan M

Arctic Ci

Iceland

Yukon

Mackenzie

Mt. McKinley △
20,320 Ft.
6,194m

Hudson
Bay

Canadian Shield

Faroe Is.

Bri

Lon

Aleutian Islands

NORTH

Rocky Mountains

Newfoundland

AMERICA

Vancouver

St. Lawrence

Great Plains

Azores

Iber
Peni

Los Angeles

Colorado

Mississippi

Appalachian Mts.

Washington D.C.

Cape Hatteras

ATLANTIC

Atla
Mt

Midway Is.

Baja
California

Gulf of Mexico

Canary
Islands

Tropic of Cancer

Hawaiian
Islands

Yucatan
Peninsula

Cuba

Hispaniola

Puerto Rico

Cape
Verde
Islands

Nig

Jamaica

Caribbean
Sea

Cape Verde

PACIFIC

Trinidad

OCEAN

Orinoco

Palmyra

Galapagos Islands

Amazon

Amazon

SOUTH

St. Helena

Equator

Basin

Kiribati

Andes

AMERICA

Marquesas Is.

Samoa
Islands

Mato Grosso
Plateau

Tonga
Is.

Cook
Islands

Tahiti

Rio de Janeiro

Tropic of Capricorn

Andes

Paraná

Easter Island

△ Mt. Aconcagua
22,831 Ft.
6,959m

Chatham Is.

Archipiélago
Juan Fernández

Buenos Aires

N

Patagonia

Falkland Is.

South
Georgia

0   1000   2000 Miles
0   1000   2000   3000 Kilometers

Copyright by Rand McNally & Co.
Robinson Projection

Tierra del Fuego

South
Sandwich Is.

Cape Horn

South
Orkney Is.

Antarctic Circle

South
Shetland Is.

Antarctic
Peninsula

Weddell
Sea

Ross
Sea

Marie
Byrd
Land

△ Vinson Massif
16,066 Ft.
4,897m

ARCTIC OCEAN

Spitsbergen
Franz Josef Land
Novaya Zemlya
North Cape
Scandinavian Peninsula
EUROPE
Moscow
Volga
Don
Alps
Balkan Peninsula
Sardinia
Sicily
Crete
Cyprus
Mediterranean Sea
Cairo
Black Sea
Caucasus
Mt. Elbrus 18,510 Ft. 5,642m
Caspian Sea
Aral Sea
Ural Mts.
Ob'
Yenisey
Lena
Siberia
Altai Mts.
ASIA
Pamir
Plateau of Tibet
Himalayas
Mt. Everest 29,035 Ft. 8,850m
Indus
Ganges
Zagros Mts.
Amur
Sea of Okhotsk
Bering Sea
Kamchatka Peninsula
Sakhalin
Gobi Desert
Beijing
Huang
Yangtze
Sea of Japan
Hokkaidō
Honshū
Kyūshū
East China Sea

Sahara Desert
AFRICA
Sahel
Red Sea
Nile
Arabian Peninsula
Arabian Sea
Mumbai (Bombay)
Deccan Plateau
Socotra
Lakshadweep
Sri Lanka
Bay of Bengal
Mekong
Hainan Island
South China Sea
Taiwan
Luzon
Mindanao
PACIFIC
Tropic of Cancer
Mariana Islands
Guam
Wake Island
OCEAN
Palau Islands
Caroline Islands
Marshall Islands
Equator

Congo
Congo Basin
Rift Valley
Zambezi
Kalahari Desert
Gulf of Guinea
Ethiopian Plateau
Kilimanjaro 19,340 Ft. 5,895m
Seychelles
Maldive Islands
INDIAN
Cocos Island
Sumatra
Java
Malay Peninsula
Borneo
Celebes
Timor
New Guinea
Solomon Islands
New Hebrides
Fiji Is.
Coral Sea
New Caledonia

Cape Town
Cape of Good Hope
Madagascar
Mauritius
Reunion
OCEAN
Great Sandy Desert
AUSTRALIA
Darling
Great Dividing Range
Cape Leeuwin
Sydney
North Island
Aoraki (Mt. Cook) 12,316 Ft. 3,754m
Tropic of Capricorn
Tasmania
South Island

Kerguelen Islands

SOUTHERN OCEAN
Queen Maud Land
Enderby Land
Wilkes Land
Antarctic Circle
Victoria Land
ANTARCTICA

Land Elevation

Meters	Feet
3,000	9,840
2,000	6,560
500	1,640
200	656
0	0

Water Depth

0	0
200	656
2,000	6,560

RAND McNALLY

A5

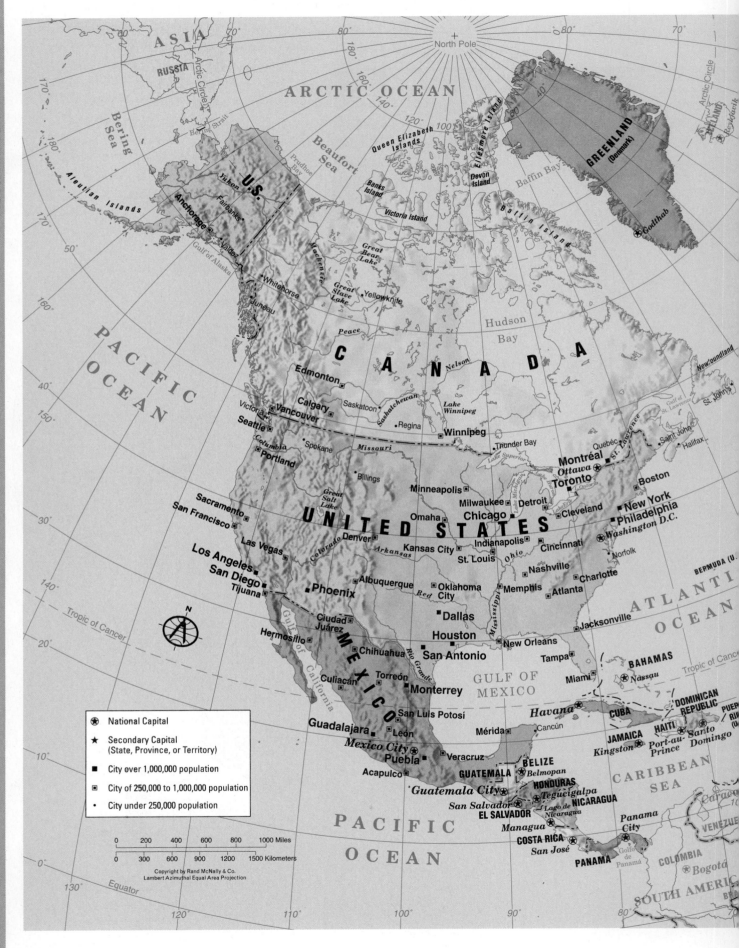

ASIA

RUSSIA

Arctic Circle

Bering Strait

Aleutian Islands

ARCTIC OCEAN

North Pole

Queen Elizabeth Islands

Ellesmere Island

Devon Island

Beaufort Sea

Banks Island

Victoria Island

Baffin Bay

Baffin Island

Arctic Circle

ICELAND

Reykjavík

GREENLAND
(Denmark)

Godthåb

U.S.

Yukon

Anchorage

Fairbanks

Valdez

Whitehorse

Juneau

Gulf of Alaska

Prudhoe Bay

Mackenzie

Great Bear Lake

Yellowknife

Great Slave Lake

Peace

Hudson Bay

Nelson

Newfoundland

St. John's

PACIFIC OCEAN

Edmonton

Calgary

C A N A D A

Saskatoon

Saskatchewan

Regina

Lake Winnipeg

Victoria

Vancouver

Seattle

Columbia

Portland

Spokane

Missouri

Winnipeg

Thunder Bay

Lake Superior

Québec

St. Lawrence

Montréal

Ottawa

Toronto

L. Ontario

Gulf of St. Lawrence

Saint John

Halifax

Boston

Sacramento

San Francisco

Great Salt Lake

Billings

Minneapolis

Milwaukee

Lake Michigan

Detroit

Chicago

Cleveland

New York

Philadelphia

UNITED STATES

Omaha

Denver

Colorado

Las Vegas

Kansas City

Arkansas

Indianapolis

Ohio

Cincinnati

Washington D.C.

St. Louis

Los Angeles

San Diego

Tijuana

Phoenix

Albuquerque

Red

Oklahoma City

Memphis

Nashville

Atlanta

Charlotte

Norfolk

BERMUDA (U.

ATLANTIC

Ciudad Juárez

Rio Grande

Dallas

Mississippi

Hermosillo

Chihuahua

San Antonio

Houston

New Orleans

Jacksonville

OCEAN

Tropic of Cancer

Gulf of California

M E X I C O

Torreón

Culiacán

Monterrey

San Luis Potosí

Tampa

Miami

GULF OF MEXICO

BAHAMAS

Nassau

Tropic of Canc

Guadalajara

León

Mexico City

Puebla

Acapulco

Mérida

Veracruz

Cancún

Havana

CUBA

BELIZE

Belmopan

GUATEMALA

HONDURAS

JAMAICA

Kingston

HAITI

Port-au-Prince

DOMINICAN REPUBLIC

Santo Domingo

PUE
RI
(U

CARIBBEAN SEA

Guatemala City

San Salvador

EL SALVADOR

Tegucigalpa

Lago de Nicaragua

NICARAGUA

Managua

Panama City

VENEZUE

PACIFIC

COSTA RICA

San José

PANAMA

Golfo de Panamá

COLOMBIA

Bogotá

Cara

OCEAN

SOUTH AMERIC

Legend

⊛ National Capital

★ Secondary Capital
(State, Province, or Territory)

■ City over 1,000,000 population

▣ City of 250,000 to 1,000,000 population

• City under 250,000 population

N

0   200   400   600   800   1000 Miles

0   300   600   900   1200   1500 Kilometers

Copyright by Rand McNally & Co.
Lambert Azimuthal Equal Area Projection

Equator

ASIA

RUSSIA

Arctic Circle

Bering Strait

Bering Sea

Aleutian Islands

180°

ARCTIC OCEAN

North Pole

Point Hope

Point Barrow

Prudhoe Bay

Beaufort Sea

Cape Bathurst

Brooks Range

U.S.

Yukon

Kuskokwim

Mt. McKinley 20,300 ft. 6,194m

Alaska Range

Anchorage

Mt. Logan 19,551 ft. 5,959m

Gulf of Alaska

Alaska Peninsula

Whitehorse

Coast Mountains

Queen Charlotte Islands

Vancouver Island

Vancouver

Queen Elizabeth Islands

Banks Island

Victoria Island

Great Bear Lake

Mackenzie

Great Slave Lake

Peace

Lake Athabasca

Edmonton

Rocky Mountains

Saskatchewan

Ellesmere Island

Devon Island

Baffin Bay

Baffin Island

Cape Adair

Cape Mercy

Foxe Basin

Péninsule d'Ungava

Hudson Bay

Churchill

Nelson

Lake Winnipeg

James Bay

Albany

Canadian Shield

Cape Farvel

GREENLAND (Denmark)

Ice Cap

ICELAND

Arctic Circle

Norwegian Sea

CANADA

Great Lakes

Lake Superior

Newfoundland

Gulf of St. Lawrence

Montréal

Ottawa

St. Lawrence

Niagara Falls

Lake Michigan

Lake Huron

Lake Erie

Lake Ontario

Chicago

Denver

Columbia

Snake

Great Salt Lake

Great Basin

Sierra Nevada

Cascade Range

Coast Ranges

Cape Blanco

Cape Mendocino

Los Angeles

Mt. Whitney 14,494 Ft. 4,418m

UNITED STATES

Colorado

Colorado Plateau

Arkansas

Great Plains

Missouri

Ozark Plateau

Red

Mississippi

Ohio

Appalachian Mts.

Coastal Plain

Cape Cod

New York

Washington D.C.

Cape Hatteras

BERMUDA (U.K.)

ATLANTIC OCEAN

PACIFIC OCEAN

Baja California

Gulf of California

Cabo San Lucas

Sierra Madre Occidental

MEXICO

Rio Grande

Houston

Sierra Madre Oriental

Mexico City

Gulf of Campeche

Yucatán Peninsula

Cape Canaveral

The Everglades

Miami

Havana

CUBA

BAHAMAS

Tropic of Cancer

DOMINICAN REPUBLIC

HAITI

PUERTO RICO (U.S.)

JAMAICA

CARIBBEAN SEA

Tropic of Cancer

GUATEMALA

BELIZE

HONDURAS

EL SALVADOR

NICARAGUA

Lago de Nicaragua

COSTA RICA

PANAMA

Golfo de Panamá

VENEZUELA

COLOMBIA

Gulf of Mexico

GULF OF MEXICO

PACIFIC OCEAN

Equator

SOUTH AMERICA

BRAZIL

Land Elevation

Meters		Feet
3,000		9,840
2,000		6,560
500		1,640
200		656
0		0

Water Depth

0		0
200		656
2,000		6,560

N

0 200 400 600 800 1000 Miles

0 300 600 900 1200 1500 Kilometers

Copyright by Rand McNally & Co.
Lambert Azimuthal Equal Area Projection

RAND McNALLY

A7

CALIFORNIA
Los Angeles
Tijuana Mexicali
Nogales
Ciudad Juárez
El Paso
ARIZONA
NEW MEXICO
110°
100°
90°
OKLAHOMA
MISSOURI
KENTUC
TENNESS
UNITED STATE
ARKANSAS
MISSISSIPPI
ALABAMA
30°
BAJA CALIFORNIA
Isla Cedros
SONORA
Hermosillo
Ciudad Obregón
CHIHUAHUA
Chihuahua
TEXAS
LOUISIANA
Houston
New Orleans
BAJA CALIFORNIA SUR
Los Mochis
DURANGO
Torreón
COAHUILA
Rio Grande
Nuevo Laredo
NUEVO LEÓN
Reynosa
Matamoros
GULF OF
MEXICO
Tropic of Cancer
La Paz
Culiacán
SINALOA
Mazatlán
Durango
ZACATECAS
MEXICO
Saltillo
Monterrey
Ciudad Victoria
TAMAULIPAS
Canal de Yucat
Zacatecas
San Luis Potosí
NAYARIT
Islas Marías
Tepic
Aguascalientes
SAN LUIS POTOSÍ
Tampico
20°
Islas Revillagigedo
Isla Roca Partida
Isla San Benedicto
Isla Socorro
Puerto Vallarta
Guadalajara
JALISCO
COLIMA
León
Irapuato
GTO.
Morelia
MICHOACÁN
Toluca
Mexico City
QRO.
Querétaro
HGO.
Pachuca
MEX.
D.F.
TLAX.
MOR.
Puebla
PUEBLA
Xalapa
Veracruz
VERACRUZ
Gulf of Campeche
Mérida
YUCATÁN
Campeche
QUINTANA ROO
Cancún
Isla Cozume
Chetumal
GUERRERO
Chilpancingo
Acapulco
Oaxaca
OAXACA
Coatzacoalcos
TABASCO
Villahermosa
CAMPECHE
Belmopan
BELIZE
Gulf of Honduras
Tuxtla Gutiérrez
CHIAPAS
Golfo de Tehuantepec
GUATEMALA
Tapachula
Guatemala City
San Salvador
EL SALVADOR
San Pedro Su
HONDURAS
Tegucigalpa
León
Managua
Lago de Nicaragua
COS
10°
PACIFIC OCEAN

⊛ National Capital

★ Secondary Capital
(State, Province, or Territory)

■ City over 1,000,000 population

▣ City of 250,000 to 1,000,000 population

• City under 250,000 population

0   100   200   300   400 Miles
0   200   400   600 Kilometers
Copyright by Rand McNally & Co.
Lambert Conformal Conic Projection

N

Isla del Mapelo
(Col.)

110°
100°
90°

VIRGINIA

NORTH CAROLINA

SOUTH CAROLINA

RGIA

FLORIDA

Lake Okeechobee

BAHAMAS

- Freeport
- *Abaco*
- Miami
- *Nassau*
- *Eleuthera*
- *Andros*
- *Cat Island*

Straits of Florida

W e s t

⊛*Havana*

Santa Clara ·

Isla de la Juventud

CUBA

⊡*Camagüey*

Holguín ·

CAYMAN ISLANDS (U.K.)

Santiago de Cuba ·

Guantánamo ·

TURKS AND CAICOS ISLANDS (U.K.)

Great Inagua

I n d i e s

Santiago ·

⊡

Santo Domingo

HAITI

⊛*Port-au-Prince*

Montego Bay ·

⊛*Kingston*

JAMAICA

DOMINICAN REPUBLIC

San Juan ⊛

PUERTO RICO (U.S.)

VIRGIN ISLANDS (U.S.)

BRITISH VIRGIN ISLANDS

ANGUILLA (U.K.)

Basseterre ⊛

SAINT KITTS AND NEVIS

MONTSERRAT (U.K.)

ANTIGUA AND BARBUDA

⊛*Saint John's*

GUADELOUPE (Fr.)

DOMINICA

Roseau ⊛

MARTINIQUE (Fr.)

Castries ⊛ **SAINT LUCIA**

SAINT VINCENT AND THE GRENADINES

Kingstown ⊛

⊛*Bridgetown* **BARBADOS**

Saint George's ⊛ **GRENADA**

Port of Spain ⊛ **TRINIDAD AND TOBAGO**

BERMUDA (U.K.)

A T L A N T I C   O C E A N

Tropic of Cancer

30°

20°

C A R I B B E A N   S E A

ARUBA (Neth.)

Curaçao

Bonaire

NETHERLANDS ANTILLES

ARAGUA

Isla de San Andrés (Col.)

10°

San José

Panama Canal

⊛*Panama City*

PANAMA

Golfo de Panamá

Isla de Coiba

⊛*Caracas*

⊛*Maracaibo*

Lago de Maracaibo

V E N E Z U E L A

Orinoco

⊛*Georgetown*

GUYANA

SURINAME

C O L O M B I A

⊛*Bogotá*

Orinoco

B R A Z I L

80°

70°

60°

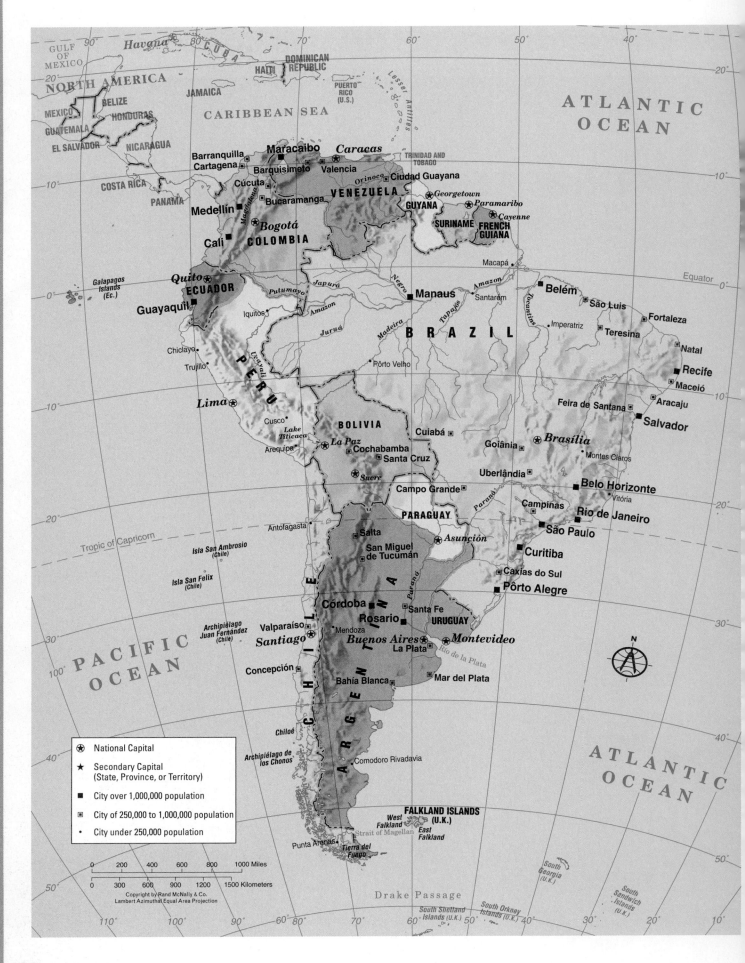

RAND M?NALLY

South America: Political

ATLANTIC OCEAN

NORTH AMERICA

GULF OF MEXICO

Havana CUBA

HAITI DOMINICAN REPUBLIC

PUERTO RICO (U.S.)

JAMAICA

CARIBBEAN SEA

MEXICO

BELIZE

GUATEMALA HONDURAS

EL SALVADOR NICARAGUA

COSTA RICA

PANAMA

Barranquilla
Cartagena

Maracaibo *Caracas*

Barquisimeto Valencia

Cúcuta *Orinoco* Ciudad Guayana

Bucaramanga **VENEZUELA**

Medellín

☆ *Bogotá*

Cali **COLOMBIA**

TRINIDAD AND TOBAGO

Georgetown *Paramaribo*

GUYANA **SURINAME** *Cayenne*

FRENCH GUIANA

Macapá

Equator

Galapagos Islands (Ec.)

Quito
ECUADOR

Guayaquil

Putumayo *Japurá* *Negro* *Amazon* Belém

Iquitos *Amazon* Manaus Santarém São Luís

Chiclayo *Juruá* *Madeira* *Tapajós* *Tocantins* Imperatriz Fortaleza

Trujillo *Ucayali* Teresina Natal

P E R U Pôrto Velho **B R A Z I L** Recife
Maceió

Lima ☆ Feira de Santana Aracaju

Cusco **BOLIVIA** Cuiabá Salvador

Lake Titicaca Goiânia ☆ *Brasília*

Arequipa *La Paz* Cochabamba Uberlândia Montes Claros

Santa Cruz Belo Horizonte

☆ *Sucre* Campo Grande Campinas Vitória

Paraná Rio de Janeiro

Antofagasta **PARAGUAY** São Paulo

Isla San Ambrosio (Chile) Salta Curitiba

Isla San Felix (Chile) San Miguel de Tucumán ☆ *Asunción* Caxias do Sul

Paraná Pôrto Alegre

Córdoba **URUGUAY**

Archipiélago Juan Fernández (Chile) Valparaíso Rosario Santa Fe

Mendoza *Buenos Aires* ☆ ☆ *Montevideo*

Santiago La Plata *Río de la Plata*

Concepción Bahía Blanca Mar del Plata

A R G E N T I N A

C H I L E

Chiloé

Archipiélago de los Chonos Comodoro Rivadavia

PACIFIC OCEAN

Tropic of Capricorn

ATLANTIC OCEAN

FALKLAND ISLANDS (U.K.)

West Falkland East Falkland

Punta Arenas Strait of Magellan

Tierra del Fuego

Drake Passage South Georgia (U.K.)

South Shetland Islands (U.K.) South Orkney Islands (U.K.) South Sandwich Islands (U.K.)

Legend:

☆ National Capital

★ Secondary Capital (State, Province, or Territory)

■ City over 1,000,000 population

▣ City of 250,000 to 1,000,000 population

• City under 250,000 population

0 200 400 600 800 1000 Miles

0 300 600 900 1200 1500 Kilometers

Copyright by Rand McNally & Co.
Lambert Azimuthal Equal Area Projection

GULF OF MEXICO
90°
80°
NORTH AMERICA
MEXICO
BELIZE
GUATEMALA
HONDURAS
Gulf of Honduras
EL SALVADOR
NICARAGUA
COSTA RICA
PANAMA
Gulf of Panama

CUBA
Greater Antilles
JAMAICA
70°
HAITI
DOMINICAN REPUBLIC
PUERTO RICO (U.S.)
Lesser Antilles
CARIBBEAN SEA

ATLANTIC OCEAN
60°
50°
40°

TRINIDAD AND TOBAGO
Cristóbal Colón Peak △ 18,948 Ft. 5,775m
Caracas ⊛
Orinoco
Llanos
VENEZUELA
GUYANA
SURINAME
FRENCH GUIANA
Cape Orange
Bogotá ⊛
COLOMBIA
20°
10°
0°

Galapagos Islands (Ec.)
ECUADOR
△ Chimborazo 20,703 Ft. 6,310m
Putumayo
Japurá
Amazon
Ilha de Marajó
Belém ■
Negro
Manaus ●
Amazon Basin
BRAZIL
Amazon
Tocantins
Equator

Juruá
Selvas
Madeira
Tapajós
São Francisco
Recife ■

Mt. Huascarán △ 22,133 Ft. 6,746m
Ucayali
PERU
Andes
Lima ⊛
Mt. Illampu △ 21,066 Ft. 6,421m
Lake Titicaca
BOLIVIA
Cordillera Oriental
Mt. Sajama △ 21,463 Ft. 6,542m
Mato Grosso Plateau
Brasília ⊛
Serra do Espinhaço

10°

PACIFIC OCEAN
Isla San Ambrosio (Chile)
Isla San Felix (Chile)
Atacama Desert
Andes
Gran Chaco
PARAGUAY
Paraná
São Paulo ■
Rio de Janeiro ■
Tropic of Capricorn

Mt. Ojos del Salado 22,615 Ft. 6,893m
CHILE
Paraná
URUGUAY
20°

Archipiélago Juan Fernández (Chile)
Santiago ⊛
△ Mt. Aconcagua 22,831 Ft. 6,959m
ARGENTINA
Buenos Aires ⊛
Pampas
Río de la Plata

N

30°

Land Elevation

Meters		Feet
3,000		9,840
2,000		6,560
500		1,640
200		656
0		0

Water Depth

0		0
200		656
2,000		6,560

Chiloé
San Matías Gulf
Península Valdés

San Jorge Gulf
Point Medanoso
Patagonia

40°

ATLANTIC OCEAN

0   200   400   600   800   1000 Miles
0   300   600   900   1200   1500 Kilometers
Copyright by Rand McNally & Co.
Lambert Azimuthal Equal Area Projection

Grand Bay
FALKLAND ISLANDS (U.K.)
West Falkland
East Falkland
Strait of Magellan
Tierra del Fuego
Cape Horn
South Georgia (U.K.)

50°

Drake Passage
South Shetland Islands (U.K.)
South Orkney Islands (U.K.)
South Sandwich Islands (U.K.)

110°   100°   90°   80°   70°   60°   50°   40°   30°   20°   10°

ATLANTIC OCEAN

NORWEGIAN SEA

Arctic Circle

Reykjavík ⊛ **ICELAND**

FAROE ISLANDS (Den.)

Trondheim •

Umeå •

NORWAY   **SWEDEN**

Bergen •

Oslo ⊛

Stockholm ⊛

Gulf of ...

Tam ...

Vänern   Vättern

Göteborg ▣

Skagerrak

DENMARK

Copenhagen ⊛

BALTIC S ...

LITHU...

Kaliningrad ▣ Rl...

Gdańsk ▣

POLAND

Aberdeen •

Glasgow ▣ ★ Edinburgh

SCOTLAND

UNITED

NORTHERN IRELAND

★ Belfast

Dublin ⊛ **IRELAND**

Irish Sea

KINGDOM

NORTH SEA

Cork •

St. George's Chann...

Liverpool ▣ Manchester ▣

WALES

Cardiff ★

Birmingham ■

ENGLAND

Thames

NETHERLANDS

Amsterdam ⊛

The Hague ⊛

Hamburg ■

Szczecin ▣

Berlin ■

GERMANY

Elbe

Oder

Warsaw ⊛

Wisła

Plymouth •

English Channel

Le Havre •

London ⊛

Strait of Dover

Brussels ⊛

BELGIUM

Rhine

Cologne ▣

Bonn •

Frankfurt ▣

Dresden ▣ Wrocław ▣

Prague ⊛

CZECH REPUBLIC

Kra...

Nantes •

FRANCE

Paris ⊛

Luxembourg ⊛

LUX.

Loire

Seine

Strasbourg ▣

Stuttgart ▣

Munich ■

Danube

Vienna ⊛

AUSTRIA

★ Bratislava

SLOVAKIA

Bay of Biscay

A Coruña •

Gijón ▣

Bilbao ▣

Bordeaux •

Toulouse ▣

Lyon ▣

Zürich ▣

Bern ⊛

Geneva ▣

SWITZERLAND

LIECH.

Rhône

Turin ■

Milan ■

Venice ▣

Po

Ljubljana ⊛

SLOVENIA

Zagreb ⊛

Belgra...

HUNGARY

Budapest ⊛

Porto ▣

Valladolid ▣

Ebro

Zaragoza ▣

ANDORRA

Marseille ▣

Nice ▣

Genoa ▣

MONACO

Florence ▣

SAN MARINO

CROATIA

BOSNIA AND HERZEGOVINA

Sarajevo ⊛

PORTUGAL

Lisbon ⊛

Tagus

Madrid ⊛

SPAIN

Barcelona ■

Valencia ▣

Córdoba ▣

Palma •

Corsica (Fr.)

ADRIATIC SEA

ITALY

Rome ⊛

VATICAN CITY

Sardinia (It.)

SERBIA **MONTENE...**

Skop...

ALBANIA

Tiranë ⊛

Ma...

D...

Seville ▣

Strait of Gibraltar

Málaga ▣

GIBRALTAR (U.K.)

Rabat ⊛

Cagliari •

Naples ■

Bari ▣

Palermo ▣

TYRRHENIAN SEA

Sicily

Catania •

IONIAN SEA

Algiers ⊛

AFRICA

MOROCCO

ALGERIA

Tunis ⊛

TUNISIA

Valletta ⊛ **MALTA**

MEDITERRA...

Legend:

⊛ National Capital

★ Secondary Capital (State, Province, or Territory)

■ City over 1,000,000 population

▣ City of 250,000 to 1,000,000 population

• City under 250,000 population

Scale:
0   100   200   300   400 Miles
0   200   400   600 Kilometers

Copyright by Rand McNally & Co.
Lambert Conformal Conic Projection

Murmansk

WHITE SEA

Arkhangel'sk

Northern Dvina

Syktyvkar

Oulu

INLAND

RUSSIA

Ob'

Pechora

Irtysh

Petrozavodsk
Lake
Onega

Perm'

Kirov

Lake
Ladoga

Helsinki

St. Petersburg

Izhevsk

Ufa

Cherepovets
Rybinsk
Res.

Nizhniy
Novgorod

Kazan'

ASIA

Tallinn

ESTONIA

Lake
Peipus

Yaroslavl'

Tver'

Riga

LATVIA

Moscow

Oka

Samara

Syr Darya

Vilnius

Vitsyebsk

Ryazan'

Penza

Volga

Tula

Bryansk

Lipetsk

Saratov

KAZAKHSTAN

Ural

Minsk

Don

Aral Sea

BELARUS

Homyel'

Voronezh

Chernobyl

Volgograd

Astrakhan'

UZBEKISTAN

Kiev

Kharkiv

Luhans'k

L'viv

Vinnytsya

UKRAINE

Dnieper

Dnipro-
petrovs'k

Volga

Amu Darya

Dniester

Donets'k

Rostov

CASPIAN

TURKMENISTAN

Kryvyy Rih

Zaporizhzhya

Mariupol'

MOLDOVA

Iaşi

Chişinău

Sea of Azov

Krasnodar

Stavropol'

Ashgabat

Cluj-Napoca

Odesa

Simferopol'

Groznyy

ROMANIA

Sevastopol'

BLACK SEA

GEORGIA

Tbilisi

Baku

SEA

Galaţi

Craiova

Bucharest

ARMENIA

AZERBAIJA

Danube

BULGARIA

Varna

AZER.

Yerevan

Sofia

Plovdiv

Tehran

Istanbul

IRAN

Thessaloníki

Ankara

TURKEY

GREECE

AEGEAN
SEA

IRAQ

Athens

Baghdad

Crete

NORTH
CYPRUS

Nicosia

SYRIA

Euphrates

Tigris

CYPRUS

Beirut LEBANON

N

40°

30°

50°

ICELAND

Surtsey

Horn

Fontur

FAROE ISLANDS
(Den.)

NORWEGIAN
SEA

Arctic Circle

Lofoten Islands

Kebnekaise
6,926 Ft.
2,111m

Torne

Lule

Umeälven

Scandinavian
Peninsula

NORWAY

Galdhøpiggen △
8,100 Ft.
2,469m

Glomma

Klarälven

Dalälven

SWEDEN

Gulf of Both

Vänern

Stockholm ⊛

ATLANTIC
OCEAN

Hebrides

Orkney
Islands

Grampian
Mts.

Cheviot
Hills

UNITED

KINGDOM

NORTH
SEA

Skagerrak

DENMARK

Vättern

Öland

Bornholm
(Den.)

Vänern

Baltic Sea

RUSS

IRELAND

Irish
Sea

Great
Britain

St. George's Channel

Thames

London ⊛

NETHERLANDS

Elbe

Berlin ⊛

Oder

Northern Eu

POLAND

Wisła

English Channel

Strait of Dover

BELGIUM

Rhine

GERMANY

Land Elevation

Meters		Feet
3,000		9,840
2,000		6,560
500		1,640
200		656
0		0

Water Depth

0		0
200		656
2,000		6,560

N

0	100	200	300	400 Miles

0	200	400	600 Kilometers

Copyright by Rand McNally & Co.
Lambert Conformal Conic Projection

LUX.

Paris ⊛

Paris
Basin

Loire

Seine

CZECH
REPUBLIC

Bohemian
Forest

SLOVAKIA

Danube

Bay of Biscay

FRANCE

Saône

Jura

SWITZERLAND

LIECH.

AUSTRIA

HUNGARY

Great Hungari
Plain

Cantabrian Mts.

Douro

Duero

Iberian Mts.

Ebro

Pyrenees

Dordogne

Massif
Central

Rhône

Mt. Blanc
15,771 Ft.
4,808m

A l p s

SLOVENIA

Drava

Po

CROATIA

Apennines

BOSNIA AND
HERZEGOVINA

Dinaric Alps

Lisbon ⊛

PORTUGAL

Iberian

Peninsula

Tagus

SPAIN

Sierra Morena

Strait of Gibraltar

ANDORRA

MONACO

Corsica
(Fr.)

SAN
MARINO

ADRIATIC SEA

Balka

SERBIA A
MONTENE

Balearic Islands

Minorca

Ibiza

Majorca

Sardinia
(It.)

Rome ⊛

ITALY

ALBANIA

MAC
DON

Pindus

GIBRALTAR
(U.K.)

△Vesuvius
4,190 Ft.
1,277m

TYRRHENIAN
SEA

IONIAN
SEA

Algiers

MEDITERRANE

Mt. Etna
10,902 Ft.
3,323m △

Sicily

MOROCCO

AFRICA

ALGERIA

TUNISIA

MALTA

Murmansk

Kola
Peninsula
Ponoy

WHITE SEA

Timan Ridge

Pechora

Mezen

Northern Dvina

Ural Mountains

Ob'

Irtysh

NLAND

Onega

Lake
Onega

Sukhona

Northern Uvals
(Uplands)

Kama

RUSSIA

ASIA

Helsinki
of Finland

Rybinsk
Res.

TONIA

Lake
Peipus

Valdai
Hills

Moscow

Oka

LATVIA

HUANIA

Plain

Central
Russian
Upland

Don

Khopar

Ural

KAZAKHSTAN

Caspian Depression

Syr Darya

Aral Sea

Neman

BELARUS

UZBEKISTAN

Amu Darya

Pripyat

Dnieper Lowland

Volga

Kiev

Donets Basin

Don

TURKMENISTAN

UKRAINE

Dnieper

Dniester

MOLDOVA

Sea of Azov

Crimean
Peninsula

CASPIAN SEA

rpathian Mts.

MANIA

sylvanian Alps

Danube

Caucasus

Mt. Elbrus
18,510 Ft.
5,642m

GEORGIA

Baku

eninsula

BLACK SEA

ARMENIA

AZERBAIJA

BULGARIA

AZER.

Istanbul

TURKEY

Tehran

IRAN

Olympus
570 Ft.
917m

REECE

AEGEAN SEA

IRAQ

Euphrates

SYRIA

N

Rhodes

30°

NORTH
CYPRUS

40°

LEBANON

50°

Tigris

30°

Crete

SEA

CYPRUS

ATLANTIC OCEAN

EUROPE

FRANCE
AUS.
UKRAINE
ROMANIA
RUSSIA
KAZ.
Aral Sea
UZBEK.
BOS.
SERB.
BUL.
Black Sea
GEORGIA
Caspian Sea
TURKMENISTAN
ITALY
ALB.
GREECE
Athens
TURKEY
ARM.
AZER.
Rome

PORTUGAL
SPAIN
Madrid
Mediterranean Sea
CYPRUS
SYRIA
LEBANON
IRAQ
IRAN

ASIA

Strait of Gibraltar
Azores (Port.)
Madeira Islands (Port.)

Algiers
Qacentina
Tunis
MALTA
ISRAEL
JORDAN
KUWAIT
Persian Gulf
QATAR
U.A.E.

Rabat
Oran
TUNISIA
Gulf of Sidra
Banghāzī
Alexandria
Cairo
Suez
Riyadh
SAUDI ARABIA

Casablanca
MOROCCO
Ghardaia
Tripoli
Asyut

Marrakec

Canary Islands (Spain)
El Aaiún
Tropic of Cancer
In Salah
LIBYA
EGYPT
Aswan
Lake Nasser
Red Sea
OMA

WESTERN SAHARA (MOROCCO)
ALGERIA
Sabhā
Port Sudan

Tamanrasset

MAURITANIA
Nouakchott
Timbuktu
MALI
NIGER
CHAD
Omdurman
Khartoum
ERITREA
Asmara
YEMEN
Gulf of Aden
Soc

CAPE VERDE
Senegal
Gao
Agadez
Lake Chad
Abéché
SUDAN
Blue Nile
Lake Tana
DJIBOUTI
Djibouti

Dakar
SENEGAL
Bamako
Niamey
BURKINA FASO
Kano
N'Djamena
ETHIOPIA
Dire Dawa
SOMALIA

GAMBIA
Niger
Ouagadougou
NIGERIA
Abuja
Waw
Addis Ababa

GUINEA-BISSAU
GUINEA
GHANA
BENIN
TOGO
Niger
Benue
CENTRAL AFRICAN REPUBLIC
Mountain Nile
Lake Turkana

Conakry
Lake Volta
Cotonou
Lagos
CAMEROON
Bangui
Uele
Congo
UGANDA
Mogadishu

Freetown
COTE D'IVOIRE
Accra
Douala
Yaoundé
Ubangi
Kisangani
Kampala
Lake Victoria
Nairobi
KENYA
INDIA OCEAN

SIERRA LEONE
LIBERIA
Malabo
EQUATORIAL GUINEA
REP. OF CONGO
DEM. REP. OF CONGO
Kigali
RWANDA
Nairobi

Monrovia
Abidjan
SAO TOME AND PRINCIPE
GABON
Libreville
Bujumbura
BURUNDI
Dodoma
Mombasa
SEYCHELL

Equator
Ascension (St. Helena)
Brazzaville
Kinshasa
Mbuji
Lake Tanganyika
TANZANIA
Dar es Salaam

Luanda
Kolwezi
Lubumbashi
MALAWI
Lake Nyasa
COMOROS
Mayotte (Fr.)
Antsiranana

ATLANTIC
St. Helena (U.K.)
Lobito
ANGOLA
Huambo
Ndola
ZAMBIA
Lilongwe
MOZAMBIQUE

OCEAN
Zambezi
Lusaka
Lake Kariba
Harare
Beira
Antananarivo
MAURITIU

Okavango
NAMIBIA
BOTSWANA
ZIMBABWE
MADAGASCAR
Reunion (Fr.)

Windhoek
Fianarantsoa

Tropic of Capricorn
Gaborone
Limpopo
Pretoria
Maputo

Johannesburg
Orange
Maseru
SWAZILAND
LESOTHO
Durban

Cape Town
SOUTH AFRICA
Port Elizabeth

Tristan da Cunha Group (St. Helena)

	National Capital
	City over 1,000,000 population
	City of 250,000 to 1,000,000 population
	City under 250,000 population

200 400 600 800 1000 Miles
300 600 900 1200 1500 Kilometers
Copyright by Rand McNally & Co.
Lambert Azimuthal Equal Area Projection

Prince Edward Islands (S. Af.)
Crozet Islands (Fr.)

RAND MᶜNALLY

ARCTIC OCEAN

ATLANTIC OCEAN

Arctic Circle

Norwegian Sea

Barents Sea

Kara Sea

ICELAND

FAROE ISLANDS (Den.)

IRELAND

UNITED KINGDOM

London

PORTUGAL

SPAIN

MOROCCO

GIBRALTAR (U.K.)

ALGERIA

TUNISIA

LIBYA

Mediterranean Sea

ITALY

FRANCE

Paris

North Sea

DENMARK

NORWAY

SWEDEN

FINLAND

ESTONIA

LATVIA

LITH.

BELARUS

POLAND

GERMANY

NETH.

BEL.

LUX.

SWITZ.

AUSTRIA

CZECH

SLOVAKIA

HUNGARY

SLOVENIA

CROATIA

BOS. HERZ.

MONT.

ALB.

MACED.

GREECE

ROMANIA

Danube

BULGARIA

Adriatic Sea

Kiev

UKRAINE

Volga

Moscow

R U S

SVALBARD (Nor.)

Spitsbergen

Franz Josef Land

Severnaya Zemlya

Novaya Zemlya

Ob'

Pechora

Yenisey

Noril'sk

Yekaterinburg

Chelyabinsk

Omsk

Novosibirsk

Barnaul

Astana

Karaganda

Semipalatinsk

Öskemen

Ishim

Irtysh

Ob'

K A Z A K H S T A N

Aral Sea

Lake Balkhash

Syr Darya

UZBEKISTAN

Bishkek

Almaty

Ürümqi

Tashkent

KYRGYZSTAN

TURKMENISTAN

Dushanbe

TAJIKISTAN

Istanbul

Izmir

Ankara

TURKEY

N. CYPRUS

CYPRUS

LEBANON

Damascus

SYRIA

ISRAEL

JORDAN

Amman

Black Sea

GEORGIA

Tbilisi

Yerevan

ARM.

AZER.

Baku

Caspian Sea

Tabriz

Tehran

Mashhad

Kabul

Islāmābād

AFGHANISTAN

Euphrates

Tigris

IRAQ

Baghdad

IRAN

Eşfahān

Kuwait

KUWAIT

Persian Gulf

SAUDI ARABIA

Riyadh

Jiddah

Red Sea

Cairo

Nile

EGYPT

SUDAN

CHAD

Blue Nile

Nile

ERITREA

ETHIOPIA

DJIBOUTI

Gulf of Aden

SOMALIA

DEM. REP. OF THE CONGO (ZAIRE)

UGANDA

RWANDA

BURUNDI

KENYA

TANZANIA

ZAMBIA

MALAWI

MOZAMBIQUE

BAHRAIN

QATAR

Abū Dhabi

U.A.E.

Muscat

OMAN

Gulf of Oman

YEMEN

Sanaa

Socotra (Yem.)

Arabian Sea

Kabul

PAKISTAN

Lahore

Amritsar

Delhi

New Delhi

Karachi

Hyderābād

Ahmadābād

Indus

Brahmaputra

Ganges

NEPAL

Kathmandu

Kānpur

Ganges

Godāvari

INDIA

Kolkata (Calcutta)

Nāgpur

Hyderābād

Mumbai (Bombay)

Bangalore

Lakshadweep (India)

Chennai (Madras)

Bay of Bengal

MALDIVES

Colombo

SRI LANKA

I N D I A N   O C E A N

N

Copyright by Rand McNally & Co.
Lambert Azimuthal Equal Area Projection

0	200	400	600	800 Miles
0	200 400 600 800			1000 Kilometers

★ National Capital

■ City over 1,000,000 population

▣ City of 250,000 to 1,000,000 population

• City under 250,000 population

New Siberian Islands

Laptev Sea

East Siberian Sea

Bering Sea

ALEUTIAN ISLANDS (U.S.)

Anadyr

Palana

Kamchatka Peninsula

Petropavlovsk-Kamchatskiy

Sea of Okhotsk

PACIFIC OCEAN

Tropic of Cancer

Yakutsk

Magadan

Sakhalin

Kuril Islands

Khabarovsk

Lake Baikal

Chita

Qiqihar

Harbin

Vladivostok

Sapporo

Hokkaido

Sea of Japan

Honshu

Tokyo

Ulaanbaatar

Changchun

Shenyang

NORTH KOREA

Seoul

SOUTH KOREA

Nagoya

JAPAN

MONGOLIA

Beijing

Pusan

Osaka

Shikoku

Kyushu

Tianjin

Jinan

Yellow Sea

Taiyuan

NORTHERN MARIANA ISLANDS (U.S.)

Lanzhou

Huang

Xi'an

Nanjing

Shanghai

East China Sea

Wuhan

Hangzhou

CHINA

Chengdu

Chang (Yangtze)

Chongqing

Fuzhou

Taipei

GUAM (U.S.)

FEDERATED STATES OF MICRONESIA

Guiyang

Guangzhou

TAIWAN

Kaohsiung

Kunming

Nanning

Hong Kong

Luzon Strait

Luzon

Philippine Sea

Hanoi

Hainan Island

Samar

PHILIPPINES

Chittagong

MYANMAR

LAOS

Gulf of Tonkin

South China Sea

Manila

PALAU

Cebu

Mindanao

Yangon

Vientiane

Da Nang

Davao

THAILAND

Mekong

VIETNAM

Sulu Sea

Bangkok

CAMBODIA

Phnom Penh

Ho Chi Minh City

Andaman Sea

Gulf of Thailand

Celebes Sea

New Guinea

PAPUA NEW GUINEA

Bandar Seri Begawan

BRUNEI

Nicobar Islands (India)

MALAYSIA

Kuala Lumpur

MALAYSIA

Borneo

Ceram

Manado

Medan

Singapore

Celebes

Sumatra

Banjarmasin

INDONESIA

Arafura Sea

Coral Sea

Gulf of Carpentaria

Palembang

Jakarta

Java Sea

Bandung

Java

Surabaya

Banda Sea

EAST TIMOR

Timor

Timor Sea

AUSTRALIA

ATLANTIC OCEAN

ARCTIC OCEAN

ICELAND

Arctic Circle

Barents Sea

Severnaya Zem.

Novaya Zemlya

Kara Sea

Yamal Pen.

FAROE ISLANDS (Den.)

IRELAND

UNITED KINGDOM

London

North Sea

DENMARK

NORWAY

SWEDEN

FINLAND

ESTONIA

LATVIA

LITH.

West Siberian Lowland

Novosibirsk

Ob

PORTUGAL

SPAIN

FRANCE

GERMANY

NETH.

BEL.

LUX.

SWITZ.

AUSTRIA

CZECH REP.

SLOVAKIA

POLAND

BELARUS

UKRAINE

MOLD.

Moscow

Volga

Ural Mountains

Ob

Irtysh

Ishim

Astana

KAZAKHSTAN

Novosibirsk

Ob

MOROCCO

GIBRALTAR (U.K.)

ANDORRA

MONACO

ITALY

SLOVENIA

CROATIA

BOS. & HER.

SERBIA & MONT.

MAC.

ALB.

HUNGARY

ROMANIA

BULGARIA

GREECE

Black Sea

Caucasus

Caspian Depression

Aral Sea

Ust-Urt Plateau

Caspian Sea

Syr Darya

Lake Balkhash

ALGERIA

TUNISIA

Mediterranean Sea

Ankara

TURKEY

Mount Ararat 16,946 Ft. 5,165m

GEORGIA

ARM.

AZER.

N. CYPRUS

CYPRUS

LEBANON

SYRIA

Tigris

ISRAEL

JORDAN

Sinai Pen.

IRAQ

Euphrates

Tehran

Dasht-e Kavir

Zagros Mts.

IRAN

Kara Kum (Desert)

Amu Darya

TURKMENISTAN

UZBEKISTAN

Tian Shan

KYRGYZSTAN

TAJIKISTAN

Pamirs

Hindu Kush

Tarim Basin

K2 (Qogir Feng) 28,250 Ft. 8,611m

Altun M

Kunlun M

LIBYA

EGYPT

Nile

Cairo

Red Sea

An-Nafud

SAUDI ARABIA

Arabian Peninsula

KUWAIT

BAHRAIN

QATAR

Persian Gulf

U.A.E.

Gulf of Oman

AFGHANISTAN

PAKISTAN

Indus

New Delhi

Great Indian Desert

HIMALAYA MTS.

NEPAL

Mt. Everest 29,035 Ft. 8,850m

CHAD

SUDAN

ERITREA

DJIBOUTI

ETHIOPIA

Gulf of Aden

Rub Al-Khali

YEMEN

OMAN

Socotra (Yem.)

Arabian Sea

Ganges

INDIA

Mumbai (Bombay)

Godavari

Deccan Plateau

Western Ghats

Eastern Ghats

Bay of Beng

DEM. REP. OF THE CONGO (ZAIRE)

UGANDA

RWANDA

BURUNDI

KENYA

SOMALIA

TANZANIA

ZAMBIA

MOZAMBIQUE

Lakshadweep (India)

N

MALDIVES

SRI LANKA

INDIAN OCEAN

0   200   400   600   800 Miles

0   200 400 600 800 1000 Kilometers

Copyright by Rand McNally & Co.
Lambert Azimuthal Equal Area Projection

Land Elevation

Meters	Feet
3,000	9,840
2,000	6,560
500	1,640
200	656
0	0

Water Depth

0	0
200	656
2,000	6,560

RUSSIA

Laptev Sea

New Siberian Islands

East Siberian Sea

Indigirka

Kolyma

Arctic Circle

Bering Sea

Aleutian Islands (U.S.)

Taymyr Peninsula

Verkhoyansk Mts.

Lena

Sea of Okhotsk

Kamchatka Peninsula

Central Siberian Uplands

Siberia

Stanovoy Range

Sakhalin

Kuril Islands

Sikhote-Alin Mts.

Amur

Greater Khingan Range

Tatar Strait

Lake Baikal

Hokkaido

PACIFIC OCEAN

Sea of Japan

Honshu

Tokyo ✷

Tropic of Cancer

Sayan Mountains

MONGOLIA

Gobi Desert

Beijing ✷

NORTH KOREA

SOUTH KOREA

Mt. Fuji 12,388 ft. 3,776m

JAPAN

Shikoku

Kyushu

Altai Mts.

Yellow Sea

Qilian Shan

Huang

Shanghai ●

East China Sea

NORTHERN MARIANA ISLANDS (U.S.)

CHINA

Qinling Shandi

Chang (Yangtze)

Xi

GUAM (U.S.)

FEDERATED STATES OF MICRONESIA

Brahmaputra

BHUTAN

TAIWAN

Philippine Sea

Salween

Irrawaddy

Mekong

Red

Gulf of Tonkin

Hainan Island

Taiwan Strait

Luzon Strait

Luzon

BANGL

NGL

MYANMAR

LAOS

South China Sea

PHILIPPINES ✷

Manila ✷

PALAU

Equator

THAILAND

VIETNAM

Mindanao

Bangkok ✷

CAMBODIA

Sulu Sea

Andaman Sea

Gulf of Thailand

Celebes Sea

New Guinea

PAPUA NEW GUINEA

Aman ands ndia)

Nicobar Islands (India)

MALAY PENINSULA

BRUNEI

MALAYSIA

Moluccas

Ceram

MALAYSIA

Celebes

Banda Sea

Arafura Sea

Str. of Malacca

Singapore ✷

Borneo

Coral Sea

Sumatra

Greater Sunda Islands

INDONESIA

EAST TIMOR

Timor

Gulf of Carpentaria

Java Sea

AUSTRALIA

Jakarta ✷

Java

Timor Sea

A21

Roman Empire About A.D. 120

ATLANTIC OCEAN

IRELAND

North Sea

Baltic Sea

BRITAIN
Wall of Antoninus
Wall of Hadrian
Deva
Eburacum
Lindum
BRITAIN
Camulodunum
Londinium

English Channel

Lugdunum Batavorum

Elbe

LOWER GERMANY
Colonia Agrippina

(Lost in 9 A.D.)

GERMANY

Vistula

Augusta Treverorum
BELGICA
Lutetia
LUGDUNENSIS
Seine
Moguntiacum

Cantabrian Sea

Liger
(Loire)

GAUL

Argentoratum
Rhine
UPPER GERMANY
Augustodunum
Vindonissa

Carpathians

Bracara Augusta
Portus Cale

Douro
Iberus
Asturica
TARRACONENSIS
Numantia
Caesar Augusta

Burdigala
AQUITANIA
Garumna (Garonne)
Lugdunum
Rhône
Tolosa
NARBONENSIS

Alps
RHAETIA
Augusta Vindelicorum
Comum
NORICUM
Vindobona
Carnuntum
Danube
Aquincum
ILLYRICUM
PANNONIA

40°
Salmantica
LUSITANIA
Emerita Augusta
Tagus
SPAIN
Toletum
Valentia
Pyrenees
Ilerda
Nemausus
Narbo
Arelate
Massilia
Mediolanum
Verona
Genua
Po
Bononia
Aquileia
Patavium
Florentia
Ravenna
Ancona
Sirmium
Siscia
Sarmizegen (Colonia Ulpia Tr
DA
Viminacium
DALMATIA
Salonae
Naissus
Narona
Serdica
Philippopoli

Olisipo

Corduba
BAETICA
Munda
Hispalis
Castulo

Guadiana

MEDITERRANEAN
Ligurian Sea
CORSICA AND SARDINIA

ITALY
Rome
Ostia
Capua
Adriatic Sea

Corcyra
EPIRUS
MACEDONIA
Dyrrhachium
Thessalonica
Demetrias

Gades
Tingis
Malaca

New Carthage
Tarraco

Balearic Islands

Carales
Tyrrhenian Sea
Pompeii
Tarentum
Brundisium

Ionian Sea

Corinth
ACHAIA
Sparta
Athens

AFRICA
MAURETANIA
Atlas Mountains
GAETULIA
Sitifis
Lambaesis
Cirta
Hippo Diarrhytus
Hippo Regius
Utica
Carthage
Theveste
Thugga
Thamugadi
Hadrumetum
Thapsus
AFRICA
NUMIDIA
Agrigentum
SICILY
Messana
Rhegium
Syracuse

Lesser Syrtis

SEA

Crete
Gortyn
CRETE AND CYRENE
Cyrene

Greater Syrtis

CYRENAI

Oea
Leptis

20°

Roman City Names and Modern Equivalents

ROMAN NAME	MODERN NAME	ROMAN NAME	MODERN NAME
Ancyra	Ankara	Londinium	London
Aquincum	Budapest	Lugdunum	Lyon
Arelate	Arles	Lugdunum Batavorum	Leiden
Augusta Treverorum	Trier, Treves	Lutetia	Paris
Augusta Vindelicorum	Augsburg	Malaca	Malaga
Augustodunum	Autun	Massilia	Marseille
Bononia	Bologna	Mazaca Caesarea	Kayseri
Burdigala	Bordeaux	Mediolanum	Milan
Caesar Augusta	Saragossa	Moguntiacum	Mainz
Camulodunum	Colchester	Nemausus	Nimes
Carales	Cagliari	Olisipo	Lisbon
Colonia Agrippina	Cologne	Patavium	Padua
Deva	Chester	Salmantica	Salamanca
Eburacum	York	Thessalonica	Salonika
Emerita Augusta	Merida	Toletum	Toledo
Gades	Cadiz	Tolosa	Toulouse
Hispalis	Seville	Valentia	Valencia
Lindum	Lincoln	Vindobona	Vienna

Legend:
- Roman Empire
- Armenia
- Parthian Empire
- Temporarily held by Rome

RAND M?NALLY

SARMATIA

Dnieper

Dniester

arnian Mts.

Danube

Tomi

Odessus

Olbia

Lake Maeotis

Tanais

Panticapaeum
Phanagoria

BLACK SEA

CAUCASUS

Dioscurias

Aral Sea

CASPIAN SEA

Byzantium
Nicomedia
Nicaea
BITHYNIA
Heraclea
Amisus
Sinope
PONTUS
Trapezus
LESSER ARMENIA

ARMENIA
(114-117 A.D.)

Artaxata

40°

Prusa
Pergamum
Ancyra
GALATIA
Halys
Mazaca Caesarea
CAPPADOCIA
Melitene
L. Thospitis
L. Matianus

ASIA
Smyrna
Sardes
LYCAONIA
Tyana
Amida
Ecbatana

sus
Laodicea
Iconium
Adana
COMMA-
GENE
SOPHENE
Edessa
Rhesaena
Nisibis
ASSYRIA
(115-117 A.D.)

Halicarnassus
PISIDIA
PAMPHYLIA
Carrhae
OSROENE
Singara
Tigris

PARTHIAN

Rhodes
LYCIA
CILICIA
Tarsus
Nicephorium
Apamea
Dura
MESOPOTAMIA
ZAGRUS MTS.

Rhodes
CYPRUS
Antioch
SYRIA
Circesium
Euphrates
Seleucia
Susa
EMPIRE

Emesa
Palmyra
Ctesiphon

Damascus

Sidon
Tyre
Caesarea
Babylon
(115-117 A.D.)

PALESTINE
Jerusalem
Gaza
PETRAEA
PERSIA

Alexandria
Pelusium
ARABIA

Petra

ARABIA

Memphis
Arsinoe

Arsinoe

Persian Gulf

Oxyrhynchus
Nile

Antinoopolis
EGYPT

Ptolemais

Red Sea

Coptos
Thebes
Syene
Berenice

30°

40°

50°

30°

40°

30°

| 0 | 100 | 200 | 300 Miles |
| 0 | 200 | 400 Kilometers | |

Copyright by Rand McNally & Co.
Equidistant Conic Projection

A25

The Ottoman, Safavid, and Mughal Empires in the 16th and 17th Centuries

ATLANTIC OCEAN

HOLY ROMAN EMPIRE

POLAND

FRANCE

PORTUGAL

SPAIN

Milan
Venice
Genoa
Naples
Otranto

Adriatic Sea

Vienna
1529,
1683
Danube
Budapest
1529
Mohács
1526
Belgrade
1521
Kosovo
1389,
1448
Nikopolis
1396
Edirne
1360
Lepanto
1571
Aegean
Sea
Bursa
1326
Söğüd
Ackerman
1484
Varna
1444
Black S
Constantinople
(Istanbul)
1453
Crimea
Anka
14
Elbis
Adan

Malaga
Granada

Algiers
Tunis
1533,
1574

Fez

Tripoli
1551

Rhodes
1522
Crete
1669
Cyprus
1571
Be

Mediterranean Sea

Jerusale
151

Cairo
1517

Nile

Dnepr

Legend:

- Ottoman Empire to 1360
- Ottoman Empire to 1481
- Ottoman Empire and its Dependencies in the 16th and 17th Centuries
- Safavid Empire in the 16th Century
- Kingdom of Babur in 1525
- Mughal Empire in 1635
- Mughal Lands Conquered after 1635
- Uzbek States in the 16th Century
- Area disputed with Safavids
- Area disputed with Uzbeks
- Area Disputed with Safavids and Uzbeks

- ○ Towns or Settlements
- ■ Main Portuguese Trade Settlements
- □ Towns with Large Portuguese Population
- Mosul 1516 Date of Control
- ■ Ottoman Capitals
- ■ Safavid Capitals
- ■ Mughal Capitals
- ✖ Chaldiran 1514 Site and Date of Important Battle

0   200   400   600   800 Miles
0   200   400   600   800   1000   1200 Kilometers
Copyright by Rand McNally & Co.
Miller Equal Area Projection

10°   0°   10°   20°   30°

MUSCOVY

Don

Ural

Volga

Don-Volga
Canal Project
1569

Azov

Aral
Sea

Syr Darya (Jaxartes)

Caspian
Sea

Urganch

Amu Darya (Oxus)

Bukhara

Samarqand

Ghujduvan
1512

abzon
1461

Darband

Tiflis

Bashkent 1473

Erivan

Chaldiran
1514

Ardabil 1501

Marv

arj Dabiq
16

Mosul
1516

Tabriz
1501

Astarabad

Mashhad

Harat 1510

Balkh

eppo
16

Qazvin

Jam
1528

Kabul

Kirmanshah
1503

Hamadan
1503

Qum 1503

KASHMIR
1586

ascus

Kashan
1503

Lahore

Baghdad
1534

Isfahan
1503

Yazd
1504

Qandahar

Multan

Panipat
1526, 1556

Basra
1546

Shiraz
1504

Kirman
1504

Delhi

Kannauj
1540

Kelat
1595

Fatihpur Sikri

Agra

Chavsa
1539

Bandar
'Abbas

Hurmuz

Lucknow

Jaunpur

Patna

Medina

Persian Gulf

Jodhpur

SIND
1591

Gulf of
Oman

Masqat

Chanderi
1572

GONDWANA

Mecca

Cambay
1572

Surat

Rissa

d
Sea

Diu
1538

Daman

BERAR
1596

Ramgir
1687

Ahmadnagar
1598

Bidar

Arabian
Sea

Bijapur
1686

Golconda
1687

Goa

Bay of
Bengal

Gulf of Aden

Mangalore

INDIAN
OCEAN

N

Cochin

Ceylon
(Sri Lanka)

Colombo

RAND McNALLY

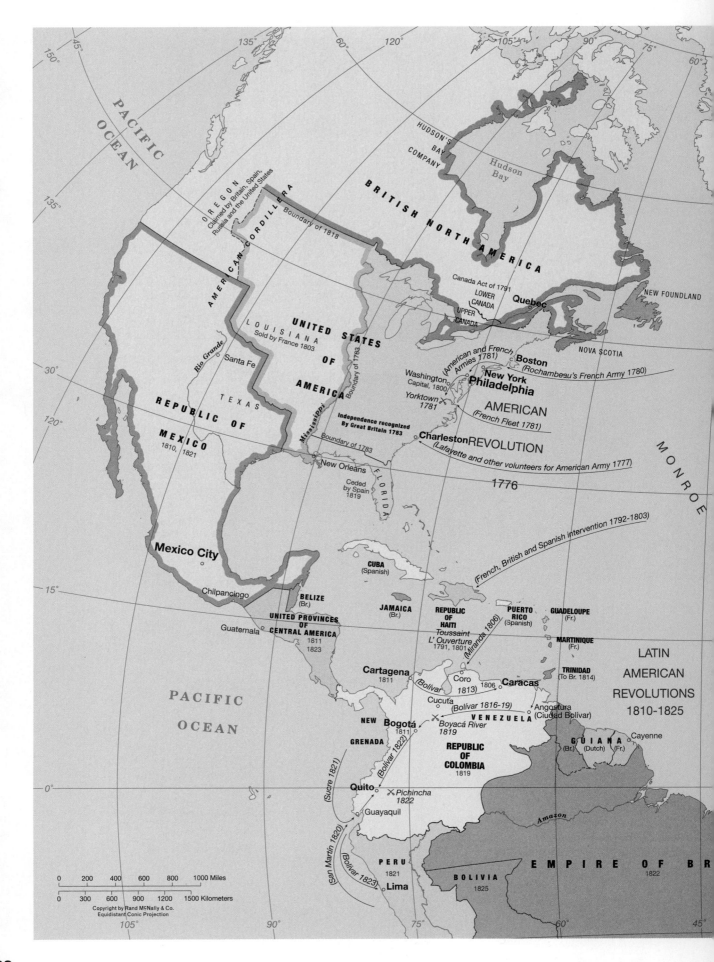

PACIFIC OCEAN

BRITISH NORTH AMERICA

HUDSON'S BAY COMPANY

Hudson Bay

NEW FOUNDLAND

Canada Act of 1791
LOWER CANADA
Quebec
UPPER CANADA

NOVA SCOTIA

OREGON
Claimed by Britain, Spain,
Russia and the United States
Boundary of 1818

AMERICAN CORDILLERA

UNITED STATES OF AMERICA

LOUISIANA
Sold by France 1803

Boundary of 1783

(American and French Armies 1781) Boston
(Rochambeau's French Army 1780)

Washington
Capital, 1800
New York
Philadelphia

Yorktown 1781

AMERICAN
(French Fleet 1781)

Rio Grande
Santa Fe

TEXAS

REPUBLIC OF MEXICO
1810, 1821

Independence recognized
By Great Britain 1783

Boundary of 1783

Mississippi

New Orleans

FLORIDA
Ceded by Spain 1819

Charleston REVOLUTION
(Lafayette and other volunteers for American Army 1777)

1776

MONROE

Mexico City

Chilpancingo

BELIZE (Br.)

UNITED PROVINCES OF CENTRAL AMERICA
1811 1823

Guatemala

CUBA (Spanish)

JAMAICA (Br.)

REPUBLIC OF HAITI
Toussaint L'Ouverture 1791, 1801

PUERTO RICO (Spanish)

GUADELOUPE (Fr.)

MARTINIQUE (Fr.)

(French, British and Spanish intervention 1792-1803)

TRINIDAD (To Br. 1814)

LATIN AMERICAN REVOLUTIONS 1810-1825

PACIFIC OCEAN

Cartagena 1811

(Bolívar)

Coro
1813

1806

Caracas

Cúcuta

(Bolívar 1816-19)

Angostura (Ciudad Bolívar)

VENEZUELA

NEW GRENADA
Bogotá 1811

(Bolívar 1822)

Boyacá River 1819

REPUBLIC OF COLOMBIA
1819

GUIANA
(Br.) (Dutch) (Fr.)
Cayenne

(Sucre 1821)

Quito
Pichincha 1822

Guayaquil

Amazon

(San Martín 1820)

(Bolívar 1823)

PERU 1821

BOLIVIA 1825

Lima

EMPIRE OF BR
1822

0 200 400 600 800 1000 Miles
0 300 600 900 1200 1500 Kilometers
Copyright by Rand McNally & Co.
Equidistant Conic Projection

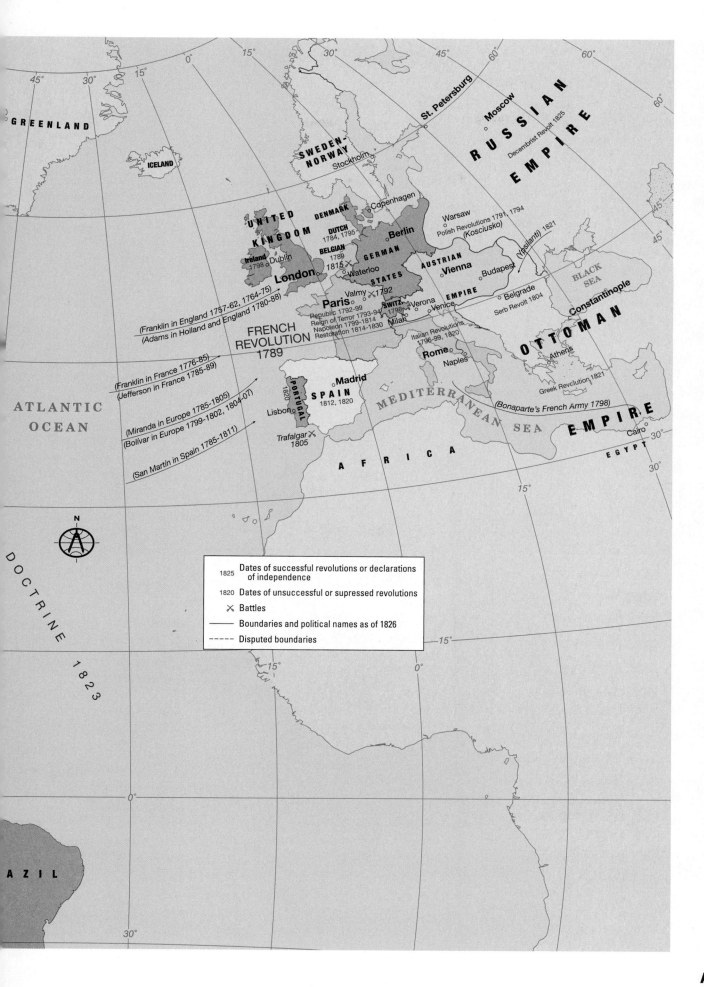

GREENLAND

ICELAND

ATLANTIC OCEAN

DOCTRINE 1823

SWEDEN-NORWAY

Stockholm

St. Petersburg

Moscow

RUSSIAN EMPIRE

Decembrist Revolt 1825

DENMARK

Copenhagen

UNITED KINGDOM

Ireland 1798 · Dublin

London

DUTCH 1784, 1795

BELGIAN 1789 1815 ✕ Waterloo

Berlin

GERMAN STATES

Warsaw
Polish Revolutions 1791, 1794 (Kosciusko)

(Ypsilanti) 1821

AUSTRIAN

Vienna

Budapest

BLACK SEA

(Franklin in England 1757-62, 1764-75)
(Adams in Holland and England 1780-88)

Valmy ✕ 1792

Paris

Republic 1792-99
Reign of Terror 1793-94
Napoleon 1799-1814
Restoration 1814-1830

SWITZ. 1798

FRENCH REVOLUTION 1789

Verona
Milan

EMPIRE

Venice

Belgrade
Serb Revolt 1804

Constantinople

OTTOMAN

(Franklin in France 1776-85)
(Jefferson in France 1785-89)

Italian Revolutions 1796-99, 1820

Rome

Naples

Athens

(Miranda in Europe 1785-1805)
(Bolívar in Europe 1799-1802, 1804-07)

Madrid

PORTUGAL 1820

SPAIN 1812, 1820

Lisbon

MEDITERRANEAN SEA

Greek Revolution 1821

(Bonaparte's French Army 1798)

EMPIRE

Cairo

(San Martín in Spain 1785-1811)

Trafalgar 1805

AFRICA

EGYPT

RAZIL

Dates of successful revolutions or declarations of independence — 1825

Dates of unsuccessful or supressed revolutions — 1820

✕ Battles

—— Boundaries and political names as of 1826

- - - Disputed boundaries

RAND McNALLY

Latin America 1800–1850

Gila

U.S. 1846-48

TEXAS

U.S. annexation, 1845

▲1836 from Mex.

Rio Grande / Bravo

U.S.,1822-25

Bahamas (Br.)

ATLANTIC OCEAN

Monterrey

Matamoros

Gulf of Mexico

MEXICO
▲1821 From Sp.
✕1823

Tampico

Havana

U.S., 1848

San Luis Potosí

U.S., 1800

U.S.,1824

Santo Domingo

PUERTO RICO

Virgin Is.(Den.)

México

Veracruz

YUCATÁN
✕1847-53

CUBA

Santiago

1844-61

✕1844

San Juan

✕ 1848

Port-au-Prince

BELIZE

JAMAICA

HAITI
1804 from Fr.
1806-20

Br., 1846

DOMINICAN REPUBLIC
▲1821 from Sp.
1844 from Haiti

Guadeloupe
1815,1822

Br.,1807-14

Martinique

GUATEMALA

HONDURAS

Guatemala.

Tegucigalpa

St Lucia

EL SALVADOR

San Salvador

León

Bluefields

Barbados

St Vincent

Grenada

Tobago

Caribbean Sea

Aruba

Bonaire

NICARAGUA

MOSQUITIA
(Miskito Indians)

Curaçao

Maracaibo

Caracas

Trinidad

(CENTRAL AMERICAN STATES)
▲1821 from Sp.
1823 from Mexico
1838 From United Provinces of Central America
✕1827-1829

San José

COSTA RICA
✕1842

Cartagena

Panama

VENEZUELA
▲1819 from Sp.
1830 from Gran Colombia

Angostura

Georgetown

Paramaribo

BRITISH GUIANA

DUTCH GUIANA

FRENCH GUIANA

Cayenne

Bogotá

Orinoco

NUEVA GRANADA
▲1819 from Sp.
1830 from Gran Colombia

Magdalena

Galápagos Is. (Ec.)

Quito

Negro

Pará

Maranhão

Ceará

ECUADOR
▲1822 from Sp.
1830 from Gran Colombia

Guayaquil

Amazon

BRAZIL
▲1822 from Port.

Pernambuca

PACIFIC OCEAN

Marañón

Ucayali

ACRE

Xingu

Tocantins

Araguaia

São Francisco

✕1831-35

Bahia

U.S., Br., Fr., 1835-36

Trujillo

PERU
▲1821 from Sp.

Callao

Lima

Cuzco

Pisco

Lake Titicaca

BOLIVIA
▲1825 from Sp.
✕1839

Mato Grosso

Minas Novas

La Paz

Diamantina

Tacna

Chuquisaca

Arica

Potosí

GRAN CHACO

Iquique

1836-39

Paraguay

Rio de Janeiro

Antofagasta

Jujuy

Salta

PARAGUAY
▲1811 from Sp.

Asunción

São Paulo

Tucumán

✕1835-45

Copiapó

CHILE
▲1818 from Sp.
✕1830

LA PLATA
▲1816 from Sp.
✕1826,1838-39

Santa Fé

Paraná

1825-28

Pôrto Alegre

Córdoba

1825-28

Valparaíso

Mendoza

1843-45

Rosario

URUGUAY
▲1814 from Sp., 1828 from Brazil
✕1836-52

Santiago

Buenos Aires

Montevideo

Br.,1828,1843

Concepción

Rio de la Plata

U.S.,1833

Fr.,1806-07,1845

Br.,1838,1845

Valdivia

PATAGONIA
(Mapuche Indians)

Br.,1833

U.S.,1831-32

Falkland Islands

South Georgia

Legend:

- Independent state
- British colony
- Dutch colony
- French colony
- Spanish colony
- U.S. colony
- Disputed area
- → Latin American military forces
- → U.S. or European intervention
- ····· Projected canals
- ▲ Independence date and colonial power
- ✕ Civil war

0   200   400   600   800   1000 Miles

0   400   800   1200   1600 Kilometers

Copyright by Rand McNally & Co.
Pseudo-Cylindrical Projection

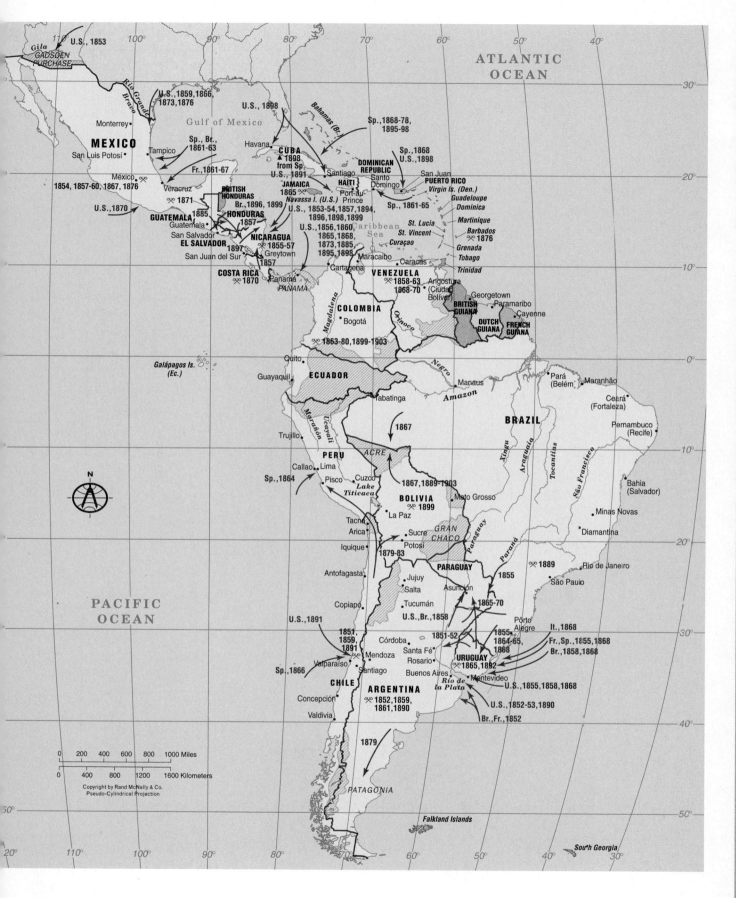

ATLANTIC OCEAN

Gila GADSDEN PURCHASE
U.S., 1853

U.S., 1859, 1866,
1873, 1876

U.S., 1898

Bahamas (Br.)

Sp., 1868-78,
1895-98

Rio Grande
Bravo

Gulf of Mexico

MEXICO
Monterrey•

Sp., Br.,
1861-63

Havana

CUBA
▲ 1898
from Sp.

Sp., 1868
U.S., 1898

Tampico•
San Luis Potosí•

Fr., 1861-67

Santiago

DOMINICAN
REPUBLIC

San Juan
PUERTO RICO

México•
1854, 1857-60, 1867, 1876

U.S., 1891

JAMAICA
1865

Santo
Domingo

Virgin Is. (Den.)

Veracruz

⚓ 1871

Navassa I. (U.S.)

HAITI
Port-au-
Prince

Sp., 1861-65

Guadeloupe
Dominica

BRITISH
HONDURAS

Br., 1896, 1899

U.S., 1853-54, 1857, 1894,
1896, 1898, 1899

Martinique

U.S., 1870

1885

HONDURAS
1857

U.S., 1856, 1860,
1865, 1868,
1873, 1885,
1895, 1898

St. Lucia
St. Vincent
Curaçao

Barbados
⚓ 1876

GUATEMALA
Guatemala•
San Salvador•

Caribbean
Sea

Grenada
Tobago

EL SALVADOR

NICARAGUA
⚓ 1855-57

Maracaibo•

Trinidad

San Juan del Sur

Greytown
1857

Cartagena•

VENEZUELA
⚓ 1858-63
1868-70

Angostura
(Ciudad
Bolívar)

1897

COSTA RICA
⚓ 1870

Panamá•
PANAMA

Georgetown

BRITISH
GUIANA

Paramaribo
Cayenne

COLOMBIA
• Bogotá

Magdalena

Orinoco

DUTCH
GUIANA

FRENCH
GUIANA

1863-80, 1899-1903

Quito•

Negro

ECUADOR

Manaus•

Pará
(Belém)

Maranhão•

*Galápagos Is.
(Ec.)*

Guayaquil•

Tabatinga•

Amazon

Ceará
(Fortaleza)•

Marañón

Ucayali

1867

BRAZIL

Pernambuco
(Recife)•

Trujillo•

ACRE

Xingu
Araguaia
Tocantins
São Francisco

Bahia
(Salvador)•

Callao•
Sp., 1864

Lima•
Pisco•

PERU

Cuzco•
*Lake
Titicaca*

1867, 1889-1903

Minas Novas•

BOLIVIA
1899

Mato
Grosso•

Diamantina•

Tacna•
Arica•

• La Paz

Sucre•

GRAN
CHACO

Paraguay

⚓ 1889

Rio de Janeiro•

Iquique•

Potosí•

1879-83

Paraná

São Paulo•

Antofagasta•

PARAGUAY

1855

Jujuy•

Asunción•

Pôrto
Alegre•

It., 1868

U.S., 1891

Salta•
Tucumán•

U.S., Br., 1858

1865-70

Fr., Sp., 1855, 1868

PACIFIC
OCEAN

1851,
1859,
1891

Córdoba•

1851-52

1855,
1864-65,
1868

Br., 1858, 1868

Sp., 1866

Mendoza•

Santa Fé•
Rosario•

URUGUAY
⚓ 1865, 1892

Valparaíso•

CHILE

Santiago•

Buenos Aires•

Montevideo•

U.S., 1855, 1858, 1868

Concepción•

ARGENTINA
⚓ 1852, 1859,
1861, 1890

*Río de
la Plata*

U.S., 1852-53, 1890

Br., Fr., 1852

Valdivia•

1879

PATAGONIA

Falkland Islands

South Georgia

0   200   400   600   800   1000 Miles

0   400   800   1200 1600 Kilometers

Copyright by Rand McNally & Co.
Pseudo-Cylindrical Projection

⊕ RAND McNALLY

RAND MCNALLY

Paris Cities of 1,000,000 or more
Constantinople Cities from 500,000 to 1,000,000
Berlin Cities from 200,000 to 500,000

20% or more of population in cities of 100,000 or more
6-10% of population in cities of 100,000 or more
5% or less of population in cities of 100,000 or more

Explanation of Figures

Population in 1850
35,800,000

(52) Railroad mileage per million of population

650,000 Pig iron production in long or metric tons

4,200,000 Ship tons in ports

Railroads

RUSSIA IN EUROPE
57,200,000
(6)
300,000

Moscow

Saint Petersburg

FINLAND
1,637,000

BALTIC SEA

KINGDOM OF
NORWAY AND SWEDEN
3,480,000
157,000
1,400,000
2,000,000

POLAND
4,850,000
(40)

MOLDAVIA
WALLACHIA
SERBIA
MONTENEGRO

OTTOMAN EMPIRE
Constantinople

HUNGARY
13,192,000
(11)

GREECE
1,035,000

DENMARK
1,415,000
(13)
1,300,000

KDM. OF PRUSSIA
Berlin

GERMAN STATES
34,300,000
(106)
600,000

AUSTRIA
17,535,000
(49)
200,000

Vienna

NETHERLANDS
3,057,000
(35)
Amsterdam
1,700,000

SWITZ.
2,393,000
(6)

ITALIAN STATES
24,348,000
(16)
70,000
Naples
2,500,000
3,000,000

NORTH SEA
1,000,000

UNITED KINGDOM
27,770,000
(240)
3,590,000
12,000,000

Glasgow
Dublin
Liverpool
Manchester
Birmingham
London
650,000

BELGIUM
4,337,000
(125)
255,000
Brussels

FRANCE
35,800,000
(52)
650,000
Paris
4,200,000

SPAIN
15,674,000
27,000
Madrid

PORTUGAL
3,980,000
Lisbon
1,300,000

ATLANTIC OCEAN

MEDITERRANEAN SEA

N

0 100 200 300 Miles
0 200 400 Kilometers

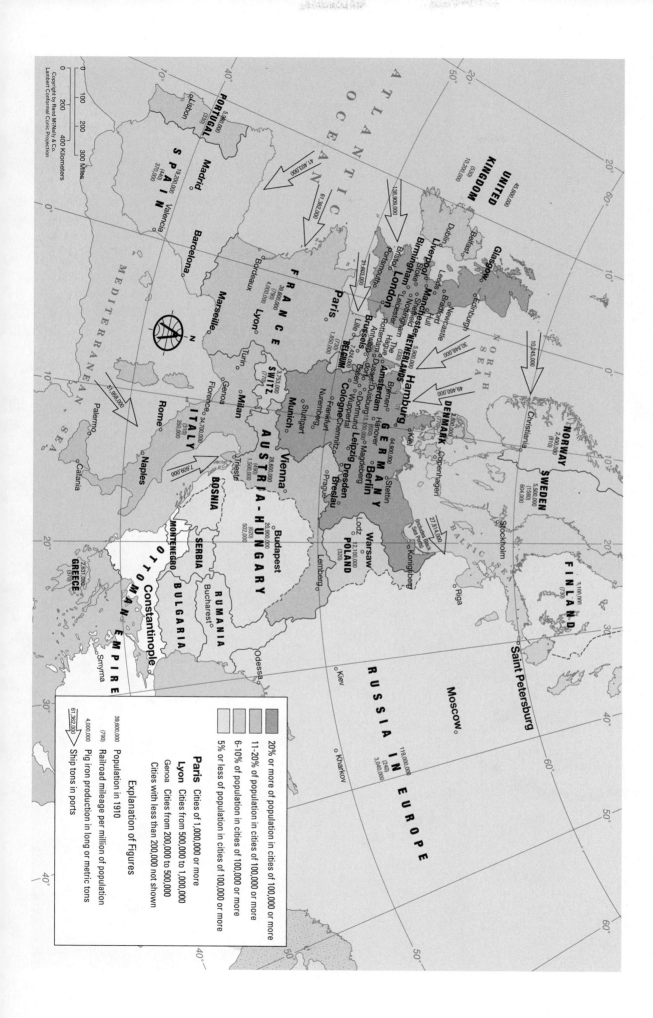

Explanation of Figures

Paris	Cities of 1,000,000 or more	
Lyon	Cities from 500,000 to 1,000,000	
Genoa	Cities from 200,000 to 500,000	
	Cities with less than 200,000 not shown	

39,600,000	Population in 1910	
(790)	Railroad mileage per million of population	
4,000,000	Pig iron production in long or metric tons	
61,362,000	Ship tons in ports	

Cities

- 20% or more of population in cities of 100,000 or more
- 11-20% of population in cities of 100,000 or more
- 6-10% of population in cities of 100,000 or more
- 5% or less of population in cities of 100,000 or more

ICELAND

ATLANTIC

OCEAN

30°

50°

40°

30°

20°

Reykjavik

20°

10°

0°

70°

10° ARCTI

Faroe Islands
(Den.)

Shetland
Islands

Hebrides

Orkney
Is.

North

Sea

Bergen

Occupied by Germany 1940

Oslo

NORWAY

SWEDEN

Åland Is.

Uppsala

Stockholm

Gulf o

Aberdeen

SCOTLAND

Glasgow   Edinburgh

Baltic

Gotland

GREAT

IRISH FREE
STATE

Dublin

Belfast

Liverpool

Manchester

Leeds

Hull

Sheffield

DENMARK
Occupied by
Germany 1940

Aalborg

Göteborg

Hälsingborg

Copenhagen

Öland

Sea

Cork

BRITAIN

WALES

Cardiff

Birmingham

ENGLAND

Oxford

Bristol

Helgoland

Kiel

Lübeck

Hamburg

Bremen

Bornholm

Stettin

MEMELAND
To Ger. 1939

LITH

Memel
Since Anne
1923 USSR

Königsberg

EAST
PRUSSIA

Kau

Plymouth

Portsmouth

London

Dover

NETHERLANDS
Occ. by Ger. 1940

Amsterdam

Rotterdam

Hanover

Magdeburg

Berlin

Potsdam

Tannenberg

Danzig

Nazi-Soviet Pact Annexed
by Germany 1939

Bialystok

Channel
Is.

English Channel

Brest

Le Havre

Dunkirk

Amiens

Lille

Brussels

BELGIUM

Occ. by
Ger. 1940

LUX.

Rhine

Essen

Cologne

GERMANY

Elbe

Leipzig

Dresden

Oder

SILESIA

Breslau

POLA

Cracow

Lubli

Rennes

Caen

Seine

Reims

Verdun

LORRAINE

SAAR

Occ. to
Germany
Plebiscite

Mainz

Frankfurt

Weimar

Mannheim

Nürnberg

Ceded at Munich 1938

Pilsen

Prague

To Pol. 1938

Przemysl

St. Nazaire

Nantes

Loire

Occupied by Germany 1940

Orléans

Fontainebleau

Paris

Dijon

ALSACE

Strasburg

Stuttgart

BAVARIA

Danube

CZECHOSLOVAKIA

Ced. at Munich 1938

Bratislava
(Pressburg)

Košice

RUTHE

Bordeaux

FRANCE

Saône

Basel

Munich

LIECH.

Innsbruck

Vienna

Anschluss 1938

AUSTRIA

Graz

Annexed by Hungary 1939

Annexed by
Hungary 1939

Bayonne

Limoges

Lyon

Grenoble

VICHY FRANCE
1940

SWITZERLAND

Berne

Zürich

Geneva

TRENTINO

Innsbruck

Ljubljana

HUNGARY

Budapest

Annexed
by Hungary
1940

TRANSYLV

RU

La Rochelle

Bay
of
Biscay

40°

Corunna

Oporto

Coimbra

Santander

Burgos

Duero

Valladolid

Salamanca

PORTUGAL

Lisbon

Tagus

SPAIN

Madrid

Toledo

Guadiana

Cordoba

Seville

Guadalquivir

Cadiz

Almeria

Granada

Tangier

Gibraltar
(To Great Britain)

SPANISH AREA

Rabat

MOROCCO

To France

Atlas

Ebro

Saragossa

Pyrenees

ANDORRA

Toulouse

Montpellier

Marseille

Nice

Barcelona

Valencia

Balearic Islands
(To Spain)

Minorca

Majorca

Cartagena

Oran

Algiers

Toulon

Turin

Milan

Verona

Genoa

Parma

Bologna

ITALY

San Remo

Ajaccio

Corsica
(To France)

Florence

SAN
MARINO

Ravenna

Ancona

Rome

Sardinia
(To Italy)

Naples

Cagliari

Palermo

SICILY

Messina

Syracuse

Tunis

Bari

Trieste

Venice

Fiume

Italy 1919

Zara DALMATIA

Split

Dubrovnik
(Ragusa)

Lagosta
(To Italy)

Zagreb

Sava

CROATIA

Drava

YUGOSLAVIA

BOSNIA

Sarajevo

MONTE
NEGRO

Cattaro

Antivari

Durazzo

Valona

ALBANIA

Tirana

Corfu

MACEDONIA

Kavo

Salonika

GREECE

Yannina

Ionian
Sea

Cephallenia

Corfu

Ionian Islands

Messolongi

Patras

Sparta

Athe

Crete

Belgrade

SERBIA

Nish

Novi
Pazar

Temisoara

Oradea

Mohacs

WAL

Danube

Sofi

B

Dard

Philippopoli

Le

Si

Mediterranean

Tyrrhenian Sea

Adriatic Sea

Gulf of
Sidra

Bengazi

CYRENAICA
To Italy

Mountains

ALGERIA

To France

TUNIS

French Protectorate

Malta
(Br.)

Tripoli

TRIPOLITANIA

To Italy

LIBYA

30°

20°

0   100   200   300 Miles

0   200   400 Kilometers

Copyright by Rand McNally & Co.
Equidistant Conic Projection

Principal status quo powers
Principal Revisionist powers
1914 Boundaries
1922 Boundaries

CEAN

Pechenga
MURMAN COAST
Murmansk

KOLA PENINSULA

White Sea

Ceded to USSR 1940

FINLAND

Dvina

Archangel

Vychegda

Pechora

Ob

Lake Onega

Lake Ladoga

Viborg
Kronstadt

gfors (nki)

nland

Leningrad (Petrograd)

Vologda

Kirov

Molotov

Sverdlovsk

Irtish

(Tallinn)

Novgorod

Yaroslavl

Chellabinsk

NIA
d by 1940

Pskov

Volga

Gorkii (Nizhni Novgorod)

Kazañ

Kama

Ufa

Tobol

Kustanai

Ishin

Akmolinsk

A

Kalinin (Tver)

MOSCOW

Oka

Riazan

Kuibyshev

Chkalov

Orsk

W Dvina

Vitebsk
Smolensk

Tula

Belaia

Magnitogorsk

Borisov

Mogilev

Orel

Ural

UNION OF SOVIET SOCIALIST REPUBLICS

Minsk

Briansk

Tambov

Penza

Saratov

Aral Sea

Pripet

Chernigov

Kursk

Voronezh

Uralsk

Zhitomir

Kiev

Dnieper

Don

Volga

Stalingrad

Czernowitz
BESSARABIA

Dniester

Kirovograd (Elizavetgrad)

Poltava

Kharkov

Prut

Kishinev

Dnepropetrovsk (Ekaterinoslav)

AVIA

Annexed by USSR 1940

A

Galatz

Odessa

Cherson

Taganrog

Rostov

Astrakhan

Sea of Azov

Kubañ

Voroshilovsk (Stavropol)

rest

DOBRUJA

Constantsa

Sevastopol

Novorossiisk (Anapa)

Krasnodar (Ekaterinodar)

Terek

Grozni

Petrovsk

CASPIAN SEA

TURKESTAN

To Bulgaria 1940

Varna

BLACK SEA

Ordzhonikidze (Vladikavkaz)

DAGHESTAN

Derbent

Krasnovodsk

Burgas

Sukhumi

REPUBLIC OF GEORGIA

Kura

REPUBLIC OF AZERBAIJAN

Baku

ple

Bosporus

Sinope

Poti

Tiflis

Batum

REPUBLIC

anbul
onstantinople)

Skutari

 Eregli

Samsun

Trebizond

Kars

OF

ARMENIA

Erivan

Lenkoran

fia

Brusa

Ankara (Angora)

Bdry of Armenia as arbitrated by President Wilson

Irmak

Tabriz

Teheran

TURKEY

Kizil

ASIA MINOR

yrna

Konia

Line of the treaty of Sèvres

L. Urmia

Aidin

Adalia

Adana

Bdry between Syria and Turkey as Established by Agree. Aug. 1921

Mosul

Makri

ALEXANDRETTA
Annexed by Turkey 1939

Aleppo

Rhodes

Nikosia

Latakia

Tigris

PERSIA

Cyprus (Br.)

Limasol

Homs

SYRIA
Fr. Mandate

Beirut

Bdry line between Fr. and Br. Mandate Territories as Established by Agree. Dec.

Baghdad

Damascus

IRAQ

EA

Acre

Independent since 1932

Euphrates

PALESTINE
Br. Mandate

Ammán

TRANS-JORDAN
Br. Mandate

endent Kingdom with sh Protective Rights

Jaffa

Jerusalem

ARABIA

KUWAIT

Kuwait

Alexandria

Port Said

Dead Sea

Persian Gulf

PT

Cairo

Nile

Red Sea

RAND McNALLY

Strait of Gibraltar

NASRIDS
Granada • Algiers
Taugiers • Ceuta • Oran • Constantine • Tunis
Fez • Tetuan • Tlemcen • Qayrawan
Rabat
MARINIDS
Marrakech
ZAYYANID **HAFSIDS**
Tripoli
Sijilmasa • Ghadamès • Surte • Barqa

Mediterranean Sea

Canary Islands

Alexandria • Jerusalem
MAMLUKS
Cairo

Tindouf • Tuat
Zawila • Auqilah • Siwa • Awjila • Asyut

Taghaza
Taurirt
Tavdeni • Ghat • Nile

Idjil
Akjoujt • Chinguetti • Murzuq • Selima • Ibrim • Daw • Aswan • Aydhab • Mecca

Tichitt • Tademakka • Bilma • Dongola • Sawakin • Red Sea

ARABIA

Awlil • Walata • Kabara • Takedda • Meroe • Berber
Ghana • Timbuktu • Gao • **KANEM-** • Darfur • Soba • Debarwa • **YEMEN**
Takrur • **MALI** • Kukiya • **BORNU** • **ALWA** • Aksum • Aden
Nioro • **SONGHAI** • Njimi • Sennar • Adefa • Gulf of Aden
Kirina • Djenné • Niger • Abesehr • Lake Tana • Zayla • Soco
Bamako • Segu • Katsina • Lake Chad • Sana • Debra • Berbera
Mali • Kangaba • Ouagadougou • **HAUSA** • Kano • **SOLOMONID** • B'rhan • **ADAL**
Kouroussa • Bobo Dioulasso • **STATES** • Zaria • Chari • **ETHIOPIA** • Harar
Kankan • Volta • Nupe • Shebele

Kong • Salaga • Oyo • Benue
Begho • Ife • Bouar • Obbia
Bono • Manso • Benin City • Igbo Ukwu
BENIN • Ke • Sanaga
Bioko

Ubangi • Victoria Nile • Lake Turkana • Mogadishu

ATLANTIC

OCEAN

Congo • Lake Albert • Kibiro • Baraawe
Lomani • Bigo • Rubaga • Tana
Ntusi • Lake Victoria • **INDIAN**
Loango • Lualaba • **SWAHILI** • Manda • **OCEAN**
Mpinda • Kasai • Uvinza • Lamu
Mbanza Kongo • Congo • **KONGO** • Gedi • Malindi
Kwango • Lake Tanganyika • **EAST AFRICAN**
Luanda • Sanga • Mombasa • Pemba • **TRADING**
Zanzibar • **STATES**
(Unguja)
Ivuna • Mafia
Bunkeya • Karonga • Rufiji • Kilwa
Lake Malawi
Lealui • Kapeni • Comoros
Zambezi • Vohema
Ingombe Ilede • Tete • Mozambique • Volhitrandria
Chedzurgwe • Hunguza • Mawudzu • **Madagascar**
Great Zimbabwe • Sena • Quelimane • Ambohimanga
GREAT ZIMBABWE • Inyanga • Sofala • Mozambique • Tananrive
Zimbabwe • Channel
Khami • Manekweni • Inhambane
Limpopo • Mapungubwe
Phalaborwa

Vaal

Orange

Legend

Southern limits of Muslim influence, about 1400

State, empire, or dynasty with Muslim leader

KONGO State or Empire

— Major trade route

HAFSIDS Dynastic group

Cataract (rapids)

Cattle

Ceramics

Copper

Tin

Foodstuffs

Glass

Gold

Iron

Ivory

Jewelry, trinkets

Kola nuts

Salt

Slaves

Textiles

0   200   400   600   800 Miles
0 200 400 600 800 1000 Kilometers
Copyright by Rand McNally & Co.
Robinson Projection

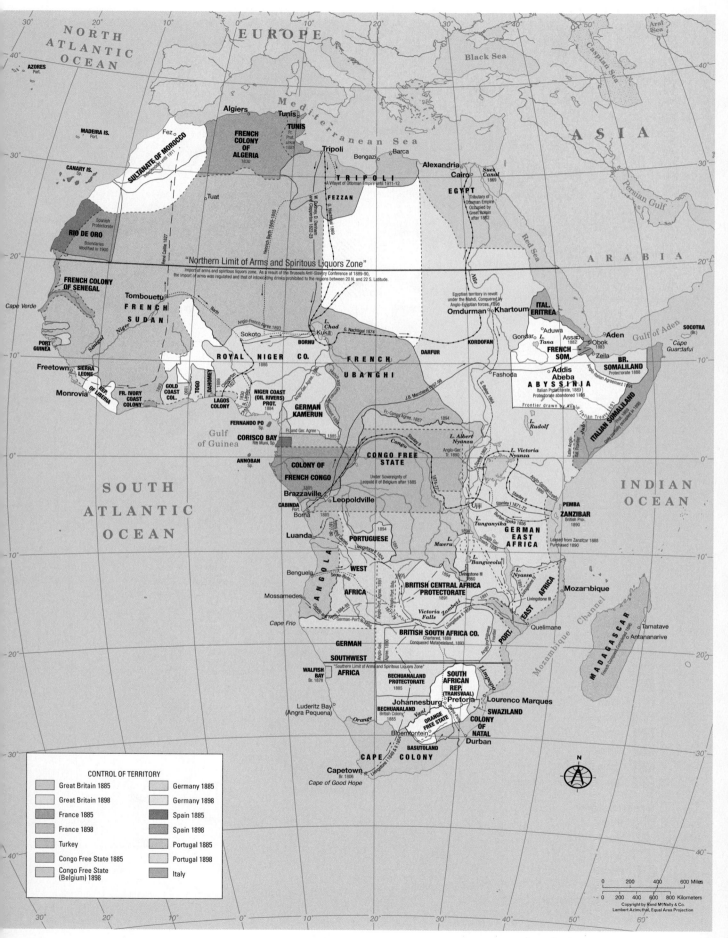

NORTH ATLANTIC OCEAN

EUROPE

Black Sea

ASIA

Aral Sea

Caspian Sea

AZORES
Port.

MADEIRA IS.
Port.

CANARY IS.
Sp.

SULTANATE OF MOROCCO
Independent until 1911

Fez

Tuat

Algiers

Tunis

TUNIS
Fr. Prot. since 1881

FRENCH COLONY OF ALGERIA
1830

Mediterranean Sea

Tripoli

Bengazi

Barca

TRIPOLI
A Vilayet of Ottoman Empire until 1911–12

FEZZAN

Alexandria

Cairo

Suez Canal
1869

EGYPT
(Tributary of Ottoman Empire, Occupied by Great Britain after 1882)

Red Sea

ARABIA

Persian Gulf

RIO DE ORO
Spanish Protectorate
Boundaries Modified in 1900

"Northern Limit of Arms and Spiritous Liquors Zone"

Import of arms and spiritous liquors zone. As a result of the Brussels Anti-Slavery Conference of 1889–90, the import of arms was regulated and that of intoxicating drinks prohibited to the regions between 20 N. and 22 S. Latitude.

Egyptian territory in revolt under the Mahdi, Conquered by Anglo-Egyptian forces, 1896

Omdurman

Khartoum

ITAL. ERITREA
Italian Protectorate 1889

Aduwa

Gondar

L. Tana

Assab
1882

Obok
1883

Zeila

Aden

Gulf of Aden

SOCOTRA
(Br.)

Cape Guardafui

Cape Verde

FRENCH COLONY OF SENEGAL

Tombouctou

FRENCH SUDAN

Niger

Sokoto

Anglo-French Agree 1893

L. Chad
Kuka

G. Nachtigal 1874

BORNU

DARFUR

KORDOFAN

FRENCH SOM.

Addis Abeba

Fashoda

ABYSSINIA
Italian Protectorate, 1889
Protectorate abandoned 1896

Frontier drawn by Anglo-Italian Treaty 1891

BR. SOMALILAND
Anglo-Italian Agreement 1894

PORT GUINEA

Freetown

SIERRA LEONE

Monrovia

REP. OF LIBERIA

FR. IVORY COAST COLONY

GOLD COAST COL.

TOGO

DAHOMEY

LAGOS COLONY

ROYAL NIGER CO.
1888

Niger Coast (Oil Rivers) PROT. 1884

FRENCH UBANGHI

J.B. Marchand 1897–98

L. Rudolf

ITALIAN SOMALILAND
Open country included in 1898
Latter Anglo-Ital Frontier

FERNANDO PO
Sp.

GERMAN KAMERUN

Fr. and Ger. Agree

Gulf of Guinea

CORISCO BAY
Rio Muni, Sp.

Fr-Congo Agree 1887

L. Albert Nyanza

Anglo-Ger. Tr. 1890

L. Victoria Nyanza

ANNOBAN
Sp.

COLONY OF FRENCH CONGO

Congo

CONGO FREE STATE

Under Sovereignty of Leopold II of Belgium after 1885

Ujiji

Stanley I 1871–72

Burton-Speke 1856

PEMBA

ZANZIBAR
British Pro. 1890

Brazzaville

Leopoldville

CABINDA
Port.

Boma

Luanda

PORTUGUESE

L. Mweru

L. Tanganyika

GERMAN EAST AFRICA
Leased from Zanzibar 1888
Purchased 1890

INDIAN OCEAN

SOUTH ATLANTIC OCEAN

Benguela

WEST

ANGOLA

AFRICA

L. Bangweolu

L. Nyassa

EAST

AFRICA

Mozambique

Mossamedes

BRITISH CENTRAL AFRICA PROTECTORATE
1891

Victoria Falls

Zambezi

Livingstone

Quelimane

Cape Frio

BRITISH SOUTH AFRICA CO.
Chartered, 1889
Conquered Matabeleland, 1893

PORT.

Mozambique Channel

MADAGASCAR
French Protectorate Confirmed 1895

Tamatave

Antananarive

GERMAN

SOUTHWEST

AFRICA

"Southern Limit of Arms and Spiritous Liquors Zone"

WALFISH BAY
Br. 1878

BECHUANALAND PROTECTORATE
1885

SOUTH AFRICAN REP. (TRANSVAAL)
Pretoria

Lourenco Marques

Limpopo

Luderitz Bay
(Angra Pequena)

Orange

BECHUANALAND
British Colony 1885

Johannesburg

Vaal

ORANGE FREE STATE

Bloemfontein

SWAZILAND

COLONY OF NATAL

Durban

BASUTOLAND

CAPE COLONY

Capetown
Br. 1806

Cape of Good Hope

N

600 Miles

800 Kilometers

Copyright by Rand McNally & Co.
Lambert Azimuthal, Equal Area Projection

CONTROL OF TERRITORY

Great Britain 1885	Germany 1885
Great Britain 1898	Germany 1898
France 1885	Spain 1885
France 1898	Spain 1898
Turkey	Portugal 1885
Congo Free State 1885	Portugal 1898
Congo Free State (Belgium) 1898	Italy

RAND McNALLY

A37

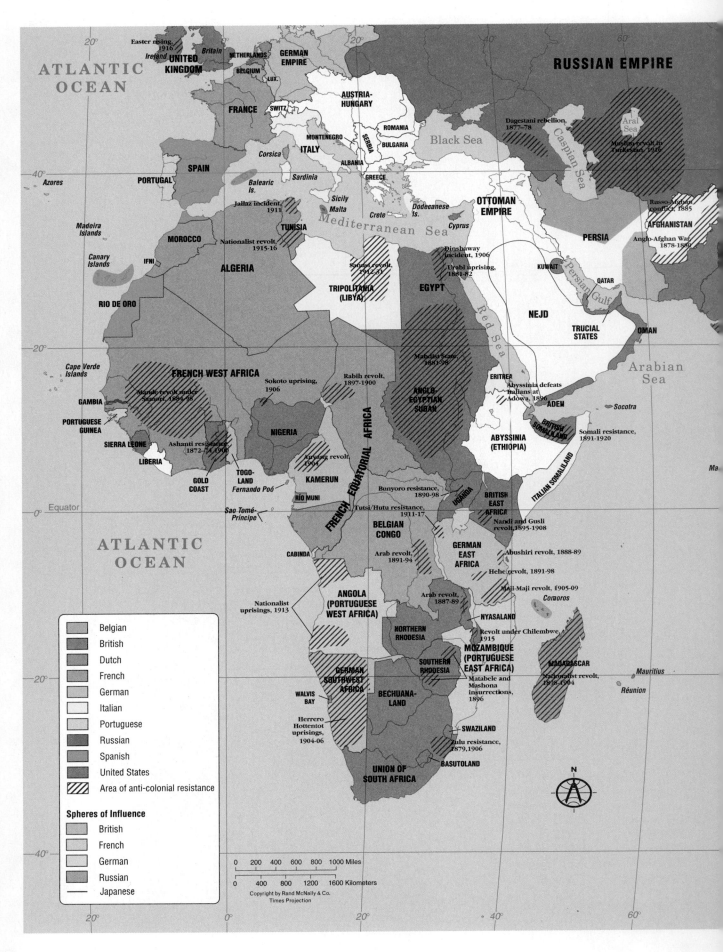

ATLANTIC OCEAN

RUSSIAN EMPIRE

Easter rising, 1916
Ireland Britain
UNITED KINGDOM
NETHERLANDS
GERMAN EMPIRE
BELGIUM
LUX.
FRANCE
SWITZ.
AUSTRIA-HUNGARY
ROMANIA
MONTENEGRO
SERBIA
BULGARIA
ITALY
ALBANIA
Corsica
GREECE
Black Sea
Dagestani rebellion, 1877-78
Aral Sea
Muslim revolt in Turkestan, 1916
Caspian Sea

SPAIN
PORTUGAL
Azores
Balearic Is.
Sardinia
Sicily
Malta
Crete
Dodecanese Is.
Cyprus
Mediterranean Sea
OTTOMAN EMPIRE
PERSIA
Russo-Afghan conflict, 1885
AFGHANISTAN
Anglo-Afghan War 1878-1880

Madeira Islands
Jallaz incident, 1911
TUNISIA
Nationalist revolt, 1915-16
MOROCCO
Canary Islands
IFNI
ALGERIA
RIO DE ORO
TRIPOLITANIA (LIBYA)
Sanusi revolt, 1912-31
EGYPT
Dinshaway incident, 1906
Urabi uprising, 1881-82
KUWAIT
NEJD
QATAR
TRUCIAL STATES
OMAN
Persian Gulf

Cape Verde Islands
FRENCH WEST AFRICA
Mande revolt under Samori, 1894-98
GAMBIA
PORTUGUESE GUINEA
SIERRA LEONE
LIBERIA
Sokoto uprising, 1906
Rabih revolt, 1897-1900
Mandist State, 1881-98
ANGLO-EGYPTIAN SUDAN
Red Sea
ERITREA
Abyssinia defeats Italians at Adowa, 1896
ADEN
BRITISH SOMALILAND
Somali resistance, 1891-1920
Arabian Sea
Socotra

Ashanti resistance 1872-74, 1900
GOLD COAST
NIGERIA
Anyang revolt, 1904
TOGOLAND
Fernando Poó
KAMERUN
RIO MUNI
São Tomé-Príncipe
FRENCH EQUATORIAL AFRICA
Bunyoro resistance, 1890-98
UGANDA
BRITISH EAST AFRICA
Nandi and Gusii revolt, 1895-1908
ABYSSINIA (ETHIOPIA)
ITALIAN SOMALILAND

Equator

ATLANTIC OCEAN

CABINDA
Tutsi/Hutu resistance, 1911-17
BELGIAN CONGO
Arab revolt, 1891-94
GERMAN EAST AFRICA
Abushiri revolt, 1888-89
Hehe revolt, 1891-98
Maji-Maji revolt, 1905-09
Comoros

Nationalist uprisings, 1913
ANGOLA (PORTUGUESE WEST AFRICA)
Arab revolt, 1887-89
NORTHERN RHODESIA
NYASALAND
Revolt under Chilembwe, 1915
MOZAMBIQUE (PORTUGUESE EAST AFRICA)
MADAGASCAR
Nationalist revolt, 1898-1904
Mauritius
Réunion

GERMAN SOUTHWEST AFRICA
SOUTHERN RHODESIA
Matabele and Mashona insurrections, 1896
WALVIS BAY
BECHUANALAND
Herrero Hottentot uprisings, 1904-06
SWAZILAND
Zulu resistance, 1879, 1906
BASUTOLAND
UNION OF SOUTH AFRICA

Legend

- Belgian
- British
- Dutch
- French
- German
- Italian
- Portuguese
- Russian
- Spanish
- United States
- Area of anti-colonial resistance

Spheres of Influence
- British
- French
- German
- Russian
- Japanese

0 200 400 600 800 1000 Miles
0 400 800 1200 1600 Kilometers
Copyright by Rand McNally & Co.
Times Projection

N

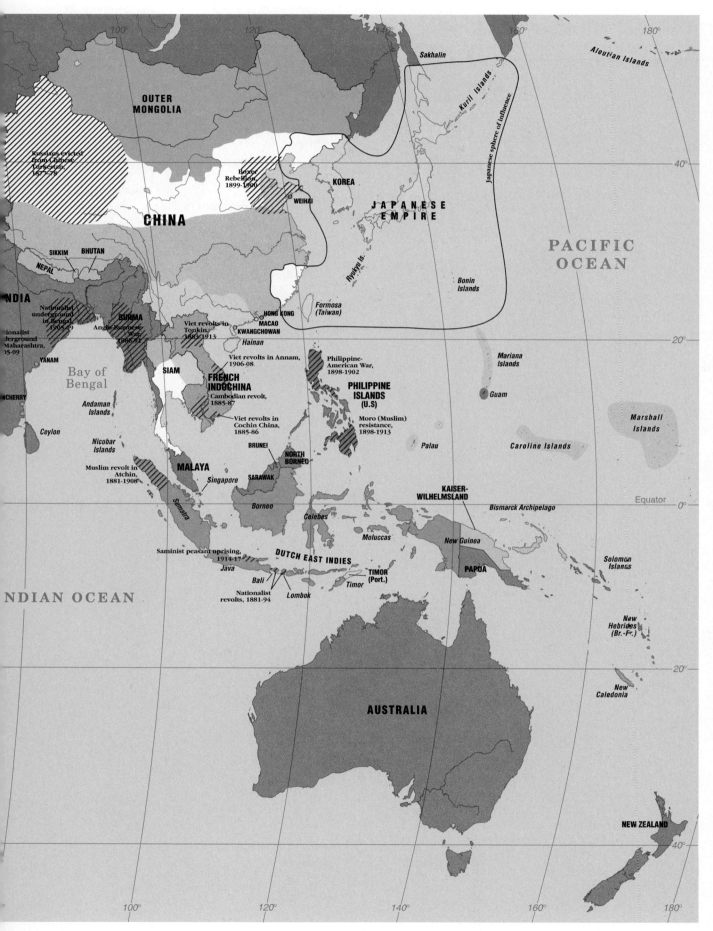

OUTER
MONGOLIA

*Russians evicted
from Chinese
Turkestan,
1877-78*

Boxer
Rebellion
1899-1900

KOREA

WEIHAI

CHINA

JAPANESE
EMPIRE

Sakhalin

Kuril Islands

Japanese sphere of influence

Aleutian Islands

PACIFIC
OCEAN

SIKKIM   BHUTAN

NEPAL

NDIA

*Nationalist
underground
in Bengal,
1905-09*

*tionalist
derground
Maharashtra,
05-09*

BURMA
*Anglo-Burmese
War,
1886-92*

*Viet revolts in
Tonkin,
1885-1913*

HONG KONG
MACAO
KWANGCHOWAN

Hainan

*Viet revolts in Annam,
1906-08*

Ryukyu Is.

Formosa
(Taiwan)

Bonin
Islands

YANAM

CHERRY

Bay of
Bengal

Andaman
Islands

Ceylon

Nicobar
Islands

SIAM

FRENCH
INDOCHINA

*Cambodian revolt,
1885-87*

*Viet revolts in
Cochin China,
1885-86*

Philippine-
American War,
1898-1902

PHILIPPINE
ISLANDS
(U.S)

Mariana
Islands

Guam

Marshall
Islands

*Muslim revolt in
Atchin,
1881-1908*

MALAYA

Singapore

BRUNEI

NORTH
BORNEO

SARAWAK

Moro (Muslim)
resistance,
1898-1913

Palau

Caroline Islands

Sumatra

Borneo

Celebes

Moluccas

KAISER-
WILHELMSLAND

New Guinea

Bismarck Archipelago

Equator

Solomon
Islands

*Saminist peasant uprising,
1914-17*

Java

DUTCH EAST INDIES

Bali

*Nationalist
revolts, 1881-94*

Lombok

TIMOR
(Port.)

Timor

PAPUA

New
Hebrides
(Br.-Fr.)

NDIAN OCEAN

New
Caledonia

AUSTRALIA

NEW ZEALAND

A39

MEDITERRANEAN SEA

Copyright by Rand McNally & Co.
Lambert Conformal Conic Projection

Ⓐ Golan Heights. Occupied and unilaterally annexed by Israel.

Ⓑ West Bank. Controlled by Israel, parts administered by the Palestinian Authority. Permanent status to be determined.

Ⓒ Gaza Strip. Administered by the Palestinian Authority following unilateral withdrawal by Israel in 2005. Permanent status to be determined.

LEBANON

Beirut

Sidon

Tyre   Litani

Golan Heights

Acre
Haifa   Sea of Galilee
    Tiberia
Nazaret   Irbid

Hader   Janin
Netanya   Nabulus

Tel Aviv-Yafo   West Bank   As Salt
    Ⓑ
Rehovot   Amman
Ashdod   Jericho
Ashqelon   Jerusalem
    Bethlehem
Gaza   Hebron
Gaza Strip Ⓒ   Dead Sea
Khan Yunus
Beersheba   Al Karak

Port Said
Pelusium Bay
Suez Canal   El Arish   Dimona
El Qantara el-Sharqiya   At Tafilah

ISRAEL   JORDAN

Ismailia   Negev Desert

Great Bitter Lake

EGYPT   Ma'an

Suez

Sinai Peninsula   Elat   Aqaba
    Gulf of Aqaba

Gulf of Suez

KAZAKHSTAN
UZBEKISTAN

TURKMENISTAN   Amu Darya

Ashgabat

Mashhad

Tehrān

IRAN   AFGHAN.

Birjand
Esfahan   Yazd
    Daryacheh-ye Hamun
Kermān
Shīrāz   Zāhedān

Bandar-e Būshehr
Bandar-e 'Abbas

Persian Gulf   Strait of Hormuz
BAHRAIN   OMAN
Manama
QATAR
Doha   Dubai   Gulf of Oman
Abu Dhabi   Muscat

UNITED ARAB EMIRATES   Tropic of Cancer   Sūr

OMAN

ARABIAN SEA

Socotra (Yem.)

INDIAN OCEAN

0   100   200   300   400 Miles
0   200   400   600 Kilometers
Copyright by Rand McNally & Co.
Lambert Conformal Conic Projection

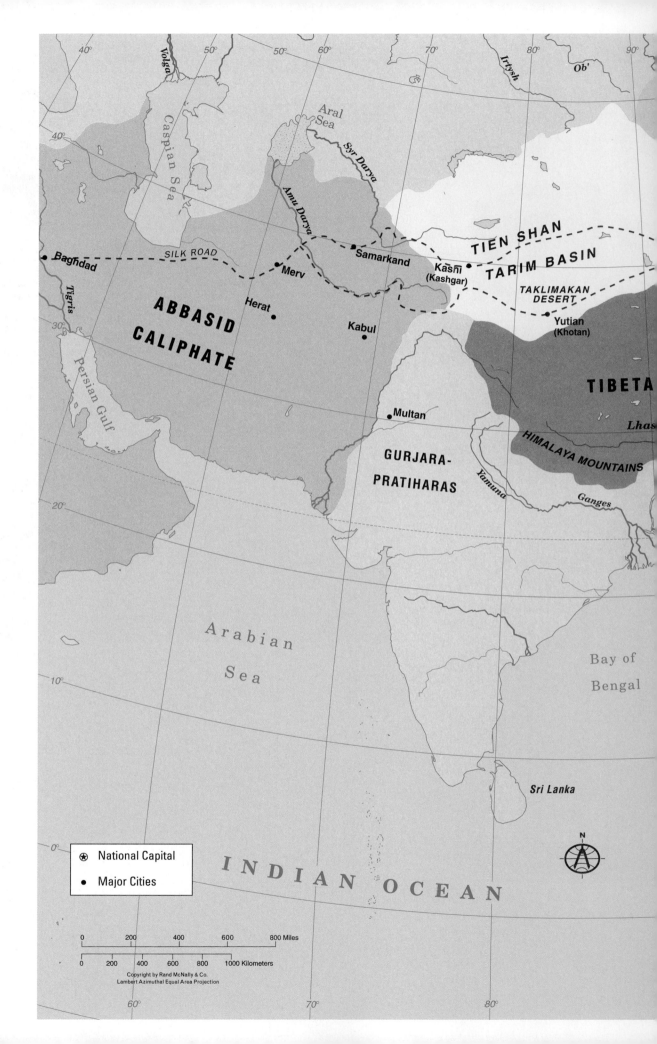

RAND M^cNALLY

A42

40° 50° 50° 60° 70° 80° 90°

Volga *Irtysh* *Ob'*

Aral Sea

Caspian Sea 40°

Syr Darya

Amu Darya

SILK ROAD

TIEN SHAN

Baghdad Samarkand TARIM BASIN

Merv Kashi (Kashgar)

Herat TAKLIMAKAN DESERT 30°

Tigris Kabul Yutian (Khotan)

ABBASID CALIPHATE

TIBETA

Persian Gulf Lhas

Multan HIMALAYA MOUNTAINS

GURJARA- PRATIHARAS *Yamuna*

Ganges 20°

Arabian

Sea Bay of

Bengal 10°

Sri Lanka

0°

⊛ National Capital N

● Major Cities I N D I A N O C E A N

0 200 400 600 800 Miles

0 200 400 600 800 1000 Kilometers

Copyright by Rand McNally & Co.
Lambert Azimuthal Equal Area Projection

60° 70° 80°

100°   110°   50°   120°   130°   140°   40°

UIGHUR EMPIRE

GOBI DESERT

GREAT WALL

PARHAE

Sea of Japan

SILLA

Heian-kyo (Kyoto)

Nara

JAPAN

30°

Dunhuang

Yellow Sea

SILK ROAD

Huang (Yellow)

Grand Canal

Yangzhou

Luoyang

Chang-an (Xi'an)

Hangzhou

East China Sea

PACIFIC OCEAN

Chang (Yangtze)

T'ANG EMPIRE (CHINA)

Taiwan

20°

...MPIRE

...ahmaputra

NAN-CHAO

Xi (West)

Guangzhou (Canton)

Philippine Islands

Mekong

CHAMPA

CHEN-LA

South China Sea

10°

SRIVIJAYA

Borneo

Celebes

Sumatra

Srivijaya (Palembang)

10°

Java

100°   110°   120°

AUSTRIA-
HUNGARY

MONT.
SERB.
ROMANIA
BULGARIA

GREECE

OTTOMAN EMPIRE

Constantinople

Black Sea

Cyprus
(Br.)

Mediterranean
Sea

Suez Canal
Cairo
Jerusalem

EGYPT

Euphrates
Tigris
Baghdad

Red Sea

Mecca

ARABIA

KUWAIT

BAHRAIN

QATAR
TRUCIAL OMAN

Persian Gulf

OMAN

ERITREA

FR. SOM.

Aden
(Br.)

HADRAMAUT

ABYSSINIA

BRITISH
SOMALILAND

ITALIAN SOMALILAND

Moscow

Dnieper

Volga

Samara

Caspian
Sea

Aral
Sea

Lake
Balkhash

Omsk

Irtysh

RUSSIAN

TURKESTAN

Bukhara
Samarkand
Tashkent

TIEN SHAN

TARIM BA

TAKLIMAKAN
DESERT

PERSIA

Tehran

Kabul

AFGHANISTAN

KASHMIR

PUNJAB

BALUCHISTAN

Indus
Delhi

SIND
RAJPUTANA

Yamuna

HIMALAYA M
NEPAL

Gang

BEN

BRITISH

ORISS

Bombay

HYDERABAD

Hyderabad

Goa
(Port.)

MYSORE

MADRAS

Madras

Ceylon

Colombo

Arabian

Sea

INDIAN OCEAN

N

	British
	French
	Dutch
	Italian
	Portuguese
	United States

0   200   400   600   800 Miles

0   200 400 600 800 1000 Kilometers

Copyright by Rand McNally & Co.
Lambert Azimuthal Equal Area Projection

EMPIRE

Lena

60°

Angara

Lake
Baikal

• Chita

Irkutsk

MANCHURIA

Amur

Sakhalin

Vladivostok

Hokkaido

Sea of
Japan

Honshu

40°

MONGOLIA

INNER MONGOLIA

GOBI DESERT

Beijing ⊛

Tianjin •

Huang (Yellow)

KOREA

Lushun
(Rus.)

Weihai
(Br.)

Qingdao
(Ger.)

Seoul ⊛

JAPANESE
EMPIRE

Tokyo ⊛

Shikoku

Kyushu

30°

CHINESE EMPIRE

Shanghai

Wuhan •

Hangzhou

Chongqing •

Chang (Yangtze)

Ryukyu Islands
(Japan)

PACIFIC

OCEAN

BET

ahmaputra

Fuzhou

20°

Taiwan
(Japan)

Xi (West)

Canton
(Guangzhou)

BHUTAN

ASSAM

Hong Kong
(Br.)

Macao
(Port.)

Luzon

PHILIPPINE

Calcutta

NDIA

BURMA

Kwangchowan
(Fr.)

ANNAM

South
China
Sea

Manila •

ISLANDS

(U.S.)

10°

Rangoon •

SIAM

Mekong

FRENCH
INDOCHINA

Mindanao

ay of
engal

Bangkok ⊛

Saigon ⊛

Andaman
Islands
(Br.)

BRITISH
NORTH
BORNEO

BRUNEI

Nicobar
Islands
(Br.)

SARAWAK

Moluccas

MALAYA

• Singapore

Borneo

Celebes

Sumatra

TIMOR
(Port.)

DUTCH EAST INDIES

10°

Batavia ⊛

Java

ARCTIC OCEAN

UNITED STATES

Bering Strait

Saint Lawrence Island

BERING SEA

EAST SIBERIAN SEA

Wrangell Island

New Siberian Islands

Novaya Sibir Island

Kotelny Island

Anadyr'

naya mlya

LAPTEV SEA

Arctic Circle

Srednekolymsk

Indigirka

Kolyma

Komandorskiye Islands

Tiksi

Seymchan

Ust'-Kamchatsk

Verkhoyansk

Kamchatka Peninsula

Petropavlovsk-Kamchatskiy

Zhigansk

Magadan

Lena

Vilyuysk

Yakutsk

SEA OF OKHOTSK

Tura

Lower Tunguska

Olëkminsk

Okha

R U S S I A

Aldan

Angara

Bodaybo

Sakhalin

Kuril Islands

Ust'-Kut

Nikolayevsk-na-Amure

Bratsk

Zeya

Komsomol'sk-na-Amure

Amur

Yuzhno-Sakhalinsk

ur

Svobodnyy

Cheremkhovo

Lake Baikal

Chita

Blagoveshchensk

Khabarovsk

La Perouse Strait

Angarsk

Irkutsk

Ulan-Ude

Birobidzhan

Hokkaidō

JAPAN

PACIFIC OCEAN

Ulan Bator

Harbin

Vladivostok

Nakhodka

MONGOLIA

N

Shenyang

NORTH KOREA

P'yongyang

SEA OF JAPAN

	National Capital
■	City over 1,000,000 population
▣	City of 250,000 to 1,000,000 population
•	City under 250,000 population

0   100   200   300   400   500 Miles

0   200   400   600   800 Kilometers

Copyright by Rand McNally & Co.
Lambert Azimuthal Equal Area Projection

RAND McNALLY

A47

Strategies for Taking Standardized Tests

This section of the textbook helps you develop and practice the skills you need to study history and to take standardized tests. Part 1, **Strategies for Studying History,** takes you through the features of the textbook and offers suggestions on how to use these features to improve your reading and study skills.

Part 2, **Test-Taking Strategies and Practice,** offers specific strategies for tackling many of the items you will find on a standardized test. It gives tips for answering multiple-choice, constructed-response, extended-response, and document-based questions. In addition, it offers guidelines for analyzing primary and secondary sources, maps, political cartoons, charts, graphs, and time lines. Each strategy is followed by a set of questions you can use for practice.

CONTENTS

Part 1: Strategies for Studying History

Reading is the central skill in the effective study of history or any other subject. You can improve your reading skills by using helpful techniques and by practicing. The better your reading skills, the more you will remember what you read. Below you will find several strategies that involve built-in features of *Modern World History: Patterns of Interaction.* Careful use of these strategies will

Preview Chapters Before You Read

Each chapter begins with a two-page chapter opener and a one-page Interact with History feature. Study these materials to help you get ready to read.

1 Read the chapter title for clues to what will be covered in the chapter.

2 Study the **Previewing Main Ideas** feature and the map. Gain more background information on chapter content by answering the questions in the feature.

3 Preview the time line and note the years covered in the chapter. Consider the important events that took place during this time period.

4 Read the **Interact with History** feature (see page S3). Study **Examining the Issues** to gain insight on a major theme addressed in the chapter.

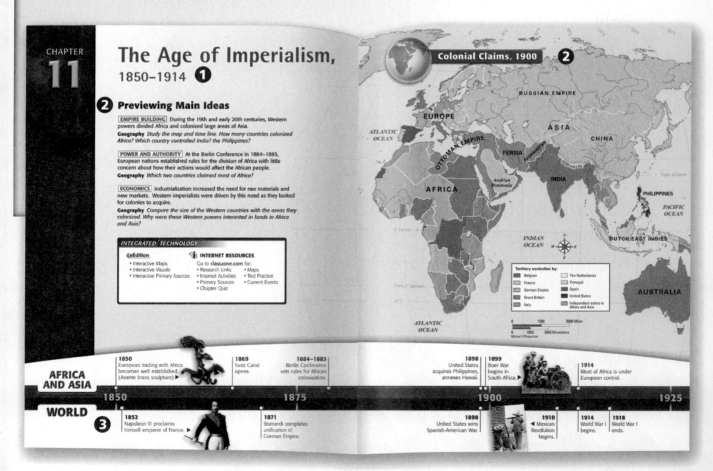

CHAPTER
11

The Age of Imperialism,
1850–1914 **1**

2 **Previewing Main Ideas**

EMPIRE BUILDING During the 19th and early 20th centuries, Western powers divided Africa and colonized large areas of Asia.
Geography *Study the map and time line. How many countries colonized Africa? Which country controlled India? The Philippines?*

POWER AND AUTHORITY At the Berlin Conference in 1884–1885, European nations established rules for the division of Africa with little concern how their actions would affect the African people.
Geography *Which two countries claimed most of Africa?*

ECONOMICS Industrialization increased the need for raw materials and new markets. Western imperialists were driven by this need as they looked for colonies to acquire.
Geography *Compare the size of the Western countries with the areas they colonized. Why were these Western powers interested in lands in Africa and Asia?*

INTEGRATED TECHNOLOGY

eEdition
• Interactive Maps
• Interactive Visuals
• Interactive Primary Sources

INTERNET RESOURCES
Go to **classzone.com** for:
• Research Links   • Maps
• Internet Activities   • Test Practice
• Primary Sources   • Current Events
• Chapter Quiz

2 Colonial Claims, 1900

RUSSIAN EMPIRE
EUROPE
ASIA
ATLANTIC OCEAN
OTTOMAN EMPIRE
PERSIA
AFGHANISTAN
CHINA
Arabian Peninsula
INDIA
AFRICA
PHILIPPINES
PACIFIC OCEAN
INDIAN OCEAN
DUTCH EAST INDIES
ATLANTIC OCEAN
AUSTRALIA

Territory controlled by:
■ Belgium   □ The Netherlands
■ France   □ Portugal
■ German Empire   ■ Spain
■ Great Britain   ■ United States
■ Italy   □ Independent states in Africa and Asia

0   1000   2000 Miles
0   1000   2000 Kilometers

AFRICA AND ASIA

1850
European trading with Africa becomes well established. (Asante brass sculpture) ▶

1869
Suez Canal opens.

1884–1885
Berlin Conference sets rules for African colonization.

1898
United States acquires Philippines, annexes Hawaii.

1899
Boer War begins in South Africa. ▶

1914
Most of Africa is under European control.

1850   1875   1900   1925

WORLD **3**

1852
Napoleon III proclaims himself emperor of France. ▶

1871
Bismarck completes unification of German Empire.

1898
United States wins Spanish-American War.

1910
◀ Mexican Revolution begins.

1914
World War I begins.

1918
World War I ends.

Preview Sections Before You Read

Each chapter consists of three, four, or five sections. These sections focus on shorter periods of time or on particular historical themes. Use the section openers to help you prepare to read.

5 Study the information under the headings **Main Idea** and **Why It Matters Now**. These features tell you what is important in the material you are about to read.

6 Preview the **Terms & Names** list. This will give you an idea of the issues and people you will read about in the section.

7 Read the paragraph under the heading **Setting the Stage**. This links the content of the section to previous sections or chapters.

8 Notice the structure of the section. **Red** heads label the major topics; **black** subheads signal smaller topics within major topics. Together, these heads provide you with a quick outline of the section.

TERMS & NAMES

- paternalism
- assimilation
- Menelik II

Interact with History

How would you react to the colonizers?

You are a young South African living in the 1880s. Gold and diamonds have recently been discovered in your country. The European colonizers need laborers to work in the mines, such as the one shown below in an 1888 photograph. Along with thousands of other South Africans, you've left your farm and rural village to work for the colonizers. Separated from your family and living in a city for the first time, you don't know what to expect.

Many Africans, such as these in a South African gold mine, left their farms and families behind to work in the mining centers. As a result, new towns developed and existing ones greatly expanded.

The migrant labor system that developed as a result of the mines would have a great impact on South African society and culture.

The European owners built railways and roads to connect the mining centers, bridging the huge distances between villages and towns in South Africa.

EXAMINING *the* ISSUES

- What advantages and disadvantages might colonizers bring?
- What does the photograph suggest about colonization?

Discuss these questions with your classmates. In your discussion, remember what you have already learned about conquests and cultural interaction. As you read about imperialism in this chapter, look for its effects on both the colonizers and the colonized.

2

Imperialism
Case Study: Nigeria

5 | **MAIN IDEA** | **WHY IT MATTERS NOW** | **TERMS & NAMES** | **6**

POWER AND AUTHORITY
Europeans embarked on a new phase of empire building that affected both Africa and the rest of the world.

Many former colonies have political problems that are the result of colonial rule.

- paternalism
- assimilation
- Menelik II

7 SETTING THE STAGE The Berlin Conference of 1884–85 was a European conference. And, although black South Africans participated in it, the Boer War was largely a European war. Europeans argued and fought among themselves over the lands of Africa. In carving up the continent, the European countries paid little or no attention to historical political divisions or to the many ethnic and language groupings in Africa. Uppermost in the minds of the Europeans was the ability to control Africa's land, its people, and its resources.

8 A New Period of Imperialism

The imperialism of the 18th and 19th centuries was conducted differently from the explorations of the 15th and 16th centuries. In the earlier period, imperial powers often did not penetrate far into the conquered areas in Asia and Africa. Nor did they always have a substantial influence on the lives of the people. During this new period of imperialism, the Europeans demanded more influence over the economic, political, and social lives of the people. They were determined to shape the economies of the lands to benefit European economies. They also wanted the people to adopt European customs.

Forms of Control Each European nation had certain policies and goals for establishing colonies. To establish control of an area, Europeans used different techniques. Over time, four forms of colonial control emerged: colony, protectorate, sphere of influence, and economic imperialism. These terms are defined and discussed in the chart on page 780. In practice, gaining control of an area might involve the use of several of these forms.

Methods of Management European rulers also developed methods of day-to-day management of the colony. Two basic methods emerged. Britain and other nations—such as the United States in its Pacific Island colonies—preferred indirect control. France and most other European nations wielded a more direct control. Later, when colonies gained independence, the management method used had an influence on the type of government chosen in the new nation.

Indirect Control Indirect control relied on existing political rulers. In some areas, the British asked a local ruler to accept British authority to rule. These local officials handled much of the daily management of the colony. In addition,

TAKING NOTES
Summarizing Use a web to record the forms and methods of European imperialism in Africa, the resistance it met with, and its impact.

Forms and methods

Imperialism in Africa

resistance   impact

Discuss these questions with your classmates. In your discussion, remember what you have already learned about conquests and cultural interaction. As you read about imperialism in this chapter, look for its effects on both the colonizers and the colonized.

Use Active Reading Strategies As You Read

Now you are ready to read the chapter. Read one section at a time, from beginning to end.

1 Ask and answer questions as you read. Look for the **Main Idea** questions in the margin. Answering these questions will show whether you understand what you have just read.

2 Try to visualize the people, places, and events you read about. Studying the pictures, maps, and other illustrations will help you do this.

3 Read to build your vocabulary. Use the marginal **Vocabulary** notes to find the meaning of unfamiliar words.

4 Look for the story behind the events. Study the boxed features for additional information and interesting sidelights on the section content.

MAIN IDEA

Summarizing

A On which continents were Indian goods being traded?

British Transport Trade Goods India became increasingly valuable to the British after they established a railroad network there. Railroads transported raw products from the interior to the ports and manufactured goods back again. Most of the raw materials were agricultural products produced on plantations. Plantation crops included tea, indigo, coffee, cotton, and jute. Another crop was opium. The British shipped opium to China and exchanged it for tea, which they then sold in England.

Trade in these crops was closely tied to international events. For example, the Crimean War in the 1850s cut off the supply of Russian jute to Scottish jute mills. This boosted the export of raw jute from Bengal, a province in India. Likewise, cotton production in India increased when the Civil War in the United States cut off supplies of cotton for British textile mills. **A**

Impact of Colonialism India both benefited from and was harmed by British colonialism. On the negative side, the British held much of the political and economic power. The British restricted Indian-owned industries such as cotton textiles. The emphasis on cash crops resulted in a loss of self-sufficiency for many villagers. The conversion to cash crops reduced food production, causing famines in the late 1800s. The British officially adopted a hands-off policy regarding Indian religious and social customs. Even so, the increased presence of missionaries and the racist attitude of most British officials threatened traditional Indian life.

On the positive side, the laying of the world's third largest railroad network was a major British achievement. When completed, the railroads enabled India to develop a modern economy and brought unity to the connected regions. Along with the railroads, a modern road network, telephone and telegraph lines, dams, bridges, and irrigation canals enabled India to modernize. Sanitation and public health improved. Schools and colleges were founded, and literacy increased. Also, British troops cleared central India of bandits and put an end to local warfare among competing local rulers.

3 **Vocabulary**
jute: a fiber used for sacks and cord

1 **MAIN IDEA**
Summarizing
A On which continents were Indian goods traded?

Western-Held Territories in Asia, 1910 **2**

Legend:
- France
- Germany
- Great Britain
- The Netherlands
- United States

GEOGRAPHY SKILLBUILDER: Interpreting Maps
1. **Region** Which nation in 1910 held the most land in colonies?
2. **Location** How is the location of India a great advantage for trade?

---

4 **Social History**

Social Class in India

In the photograph at right, a British officer is waited on by Indian servants. This reflects the class system in India.

British Army
Social class determined the way of life for the British Army in India. Upper-class men served as officers. Lower-class British served at lesser rank and did not advance past the rank of sergeant. Only men with the rank of sergeant and above were allowed to bring their wives to India.

Each English officer's wife attempted to re-create England in the home setting. Like a general, she directed an army of 20 to 30 servants.

Indian Servants
Caste determined Indian occupations. Castes were divided into four broad categories called varna. Indian civil servants were of the third varna. House and personal servants were of the fourth varna.

Even within the varna, jobs were strictly regulated, which is why such large servant staffs were required. For example, in the picture here, both servants were of the same varna. However, the person washing the British officer's feet was of a different caste than the person doing the fanning.

 2

The Sepoy Mutiny

By 1850, the British controlled most of the Indian subcontinent. However, there were many pockets of discontent. Many Indians believed that in addition to controlling their land, the British were trying to convert them to Christianity. The Indian people also resented the constant racism that the British expressed toward them.

Indians Rebel As economic problems increased for Indians, so did their feelings of resentment and nationalism. In 1857, gossip spread among the sepoys, the Indian soldiers, that the cartridges of their new Enfield rifles were greased with beef and pork fat. To use the cartridges, soldiers had to bite off the ends. Both Hindus, who consider the cow sacred, and Muslims, who do not eat pork, were outraged by the news.

A garrison commander was shocked when 85 of the 90 sepoys refused to accept the cartridges. The British handled the crisis badly. The soldiers who had disobeyed were jailed. The next day, on May 10, 1857, the sepoys rebelled. They marched to Delhi, where they were joined by Indian soldiers stationed there. They captured the city of Delhi. From Delhi, the rebellion spread to northern and central India.

Some historians have called this outbreak the **Sepoy Mutiny**. The uprising spread over much of northern India. Fierce fighting took place. Both British and sepoys tried to slaughter each other's armies. The East India Company took more than a year to regain control of the country. The British government sent troops to help them. **B**

The Indians could not unite against the British due to weak leadership and serious splits between Hindus and Muslims. Hindus did not want the Muslim Mughal Empire restored. Indeed, many Hindus preferred British rule to Muslim rule. Most of the princes and maharajahs who had made alliances with the East India

MAIN IDEA
Recognizing Effects
B Look back at Elphinstone's comment on page 791. Did the Sepoy Mutiny prove him correct?

Review and Summarize What You Have Read

When you finish reading a section, review and summarize what you have read. If necessary, go back and reread information that was not clear the first time through.

❺ Reread the red heads and black subheads for a quick summary of the major points covered in the section

❻ Study any charts, graphs, or maps in the section. These visual materials usually provide a condensed version of information in the section.

❼ Review the visuals—photographs, charts, graphs, maps, and time lines—and any illustrated boxed features and note how they relate to the section content.

❽ Complete all the questions in the **Section Assessment.** This will help you think critically about what you have just read.

British Take the Malayan Peninsula To compete with the Dutch, the British sought a trading base that would serve as a stop for their ships that traveled the India-China sea routes. They found a large, sheltered harbor on Singapore, an island just off the tip of the Malay Peninsula. The opening of the Suez Canal and the increased demand for tin and rubber combined to make Singapore one of the world's busiest ports.

Britain also gained colonies in Malaysia and in Burma (modern Myanmar). Malaysia had large deposits of tin and became the world's leading rubber exporter. Needing workers to mine the tin and tap the rubber trees, Britain encouraged Chinese to immigrate to Malaysia. Chinese flocked to the area. As a result of such immigration, the Malays soon became a minority in their own country. Conflict between the resident Chinese and the native Malays remains unresolved today. **Ⓐ**

MAIN IDEA
Analyzing Motives
Ⓐ Why do you think so many Chinese moved to Malaysia?

French Control Indochina The French had been active in Southeast Asia since the 17th century. They even helped the Nguyen (nuh•WIN) dynasty rise to power in Vietnam. In the 1840s, during the rule of an anti-Christian Vietnamese emperor, seven French missionaries were killed. Church leaders and capitalists who wanted a larger share of the overseas market demanded military intervention. Emperor Napoleon III ordered the French army to invade southern Vietnam. Later, the French added Laos, Cambodia, and northern Vietnam to the territory. The combined states would eventually be called French Indochina.

Using direct colonial management, the French themselves filled all important positions in the government bureaucracy. They did not encourage local industry. Four times as much land was devoted to rice production. However, the peasants' consumption of rice decreased because much of the rice was exported. Anger over this reduction set the stage for Vietnamese resistance against the French.

Colonial Impact In Southeast Asia, colonization brought mixed results. Economies grew based on cash crops or goods that could be sold on the world market. Roads, harbors, and rail systems improved communication and transportation but mostly benefited European business. However, education, health, and sanitation did improve.

Unlike other colonial areas, millions of people from other areas of Asia and the world migrated to work on plantations and in the mines in Southeast Asia. The region became a melting pot of Hindus, Muslims, Christians, and Buddhists. The resulting cultural changes often led to racial and religious clashes that are still seen today.

❺ Siam Remains Independent

While its neighbors on all sides fell under the control of imperialists, Siam (present-day Thailand) maintained its independence throughout the colonial period. Siam lay between British-controlled Burma and French Indochina. (See map above.) France and Britain each aimed to prevent the other from gaining control of Siam. Knowing this, Siamese kings skillfully promoted Siam as a neutral zone between the two powers.

Colonies in Southeast Asia, 1895 **❻**

- British
- Dutch
- French
- Portuguese
- Spanish
- Independent state

GEOGRAPHY SKILLBUILDER: Interpreting Maps
1. **Location** What was Siam's location relative to the nearest European colonies?
2. **Region** Which European country could access both the Indian and the Pacific oceans from its colony?

Then in 1890, the McKinley Tariff Act passed by the U.S. government set off a crisis in the islands. The act eliminated the tariffs on all sugar entering the United States. Now, sugar from Hawaii was no longer cheaper than sugar produced elsewhere. That change cut into the sugar producers' profits. Some U.S. business leaders pushed for annexation of Hawaii, or the adding of the territory to the United States. Making Hawaii a part of the United States meant that Hawaiian sugar could be sold for greater profits because American producers got an extra two cents a pound from the U.S. government.

About the same time, the new Hawaiian ruler, Queen Liliuokalani (luh•LEE•uh•oh•kuh•LAH•nee), took the throne. In 1893, she called for a new constitution that would increase her power. It would also restore the political power of Hawaiians at the expense of wealthy planters. To prevent this from happening, a group of American businessmen hatched a plot to overthrow the Hawaiian monarchy. In 1893, Queen Liliuokalani was removed from power.

In 1894, Sanford B. Dole, a wealthy plantation owner and politician, was named president of the new Republic of Hawaii. The president of the new republic asked the United States to annex it. At first, President Cleveland refused. In 1898, however, the Republic of Hawaii was annexed by the United States.

The period of imperialism was a time of great power and domination of others by mostly European powers. As the 19th century closed, the lands of the world were all claimed. The European powers now faced each other with competing claims. Their battles would become the focus of the 20th century.

History Makers **❼**

Queen Liliuokalani
1838–1917
Liliuokalani was Hawaii's only queen and the last monarch of Hawaii. She bitterly regretted her brother's loss of power to American planters and worked to regain power for the Hawaiian monarchy. As queen, she refused to renew a treaty signed by her brother that would have given commercial privileges to foreign businessmen. It was a decision that would cost her the crown.

INTEGRATED TECHNOLOGY
RESEARCH LINKS For more on Queen Liliuokalani, go to classzone.com

---

SECTION ❺ ASSESSMENT **❽**

TERMS & NAMES 1. For each term or name, write a sentence explaining its significance.
- Pacific Rim
- King Mongkut
- Emilio Aguinaldo
- annexation
- Queen Liliuokalani

USING YOUR NOTES
2. Which Western power do you think had the most negative impact on its colonies?

Western powers in Southeast Asia

MAIN IDEAS
3. How were the Dutch East India Trading Company and the British East India Company similar?
4. What changes took place in Southeast Asia as a result of colonial control?
5. Why did some groups believe that the United States should colonize like the Europeans?

CRITICAL THINKING & WRITING
6. **DRAWING CONCLUSIONS** How did the reforms of the Siamese kings help Siam remain independent?
7. **ANALYZING BIAS** What does President McKinley's desire to "uplift and Christianize" the Filipinos suggest about his perception of the people?
8. **ANALYZING MOTIVES** Why do you think Sanford Dole wanted the United States to annex Hawaii?
9. **WRITING ACTIVITY** ECONOMICS Compose a letter to the editor expressing a Hawaiian's view on the U.S. businessmen who pushed for the annexation of Hawaii for economic gain.

CONNECT TO TODAY DRAWING A BAR GRAPH
Research to find out about the economic situation of Southeast Asian countries today. Rank the economies and present your findings in a **bar graph.**

Part 2: Test-Taking Strategies and Practice

You can improve your test-taking skills by practicing the strategies discussed in this section. First, read the tips on the left-hand page. Then apply them to the practice items on the right-hand page.

Multiple Choice

A multiple-choice question consists of a stem and a set of alternatives. The stem usually is in the form of a question or an incomplete sentence. One of the alternatives correctly answers the question or completes the sentence.

❶ Read the stem carefully and try to answer the question or complete the sentence before looking at the alternatives.

❷ Look for key words in the stem. They may direct you to the correct answer.

❸ Read each alternative with the stem. Don't make your final decision on the correct answer until you have read all of the alternatives.

❹ Eliminate alternatives that you know are wrong.

❺ Carefully consider questions that include *all of the above* as an alternative.

❻ Look for modifiers to help you rule out incorrect alternatives.

❼ Take great care with questions that are stated negatively.

stem

❶ 1. One (negative) impact of European colonialism in Africa was the

Negative is the key word here. All the alternatives ❷ deal with the effect of colonization on Africa, but only one describes a negative impact.

alternatives ❸

A. decrease in local warfare.

B. increase in life expectancy.

C. construction of communications systems across the continent.

D. division of the continent along artificial boundary lines.

2. What parts of Africa south of the Sahara were independent by 1913?

A. Algeria and Morocco

You can eliminate **A** if ❹ you remember that Algeria and Morocco are not located south of the Sahara.

B. Ethiopia and Liberia

C. Nigeria and Gambia

D. all of the above

If you select this answer, ❺ be sure that all the alternatives are correct.

3. African efforts to resist European imperialism

A. (often) failed.

B. were (always) successful.

C. (all) failed.

D. (never) occurred.

Absolute words like *all, always, never, only,* and *alone* frequently ❻ signal an incorrect answer. Qualifiers such as *often, some,* or *usually* are more likely correct.

4. All of the following are motives that drove Europeans to colonize Africa *except*

Eliminate incorrect ❼ alternatives by identifying those that *are* motives for European colonization.

A. economic competition.

B. racist attitudes.

C. the desire to spread Islam.

D. a sense of national pride.

answers: 1 (D); 2 (B); 3 (A); 4 (C)

Directions: Read each question carefully and choose the *best* answer from the four alternatives.

1. Which of the following is *not* a reason why the Renaissance began in Italy?

    A. Italy had several thriving cities.

    B. The Black Death did not strike Italy.

    C. Italian merchants gained in wealth and power.

    D. Italy could draw on its classical Roman heritage.

2. Reformation teachings were adopted by

    A. the Catholic Church.

    B. all the countries in Europe.

    C. some countries in Europe.

    D. common people, but not rulers.

3. Akbar differed from Aurangzeb in that he

    A. extended the boundaries of the Mughal Empire.

    B. followed Western ways.

    C. defended religious freedom.

    D. all of the above

4. During the 1700s, the Atlantic slave trade was dominated by the

    A. Dutch.

    B. English.

    C. Portuguese.

    D. Spanish.

Primary Sources

Primary sources are written or made by people who were at historical events, either as observers or participants. Primary sources include journals, diaries, letters, speeches, newspaper articles, autobiographies, wills, deeds, and financial records.

1 Look at the source line to learn about the document and its author. Consider the reliability of the information in the document.

2 Skim the document to get an idea of what it is about. (This source expresses Mao Zedong's economic and social goals for China under communism.)

3 Note any special punctuation. Ellipses, for example, indicate that words or sentences have been removed from the original text.

4 Use active reading strategies. For instance, ask and answer questions on the content as you read.

5 Use context clues to help you understand difficult or unfamiliar words. (From the context, you realize that *confiscate* means "take control of.")

6 Before rereading the document, skim the questions. This will help you focus your reading and more easily locate answers.

answers: 1 (A); 2 (B)

New Policies in China

We must establish in China a republic that is politically new-democratic as well as economically new-democratic.

Big banks and big industrial and commercial enterprises shall be owned by this republic. . . . **3**

The state-operated enterprises of the new-democratic republic are socialist in character and constitute the leading force in the national economy. . . . **2 4**

This republic will . . . confiscate the land of landlords and **5** distribute it to those peasants having no land or only a little land. . . .

China's economy . . . must never be "monopolist by a few"; we must never let . . . capitalists and landlords "dominate the livelihood of the people"; we must never establish a capitalist society of the European-American type, nor allow the old semi-feudal society to remain.

—Mao Zedong, *On New Democracy* (1940)

Mao Zedong was the leader of the Communists who began fighting to gain control of China's government in the late 1920s. **1**

1. Which part of the economy does Mao suggest is the most important?

A. State-run large enterprises

B. Retail stores

C. Farms

D. Small private businesses

6

2. Which sentence expresses the main idea shared by these paragraphs?

A. Private property will be respected.

B. China's government will make economic decisions.

C. China will follow the examples of Europe and the United States.

D. China's economy will depend on farming.

Directions: Use this passage, taken from the English Bill of Rights, and your knowledge of world history to answer questions 1 through 4.

A Declaration of English Rights

The . . . lords spiritual and temporal, and commons, . . . being now assembled in a full and free representative of this nation, . . . declare:

1. That the pretended power of suspending of laws, or the execution of laws, by regal authority, without consent of parliament, is illegal. . . .

4. That levying money for or to the use of the crown . . . , without grant of parliament, . . . is illegal.

5. That it is the right of the subjects to petition the King, and all commitments and prosecutions for such petitioning are illegal.

6. That the raising or keeping a standing army within the kingdom in time of peace, unless it be with consent of parliament, is against the law. . . .

9. That the freedom of speech, and debates or proceedings in parliament, ought not to be impeached or questioned in any court or place out of parliament.

10. That excessive bail ought not to be required, nor excessive fines imposed; nor cruel and unusual punishments inflicted.

—*Declaration of Rights,* 1689 (English Bill of Rights)

1. Article 4 of the Bill of Rights says that the King cannot

   A. raise and keep a standing army.

   B. impose a tax without Parliament's consent.

   C. spend money without Parliament's consent.

   D. prosecute a person for petitioning the crown.

2. The Declaration of Rights was aimed at limiting the power of the

   A. Parliament.

   B. nobles and clergy.

   C. rising middle class.

   D. King.

3. In the "Glorious Revolution," the English issued the Declaration of Rights and

   A. replaced James II with William and Mary.

   B. unseated James II and declared a republic.

   C. won their independence.

   D. approved the Constitution.

4. Which of the rights mentioned in this passage also appears in the United States Bill of Rights?

   A. freedom of religion

   B. right to bear arms

   C. right to a speedy trial

   D. limits on fines and punishments

Secondary Sources

Secondary sources are written or made by people who were not at the original events. They often combine information from several primary sources. The most common types of written secondary sources are biographies and history books.

1 Read the title to preview the content of the passage. (The title here signals that the passage is about a person named Malinche who seems to be controversial.)

2 Skim the passage to locate the main idea—the central point that is supported by other details.

3 Notice words and phrases that clarify the sequence of events.

4 Read actively by asking and answering questions about what you read. (You might ask yourself: "Why did opinions of Malinche change over time?")

5 Before rereading the passage, review the questions to identify the information you need to find.

1 **Malinche, Heroine or Traitor?**

The origins of the Native American woman Malinche are unknown. What is clear is that in 1519—when she was perhaps 15 years old—she was given with 19 other young women to Hernando Cortés, who had recently landed in Mexico. **2** Malinche greatly aided Cortés's conquest of the Aztecs. She spoke both Nahuatl—the language of the Aztecs—and Mayan. Over time, she also learned Spanish and became Cortés's chief translator. She also advised Cortés on the tricky politics of Mexico's Native American peoples.

The Spanish conquistadors reportedly admired and honored Malinche, calling her Doña Marina. And for many centuries, she **3** was seen as a praiseworthy figure. In the 1800s, though, people came to view her harshly. Writers and artists portrayed her as a traitor to her people. This criticism of Malinche began after Mexico won its independence from Spain, and reflected anti-Spanish feeling. Today, however, she is once again seen favorably. **4**

1. Which of the following statements about Malinche is a fact?

A. She spoke three languages.

B. She was a traitor.

C. She was a heroine.

D. She hated the Spanish.

> Remember that a fact is a verifiable statement. An opinion is a statement of someone's belief about something.

2. Based on this account, which person or group would be most likely to view Malinche as a traitor?

> These words signal that you have to make inferences from information in the passage.

A. Cortés and the conquistadors

B. a supporter of Mexican independence in the 1800s

C. one of the 19 other women who were with her in 1519

D. a historian writing about her today

answers: 1 (A); 2 (B)

Directions: Use the passage and your knowledge of world history to answer questions 1 through 4.

Entangling Alliances

[England's] Lord Palmerston . . . secured an international treaty guaranteeing Belgium as an "independent and perpetually neutral state." The treaty was signed . . . by England, France, Russia, [Germany], and Austria.

Ever since 1892, when France and Russia had joined in military alliance, it was clear that four of the five signatories of the Belgian treaty would be automatically engaged—two against two—in the war for which [the German military commanders] had to plan. . . . Under the terms of the Austro-German alliance, Germany was obliged to support Austria in any conflict with Russia. Under the terms of the alliance between France and Russia, both parties were obliged to move against Germany if either became involved in a "defensive war" with Germany. These arrangements made it inevitable that in any war in which she engaged, Germany would have to fight on two fronts against both Russia and France.

What part England would play was uncertain; she might remain neutral; she might, if given cause, come in against Germany.

— Barbara Tuchman, *The Guns of August* (1962)

1. The system of tangled alliances described here helped lead to

   A. the French Revolution.

   B. the Napoleonic Wars.

   C. World War I.

   D. World War II.

3. If Austria went to war, which country could it depend on for support?

   A. Germany

   B. France

   C. Russia

   D. England

2. The small country of Belgium was in danger if war broke out in Europe because it was located between

   A. England and France.

   B. France and Germany.

   C. Germany and Austria.

   D. Austria and Russia.

4. What event set off a chain reaction within this alliance system that led to World War I?

   A. Germany's invasion of Belgium

   B. Germany's invasion of Poland

   C. the Communist revolution in Russia

   D. the assassination of Archduke Franz Ferdinand

Political Cartoons

Political cartoons use a combination of words and images to express a point of view on political issues. They are useful primary sources, because they reflect the opinions of the time.

1 Identify the subject of the cartoon. Titles and captions often provide clues to the subject matter.

2 Use labels to help identify the people, places, and events represented in the cartoon.

3 Note where and when the cartoon was published for more information on people, places, and events.

4 Identify any important symbols—ideas or images that stand for something else—in the cartoon.

5 Analyze the point of view presented in the cartoon. The use of caricature—the exaggeration of physical features—often signals how the cartoonist feels.

6 Interpret the cartoonist's message.

1 "NEXT!"

Daniel Fitzpatrick/St. Louis Post-Dispatch, August 24, 1939.

4 The cartoonist uses the swastika, the symbol of the Nazi Party, to represent Germany.

5 The swastika looks like a huge, menacing machine, which can easily overrun the Polish landscape.

2 The label *Poland* indicates the location of the subject addressed in the cartoon.

6 The cartoonist suggests that Poland will be the German war machine's next victim.

3 The date of the publication, 1939, suggests that the cartoon might concern the beginning of World War II.

1. The machine-like swastika in the cartoon represents

A. Nazi Germany.

B. the Soviet Union.

C. Napoleon's empire.

D. the Polish military.

2. Which sentence *best* summarizes the cartoonist's message?

A. Germany must beware of Poland.

B. Poland is in danger of civil war.

C. Germany and Poland are military giants.

D. Poland will be Germany's next victim.

answers: 1 (A); 2 (D)

Directions: Use the cartoon and your knowledge of world history to answer questions 1 through 4.

Steve Sack, *Minneapolis Star-Tribune,* January 1, 1992

1. What leader from the Middle East does the cartoon portray?

   A. Iraq's Saddam Hussein

   B. Egypt's Hosni Mubarak

   C. Syria's Hafez al-Assad

   D. Libya's Muammar al-Qaddafi

2. How has the cartoonist drawn this leader?

   A. as a soldier

   B. as a poor person

   C. as Count Dracula

   D. as Frankenstein's monster

3. The countries identified in the cartoon include

   A. Saudi Arabia and Kuwait.

   B. West Germany and China.

   C. the United States and the Soviet Union.

   D. France and Japan.

4. The most appropriate title for this cartoon would be

   A. "A Monster Walks at Night."

   B. "They've Created a Monster."

   C. "The Monster of the Middle East."

   D. "They've Made a Mistake."

Charts

Charts present information in a visual form. History textbooks use several types of charts, including tables, flow charts, Venn diagrams, and infographics. The chart most commonly found in standardized tests is the table. This organizes information in columns and rows for easy viewing.

1 Read the title and identify the broad subject of the chart.

2 Read the column and row headings and any other labels. These will provide more details about the subject of the chart.

3 Note how the information in the chart is organized.

4 Compare and contrast the information from column to column and row to row.

5 Try to draw conclusions from the information in the chart.

6 Read the questions and then study the chart again.

1 This chart is about the number of people who immigrated to different countries.

4 Notice that the years covered in the table are not the same for all countries.

Immigration to Selected Countries

Country	Period	Number of Immigrants
Argentina	1856–1932	6,405,000
Australia	1861–1932	2,913,000
Brazil	1821–1932	4,431,000
British West Indies	1836–1932	1,587,000
Canada	1821–1932	5,206,000
Cuba	1901–1932	857,000
Mexico	1911–1931	226,000
New Zealand	1851–1932	594,000
South Africa	1881–1932	852,000
United States	1821–1932	34,244,000
Uruguay	1836–1932	713,000

Source: Alfred W. Crosby, Jr., *The Columbian Exchange: Biological and Cultural Consequences of 1492*

3 This chart organizes the countries alphabetically. In some charts, information is organized according to years or the value of the numbers displayed.

5 Think about what the countries with the highest number of immigrants have in common.

6

1. The country that received the vast majority of immigrants was

   A. Argentina.
   B. Brazil.
   C. Canada.
   D. the United States.

2. The Latin American country that received the most immigrants was

   A. Argentina.
   B. Brazil.
   C. Cuba.
   D. Uruguay.

answers: 1 (D); 2 (A)

STRATEGIES FOR TAKING STANDARDIZED TESTS

Directions: Use the chart and your knowledge of world history to answer questions 1 through 4.

Crude Steel Production for Selected Countries (in Thousands of Metric Tons)							
Year	China	Germany*	Japan	Korea	Russia/ USSR	United Kingdom	United States
1900	—	6,646	1	—	2,214	4,979	10,351
1910	—	13,699	250	—	3,444	6,476	26,512
1920	—	8,538	845	—	162	9,212	42,807
1930	—	11,511	2,289	—	5,761	7,443	41,351
1940	—	19,141	7,528	—	19,000	13,183	60,765
1950	61	12,121	4,839	—	27,300	16,553	87,848
1960	1,866	34,100	22,138	—	65,292	24,695	91,920
1970	1,779	45,041	93,322	—	115,886	28,314	119,310
1980	3,712	43,838	111,935	8,558	148,000	11,278	101,457
1990	6,535	44,022	110,339	23,125	154,414	17,896	89,276
2000	127,200	46,400	106,400	43,100	59,100	15,200	101,500

* Figures from 1950 through 1990 are West Germany only.

Source: International Iron and Steel Institute; Japan Iron and Steel Federation

1. Which country produced the most crude steel in 1900?

   A. Germany

   B. Russia/USSR

   C. United Kingdom

   D. United States

2. Japanese crude steel production most likely dropped from 1940 to 1950 due to

   A. growing competition from Korea and the USSR.

   B. rising production in China.

   C. damage to the industry suffered in World War II.

   D. mergers with American companies.

3. By 2000, the largest share of crude steel was being produced by countries in

   A. Africa.

   B. Asia.

   C. Europe.

   D. North America.

4. What country rose from no crude steel production to be the world's largest producer in 50 years?

   A. China

   B. Germany

   C. Korea

   D. United Kingdom

Line and Bar Graphs

Graphs show statistics in a visual form. Line graphs are particularly useful for showing changes over time. Bar graphs make it easy to compare numbers or sets of numbers.

1 Read the title and identify the broad subject of the graph.

2 Study the labels on the vertical and horizontal axes to see the kinds of information presented in the graph. Note the intervals between amounts and between dates. This will help you read the graph more efficiently.

3 Look at the source line and evaluate the reliability of the information in the graph.

4 If the graph presents information over time, look for trends—generalizations you can make about changes over time.

5 Draw conclusions and make inferences based on information in the graph.

6 Read the questions carefully and then study the graph again.

1 Exports of English Manufactured Goods, 1699–1774

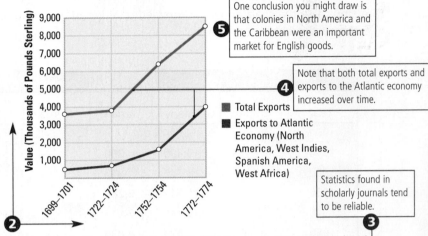

One conclusion you might draw is that colonies in North America and the Caribbean were an important market for English goods.

Note that both total exports and exports to the Atlantic economy increased over time.

Statistics found in scholarly journals tend to be reliable.

Source: R. Davis, "English Foreign Trade, 1700–1774," *Economic History Review* (1962)

6 1. Which statement *best* describes the change in proportion of Atlantic economy exports to total exports?

A. It started small and remained small.

B. It started large and remained large.

C. It grew over time.

D. It decreased over time.

1 Nations with High Foreign Debt, 2000

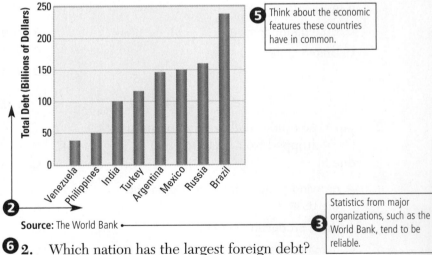

Think about the economic features these countries have in common.

Statistics from major organizations, such as the World Bank, tend to be reliable.

Source: The World Bank

6 2. Which nation has the largest foreign debt?

A. Venezuela

B. Brazil

C. Mexico

D. Russia

answers: 1 (C); 2 (B)

STRATEGIES FOR TAKING STANDARDIZED TESTS

Directions: Use the graphs and your knowledge of world history to answer questions 1 through 4.

Japan: Gross Domestic Product, 1984–2000

Source: *Annual Report on National Accounts 2002,* Cabinet Office of the Government of Japan

Unemployment Rates for Selected Countries, 2002

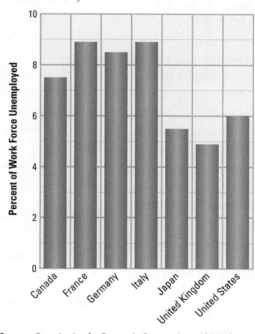

Source: Organization for Economic Cooperation and Development

1. Which of the following periods saw a decline in the gross domestic product of Japan?

   A. 1984 to 1988

   B. 1988 to 1992

   C. 1990 to 1994

   D. 1994 to 1998

2. From 1986 to 1994, Japan's gross domestic product

   A. more than doubled.

   B. more than tripled.

   C. grew by about five times.

   D. grew nearly ten times.

3. Which of these countries had the lowest unemployment rate in 2002?

   A. Italy

   B. Japan

   C. United Kingdom

   D. United States

4. In 2002, France's unemployment rate stood at

   A. about 9 percent

   B. well over 9 percent.

   C. about 7 percent.

   D. less than 7 percent.

Pie Graphs

A pie, or circle, graph shows relationships among the parts of a whole. These parts look like slices of a pie. The size of each slice is proportional to the percentage of the whole that it represents.

❶ Read the title and identify the broad subject of the pie graph.

❷ Look at the legend to see what each slice of the pie represents.

❸ Look at the source line and evaluate the reliability of the information in the graph.

❹ Compare the slices of the pie and try to make generalizations and draw conclusions from your comparisons.

❺ Read the questions carefully.

❻ Eliminate choices that you know are wrong and then select the best answer from the remaining choices.

2 A greater share of the world's population lives in Latin America and the Caribbean than lives in

A. Africa.

B. Europe.

C. North America.

D. Asia.

❶ World Population by Region, 2002

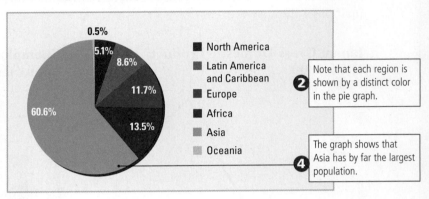

Note that each region is shown by a distinct color in the pie graph. **❷**

The Population Reference Bureau specializes in studies of United States and international population data. **❸**

Source: Population Reference Bureau

The graph shows that Asia has by far the largest population. **❹**

❺ **1.** Which region accounts for the smallest share of the world population?

A. Africa

B. North America

C. Latin America and the Caribbean

D. Oceania

2. A greater share of the world's population lives in Latin America and the Caribbean than lives in

A. Africa.

B. Europe.

C. North America.

D. Asia.

❻ For this question, find the "pie slices" for each of the regions listed in the alternatives. Compare each one to the "pie slice" for Latin America and the Caribbean.

answers: 1 (D); 2 (C)

Directions: Use the pie graph and your knowledge of world history to answer questions 1 through 4.

World Energy Consumption by Region

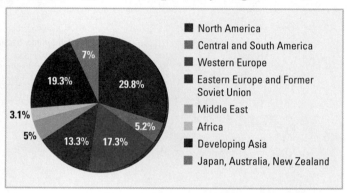

Source: "Earth Pulse," *National Geographic* (March 2001)

1. Energy consumption statistics for Russia are included in the region called

   A. North America.

   B. Western Europe.

   C. Eastern Europe and former Soviet Union.

   D. Developing Asia.

2. Which region uses the highest proportion of energy?

   A. North America

   B. Western Europe

   C. Eastern Europe and former Soviet Union

   D. Developing Asia

3. The word *Developing* in the legend refers to countries that are

   A. growing in population.

   B. adopting new methods of agriculture.

   C. developing nuclear weapons.

   D. moving toward industrial economies.

4. Japan, Australia, and New Zealand are grouped together because they are in the same part of the world and

   A. have roughly equal populations.

   B. have advanced industrial economies.

   C. rely on fishing for food.

   D. rely on other countries for economic aid.

Political Maps

Political maps show countries and the political divisions within them—states or provinces, for example. They also show the location of major cities. In addition, political maps often show some physical features, such as mountain ranges, oceans, seas, lakes, and rivers.

1 Read the title of the map to identify the subject and purpose of the map.

2 Review the labels on the map. They also will reveal information about the map's subject and purpose.

3 Study the legend to find the meaning of the symbols used on the map.

4 Use the scale to estimate distances between places shown on the map.

5 Use the compass rose to determine the direction on the map.

6 Read the questions, and then carefully study the map to determine the answers.

1 Canada in 1871

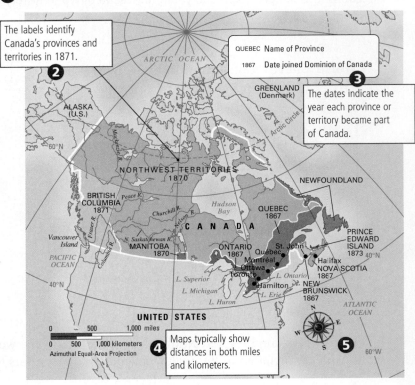

The labels identify Canada's provinces and territories in 1871.

QUEBEC Name of Province
1867   Date joined Dominion of Canada

The dates indicate the year each province or territory became part of Canada.

Maps typically show distances in both miles and kilometers.

1. All of the following provinces were part of Canada in 1867 *except*

A. New Brunswick.

B. Manitoba.

C. Ontario.

D. Quebec.

2. About how long is the United States-Canada border from western Lake Superior to the Pacific Ocean?

Use the scale to answer questions like this.

A. 900 miles

B. 1,200 miles

C. 1,500 miles

D. 1,800 miles

answers: 1 (B); 2 (C)

Directions: Use the map and your knowledge of world history to answer questions 1 through 4.

Empires in South and Southwest Asia, 1500–1660

1. All of the following cities were within the Ottoman Empire *except*

   A. Cairo.

   B. Damascus.

   C. Isfahan.

   D. Constantinople.

2. Which empire controlled part of Europe?

   A. Ottoman

   B. Safavid

   C. Mughal

   D. All of the above

3. In all of these empires, the dominant religion was

   A. Buddhism.

   B. Christianity.

   C. Islam.

   D. Hinduism.

4. Which city was within the Mughal Empire by 1530?

   A. Bombay

   B. Delhi

   C. Madras

   D. Pondicherry

Thematic Maps

A thematic map, or special-purpose map, focuses on a particular topic. The movements of peoples, a country's natural resources, and major battles in a war are all topics you might see illustrated on a thematic map.

1 Read the title to determine the subject and purpose of the map.

2 Examine the labels on the map to find more information on the map's subject and purpose.

3 Study the legend to find the meaning of the symbols and colors used on the map.

4 Look at the colors and symbols on the map to try to identify patterns.

5 Read the questions, and then carefully study the map to determine the answers.

1 Japan, 1850–1914

Notice that Japan controlled Korea and exercised influence over a considerable part of China.

Legend:
- Japan, c. 1850
- Gained by Japan by 1914
- Japanese sphere of influence
- Industrial area
- ☐ Trading ports
- ✷ Battles in Sino-Japanese War
- ✷ Battles in Russo-Japanese War

The colors indicate the spread of Japan's territories and influence over time. The symbols show Japanese trading ports and industrial centers and the battles that Japan fought in different wars.

1. Which city was the site of battles in both the Sino-Japanese War and the Russo-Japanese War?

A. Mukden

B. Port Arthur

C. Pusan

D. Tokyo

2. Which of the following was a major Japanese industrial center?

A. Shanghai

B. Seoul

C. Nagoya

D. Amoy

answers: 1 (B); 2 (C)

S22

Directions: Use the map and your knowledge of world history to answer questions 1 through 4.

European Empires in North America, 1700

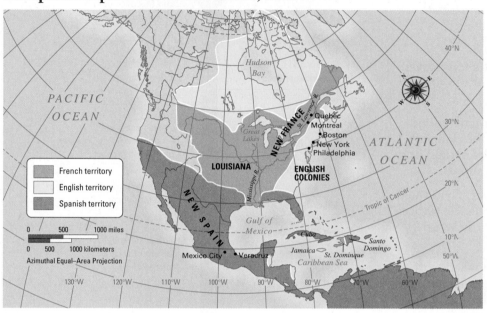

1. Which European power held lands along the shores of Hudson Bay?

   A. England

   B. France

   C. Spain

   D. All of the above

2. The land around the Great Lakes was controlled by

   A. England.

   B. France.

   C. Spain.

   D. all of the above

3. Which of the following statements about the English colonial empire in North America is *not* true?

   A. English lands shared borders with both French and Spanish lands.

   B. English lands did not stretch as far west as those held by Spain.

   C. England held no land on the Pacific Coast of North America.

   D. England held no lands east of 60° W longitude.

4. All of the following could be considered ports *except*

   A. Boston.

   B. Mexico City.

   C. Quebec.

   D. Veracruz.

Time Lines

A time line is a type of chart that lists events in the order in which they occurred. In other words, time lines are a visual method of showing what happened when.

1 Read the title to discover the subject of the time line.

2 Identify the time period covered by the time line by noting the earliest and latest dates shown.

3 Read the events and their dates in sequence. Notice the intervals between events.

4 Use your knowledge of history to develop a fuller picture of the events listed in the time line. For example, place the events in a broader context by considering what was happening elsewhere in the world.

5 Use the information you have gathered from these strategies to answer the questions.

1 The End of Colonialism in Africa

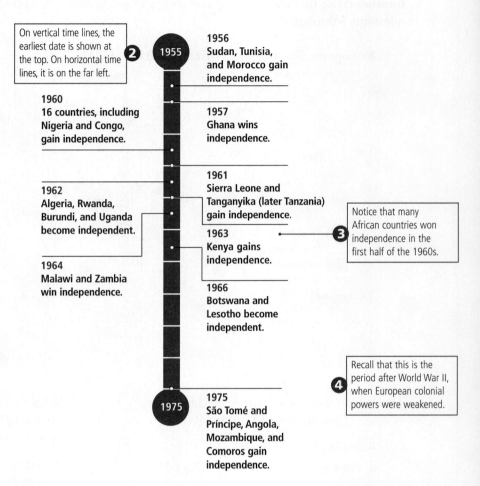

On vertical time lines, the earliest date is shown at the top. On horizontal time lines, it is on the far left.

2 1955

1956
Sudan, Tunisia, and Morocco gain independence.

1960
16 countries, including Nigeria and Congo, gain independence.

1957
Ghana wins independence.

1961
Sierra Leone and Tanganyika (later Tanzania) gain independence.

1962
Algeria, Rwanda, Burundi, and Uganda become independent.

1963
Kenya gains independence.

Notice that many African countries won independence in the first half of the 1960s. **3**

1964
Malawi and Zambia win independence.

1966
Botswana and Lesotho become independent.

Recall that this is the period after World War II, when European colonial powers were weakened. **4**

1975

1975
São Tomé and Príncipe, Angola, Mozambique, and Comoros gain independence.

1. The first countries to win independence were all located in

A. North Africa.

B. West Africa.

C. East Africa.

D. Southern Africa.

2. Which of the following titles *best* describes events in the 1960s?

A. The Rise of Communism

B. The Rise of Colonialism

C. The Decade of Independence

D. The Decade of Suffering

answers: 1 (A); 2 (C)

Directions: Use the time line and your knowledge of world history to answer questions 1 through 4.

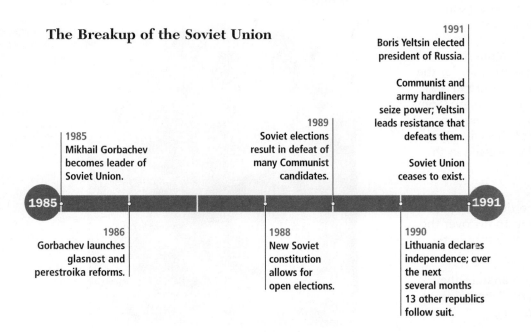

The Breakup of the Soviet Union

1985
Mikhail Gorbachev becomes leader of Soviet Union.

1986
Gorbachev launches glasnost and perestroika reforms.

1988
New Soviet constitution allows for open elections.

1989
Soviet elections result in defeat of many Communist candidates.

1990
Lithuania declares independence; over the next several months 13 other republics follow suit.

1991
Boris Yeltsin elected president of Russia.

Communist and army hardliners seize power; Yeltsin leads resistance that defeats them.

Soviet Union ceases to exist.

1. What event was a direct result of the new constitution that took effect in 1988?

   A. Gorbachev launched glasnost and perestroika reforms.

   B. Many communist candidates lost elections.

   C. Communist hardliners seized power.

   D. Several Soviet republics declared independence.

2. When did Lithuania declare its independence from the Soviet Union?

   A. 1988

   B. 1989

   C. 1990

   D. 1991

3. What was the result of the hardliners' attempt to seize power in 1991?

   A. They prevented the collapse of the Soviet Union.

   B. Leaders in other communist countries joined their cause.

   C. Gorbachev defeated Yeltsin in a struggle for power.

   D. They failed to gain control, and the country rapidly fell apart.

4. For much of the time it existed, the Soviet Union was engaged with the United States in a long conflict called

   A. World War I.

   B. World War II.

   C. the Gulf War.

   D. the Cold War.

Constructed Response

Constructed-response questions focus on various kinds of documents. Each document usually is accompanied by a series of questions. These questions call for short answers that, for the most part, can be found directly in the document. Some answers, however, require knowledge of the subject or time period addressed in the document.

1 Read the title of the document to discover the subject addressed in the questions.

2 Study and analyze the document. Take notes on what you see.

3 Read the questions carefully, and then study the document again to locate the answers.

4 Carefully write your answers. Unless the directions say otherwise, your answers need not be complete sentences.

1 **Mohandas Gandhi Leads the Salt March, 1930**

2 Constructed-response questions use a wide range of documents including short passages, cartoons, charts, graphs, maps, time lines, posters, and other visual materials. This document is a photograph of Mohandas K. Gandhi leading a demonstration.

Copyright © Hulton Archive.

Mohandas K. Gandhi, accompanied by the poet Sarojini Naidu, leads a protest march against the Salt Acts.

3 **1.** What demonstration is Mohandas Gandhi shown leading in the photograph?

4 the Salt March of 1930

2. What was this demonstration about?

It was a demonstration against the Salt Acts, which required Indians to buy salt only from the British government and to pay sales taxes on their salt purchases.

3. What principle did Gandhi follow in his campaign to win Indian independence? Describe the tactics he used to put this principle into action.

Passive resistance, civil disobedience, or nonviolence. He led peaceful demonstrations against unjust laws, organized boycotts of British goods, and encouraged people not to cooperate with the British government.

Directions: Use the passage and your knowledge of world history to answer questions 1 through 3. Your answers need not be in complete sentences.

A New South Africa

. . . [W]e all carried [pain] in our hearts as we saw our country tear itself apart in terrible conflict, and as we saw it spurned, outlawed and isolated by the peoples of the world, precisely because it has become the universal base of the [destructive] ideology and practice of racism and racial oppression. . . .

We have, at last, achieved our political emancipation. We pledge ourselves to liberate all our people from the continuing bondage of poverty, deprivation, suffering, gender, and other discrimination. . . . We enter into a covenant that we shall build the society in which all South Africans, both black and white, will be able to walk tall, without any fear in their hearts, assured of their inalienable right to human dignity—a rainbow nation at peace with itself and the world. . . .

Never, never and never again shall it be that this beautiful land will again experience the oppression of one by another and suffer the indignity of being the skunk of the world.

—Nelson Mandela, Inaugural Address as President of South Africa (1994)

1. What was the name of the government policy that Nelson Mandela called the "[destructive ideology] and practice of racism and racial oppression"?

2. How did other nations outlaw and isolate South Africa?

3. Why was Mandela's election as president significant?

Extended Response

Extended-response questions, like constructed-response questions, usually focus on a document of some kind. However, they are more complex and require more time to complete than short-answer constructed-response questions. Some extended-response questions ask you to present the information in the document in a different form. Others require you to complete a chart, graph, or diagram. Still others ask you to write an essay, a report, or some other piece of extended writing. In most standardized tests, documents are accompanied by only one extended-response question.

1 Read the title of the document to get an idea of the subject. (This document concerns the Industrial Revolution.)

2 Carefully read the extended-response questions. (Question 1 asks you to complete a chart. Question 2 assumes that the chart is complete and asks you to write a short essay based on information in the chart.)

3 Study and analyze the document.

4 Sometimes the question gives you a partial answer. Analyze that answer to determine what kind of information your answers should contain.

5 If the question requires an extended piece of writing, jot down ideas in outline form. Use this outline to write your answer.

1 Inventions of the Industrial Revolution

3 Like constructed-response questions, extended-response questions use a wide range of documents. This document is a chart of several inventions developed during the Industrial Revolution.

Invention	Impact
Flying shuttle, spinning jenny, water frame, spinning mule, power loom	Made it possible to quickly spin thread and weave cloth; led to the spread of factories **4**
Cotton gin	Made it faster to clean seeds from cotton; spurred increase in cotton production
Macadam road, steamboat, locomotive	Made transportation by land and water faster; made transportation of larger loads possible; railroads boosted demand for coal and iron, spurring those industries
Mechanical reaper	Made harvesting easier; increased wheat production

2

1. In the right-hand column of the chart, briefly describe the impact of the inventions listed in the left-hand column. The first entry has been completed for you.

2. The chart shows how certain inventions contributed to the development of the Industrial Revolution. Write a short essay describing the impact of the Industrial Revolution on society.

5 Sample Response The best essays will point out that developments in agriculture reduced the need for labor on the land. Many farm workers left the country seeking work in factories in the cities. As a result, cities grew much larger. However, lack of sanitation and poor quality buildings made cities unhealthy, and sometimes dangerous, places to live. Life for factory workers was made worse because they worked long hours under dreadful conditions. Society split into clear social classes, with an upper class of landowners and aristocrats, a growing middle class of merchants and factory owners, and a large, generally poor lower class. Over the long term, though, working and living conditions improved for the working class, in part because factory-produced goods were cheaper.

Directions: Use the passage and your knowledge of world history to answer question 1.

Sold Into Slavery

One day, when all our people were gone out to their work as usual and only I and my dear sister were left to mind the house, two men and a woman got over our walls, and in a moment seized us both, and without giving us time to cry out or make resistance they stopped our mouths and ran off with us into the nearest wood. . . .

The first object which saluted my eyes when I arrived on the coast was the sea, and a slave ship which was then riding at anchor and waiting for its cargo. These filled me with astonishment, which was soon converted into terror when I was carried on board. . . .

I was soon put down under the decks, and there I received such a salutation in my nostrils as I had never experienced in my life: so that with the loathsomeness of the stench and crying together, I became so sick and low that I was not able to eat, nor had I the least desire to taste anything.

—Olaudah Equiano, *The Interesting Narrative of Olaudah Equiano* (1789)

1. Write a short essay explaining the development and operation of the Atlantic slave trade.

Document-Based Questions

A document-based question (DBQ) requires you to analyze and interpret a variety of documents. These documents often are accompanied by short-answer questions. You use these answers and information from the documents to write an essay on a specified subject.

1 Read the "Historical Context" section to get a sense of the issue addressed in the question.

2 Read the "Task" section and note the action words. This will help you understand exactly what the essay question requires.

3 Study and analyze each document. Consider what connection the documents have to the essay question. Take notes on your ideas.

4 Read and answer the document-specific questions. Think about how these questions connect to the essay topic.

Introduction

1 **Historical Context:** During World War II, the United States and the Soviet Union joined together as allies to defeat Nazi Germany. Soon after the war ended, however, they became enemies in the long conflict called the Cold War.

2 **Task:** (Identify) the postwar developments that led to the Cold War, and (discuss) the impact the Cold War had on world affairs.

Part 1: Short Answer

Study each document carefully and answer the questions that follow.

3 **Document 1: The Cold War—1946–1961**

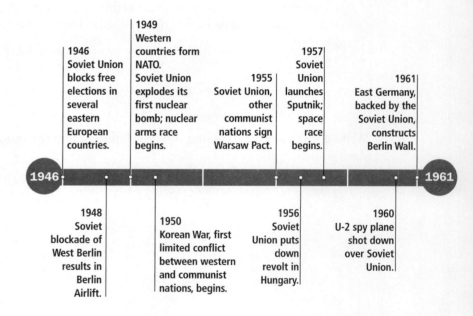

1946
Soviet Union blocks free elections in several eastern European countries.

1949
Western countries form NATO. Soviet Union explodes its first nuclear bomb; nuclear arms race begins.

1955
Soviet Union, other communist nations sign Warsaw Pact.

1957
Soviet Union launches Sputnik; space race begins.

1961
East Germany, backed by the Soviet Union, constructs Berlin Wall.

1946 — **1961**

1948
Soviet blockade of West Berlin results in Berlin Airlift.

1950
Korean War, first limited conflict between western and communist nations, begins.

1956
Soviet Union puts down revolt in Hungary.

1960
U-2 spy plane shot down over Soviet Union.

4 **What impact did the launching of Sputnik have on United States-Soviet relations?**

It led to the space race the struggle between the United States and the Soviet Union for control of outer space.

Document 2: The Iron Curtain

From Stettin in the Baltic to Trieste in the Adriatic, an iron curtain has descended across the Continent. Behind that line lie all the capitals of the ancient states of Central and Eastern Europe. . . . All these famous cities and the populations around them lie in what I must call the Soviet sphere and all are subject in one form or another, not only to Soviet influence but to a very high, and in many cases, increasing measure of control from Moscow. . . . The Communist parties, which were very small in all these Eastern States of Europe, have been raised to pre-eminence and power far beyond their numbers and are seeking everywhere to obtain totalitarian control.

—Winston Churchill, Speech at Westminster College, Fulton, Missouri 1946

What did the Iron Curtain represent to Winston Churchill?

The barrier that separated Soviet-dominated Eastern Europe from free, democratic Western Europe.

Document 3: United States Military Spending, 1946–1959

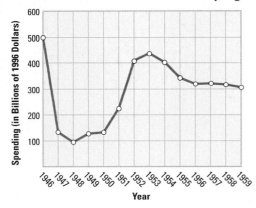

Source: Center for Defense Information

What trend in United States military spending is shown in the graph?

United States military spending fell dramatically in the immediate postwar years. However, it rose markedly in the early 1950s, then leveled off, but remained considerably higher than in the immediate postwar years.

5 **Part 2: Essay**

Using information from the documents, your answers to the questions in Part 1, and your knowledge of world history, write an essay that identifies the postwar developments that led to the Cold War and discusses the impact the Cold War had on world affairs. **6**

5 Carefully read the essay question. Then write an outline for your essay.

6 Write your essay. Be sure that it has an introductory paragraph that introduces your argument, main body paragraphs that explain it, and a concluding paragraph that restates your position. In your essay, include quotations or details from specific documents to support your ideas. Add other supporting facts or details that you know from your study of world history.

Sample Response The best essays will point out such developments as the imposition of Soviet control in Eastern Europe (Documents 1 and 2), the blockade of Berlin and the Berlin Airlift (Document 1), and the formation of eastern and western military alliances (Document 1). Essays also will point out that the Cold War led to a division of Europe and much of the rest of the world between countries that sided with the United States and those that allied with the Soviet Union. Increased military spending (Document 3) related to the nuclear arms race (Document 1) made this division potentially dangerous.

Introduction

Historical Context: For many centuries, kings and queens ruled the countries of Europe. Their power was supported by nobles and armies. European society began to change, however, and in the late 1700s, those changes produced a violent upheaval in France.

Task: Discuss how social conflict and intellectual movements contributed to the French Revolution and why the Revolution turned radical.

Part 1: Short Answer

Study each document carefully and answer the questions that follow.

Document 1: Social Classes in Pre-Revolutionary France

LE GRAND ABUS

What do the peasant woman, the noblewoman, and the nun represent? Why is the peasant woman shown carrying the noblewoman and the nun?

Engraving: *Le Grand Abus.* Engraving of a cartoon held in the collection of M. de baron de Vinck d'Orp of Brussels/Mary Evans Picture Library, London.

Document 2: A Declaration of Rights

1. Men are born and remain free and equal in rights. Social distinctions may be founded only upon the general good.

2. The aim of all political association is the preservation of the natural . . . rights of man. These rights are liberty, property, security, and resistance to oppression. . . .

6. Law is the expression of the general will. Every citizen has a right to participate personally, or through his representative, in its foundation. It must be the same for all, whether it protects or punishes. All citizens, being equal in the eyes of the law, are equally eligible to all dignities and to all public positions and occupations, according to their abilities, and without distinction except that of their virtues and talents.

—*Declaration of the Rights of Man and of the Citizen* (1789)

How do these statements reflect the ideals of the Enlightenment?

Document 3: The French Revolution—Major Events

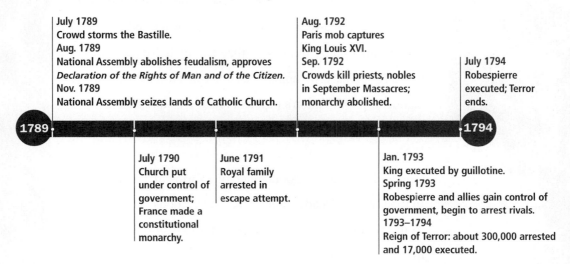

July 1789
Crowd storms the Bastille.
Aug. 1789
National Assembly abolishes feudalism, approves *Declaration of the Rights of Man and of the Citizen.*
Nov. 1789
National Assembly seizes lands of Catholic Church.

Aug. 1792
Paris mob captures King Louis XVI.
Sep. 1792
Crowds kill priests, nobles in September Massacres; monarchy abolished.

July 1794
Robespierre executed; Terror ends.

1789

1794

July 1790
Church put under control of government; France made a constitutional monarchy.

June 1791
Royal family arrested in escape attempt.

Jan. 1793
King executed by guillotine.
Spring 1793
Robespierre and allies gain control of government, begin to arrest rivals.
1793–1794
Reign of Terror: about 300,000 arrested and 17,000 executed.

The French Revolution was moderate at first but quickly became radical. How does the information in the time line illustrate this?

Part 2: Essay

Using information from the documents, your answers to the questions in Part 1, and your knowledge of world history, write an essay discussing how social conflict and intellectual movements contributed to the French Revolution and why the Revolution turned radical.

"Everyone has the right to take part in the government of his [or her] country."

Universal Declaration of Human Rights
United Nations, 1948

In 2001, citizens of one of the newest nations in the world—East Timor in Southeast Asia—cast ballots to establish a democratic government. The East Timorese had been waiting a long time for that day. After more than 400 years of Portuguese domination, and 25 years under military occupation by Indonesia, they finally had a free land.

As Americans, we applaud as other countries embrace democracy. Our nation's political ideals as expressed in our most treasured political documents—the Declaration of Independence and the Constitution—have inspired people around the world to adopt democratic forms of government. In the last two decades, democratic revolutions have transformed many countries. Additional millions of people now live under democratic rule.

As you read this book, you will learn about the people and events that have shaped our modern world. You will also follow the centuries-long struggle for individual freedom. To help understand today's world, we need to understand why democracy matters. We need to know how the idea of democracy has become a reality for so many people in the world, and a goal for others.

1

The Rise of Democratic Ideas

Previewing Main Ideas

POWER AND AUTHORITY People living in groups recognize the need for government, or a system for exercising authority. For much of history, people lived under authoritarian rulers, such as kings. With the rise of democratic ideas, people came to demand a role in governing themselves.

Geography *Study the time line. Identify two events that illustrate a move toward democratic rule.*

REVOLUTION In the Glorious Revolution, the English established the right to limit a ruler's power. This Revolution and Enlightenment ideas sparked a rebellion of the American colonies against British rule. In turn, the American Revolution helped spur the French Revolution.

Geography *Study the map key. How many years separate the English Bill of Rights from the establishment of democracy in the United States?*

CULTURAL INTERACTION Democratic ideas developed first in ancient Athens and later in Rome. They then spread to England and England's American colonies. Eventually, democratic movements sprang up throughout the world, inspired by the U.S. Constitution.

Geography *What can be said about the size of the early areas where democracy developed as compared to later sites?*

INTEGRATED TECHNOLOGY

eEdition
- Interactive Maps
- Interactive Visuals
- Interactive Primary Sources

VIDEO *Patterns of Interaction: The Rise of the Persians and the Inca*

INTERNET RESOURCES

Go to **classzone.com** for:
- Research Links
- Maps
- Internet Activities
- Test Practice
- Primary Sources
- Current Events
- Chapter Quiz

---

c. 1200 B.C.
Moses brings Ten Commandments to the Hebrews. ▶

509 B.C.
Romans choose representative government.

WORLD

1200 B.C.

200 B.C.

461 B.C.
Pericles begins reform in Greece. ▶

Origins of Democracy

NORTH
AMERICA

ATLANTIC
OCEAN

Gulf of
Mexico

0   150   300 Miles

0 150 300 Kilometers
Lambert Equal-Area Projection

40°N

58°N

42°N

ATLANTIC

OCEAN

N
W   E
S

North
Sea

Baltic Sea

EUROPE

Adriatic Sea

Rome

Athens

Mediterranean Sea

16°E

8°E

0   300   600 Miles

0   300   600 Kilometers
Azimuthal Equidistant Projection

- ■ Athens, first democracy, 508 B.C.
- ■ Rome, first republic, 509 B.C.
- England, English Bill of Rights, 1689
- United States, first modern democracy, 1789
- France, monarchy replaced by republic, 1792

A.D. 533
Justinian's legal
code completed.

A.D. 1690
◄ John Locke proposes
government by the
consent of the governed.

A.D. 1787
U.S. Constitution
is written.

A.D. 200   A.D. 1000   A.D. 1800

A.D. 1215
Magna Carta limits
◄ English monarchy.

A.D. 1790
French National Assembly
issues the Declaration of
the Rights of Man.

3

Why would people risk their lives for democracy?

The young man in the photograph faces arrest, possibly jail, or even worse, death for supporting a pro-democracy movement in Hong Kong, China, in 2002. This was neither the first nor the last time that people have rebelled against tyranny. In countless incidents around the world, men and women have taken a stand to support political movements that promise to bring democracy to their lands. Over the centuries, millions of people have died for the cause of democracy.

▲ A member of a political group called the April 5th Movement protests the loss of democracy in Hong Kong.

EXAMINING *the* ISSUES

- **How do the personal freedoms associated with democracy affect the quality of a person's life?**

- **How can people bring democracy into their lives?**

Discuss these questions with your classmates. In your discussion, first think about what you value most in life, and why. Then imagine what people who do not live in a democratic country might value and what they might do to protect or gain those things they value.

As you read about the rise of democratic ideas in this prologue, think about how these ideas are expressed today.

The Legacy of Ancient Greece and Rome

MAIN IDEA	WHY IT MATTERS NOW	TERMS & NAMES
POWER AND AUTHORITY The Greeks developed democracy, and the Romans added representative government.	Representation and citizen participation are important features of democratic governments around the world.	• government • monarchy • aristocracy • oligarchy • democracy • direct democracy • republic • senate

SETTING THE STAGE Throughout history, people have recognized the need for a system for exercising authority and control in their society. Small bands of people often did not need a formal organization. Councils of elders, for example, worked together to control a group. However, most people in larger groups lived under rulers, such as chieftains, kings, or pharaohs, who often had total power. Over the course of thousands of years, people began to believe that even in large groups they could govern themselves without a powerful ruler.

Athens Builds a Limited Democracy

About 2000 B.C., the Greeks established cities in the small fertile valleys along Greece's rocky coast. Each city-state had its own **government**, a system for controlling the society.

The Greek city-states adopted many styles of government. In some, a single person called a king or monarch ruled in a government called a **monarchy**. Others adopted an **aristocracy** (AR•uh•STAHK• ruh•see), a government ruled by a small group of noble, land-owning families. Later, as trade expanded, a new class of wealthy merchants emerged in some cities. Sometimes these groups took power or shared it with the nobility. They formed an **oligarchy**, a government ruled by a few powerful people.

Ancient Greek civilization claims the distinction of developing the first democracy in a country. In fact, the word **democracy**, meaning "rule of the people," comes from the Greek words *demos,* meaning "people," and *kratos,* meaning "power."

Building Democracy Athens was the largest and most powerful city-state to emerge in Greece. In Athens, citizens participated in governmental decision making. Citizens were adult male residents who enjoyed certain rights and responsibilities. Each year, an assembly of citizens elected three nobles to rule the city-state. After a year of service, the nobles became part of a larger council of advisers.

Around 600 B.C., Athens suffered severe economic problems. In order to pay their debts, poor farmers pledged part of their crops to wealthy landowners. They later pledged their land. Then, they sold themselves into slavery and were not able to leave the land. Eventually, a strong leader stepped in to deal with the political and economic crisis.

TAKING NOTES

Determining Main Ideas Use a web diagram to record the contributions of Greece and Rome to democracy.

Government

Every society must create ways to regulate the behaviors of its members. Government consists of the people and institutions with the authority to establish and enforce rules for society. The rules are designed to keep order within the society, to promote the behaviors that the society approves of, and to protect the society from outside dangers. The government has the authority to administer punishments if the rules are broken. Different societies have forms of government that may feature different types of leaders, lawmakers, and enforcers, such as police or the military.

Major Forms of Government

Monarchy

- State ruled by a king
- Rule is hereditary
- Some rulers claim divine right

Aristocracy

- State ruled by nobility
- Rule is hereditary and based on family ties, social rank, wealth
- Social status and wealth support rulers' authority

Oligarchy

- State ruled by a small group of citizens
- Rule is based on wealth or ability
- Ruling group controls military

Direct Democracy

- State ruled by its citizens
- Rule is based on citizenship
- Majority rule decides vote

Igbo

MALI
NIGER
Niamey
BURKINA FASO
CHAD
N'Djamena
NIGERIA
GHANA
TOGO
BENIN
Abuja
Accra
Lomé
CAMEROON
Yaoundé
EQUATORIAL GUINEA
GABON

■ Igbo lands

One Early Democracy: The Igbo People

The Igbo (IHG•boh) people—also called Ibo—of southern Nigeria in Africa practiced a form of democracy as early as the ninth century. Igbo village government was made up of a council of elders and a village assembly. In the council, any adult male could take part in discussion, although the elders made the final decisions. In the assembly, everyone—young or old, rich or poor—had the right to speak. This practice encouraged a spirit of equality among the Igbo.

INTEGRATED / TECHNOLOGY

RESEARCH LINKS For more on forms of government, go to **classzone.com**

CURRENT WORLD GOVERNMENTS

Traditional Monarchies 5.2%
Protectorates (countries under the protection of others) 1%
Limited Democracies 8.3%
Democracies 62%
Authoritarian/ Totalitarian Regimes (often one-party states or dictatorships) 23.4%

Democracy Facts

- Theoretically, 40,000 people could attend the Greek Assembly. In practice, about 6,000 people attended.
- In 1215, King John of England granted the Magna Carta, which largely influenced subsequent democratic thought.
- In the 1970s, there were 40 democratic governments worldwide.
- In 2002, over 120 established and emerging democracies met to discuss their common issues.

Source: adapted from *Democracy's Century*, Freedom House online (2003)

Connect *to* Today

1. **Categorizing** In which forms of government is rule based on wealth or property ownership?

   See Skillbuilder Handbook, page R9.

2. **Hypothesizing** How might the mass media in modern life help make democracy an achievable form of government?

Reforms of Solon In 594 B.C., Solon (SO•luhn), a respected statesman, passed a law outlawing slavery based on debt and canceled the farmers' debts. This simple act enabled Athens to avoid revolution or civil war.

Solon continued his policies of political reform. He established four classes of citizenship based on wealth rather than heredity. Only citizens of the three higher classes were able to hold public office. Yet, even the lowest class of citizens could vote in the assembly. All free adult males were citizens. Solon also created a new Council of Four Hundred. This body prepared business for the already existing council. Solon also introduced the legal concept that any citizen could bring charges against wrongdoers.

Although these acts increased participation in government, Athens was still limited as a democracy. Only citizens could participate in government, and only about one-tenth of the population were citizens at the time. Athenian law denied citizenship to women, slaves, and foreign residents. Slaves formed about one-third of the Athenian population.

Cleisthenes Enacts More Reforms Beginning in 508 B.C., the Athenian leader Cleisthenes (KLYS•thuh•neez) introduced further reforms. Because of his reforms, Cleisthenes is generally regarded as the founder of democracy in Athens. He worked to make Athens a full democracy by reorganizing the assembly to balance the power of the rich and poor. He also increased the power of the assembly by allowing all citizens to submit laws for debate and passage. Cleisthenes then created the Council of Five Hundred.

MAIN IDEA

Summarizing

A Why is Cleisthenes generally considered the founder of Athenian democracy?

The Council proposed laws and counseled the assembly. Council members were chosen at random from among the citizens. These reforms allowed Athenian citizens to participate in a limited democracy. However, still only one-fifth of Athenian residents were actual citizens. **A**

History Makers

Solon
630?–560? B.C.

Solon is known as one of the Seven Wise Men of Greece. Solon began a series of political reforms that greatly increased citizen participation in Athenian government. He said that he "stood with a strong shield before both parties [the common people and the powerful] and allowed neither to win an unfair victory." His reforms, unfortunately, did not please either the wealthy or the poor.

Solon left Athens for ten years to travel. He spent that period warning people wherever he traveled against rulers who would not uphold his reforms.

INTEGRATED TECHNOLOGY

RESEARCH LINKS For more on Solon, go to **classzone.com**

Greek Democracy Changes

From 490 to 479 B.C., the Greeks fought Persian invaders who were attempting to conquer Greece. The Greek city-states fought side by side as allies and defeated the Persian forces.

The Athenians maintained democracy during the Persian Wars by holding public debates about how to defend their city. After Persia's defeat, Athens continued to develop democracy. A wise and able statesman named Pericles led Athens for 32 years, from 461 to 429 B.C.

Pericles Strengthens Democracy Pericles strengthened Greek democracy by increasing the number of paid public officials and by paying jurors. This enabled poorer citizens to participate in the government. Through greater citizen participation, Athens evolved into a **direct democracy**. This is a form of government in which citizens rule and make laws directly rather than through representatives. In Athens, more citizens were actively involved in government than in any other city-state. In a speech, Pericles expressed his great pride in Athenian democracy when he said, "Our constitution is called a democracy because power is in the hands not of a minority but of the whole people."

Democracy ended in Greece after a war between the two strongest city-states, Athens and Sparta. Macedonia, a nearby state, invaded Greece and defeated the weakened city-states.

Greek Philosophers Use Reason During the fourth century B.C. in Athens, several great thinkers appeared. They used logic and reason to investigate the nature of the universe, human society, and morality. These Greek thinkers based their philosophy on the following assumptions: (1) The universe (land, sky, and sea) is put together in an orderly way and is subject to absolute and unchanging laws; and (2) people can understand these laws through logic and reason. The Greeks' respect for human intelligence and the power of reason had allowed the ideas of democracy to flourish.

The first of these great philosophers was Socrates (SAHK•ruh•TEEZ). He encouraged his students to examine their most closely held beliefs. He used a question-and-answer approach that became known as the Socratic method. Socrates' greatest pupil was Plato (PLAY•toh). In his famous work *The Republic,* Plato set forth his vision of a perfectly governed society. He wanted society governed not by the richest and most powerful but by the wisest, whom he called philosopher-kings.

Plato's student Aristotle (AR•ih•STAHT•uhl) examined the nature of the world and of human belief, thought, and knowledge. In *Politics,* he wrote, "Man is by nature a political animal; it is his nature to live in a state."

Legacy of Greece Greece set lasting standards in government and philosophy. The Greeks used reason and intelligence to discover patterns and explanations of the world that they called natural laws. The Greeks did not wish to be subject to authoritarian rulers. So they developed direct democracy in order that citizens could actively participate in political decisions. They also were the first to develop three branches of government—a legislative branch to pass laws, an executive branch to carry out the laws, and a judicial branch to settle disputes about the laws. (The chart below compares democracy in ancient Athens and in the United States.)

MAIN IDEA

Analyzing Primary Sources
B What does Plato believe needs to happen to bring peace and harmony to cities and to the human race?

Athenian and United States Democracy

Athenian Democracy	Both	U.S. Democracy
• Citizens: male; at least 18 years old; with citizen parents	• Political power exercised by citizens	• Citizens: born in United States or completed citizenship process
• Laws voted on and proposed directly by assembly of all citizens	• Three branches of government	• Representatives elected to propose and vote on laws
• Leader chosen by lot	• Legislative branch passes laws	• Elected president
• Executive branch: a council of 500 men	• Executive branch carries out laws	• Executive branch made up of elected and appointed officials
• Juries varied in size	• Judicial branch conducts trials with paid jurors	• Juries composed of 12 jurors
• No attorneys; no appeals; one-day trials		• Defendants and plaintiffs have attorneys; long appeals process

Juries in Athens

Jury duty was one of the most important civic functions of a citizen of Athens. Juries ranged in size from at least 201 to as many as 2,500 men. (Athenian women were not allowed to serve as jurors.) The jurors would hear both sides of a legal case. Then they would render their verdict by casting bronze ballots in a large ballot box.

▲ Selecting a Jury

Each potential juror was given a bronze ticket inscribed with his name. After the tickets had been placed in a basket, jurors were randomly selected.

solid ballot

hollow ballot

◄ Making a Decision

These round disks are ballots. A hollow ballot was cast for a guilty vote, while a solid ballot indicated a vote in favor of the defendant. (The detail from a Greek drinking cup pictured above shows ballots being cast in a ballot box.)

► Deciding on a Punishment

Citizens could vote to ostracize, or banish, a leader from Athens for ten years to prevent a person from gaining too much power. The person's name was inscribed on a pottery fragment called an ostrakon. This one bears the name of Pericles.

ballot box

SKILLBUILDER: Interpreting Visual Sources
1. **Comparing and Contrasting** *In what ways are the jury practices of Athens similar to those of the United States? How are they different?*
2. **Forming and Supporting Opinions** *What advantages or disadvantages do you see in the number of jurors on an Athenian jury?*

Rome Develops a Republic

While Greece was in decline, a new civilization to the west was developing. From about 1000 to 500 B.C., the earliest Romans—the Latins—battled with Greeks and Etruscans for control of the Italian peninsula. The Romans were the victors.

From Kingdom to Republic Beginning about 600 B.C., a series of kings ruled Rome. Then, in 509 B.C., a group of Roman aristocrats overthrew a harsh king. They set up a new government, calling it a **republic**. A republic is a form of government in which power rests with citizens who have the right to elect the leaders who make governmental decisions. It is an indirect democracy, in contrast to the direct democracy in which all citizens participate directly in the government. In Rome, as in Greece, citizenship with voting rights was granted only to free-born males. **C**

MAIN IDEA

Contrasting
C How does an indirect democracy differ from a direct democracy?

In the early republic, two groups struggled for power. The patricians were aristocratic landowners who held most of the power. The plebeians were common farmers, artisans, and merchants. The patricians inherited their power and social status. They claimed that their ancestry gave them the authority to make laws for Rome and its people. The plebeians were citizens of Rome with the right to vote. But they were barred by law from holding most important government positions. In time, plebeian pressure on the patricians gained them political power.

Twelve Tables An important victory for the plebeians was forcing creation of a written law code. With laws unwritten, patrician officials often interpreted the law to suit themselves. In 451 B.C., a group of ten officials began writing down Rome's laws. They had the laws carved on 12 tables, or tablets, and publicly displayed. The Twelve Tables established the idea that all free citizens had the right to protection of the law and that laws would be fairly administered.

Republican Government Like the Athenians, the Romans had established a government with separate branches. Two officials called consuls commanded the army and directed the government. Their term of office was only one year. The legislative branch was made up of a **senate** and two assemblies. Patricians made up the senate. It controlled foreign and financial policies and advised the consuls. The two assemblies included other classes of citizens. In times of crisis, the republic also provided for a dictator, a leader who had absolute power to make laws and command the army. The dictator was limited to a six-month term.

For hundreds of years after the founding of the republic, Rome expanded its territories through conquest and trade. But expansion created problems. For decades, Rome alternated between the chaos of civil war and the authoritarian rule of a series of dictators. Eventually, the republic collapsed. In 27 B.C., Rome came under the rule of an emperor.

Roman Law

Rome had become a great power not only by conquering other lands but also by bringing the conquered peoples into its system. The Romans tried to create a system of laws that could be applied throughout the Roman Empire. Like the

History Makers

Justinian
482–565

Justinian believed that "imperial majesty should not only be adorned with military might but also graced with laws, so that in times of peace and war alike the state may be governed aright."

To regulate the Byzantine Empire, Justinian set up a panel of legal experts to comb through hundreds of years of Roman law and opinion. The panel's task was to create a single, uniform legal code for Justinian's "New Rome."

The Justinian Code has had a profound impact on the law of most Western countries.

INTEGRATED / TECHNOLOGY

INTERNET ACTIVITY Create a table comparing some of Justinian's laws with similar ones in the United States. Go to **classzone.com** for your research.

Greeks, they believed that laws should be based on principles of reason and justice and should protect citizens and their property. This idea applied to all people regardless of their nationality. It had a great influence on the development of democracy throughout the Western world.

Some important principles of Roman law were
- All citizens had the right to equal treatment under the law.
- A person was considered innocent until proven guilty.
- The burden of proof rested with the accuser rather than the accused.
- Any law that seemed unreasonable or grossly unfair could be set aside.

▲ A coin from 137 B.C. shows a Roman citizen taking part in the democratic process by voting.

A Written Legal Code Another major characteristic of Roman government was its regard for written law as exemplified by the creation of the Twelve Tables in 451 B.C. Nearly 1,000 years later, in A.D. 528, Emperor Justinian ordered the compilation of all Roman laws since the earlier code. After its completion, this new code consisted of four works. *The Code* contained nearly 5,000 Roman laws. *The Digest* was a summary of legal opinions. *The Institutes* served as a textbook for law students. *The Novellae* contained laws passed after 534. The Code of Justinian later became a guide on legal matters throughout Western Europe. Written laws helped establish the idea of "a government of laws, not of men," in which even rulers and other powerful persons could be held accountable for their actions.

Legacy of Rome Rome gave the world the idea of a republic. Rome also adopted from the Greeks the notion that an individual is a citizen in a state rather than the subject of a ruler. Perhaps Rome's greatest and most lasting legacy was its written legal code and the idea that this code should be applied equally and impartially to all citizens. Rome preserved and added to Greece's idea of democracy and passed on the early democratic tradition to civilizations that followed. **D**

MAIN IDEA

Recognizing Effects

D How did Rome influence the development of democracy in the Western world?

SECTION ① **ASSESSMENT**

TERMS & NAMES 1. For each term or name, write a sentence explaining its significance.
- government   • monarchy   • aristocracy   • oligarchy   • democracy   • direct democracy   • republic   • senate

USING YOUR NOTES	MAIN IDEAS	CRITICAL THINKING & WRITING
2. Which contribution, shown on your web diagram, do you think had the greatest impact on the modern world?	3. How does an aristocracy differ from an oligarchy? 4. What steps did Cleisthenes take to strengthen democracy in Athens? 5. What are the four basic principles of Roman law?	6. **DRAWING CONCLUSIONS** How do the steps taken by leaders of Athens reflect a turn toward democracy? 7. **FORMING AND SUPPORTING OPINIONS** Was Athenian democracy under Pericles truly a democracy? Explain. 8. **SYNTHESIZING** Which characteristic of the government under the Roman Republic had the greatest impact on the democratic tradition? 9. **WRITING ACTIVITY** POWER AND AUTHORITY Write a **dialogue** between a Roman citizen and a Greek citizen each arguing that their style of democracy is a better form of government.

CONNECT TO TODAY CREATING AN ORAL REPORT
New England town meetings are similar to the kind of democracy practiced in Ancient Greece. Research New England town meetings and prepare an **oral report** on your findings.

Judeo-Christian Tradition

MAIN IDEA	WHY IT MATTERS NOW	TERMS & NAMES
CULTURAL INTERACTION Judaism and Christianity taught individual worth, ethical values, and the need to fight injustice.	These ideals continue to be important to democracy today.	• Judaism • Ten Commandments • Christianity • Islam • Roman Catholic Church • Renaissance • Reformation

SETTING THE STAGE Ideas from three monotheistic religions helped shape democratic traditions. Judaism, Christianity, and Islam all began in a small corner of southwest Asia, and later spread across the world. Their ideas about the worth of individuals and the responsibility of individuals to the community had a strong impact on the development of democracy. More ideas about the value of the individual and the questioning of authority emerged during the periods of the Renaissance and the Reformation.

TAKING NOTES

Clarifying Use a chart to list one contribution to democracy with each item on the list.

Category	Contribution
Judaism	
Christianity	
Islam	
Renaissance	
Reformation	

Judaism

Much of what we know about the early history of the Hebrews, later called the Jews, is contained in the first five books of the Hebrew Bible, the Torah. In the Torah, God chose Abraham to be the "father," or ancestor, of the Hebrew people. God commanded Abraham to move his people to Canaan, an area on the east coast of the Mediterranean Sea. This occurred around 1800 B.C.

Created in God's Image Other groups around the Hebrews were polytheists, people who believed in more than one God. The Hebrews, however, were monotheists. They believed in one God. This God was perfect, all-knowing, all-powerful, and eternal. Earlier, people had generally thought that what the gods wanted from human beings was the performance of rituals and sacrifices in their honor. The Hebrews believed that it was God's wish for people to live moral lives. The religion of the Hebrews was called **Judaism**.

The Hebrew Bible (the Old Testament, to Christians) states that human beings are created in God's image. The Hebrews interpreted this to mean that each human being has a divine spark that gives him or her a dignity that can never be taken away. For the Greeks and Romans, the individual had dignity because of his or her ability to reason. For the Hebrews, each person had dignity simply by being a child of God.

The Hebrews believed that God had given human beings moral freedom—the capacity to choose between good and evil. Therefore, each person was responsible for the choices he or she made. These beliefs led to a new emphasis on the worth of the individual.

Jewish Law Teaches Morality Like the Greeks, the Romans, and other ancient peoples, the Jews had a written code of laws. The Bible states that God gave this code to their leader Moses in the form of the **Ten Commandments** and other laws. This event occurred sometime between 1300 and 1200 B.C. Unlike the laws of other peoples, the Hebrews' code focused more on morality and ethics and less on politics. The code included rules of social and religious behavior to which even rulers were subject. While the Hebrew code of justice was strict, it was softened by expressions of God's mercy.

An expansion of the religious thought of the Jews occurred with the emergence of prophets in the eighth century B.C. The prophets were leaders and teachers who were believed by the Jews to be messengers from God. The prophets attacked war, oppression, and greed in statements such as these from the Hebrew Bible:

> **PRIMARY SOURCE**
> He has told you, O mortal, what is good; and what does the Lord require of you but to do justice, and to love kindness, and to walk humbly with your God?
>
> **MICAH** 6:8

The prophets strengthened the Jews' social conscience, which has become part of the Western tradition. The Jews believed that it is the responsibility of every person to oppose injustice and oppression and that the community should assist the unfortunate. The prophets held out the hope that life on earth could be improved, that poverty and injustice need not exist, and that individuals are capable of living according to high moral standards.

MAIN IDEA

Clarifying
What did the prophets teach about injustice and oppression?

> Analyzing Primary Sources

The Ten Commandments

The Ten Commandments are the ten orders or laws given by God to Moses on Mount Sinai. These orders serve as the basis for Jewish laws.

PRIMARY SOURCE

1. I am the Lord your God. . . You shall have no other gods besides me.
2. You shall not make for yourself a sculptured image. . .
3. You shall not swear falsely by the name of the Lord your God.
4. Remember the Sabbath day and keep it holy.
5. Honor your father and your mother. . .
6. You shall not murder.
7. You shall not commit adultery.
8. You shall not steal.
9. You shall not bear false witness against your neighbor.
10. You shall not covet. . . anything that is your neighbor's.

Exodus 20:2–14

▲ An engraving from the 19th century shows Moses with the Ten Commandments.

DOCUMENT-BASED QUESTIONS

1. **Comparing** Do the first four commandments concern themselves more with the Hebrews' relationship with God or with one another?
2. **Contrasting** What do the last six commandments have in common that distinguish them from the first four?

North Sea

BRITAIN

Rhine R.

Danube R.

Christian areas, 325
Additional Christian areas, 500
Boundary of Roman Empire, 395

ATLANTIC
OCEAN

GAUL

Black Sea

ITALY
Rome

Constantinople
Nicaea

SPAIN

40°N

GREECE

ANATOLIA

ARMENIA

Caspian Sea

Corinth

Mediterranean

Hippo

Sea

Antioch
SYRIA

JUDEA

Jerusalem

N

Alexandria

0   500 Miles

EGYPT

Persian Gulf

0   1,000 Kilometers

Nile R.

Red Sea

GEOGRAPHY SKILLBUILDER: Interpreting Maps
1. **Location** *Where was Christianity most widespread in* A.D. *325?*
2. **Region** *What was the extent (north to south, east to west) of Christianity's spread by* A.D. *500?*

Christianity

As Rome expanded, its power spread throughout the Mediterranean. It took control of Judea, homeland of the Jews, around 63 B.C. By 6 B.C., the Romans ruled Judea directly as a part of their empire.

According to the New Testament, Jesus of Nazareth was born around 6 to 4 B.C. He was both a Jew and a Roman subject. He began his public ministry at the age of 30. His preaching contained many ideas from Jewish tradition, such as monotheism and the principles of the Ten Commandments. Jesus emphasized God's personal relationship to each human being.

The Teachings of Christianity Jesus' ideas went beyond traditional morality. He stressed the importance of people's love for God, their neighbors, their enemies, and themselves. In the Sermon on the Mount, Jesus told the people, "I say unto you, Love your enemies, bless them that curse you, do good to them that hate you, and pray for them which despitefully use you, and persecute you." He also taught that God would eventually end wickedness in the world and would establish an eternal kingdom in which he would reign. People who sincerely repented their sins would find life after death in this kingdom.

About A.D. 29, Jesus visited Jerusalem. Because some referred to him as the "king of the Jews," the Roman governor considered him a political threat. Jesus was put to death by crucifixion. According to Jesus' followers, he rose from the dead three days later and ascended into heaven. His followers believed he was the Messiah, or savior. Jesus came to be referred to as Jesus Christ. *Christos* is a Greek word meaning "messiah" or "savior." The word **Christianity**, the name of the religion founded by Jesus, was derived from the name Christ.

Vocabulary
An *apostle* is one
of the followers of
Jesus who preached
and spread his
teaching.

The Spread of Christianity In the first century after Jesus' death, his followers began to teach this new religion based on his message. Christianity spread slowly but steadily across the Roman Empire. One man, the apostle Paul, had enormous influence on Christianity's development.

Paul preached in cities around the eastern Mediterranean. He stressed that Jesus was the son of God and that he had died for people's sins. Paul declared that Christianity was a universal religion. It should welcome all converts, Jew and non-Jew. He said, "There is neither Jew nor Greek, there is neither slave nor free, there is neither male nor female; for you are all one in Christ Jesus." He stressed the essential equality of all human beings, a belief central to democracy.

Rome Spreads Judeo-Christian Ideas In the beginning, the Roman Empire was hostile to the beliefs of Judaism and Christianity. Yet it was the empire that helped spread the ideas of these religions in two ways. The first way was indirect. After the Jews began to rebel against the Romans in the first century, many were exiled from their homeland. This movement continued the dispersal of the Jews called the Diaspora. The Jews then fled to many parts of the world, where they shared their beliefs that all people had the right to be treated with justice and dignity.

MAIN IDEA

Summarizing
Ⓑ How were
Judeo-Christian
ideas spread
throughout the
Roman Empire?

The second way the empire spread Judeo-Christian ideas was more direct. Despite Roman persecution of Christians, Christianity became a powerful religion throughout the empire and beyond. By 380, it had become the official religion of the empire. Eventually it took root in Europe, the Near East, and northern Africa. Ⓑ

Islam

Another monotheistic religion that taught equality of all persons and individual worth also developed in southwest Asia in the early 600s. **Islam** was based on the teachings of the prophet Muhammad. Muhammad's teachings, which are the revealed word of God (Allah in Arabic), are found in the holy book called the Qur'an. He emphasized the dignity of all human beings and the brotherhood of all people. A belief in the bond of community and the unity of all people led to a tolerance of different groups within the community.

▲ An illustrated page of the Qur'an from the 9th century

Followers of Islam are called Muslims. Muslims were required by their religion to offer charity and help to those in need. Under Muslim law, rulers had to obey the same laws as those they ruled. In lands controlled by Muslims, the Muslims were required to show tolerance for the religious practices of Jews and Christians.

The Legacy of Monotheistic Religions Several ideals crucial to the shaping of a democratic outlook emerged from the early monotheistic religions of southwest Asia. They include the following:

• the duty of the individual and the community to combat oppression
• the worth of the individual
• the equality of people before God

These ideas would form part of the basis of democratic thinking. More ideas about the value of the individual and about the questioning of authority would surface during the Renaissance and Reformation.

The Rise of Democratic Ideas **15**

Printing Spreads Ideas

The development of a movable type printing press around 1440, shown above in a 16th-century French woodcut, revolutionized the sharing of ideas. The press made it possible to print books quickly and cheaply. This fueled Renaissance learning because scholars could read each other's works soon after they were written. The ideas of the Renaissance and, later, of the Enlightenment were spread through the printed word.

The spread of reading matter made literacy for large numbers of people suddenly possible. And an informed citizenry contributed to the rise of democracy. These informed citizens began to question authority. This ultimately spurred democratic revolutions in America and France in the late 1700s.

Renaissance and Reformation

The **Roman Catholic Church** developed from Roman Christianity. By the Middle Ages, it had become the most powerful institution in Europe. It influenced all aspects of life—religious, social, and political. It was strongly authoritarian in structure, that is, it expected unquestioned obedience to its authority.

Renaissance Revives Classical Ideas In the 1300s, a brilliant cultural movement arose in Italy. Over the next 300 years, it spread to the rest of Europe, helped by the development of the printing press. This movement was called the **Renaissance**, from the French word for "rebirth." The Renaissance was marked by renewed interest in classical culture. This included the restoration of old monuments and works of art and the rediscovery of forgotten Greek and Latin manuscripts. Renaissance thinkers were interested in earthly life for its own sake. They rejected the medieval view that life was only a preparation for the afterlife.

Renaissance education was intended to prepare some men for public service rather than just for service to the Church. Scholars placed increasing value on subjects concerned with humankind and culture. The study of classical texts led to an intellectual movement that encouraged ideas about human potential and achievement. Some Christian writers were critical of the failure of the Church to encourage people to live a life that was moral and ethical. They also discussed ways in which the lives of all in society could improve.

Renaissance thinkers and writers began to explore ideas about political power and the role of government in the lives of ordinary people. The Greek and Roman ideas about democracy were quite different from the oligarchic governments they were experiencing.

During the Renaissance, individualism became deeply rooted in Western culture. Artists expressed it by seeking to capture individual character. Explorers and conquerors demonstrated it by venturing into uncharted seas and by carving out vast empires in the Americas. It also was shown by merchant-capitalists, who amassed huge fortunes by taking great economic risks.

Vocabulary
Individualism is the belief in the importance of the individual and in the virtues of self-reliance and personal independence.

The Reformation Challenges Church Power Although Christianity remained a strong force in Europe during the Renaissance, people began to be more critical of the Church. The spirit of questioning that started during the Renaissance came to full bloom in the **Reformation**. The Reformation was a religious reform movement that began in the 16th century. Those who wanted to reform the Catholic Church were called Protestants, because they protested against the power and abuses of the Church. Reformers stressed the importance of a direct relationship with God.

The Reformation started in Germany. In 1517, a monk and teacher named Martin Luther criticized the Church's practice of selling pardons for sins. Soon, Luther went further. He contradicted the Church's position that salvation came through faith and good works. He said people could be saved only through faith in God. What began as a reform movement ended up as a new division of Christianity—Protestantism.

Vocabulary
A *pardon* is a cancellation of punishment still due for a sin that has been forgiven.

Because Protestantism encouraged people to make their own religious judgments, Protestants began to have differences of belief. They then established new churches in addition to the already-formed Lutheran Church. These included the Anglican, Presbyterian, and Calvinist churches.

Catholics and Protestants differed on many issues. The Catholic Church claimed the right to interpret the Bible for all Christians. Protestants called on believers to interpret the Bible for themselves. The Catholic Church said the only way to salvation was through the Church. Protestants said that the clergy had no special powers; people could find individual paths to God. The Protestant emphasis on private judgment in religious matters—on a sense of conviction rather than a reliance on authority—strengthened the importance of the individual even more. It also led to a questioning of political authority. (See History in Depth on this page.)

Legacy of the Renaissance and Reformation The Reformation and the other changes that swept Europe during and after the Middle Ages greatly influenced the shaping of the modern world. By challenging the authority of monarchs and popes, the Reformation indirectly contributed to the growth of democracy. Also, by calling on believers to read and interpret the Bible for themselves, it introduced individuals to reading and exposed them to more than just religious ideas.

Both the Renaissance and the Reformation placed emphasis on the importance of the individual. This was an important idea in the democratic revolutions that followed and in the growth of political liberty in modern times. **C**

History *in* Depth

The Peasants' Revolt
Luther questioned Church authority. But peasants in southern Germany took Luther's example further. In 1524, they questioned political and social authority. They wanted an end to serfdom, or being forced to serve a master. They stormed the castles of the nobles, forcing them, at least initially, to give in to their demands.

It was the largest mass uprising in the history of Germany. The peasants looked to Luther to support their rights, but Luther supported the nobles instead. As many as 100,000 peasants were killed during the rebellion.

MAIN IDEA
Synthesizing
C How did the Renaissance and the Reformation shape ideas about democracy?

SECTION 2 ASSESSMENT

TERMS & NAMES 1. For each term or name, write a sentence explaining its significance.
• Judaism • Ten Commandments • Christianity • Islam • Roman Catholic Church • Renaissance • Reformation

USING YOUR NOTES
2. How do the contributions listed on your chart support the ideals of democracy?

Category	Contri-bution
Judaism	
Christianity	
Islam	
Renaissance	
Reformation	

MAIN IDEAS
3. How are the Ten Commandments different from the laws of other groups?

4. Which of the Christian teachings supports the central idea of democracy?

5. How did the Reformation indirectly contribute to the growth of democracy?

CRITICAL THINKING & WRITING
6. **COMPARING** What ideas crucial to the shaping of democracy did Judaism and Christianity share?

7. **DRAWING CONCLUSIONS** How did the Reformation promote the idea of individualism?

8. **SYNTHESIZING** How did the printing press help promote the ideas of democracy?

9. **WRITING ACTIVITY** CULTURAL INTERACTION Write a **summary paragraph** that illustrates how the Judeo-Christian view of reason and faith, and the duties of the individual and community contributed to the development of democratic thought.

CONNECT TO TODAY CREATING A COLLAGE

Using newspapers or magazines, create a **collage** showing modern nations practicing ideas of democracy. You might include headlines, pictures, or articles about equality of all people and community efforts to combat oppression.

Democracy Develops in England

MAIN IDEA	WHY IT MATTERS NOW	TERMS & NAMES
POWER AND AUTHORITY England began to develop democratic institutions that limited the power of the monarchy.	Democratic traditions developed in England have influenced many countries, including the United States.	• common law • Magna Carta • due process of law • Parliament • divine right • Glorious Revolution • constitutional monarchy • bill of rights

SETTING THE STAGE The idea of democracy developed gradually over the centuries, as you read in previous sections. From its beginnings in the city-states of ancient Greece, democracy moved to Rome. There, the Romans adapted democratic ideas to establish a republican form of government. Judaism and Christianity spread the ideas of individual worth and responsibility to community. Democracy finally took root and found permanence in England in the late Middle Ages.

TAKING NOTES

Following Chronological Order Use a time line to show the main events in the development of democracy in England.

Reforms in Medieval England

In 1066, William, duke of Normandy in France, invaded England and defeated the Anglo-Saxons at the Battle of Hastings. William then claimed the English throne. This set in motion events that led to: (1) the end of feudalism—the political and economic system of the Middle Ages, (2) the beginnings of centralized government in England, and (3) the development of democracy there. One of William's descendants was Henry II, who ruled from 1154 to 1189. He controlled most of the western half of France, as well as all of England. A man of great wisdom and vigor, Henry is considered one of the most gifted statesmen of the 12th century.

▼ King John of England

Juries and Common Law One of Henry's greatest achievements was the development of the jury trial as a means of administering royal justice. Before then, people were tried in courts of feudal lords. In such courts, the accused would usually have to survive a duel or some physically painful or dangerous ordeal to be set free.

With Henry's innovation, a royal judge would visit each shire, or county, at least once a year. First, the judge would review the crime that had been committed. Then he would ask 12 men, often neighbors of the accused, to answer questions about the facts of the case. These people were known as a jury. Unlike modern juries, they did not decide guilt or innocence. People came to prefer the jury trial to the feudal-court trial because they found it more just.

Legal decisions made by royal justices were used as precedents in new cases. Gradually, England was unified under a single legal system. This was called "common law" because it was common to the whole kingdom. Unlike Roman law, which expressed the will of a ruler or a lawmaker, **common law** reflected customs and principles established over time. Common law became the basis of the legal systems in many English-speaking countries, including the United States.

The Magna Carta When Henry II died, his son Richard the Lion-Hearted assumed the throne. Richard's brother John, an unpopular king, followed him. King John fought a costly and unsuccessful war with France. Not only did England lose many of its land holdings in France, but John also tried to raise taxes to pay for the war. This led to conflict between the English nobles and the king. In 1215 the angry nobles rebelled and forced John to grant guarantees of certain traditional political rights. They presented their demands to him in written form as the **Magna Carta** (Great Charter).

The Magna Carta is the major source of traditional English respect for individual rights and liberties. Basically, it was a contract between the king and nobles of England. However, the Magna Carta contained certain important principles that limited the power of the English monarch over all his English subjects. It implied the idea that monarchs had no right to rule in any way they pleased. They had to govern according to law.

> Analyzing Primary Sources

The Magna Carta

The Magna Carta is considered one of the cornerstones of democratic government. The underlying principle of the document is the idea that all must obey the law, even the king. Its guaranteed rights are an important part of modern liberties and justice.

PRIMARY SOURCE

38. No bailiff [officer of the court] for the future shall, upon his own unsupported complaint, put anyone to his "law," without credible witnesses brought for this purpose.

39. No freeman shall be taken or imprisoned . . . or exiled or in any way destroyed, nor will we [the king] go upon him nor send upon him, except by the lawful judgement of his peers or by the law of the land.

40. To no one will we sell, to no one will we refuse or delay, right or justice.

45. We will appoint as justices, constables, sheriffs, or bailiffs only such as know the law of the realm and mean to observe it well.

DOCUMENT-BASED QUESTIONS

1. **Analyzing Motives** Why might the English nobles have insisted on the right listed in number 45?
2. **Making Inferences** Which of the statements is a forerunner to the right to a speedy public trial guaranteed in the Sixth Amendment of the U.S. Constitution?

The Magna Carta had 63 clauses. Two established basic legal rights for individuals. Clause 12 declared that taxes "shall be levied in our kingdom only by the common consent of our kingdom." This meant that the king had to ask for popular consent before he could tax. Clause 39 declared, "No man shall be arrested or imprisoned . . . except by the lawful judgment of his peers or by the law of the land." This meant that a person had the right to a jury trial and to the protection of the law. This right—to have the law work in known, orderly ways—is called **due process of law**. In other words, the king could not willfully, or arbitrarily, punish his subjects. **A**

Over the centuries, the principles of the Magna Carta were extended to protect the liberties of all the English people. Clause 12, for example, was later interpreted to mean that the king could not levy taxes without the consent of **Parliament**, England's national legislature. The principle of "no taxation without representation" was a rallying cry, over five centuries later, of the American Revolution.

Model Parliament Even before the Norman Conquest, Anglo-Saxon kings had discussed important issues with members of the nobility who acted as a council of advisers. This practice continued through the centuries. In 1295, King John's grandson, Edward I, needed money to pay for yet another war in France. He wanted wide support for the war. So he called together not only the lords but also lesser knights and some burgesses, or leading citizens of the towns. Edward explained his action by saying, "What affects all, by all should be approved." Historians refer to this famous gathering as the Model Parliament, because it established a standard for later parliaments. The Model Parliament voted on taxes and helped Edward make reforms and consolidate laws.

By the mid-1300s, the knights and burgesses had gained an official role in the government. They had formed an assembly of their own—the House of Commons, which was the lower house of Parliament. Nobles and bishops met separately in the upper house, the House of Lords. Because the great majority of English people had no part in Parliament, it was not truly a democratic body. Even so, its existence limited the power of the monarch and established the principle of representation.

MAIN IDEA

Drawing Conclusions

A How did the principle of rule by law, as implied in the Magna Carta, limit the power of the king?

▼ The House of Commons meeting in its chamber

Parliament Grows Stronger

Over the next few centuries, Parliament's "power of the purse," or its right to approve certain expenses, gave it strong influence in governing. The House of Commons, which controlled those purse strings, was gradually becoming the equal of the House of Lords. Parliament increasingly viewed itself as a partner with the monarch in governing. It voted on taxes, passed laws, and advised on royal policies.

Conflict With the Monarch The struggle to limit the power of the monarchy continued over the centuries. In the 1600s, monarchs on the European continent were asserting greater authority over lords than they had during the Middle Ages. These kings claimed not just the right to rule but the right to rule with absolute power. They claimed that a king's power came from God. This assertion was known as the theory of the **divine right** of kings. Advocates of divine right said that monarchs were chosen by God and responsible only to God.

Elizabeth I, the last Tudor monarch of England, died in 1603, without a child. She was succeeded by a new line of monarchs, the Stuarts, who were relatives from Scotland. The Stuarts were strong believers in divine right. King James VI of Scotland became James I, the first Stuart king of England. Because he came from Scotland and knew little of English laws and institutions, he clashed with Parliament over the rights of the people.

Three issues caused conflict. First, religious reformers known as Puritans were trying to change the Church of England, or Anglican Church, through legislation. They wanted to simplify, or purify, Church doctrines and ceremonies. They felt the Church of England was still too much like the Roman Catholic Church, from which it had separated. The Puritans entered an ongoing battle with James, the official head of the Church.

Second, James used the Star Chamber, a royal court of law, to administer justice. He ignored parliamentary courts, which used common law. The people began to accuse the king of tyranny. Third, and most important, was the issue of money. Elizabeth had left James a large debt. In addition, he wanted more money in order to have an extravagant court and to wage war. Parliament declined to grant him any additional funds. James then ignored Parliament and tried to raise money by other means. Ⓑ

Parliament Overthrows the King The troubles under James became explosions under his son, Charles I, who became king in 1625. Like James, Charles needed funds. He asked Parliament for money in 1628. In return for granting revenue from taxes, Parliament tried to limit royal power further. It sought to force Charles to accept the Petition of Right.

The Petition of Right went against theories of absolute monarchy. It is viewed as a landmark in constitutional history. It demanded an end to
- taxing without Parliament's consent
- imprisoning citizens illegally
- housing troops in citizens' homes
- maintaining military government in peacetime

Charles agreed to sign the petition in order to get the funds he wanted. Later, he ignored the commitments secured in the document.

Charles dismissed Parliament in 1629 and refused to convene it again. When the Scots invaded England in 1640, Charles was forced to call Parliament to get funds to defend the country. In a show of independence, Parliament refused to discuss money until Charles considered how he had wronged Parliament. Parliament passed laws to reduce the power of the monarchy, angering the king. Grievances continued to grow. Eventually, in 1642, the English Civil War broke out. Royalists, who upheld the monarchy, were opposed by antiroyalists, who supported Parliament.

After years of conflict, antiroyalist forces, commanded by Puritan leader Oliver Cromwell, won control of the government. Charles was condemned as a "tyrant, murderer, and public enemy" and, in 1649, was executed.

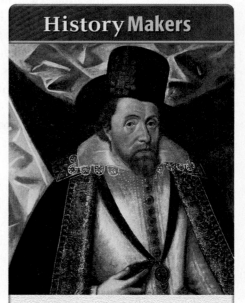

History Makers

James I
1566–1625

As king, James believed he had absolute authority to govern England as he saw fit. Royal authority came directly from God, and kings were answerable only to God, not to the people or Parliament.

In a speech to Parliament in 1609, James declared:

The state of monarchy is the supremest thing upon earth . . . Kings are justly called Gods, for that they exercise a manner or resemblance of divine power upon earth . . . [T]o dispute what God may do, is blasphemy . . . so is it sedition in subjects, to dispute what a king may do.

James had passed down these views to a son a decade earlier in *Basilicon Doron*, a book of instructions he wrote on the ways of kingship.

The Rise of Democratic Ideas **21**

Establishment of Constitutional Monarchy

After Charles's execution, Cromwell established a republic called the Commonwealth of England. He spent several years crushing a series of uprisings against his rule. He was opposed both by supporters of monarchy and by more extreme Puritans. Cromwell became unhappy with Parliament's failure to enact his religious, social, and economic reforms. In 1653 he dissolved Parliament and created a government called the Protectorate. He named himself Lord Protector, in effect becoming a military dictator.

Cromwell's rule was increasingly authoritarian, and he became extremely unpopular. Most of the English were not unhappy at his death in 1658.

The Restoration Cromwell's son Richard succeeded him as Lord Protector. He was not a strong ruler, and the military dictatorship continued to be unpopular. Cromwell resigned in 1659. In 1660, a new Parliament restored the monarchy and invited Charles Stuart, the son of Charles I, to take the throne. This period was called the Restoration, because the monarchy was restored to the throne. Yet Parliament retained the powers it had gained during the struggles of the previous two decades. For example, the monarch could not tax without Parliament's consent. **C**

In addition, Parliament continued to try to limit the monarchy and to expand rights. In 1679 it passed the Habeas Corpus Amendment Act. *Habeas corpus* is a Latin term meaning "you are ordered to have the body." When someone is arrested, the police must produce the person in court. That person must be informed of what he or she is accused of having done. The court then decides if there is reason to hold the accused. Habeas corpus prevents authorities from detaining a person wrongfully or unjustly. (This right is still important in democracies today. It is mentioned in the U.S. Constitution.)

Glorious Revolution When Charles II died in 1685, his younger brother became King James II. James was a Roman Catholic and a believer in the divine right of kings. English Protestants were afraid that he wanted to make Catholicism the official religion. They hoped that when James died, his Protestant daughter, Mary, would become queen. But James's wife gave birth to a son in 1688. Because a male heir to the throne took precedence, or came before, a female, it appeared that rule by Catholic monarchs would continue. This was unacceptable to most of the English people.

Parliament withdrew its support from James and offered the English throne to his daughter, Mary, and her husband, William of Orange, ruler of the Netherlands, both Protestants. William invaded England, and James fled to France. In 1689 William and Mary were crowned co-rulers of England. The **Glorious Revolution**, as it came to be called, was a turning point in English constitutional history. Parliament had established its right to limit the English monarch's power and to control succession to the throne. England was now a **constitutional monarchy**, in which the powers of the ruler are restricted by the constitution and the laws of the country.

MAIN IDEA

Analyzing Causes
C What caused Parliament to restore the monarchy?

Global Impact

Prelude to the American Revolution

James II's unpopularity extended across the Atlantic Ocean to England's American colonies.

In 1684, a royal court took away the charter of the Massachusetts Bay Colony. James had decided to create a union of all colonies from New Jersey to New Hampshire. He appointed Sir Edmund Andros as royal governor of the Dominion of New England. Andros abolished elective assemblies, declared town meetings illegal, and collected taxes the people had never voted on.

When word of the Glorious Revolution reached America, the colonists overthrew Andros in their own version of the revolt. This action may have contributed to the colonists' belief that it was their right to overthrow an unjust king.

English Bill of Rights In 1689, William and Mary accepted from Parliament a <u>bill of rights</u>, or formal summary of the rights and liberties believed essential to the people. The English Bill of Rights limited the monarchy's power and protected free speech in Parliament.

The Bill of Rights did not allow the monarch to suspend laws, to tax without Parliament's consent, or to raise an army in peacetime without approval from Parliament. It assured the people the right to petition the king to seek remedies for grievances against government. Excessive bail and cruel and unusual punishment were forbidden. And foremost, the Bill of Rights declared:

▲ William and Mary became rulers of England in 1689.

PRIMARY SOURCE
. . . that for redress of all grievances, and for the amending, strengthening, and preserving of the laws, parliament ought to be held frequently.

English Bill of Rights

England's Legacy England's Glorious Revolution and the bill of rights that it produced had a great impact. English citizens were guaranteed the rule of law, parliamentary government, individual liberties, and a constitutional monarchy. This completed a process begun with the Magna Carta. The Bill of Rights also set an example for England's American colonists when they considered grievances against Britain nearly 100 years later. These legal and political developments, along with the ideas of the Enlightenment, would give rise to democratic revolutions in America and France in the late 18th century. **D**

MAIN IDEA

Summarizing
D What was England's legacy to democracy?

SECTION ③ **ASSESSMENT**

TERMS & NAMES 1. For each term or name, write a sentence explaining its significance.
• common law • Magna Carta • due process of law • Parliament • divine right • Glorious Revolution • constitutional monarchy • bill of rights

USING YOUR NOTES	MAIN IDEAS	CRITICAL THINKING & WRITING
2. Which of the events listed do you think was the most important? Explain.	3. What were three eventual consequences of William the Conqueror's victory at Hastings? 4. What important legal practice dates back to Henry II? 5. Why did Parliament invite William and Mary to rule England in 1689?	6. **RECOGNIZING EFFECTS** What impact did the English common law have on the United States? 7. **COMPARING** Why was Oliver Cromwell's rule like that of an absolute monarch? 8. **SUMMARIZING** What were the main achievements of the Glorious Revolution? 9. **WRITING ACTIVITY** POWER AND AUTHORITY Think of yourself as an adviser to King John. Write him a **letter** in which you argue for or against accepting the Magna Carta. Tell the king the advantages and disadvantages of agreeing to the demands of the nobles.

CONNECT TO TODAY **COMPARING HISTORICAL DOCUMENTS**
Locate a copy of the Magna Carta and a copy of the Bill of Rights of the U.S. Constitution. Study both documents and create a **table** showing where the U.S. Bill of Rights reflects the ideas of the Magna Carta.

The Enlightenment and Democratic Revolutions

MAIN IDEA	WHY IT MATTERS NOW	TERMS & NAMES
REVOLUTION Enlightenment ideas helped bring about the American and French revolutions.	These revolutions and the documents they produced have inspired other democratic movements.	• Enlightenment • representative • social contract government • natural rights • federal system • separation of • United Nations powers

SETTING THE STAGE The Renaissance continued to affect European thinking throughout the 17th century. The Renaissance emphasis on the individual and on expanding human potential were especially influential. At the same time, Europeans began to explore their physical world. They extended the boundaries of the known world in what came to be called the Age of Exploration. New ideas and discoveries had a great impact on Europeans' understanding of themselves and the world.

TAKING NOTES

Outlining Use an outline to organize the main ideas and details.

I. Enlightenment Thinkers and Ideas
   A.
   B.
II. The Beginnings of Democracy in America
   A.
   B.
III. The French Revolution

Enlightenment Thinkers and Ideas

During the 17th and 18th centuries, an intellectual movement called the **Enlightenment** developed. Enlightenment thinkers tried to apply the principles of reason and the methods of science to all aspects of society. They built upon the long history of Western thought.

The philosophers of ancient Greece had established the idea of natural laws that could be discovered by careful observation and reasoned inquiry. Christianity contributed the belief in the equality of all human beings. (This belief would later lead to the principle of equal rights in society.) During the Renaissance, thinkers had focused on worldly concerns. They criticized medieval philosophy for concentrating on questions that seemed unrelated to human conditions.

The Scientific Revolution of the 1500s and 1600s was an even more immediate source of Enlightenment thought. It stimulated new ideas about society and government. The Scientific Revolution caused thinkers to rely on rational thought rather than just accept traditional beliefs. Enlightenment thinkers praised both Isaac Newton's discovery of the mechanical laws that govern the universe and the scientific method that made such a discovery possible. These thinkers wanted to apply the scientific method, which relied on observation and testing of theories, to human affairs. They hoped to use reason to discover natural laws that governed society just as scientists had used it to discover physical laws.

Hobbes and Locke The English philosophers Thomas Hobbes and John Locke were important Enlightenment thinkers. Both considered human nature and the role of government. In his masterpiece of political theory, *Leviathan* (1651), Hobbes stated that people were by nature selfish and ambitious. He thought the type of government needed to control selfish ambitions was absolute monarchy.

In a kind of **social contract,** or agreement among members of society, people submitted to an authoritarian ruler to prevent disorder. Although Hobbes was a monarchist, his idea of a social contract was important for the development of democracy.

Locke held a more positive view of human nature. His book *Two Treatises of Government* was published in 1690, the year after the Glorious Revolution. Locke argued that the English people had been justified in overthrowing James II. The government had failed under James to perform its most fundamental duty—protecting the rights of the people. Locke said that all human beings had, by nature, the right to life, liberty, and property. In order to protect these **natural rights**, they formed governments. The people had an absolute right, he said, to rebel against a government that violated or failed to protect their rights.

Locke believed that a government's power comes from the people, not from God. Thus, Locke provided a strong argument against the divine right of kings. Locke's ideas about self-government inspired people and became cornerstones of modern democratic thought. **A**

MAIN IDEA

Summarizing

A What was John Locke's argument against the divine right of kings?

Vocabulary

A *freethinker* is one who rejects dogma and authority.

Voltaire and Rousseau Other thinkers of the Enlightenment admired the democratic nature of English institutions. They themselves, however, lived under absolute monarchs. Voltaire was a brilliant 18th-century French historian. He argued in favor of tolerance, freedom of religion, and free speech. The French government and Christianity were often targets of his criticism.

Perhaps the most freethinking of all Enlightenment philosophers was Jean-Jacques Rousseau. His most famous work was *The Social Contract* (1762). In it, Rousseau advocated democracy. Unlike Hobbes, he called the social contract an agreement among free individuals to create a government that would respond to the people's will:

PRIMARY SOURCE
The problem is to find a form of association which will defend and protect with the whole common force the person and goods of each associate, and in which each, while uniting himself with all, may still obey himself alone, and remain as free as before.

JEAN-JACQUES ROUSSEAU, *The Social Contract*

For Rousseau, the only legitimate, or authentic, government came from the consent of the governed. The people, he hoped, would follow their consciences to vote for, or choose, what was best for the community as a whole.

Montesquieu Another French philosopher, Baron de Montesquieu, also recognized liberty as a natural right. In *The Spirit of the Laws* (1748), Montesquieu pointed out that any person or group in power will try to increase its power. Like Aristotle, Montesquieu searched for a way to control government. He concluded that liberty could best be safeguarded by a **separation of powers**, that is, by dividing government into three separate branches. These branches were (1) a legislature to make laws, (2) an executive to enforce them, and (3) courts to interpret them. The United States and many other democratic countries use this basic plan.

The Beginnings of Democracy in America

The ideas of the Enlightenment had a strong impact on Britain's North American colonies. By the mid-1700s, 13 British colonies had been established in North America. They were administered by the British government. To the north and west of Britain's colonies was New France, a French colony. In 1754, Britain and France went to war for control of North America. The war was called the French and Indian War. France and England also fought in Europe. There the conflict was known as the Seven Years' War.

Americans Protest British Policies The American colonists helped Britain defeat France in the French and Indian War, which ended in 1763. The war had been very costly, however, and further expenses lay ahead. Britain believed its colonies should pay some of the cost because they shared some of the benefits. To protect the newly acquired territory, the British needed to keep even more soldiers in America. To raise money, Britain sought to tax the colonists. The British Parliament passed the Stamp Act in 1765. It was the first in a series of such tax measures.

The colonists, who were not represented in Parliament, protested what they viewed as a violation of their rights as British citizens—there should be no taxation without representation. The colonists also resented the British for preventing them from settling on land west of the Appalachian Mountains. They felt that the French and Indian War had been fought to allow westward expansion.

Americans Win Independence The colonists opposed each tax measure Parliament imposed. Eventually, to protect their economic and political rights, the colonists united and began to arm themselves against what they called British oppression. The colonists' fight for independence from Great Britain, the American Revolution, began with the Battle of Lexington and Concord on April 19, 1775. The Americans issued a Declaration of Independence on July 4, 1776. In it, they declared to King George III of England and to the world why they should be free of British rule. The ideas of the Enlightenment—especially Locke's ideas that governments are created by the people to protect their rights—strongly influenced the writers of the Declaration. After five more years of war, the British army surrendered in 1781. The Americans had won their independence.

For several years, the new nation existed as a loose federation, or union, of states under a plan of government called the Articles of Confederation. Americans had wanted a weak central government. They feared that a strong government would lead to the kind of tyranny they had rebelled against. The Articles established one body, the Congress. But it was too weak. It did not have the power to collect taxes to pay war debt or to finance the government.

Enlightenment Ideas Shape the Constitution In the summer of 1787, a group of American leaders met in Philadelphia. They had been chosen by their state legislatures to frame, or work out, a better plan of government. The result of their efforts was the Constitution of the United States. This document has served as an inspiration and a model for new democracies around the world for more than 200

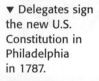
▼ Delegates sign the new U.S. Constitution in Philadelphia in 1787.

years. Creating the Constitution was not an easy task, however. There was great debate over a very basic question: Is it possible to establish a government that is strong and stable but not tyrannical? The answer that the framers reached was yes—such a government was possible if they created a system in which power and responsibility were shared in a balanced way.

First, the framers agreed to set up a **representative government**, one in which citizens elect representatives to make laws and policies for them. This was to ensure that the power to govern ultimately rested with the people, as advocated by Rousseau. Yet, unlike Rousseau, they selected an indirect form of government over direct democracy. The Romans, too, had chosen an indirect democracy when they established a republic.

Second, the framers created a **federal system**. The powers of government were to be divided between the federal, or central, government and the states, or local, governments.

MAIN IDEA

Recognizing Effects

B What Enlightenment ideas influenced the U.S. Constitution?

Third, within the federal government, the framers set up a separation of powers based on the writings of Montesquieu. Power was divided among the executive, legislative, and judicial branches. This provided a system of checks and balances to prevent any branch from having too much power. James Madison played an important role in the constitutional debates. (See History Makers on this page.) **B**

The French Revolution

During the 1700s, the impulse toward democracy had also been stirring in France. Under Louis XIV, who ruled from 1643 to 1715, France experienced the excesses of absolute monarchy. He left unresolved problems, massive debts, and growing unrest for his heirs—Louis XV and Louis XVI.

Causes of the Revolution Louis XVI came to the throne at the age of 19 in 1774. He was a well-intentioned but weak leader often dominated by his wife, Marie Antoinette. She was Austrian by birth and unpopular with the French people. France's problems, however, went deeper than the monarchy. The clergy and the nobility enjoyed many privileges. Even though the monarchy was deeply in debt, only commoners paid taxes. Many historians say that the French Revolution was fought to balance the inequalities in French society.

During the 18th century, Enlightenment ideas caused people to rethink the structure of society. The French middle class and some nobles were strongly impressed with ideas such as the social contract and freedom of speech. They were also inspired by the example of the American people throwing off an oppressive government in the 1770s. French peasants, too, were dissatisfied and restless. There had been poor harvests in the late 1780s. The people were hungry and felt that neither the king nor the nobility cared about their plight.

Early Reforms of the Revolution In 1789, Louis XVI's government was about to go bankrupt. In desperation, Louis sought to raise taxes. He called the Estates-General into session. This representative assembly had not been called to meet since 1614. The commoners in the Estates-General, however, felt their class was not fairly represented. They left in protest and formed the National Assembly.

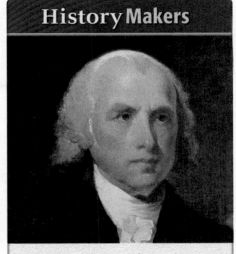

History Makers

James Madison
1751–1836

As a young man, James Madison was strongly influenced by the Enlightenment. When the Constitutional Convention was called, he spent a year preparing by reading the works of Locke, Montesquieu, Voltaire, and other Enlightenment philosophers.

Madison is known as the Father of the Constitution. He designed the plan that included the three branches of government. He also helped to create the federal system. Madison kept careful records of the debates at the convention so that future Americans could know how the delegates made their decisions. Later, he served as the fourth president of the United States.

▲ During the Reign of Terror, thousands of people suspected of not supporting the French Revolution were beheaded.

Eventually, members of other classes joined them. In the meantime, on July 14, 1789, the people of Paris stormed the Bastille, a much-hated prison in Paris that symbolized autocratic rule. Peasant uprisings then spread from Paris throughout the country. The fight to win democratic freedoms for the people, the French Revolution, had begun.

The National Assembly made many reforms. It adopted the Declaration of the Rights of Man and of the Citizen. This document was influenced by Enlightenment ideas and the American Declaration of Independence. It guaranteed the rights of "liberty, property, security, and resistance to oppression" to all people. The National Assembly also drafted a constitution that made France a limited monarchy. It reorganized the Catholic Church in France and redistributed its land. It reformed the court system. Believing its work done, it disbanded in 1791 so that a newly elected Legislative Assembly could take over.

Democratic Reforms Undone The new French assembly was not accepted by the king, the aristocracy, or many Catholics. Also, European countries that had absolute monarchs feared the spread of democratic ideas. They went to war with France, hoping to undo the new French republic. The country was in a state of crisis. In 1792, the royal family was imprisoned. A new legislature, even more radical, took charge. A period called the Reign of Terror followed. People thought to be opponents of the revolution were killed for their beliefs. Included among them were the king and queen. Finally, in 1799, a military leader, Napoleon Bonaparte, took control of France and created a dictatorship. **C**

Not until the mid-1800s did democracy develop in France. The French Revolution illustrates why democracy is hard to achieve. It is not enough to promise equality and freedom or to have representative government. For democracy to work, a society must have rule by law, protections for both civil rights and civil liberties, tolerance of dissent, and acceptance of majority decisions by the minority.

MAIN IDEA

Recognizing Effects
C What factors brought an end to the French Republic?

The Struggle for Democracy Continues

It took centuries for the ideas of democracy to develop and take hold in the world. Today, most people view democracy as the preferred form of government. Even some authoritarian governments voice agreement with the idea of democracy. Generally, however, they do not follow through with democratic actions.

The United Nations Promotes Democracy Before the end of World War II in 1945, a new international organization called the <u>United Nations</u> was established. Its goal was to work for world peace and the betterment of humanity. One branch of the UN, the General Assembly, is a kind of democracy. There, nations discuss problems, hoping to settle conflicts peacefully. Each nation has equal representation. The UN's charter is based on the traditions of democracy. The UN's authority comes from the nations of the world. The charter reaffirms basic human rights, the need for justice and the rule of law, and the desire for social progress.

One of the UN's most important contributions is the Universal Declaration of Human Rights. The General Assembly adopted the Declaration in 1948. This document draws on democratic ideas. It sets a worldwide standard for basic social, political, and economic rights. Included are the right to life, liberty, and security. Also stated are the rights to equal protection under the law, free movement, and free association and assembly with other people. To these rights were added social and economic rights: the rights to work, to rest and leisure, and to education. The declaration's purpose is to serve as an international code of conduct.

New Movements Toward Democracy In many places in the world, the ideals of the UN's Universal Declaration of Human Rights have yet to be wholly achieved. Nations are struggling to move toward more democratic government. But it is not easy to establish democratic policies where, for example, dictatorship has been the rule. Still, beginnings have been made in a number of countries.

In the early 1990s, the breakup of the Soviet Union enabled 15 new republics to assert their people's national identity and interests. In South Africa, after many years of apartheid, or racial segregation, a democratic, all-race government was established. In 2002, East Timor regained its independence following a UN-sponsored referendum. It had been seized nearly 30 years earlier by Indonesia.

There is no guarantee democracy can be achieved in any particular time and place. Nor is it guaranteed that once achieved, democracy will not be lost if people are not constantly watchful. Yet, as you read the history that follows, you will see that the idea of democracy has survived wars and oppression. It is an idea whose strength comes from the people. **D**

Global Impact

Revolutions of 1989

Democratic revolutions swept Eastern Europe in 1989. Reforms in the Soviet Union opened the door for more freedoms throughout Communist-controlled Eastern Europe. In April 1989, Poland held its first free election since the Communists seized control during World War II.

Hungary also launched a sweeping reform program. It then began to admit East Germans who claimed to be tourists but actually planned to escape to freedom. Soon, demonstrations began in East Germany, leading to the tearing down of the Berlin Wall. Eventually, the Communists fell from power, and East and West Germany voted to reunite.

MAIN IDEA

Forming and Supporting Opinions

D Why do you think people and nations continue to struggle toward more democratic government? Explain.

SECTION **4** **ASSESSMENT**

TERMS & NAMES 1. For each term or name, write a sentence explaining its significance.
• Enlightenment • social contract • natural rights • separation of powers • representative government • federal system • United Nations

USING YOUR NOTES	MAIN IDEAS	CRITICAL THINKING & WRITING
2. Which Enlightenment idea do you think contributed most to the democratic revolutions in America and France? Why?	3. What were natural rights?	6. **RECOGNIZING EFFECTS** How did the writers of the U.S. Constitution adapt the political theories of the Enlightenment?
	4. What was Rousseau's idea of government?	7. **COMPARING AND CONTRASTING** In what ways was the French Revolution similar to and different from the American Revolution?
	5. What political rights are set forth in the Universal Declaration of Human Rights?	8. **DEVELOPING HISTORICAL PERSPECTIVE** Why has the idea of democracy survived wars and oppression?
		9. **WRITING ACTIVITY** REVOLUTION Prepare a series of **slogans** that could be displayed at a pro-democracy rally during either the American or the French revolutions.

I. Enlightenment Thinkers and Ideas
A.
B.
II. The Beginnings of Democracy in America
A.
B.
III. The French Revolution

INTEGRATED TECHNOLOGY **INTERNET ACTIVITY**

Use the Internet to research new members of the United Nations since 1990. Prepare a **chart** showing the name of the nation, the date of its admission into the UN, and its form of government.

INTERNET KEYWORD
United Nations members

Prologue Assessment

TERMS & NAMES

Briefly explain the importance of each of the following to the rise of democratic ideas.

1. aristocracy
2. monarchy
3. direct democracy
4. republic
5. due process of law
6. divine right
7. social contract
8. representative government

MAIN IDEAS

The Legacy of Ancient Greece and Rome Section 1 (pages 5–11)

9. What changes did Pericles introduce into Greek government to make it more democratic?
10. How is a republic different from direct democracy?
11. What does the phrase "government of laws, not of men" mean?

Judeo-Christian Tradition Section 2 (pages 12–17)

12. What did the Hebrew tradition teach about the responsibilities of the individual and community to combat injustice?
13. How did the Reformation contribute to the growth of democracy?

Democracy Develops in England Section 3 (pages 18–23)

14. How does common law differ from Roman law?
15. Name two basic individual rights guaranteed in the Magna Carta.

16. In what three ways was the power of the English monarch limited by the English Bill of Rights?

The Enlightenment and Democratic Revolutions
Section 4 (pages 24–29)

17. What question did the framers of the American Constitution have to deal with, and what was the answer?
18. What is required in a society for democracy to work?

CRITICAL THINKING

1. USING YOUR NOTES

In a chart, show the Enlightenment ideas about government with which each philosopher is connected.

Philosopher	Idea

2. EVALUATING COURSES OF ACTION

POWER AND AUTHORITY   For what reasons would a nation in today's world choose representative democracy rather than direct democracy?

3. SYNTHESIZING

What do the basic ideals of monotheistic religions and the ideals of democracy have in common?

4. DRAWING CONCLUSIONS

How did the Magna Carta, the Petition of Right, and the English Bill of Rights advance the ideals of democracy?

5. ANALYZING CAUSES AND RECOGNIZING EFFECTS

CULTURAL INTERACTION   What impact did Enlightenment ideas have on the spread of democracy in the 18th century?

VISUAL SUMMARY

The Rise of Democratic Ideas

Greece
- direct democracy

Rome
- representative democracy

United States
- U.S. Constitution
- Bill of Rights

France
- Declaration of the Rights of Man and of the Citizen

DEMOCRACY
- rule of law
- code of laws
- value of individuals
- consent of the governed
- citizen participation

Judeo-Christian
- individual worth
- equality of all
- community concern

England
- common law
- Bill of Rights
- due process

Renaissance & Reformation
- natural laws
- challenge authority

Enlightenment
- social contract
- natural rights
- separation of powers

In the following selection from *Politics,* Aristotle presents his views on where the power of the state should reside. Use the quotation and your knowledge of world history to answer questions 1 and 2.
Additional Test Practice pp. S1–S33

PRIMARY SOURCE

Where ought the sovereign power of the state to reside? . . . The state aims to consist as far as possible of those who are alike and equal, a condition found chiefly among the middle section. . . . The middle class is also the steadiest element, the least eager for change. They neither covet, like the poor the possessions of others, nor do others covet theirs, as the poor covet those of the rich. . . . Tyranny often emerges from an over-enthusiastic democracy or from an oligarchy, but much more rarely from middle class constitutions

ARISTOTLE, *Politics*

1. With which group does Aristotle say political power is best located?
   A. the rich
   B. the middle class
   C. the poor
   D. the oligarchy

2. According to Aristotle what causes tyranny?
   A. the middle class
   B. the rich
   C. the poor
   D. over-enthusiastic democracy

Use the graph and your knowledge of world history to answer question 3.

3. How does the percentage of voters participating in United States elections compare to that of other nations?
   A. It is slightly higher than all but two nations.
   B. It is slightly lower than all but two nations.
   C. It is much lower than most nations.
   D. It is not possible to tell from the graph.

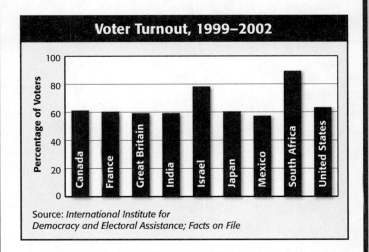

Voter Turnout, 1999–2002

Source: *International Institute for Democracy and Electoral Assistance; Facts on File*

INTEGRATED / TECHNOLOGY

TEST PRACTICE Go to **classzone.com**
- Diagnostic tests
- Tutorials
- Strategies
- Additional practice

ALTERNATIVE ASSESSMENT

1. Interact *with* History

On page 4, you were asked to think about why people would risk arrest, jail, or even death to have or preserve democracy. Imagine yourself as a television news reporter. Write at least five questions that you would ask the young man in the photograph on that page. Compare your questions with those of at least one other person in your class.

2. WRITING ABOUT HISTORY

REVOLUTION Write an **editorial** supporting or rejecting the idea that the only way to gain democracy in a country that does not have a democratic government is to wage a revolution.

Consider the following:
- No established government willingly gives up power.
- Complete change of government will only occur with the support of the people.
- Rule of law is basic to any democratic government.

INTEGRATED / TECHNOLOGY

Creating a Database

Democratic ideas continue to have enormous appeal throughout the world. During recent decades, democratic institutions were adopted in Brazil, Mexico, South Africa, and some countries of the former Soviet Union. Working with a team, use the Internet or your library to research changes that have taken place in the countries listed above. Then create a database comparing steps toward democracy in each country. The database might include the following:
- adoption of democratic election practices
- enforcement of laws regarding freedom of speech and the press
- peaceful transfer of power to democratically elected leaders
- the military's retreat from politics

Beginnings of the Modern World
1300–1800

Seeking new land and new markets, European explorers sailed around the world. This painting by Theodore Gudin depicts French explorer La Salle's Louisiana expedition of 1684.

Comparing & Contrasting

Methods of Government
In Unit 1, you will learn about different methods of ruling a nation or empire. At the end of the unit, you will have a chance to compare and contrast the governments you have studied. (See pages 144–149.)

CHAPTER

1

European Renaissance and Reformation, 1300–1600

Previewing Main Ideas

CULTURAL INTERACTION Trade with the East and the rediscovery of ancient manuscripts caused Europeans to develop new ideas about culture and art. This period was called the "Renaissance," which means rebirth.

Geography *Study the time line and the map. In which countries did the Renaissance begin?*

RELIGIOUS AND ETHICAL SYSTEMS Martin Luther began a movement to reform practices in the Catholic Church that he believed were wrong. That movement, the Reformation, led to the founding of non-Catholic churches.

Geography *Locate Wittenberg, the city where the Reformation began. What geographical features helped the Reformation spread from there?*

REVOLUTION The invention of the printing press allowed books and pamphlets to be made faster and more cheaply. This new technology helped spread the revolutionary ideas of the Renaissance and Reformation.

Geography *Printing spread from Mainz to other parts of Europe. How might the location of Mainz have helped the spread of printing?*

INTEGRATED TECHNOLOGY

eEdition
- Interactive Maps
- Interactive Visuals
- Interactive Primary Sources

INTERNET RESOURCES
Go to **classzone.com** for:
- Research Links
- Internet Activities
- Primary Sources
- Chapter Quiz
- Maps
- Test Practice
- Current Events

EUROPE

1300
In the 1300s the Renaissance begins in Italian city-states such as Florence, Milan, and Mantua.

1434
◄ Medici family takes control of Florence. (bust of Lorenzo Medici)

1300

1400

WORLD

1324
Mali king Mansa Musa makes a pilgrimage to Mecca.

1368
◄ Hongwu founds Ming Dynasty in China. (vase from that period)

1405
Chinese explorer Zheng He begins exploration of Asia and Africa.

Europe, 1500

SCOTLAND

IRELAND

ENGLAND

London

North Sea

NORWAY-DENMARK

SWEDEN

Baltic Sea

TEUTONIC ORDER

LITHUANIA

ATLANTIC OCEAN

Rotterdam

FLANDERS

BRANDENBURG

Wittenberg

POLAND

HOLY ROMAN EMPIRE

Mainz

Worms

Prague

Paris

Nantes

FRANCE

Augsburg

SWISS CONFEDERATION

Geneva

Trent

Milan

Mantua

AUSTRIA

HUNGARY

VENETIAN REPUBLIC

Adriatic Sea

OTTOMAN EMPIRE

MONTENEGRO

— Boundary of the Holy Roman Empire

PORTUGAL

Madrid

SPAIN

AVIGNON (Papal State)

CORSICA

Florence

PAPAL STATES

Rome

Naples

KINGDOM OF NAPLES

SARDINIA

Mediterranean Sea

KINGDOM OF SICILY

N
W E
S

0   150   300 Miles
0   300   600 Kilometers
Conic Projection

1455
Gutenberg Bible printed in Mainz. ▶

1517
Martin Luther begins the Reformation in Wittenberg.

1534
English king Henry VIII starts the Church of England.

1563
Council of Trent mandates reforms in Catholic Church.

1500

1600

1453
Ottoman Turks capture Constantinople.

1492
Columbus reaches the Americas.

1526
Babur establishes Mughal Empire in India. (Mughal noble) ▶

What can you learn from art?

You work at a museum that is considering buying this painting by Jan van Eyck. It is a portrait of Chancellor Rolin, a powerful government official in Burgundy (later part of France). Before deciding, the museum director wants to know what this painting can teach the public about the Renaissance.

1 Classical Art Renaissance artists admired classical art. The columns show classical style.

2 Perspective Van Eyck used the technique of perspective, which shows distant objects as smaller than close ones. He also used oil paints, a new invention.

3 Religion This painting portrays the infant Jesus and his mother Mary in 15th-century Europe. Such a depiction shows the continuing importance of religion during the Renaissance.

4 The Individual Renaissance artists portrayed the importance of individuals. Chancellor Rolin is wearing a fur-trimmed robe that shows his high status.

5 Beauty Van Eyck included many details simply to add beauty. These include the design on the floor, the folds of Mary's cloak, and the scenery outside.

▲ *The Madonna of Chancellor Rolin* (about 1435), Jan van Eyck

EXAMINING *the* ISSUES

- **What can you infer about the setting of the painting?**
- **What details in the painting give you an idea of the role of religion in society?**

As a class, discuss these questions to see what you can learn about this art. Also recall what you know about art in such places as Egypt and India. As you read about the Renaissance, notice what the art of that time reveals about European society.

Italy: Birthplace of the Renaissance

1

MAIN IDEA	WHY IT MATTERS NOW	TERMS & NAMES
REVOLUTION The Italian Renaissance was a rebirth of learning that produced many great works of art and literature.	Renaissance art and literature still influence modern thought and modern art.	• Renaissance • patron • humanism • perspective • secular • vernacular

SETTING THE STAGE During the late Middle Ages, Europe suffered from both war and plague. Those who survived wanted to celebrate life and the human spirit. They began to question institutions of the Middle Ages, which had been unable to prevent war or to relieve suffering brought by the plague. Some people questioned the Church, which taught Christians to endure suffering while they awaited their rewards in heaven. In northern Italy, writers and artists began to express this new spirit and to experiment with different styles. These men and women would greatly change how Europeans saw themselves and their world.

Italy's Advantages

This movement that started in Italy caused an explosion of creativity in art, writing, and thought that lasted approximately from 1300 to 1600. Historians call this period the **Renaissance** (REHN•ih•SAHNS). The term means rebirth, and in this context, it refers to a revival of art and learning. The educated men and women of Italy hoped to bring back to life the culture of classical Greece and Rome. Yet in striving to revive the past, the people of the Renaissance created something new. The contributions made during this period led to innovative styles of art and literature. They also led to new values, such as the importance of the individual.

The Renaissance eventually spread from northern Italy to the rest of Europe. Italy had three advantages that made it the birthplace of the Renaissance: thriving cities, a wealthy merchant class, and the classical heritage of Greece and Rome.

City-States Overseas trade, spurred by the Crusades, had led to the growth of large city-states in northern Italy. The region also had many sizable towns. Thus, northern Italy was urban while the rest of Europe was still mostly rural. Since cities are often places where people exchange ideas, they were an ideal breeding ground for an intellectual revolution.

In the 1300s, the bubonic plague struck these cities hard, killing up to 60 percent of the population. This brought economic changes. Because there were fewer laborers, survivors could demand higher wages. With few opportunities to expand business, merchants began to pursue other interests, such as art.

Merchants and the Medici A wealthy merchant class developed in each Italian city-state. Because city-states like Milan and Florence were relatively small, a high percentage of citizens could be intensely involved in political life.

TAKING NOTES
Outlining Use an outline to organize main ideas and details.

Italian Renaissance
I. Italy's advantages
A.
B.
II. Classical and worldly values

Merchants dominated politics. Unlike nobles, merchants did not inherit social rank. To succeed in business, they used their wits. As a result, many successful merchants believed they deserved power and wealth because of their individual merit. This belief in individual achievement became important during the Renaissance.

Since the late 1200s, the city-state of Florence had a republican form of government. But during the Renaissance, Florence came under the rule of one powerful banking family, the Medici (MEHD•ih•chee). The Medici family bank had branch offices throughout Italy and in the major cities of Europe. Cosimo de Medici was the wealthiest European of his time. In 1434, he won control of Florence's government. He did not seek political office for himself, but influenced members of the ruling council by giving them loans. For 30 years, he was dictator of Florence.

Cosimo de Medici died in 1464, but his family continued to control Florence. His grandson, Lorenzo de Medici, came to power in 1469. Known as Lorenzo the Magnificent, he ruled as a dictator yet kept up the appearance of having an elected government.

Looking to Greece and Rome Renaissance scholars looked down on the art and literature of the Middle Ages. Instead, they wanted to return to the learning of the Greeks and Romans. They achieved this in several ways. First, the artists and scholars of Italy drew inspiration from the ruins of Rome that surrounded them. Second, Western scholars studied ancient Latin manuscripts that had been preserved in monasteries. Third, Christian scholars in Constantinople fled to Rome with Greek manuscripts when the Turks conquered Constantinople in 1453. **A**

MAIN IDEA

Analyzing Causes
A What three advantages fostered the Renaissance in Italy?

Classical and Worldly Values

As scholars studied these manuscripts, they became more influenced by classical ideas. These ideas helped them to develop a new outlook on life and art.

Classics Lead to Humanism The study of classical texts led to **humanism**, an intellectual movement that focused on human potential and achievements. Instead of trying to make classical texts agree with Christian teaching as medieval scholars had, humanists studied them to understand ancient Greek values. Humanists influenced artists and architects to carry on classical traditions. Also, humanists popularized the study of subjects common to classical education, such as history, literature, and philosophy. These subjects are called the humanities.

Worldly Pleasures In the Middle Ages, some people had demonstrated their piety by wearing rough clothing and eating plain foods. However, humanists suggested that a person might enjoy life without offending God. In Renaissance Italy, the wealthy enjoyed material luxuries, good music, and fine foods.

Most people remained devout Catholics. However, the basic spirit of Renaissance society was **secular**—worldly rather than spiritual and concerned with the here and now. Even church leaders became more worldly. Some lived in beautiful mansions, threw lavish banquets, and wore expensive clothes.

Patrons of the Arts Church leaders during the Renaissance beautified Rome and other cities by spending huge amounts of money for art. They became **patrons** of the

Vocabulary
The words *humanist* and *humanities* come from the Latin word *humanitas,* which refers to the literary culture that every educated person should possess.

arts by financially supporting artists. Renaissance merchants and wealthy families also were patrons of the arts. By having their portraits painted or by donating art to the city to place in public squares, the wealthy demonstrated their own importance.

The Renaissance Man Renaissance writers introduced the idea that all educated people were expected to create art. In fact, the ideal individual strove to master almost every area of study. A man who excelled in many fields was praised as a "universal man." Later ages called such people "Renaissance men."

Baldassare Castiglione (KAHS•teel•YOH•nay) wrote a book called *The Courtier* (1528) that taught how to become such a person. A young man should be charming, witty, and well educated in the classics. He should dance, sing, play music, and write poetry. In addition, he should be a skilled rider, wrestler, and swordsman.

The Renaissance Woman According to *The Courtier*, upper-class women also should know the classics and be charming. Yet they were not expected to seek fame. They were expected to inspire art but rarely to create it. Upper-class Renaissance women were better educated than medieval women. However, most Renaissance women had little influence in politics.

MAIN IDEA

Comparing

B How were expectations for Renaissance men and Renaissance women similar?

A few women, such as Isabella d'Este, did exercise power. Born into the ruling family of the city-state of Ferrara, she married the ruler of another city-state, Mantua. She brought many Renaissance artists to her court and built a famous art collection. She was also skilled in politics. When her husband was taken captive in war, she defended Mantua and won his release. **B**

> Analyzing Primary Sources

The Renaissance Man

In *The Courtier*, Baldassare Castiglione described the type of accomplished person who later came to be called the Renaissance man.

PRIMARY SOURCE

Let the man we are seeking be very bold, stern, and always among the first, where the enemy are to be seen; and in every other place, gentle, modest, reserved, above all things avoiding ostentation [showiness] and that impudent [bold] self-praise by which men ever excite hatred and disgust in all who hear them. . . .

I would have him more than passably accomplished in letters, at least in those studies that are called the humanities, and conversant not only with the Latin language but with Greek, for the sake of the many different things that have been admirably written therein. Let him be well versed in the poets, and not less in the orators and historians, and also proficient in writing verse and prose.

BALDASSARE CASTIGLIONE, *The Courtier*

The Renaissance Woman

Although Renaissance women were not expected to create art, wealthy women often were patrons of artists, as this letter by Isabella d'Este demonstrates.

PRIMARY SOURCE

To Master Leonardo da Vinci, the painter: Hearing that you are settled at Florence, we have begun to hope that our cherished desire to obtain a work by your hand might be at length realized. When you were in this city and drew our portrait in carbon, you promised us that you would some day paint it in colors. But because this would be almost impossible, since you are unable to come here, we beg you to keep your promise by converting our portrait into another figure, which would be still more acceptable to us; that is to say, a youthful Christ of about twelve years . . . executed with all that sweetness and charm of atmosphere which is the peculiar excellence of your art. *Mantua, May 14, 1504*

ISABELLA D'ESTE, *Letters*

DOCUMENT-BASED QUESTIONS

1. **Drawing Conclusions** *Do the qualities called for in the ideal Renaissance man and woman seem to emphasize the individual or the group?*
2. **Making Inferences** *Isabella d'Este's portrait was painted by Titian, and Castiglione's by Raphael, two famous painters. What does this tell you about the subjects' social status?*

The Renaissance Revolutionizes Art

Supported by patrons like Isabella d'Este, dozens of artists worked in northern Italy. As the Renaissance advanced, artistic styles changed. Medieval artists had used religious subjects to convey a spiritual ideal. Renaissance artists often portrayed religious subjects, but they used a realistic style copied from classical models. Greek and Roman subjects also became popular. Renaissance painters used the technique of **perspective**, which shows three dimensions on a flat surface.

Realistic Painting and Sculpture Following the new emphasis on individuals, painters began to paint prominent citizens. These realistic portraits revealed what was distinctive about each person. In addition, artists such as the sculptor, poet, architect, and painter Michelangelo (MY•kuhl•AN•juh•LOH) Buonarroti used a realistic style when depicting the human body. **C**

Donatello (DAHN•uh•TEHL•oh) also made sculpture more realistic by carving natural postures and expressions that reveal personality. He revived a classical form in his statue of David, a boy who, according to the Bible, became a great king. Donatello's statue was created in the late 1460s. It was the first European sculpture of a large, free-standing nude since ancient times. For sculptors of the period, including Michelangelo, David (page 44) was a favorite subject.

MAIN IDEA

Synthesizing
C What major change did a belief in individual merit bring about in art?

> Analyzing Art

Perspective

Perspective creates the appearance of three dimensions. Classical artists had used perspective, but medieval artists abandoned the technique. In the 1400s, Italian artists rediscovered it.

Perspective is based on an optical illusion. As parallel lines stretch away from a viewer, they seem to draw together, until they meet at a spot on the horizon called the vanishing point. The use of perspective was a feature of most Western painting for the next 450 years.

Vanishing Point

Horizon

Marriage of the Virgin (1504), Raphael

SKILLBUILDER: Interpreting Visual Sources
Contrasting *What is the major difference between the figures in the background of the painting and the figures in the foreground? What is the effect of this difference?*

Leonardo, Renaissance Man Leonardo da Vinci (LAY•uh•NAHR•doh duh•VIHN•chee) was a painter, sculptor, inventor, and scientist. A true "Renaissance man," he was interested in how things worked. He studied how a muscle moves and how veins are arranged in a leaf. He filled his notebooks with observations and sketches. Then he incorporated his findings in his art.

Among his many masterpieces, Leonardo painted one of the best-known portraits in the world, the *Mona Lisa* (page 44). The woman in the portrait seems so real that many writers have tried to explain the thoughts behind her smile. Leonardo also produced a famous religious painting, *The Last Supper*. It shows the personalities of Jesus' disciples through facial expressions.

Raphael Advances Realism Raphael (RAHF•ee•uhl) Sanzio was younger than Michelangelo and Leonardo. He learned from studying their works. One of Raphael's favorite subjects was the Madonna and child. Raphael often portrayed their expressions as gentle and calm. He was famous for his use of perspective.

In his greatest achievement, Raphael filled the walls of Pope Julius II's library with paintings. One of these, *School of Athens* (page 45), conveys the classical influence on the Renaissance. Raphael painted famous Renaissance figures, such as Michelangelo, Leonardo, and himself, as classical philosophers and their students.

Anguissola and Gentileschi Renaissance society generally restricted women's roles. However, a few Italian women became notable painters. Sofonisba Anguissola (ahng•GWEES•soh•lah) was the first woman artist to gain an international reputation. She is known for her portraits of her sisters and of prominent people such as King Philip II of Spain. Artemisia Gentileschi (JAYN•tee•LEHS•kee) was another accomplished artist. She trained with her painter father and helped with his work. In her own paintings, Gentileschi painted pictures of strong, heroic women.

Renaissance Writers Change Literature

Renaissance writers produced works that reflected their time, but they also used techniques that writers rely on today. Some followed the example of the medieval writer Dante. He wrote in the **vernacular**, his native language, instead of Latin. Dante's native language was Italian. In addition, Renaissance writers wrote either for self-expression or to portray the individuality of their subjects. In these ways, writers of the Renaissance began trends that modern writers still follow.

Petrarch and Boccaccio Francesco Petrarch (PEE•trahrk) was one of the earliest and most influential humanists. Some have called him the father of Renaissance humanism. He was also a great poet. Petrarch wrote both in Italian and in Latin. In

Italian, he wrote sonnets—14-line poems. They were about a mysterious woman named Laura, who was his ideal. (Little is known of Laura except that she died of the plague in 1348.) In classical Latin, he wrote letters to many important friends.

The Italian writer Giovanni Boccaccio (boh•KAH•chee•oh) is best known for the *Decameron,* a series of realistic, sometimes off-color stories. The stories are supposedly told by a group of worldly young people waiting in a rural villa to avoid the plague sweeping through Florence:

PRIMARY SOURCE
In the year of Our Lord 1348 the deadly plague broke out in the great city of Florence, most beautiful of Italian cities. Whether through the operation of the heavenly bodies or because of our own iniquities [sins] which the just wrath of God sought to correct, the plague had arisen in the East some years before, causing the death of countless human beings. It spread without stop from one place to another, until, unfortunately, it swept over the West. Neither knowledge nor human foresight availed against it, though the city was cleansed of much filth by chosen officers in charge and sick persons were forbidden to enter it, while advice was broadcast for the preservation of health.

GIOVANNI BOCCACCIO, Preface, *Decameron*

The *Decameron* presents both tragic and comic views of life. In its stories, the author uses cutting humor to illustrate the human condition. Boccaccio presents his characters in all of their individuality and all their folly.

Machiavelli Advises Rulers *The Prince* (1513) by Niccolò Machiavelli (MAK•ee•uh•VEHL•ee) also examines the imperfect conduct of human beings. It does so by taking the form of a political guidebook. In *The Prince,* Machiavelli examines how a ruler can gain power and keep it in spite of his enemies. In answering this question, he began with the idea that most people are selfish, fickle, and corrupt.

To succeed in such a wicked world, Machiavelli said, a prince must be strong as a lion and shrewd as a fox. He might have to trick his enemies and even his own people for the good of the state. In *The Prince,* Machiavelli was not concerned with what was morally right, but with what was politically effective.

He pointed out that most people think it is praiseworthy in a prince to keep his word and live with integrity. Nevertheless, Machiavelli argued that in the real world of power and politics a prince must sometimes mislead the people and lie to his opponents. As a historian and political thinker, Machiavelli suggested that in order for a prince to accomplish great things, he must be crafty enough to not only overcome the suspicions but also gain the trust of others:

PRIMARY SOURCE
From this arises the question whether it is better to be loved more than feared, or feared more than loved. The reply is, that one ought to be both feared and loved, but as it is difficult for the two to go together, it is much safer to be feared than loved, if one of the two has to be wanting. For it may be said of men in general that they are ungrateful, voluble [changeable], dissemblers [liars], anxious to avoid danger, and covetous of gain; as long as you benefit them, they are entirely yours; they offer you their blood, their goods, their life, and their children, as I have before said, when the necessity is remote; but when it approaches, they revolt. And the prince who has relied solely on their words, without making preparations, is ruined.

NICCOLÒ MACHIAVELLI, *The Prince*

MAIN IDEA

Analyzing Primary Sources
D Does Machiavelli think that a prince should prefer to be loved or feared? Why?

Vittoria Colonna The women writers who gained fame during the Renaissance usually wrote about personal subjects, not politics. Yet, some of them had great influence. Vittoria Colonna (1492–1547) was born of a noble family. In 1509, she married the Marquis of Pescara. He spent most of his life away from home on military campaigns.

Vittoria Colonna exchanged sonnets with Michelangelo and helped Castiglione publish *The Courtier.* Her own poems express personal emotions. When her husband was away at the Battle of Ravenna in 1512, she wrote to him:

PRIMARY SOURCE
But now in this perilous assault,
in this horrible, pitiless battle
that has so hardened my mind and heart,
your great valor has shown you an equal
to Hector and Achilles. But what good is
this to me, sorrowful, abandoned? . . .
Your uncertain enterprises do not hurt you;
but we who wait, mournfully grieving,
are wounded by doubt and fear.
You men, driven by rage, considering nothing
but your honor, commonly go off, shouting,
with great fury, to confront danger.
We remain, with fear in our heart and
grief on our brow for you; sister longs for
brother, wife for husband, mother for son.

VITTORIA COLONNA, *Poems*

Toward the end of the 15th century, Renaissance ideas began to spread north from Italy. As you will read in Section 2, northern artists and thinkers adapted Renaissance ideals in their own ways.

Global Patterns

Other Renaissances

In addition to the Italian Renaissance, there have been rebirths and revivals in other places around the world. For example, the Tang (618–907) and Song (960–1279) dynasties in China saw periods of great artistic and technological advances.

Like the Italian Renaissance, the achievements of the Tang and the Song had roots in an earlier time, the Han Dynasty (202 B.C. to A.D. 220). After the Han collapsed, China experienced turmoil.

When order was restored, Chinese culture flourished. The Chinese invented gunpowder and printing. Chinese poets wrote literary masterpieces. Breakthroughs were made in architecture, painting, and pottery. The Song painting above, *Waiting for Guests by Lamplight,* was done with ink and color on silk.

SECTION 1 ASSESSMENT

TERMS & NAMES 1. For each term or name, write a sentence explaining its significance.
• Renaissance • humanism • secular • patron • perspective • vernacular

USING YOUR NOTES
2. Which of Italy's advantages was most important? Why?

Italian Renaissance
I. Italy's advantages
   A.
   B.
II. Classical and
   worldly values

MAIN IDEAS
3. What are some of the characteristics of the "Renaissance man" and "Renaissance woman"?

4. How did Italy's cities help to make it the birthplace of the Renaissance?

5. What was the attitude of Church leaders and the wealthy toward the arts? Why?

CRITICAL THINKING & WRITING
6. **DRAWING CONCLUSIONS** How did study of the classics influence branches of learning such as history, literature, and philosophy?

7. **MAKING INFERENCES** How is the humanism of the Renaissance reflected in its art? Explain with examples.

8. **COMPARING** What were the differences between the Middle Ages and the Renaissance in the attitude toward worldly pleasures?

9. **WRITING ACTIVITY** REVOLUTION How did the Renaissance revolutionize European art and thought? Support your opinions in a three-paragraph **essay**.

CONNECT TO TODAY WRITING A DESCRIPTION

In a book on modern art, find an artist who worked in more than one medium, such as painting and sculpture. Write a **description** of one of the artist's works in each medium.

Renaissance Ideas Influence Renaissance Art

The Renaissance in Italy produced extraordinary achievements in many different forms of art, including painting, architecture, sculpture, and drawing. These art forms were used by talented artists to express important ideas and attitudes of the age.

The value of humanism is shown in Raphael's *School of Athens*, a depiction of the greatest Greek philosophers. The realism of Renaissance art is seen in a portrait such as the *Mona Lisa*, which is an expression of the subject's unique features and personality. And Michelangelo's *David* shares stylistic qualities with ancient Greek and Roman sculpture.

INTEGRATED / TECHNOLOGY

RESEARCH LINKS For more on Renaissance art, go to **classzone.com**

▼ Classical and Renaissance Sculpture

Michelangelo Influenced by classical statues, Michelangelo sculpted *David* from 1501 to 1504. Michelangelo portrayed the biblical hero in the moments just before battle. David's posture is graceful, yet his figure also displays strength. The statue, which is 18 feet tall, towers over the viewer.

▲ Portraying Individuals

Da Vinci The *Mona Lisa* (c. 1504–1506) is thought to be a portrait of Lisa Gherardini, who, at 16, married Francesco del Giocondo, a wealthy merchant of Florence who commissioned the portrait. Mona Lisa is a shortened form of Madonna Lisa (Madam, or My Lady, Lisa). Renaissance artists showed individuals as they really looked.

▲ The Importance of Ancient Greece

Raphael The painting *School of Athens* (1508) for the pope's apartments in the Vatican shows that the scholars of ancient Greece were highly honored. Under the center arch stand Plato and Aristotle. To their right, Socrates argues with several young men. Toward the front, Pythagoras draws a lesson on a slate and Ptolemy holds a globe.

▲ Renaissance Science and Technology

Da Vinci Leonardo da Vinci filled his notebooks with observations and sketches of new inventions. This drawing from his notebooks shows a design for a spiral screw to achieve vertical flight. Leonardo's drawing anticipated the helicopter.

Connect *to* Today

1. **Clarifying** How do the works of Renaissance artists and architects reflect Renaissance ideas? Explain.

   See Skillbuilder Handbook, page R4.

2. **Synthesizing** Look through books on architecture to find examples of American architects who were influenced by the architects and buildings of the Italian Renaissance. Share your findings with the class.

45

The Northern Renaissance

MAIN IDEA	WHY IT MATTERS NOW	TERMS & NAMES
CULTURAL INTERACTION In the 1400s, the ideas of the Italian Renaissance began to spread to Northern Europe.	Renaissance ideas such as the importance of the individual are a strong part of modern thought.	• utopia • William Shakespeare • Johann Gutenberg

SETTING THE STAGE The work of such artists as Leonardo da Vinci, Michelangelo, and Raphael showed the Renaissance spirit. All three artists demonstrated an interest in classical culture, a curiosity about the world, and a belief in human potential. Humanist writers expanded ideas about individuality. These ideas impressed scholars, students, and merchants who visited Italy. By the late 1400s, Renaissance ideas had spread to Northern Europe—especially England, France, Germany, and Flanders (now part of France and the Netherlands).

TAKING NOTES

Following Chronological Order
On a time line, note important events of the Northern Renaissance.

The Northern Renaissance Begins

By 1450 the population of northern Europe, which had declined due to bubonic plague, was beginning to grow again. When the destructive Hundred Years' War between France and England ended in 1453, many cities grew rapidly. Urban merchants became wealthy enough to sponsor artists. This happened first in Flanders, which was rich from long-distance trade and the cloth industry. Then, as wealth increased in other parts of Northern Europe, patronage of artists increased as well.

As Section 1 explained, Italy was divided into city-states. In contrast, England and France were unified under strong monarchs. These rulers often sponsored the arts by purchasing paintings and by supporting artists and writers. For example, Francis I of France invited Leonardo da Vinci to retire in France, and hired Italian artists and architects to rebuild and decorate his castle at Fontainebleau (FAHN•tihn•BLOH). The castle became a showcase for Renaissance art.

As Renaissance ideas spread out of Italy, they mingled with northern traditions. As a result, the northern Renaissance developed its own character. For example, the artists were especially interested in realism. The Renaissance ideal of human dignity inspired some northern humanists to develop plans for social reform based on Judeo-Christian values.

Artistic Ideas Spread

In 1494, a French king claimed the throne of Naples in southern Italy and launched an invasion through northern Italy. As the war dragged on, many Italian artists and writers left for a safer life in Northern Europe. They brought with them the styles and techniques of the Italian Renaissance. In addition, Northern European artists who studied in Italy carried Renaissance ideas back to their homelands.

German Painters Perhaps the most famous person to do this was the German artist Albrecht Dürer (DYUR•uhr). He traveled to Italy to study in 1494. After returning to Germany, Dürer produced woodcuts and engravings. Many of his prints portray religious subjects. Others portray classical myths or realistic landscapes. The popularity of Dürer's work helped to spread Renaissance styles.

Dürer's emphasis upon realism influenced the work of another German artist, Hans Holbein (HOHL•byn) the Younger. Holbein specialized in painting portraits that are almost photographic in detail. He emigrated to England where he painted portraits of King Henry VIII and other members of the English royal family.

Flemish Painters The support of wealthy merchant families in Flanders helped to make Flanders the artistic center of northern Europe. The first great Flemish Renaissance painter was Jan van Eyck (yahn van YK). Van Eyck used recently developed oil-based paints to develop techniques that painters still use. By applying layer upon layer of paint, van Eyck was able to create a variety of subtle colors in clothing and jewels. Oil painting became popular and spread to Italy.

In addition to new techniques, van Eyck's paintings display unusually realistic details and reveal the personality of their subjects. His work influenced later artists in Northern Europe.

Flemish painting reached its peak after 1550 with the work of Pieter Bruegel (BROY•guhl) the Elder. Bruegel was also interested in realistic details and individual people. He was very skillful in portraying large numbers of people. He captured scenes from everyday peasant life such as weddings, dances, and harvests. Bruegel's rich colors, vivid details, and balanced use of space give a sense of life and feeling. **A**

MAIN IDEA
Summarizing
A What techniques does Bruegel use to give life to his paintings?

> Analyzing Art

Peasant Life

The Flemish painter Pieter Bruegel's paintings provide information about peasant life in the 1500s. *Peasant Wedding* (1568) portrays a wedding feast.

- **The Bride** The bride sits under the paper crown hanging on the green cloth.
- **The Servers** Men who may be her brothers are passing out plates.
- **The Guests** Several children have come to the party.
- **The Musicians** They are carrying bagpipes. One glances hungrily at the food.

SKILLBUILDER:
Interpreting Visual Sources
Forming Generalizations
In what ways does this painting present a snapshot of peasant life?

Northern Writers Try to Reform Society

Italian humanists were very interested in reviving classical languages and classical texts. When the Italian humanist ideas reached the north, people used them to examine the traditional teachings of the Church. The northern humanists were critical of the failure of the Christian Church to inspire people to live a Christian life. This criticism produced a new movement known as Christian humanism. The focus of Christian humanism was the reform of society. Of particular importance to humanists was education. The humanists promoted the education of women and founded schools attended by both boys and girls.

Christian Humanists The best known of the Christian humanists were Desiderius Erasmus (DEHZ•ih•DEER•ee•uhs ih•RAZ•muhs) of Holland and Thomas More of England. The two were close friends.

In 1509, Erasmus wrote his most famous work, *The Praise of Folly*. This book poked fun at greedy merchants, heartsick lovers, quarrelsome scholars, and pompous priests. Erasmus believed in a Christianity of the heart, not one of ceremonies or rules. He thought that in order to improve society, all people should study the Bible.

Thomas More tried to show a better model of society. In 1516, he wrote the book *Utopia*. In Greek, **utopia** means "no place." In English it has come to mean an ideal place as depicted in More's book. The book is about an imaginary land where greed, corruption, and war have been weeded out. In Utopia, because there was little greed, Utopians had little use for money:

▼ Christian humanist Thomas More

PRIMARY SOURCE

Gold and silver, of which money is made, are so treated . . . that no one values them more highly than their true nature deserves. Who does not see that they are far inferior to iron in usefulness since without iron mortals cannot live any more than without fire and water?

THOMAS MORE, *Utopia*

More wrote in Latin. As his work became popular, More's works were translated into a variety of languages including French, German, English, Spanish, and Italian.

Women's Reforms During this period the vast majority of Europeans were unable to read or write. Those families who could afford formal schooling usually sent only their sons. One woman spoke out against this practice. Christine de Pizan was highly educated for the time and was one of the first women to earn a living as a writer. Writing in French, she produced many books, including short stories, biographies, novels, and manuals on military techniques. She frequently wrote about the objections men had to educating women. In one book, *The Book of The City of Ladies,* she wrote:

▼ Christine de Pizan is best known for her works defending women.

PRIMARY SOURCE B

I am amazed by the opinion of some men who claim that they do not want their daughters, wives, or kinswomen to be educated because their mores [morals] would be ruined as a result. . . . Here you can clearly see that not all opinions of men are based on reason and that these men are wrong.

CHRISTINE DE PIZAN, *The Book of The City of Ladies*

Christine de Pizan was one of the first European writers to question different treatment of boys and girls. However, her goal of formal education for children of both sexes would not be achieved for several centuries.

MAIN IDEA

Analyzing Primary Sources

B What does de Pizan argue for in this passage?

The Elizabethan Age

The Renaissance spread to England in the mid-1500s. The period was known as the Elizabethan Age, after Queen Elizabeth I. Elizabeth reigned from 1558 to 1603. She was well educated and spoke French, Italian, Latin, and Greek. She also wrote poetry and music. As queen she did much to support the development of English art and literature.

William Shakespeare The most famous writer of the Elizabethan Age was <u>William Shakespeare</u>. Many people regard him as the greatest playwright of all time. Shakespeare was born in 1564 in Stratford-upon-Avon, a small town about 90 miles northwest of London. By 1592 he was living in London and writing poems and plays, and soon he would be performing at the Globe Theater.

Like many Renaissance writers, Shakespeare revered the classics and drew on them for inspiration and plots. His works display a masterful command of the English language and a deep understanding of human beings. He revealed the souls of men and women through scenes of dramatic conflict. Many of these plays examine human flaws. However, Shakespeare also had one of his characters deliver a speech that expresses the Renaissance's high view of human nature:

PRIMARY SOURCE

What a piece of work is a man, how noble in reason, how infinite in faculties, in form and moving, how express and admirable; in action how like an angel, in apprehension [understanding] how like a god: the beauty of the world, the paragon of animals.

WILLIAM SHAKESPEARE, *Hamlet (Act 2, Scene 2)*

MAIN IDEA

Summarizing

C What are two ways in which Shakespeare's work showed Renaissance influences?

Shakespeare's most famous plays include the tragedies *Macbeth, Hamlet, Othello, Romeo and Juliet,* and *King Lear,* and the comedies *A Midsummer Night's Dream* and *The Taming of the Shrew.* **C**

Connect *to* Today

Shakespeare's Popularity

Even though he has been dead for about 400 years, Shakespeare is one of the favorite writers of filmmakers. His works are produced both in period costumes and in modern attire. The themes or dialogue have been adapted for many films, including some in foreign languages. The posters at the right illustrate *Othello* (done in period costume); *Romeo and Juliet* in a modern setting; a Japanese film, *Ran,* an adaptation of *King Lear;.* and *10 Things I Hate About You,* an adaptation of *The Taming of the Shrew.*

Printing Spreads Renaissance Ideas

The Chinese invented block printing, in which a printer carved words or letters on a wooden block, inked the block, and then used it to print on paper. Around 1045, Bi Sheng invented movable type, or a separate piece of type for each character in the language. The Chinese writing system contains thousands of different characters, so most Chinese printers found movable type impractical. However, the method would prove practical for Europeans because their languages have a very small number of letters in their alphabets.

Gutenberg Improves the Printing Process During the 13th century, block-printed items reached Europe from China. European printers began to use block printing to create whole pages to bind into books. However, this process was too slow to satisfy the Renaissance demand for knowledge, information, and books.

Around 1440 **Johann Gutenberg**, a craftsman from Mainz, Germany, developed a printing press that incorporated a number of technologies in a new way. The process made it possible to produce books quickly and cheaply. Using this improved process, Gutenberg printed a complete Bible, the Gutenberg Bible, in about 1455. It was the first full-sized book printed with movable type. **D**

The printing press enabled a printer to produce hundreds of copies of a single work. For the first time, books were cheap enough that many people could buy them. At first printers produced mainly religious works. Soon they began to provide books on other subjects such as travel guides and medical manuals.

MAIN IDEA
Recognizing Effects
D What were the major effects of the invention of the printing press?

Global Impact

The Printing Press

Many inventions are creative combinations of known technologies. In 1452, Johann Gutenberg combined known technologies from Europe and Asia with his idea for molding movable type to create a printing press that changed the world.

Screw-type Press An adaptation of Asian olive-oil presses made a workable printing press.

Movable Type Letters that could be put together in any fashion and reused was a Chinese idea.

Paper Using paper mass-produced by Chinese techniques, rather than vellum (calf or lambskin), made printing books possible.

Ink Oil-based inks from 10th-century Europe worked better on type than tempera ink.

A copyist took five months to produce a single book.

5 months → 1 book

One man and a printing press could produce 500 books in the same amount of time.

5 months → 500 books

SKILLBUILDER: Interpreting Graphics
1. **Drawing Conclusions** About how many books could a printing press produce in a month?
2. **Making Inferences** Which areas of the world contributed technologies to Gutenberg's printing press?

The Legacy of the Renaissance

The European Renaissance was a period of great artistic and social change. It marked a break with the medieval-period ideals focused around the Church. The Renaissance belief in the dignity of the individual played a key role in the gradual rise of democratic ideas. Furthermore, the impact of the movable-type printing press was tremendous. Some historians have suggested that its effects were even more dramatic than the arrival of personal computers in the 20th century. Below is a summary of the changes that resulted from the Renaissance.

Changes in the Arts

- Art drew on techniques and styles of classical Greece and Rome.
- Paintings and sculptures portrayed individuals and nature in more realistic and lifelike ways.
- Artists created works that were secular as well as those that were religious.
- Writers began to use vernacular languages to express their ideas.
- The arts praised individual achievement.

Changes in Society

- Printing changed society by making more information available and inexpensive enough for society at large.
- A greater availability of books prompted an increased desire for learning and a rise in literacy throughout Europe.
- Published accounts of new discoveries, maps, and charts led to further discoveries in a variety of fields.
- Published legal proceedings made the laws clear so that people were more likely to understand their rights.
- Christian humanists' attempts to reform society changed views about how life should be lived.
- People began to question political structures and religious practices.

Renaissance ideas continued to influence European thought—including religious thought—as you will see in Section 3.

SECTION 2 ASSESSMENT

TERMS & NAMES 1. For each term or name, write a sentence explaining its significance.
- utopia
- William Shakespeare
- Johann Gutenberg

USING YOUR NOTES

2. Which of the events listed do you think was most important? Explain.

1400   1600

MAIN IDEAS

3. How did Albrecht Dürer's work reflect the influence of the Italian Renaissance?

4. What was one way the Renaissance changed society?

5. Why was the invention of the printing press so important?

CRITICAL THINKING & WRITING

6. **COMPARING** How were the works of German painters different from those of the Flemish painters? Give examples.

7. **ANALYZING MOTIVES** What reasons did humanists give for wanting to reform society? Explain.

8. **RECOGNIZING EFFECTS** How did the availability of cheap books spread learning?

9. **WRITING ACTIVITY** [CULTURAL INTERACTION] Reread the primary source quotation from Christine de Pizan on page 48. Write a one paragraph **opinion piece** about the ideas expressed there.

INTEGRATED TECHNOLOGY INTERNET ACTIVITY

Use the Internet to find information on the number of books published in print and those published electronically last year. Create a **pie graph** showing the results of your research.

INTERNET KEYWORD
book publishing statistics

Social History

City Life in Renaissance Europe

Throughout the 1500s, the vast majority of Europeans—more than 75 percent—lived in rural areas. However, the capital and port cities of most European countries experienced remarkable growth during this time. The population of London, for example, stood at about 200,000 in 1600, making it perhaps the largest city in Europe. In London, and in other large European cities, a distinctively urban way of life developed in the Renaissance era.

INTEGRATED TECHNOLOGY

RESEARCH LINKS For more on life in Renaissance Europe, go to **classzone.com**

▼ Joblessness

Many newcomers to London struggled to find jobs and shelter. Some turned to crime to make a living. Others became beggars. However, it was illegal for able-bodied people to beg. To avoid a whipping or prison time, beggars had to be sick or disabled.

▲ Entertainment

Performances at playhouses like the Globe often were wild affairs. If audiences did not like the play, they booed loudly, pelted the stage with garbage, and sometimes attacked the actors.

▼ Sanitation

This small pomander (POH•man•durh), a metal container filled with spices, was crafted in the shape of orange segments. Well-to-do Londoners held pomanders to their noses to shield themselves from the stench of the rotting garbage that littered the streets.

▼ Food

A typical meal for wealthy Londoners might include fish, several kinds of meat, bread, and a variety of vegetables, served on silver or pewter tableware. The diet of the poor was simpler. They rarely ate fish, meat, or cheese. Usually, their meals consisted of a pottage—a kind of soup—of vegetables. And the poor ate their meals from a trencher, a hollowed-out slab of stale bread or wood.

▼ Transportation

Many of London's streets were so narrow that walking was the only practical means of transportation. Often, however, the quickest way to get from here to there in the city was to take the river. Boat traffic was especially heavy when the playhouses were open. On those days, as many as 4,000 people crossed the Thames from the city to Southwark, where most of the theaters were located.

COST OF LIVING IN RENAISSANCE LONDON

These tables show what typical Londoners earned and spent in the late 1500s. The basic denominations in English currency at the time were the pound (£), the shilling, and the penny (12 pence equaled 1 shilling, and 20 shillings equaled 1 pound). The pound of the late 1500s is roughly equivalent to $400 in today's U.S. currency.

Typical Earnings

Merchant	£100 per year
Skilled Worker	£13 per year (about 5 shillings/week)
Unskilled Worker	£5 per year (about 4 pence/day)
Servant	£1 to £2 per year (plus food and lodging)

Typical Prices

Lodging	4 to 8 pence a week
Beef	3 pence per lb
Chickens	1 penny each
Eggs	2 pence per dozen
Apples	1 penny per dozen
Onions	1/2 penny a sack
Various Spices	10 to 11 shillings per lb

Connect *to* Today

1. **Making Inferences** Study the images and captions as well as the information in the Data File. What inferences about the standard of living of London's wealthy citizens can you make from this information? How did it compare to the standard of living of London's common people?

   📁 See Skillbuilder Handbook, page R9.

2. **Comparing** How does diet in the United States today compare to the diet of Renaissance Europeans? Cite specific examples in your answer.

Luther Leads the Reformation

MAIN IDEA	WHY IT MATTERS NOW	TERMS & NAMES
REVOLUTION Martin Luther's protest over abuses in the Catholic Church led to the founding of Protestant churches.	Nearly one-fifth of the Christians in today's world are Protestants.	• indulgence • Peace of • Reformation Augsburg • Lutheran • annul • Protestant • Anglican

SETTING THE STAGE By the tenth century, the Roman Catholic Church had come to dominate religious life in Northern and Western Europe. However, the Church had not won universal approval. Over the centuries, many people criticized its practices. They felt that Church leaders were too interested in worldly pursuits, such as gaining wealth and political power. Even though the Church made some reforms during the Middle Ages, people continued to criticize it. Prompted by the actions of one man, that criticism would lead to rebellion.

TAKING NOTES
Recognizing Effects
Use a chart to identify the effects of Martin Luther's protests.

cause:
Luther
protests
abuses
→ effect 1
→ effect 2
→ effect 3

Causes of the Reformation

By 1500, additional forces weakened the Church. The Renaissance emphasis on the secular and the individual challenged Church authority. The printing press spread these secular ideas. In addition, some rulers began to challenge the Church's political power. In Germany, which was divided into many competing states, it was difficult for the pope or the emperor to impose central authority. Finally, northern merchants resented paying church taxes to Rome. Spurred by these social, political, and economic forces, a new movement for religious reform began in Germany. It then swept much of Europe.

Criticisms of the Catholic Church Critics of the Church claimed that its leaders were corrupt. The popes who ruled during the Renaissance patronized the arts, spent extravagantly on personal pleasure, and fought wars. Pope Alexander VI,

Causes of the Reformation

Social	Political	Economic	Religious
• The Renaissance values of humanism and secularism led people to question the Church. • The printing press helped to spread ideas critical of the Church.	• Powerful monarchs challenged the Church as the supreme power in Europe. • Many leaders viewed the pope as a foreign ruler and challenged his authority.	• European princes and kings were jealous of the Church's wealth. • Merchants and others resented having to pay taxes to the Church.	• Some Church leaders had become worldly and corrupt. • Many people found Church practices such as the sale of indulgences unacceptable.

for example, admitted that he had fathered several children. Many popes were too busy pursuing worldly affairs to have much time for spiritual duties.

The lower clergy had problems as well. Many priests and monks were so poorly educated that they could scarcely read, let alone teach people. Others broke their priestly vows by marrying, and some drank to excess or gambled.

Early Calls for Reform Influenced by reformers, people had come to expect higher standards of conduct from priests and church leaders. In the late 1300s and early 1400s, John Wycliffe of England and Jan Hus of Bohemia had advocated Church reform. They denied that the pope had the right to worldly power. They also taught that the Bible had more authority than Church leaders did. In the 1500s, Christian humanists like Desiderius Erasmus and Thomas More added their voices to the chorus of criticism. In addition, many Europeans were reading religious works and forming their own opinions about the Church. The atmosphere in Europe was ripe for reform by the early 1500s.

Luther Challenges the Church

Martin Luther's parents wanted him to be a lawyer. Instead, he became a monk and a teacher. From 1512 until his death, he taught scripture at the University of Wittenberg in the German state of Saxony. All he wanted was to be a good Christian, not to lead a religious revolution.

The 95 Theses In 1517, Luther decided to take a public stand against the actions of a friar named Johann Tetzel. Tetzel was raising money to rebuild St. Peter's Cathedral in Rome. He did this by selling indulgences. An **indulgence** was a pardon. It released a sinner from performing the penalty that a priest imposed for sins. Indulgences were not supposed to affect God's right to judge. Unfortunately, Tetzel gave people the impression that by buying indulgences, they could buy their way into heaven.

Luther was troubled by Tetzel's tactics. In response, he wrote 95 Theses, or formal statements, attacking the "pardon-merchants." On October 31, 1517, he posted these statements on the door of the castle church in Wittenberg and invited other scholars to debate him. Someone copied Luther's words and took them to a printer. Quickly, Luther's name became known all over Germany. His actions began the **Reformation**, a movement for religious reform. It led to the founding of Christian churches that did not accept the pope's authority.

Luther's Teachings Soon Luther went beyond criticizing indulgences. He wanted full reform of the Church. His teachings rested on three main ideas:

- People could win salvation only by faith in God's gift of forgiveness. The Church taught that faith and "good works" were needed for salvation.
- All Church teachings should be clearly based on the words of the Bible. Both the pope and Church traditions were false authorities.
- All people with faith were equal. Therefore, people did not need priests to interpret the Bible for them. **(A)**

MAIN IDEA

Summarizing
(A) What were the main points of Luther's teachings?

The Response to Luther

Luther was astonished at how rapidly his ideas spread and attracted followers. Many people had been unhappy with the Church for political and economic reasons. They saw Luther's protests as a way to challenge Church control.

The Pope's Threat Initially, Church officials in Rome viewed Luther simply as a rebellious monk who needed to be punished by his superiors. However, as Luther's ideas became more popular, the pope realized that this monk was a serious threat. In one angry reply to Church criticism, Luther actually suggested that Christians drive the pope from the Church by force.

In 1520, Pope Leo X issued a decree threatening Luther with excommunication unless he took back his statements. Luther did not take back a word. Instead, his students at Wittenberg gathered around a bonfire and cheered as he threw the pope's decree into the flames. Leo excommunicated Luther.

Vocabulary
Excommunication is the taking away of a person's right to membership in the Church.

The Emperor's Opposition Holy Roman Emperor Charles V, a devout Catholic, also opposed Luther's teaching. Charles controlled a vast empire, including the German states. He summoned Luther to the town of Worms (vawrmz) in 1521 to stand trial. Told to recant, or take back his statements, Luther refused:

> **PRIMARY SOURCE**
> I am bound by the Scriptures I have quoted and my conscience is captive to the Word of God. I cannot and I will not retract anything, since it is neither safe nor right to go against conscience. I cannot do otherwise, here I stand, may God help me. Amen.
>
> **MARTIN LUTHER,** quoted in *The Protestant Reformation* by Lewis W. Spitz

A month after Luther made that speech, Charles issued an imperial order, the Edict of Worms. It declared Luther an outlaw and a heretic. According to this edict, no one in the empire was to give Luther food or shelter. All his books were to be burned. However, Prince Frederick the Wise of Saxony disobeyed the emperor. For almost a year after the trial, he sheltered Luther in one of his castles. While there, Luther translated the New Testament into German.

Vocabulary
A *heretic* is a person who holds beliefs that differ from official Church teachings.

Luther returned to Wittenberg in 1522. There he discovered that many of his ideas were already being put into practice. Instead of continuing to seek reforms in the Catholic Church, Luther and his followers had become a separate religious group, called **Lutherans**.

The Peasants' Revolt Some people began to apply Luther's revolutionary ideas to society. In 1524, German peasants, excited by reformers' talk of Christian freedom, demanded an end to serfdom. Bands of angry peasants went about the countryside raiding monasteries, pillaging, and burning. The revolt horrified Luther. He wrote a pamphlet urging the German princes to show the peasants no mercy. The princes' armies crushed the revolt, killing as many as 100,000 people. Feeling betrayed, many peasants rejected Luther's religious leadership. **B**

Germany at War In contrast to the bitter peasants, many northern German princes supported Lutheranism. While some princes genuinely shared Luther's beliefs, others liked Luther's ideas for selfish reasons. They saw his teachings as a good excuse to seize Church property and to assert their independence from Charles V.

In 1529, German princes who remained loyal to the pope agreed to join forces against Luther's ideas. Those princes who supported Luther signed a protest against that agreement. These protesting princes came to be known as Protestants. Eventually, the term **Protestant** was applied to Christians who belonged to non-Catholic churches.

MAIN IDEA

Analyzing Causes
B Why did Luther's ideas encourage the German peasants to revolt?

Protestantism

Protestantism is a branch of Christianity. It developed out of the Reformation, the 16th-century protest in Europe against beliefs and practices of the Catholic Church. Three distinct branches of Protestantism emerged at first. They were Lutheranism, based on the teachings of Martin Luther in Germany; Calvinism, based on the teachings of John Calvin in Switzerland; and Anglicanism, which was established by King Henry VIII in England. Protestantism spread throughout Europe in the 16th century, and later, the world. As differences in beliefs developed, new denominations formed.

The Division of Christianity

The Early Christian Church → Eastern Orthodoxy

East-West Schism (1054)

Roman Catholicism

The Reformation (16th Century)

Protestantism → Lutheranism

Anglicanism → Episcopalian, Baptist, Methodist, Pentecostal

Calvinism → Presbyterian, Reformed

Religious Beliefs and Practices in the 16th Century

	Roman Catholicism	Lutheranism	Calvinism	Anglicanism
Leadership	Pope is head of the Church	Ministers lead congregations	Council of elders govern each church	English monarch is head of the Church
Salvation	Salvation by faith and good works	Salvation by faith alone	God has predetermined who will be saved	Salvation by faith alone
Bible	Church and Bible tradition are sources of revealed truth	Bible is sole source of revealed truth	Bible is sole source of revealed truth	Bible is sole source of revealed truth
Worship Service	Worship service based on ritual	Worship service focused on preaching and ritual	Worship service focused on preaching	Worship service based on ritual and preaching
Interpretation of Beliefs	Priests interpret Bible and Church teachings for believers	Believers interpret the Bible for themselves	Believers interpret the Bible for themselves	Believers interpret the Bible using tradition and reason

RESEARCH LINKS For more on Protestantism, go to **classzone.com**

> **DATA FILE**

PROTESTANTISM TODAY

Membership:
- Nearly 400 million Protestants worldwide
- About 65 million Protestants in the United States

Branches:
- More than 465 major Protestant denominations worldwide
- Major denominational families worldwide: Anglican, Assemblies of God, Baptist, Methodist, Lutheran, and Presbyterian
- More than 250 denominations in the United States
- About 40 denominations with more than 400,000 members each in the United States

Religious Adherents in the United States:

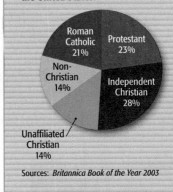

Roman Catholic 21%
Protestant 23%
Non-Christian 14%
Independent Christian 28%
Unaffiliated Christian 14%

Sources: *Britannica Book of the Year 2003*

Connect *to* Today

1. **Comparing** Which of the branches on the chart at left are most different and which are most similar?

    See Skillbuilder Handbook, page R7.

2. **Developing Historical Perspective** Do research on Protestantism. Select a denomination not shown on this page and write a paragraph tracing its roots to Reformation Protestantism.

Still determined that his subjects should remain Catholic, Charles V went to war against the Protestant princes. Even though he defeated them in 1547, he failed to force them back into the Catholic Church. In 1555, Charles, weary of fighting, ordered all German princes, both Protestant and Catholic, to assemble in the city of Augsburg. There the princes agreed that each ruler would decide the religion of his state. This famous religious settlement was known as the **Peace of Augsburg**.

England Becomes Protestant

The Catholic Church soon faced another great challenge to its authority, this time in England. Unlike Luther, the man who broke England's ties to the Roman Catholic Church did so for political and personal, not religious, reasons.

Henry VIII Wants a Son When Henry VIII became king of England in 1509, he was a devout Catholic. Indeed, in 1521, Henry wrote a stinging attack on Luther's ideas. In recognition of Henry's support, the pope gave him the title "Defender of the Faith." Political needs, however, soon tested his religious loyalty. He needed a male heir. Henry's father had become king after a long civil war. Henry feared that a similar war would start if he died without a son as his heir. He and his wife, Catherine of Aragon, had one living child—a daughter, Mary—but no woman had ever successfully claimed the English throne.

By 1527, Henry was convinced that the 42-year-old Catherine would have no more children. He wanted to divorce her and take a younger queen. Church law did not allow divorce. However, the pope could **annul**, or set aside, Henry's marriage if proof could be found that it had never been legal in the first place. In 1527, Henry asked the pope to annul his marriage, but the pope turned him down. The pope did not want to offend Catherine's powerful nephew, the Holy Roman Emperor Charles V.

The Reformation Parliament Henry took steps to solve his marriage problem himself. In 1529, he called Parliament into session and asked it to pass a set of laws

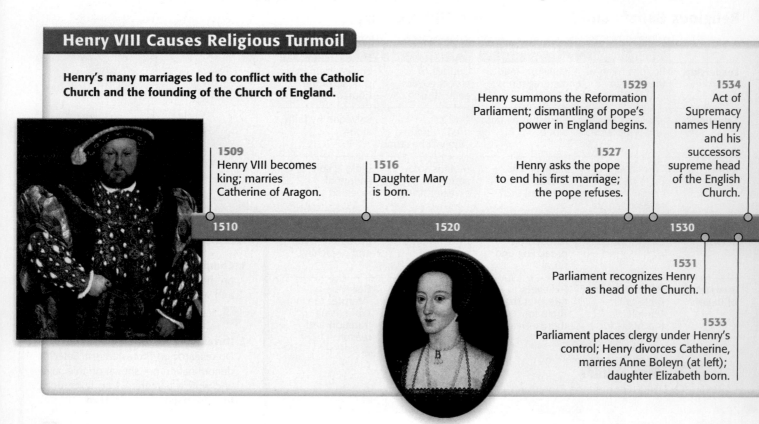

Henry VIII Causes Religious Turmoil

Henry's many marriages led to conflict with the Catholic Church and the founding of the Church of England.

1509
Henry VIII becomes king; marries Catherine of Aragon.

1516
Daughter Mary is born.

1527
Henry asks the pope to end his first marriage; the pope refuses.

1529
Henry summons the Reformation Parliament; dismantling of pope's power in England begins.

1534
Act of Supremacy names Henry and his successors supreme head of the English Church.

1531
Parliament recognizes Henry as head of the Church.

1533
Parliament places clergy under Henry's control; Henry divorces Catherine, marries Anne Boleyn (at left); daughter Elizabeth born.

1510   1520   1530

that ended the pope's power in England. This Parliament is known as the Reformation Parliament.

In 1533, Henry secretly married Anne Boleyn (BUL•ihn), who was in her twenties. Shortly after, Parliament legalized Henry's divorce from Catherine. In 1534, Henry's break with the pope was completed when Parliament voted to approve the Act of Supremacy. This called on people to take an oath recognizing the divorce and accepting Henry, not the pope, as the official head of England's Church.

The Act of Supremacy met some opposition. Thomas More, even though he had strongly criticized the Church, remained a devout Catholic. His faith, he said, would not allow him to accept the terms of the act and he refused to take the oath. In response, Henry had him arrested and imprisoned in the Tower of London. In 1535, More was found guilty of high treason and executed.

Consequences of Henry's Changes Henry did not immediately get the male heir he sought. After Anne Boleyn gave birth to a daughter, Elizabeth, she fell out of Henry's favor. Eventually, she was charged with treason. Like Thomas More, she was imprisoned in the Tower of London. She was found guilty and beheaded in 1536. Almost at once, Henry took a third wife, Jane Seymour. In 1537, she gave him a son named Edward. Henry's happiness was tempered by his wife's death just two weeks later. Henry married three more times. None of these marriages, however, produced children.

After Henry's death in 1547, each of his three children ruled England in turn. This created religious turmoil. Henry's son, Edward, became king when he was just nine years old. Too young to rule alone, Edward VI was guided by adult advisers. These men were devout Protestants, and they introduced Protestant reforms to the English Church. Almost constantly in ill health, Edward reigned for just six years. Mary, the daughter of Catherine of Aragon, took the throne in 1553. She was a Catholic who returned the English Church to the rule of the pope. Her efforts met with considerable resistance, and she had many Protestants executed. When Mary died in 1558, Elizabeth, Anne Boleyn's daughter, inherited the throne.

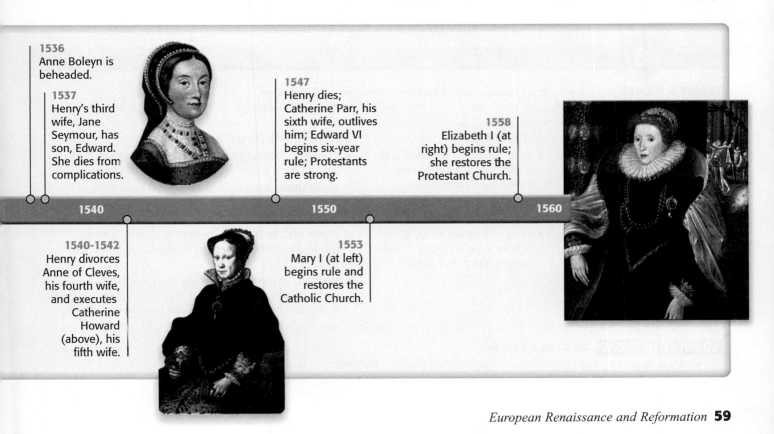

1536
Anne Boleyn is beheaded.

1537
Henry's third wife, Jane Seymour, has son, Edward. She dies from complications.

1547
Henry dies; Catherine Parr, his sixth wife, outlives him; Edward VI begins six-year rule; Protestants are strong.

1558
Elizabeth I (at right) begins rule; she restores the Protestant Church.

1540   1550   1560

1540-1542
Henry divorces Anne of Cleves, his fourth wife, and executes Catherine Howard (above), his fifth wife.

1553
Mary I (at left) begins rule and restores the Catholic Church.

Elizabeth I
1533–1603

Elizabeth I, like her father, had a robust nature and loved physical activity. She had a particular passion for dancing. Her fondness for exercise diminished little with age, and she showed amazing energy and strength well into her sixties.

Elizabeth also resembled her father in character and temperament. She was stubborn, strong-willed, and arrogant, and she expected to be obeyed without question. And Elizabeth had a fierce and unpredictable temper. To her subjects, Elizabeth was an object of both fear and love. She was their "most dread sovereign lady."

Elizabeth Restores Protestantism Elizabeth I was determined to return her kingdom to Protestantism. In 1559, Parliament followed Elizabeth's wishes and set up the Church of England, or **Anglican** Church, with Elizabeth as its head. This was to be the only legal church in England.

Elizabeth decided to establish a state church that moderate Catholics and moderate Protestants might both accept. To please Protestants, priests in the Church of England were allowed to marry. They could deliver sermons in English, not Latin. To please Catholics, the Church of England kept some of the trappings of the Catholic service such as rich robes. In addition, church services were revised to be somewhat more acceptable to Catholics. **C**

Elizabeth Faces Other Challenges By taking this moderate approach, Elizabeth brought a level of religious peace to England. Religion, however, remained a problem. Some Protestants pushed for Elizabeth to make more far-reaching church reforms. At the same time, some Catholics tried to overthrow Elizabeth and replace her with her cousin, the Catholic Mary Queen of Scots. Elizabeth also faced threats from Philip II, the Catholic king of Spain.

Elizabeth faced other difficulties. Money was one problem. In the late 1500s, the English began to think about building an American empire as a new source of income. While colonies strengthened England economically, they did not enrich the queen directly. Elizabeth's constant need for money would carry over into the next reign and lead to bitter conflict between the monarch and Parliament. You will read more about Elizabeth's reign in Chapter 5. In the meantime, the Reformation gained ground in other European countries.

MAIN IDEA

Recognizing Effects
C How did Henry VIII's marriages and divorces cause religious turmoil in England?

SECTION 3 ASSESSMENT

TERMS & NAMES 1. For each term or name, write a sentence explaining its significance.
• indulgence • Reformation • Lutheran • Protestant • Peace of Augsburg • annul • Anglican

USING YOUR NOTES
2. Which effect do you think had the most permanent impact? Explain.

```
cause:          effect 1
Luther
protests        effect 2
abuses
                effect 3
```

MAIN IDEAS
3. What political, economic, and social factors helped bring about the Reformation?

4. From where did the term *Protestantism* originate?

5. What impact did Henry VIII's actions have on England in the second half of the 1500s?

CRITICAL THINKING & WRITING
6. **DRAWING CONCLUSIONS** Explain how Elizabeth I was able to bring a level of religious peace to England.

7. **COMPARING** Do you think Luther or Henry VIII had a better reason to break with the Church? Provide details to support your answer.

8. **ANALYZING MOTIVES** How did the Catholic Church respond to Luther's teachings? Why do you think this was so?

9. **WRITING ACTIVITY** REVOLUTION Imagine Martin Luther and a leader of the Catholic Church are squaring off in a public debate. Write a brief **dialogue** between the two.

CONNECT TO TODAY CREATING A GRAPHIC
Use library resources to find information on the countries in which Protestantism is a major religion. Use your findings to create a **graphic** that makes a comparison among those countries.

The Reformation Continues

4

MAIN IDEA	WHY IT MATTERS NOW	TERMS & NAMES
RELIGIOUS AND ETHICAL SYSTEMS As Protestant reformers divided over beliefs, the Catholic Church made reforms.	Many Protestant churches began during this period, and many Catholic schools are the result of reforms in the Church.	• predestination • Catholic Reformation • Calvinism • theocracy • Jesuits • Presbyterian • Council of • Anabaptist Trent

SETTING THE STAGE Under the leadership of Queen Elizabeth I, the Anglican Church, though Protestant, remained similar to the Catholic Church in many of its doctrines and ceremonies. Meanwhile, other forms of Protestantism were developing elsewhere in Europe. Martin Luther had launched the Reformation in northern Germany, but reformers were at work in other countries. In Switzerland, another major branch of Protestantism emerged. Based mainly on the teachings of John Calvin, a French follower of Luther, it promoted unique ideas about the relationship between people and God.

Calvin Continues the Reformation

Religious reform in Switzerland was begun by Huldrych Zwingli (HUL•drykh ZWIHNG•lee), a Catholic priest in Zurich. He was influenced both by the Christian humanism of Erasmus and by the reforms of Luther. In 1520, Zwingli openly attacked abuses in the Catholic Church. He called for a return to the more personal faith of early Christianity. He also wanted believers to have more control over the Church.

Zwingli's reforms were adopted in Zurich and other cities. In 1531, a bitter war between Swiss Protestants and Catholics broke out. During the fighting, Zwingli met his death. Meanwhile, John Calvin, then a young law student in France with a growing interest in Church doctrine, was beginning to clarify his religious beliefs.

Calvin Formalizes Protestant Ideas When Martin Luther posted his 95 Theses in 1517, John Calvin had been only eight years old. But Calvin grew up to have as much influence in the spread of Protestantism as Luther did. He would give order to the faith Luther had begun.

In 1536, Calvin published *Institutes of the Christian Religion*. This book expressed ideas about God, salvation, and human nature. It was a summary of Protestant theology, or religious beliefs. Calvin wrote that men and women are sinful by nature. Taking Luther's idea that humans cannot earn salvation, Calvin went on to say that God chooses a very few people to save. Calvin called these few the "elect." He believed that God has known since the beginning of time who will be saved. This doctrine is called **predestination**. The religion based on Calvin's teachings is called **Calvinism**.

TAKING NOTES

Comparing Use a chart to compare the ideas of the reformers who came after Luther.

Reformers	Ideas
Zwingli	
Calvin	
Anabaptists	
Catholic Reformers	

John Calvin
1509–1564

A quiet boy, Calvin grew up to study law and philosophy at the University of Paris. In the 1530s, he was influenced by French followers of Luther. When King Francis I ordered Protestants arrested, Calvin fled. Eventually, he moved to Geneva.

Because Calvin and his followers rigidly regulated morality in Geneva, Calvinism is often described as strict and grim. But Calvin taught that people should enjoy God's gifts. He wrote that it should not be "forbidden to laugh, or to enjoy food, or to add new possessions to old."

Calvin Leads the Reformation in Switzerland Calvin believed that the ideal government was a **theocracy**, a government controlled by religious leaders. In 1541, Protestants in Geneva, Switzerland, asked Calvin to lead their city.

When Calvin arrived there in the 1540s, Geneva was a self-governing city of about 20,000 people. He and his followers ran the city according to strict rules. Everyone attended religion class. No one wore bright clothing or played card games. Authorities would imprison, excommunicate, or banish those who broke such rules. Anyone who preached different doctrines might be burned at the stake. Yet, to many Protestants, Calvin's Geneva was a model city of highly moral citizens.

Calvinism Spreads One admiring visitor to Geneva was a Scottish preacher named John Knox. When he returned to Scotland in 1559, Knox put Calvin's ideas to work. Each community church was governed by a group of laymen called elders or presbyters (PREHZ•buh•tuhrs). Followers of Knox became known as **Presbyterians**. In the 1560s, Protestant nobles led by Knox made Calvinism Scotland's official religion. They also deposed their Catholic ruler, Mary Queen of Scots, in favor of her infant son, James.

Elsewhere, Swiss, Dutch, and French reformers adopted the Calvinist form of church organization. One reason Calvin is considered so influential is that many Protestant churches today trace their roots to Calvin. Over the years, however, many of them have softened Calvin's strict teachings.

In France, Calvin's followers were called Huguenots. Hatred between Catholics and Huguenots frequently led to violence. The most violent clash occurred in Paris on August 24, 1572—the Catholic feast of St. Bartholomew's Day. At dawn, Catholic mobs began hunting for Protestants and murdering them. The massacres spread to other cities and lasted six months. Scholars believe that as many as 12,000 Huguenots were killed.

Other Protestant Reformers

Protestants taught that the Bible is the source of all religious truth and that people should read it to discover those truths. As Christians interpreted the Bible for themselves, new Protestant groups formed over differences in belief. **A**

The Anabaptists One such group baptized only those persons who were old enough to decide to be Christian. They said that persons who had been baptized as children should be rebaptized as adults. These believers were called **Anabaptists**, from a Greek word meaning "baptize again." The Anabaptists also taught that church and state should be separate, and they refused to fight in wars. They shared their possessions.

Viewing Anabaptists as radicals who threatened society, both Catholics and Protestants persecuted them. But the Anabaptists survived and became the forerunners of the Mennonites and the Amish. Their teaching influenced the later Quakers and Baptists, groups who split from the Anglican Church.

Women's Role in the Reformation Many women played prominent roles in the Reformation, especially during the early years. For example, the sister of King

MAIN IDEA

Analyzing Causes
A How did Protestant teaching lead to the forming of new groups?

Religions in Europe, 1560
INTERACTIVE

North Sea

Baltic Sea

ATLANTIC OCEAN

SCOTLAND
· Edinburgh

IRELAND

ENGLAND
· London

DENMARK–NORWAY

SWEDEN

POLAND-LITHUANIA

NETHERLANDS

· Munster

GERMAN STATES

· Wittenburg

FRANCE

· Paris

· Worms

AUSTRIA

HUNGARY

· Vienna

SWISS CONFEDERATION

Augsburg ·

Geneva ·

ITALIAN STATES

· Venice

PORTUGAL

Avignon ·

SPAIN

· Madrid

· Barcelona

PAPAL STATES

· Rome

OTTOMAN EMPIRE

· Seville

NAPLES

Naples ·

· Constantinople

Mediterranean Sea

50° N

42° N

16° W

8° W

0°

8° E

16° E

24° E

0 200 Miles
0 400 Kilometers

N

Spread of Protestantism

NORWAY

SWEDEN

SCOTLAND

IRELAND

DENMARK

PRUSSIA

ENGLAND
· London

BRANDENBURG

POLAND-LITHUANIA

FLANDERS

· Wittenberg

HOLY ROMAN EMPIRE

AUSTRIA

FRANCE

SWISS CONFEDERATION

Geneva ·

VENETIAN REPUBLIC

OTTOMAN EMPIRE

PAPAL STATES

CORSICA

KINGDOM OF NAPLES

PORTUGAL

SPAIN

SARDINIA

KINGDOM OF SICILY

58° N

50° N

42° N

34° N

16° W

8° W

0°

8° E

16° E

24° E

N

0 400 Miles
0 800 Kilometers

Spread of Religion
→ Lutheran
→ Anglican
→ Calvinist

Dominant Religion
- Roman Catholic
- Lutheran
- Anglican
- Calvinist
- Eastern Orthodox
- Islam
- Mixture of Calvinist, Lutheran, and Roman Catholic

Minority Religion
- Roman Catholic
- Lutheran
- Calvinist
- Islam
- Anabaptist

GEOGRAPHY SKILLBUILDER: Interpreting Maps

1. **Region** *Which European countries became mostly Protestant and which remained mostly Roman Catholic?*
2. **Location** *Judging from the way the religions were distributed, where would you expect religious conflicts to take place? Explain.*

▲ Although Catholic, Marguerite of Navarre supported the call for reform in the Church.

Francis I, Marguerite of Navarre, protected John Calvin from being executed for his beliefs while he lived in France. Other noblewomen also protected reformers. The wives of some reformers, too, had influence. Katherina Zell, married to Matthew Zell of Strasbourg, once scolded a minister for speaking harshly of another reformer. The minister responded by saying that she had "disturbed the peace." She answered his criticism sharply:

PRIMARY SOURCE
Do you call this disturbing the peace that instead of spending my time in frivolous amusements I have visited the plague-infested and carried out the dead? I have visited those in prison and under sentence of death. Often for three days and three nights I have neither eaten nor slept. I have never mounted the pulpit, but I have done more than any minister in visiting those in misery.

KATHERINA ZELL, quoted in *Women of the Reformation*

Katherina von Bora played a more typical, behind-the-scenes role as Luther's wife. Katherina was sent to a convent at about age ten, and had become a nun. Inspired by Luther's teaching, she fled the convent. After marrying Luther, Katherina had six children. She also managed the family finances, fed all who visited their house, and supported her husband's work. She respected Luther's position but argued with him about woman's equal role in marriage.

As Protestant religions became more firmly established, their organization became more formal. Male religious leaders narrowly limited women's activities to the home and discouraged them from being leaders in the church. In fact, it was Luther who said, "God's highest gift on earth is a pious, cheerful, God-fearing, home-keeping wife." **B**

MAIN IDEA

Making Inferences
B Why was it easier for women to take part in the earlier stages of the Reformation than in the later stages?

The Catholic Reformation

While Protestant churches won many followers, millions remained true to Catholicism. Helping Catholics to remain loyal was a movement within the Catholic Church to reform itself. This movement is now known as the **Catholic Reformation**. Historians once referred to it as the Counter Reformation. Important leaders in this movement were reformers, such as Ignatius (ihg•NAY•shuhs) of Loyola, who founded new religious orders, and two popes—Paul III and Paul IV—who took actions to reform and renew the Church from within.

Ignatius of Loyola Ignatius grew up in his father's castle in Loyola, Spain. The great turning point in his life came in 1521 when he was injured in a war. While recovering, he thought about his past sins and about the life of Jesus. His daily devotions, he believed, cleansed his soul. In 1522, Ignatius began writing a book called *Spiritual Exercises* that laid out a day-by-day plan of meditation, prayer, and study. In it, he compared spiritual and physical exercise:

PRIMARY SOURCE
Just as walking, traveling, and running are bodily exercises, preparing the soul to remove ill-ordered affections, and after their removal seeking and finding the will of God with respect to the ordering of one's own life and the salvation of one's soul, are Spiritual Exercises.

IGNATIUS OF LOYOLA, *Spiritual Exercises*

▲ Church leaders consult on reforms at the Council of Trent in this 16th-century painting.

For the next 18 years, Ignatius gathered followers. In 1540, the pope created a religious order for his followers called the Society of Jesus. Members were called **Jesuits** (JEHZH•oo•ihts). The Jesuits focused on three activities. First, they founded schools throughout Europe. Jesuit teachers were well-trained in both classical studies and theology. The Jesuits' second mission was to convert non-Christians to Catholicism. So they sent out missionaries around the world. Their third goal was to stop the spread of Protestantism. The zeal of the Jesuits overcame the drift toward Protestantism in Poland and southern Germany.

Reforming Popes Two popes took the lead in reforming the Catholic Church. Paul III, pope from 1534 to 1549, took four important steps. First, he directed a council of cardinals to investigate indulgence selling and other abuses in the Church. Second, he approved the Jesuit order. Third, he used the Inquisition to seek out heresy in papal territory. Fourth, and most important, he called a council of Church leaders to meet in Trent, in northern Italy.

Vocabulary
The *Inquisition* was a papal judicial process established to try and punish those thought to be heretics.

From 1545 to 1563, at the **Council of Trent**, Catholic bishops and cardinals agreed on several doctrines:

- The Church's interpretation of the Bible was final. Any Christian who substituted his or her own interpretation was a heretic.
- Christians needed faith and good works for salvation. They were not saved by faith alone, as Luther argued.
- The Bible and Church tradition were equally powerful authorities for guiding Christian life.
- Indulgences were valid expressions of faith. But the false selling of indulgences was banned.

The next pope, Paul IV, vigorously carried out the council's decrees. In 1559, he had officials draw up a list of books considered dangerous to the Catholic faith. This list was known as the Index of Forbidden Books. Catholic bishops throughout Europe were ordered to gather up the offensive books (including Protestant Bibles) and burn them in bonfires. In Venice alone, followers burned 10,000 books in one day.

Global Impact

Jesuit Missionaries

The work of Jesuit missionaries has had a lasting impact around the globe. By the time Ignatius died in 1556, about a thousand Jesuits had brought his ministry to Europe, Africa, Asia, and the Americas. Two of the most famous Jesuit missionaries of the 1500s were Francis Xavier, who worked in India and Japan, and Matteo Ricci, who worked in China.

One reason the Jesuits had such an impact is that they founded schools throughout the world. For example, the Jesuits today run about 45 high schools and 28 colleges and universities in the United States. Four of these are Georgetown University (shown above), Boston College, Marquette University, and Loyola University of Chicago.

The Legacy of the Reformation

The Reformation had an enduring impact. Through its religious, social, and political effects, the Reformation set the stage for the modern world. It also ended the Christian unity of Europe and left it culturally divided.

Religious and Social Effects of the Reformation Despite religious wars and persecutions, Protestant churches flourished and new denominations developed. The Roman Catholic Church itself became more unified as a result of the reforms started at the Council of Trent. Both Catholics and Protestants gave more emphasis to the role of education in promoting their beliefs. This led to the founding of parish schools and new colleges and universities throughout Europe.

Some women reformers had hoped to see the status of women in the church and society improve as a result of the Reformation. But it remained much the same both under Protestantism and Roman Catholicism. Women were still mainly limited to the concerns of home and family.

Political Effects of the Reformation As the Catholic Church's moral and political authority declined, individual monarchs and states gained power. This led to the development of modern nation-states. In the 1600s, rulers of nation-states would seek more power for themselves and their countries through warfare, exploration, and expansion.

The Reformation's questioning of beliefs and authority also laid the groundwork for the Enlightenment. As you will read in Chapter 6, this intellectual movement would sweep Europe in the late 18th century. It led some to reject all religions and others to call for the overthrow of existing governments.

SECTION 4 ASSESSMENT

TERMS & NAMES 1. For each term or name, write a sentence explaining its significance.
• predestination • Calvinism • theocracy • Presbyterian • Anabaptist • Catholic Reformation • Jesuits • Council of Trent

USING YOUR NOTES
2. Which Catholic reform do you think had the most impact?

Reformers	Ideas
Zwingli	
Calvin	
Anabaptists	
Catholic Reformers	

MAIN IDEAS
3. What was Calvin's idea of the "elect" and their place in society?
4. What role did noblewomen play in the Reformation?
5. What were the goals of the Jesuits?

CRITICAL THINKING & WRITING
6. **DRAWING CONCLUSIONS** How did the Reformation set the stage for the modern world? Give examples.
7. **MAKING INFERENCES** Why do you think the Church wanted to forbid people to read certain books?
8. **COMPARING** How did steps taken by Paul III and Paul IV to reform the Catholic Church differ from Protestant reforms? Support your answer with details from the text.
9. **WRITING ACTIVITY** [RELIGIOUS AND ETHICAL SYSTEMS] Write a two-paragraph **essay** on whether church leaders should be political rulers.

CONNECT TO TODAY PRESENTING AN ORAL REPORT
Research the religious origins of a university in the United States. Then present your findings to the class in an **oral report.**

INTERACTIVE

The Reformation

Martin Luther's criticisms of the Catholic Church grew sharper over time. Some Catholics, in turn, responded with personal attacks on Luther. In recent times, historians have focused less on the theological and personal issues connected with the Reformation. Instead, many modern scholars analyze the political, social, and economic conditions that contributed to the Reformation.

A PRIMARY SOURCE

Martin Luther

In 1520, Martin Luther attacked the whole system of Church government and sent the pope the following criticism of the Church leaders who served under him in Rome.

——

The Roman Church has become the most licentious [sinful] den of thieves. . . . They err who ascribe to thee the right of interpreting Scripture, for under cover of thy name they seek to set up their own wickedness in the Church, and, alas, through them Satan has already made much headway under thy predecessors. In short, believe none who exalt thee, believe those who humble thee.

B SECONDARY SOURCE

Steven Ozment

In 1992, historian Steven Ozment published *Protestants: The Birth of a Revolution*. Here, he comments on some of the political aspects of the Reformation.

——

Beginning as a protest against arbitrary, self-aggrandizing, hierarchical authority in the person of the pope, the Reformation came to be closely identified in the minds of contemporaries with what we today might call states' rights or local control. To many townspeople and villagers, Luther seemed a godsend for their struggle to remain politically free and independent; they embraced his Reformation as a conserving political force, even though they knew it threatened to undo traditional religious beliefs and practices.

C SECONDARY SOURCE

G. R. Elton

In *Reformation Europe*, published in 1963, historian G. R. Elton notes the role of geography and trade in the spread of Reformation ideas.

——

Could the Reformation have spread so far and so fast if it had started anywhere but in Germany? The fact that it had its beginnings in the middle of Europe made possible a very rapid radiation in all directions. . . . Germany's position at the center of European trade also helped greatly. German merchants carried not only goods but Lutheran ideas and books to Venice and France; the north German Hanse [a trade league] transported the Reformation to the Scandinavian countries.

D PRIMARY SOURCE

Hans Brosamer

"Seven-Headed Martin Luther" (1529) The invention of the printing press enabled both Protestants and Catholics to engage in a war of words and images. This anti-Luther illustration by German painter Hans Brosamer depicted Martin Luther as a seven-headed monster—doctor, monk, infidel, preacher, fanatic swarmed by bees, self-appointed pope, and thief Barabbas from the Bible.

Sieben Köpffe Martini Luthers
Vom Hochwirdigen Sacrament des Altars / Durch Doctor Jo. Cocleus.

Martinus Luther Siebenkopff.

Document-Based QUESTIONS

1. In what way does Luther's letter (Source A) support the point of view of the historian in Source B?

2. Based on Source C, why was Germany's location important to the spread of Reformation ideas?

3. Why might Hans Brosamer's woodcut (Source D) be an effective propaganda weapon against Martin Luther?

VISUAL SUMMARY

European Renaissance and Reformation

The Renaissance and the Reformation bring dramatic changes to social and cultural life in Europe.

1. Italy: Birthplace of the Renaissance

- A period of intellectual and artistic creativity begins in Italy around the 1300s.
- Artists and writers revive techniques, styles, and subjects from classical Greece and Rome and celebrate human achievements.

2. The Northern Renaissance

- Renaissance ideas spread to Northern Europe, where German and Flemish artists create distinctive works of art.
- Thousands of books and pamphlets created on printing presses spread political, social, and artistic ideas.

3. Luther Leads the Reformation

- Martin Luther starts a movement for religious reform and challenges the authority of the Catholic Church.
- King Henry VIII breaks ties with the Catholic Church and starts the Church of England.

4. The Reformation Continues

- Protestant groups divide into several denominations, including the Calvinists and the Anabaptists.
- The Catholic Church introduces its own reforms.

TERMS & NAMES

For each term or name below, briefly explain its connection to European history from 1300 to 1600.

1. Renaissance
2. vernacular
3. utopia
4. Reformation
5. Protestant
6. Peace of Augsburg
7. Catholic Reformation
8. Council of Trent

MAIN IDEAS

Italy: Birthplace of the Renaissance Section 1 (pages 37–45)

9. How did the merchant class in northern Italy influence the Renaissance?

10. In what ways did literature and the arts change during the Renaissance?

The Northern Renaissance Section 2 (pages 46–53)

11. What did northern European rulers do to encourage the spread of Renaissance ideas?

12. How were the Christian humanists different from the humanists of the Italian Renaissance?

Luther Leads the Reformation Section 3 (pages 54–60)

13. On what three teachings did Martin Luther rest his Reformation movement?

14. Why did the Holy Roman emperor go to war against Protestant German princes?

15. Why did Henry VIII create his own church? Refer to the time line on pages 58–59.

The Reformation Continues Section 4 (pages 61–67)

16. In what ways was John Calvin's church different from the Lutheran Church?

17. What was the goal of the Catholic Reformation?

18. What are three legacies of the Reformation?

CRITICAL THINKING

1. USING YOUR NOTES

In a diagram, show how the Reformation led to great changes in European ideas and institutions.

Effects of the Reformation

| Religious | Political | Social |

2. ANALYZING ISSUES

REVOLUTION What role did the printing press play in the spread of the Reformation and the spread of democracy?

3. RECOGNIZING EFFECTS

CULTURAL INTERACTION How did the Renaissance and Reformation expand cultural interaction both within Europe and outside of it?

4. DEVELOPING HISTORICAL PERSPECTIVE

What conditions needed to exist before the Renaissance could occur?

5. SYNTHESIZING

How did views of the role of women change in the Renaissance period?

Use the quotation and your knowledge of world history to answer questions 1 and 2.
Additional Test Practice, pp. S1–S33

PRIMARY SOURCE

A prince must also show himself a lover of merit [excellence], give preferment [promotion] to the able, and honour those who excel in every art. Moreover he must encourage his citizens to follow their callings [professions] quietly, whether in commerce, or agriculture, or any other trade that men follow. . . . [The prince] should offer rewards to whoever does these things, and to whoever seeks in any way to improve his city or state.

NICCOLÒ MACHIAVELLI, *The Prince*

1. Which phrase best describes the advice given by Machiavelli?

  A. Rule with an iron hand in a velvet glove.

  B. Do not give your subjects any freedoms.

  C. Reward hard work and patriotism.

  D. To retain your rule, you must interfere in the lives of your subjects.

2. In his book *The Prince,* the writer of this advice also suggested

  A. the pope should listen to the calls for reform of the Church.

  B. a prince might have to trick his people for the good of the state.

  C. merchants should try to take control of the cities away from the prince.

  D. the prince should reform society by establishing a utopia.

Use this drawing of a machine from the notebooks of Leonardo da Vinci and your knowledge of world history to answer question 3.

3. The principles upon which this machine is based evolved into what modern machine?

  A. food blender

  B. a fan

  C. a well-digging machine

  D. helicopter

INTEGRATED TECHNOLOGY

TEST PRACTICE Go to **classzone.com**

- Diagnostic tests
- Tutorials
- Strategies
- Additional practice

ALTERNATIVE ASSESSMENT

1. Interact *with* History

On page 36, you looked at a painting and discussed what you learned about Renaissance society from that painting. Now choose one other piece of art from the chapter. Explain what you can learn about Renaissance or Reformation society from that piece of art.

2. WRITING ABOUT HISTORY

RELIGIOUS AND ETHICAL SYSTEMS Study the information about Protestantism in the Analyzing Key Concepts on page 57. Write a three-paragraph **essay** analyzing the effects Protestantism had on the Christian Church.

- Examine its impact on the number of denominations.
- Explain the different beliefs and practices it promoted.

INTEGRATED TECHNOLOGY

Writing an Internet-based Research Paper

Go to the *Web Research Guide* at **classzone.com** to learn about conducting research on the Internet. Then, working with a partner, use the Internet to research major religious reforms of the 20th century. You might search for information on changes in the Catholic Church as a result of Vatican II, or major shifts in the practices or doctrines of a branch of Hinduism, Islam, Judaism, or Protestantism. Compare the 20th-century reforms with those of the Protestant Reformation. Present the results of your research in a well-organized paper. Be sure to

- apply a search strategy when using directories and search engines to locate Web resources.
- judge the usefulness and reliability of each Web site.
- correctly cite your Web sources.
- peer-edit for organization and correct use of language.

The Muslim World Expands, 1300–1700

Previewing Main Ideas

EMPIRE BUILDING Three of the great empires of history—the Ottomans in Turkey, the Safavids in Persia, and the Mughals in India—emerged in the Muslim world between the 14th and the 18th centuries.

Geography *Locate the empires on the map. Which of the empires was the largest? Where was it located?*

CULTURAL INTERACTION As powerful societies moved to expand their empires, Turkish, Persian, Mongol, and Arab ways of life blended. The result was a flowering of Islamic culture that peaked in the 16th century.

Geography *The Ottoman Empire included cultures from which continents?*

POWER AND AUTHORITY The rulers of all three great Muslim empires of this era based their authority on Islam. They based their power on strong armies, advanced technology, and loyal administrative officers.

Geography *Study the time line and the map. When was the Mughal Empire founded? Where was Babur's empire located?*

INTEGRATED TECHNOLOGY

eEdition
- Interactive Maps
- Interactive Visuals
- Interactive Primary Sources

INTERNET RESOURCES
Go to **classzone.com** for:
- Research Links
- Internet Activities
- Primary Sources
- Chapter Quiz
- Maps
- Test Practice
- Current Events

MUSLIM WORLD

1300
Osman founds Ottoman state. ▶

1398
Timur the Lame destroys Delhi.

1453
Ottomans capture Constantinople.

1300   1400

WORLD

1325
Aztecs build Tenochtitlán. (ornament of an Aztec snake god) ▶

1455
◀ Gutenberg prints the Bible.

Empire Builders, 1683

EUROPE

Vienna
ALPS
Rome
Baltic Sea
Black Sea
CAUCASUS MTS.
Caspian Sea
Aral Sea

ASIA

Constantinople
Aleppo
Tehran
Kabul
Algiers
Tunis
Baghdad
Esfahan
ATLAS MOUNTAINS
Mediterranean Sea
Damascus
Jerusalem
ZAGROS MTS.
HIMALAYAS
Tripoli
Alexandria
Delhi
Ganges R.
Agra
Persian Gulf
Ormuz (Hormuz)
Benares

AFRICA

Nile R.
Medina
Red Sea
Mecca

Euphrates
Tigris

Arabian Sea

Bay of Bengal

- Mughal Empire
- Ottoman Empire
- Safavid Empire

0   500   1,000 Miles
0 500 1,000 Kilometers
Polyconic Projection

N
W   E
S

0° Equator

INDIAN OCEAN

1501
Safavids
conquer
Persia.

1526
Babur founds
Mughal Empire.

1587
Shah Abbas I
rules Safavid
Empire.

1632
◄ Shah Jahan orders
construction of
Taj Mahal at Agra.

1500   **1600**   **1700**

1522
Magellan's crew sails
around the world.

1603
Tokugawa regime
begins in Japan.

1607
British settle in North
America at Jamestown.

How do you govern a diverse empire?

Your father is a Safavid shah, the ruler of a growing empire. With a well-trained army and modern weapons, he has easily conquered most of the surrounding area. Because you are likely to become the next ruler, you are learning all you can about how to rule. You wonder what is best for the empire. Should conquered people be given the freedom to practice a religion that is different from your own and to follow their own traditions? Or would it be better to try and force them to accept your beliefs and way of life—or even to enslave them?

INTER*ACTIVE*

1 The shah entertains the emperor of a neighboring land. Both lands have great diversity of people and cultures.

2 Distinctive headgear marks the status of military leaders and scholars gathered from all parts of the empire.

3 Clothing, music, dancing, and food reflect the customs of several groups within the empire.

4 People in the court, from the servants to the members of the court, mirror the empire's diversity.

EXAMINING *the* ISSUES

- **What problems might conquered people present for their conqueror?**

- **In what ways might a conqueror integrate conquered people into the society?**

As a class, discuss the ways other empires—such as those of Rome, Assyria, and Persia—treated their conquered peoples. As you read about the three empires featured in this chapter, notice how the rulers dealt with empires made up of different cultures.

The Ottomans Build a Vast Empire

MAIN IDEA	WHY IT MATTERS NOW	TERMS & NAMES
EMPIRE BUILDING The Ottomans established a Muslim empire that combined many cultures and lasted for more than 600 years.	Many modern societies, from Algeria to Turkey, had their origins under Ottoman rule.	• ghazi • Ottoman • sultan • Timur the Lame	• Mehmed II • Suleyman the Lawgiver • *devshirme* • janissary

SETTING THE STAGE By 1300, the Byzantine Empire was declining, and the Mongols had destroyed the Turkish Seljuk kingdom of Rum. Anatolia was inhabited mostly by the descendants of nomadic Turks. These militaristic people had a long history of invading other countries. Loyal to their own groups, they were not united by a strong central power. A small Turkish state occupied land between the Byzantine Empire and that of the Muslims. From this place, a strong leader would emerge to unite the Turks into what eventually would become an immense empire stretching across three continents.

Turks Move into Byzantium

Many Anatolian Turks saw themselves as **ghazis** (GAH•zees), or warriors for Islam. They formed military societies under the leadership of an emir, a chief commander, and followed a strict Islamic code of conduct. They raided the territories of people who lived on the frontiers of the Byzantine Empire.

Osman Establishes a State The most successful ghazi was Osman. People in the West called him Othman and named his followers **Ottomans**. Osman built a small Muslim state in Anatolia between 1300 and 1326. His successors expanded it by buying land, forming alliances with some emirs, and conquering others.

The Ottomans' military success was largely based on the use of gunpowder. They replaced their archers on horseback with musket-carrying foot soldiers. They also were among the first people to use cannons as weapons of attack. Even heavily walled cities fell to an all-out attack by the Turks.

The second Ottoman leader, Orkhan I, was Osman's son. He felt strong enough to declare himself **sultan**, meaning "overlord" or "one with power." And in 1361, the Ottomans captured Adrianople (ay•dree•uh•NOH•puhl), the second most important city in the Byzantine Empire. A new Turkish empire was on the rise.

The Ottomans acted wisely toward the people they conquered. They ruled through local officials appointed by the sultan and often improved the lives of the peasants. Most Muslims were required to serve in Turkish armies and make contributions required by their faith. Non-Muslims did not have to serve in the army but had to pay for their exemption with a small tax.

TAKING NOTES

Comparing List the main rulers of the Ottoman Empire and their successes.

Rulers	Successes

Timur the Lame Halts Expansion The rise of the Ottoman Empire was briefly interrupted in the early 1400s by a rebellious warrior and conqueror from Samarkand in Central Asia. Permanently injured by an arrow in the leg, he was called Timur-i-Lang, or **Timur the Lame**. Europeans called him Tamerlane. Timur burned the powerful city of Baghdad in present-day Iraq to the ground. He crushed the Ottoman forces at the Battle of Ankara in 1402. This defeat halted the expansion of their empire.

Powerful Sultans Spur Dramatic Expansion

Soon Timur turned his attention to China. When he did, war broke out among the four sons of the Ottoman sultan. Mehmed I defeated his brothers and took the throne. His son, Murad II, defeated the Venetians, invaded Hungary, and overcame an army of Italian crusaders in the Balkans. He was the first of four powerful sultans who led the expansion of the Ottoman Empire through 1566.

Mehmed II Conquers Constantinople Murad's son **Mehmed II**, or Mehmed the Conqueror, achieved the most dramatic feat in Ottoman history. By the time Mehmed took power in 1451, the ancient city of Constantinople had shrunk from a population of a million to a mere 50,000. Although it controlled no territory outside its walls, it still dominated the Bosporus Strait. Controlling this waterway meant that it could choke off traffic between the Ottomans' territories in Asia and in the Balkans.

Mehmed II decided to face this situation head-on. "Give me Constantinople!" he thundered, shortly after taking power at age 21. Then, in 1453, he launched his attack.

Ottoman Empire, 1451–1566
INTER**ACTIVE**

| | Ottoman Empire, 1451 |
| Acquisitions to 1481 |
| Acquisitions to 1521 |
| Acquisitions to 1566 |

GEOGRAPHY SKILLBUILDER: Interpreting Maps
1. **Location** *To which waterways did the Ottoman Empire have access?*
2. **Movement** *In which time period did the Ottoman Empire gain the most land?*

The Conquest of Constantinople

Kritovoulos, a Greek who served in the Ottoman administration, recorded the following about the Ottoman takeover of Constantinople. The second source, the French miniature at the right, shows a view of the siege of Constantinople.

PRIMARY SOURCE

After this the Sultan entered the City and looked about to see its great size, its situation, its grandeur and beauty, its teeming population, its loveliness, and the costliness of its churches and public buildings and of the private houses and community houses and those of the officials. . . .

When he saw what a large number had been killed and the ruin of the buildings, and the wholesale ruin and destruction of the City, he was filled with compassion and repented not a little at the destruction and plundering. Tears fell from his eyes as he groaned deeply and passionately: "What a city we have given over to plunder and destruction."

KRITOVOULOS, *History of Mehmed the Conqueror*

DOCUMENT-BASED QUESTIONS

1. **Comparing and Contrasting** *In what details do the two sources agree? disagree?*
2. **Making Inferences** *Why do you think the sultan wept over the destruction?*

Mehmed's Turkish forces began firing on the city walls with mighty cannons. One of these was a 26-foot gun that fired 1,200-pound boulders. A chain across the Golden Horn between the Bosporus Strait and the Sea of Marmara kept the Turkish fleet out of the city's harbor. Finally, one night Mehmed's army tried a daring tactic. They dragged 70 ships over a hill on greased runners from the Bosporus to the harbor. Now Mehmed's army was attacking Constantinople from two sides. The city held out for over seven weeks, but the Turks finally found a break in the wall and entered the city.

Mehmed the Conqueror, as he was now called, proved to be an able ruler as well as a magnificent warrior. He opened Constantinople to new citizens of many religions and backgrounds. Jews, Christians, and Muslims, Turks and non-Turks all flowed in. They helped rebuild the city, which was now called Istanbul. **A**

MAIN IDEA

Analyzing Motives
A Why was taking Constantinople so important to Mehmed II?

Ottomans Take Islam's Holy Cities Mehmed's grandson, Selim the Grim, came to power in 1512. He was an effective sultan and a great general. In 1514, he defeated the Safavids (suh•FAH•vihdz) of Persia at the Battle of Chaldiran. Then he swept south through Syria and Palestine and into North Africa. At the same time that Cortez was toppling the Aztec Empire in the Americas, Selim's empire took responsibility for Mecca and Medina. Finally he took Cairo, the intellectual center of the Muslim world. The once-great civilization of Egypt had become just another province in the growing Ottoman Empire.

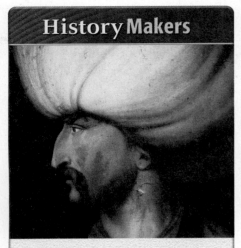

**Suleyman the Lawgiver
1494–1566**

In the halls of the U.S. Congress are images of some of the greatest lawgivers of all time. Included in that group are such persons as Thomas Jefferson, Moses, and Suleyman.

Suleyman's law code prescribed penalties for various criminal acts and for bureaucratic and financial corruption. He also sought to reduce bribes, did not allow imprisonment without a trial, and rejected promotions that were not based on merit. He also introduced the idea of a balanced budget for governments.

INTEGRATED / TECHNOLOGY

RESEARCH LINKS For more on Suleyman, go to **classzone.com**

Suleyman the Lawgiver

The Ottoman Empire didn't reach its peak size and grandeur until the reign of Selim's son, Suleyman I (SOO•lay•mahn). Suleyman came to the throne in 1520 and ruled for 46 years. His own people called him **Suleyman the Lawgiver**. He was known in the West, though, as Suleyman the Magnificent. This title was a tribute to the splendor of his court and to his cultural achievements.

The Empire Reaches Its Limits Suleyman was a superb military leader. He conquered the important European city of Belgrade in 1521. The next year, Turkish forces captured the island of Rhodes in the Mediterranean and now dominated the whole eastern Mediterranean.

Applying their immense naval power, the Ottomans captured Tripoli on the coast of North Africa. They continued conquering peoples along the North African coastline. Although the Ottomans occupied only the coastal cities of North Africa, they managed to control trade routes to the interior of the continent.

In 1526, Suleyman advanced into Hungary and Austria, throwing central Europe into a panic. Suleyman's armies then pushed to the outskirts of Vienna, Austria. Reigning from Istanbul, Suleyman had waged war with central Europeans, North Africans, and Central Asians. He had become the most powerful monarch on earth. Only Charles V, head of the Hapsburg Empire in Europe, came close to rivaling his power.

Highly Structured Social Organization Binding the Ottoman Empire together in a workable social structure was Suleyman's crowning achievement. The massive empire required an efficient government structure and social organization. Suleyman created a law code to handle both criminal and civil actions. He also simplified and limited taxes, and systematized and reduced government bureaucracy. These changes bettered the lives of most citizens and helped earn Suleyman the title of Lawgiver.

The sultan's 20,000 personal slaves staffed the palace bureaucracy. The slaves were acquired as part of a policy called *devshirme* (dehv•SHEER•meh). Under the **devshirme** system, the sultan's army drafted boys from the peoples of conquered Christian territories. The army educated them, converted them to Islam, and trained them as soldiers. An elite force of 30,000 soldiers known as **janissaries** was trained to be loyal to the sultan only. Their superb discipline made them the heart of the Ottoman war machine. In fact, Christian families sometimes bribed officials to take their children into the sultan's service, because the brightest ones could rise to high government posts or military positions. **B**

As a Muslim, Suleyman was required to follow Islamic law. In accordance with Islamic law, the Ottomans granted freedom of worship to other religious communities, particularly to Christians and Jews. They treated these communities as *millets,* or nations. They allowed each *millet* to follow its own religious laws and practices. The head of the *millets* reported to the sultan and his staff. This system kept conflict among people of the various religions to a minimum.

MAIN IDEA

Making Inferences
B What were the advantages of the *devshirme* system to the sultan?

Cultural Flowering Suleyman had broad interests, which contributed to the cultural achievements of the empire. He found time to study poetry, history, geography, astronomy, mathematics, and architecture. He employed one of the world's finest architects, Sinan, who was probably from Albania. Sinan's masterpiece, the Mosque of Suleyman, is an immense complex topped with domes and half domes. It includes four schools, a library, a bath, and a hospital.

MAIN IDEA

Comparing

C Which cultural achievements of Suleyman's reign were similar to the European Renaissance?

Art and literature also flourished under Suleyman's rule. This creative period was similar to the European Renaissance. Painters and poets looked to Persia and Arabia for models. The works that they produced used these foreign influences to express original Ottoman ideas in the Turkish style. They are excellent examples of cultural blending. **C**

▲ Sinan's Mosque of Suleyman in Istanbul is the largest mosque in the Ottoman Empire.

The Empire Declines Slowly

Despite Suleyman's magnificent social and cultural achievements, the Ottoman Empire was losing ground. Suleyman killed his ablest son and drove another into exile. His third son, the incompetent Selim II, inherited the throne.

Suleyman set the pattern for later sultans to gain and hold power. It became customary for each new sultan to have his brothers strangled. The sultan would then keep his sons prisoner in the harem, cutting them off from education or contact with the world. This practice produced a long line of weak sultans who eventually brought ruin on the empire. However, the Ottoman Empire continued to influence the world into the early 20th century.

SECTION 1 ASSESSMENT

TERMS & NAMES 1. For each term or name, write a sentence explaining its significance.
• ghazi   • Ottoman   • sultan   • Timur the Lame   • Mehmed II   • Suleyman the Lawgiver   • *devshirme*   • janissary

USING YOUR NOTES

2. Which do you consider more significant to the Ottoman Empire, the accomplishments of Mehmed II or those of Selim the Grim? Explain.

Rulers	Successes

MAIN IDEAS

3. By what means did the early Ottomans expand their empire?

4. Why was Suleyman called the Lawgiver?

5. How powerful was the Ottoman Empire compared to other empires of the time?

CRITICAL THINKING & WRITING

6. **EVALUATING DECISIONS** Do you think that the Ottomans were wise in staffing their military and government with slaves? Explain.

7. **EVALUATING COURSES OF ACTION** How did Suleyman's selection of a successor eventually spell disaster for the Ottoman Empire?

8. **ANALYZING MOTIVES** Do you think that Suleyman's religious tolerance helped or hurt the Ottoman Empire?

9. **WRITING ACTIVITY** [EMPIRE BUILDING] Using the description of Mehmed II's forces taking Constantinople, write a **newspaper article** describing the action.

CONNECT TO TODAY CREATING A TIME LINE

Create a **time line** showing events in the decline of the Ottoman Empire and the creation of the modern nation of Turkey.

Cultural Blending

CASE STUDY: The Safavid Empire

MAIN IDEA	WHY IT MATTERS NOW	TERMS & NAMES
CULTURAL INTERACTION The Safavid Empire produced a rich and complex blended culture in Persia.	Modern Iran, which plays a key role in global politics, descended from the culturally diverse Safavid Empire.	• Safavid • Isma'il • shah • Shah Abbas • Esfahan

SETTING THE STAGE Throughout the course of world history, cultures have interacted with each other. Often such interaction has resulted in the mixing of different cultures in new and exciting ways. This process is referred to as cultural blending. The **Safavid** Empire, a Shi'ite Muslim dynasty that ruled in Persia between the 16th and 18th centuries, provides a striking example of how inter-action among peoples can produce a blending of cultures. This culturally diverse empire drew from the traditions of Persians, Ottomans, and Arabs.

TAKING NOTES

Drawing Conclusions
Identify examples of cultural blending in the Safavid Empire.

Patterns of Cultural Blending

Each time a culture interacts with another, it is exposed to ideas, technologies, foods, and ways of life not exactly like its own. Continental crossroads, trade routes, ports, and the borders of countries are places where cultural blending commonly begins. Societies that are able to benefit from cultural blending are those that are open to new ways and are willing to adapt and change. The blended ideas spread throughout the culture and produce a new pattern of behavior. Cultural blending has several basic causes.

Causes of Cultural Blending Cultural change is most often prompted by one or more of the following four activities:

- migration
- pursuit of religious freedom or conversion
- trade
- conquest

The blending that contributed to the culture of the Ottomans, which you just read about in Section 1, depended on some of these activities. Surrounded by the peoples of Byzantium, the Turks were motivated to win territory for their empire. The Ottoman Empire's location on a major trading route created many opportunities for contact with different cultures. Suleyman's interest in learning and culture prompted him to bring the best foreign artists and scholars to his court. They brought new ideas about art, literature, and learning to the empire.

Results of Cultural Blending Cultural blending may lead to changes in language, religion, styles of government, the use of technology, and military tactics.

Cultural Blending			
Location	**Interacting Cultures**	**Reason for Interaction**	**Some Results of Interaction**
India—1000 B.C.	Aryan and Dravidian Indian Arab, African, Indian	Migration	Vedic culture, forerunner of Hinduism
East Africa—A.D. 700	Islamic, Christian	Trade, religious conversion	New trade language, Swahili
Russia—A.D. 1000	Christian and Slavic	Religious conversion	Eastern Christianity, Russian identity
Mexico—A.D. 1500	Spanish and Aztec	Conquest	Mestizo culture, Mexican Catholicism
United States—A.D. 1900	European, Asian, Caribbean	Migration, religious freedom	Cultural diversity

SKILLBUILDER: Interpreting Charts
1. **Determining Main Ideas** *What are the reasons for interaction in the Americas?*
2. **Hypothesizing** *What are some aspects of cultural diversity?*

These changes often reflect unique aspects of several cultures. For example:

- **Language** Sometimes the written characters of one language are used in another, as in the case of written Chinese characters used in the Japanese language. In the Safavid Empire, the language spoken was Persian. But after the area converted to Islam, a significant number of Arabic words appeared in the Persian language.
- **Religion and ethical systems** Buddhism spread throughout Asia. Yet the Buddhism practiced by Tibetans is different from Japanese Zen Buddhism.
- **Styles of government** The concept of a democratic government spread to many areas of the globe. Although the basic principles are similar, it is not practiced exactly the same way in each country.
- **Racial or ethnic blending** One example is the mestizo, people of mixed European and Indian ancestry who live in Mexico.
- **Arts and architecture** Cultural styles may be incorporated or adapted into art or architecture. For example, Chinese artistic elements are found in Safavid Empire tiles and carpets as well as in European paintings.

MAIN IDEA

Recognizing Effects

A Which of the effects of cultural blending do you think is the most significant? Explain.

The chart above shows other examples of cultural blending that have occurred over time in various areas of the world. **A**

▼ Grandson of Isma'il, Shah Abbas led the Safavid Empire during its Golden Age.

CASE STUDY: The Safavid Empire

The Safavids Build an Empire

Conquest and ongoing cultural interaction fueled the development of the Safavid Empire. Originally, the Safavids were members of an Islamic religious brotherhood named after their founder, Safi al-Din. In the 15th century, the Safavids aligned themselves with the Shi'a branch of Islam.

The Safavids were also squeezed geographically between the Ottomans and Uzbek tribespeople and the Mughal Empire. (See the map on page 80.) To protect themselves from these potential enemies, the Safavids concentrated on building a powerful army.

Isma'il Conquers Persia The Safavid military became a force to reckon with. In 1499, a 12-year-old named **Isma'il** (ihs•MAH•eel) began to seize most of what is now Iran. Two years later he completed the task.

Safavid Empire, 1683

RUSSIA

Azov

Aral Sea

Caspian Sea

CAUCASUS MTS.

Trabzon

Chaldiran

Tabriz

Mosul

Tigris R.

Euphrates R.

MESOPOTAMIA

Baghdad

ARABIA

Basra

Tehran

Persian Gulf

Shiraz

Ormuz (Hormuz)

Esfahan

PERSIA

Herat

Amu Darya

UZBEKS

40° N

Legend:
- Ottoman Empire
- Safavid Empire
- Mughal Empire

N

0   500 Miles

0   1,000 Kilometers

Tropic of Cancer

GEOGRAPHY SKILLBUILDER: Interpreting Maps
1. **Movement** *What waterways might have enabled the Safavids to interact with other cultures?*
2. **Location** *Why might the Safavids not have expanded further?*

To celebrate his achievement, he took the ancient Persian title of **shah**, or king. He also established Shi'a Islam as the state religion.

Isma'il became a religious tyrant. Any citizen who did not convert to Shi'ism was put to death. Isma'il destroyed the Sunni population of Baghdad in his confrontation with the Ottomans. Their leader, Selim the Grim, later ordered the execution of all Shi'a in the Ottoman Empire. As many as 40,000 died. Their final face-off took place at the Battle of Chaldiran in 1514. Using artillery, the Ottomans pounded the Safavids into defeat. Another outcome of the battle was to set the border between the two empires. It remains the border today between Iran and Iraq.

Isma'il's son Tahmasp learned from the Safavids' defeat at Chaldiran. He adopted the use of artillery with his military forces. He expanded the Safavid Empire up to the Caucasus Mountains, northeast of Turkey, and brought Christians under Safavid rule. Tahmasp laid the groundwork for the golden age of the Safavids. **B**

MAIN IDEA

Drawing Conclusions
B How did Tahmasp's cultural borrowing lead to the expansion of the Safavid Empire?

A Safavid Golden Age

Shah Abbas, or Abbas the Great, took the throne in 1587. He helped create a Safavid culture and golden age that drew from the best of the Ottoman, Persian, and Arab worlds.

Reforms Shah Abbas reformed aspects of both military and civilian life. He limited the power of the military and created two new armies that would be loyal to him alone. One of these was an army of Persians. The other was a force that Abbas recruited from the Christian north and modeled after the Ottoman janissaries. He equipped both of these armies with modern artillery.

Abbas also reformed his government. He punished corruption severely and promoted only officials who proved their competence and loyalty. He hired foreigners from neighboring countries to fill positions in the government.

To convince European merchants that his empire was tolerant of other religions, Abbas brought members of Christian religious orders into the empire. As a result, Europeans moved into the land. Then industry, trade, and art exchanges grew between the empire and European nations.

A New Capital The Shah built a new capital at **Esfahan**. With a design that covered four and a half miles, the city was considered one of the most beautiful in the world. It was a showplace for the many artisans, both foreign and Safavid, who worked on the buildings and the objects in them. For example, 300 Chinese potters produced glazed building tiles for the buildings in the city, and Armenians wove carpets.

Art Works Shah Abbas brought hundreds of Chinese artisans to Esfahan. Working with Safavid artists, they produced intricate metalwork, miniature paintings, calligraphy, glasswork, tile work, and pottery. This collaboration gave rise to artwork that blended Chinese and Persian ideas. These decorations beautified the many mosques, palaces, and marketplaces.

Carpets The most important result of Western influence on the Safavids, however, may have been the demand for Persian carpets. This demand helped change carpet weaving from a local craft to a national industry. In the beginning, the carpets reflected traditional Persian themes. As the empire became more culturally blended, the designs incorporated new themes. In the 16th century, Shah Abbas sent artists to Italy to study under the Renaissance artist Raphael. Rugs then began to reflect European designs. **C**

MAIN IDEA

Comparing
C In what ways were Shah Abbas and Suleyman the Lawgiver similar?

▲ The Masjid-e-Imam mosque in Esfahan is a beautiful example of the flowering of the arts in the Safavid Empire.

The Dynasty Declines Quickly

In finding a successor, Shah Abbas made the same mistake the Ottoman monarch Suleyman made. He killed or blinded his ablest sons. His incompetent grandson, Safi, succeeded Abbas. This pampered young prince led the Safavids down the same road to decline that the Ottomans had taken, only more quickly.

In 1736, however, Nadir Shah Afshar conquered land all the way to India and created an expanded empire. But Nadir Shah was so cruel that one of his own troops assassinated him. With Nadir Shah's death in 1747, the Safavid Empire fell apart.

At the same time that the Safavids flourished, cultural blending and conquest led to the growth of a new empire in India, as you will learn in Section 3.

SECTION ② **ASSESSMENT**

TERMS & NAMES 1. For each term or name, write a sentence explaining its significance.
• Safavid   • Isma'il   • shah   • Shah Abbas   • Esfahan

USING YOUR NOTES	MAIN IDEAS	CRITICAL THINKING & WRITING
2. What are some examples of cultural blending in the Safavid Empire?	3. What are the four causes of cultural blending? 4. What reforms took place in the Safavid Empire under Shah Abbas? 5. Why did the Safavid Empire decline so quickly?	6. **FORMING OPINIONS** Which of the results of cultural blending do you think has the most lasting effect on a country? Explain. 7. **DRAWING CONCLUSIONS** How did the location of the Safavid Empire contribute to the cultural blending in the empire? 8. **ANALYZING MOTIVES** Why might Isma'il have become so intolerant of the Sunni Muslims? 9. **WRITING ACTIVITY** [CULTURAL INTERACTION] Write a **letter** from Shah Abbas to a Chinese artist persuading him to come teach and work in the Safavid Empire.

Cultural Blending

INTEGRATED TECHNOLOGY **INTERNET ACTIVITY**
Use the Internet to research the charge that Persian rugs are largely made by children under the age of 14. Write a television documentary **script** detailing your research results.

INTERNET KEYWORD
child labor rug making

The Mughal Empire in India

MAIN IDEA	WHY IT MATTERS NOW	TERMS & NAMES
POWER AND AUTHORITY The Mughal Empire brought Turks, Persians, and Indians together in a vast empire.	The legacy of great art and deep social division left by the Mughal Empire still influences southern Asia.	• Mughal • Sikh • Babur • Shah Jahan • Akbar • Taj Mahal • Aurangzeb

SETTING THE STAGE The Gupta Empire crumbled in the late 400s. First, Huns invaded. Then, beginning in the 700s, warlike Muslim tribes from Central Asia carved northwestern India into many small kingdoms. The people who invaded descended from Muslim Turks and Afghans. Their leader was a descendant of Timur the Lame and of the Mongol conqueror Genghis Khan. They called themselves **Mughals**, which means "Mongols." The land they invaded had been through a long period of turmoil.

TAKING NOTES

Following Chronological Order Create a time line of the Mughal emperors and their successes.

1494
|————|————|
Babur

Early History of the Mughals

The 8th century began with a long clash between Hindus and Muslims in this land of many kingdoms. For almost 300 years, the Muslims were able to advance only as far as the Indus River valley. Starting around the year 1000, however, well-trained Turkish armies swept into India. Led by Sultan Mahmud (muh•MOOD) of Ghazni, they devastated Indian cities and temples in 17 brutal campaigns. These attacks left the region weakened and vulnerable to other conquerors. Delhi eventually became the capital of a loose empire of Turkish warlords called the Delhi Sultanate. These sultans treated the Hindus as conquered people.

Delhi Sultanate Between the 13th and 16th centuries, 33 different sultans ruled this divided territory from their seat in Delhi. In 1398, Timur the Lame destroyed Delhi. The city was so completely devastated that according to one witness, "for months, not a bird moved in the city." Delhi eventually was rebuilt. But it was not until the 16th century that a leader arose who would unify the empire.

Babur Founds an Empire In 1494, an 11-year-old boy named **Babur** inherited a kingdom in the area that is now Uzbekistan and Tajikistan. It was only a tiny kingdom, and his elders soon took it away and drove him south. But Babur built up an army. In the years that followed, he swept down into India and laid the foundation for the vast Mughal Empire.

Babur was a brilliant general. In 1526, for example, he led 12,000 troops to victory against an army of 100,000 commanded by a sultan of Delhi. A year later, Babur also defeated a massive rajput army. After Babur's death, his incompetent son, Humayun, lost most of the territory Babur had gained. Babur's 13-year-old grandson took over the throne after Humayun's death.

Akbar's Golden Age

Babur's grandson was called <u>Akbar</u>, which means "Great." Akbar certainly lived up to his name, ruling India with wisdom and tolerance from 1556 to 1605.

A Military Conqueror Akbar recognized military power as the root of his strength. In his opinion, A king must always be aggressive so that his neighbors will not try to conquer him.

Like the Safavids and the Ottomans, Akbar equipped his armies with heavy artillery. Cannons enabled him to break into walled cities and extend his rule into much of the Deccan plateau. In a brilliant move, he appointed some rajputs as officers. In this way he turned potential enemies into allies. This combination of military power and political wisdom enabled Akbar to unify a land of at least 100 million people—more than in all of Europe put together.

A Liberal Ruler Akbar was a genius at cultural blending. A Muslim, he continued the Islamic tradition of religious freedom. He permitted people of other religions to practice their faiths. He proved his tolerance by marrying Hindu princesses without forcing them to convert. He allowed his wives to practice their religious rituals in the palace. He proved his tolerance again by abolishing both the tax on Hindu pilgrims and the hated *jizya*, or tax on non-Muslims. He even appointed a Spanish Jesuit to tutor his second son.

Growth of the Mughal Empire, 1526–1707

- ■ Mughal Empire, 1526 (Babur)
- ■ Added by 1605 (Akbar)
- ■ Added by 1707 (Aurangzeb)

GEOGRAPHY SKILLBUILDER: Interpreting Maps
1. **Movement** *During which time period was the most territory added to the Mughal Empire?*
2. **Human-Environment Interaction** *What landform might have prevented the empire from expanding farther east?*

Akbar governed through a bureaucracy of officials. Natives and foreigners, Hindus and Muslims, could all rise to high office. This approach contributed to the quality of his government. Akbar's chief finance minister, Todar Mal, a Hindu, created a clever—and effective—taxation policy. He levied a tax similar to the present-day U.S. graduated income tax, calculating it as a percentage of the value of the peasants' crops. Because this tax was fair and affordable, the number of peasants who paid it increased. This payment brought in much needed money for the empire. **A**

Akbar's land policies had more mixed results. He gave generous land grants to his bureaucrats. After they died, however, he reclaimed the lands and distributed them as he saw fit. On the positive side, this policy prevented the growth of feudal aristocracies. On the other hand, it did not encourage dedication and hard work by the Mughal officials. Their children would not inherit the land or benefit from their parents' work. So the officials apparently saw no point in devoting themselves to their property.

MAIN IDEA

Comparing

A In what ways were Akbar's attitudes toward religion similar to those of Suleyman the Lawgiver?

A Flowering of Culture As Akbar extended the Mughal Empire, he welcomed influences from the many cultures in the empire. This cultural blending affected art, education, politics, and language. Persian was the language of Akbar's court and of high culture. The common people, however, spoke Hindi, a language derived from Sanskrit. Hindi remains one of the most widely spoken languages in India today. Out of the Mughal armies, where soldiers of many backgrounds rubbed shoulders, came yet another new language. This language was Urdu, which means "from the soldier's camp." A blend of Arabic, Persian, and Hindi, Urdu is today the official language of Pakistan.

The Arts and Literature The arts flourished at the Mughal court, especially in the form of book illustrations. These small, highly detailed, and colorful paintings were called miniatures. They were brought to a peak of perfection in the Safavid Empire (see section 2). Babur's son, Humayun, brought two masters of this art to his court to teach it to the Mughals. Some of the most famous Mughal miniatures adorned the *Akbarnamah* ("Book of Akbar"), the story of the great emperor's campaigns and deeds. Indian art drew from traditions developed earlier in Rajput kingdoms.

Hindu literature also enjoyed a revival in Akbar's time. The poet Tulsi Das, for example, was a contemporary of Akbar's. He retold the epic love story of Rama and Sita from the fourth century B.C. Indian poem the *Ramayana* (rah•MAH•yuh•nuh) in Hindi. This retelling, the *Ramcaritmanas,* is now even more popular than the original.

Architecture Akbar devoted himself to architecture, too. The style developed under his reign is still known as Akbar period architecture. Its massive but graceful structures are decorated with intricate stonework that portrays Hindu themes. The capital city of Fatehpur Sikri is one of the most important examples of this type of architecture. Akbar had this red-sandstone city built to thank a Sufi saint, Sheik Salim Chisti, who had predicted the birth of his first son. **B**

MAIN IDEA

Drawing Conclusions
B How was Akbar able to build such an immense empire?

Akbar's Successors

With Akbar's death in 1605, the Mughal court changed to deal with the changing times. The next three emperors each left his mark on the Mughal Empire.

Jahangir and Nur Jahan Akbar's son called himself Jahangir (juh•hahn•GEER) —"Grasper of the World." However, for most of his reign, he left the affairs of state to his wife, who ruled with an iron hand.

Jahangir's wife was the Persian princess Nur Jahan. She was a brilliant politician who perfectly understood the use of power. As the real ruler of India, she installed her father as prime minister in the Mughal court. She saw Jahangir's son Khusrau as her ticket to future power. But when Khusrau rebelled against his father, Nur Jahan removed him. She then shifted her favor to another son.

This rejection of Khusrau affected more than the political future of the empire. It was also the basis of a long and bitter religious conflict. Jahangir tried to promote Islam in the Mughal state, but was tolerant of other religions. When Khusrau

Connect *to* Today

Women Leaders of the Indian Subcontinent

Since World War II, the subcontinent of India has seen the rise of several powerful women. Unlike Nur Jahan, however, they achieved power on their own—not through their husbands.

Indira Gandhi headed the Congress Party and dominated Indian politics for almost 30 years. She was elected prime minister in 1966 and again in 1980. Gandhi was assassinated in 1984 by Sikh separatists.

Benazir Bhutto took charge of the Pakistan People's Party after her father was executed by his political enemies. She won election as her country's prime minister in 1988, the first woman to run a modern Muslim state. She was reelected in 1993.

Chandrika Bandaranaike Kumaratunga is the president of Sri Lanka. She was elected in 1994 with 62 percent of the votes cast. She survived an assassination attempt in 1999 and was reelected.

Khaleda Zia became Bangladesh's first woman prime minister in 1991. She was reelected several times, the last time in 2001. She has made progress in empowering women and girls in her nation.

Indira Gandhi

Benazir Bhutto

Chandrika Bandaranaike Kumaratunga

Khaleda Zia

---

rebelled, he turned to the **Sikhs**. This was a nonviolent religious group whose doctrines contained elements similar to Hinduism, and Sufism (Islamic mysticism). However, the Sikhs see themselves as an independent tradition and not an offshoot of another religion. Their leader, Guru Arjun, sheltered Khusrau and defended him. In response, the Mughal rulers had Arjun arrested and tortured to death. The Sikhs became the target of the Mughals' particular hatred. **C**

MAIN IDEA

Analyzing Causes
C How did the Mughals' dislike of the Sikhs develop?

Shah Jahan Jahangir's son and successor, **Shah Jahan**, could not tolerate competition and secured his throne by assassinating all his possible rivals. He had a great passion for two things: beautiful buildings and his wife Mumtaz Mahal (moom•TAHZ mah•HAHL). Nur Jahan had arranged this marriage between Jahangir's son and her niece for political reasons. Shah Jahan, however, fell genuinely in love with his Persian princess.

In 1631, Mumtaz Mahal died at age 39 while giving birth to her 14th child. To enshrine his wife's memory, he ordered that a tomb be built "as beautiful as she was beautiful." Fine white marble and fabulous jewels were gathered from many parts of Asia. This memorial, the **Taj Mahal**, has been called one of the most beautiful buildings in the world. Its towering marble dome and slender minaret towers look like lace and seem to change color as the sun moves across the sky.

The People Suffer But while Shah Jahan was building gardens, monuments, and forts, his country was suffering. There was famine in the land. Furthermore, farmers needed tools, roads, and ways of irrigating their crops and dealing with India's harsh environment. What they got instead were taxes and more taxes to support the building of monuments, their rulers' extravagant living, and war.

The Muslim World Expands **85**

▲ Mirrored in a reflecting pool is the Taj Mahal, a monument to love and the Mughal Empire.

Building the Taj Mahal

Some 20,000 workers labored for 22 years to build the famous tomb. It is made of white marble brought from 250 miles away. The minaret towers are about 130 feet high. The building itself is 186 feet square.

The design of the building is a blend of Hindu and Muslim styles. The pointed arches are of Muslim design, and the perforated marble windows and doors are typical of a style found in Hindu temples.

The inside of the building is a glittering garden of thousands of carved marble flowers inlaid with tiny precious stones. One tiny flower, one inch square, had 60 different inlays.

INTEGRATED TECHNOLOGY

INTERNET ACTIVITY Use the Internet to take a virtual trip to the Taj Mahal. Create a brochure about the building. Go to **classzone.com** for your research.

All was not well in the royal court either. When Shah Jahan became ill in 1657, his four sons scrambled for the throne. The third son, **Aurangzeb** (AWR•uhng•zehb), moved first and most decisively. In a bitter civil war, he executed his older brother, who was his most serious rival. Then he arrested his father and put him in prison, where he died several years later. After Shah Jahan's death, a mirror was found in his room, angled so that he could look out at the reflection of the Taj Mahal.

Aurangzeb's Reign A master at military strategy and an aggressive empire builder, Aurangzeb ruled from 1658 to 1707. He expanded the Mughal holdings to their greatest size. However, the power of the empire weakened during his reign.

This loss of power was due largely to Aurangzeb's oppression of the people. He rigidly enforced Islamic laws, outlawing drinking, gambling, and other activities viewed as vices. He appointed censors to police his subjects' morals and make sure they prayed at the appointed times. He also tried to erase all the gains Hindus had made under Akbar. For example, he brought back the hated tax on non-Muslims and dismissed Hindus from high positions in his government. He banned the construction of new temples and had Hindu monuments destroyed. Not surprisingly, these actions outraged the Hindus.

The Hindu rajputs, whom Akbar had converted from potential enemies to allies, rebelled. Aurangzeb defeated them repeatedly, but never completely. In the southwest, a Hindu warrior community called Marathas founded their own state. Aurangzeb captured their leader but could never conquer them. Meanwhile, the Sikhs transformed themselves into a brotherhood of warriors. They began building a state in the Punjab, an area in northwest India.

Aurangzeb levied oppressive taxes to pay for the wars against the increasing numbers of enemies. He had done away with all taxes not authorized by Islamic law, so he doubled the taxes on Hindu merchants. This increased tax burden deepened the Hindus' bitterness and led to further rebellion. As a result, Aurangzeb needed to raise more money to increase his army. The more territory he conquered, the more desperate his situation became. **D**

MAIN IDEA

Recognizing Effects

D How did Aurangzeb's personal qualities and political policies affect the Mughal Empire?

The Empire's Decline and Decay

By the end of Aurangzeb's reign, he had drained the empire of its resources. Over 2 million people died in a famine while Aurangzeb was away waging war. Most of his subjects felt little or no loyalty to him.

As the power of the central state weakened, the power of local lords grew. After Aurangzeb's death, his sons fought a war of succession. In fact, three emperors reigned in the first 12 years after Aurangzeb died. By the end of this period, the Mughal emperor was nothing but a wealthy figurehead. He ruled not a united empire but a patchwork of independent states.

As the Mughal Empire rose and fell, Western traders slowly built their own power in the region. The Portuguese were the first Europeans to reach India. In fact, they arrived just before Babur did. Next came the Dutch, who in turn gave way to the French and the English. However, the great Mughal emperors did not feel threatened by the European traders. In 1661, Aurangzeb casually handed them the port of Bombay. Aurangzeb had no idea that he had given India's next conquerors their first foothold in a future empire.

SECTION 3 ASSESSMENT

TERMS & NAMES 1. For each term or name, write a sentence explaining its significance.
• Mughal   • Babur   • Akbar   • Sikh   • Shah Jahan   • Taj Mahal   • Aurangzeb

USING YOUR NOTES	MAIN IDEAS	CRITICAL THINKING & WRITING
2. Which of the Mughal emperors on your time line had a positive effect on the empire? Which had negative effects?	3. How did Akbar demonstrate tolerance in his empire? 4. What pattern is seen in the ways individuals came to power in the Mughal Empire? 5. Why did the empire weaken under the rule of Aurangzeb?	6. **CLARIFYING** Why were Akbar's tax policies so successful? 7. **MAKING INFERENCES** Why was Nur Jahan able to hold so much power in Jahangir's court? 8. **EVALUATING COURSES OF ACTION** Why were the policies of Aurangzeb so destructive to the Mughal Empire? 9. **WRITING ACTIVITY** POWER AND AUTHORITY Write a **compare-and-contrast essay** on the policies of Akbar and Aurangzeb. Use references from the text in your response.

CONNECT TO TODAY **CREATING A BIOGRAPHY**

Select one of the women leaders in Connect to Today on page 85. Research her life and write a short **biography** of her.

Cultural Blending in Mughal India

As you have read, Mughal India enjoyed a golden age under Akbar. Part of Akbar's success—indeed, the success of the Mughals—came from his religious tolerance. India's population was largely Hindu, and the incoming Mughal rulers were Muslim. The Mughal emperors encouraged the blending of cultures to create a united India.

This cultural integration can be seen in the art of Mughal India. Muslim artists focused heavily on art with ornate patterns of flowers and leaves, called arabesque or geometric patterns. Hindu artists created naturalistic and often ornate artworks. These two artistic traditions came together and created a style unique to Mughal India. As you can see, the artistic collaboration covered a wide range of art forms.

INTEGRATED / TECHNOLOGY

RESEARCH LINKS For more on art in Mughal India, go to **classzone.com**

▼ Decorative Arts

Decorative work on items from dagger handles to pottery exhibits the same cultural blending as other Mughal art forms. This dagger handle shows some of the floral and geometric elements common in Muslim art, but the realistic depiction of the horse comes out of the Hindu tradition.

▼ Architecture

Mughal emperors brought to India a strong Muslim architectural tradition. Indian artisans were extremely talented with local building materials—specifically, marble and sandstone. Together, they created some of the most striking and enduring architecture in the world, like Humayun's Tomb shown here.

▼ Painting

Mughal painting was largely a product of the royal court. Persian artists brought to court by Mughal emperors had a strong influence, but Mughal artists quickly developed their own characteristics. The Mughal style kept aspects of the Persian influence—particularly the flat aerial perspective. But, as seen in this colorful painting, the Indian artists incorporated more naturalism and detail from the world around them.

▲ Fabrics

Mughal fabrics included geometric patterns found in Persian designs, but Mughal weavers, like other Mughal artisans, also produced original designs. Themes that were common in Mughal fabrics were landscapes, animal chases, floral latticeworks, and central flowering plants like the one on this tent hanging.

Connect *to* Today

1. **Clarifying** What does the art suggest about the culture of Mughal India?

   📖 See Skillbuilder Handbook, page R4.

2. **Forming and Supporting Opinions** What are some modern examples of cultural blending in art? What elements of each culture are represented in the artwork? Consider other art forms, such as music and literature, as well.

Chapter 2 Assessment

TERMS & NAMES

Briefly explain the importance of each of the following to the Ottoman, Safavid, or Mughal empires.

1. Suleyman the Lawgiver
2. *devshirme*
3. janissary
4. shah
5. Shah Abbas
6. Akbar
7. Sikh
8. Taj Mahal

MAIN IDEAS

The Ottomans Build a Vast Empire
Section 1 (pages 73–77)

9. Why were the Ottomans such successful conquerors?
10. How did Mehmed the Conqueror show his tolerance of other cultures?
11. Why was Selim's capture of Mecca, Medina, and Cairo so significant?

Case Study: Cultural Blending Section 2 (pages 78–81)

12. What are some of the causes of cultural blending in the Safavid Empire?
13. In what ways did the Safavids weave foreign ideas into their culture?

The Mughal Empire in India Section 3 (pages 82–89)

14. In what ways did Akbar defend religious freedom during his reign?
15. How did Akbar's successors promote religious conflict in the empire?

CRITICAL THINKING

1. USING YOUR NOTES

In a diagram, compare and contrast the Mughal Empire under Akbar, the Safavid Empire under Shah Abbas, and the Ottoman Empire under Suleyman I.

	Government Reforms	Cultural Blending
Akbar		
Abbas		
Suleyman		

2. EVALUATING COURSES OF ACTION

POWER AND AUTHORITY How did the use of artillery change the way empires in this chapter and lands that bordered them reacted to each other?

3. RECOGNIZING EFFECTS

CULTURAL INTERACTION What impact did religion have on governing each of the three empires in this chapter?

4. EVALUATING DECISIONS

EMPIRE BUILDING What was the value of treating conquered peoples in a way that did not oppress them?

5. MAKING INFERENCES

Why do you think the three empires in this chapter did not unite into one huge empire? Give reasons for your answer.

6. MAKING INFERENCES

Conquest of new territories contributed to the growth of the Muslim empires you read about in this chapter. How might it have also hindered this growth?

VISUAL SUMMARY

The Muslim World Expands

Muslims control Middle East, India, North Africa, and parts of Europe.

Ottoman Empire

- Move into Byzantium
- Take Constantinople
- Add Syria and Palestine
- Use janissaries and *devshirme* to control the empire

Safavid Empire

- Take old Persian Empire
- Expand to Caucasus Mountains
- Build a new capital
- Use janissary-style army to control the empire

Mughal Empire

- Delhi Sultanate loosely controls Indian subcontinent
- Babur lays groundwork for an empire
- Akbar controls most of sub-continent in empire
- Aurangzeb expands empire to its largest size

Use the graphs and your knowledge of world history to answer questions 1 and 2.
Additional Test Practice, pp. S1–S33

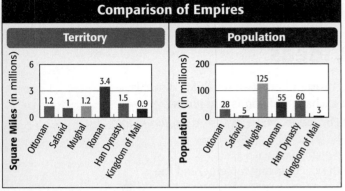

Source: Atlas of World Population History

1. Which empire was most densely populated?

A. Han

B. Roman

C. Mughal

D. Mali

2. Of the three Asian Muslim empires shown on the graph, which one had the smallest territory?

A. Ottoman

B. Safavid

C. Mughal

D. Mali

Use the quotation from Kritovoulos, a Greek historian and a governor in the court of Mehmed II, and your knowledge of world history to answer question 3.

PRIMARY SOURCE

When the Sultan [Mehmed] had captured the City of Constantinople, almost his very first care was to have the City repopulated. He also undertook the further care and repairs of it. He sent an order in the form of an imperial command to every part of his realm, that as many inhabitants as possible be transferred to the City, not only Christians but also his own people and many of the Hebrews.

KRITOVOULOS, *History of Mehmed the Conqueror*

3. What groups of people were to be sent to Constantinople?

A. Hebrews and Christians

B. Christians and Turks

C. Christians, Hebrews, and Turkish Muslims

D. Imperial armies

INTEGRATED TECHNOLOGY

TEST PRACTICE Go to **classzone.com**

• Diagnostic tests   • Strategies

• Tutorials   • Additional practice

ALTERNATIVE ASSESSMENT

1. Interact *with* History

On page 72, you considered how you might treat the people you conquered. Now that you have learned more about three Muslim empires, in what ways do you think you would change your policies? Discuss your thoughts with a small group of classmates.

2. WRITING ABOUT HISTORY

Think about the experience of being a janissary in the court of Suleyman the Lawgiver. Write a **journal entry** about your daily activities. Consider the following:

• how a janissary was recruited

• what jobs or activities a janissary may have done

• the grandeur of the court of Suleyman

INTEGRATED TECHNOLOGY

Creating a Database

The three empires discussed in this chapter governed many religious and ethnic groups. Gather information on the religious and ethnic makeup of the modern nations of the former Ottoman, Safavid, and Mughal empires. Organize the information in a population database.

• Create one table for each empire.

• Make row headings for each modern nation occupying the lands of that empire.

• Make column headings for each ethnic group and each religious group.

• Insert the most recent population figures or percentages for each group.

• Use the final column to record the population total for each modern nation.

An Age of Explorations and Isolation, 1400–1800

Previewing Main Ideas

CULTURAL INTERACTION Asians resisted European influence, but this cultural interaction did produce an exchange of goods and ideas.
Geography *Study the map. What European power first sent explorers into the Indian Ocean?*

ECONOMICS The desire for wealth was a driving force behind the European exploration of the East. Europeans wanted to control trade with Asian countries.
Geography *How did the voyages of Bartolomeu Dias and Vasco da Gama compare in length?*

SCIENCE AND TECHNOLOGY Europeans were able to explore faraway lands after they improved their sailing technology.
Geography *Look at the map and time line. What country sent the first expedition to explore the Indian Ocean in the 15th century?*

INTEGRATED TECHNOLOGY

eEdition
- Interactive Maps
- Interactive Visuals
- Interactive Primary Sources

INTERNET RESOURCES
Go to **classzone.com** for:
- Research Links
- Internet Activities
- Primary Sources
- Chapter Quiz
- Maps
- Test Practice
- Current Events

EUROPE AND ASIA

1405
Zheng He takes first voyage.

1419
Prince Henry ▶ founds navigation school.

1494
Spain and Portugal sign Treaty of Tordesillas.

1400

1500

WORLD

1453
◀ Ottomans capture Constantinople.

1464
Songhai Empire begins in West Africa.

1511
First enslaved Africans arrive in the Americas.

Early Explorations, 1400s

ATLANTIC OCEAN

EUROPE

ENGLAND
London
NETHERLANDS
Amsterdam
Paris
FRANCE
Venice
PORTUGAL
Lisbon
Madrid
SPAIN
Seville
Ceuta
Madeira
Canary Is.
30°N
Mediterranean Sea
Cairo

ASIA

Beijing
Nanjing
CHINA

AFRICA

Jiddah
Aden
Hormuz
Bombay
Goa
Calicut
Arabian Sea

Mogadishu
Malindi
Mombasa
Kilwa
Mozambique
Sofala

Cape Verde Is.

0° Equator

INDIAN OCEAN

Malacca

30°S

Cape of Good Hope

ATLANTIC OCEAN

N
W   E
S

- - - Dias, 1487–1488
——— da Gama, (1st voyage) 1497–1498
——— Zheng He, (7 voyages) 1405–1433

0   500   1000 Miles
0   500 1000 Kilometers
Winkel II Projection

1603
Tokugawa shoguns rule Japan.

1619
Dutch open trade with Java.

1644
Manchus establish Qing Dynasty in China.

1793
Britain seeks to trade with China.

1600

1700

1800

1608
◄ Samuel de Champlain founds Quebec. (French flag)

1776
◄ American colonies declare independence from Britain. (George Washington)

Would you sail into the unknown?

It is a gray morning in 1430. You are standing on a dock in the European country of Portugal, staring out at the mysterious Atlantic Ocean. You have been asked to go on a voyage of exploration. Yet, like most people at the time, you have no idea what lies beyond the horizon. The maps that have been drawn show some of the dangers you might face. And you've heard the terrifying stories of sea monsters and shipwrecks (see map below). You also have heard that riches await those who help explore and claim new lands. Now, you must decide whether to go.

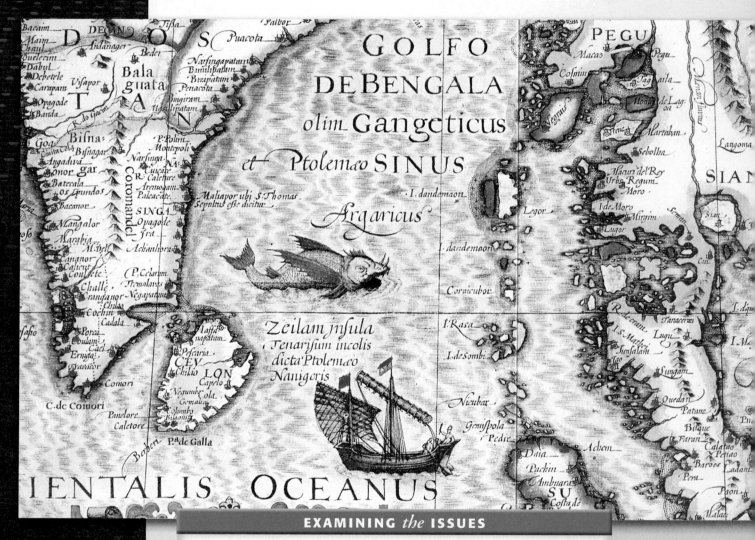

EXAMINING *the* ISSUES

- **What possible rewards might come from exploring the seas for new lands?**

- **What are the risks involved in embarking on a voyage into the unknown?**

Discuss these questions with your classmates. In your discussion, recall what you have learned about the lands beyond Europe and what they have to offer. As you read about the age of explorations and isolation, see why Europeans explored and what they achieved.

Europeans Explore the East

MAIN IDEA	WHY IT MATTERS NOW	TERMS & NAMES
SCIENCE AND TECHNOLOGY Advances in sailing technology enabled Europeans to explore other parts of the world.	European exploration was an important step toward the global interaction existing in the world today.	• Bartolomeu Dias • Prince Henry • Vasco da Gama • Treaty of Tordesillas • Dutch East India Company

SETTING THE STAGE By the early 1400s, Europeans were ready to venture beyond their borders. As Chapter 1 explained, the Renaissance encouraged, among other things, a new spirit of adventure and curiosity. This spirit of adventure, along with several other important reasons, prompted Europeans to explore the world around them. This chapter and the next one describe how these explorations began a long process that would bring together the peoples of many different lands and permanently change the world.

For "God, Glory, and Gold"

Europeans had not been completely isolated from the rest of the world before the 1400s. Beginning around 1100, European crusaders battled Muslims for control of the Holy Lands in Southwest Asia. In 1275, the Italian trader Marco Polo reached the court of Kublai Khan in China. For the most part, however, Europeans had neither the interest nor the ability to explore foreign lands. That changed by the early 1400s. The desire to grow rich and to spread Christianity, coupled with advances in sailing technology, spurred an age of European exploration.

Europeans Seek New Trade Routes The desire for new sources of wealth was the main reason for European exploration. Through overseas exploration, merchants and traders hoped ultimately to benefit from what had become a profitable business in Europe: the trade of spices and other luxury goods from Asia. The people of Europe had been introduced to these items during the Crusades, the wars fought between Christians and Muslims from 1096 to 1270. After the Crusades ended, Europeans continued to demand such spices as nutmeg, ginger, cinnamon, and pepper, all of which added flavor to the bland foods of Europe. Because demand for these goods was greater than the supply, merchants could charge high prices and thus make great profits.

The Muslims and the Italians controlled the trade of goods from East to West. Muslims sold Asian goods to Italian merchants, who controlled trade across the land routes of the Mediterranean region. The Italian merchants resold the items at increased prices to merchants

▼ This early globe depicts the Europeans' view of Europe and Africa around 1492.

TAKING NOTES

Following Chronological Order On a time line, note the important events in the European exploration of the East.

1400

1800

throughout Europe. Other European traders did not like this arrangement. Paying such high prices to the Italians severely cut into their own profits. By the 1400s, European merchants—as well as the new monarchs of England, Spain, Portugal, and France—sought to bypass the Italian merchants. This meant finding a sea route directly to Asia.

The Spread of Christianity The desire to spread Christianity also motivated Europeans to explore. The Crusades had left Europeans with a taste for spices, but more significantly with feelings of hostility between Christians and Muslims. European countries believed that they had a sacred duty not only to continue fighting Muslims, but also to convert non-Christians throughout the world.

Europeans hoped to obtain popular goods directly from the peoples of Asia. They also hoped to Christianize them. **Bartolomeu Dias**, an early Portuguese explorer, explained his motives: "To serve God and His Majesty, to give light to those who were in darkness and to grow rich as all men desire to do." **A**

Technology Makes Exploration Possible While "God, glory, and gold" were the primary motives for exploration, advances in technology made the voyages of discovery possible. During the 1200s, it would have been nearly impossible for a European sea captain to cross 3,000 miles of ocean and return again. The main problem was that European ships could not sail against the wind. In the 1400s, shipbuilders designed a new vessel, the caravel. The caravel was sturdier than earlier vessels. In addition, triangular sails adopted from the Arabs allowed it to sail effectively against the wind.

Europeans also improved their navigational techniques. To better determine their location at sea, sailors used the astrolabe, which the Muslims had perfected. The astrolabe was a brass circle with carefully adjusted rings marked off in degrees. Using the rings to sight the stars, a sea captain could calculate latitude, or how far north or south of the equator the ship was. Explorers were also able to more accurately track direction by using a magnetic compass, a Chinese invention.

MAIN IDEA

Summarizing

A How might the phrase "God, glory, and gold" summarize the Europeans' motives for exploration?

History Makers

Prince Henry
1394–1460

For his role in promoting Portuguese exploration, historians call Prince Henry "the Navigator." Although he never went on voyages of discovery, Henry was consumed by the quest to find new lands and to spread Christianity. A devout Catholic, he wanted "to make increase in the faith of our lord Jesus Christ and bring to him all the souls that should be saved."

To that end, Henry used his own fortune to organize more than 14 voyages along the western coast of Africa, which was previously unexplored by Europeans. As a result, Henry died in debt. The Portuguese crown spent more than 60 years paying off his debts.

INTEGRATED / TECHNOLOGY

RESEARCH LINKS For more on Prince Henry, go to **classzone.com**

Portugal Leads the Way

The leader in developing and applying these sailing innovations was Portugal. Located on the Atlantic Ocean at the southwest corner of Europe, Portugal was the first European country to establish trading outposts along the west coast of Africa. Eventually, Portuguese explorers pushed farther east into the Indian Ocean.

The Portuguese Explore Africa Portugal took the lead in overseas exploration in part due to strong government support. The nation's most enthusiastic supporter of exploration was **Prince Henry**, the son of Portugal's king. Henry's dreams of overseas exploration began in 1415 when he helped conquer the Muslim city of Ceuta in North Africa. There, he had his first glimpse of the dazzling wealth that lay beyond Europe. In Ceuta, the Portuguese invaders found exotic stores filled with pepper, cinnamon, cloves, and other spices. In addition, they encountered large supplies of gold, silver, and jewels.

The Tools of Exploration

Out on the open seas, winds easily blew ships off course. With only the sun, moon, and stars to guide them, few sailors willingly ventured beyond the sight of land. In order to travel to distant places, European inventors and sailors experimented with new tools for navigation and new designs for sailing ships, often borrowing from other cultures.

INTEGRATED *TECHNOLOGY*
RESEARCH LINKS For more on the tools of exploration, go to **classzone.com**

▲ Here, a French mariner uses an early navigation instrument that he has brought ashore to fix his ship's position. It was difficult to make accurate calculations aboard wave-tossed vessels.

1 The average caravel was 65 feet long. This versatile ship had triangular sails for maneuverability and square sails for power.

2 The large cargo area could hold the numerous supplies needed for long voyages.

3 Its shallow draft (depth of the ship's keel below the water) allowed it to explore close to the shore.

◀ The sextant replaced the astrolabe in the mid-1700s as the instrument for measuring the height of the stars above the horizon—to determine latitude and longitude.

▲ This 17th-century compass is typical of those taken by navigators on voyages of exploration. The compass was invented by the Chinese.

Connect *to* Today

1. **Analyzing Motives** Why did inventors and sailors develop better tools for navigation?
   See Skillbuilder Handbook, page R16.

2. **Summarizing** What types of navigational or other tools do sailors use today? Choose one type of tool and write a brief explanation of what it does.

A Ship's Rations

The captain of a 17th-century sailing vessel, with a crew of 190 sailors, would normally order the following food items for a three-month trip:

- 8,000 pounds of salt beef; 2,800 pounds of salt pork; 600 pounds of salt cod; a few beef tongues
- 15,000 brown biscuits; 5,000 white biscuits
- 30 bushels of oatmeal; 40 bushels of dried peas; 1 1/2 bushels of mustard seed
- 1 barrel of salt; 1 barrel of flour
- 11 small wooden casks of butter; 1 large cask of vinegar
- 10,500 gallons of beer; 3,500 gallons of water; 2 large casks of cider

INTEGRATED / TECHNOLOGY

INTERNET ACTIVITY Research food services aboard a modern U.S. warship and prepare a menu for a typical meal. Go to **classzone.com** for your research.

Henry returned to Portugal determined to reach the source of these treasures in the East. The prince also wished to spread the Christian faith. In 1419, Henry founded a navigation school on the southwestern coast of Portugal. Mapmakers, instrument makers, shipbuilders, scientists, and sea captains gathered there to perfect their trade.

Within several years, Portuguese ships began sailing down the western coast of Africa. By the time Henry died in 1460, the Portuguese had established a series of trading posts along western Africa's shores. There, they traded with Africans for such profitable items as gold and ivory. Eventually, they traded for African captives to be used as slaves. Having established their presence along the African coast, Portuguese explorers plotted their next move. They would attempt to find a sea route to Asia.

Portuguese Sailors Reach Asia The Portuguese believed that to reach Asia by sea, they would have to sail around the southern tip of Africa. In 1488, Portuguese captain Bartolomeu Dias ventured far down the coast of Africa until he and his crew reached the tip. As they arrived, a huge storm rose and battered the fleet for days. When the storm ended, Dias realized his ships had been blown around the tip to the other side. Dias explored the southeast coast of Africa and then considered sailing to India. However, his crew was exhausted and food supplies were low. As a result, the captain returned home.

With the tip of Africa finally rounded, the Portuguese continued pushing east. In 1497, Portuguese explorer **Vasco da Gama** began exploring the east African coast. In 1498, he reached the port of Calicut, on the southwestern coast of India. Da Gama and his crew were amazed by the spices, rare silks, and precious gems that filled Calicut's shops. The Portuguese sailors filled their ships with such spices as pepper and cinnamon and returned to Portugal in 1499. Their cargo was worth 60 times the cost of the voyage. Da Gama's remarkable voyage of 27,000 miles had given Portugal a direct sea route to India.

Spain Also Makes Claims

As the Portuguese were establishing trading posts along the west coast of Africa, Spain watched with increasing envy. The Spanish monarchs also desired a direct sea route to Asia.

In 1492, an Italian sea captain, Christopher Columbus, convinced Spain to finance a bold plan: finding a route to Asia by sailing west across the Atlantic Ocean. In October of that year, Columbus reached an island in the Caribbean. He was mistaken in his thought that he had reached the East Indies. But his voyage would open the way for European colonization of the Americas—a process that would forever change the world. The immediate impact of Columbus's voyage, however, was to increase tensions between Spain and Portugal.

The Portuguese believed that Columbus had indeed reached Asia. Portugal suspected that Columbus had claimed for Spain lands that Portuguese sailors might have reached first. The rivalry between Spain and Portugal grew more tense. In 1493, Pope Alexander VI stepped in to keep peace between the two nations. He suggested an imaginary dividing line, drawn north to south, through the Atlantic Ocean. All lands to the west of the line, known as the Line of Demarcation, would be Spain's. These lands included most of the Americas. All lands to the east of the line would belong to Portugal.

MAIN IDEA

Analyzing Issues

B How did the Treaty of Tordesillas ease tensions between Spain and Portugal?

Portugal complained that the line gave too much to Spain. So it was moved farther west to include parts of modern-day Brazil for the Portuguese. In 1494, Spain and Portugal signed the **Treaty of Tordesillas**, in which they agreed to honor the line. The era of exploration and colonization was about to begin in earnest. **B**

Trading Empires in the Indian Ocean

With da Gama's voyage, Europeans had finally opened direct sea trade with Asia. They also opened an era of violent conflict in the East. European nations scrambled to establish profitable trading outposts along the shores of South and Southeast Asia. And all the while they battled the region's inhabitants, as well as each other.

Portugal's Trading Empire In the years following da Gama's voyage, Portugal built a bustling trading empire throughout the Indian Ocean. As the Portuguese moved into the region, they took control of the spice trade from Muslim merchants. In 1509, Portugal extended its control over the area when it defeated a Muslim fleet off the coast of India, a victory made possible by the cannons they had added aboard their ships.

Portugal strengthened its hold on the region by building a fort at Hormuz in 1514. It established control of the Straits of Hormuz, connecting the Persian Gulf and Arabian Sea, and helped stop Muslim traders from reaching India.

In 1510, the Portuguese captured Goa, a port city on India's west coast. They made it the capital of their trading empire. They then sailed farther east to Indonesia, also known as the East Indies. In 1511, a Portuguese fleet attacked the city of Malacca on the west coast of the Malay Peninsula. In capturing the town, the Portuguese seized control of the Strait of Malacca. Seizing this waterway gave them control of the Moluccas. These were islands so rich in spices that they became known as the Spice Islands.

In convincing his crew to attack Malacca, Portuguese sea captain Afonso de Albuquerque stressed his country's intense desire to crush the Muslim-Italian domination over Asian trade:

MAIN IDEA

Analyzing Primary Sources

C What did de Albuquerque see as the outcome of a Portuguese victory at Malacca?

PRIMARY SOURCE C

If we deprive them [Muslims] of this their ancient market there, there does not remain for them a single port in the whole of these parts, where they can carry on their trade in these things. . . . I hold it as very certain that if we take this trade of Malacca away out of their hands, Cairo and Mecca are entirely ruined, and to Venice will no spiceries . . . [be] . . . conveyed except that which her merchants go and buy in Portugal.

AFONSO DE ALBUQUERQUE, from *The Commentaries of the Great Afonso Dalbuquerque*

Portugal did break the old Muslim-Italian domination on trade from the East, much to the delight of European consumers. Portuguese merchants brought back goods from Asia at about one-fifth of what they cost when purchased through the Arabs and Italians. As a result, more Europeans could afford these items.

Europeans in the East, 1487–1700
INTERACTIVE

European territories
- Dutch
- English
- French
- Portuguese
- Spanish

European trading posts
- Dutch
- English
- French
- Portuguese
- Spanish

Dias's route Aug. 1487– Feb. 1488
Da Gama's route July 1497–May 1498

GEOGRAPHY SKILLBUILDER: Interpreting Maps
1. **Place** *Why would a fort at Hormuz help the Portuguese to stop trade between the Arabian Peninsula and India?*
2. **Region** *Where was the Dutch influence the greatest?*

In time, Portugal's success in Asia attracted the attention of other European nations. As early as 1521, a Spanish expedition led by Ferdinand Magellan arrived in the Philippines. Spain claimed the islands and began settling them in 1565. By the early 1600s, the rest of Europe had begun to descend upon Asia. They wanted to establish their own trade empires in the East.

Other Nations Challenge the Portuguese Beginning around 1600, the English and Dutch began to challenge Portugal's dominance over the Indian Ocean trade. The Dutch Republic, also known as the Netherlands, was a small country situated along the North Sea in northwestern Europe. Since the early 1500s, Spain had ruled the area. In 1581, the people of the region declared their independence from Spain and established the Dutch Republic.

In a short time, the Netherlands became a leading sea power. By 1600, the Dutch owned the largest fleet of ships in the world—20,000 vessels. Pressure from Dutch and also English fleets eroded Portuguese control of the Asian region. The Dutch and English then battled one another for dominance of the area.

Both countries had formed an East India Company to establish and direct trade throughout Asia. These companies had the power to mint money, make treaties, and even raise their own armies. The **Dutch East India Company** was richer and more powerful than England's company. As a result, the Dutch eventually drove out the English and established their dominance over the region. **D**

Dutch Trade Outposts In 1619, the Dutch established their trading headquarters at Batavia on the island of Java. From there, they expanded west to

MAIN IDEA

Analyzing Issues
D How were the Dutch able to dominate the Indian Ocean trade?

conquer several nearby islands. In addition, the Dutch seized both the port of Malacca and the valuable Spice Islands from Portugal. Throughout the 1600s, the Netherlands increased its control over the Indian Ocean trade. With so many goods from the East traveling to the Netherlands, the nation's capital, Amsterdam, became a leading commercial center. By 1700, the Dutch ruled much of Indonesia and had trading posts in several Asian countries. They also controlled the Cape of Good Hope on the southern tip of Africa, which was used as a resupply stop.

British and French Traders By 1700 also, Britain and France had gained a foothold in the region. Having failed to win control of the larger area, the English East India Company focused much of its energy on establishing outposts in India. There, the English developed a successful business trading Indian cloth in Europe. In 1664, France also entered the Asia trade with its own East India Company. It struggled at first, as it faced continual attacks by the Dutch. Eventually, the French company established an outpost in India in the 1720s. However, it never showed much of a profit.

As the Europeans battled for a share of the profitable Indian Ocean trade, their influence inland in Southeast Asia remained limited. European traders did take control of many port cities in the region. But their impact rarely spread beyond the ports. From 1500 to about 1800, when Europeans began to conquer much of the region, the peoples of Asia remained largely unaffected by European contact. As the next two sections explain, European traders who sailed farther east to seek riches in China and Japan had even less success in spreading Western culture. **E**

Connect to Today

Trading Partners

Global trade is important to the economies of Asian countries now just as it was when the region first began to export spices, silks, and gems centuries ago. Today, a variety of products, including automobiles and electronic goods, as well as tea and textiles, are shipped around the world. (Hong Kong harbor is pictured.)

Regional trade organizations help to strengthen economic cooperation among Asian nations and promote international trade. They include the Association of Southeast Asian Nations (ASEAN) and the South Asian Association of Regional Co-operation (SAARC).

MAIN IDEA

Recognizing Effects

E How did the arrival of Europeans affect the peoples of the East in general?

SECTION 1 ASSESSMENT

TERMS & NAMES 1. For each term or name, write a sentence explaining its significance.
• Bartolomeu Dias   • Prince Henry   • Vasco da Gama   • Treaty of Tordesillas   • Dutch East India Company

USING YOUR NOTES	MAIN IDEAS	CRITICAL THINKING & WRITING
2. Which event in the European exploration of the East is the most significant? Explain with references from the text. 	3. What role did the Renaissance play in launching an age of exploration? 4. What was Prince Henry's goal and who actually achieved it? 5. What European countries were competing for Asian trade during the age of exploration?	6. **MAKING INFERENCES** What did the Treaty of Tordesillas reveal about Europeans' attitudes toward non-European lands and peoples? 7. **ANALYZING MOTIVES** What were the motives behind European exploration in the 1400s? Explain. 8. **RECOGNIZING EFFECTS** In what ways did Europeans owe some of their sailing technology to other peoples? 9. **WRITING ACTIVITY** **SCIENCE AND TECHNOLOGY** Review "The Tools of Exploration" on page 97. Write a one-paragraph **opinion piece** on which technological advancement was the most important for European exploration.

CONNECT TO TODAY **WRITING A DESCRIPTION**
Research the Global Positioning System (GPS). Then write a brief **description** of this modern navigation system.

China Limits European Contacts

MAIN IDEA	WHY IT MATTERS NOW	TERMS & NAMES
CULTURAL INTERACTION Advances under the Ming and Qing dynasties left China uninterested in European contact.	China's independence from the West continues today, even as it forges new economic ties with the outside world.	• Ming Dynasty • Hongwu • Yonglo • Zheng He • Manchus • Qing Dynasty • Kangxi

SETTING THE STAGE The European voyages of exploration had led to opportunities for trade. Europeans made healthy profits from trade in the Indian Ocean region. They began looking for additional sources of wealth. Soon, European countries were seeking trade relationships in East Asia, first with China and later with Japan. By the time Portuguese ships dropped anchor off the Chinese coast in 1514, the Chinese had driven out their Mongol rulers and had united under a new dynasty.

TAKING NOTES

Summarizing Use a chart to summarize relevant facts about each emperor.

Emperor	Facts
1.	1.
2.	2.
3.	3.

China Under the Powerful Ming Dynasty

China had become the dominant power in Asia under the **Ming Dynasty** (1368–1644). In recognition of China's power, vassal states from Korea to Southeast Asia paid their Ming overlords regular tribute, which is a payment by one country to another to acknowledge its submission. China expected Europeans to do the same. Ming rulers were not going to allow outsiders from distant lands to threaten the peace and prosperity the Ming had brought to China when they ended Mongol rule.

The Rise of the Ming A peasant's son, **Hongwu**, commanded the rebel army that drove the Mongols out of China in 1368. That year, he became the first Ming emperor. Hongwu continued to rule from the former Yuan capital of Nanjing in the south. (See the map on page 93.) He began reforms designed to restore agricultural lands devastated by war, erase all traces of the Mongol past, and promote China's power and prosperity. Hongwu's agricultural reforms increased rice production and improved irrigation. He also encouraged fish farming and growing commercial crops, such as cotton and sugar cane.

Hongwu used respected traditions and institutions to bring stability to China. For example, he encouraged a return to Confucian moral standards. He improved imperial administration by restoring the merit-based civil service examination system. Later in his rule, however, when problems developed, Hongwu became a ruthless tyrant. Suspecting plots against his rule everywhere, he conducted purges of the government, killing thousands of officials.

Hongwu's death in 1398 led to a power struggle. His son **Yonglo** (yung•lu) emerged victorious. Yonglo continued many of his father's policies, although he moved the royal court to Beijing. (See the Forbidden City feature on page 104.)

▼ Porcelain vase from the Ming Dynasty

Zheng He's Treasure Ship

85 FEET 400 FEET

◄ Zheng He's treasure ship compared with Christopher Columbus's *Santa Maria*

Yonglo also had a far-ranging curiosity about the outside world. In 1405, before Europeans began to sail beyond their borders, he launched the first of seven voyages of exploration. He hoped they would impress the world with the power and splendor of Ming China. He also wanted to expand China's tribute system.

The Voyages of Zheng He A Chinese Muslim admiral named <u>Zheng He</u> (jung huh) led all of the seven voyages. His expeditions were remarkable for their size. Everything about them was large—distances traveled, fleet size, and ship measurements. The voyages ranged from Southeast Asia to eastern Africa. From 40 to 300 ships sailed in each expedition. Among them were fighting ships, storage vessels, and huge "treasure" ships measuring more than 400 feet long. The fleet's crews numbered over 27,000 on some voyages. They included sailors, soldiers, carpenters, interpreters, accountants, doctors, and religious leaders. Like a huge floating city, the fleet sailed from port to port along the Indian Ocean.

Everywhere Zheng He went, he distributed gifts including silver and silk to show Chinese superiority. As a result, more than 16 countries sent tribute to the Ming court. Even so, Chinese scholar-officials complained that the voyages wasted valuable resources that could be used to defend against barbarians' attacks on the northern frontier. After the seventh voyage, in 1433, China withdrew into isolation. **A**

MAIN IDEA

Making Inferences
A What do you think the people of other countries thought about China after one of Zheng He's visits?

Ming Relations with Foreign Countries China's official trade policies in the 1500s reflected its isolation. To keep the influence of outsiders to a minimum, only the government was to conduct foreign trade, and only through three coastal ports, Canton, Macao, and Ningbo. In reality, trade flourished up and down the coast. Profit-minded merchants smuggled cargoes of silk, porcelain, and other valuable goods out of the country into the eager hands of European merchants. Usually, Europeans paid for purchases with silver, much of it from mines in the Americas.

Demand for Chinese goods had a ripple effect on the economy. Industries such as silk-making and ceramics grew rapidly. Manufacturing and commerce increased. But China did not become highly industrialized for two main reasons. First, the idea of commerce offended China's Confucian beliefs. Merchants, it was said, made their money "supporting foreigners and robbery." Second, Chinese economic policies traditionally favored agriculture. Taxes on agriculture stayed low. Taxes on manufacturing and trade skyrocketed.

Christian missionaries accompanied European traders into China. They brought Christianity and knowledge of European science and technology, such as the clock. The first missionary to have an impact was an Italian Jesuit named Matteo Ricci. He

The Forbidden City

When Yonglo moved the Chinese capital to Beijing, he ordered the building of a great palace complex to symbolize his power and might. Construction took 14 years, from 1406 to 1420. Red walls 35 feet in height surrounded the complex, which had dozens of buildings, including palaces and temples. The complex became known as the Forbidden City because commoners and foreigners were not allowed to enter.

1

▲ Hall of Supreme Harmony

Taihe Hall, or the Hall of Supreme Harmony, is the largest building in the compound. It measures 201 by 122 feet and stands about 125 feet high. This hall was used for important ceremonies, such as those marking the emperor's birthday or the day the crown prince took the throne.

2

▲ Hall of Central Harmony

Zhonge Hall, or the Hall of Central Harmony, was a smaller square building between the two main halls. It was a sort of private office where the emperor could stop to rest on his way to ceremonies.

▼ Nine-Dragon Wall

This wall, or screen, of glazed tiles shows nine dragons playing with pearls against a background of sea and sky. From ancient times, the dragon was the symbol of the imperial family. This is the largest of three famous nine-dragon screens that exist in China.

3

SKILLBUILDER: Interpreting Visuals
1. **Analyzing Motives** *Why do you think the emperor wanted to keep common people out of the Forbidden City?*
2. **Drawing Conclusions** *What aspects of the Forbidden City helped to convey the power of the emperor?*

gained special favor at the Ming court through his intelligence and fluency in Chinese. Still, many educated Chinese opposed the European and Christian presence.

Manchus Found the Qing Dynasty

By 1600, the Ming had ruled for more than 200 years, and the dynasty was weakening. Its problems grew—ineffective rulers, corrupt officials, and a government that was out of money. Higher taxes and bad harvests pushed millions of peasants toward starvation. Civil strife and rebellion followed.

Northeast of the Great Wall lay Manchuria. In 1644, the **Manchus** (MAN•chooz), the people of that region, invaded China and the Ming Dynasty collapsed. The Manchus seized Beijing, and their leader became China's new emperor. As the Mongols had done in the 1300s, the Manchus took a Chinese name for their dynasty, the **Qing** (chihng) **Dynasty**. They would rule for more than 260 years and expand China's borders to include Taiwan, Chinese Central Asia, Mongolia, and Tibet.

China Under the Qing Many Chinese resisted rule by the non-Chinese Manchus. Rebellions flared up periodically for decades. The Manchus, however, slowly earned the people's respect. They upheld China's traditional Confucian beliefs and social structures. They made the country's frontiers safe and restored China's prosperity. Two powerful Manchu rulers contributed greatly to the acceptance of the new dynasty.

The first, **Kangxi** (kahng•shee), became emperor in 1661 and ruled for some 60 years. He reduced government expenses and lowered taxes. A scholar and patron of the arts, Kangxi gained the support of intellectuals by offering them government positions. He also enjoyed the company of the Jesuits at court. They told him about developments in science, medicine, and mathematics in Europe. Under his grandson Qian-long (chyahn•lung), who ruled from 1736 to 1795, China reached its greatest size and prosperity. An industrious emperor like his grandfather, Qian-long often rose at dawn to work on the empire's problems. These included armed nomads on its borders and the expanding presence of European missionaries and merchants in China.

Manchus Continue Chinese Isolation To the Chinese, their country—called the Middle Kingdom—had been the cultural center of the universe for 2,000 years. If foreign states wished to trade with China, they would have to follow Chinese rules. These rules included trading only at special ports and paying tribute.

The Dutch were masters of the Indian Ocean trade by the time of Qian-long. They accepted China's restrictions. Their diplomats paid tribute to the emperor through gifts and by performing the required "kowtow" ritual. This ritual involved kneeling in front of the emperor and touching one's head to the ground nine times. As a result, the Chinese accepted the Dutch as trading partners. The Dutch returned home with traditional porcelains and silk, as well as a new trade item, tea. By 1800, tea would make up 80 percent of shipments to Europe. **B**

Great Britain also wanted to increase trade with China. But the British did not like China's trade restrictions. In 1793, Lord George Macartney delivered a letter from King George III to Qian-long. It asked for a better trade arrangement,

History Makers

Kangxi
1654–1722

The emperor Kangxi had too much curiosity to remain isolated in the Forbidden City. To calm the Chinese in areas devastated by the Manchu conquest, Kangxi set out on a series of "tours."

On tours I learned about the common people's grievances by talking with them. . . . I asked peasants about their officials, looked at their houses, and discussed their crops.

In 1696, with Mongols threatening the northern border, Kangxi exhibited leadership unheard of in later Ming times. Instead of waiting in the palace for reports, he personally led 80,000 troops to victory over the Mongols.

MAIN IDEA

Making Inferences
B Why do you think the kowtow ritual was so important to the Chinese emperor?

An Age of Explorations and Isolation **105**

including Chinese acceptance of British manufactured goods. Macartney refused to kowtow, and Qian-long denied Britain's request. As the emperor made clear in a letter to the king, China was self-sufficient and did not need the British:

PRIMARY SOURCE
There is nothing we lack, as your principal envoy and others have themselves observed. We have never set much store on strange or ingenious objects, nor do we need any more of your country's manufactures.

QIAN-LONG, from a letter to King George III of Great Britain

In the 1800s, the British, Dutch, and others would attempt to chip away at China's trade restrictions until the empire itself began to crack, as Chapter 12 will describe.

Korea Under the Manchus In 1636, even before they came to power in China, the Manchus conquered nearby Korea and made it a vassal state. Although Korea remained independent, it existed in China's shadow. Koreans organized their government according to Confucian principles. They also adopted China's technology, its culture, and especially its policy of isolation.

When the Manchus established the Qing dynasty, Korea's political relationship with China did not change. But Korea's attitude did. The Manchu invasion, combined with a Japanese attack in the 1590s, provoked strong feelings of nationalism in the Korean people. This sentiment was most evident in their art. Instead of traditional Chinese subjects, many artists chose to show popular Korean scenes.

Social History

China's Population Boom

China's population grew dramatically from 1650 to 1900. General peace and increased agricultural productivity were the causes.

The Growth of Early Modern China

Population (in millions)

500
400
300
200
100

1650 1700 1750 1800 1850 1900

▲ A Chinese family prepares for a wedding in the 1800s.

SKILLBUILDER: Interpreting Graphs
Comparing *By what percentage did China's population increase between 1650 and 1900?*

Life in Ming and Qing China

In the 1600s and 1700s, there was general peace and prosperity in China. Life improved for most Chinese.

Families and the Role of Women Most Chinese families had farmed the land the same way their ancestors had. However, during the Qing Dynasty, irrigation and fertilizer use increased. Farmers grew rice and new crops, such as corn and sweet potatoes, brought by Europeans from the Americas. As food production increased, nutrition improved and families expanded. A population explosion followed.

These expanded Chinese families favored sons over daughters. Only a son was allowed to perform vital religious rituals. A son also would raise his own family under his parents' roof, assuring aging parents of help with the farming. As a result, females were not valued, and many female infants were killed. Although men dominated the household and their wives, women had significant responsibilities. Besides working in the fields, they supervised the children's education and managed the family's finances. While most women were forced to remain secluded in their homes, some found outside jobs such as working as midwives or textile workers.

Vocabulary
A *midwife* is a woman trained to assist women in childbirth.

Cultural Developments The culture of early modern China was based mainly on traditional forms. The great masterpiece of traditional Chinese fiction was written during this period. *Dream of the Red Chamber* by Cao Zhan examines upper class Manchu society in the 1700s. Most artists of the time painted in traditional styles, which valued technique over creativity. In pottery, technical skill as well as experimentation led to the production of high-quality ceramics, including porcelain. Drama was a popular entertainment, especially in rural China where literacy rates were low. Plays that presented Chinese history and cultural heroes entertained and also helped unify Chinese society by creating a national culture. **C**

MAIN IDEA

Making Inferences
C What was the effect of the emphasis on tradition in early modern China?

While China preserved its traditions in isolation, another civilization that developed in seclusion—the Japanese—was in conflict, as you will read in Section 3.

▲ These 12th-century Chinese women work outside the home making silk.

SECTION 2 ASSESSMENT

TERMS & NAMES 1. For each term or name, write a sentence explaining its significance.
• Ming Dynasty   • Hongwu   • Yonglo   • Zheng He   • Manchus   • Qing Dynasty   • Kangxi

USING YOUR NOTES	MAIN IDEAS	CRITICAL THINKING & WRITING
2. Which of these emperors was most influential? Explain with text references.	3. How did Beijing become the capital of China?	6. **MAKING DECISIONS** Do you think Lord George Macartney should have kowtowed to Emperor Qian-long? Why?
	4. What evidence indicates that China lost interest in contacts abroad after 1433?	7. **ANALYZING CAUSES** What factors, both within China and outside its borders, contributed to the downfall of the Ming Dynasty?
	5. What did Christian missionaries bring to China?	8. **DRAWING CONCLUSIONS** What was Korea's relationship with China under the Qing Dynasty?

USING YOUR NOTES table:

Emperor	Facts
1.	1.
2.	2.
3.	3.

9. **WRITING ACTIVITY** [CULTURAL INTERACTION] Choose one emperor of China and write a one-paragraph **biography** using the information you listed in your Taking Notes chart and from the text.

CONNECT TO TODAY WRITING AN ESSAY

Learn more about popular culture in China today. Then write a two-paragraph **expository essay** on some form of popular entertainment in the arts or sports.

Japan Returns to Isolation

MAIN IDEA	WHY IT MATTERS NOW	TERMS & NAMES
ECONOMICS The Tokugawa regime unified Japan and began 250 years of isolation, autocracy, and economic growth.	Even now, Japan continues to limit and control dealings with foreigners, especially in the area of trade.	• daimyo • Oda Nobunaga • Toyotomi Hideyoshi • Tokugawa Shogunate • haiku • kabuki

SETTING THE STAGE In the 1300s, the unity that had been achieved in Japan in the previous century broke down. Shoguns, or military leaders, in the north and south fiercely fought one another for power. Although these two rival courts later came back together at the end of the century, a series of politically weak shoguns let control of the country slip from their grasp. The whole land was torn by factional strife and economic unrest. It would be centuries before Japan would again be unified.

TAKING NOTES

Comparing Use a chart to compare the achievements of the daimyos who unified Japan.

Daimyo	Achievements

A New Feudalism Under Strong Leaders

In 1467, civil war shattered Japan's old feudal system. The country collapsed into chaos. Centralized rule ended. Power drained away from the shogun to territorial lords in hundreds of separate domains.

Local Lords Rule A violent era of disorder followed. This time in Japanese history, which lasted from 1467 to 1568, is known as the Sengoku, or "Warring States," period. Powerful samurai seized control of old feudal estates. They offered peasants and others protection in return for their loyalty. These warrior-chieftains, called **daimyo** (DY•mee•OH), became lords in a new kind of Japanese feudalism. Daimyo meant "great name." Under this system, security came from this group of powerful warlords. The emperor at Kyoto became a figurehead, having a leadership title but no actual power.

The new Japanese feudalism resembled European feudalism in many ways. The daimyo built fortified castles and created small armies of samurai on horses. Later they added foot soldiers with muskets (guns) to their ranks. Rival daimyo often fought each other for territory. This led to disorder throughout the land.

New Leaders Restore Order A number of ambitious daimyo hoped to gather enough power to take control of the entire country. One, the brutal and ambitious **Oda Nobunaga** (oh•dah noh•boo•nah•gah), defeated his rivals and seized the imperial capital Kyoto in 1568.

Following his own motto "Rule the empire by force," Nobunaga sought to eliminate his remaining enemies. These included rival daimyo as well as wealthy Buddhist monasteries aligned with them. In 1575, Nobunaga's 3,000 soldiers armed with muskets crushed an enemy force of samurai cavalry. This was the first time firearms had been used effectively in battle in Japan. However,

A samurai warrior ▼

Land controlled by Tokugawa or related households
Five highways
Daimyo boundary

Hokkaido

Sea of Japan

KOREA

Honshu

Kyoto
Edo (Tokyo)
Osaka

Kyushu

Nagasaki

Shikoku

PACIFIC OCEAN

0   200 Miles
0   400 Kilometers

▲ Himeji Castle, completed in the 17th century, is near Kyoto.

GEOGRAPHY SKILLBUILDER: Interpreting Maps
1. **Place** *Why might Edo have been a better site for a capital in the 17th century than Kyoto?*
2. **Region** *About what percentage of Japan was controlled by Tokugawa or related households when Tokugawa Ieyasu took power in the early 1600s?*

Nobunaga was not able to unify Japan. He committed *seppuku,* the ritual suicide of a samurai, in 1582, when one of his own generals turned on him.

Nobunaga's best general, **Toyotomi Hideyoshi** (toh•you•toh•mee hee•deh•yoh•shee), continued his fallen leader's mission. Hideyoshi set out to destroy the daimyo that remained hostile. By 1590, by combining brute force with shrewd political alliances, he controlled most of the country. Hideyoshi did not stop with Japan. With the idea of eventually conquering China, he invaded Korea in 1592 and began a long campaign against the Koreans and their Ming Chinese allies. When Hideyoshi died in 1598, his troops withdrew from Korea.

Tokugawa Shogunate Unites Japan One of Hideyoshi's strongest daimyo allies, Tokugawa Ieyasu (toh•koo•gah•wah ee•yeh•yah•soo), completed the unification of Japan. In 1600, Ieyasu defeated his rivals at the Battle of Sekigahara. His victory earned him the loyalty of daimyo throughout Japan. Three years later, Ieyasu became the sole ruler, or shogun. He then moved Japan's capital to his power base at Edo, a small fishing village that would later become the city of Tokyo.

Japan was unified, but the daimyo still governed at the local level. To keep them from rebelling, Ieyasu required that they spend every other year in the capital. Even when they returned to their lands, they had to leave their families behind as hostages in Edo. Through this "alternate attendance policy" and other restrictions, Ieyasu tamed the daimyo. This was a major step toward restoring centralized government to Japan. As a result, the rule of law overcame the rule of the sword. **A**

MAIN IDEA

Drawing Conclusions

A How would the "alternate attendance policy" restrict the daimyo?

An Age of Explorations and Isolation **109**

Ieyasu founded the **Tokugawa Shogunate**, which would hold power until 1867. On his deathbed in 1616, Ieyasu advised his son, Hidetada, "Take care of the people. Strive to be virtuous. Never neglect to protect the country." Most Tokugawa shoguns followed that advice. Their rule brought a welcome order to Japan.

Vocabulary
A *shogunate* is the administration or rule of a shogun.

Life in Tokugawa Japan

Japan enjoyed more than two and a half centuries of stability, prosperity, and isolation under the Tokugawa shoguns. Farmers produced more food, and the population rose. Still, the vast majority of peasants, weighed down by heavy taxes, led lives filled with misery. The people who prospered in Tokugawa society were the merchant class and the wealthy. However, everyone, rich and poor alike, benefited from a flowering of Japanese culture during this era.

Society in Tokugawa Japan Tokugawa society was very structured. The emperor had the top rank but was just a figurehead. The actual ruler was the shogun, who was the supreme military commander. Below him were the daimyo, the powerful landholding samurai. Samurai warriors came next. The peasants and artisans followed them. Peasants made up about four-fifths of the population. Merchants were at the bottom, but they gradually became more important as the Japanese economy expanded.

In Japan, as in China, Confucian values influenced ideas about society. According to Confucius, the ideal society depended on agriculture, not commerce. Farmers, not merchants, made ideal citizens. In the real world of Tokugawa Japan, however, peasant farmers bore the main tax burden and faced more difficulties than any other class. Many of them abandoned farm life and headed for the expanding towns and cities. There, they mixed with samurai, artisans, and merchants.

By the mid-1700s, Japan began to shift from a rural to an urban society. Edo had grown from a small village in 1600 to perhaps the largest city in the world. Its population was more than one million. The rise of large commercial centers also increased employment opportunities for women. Women found jobs in entertainment, textile manufacturing, and publishing. Still, the majority of Japanese women led sheltered and restricted lives as peasant wives. They worked in the fields, managed the household, cared for the children, and each woman obeyed her husband without question.

Culture Under the Tokugawa Shogunate Traditional culture continued to thrive. Samurai attended ceremonial *noh* dramas, which were based on tragic themes. They read tales of ancient warriors and their courage in battle. In their homes, they hung paintings that showed scenes from classical literature. But traditional entertainment faced competition in the cities from new styles of literature, drama, and art.

Townspeople read a new type of fiction, realistic stories about self-made merchants or the hardships of life. The people also read **haiku** (HY•koo), 5-7-5-syllable, 3-line verse poetry. This poetry presents images rather than ideas. For example, Matsuo Basho, the greatest haiku poet, wrote before his death in 1694:

PRIMARY SOURCE Ⓑ
On a journey, ailing—
My dreams roam about
Over a withered moor.
MATSUO BASHO, from *Matsuo Basho*

Tabi ni yande
Yume wa Kareno o
Kakemeguru

MATSUO BASHO, in Japanese

MAIN IDEA

Analyzing Primary Sources
Ⓑ How is Matsuo Basho's haiku a poem about death?

Townspeople also attended **kabuki** theater. Actors in elaborate costumes, using music, dance, and mime, performed skits about modern life. The paintings the people enjoyed were often woodblock prints showing city life.

Connect *to* Today

Kabuki Theater

Kabuki is a traditional form of Japanese theater. It makes use of extravagant costumes, masklike makeup, and exaggerated postures and gestures. The illustrations to the right show a contemporary actor and a 19th-century performer playing warriors.

Although kabuki was created by a woman, all roles, both male and female, are performed by men. Kabuki plays are about grand historical events or the everyday life of people in Tokugawa Japan.

For 400 years, kabuki has provided entertainment for the Japanese people. And more recently, kabuki has been performed for audiences around the world, including the United States. Major centers for kabuki theater in Japan are Tokyo, Kyoto, and Osaka.

Contact Between Europe and Japan

Europeans began coming to Japan in the 16th century, during the Warring States period. Despite the severe disorder in the country, the Japanese welcomed traders and missionaries, from Portugal and, later, other European countries. These newcomers introduced fascinating new technologies and ideas. Within a century, however, the aggressive Europeans had worn out their welcome.

Portugal Sends Ships, Merchants, and Technology to Japan The Japanese first encountered Europeans in 1543, when shipwrecked Portuguese sailors washed up on the shores of southern Japan. Portuguese merchants soon followed. They hoped to involve themselves in Japan's trade with China and Southeast Asia. The Portuguese brought clocks, eyeglasses, tobacco, firearms, and other unfamiliar items from Europe. Japanese merchants, eager to expand their markets, were happy to receive the newcomers and their goods. **C**

The daimyo, too, welcomed the strangers. They were particularly interested in the Portuguese muskets and cannons, because every daimyo sought an advantage over his rivals. One of these warlords listened intently to a Japanese observer's description of a musket:

> **PRIMARY SOURCE**
> In their hands they carried something two or three feet long, straight on the outside with a passage inside, and made of a heavy substance. . . . This thing with one blow can smash a mountain of silver and a wall of iron. If one sought to do mischief in another man's domain and he was touched by it, he would lose his life instantly.
> **ANONYMOUS JAPANESE WRITER**, quoted in *Sources of Japanese Tradition* (1958)

The Japanese purchased weapons from the Portuguese and soon began their own production. Firearms forever changed the time-honored tradition of the Japanese warrior, whose principal weapon had been the sword. Some daimyo recruited and trained corps of peasants to use muskets. Many samurai, who retained the sword as their principal weapon, would lose their lives to musket fire in future combat.

MAIN IDEA

Analyzing Motives
C Why did Europeans want to open trade with Japan?

An Age of Explorations and Isolation **111**

The cannon also had a huge impact on warfare and life in Japan. Daimyo had to build fortified castles to withstand the destructive force of cannonballs. (See the photograph of Himeji Castle on page 109.) The castles attracted merchants, artisans, and others to surrounding lands. Many of these lands were to grow into the towns and cities of modern Japan, including Edo (Tokyo), Osaka, Himeji, and Nagoya.

Christian Missionaries in Japan In 1549, Christian missionaries began arriving in Japan. The Japanese accepted the missionaries in part because they associated them with the muskets and other European goods that they wanted to purchase. However, the religious orders of Jesuits, Franciscans, and Dominicans came to convert the Japanese.

Francis Xavier, a Jesuit, led the first mission to Japan. He wrote that the Japanese were "very sociable. . . and much concerned with their honor, which they prize above everything else." Francis Xavier baptized about a hundred converts before he left Japan. By the year 1600, other European missionaries had converted about 300,000 Japanese to Christianity.

The success of the missionaries upset Tokugawa Ieyasu. He found aspects of the Christian invasion troublesome. Missionaries, actively seeking converts, scorned traditional Japanese beliefs and sometimes involved themselves in local politics. At first, Ieyasu did not take any action. He feared driving off the Portuguese, English, Spanish, and Dutch traders who spurred Japan's economy. By 1612, however, the shogun had come to fear religious uprisings more. He banned Christianity and focused on ridding his country of all Christians.

Ieyasu died in 1616, but repression of Christianity continued off and on for the next two decades under his successors. In 1637, the issue came to a head. An uprising in southern Japan of some 30,000 peasants, led by dissatisfied samurai, shook the Tokugawa shogunate. Because so many of the rebels were Christian, the shogun decided that Christianity was at the root of the rebellion. After that, the shoguns ruthlessly persecuted Christians. European missionaries were killed or driven out of Japan. All Japanese were forced to demonstrate faithfulness to some branch of Buddhism. These policies eventually eliminated Christianity in Japan and led to the formation of an exclusion policy. **D**

▼ Japanese merchants and Jesuit missionaries await the arrival of a Portuguese ship at Nagasaki in the 1500s in this painting on wood panels.

MAIN IDEA

Comparing
D How was the treatment of Europeans different in Japan and China? How was it similar?

The Closed Country Policy

The persecution of Christians was part of an attempt to control foreign ideas. When Europeans first arrived, no central authority existed to contain them. The strong leaders who later took power did not like the introduction of European ideas and ways, but they valued European trade. As time passed, the Tokugawa shoguns realized that they could safely exclude both the missionaries and the merchants. By 1639, they had sealed Japan's borders and instituted a "closed country policy."

Japan in Isolation Most commercial contacts with Europeans ended. One port, Nagasaki, remained open to foreign traders. But only Dutch and Chinese merchants were allowed into the port. Earlier, the English had left Japan voluntarily; the Spanish and the Portuguese had been expelled. Since the Tokugawa shoguns controlled Nagasaki, they now had a monopoly on foreign trade, which continued to be profitable.

For more than 200 years, Japan remained basically closed to Europeans. In addition, the Japanese were forbidden to leave, so as not to bring back foreign ideas. Japan would continue to develop, but as a self-sufficient country, free from European attempts to colonize or to establish their presence.

Europeans had met with much resistance in their efforts to open the East to trade. But expansion to the West, in the Americas, as you will learn in Chapter 4, would prove much more successful for European traders, missionaries, and colonizers.

History *in* Depth

Zen Buddhism

The form of Buddhism that had the greatest impact on Japanese culture was Zen Buddhism. It especially influenced the samurai.

Zen Buddhists sought spiritual enlightenment through meditation. Strict discipline of mind and body was the Zen path to wisdom. Zen monks would sit in meditation for hours, as shown in the sculpture above. If they showed signs of losing concentration, a Zen master might shout at them or hit them with a stick.

SECTION 3 ASSESSMENT

TERMS & NAMES 1. For each term or name, write a sentence explaining its significance.
• daimyo   • Oda Nobunaga   • Toyotomi Hideyoshi   • Tokugawa Shogunate   • haiku   • kabuki

USING YOUR NOTES

2. Which contribution by a daimyo was the most significant? Why?

Daimyo	Achievements

MAIN IDEAS

3. What happened during the period of the "Warring States"?

4. What was the structure of society in Tokugawa Japan?

5. What were the new styles of drama, art, and literature in Tokugawa Japan?

CRITICAL THINKING & WRITING

6. **DRAWING CONCLUSIONS** Why do you think that the emperor had less power than a shogun?

7. **ANALYZING CAUSES** Why did the Japanese policy toward Christians change from acceptance to repression?

8. **FORMING OPINIONS** Do you think Japan's closed country policy effectively kept Western ideas and customs out of Japan?

9. **WRITING ACTIVITY** CULTURAL INTERACTION Write a two-paragraph **comparison** of the similarities and differences between the roles of women in China (discussed on page 107) and in Japan (page 110).

INTEGRATED/TECHNOLOGY **INTERNET ACTIVITY**
Use the Internet to find information on the Japanese government today. Then create an **organizational chart** showing the structure of the government.

INTERNET KEYWORD
country profiles

VISUAL SUMMARY

An Age of Explorations and Isolation

Explorations

1405 **Zheng He of China** launches voyages of exploration to Southeast Asia, India, Arabia, and eastern Africa.

1500s **The Portuguese** establish trading outposts throughout Asia and gain control of the spice trade.

1600s **The Dutch** drive out the Portuguese and establish their own trading empire in the East. (Below, a Dutch ship is pictured on a plate made in China for European trade.)

Europeans sail farther east to China and Japan in search of more trade; both nations ultimately reject European advances.

Isolation

1433 **China** abandons its voyages of exploration.

1500s **The Chinese** severely restrict trade with foreigners.

1612 **Japan** outlaws Christianity and drives out Christian missionaries.

1630s **The Japanese** institute a "closed country policy" and remain isolated from Europe for 200 years.

TERMS & NAMES

For each term or name below, briefly explain its importance to European exploration and the development of China and Japan.

1. Bartolomeu Dias
2. Vasco da Gama
3. Treaty of Tordesillas
4. Dutch East India Company
5. Ming Dynasty
6. Manchus
7. Qing Dynasty
8. Oda Nobunaga
9. Toyotomi Hideyoshi
10. Tokugawa Shogunate

MAIN IDEAS

Europeans Explore the East Section 1 (pages 95–101)

11. What factors helped spur European exploration?
12. What role did Portugal's Prince Henry play in overseas exploration?
13. What was the significance of Dias's voyage? da Gama's voyage?
14. Why were the Dutch so successful in establishing a trading empire in the Indian Ocean?

China Limits European Contacts Section 2 (pages 102–107)

15. Why did China not undergo widespread industrialization?
16. What did Christian missionaries bring to China?
17. What are five reasons the Ming Dynasty fell to civil disorder?

Japan Returns to Isolation Section 3 (pages 108–113)

18. Why was the time between 1467 and 1568 called the period of the "Warring States"?
19. What was the difference between the Confucian ideal of society and the real society of Japan?
20. How did the Japanese express themselves culturally under the Tokugawa shoguns?

CRITICAL THINKING

1. USING YOUR NOTES
In a time line, trace the events that led to Japan's expulsion of European Christians.

2. RECOGNIZING EFFECTS
How might a Chinese emperor's leadership be affected by living in the Forbidden City? Explain and support your opinion.

3. ANALYZING ISSUES
SCIENCE AND TECHNOLOGY Of the technological advances that helped spur European exploration, which do you think was the most important? Why?

4. ANALYZING CAUSES
CULTURAL INTERACTION What caused Japan to institute a policy of isolation? Defend your viewpoint with text references.

5. SUMMARIZING
ECONOMICS How did the Manchus earn the respect of the Chinese? Support your answer with details from the chapter.

Use the quotation and your knowledge of world history to answer questions 1 and 2.
Additional Test Practice, pp. S1–S33

PRIMARY SOURCE

But I was careful not to refer to these Westerners as "Great Officials," and corrected Governor Liu Yin-shu when he referred to the Jesuits Regis and Fridelli . . . as if they were honored imperial commissioners. For even though some of the Western methods are different from our own, and may even be an improvement, there is little about them that is new. The principles of mathematics all derive from the Book of Changes, and the Western methods are Chinese in origin: this algebra—"A-erh-chu-pa-erh"—springs from an Eastern word. And though it was indeed the Westerners who showed us something our ancient calendar experts did not know—namely how to calculate the angles of the northern pole—this but shows the truth of what Chu Hsi arrived at through his investigation of things: the earth is like the yolk within an egg.

KANGXI, quoted in *Emperor of China: Self-Portrait of K'Ang-Hsi*

1. Which phrase best describes Kangxi's thoughts about Europeans, or "Westerners"?

   A. Westerners use methods that are inferior to Chinese methods.

   B. Westerners would make good trading partners.

   C. Westerners use methods that are based on Chinese methods.

   D. There are too many Westerners in China.

2. What can be inferred about Kangxi's beliefs about China?

   A. China needs the assistance of Westerners.

   B. China is superior to countries of the West.

   C. China has many problems.

   D. China is destined to rule the world.

Use this map produced by German cartographer Henricus Martellus in about 1490 and your knowledge of world history to answer question 3.

3. Which of these statements about Martellus's map is not accurate?

   A. Martellus shows Europe, Africa, and Asia.

   B. Martellus's map includes the oceans.

   C. Martellus shows North America.

   D. Martellus's map has many ports marked on the western coast of Africa.

INTEGRATED / TECHNOLOGY

TEST PRACTICE Go to **classzone.com**

- Diagnostic tests
- Tutorials
- Strategies
- Additional practice

ALTERNATIVE ASSESSMENT

1. Interact *with* History

On page 94, you decided whether or not you would sail into the unknown. Now that you have read the chapter, reevaluate your decision. If you decided to go, did what you read reaffirm your decision? Why or why not? If you chose not to go, explain what your feelings are now. Discuss your answers within a small group.

2. WRITING ABOUT HISTORY

Imagine you are the Jesuit missionary Matteo Ricci. Write an **expository essay** describing your impressions of Chinese rule and culture. Consider the following in the essay:

- Matteo Ricci's values
- Chinese culture as compared with Western Christian culture

INTEGRATED / TECHNOLOGY

Planning a Television Special

Use the Internet, books, and other reference materials to create a script for a television special "The Voyages of Zheng He." The script should address the historical context of Zheng He's voyages and their impact on China and the lands visited. The script should include narration, sound, re-creations, and locations. In researching, consider the following:

- biographical data on Zheng He
- information on the ships, crews, and cargo
- descriptions of the voyages
- music and visuals

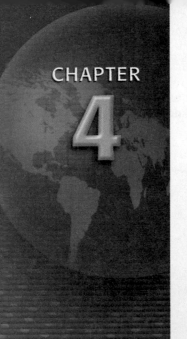

The Atlantic World,
1492–1800

Previewing Main Ideas

CULTURAL INTERACTION The voyages of Columbus prompted a worldwide exchange of everything from religious and political ideas to new foods and plants.

Geography *According to the map, what lands were included in the viceroyalty of New Spain in 1700?*

ECONOMICS The vast wealth to be had from colonizing the Americas sealed the fate of millions of Native Americans and Africans who were forced to work in mines and on plantations.

Geography *On which coast of the Americas would enslaved persons from Africa have arrived?*

EMPIRE BUILDING Over the span of several centuries, Europeans conquered the Americas' native inhabitants and built powerful American empires.

Geography *What two major Native American empires did the Spanish conquer in the sixteenth century?*

INTEGRATED TECHNOLOGY

eEdition
• Interactive Maps
• Interactive Visuals
• Interactive Primary Sources

VIDEO *Patterns of Interaction: The Impact of Potatoes and Sugar*

INTERNET RESOURCES
Go to **classzone.com** for:
• Research Links   • Maps
• Internet Activities   • Test Practice
• Primary Sources   • Current Events
• Chapter Quiz

AMERICAS

1492
Columbus makes first voyage.

1521
Cortés conquers Aztec Empire. ▶

1533
Pizarro conquers Incan Empire.

1607
English found Jamestown.

1500

1600

WORLD

1494
Spain and Portugal sign Treaty of Tordesillas.

1547
Ivan the Terrible assumes throne of Russia.

1603
◀ Tokugawa shoguns rule Japan.

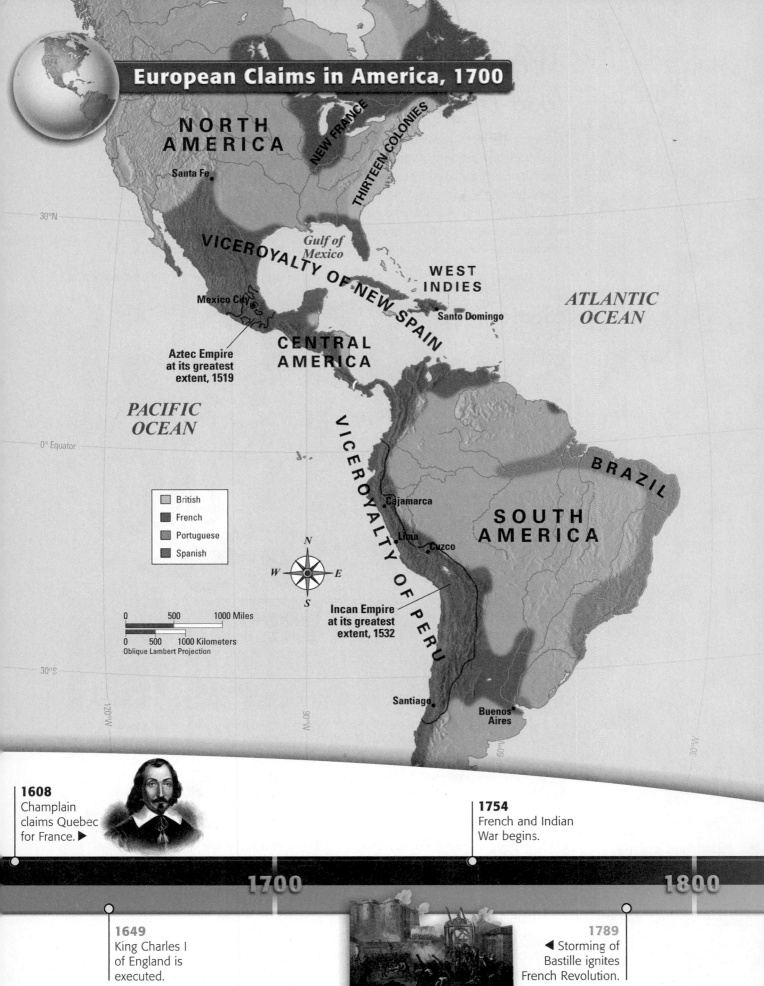

European Claims in America, 1700

NORTH AMERICA

NEW FRANCE

THIRTEEN COLONIES

Santa Fe

30°N

VICEROYALTY OF NEW SPAIN

Gulf of Mexico

WEST INDIES

ATLANTIC OCEAN

Mexico City

Santo Domingo

Aztec Empire at its greatest extent, 1519

CENTRAL AMERICA

PACIFIC OCEAN

0° Equator

VICEROYALTY OF PERU

Cajamarca

BRAZIL

SOUTH AMERICA

Lima
Cuzco

British
French
Portuguese
Spanish

N
W   E
S

0   500   1000 Miles
0   500   1000 Kilometers
Oblique Lambert Projection

Incan Empire at its greatest extent, 1532

30°S

120°W

90°W

Santiago

Buenos Aires

60°W

30°W

1608
Champlain claims Quebec for France. ▶

1754
French and Indian War begins.

1700

1800

1649
King Charles I of England is executed.

1789
◀ Storming of Bastille ignites French Revolution.

What might you gain or lose by joining the fight?

You are a Native American living in central Mexico in 1520. Suddenly you are faced with a decision that may change your life forever. Invaders, known as the Spanish, are engaged in a fierce battle with the nearby Aztecs, who are cruel and harsh rulers. Like many of your people, you hate the powerful Aztecs and hope for their defeat. The newcomers, however, are equally frightening. They ride on large beasts and fire loud, deadly weapons. You wonder whether you should follow the example of your friends and join the fight, or not fight at all.

▲ This 16th-century painting by an Indian artist depicts a battle on the left between the Aztecs and Spanish. The right side shows the Spanish with their main Indian allies, the Tlaxcalans.

EXAMINING *the* ISSUES

- **What are the advantages and disadvantages of not fighting?**

- **Which might be the lesser of two evils—supporting the Aztecs, whom you know as oppressors, or the fierce invaders, about whom you know almost nothing?**

Discuss these questions with your classmates. In your discussion, examine whether invading armies throughout history have made life better or worse for people in the areas they conquer. As you read about colonization in the Americas, learn the outcome of the battle between the Aztecs and the Spanish.

Spain Builds an American Empire

1

MAIN IDEA	WHY IT MATTERS NOW	TERMS & NAMES
EMPIRE BUILDING The voyages of Columbus prompted the Spanish to establish colonies in the Americas.	Throughout the Americas, Spanish culture, language, and descendants are the legacy of this period.	• Christopher Columbus • colony • Hernando Cortés • conquistador • Francisco Pizarro • Atahualpa • mestizo • *encomienda*

SETTING THE STAGE Competition for wealth in Asia among European nations was fierce. This competition prompted a Genoese sea captain named **Christopher Columbus** to make a daring voyage from Spain in 1492. Instead of sailing south around Africa and then east, Columbus sailed west across the Atlantic in search of an alternate trade route to Asia and its riches. Columbus never reached Asia. Instead, he stepped onto an island in the Caribbean. That event would bring together the peoples of Europe, Africa, and the Americas.

The Voyages of Columbus

The *Niña, Pinta,* and *Santa María* sailed out of a Spanish port around dawn on August 3, 1492. In a matter of months, Columbus's fleet would reach the shores of what Europeans saw as an astonishing new world.

First Encounters In the early hours of October 12, 1492, the long-awaited cry came. A lookout aboard the *Pinta* caught sight of a shoreline in the distance. *"Tierra! Tierra!"* he shouted. "Land! Land!" By dawn, Columbus and his crew were ashore. Thinking he had successfully reached the East Indies, Columbus called the surprised inhabitants who greeted him, *los indios*. The term translated into "Indian," a word mistakenly applied to all the native peoples of the Americas. In his journal, Columbus recounted his first meeting with the native peoples:

PRIMARY SOURCE
I presented them with some red caps, and strings of glass beads to wear upon the neck, and many other trifles of small value, wherewith they were much delighted, and became wonderfully attached to us. Afterwards they came swimming to the boats where we were, bringing parrots, balls of cotton thread, javelins, and many other things which they exchanged for articles we gave them . . . in fact they accepted anything and gave what they had with the utmost good will.

CHRISTOPHER COLUMBUS, *Journal of Columbus*

Columbus had miscalculated where he was. He had not reached the East Indies. Scholars believe he landed instead on an island in the Bahamas in the Caribbean Sea. The natives there were not Indians, but a group who called themselves the Taino. Nonetheless, Columbus claimed the island for Spain. He named it San Salvador, or "Holy Savior."

TAKING NOTES
Following Chronological Order Use a diagram to trace the major events in the establishment of Spain's empire in the Americas.

Columbus arrives in Americas, 1492

▲ *Portrait of a Man Called Christopher Columbus* (1519) by Sebastiano del Piombo

Columbus, like other explorers, was interested in gold. Finding none on San Salvador, he explored other islands, staking his claim to each one. "It was my wish to bypass no island without taking possession," he wrote.

In early 1493, Columbus returned to Spain. The reports he relayed about his journey delighted the Spanish monarchs. Spain's rulers, who had funded his first voyage, agreed to finance three more trips. Columbus embarked on his second voyage to the Americas in September of 1493. He journeyed no longer as an explorer, but as an empire builder. He commanded a fleet of some 17 ships that carried over 1,000 soldiers, crewmen, and colonists. The Spanish intended to transform the islands of the Caribbean into **colonies**, or lands that are controlled by another nation. Over the next two centuries, other European explorers began sailing across the Atlantic in search of new lands to claim.

Other Explorers Take to the Seas In 1500, the Portuguese explorer Pedro Álvares Cabral reached the shores of modern-day Brazil and claimed the land for his country. A year later, Amerigo Vespucci (vehs•POO•chee), an Italian in the service of Portugal, also traveled along the eastern coast of South America. Upon his return to Europe, he claimed that the land was not part of Asia, but a "new" world. In 1507, a German mapmaker named the new continent "America" in honor of Amerigo Vespucci.

In 1519, Portuguese explorer Ferdinand Magellan led the boldest exploration yet. Several years earlier, Spanish explorer Vasco Núñez de Balboa had marched through modern-day Panama and had become the first European to gaze upon the Pacific Ocean. Soon after, Magellan convinced the king of Spain to fund his voyage into the newly discovered ocean.

With about 250 men and five ships, Magellan sailed around the southern end of South America and into the waters of the Pacific. The fleet sailed for months without seeing land, except for some small islands. Food supplies soon ran out.

After exploring the island of Guam, Magellan and his crew eventually reached the Philippines. Unfortunately, Magellan became involved in a local war there and was killed. His crew, greatly reduced by disease and starvation, continued sailing west toward home. Out of Magellan's original crew, only 18 men and one ship arrived back in Spain in 1522, nearly three years after they had left. They were the first persons to circumnavigate, or sail around, the world. **A**

MAIN IDEA

Making Inferences
A What was the significance of Magellan's voyage?

Spanish Conquests in Mexico

In 1519, as Magellan embarked on his historic voyage, a Spaniard named **Hernando Cortés** landed on the shores of Mexico. After colonizing several Caribbean islands, the Spanish had turned their attention to the American mainland. Cortés marched inland, looking to claim new lands for Spain. Cortés and the many other Spanish explorers who followed him were known as **conquistadors** (conquerors). Lured by rumors of vast lands filled with gold and silver, conquistadors carved out colonies in regions that would become Mexico, South America, and the United States. The Spanish were the first European settlers in the Americas. As a result of their colonization, the Spanish greatly enriched their empire and left a mark on the cultures of North and South America that exists today.

European Exploration of the Americas, 1492–1682

INTERACTIVE

GREENLAND

ICELAND

Hudson 1610

Hudson 1609

Cabot 1497

ENGLAND

Cartier 1534–35

EUROPE

FRANCE

Hudson
Bay

40° N

NORTH
AMERICA

Marquette 1673

Smith 1606–07, Mayflower 1620

PORTUGAL

SPAIN

Plymouth

LaSalle 1682

Coronado
1540–42

De Soto
1539–42

Jamestown

ATLANTIC
OCEAN

Santa Fe

Cabrillo
1542–43

St. Augustine

Ponce de León
1512–13

CANARY
ISLANDS

MADEIRA

Cabeza de Vaca
1535–36

Gulf
of Mexico

HISPANIOLA

Verrazzano 1524

AFRICA

CUBA

Columbus 1492

Cortés 1519

Veracruz

Santo Domingo

Columbus 1493–95

Tenochtitlán
(Mexico City)

Caribbean   Sea

Columbus 1502–03

PACIFIC
OCEAN

Balboa
1510–13

Columbus 1498

Cabral 1500

Magellan 1519

Magellan's Crew 1522

Pizarro
1530–33

Vespucci
1499

0° Equator

N

0   1,000 Miles

0   2,000 Kilometers

Explorers' Routes

← Spanish
← Portuguese
← French
← English
← Dutch

SOUTH
AMERICA

Magellan 1519

120° W

80° W

40° W

0°

40° S

GEOGRAPHY SKILLBUILDER: Interpreting Maps

1. **Movement** *How many different voyages did Columbus make to the Americas?*
2. **Region** *Which general region did the Spanish and Portuguese explore? Where did the English, Dutch, and French explore?*

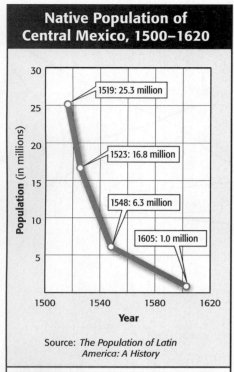

Native Population of Central Mexico, 1500–1620

1519: 25.3 million
1523: 16.8 million
1548: 6.3 million
1605: 1.0 million

Population (in millions)

Year

Source: *The Population of Latin America: A History*

SKILLBUILDER: Interpreting Graphs
1. **Drawing Conclusions** *By what percentage did the native population decrease between 1519 and 1605?*
2. **Making Inferences** *How did the sharp decline in the native population, due greatly to disease, affect the Spaniards' attempts to conquer the region?*

Cortés Conquers the Aztecs Soon after landing in Mexico, Cortés learned of the vast and wealthy Aztec Empire in the region's interior. After marching for weeks through difficult mountain passes, Cortés and his force of roughly 600 men finally reached the magnificent Aztec capital of Tenochtitlán (teh•NAWCH•tee•TLAHN). The Aztec emperor, Montezuma II, was convinced at first that Cortés was a god wearing armor. He agreed to give the Spanish explorer a share of the empire's existing gold supply. The conquistador was not satisfied. Cortés admitted that he and his comrades had a "disease of the heart that only gold can cure."

In the late spring of 1520, some of Cortés's men killed many Aztec warriors and chiefs while they were celebrating a religious festival. In June of 1520, the Aztecs rebelled against the Spanish intruders and drove out Cortés's forces.

The Spaniards, however, struck back. Despite being greatly outnumbered, Cortés and his men conquered the Aztecs in 1521. Several factors played a key role in the stunning victory. First, the Spanish had the advantage of superior weaponry. Aztec arrows were no match for the Spaniards' muskets and cannons.

Second, Cortés was able to enlist the help of various native groups. With the aid of a native woman translator named Malinche, Cortés learned that some natives resented the Aztecs. They hated their harsh practices, including human sacrifice. Through Malinche, Cortés convinced these natives to fight on his side.

Finally, and most important, the natives could do little to stop the invisible warrior that marched alongside the Spaniards—disease. Measles, mumps, smallpox, and typhus were just some of the diseases Europeans were to bring with them to the Americas. Native Americans had never been exposed to these diseases. Thus, they had developed no natural immunity to them. As a result, they died by the hundreds of thousands. By the time Cortés launched his counterattack, the Aztec population had been greatly reduced by smallpox and measles. In time, European disease would truly devastate the natives of central Mexico, killing millions of them. **B**

MAIN IDEA
Summarizing
B What factors enabled the Spanish to defeat the Aztecs?

Spanish Conquests in Peru

In 1532, another conquistador, <u>**Francisco Pizarro**</u>, marched a small force into South America. He conquered the Incan Empire.

Pizarro Subdues the Inca Pizarro and his army of about 200 met the Incan ruler, <u>**Atahualpa**</u> (AH•tuh•WAHL•puh), near the city of Cajamarca. Atahualpa, who commanded a force of about 30,000, brought several thousand mostly unarmed men for the meeting. The Spaniards waited in ambush, crushed the Incan force, and kidnapped Atahualpa.

Atahualpa offered to fill a room once with gold and twice with silver in exchange for his release. However, after receiving the ransom, the Spanish strangled the Incan king. Demoralized by their leader's death, the remaining Incan force retreated from Cajamarca. Pizarro then marched on the Incan capital, Cuzco. He captured it without a struggle in 1533.

As Cortés and Pizarro conquered the civilizations of the Americas, fellow conquistadors defeated other native peoples. Spanish explorers also conquered the Maya in Yucatan and Guatemala. By the middle of the 16th century, Spain had created an American empire. It included New Spain (Mexico and parts of Guatemala), as well as other lands in Central and South America and the Caribbean.

Spain's Pattern of Conquest In building their new American empire, the Spaniards drew from techniques used during the *reconquista* of Spain. When conquering the Muslims, the Spanish lived among them and imposed their Spanish culture upon them. The Spanish settlers to the Americas, known as *peninsulares,* were mostly men. As a result, relationships between Spanish settlers and native women were common. These relationships created a large **mestizo**—or mixed Spanish and Native American—population.

Although the Spanish conquerors lived among the native people, they also oppressed them. In their effort to exploit the land for its precious resources, the Spanish forced Native Americans to work within a system known as **encomienda**. Under this system, natives farmed, ranched, or mined for Spanish landlords. These landlords had received the rights to the natives' labor from Spanish authorities. The holders of *encomiendas* promised the Spanish rulers that they would act fairly and respect the workers. However, many abused the natives and worked many laborers to death, especially inside dangerous mines.

The Portuguese in Brazil One area of South America that remained outside of Spanish control was Brazil. In 1500, Cabral claimed the land for Portugal. During the 1530s, colonists began settling Brazil's coastal region. Finding little gold or silver, the settlers began growing sugar. Clearing out huge swaths of forest land, the Portuguese built giant sugar plantations. The demand for sugar in Europe was great, and the colony soon enriched Portugal. In time, the colonists pushed farther west into Brazil. They settled even more land for the production of sugar.

History Makers

Francisco Pizarro
1475?–1541

Pizarro was the son of an infantry captain and a young peasant woman. His parents never married. Raised by his mother's poor family, he never learned to read. Ambitious, brave, and ruthless, he determined to make his fortune as an explorer and conqueror.

Embarked on a voyage of conquest down the west coast of South America, Pizarro was ordered by the governor of Panama to abandon the expedition to prevent the loss of lives. Pizarro took his sword and drew a line in the dust, inviting those of his followers who desired wealth and fame to cross the line and follow him. Thus began the conquest of Peru.

Pizarro founded the city of Lima, Peru's capital, in 1535. He became governor of Peru and encouraged settlers from Spain.

Atahualpa
1502?–1533

Atahualpa was the last ruler of the Incan empire in Peru. After Atahualpa was captured and held for ransom by the Spanish, the Incan people throughout the empire brought gold and silver that the Spanish then had melted down into bullion and ingots. They accumulated 24 tons of gold and silver, the richest ransom in history.

The Spanish executed Atahualpa despite the ransom paid by his people. As he was about to be burned at the stake, the Spanish offered him a more merciful death by strangulation if he agreed to convert to Christianity, which he did. Thus died the last emperor of the Inca.

INTEGRATED TECHNOLOGY

INTERNET ACTIVITY Create a poster about the ransom paid by the Incan people to rescue Atahualpa. Go to **classzone.com** for your research.

This U.S. postage ▶ stamp was issued in 1940 to celebrate the 400th anniversary of the Coronado expedition.

Spain's Influence Expands

Spain's American colonies helped make it the richest, most powerful nation in the world during much of the 16th century. Ships filled with treasures from the Americas continually sailed into Spanish harbors. This newfound wealth helped usher in a golden age of art and culture in Spain. (See Chapter 5.)

Throughout the 16th century, Spain also increased its military might. To protect its treasure-filled ships, Spain built a powerful navy. The Spanish also strengthened their other military forces, creating a skillful and determined army. For a century and a half, Spain's army seldom lost a battle. Meanwhile, Spain enlarged its American empire by settling in parts of what is now the United States.

Conquistadors Push North Dreams of new conquests prompted Spain to back a series of expeditions into the southwestern United States. The Spanish actually had settled in parts of the United States before they even dreamed of building an empire on the American mainland. In 1513, Spanish explorer Juan Ponce de León landed on the coast of modern-day Florida and claimed it for Spain.

By 1540, after building an empire that stretched from Mexico to Peru, the Spanish once again looked to the land that is now the United States. In 1540–1541, Francisco Vásquez de Coronado led an expedition throughout much of present-day Arizona, New Mexico, Texas, Oklahoma, and Kansas. He was searching for another wealthy empire to conquer. Coronado found little gold amidst the dry deserts of the Southwest. As a result, the Spanish monarchy assigned mostly priests to explore and colonize the future United States.

Catholic priests had accompanied conquistadors from the very beginning of American colonization. The conquistadors had come in search of wealth. The priests who accompanied them had come in search of converts. In the winter of 1609–1610, Pedro de Peralta, governor of Spain's northern holdings, called New Mexico, led settlers to a tributary on the upper Rio Grande. They built a capital called Santa Fe, or "Holy Faith." In the next two decades, a string of Christian missions arose among the Pueblo, the native inhabitants of the region. Scattered missions, forts, and small ranches dotted the lands of New Mexico. These became the headquarters for advancing the Catholic religion. **C**

MAIN IDEA

Contrasting
C How did Spain's colony in New Mexico differ from its colonies in New Spain?

Opposition to Spanish Rule

Spanish priests worked to spread Christianity in the Americas. They also pushed for better treatment of Native Americans. Priests spoke out against the cruel treatment of natives. In particular, they criticized the harsh pattern of labor that emerged under the *encomienda* system. "There is nothing more detestable or more cruel," Dominican monk Bartolomé de Las Casas wrote, "than the tyranny which the Spaniards use toward the Indians for the getting of pearl [riches]."

African Slavery and Native Resistance The Spanish government abolished the *encomienda* system in 1542. To meet the colonies' need for labor, Las Casas suggested Africans. "The labor of one . . . [African] . . . [is] more valuable than that of four Indians," he said. The priest later changed his view and denounced African slavery. However, others promoted it.

Opposition to the Spanish method of colonization came not only from Spanish priests, but also from the natives themselves. Resistance to Spain's attempt at domination began shortly after the Spanish arrived in the Caribbean. In November of 1493, Columbus encountered resistance in his attempt to conquer the present-day island of St. Croix. Before finally surrendering, the inhabitants defended themselves by firing poison arrows.

As late as the end of the 17th century, natives in New Mexico fought Spanish rule. Although they were not risking their lives in silver mines, the natives still felt the weight of Spanish force. In converting the natives, Spanish priests and soldiers burned their sacred objects and prohibited native rituals. The Spanish also forced natives to work for them and sometimes abused them physically.

MAIN IDEA

Analyzing Causes
D Why did the natives of New Mexico revolt against Spanish settlers?

In 1680, Popé, a Pueblo ruler, led a well-organized rebellion against the Spanish. The rebellion involved more than 8,000 warriors from villages all over New Mexico. The native fighters drove the Spanish back into New Spain. For the next 12 years, until the Spanish regained control of the area, the southwest region of the future United States once again belonged to its original inhabitants. **D**

By this time, however, the rulers of Spain had far greater concerns. The other nations of Europe had begun to establish their own colonies in the Americas.

SECTION 1 ASSESSMENT

TERMS & NAMES 1. For each term or name, write a sentence explaining its significance.
• Christopher Columbus • colony • Hernando Cortés • conquistador • Francisco Pizarro • Atahualpa • mestizo • *encomienda*

USING YOUR NOTES

2. Which of these events do you think had the greatest impact?

Columbus arrives in Americas, 1492

MAIN IDEAS

3. What process did Columbus and his followers begin?

4. Why were most of the Spanish explorers drawn to the Americas?

5. Which country was the richest and most powerful in the 16th century, and why?

CRITICAL THINKING & WRITING

6. ANALYZING PRIMARY SOURCES Reread the primary source on page 119. How might Columbus's view of the Taino have led the Spanish to think they could take advantage of and impose their will on the natives?

7. COMPARING What might have been some similarities in character between Cortés and Pizarro?

8. CLARIFYING Through what modern-day states did Coronado lead his expedition?

9. WRITING ACTIVITY [EMPIRE BUILDING] Write a **dialogue** in which a Native American and a conquistador debate the merits of Spain's colonization of the Americas.

CONNECT TO TODAY MAKING A DATABASE

Use library resources to compile a **database** of places and geographical features in the Americas named after Columbus. Display your list in the classroom.

INTERACTIVE

The Legacy of Columbus

In the years and centuries since Christopher Columbus's historic journeys, people still debate the legacy of his voyages. Some argue they were the heroic first steps in the creation of great and democratic societies. Others claim they were the beginnings of an era of widespread cruelty, bloodshed, and epidemic disease.

A SECONDARY SOURCE

Samuel Eliot Morison

Morison, a strong supporter of Columbus, laments that the sea captain died without realizing the true greatness of his deeds.

——

One only wishes that the Admiral might have been afforded the sense of fulfillment that would have come from foreseeing all that flowed from his discoveries; that would have turned all the sorrows of his last years to joy. The whole history of the Americas stems from the Four Voyages of Columbus; and as the Greek city-states looked back to the deathless gods as their founders, so today a score of independent nations and dominions unite in homage to Christopher, the stout-hearted son of Genoa, who carried Christian civilization across the Ocean Sea.

B PRIMARY SOURCE

Bartolomé de Las Casas

Las Casas was an early Spanish missionary who watched fellow Spaniards unleash attack dogs on Native Americans.

——

Their other frightening weapon after the horses: twenty hunting greyhounds. They were unleashed and fell on the Indians at the cry of *Tómalo!* ["Get them!"]. Within an hour they had preyed on one hundred of them. As the Indians were used to going completely naked, it is easy to imagine what the fierce greyhounds did, urged to bite naked bodies and skin much more delicate than that of the wild boars they were used to. . . . This tactic, begun here and invented by the devil, spread throughout these Indies and will end when there is no more land nor people to subjugate and destroy in this part of the world.

C SECONDARY SOURCE

Suzan Shown Harjo

Harjo, a Native American, disputes the benefits that resulted from Columbus's voyages and the European colonization of the Americas that followed.

——

Columbus Day, never on Native America's list of favorite holidays, became somewhat tolerable as its significance diminished to little more than a good shopping day. But this next long year [1992] of Columbus hoopla will be tough to take amid the spending sprees and horn blowing to tout a five-century feeding frenzy that has left Native people and this red quarter of Mother Earth in a state of emergency. For Native people, this half millennium of land grabs and one-cent treaty sales has been no bargain.

D PRIMARY SOURCE

Anonymous

Contemporary with the Spanish conquest of the Americas, this illustration depicts a medicine man tending to an Aztec suffering from smallpox, which killed millions of Native Americans.

Document-Based QUESTIONS

1. Based on Source A, was the legacy of Columbus a positive or negative thing?

2. In what ways do Sources B and C agree about Columbus?

3. Which aspect of the legacy of Columbus does the illustration in Source D show?

4. If you had to construct a balance sheet on Columbus, would you come up with a positive or negative balance? On a poster board, make up a list of positive and negative elements, and display your chart in the classroom.

126

European Nations Settle North America

MAIN IDEA	WHY IT MATTERS NOW	TERMS & NAMES
EMPIRE BUILDING Several European nations fought for control of North America, and England emerged victorious.	The English settlers in North America left a legacy of law and government that guides the United States today.	• New France • Jamestown • Pilgrims • Puritans	• New Netherland • French and Indian War • Metacom

SETTING THE STAGE Spain's successful colonization efforts in the Americas did not go unnoticed. Other European nations, such as England, France, and the Netherlands, soon became interested in obtaining their own valuable colonies. The Treaty of Tordesillas, signed in 1494, had divided the newly discovered lands between Spain and Portugal. However, other European countries ignored the treaty. They set out to build their own empires in the Americas. This resulted in a struggle for North America.

Competing Claims in North America

Magellan's voyage showed that ships could reach Asia by way of the Pacific Ocean. Spain claimed the route around the southern tip of South America. Other European countries hoped to find an easier and more direct route to the Pacific. If it existed, a northwest trade route through North America to Asia would become highly profitable. Not finding the route, the French, English, and Dutch instead established colonies in North America.

Explorers Establish New France The early French explorers sailed west with dreams of reaching the East Indies. One explorer was Giovanni da Verrazzano (VEHR•uh•ZAHN•noh), an Italian in the service of France. In 1524, he sailed to North America in search of a sea route to the Pacific. While he did not find the route, Verrazzano did discover what is today New York harbor. Ten years later, the Frenchman Jacques Cartier (kahr•TYAY) reached a gulf off the eastern coast of Canada that led to a broad river. Cartier named it the St. Lawrence. He followed it inward until he reached a large island dominated by a mountain. He named the island Mont Real (Mount Royal), which later became known as Montreal. In 1608, another French explorer, Samuel de Champlain, sailed up the St. Lawrence with about 32 colonists. They founded Quebec, which became the base of France's colonial empire in North America, known as **New France**.

Then the French penetrated the North American continent. In 1673, French Jesuit priest Jacques Marquette and trader Louis Joliet explored the Great Lakes and the upper Mississippi River. Nearly 10 years later, Sieur de La Salle explored the lower Mississippi. He claimed the entire river valley for France. He named it Louisiana in honor of the French king, Louis XIV. By the early 1700s, New France covered much of what is now the midwestern United States and eastern Canada.

TAKING NOTES

Clarifying Use a chart to record information about early settlements.

Name of Settlement	General Location
New France	
New Netherland	
Massachusetts Bay	

A Trading Empire France's North American empire was immense. But it was sparsely populated. By 1760, the European population of New France had grown to only about 65,000. A large number of French colonists had no desire to build towns or raise families. These settlers included Catholic priests who sought to convert Native Americans. They also included young, single men engaged in what had become New France's main economic activity, the fur trade. Unlike the English, the French were less interested in occupying territories than they were in making money off the land. **Ⓐ**

MAIN IDEA

Summarizing
Ⓐ Why were France's North American holdings so sparsely populated?

The English Arrive in North America

The explorations of the Spanish and French inspired the English. In 1606, a company of London investors received from King James a charter to found a colony in North America. In late 1606, the company's three ships, and more than 100 settlers, pushed out of an English harbor. About four months later, in 1607, they reached the coast of Virginia. The colonists claimed the land as theirs. They named the settlement **Jamestown** in honor of their king.

The Settlement at Jamestown The colony's start was disastrous. The settlers were more interested in finding gold than in planting crops. During the first few years, seven out of every ten people died of hunger, disease, or battles with the Native Americans.

Despite their nightmarish start, the colonists eventually gained a foothold in their new land. Jamestown became England's first permanent settlement in North America. The colony's outlook improved greatly after farmers there discovered tobacco. High demand in England for tobacco turned it into a profitable cash crop.

Puritans Create a "New England" In 1620, a group known as **Pilgrims** founded a second English colony, Plymouth, in Massachusetts. Persecuted for their religious beliefs in England, these colonists sought religious freedom. Ten years later, a group known as **Puritans** also sought religious freedom from England's Anglican Church. They established a larger colony at nearby Massachusetts Bay.

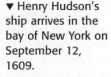

▼ Henry Hudson's ship arrives in the bay of New York on September 12, 1609.

The Puritans wanted to build a model community that would set an example for other Christians to follow. Although the colony experienced early difficulties, it gradually took hold. This was due in large part to the numerous families in the colony, unlike the mostly single, male population in Jamestown.

The Dutch Found New Netherland Following the English and French into North America were the Dutch. In 1609, Henry Hudson, an Englishman in the service of the Netherlands, sailed west. He was searching for a northwest sea route to Asia. Hudson did not find a route. He did, however, explore three waterways that were later named for him—the Hudson River, Hudson Bay, and Hudson Strait.

The Dutch claimed the region along these waterways. They established a fur trade with the Iroquois Indians. They built trading posts along the Hudson River at Fort Orange (now Albany) and on Manhattan Island. Dutch merchants formed the Dutch West India Company. In 1621, the Dutch government granted the company permission to colonize the region and expand the fur trade. The Dutch holdings in North America became known as **New Netherland**.

Although the Dutch company profited from its fur trade, it was slow to attract Dutch colonists. To encourage settlers, the colony opened its doors to a variety of peoples. Gradually more Dutch, as well as Germans, French, Scandinavians, and other Europeans, settled the area. **B**

Colonizing the Caribbean During the 1600s, the nations of Europe also colonized the Caribbean. The French seized control of present-day Haiti, Guadeloupe, and Martinique. The English settled Barbados and Jamaica. In 1634, the Dutch captured what are now the Netherlands Antilles and Aruba from Spain.

On these islands, the Europeans built huge cotton and sugar plantations. These products, although profitable, demanded a large and steady supply of labor. Enslaved Africans eventually would supply this labor.

MAIN IDEA

Contrasting

B How were the Dutch and French colonies different from the English colonies in North America?

The Struggle for North America

As they expanded their settlements in North America, the nations of France, England, and the Netherlands battled each other for colonial supremacy.

The English Oust the Dutch To the English, New Netherland separated their northern and southern colonies. In 1664, the English king, Charles II, granted his brother, the Duke of York, permission to drive out the Dutch. When the duke's fleet arrived at New Netherland, the Dutch surrendered without firing a shot. The Duke of York claimed the colony for England and renamed it New York.

With the Dutch gone, the English colonized the Atlantic coast of North America. By 1750, about 1.2 million English settlers lived in 13 colonies from Maine to Georgia.

England Battles France The English soon became hungry for more land for their colonial population. So they pushed farther west into the continent. By doing so, they collided with France's North American holdings. As their colonies expanded, France and England began to interfere with each other. It seemed that a major conflict was on the horizon.

In 1754 a dispute over land claims in the Ohio Valley led to a war between the British and French on the North

History *in* Depth

Pirates

The battle for colonial supremacy occurred not only on land, but also on the sea. Acting on behalf of their government, privately owned armed ships, known as privateers, attacked merchant ships of enemy nations and sank or robbed them.

Also patrolling the high seas were pirates. They attacked ships for their valuables and did not care what nation the vessels represented. One of the best-known pirates was Edward B. Teach, whose prominent beard earned him the nickname Blackbeard. According to one account, Blackbeard attempted to frighten his victims by sticking "lighted matches under his hat, which appeared on both sides of his face and eyes, naturally fierce and wild."

1754

1763

Disputed
English
French
Spanish

English
French
Russian
Spanish

GEOGRAPHY SKILLBUILDER: Interpreting Maps
1. **Region** *Which nation claimed the largest area of the present-day United States in 1754?*
2. **Place** *How did Britain's North American empire change by 1763?*

American continent. The conflict became known as the **French and Indian War**. The war became part of a larger conflict known as the Seven Years' War. Britain and France, along with their European allies, also battled for supremacy in Europe, the West Indies, and India.

In North America, the British colonists, with the help of the British Army, defeated the French in 1763. The French surrendered their North American holdings. As a result of the war, the British seized control of the eastern half of North America.

Native Americans Respond

As in Mexico and South America, the arrival of Europeans in the present-day United States had a great impact on Native Americans. European colonization brought mostly disaster for the lands' original inhabitants.

A Strained Relationship French and Dutch settlers developed a mostly cooperative relationship with the Native Americans. This was due mainly to the mutual benefits of the fur trade. Native Americans did most of the trapping and then traded the furs to the French for such items as guns, hatchets, mirrors, and beads. The Dutch also cooperated with Native Americans in an effort to establish a fur-trading enterprise.

The groups did not live together in complete harmony. Dutch settlers fought with various Native American groups over land claims and trading rights. For the most part, however, the French and Dutch colonists lived together peacefully with their North American hosts. **C**

MAIN IDEA

Analyzing Issues
C Why were the Dutch and French able to coexist in relative peace with the Native Americans?

The same could not be said of the English. Early relations between English settlers and Native Americans were cooperative. However, they quickly worsened over the issues of land and religion. Unlike the French and Dutch, the English sought to populate their colonies in North America. This meant pushing the natives off their land. The English colonists seized more land for their population—and to grow tobacco.

MAIN IDEA

Identifying Problems

D Why did the issues of land and religion cause strife between Native Americans and settlers?

Religious differences also heightened tensions. The English settlers considered Native Americans heathens, people without a faith. Over time, many Puritans viewed Native Americans as agents of the devil and as a threat to their godly society. Native Americans developed a similarly harsh view of the European invaders. **D**

Settlers and Native Americans Battle The hostility between the English settlers and Native Americans led to warfare. As early as 1622, the Powhatan tribe attacked colonial villages around Jamestown and killed about 350 settlers. During the next few years, the colonists struck back and massacred hundreds of Powhatan.

One of the bloodiest conflicts between colonists and Native Americans was known as King Philip's War. It began in 1675 when the Native American ruler **Metacom** (also known as King Philip) led an attack on colonial villages throughout Massachusetts. In the months that followed, both sides massacred hundreds of victims. After a year of fierce fighting, the colonists defeated the natives. During the 17th century, many skirmishes erupted throughout North America.

Natives Fall to Disease More destructive than the Europeans' weapons were their diseases. Like the Spanish in Central and South America, the Europeans who settled North America brought with them several diseases. The diseases devastated the native population in North America.

In 1616, for example, an epidemic of smallpox ravaged Native Americans living along the New England coast. The population of one tribe, the Massachusett, dropped from 24,000 to 750 by 1631. From South Carolina to Missouri, nearly whole tribes fell to smallpox, measles, and other diseases.

One of the effects of this loss was a severe shortage of labor in the colonies. In order to meet their growing labor needs, European colonists soon turned to another group: Africans, whom they would enslave by the million.

SECTION 2 ASSESSMENT

TERMS & NAMES 1. For each term or name, write a sentence explaining its significance.
• New France   • Jamestown   • Pilgrims   • Puritans   • New Netherland   • French and Indian War   • Metacom

USING YOUR NOTES

2. What did these settlements have in common?

Name of Settlement	General Location	Reasons Settled
New France		
New Netherland		
Massachusetts Bay		

MAIN IDEAS

3. What was a basic difference between French and English attitudes about the land they acquired in North America?

4. What was the main result of the French and Indian War?

5. What were some of the results for Native Americans of European colonization of North America?

CRITICAL THINKING & WRITING

6. **MAKING INFERENCES** What may have been one reason the English eventually beat the French in North America?

7. **DRAWING CONCLUSIONS** What need drove the English farther west into the North American continent?

8. **COMPARING** In what ways did the colonies at Jamestown and Massachusetts Bay differ?

9. **WRITING ACTIVITY** EMPIRE BUILDING What were some of the grievances of Native Americans toward English colonists? Make a bulleted **list** of Native American complaints to display in the classroom.

INTEGRATED TECHNOLOGY INTERNET ACTIVITY

Use the Internet to research French Cajun culture in Louisiana. Make a **poster** displaying your findings.

INTERNET KEYWORD
Cajun

The Atlantic Slave Trade

MAIN IDEA	WHY IT MATTERS NOW	TERMS & NAMES
CULTURAL INTERACTION To meet their growing labor needs, Europeans enslaved millions of Africans in the Americas.	Descendants of enslaved Africans represent a significant part of the Americas' population today.	• Atlantic slave trade • middle passage • triangular trade

SETTING THE STAGE Sugar plantations and tobacco farms required a large supply of workers to make them profitable for their owners. European owners had planned to use Native Americans as a source of cheap labor. But millions of Native Americans died from disease, warfare, and brutal treatment. Therefore, the Europeans in Brazil, the Caribbean, and the southern colonies of North America soon turned to Africa for workers. This demand for cheap labor resulted in the brutalities of the slave trade.

TAKING NOTES

Recognizing Effects Use a diagram like the one below to list effects of the Atlantic slave trade.

Consequences of the slave trade
  I. in Africa
     A.
     B.
  II. in the Americas
     A.
     B.

The Causes of African Slavery

Beginning around 1500, European colonists in the Americas who needed cheap labor began using enslaved Africans on plantations and farms.

Slavery in Africa Slavery had existed in Africa for centuries. In most regions, it was a relatively minor institution. The spread of Islam into Africa during the seventh century, however, ushered in an increase in slavery and the slave trade. Muslim rulers in Africa justified enslavement with the Muslim belief that non-Muslim prisoners of war could be bought and sold as slaves. As a result, between 650 and 1600, Muslims transported about 17 million Africans to the Muslim lands of North Africa and Southwest Asia.

In most African and Muslim societies, slaves had some legal rights and an opportunity for social mobility. In the Muslim world, a few slaves even occupied positions of influence and power. Some served as generals in the army. In African societies, slaves could escape their bondage in numerous ways, including marrying into the family they served.

The Demand for Africans The first Europeans to explore Africa were the Portuguese during the 1400s. Initially, Portuguese traders were more interested in trading for gold than for captured Africans. That changed with the colonization of the Americas, as natives began dying by the millions.

Europeans saw advantages in using Africans in the Americas. First, many Africans had been exposed to European diseases and had built up some immunity. Second, many Africans had experience in farming and could be taught plantation work. Third, Africans were less likely to escape because they did not know their way around the new land. Fourth, their skin color made it easier to catch them if they escaped and tried to live among others.

MAIN IDEA

Analyzing Motives

A What advantages did Europeans see in enslaving Africans?

In time, the buying and selling of Africans for work in the Americas—known as the **Atlantic slave trade**—became a massive enterprise. Between 1500 and 1600, nearly 300,000 Africans were transported to the Americas. During the next century, that number climbed to almost 1.3 million. By the time the Atlantic slave trade ended around 1870, Europeans had imported about 9.5 million Africans to the Americas. **A**

Spain and Portugal Lead the Way The Spanish took an early lead in importing Africans to the Americas. Spain moved on from the Caribbean and began to colonize the American mainland. As a result, the Spanish imported and enslaved thousands more Africans. By 1650, nearly 300,000 Africans labored throughout Spanish America on plantations and in gold and silver mines.

By this time, however, the Portuguese had surpassed the Spanish in the importation of Africans to the Americas. During the 1600s, Brazil dominated the European sugar market. As the colony's sugar industry grew, so too did European colonists' demand for cheap labor. During the 17th century, more than 40 percent of all Africans brought to the Americas went to Brazil.

Slavery Spreads Throughout the Americas

As the other European nations established colonies in the Americas, their demand for cheap labor grew. Thus, they also began to import large numbers of Africans.

England Dominates the Slave Trade As England's presence in the Americas grew, it came to dominate the Atlantic slave trade. From 1690 until England abolished the slave trade in 1807, it was the leading carrier of enslaved Africans. By the time the slave trade ended, the English had transported nearly 1.7 million Africans to their colonies in the West Indies.

African slaves were also brought to what is now the United States. In all, nearly 400,000 Africans were sold to Britain's North American colonies. Once in North America, however, the slave population steadily grew. By 1830, roughly 2 million slaves toiled in the United States.

History *in* Depth

Slavery

Slavery probably began with the development of farming about 10,000 years ago. Farmers used prisoners of war to work for them.

Slavery has existed in societies around the world. People were enslaved in civilizations from Egypt to China to India. The picture at the right shows slaves working in a Roman coal mine.

Race was not always a factor in slavery. Often, slaves were captured prisoners of war, or people of a different nationality or religion.

However, the slavery that developed in the Americas was based largely on race. Europeans viewed black people as naturally inferior. Because of this, slavery in the Americas was hereditary.

African Cooperation and Resistance Many African rulers and merchants played a willing role in the Atlantic slave trade. Most European traders, rather than travel inland, waited in ports along the coasts of Africa. African merchants, with the help of local rulers, captured Africans to be enslaved. They then delivered them to the Europeans in exchange for gold, guns, and other goods. **B**

As the slave trade grew, some African rulers voiced their opposition to the practice. Nonetheless, the slave trade steadily grew. Lured by its profits, many African rulers continued to participate. African merchants developed new trade routes to avoid rulers who refused to cooperate.

MAIN IDEA

Analyzing Issues
B Why did many African rulers participate in the Atlantic slave trade?

A Forced Journey

After being captured, African men and women were shipped to the Americas as part of a profitable trade network. Along the way, millions of Africans died.

The Triangular Trade Africans transported to the Americas were part of a transatlantic trading network known as the **triangular trade**. Over one trade route, Europeans transported manufactured goods to the west coast of Africa. There, traders exchanged these goods for captured Africans. The Africans were then transported across the Atlantic and sold in the West Indies. Merchants bought sugar, coffee, and tobacco in the West Indies and sailed to Europe with these products.

On another triangular route, merchants carried rum and other goods from the New England colonies to Africa. There they exchanged their merchandise for Africans. The traders transported the Africans to the West Indies and sold them for sugar and molasses. They then sold these goods to rum producers in New England.

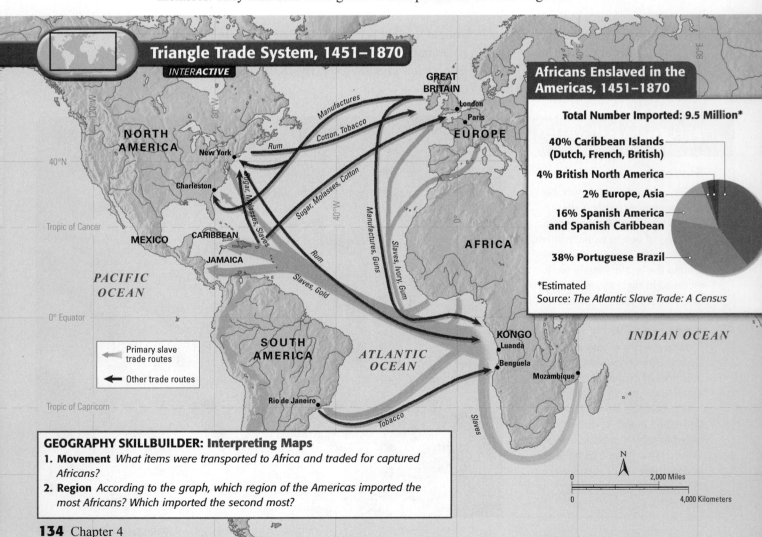

Triangle Trade System, 1451–1870
INTERACTIVE

Africans Enslaved in the Americas, 1451–1870

Total Number Imported: 9.5 Million*

- 40% Caribbean Islands (Dutch, French, British)
- 4% British North America
- 2% Europe, Asia
- 16% Spanish America and Spanish Caribbean
- 38% Portuguese Brazil

*Estimated
Source: *The Atlantic Slave Trade: A Census*

Primary slave trade routes

Other trade routes

GEOGRAPHY SKILLBUILDER: Interpreting Maps
1. **Movement** *What items were transported to Africa and traded for captured Africans?*
2. **Region** *According to the graph, which region of the Americas imported the most Africans? Which imported the second most?*

The Horrors of the Middle Passage

One African, Olaudah Equiano, recalled the inhumane conditions on his trip from West Africa to the West Indies at age 12 in 1762.

PRIMARY SOURCE

I was soon put down under the decks, and there I received such a salutation [greeting] in my nostrils as I never experienced in my life; so that, with the loathsomeness of the stench, and crying together, I became so sick and low that I was not able to eat . . . but soon, to my grief, two of the white men offered me eatables; and on my refusing to eat, one of them held me fast by the hands, and laid me across . . . the windlass, while the other flogged me severely.

OLAUDAH EQUIANO, quoted in
Eyewitness: The Negro in American History

This diagram of a British slave ship shows how slave traders packed Africans onto slave ships in the hold below decks for the brutal middle passage.

DOCUMENT-BASED QUESTIONS

1. **Making Inferences** *Why might the white men have forced Equiano to eat?*
2. **Drawing Conclusions** *What does the diagram of the slave ship suggest about conditions on board?*

Various other transatlantic routes existed. The "triangular" trade encompassed a network of trade routes crisscrossing the northern and southern colonies, the West Indies, England, Europe, and Africa. The network carried a variety of traded goods.

The Middle Passage The voyage that brought captured Africans to the West Indies and later to North and South America was known as the **middle passage**. It was considered the middle leg of the transatlantic trade triangle. Sickening cruelty characterized this journey. In African ports, European traders packed Africans into the dark holds of large ships. On board, Africans endured whippings and beatings from merchants, as well as diseases that swept through the vessel. Numerous Africans died from disease or physical abuse aboard the slave ships. Many others committed suicide by drowning. Scholars estimate that roughly 20 percent of the Africans aboard each slave ship perished during the brutal trip.

Slavery in the Americas

Africans who survived their ocean voyage faced a difficult life in the Americas. Forced to work in a strange land, enslaved Africans coped in a variety of ways.

A Harsh Life Upon arriving in the Americas, captured Africans usually were auctioned off to the highest bidder. After being sold, slaves worked in mines or fields or as domestic servants. Slaves lived a grueling existence. Many lived on little food in small, dreary huts. They worked long days and suffered beatings. In much of the Americas, slavery was a lifelong condition, as well as a hereditary one.

Resistance and Rebellion To cope with the horrors of slavery, Africans developed a way of life based on their cultural heritage. They kept alive such things as their musical traditions as well as the stories of their ancestors.

Slaves also found ways to resist. They made themselves less productive by breaking tools, uprooting plants, and working slowly. Thousands also ran away.

Some slaves pushed their resistance to open revolt. As early as 1522, about 20 slaves on Hispaniola attacked and killed several Spanish colonists. Larger revolts occurred throughout Spanish settlements during the 16th century.

Occasional uprisings also occurred in Brazil, the West Indies, and North America. In 1739, a group of slaves in South Carolina led an uprising known as the Stono Rebellion. Uprisings continued into the 1800s.

Consequences of the Slave Trade

The Atlantic slave trade had a profound impact on both Africa and the Americas. In Africa, numerous cultures lost generations of their fittest members—their young and able—to European traders and plantation owners. In addition, countless African families were torn apart. Many of them were never reunited. The slave trade devastated African societies in another way: by introducing guns into the continent.

While they were unwilling participants in the growth of the colonies, African slaves contributed greatly to the economic and cultural development of the Americas. Their greatest contribution was their labor. Without their back-breaking work, colonies such as those on Haiti and Barbados may not have survived. In addition to their muscle, enslaved Africans brought their expertise, especially in agriculture. They also brought their culture. Their art, music, religion, and food continue to influence American societies.

The influx of so many Africans to the Americas also has left its mark on the very population itself. From the United States to Brazil, many of the nations of the Western Hemisphere today have substantial African-American populations. Many Latin American countries have sizable mixed-race populations.

As the next section explains, Africans were not the only cargo transported across the Atlantic during the colonization of the Americas. The settlement of the Americas brought many different items from Europe, Asia, and Africa to North and South America. It also introduced items from the Americas to the rest of the world.

SECTION 3 ASSESSMENT

TERMS & NAMES 1. For each term or name, write a sentence explaining its significance.
• Atlantic slave trade   • triangular trade   • middle passage

USING YOUR NOTES

2. What seems to have been the most important consequence? Explain.

Consequences of the slave trade
   I. in Africa
      A.
      B.
   II. in the Americas
      A.
      B.

MAIN IDEAS

3. What effect did the spread of Islam have on the slave trade?

4. How did enslaved Africans resist their bondage?

5. How did African slaves contribute to the development of the Americas?

CRITICAL THINKING & WRITING

6. **COMPARING AND CONTRASTING** How was slavery in the Americas different from slavery in Africa?

7. **SYNTHESIZING** What does the percentage of enslaved Africans imported to the Caribbean Islands and Brazil suggest about the racial makeup of these areas?

8. **MAKING INFERENCES** Why do you think the slave trade flourished for so long?

9. **WRITING ACTIVITY** [CULTURAL INTERACTION] Imagine you are an African ruler. Write a **letter** to a European leader in which you try to convince him or her to stop participating in the slave trade.

CONNECT TO TODAY MAKING A MAP

Research which of the original 13 colonies had the greatest numbers of slaves in the late 18th century. Then make a **map** of the colonies in which you show the numbers for each state.

The Columbian Exchange and Global Trade

MAIN IDEA	WHY IT MATTERS NOW	TERMS & NAMES
ECONOMICS The colonization of the Americas introduced new items into the Eastern and Western hemispheres.	This global exchange of goods permanently changed Europe, Asia, Africa, and the Americas.	• Columbian Exchange • capitalism • joint-stock company • mercantilism • favorable balance of trade

SETTING THE STAGE The colonization of the Americas dramatically changed the world. It prompted both voluntary and forced migration of millions of people. It led to the establishment of new and powerful societies. Other effects of European settlement of the Americas were less noticeable but equally important. Colonization resulted in the exchange of new items that greatly influenced the lives of people throughout the world. The new wealth from the Americas resulted in new business and trade practices in Europe.

The Columbian Exchange

The global transfer of foods, plants, and animals during the colonization of the Americas is known as the **Columbian Exchange**. Ships from the Americas brought back a wide array of items that Europeans, Asians, and Africans had never before seen. They included such plants as tomatoes, squash, pineapples, tobacco, and cacao beans (for chocolate). And they included animals such as the turkey, which became a source of food in the Eastern Hemisphere.

Perhaps the most important items to travel from the Americas to the rest of the world were corn and potatoes. Both were inexpensive to grow and nutritious. Potatoes, especially, supplied many essential vitamins and minerals. Over time, both crops became an important and steady part of diets throughout the world. These foods helped people live longer. Thus they played a significant role in boosting the world's population. The planting of the first white potato in Ireland and the first sweet potato in China probably changed more lives than the deeds of 100 kings.

Traffic across the Atlantic did not flow in just one direction, however. Europeans introduced various livestock animals into the Americas. These included horses, cattle, sheep, and pigs. Foods from Africa (including some that originated in Asia) migrated west in European ships. They included bananas, black-eyed peas, and yams. Grains introduced to the Americas included wheat, rice, barley, and oats.

Some aspects of the Columbian Exchange had a tragic impact on many Native Americans. Disease was just as much a part of the Columbian Exchange as goods and food. The diseases Europeans brought with them, which included smallpox and measles, led to the deaths of millions of Native Americans.

TAKING NOTES

Recognizing Effects Use a chart to record information about the Columbian Exchange.

Food/ Livestock/ Disease	Place of Origin	Effect
Potato		
Horse		
Smallpox		

The Columbian Exchange

Few events transformed the world like the Columbian Exchange. This global transfer of plants, animals, disease, and especially food brought together the Eastern and Western hemispheres and touched, in some way, nearly all the peoples of the world.

Frightening Foods

Several foods from the Americas that we now take for granted at first amazed and terrified Europeans. Early on, people thought the tomato was harmful to eat. One German official warned that the tomato "should not be taken internally." In 1619, officials in Burgundy, France, banned potatoes, explaining that "too frequent use of them caused the leprosy." In 1774, starving peasants in Prussia refused to eat the spud.

"The culinary life we owe Columbus is a progressive dinner in which the whole human race takes part but no one need leave home to sample all the courses."

Raymond Sokolov

The Columbian Exchange

Patterns of Interaction

The Geography of Food: The Impact of Potatoes and Sugar

Think about your favorite foods. Chances are that at least one originated in a distant land. Throughout history, the introduction of new foods into a region has dramatically changed lives—for better and worse. Dependence on the potato, for example, led to a famine in Ireland. This prompted a massive migration of Irish people to other countries. In the Americas, the introduction of sugar led to riches for some and enslavement for many others.

Connect to Today

1. **Forming Opinions** Have students work in small groups to pose and answer questions about the beneficial and harmful aspects of the Columbian Exchange.

   See Skillbuilder Handbook, page R:

2. **Comparing and Contrasting** Find what major items are exchanged traded between the United States either Asia, Africa, or Europe. How the items compare with those of Columbian Exchange? Report you findings to the class.

A Spanish missionary in Mexico described the effects of smallpox on the Aztecs:

PRIMARY SOURCE
There was a great havoc. Very many died of it. They could not walk. . . . They could not move; they could not stir; they could not change position, nor lie on one side; nor face down, nor on their backs. And if they stirred, much did they cry out. Great was its destruction.

BERNARDINO DE SAHAGUN, quoted in *Seeds of Change*

Other diseases Europeans brought with them included influenza, typhus, malaria, and diphtheria. **A**

Global Trade

The establishment of colonial empires in the Americas influenced the nations of Europe in still other ways. New wealth from the Americas was coupled with a dramatic growth in overseas trade. The two factors together prompted a wave of new business and trade practices in Europe during the 16th and 17th centuries. These practices, many of which served as the root of today's financial dealings, dramatically changed the economic atmosphere of Europe.

The Rise of Capitalism One aspect of the European economic revolution was the growth of **capitalism**. Capitalism is an economic system based on private ownership and the investment of resources, such as money, for profit. No longer were governments the sole owners of great wealth. Due to overseas colonization and trade, numerous merchants had obtained great wealth. These merchants continued to invest their money in trade and overseas exploration. Profits from these investments enabled merchants and traders to reinvest even more money in other enterprises. As a result, businesses across Europe grew and flourished.

The increase in economic activity in Europe led to an overall increase in many nations' money supply. This in turn brought on inflation, or the steady rise in the price of goods. Inflation occurs when people have more money to spend and thus demand more goods and services. Because the supply of goods is less than the demand for them, the goods become both scarce and more valuable. Prices then rise. At this time in Europe, the costs of many goods rose. Spain, for example, endured a crushing bout of inflation during the 1600s, as boatloads of gold and silver from the Americas greatly increased the nation's money supply.

Joint-Stock Companies Another business venture that developed during this period was known as the **joint-stock company**. The joint-stock company worked much like the modern-day corporation, with investors buying shares of stock in a company. It involved a number of people combining their wealth for a common purpose.

MAIN IDEA

Making Inferences

A Why is the Columbian Exchange considered a significant event?

Three Worlds Meet, 1492–1700

1492 (Europeans)
Columbus embarks on voyage.

1511 (Africans)
Africans begin working as slaves in the Americas.

1521 (Americans)
The Aztec Empire in Mexico is conquered by Hernando Cortés.

1533 (Americans)
The Inca Empire in South America falls to Francisco Pizarro.

1630 (Europeans)
Puritans establish the Massachusetts Bay Colony in North America.

1650 (Africans)
The number of Africans toiling in Spanish America reaches 300,000.

1675 (Americans)
Native Americans battle colonists in King Philip's War.

Mercantilism

As you have read, mercantilism was an economic theory practiced in Europe from the 16th to the 18th centuries. Economists of the period believed that a country's power came from its wealth. Thus, a country would do everything possible to acquire more gold, preferably at the expense of its rivals. A mercantilist country primarily sought gold in two ways: establishing and exploiting colonies, and establishing a favorable balance of trade with a rival country. In the example to the right, England is the home country, America is England's colony, and France is England's rival.

1 **England** wants gold.

2 **England** establishes a colony: **America.**

3 **America** does not have gold, but can produce cotton.

6 **England** gets gold and depletes **France's** gold reserves.

5 **England** sells finished cloth to **America,** and to England's rival, France.

4 **England** buys cotton cheap and does not allow **America** to produce cloth.

SKILLBUILDER: Interpreting Charts
Identifying Problems and Solutions Under the mercantilism model, how might France try to acquire gold and become more powerful than England?

In Europe during the 1500s and 1600s, that common purpose was American colonization. It took large amounts of money to establish overseas colonies. Moreover, while profits may have been great, so were risks. Many ships, for instance, never completed the long and dangerous ocean voyage. Because joint-stock companies involved numerous investors, the individual members paid only a fraction of the total colonization cost. If the colony failed, investors lost only their small share. If the colony thrived, the investors shared in the profits. It was a joint-stock company that was responsible for establishing Jamestown, England's first North American colony. **B**

MAIN IDEA

Making Inferences
B Why would a joint-stock company be popular with investors in over-seas colonies?

The Growth of Mercantilism

During this time, the nations of Europe adopted a new economic policy known as **mercantilism**. The theory of mercantilism (shown above) held that a country's power depended mainly on its wealth. Wealth, after all, allowed nations to build strong navies and purchase vital goods. As a result, the goal of every nation became the attainment of as much wealth as possible.

Balance of Trade According to the theory of mercantilism, a nation could increase its wealth and power in two ways. First, it could obtain as much gold and silver as possible. Second, it could establish a **favorable balance of trade**, in which it sold more goods than it bought. A nation's ultimate goal under mercantilism was to become self-sufficient, not dependent on other countries for goods. An English author of the time wrote about the new economic idea of mercantilism:

PRIMARY SOURCE
Although a Kingdom may be enriched by gifts received, or by purchases taken from some other Nations . . . these are things uncertain and of small consideration when they happen. The ordinary means therefore to increase our wealth and treasure is by Foreign Trade, wherein we must ever observe this rule: to sell more to strangers yearly than we consume of theirs in value.

THOMAS MUN, quoted in *World Civilizations*

Mercantilism went hand in hand with colonization, for colonies played a vital role in this new economic practice. Aside from providing silver and gold, colonies provided raw materials that could not be found in the home country, such as wood or furs. In addition to playing the role of supplier, the colonies also provided a market. The home country could sell its goods to its colonies. **C**

MAIN IDEA

Summarizing
C What role did colonies play in mercantilism?

Economic Revolution Changes European Society The economic changes that swept through much of Europe during the age of American colonization also led to changes in European society. The economic revolution spurred the growth of towns and the rise of a class of merchants who controlled great wealth.

The changes in European society, however, only went so far. While towns and cities grew in size, much of Europe's population continued to live in rural areas. And although merchants and traders enjoyed social mobility, the majority of Europeans remained poor. More than anything else, the economic revolution increased the wealth of European nations. In addition, mercantilism contributed to the creation of a national identity. Also, as Chapter 5 will describe, the new economic practices helped expand the power of European monarchs, who became powerful rulers.

SECTION 4 ASSESSMENT

TERMS & NAMES 1. For each term or name, write a sentence explaining its significance.
• Columbian Exchange   • capitalism   • joint-stock company   • mercantilism   • favorable balance of trade

USING YOUR NOTES	MAIN IDEAS	CRITICAL THINKING & WRITING
2. Which effect do you think had the greatest impact on history?	3. What were some of the food items that traveled from the Americas to the rest of the world?	6. **MAKING INFERENCES** Why were colonies considered so important to the nations of Europe?

USING YOUR NOTES

2. Which effect do you think had the greatest impact on history?

Food/ Livestock/ Disease	Place of Origin	Effect
Potato		
Horse		
Smallpox		

MAIN IDEAS

3. What were some of the food items that traveled from the Americas to the rest of the world?

4. What food and livestock from the rest of the world traveled to the Americas?

5. What were some of the effects on European society of the economic revolution that took place in the 16th and 17th centuries?

CRITICAL THINKING & WRITING

6. **MAKING INFERENCES** Why were colonies considered so important to the nations of Europe?

7. **DRAWING CONCLUSIONS** Why might establishing overseas colonies have justified high profits for those who financed the colonies?

8. **COMPARING** What were some of the positive and negative consequences of the Columbian Exchange?

9. **WRITING ACTIVITY** ECONOMICS Do you think the economic changes in Europe during the era of American colonization qualify as a revolution? Why or why not? Support your opinions in a two-paragraph **essay.**

CONNECT TO TODAY MAKING A POSTER

Research one crop that developed in the Americas (such as corn or potatoes) and its impact on the world today. Show your findings in a **poster.**

TERMS & NAMES

For each term or name below, briefly explain its connection to the Atlantic world from 1492 to 1800.

1. conquistador
2. *encomienda*
3. Jamestown
4. French and Indian War
5. Atlantic slave trade
6. triangular trade
7. Columbian Exchange
8. mercantilism

MAIN IDEAS

Spain Builds an American Empire Section 1
(pages 119–126)

9. Why did Columbus set sail westward?
10. What were three goals of the Spanish in the Americas?
11. Why did Popé lead a rebellion against the Spanish?

European Nations Settle North America Section 2
(pages 127–131)

12. What did the Europeans mostly grow in their Caribbean colonies?
13. What was the result of the French and Indian War?

The Atlantic Slave Trade Section 3 (pages 132–136)

14. What factors led European colonists to use Africans to resupply their labor force?
15. What were the conditions on board a slave ship?
16. What were several ways in which enslaved Africans resisted their treatment in the Americas?

The Columbian Exchange and Global Trade Section 4
(pages 137–141)

17. Why was the introduction of corn and potatoes to Europe and Asia so significant?
18. What was the economic policy of mercantilism?

CRITICAL THINKING

1. USING YOUR NOTES

Use the chart to identify which nation sponsored each explorer and the regions he explored.

Explorer	Nation	Regions
Cabral		
Magellan		
Cartier		

2. DRAWING CONCLUSIONS

EMPIRE BUILDING What factors helped the Europeans conquer the Americas? Which was the most important? Why?

3. RECOGNIZING EFFECTS

ECONOMICS Explain the statement, "Columbus's voyage began a process that changed the world forever." Consider all the peoples and places American colonization affected economically.

4. COMPARING AND CONTRASTING

CULTURAL INTERACTION What might have been some of the differences in the Europeans' and Native Americans' views of colonization?

5. SYNTHESIZING

How did enslaved Africans help create the societies in the New World?

VISUAL SUMMARY

The Atlantic World

Global Interaction

Europeans

- Beginning around 1500, the Spanish and Portuguese colonize Central and South America and establish prosperous overseas empires.
- Throughout the 1600s and 1700s, the English, French, and Dutch battle for control of North America, with the English emerging victorious.

Native Americans

- Between 1521 and 1533, the once mighty Aztec and Incan empires fall to the invading Spanish.
- Throughout the Americas, the native population is devastated by European conquests and diseases.

Africans

- Beginning around 1500, millions of Africans are taken from their homeland and forced to labor as slaves in the Americas.
- Africans eventually become an important part of the Americas, as they populate the various regions and share aspects of their culture.

Use the quotation and your knowledge of world history to answer questions 1 and 2.
Additional Test Practice, pp. S1–S33

PRIMARY SOURCE

Where there is a vacant place, there is liberty for . . . [Christians] to come and inhabit, though they neither buy it nor ask their leaves. . . . Indeed, no nation is to drive out another without special commission from Heaven . . . unless the natives do unjustly wrong them, and will not recompense the wrongs done in a peaceable fort [way]. And then they may right themselves by lawful war and subdue the country unto themselves.

JOHN COTTON, from "God's Promise to His Plantation"

1. What do you think Native Americans might have said about Cotton's statement that America was a "vacant place"?

   A. agreed that the continent was largely empty

   B. discussed development plans with him

   C. pointed out that they inhabited the land

   D. offered to sell the land to him

2. How might the last part of Cotton's statement have helped the Puritans justify taking land from the Native Americans?

   A. Puritans could claim natives had wronged them.

   B. Natives could claim Puritans had wronged them.

   C. Puritans believed war was wrong in all circumstances.

   D. Native Americans were willing to negotiate their grievances.

Use the Aztec drawing below and your knowledge of world history to answer question 3.

3. How does the artist depict the clash of Aztec and Spanish cultures?

   A. meeting to negotiate peace

   B. meeting as warriors

   C. engaging in a sports competition

   D. meeting as friends

INTEGRATED TECHNOLOGY

TEST PRACTICE Go to **classzone.com**

• Diagnostic tests   • Strategies

• Tutorials   • Additional practice

ALTERNATIVE ASSESSMENT

1. Interact *with* History

On page 118 you examined the choices some Native Americans faced during the invasion by Spanish conquistadors. Now that you have read the chapter, rethink the choice you made. If you chose to side with the Spaniards, would you now change your mind? Why? If you decided to fight with the Aztecs, what are your feelings now? Discuss your thoughts and opinions with a small group.

2. WRITING ABOUT HISTORY

An English colony would have looked strange and different to a Native American of the time. Write a **paragraph** describing an English colony of the 17th century. In your paragraph, provide details about the following:

• clothes

• food

• shelter

• weapons

INTEGRATED TECHNOLOGY

Participating in a WebQuest

Introduction The Columbian Exchange marked the beginning of worldwide trade. Imagine that you are an exporter of a product and want to know how tariffs will affect your sales in various countries.

Task Collect and organize data about a particular product, including how much of the product various countries import and the tariff each country imposes.

Process and Resources With a team of four other students, use the Internet to research your product. Internet keyword: *customs tariffs various countries.* Identify at least five countries that import the product. Organize your findings in a spreadsheet.

Evaluation and Conclusion How did this project contribute to your understanding of global trade? How do you think tariffs will affect demand for your product in each country?

Four Governments

In Unit 1, you studied how cultures around the world organized and governed themselves. The next six pages focus on four of those governments—the Incan Empire, Italian city-states, Tokugawa Japan, and the Ottoman Empire. How they functioned and the physical symbols they used to communicate their power are important themes. The chart below identifies some key characteristics of the four different governments, and the map locates them in time and place. Take notes on the similarities and differences between the four governments.

Key Characteristics			
Incan Empire	**Italian City-States**	**Tokugawa Japan**	**Ottoman Empire**
Title of Ruler • Inca	• varied by city: some had title of nobility, others of an elected position	• Shogun; emperor was a figurehead only	• Sultan
Ruling Structure • monarchical	• oligarchic	• militaristic	• bureaucratic
Basis of Authority • ruler believed to be descendant of the Sun god	• inheritance or social status supported by financial influence	• absolute loyalty and devoted service of samurai to their daimyo	• military power
Distinctive Feature of Government • Officials reported from the village level up to the king. • Members of an ethnic group, or *mitimas,* were moved from their homes to other areas to increase agricultural output or put down rebellions. • Children of Inca, local officials, and some others were taken to Cuzco for training.	• Power was in the hands of the ruling family or of a few wealthy families of bankers and merchants. • Many cities had constitutions and elected assemblies with little power.	• Daimyo were the shogun's vassals and local administrators. • Shogun controlled daimyo's marriage alliances and the number of samurai each had. • To ensure cooperation, daimyo's families were held hostage at court while daimyos administered their home regions.	• Sultan owned everything of value (such as land and labor); his bureaucracy was in charge of managing and protecting it. • Members of the bureaucracy derived status from the sultan but were his slaves along with their families. • Heads of *millets* governed locally.

SKILLBUILDER: Interpreting Charts
Drawing Conclusions *How did the rulers of most of these governments keep themselves in power?*

Monarchy in the Incan Empire, 1438–1535

The Incan monarchy was different from European monarchies. In the Incan Empire, all people worked for the state, either as farmers, or artisans making cloth, for example. Men also served as road builders, as messengers, or as soldiers. The state provided clothing, food, and any necessities in short supply. Every year, the amount of land every family had was reviewed to make sure it could produce enough food to live on.

SOUTH AMERICA

Oligarchy in the Italian City-States, 1000–1870

Oligarchy is government by a small group of people. In Venice, citizens elected a great council, but real power was held by the senate, which made all decisions. Only members of 125 to 150 wealthy and cultured families were eligible for membership.

Militarism in Tokugawa Japan, 1603–1867

A militaristic government is run by the military. All those in power under the Tokugawa shoguns were samurai. As the samurais' work became more administrative than military, the Tokugawa rulers encouraged cultural pursuits such as poetry, calligraphy, and the tea ceremony to keep warlike tendencies in check.

EUROPE

ASIA

Sea of Japan

40°N

Mediterranean Sea

AFRICA

Bureaucracy in the Ottoman Empire, 1451–1922

A bureaucratic government is organized into departments and offices staffed by workers who perform limited tasks. Because of the size of the empire, the Ottoman bureaucracy required tens of thousands of civil servants. The empire also supported and encouraged the arts.

PACIFIC OCEAN

INDIAN OCEAN

0°

Comparing & Contrasting

1. In what ways did the Incan government resemble the Ottoman bureaucracy?

2. What similarities and differences were there in the way the sultans and shoguns controlled government officials?

3. What characteristic did the ruling class of the Italian city-states and Tokugawa Japan have in common?

40°S

Structures of Government

All of the governments have officials at different levels with varying degrees of power and responsibility. Compare the governmental structure of the Ottoman bureaucracy with that of Tokugawa Shogunate's militaristic government using the charts below.

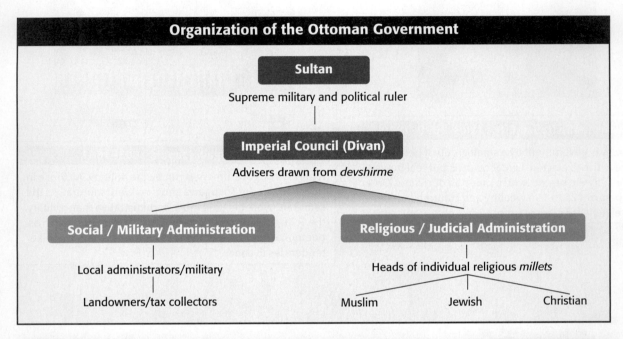

Organization of the Ottoman Government

Sultan
Supreme military and political ruler

Imperial Council (Divan)
Advisers drawn from *devshirme*

Social / Military Administration
Local administrators/military
Landowners/tax collectors

Religious / Judicial Administration
Heads of individual religious *millets*
Muslim   Jewish   Christian

Organization of the Tokugawa Shogunate

Emperor
Held highest rank in society but had no political power

Shogun
Actual ruler

Daimyo
Large landowners

Samurai Warriors
Loyal to daimyo and shogun

Peasants
Four-fifths of the population

Merchants
Low status gradually gained influence

Artisans
Craftspeople such as artists and blacksmiths

SKILLBUILDER: Interpreting Charts
1. **Clarifying** *To whom were the heads of the* millets *answerable?*
2. **Drawing Conclusions** *How might the samurai's loyalty to his daimyo conflict with his loyalty to the shogun?*

Artifacts of Power

The everyday objects used by members of government often serve a symbolic purpose. Note how the objects below communicated the rank and importance of the person who used them. Examine them and consider the effect they probably had on the people who saw them.

◄ **Japanese Sword**
Beautiful weapons and armor were symbols of status and power in Tokugawa Japan. Swords were the special weapons of the samurai, who were the only people allowed to carry arms. Daimyo had artisans make fine swords with expensively decorated hilts and scabbards for ceremonial occasions.

◄**Incan Headdress**
All of the people in the Incan Empire were required to wear the clothing of their particular ethnic group. The patterns on clothes and headdresses immediately identified a person's place of birth and social rank.

Italian Medici Pitcher ▲
As well as being great patrons of the fine arts, wealthy Italians surrounded themselves with luxurious practical objects. Even ordinary items, like a pitcher, were elaborately made of expensive materials.

Comparing & Contrasting

1. How did the role of the sultan compare with the role of the Japanese emperor?

2. What message were expensive personal items meant to convey?

3. How does a household item like the pitcher differ from a sword or headdress as a symbol of power?

Architecture of Government

A ruler's castle or palace was a luxurious and safe home where he was surrounded by vassals who protected him. It was also a center of government where his administrators carried on their work under his supervision. Castles and palaces are a show of greatness. Large rooms that accommodate many guests demonstrate the ruler's authority over many people. Rich decorations display the ruler's wealth, refinement, and superior rank.

Japanese Palace ▶
Osaka Castle was originally built by Toyotami Hideyoshi and has been rebuilt twice since then due to fire. It is surrounded by gardens, and the interior was known for its wall paintings and painted screens. During the Tokugawa period, the city of Osaka was a center of trade for agricultural and manufactured goods. The city was governed directly by the shoguns who owned the castle.

◀ Ottoman Palace
Topkapi Palace in modern Istanbul, Turkey, was the home of the Ottoman sultans. The buildings were built around several courtyards. Within the outer walls were gardens, a school for future officials, the treasury, and an arsenal. Elaborate paintings, woodwork, and tile designs decorated the walls and ceilings of rooms used by the sultan and his high officials.

Descriptions of Government

The following passages were written by writers who were reflecting not only on the past, but also on places and events they had personally witnessed.

INTERACTIVE

Machiavelli

In this excerpt from *The Discourses,* Italian writer Niccolò Machiavelli discusses six types of government—three good and three bad.

[T]he three bad ones result from the degradation of the other three. . . . Thus monarchy becomes tyranny; aristocracy degenerates into oligarchy; and the popular government lapses readily into licentiousness [lack of restraint].

  [S]agacious legislators . . . have chosen one that should partake of all of them, judging that to be the most stable and solid. In fact, when there is combined under the same constitution a prince, a nobility, and the power of the people, then these three powers will watch and keep each other reciprocally in check.

DOCUMENT-BASED QUESTION
Why does Machiavelli think a combined government is the best type of government?

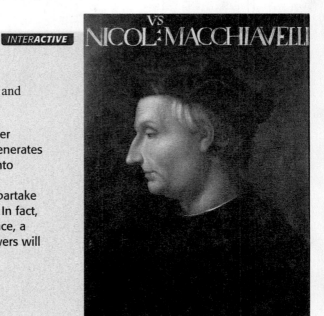

VS
NICOL:MACCHIAVELLI

INTERACTIVE

Garcilaso de la Vega

This description of government administration comes from Garcilaso's history of the Inca.

[Local administrators] were obliged each lunar month to furnish their superiors . . . with a record of the births and deaths that had occurred in the territory administered by them. . . .

  [E]very two years . . . the wool from the royal herds was distributed in every village, in order that each person should be decently clothed during his entire life. It should be recalled that . . . the people . . . possessed only very few cattle, whereas the Inca's and the Sun's herds were . . . numerous. . . . Thus everyone was always provided with clothing, shoes, food, and all that is necessary in life.

DOCUMENT-BASED QUESTION
What and how did the Incan authorities provide for the common people's needs?

Comparing & Contrasting

1. How do Osaka Castle and Topkapi Palace project the importance of their owners? Explain.
2. Does Machiavelli favor a system of government that would provide directly for people's needs? Explain.

EXTENSION ACTIVITY

Use the library to get some additional information about the government structure of the Incan Empire and Renaissance Venice. Then draw an organizational chart for each of those governments like the charts on page 146.

Absolutism to Revolution
1500–1900

On July 14, 1789, an angry French mob attacked the Bastille, a state prison in Paris, because they were looking for arms and gunpowder. The capture of this prison is considered the beginning of the French Revolution.

Comparing & Contrasting

Political Revolutions

In Unit 2, you will learn that new ideas about human rights and government led to political revolutions in many countries during the late 1700s and the 1800s. At the end of the unit, you will have a chance to compare and contrast those revolutions. (See pages 272–277.)

Absolute Monarchs in Europe, 1500–1800

Previewing Main Ideas

POWER AND AUTHORITY As feudalism declined, stronger national kingdoms in Spain, France, Austria, Prussia, and Russia emerged under the control of absolute rulers.

Geography *Study the map. What large empire was surrounded by many of these national kingdoms?*

ECONOMICS Absolute rulers wanted to control their countries' economies so that they could free themselves from limitations imposed by the nobility. In France, Louis XIV's unrestrained spending left his country with huge debts.

Geography *What other evidence of unrestrained spending by an absolute ruler does the time line suggest?*

REVOLUTION In Great Britain, Parliament and the British people challenged the monarch's authority. The overthrow of the king led to important political changes.

Geography *Study the map and the time line. Which British Stuart lands were most affected by the event occurring in 1649?*

INTEGRATED TECHNOLOGY

eEdition
- Interactive Maps
- Interactive Visuals
- Interactive Primary Sources

INTERNET RESOURCES
Go to **classzone.com** for:
- Research Links
- Maps
- Internet Activities
- Test Practice
- Primary Sources
- Current Events
- Chapter Quiz

EUROPE

1500 1600

1588
◄ British defeat Philip II's Spanish Armada.

WORLD

1521
Cortés conquers Aztec Empire.

1533
Pizarro conquers Incan Empire. ►

1603
Tokugawa shoguns rule Japan.

Europe, 1650

Legend:
- Austrian Hapsburg lands
- British Stuart lands
- French Bourbon lands
- Prussian lands
- Russian lands
- Spanish Hapsburg lands
- —— Boundary of Holy Roman Empire

0   250   500 Miles
0   250   500 Kilometers
Conic Projection

60°N

15°W

45°N

SWEDEN

DENMARK - NORWAY

North Sea

Baltic Sea

INGRIA
ESTONIA
LIVONIA
LITHUANIA

RUSSIA

Moscow

SCOTLAND

IRELAND

ENGLAND

London

ATLANTIC OCEAN

UNITED NETHERLANDS

Hamburg

Amsterdam

Utrecht

SPANISH NETH.

BRANDENBURG

Magdeburg

Danzig

PRUSSIA

Warsaw

POLAND

Kiev

HOLY ROMAN EMPIRE

Paris

FRANCHE-COMTÉ

Augsburg

Prague

AUSTRIA

Vienna

Nantes

CHAROLAIS

FRANCE

SWISS CONFED.

Milan

ITALIAN STATES

HUNGARY

Black Sea

PORTUGAL

Lisbon

Madrid

SPAIN

Balearic Is.

CORSICA

PAPAL STATES

Rome

SARDINIA (SPAIN)

Adriatic Sea

Naples

KINGDOM OF NAPLES

O T T O M A N   E M P I R E

Mediterranean Sea

1643
Louis XIV begins to rule France.

1649
Puritans under Oliver Cromwell (at right) execute English king.

1696
Peter the Great becomes sole czar of Russia.

1756
Prussian king Frederick the Great begins Seven Years' War against Austria.

1700

1800

1631
Shah Jahan orders construction of Taj Mahal. ▶

1776
American colonists declare their independence from England.

What are the benefits and drawbacks of having an absolute ruler?

You live under the most powerful monarch in 17th-century Europe, Louis XIV of France, shown below. As Louis's subject, you feel proud and well protected because the French army is the strongest in Europe. But Louis's desire to gain lands for France and battle enemies has resulted in costly wars. And he expects you and his other subjects to pay for them.

INTER**ACTIVE**

1 Louis XIV uses his clothing to demonstrate his power and status, as his portrait shows. The gold flower on his robe is the symbol of French kings.

2 Louis's love of finery is apparent not only in his clothing but also in the ornate setting for this painting. As absolute ruler, Louis imposes taxes to pay for the construction of a magnificent new palace and to finance wars.

3 The government of Louis XIV enforces laws and provides security. His sword, scepter, and crown symbolize the power he wields. Yet the French people have no say in what laws are passed or how they are enforced.

EXAMINING *the* ISSUES

- What might people gain from having a ruler whose power is total, or absolute?

- What factors might weaken the power of an absolute monarch?

As a class, discuss these questions. You may want to refer to earlier rulers, such as those of the Roman, Ottoman, and Carolingian empires. As you read about absolute monarchs in Europe, notice what strengthened and weakened their power.

Spain's Empire and European Absolutism

MAIN IDEA	WHY IT MATTERS NOW	TERMS & NAMES
ECONOMICS During a time of religious and economic instability, Philip II ruled Spain with a strong hand.	When faced with crises, many heads of government take on additional economic or political powers.	• Philip II • divine right • absolute monarch

SETTING THE STAGE As you learned in Chapter 2, from 1520 to 1566, Suleyman I exercised great power as sultan of the Ottoman Empire. A European monarch of the same period, Charles V, came close to matching Suleyman's power. As the Hapsburg king, Charles inherited Spain, Spain's American colonies, parts of Italy, and lands in Austria and the Netherlands. As the elected Holy Roman emperor, he ruled much of Germany. It was the first time since Charlemagne that a European ruler controlled so much territory.

A Powerful Spanish Empire

A devout Catholic, Charles not only fought Muslims but also opposed Lutherans. In 1555, he unwillingly agreed to the Peace of Augsburg, which allowed German princes to choose the religion for their territory. The following year, Charles V divided his immense empire and retired to a monastery. To his brother Ferdinand, he left Austria and the Holy Roman Empire. His son, **Philip II**, inherited Spain, the Spanish Netherlands, and the American colonies.

Philip II's Empire Philip was shy, serious, and—like his father—deeply religious. He was also very hard working. Yet Philip would not allow anyone to help him. Deeply suspicious, he trusted no one for long. As his own court historian wrote, "His smile and his dagger were very close."

Perhaps above all, Philip could be aggressive for the sake of his empire. In 1580, the king of Portugal died without an heir. Because Philip was the king's nephew, he seized the Portuguese kingdom. Counting Portuguese strongholds in Africa, India, and the East Indies, he now had an empire that circled the globe.

Philip's empire provided him with incredible wealth. By 1600, American mines had supplied Spain with an estimated 339,000 pounds of gold. Between 1550 and 1650, roughly 16,000 tons of silver bullion were unloaded from Spanish galleons, or ships. The king of Spain claimed between a fourth and a fifth of every shipload of treasure as his royal share. With this wealth, Spain was able to support a large standing army of about 50,000 soldiers.

Defender of Catholicism When Philip assumed the throne, Europe was experiencing religious wars caused by the Reformation. However, religious conflict was not new to Spain. The Reconquista, the campaign to drive Muslims from Spain, had been completed only 64 years before. In addition, Philip's great-grandparents

TAKING NOTES

Clarifying Use a chart to list the conditions that allowed European monarchs to gain power.

Absolute Monarchs in Europe **155**

Route of the Armada
Route of the English fleet
Some shipwreck sites
Spanish Hapsburg lands

SCOTLAND

IRELAND

ATLANTIC
OCEAN

ENGLAND

London

Plymouth

Dover

North
Sea

SPANISH
NETHERLANDS

Calais

English
Channel

0   200 Miles

0   400 Kilometers

Bay of
Biscay

FRANCE

La Coruña

Santander
Late September, 1588

PORTUGAL

Lisbon
Late May, 1588

SPAIN

In the summer of 1588, Philip II sent about 130 ships carrying 19,000 soldiers to the English Channel. English warships, however, outmaneuvered the Spanish vessels and bombarded the Armada with their heavier long-range cannons.

ENGLAND

0   50 Miles

0   100 Kilometers

Major battles

London

Dover

Aug. 8

Calais

Gravelines

SP.
NETH.

Plymouth

Portland Bill

Isle of Wight

Aug. 2

Aug. 3

Aug. 4

July 31

English Channel

FRANCE

GEOGRAPHY SKILLBUILDER:
Interpreting Maps

1. **Location** *Off what English town did the first clash between the Spanish Armada and the English fleet take place?*
2. **Movement** *Why do you think the Spanish captains chose to sail north around Scotland rather than take the more direct route home back through the English Channel?*

Isabella and Ferdinand had used the Inquisition to investigate suspected heretics, or nonbelievers in Christianity.

Philip believed it was his duty to defend Catholicism against the Muslims of the Ottoman Empire and the Protestants of Europe. In 1571, the pope called on all Catholic princes to take up arms against the mounting power of the Ottoman Empire. Philip responded like a true crusader. More than 200 Spanish and Venetian ships defeated a large Ottoman fleet in a fierce battle near Lepanto. In 1588, Philip launched the Spanish Armada in an attempt to punish Protestant England and its queen, Elizabeth I. Elizabeth had supported Protestant subjects who had rebelled against Philip. However, his fleet was defeated. (See map opposite.)

MAIN IDEA

Making Inferences

Ⓐ What did Philip want his palace to demonstrate about his monarchy?

Although this setback seriously weakened Spain, its wealth gave it the appearance of strength for a while longer. Philip's gray granite palace, the Escorial, had massive walls and huge gates that demonstrated his power. The Escorial also reflected Philip's faith. Within its walls stood a monastery as well as a palace. Ⓐ

Golden Age of Spanish Art and Literature

Spain's great wealth did more than support navies and build palaces. It also allowed monarchs and nobles to become patrons of artists. During the 16th and 17th centuries, Spain experienced a golden age in the arts. The works of two great painters show both the faith and the pride of Spain during this period.

El Greco and Velázquez Born in Crete, El Greco (GREHK•oh) spent much of his adult life in Spain. His real name was Domenikos Theotokopoulos, but Spaniards called him El Greco, meaning "the Greek." El Greco's art often puzzled the people of his time. He chose brilliant, sometimes clashing colors, distorted the human figure, and expressed emotion symbolically in his paintings. Although unusual, El Greco's techniques showed the deep Catholic faith of Spain. He painted saints and martyrs as huge, long-limbed figures that have a supernatural air.

The paintings of Diego Velázquez (vuh•LAHS•kehs), on the other hand, reflected the pride of the Spanish monarchy. Velázquez, who painted 50 years after El Greco, was the court painter to Philip IV of Spain. He is best known for his portraits of the royal family and scenes of court life. Like El Greco, he was noted for using rich colors.

Don Quixote The publication of *Don Quixote de la Mancha* in 1605 is often called the birth of the modern European novel. In this book, Miguel de Cervantes (suhr•VAN•teez) wrote about a poor Spanish nobleman who went a little crazy after reading too many books about heroic knights.

▼ In *Las Meninas (The Maids of Honor)*, Velázquez depicts King Philip IV's daughter and her attendants.

Hoping to "right every manner of wrong," Don Quixote rode forth in a rusty suit of armor, mounted on a feeble horse. At one point, he mistook some windmills for giants:

PRIMARY SOURCE
He rushed with [his horse's] utmost speed upon the first windmill he could come at, and, running his lance into the sail, the wind whirled about with such swiftness, that the rapidity of the motion presently broke the lance into shivers, and hurled away both knight and horse along with it, till down he fell, rolling a good way off in the field.

MIGUEL DE CERVANTES, *Don Quixote de la Mancha*

Some critics believe that Cervantes was mocking chivalry, the knightly code of the Middle Ages. Others maintain that the book is about an idealistic person who longs for the romantic past because he is frustrated with his materialistic world.

The Spanish Empire Weakens

Certainly, the age in which Cervantes wrote was a materialistic one. The gold and silver coming from the Americas made Spain temporarily wealthy. However, such treasure helped to cause long-term economic problems.

Inflation and Taxes One of these problems was severe inflation, which is a decline in the value of money, accompanied by a rise in the prices of goods and services. Inflation in Spain had two main causes. First, Spain's population had been growing. As more people demanded food and other goods, merchants were able to raise prices. Second, as silver bullion flooded the market, its value dropped. People needed more and more amounts of silver to buy things.

Spain's economic decline also had other causes. When Spain expelled the Jews and Moors (Muslims) around 1500, it lost many valuable artisans and business-people. In addition, Spain's nobles did not have to pay taxes. The tax burden fell on the lower classes. That burden prevented them from accumulating enough wealth to start their own businesses. As a result, Spain never developed a middle class.

Global Impact

Tulip Mania

Tulips came to Europe from Turkey around 1550. People went wild over the flowers and began to buy rare varieties. However, the supply of tulips could not meet the demand, and prices began to rise. Soon people were spending all their savings on bulbs and taking out loans so that they could buy more.

Tulip mania reached a peak between 1633 and 1637. Soon after, tulip prices sank rapidly. Many Dutch families lost property and were left with bulbs that were nearly worthless.

Making Spain's Enemies Rich Guilds that had emerged in the Middle Ages still dominated business in Spain. Such guilds used old-fashioned methods. This made Spanish cloth and manufactured goods more expensive than those made elsewhere. As a result, Spaniards bought much of what they needed from France, England, and the Netherlands. Spain's great wealth flowed into the pockets of foreigners, who were mostly Spain's enemies.

To finance their wars, Spanish kings borrowed money from German and Italian bankers. When shiploads of silver came in, the money was sent abroad to repay debts. The economy was so feeble that Philip had to declare the Spanish state bankrupt three times. **B**

The Dutch Revolt In the Spanish Netherlands, Philip had to maintain an army to keep his subjects under control. The Dutch had little in common with their Spanish rulers. While Spain was Catholic, the Netherlands had many Calvinist congregations. Also, Spain had a sluggish economy, while the Dutch had a prosperous middle class.

Philip raised taxes in the Netherlands and took steps to crush Protestantism. In response, in 1566, angry Protestant mobs swept through Catholic churches. Philip then sent an

MAIN IDEA

Identifying Problems
B Why didn't Spain's economy benefit from the gold and silver from the Americas?

army under the Spanish duke of Alva to punish the rebels. On a single day in 1568, the duke executed 1,500 Protestants and suspected rebels.

The Dutch continued to fight the Spanish for another 11 years. Finally, in 1579, the seven northern provinces of the Netherlands, which were largely Protestant, united and declared their independence from Spain. They became the United Provinces of the Netherlands. The ten southern provinces (present-day Belgium) were Catholic and remained under Spanish control.

The Independent Dutch Prosper

The United Provinces of the Netherlands was different from other European states of the time. For one thing, the people there practiced religious toleration. In addition, the United Provinces was not a kingdom but a republic. Each province had an elected governor, whose power depended on the support of merchants and landholders.

Dutch Art During the 1600s, the Netherlands became what Florence had been during the 1400s. It boasted not only the best banks but also many of the best artists in Europe. As in Florence, wealthy merchants sponsored many of these artists.

Rembrandt van Rijn (REHM•BRANT vahn RYN) was the greatest Dutch artist of the period. Rembrandt painted portraits of wealthy middle-class merchants. He also produced group portraits. In *The Night Watch* (shown below), he portrayed a group of city guards. Rembrandt used sharp contrasts of light and shadow to draw attention to his focus.

Another artist fascinated with the effects of light and dark was Jan Vermeer (YAHN vuhr•MEER). Like many other Dutch artists, he chose domestic, indoor settings for his portraits. He often painted women doing such familiar activities as pouring milk from a jug or reading a letter. The work of both Rembrandt and Vermeer reveals how important merchants, civic leaders, and the middle class in general were in 17th-century Netherlands.

◄ In *The Night Watch,* Rembrandt showed the individuality of each man by capturing distinctive facial expressions and postures.

Dutch Trading Empire The stability of the government allowed the Dutch people to concentrate on economic growth. The merchants of Amsterdam bought surplus grain in Poland and crammed it into their warehouses. When they heard about poor harvests in southern Europe, they shipped the grain south while prices were highest. The Dutch had the largest fleet of ships in the world—perhaps 4,800 ships in 1636. This fleet helped the Dutch East India Company (a trading company controlled by the Dutch government) to dominate the Asian spice trade and the Indian Ocean trade. Gradually, the Dutch replaced the Italians as the bankers of Europe.

Absolutism in Europe

Even though Philip II lost his Dutch possessions, he was a forceful ruler in many ways. He tried to control every aspect of his empire's affairs. During the next few centuries, many European monarchs would also claim the authority to rule without limits on their power.

The Theory of Absolutism These rulers wanted to be **absolute monarchs**, kings or queens who held all of the power within their states' boundaries. Their goal was to control every aspect of society. Absolute monarchs believed in **divine right**, the idea that God created the monarchy and that the monarch acted as God's representative on Earth. An absolute monarch answered only to God, not to his or her subjects. **C**

MAIN IDEA

Drawing Conclusions
C How was Philip II typical of an absolute monarch?

> ## Analyzing Key Concepts

Absolutism

Absolutism was the political belief that one ruler should hold all of the power within the boundaries of a country. Although practiced by several monarchs in Europe during the 16th through 18th centuries, absolutism has been used in many regions throughout history. In ancient times, Shi Huangdi in China, Darius in Persia, and the Roman caesars were all absolute rulers. (See Chapters 4, 5, and 6.)

SKILLBUILDER: Interpreting Charts

1. **Making Inferences** *Why do you think absolute rulers controlled social gatherings?*
   See Skillbuilder Handbook, page R10.

2. **Hypothesizing** *Today several nations of the world (such as Saudi Arabia) have absolute rulers. Judging from what you know of past causes of absolutism, why do you think absolute rulers still exist today?*

Causes

- Religious and territorial conflicts created fear and uncertainty.
- The growth of armies to deal with conflicts caused rulers to raise taxes to pay troops.
- Heavy taxes led to additional unrest and peasant revolts.

ABSOLUTISM

Effects

- Rulers regulated religious worship and social gatherings to control the spread of ideas.
- Rulers increased the size of their courts to appear more powerful.
- Rulers created bureaucracies to control their countries' economies.

Growing Power of Europe's Monarchs As Europe emerged from the Middle Ages, monarchs grew increasingly powerful. The decline of feudalism, the rise of cities, and the growth of national kingdoms all helped to centralize authority. In addition, the growing middle class usually backed monarchs, because they promised a peaceful, supportive climate for business. Monarchs used the wealth of colonies to pay for their ambitions. Church authority also broke down during the late Middle Ages and the Reformation. That opened the way for monarchs to assume even greater control. In 1576, Jean Bodin, an influential French writer, defined absolute rule:

PRIMARY SOURCE
The first characteristic of the sovereign prince is the power to make general and special laws, but—and this qualification is important—without the consent of superiors, equals, or inferiors. If the prince requires the consent of superiors, then he is a subject himself; if that of equals, he shares his authority with others; if that of his subjects, senate or people, he is not sovereign.

JEAN BODIN, *Six Books on the State*

Crises Lead to Absolutism The 17th century was a period of great upheaval in Europe. Religious and territorial conflicts between states led to almost continuous warfare. This caused governments to build huge armies and to levy even heavier taxes on an already suffering population. These pressures in turn brought about widespread unrest. Sometimes peasants revolted.

In response to these crises, monarchs tried to impose order by increasing their own power. As absolute rulers, they regulated everything from religious worship to social gatherings. They created new government bureaucracies to control their countries' economic life. Their goal was to free themselves from the limitations imposed by the nobility and by representative bodies such as Parliament. Only with such freedom could they rule absolutely, as did the most famous monarch of his time, Louis XIV of France. You'll learn more about him in the next section.

SECTION 1 ASSESSMENT

TERMS & NAMES 1. For each term or name, write a sentence explaining its significance.
• Philip II   • absolute monarch   • divine right

USING YOUR NOTES
2. Which condition is probably most necessary for a monarch to gain power? Why?

MAIN IDEAS
3. What is the significance of England's defeat of the Spanish Armada?
4. Why did the Dutch revolt against Spain?
5. Why did absolute monarchs believe that they were justified in exercising absolute power?

CRITICAL THINKING & WRITING
6. **DRAWING CONCLUSIONS** What does the art described in this section reveal about the cultures of Spain and the Netherlands?
7. **ANALYZING CAUSES** What role did religion play in the struggle between the Spanish and the Dutch?
8. **MAKING INFERENCES** How did the lack of a middle class contribute to the decline of Spain's economy?
9. **WRITING ACTIVITY** ECONOMICS Write a **comparison-contrast paragraph** on the economies of Spain and the Netherlands around 1600.

INTEGRATED / TECHNOLOGY **INTERNET ACTIVITY**
Use the Internet to identify the religious affiliations of people in Spain and in the Netherlands today. Create a **graph** for each country showing the results of your research.

INTERNET KEYWORD
religion in Spain; religion in the Netherlands

The Reign of Louis XIV

MAIN IDEA	WHY IT MATTERS NOW	TERMS & NAMES
POWER AND AUTHORITY After a century of war and riots, France was ruled by Louis XIV, the most powerful monarch of his time.	Louis's abuse of power led to revolution that would inspire the call for democratic government throughout the world.	• Edict of Nantes • Cardinal Richelieu • skepticism • Louis XIV	• intendant • Jean Baptiste Colbert • War of the Spanish Succession

SETTING THE STAGE In 1559, King Henry II of France died, leaving four young sons. Three of them ruled, one after the other, but all proved incompetent. The real power behind the throne during this period was their mother, Catherine de Médicis. Catherine tried to preserve royal authority, but growing conflicts between Catholics and Huguenots—French Protestants—rocked the country. Between 1562 and 1598, Huguenots and Catholics fought eight religious wars. Chaos spread through France.

Religious Wars and Power Struggles

In 1572, the St. Bartholomew's Day Massacre in Paris sparked a six-week, nationwide slaughter of Huguenots. The massacre occurred when many Huguenot nobles were in Paris. They were attending the marriage of Catherine's daughter to a Huguenot prince, Henry of Navarre. Most of these nobles died, but Henry survived.

Henry of Navarre Descended from the popular medieval king Louis IX, Henry was robust, athletic, and handsome. In 1589, when both Catherine and her last son died, Prince Henry inherited the throne. He became Henry IV, the first king of the Bourbon dynasty in France. As king, he showed himself to be decisive, fearless in battle, and a clever politician.

Many Catholics, including the people of Paris, opposed Henry. For the sake of his war-weary country, Henry chose to give up Protestantism and become a Catholic. Explaining his conversion, Henry reportedly declared, "Paris is well worth a mass."

In 1598, Henry took another step toward healing France's wounds. He declared that the Huguenots could live in peace in France and set up their own houses of worship in some cities. This declaration of religious toleration was called the **Edict of Nantes**.

Aided by an adviser who enacted wise financial policies, Henry devoted his reign to rebuilding France and its prosperity. He restored the French monarchy to a strong position. After a generation of war, most French people welcomed peace. Some people, however, hated Henry for his religious compromises. In 1610, a fanatic leaped into the royal carriage and stabbed Henry to death.

TAKING NOTES
Following Chronological Order Use a time line to list the major events of Louis XIV's reign.

1643 — 1715

Louis XIII and Cardinal Richelieu After Henry IV's death, his son Louis XIII reigned. Louis was a weak king, but in 1624, he appointed a strong minister who made up for all of Louis's weaknesses.

<u>Cardinal Richelieu</u> (RIHSH•uh•LOO) became, in effect, the ruler of France. For several years, he had been a hard-working leader of the Catholic church in France. Although he tried sincerely to lead according to moral principles, he was also ambitious and enjoyed exercising authority. As Louis XIII's minister, he was able to pursue his ambitions in the political arena.

Richelieu took two steps to increase the power of the Bourbon monarchy. First, he moved against Huguenots. He believed that Protestantism often served as an excuse for political conspiracies against the Catholic king. Although Richelieu did not take away the Huguenots' right to worship, he forbade Protestant cities to have walls. He did not want them to be able to defy the king and then withdraw behind strong defenses.

Second, he sought to weaken the nobles' power. Richelieu ordered nobles to take down their fortified castles. He increased the power of government agents who came from the middle class. The king relied on these agents, so there was less need to use noble officials.

Richelieu also wanted to make France the strongest state in Europe. The greatest obstacle to this, he believed, was the Hapsburg rulers, whose lands surrounded France. The Hapsburgs ruled Spain, Austria, the Netherlands, and parts of the Holy Roman Empire. To limit Hapsburg power, Richelieu involved France in the Thirty Years' War. **Ⓐ**

MAIN IDEA

Making Inferences

Ⓐ How did Richelieu's actions toward Huguenots and the nobility strengthen the monarchy?

▲ Cardinal Richelieu probably had himself portrayed in a standing position in this painting to underscore his role as ruler.

Writers Turn Toward Skepticism

As France regained political power, a new French intellectual movement developed. French thinkers had witnessed the religious wars with horror. What they saw turned them toward <u>skepticism</u>, the idea that nothing can ever be known for certain. These thinkers expressed an attitude of doubt toward churches that claimed to have the only correct set of doctrines. To doubt old ideas, skeptics thought, was the first step toward finding truth.

Montaigne and Descartes Michel de Montaigne lived during the worst years of the French religious wars. After the death of a dear friend, Montaigne thought deeply about life's meaning. To communicate his ideas, Montaigne developed a new form of literature, the essay. An essay is a brief work that expresses a person's thoughts and opinions.

In one essay, Montaigne pointed out that whenever a new belief arose, it replaced an old belief that people once accepted as truth. In the same way, he went on, the new belief would also probably be replaced by some different idea in the future. For these reasons, Montaigne believed that humans could never have absolute knowledge of what is true.

Another French writer of the time, René Descartes, was a brilliant thinker. In his *Meditations on First Philosophy,* Descartes examined the skeptical argument that one could never be certain of anything. Descartes used his observations and his reason to answer such arguments. In doing so, he created a philosophy that influenced modern thinkers and helped to develop the scientific method. Because of

Although Louis XIV stood only 5 feet 5 inches tall, his erect and dignified posture made him appear much taller. (It also helped that he wore high-heeled shoes.)

Louis had very strong likes and dislikes. He hated cities and loved to travel through France's countryside. The people who traveled with him were at his mercy, however, for he allowed no stopping except for his own comfort.

It is small wonder that the vain Louis XIV liked to be called the Sun King. He believed that, as with the sun, all power radiated from him.

INTEGRATED/TECHNOLOGY

RESEARCH LINKS For more on Louis XIV, go to **classzone.com**

this, he became an important figure in the Enlightenment, which you will read about in Chapter 6.

Louis XIV Comes to Power

The efforts of Henry IV and Richelieu to strengthen the French monarchy paved the way for the most powerful ruler in French history—**Louis XIV**. In Louis's view, he and the state were one and the same. He reportedly boasted, *"L'état, c'est moi,"* meaning "I am the state." Although Louis XIV became the strongest king of his time, he was only a four-year-old boy when he began his reign.

Louis, the Boy King When Louis became king in 1643 after the death of his father, Louis XIII, the true ruler of France was Richelieu's successor, Cardinal Mazarin (MAZ•uh•RAN). Mazarin's greatest triumph came in 1648, with the ending of the Thirty Years' War.

Many people in France, particularly the nobles, hated Mazarin because he increased taxes and strengthened the central government. From 1648 to 1653, violent anti-Mazarin riots tore France apart. At times, the nobles who led the riots threatened the young king's life. Even after the violence was over, Louis never forgot his fear or his anger at the nobility. He determined to become so strong that they could never threaten him again.

In the end, the nobles' rebellion failed for three reasons. Its leaders distrusted one another even more than they distrusted Mazarin. In addition, the government used violent repression. Finally, peasants and townspeople grew weary of disorder and fighting. For many years afterward, the people of France accepted the oppressive laws of an absolute king. They were convinced that the alternative—rebellion—was even worse. **B**

Louis Weakens the Nobles' Authority When Cardinal Mazarin died in 1661, the 22-year-old Louis took control of the government himself. He weakened the power of the nobles by excluding them from his councils. In contrast, he increased the power of the government agents called **intendants**, who collected taxes and administered justice. To keep power under central control, he made sure that local officials communicated regularly with him.

Economic Growth Louis devoted himself to helping France attain economic, political, and cultural brilliance. No one assisted him more in achieving these goals than his minister of finance, **Jean Baptiste Colbert** (kawl•BEHR). Colbert believed in the theory of mercantilism. To prevent wealth from leaving the country, Colbert tried to make France self-sufficient. He wanted it to be able to manufacture everything it needed instead of relying on imports.

To expand manufacturing, Colbert gave government funds and tax benefits to French companies. To protect France's industries, he placed a high tariff on goods from other countries. Colbert also recognized the importance of colonies, which provided raw materials and a market for manufactured goods. The French government encouraged people to migrate to France's colony in Canada. There the fur trade added to French trade and wealth.

MAIN IDEA

Recognizing Effects
B What effects did the years of riots have on Louis XIV? on his subjects?

Vocabulary
mercantilism: the economic theory that nations should protect their home industries and export more than they import

After Colbert's death, Louis announced a policy that slowed France's economic progress. In 1685, he canceled the Edict of Nantes, which protected the religious freedom of Huguenots. In response, thousands of Huguenot artisans and business people fled the country. Louis's policy thus robbed France of many skilled workers.

The Sun King's Grand Style

In his personal finances, Louis spent a fortune to surround himself with luxury. For example, each meal was a feast. An observer claimed that the king once devoured four plates of soup, a whole pheasant, a partridge in garlic sauce, two slices of ham, a salad, a plate of pastries, fruit, and hard-boiled eggs in a single sitting! Nearly 500 cooks, waiters, and other servants worked to satisfy his tastes.

Louis Controls the Nobility Every morning, the chief valet woke Louis at 8:30. Outside the curtains of Louis's canopy bed stood at least 100 of the most privileged nobles at court. They were waiting to help the great king dress. Only four would be allowed the honor of handing Louis his slippers or holding his sleeves for him.

Meanwhile, outside the bedchamber, lesser nobles waited in the palace halls and hoped Louis would notice them. A kingly nod, a glance of approval, a kind word—these marks of royal attention determined whether a noble succeeded or failed. A duke recorded how Louis turned against nobles who did not come to court to flatter him:

▼ Though full of errors, Saint-Simon's memoirs provide valuable insight into Louis XIV's character and life at Versailles.

MAIN IDEA

Analyzing Primary Sources
Ⓒ How did Louis's treatment of the nobles reflect his belief in his absolute authority?

PRIMARY SOURCE Ⓒ

He looked to the right and to the left, not only upon rising but upon going to bed, at his meals, in passing through his apartments, or his gardens. . . . He marked well all absentees from the Court, found out the reason of their absence, and never lost an opportunity of acting toward them as the occasion might seem to justify. . . . When their names were in any way mentioned, "I do not know them," the King would reply haughtily.

DUKE OF SAINT-SIMON, *Memoirs of Louis XIV and the Regency*

Having the nobles at the palace increased royal authority in two ways. It made the nobility totally dependent on Louis. It also took them from their homes, thereby giving more power to the intendants. Louis required hundreds of nobles to live with him at the splendid palace he built at Versailles, about 11 miles southwest of Paris.

As you can see from the pictures on the following page, everything about the Versailles palace was immense. It faced a huge royal courtyard dominated by a statue of Louis XIV. The palace itself stretched for a distance of about 500 yards. Because of its great size, Versailles was like a small royal city. Its rich decoration and furnishings clearly showed Louis's wealth and power to everyone who came to the palace.

Patronage of the Arts Versailles was a center of the arts during Louis's reign. Louis made opera and ballet more popular. He even danced the title role in the ballet *The Sun King*. One of his favorite writers was Molière (mohl•YAIR), who wrote some of the funniest plays in French literature. Molière's comedies include *Tartuffe,* which mocks religious hypocrisy.

Not since Augustus of Rome had there been a European monarch who supported the arts as much as Louis. Under Louis, the chief purpose of art was no longer to glorify God, as it had been in the Middle Ages. Nor was its purpose to glorify human potential, as it had been in the Renaissance. Now the purpose of art was to glorify the king and promote values that supported Louis's absolute rule.

The Palace at Versailles

Louis XIV's palace at Versailles was proof of his absolute power. Only a ruler with total control over his country's economy could afford such a lavish palace. It cost an estimated $2.5 billion in 2003 dollars. Louis XIV was also able to force 36,000 laborers and 6,000 horses to work on the project.

Many people consider the Hall of Mirrors the most beautiful room in the palace. Along one wall are 17 tall mirrors. The opposite wall has 17 windows that open onto the gardens. The hall has gilded statues, crystal chandeliers, and a painted ceiling.

It took so much water to run all the fountains at once that it was done only for special events. On other days, when the king walked in the garden, servants would turn on fountains just before he reached them. The fountains were turned off after he walked away.

The gardens at Versailles remain beautiful today. Originally, Versailles was built with:
• 5,000 acres of gardens, lawns, and woods
• 1,400 fountains

SKILLBUILDER: Interpreting Visuals
1. **Analyzing Motives** *Why do you think Louis XIV believed he needed such a large and luxurious palace? Explain what practical and symbolic purposes Versailles might have served.*
2. **Developing Historical Perspective** *Consider the amount of money and effort that went into the construction of this extravagant palace. What does this reveal about the way 17th-century French society viewed its king?*

Louis Fights Disastrous Wars

Under Louis, France was the most powerful country in Europe. In 1660, France had about 20 million people. This was four times as many as England and ten times as many as the Dutch republic. The French army was far ahead of other states' armies in size, training, and weaponry.

Attempts to Expand France's Boundaries In 1667, just six years after Mazarin's death, Louis invaded the Spanish Netherlands in an effort to expand France's boundaries. Through this campaign, he gained 12 towns. Encouraged by his success, he personally led an army into the Dutch Netherlands in 1672. The Dutch saved their country by opening the dikes and flooding the countryside. This was the same tactic they had used in their revolt against Spain a century earlier. The war ended in 1678 with the Treaty of Nijmegen. France gained several towns and a region called Franche-Comté.

Louis decided to fight additional wars, but his luck had run out. By the end of the 1680s, a Europeanwide alliance had formed to stop France. By banding together, weaker countries could match France's strength. This defensive strategy was meant to achieve a balance of power, in which no single country or group of countries could dominate others.

In 1689, the Dutch prince William of Orange became the king of England. He joined the League of Augsburg, which consisted of the Austrian Hapsburg emperor, the kings of Sweden and Spain, and the leaders of several smaller European states. Together, these countries equaled France's strength.

France at this time had been weakened by a series of poor harvests. That, added to the constant warfare, brought great suffering to the French people. So, too, did new taxes, which Louis imposed to finance his wars. **D**

MAIN IDEA

Recognizing Effects

D How did Louis's wars against weaker countries backfire?

War of the Spanish Succession Tired of hardship, the French people longed for peace. What they got was another war. In 1700, the childless king of Spain, Charles II, died after promising his throne to Louis XIV's 16-year-old grandson, Philip of Anjou. The two greatest powers in Europe, enemies for so long, were now both ruled by the French Bourbons.

Other countries felt threatened by this increase in the Bourbon dynasty's power. In 1701, England, Austria, the Dutch Republic, Portugal, and several German and Italian states joined together to prevent the union of the French and Spanish thrones. The long struggle that followed is known as the **War of the Spanish Succession**.

The costly war dragged on until 1714. The Treaty of Utrecht was signed in that year. Under its terms, Louis's grandson was allowed to remain king of Spain so long as the thrones of France and Spain were not united.

The big winner in the war was Great Britain. From Spain, Britain took Gibraltar, a fortress that controlled the entrance to the Mediterranean. Spain also granted a British company an *asiento*, permission to send enslaved Africans to Spain's American colonies. This increased Britain's involvement in trading enslaved Africans.

▼ The painting below shows the Battle of Denain, one of the last battles fought during the War of the Spanish Succession.

Debt of the Royal Family, 1643–1715

A livre is equal to approximately $10.50 in 1992 U.S. dollars.
Source: *Early Modern France 1560–1715*

SKILLBUILDER: Interpreting Charts
1. **Comparing** *How many times greater was the royal debt in 1715 than in 1643?*
2. **Synthesizing** *What was the royal debt of 1715 equal to in 1992 dollars?*

In addition, France gave Britain the North American territories of Nova Scotia and Newfoundland, and abandoned claims to the Hudson Bay region. The Austrian Hapsburgs took the Spanish Netherlands and other Spanish lands in Italy. Prussia and Savoy were recognized as kingdoms.

Louis's Death and Legacy Louis's last years were more sad than glorious. Realizing that his wars had ruined France, he regretted the suffering he had brought to his people. He died in bed in 1715. News of his death prompted rejoicing throughout France. The people had had enough of the Sun King.

Louis left a mixed legacy to his country. On the positive side, France was certainly a power to be reckoned with in Europe. France ranked above all other European nations in art, literature, and statesmanship during Louis's reign. In addition, France was considered the military leader of Europe. This military might allowed France to develop a strong empire of colonies, which provided resources and goods for trade.

On the negative side, constant warfare and the construction of the Palace of Versailles plunged France into staggering debt. Also, resentment over the tax burden imposed on the poor and Louis's abuse of power would plague his heirs—and eventually lead to revolution.

Absolute rule didn't die with Louis XIV. His enemies in Prussia and Austria had been experimenting with their own forms of absolute monarchy, as you will learn in Section 3.

SECTION 2 ASSESSMENT

TERMS & NAMES 1. For each term or name, write a sentence explaining its significance.
• Edict of Nantes • Cardinal Richelieu • skepticism • Louis XIV • intendant • Jean Baptiste Colbert • War of the Spanish Succession

USING YOUR NOTES
2. Which events on your time line strengthened the French monarchy? Which weakened it?

1643   1715

MAIN IDEAS
3. What impact did the French religious wars have on French thinkers?
4. How did Jean Baptiste Colbert intend to stimulate economic growth in France?
5. What was the result of the War of the Spanish Succession?

CRITICAL THINKING & WRITING
6. **SUPPORTING OPINIONS** Many historians think of Louis XIV as the perfect example of an absolute monarch. Do you agree? Explain why or why not.
7. **RECOGNIZING EFFECTS** How did the policies of Colbert and Louis XIV affect the French economy? Explain both positive and negative effects.
8. **SYNTHESIZING** To what extent did anti-Protestantism contribute to Louis's downfall?
9. **WRITING ACTIVITY** [POWER AND AUTHORITY] Write a **character sketch** of Louis XIV. Discuss his experiences and character traits.

CONNECT TO TODAY CREATING AN ORAL PRESENTATION
Research to find out what happened to Versailles after Louis's death and what its function is today. Then present your findings in an **oral presentation.**

Central European Monarchs Clash

POWER AND AUTHORITY After a period of turmoil, absolute monarchs ruled Austria and the Germanic state of Prussia.

Prussia built a strong military tradition in Germany that contributed in part to world wars in the 20th century.

- Thirty Years' War
- Maria Theresa
- Frederick the Great
- Seven Years' War

SETTING THE STAGE For a brief while, the German rulers appeared to have settled their religious differences through the Peace of Augsburg (1555). They had agreed that the faith of each prince would determine the religion of his subjects. Churches in Germany could be either Lutheran or Catholic, but not Calvinist. The peace was short-lived—soon to be replaced by a long war. After the Peace of Augsburg, the Catholic and Lutheran princes of Germany watched each other suspiciously.

The Thirty Years' War

Both the Lutheran and the Catholic princes tried to gain followers. In addition, both sides felt threatened by Calvinism, which was spreading in Germany and gaining many followers. As tension mounted, the Lutherans joined together in the Protestant Union in 1608. The following year, the Catholic princes formed the Catholic League. Now, it would take only a spark to set off a war.

Bohemian Protestants Revolt That spark came in 1618. The future Holy Roman emperor, Ferdinand II, was head of the Hapsburg family. As such, he ruled the Czech kingdom of Bohemia. The Protestants in Bohemia did not trust Ferdinand, who was a foreigner and a Catholic. When he closed some Protestant churches, the Protestants revolted. Ferdinand sent an army into Bohemia to crush the revolt. Several German Protestant princes took this chance to challenge their Catholic emperor.

Thus began the **Thirty Years' War**, a conflict over religion and territory and for power among European ruling families. The war can be divided into two main phases: the phase of Hapsburg triumphs and the phase of Hapsburg defeats.

Hapsburg Triumphs The Thirty Years' War lasted from 1618 to 1648. During the first 12 years, Hapsburg armies from Austria and Spain crushed the troops hired by the Protestant princes. They succeeded in putting down the Czech uprising. They also defeated the German Protestants who had supported the Czechs.

Ferdinand II paid his army of 125,000 men by allowing them to plunder, or rob, German villages. This huge army destroyed everything in its path.

Hapsburg Defeats The Protestant Gustavus Adolphus of Sweden and his disciplined army of 23,000 shifted the tide of war in 1630. They drove the Hapsburg

TAKING NOTES

Comparing Use a chart to compare Maria Theresa with Frederick the Great. Compare their years of reign, foreign policy, and success in war.

Maria Theresa	Frederick the Great

armies out of northern Germany. However, Gustavus Adolphus was killed in battle in 1632.

Cardinal Richelieu and Cardinal Mazarin of France dominated the remaining years of the war. Although Catholic, these two cardinals feared the Hapsburgs more than the Protestants. They did not want other European rulers to have as much power as the French king. Therefore, in 1635, Richelieu sent French troops to join the German and Swedish Protestants in their struggle against the Hapsburg armies.

Peace of Westphalia The war did great damage to Germany. Its population dropped from 20 million to about 16 million. Both trade and agriculture were disrupted, and Germany's economy was ruined. Germany had a long, difficult recovery from this devastation. That is a major reason it did not become a unified state until the 1800s.

The Peace of Westphalia (1648) ended the war. The treaty had these important consequences:

- weakened the Hapsburg states of Spain and Austria;
- strengthened France by awarding it German territory;
- made German princes independent of the Holy Roman emperor;
- ended religious wars in Europe;
- introduced a new method of peace negotiation whereby all participants meet to settle the problems of a war and decide the terms of peace. This method is still used today. **A**

Beginning of Modern States The treaty thus abandoned the idea of a Catholic empire that would rule most of Europe. It recognized Europe as a group of equal, independent states. This marked the beginning of the modern state system and was the most important result of the Thirty Years' War.

MAIN IDEA

Drawing Conclusions

A Judging from their actions, do you think the two French cardinals were motivated more by religion or politics? Why?

Europe After the Thirty Years' War, 1648

INTERACTIVE

The Holy Roman Empire

Population Losses

Up to 15%   34–66%
15–33%   Over 66%   The Holy Roman Empire

GEOGRAPHY SKILLBUILDER: Interpreting Maps

1. **Place** *Name at least five modern European countries that existed at the end of the Thirty Years' War.*
2. **Region** *Refer to the inset map. Which regions lost the most population in the Thirty Years' War?*

170

States Form in Central Europe

Strong states formed more slowly in central Europe than in western Europe. The major powers of this region were the kingdom of Poland, the Holy Roman Empire, and the Ottoman Empire. None of them was very strong in the mid-1600s.

Economic Contrasts with the West One reason for this is that the economy of central Europe developed differently from that of western Europe. During the late Middle Ages, serfs in western Europe slowly won freedom and moved to towns. There, they joined middle-class townspeople, who gained economic power because of the commercial revolution and the development of capitalism.

By contrast, the landowning aristocracy in central Europe passed laws restricting the ability of serfs to gain freedom and move to cities. These nobles wanted to keep the serfs on the land, where they could produce large harvests. The nobles could then sell the surplus crops to western European cities at great profit.

Several Weak Empires The landowning nobles in central Europe not only held down the serfs but also blocked the development of strong kings. For example, the Polish nobility elected the Polish king and sharply limited his power. They allowed the king little income, no law courts, and no standing army. As a result, there was not a strong ruler who could form a unified state.

The two empires of central Europe were also weak. Although Suleyman the Magnificent had conquered Hungary and threatened Vienna in 1529, the Ottoman Empire could not take its European conquest any farther. From then on, the Ottoman Empire declined from its peak of power.

In addition, the Holy Roman Empire was seriously weakened by the Thirty Years' War. No longer able to command the obedience of the German states, the Holy Roman Empire had no real power. These old, weakened empires and kingdoms left a power vacuum in central Europe. In the late 1600s, two German-speaking families decided to try to fill this vacuum by becoming absolute rulers themselves.

Austria Grows Stronger One of these families was the Hapsburgs of Austria. The Austrian Hapsburgs took several steps to become absolute monarchs. First, during the Thirty Years' War, they reconquered Bohemia. The Hapsburgs wiped out Protestantism there and created a new Czech nobility that pledged loyalty to them. Second, after the war, the Hapsburg ruler centralized the government and created a standing army. Third, by 1699, the Hapsburgs had retaken Hungary from the Ottoman Empire.

In 1711, Charles VI became the Hapsburg ruler. Charles's empire was a difficult one to rule. Within its borders lived a diverse assortment of people—Czechs, Hungarians, Italians, Croatians, and Germans. Only the fact that one Hapsburg ruler wore the Austrian, Hungarian, and Bohemian crowns kept the empire together.

Maria Theresa Inherits the Austrian Throne How could the Hapsburgs make sure that they continued to rule all those lands? Charles VI spent his entire reign working out an answer to this problem. With endless arm-twisting, he persuaded other leaders of Europe to sign an agreement that declared they would recognize Charles's eldest daughter as the heir to all his Hapsburg territories. That heir was a young woman named **Maria Theresa**. In theory, this agreement guaranteed Maria Theresa a peaceful reign. Instead, she faced years of war. Her main enemy was Prussia, a state to the north of Austria. (See map opposite.)

▼ The imperial crest of the Hapsburgs shows a double-headed eagle with a crown.

Maria Theresa
1717–1780

An able ruler, Maria Theresa also devoted herself to her children, whom she continued to advise even after they were grown. Perhaps her most famous child was Marie Antoinette, wife of Louis XVI of France.

As the Austrian empress, Maria Theresa decreased the power of the nobility. She also limited the amount of labor that nobles could force peasants to do. She argued: "The peasantry must be able to sustain itself."

Frederick the Great
1712–1786

Although they reigned during the same time, Frederick the Great and Maria Theresa were very different. Where Maria was religious, Frederick was practical and atheistic. Maria Theresa had a happy home life and a huge family, while Frederick died without a son to succeed him.

An aggressor in foreign affairs, Frederick once wrote that "the fundamental role of governments is the principle of extending their territories." Frederick earned the title "the Great" by achieving his goals for Prussia.

INTEGRATED TECHNOLOGY

INTERNET ACTIVITY Create a family tree showing Maria Theresa's parents and children. Go to **classzone.com** for your research.

Prussia Challenges Austria

Like Austria, Prussia rose to power in the late 1600s. Like the Hapsburgs of Austria, Prussia's ruling family, the Hohenzollerns, also had ambitions. Those ambitions threatened to upset central Europe's delicate balance of power.

The Rise of Prussia The Hohenzollerns built up their state from a number of small holdings, beginning with the German states of Brandenburg and Prussia. In 1640, a 20-year-old Hohenzollern named Frederick William inherited the title of elector of Brandenburg. After seeing the destruction of the Thirty Years' War, Frederick William, later known as the Great Elector, decided that having a strong army was the only way to ensure safety.

To protect their lands, the Great Elector and his descendants moved toward absolute monarchy. They created a standing army, the best in Europe. They built it to a force of 80,000 men. To pay for the army, they introduced permanent taxation. Beginning with the Great Elector's son, they called themselves kings. They also weakened the representative assemblies of their territories.

Prussia's landowning nobility, the Junkers (YUNG•kuhrz), resisted the king's growing power. However, in the early 1700s, King Frederick William I bought their cooperation. He gave the Junkers the exclusive right to be officers in his army. As a result, Prussia became a rigidly controlled, highly militarized society. **B**

Frederick the Great Frederick William worried that his son, Frederick, was not military enough to rule. The prince loved music, philosophy, and poetry. In 1730, when he and a friend tried to run away, they were caught. To punish Frederick, the king ordered him to witness his friend's beheading. Despite such bitter memories, Frederick II, known as **Frederick the Great**, followed his father's military policies when he came to power. However, he also softened some of his father's laws. With regard to domestic affairs, he encouraged religious toleration and legal reform. According to his theory of government, Frederick believed that a ruler should be like a father to his people:

MAIN IDEA

Clarifying
B What steps did the Prussian monarchs take to become absolute monarchs?

PRIMARY SOURCE
A prince . . . is only the first servant of the state, who is obliged to act with probity [honesty] and prudence. . . . As the sovereign is properly the head of a family of citizens, the father of his people, he ought on all occasions to be the last refuge of the unfortunate.

FREDERICK II, *Essay on Forms of Government*

War of the Austrian Succession In 1740, Maria Theresa succeeded her father, just five months after Frederick II became king of Prussia. Frederick wanted the Austrian land of Silesia, which bordered Prussia. Silesia produced iron ore, textiles, and food products. Frederick underestimated Maria Theresa's strength. He assumed that because she was a woman, she would not be forceful enough to defend her lands. In 1740, he sent his army to occupy Silesia, beginning the War of the Austrian Succession. **C**

MAIN IDEA

Clarifying

C Why would iron ore, agricultural lands, and textiles be helpful acquisitions for Frederick the Great?

Even though Maria Theresa had recently given birth, she journeyed to Hungary. There she held her infant in her arms as she asked the Hungarian nobles for aid. Even though the nobles resented their Hapsburg rulers, they pledged to give Maria Theresa an army. Great Britain also joined Austria to fight its longtime enemy France, which was Prussia's ally. Although Maria Theresa did stop Prussia's aggression, she lost Silesia in the Treaty of Aix-la-Chapelle in 1748. With the acquisition of Silesia, Prussia became a major European power.

The Seven Years' War Maria Theresa decided that the French kings were no longer Austria's chief enemies. She made an alliance with them. The result was a diplomatic revolution. When Frederick heard of her actions, he signed a treaty with Britain—Austria's former ally. Now, Austria, France, Russia, and others were allied against Britain and Prussia. Not only had Austria and Prussia switched allies, but for the first time, Russia was playing a role in European affairs.

In 1756, Frederick attacked Saxony, an Austrian ally. Soon every great European power was involved in the war. Fought in Europe, India, and North America, the war lasted until 1763. It was called the **Seven Years' War**. The war did not change the territorial situation in Europe.

It was a different story on other continents. Both France and Britain had colonies in North America and the West Indies. Both were competing economically in India. The British emerged as the real victors in the Seven Years' War. France lost its colonies in North America, and Britain gained sole economic domination of India. This set the stage for further British expansion in India in the 1800s, as you will see in Chapter 11.

SECTION 3 ASSESSMENT

TERMS & NAMES 1. For each term or name, write a sentence explaining its significance.
• Thirty Years' War   • Maria Theresa   • Frederick the Great   • Seven Years' War

USING YOUR NOTES

2. In what ways were the rulers similar?

Maria Theresa	Frederick the Great

MAIN IDEAS

3. What were the major conflicts in the Thirty Years' War?

4. What steps did the Austrian Hapsburgs take toward becoming absolute monarchs?

5. What countries were allies during the Seven Years' War?

CRITICAL THINKING & WRITING

6. **RECOGNIZING EFFECTS** How did the Peace of Westphalia lay the foundations of modern Europe?

7. **ANALYZING MOTIVES** Why did Maria Theresa make an alliance with the French kings, Austria's chief enemies?

8. **DRAWING CONCLUSIONS** Based on Frederick's assumption about Maria Theresa at the outset of the War of the Austrian Succession, what conclusions can you draw about how men viewed women in 1700s Europe?

9. **WRITING ACTIVITY** POWER AND AUTHORITY Write an **outline** for a lecture on "How to Increase Royal Power and Become an Absolute Monarch."

CONNECT TO TODAY CREATING A POSTER

Today much of western Europe belongs to an organization called the European Union (EU). Find out which countries belong to the EU and how they are linked economically and politically. Present your findings—including maps, charts, and pictures—in a **poster**.

Absolute Rulers of Russia

MAIN IDEA	WHY IT MATTERS NOW	TERMS & NAMES
POWER AND AUTHORITY Peter the Great made many changes in Russia to try to make it more like western Europe.	Many Russians today debate whether to model themselves on the West or to focus on traditional Russian culture.	• Ivan the Terrible • Peter the Great • boyar • westernization

SETTING THE STAGE Ivan III of Moscow, who ruled Russia from 1462 to 1505, accomplished several things. First, he conquered much of the territory around Moscow. Second, he liberated Russia from the Mongols. Third, he began to centralize the Russian government. Ivan III was succeeded by his son, Vasily, who ruled for 28 years. Vasily continued his father's work of adding territory to the growing Russian state. He also increased the power of the central government. This trend continued under his son, Ivan IV, who would become an absolute ruler.

TAKING NOTES

Summarizing Use a cluster diagram to list the important events of Peter the Great's reign.

Peter the Great

The First Czar

Ivan IV, called **Ivan the Terrible**, came to the throne in 1533 when he was only three years old. His young life was disrupted by struggles for power among Russia's landowning nobles, known as **boyars**. The boyars fought to control young Ivan. When he was 16, Ivan seized power and had himself crowned czar. This title meant "caesar," and Ivan was the first Russian ruler to use it officially. He also married the beautiful Anastasia, related to an old boyar family, the Romanovs.

The years from 1547 to 1560 are often called Ivan's "good period." He won great victories, added lands to Russia, gave Russia a code of laws, and ruled justly.

Rule by Terror Ivan's "bad period" began in 1560 after Anastasia died. Accusing the boyars of poisoning his wife, Ivan turned against them. He organized his own police force, whose chief duty was to hunt down and murder people Ivan considered traitors. The members of this police force dressed in black and rode black horses.

Using these secret police, Ivan executed many boyars, their families, and the peasants who worked their lands. Thousands of people died. Ivan seized the boyars' estates and gave them to a new class of nobles, who had to remain loyal to him or lose their land.

Eventually, Ivan committed an act that was both a personal tragedy and a national disaster. In 1581, during a violent quarrel, he killed his oldest son and heir. When Ivan died three years later, only his weak second son was left to rule.

Rise of the Romanovs Ivan's son proved to be physically and mentally incapable of ruling. After he died without an heir, Russia experienced a period of

MAIN IDEA

Recognizing Effects

A What were the long-term effects of Ivan's murder of his oldest son?

turmoil known as the Time of Troubles. Boyars struggled for power, and heirs of czars died under mysterious conditions. Several impostors tried to claim the throne.

Finally, in 1613, representatives from many Russian cities met to choose the next czar. Their choice was Michael Romanov, grandnephew of Ivan the Terrible's wife, Anastasia. Thus began the Romanov dynasty, which ruled Russia for 300 years (1613–1917). **A**

Peter the Great Comes to Power

Over time, the Romanovs restored order to Russia. They strengthened government by passing a law code and putting down a revolt. This paved the way for the absolute rule of Czar Peter I. At first, Peter shared the throne with his half-brother. However, in 1696, Peter became sole ruler of Russia. He is known to history as **Peter the Great**, because he was one of Russia's greatest reformers. He also continued the trend of increasing the czar's power.

Russia Contrasts with Europe When Peter I came to power, Russia was still a land of boyars and serfs. Serfdom in Russia lasted into the mid-1800s, much longer than it did in western Europe. Russian landowners wanted serfs to stay on the land and produce large harvests. The landowners treated the serfs like property. When a Russian landowner sold a piece of land, he sold the serfs with it. Landowners could give away serfs as presents or to pay debts. It was also against the law for serfs to run away from their owners.

Most boyars knew little of western Europe. In the Middle Ages, Russia had looked to Constantinople, not to Rome, for leadership. Then Mongol rule had cut Russia off from the Renaissance and the Age of Exploration. Geographic barriers also isolated Russia. Its only seaport, Archangel in northern Russia, was choked with ice much of the year. The few travelers who reached Moscow were usually Dutch or German, and they had to stay in a separate part of the city.

Religious differences widened the gap between western Europe and Russia. The Russians had adopted the Eastern Orthodox branch of Christianity. Western Europeans were mostly Catholics or Protestants, and the Russians viewed them as heretics and avoided them. **B**

Peter Visits the West In the 1680s, people in the German quarter of Moscow were accustomed to seeing the young Peter striding through their neighborhood on his long legs. (Peter was more than six and a half feet tall.) He was fascinated by the modern tools and machines in the foreigners' shops. Above all, he had a passion for ships and the sea. The young czar believed that Russia's future depended on having a warm-water port. Only then could Russia compete with the more modern states of western Europe.

Peter was 24 years old when he became the sole ruler of Russia. In 1697, just one year later, he embarked on the "Grand Embassy," a long visit to western Europe. One of Peter's goals was to learn about European customs and manufacturing techniques. Never before had a czar traveled among Western "heretics."

History Makers

Peter the Great
1672–1725

Peter the Great had the mind of a genius, the body of a giant, and the ferocious temper of a bear. He was so strong that he was known to take a heavy silver plate and roll it up as if it were a piece of paper. If someone annoyed him, he would knock the offender unconscious.

The painting above represents Peter as he looked when he traveled through western Europe. He dressed in the plain clothes of an ordinary worker to keep his identity a secret.

INTEGRATED TECHNOLOGY

RESEARCH LINKS For more on Peter the Great, go to **classzone.com**

Peter Rules Absolutely

Inspired by his trip to the West, Peter resolved that Russia would compete with Europe on both military and commercial terms. Peter's goal of **westernization**, of using western Europe as a model for change, was not an end in itself. Peter saw it as a way to make Russia stronger.

Peter's Reforms Although Peter believed Russia needed to change, he knew that many of his people disagreed. As he said to one official, "For you know yourself that, though a thing be good and necessary, our people will not do it unless forced to." To force change upon his state, Peter increased his powers as an absolute ruler. **C**

Peter brought the Russian Orthodox Church under state control. He abolished the office of patriarch, head of the Church. He set up a group called the Holy Synod to run the Church under his direction.

Like Ivan the Terrible, Peter reduced the power of the great landowners. He recruited men from lower-ranking families. He then promoted them to positions of authority and rewarded them with grants of land.

To modernize his army, Peter hired European officers, who drilled his soldiers in European tactics with European weapons. Being a soldier became a lifetime job. By the time of Peter's death, the Russian army numbered 200,000 men. To pay for this huge army, Peter imposed heavy taxes.

Westernizing Russia As part of his attempts to westernize Russia, Peter undertook the following:

- introduced potatoes, which became a staple of the Russian diet
- started Russia's first newspaper and edited its first issue himself
- raised women's status by having them attend social gatherings
- ordered the nobles to give up their traditional clothes for Western fashions
- advanced education by opening a school of navigation and introducing schools for the arts and sciences

MAIN IDEA

Analyzing Bias
C Judging from this remark, what was Peter's view of his people?

The Expansion of Russia, 1500–1800
INTER**ACTIVE**

- 1462
- Acquisitions to 1505
- Acquisitions to 1584
- Acquisitions to 1682
- Acquisitions to 1725
- Acquisitions to 1796

GEOGRAPHY SKILLBUILDER: Interpreting Maps
1. **Location** Locate the territories that Peter added to Russia during his reign, from 1682 to 1725. What bodies of water did Russia gain access to because of these acquisitions?
2. **Region** Who added a larger amount of territory to Russia—Ivan III, who ruled from 1462 to 1505, or Peter the Great?

Peter believed that education was a key to Russia's progress. In former times, subjects were forbidden under pain of death to study the sciences in foreign lands. Now subjects were not only permitted to leave the country, many were forced to do it.

Establishing St. Petersburg To promote education and growth, Peter wanted a seaport that would make it easier to travel to the West. Therefore, Peter fought Sweden to gain a piece of the Baltic coast. After 21 long years of war, Russia finally won the "window on Europe" that Peter had so desperately wanted.

Actually, Peter had secured that window many years before Sweden officially surrendered it. In 1703, he began building a new city on Swedish lands occupied by Russian troops. Although the swampy site was unhealthful, it seemed ideal to Peter. Ships could sail down the Neva River into the Baltic Sea and on to western Europe. Peter called the city St. Petersburg, after his patron saint.

To build a city on a desolate swamp was no easy matter. Every summer, the army forced thousands of luckless serfs to leave home and work in St. Petersburg. An estimated 25,000 to 100,000 people died from the terrible working conditions and widespread diseases. When St. Petersburg was finished, Peter ordered many Russian nobles to leave the comforts of Moscow and settle in his new capital. In time, St. Petersburg became a busy port. **D**

For better or for worse, Peter the Great had tried to westernize and reform the culture and government of Russia. To an amazing extent he had succeeded. By the time of his death in 1725, Russia was a power to be reckoned with in Europe. Meanwhile, another great European power, England, had been developing a form of government that limited the power of absolute monarchs, as you will see in Section 5.

MAIN IDEA
Synthesizing
D Which of Peter's actions in building St. Petersburg show his power as an absolute monarch?

SECTION 4 ASSESSMENT

TERMS & NAMES 1. For each term or name, write a sentence explaining its significance.
• Ivan the Terrible   • boyar   • Peter the Great   • westernization

USING YOUR NOTES

2. Which event had the most impact on modern Russia? Why?

Peter the Great

MAIN IDEAS

3. How did Ivan the Terrible deal with his enemies during his "bad period"?

4. Why did Peter the Great believe that Russia's future depended on having a warm-water port?

5. What were some of the ways Peter tried to westernize Russia?

CRITICAL THINKING & WRITING

6. **SUPPORTING OPINIONS** Who do you think was more of an absolute monarch: Ivan the Terrible or Peter the Great?

7. **DRAWING CONCLUSIONS** Which class of Russian society probably didn't benefit from Peter's reforms? Why?

8. **HYPOTHESIZING** How might Peter's attempts at westernization have affected his people's opinion of Christians in western Europe?

9. **WRITING ACTIVITY** POWER AND AUTHORITY Write a one-paragraph **expository essay** explaining which of Peter the Great's actions reveal that he saw himself as the highest authority in Russia.

CONNECT TO TODAY STAGING A DEBATE

Peter the Great's reforms were a first step toward Russia's westernization. Today the country continues the process by experimenting with democratization. Research to find out how Russia has fared as a democracy. Then stage a **debate** to argue whether the experiment is working.

Surviving the Russian Winter

Much of Russia has severe winters. In Moscow, snow usually begins to fall in mid-October and lasts until mid-April. Siberia has been known to have temperatures as low as -90°F. Back in the 18th century, Russians did not have down parkas or high-tech insulation for their homes. But they had other ways to cope with the climate.

For example, in the 18th century, Russian peasants added potatoes and corn to their diet. During the winter, these nutritious foods were used in soups and stews. Such dishes were warming and provided plenty of calories to help fight off the cold.

INTEGRATED / TECHNOLOGY

RESEARCH LINKS For more on Russian winters, go to **classzone.com**

Silver Samovar ▶

In the mid-18th century, samovars were invented in Russia. These large, often elaborately decorated urns were used to boil water for tea. Fire was kept burning in a tube running up the middle of the urn—keeping the water piping hot.

◀ Crimean Dress

These people are wearing the traditional dress of tribes from the Crimean Peninsula, a region that Russia took over in the 1700s. Notice the heavy hats, the fur trim on some of the robes, and the leggings worn by those with shorter robes. All these features help to conserve body heat.

▼ Troika

To travel in winter, the wealthy often used sleighs called troikas. *Troika* means "group of three"; the name comes from the three horses that draw this kind of sleigh. The middle horse trotted while the two outside horses galloped.

Winter Festival ▶

Russians have never let their climate stop them from having fun outdoors. Here, they are shown enjoying a Shrovetide festival, which occurs near the end of winter. Vendors sold food such as blinis (pancakes with sour cream). Entertainments included ice skating, dancing bears, and magic shows.

The people in the foreground are wearing heavy fur coats. Otter fur was often used for winter clothing. This fur is extremely thick and has about one million hairs per square inch.

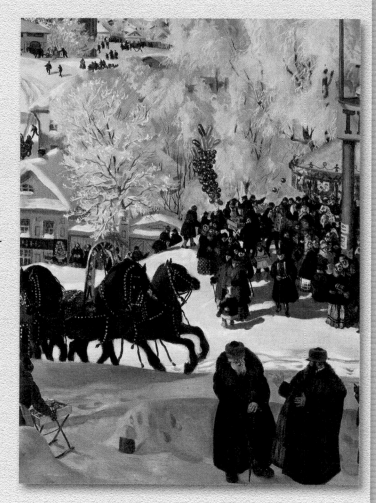

▼ Wooden House

Wooden houses, made of logs, were common in Russia during Peter the Great's time. To insulate the house from the wind, people stuffed moss between the logs. Russians used double panes of glass in their windows. For extra protection, many houses had shutters to cover the windows. The roofs were steep so snow would slide off.

> **DATA FILE**

FROSTY FACTS

- According to a 2001 estimate, Russian women spend about $500 million a year on fur coats and caps.

- The record low temperature in Asia of -90°F was reached twice, first in Verkhoyansk, Russia, in 1892 and then in Oimekon, Russia, in 1933.

- The record low temperature in Europe of -67°F was recorded in Ust'Shchugor, Russia.

- One reason for Russia's cold climate is that most of the country lies north of the 45° latitude line, closer to the North Pole than to the Equator.

Average High Temperature for January, Russian Cities

Moscow, Russia	Perm, Russia	Rostov, Russia
21°F	12°F	29°F

Source: *Worldclimate.com*

Average High Temperature for January, U.S. Cities

Los Angeles, California	Minneapolis, Minnesota	New York, New York
66°F	21°F	38°F

Source: *Worldclimate.com*

Connect *to* Today

1. Making Inferences In the 18th century, how did Russians use their natural resources to help them cope with the climate?

See Skillbuilder Handbook, page R10.

2. Comparing and Contrasting How has coping with winter weather changed from 18th-century Russia to today's world? How has it stayed the same?

Parliament Limits the English Monarchy

MAIN IDEA	WHY IT MATTERS NOW	TERMS & NAMES
REVOLUTION Absolute rulers in England were overthrown, and Parliament gained power.	Many of the government reforms of this period contributed to the democratic tradition of the United States.	• Charles I • English Civil War • Oliver Cromwell • Restoration • *habeas corpus* • Glorious Revolution • constitutional monarchy • cabinet

SETTING THE STAGE During her reign, Queen Elizabeth I of England had had frequent conflicts with Parliament. Many of the arguments were over money, because the treasury did not have enough funds to pay the queen's expenses. By the time Elizabeth died in 1603, she had left a huge debt for her successor to deal with. Parliament's financial power was one obstacle to English rulers' becoming absolute monarchs. The resulting struggle between Parliament and the monarchy would have serious consequences for England.

Monarchs Defy Parliament

TAKING NOTES

Analyzing Causes Use a chart to list the causes of each monarch's conflicts with Parliament.

Monarch	Conflicts with Parliament
James I	
Charles I	
James II	

Elizabeth had no child, and her nearest relative was her cousin, James Stuart. Already king of Scotland, James Stuart became King James I of England in 1603. Although England and Scotland were not united until 1707, they now shared a ruler.

James's Problems James inherited the unsettled issues of Elizabeth's reign. His worst struggles with Parliament were over money. In addition, James offended the Puritan members of Parliament. The Puritans hoped he would enact reforms to purify the English church of Catholic practices. Except for agreeing to a new translation of the Bible, however, he refused to make Puritan reforms.

Charles I Fights Parliament In 1625, James I died. **Charles I**, his son, took the throne. Charles always needed money, in part because he was at war with both Spain and France. Several times when Parliament refused to give him funds, he dissolved it.

By 1628, Charles was forced to call Parliament again. This time it refused to grant him any money until he signed a document that is known as the Petition of Right. In this petition, the king agreed to four points:

• He would not imprison subjects without due cause.
• He would not levy taxes without Parliament's consent.
• He would not house soldiers in private homes.
• He would not impose martial law in peacetime.

After agreeing to the petition, Charles ignored it. Even so, the petition was important. It set forth the idea that the law was higher than the king. This idea contradicted theories of absolute monarchy. In 1629, Charles dissolved Parliament and refused to call it back into session. To get money, he imposed all kinds of fees and fines on the English people. His popularity decreased year by year.

English Civil War

Charles offended Puritans by upholding the rituals of the Anglican Church. In addition, in 1637, Charles tried to force the Presbyterian Scots to accept a version of the Anglican prayer book. He wanted both his kingdoms to follow one religion. The Scots rebelled, assembled a huge army, and threatened to invade England. To meet this danger, Charles needed money—money he could get only by calling Parliament into session. This gave Parliament a chance to oppose him.

War Topples a King During the autumn of 1641, Parliament passed laws to limit royal power. Furious, Charles tried to arrest Parliament's leaders in January 1642, but they escaped. Equally furious, a mob of Londoners raged outside the palace. Charles fled London and raised an army in the north of England, where people were loyal to him.

From 1642 to 1649, supporters and opponents of King Charles fought the **English Civil War**. Those who remained loyal to Charles were called Royalists or Cavaliers. On the other side were Puritan supporters of Parliament. Because these men wore their hair short over their ears, Cavaliers called them Roundheads.

At first neither side could gain a lasting advantage. However, by 1644 the Puritans found a general who could win—**Oliver Cromwell**. In 1645, Cromwell's New Model Army began defeating the Cavaliers, and the tide turned toward the Puritans. In 1647, they held the king prisoner.

In 1649, Cromwell and the Puritans brought Charles to trial for treason against Parliament. They found him guilty and sentenced him to death. The execution of Charles was revolutionary. Kings had often been overthrown, killed in battle, or put to death in secret. Never before, however, had a reigning monarch faced a public trial and execution.

Cromwell's Rule Cromwell now held the reins of power. In 1649, he abolished the monarchy and the House of Lords. He established a commonwealth, a republican form of government. In 1653, Cromwell sent home the remaining members of Parliament. Cromwell's associate John Lambert drafted a constitution, the first written constitution of any modern European state. However, Cromwell eventually tore up the document and became a military dictator. **A**

MAIN IDEA

Comparing
A What did Cromwell's rule have in common with an absolute monarchy?

Cromwell almost immediately had to put down a rebellion in Ireland. English colonization of Ireland had begun in the 1100s under Henry II. Henry VIII and his children had brought the country firmly under English rule in the 1500s. In 1649, Cromwell landed on Irish shores with an army and crushed the uprising. He seized the lands and homes of the Irish and gave them to English soldiers. Fighting, plague, and famine killed hundreds of thousands.

Puritan Morality In England, Cromwell and the Puritans sought to reform society. They made laws that promoted Puritan morality and abolished activities they found sinful, such as the theater, sporting events, and dancing. Although he was a strict

▼ This engraving depicts the beheading of Charles I.

The English Civil War, 1642–1645

December 1642

SCOTLAND

North Sea

IRELAND

ENGLAND

Edgehill
Oct. 1642 ✳

London ●

50°N

December 1643

SCOTLAND

North Sea

IRELAND

Adwalton Moor
June 1643 ✳

ENGLAND

London ●

December 1644

SCOTLAND

IRELAND

Marston Moor
July 1644 ✳

ENGLAND

London ●

N

58°N   0   250 Miles
0   500 Kilometers

58°N

December 1645

SCOTLAND

IRELAND

ENGLAND

Naseby
June 1645 ✳

London ●

50°N

■ Area controlled by Puritans
■ Area controlled by Royalists
✳ Battle

GEOGRAPHY SKILLBUILDER: Interpreting Maps
1. **Movement** *Explain which side gained and which side lost territory during each year from 1643 to 1645.*
2. **Place** *Which side maintained control of London? Why would this be important?*

Puritan, Cromwell favored religious toleration for all Christians except Catholics. He even allowed Jews to return; they had been expelled from England in 1290.

Restoration and Revolution

Oliver Cromwell ruled until his death in 1658. Shortly afterward, the government he had established collapsed, and a new Parliament was selected. The English people were sick of military rule. In 1659, Parliament voted to ask the older son of Charles I to rule England.

Charles II Reigns When Prince Charles entered London in 1660, crowds shouted joyfully and bells rang. On this note of celebration, the reign of Charles II began. Because he restored the monarchy, the period of his rule is called the **Restoration**.

During Charles II's reign, Parliament passed an important guarantee of freedom, **habeas corpus**. *Habeas corpus* is Latin meaning "to have the body." This 1679 law gave every prisoner the right to obtain a writ or document ordering that the prisoner be brought before a judge to specify the charges against the prisoner. The judge would decide whether the prisoner should be tried or set free. Because of the Habeas Corpus Act, a monarch could not put someone in jail simply for opposing the ruler. Also, prisoners could not be held indefinitely without trials.

In addition, Parliament debated who should inherit Charles's throne. Because Charles had no legitimate child, his heir was his brother James, who was Catholic. A group called the Whigs opposed James, and a group called the Tories supported him. These two groups were the ancestors of England's first political parties.

James II and the Glorious Revolution In 1685, Charles II died, and James II became king. James soon offended his subjects by displaying his Catholicism. Violating English law, he appointed several Catholics to high office. When Parliament protested, James dissolved it. In 1688, James's second wife gave birth to a son. English Protestants became terrified at the prospect of a line of Catholic kings.

James had an older daughter, Mary, who was Protestant. She was also the wife of William of Orange, a prince of the Netherlands. Seven members of Parliament invited William and Mary to overthrow James for the sake of Protestantism. When William led his army to London in 1688, James fled to France. This bloodless overthrow of King James II is called the **Glorious Revolution**. **B**

MAIN IDEA

Contrasting
B How was the overthrow of James II different from the overthrow of Charles I?

Limits on Monarch's Power

At their coronation, William and Mary vowed to recognize Parliament as their partner in governing. England had become not an absolute monarchy but a **constitutional monarchy**, where laws limited the ruler's power.

Bill of Rights To make clear the limits of royal power, Parliament drafted a Bill of Rights in 1689. This document listed many things that a ruler could not do:

- no suspending of Parliament's laws
- no levying of taxes without a specific grant from Parliament
- no interfering with freedom of speech in Parliament
- no penalty for a citizen who petitions the king about grievances

William and Mary consented to these and other limits on their royal power.

Cabinet System Develops After 1688, no British monarch could rule without the consent of Parliament. At the same time, Parliament could not rule without the consent of the monarch. If the two disagreed, government came to a standstill.

During the 1700s, this potential problem was remedied by the development of a group of government ministers, or officials, called the **cabinet**. These ministers acted in the ruler's name but in reality represented the major party of Parliament. Therefore, they became the link between the monarch and the majority party in Parliament.

Over time, the cabinet became the center of power and policymaking. Under the cabinet system, the leader of the majority party in Parliament heads the cabinet and is called the prime minister. This system of English government continues today.

SECTION 5 ASSESSMENT

TERMS & NAMES 1. For each term or name, write a sentence explaining its significance.
- Charles I • English Civil War • Oliver Cromwell • Restoration • *habeas corpus* • Glorious Revolution • constitutional monarchy • cabinet

USING YOUR NOTES

2. What patterns do you see in the causes of these conflicts?

Monarch	Conflicts with Parliament
James I	
Charles I	
James II	

MAIN IDEAS

3. Why was the death of Charles I revolutionary?

4. What rights were guaranteed by the Habeas Corpus Act?

5. How does a constitutional monarchy differ from an absolute monarchy?

CRITICAL THINKING & WRITING

6. **EVALUATING DECISIONS** In your opinion, which decisions by Charles I made his conflict with Parliament worse? Explain.

7. **MAKING INFERENCES** Why do you think James II fled to France when William of Orange led his army to London?

8. **SYNTHESIZING** What conditions in England made the execution of one king and the overthrow of another possible?

9. **WRITING ACTIVITY** REVOLUTION Write a **persuasive essay** for an underground newspaper designed to incite the British people to overthrow Charles I.

CONNECT TO TODAY DRAWING A POLITICAL CARTOON

Yet another revolution threatens the monarchy today in Great Britain. Some people would like to see the monarchy ended altogether. Find out what you can about the issue and choose a side. Represent your position on the issue in an original **political cartoon.**

VISUAL SUMMARY

Absolute Monarchs in Europe

Long-Term Causes

- decline of feudalism
- rise of cities and support of middle class
- growth of national kingdoms
- loss of Church authority

Immediate Causes

- religious and territorial conflicts
- buildup of armies
- need for increased taxes
- revolts by peasants or nobles

European Monarchs Claim Divine Right to Rule Absolutely

Immediate Effects

- regulation of religion and society
- larger courts
- huge building projects
- new government bureaucracies appointed by the government
- loss of power by nobility and legislatures

Long-Term Effects

- revolution in France
- western European influence on Russia
- English political reforms that influence U.S. democracy

TERMS & NAMES

For each term or name below, briefly explain its connection to European history from 1500 to 1800.

1. absolute monarch
2. divine right
3. Louis XIV
4. War of the Spanish Succession
5. Thirty Years' War
6. Seven Years' War
7. Peter the Great
8. English Civil War
9. Glorious Revolution
10. constitutional monarchy

MAIN IDEAS

Spain's Empire and European Absolutism Section 1 (pages 155–161)

11. What three actions demonstrated that Philip II of Spain saw himself as a defender of Catholicism?
12. According to French writer Jean Bodin, should a prince share power with anyone else? Explain why or why not.

The Reign of Louis XIV Section 2 (pages 162–168)

13. What strategies did Louis XIV use to control the French nobility?
14. In what ways did Louis XIV cause suffering to the French people?

Central European Monarchs Clash Section 3 (pages 169–173)

15. What were six results of the Peace of Westphalia?
16. Why did Maria Theresa and Frederick the Great fight two wars against each other?

Absolute Rulers of Russia Section 4 (pages 174–179)

17. What were three differences between Russia and western Europe?
18. What was Peter the Great's primary goal for Russia?

Parliament Limits the English Monarchy Section 5 (pages 180–183)

19. List the causes, participants, and outcome of the English Civil War.
20. How did Parliament try to limit the power of the English monarchy?

CRITICAL THINKING

1. USING YOUR NOTES

POWER AND AUTHORITY In a chart, list actions that absolute monarchs took to increase their power. Then identify the monarchs who took these actions.

Actions of Absolute Rulers	Monarchs Who Took Them

2. DRAWING CONCLUSIONS

ECONOMICS What benefits might absolute monarchs hope to gain by increasing their countries' territory?

3. DEVELOPING HISTORICAL PERSPECTIVE

What conditions fostered the rise of absolute monarchs in Europe?

4. COMPARING AND CONTRASTING

Compare the reign of Louis XIV with that of Peter the Great. Which absolute ruler had a more lasting impact on his country? Explain why.

5. HYPOTHESIZING

Would Charles I have had a different fate if he had been king of another country in western or central Europe? Why or why not?

Use the excerpt from the English Bill of Rights passed in 1689 and your knowledge of world history to answer questions 1 and 2.
Additional Test Practice, pp. S1–S33.

PRIMARY SOURCE

That the pretended power of suspending [canceling] of laws or the execution [carrying out] of laws by regal authority without consent of Parliament is illegal; . . .

That it is the right of the subjects to petition [make requests of] the king, and all commitments [imprisonments] and prosecutions for such petitioning are illegal;

That the raising or keeping a standing army within the kingdom in time of peace, unless it be with consent of Parliament, is against the law; . . .

That election of members of Parliament ought to be free [not restricted].

English Bill of Rights

1. According to the excerpt, which of the following is illegal?

A. the enactment of laws without Parliament's permission

B. the unrestricted election of members of Parliament

C. the right of subjects to make requests of the king

D. keeping a standing army in time of peace with Parliament's consent

2. The English Bill of Rights was passed as a means to

A. limit Parliament's power.

B. increase Parliament's power.

C. overthrow the monarch.

D. increase the monarch's power.

Use the map and your knowledge of world history to answer question 3.

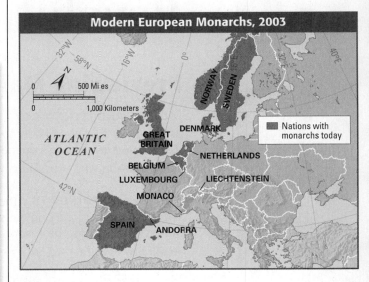

Modern European Monarchs, 2003

3. Of the countries that you studied in this chapter, which have monarchs today?

A. Spain, Great Britain, the Netherlands

B. Liechtenstein, Monaco

C. Luxembourg, Andorra

D. Great Britain, Norway, Sweden

INTEGRATED TECHNOLOGY

TEST PRACTICE Go to **classzone.com**

- Diagnostic tests
- Tutorials
- Strategies
- Additional practice

ALTERNATIVE ASSESSMENT

1. Interact with History

On page 154, you thought about the advantages and disadvantages of absolute power. Now that you have read the chapter, what do you consider to be the main advantage and the main disadvantage of being an absolute ruler?

2. WRITING ABOUT HISTORY

[REVOLUTION] Reread the information on Oliver Cromwell. Then write a **History Maker,** like the ones you've seen throughout this textbook, on Cromwell as a leader of a successful revolution. Be sure to

- include biographical information about Cromwell.
- discuss his effectiveness as a leader.
- use vivid language to hold your reader's attention.

INTEGRATED TECHNOLOGY

Creating a Television News Report

Use a video recorder to tape a television news report on the trial of Charles I. Role-play an announcer reporting a breaking news story. Relate the facts of the trial and interview key participants, including:

- a member of Parliament
- a Puritan
- a Royalist
- Charles I

CHAPTER

6

Enlightenment and Revolution, 1550–1789

Previewing Main Ideas

SCIENCE AND TECHNOLOGY The Scientific Revolution began when astronomers questioned how the universe operates. By shattering long-held views, these astronomers opened a new world of discovery.

Geography *In what Russian city did Enlightenment ideas bloom?*

POWER AND AUTHORITY The thinkers of the Enlightenment challenged old ideas about power and authority. Such new ways of thinking led to, among other things, the American Revolution.

Geography *Where had Enlightenment ideas spread outside Europe?*

REVOLUTION Between the 16th and 18th centuries, a series of revolutions helped to usher in the modern era in Western history. Revolutions in both thought and action forever changed European and American society.

Geography *What city in Brandenburg-Prussia was an Enlightenment center?*

INTEGRATED TECHNOLOGY

eEdition
• Interactive Maps
• Interactive Visuals
• Interactive Primary Sources

INTERNET RESOURCES
Go to **classzone.com** for:
• Research Links • Maps
• Internet Activities • Test Practice
• Primary Sources • Current Events
• Chapter Quiz

EUROPE AND NORTH AMERICA

1543
Copernicus publishes heliocentric theory.

1609
◄ Galileo observes heavens through a telescope similar to this one.

1500

1600

WORLD

1556
◄ Golden Age of Mughal Empire begins in India. (portrait of Mughal princess)

1603
Tokugawa Ieyasu becomes ruler of all Japan.

186

Centers of Enlightenment, c. 1740

British North American Colonies

Boston
Philadelphia

N

0   150   300 Miles
0   150 300 Kilometers
Conic Projection

NORWAY
SWEDEN
St. Petersburg
Stockholm

RUSSIA

Edinburgh

IRELAND
Dublin

North Sea

Copenhagen
DENMARK

EAST PRUSSIA

GREAT BRITAIN

UNITED NETHERLANDS

London

Amsterdam

BRANDENBURG-PRUSSIA
Berlin

POLAND

AUSTRIAN NETH.

SAXONY

SMALL GERMAN STATES

Paris

FRANCE

SWITZERLAND

AUSTRIA
Vienna

HUNGARY

SAVOY

ITALIAN STATES

PAPAL STATES

OTTOMAN EMPIRE

Baltic Sea

PORTUGAL
Lisbon

SPAIN
Madrid

N
W   E
S

SARDINIA (SAVOY)

Adriatic Sea

KINGDOM OF THE TWO SICILIES

◆ Enlightenment Centers

Mediterranean Sea

0   250   500 Miles
0   250   500 Kilometers
Conic Projection

1687
Newton publishes treatise on law of gravity.

1776
◄ With Liberty Bell symbolizing their freedom, American colonies declare independence.

1789
Revolution erupts in France.

1700

1800

1644
Manchus invade China and establish Qing Dynasty. (Qing ruler Lohan) ▶

1722
Chinese emperor Kangxi dies after a 61-year reign.

1776
Tukolor Kingdom arises in the former Songhai region of West Africa.

How would you react to a revolutionary idea?

You are a university student during the late 1600s, and it seems that the world as you know it has turned upside down. An English scientist named Isaac Newton has just theorized that the universe is not a dark mystery but a system whose parts work together in ways that can be expressed mathematically. This is just the latest in a series of arguments that have challenged old ways of thinking in fields from astronomy to medicine. Many of these ideas promise to open the way for improving society. And yet they are such radical ideas that many people refuse to accept them.

▲ This painting by English artist Joseph Wright depicts adults and children gazing at a miniature planetarium and its new ideas about the universe.

EXAMINING *the* ISSUES

- **Why might people have difficulty accepting new ideas or ways of thinking?**

- **What are the risks of embracing a different idea? What are some risks of always refusing to do so?**

Meet in small groups and discuss these questions. As you discuss these and other issues, recall other times in history when people expressed ideas that were different from accepted ones. As you read this chapter, watch for the effects of revolutionary ideas, beliefs, and discoveries.

The Scientific Revolution

MAIN IDEA	WHY IT MATTERS NOW	TERMS & NAMES
SCIENCE AND TECHNOLOGY In the mid-1500s, scientists began to question accepted beliefs and make new theories based on experimentation.	Such questioning led to the development of the scientific method still in use today.	• geocentric theory • Scientific Revolution • heliocentric theory • Galileo Galilei • scientific method • Isaac Newton

SETTING THE STAGE As you recall, the period between 1300 and 1600 was a time of great change in Europe. The Renaissance, a rebirth of learning and the arts, inspired a spirit of curiosity in many fields. Scholars began to question ideas that had been accepted for hundreds of years. Meanwhile, the religious movement known as the Reformation prompted followers to challenge accepted ways of thinking about God and salvation. While the Reformation was taking place, another revolution in European thought had begun, one that would permanently change how people viewed the physical world.

The Roots of Modern Science

Before 1500, scholars generally decided what was true or false by referring to an ancient Greek or Roman author or to the Bible. Few European scholars challenged the scientific ideas of the ancient thinkers or the church by carefully observing nature for themselves.

The Medieval View During the Middle Ages, most scholars believed that the earth was an immovable object located at the center of the universe. According to that belief, the moon, the sun, and the planets all moved in perfectly circular paths around the earth. Common sense seemed to support this view. After all, the sun appeared to be moving around the earth as it rose in the morning and set in the evening.

This earth-centered view of the universe was called the **geocentric theory**. The idea came from Aristotle, the Greek philosopher of the fourth century B.C. The Greek astronomer Ptolemy (TOL•a•mee) expanded the theory in the second century A.D. In addition, Christianity taught that God had deliberately placed the earth at the center of the universe. Earth was thus a special place on which the great drama of life unfolded.

A New Way of Thinking Beginning in the mid-1500s, a few scholars published works that challenged the ideas of the ancient thinkers and the church. As these scholars replaced old assumptions with new theories, they launched a change in European thought that historians call the **Scientific Revolution**. The Scientific Revolution was a new way of thinking about the natural world. That way was based upon careful observation and a willingness to question accepted beliefs.

TAKING NOTES
Analyzing Causes Use a diagram to list the events and circumstances that led to the Scientific Revolution.

Causes of the Scientific Revolution

A combination of discoveries and circumstances led to the Scientific Revolution and helped spread its impact. During the Renaissance, European explorers traveled to Africa, Asia, and the Americas. Such lands were inhabited by peoples and animals previously unknown in Europe. These discoveries opened Europeans to the possibility that there were new truths to be found. The invention of the printing press during this period helped spread challenging ideas—both old and new— more widely among Europe's thinkers.

The age of European exploration also fueled a great deal of scientific research, especially in astronomy and mathematics. Navigators needed better instruments and geographic measurements, for example, to determine their location in the open sea. As scientists began to look more closely at the world around them, they made observations that did not match the ancient beliefs. They found they had reached the limit of the classical world's knowledge. Yet, they still needed to know more.

A Revolutionary Model of the Universe

An early challenge to accepted scientific thinking came in the field of astronomy. It started when a small group of scholars began to question the geocentric theory.

The Heliocentric Theory Although backed by authority and common sense, the geocentric theory did not accurately explain the movements of the sun, moon, and planets. This problem troubled a Polish cleric and astronomer named Nicolaus Copernicus (koh•PUR•nuh•kuhs). In the early 1500s, Copernicus became interested in an old Greek idea that the sun stood at the center of the universe. After studying planetary movements for more than 25 years, Copernicus reasoned that indeed, the stars, the earth, and the other planets revolved around the sun.

Copernicus's **heliocentric**, or sun-centered, **theory** still did not completely explain why the planets orbited the way they did. He also knew that most scholars and clergy would reject his theory because it contradicted their religious views.

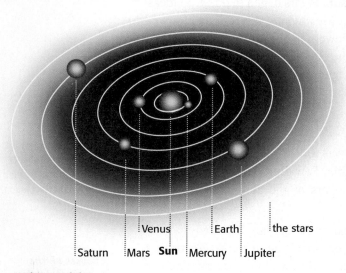

▲ This model shows how Copernicus saw the planets revolving around the sun.

Saturn Mars **Sun** Mercury Jupiter
Venus Earth the stars

Fearing ridicule or persecution, Copernicus did not publish his findings until 1543, the last year of his life. He received a copy of his book, *On the Revolutions of the Heavenly Bodies,* on his deathbed.

While revolutionary, Copernicus's book caused little stir at first. Over the next century and a half, other scientists built on the foundations he had laid. A Danish astronomer, Tycho Brahe (TEE•koh brah), carefully recorded the movements of the planets for many years. Brahe produced mountains of accurate data based on his observations. However, it was left to his followers to make mathematical sense of them.

After Brahe's death in 1601, his assistant, a brilliant mathematician named Johannes Kepler, continued his work. After studying Brahe's data, Kepler concluded that certain mathematical laws govern planetary motion. One of these laws showed that the planets revolve around the sun in elliptical orbits instead of circles, as was previously thought. Kepler's laws showed that Copernicus's basic ideas were true. They demonstrated mathematically that the planets revolve around the sun. **Ⓐ**

MAIN IDEA

Recognizing Effects
Ⓐ How did Kepler's findings support the helio-centric theory?

Galileo's Discoveries An Italian scientist named <u>Galileo Galilei</u> built on the new theories about astronomy. As a young man, Galileo learned that a Dutch lens maker had built an instrument that could enlarge far-off objects. Galileo built his own telescope and used it to study the heavens in 1609.

Then, in 1610, he published a small book called *Starry Messenger,* which described his astonishing observations. Galileo announced that Jupiter had four moons and that the sun had dark spots. He also noted that the earth's moon had a rough, uneven surface. This shattered Aristotle's theory that the moon and stars were made of a pure, perfect substance. Galileo's observations, as well as his laws of motion, also clearly supported the theories of Copernicus.

Conflict with the Church Galileo's findings frightened both Catholic and Protestant leaders because they went against church teaching and authority. If people believed the church could be wrong about this, they could question other church teachings as well.

In 1616, the Catholic Church warned Galileo not to defend the ideas of Copernicus. Although Galileo remained publicly silent, he continued his studies. Then, in 1632, he published *Dialogue Concerning the Two Chief World Systems.* This book presented the ideas of both Copernicus and Ptolemy, but it clearly showed that Galileo supported the Copernican theory. The pope angrily summoned Galileo to Rome to stand trial before the Inquisition.

Galileo stood before the court in 1633. Under the threat of torture, he knelt before the cardinals and read aloud a signed confession. In it, he agreed that the ideas of Copernicus were false.

▲ Galileo stands before the papal court.

MAIN IDEA

Analyzing Primary Sources

B In what two ways does Galileo seek to appease the Church?

PRIMARY SOURCE B
With sincere heart and unpretended faith I abjure, curse, and detest the aforesaid errors and heresies [of Copernicus] and also every other error . . . contrary to the Holy Church, and I swear that in the future I will never again say or assert . . . anything that might cause a similar suspicion toward me.

GALILEO GALILEI, quoted in
The Discoverers

Galileo was never again a free man. He lived under house arrest and died in 1642 at his villa near Florence. However, his books and ideas still spread all over Europe. (In 1992, the Catholic Church officially acknowledged that Galileo had been right.)

The Scientific Method

The revolution in scientific thinking that Copernicus, Kepler, and Galileo began eventually developed into a new approach to science called the <u>scientific method</u>. The scientific method is a logical procedure for gathering and testing ideas. It begins with a problem or question arising from an observation. Scientists next form a hypothesis, or unproved assumption. The hypothesis is then tested in an experiment or on the basis of data. In the final step, scientists analyze and interpret their data to reach a new conclusion. That conclusion either confirms or disproves the hypothesis.

Major Steps in the Scientific Revolution

1566 Marie de Coste Blanche publishes *The Nature of the Sun and Earth.*

1609 Kepler publishes first two laws of planetary motion.

1610 Galileo publishes *Starry Messenger.*

1520   1570   1620

1543 Copernicus publishes heliocentric theory.

Vesalius publishes human anatomy textbook.

1590 Janssen invents microscope.

1620 Bacon's book *Novum Organum* (New Instrument) encourages experimental method.

▲ Nicolaus Copernicus began the Scientific Revolution with his heliocentric theory.

Bacon and Descartes The scientific method did not develop overnight. The work of two important thinkers of the 1600s, Francis Bacon and René Descartes (day•KAHRT), helped to advance the new approach.

Francis Bacon, an English statesman and writer, had a passionate interest in science. He believed that by better understanding the world, scientists would generate practical knowledge that would improve people's lives. In his writings, Bacon attacked medieval scholars for relying too heavily on the conclusions of Aristotle and other ancient thinkers. Instead of reasoning from abstract theories, he urged scientists to experiment and then draw conclusions. This approach is called empiricism, or the experimental method.

In France, René Descartes also took a keen interest in science. He developed analytical geometry, which linked algebra and geometry. This provided an important new tool for scientific research.

Like Bacon, Descartes believed that scientists needed to reject old assumptions and teachings. As a mathematician, however, he approached gaining knowledge differently than Bacon. Rather than using experimentation, Descartes relied on mathematics and logic. He believed that everything should be doubted until proved by reason. The only thing he knew for certain was that he existed—because, as he wrote, "I think, therefore I am." From this starting point, he followed a train of strict reasoning to arrive at other basic truths. **C**

Modern scientific methods are based on the ideas of Bacon and Descartes. Scientists have shown that observation and experimentation, together with general laws that can be expressed mathematically, can lead people to a better understanding of the natural world.

MAIN IDEA

Contrasting
C How did Descartes's approach to science differ from Bacon's?

Newton Explains the Law of Gravity

By the mid-1600s, the accomplishments of Copernicus, Kepler, and Galileo had shattered the old views of astronomy and physics. Later, the great English scientist **Isaac Newton** helped to bring together their breakthroughs under a single theory of motion.

Changing Idea: Scientific Method	
Old Science	**New Science**
Scholars generally relied on ancient authorities, church teachings, common sense, and reasoning to explain the physical world.	In time, scholars began to use observation, experimentation, and scientific reasoning to gather knowledge and draw conclusions about the physical world.

1628 Harvey reveals how human heart functions.

1637 Descartes's book *Discourse on Method* sets forth his scientific method of reasoning from the basis of doubt.

1662 Boyle discovers mathematical relationship between the pressure and volume of gases, known as Boyle's law.

1674 Leeuwenhoek observes bacteria through microscope.

1714 Fahrenheit invents mercury thermometer.

1620   1670   1720

1633 Galileo faces Inquisition for support of Copernicus's theory.

1643 Torricelli invents barometer.

1666 France establishes Academy of Sciences.

1660 England establishes Royal Society to support scientific study.

1687 Newton publishes law of gravity.

▲ Isaac Newton's law of gravity explained how the same physical laws governed motion both on earth and in the heavens.

Newton studied mathematics and physics at Cambridge University. By the time he was 26, Newton was certain that all physical objects were affected equally by the same forces. Newton's great discovery was that the same force ruled motion of the planets and all matter on earth and in space. The key idea that linked motion in the heavens with motion on the earth was the law of universal gravitation. According to this law, every object in the universe attracts every other object. The degree of attraction depends on the mass of the objects and the distance between them.

In 1687, Newton published his ideas in a work called *The Mathematical Principles of Natural Philosophy*. It was one of the most important scientific books ever written. The universe he described was like a giant clock. Its parts all worked together perfectly in ways that could be expressed mathematically. Newton believed that God was the creator of this orderly universe, the clockmaker who had set everything in motion. **D**

MAIN IDEA

Clarifying

D Why was the law of gravitation important?

The Scientific Revolution Spreads

As astronomers explored the secrets of the universe, other scientists began to study the secrets of nature on earth. Careful observation and the use of the scientific method eventually became important in many different fields.

Scientific Instruments Scientists developed new tools and instruments to make the precise observations that the scientific method demanded. The first microscope was invented by a Dutch maker of eyeglasses, Zacharias Janssen (YAHN•suhn), in 1590. In the 1670s, a Dutch drapery merchant and amateur scientist named Anton van Leeuwenhoek (LAY•vuhn•HUK) used a microscope to observe bacteria swimming in tooth scrapings. He also examined red blood cells for the first time.

In 1643, one of Galileo's students, Evangelista Torricelli (TAWR•uh•CHEHL•ee), developed the first mercury barometer, a tool for measuring atmospheric pressure and predicting weather. In 1714, the German physicist Gabriel Fahrenheit (FAR•uhn•HYT) made the first thermometer to use mercury in glass. Fahrenheit's thermometer showed water freezing at 32°. A Swedish astronomer, Anders Celsius (SEHL•see•uhs), created another scale for the mercury thermometer in 1742. Celsius's scale showed freezing at 0°.

Medicine and the Human Body During the Middle Ages, European doctors had accepted as fact the writings of an ancient Greek physician named Galen. However, Galen had never dissected the body of a human being. Instead, he had studied the anatomy of pigs and other animals. Galen assumed that human anatomy was much the same. A Flemish physician named Andreas Vesalius proved Galen's assumptions wrong. Vesalius dissected human corpses and published his observations. His

The famous Dutch painter Rembrandt painted *Anatomy Lesson of Dr. Tulp* in 1632 from an actual anatomy lesson. The corpse was that of a criminal.

book, *On the Structure of the Human Body* (1543), was filled with detailed drawings of human organs, bones, and muscle.

In the late 1700s, British physician Edward Jenner introduced a vaccine to prevent smallpox. Inoculation using live smallpox germs had been practiced in Asia for centuries. While beneficial, this technique could also be dangerous. Jenner discovered that inoculation with germs from a cattle disease called cowpox gave permanent protection from smallpox for humans. Because cowpox was a much milder disease, the risks for this form of inoculation were much lower. Jenner used cowpox to produce the world's first vaccination.

Vocabulary
Inoculation is the act of injecting a germ into a person's body so as to create an immunity to the disease.

Discoveries in Chemistry Robert Boyle pioneered the use of the scientific method in chemistry. He is considered the founder of modern chemistry. In a book called *The Sceptical Chymist* (1661), Boyle challenged Aristotle's idea that the physical world consisted of four elements—earth, air, fire, and water. Instead, Boyle proposed that matter was made up of smaller primary particles that joined together in different ways. Boyle's most famous contribution to chemistry is Boyle's law. This law explains how the volume, temperature, and pressure of gas affect each other.

The notions of reason and order, which spurred so many breakthroughs in science, soon moved into other fields of life. Philosophers and scholars across Europe began to rethink long-held beliefs about the human condition, most notably the rights and liberties of ordinary citizens. These thinkers helped to usher in a movement that challenged the age-old relationship between a government and its people, and eventually changed forever the political landscape in numerous societies.

SECTION ❶ **ASSESSMENT**

TERMS & NAMES 1. For each term or name, write a sentence explaining its significance.
• geocentric theory   • Scientific Revolution   • heliocentric theory   • Galileo Galilei   • scientific method   • Isaac Newton

USING YOUR NOTES	**MAIN IDEAS**	**CRITICAL THINKING & WRITING**
2. Which event or circumstance do you consider to be the most significant? Why?	3. Before the 1500s, who and what were the final authorities with regard to most knowledge? 4. How did the heliocentric theory of the universe differ from the geocentric theory? 5. What are the main steps of the scientific method?	6. **DRAWING CONCLUSIONS** "If I have seen farther than others," said Newton, "it is because I have stood on the shoulders of giants." Could this be said of most scientific accomplishments? Explain. 7. **ANALYZING MOTIVES** Why might institutions of authority tend to reject new ideas? 8. **FORMING AND SUPPORTING OPINIONS** Do you agree with Galileo's actions during his Inquisition? Explain. 9. **WRITING ACTIVITY** ⟨SCIENCE AND TECHNOLOGY⟩ Create a television **script** for a discovery of the Scientific Revolution. Include key people, ideas, and accomplishments.

Causes of the Scientific Revolution

CONNECT TO TODAY **CREATING A GRAPHIC**

Research a modern-day invention or new way of thinking and then describe it and its impact on society to the class in a **poster** or **annotated diagram**.

The Enlightenment in Europe

MAIN IDEA	WHY IT MATTERS NOW	TERMS & NAMES
POWER AND AUTHORITY A revolution in intellectual activity changed Europeans' view of government and society.	The various freedoms enjoyed in many countries today are a result of Enlightenment thinking.	• Enlightenment • social contract • John Locke • philosophe • Voltaire • Montesquieu • Rousseau • Mary Wollstonecraft

SETTING THE STAGE In the wake of the Scientific Revolution, and the new ways of thinking it prompted, scholars and philosophers began to reevaluate old notions about other aspects of society. They sought new insight into the underlying beliefs regarding government, religion, economics, and education. Their efforts spurred the **Enlightenment**, a new intellectual movement that stressed reason and thought and the power of individuals to solve problems. Known also as the Age of Reason, the movement reached its height in the mid-1700s and brought great change to many aspects of Western civilization.

Two Views on Government

The Enlightenment started from some key ideas put forth by two English political thinkers of the 1600s, Thomas Hobbes and John Locke. Both men experienced the political turmoil of England early in that century. However, they came to very different conclusions about government and human nature.

Hobbes's Social Contract Thomas Hobbes expressed his views in a work called *Leviathan* (1651). The horrors of the English Civil War convinced him that all humans were naturally selfish and wicked. Without governments to keep order, Hobbes said, there would be "war . . . of every man against every man," and life would be "solitary, poor, nasty, brutish, and short."

Hobbes argued that to escape such a bleak life, people had to hand over their rights to a strong ruler. In exchange, they gained law and order. Hobbes called this agreement by which people created a government the **social contract**. Because people acted in their own self-interest, Hobbes said, the ruler needed total power to keep citizens under control. The best government was one that had the awesome power of a leviathan (sea monster). In Hobbes's view, such a government was an absolute monarchy, which could impose order and demand obedience.

TAKING NOTES
Outlining Use an outline to organize main ideas and details.

Enlightenment in Europe
  I. Two Views on Government
    A.
    B.
  II. The Philosophes Advocate Reason
    A.
    B.

Changing Idea: The Right to Govern	
Old Idea	**New Idea**
A monarch's rule is justified by divine right.	A government's power comes from the consent of the governed.

Locke's Natural Rights The philosopher **John Locke** held a different, more positive, view of human nature. He believed that people could learn from experience and improve themselves. As reasonable beings, they had the natural ability to govern their own affairs and to look after the welfare of society. Locke criticized absolute monarchy and favored the idea of self-government.

According to Locke, all people are born free and equal, with three natural rights—life, liberty, and property. The purpose of government, said Locke, is to protect these rights. If a government fails to do so, citizens have a right to overthrow it. Locke's theory had a deep influence on modern political thinking. His belief that a government's power comes from the consent of the people is the foundation of modern democracy. The ideas of government by popular consent and the right to rebel against unjust rulers helped inspire struggles for liberty in Europe and the Americas. **A**

MAIN IDEA

Contrasting

A How does Locke's view of human nature differ from that of Hobbes?

The Philosophes Advocate Reason

History Makers

Voltaire
1694–1778

Voltaire befriended several European monarchs and nobles. Among them was the Prussian king Frederick II. The two men seemed like ideal companions. Both were witty and preferred to dress in shabby, rumpled clothes.

Their relationship eventually soured, however. Voltaire disliked editing Frederick's mediocre poetry, while Frederick suspected Voltaire of shady business dealings. Voltaire eventually described the Prussian king as "a nasty monkey, perfidious friend, [and] wretched poet." Frederick in turn called Voltaire a "miser, dirty rogue, [and] coward."

INTEGRATED / TECHNOLOGY

RESEARCH LINKS For more on Voltaire, go to **classzone.com**

The Enlightenment reached its height in France in the mid-1700s. Paris became the meeting place for people who wanted to discuss politics and ideas. The social critics of this period in France were known as **philosophes** (FIHL•uh•SAHFS), the French word for philosophers. The philosophes believed that people could apply reason to all aspects of life, just as Isaac Newton had applied reason to science. Five concepts formed the core of their beliefs:

1. **Reason** Enlightened thinkers believed truth could be discovered through reason or logical thinking.
2. **Nature** The philosophes believed that what was natural was also good and reasonable.
3. **Happiness** The philosophes rejected the medieval notion that people should find joy in the hereafter and urged people to seek well-being on earth.
4. **Progress** The philosophes stressed that society and humankind could improve.
5. **Liberty** The philosophes called for the liberties that the English people had won in their Glorious Revolution and Bill of Rights.

Voltaire Combats Intolerance Probably the most brilliant and influential of the philosophes was François Marie Arouet. Using the pen name **Voltaire**, he published more than 70 books of political essays, philosophy, and drama.

Voltaire often used satire against his opponents. He made frequent targets of the clergy, the aristocracy, and the government. His sharp tongue made him enemies at the French court, and twice he was sent to prison. After his second jail term, Voltaire was exiled to England for more than two years.

Although he made powerful enemies, Voltaire never stopped fighting for tolerance, reason, freedom of religious belief, and freedom of speech. He used his quill pen as if it were a deadly weapon in a thinker's war against humanity's worst enemies—intolerance, prejudice, and superstition. He summed up his staunch defense of liberty in one of his most famous quotes: "I do not agree with a word you say but will defend to the death your right to say it."

Vocabulary
Satire is the use of irony, sarcasm, or wit to attack folly, vice, or stupidity.

Montesquieu and the Separation of Powers Another influential French writer, the Baron de **Montesquieu** (MAHN•tuh•SKYOO), devoted himself to the study of political liberty. Montesquieu believed that Britain was the best-governed and most politically balanced country of his own day. The British king and his ministers held executive power. They carried out the laws of the state. The members of Parliament held legislative power. They made the laws. The judges of the English courts held judicial power. They interpreted the laws to see how each applied to a specific case. Montesquieu called this division of power among different branches separation of powers.

Montesquieu oversimplified the British system. It did not actually separate powers this way. His idea, however, became a part of his most famous book, *On the Spirit of Laws* (1748). In his book, Montesquieu proposed that separation of powers would keep any individual or group from gaining total control of the government. "Power," he wrote, "should be a check to power." This idea later would be called checks and balances.

MAIN IDEA

Analyzing Issues
Ⓑ What advantages did Montesquieu see in the separation of powers?

Montesquieu's book was admired by political leaders in the British colonies of North America. His ideas about separation of powers and checks and balances became the basis for the United States Constitution. Ⓑ

Rousseau: Champion of Freedom A third great philosophe, Jean Jacques **Rousseau** (roo•SOH), was passionately committed to individual freedom. The son of a poor Swiss watchmaker, Rousseau won recognition as a writer of essays. A strange, brilliant, and controversial figure, Rousseau strongly disagreed with other

> Analyzing Primary Sources

Laws Protect Freedom

Both Montesquieu and Rousseau believed firmly that fair and just laws—not monarchs or unrestrained mobs—should govern society. Here, Rousseau argues that laws established by and for the people are the hallmark of a free society.

Laws Ensure Security

While laws work to protect citizens from abusive rulers, Montesquieu argues that they also guard against anarchy and mob rule.

PRIMARY SOURCE

I . . . therefore give the name "Republic" to every state that is governed by laws, no matter what the form of its administration may be: for only in such a case does the public interest govern, and the *res republica* rank as a *reality*. . . . Laws are, properly speaking, only the conditions of civil association. The people, being subject to the laws, ought to be their author: the conditions of the society ought to be regulated . . . by those who come together to form it.

JEAN JACQUES ROUSSEAU, *The Social Contract*

PRIMARY SOURCE

It is true that in democracies the people seem to act as they please; but political liberty does not consist in an unlimited freedom. . . . We must have continually present to our minds the difference between independence and liberty. Liberty is a right of doing whatever the laws permit, and if a citizen could do what they [the laws] forbid he would be no longer possessed of liberty, because all his fellow-citizens would have the same power.

BARON DE MONTESQUIEU, *The Spirit of Laws*

DOCUMENT-BASED QUESTIONS

1. **Analyzing Issues** *Why should citizens be the authors of society's laws, according to Rousseau?*
2. **Making Inferences** *Why does Montesquieu believe that disobeying laws leads to a loss of liberty?*

Enlightenment thinkers on many matters. Most philosophes believed that reason, science, and art would improve life for all people. Rousseau, however, argued that civilization corrupted people's natural goodness. "Man is born free, and everywhere he is in chains," he wrote.

Rousseau believed that the only good government was one that was freely formed by the people and guided by the "general will" of society—a direct democracy. Under such a government, people agree to give up some of their freedom in favor of the common good. In 1762, he explained his political philosophy in a book called *The Social Contract.*

Rousseau's view of the social contract differed greatly from that of Hobbes. For Hobbes, the social contract was an agreement between a society and its government. For Rousseau, it was an agreement among free individuals to create a society and a government.

Like Locke, Rousseau argued that legitimate government came from the consent of the governed. However, Rousseau believed in a much broader democracy than Locke had promoted. He argued that all people were equal and that titles of nobility should be abolished. Rousseau's ideas inspired many of the leaders of the French Revolution who overthrew the monarchy in 1789.

Beccaria Promotes Criminal Justice An Italian philosophe named Cesare Bonesana Beccaria (BAYK•uh•REE•ah) turned his thoughts to the justice system. He believed that laws existed to preserve social order, not to avenge crimes. Beccaria regularly criticized common abuses of justice. They included torturing of witnesses and suspects, irregular proceedings in trials, and punishments that were arbitrary or cruel. He argued that a person accused of a crime should receive a speedy trial, and that torture should never be used. Moreover, he said, the degree of punishment should be based on the seriousness of the crime. He also believed that capital punishment should be abolished.

Beccaria based his ideas about justice on the principle that governments should seek the greatest good for the greatest number of people. His ideas influenced criminal law reformers in Europe and North America.

Major Ideas of the Enlightenment

Idea	Thinker	Impact
Natural rights—life, liberty, property	Locke	Fundamental to U.S. Declaration of Independence
Separation of powers	Montesquieu	France, United States, and Latin American nations use separation of powers in new constitutions
Freedom of thought and expression	Voltaire	Guaranteed in U.S. Bill of Rights and French Declaration of the Rights of Man and Citizen; European monarchs reduce or eliminate censorship
Abolishment of torture	Beccaria	Guaranteed in U.S. Bill of Rights; torture outlawed or reduced in nations of Europe and the Americas
Religious freedom	Voltaire	Guaranteed in U.S. Bill of Rights and French Declaration of the Rights of Man and Citizen; European monarchs reduce persecution
Women's equality	Wollstonecraft	Women's rights groups form in Europe and North America

SKILLBUILDER: Interpreting Charts
1. **Analyzing Issues** *What important documents reflect the influence of Enlightenment ideas?*
2. **Forming Opinions** *Which are the two most important Enlightenment ideas? Support your answer with reasons.*

Women and the Enlightenment

The philosophes challenged many assumptions about government and society. But they often took a traditional view toward women. Rousseau, for example, developed many progressive ideas about education. However, he believed that a girl's education should mainly teach her how to be a helpful wife and mother. Other male social critics scolded women for reading novels because they thought it encouraged idleness and wickedness. Still, some male writers argued for more education for women and for women's equality in marriage.

Women writers also tried to improve the status of women. In 1694, the English writer Mary Astell published *A Serious Proposal to the Ladies.* Her book addressed the lack of educational opportunities for women. In later writings, she used Enlightenment arguments about government to criticize the unequal relationship between men and women in marriage. She wrote, "If absolute sovereignty be not necessary in a state, how comes it to be so in a family? . . . If all men are born free, how is it that all women are born slaves?"

During the 1700s, other women picked up these themes. Among the most persuasive was **Mary Wollstonecraft**, who published an essay called *A Vindication of the Rights of Woman* in 1792. In the essay, she disagreed with Rousseau that women's education should be secondary to men's. Rather, she argued that women, like men, need education to become virtuous and useful. Wollstonecraft also urged women to enter the male-dominated fields of medicine and politics. **C**

MAIN IDEA

Drawing Conclusions

C Why do you think the issue of education was important to both Astell and Wollstonecraft? .

Women made important contributions to the Enlightenment in other ways. In Paris and other European cities, wealthy women helped spread Enlightenment ideas through social gatherings called salons, which you will read about later in this chapter.

One woman fortunate enough to receive an education in the sciences was Emilie du Châtelet (shah•tlay). Du Châtelet was an aristocrat trained as a mathematician and physicist. By translating Newton's work from Latin into French, she helped stimulate interest in science in France.

History Makers

Mary Wollstonecraft
1759–1797

A strong advocate of education for women, Wollstonecraft herself received little formal schooling. She and her two sisters taught themselves by studying books at home. With her sisters, she briefly ran a school. These experiences shaped much of her thoughts about education.

Wollstonecraft eventually took a job with a London publisher. There, she met many leading radicals of the day. One of them was her future husband, the writer William Godwin. Wollstonecraft died at age 38, after giving birth to their daughter, Mary. This child, whose married name was Mary Wollstonecraft Shelley, went on to write the classic novel *Frankenstein*.

INTEGRATED TECHNOLOGY

RESEARCH LINKS For more on Mary Wollstonecraft, go to **classzone.com**

Legacy of the Enlightenment

Over a span of a few decades, Enlightenment writers challenged long-held ideas about society. They examined such principles as the divine right of monarchs, the union of church and state, and the existence of unequal social classes. They held these beliefs up to the light of reason and found them in need of reform.

The philosophes mainly lived in the world of ideas. They formed and popularized new theories. Although they encouraged reform, they were not active revolutionaries. However, their theories eventually inspired the American and French revolutions and other revolutionary movements in the 1800s. Enlightenment thinking produced three other long-term effects that helped shape Western civilization.

Belief in Progress The first effect was a belief in progress. Pioneers such as Galileo and Newton had discovered the key for unlocking the mysteries of nature in the 1500s and 1600s. With the door thus opened, the growth of scientific knowledge seemed to quicken in the 1700s. Scientists made key new discoveries in chemistry, physics, biology, and mechanics. The successes of the Scientific Revolution gave people the confidence that human reason could solve social problems. Philosophes and reformers urged an end to the practice of slavery and argued for greater social equality, as well as a more democratic style of government.

A More Secular Outlook A second outcome was the rise of a more secular, or non-religious, outlook. During the Enlightenment, people began to question openly their religious beliefs and the teachings of the church. Before the Scientific Revolution, people accepted the mysteries of the universe as the workings of God. One by one, scientists discovered that these mysteries could be explained mathematically. Newton himself was a deeply religious man, and he sought to reveal God's majesty through his work. However, his findings often caused people to change the way they thought about God.

Meanwhile, Voltaire and other critics attacked some of the beliefs and practices of organized Christianity. They wanted to rid religious faith of superstition and fear and promote tolerance of all religions.

Importance of the Individual Faith in science and in progress produced a third outcome, the rise of individualism. As people began to turn away from the church and royalty for guidance, they looked to themselves instead.

The philosophes encouraged people to use their own ability to reason in order to judge what was right or wrong. They also emphasized the importance of the individual in society. Government, they argued, was formed by individuals to promote their welfare. The British thinker Adam Smith extended the emphasis on the individual to economic thinking. He believed that individuals acting in their own self-interest created economic progress. Smith's theory is discussed in detail in Chapter 9.

During the Enlightenment, reason took center stage. The greatest minds of Europe followed each other's work with interest and often met to discuss their ideas. Some of the kings and queens of Europe were also very interested. As you will learn in Section 3, they sought to apply some of the philosophes' ideas to create progress in their countries.

SECTION 2 ASSESSMENT

TERMS & NAMES 1. For each term or name, write a sentence explaining its significance.
• Enlightenment • social contract • John Locke • philosophe • Voltaire • Montesquieu • Rousseau • Mary Wollstonecraft

USING YOUR NOTES	MAIN IDEAS	CRITICAL THINKING & WRITING

2. Which impact of the Enlightenment do you consider most important? Why?
 	
Enlightenment in Europe
I. Two Views on Government
  A.
  B.
II. The Philosophes Advocate Reason
  A.
  B.
	3. What are the natural rights with which people are born, according to John Locke?
	
	4. Who were the philosophes and what did they advocate?
	
	5. What was the legacy of the Enlightenment?
		6. **SYNTHESIZING** Explain how the following statement reflects Enlightenment ideas: "Power should be a check to power."
		
		7. **ANALYZING ISSUES** Why might some women have been critical of the Enlightenment?
		
		8. **DRAWING CONCLUSIONS** Do you think the philosophes were optimistic about the future of humankind? Explain.
		
		9. **WRITING ACTIVITY** POWER AND AUTHORITY Compare the views of Hobbes, Locke, and Rousseau on government. Then write one **paragraph** about how their ideas reflect their understanding of human behavior.

CONNECT TO TODAY PRESENTING AN ORAL REPORT

Identify someone considered a modern-day social critic. Explore the person's beliefs and methods and present your findings to the class in a brief **oral report.**

European Values During the Enlightenment

Writers and artists of the Enlightenment often used satire to comment on European values. Using wit and humor, they ridiculed various ideas and customs. Satire allowed artists to explore human faults in a way that is powerful but not preachy. In the two literary excerpts and the painting below, notice how the writer or artist makes his point.

A PRIMARY SOURCE

Voltaire

Voltaire wrote *Candide* (1759) to attack a philosophy called Optimism, which held that all is right with the world. The hero of the story, a young man named Candide, encounters the most awful disasters and human evils. In this passage, Candide meets a slave in South America, who explains why he is missing a leg and a hand.

———

"When we're working at the sugar mill and catch our finger in the grinding-wheel, they cut off our hand. When we try to run away, they cut off a leg. I have been in both of these situations. This is the price you pay for the sugar you eat in Europe. . . .

"The Dutch fetishes [i.e., missionaries] who converted me [to Christianity] tell me every Sunday that we are all the sons of Adam, Whites and Blacks alike. I'm no genealogist, but if these preachers are right, we are all cousins born of first cousins. Well, you will grant me that you can't treat a relative much worse than this."

B PRIMARY SOURCE

Jonathan Swift

The narrator of *Gulliver's Travels* (1726), an English doctor named Lemuel Gulliver, takes four disastrous voyages that leave him stranded in strange lands. In the following passage, Gulliver tries to win points with the king of Brobdingnag—a land of giants—by offering to show him how to make guns and cannons.

———

The king was struck with horror at the description I had given of those terrible engines. . . . He was amazed how so impotent and grovelling an insect as I (these were his expressions) could entertain such inhuman ideas, and in so familiar a manner as to appear wholly unmoved at all the scenes of blood and desolation, which I had painted as the common effects of those destructive machines; whereof, he said, some evil genius, enemy to mankind, must have been the first contriver [inventor].

C PRIMARY SOURCE

William Hogarth

The English artist William Hogarth often used satire in his paintings. In this painting, *Canvassing for Votes,* he comments on political corruption. While the candidate flirts with the ladies on the balcony, his supporters offer a man money for his vote.

Document-Based QUESTIONS

1. What is the main point that Voltaire is making in Source A? What technique does he use to reinforce his message?

2. What does the king's reaction in Source B say about Swift's view of Europe's military technology?

3. Why might Hogarth's painting in Source C be difficult for modern audiences to understand? Does this take away from his message?

The Enlightenment Spreads

MAIN IDEA	WHY IT MATTERS NOW	TERMS & NAMES
POWER AND AUTHORITY Enlightenment ideas spread through the Western world and profoundly influenced the arts and government.	An "enlightened" problem-solving approach to government and society prevails in modern civilization today.	• salon • baroque • neoclassical • enlightened despot • Catherine the Great

SETTING THE STAGE The philosophes' views about society often got them in trouble. In France it was illegal to criticize either the Catholic Church or the government. Many philosophes landed in jail or were exiled. Voltaire, for example, experienced both punishments. Nevertheless, the Enlightenment spread throughout Europe with the help of books, magazines, and word of mouth. In time, Enlightenment ideas influenced everything from the artistic world to the royal courts across the continent.

TAKING NOTES

Summarizing Use a web diagram to list examples of each concept related to the spread of ideas.

A World of Ideas

In the 1700s, Paris was the cultural and intellectual capital of Europe. Young people from around Europe—and also from the Americas—came to study, philosophize, and enjoy the culture of the bustling city. The brightest minds of the age gathered there. From their circles radiated the ideas of the Enlightenment.

The buzz of Enlightenment ideas was most intense in the mansions of several wealthy women of Paris. There, in their large drawing rooms, these hostesses held regular social gatherings called **salons**. At these events, philosophers, writers, artists, scientists, and other great intellects met to discuss ideas.

Diderot's *Encyclopedia* The most influential of the salon hostesses in Voltaire's time was Marie-Thérèse Geoffrin (zhuh•frehn). She helped finance the project of a leading philosophe named Denis Diderot (DEE•duh•ROH). Diderot created a large set of books to which many leading scholars of Europe contributed articles and essays. He called it *Encyclopedia* and began publishing the first volumes in 1751.

The Enlightenment views expressed in the articles soon angered both the French government and the Catholic Church. Their censors banned the work. They said it undermined royal authority, encouraged a spirit of revolt, and fostered "moral corruption, irreligion, and unbelief." Nonetheless, Diderot continued publishing his *Encyclopedia*.

The salons and the *Encyclopedia* helped spread Enlightenment ideas to educated people all over Europe. Enlightenment ideas also eventually spread through newspapers, pamphlets, and even political songs. Enlightenment ideas about government and equality attracted the attention of a growing literate middle class, which could afford to buy many books and support the work of artists.

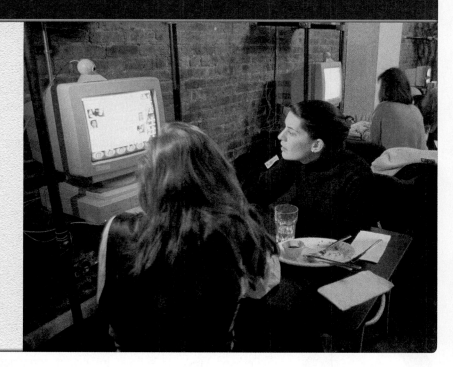

New Artistic Styles

The Enlightenment ideals of order and reason were reflected in the arts—music, literature, painting, and architecture.

Neoclassical Style Emerges European art of the 1600s and early 1700s had been dominated by the style called **baroque**, which was characterized by a grand, ornate design. Baroque styles could be seen in elaborate palaces such as Versailles (see page 166) and in numerous paintings.

Under the influence of the Enlightenment, styles began to change. Artists and architects worked in a simple and elegant style that borrowed ideas and themes from classical Greece and Rome. The artistic style of the late 1700s is therefore called **neoclassical** ("new classical").

Changes in Music and Literature Music styles also changed to reflect Enlightenment ideals. The music scene in Europe had been dominated by such composers as Johann Sebastian Bach of Germany and George Friedrich Handel of England. These artists wrote dramatic organ and choral music. During the Enlightenment, a new, lighter, and more elegant style of music known as *classical* emerged. Three composers in Vienna, Austria, rank among the greatest figures of the classical period in music. They were Franz Joseph Haydn, Wolfgang Amadeus Mozart, and Ludwig van Beethoven.

Writers in the 18th century also developed new styles and forms of literature. A number of European authors began writing novels, which are lengthy works of prose fiction. Their works had carefully crafted plots, used suspense, and explored characters' thoughts and feelings. These books were popular with a wide middle-class audience, who liked the entertaining stories written in everyday language. Writers, including many women, turned out a flood of popular novels in the 1700s.

Samuel Richardson's *Pamela* is often considered the first true English novel. It tells the story of a young servant girl who refuses the advances of her master. Another English masterpiece, *Tom Jones,* by Henry Fielding, tells the story of an orphan who travels all over England to win the hand of his lady.

Enlightenment and Monarchy

From the salons, artists' studios, and concert halls of Europe, the Enlightenment spirit also swept through Europe's royal courts. Many philosophes, including Voltaire, believed that the best form of government was a monarchy in which the ruler respected the people's rights. The philosophes tried to convince monarchs to rule justly. Some monarchs embraced the new ideas and made reforms that reflected the Enlightenment spirit. They became known as **enlightened despots**. Despot means "absolute ruler."

The enlightened despots supported the philosophes' ideas. But they also had no intention of giving up any power. The changes they made were motivated by two desires: they wanted to make their countries stronger and their own rule more effective. The foremost of Europe's enlightened despots were Frederick II of Prussia, Holy Roman Emperor Joseph II of Austria, and Catherine the Great of Russia. **Ⓐ**

Frederick the Great Frederick II, the king of Prussia from 1740 to 1786, committed himself to reforming Prussia. He granted many religious freedoms, reduced censorship, and improved education. He also reformed the justice system and abolished the use of torture. However, Frederick's changes only went so far. For example, he believed that serfdom was wrong, but he did nothing to end it since he needed the support of wealthy landowners. As a result, he never tried to change the existing social order.

Perhaps Frederick's most important contribution was his attitude toward being king. He called himself "the first servant of the state." From the beginning of his reign, he made it clear that his goal was to serve and strengthen his country. This attitude was clearly one that appealed to the philosophes.

Joseph II The most radical royal reformer was Joseph II of Austria. The son and successor of Maria Theresa, Joseph II ruled Austria from 1780 to 1790. He introduced legal reforms and freedom of the press. He also supported freedom of worship, even for Protestants, Orthodox Christians, and Jews. In his most radical reform, Joseph abolished serfdom and ordered that peasants be paid for their labor with cash. Not surprisingly, the nobles firmly resisted this change. Like many of Joseph's reforms, it was undone after his death.

▲ Joseph II

Catherine the Great The ruler most admired by the philosophes was Catherine II, known as **Catherine the Great**. She ruled Russia from 1762 to 1796. The well-educated empress read the works of philosophes, and she exchanged many letters with Voltaire. She ruled with absolute authority but also sought to reform Russia.

In 1767, Catherine formed a commission to review Russia's laws. She presented it with a brilliant proposal for reforms based on the ideas of Montesquieu and Beccaria. Among other changes, she recommended allowing religious toleration and abolishing torture and capital punishment. Her commission, however, accomplished none of these lofty goals.

Catherine eventually put in place limited reforms, but she did little to improve the life of the Russian peasants. Her views about enlightened ideas changed after a massive uprising of serfs in 1773. With great brutality, Catherine's army crushed the

MAIN IDEA

Analyzing Motives
Ⓐ Why did the enlightened despots undertake reforms?

Vocabulary
Serfdom was a system in which peasants were forced to live and work on a landowner's estate.

Changing Idea: Relationship Between Ruler and State	
Old Idea	**New Idea**
The state and its citizens exist to serve the monarch. As Louis XIV reportedly said, "I am the state."	The monarch exists to serve the state and support citizens' welfare. As Frederick the Great said, a ruler is only "the first servant of the state."

rebellion. Catherine had previously favored an end to serfdom. However, the revolt convinced her that she needed the nobles' support to keep her throne. Therefore, she gave the nobles absolute power over the serfs. As a result, Russian serfs lost their last traces of freedom. **B**

Catherine Expands Russia Peter the Great, who ruled Russia in the early 1700s, had fought for years to win a port on the Baltic Sea. Likewise, Catherine sought access to the Black Sea. In two wars with the Ottoman Turks, her armies finally won control of the northern shore of the Black Sea. Russia also gained the right to send ships through Ottoman-controlled straits leading from the Black Sea to the Mediterranean Sea.

Catherine also expanded her empire westward into Poland. In Poland, the king was relatively weak, and independent nobles held the most power. The three neighboring powers—Russia, Prussia, and Austria—each tried to assert their influence over the country. In 1772, these land-hungry neighbors each took a piece of Poland in what is called the First Partition of Poland. In further partitions in 1793 and 1795, they grabbed up the rest of Poland's territory. With these partitions, Poland disappeared as an independent country for more than a century.

By the end of her remarkable reign, Catherine had vastly enlarged the Russian empire. Meanwhile, as Russia was becoming an international power, another great power, Britain, faced a challenge from its North American colonies. Inspired by Enlightenment ideas, colonial leaders decided to do the unthinkable: break away from their ruling country and found an independent republic.

MAIN IDEA

Synthesizing

B How accurately does the term enlightened despot describe Catherine the Great? Explain.

History Makers

**Catherine the Great
1729–1796**

The daughter of a minor German prince, Catherine was 15 when she was handed over to marry the Grand Duke Peter, heir to the Russian throne.

Peter was mentally unstable. Catherine viewed her husband's weakness as her chance for power. She made important friends among Russia's army officers and became known as the most intelligent and best-informed person at court. In 1762, only months after her husband became czar, Catherine had him arrested and confined. Soon afterward, Peter conveniently died, probably by murder.

SECTION 3 ASSESSMENT

TERMS & NAMES 1. For each term or name, write a sentence explaining its significance.
• salon   • baroque   • neoclassical   • enlightened despot   • Catherine the Great

USING YOUR NOTES

2. What are two generalizations you could make about the spread of Enlightenment ideas?

art and literature — monarchy

Spread of Enlightenment Ideas

circulation of ideas

MAIN IDEAS

3. What were the defining aspects of neoclassical art?

4. What new form of literature emerged during the 18th century and what were its main characteristics?

5. Why were several rulers in 18th century Europe known as enlightened despots?

CRITICAL THINKING & WRITING

6. **DRAWING CONCLUSIONS** What advantages did salons have over earlier forms of communication in spreading ideas?

7. **ANALYZING ISSUES** In what way were the enlightened despots less than true reformers? Cite specific examples from the text.

8. **MAKING INFERENCES** How did the *Encyclopedia* project reflect the age of Enlightenment?

9. **WRITING ACTIVITY** POWER AND AUTHORITY Imagine you are a public relations consultant for an enlightened despot. Write a **press release** explaining why your client is "Most Enlightened Despot of the 1700s."

INTEGRATED TECHNOLOGY INTERNET ACTIVITY

Use the Internet to find out more about a composer or writer mentioned in this section. Then write a brief **character sketch** on that artist, focusing on interesting pieces of information about his or her life.

INTERNET KEYWORDS
biography European Enlightenment

The American Revolution

MAIN IDEA	WHY IT MATTERS NOW	TERMS & NAMES
REVOLUTION Enlightenment ideas helped spur the American colonies to shed British rule and create a new nation.	The revolution created a republic, the United States of America, that became a model for many nations of the world.	• Declaration of Independence • checks and balances • Thomas Jefferson • federal system • Bill of Rights

SETTING THE STAGE Philosophes such as Voltaire considered England's government the most progressive in Europe. The Glorious Revolution of 1688 had given England a constitutional monarchy. In essence, this meant that various laws limited the power of the English king. Despite the view of the philosophes, however, a growing number of England's colonists in North America accused England of tyrannical rule. Emboldened by Enlightenment ideas, they would attempt to overthrow what was then the mightiest power on earth and create their own nation.

TAKING NOTES

Identifying Problems and Solutions Use a chart to list the problems American colonists faced in shaping their republic and solutions they found.

Problem	Solution
1.	1.
2.	2.
3.	3.

Britain and Its American Colonies

Throughout the 1600s and 1700s, British colonists had formed a large and thriving settlement along the eastern shore of North America. When George III became king of Great Britain in 1760, his North American colonies were growing by leaps and bounds. Their combined population soared from about 250,000 in 1700 to 2,150,000 in 1770, a nearly ninefold increase. Economically, the colonies thrived on trade with the nations of Europe.

Along with increasing population and prosperity, a new sense of identity was growing in the colonists' minds. By the mid-1700s, colonists had been living in America for nearly 150 years. Each of the 13 colonies had its own government, and people were used to a great degree of independence. Colonists saw themselves less as British and more as Virginians or Pennsylvanians. However, they were still British subjects and were expected to obey British law.

In 1651, the British Parliament passed a trade law called the Navigation Act. This and subsequent trade laws prevented colonists from selling their most valuable products to any country except Britain. In addition, colonists had to pay high taxes on imported French and Dutch goods. Nonetheless, Britain's policies benefited both the colonies and the motherland. Britain bought American raw materials for low prices and sold manufactured goods to the colonists. And despite various British trade restrictions, colonial merchants also thrived. Such a spirit of relative harmony, however, soon would change.

▼ This French snuffbox pictures (left to right) Voltaire, Rousseau, and colonial statesman Benjamin Franklin.

Americans Win Independence

In 1754, war erupted on the North American continent between the English and the French. As you recall, the French had also colonized parts of North America throughout the 1600s and 1700s. The conflict was known as the French and Indian War. (The name stems from the fact that the French enlisted numerous Native American tribes to fight on their side.) The fighting lasted until 1763, when Britain and her colonists emerged victorious—and seized nearly all French land in North America.

The victory, however, only led to growing tensions between Britain and its colonists. In order to fight the war, Great Britain had run up a huge debt. Because American colonists benefited from Britain's victory, Britain expected the colonists to help pay the costs of the war. In 1765, Parliament passed the Stamp Act. According to this law, colonists had to pay a tax to have an official stamp put on wills, deeds, newspapers, and other printed material. **A**

American colonists were outraged. They had never paid taxes directly to the British government before. Colonial lawyers argued that the stamp tax violated colonists' natural rights, and they accused the government of "taxation without representation." In Britain, citizens consented to taxes through their representatives in Parliament. The colonists, however, had no representation in Parliament. Thus, they argued they could not be taxed.

Growing Hostility Leads to War Over the next decade, hostilities between the two sides increased. Some colonial leaders favored independence from Britain. In 1773, to protest an import tax on tea, a group of colonists dumped a large load of British tea into Boston Harbor. George III, infuriated by the "Boston Tea Party," as it was called, ordered the British navy to close the port of Boston.

Such harsh tactics by the British made enemies of many moderate colonists. In September 1774, representatives from every colony except Georgia gathered in Philadelphia to form the First Continental Congress. This group protested the treatment of Boston. When the king paid little attention to their complaints, the colonies decided to form the Second Continental Congress to debate their next move.

On April 19, 1775, British soldiers and American militiamen exchanged gunfire on the village green in Lexington, Massachusetts. The fighting spread to nearby Concord. The Second Continental Congress voted to raise an army and organize for battle under the command of a Virginian named George Washington. The American Revolution had begun.

The Influence of the Enlightenment Colonial leaders used Enlightenment ideas to justify independence. The colonists had asked for the same political rights as people in Britain, they said, but the king had stubbornly refused. Therefore, the colonists were justified in rebelling against a tyrant who had broken the social contract.

In July 1776, the Second Continental Congress issued the **Declaration of Independence**. This document, written by political leader **Thomas Jefferson**,

MAIN IDEA

Analyzing Causes

A How did the French and Indian War lead to the Stamp Act?

History Makers

Thomas Jefferson
1743–1826

The author of the Declaration of Independence, Thomas Jefferson of Virginia, was a true figure of the Enlightenment. As a writer and statesman, he supported free speech, religious freedom, and other civil liberties. At the same time, he was also a slave owner.

Jefferson was a man of many talents. He was an inventor as well as one of the great architects of early America. He designed the Virginia state capitol building in Richmond and many buildings for the University of Virginia. Of all his achievements, Jefferson wanted to be most remembered for three: author of the Declaration of Independence, author of the Statute of Virginia for Religious Freedom, and founder of the University of Virginia.

INTEGRATED / TECHNOLOGY

INTERNET ACTIVITY Create a time line of Jefferson's major achievements. Go to **classzone.com** for your research.

Changing Idea: Colonial Attachment to Britain	
Old Idea	**New Idea**
American colonists considered themselves to be subjects of the British king.	After a long train of perceived abuses by the king, the colonists asserted their right to declare independence.

was firmly based on the ideas of John Locke and the Enlightenment. The Declaration reflected these ideas in its eloquent argument for natural rights. "We hold these truths to be self-evident," states the beginning of the Declaration, "that all men are created equal, that they are endowed by their Creator with certain unalienable rights, that among these are life, liberty, and the pursuit of happiness."

Since Locke had asserted that people had the right to rebel against an unjust ruler, the Declaration of Independence included a long list of George III's abuses. The document ended by declaring the colonies' separation from Britain. The colonies, the Declaration said, "are absolved from all allegiance to the British crown."

Success for the Colonists The British were not about to let their colonies leave without a fight. Shortly after the publication of the Declaration of Independence, the two sides went to war. At first glance, the colonists seemed destined to go down in quick defeat. Washington's ragtag, poorly trained army faced the well-trained forces of the most powerful country in the world. In the end, however, the Americans won their war for independence.

Several reasons explain the colonists' success. First, the Americans' motivation for fighting was much stronger than that of the British, since their army was defending their homeland. Second, the overconfident British generals made several mistakes. Third, time itself was on the side of the Americans. The British could win battle after battle, as they did, and still lose the war. Fighting an overseas war, 3,000 miles from London, was terribly expensive. After a few years, tax-weary British citizens called for peace.

Finally, the Americans did not fight alone. Louis XVI of France had little sympathy for the ideals of the American Revolution. However, he was eager to weaken France's rival, Britain. French entry into the war in 1778 was decisive. In 1781, combined forces of about 9,500 Americans and 7,800 French trapped a British army commanded by Lord Cornwallis near Yorktown, Virginia. Unable to escape, Cornwallis eventually surrendered. The Americans had shocked the world and won their independence.

North America, 1783

British
French
Russian
Spanish
U.S. and Great Britain
U.S. and Spain

GEOGRAPHY SKILLBUILDER: Interpreting Maps
1. **Region** *What feature formed the western border of the United States?*
2. **Human-Environment Interaction** *What European countries had claims on the North American continent in 1783?*

Democracy

Ancient Greece and Rome were strong influences on the framers of the U.S. system of government. Democracy as it is practiced today, however, is different from the Greek and Roman models.

The most famous democracy today is the United States. The type of government the United States uses is called a federal republic. "Federal" means power is divided between the national and state governments. In a republic, the people vote for their representatives. Two key components of democracy in the United States are the Constitution and voting.

Enlightenment Ideas and the U.S. Constitution

Many of the ideas contained in the Constitution are built on the ideas of Enlightenment thinkers.

Enlightenment Idea	U.S. Constitution
Locke A government's power comes from the consent of the people.	• Preamble begins "We the people of the United States" to establish legitimacy. • Creates representative government • Limits government powers
Montesquieu Separation of powers	• Federal system of government • Powers divided among three branches • System of checks and balances
Rousseau Direct democracy	• Public election of president and Congress
Voltaire Free speech, religious toleration	• Bill of Rights provides for freedom of speech and religion.
Beccaria Accused have rights, no torture	• Bill of Rights protects rights of accused and prohibits cruel and unusual punishment.

Who Votes?

Voting is an essential part of democracy. Universal suffrage means that all adult citizens can vote. Universal suffrage is part of democracy in the United States today, but that was not always the case. This chart shows how the United States gradually moved toward giving all citizens the right to vote.

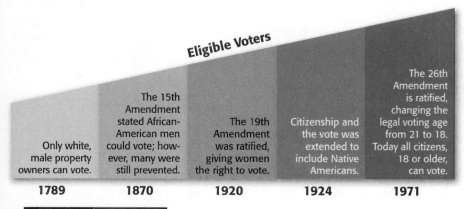

Eligible Voters

1789	**1870**	**1920**	**1924**	**1971**
Only white, male property owners can vote.	The 15th Amendment stated African-American men could vote; however, many were still prevented.	The 19th Amendment was ratified, giving women the right to vote.	Citizenship and the vote was extended to include Native Americans.	The 26th Amendment is ratified, changing the legal voting age from 21 to 18. Today all citizens, 18 or older, can vote.

INTEGRATED TECHNOLOGY

RESEARCH LINKS For more on democracy, go to **classzone.com**

> DATA FILE

U.S. Constitution
• There have been 27 amendments to the Constitution since its creation.
• The U.S. Constitution has been used by many other countries as a model for their constitutions.
• In 2002, over 120 established and emerging democracies met to discuss their common issues.

Voting
• In the 2000 U.S. presidential election, only 36.1 percent of people between 18 and 24 years old voted.
• Some countries, such as Australia, fine citizens for not voting. Australia's voter turnout has been over 90 percent since 1925.

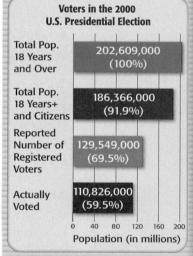

Voters in the 2000 U.S. Presidential Election

Total Pop. 18 Years and Over	202,609,000 (100%)
Total Pop. 18 Years+ and Citizens	186,366,000 (91.9%)
Reported Number of Registered Voters	129,549,000 (69.5%)
Actually Voted	110,826,000 (59.5%)

0   40   80   120   160   200
Population (in millions)

Source: U.S. Census Bureau, Current Population Survey, November 2000.

Connect *to* Today

1. **Synthesizing** If so much of the U.S. Constitution can be found in European ideas, why were the framers of the U.S. Constitution so important?
   See Skillbuilder Handbook, Page R21.

2. **Hypothesizing** Why is it important that every citizen has, and exercises, his or her right to vote?

The French Revolution

The American Revolution inspired the growing number of French people who sought reform in their own country. They saw the new government of the United States as the fulfillment of Enlightenment ideals, and longed for such a government in France.

The Declaration of Independence was widely circulated and admired in France. French officers like the Marquis de Lafayette (shown here), who fought for American independence, captivated his fellow citizens with accounts of the war. One Frenchman remarked about this time period, "We talked of nothing but America." Less than a decade after the American Revolution ended, an armed struggle to topple the government would begin in France.

Americans Create a Republic

Shortly after declaring their independence, the 13 individual states recognized the need for a national government. As victory became certain, all 13 states ratified a constitution in 1781. This plan of government was known as the Articles of Confederation. The Articles established the United States as a republic, a government in which citizens rule through elected representatives.

A Weak National Government To protect their authority, the 13 states created a loose confederation in which they held most of the power. Thus, the Articles of Confederation deliberately created a weak national government. There were no executive or judicial branches. Instead, the Articles established only one body of government, the Congress. Each state, regardless of size, had one vote in Congress. Congress could declare war, enter into treaties, and coin money. It had no power, however, to collect taxes or regulate trade. Passing new laws was difficult because laws needed the approval of 9 of the 13 states.

These limits on the national government soon produced many problems. Although the new national government needed money to operate, it could only request contributions from the states. Angry Revolutionary War veterans bitterly complained that Congress still owed them back pay for their services. Meanwhile, several states issued their own money. Some states even put tariffs on goods from neighboring states. **B**

A New Constitution Colonial leaders eventually recognized the need for a strong national government. In February 1787, Congress approved a Constitutional Convention to revise the Articles of Confederation. The Constitutional Convention held its first session on May 25, 1787. The 55 delegates were experienced statesmen who were familiar with the political theories of Locke, Montesquieu, and Rousseau.

Although the delegates shared basic ideas on government, they sometimes disagreed on how to put them into practice. For almost four months the delegates argued over important questions. Who should be represented in Congress? How many representatives should each state have? The delegates' deliberations produced not only compromises but also new approaches to governing. Using the political ideas of the Enlightenment, the delegates created a new system of government.

The Federal System Like Montesquieu, the delegates distrusted a powerful central government controlled by one person or group. They therefore established

MAIN IDEA

Making Inferences
B What was the main cause of the nation's problems under the Articles?

three separate branches—legislative, executive, and judicial. This setup provided a built-in system of **checks and balances**, with each branch checking the actions of the other two. For example, the president received the power to veto legislation passed by Congress. However, the Congress could override a presidential veto with the approval of two-thirds of its members.

Although the Constitution created a strong central government, it did not eliminate local governments. Instead, the Constitution set up a **federal system** in which power was divided between national and state governments.

The Bill of Rights The delegates signed the new Constitution on September 17, 1787. In order to become law, however, the Constitution required approval by conventions in at least 9 of the 13 states. These conventions were marked by sharp debate. Supporters of the Constitution were called Federalists. They argued in their famous work, the *Federalist Papers*, that the new government would provide a better balance between national and state powers. Their opponents, the Antifederalists, feared that the Constitution gave the central government too much power. They also wanted a bill of rights to protect the rights of individual citizens. **C**

MAIN IDEA

Analyzing Issues

C What were the opposing views regarding ratification of the Constitution?

In order to gain support, the Federalists promised to add a bill of rights to the Constitution. This promise cleared the way for approval. Congress formally added to the Constitution the ten amendments known as the **Bill of Rights**. These amendments protected such basic rights as freedom of speech, press, assembly, and religion. Many of these rights had been advocated by Voltaire, Rousseau, and Locke.

The Constitution and Bill of Rights marked a turning point in people's ideas about government. Both documents put Enlightenment ideas into practice. They expressed an optimistic view that reason and reform could prevail and that progress was inevitable. Such optimism swept across the Atlantic. However, the monarchies and the privileged classes didn't give up power and position easily. As Chapter 7 explains, the struggle to attain the principles of the Enlightenment led to violent revolution in France.

▼ Early copy of the U.S. Constitution

SECTION 4 ASSESSMENT

TERMS & NAMES 1. For each term or name, write a sentence explaining its significance.
• Declaration of Independence • Thomas Jefferson • checks and balances • federal system • Bill of Rights

USING YOUR NOTES

2. Which of the solutions that you recorded represented a compromise?

Problem	Solution
1.	1.
2.	2.
3.	3.

MAIN IDEAS

3. Why did the colonists criticize the Stamp Act as "taxation without representation"?

4. How did John Locke's notion of the social contract influence the American colonists?

5. Why were the colonists able to achieve victory in the American Revolution?

CRITICAL THINKING & WRITING

6. **MAKING INFERENCES** Why might it be important to have a Bill of Rights that guarantees basic rights of citizens?

7. **FORMING AND SUPPORTING OPINIONS** Do you think the American Revolution would have happened if there had not been an Age of Enlightenment?

8. **ANALYZING CAUSES** Why do you think the colonists at first created such a weak central government?

9. **WRITING ACTIVITY** [REVOLUTION] Summarize in several **paragraphs** the ideas from the American Revolution concerning separation of powers, basic rights of freedom, and popular sovereignty.

CONNECT TO TODAY CELEBRATING AMERICA'S BIRTHDAY

Create a **birthday poster** to present to the United States this July 4th. The poster should include images or quotes that demonstrate the ideals upon which the nation was founded.

Chapter 6 Assessment

TERMS & NAMES

For each term or name below, briefly explain its connection to European history from 1550–1789.

1. heliocentric theory
2. Isaac Newton
3. social contract
4. philosophe
5. salon
6. enlightened despot
7. Declaration of Independence
8. federal system

MAIN IDEAS

The Scientific Revolution Section 1 (pages 189–194)

9. According to Ptolemy, what was the earth's position in the universe? How did Copernicus's view differ?
10. What are the four steps in the scientific method?
11. What four new instruments came into use during the Scientific Revolution? What was the purpose of each one?

The Enlightenment in Europe Section 2 (pages 195–201)

12. How did the ideas of Hobbes and Locke differ?
13. What did Montesquieu admire about the government of Britain?
14. How did the Enlightenment lead to a more secular outlook?

The Enlightenment Spreads Section 3 (pages 202–205)

15. What were three developments in the arts during the Enlightenment?
16. What sorts of reforms did the enlightened despots make?

The American Revolution Section 4 (pages 206–211)

17. Why did the Articles of Confederation result in a weak national government?
18. How did the writers of the U.S. Constitution put into practice the idea of separation of powers? A system of checks and balances?

CRITICAL THINKING

1. USING YOUR NOTES

List in a table important new ideas that arose during the Scientific Revolution and Enlightenment. In the right column, briefly explain why each idea was revolutionary.

New Idea	Why Revolutionary

2. RECOGNIZING EFFECTS

SCIENCE AND TECHNOLOGY What role did technology play in the Scientific Revolution?

3. ANALYZING ISSUES

POWER AND AUTHORITY How did the U.S. Constitution reflect the ideas of the Enlightenment? Refer to specific Enlightenment thinkers to support your answer.

4. CLARIFYING

How did the statement by Prussian ruler Frederick the Great that a ruler is only "the first servant of the state" highlight Enlightenment ideas about government?

VISUAL SUMMARY

Enlightenment and Revolution, 1550–1789

Scientific Revolution

- Heliocentric theory challenges geocentric theory.
- Mathematics and observation support heliocentric theory.
- Scientific method develops.
- Scientists make discoveries in many fields.

A new way of thinking about the world develops, based on observation and a willingness to question assumptions.

Enlightenment

- People try to apply the scientific approach to aspects of society.
- Political scientists propose new ideas about government.
- Philosophes advocate the use of reason to discover truths.
- Philosophes address social issues through reason.

Enlightenment writers challenge many accepted ideas about government and society.

Spread of Ideas

- Enlightenment ideas appeal to thinkers and artists across Europe.
- Salons help spread Enlightenment thinking.
- Ideas spread to literate middle class.
- Enlightened despots attempt reforms.

Enlightenment ideas sweep through European society and to colonial America.

American Revolution

- Enlightenment ideas influence colonists.
- Britain taxes colonists after French and Indian War.
- Colonists denounce taxation without representation.
- War begins in Lexington and Concord.

Colonists declare independence, defeat Britain, and establish republic.

Use the quotation and your knowledge of world history to answer questions 1 and 2.
Additional Test Practice, pp. S1–S33

PRIMARY SOURCE

> We the People of the United States, in order to form a more perfect Union, establish Justice, insure domestic Tranquility, provide for the common defense, promote the general Welfare, and secure the Blessings of Liberty to ourselves and our Posterity, do ordain and establish this Constitution of the United States of America.
>
> Preamble, *Constitution of the United States of America*

1. All of the following are stated objectives of the Constitution except

    A. justice.

    B. liberty.

    C. defense.

    D. prosperity.

2. With whom does the ultimate power in society lie, according to the Constitution?

    A. the church

    B. the military

    C. the citizens

    D. the monarchy

Use this engraving, entitled *The Sleep of Reason Produces Monsters,* and your knowledge of world history to answer question 3.

3. Which of the following statements best summarizes the main idea of this Enlightenment engraving?

    A. Nothing good comes from relaxation or laziness.

    B. A lack of reason fosters superstition and irrational fears.

    C. Dreams are not restricted by the boundaries of reason.

    D. Rulers that let down their guard risk rebellion and overthrow.

INTEGRATED TECHNOLOGY

TEST PRACTICE Go to **classzone.com**

- Diagnostic tests
- Tutorials
- Strategies
- Additional practice

ALTERNATIVE ASSESSMENT

1. Interact *with* History

On page 188, you examined how you would react to a different or revolutionary idea or way of doing things. Now that you have read the chapter, consider how such breakthroughs impacted society. Discuss in a small group what you feel were the most significant new ideas or procedures and explain why.

2. WRITING ABOUT HISTORY

REVOLUTION Re-examine the material on the Scientific Revolution. Then write a three paragraph **essay** summarizing the difference in scientific understanding before and after the various scientific breakthroughs. Focus on

- the ultimate authority on many matters before the Scientific Revolution.
- how and why that changed after the Revolution.

INTEGRATED TECHNOLOGY

Writing an Internet-based Research Paper

Go to the *Web Research Guide* at **classzone.com** to learn about conducting research on the Internet. Use the Internet to explore a recent breakthrough in science or medicine. Look for information that will help you explain why the discovery is significant and how the new knowledge changes what scientists had thought about the topic.

In a well-organized paper, compare the significance of the discovery you are writing about with major scientific or medical discoveries of the Scientific Revolution. Be sure to

- apply a search strategy when using directories and search engines to locate Web resources.
- judge the usefulness of each Web site.
- correctly cite your Web resources.
- revise and edit for correct use of language.

The French Revolution and Napoleon, 1789–1815

Previewing Main Ideas

ECONOMICS The gap between rich and poor in France was vast. The inequalities of the economy of France were a major cause of the French Revolution.

Geography *Why do you think the royal palace at Versailles became a focal point for the anger of the poor people of Paris during the Revolution?*

REVOLUTION Driven by the example of the American Revolution and such Enlightenment ideas as liberty, equality, and democracy, the French ousted the government of Louis XVI and established a new political order.

Geography *Why do you think some historians cite the "wind from America" as a cause of the French Revolution?*

POWER AND AUTHORITY After seizing power in 1799, Napoleon conquered a huge empire that included much of Western Europe. His attempt to conquer Russia, however, led to his downfall.

Geography *What challenges and hazards of invading Russia might be inferred from the map?*

INTEGRATED TECHNOLOGY

eEdition
- Interactive Maps
- Interactive Visuals
- Interactive Primary Sources

INTERNET RESOURCES
Go to **classzone.com** for:
- Research Links
- Internet Activities
- Primary Sources
- Chapter Quiz
- Maps
- Test Practice
- Current Events

1789
Storming of the Bastille ignites the French Revolution.

1793
King Louis XVI is executed by guillotine; Reign of Terror begins. ▶

1796
Directory appoints Napoleon commander of French forces in Italy.

EUROPE

1789

WORLD

1789
George Washington is inaugurated as first U.S. president. ▶

1795
Great Britain seizes the Cape Colony in South Africa from the Dutch.

Napoleon's Empire, 1810

Legend:
- French Empire
- Countries allied with Napoleon
- Countries controlled by Napoleon
- Countries at war with Napoleon

KINGDOM OF DENMARK AND NORWAY

KINGDOM OF SWEDEN

Baltic Sea

REP. OF DANZIG

PRUSSIA

RUSSIAN EMPIRE

Berlin

Warsaw

GRAND DUCHY OF WARSAW

UNITED KINGDOM OF GREAT BRITAIN AND IRELAND

North Sea

London

Brussels

Amiens

Paris

Versailles

CONFEDERATION OF THE RHINE

Elbe River

Prague

Vienna

AUSTRIAN EMPIRE

ATLANTIC OCEAN

FRENCH EMPIRE

HELVETIC REPUBLIC

Danube River

Milan

KINGDOM OF ITALY

Marseille

ILLYRIAN PROVINCES

Adriatic Sea

OTTOMAN EMPIRE

Black Sea

PORTUGAL

Madrid

Lisbon

SPAIN

Barcelona

CORSICA

Rome

MONTENEGRO

Naples

KINGDOM OF NAPLES

KINGDOM OF SARDINIA

Mediterranean Sea

KINGDOM OF SICILY

| 0 | 250 | 500 Miles |
| 0 | 250 | 500 Kilometers |

Conic Projection

1799
Napoleon overthrows the Directory through a coup d'état.

1804
Napoleon crowns himself emperor, begins to create a vast European empire. ▶

1815
Napoleon is defeated at the Battle of Waterloo.

1800

1815

1800
Opium trade begins in China.

1804
Saint Domingue gains independence.
(Toussaint L'Ouverture) ▶

1810
Padre Hidalgo calls for Mexican independence.

1814
War of 1812 between Great Britain and the United States ends.

How would you change an unjust government?

You are living in France in the late 1700s. Your parents are merchants who earn a good living. However, after taxes they have hardly any money left. You know that other people, especially the peasants in the countryside, are even worse off than you. At the same time, the nobility lives in luxury and pays practically no taxes.

Many people in France are desperate for change. But they are uncertain how to bring about that change. Some think that representatives of the people should demand fair taxes and just laws. Others support violent revolution. In Paris, that revolution seems to have begun. An angry mob has attacked and taken over the Bastille, a royal prison. You wonder what will happen next.

1 One of the mob leaders triumphantly displays the keys to the Bastille.

2 Although they were in search of gunpowder and firearms, the conquerors of the Bastille took whatever they could find.

3 One man drags the royal standard behind him.

▲ The conquerors of the Bastille parade outside City Hall in Paris.

EXAMINING *the* ISSUES

- **How would you define an unjust government?**

- **What, if anything, would lead you to take part in a violent revolution?**

Discuss these questions with your classmates. In your discussion, remember what you've learned about the causes of revolutionary conflicts such as the American Revolution and the English Civil War. As you read about the French Revolution in this chapter, see what changes take place and how these changes came about.

The French Revolution Begins

MAIN IDEA	WHY IT MATTERS NOW	TERMS & NAMES
ECONOMICS Economic and social inequalities in the Old Regime helped cause the French Revolution.	Throughout history, economic and social inequalities have at times led peoples to revolt against their governments.	• Old Regime • estate • Louis XVI • Marie Antoinette • Estates-General • National Assembly • Tennis Court Oath • Great Fear

SETTING THE STAGE In the 1700s, France was considered the most advanced country of Europe. It had a large population and a prosperous foreign trade. It was the center of the Enlightenment, and France's culture was widely praised and imitated by the rest of the world. However, the appearance of success was deceiving. There was great unrest in France, caused by bad harvests, high prices, high taxes, and disturbing questions raised by the Enlightenment ideas of Locke, Rousseau, and Voltaire.

The Old Order

In the 1770s, the social and political system of France—the **Old Regime**—remained in place. Under this system, the people of France were divided into three large social classes, or **estates**.

The Privileged Estates Two of the estates had privileges, including access to high offices and exemptions from paying taxes, that were not granted to the members of the third. The Roman Catholic Church, whose clergy formed the First Estate, owned 10 percent of the land in France. It provided education and relief services to the poor and contributed about 2 percent of its income to the government. The Second Estate was made up of rich nobles. Although they accounted for just 2 percent of the population, the nobles owned 20 percent of the land and paid almost no taxes. The majority of the clergy and the nobility scorned Enlightenment ideas as radical notions that threatened their status and power as privileged persons.

The Third Estate About 97 percent of the people belonged to the Third Estate. The three groups that made up this estate differed greatly in their economic conditions. The first group—the bourgeoisie (BUR•zhwah•ZEE), or middle class—were bankers, factory owners, merchants, professionals, and skilled artisans. Often, they were well educated and believed strongly in the Enlightenment ideals of liberty and equality. Although some of the bourgeoisie were as rich as nobles, they paid high taxes and, like the rest of the Third Estate, lacked privileges. Many felt that their wealth entitled them to a greater degree of social status and political power.

The workers of France's cities formed the second, and poorest, group within the Third Estate. These urban workers included tradespeople, apprentices, laborers, and domestic servants. Paid low wages and frequently out of work, they often

TAKING NOTES

Analyzing Causes
Use a web diagram to identify the causes of the French Revolution.

Causes of Revolution

The French Revolution and Napoleon **217**

The Three Estates

A First Estate
- made up of clergy of Roman Catholic Church
- scorned Enlightenment ideas

B Second Estate
- made up of rich nobles
- held highest offices in government
- disagreed about Enlightenment ideas

C Third Estate
- included bourgeoisie, urban lower class, and peasant farmers
- had no power to influence government
- embraced Enlightenment ideas
- resented the wealthy First and Second Estates.

A FAUT ESPERER Q'EU JEU LA FINIRA BEN TOT.

Population of France, 1787

97% (Third Estate)

less than 1% (First Estate)

2% (Second Estate)

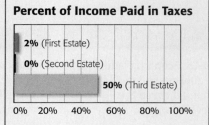

Percent of Income Paid in Taxes

- 2% (First Estate)
- 0% (Second Estate)
- 50% (Third Estate)

0% 20% 40% 60% 80% 100%

SKILLBUILDER: Interpreting Charts and Political Cartoons
1. **Drawing Conclusions** *How do the chart and the graphs help explain the political cartoon?*
2. **Making Inferences** *Why might the First and Second Estates be opposed to change?*

went hungry. If the cost of bread rose, mobs of these workers might attack grain carts and bread shops to steal what they needed.

Peasants formed the largest group within the Third Estate, more than 80 percent of France's 26 million people. Peasants paid about half their income in dues to nobles, tithes to the Church, and taxes to the king's agents. They even paid taxes on such basic staples as salt. Peasants and the urban poor resented the clergy and the nobles for their privileges and special treatment. The heavily taxed and discontented Third Estate was eager for change.

Vocabulary
tithe: a church tax, normally about one-tenth of a family's income

The Forces of Change

In addition to the growing resentment among the lower classes, other factors contributed to the revolutionary mood in France. New ideas about government, serious economic problems, and weak and indecisive leadership all helped to generate a desire for change.

Enlightenment Ideas New views about power and authority in government were spreading among the Third Estate. Members of the Third Estate were inspired by the success of the American Revolution. They began questioning long-standing notions about the structure of society. Quoting Rousseau and Voltaire, they began to demand equality, liberty, and democracy. The Comte D'Antraigues, a friend of Rousseau, best summed up their ideas on what government should be:

PRIMARY SOURCE
The Third Estate is the People and the People is the foundation of the State; it is in fact the State itself; the . . . People is everything. Everything should be subordinated to it. . . . It is in the People that all national power resides and for the People that all states exist.

COMTE D'ANTRAIGUES, quoted in *Citizens: A Chronicle of the French Revolution*

Economic Troubles By the 1780s, France's once prosperous economy was in decline. This caused alarm, particularly among the merchants, factory owners, and bankers of the Third Estate. On the surface, the economy appeared to be sound, because both production and trade were expanding rapidly. However, the heavy burden of taxes made it almost impossible to conduct business profitably within France. Further, the cost of living was rising sharply. In addition, bad weather in the 1780s caused widespread crop failures, resulting in a severe shortage of grain. The price of bread doubled in 1789, and many people faced starvation.

During the 1770s and 1780s, France's government sank deeply into debt. Part of the problem was the extravagant spending of **Louis XVI** and his queen, **Marie Antoinette**. Louis also inherited a considerable debt from previous kings. And he borrowed heavily in order to help the American revolutionaries in their war against Great Britain, France's chief rival. This nearly doubled the government's debt. In 1786, when bankers refused to lend the government any more money, Louis faced serious problems.

A Weak Leader Strong leadership might have solved these and other problems. Louis XVI, however, was indecisive and allowed matters to drift. He paid little attention to his government advisers, and had little patience for the details of governing. The queen only added to Louis's problems. She often interfered in the government, and frequently offered Louis poor advice. Further, since she was a member of the royal family of Austria, France's long-time enemy, Marie Antoinette had been unpopular from the moment she set foot in France. Her behavior only made the situation worse. As queen, she spent so much money on gowns, jewels, gambling, and gifts that she became known as "Madame Deficit."

Rather than cutting expenses, Louis put off dealing with the emergency until he practically had no money left. His solution was to impose taxes on the nobility. However, the Second Estate forced him to call a meeting of the **Estates-General**—an assembly of representatives from all three estates—to approve this new tax. The meeting, the first in 175 years, was held on May 5, 1789, at Versailles.

Vocabulary
deficit: debt

History Makers

Louis XVI
1754–1793

Louis XVI's tutors made little effort to prepare him for his role as king—and it showed. He was easily bored with affairs of state, and much preferred to spend his time in physical activities, particularly hunting. He also loved to work with his hands, and was skilled in several trades, including lock-making, metalworking, and bricklaying.

Despite these shortcomings, Louis was well intentioned and sincerely wanted to improve the lives of the common people. However, he lacked the ability to make decisions and the determination to see policies through. When he did take action, it often was based on poor advice from ill-informed members of his court. As one politician of the time noted, "His reign was a succession of feeble attempts at doing good, shows of weakness, and clear evidence of his inadequacy as a leader."

Marie Antoinette
1755–1793

Marie Antoinette was a pretty, lighthearted, charming woman. However, she was unpopular with the French because of her spending and her involvement in controversial court affairs. She referred to Louis as "the poor man" and sometimes set the clock forward an hour to be rid of his presence.

Marie Antoinette refused to wear the tight-fitting clothing styles of the day and introduced a loose cotton dress for women. The elderly, who viewed the dress as an undergarment, thought that her clothing was scandalous. The French silk industry was equally angry.

In constant need of entertainment, Marie Antoinette often spent hours playing cards. One year she lost the equivalent of $1.5 million by gambling in card games.

INTEGRATED TECHNOLOGY

RESEARCH LINKS For more on Louis XVI and Marie Antoinette, go to **classzone.com**

The French Revolution and Napoleon **219**

Dawn of the Revolution

The clergy and the nobles had dominated the Estates-General throughout the Middle Ages and expected to do so in the 1789 meeting. Under the assembly's medieval rules, each estate's delegates met in a separate hall to vote, and each estate had one vote. The two privileged estates could always outvote the Third Estate.

The National Assembly The Third Estate delegates, mostly members of the bourgeoisie whose views had been shaped by the Enlightenment, were eager to make changes in the government. They insisted that all three estates meet together and that each delegate have a vote. This would give the advantage to the Third Estate, which had as many delegates as the other two estates combined. Ⓐ

MAIN IDEA

Analyzing Motives
Ⓐ Why did the Third Estate propose a change in the Estates-General's voting rules?

Siding with the nobles, the king ordered the Estates-General to follow the medieval rules. The delegates of the Third Estate, however, became more and more determined to wield power. A leading spokesperson for their viewpoint was a clergyman sympathetic to their cause, Emmanuel-Joseph Sieyès (syay•YEHS). In a dramatic speech, Sieyès suggested that the Third Estate delegates name themselves the **National Assembly** and pass laws and reforms in the name of the French people.

After a long night of excited debate, the delegates of the Third Estate agreed to Sieyès's idea by an overwhelming majority. On June 17, 1789, they voted to establish the National Assembly, in effect proclaiming the end of absolute monarchy and the beginning of representative government. This vote was the first deliberate act of revolution.

Three days later, the Third Estate delegates found themselves locked out of their meeting room. They broke down a door to an indoor tennis court, pledging to stay until they had drawn up a new constitution. This pledge became known as the **Tennis Court Oath**. Soon after, nobles and members of the clergy who favored reform joined the Third Estate delegates. In response to these events, Louis stationed his mercenary army of Swiss guards around Versailles.

Vocabulary
mercenary army: a group of soldiers who will work for any country or employer that will pay them

Storming the Bastille In Paris, rumors flew. Some people suggested that Louis was intent on using military force to dismiss the National Assembly. Others charged that the foreign troops were coming to Paris to massacre French citizens.

▼ The attack on the Bastille claimed the lives of about 100 people.

People began to gather weapons in order to defend the city against attack. On July 14, a mob searching for gunpowder and arms stormed the Bastille, a Paris prison. The mob overwhelmed the guard and seized control of the building. The angry attackers hacked the prison commander and several guards to death, and then paraded around the streets with the dead men's heads on pikes.

The fall of the Bastille became a great symbolic act of revolution to the French people. Ever since, July 14—Bastille Day—has been a French national holiday, similar to the Fourth of July in the United States.

A Great Fear Sweeps France

Before long, rebellion spread from Paris into the countryside. From one village to the next, wild rumors circulated that the nobles were hiring outlaws to terrorize the peasants. A wave of senseless panic called the **Great Fear** rolled through France. The peasants soon became outlaws themselves. Armed with pitchforks and other farm tools, they broke into nobles' manor houses and destroyed the old legal papers that bound them to pay feudal dues. In some cases, the peasants simply burned down the manor houses.

In October 1789, thousands of Parisian women rioted over the rising price of bread. Brandishing knives, axes, and other weapons, the women marched on Versailles. First, they demanded that the National Assembly take action to provide bread. Then they turned their anger on the king and queen. They broke into the palace, killing some of the guards. The women demanded that Louis and Marie Antoinette return to Paris. After some time, Louis agreed.

A few hours later the king, his family, and servants left Versailles, never again to see the magnificent palace. Their exit signaled the change of power and radical reforms about to overtake France. **B**

MAIN IDEA

Recognizing Effects

B How did the women's march mark a turning point in the relationship between the king and the people?

Social History

Bread

Bread was a staple of the diet of the common people of France. Most families consumed three or four 4-pound loaves a day. And the purchase of bread took about half of a worker's wages—when times were good. So, when the price of bread jumped dramatically, as it did in the fall of 1789, people faced a real threat of starvation.

On their march back from Versailles, the women of Paris happily sang that they were bringing "the baker, the baker's wife, and the baker's lad" with them. They expected the "baker"—Louis—to provide the cheap bread that they needed to live.

SECTION 1 ASSESSMENT

TERMS & NAMES 1. For each term or name, write a sentence explaining its significance.
• Old Regime • estates • Louis XVI • Marie Antoinette • Estates-General • National Assembly • Tennis Court Oath • Great Fear

USING YOUR NOTES

2. Select one of the causes you listed and explain how it contributed to the French Revolution.

Causes of Revolution

MAIN IDEAS

3. Why were members of the Third Estate dissatisfied with life under the Old Regime?

4. How did Louis XVI's weak leadership contribute to the growing crisis in France?

5. How did the purpose of the meeting of the Estates-General in 1789 change?

CRITICAL THINKING & WRITING

6. **FORMING AND SUPPORTING OPINIONS** Do you think that changes in the French government were inevitable? Explain.

7. **ANALYZING MOTIVES** Why do you think some members of the First and Second Estates joined the National Assembly and worked to reform the government?

8. **COMPARING AND CONTRASTING** How were the storming of the Bastille and the women's march on Versailles similar? How were they different?

9. **WRITING ACTIVITY** POWER AND AUTHORITY In the role of a member of the Third Estate, write a brief **speech** explaining why the French political system needs to change.

CONNECT TO TODAY CREATING A COLLAGE

Conduct research on how Bastille Day is celebrated in France today. Use your findings to create an **annotated collage** titled "Celebrating the Revolution."

The French Revolution and Napoleon **221**

Revolution Brings Reform and Terror

MAIN IDEA	WHY IT MATTERS NOW	TERMS & NAMES
REVOLUTION The revolutionary government of France made reforms but also used terror and violence to retain power.	Some governments that lack the support of a majority of their people still use fear to control their citizens.	• Legislative Assembly • émigré • sans-culotte • Jacobin	• guillotine • Maximilien Robespierre • Reign of Terror

SETTING THE STAGE Peasants were not the only members of French society to feel the Great Fear. Nobles and officers of the Church were equally afraid. Throughout France, bands of angry peasants struck out against members of the upper classes, attacking and destroying many manor houses. In the summer of 1789, a few months before the women's march to Versailles, some nobles and members of clergy in the National Assembly responded to the uprisings in an emotional late-night meeting.

TAKING NOTES

Recognizing Effects
Use a flow chart to identify the major events that followed the creation of the Constitution of 1791.

Assembly
Creates a
Constitution

The Assembly Reforms France

Throughout the night of August 4, 1789, noblemen made grand speeches, declaring their love of liberty and equality. Motivated more by fear than by idealism, they joined other members of the National Assembly in sweeping away the feudal privileges of the First and Second Estates, thus making commoners equal to the nobles and the clergy. By morning, the Old Regime was dead.

The Rights of Man Three weeks later, the National Assembly adopted a statement of revolutionary ideals, the Declaration of the Rights of Man and of the Citizen. Reflecting the influence of the Declaration of Independence, the document stated that "men are born and remain free and equal in rights." These rights included "liberty, property, security, and resistance to oppression." The document also guaranteed citizens equal justice, freedom of speech, and freedom of religion.

In keeping with these principles, revolutionary leaders adopted the expression "Liberty, Equality, Fraternity" as their slogan. Such sentiments, however, did not apply to everyone. When writer Olympe de Gouges (aw•LIMP duh GOOZH) published a declaration of the rights of women, her ideas were rejected. Later, in 1793, she was declared an enemy of the Revolution and executed.

A State-Controlled Church Many of the National Assembly's early reforms focused on the Church. The assembly took over Church lands and declared that Church officials and priests were to be elected and paid as state officials. Thus, the Catholic Church lost both its lands and its political independence. The reasons for the assembly's actions were largely economic. Proceeds from the sale of Church lands helped pay off France's huge debt.

The assembly's actions alarmed millions of French peasants, who were devout Catholics. The effort to make the Church a part of the state offended them, even

◄ One of the people who stopped Louis from escaping said that he recognized the king from his portrait on a French bank note.

though it was in accord with Enlightenment philosophy. They believed that the pope should rule over a church independent of the state. From this time on, many peasants opposed the assembly's reforms.

Louis Tries to Escape As the National Assembly restructured the relationship between church and state, Louis XVI pondered his fate as a monarch. Some of his advisers warned him that he and his family were in danger. Many supporters of the monarchy thought France unsafe and left the country. Then, in June 1791, the royal family tried to escape from France to the Austrian Netherlands. As they neared the border, however, they were apprehended and returned to Paris under guard. Louis's attempted escape increased the influence of his radical enemies in the government and sealed his fate.

Divisions Develop

For two years, the National Assembly argued over a new constitution for France. By 1791, the delegates had made significant changes in France's government and society.

A Limited Monarchy In September 1791, the National Assembly completed the new constitution, which Louis reluctantly approved. The constitution created a limited constitutional monarchy. It stripped the king of much of his authority. It also created a new legislative body—the <u>**Legislative Assembly**</u>. This body had the power to create laws and to approve or reject declarations of war. However, the king still held the executive power to enforce laws.

Factions Split France Despite the new government, old problems, such as food shortages and government debt, remained. The question of how to handle these problems caused the Legislative Assembly to split into three general groups, each of which sat in a different part of the meeting hall. Radicals, who sat on the left side of the hall, opposed the idea of a monarchy and wanted sweeping changes in the way the government was run. Moderates sat in the center of the hall and wanted some changes in government, but not as many as the radicals. Conservatives sat on the right side of the hall. They upheld the idea of a limited monarchy and wanted few changes in government. **A**

MAIN IDEA

Recognizing Effects

A How did differences of opinion on how to handle such issues as food shortages and debt affect the Legislative Assembly?

Connect *to* Today

Left, Right, and Center

The terms we use today to describe where people stand politically derive from the factions that developed in the Legislative Assembly in 1791.

- People who want to radically change government are called left wing or are said to be on the left.
- People with moderate views often are called centrist or are said to be in the center.
- People who want few or no changes in government often are called right wing or are said to be on the right.

The French Revolution and Napoleon **223**

In addition, factions outside the Legislative Assembly wanted to influence the direction of the government too. **Émigrés** (EHM•ih•GRAYZ), nobles and others who had fled France, hoped to undo the Revolution and restore the Old Regime. In contrast, some Parisian workers and small shopkeepers wanted the Revolution to bring even greater changes to France. They were called **sans-culottes** (SANZ kyoo•LAHTS), or "those without knee breeches." Unlike the upper classes, who wore fancy knee-length pants, sans-culottes wore regular trousers. Although they did not have a role in the assembly, they soon discovered ways to exert their power on the streets of Paris.

War and Execution

Monarchs and nobles in many European countries watched the changes taking place in France with alarm. They feared that similar revolts might break out in their own countries. In fact, some radicals were keen to spread their revolutionary ideas across Europe. As a result, some countries took action. Austria and Prussia, for example, urged the French to restore Louis to his position as an absolute monarch. The Legislative Assembly responded by declaring war in April 1792.

France at War The war began badly for the French. By the summer of 1792, Prussian forces were advancing on Paris. The Prussian commander threatened to destroy Paris if the revolutionaries harmed any member of the royal family. This enraged the Parisians. On August 10, about 20,000 men and women invaded the Tuileries, the palace where the royal family was staying. The mob massacred the royal guards and imprisoned Louis, Marie Antoinette, and their children.

Shortly after, the French troops defending Paris were sent to reinforce the French army in the field. Rumors began to spread that supporters of the king held in Paris prisons planned to break out and seize control of the city. Angry and fearful citizens responded by taking the law into their own hands. For several days in early September, they raided the prisons and murdered over 1,000 prisoners. Many nobles, priests, and royalist sympathizers fell victim to the angry mobs in these September Massacres. **B**

Under pressure from radicals in the streets and among its members, the Legislative Assembly set aside the Constitution of 1791. It declared the king deposed, dissolved the assembly, and called for the election of a new legislature. This new governing body, the National Convention, took office on September 21. It quickly abolished the monarchy and declared France a republic. Adult male citizens were granted the right to vote and hold office. Despite the important part they had already played in the Revolution, women were not given the vote.

Jacobins Take Control Most of the people involved in the governmental changes in September 1792 were members of a radical political organization, the Jacobin (JAK•uh•bihn) Club. One of the most prominent **Jacobins**, as club members were called, was Jean-Paul Marat (mah•RAH). During the Revolution, he edited a newspaper called *L'Ami du Peuple* (Friend of the People). In his fiery editorials, Marat called for

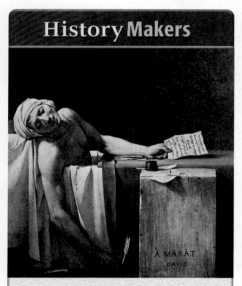

History Makers

A. MARAT. DAVID.

Jean-Paul Marat
1743–1793

Marat was a thin, high-strung, sickly man whose revolutionary writings stirred up the violent mood in Paris. Because he suffered from a painful skin disease, he often found comfort by relaxing in a cold bath—even arranging things so that he could work in his bathtub!

During the summer of 1793, Charlotte Corday, a supporter of a rival faction whose members had been jailed, gained an audience with Marat by pretending to have information about traitors. Once inside Marat's private chambers, she fatally stabbed him as he bathed. For her crime, Corday went to the guillotine.

MAIN IDEA

Analyzing Causes
B What did the September Massacres show about the mood of the people?

The Guillotine

If you think the guillotine was a cruel form of capital punishment, think again. Dr. Joseph Ignace Guillotin proposed a machine that satisfied many needs—it was efficient, humane, and democratic. A physician and member of the National Assembly, Guillotin claimed that those executed with the device "wouldn't even feel the slightest pain."

Prior to the guillotine's introduction in 1792, many French criminals had suffered through horrible punishments in public places. Although public punishments continued to attract large crowds, not all spectators were pleased with the new machine. Some witnesses felt that death by the guillotine occurred much too quickly to be enjoyed by an audience.

INTEGRATED/ TECHNOLOGY

RESEARCH LINKS For more on the guillotine, go to **classzone.com**

Once the executioner cranked the blade to the top, a mechanism released it. The sharp weighted blade fell, severing the victim's head from his or her body.

Some doctors believed that a victim's head retained its hearing and eyesight for up to 15 minutes after the blade's deadly blow. All remains were eventually gathered and buried in simple graves.

Tricoteuses, or "woman knitters," were regular spectators at executions and knitted stockings for soldiers as they sat near the base of the scaffold.

Before each execution, bound victims traveled from the prison to the scaffold in horse-drawn carts during a one and one-half hour procession through city streets.

Beheading by Class

More than 2,100 people were executed during the last 132 days of the Reign of Terror. The pie graph below displays the breakdown of beheadings by class.

- ■ First Estate
- ■ Second Estate
- ■ Third Estate

Connect *to* Today

1. **Synthesizing** In what ways was the guillotine an efficient means of execution?

   See Skillbuilder Handbook, page R21.

2. **Comparing** France continued to use the guillotine until 1977. Four years later, France abolished capital punishment. Conduct research to identify countries where capital punishment is still used. Use your findings to create a map titled "Countries Using Capital Punishment."

225

the death of all those who continued to support the king. Georges Danton (zhawrzh dahn•TAWN), a lawyer, was among the club's most talented and passionate speakers. He also was known for his devotion to the rights of Paris's poor people.

The National Convention had reduced Louis XVI's role from that of a king to that of a common citizen and prisoner. Now, guided by radical Jacobins, it tried Louis for treason. The Convention found him guilty, and, by a very close vote, sentenced him to death. On January 21, 1793, the former king walked with calm dignity up the steps of the scaffold to be beheaded by a machine called the **guillotine** (GIHL•uh•TEEN). (See the Science & Technology feature on page 225.)

The War Continues The National Convention also had to contend with the continuing war with Austria and Prussia. At about the time the Convention took office, the French army won a stunning victory against the Austrians and Prussians at the Battle of Valmy. Early in 1793, however, Great Britain, Holland, and Spain joined Prussia and Austria against France. Forced to contend with so many enemies, the French suffered a string of defeats. To reinforce the French army, Jacobin leaders in the Convention took an extreme step. At their urging, in February 1793 the Convention ordered a draft of 300,000 French citizens between the ages of 18 and 40. By 1794, the army had grown to 800,000 and included women.

The Terror Grips France

Foreign armies were not the only enemies of the French republic. The Jacobins had thousands of enemies within France itself. These included peasants who were horrified by the king's execution, priests who would not accept government control, and rival leaders who were stirring up rebellion in the provinces. How to contain and control these enemies became a central issue.

Robespierre Assumes Control In the early months of 1793, one Jacobin leader, **Maximilien Robespierre** (ROHBZ•peer), slowly gained power. Robespierre and his supporters set out to build a "republic of virtue" by wiping out every trace of France's past. Firm believers in reason, they changed the calendar, dividing the year into 12 months of 30 days and renaming each month. This calendar had no Sundays because the radicals considered religion old-fashioned and dangerous. They even closed all churches in Paris, and cities and towns all over France soon did the same.

In July 1793, Robespierre became leader of the Committee of Public Safety. For the next year, Robespierre governed France virtually as a dictator, and the period of his rule became known as the **Reign of Terror**. The Committee of Public Safety's chief task was to protect the Revolution from its enemies. Under Robespierre's leadership, the committee often had these "enemies" tried in the morning and guillotined in the afternoon. Robespierre justified his use of terror by suggesting that it enabled French citizens to remain true to the ideals of the Revolution. He also saw a connection between virtue and terror:

PRIMARY SOURCE C
The first maxim of our politics ought to be to lead the people by means of reason and the enemies of the people by terror. If the basis of popular government in time of peace is virtue, the basis of popular government in time of revolution is both virtue and terror: virtue without which terror is murderous, terror without which virtue is powerless. Terror is nothing else than swift, severe, indomitable justice; it flows, then, from virtue.
MAXIMILIEN ROBESPIERRE, "On the Morals and Political Principles of Domestic Policy" (1794)

MAIN IDEA

Analyzing Primary Sources
C How did Robespierre justify the use of terror?

The "enemies of the Revolution" who troubled Robespierre the most were fellow radicals who challenged his leadership. In 1793 and 1794, many of those who had led the Revolution received death sentences. Their only crime was that they were considered less radical than Robespierre. By early 1794, even Georges Danton found himself in danger. Danton's friends in the National Convention, afraid to defend him, joined in condemning him. On the scaffold, he told the executioner, "Don't forget to show my head to the people. It's well worth seeing."

The Terror claimed not only the famous, such as Danton and Marie Antoinette, the widowed queen. Thousands of unknown people also were sent to their deaths, often on the flimsiest of charges. For example, an 18-year-old youth was sentenced to die for cutting down a tree that had been planted as a symbol of liberty. Perhaps as many as 40,000 were executed during the Terror. About 85 percent were peasants or members of the urban poor or middle class—for whose benefit the Revolution had been launched.

▲ At his trial, Georges Danton defended himself so skillfully that the authorities eventually denied him the right to speak.

End of the Terror

In July 1794, fearing for their own safety, some members of the National Convention turned on Robespierre. They demanded his arrest and execution. The Reign of Terror, the radical phase of the French Revolution, ended on July 28, 1794, when Robespierre went to the guillotine.

French public opinion shifted dramatically after Robespierre's death. People of all classes had grown weary of the Terror. They were also tired of the skyrocketing prices for bread, salt, and other necessities of life. In 1795, moderate leaders in the National Convention drafted a new plan of government, the third since 1789. It placed power firmly in the hands of the upper middle class and called for a two-house legislature and an executive body of five men, known as the Directory. These five were moderates, not revolutionary idealists. Some of them were corrupt and made themselves rich at the country's expense. Even so, they gave their troubled country a period of order. They also found the right general to command France's armies—Napoleon Bonaparte.

SECTION 2 ASSESSMENT

TERMS & NAMES 1. For each term or name, write a sentence explaining its significance.
• Legislative Assembly • émigré • sans-culotte • Jacobin • guillotine • Maximilien Robespierre • Reign of Terror

USING YOUR NOTES	MAIN IDEAS	CRITICAL THINKING & WRITING
2. Do you think this chain of events could have been changed in any way? Explain. Assembly Creates a Constitution	3. What major reforms did the National Assembly introduce? 4. What did the divisions in the Legislative Assembly say about the differences in French society? 5. How did the Reign of Terror come to an end?	6. **SYNTHESIZING** How did the slogan "Liberty, Equality, Fraternity" sum up the goals of the Revolution? 7. **COMPARING AND CONTRASTING** What similarities and differences do you see between the political factions in the Legislative Assembly and those in the U.S. government today? 8. **ANALYZING CAUSES** What factors led to Robespierre becoming a dictator? 9. **WRITING ACTIVITY** REVOLUTION Working in small teams, write short **biographies** of three revolutionary figures mentioned in this section.

INTEGRATED TECHNOLOGY **INTERNET ACTIVITY**

Use the Internet to conduct research on governments that use terrorism against their own people. Prepare an **oral report** on the methods these countries use.

INTERNET KEYWORD
human rights

INTER*ACTIVE*

The French Revolution

Over time, people have expressed a wide variety of opinions about the causes and outcomes of the French Revolution. The following excerpts, dating from the 1790s to 1859, illustrate this diversity of opinion.

Ⓐ SECONDARY SOURCE

Charles Dickens

In 1859, the English writer Dickens wrote *A Tale of Two Cities,* a novel about the French Revolution for which he did much research. In the following scene, Charles Darnay—an aristocrat who gave up his title because he hated the injustices done to the people—has returned to France and been put on trial.

His judges sat upon the bench in feathered hats; but the rough red cap and tricolored cockade was the headdress otherwise prevailing. Looking at the jury and the turbulent audience, he might have thought that the usual order of things was reversed, and that the felons were trying the honest men. The lowest, cruelest, and worst populace of a city, never without its quantity of low, cruel, and bad, were the directing spirits of the scene. . . .

Charles Evrémonde, called Darnay, was accused by the public prosecutor as an emigrant, whose life was forfeit to the Republic, under the decree which banished all emigrants on pain of Death. It was nothing that the decree bore date since his return to France. There he was, and there was the decree; he had been taken in France, and his head was demanded.

"Take off his head!" cried the audience. "An enemy to the Republic!"

▶ In this illustration from *A Tale of Two Cities,* Sidney Carton goes to the guillotine in Darnay's place.

Ⓑ PRIMARY SOURCE

Edmund Burke

Burke, a British politician, was one of the earliest and most severe critics of the French Revolution. In 1790, he expressed this opinion.

[The French have rebelled] against a mild and lawful monarch, with more fury, outrage, and insult, than ever any people has been known to rise against the most illegal usurper, or the most [bloodthirsty] tyrant. . . .

They have found their punishment in their success. Laws overturned; tribunals subverted; . . . the people impoverished; a church pillaged, and . . . civil and military anarchy made the constitution of the kingdom. . . .

Were all these dreadful things necessary?

Ⓒ PRIMARY SOURCE

Thomas Paine

In 1790, Paine—a strong supporter of the American Revolution—defended the French Revolution against Burke and other critics.

It is no longer the paltry cause of kings or of this or of that individual, that calls France and her armies into action. It is the great cause of all. It is the establishment of a new era, that shall blot despotism from the earth, and fix, on the lasting principles of peace and citizenship, the great Republic of Man.

The scene that now opens itself to France extends far beyond the boundaries of her own dominions. Every nation is becoming her ally, and every court has become her enemy. It is now the cause of all nations, against the cause of all courts.

Document-Based QUESTIONS

1. In your own words, summarize the attitude toward the French Revolution expressed in each of these excerpts.

2. Why might Edmund Burke (Source B) be so against the French Revolution?

3. In Source C, what is the distinction Thomas Paine is making between nations and courts?

Napoleon Forges an Empire

MAIN IDEA	WHY IT MATTERS NOW	TERMS & NAMES
POWER AND AUTHORITY Napoleon Bonaparte, a military genius, seized power in France and made himself emperor.	In times of political turmoil, military dictators often seize control of nations.	• Napoleon Bonaparte • coup d'état • plebiscite • lycée • concordat • Napoleonic Code • Battle of Trafalgar

SETTING THE STAGE Napoleon Bonaparte was quite a short man—just five feet three inches tall. However, he cast a long shadow over the history of modern times. He would come to be recognized as one of the world's greatest military geniuses, along with Alexander the Great of Macedonia, Hannibal of Carthage, and Julius Caesar of Rome. In only four years, from 1795 to 1799, Napoleon rose from a relatively obscure position as an officer in the French army to become master of France.

Napoleon Seizes Power

Napoleon Bonaparte was born in 1769 on the Mediterranean island of Corsica. When he was nine years old, his parents sent him to a military school. In 1785, at the age of 16, he finished school and became a lieutenant in the artillery. When the Revolution broke out, Napoleon joined the army of the new government.

Hero of the Hour In October 1795, fate handed the young officer a chance for glory. When royalist rebels marched on the National Convention, a government official told Napoleon to defend the delegates. Napoleon and his gunners greeted the thousands of royalists with a cannonade. Within minutes, the attackers fled in panic and confusion. Napoleon Bonaparte became the hero of the hour and was hailed throughout Paris as the savior of the French republic.

In 1796, the Directory appointed Napoleon to lead a French army against the forces of Austria and the Kingdom of Sardinia. Crossing the Alps, the young general swept into Italy and won a series of remarkable victories. Next, in an attempt to protect French trade interests and to disrupt British trade with India, Napoleon led an expedition to Egypt. But he was unable to repeat the successes he had achieved in Europe. His army was pinned down in Egypt, and the British admiral Horatio Nelson defeated his naval forces. However, Napoleon managed to keep stories about his setbacks out of the newspapers and thereby remained a great hero to the people of France.

Coup d'État By 1799, the Directory had lost control of the political situation and the confidence of the French people. When Napoleon returned from Egypt, his friends urged him to seize political power. Napoleon took action in early November 1799. Troops under his command surrounded the national legislature and drove out most of its members. The lawmakers who remained then voted to

TAKING NOTES

Following Chronological Order On a time line, note the events that led to Napoleon's crowning as emperor of France.

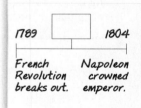

1789   *1804*

French Revolution breaks out.   *Napoleon crowned emperor.*

Napoleon Bonaparte
1769–1821

Because of his small stature and thick Corsican accent, Napoleon was mocked by his fellow students at military school. Haughty and proud, Napoleon refused to grace his tormentors' behavior with any kind of response. He simply ignored them, preferring to lose himself in his studies. He showed a particular passion for three subjects—classical history, geography, and mathematics.

In 1784, Napoleon was recommended for a career in the army and he transferred to the Ecole Militaire (the French equivalent of West Point) in Paris. There, he proved to be a fairly poor soldier, except when it came to artillery. His artillery instructor quickly noticed Napoleon's abilities: "He is most proud, ambitious, aspiring to everything. This young man merits our attention."

---

dissolve the Directory. In its place, they established a group of three consuls, one of whom was Napoleon. Napoleon quickly took the title of first consul and assumed the powers of a dictator. A sudden seizure of power like Napoleon's is known as a *coup*—from the French phrase **coup d'état** (KOO day•TAH), or "blow to the state." **A**

At the time of Napoleon's coup, France was still at war. In 1799, Britain, Austria, and Russia joined forces with one goal in mind, to drive Napoleon from power. Once again, Napoleon rode from Paris at the head of his troops. Eventually, as a result of war and diplomacy, all three nations signed peace agreements with France. By 1802, Europe was at peace for the first time in ten years. Napoleon was free to focus his energies on restoring order in France.

MAIN IDEA

Analyzing Causes
A How was Napoleon able to become a dictator?

Napoleon Rules France

At first, Napoleon pretended to be the constitutionally chosen leader of a free republic. In 1800, a **plebiscite** (PLEHB•ih•SYT), or vote of the people, was held to approve a new constitution. Desperate for strong leadership, the people voted overwhelmingly in favor of the constitution. This gave all real power to Napoleon as first consul.

Restoring Order at Home Napoleon did not try to return the nation to the days of Louis XVI. Rather, he kept many of the changes that had come with the Revolution. In general, he supported laws that would both strengthen the central government and achieve some of the goals of the Revolution.

His first task was to get the economy on a solid footing. Napoleon set up an efficient method of tax collection and established a national banking system. In addition to ensuring the government a steady supply of tax money, these actions promoted sound financial management and better control of the economy. Napoleon also took steps to end corruption and inefficiency in government. He dismissed corrupt officials and, in order to provide the government with trained officials, set up **lycées**, or government-run public schools. These lycées were open to male students of all backgrounds. Graduates were appointed to public office on the basis of merit rather than family connections.

One area where Napoleon disregarded changes introduced by the Revolution was religion. Both the clergy and many peasants wanted to restore the position of the Church in France. Responding to their wishes, Napoleon signed a **concordat**, or agreement, with Pope Pius VII. This established a new relationship between church and state. The government recognized the influence of the Church, but rejected Church control in national affairs. The concordat gained Napoleon the support of the organized Church as well as the majority of the French people.

Napoleon thought that his greatest work was his comprehensive system of laws, known as the **Napoleonic Code**. This gave the country a uniform set of laws and eliminated many injustices. However, it actually limited liberty and promoted order and authority over individual rights. For example, freedom of speech and of the press, established during the Revolution, were restricted under the code. The code also restored slavery in the French colonies of the Caribbean.

Napoleon Crowned as Emperor In 1804, Napoleon decided to make himself emperor, and the French voters supported him. On December 2, 1804, dressed in a splendid robe of purple velvet, Napoleon walked down the long aisle of Notre Dame Cathedral in Paris. The pope waited for him with a glittering crown. As thousands watched, the new emperor took the crown from the pope and placed it on his own head. With this gesture, Napoleon signaled that he was more powerful than the Church, which had traditionally crowned the rulers of France. **B**

MAIN IDEA

Analyzing Motives
B Why do you think Napoleon crowned himself emperor?

Napoleon Creates an Empire

Napoleon was not content simply to be master of France. He wanted to control the rest of Europe and to reassert French power in the Americas. He envisioned his western empire including Louisiana, Florida, French Guiana, and the French West Indies. He knew that the key to this area was the sugar-producing colony of Saint Domingue (now called Haiti) on the island of Hispaniola.

Loss of American Territories In 1789, when the ideas of the Revolution reached the planters in Saint Domingue, they demanded that the National Assembly give them the same privileges as the people of France. Eventually, enslaved Africans in the colony demanded their rights too—in other words, their freedom. A civil war erupted, and enslaved Africans under the leadership of Toussaint L'Ouverture seized control of the colony. In 1801, Napoleon decided to take back the colony and restore its productive sugar industry. However, the French forces were devastated by disease. And the rebels proved to be fierce fighters.

After the failure of the expedition to Saint Domingue, Napoleon decided to cut his losses in the Americas. He offered to sell all of the Louisiana Territory to the United States, and in 1803 President Jefferson's administration agreed to purchase the land for $15 million. Napoleon saw a twofold benefit to the sale. First, he would gain money to finance operations in Europe. Second, he would punish the British. "The sale assures forever the power of the United States," he observed, "and I have given England a rival who, sooner or later, will humble her pride." **C**

MAIN IDEA

Recognizing Effects
C What effects did Napoleon intend the sale of Louisiana to have on France? on the United States? on Britain?

Conquering Europe Having abandoned his imperial ambitions in the New World, Napoleon turned his attention to Europe. He had already annexed the Austrian Netherlands and parts of Italy to France and set up a puppet government in Switzerland. Now he looked to expand his influence further. Fearful of his ambitions, the British persuaded Russia, Austria, and Sweden to join them against France.

Napoleon met this challenge with his usual boldness. In a series of brilliant battles, he crushed the opposition. (See the map on page 232.) The commanders of the enemy armies could never predict his next move and often took heavy losses. After the Battle of Austerlitz in 1805, Napoleon issued a proclamation expressing his pride in his troops:

▼ This painting by Jacques Louis David shows Napoleon in a heroic pose.

PRIMARY SOURCE
Soldiers! I am pleased with you. On the day of Austerlitz, you justified everything that I was expecting of [you]. . . . In less than four hours, an army of 100,000 men, commanded by the emperors of Russia and Austria, was cut up and dispersed. . . . 120 pieces of artillery, 20 generals, and more than 30,000 men taken prisoner—such are the results of this day which will forever be famous. . . . And it will be enough for you to say, "I was at Austerlitz," to hear the reply: "There is a brave man!"

NAPOLEON, quoted in *Napoleon* by André Castelot

French Empire
Controlled by Napoleon
✷ French victory
✩ French defeat
British blockade

KINGDOM OF DENMARK AND NORWAY

KINGDOM OF SWEDEN

Moscow (1812)

Borodino (1812)

Baltic Sea

REP. OF DANZIG

Neman R.

Friedland (1807)

RUSSIAN EMPIRE

UNITED KINGDOM OF GREAT BRITAIN AND IRELAND

North Sea

PRUSSIA

Berlin

GRAND DUCHY OF WARSAW

London

CONFEDERATION OF THE RHINE

Leipzig (1813)

ATLANTIC OCEAN

Brussels
Amiens

Jena (1806)

Austerlitz (1805)

Paris
Versailles

Seine R.

Elbe R.

Rhine R.

Ulm (1805)

Wagram (1809)
Aspern (1809)

AUSTRIAN EMPIRE

Loire R.

HELVETIC REPUBLIC

Vienna

La Coruña (1809)

Vitoria (1813)

Ebro R.

Milan
KINGDOM OF ITALY

ILLYRIAN PROVINCES

Danube R.

Black Sea

PORTUGAL

Talavera (1809)

Madrid (1808)

Marseille

Po R.

Adriatic Sea

Tagus R.

CORSICA

Rome

MONTENEGRO

SPAIN

Valencia (1808)

SARDINIA

Naples

KINGDOM OF NAPLES

OTTOMAN EMPIRE

Trafalgar (1805)

Gibraltar

Mediterranean Sea

SICILY

0   500 Miles
0   1,000 Kilometers

N

Battle of Trafalgar, Oct. 21, 1805

British fleet
French and Spanish fleet
British thrust

Villeneuve

Nelson

Álava

Collingwood

By dividing Villeneuve's formation, Admiral Nelson captured nearly two-thirds of the enemy fleet.

Battle of Austerlitz, Dec. 2, 1805

French forces
Allied Russian, Prussian, and Austrian forces
French thrust
Allied thrust

Bagration

Bernadotte
Lannes

Austerlitz

Soult

Pratzen Plateau

Kollowrat

NAPOLEON (About 70,000 troops)

Doctorov

CZAR ALEXANDER I (About 85,000 troops)

Goldbach Creek

Davout

N

0   2 Miles
0   4 Kilometers

By drawing an Allied attack on his right flank, Napoleon was able to split the Allied line at its center.

GEOGRAPHY SKILLBUILDER: Interpreting Maps
1. **Region** What was the extent of the lands under Napoleon's control?
2. **Location** Where was the Battle of Trafalgar fought? What tactic did Nelson use in the battle, and why was it successful?

In time, Napoleon's battlefield successes forced the rulers of Austria, Prussia, and Russia to sign peace treaties. These successes also enabled him to build the largest European empire since that of the Romans. France's only major enemy left undefeated was the great naval power, Britain.

The Battle of Trafalgar In his drive for a European empire, Napoleon lost only one major battle, the **Battle of Trafalgar** (truh•FAL•guhr). This naval defeat, however, was more important than all of his victories on land. The battle took place in 1805 off the southwest coast of Spain. The British commander, Horatio Nelson, was as brilliant in warfare at sea as Napoleon was in warfare on land. In a bold maneuver, he split the larger French fleet, capturing many ships. (See the map inset on the opposite page.)

The destruction of the French fleet had two major results. First, it ensured the supremacy of the British navy for the next 100 years. Second, it forced Napoleon to give up his plans of invading Britain. He had to look for another way to control his powerful enemy across the English Channel. Eventually, Napoleon's extravagant efforts to crush Britain would lead to his own undoing.

The French Empire During the first decade of the 1800s, Napoleon's victories had given him mastery over most of Europe. By 1812, the only areas of Europe free from Napoleon's control were Britain, Portugal, Sweden, and the Ottoman Empire. In addition to the lands of the French Empire, Napoleon also controlled numerous supposedly independent countries. (See the map on the opposite page.) These included Spain, the Grand Duchy of Warsaw, and a number of German kingdoms in Central Europe. The rulers of these countries were Napoleon's puppets; some, in fact, were members of his family. Furthermore, the powerful countries of Russia, Prussia, and Austria were loosely attached to Napoleon's empire through alliances. Although not totally under Napoleon's control, they were easily manipulated by threats of military action. **D**

The French Empire was huge but unstable. Napoleon was able to maintain it at its greatest extent for only five years—from 1807 to 1812. Then it quickly fell to pieces. Its sudden collapse was caused in part by Napoleon's actions.

MAIN IDEA

Drawing Conclusions

D By 1805, how successful had Napoleon been in his efforts to build an empire?

SECTION 3 **ASSESSMENT**

TERMS & NAMES 1. For each term or name, write a sentence explaining its significance.
• Napoleon Bonaparte   • coup d'état   • plebiscite   • lycée   • concordat   • Napoleonic Code   • Battle of Trafalgar

USING YOUR NOTES

2. Which of these events do you think had the greatest impact on Napoleon's rise to power?

1789   1804

French   Napoleon
Revolution   crowned
breaks out.   emperor.

MAIN IDEAS

3. How did Napoleon become a hero in France?

4. What did Napoleon consider his greatest triumph in domestic policy?

5. How was Napoleon able to control the countries neighboring the French Empire?

CRITICAL THINKING & WRITING

6. **FORMING OPINIONS** In your opinion, was Napoleon the creator or the creation of his times?

7. **ANALYZING ISSUES** Napoleon had to deal with forces both inside and outside the French Empire. In your judgment, which area was more important to control?

8. **MAKING INFERENCES** If you had been a member of the bourgeoisie, would you have been satisfied with the results of Napoleon's actions? Explain.

9. **WRITING ACTIVITY** POWER AND AUTHORITY Look at the painting on page 231. Write a **paragraph** discussing why the painter portrayed Napoleon in this fashion.

CONNECT TO TODAY CREATING A VENN DIAGRAM

Identify and conduct research on a present-day world leader who has used dictatorial powers to rule his or her country. Use your findings to create a **Venn diagram** comparing this leader's use of power to Napoleon's use of power.

4

Napoleon's Empire Collapses

MAIN IDEA	WHY IT MATTERS NOW	TERMS & NAMES
POWER AND AUTHORITY Napoleon's conquests aroused nationalistic feelings across Europe and contributed to his downfall.	In the 1990s, nationalistic feelings contributed to the breakup of nations such as Yugoslavia.	• blockade • Continental System • guerrilla • Peninsular War	• scorched-earth policy • Waterloo • Hundred Days

SETTING THE STAGE Napoleon worried about what would happen to his vast empire after his death. He feared it would fall apart unless he had an heir whose right to succeed him was undisputed. His wife, Josephine, had failed to bear him a child. He, therefore, divorced her and formed an alliance with the Austrian royal family by marrying Marie Louise, the grandniece of Marie Antoinette. In 1811, Marie Louise gave birth to a son, Napoleon II, whom Napoleon named king of Rome.

TAKING NOTES
Recognizing Effects
Use a chart to identify Napoleon's three mistakes and the impact they had on the French Empire.

Napoleon's Mistakes	Effect on Empire

Napoleon's Costly Mistakes

Napoleon's own personality proved to be the greatest danger to the future of his empire. His desire for power had raised him to great heights, and the same love of power led him to his doom. In his efforts to extend the French Empire and crush Great Britain, Napoleon made three disastrous mistakes.

The Continental System In November 1806, Napoleon set up a **blockade**—a forcible closing of ports—to prevent all trade and communication between Great Britain and other European nations. Napoleon called this policy the **Continental System** because it was supposed to make continental Europe more self-sufficient. Napoleon also intended it to destroy Great Britain's commercial and industrial economy.

▼ "Little Johnny Bull"—Great Britain—waves a sword at Napoleon as the emperor straddles the globe.

Napoleon's blockade, however, was not nearly tight enough. Aided by the British, smugglers managed to bring cargo from Britain into Europe. At times, Napoleon's allies also disregarded the blockade. Even members of Napoleon's family defied the policy, including his brother, Louis, whom he had made king of Holland. While the blockade weakened British trade, it did not destroy it. In addition, Britain responded with its own blockade. And because the British had a stronger navy, they were better able than the French to make the blockade work.

To enforce the blockade, the British navy stopped neutral ships bound for the continent and forced them to sail to a British port to be searched and taxed. American ships were among those stopped by the British navy. Angered, the U.S.

A STOPPAGE to a STRIDE over the GLOBE

Congress declared war on Britain in 1812. Even though the War of 1812 lasted two years, it was only a minor inconvenience to Britain in its struggle with Napoleon.

The Peninsular War In 1808, Napoleon made a second costly mistake. In an effort to get Portugal to accept the Continental System, he sent an invasion force through Spain. The Spanish people protested this action. In response, Napoleon removed the Spanish king and put his own brother, Joseph, on the throne. This outraged the Spanish people and inflamed their nationalistic feelings. The Spanish, who were devoutly Catholic, also worried that Napoleon would attack the Church. They had seen how the French Revolution had weakened the Catholic Church in France, and they feared that the same thing would happen to the Church in Spain.

For six years, bands of Spanish peasant fighters, known as **guerrillas**, struck at French armies in Spain. The guerrillas were not an army that Napoleon could defeat in open battle. Rather, they worked in small groups that ambushed French troops and then fled into hiding. The British added to the French troubles by sending troops to aid the Spanish. Napoleon lost about 300,000 men during this **Peninsular War**—so called because Spain lies on the Iberian Peninsula. These losses weakened the French Empire.

In Spain and elsewhere, nationalism, or loyalty to one's own country, was becoming a powerful weapon against Napoleon. People who had at first welcomed the French as their liberators now felt abused by a foreign conqueror. Like the Spanish guerrillas, Germans and Italians and other conquered peoples turned against the French. **A**

The Invasion of Russia Napoleon's most disastrous mistake of all came in 1812. Even though Alexander I had become Napoleon's ally, the Russian czar refused to stop selling grain to Britain. In addition, the French and Russian rulers suspected each other of having competing designs on Poland. Because of this breakdown in their alliance, Napoleon decided to invade Russia.

In June 1812, Napoleon and his Grand Army of more than 420,000 soldiers marched into Russia. As Napoleon advanced, Alexander pulled back his troops, refusing to be lured into an unequal battle. On this retreat, the Russians practiced a **scorched-earth policy**. This involved burning grain fields and slaughtering livestock so as to leave nothing for the enemy to eat.

MAIN IDEA

Recognizing Effects

A How could the growing feelings of nationalism in European countries hurt Napoleon?

▼ Francisco Goya's painting *The Third of May, 1808* shows a French firing squad executing Spanish peasants suspected of being guerrillas.

235

Napoleon's Russian Campaign, 1812

June 1812 Napoleon and his troops march across the Neman River and into Russia. **422,000**

Napoleon sends troops to Polotsk to protect his left flank. 50,000

Reduced by desertion, disease, starvation, and capture, an army of 175,000 arrives in Smolensk. Another 30,000 die there. 175,000

Sept. 7, 1812 Napoleon's army fights the Battle of Borodino and suffers 30,000 casualties. **130,000**

Sept. 14, 1812 Napoleon enters Moscow to find it in ashes, torched by the czar. He waits, hoping to induce the czar to surrender.

Oct. 18, 1812 Frustrated and starving, having waited too long for the czar, the 100,000 survivors of the Grand Army begin their hellish retreat through the cruel Russia winter.

November 1812 The army returns to Smolensk and finds famine. The remaining 24,000 march on, abandoning their wounded. **37,000**

Dec. 6, 1812 Troops march for the Neman River. Only 10,000 make it out of Russia. **28,000**

The 30,000 in Polotsk join the 20,000 survivors. Thousands drown while crossing the Berezina River. **50,000**

RUSSIA

PRUSSIA

GRAND DUCHY OF WARSAW

Western Dvina River · Neman River · Berezina River · Dnieper River · Moscow R. · Oka R.

Kovno · Vilna · Molodechno · Borisov · Minsk · Glubokoye · Polotsk · Vitebsk · Smolensk · Vyazma · Borodino · Maloyaroslavets · Moscow

→ Advancing troops
← Retreating troops
👤 = 10,000 soldiers
👤 = 10,000 lost troops

0 — 100 Miles
0 — 200 Kilometers

GEOGRAPHY SKILLBUILDER: Interpreting Maps
1. **Movement** How long did it take the Grand Army to cover the distance between the Russian border and Moscow?
2. **Place** Why was it a mistake for Napoleon to stay in Moscow until mid-October?

On September 7, 1812, the two armies finally clashed in the Battle of Borodino. (See the map on this page.) After several hours of indecisive fighting, the Russians fell back, allowing Napoleon to move on Moscow. When Napoleon entered Moscow seven days later, the city was in flames. Rather than surrender Russia's "holy city" to the French, Alexander had destroyed it. Napoleon stayed in the ruined city until the middle of October, when he decided to turn back toward France.

As the snows—and the temperature—began to fall in early November, Russian raiders mercilessly attacked Napoleon's ragged, retreating army. Many soldiers were killed in these clashes or died of their wounds. Still more dropped in their tracks from exhaustion, hunger, and cold. Finally, in the middle of December, the last survivors straggled out of Russia. The retreat from Moscow had devastated the Grand Army—only 10,000 soldiers were left to fight.

Napoleon's Downfall

Napoleon's enemies were quick to take advantage of his weakness. Britain, Russia, Prussia, and Sweden joined forces against him. Austria also declared war on Napoleon, despite his marriage to Marie Louise. All of the main powers of Europe were now at war with France.

Napoleon Suffers Defeat In only a few months, Napoleon managed to raise another army. However, most of his troops were untrained and ill prepared for battle. He faced the allied armies of the European powers outside the German city of Leipzig (LYP•sihg) in October 1813. The allied forces easily defeated his inexperienced army and French resistance crumbled quickly. By January of 1814, the allied armies were pushing steadily toward Paris. Some two months later, King

Frederick William III of Prussia and Czar Alexander I of Russia led their troops in a triumphant parade through the French capital.

Napoleon wanted to fight on, but his generals refused. In April 1814, he accepted the terms of surrender and gave up his throne. The victors gave Napoleon a small pension and exiled, or banished, him to Elba, a tiny island off the Italian coast. The allies expected no further trouble from Napoleon, but they were wrong.

The Hundred Days Louis XVI's brother assumed the throne as Louis XVIII. (The executed king's son, Louis XVII, had died in prison in 1795.) However, the new king quickly became unpopular among his subjects, especially the peasants. They suspected him of wanting to undo the Revolution's land reforms.

MAIN IDEA
Analyzing Motives
B Why do you think the French people welcomed back Napoleon so eagerly?

The news of Louis's troubles was all the incentive Napoleon needed to try to regain power. He escaped from Elba and, on March 1, 1815, landed in France. Joyous crowds welcomed him on the march to Paris. And thousands of volunteers swelled the ranks of his army. Within days, Napoleon was again emperor of France. **B**

In response, the European allies quickly marshaled their armies. The British army, led by the Duke of Wellington, prepared for battle near the village of **Waterloo** in Belgium. On June 18, 1815, Napoleon attacked. The British army defended its ground all day. Late in the afternoon, the Prussian army arrived. Together, the British and the Prussian forces attacked the French. Two days later, Napoleon's exhausted troops gave way, and the British and Prussian forces chased them from the field.

This defeat ended Napoleon's last bid for power, called the **Hundred Days**. Taking no chances this time, the British shipped Napoleon to St. Helena, a remote island in the South Atlantic. There, he lived in lonely exile for six years, writing his memoirs. He died in 1821 of a stomach ailment, perhaps cancer.

Without doubt, Napoleon was a military genius and a brilliant administrator. Yet all his victories and other achievements must be measured against the millions of lives that were lost in his wars. The French writer Alexis de Tocqueville summed up Napoleon's character by saying, "He was as great as a man can be without virtue." Napoleon's defeat opened the door for the freed European countries to establish a new order.

▲ British soldiers who fought at the battle of Waterloo received this medal.

SECTION 4 ASSESSMENT

TERMS & NAMES 1. For each term or name, write a sentence explaining its significance.
• blockade   • Continental System   • guerrilla   • Peninsular War   • scorched-earth policy   • Waterloo   • Hundred Days

USING YOUR NOTES

2. Which of Napoleon's mistakes was the most serious? Why?

Napoleon's Mistakes	Effect on Empire

MAIN IDEAS

3. How did Great Britain combat Napoleon's naval blockade?

4. Why did Napoleon have trouble fighting the enemy forces in the Peninsular War?

5. Why was Napoleon's delay of the retreat from Moscow such a great blunder?

CRITICAL THINKING & WRITING

6. **ANALYZING MOTIVES** Why did people in other European countries resist Napoleon's efforts to build an empire?

7. **EVALUATING COURSES OF ACTION** Napoleon had no choice but to invade Russia. Do you agree with this statement? Why or why not?

8. **FORMING AND SUPPORTING OPINIONS** Do you think that Napoleon was a great leader? Explain.

9. **WRITING ACTIVITY** [POWER AND AUTHORITY] In the role of a volunteer in Napoleon's army during the Hundred Days, write a **letter** to a friend explaining why you are willing to fight for the emperor.

CONNECT TO TODAY CREATING A MAP

Conduct research on how nationalist feelings affect world affairs today. Create a **map** showing the areas of the world where nationalist movements are active. Annotate the map with explanations of the situation in each area.

The Congress of Vienna

MAIN IDEA	WHY IT MATTERS NOW	TERMS & NAMES
POWER AND AUTHORITY After exiling Napoleon, European leaders at the Congress of Vienna tried to restore order and reestablish peace.	International bodies such as the United Nations play an active role in trying to maintain world peace and stability today.	• Congress of Vienna • Klemens von Metternich • balance of power • legitimacy • Holy Alliance • Concert of Europe

SETTING THE STAGE European heads of government were looking to establish long-lasting peace and stability on the continent after the defeat of Napoleon. They had a goal of the new European order—one of collective security and stability for the entire continent. A series of meetings in Vienna, known as the **Congress of Vienna**, were called to set up policies to achieve this goal. Originally, the Congress of Vienna was scheduled to last for four weeks. Instead, it went on for eight months.

TAKING NOTES

Recognizing Effects
Use a chart to show how the three goals of Metternich's plan at the Congress of Vienna solved a political problem.

Metternich's Plan	
Problem	Solution

Metternich's Plan for Europe

Most of the decisions made in Vienna during the winter of 1814–1815 were made in secret among representatives of the five "great powers"—Russia, Prussia, Austria, Great Britain, and France. By far the most influential of these representatives was the foreign minister of Austria, Prince **Klemens von Metternich** (MEHT•uhr•nihk).

Metternich distrusted the democratic ideals of the French Revolution. Like most other European aristocrats, he felt that Napoleon's behavior had been a natural outcome of experiments with democracy. Metternich wanted to keep things as they were and remarked, "The first and greatest concern for the immense majority of every nation is the stability of laws—never their change." Metternich had three goals at the Congress of Vienna. First, he wanted to prevent future French aggression by surrounding France with strong countries. Second, he wanted to restore a **balance of power**, so that no country would be a threat to others. Third, he wanted to restore Europe's royal families to the thrones they had held before Napoleon's conquests.

The Containment of France The Congress took the following steps to make the weak countries around France stronger:

- The former Austrian Netherlands and Dutch Republic were united to form the Kingdom of the Netherlands.
- A group of 39 German states were loosely joined as the newly created German Confederation, dominated by Austria.
- Switzerland was recognized as an independent nation.
- The Kingdom of Sardinia in Italy was strengthened by the addition of Genoa.

▲ Delegates at the Congress of Vienna study a map of Europe.

These changes enabled the countries of Europe to contain France and prevent it from overpowering weaker nations. (See the map on page 240.)

Balance of Power Although the leaders of Europe wanted to weaken France, they did not want to leave it powerless. If they severely punished France, they might encourage the French to take revenge. If they broke up France, then another country might become so strong that it would threaten them all. Thus, the victorious powers did not exact a great price from the defeated nation. As a result, France remained a major but diminished European power. Also, no country in Europe could easily overpower another.

Legitimacy The great powers affirmed the principle of **legitimacy**—agreeing that as many as possible of the rulers whom Napoleon had driven from their thrones be restored to power. The ruling families of France, Spain, and several states in Italy and Central Europe regained their thrones. The participants in the Congress of Vienna believed that the return of the former monarchs would stabilize political relations among the nations.

The Congress of Vienna was a political triumph in many ways. For the first time, the nations of an entire continent had cooperated to control political affairs. The settlements they agreed upon were fair enough that no country was left bearing a grudge. Therefore, the Congress did not sow the seeds of future wars. In that sense, it was more successful than many other peace meetings in history.

MAIN IDEA

Drawing Conclusions

Ⓐ In what ways was the Congress of Vienna a success?

By agreeing to come to one another's aid in case of threats to peace, the European nations had temporarily ensured that there would be a balance of power on the continent. The Congress of Vienna, then, created a time of peace in Europe. It was a lasting peace. None of the five great powers waged war on one another for nearly 40 years, when Britain and France fought Russia in the Crimean War. Ⓐ

Political Changes Beyond Vienna

The Congress of Vienna was a victory for conservatives. Kings and princes resumed power in country after country, in keeping with Metternich's goals. Nevertheless, there were important differences from one country to another. Britain and France now had constitutional monarchies. Generally speaking, however, the governments in Eastern and Central Europe were more conservative. The rulers of Russia, Prussia, and Austria were absolute monarchs.

Europe, 1810
INTERACTIVE

KINGDOM OF DENMARK AND NORWAY
KINGDOM OF SWEDEN
UNITED KINGDOM OF GREAT BRITAIN AND IRELAND
North Sea
Baltic Sea
PRUSSIA
RUSSIAN EMPIRE
London
Berlin
GRAND DUCHY OF WARSAW
Brussels
Amiens
CONFEDERATION OF THE RHINE
Versailles • Paris
ATLANTIC OCEAN
FRENCH EMPIRE
SWITZ.
Vienna
AUSTRIAN EMPIRE
Milan
ITALY
ILLYRIAN PROVINCES
PORTUGAL
Madrid
CORSICA
Rome
KINGDOM OF NAPLES
OTTOMAN EMPIRE
SPAIN
SARDINIA
Naples
Gibraltar
Mediterranean Sea
SICILY
N
0   400 Miles
0   800 Kilometers

- French Empire
- Countries controlled by Napoleon
- Countries allied with Napoleon
- Countries at war with Napoleon
- Neutral countries

Europe, 1817
INTERACTIVE

KINGDOM OF NORWAY AND SWEDEN
UNITED KINGDOM OF GREAT BRITAIN AND IRELAND
North Sea
DENMARK
Baltic Sea
NETHERLANDS
HANOVER
PRUSSIA
London
Berlin
SAXONY
RUSSIAN EMPIRE
Brussels
Amiens • Paris
Versailles
ATLANTIC OCEAN
FRANCE
BAVARIA
SWITZ.
Milan
Vienna
AUSTRIAN EMPIRE
PARMA
MODENA
LUCCA
TUSCANY
PAPAL STATES
PORTUGAL
Madrid
KINGDOM OF SARDINIA
CORSICA
Rome
Naples
OTTOMAN EMPIRE
SPAIN
Gibraltar
Mediterranean Sea
KINGDOM OF THE TWO SICILIES
N
0   400 Miles
0   800 Kilometers

- Small German states
- Boundary of the German Confederation

GEOGRAPHY SKILLBUILDER: Interpreting Maps
1. **Region** What parts of Napoleon's French Empire did France lose as a result of the Congress of Vienna?
2. **Region** In what sense did the territorial changes of 1815 reflect a restoration of order and balance?

Conservative Europe The rulers of Europe were very nervous about the legacy of the French Revolution. They worried that the ideals of liberty, equality, and fraternity might encourage revolutions elsewhere. Late in 1815, Czar Alexander I, Emperor Francis I of Austria, and King Frederick William III of Prussia signed an agreement called the **Holy Alliance**. In it, they pledged to base their relations with other nations on Christian principles in order to combat the forces of revolution. Finally, a series of alliances devised by Metternich, called the **Concert of Europe**, ensured that nations would help one another if any revolutions broke out.

Across Europe, conservatives held firm control of the governments, but they could not contain the ideas that had emerged during the French Revolution. France after 1815 was deeply divided politically. Conservatives were happy with the monarchy of Louis XVIII and were determined to make it last. Liberals, however, wanted the king to share more power with the legislature. And many people in the lower classes remained committed to the ideals of liberty, equality, and fraternity. Similarly, in other countries there was an explosive mixture of ideas and factions that would contribute directly to revolutions in 1830 and 1848. **B**

Despite their efforts to undo the French Revolution, the leaders at the Congress of Vienna could not turn back the clock. The Revolution had given Europe its first experiment in democratic government. Although the experiment had failed, it had set new political ideas in motion. The major political upheavals of the early 1800s had their roots in the French Revolution.

Revolution in Latin America The actions of the Congress of Vienna had consequences far beyond events in Europe. When Napoleon deposed the king of Spain during the Peninsular War, liberal Creoles (colonists born in Spanish America)

MAIN IDEA

Making Inferences

B What seeds of democracy had been sown by the French Revolution?

seized control of many colonies in the Americas. When the Congress of Vienna restored the king to the Spanish throne, royalist *peninsulares* (colonists born in Spain) tried to regain control of these colonial governments. The Creoles, however, attempted to retain and expand their power. In response, the Spanish king took steps to tighten control over the American colonies.

This action angered the Mexicans, who rose in revolt and successfully threw off Spain's control. Other Spanish colonies in Latin America also claimed independence. At about the same time, Brazil declared independence from Portugal. (See Chapter 8.)

Long-Term Legacy The Congress of Vienna left a legacy that would influence world politics for the next 100 years. The continent-wide efforts to establish and maintain a balance of power diminished the size and the power of France. At the same time, the power of Britain and Prussia increased.

Nationalism began to spread in Italy, Germany, Greece, and to other areas that the Congress had put under foreign control. Eventually, the nationalistic feelings would explode into revolutions, and new nations would be formed. European colonies also responded to the power shift. Spanish colonies took advantage of the events in Europe to declare their independence and break away from Spain.

At the same time, ideas about the basis of power and authority had changed permanently as a result of the French Revolution. More and more, people saw democracy as the best way to ensure equality and justice for all. The French Revolution, then, changed the social attitudes and assumptions that had dominated Europe for centuries. A new era had begun. **C**

MAIN IDEA

Recognizing Effects

C How did the French Revolution affect not only Europe but also other areas of the world?

Connect *to* Today

Congress of Vienna and the United Nations

The Congress of Vienna and the Concert of Europe tried to keep the world safe from war. The modern equivalent of these agreements is the United Nations (UN), an international organization established in 1945 and continuing today, whose purpose is to promote world peace.

Like the Congress of Vienna, the United Nations was formed by major powers after a war—World War II. These powers agreed to cooperate to reduce tensions and bring greater harmony to international relations. Throughout its history, the United Nations has used diplomacy as its chief method of keeping the peace.

INTEGRATED / TECHNOLOGY

INTERNET ACTIVITY Create a graphic organizer to show the major agencies and functions of the United Nations. Go to **classzone.com** for your research.

SECTION 5 ASSESSMENT

TERMS & NAMES 1. For each term or name, write a sentence explaining its significance.
• Congress of Vienna   • Klemens von Metternich   • balance of power   • legitimacy   • Holy Alliance   • Concert of Europe

USING YOUR NOTES	MAIN IDEAS	CRITICAL THINKING & WRITING
2. What was the overall effect of Metternich's plan on France? 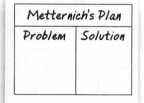	3. What were the three points of Metternich's plan for Europe? 4. Why was the Congress of Vienna considered a success? 5. What was the long-term legacy of the Congress of Vienna?	6. **DRAWING CONCLUSIONS** From France's point of view, do you think the Congress of Vienna's decisions were fair? 7. **ANALYZING ISSUES** Why did liberals and conservatives differ over who should have power? 8. **MAKING INFERENCES** What do you think is meant by the statement that the French Revolution let the "genie out of the bottle"? 9. **WRITING ACTIVITY** **POWER AND AUTHORITY** In the role of a newspaper editor in the early 1800s, write an **editorial**—pro or con—on the Congress of Vienna and its impact on politics in Europe.

Metternich's Plan

Problem	Solution

CONNECT TO TODAY CREATING A SCRAPBOOK

Work in pairs to locate recent articles in newspapers and magazines on the peacekeeping efforts of the UN. Photocopy or clip the articles and use them to create a scrapbook titled "The UN as Peacekeeper."

VISUAL SUMMARY

The French Revolution and Napoleon

Long-Term Causes

- Social and economic injustices of the Old Regime
- Enlightenment ideas—liberty and equality
- Example furnished by the American Revolution

Immediate Causes

- Economic crisis—famine and government debt
- Weak leadership
- Discontent of the Third Estate

Revolution

- Fall of the Bastille
- National Assembly
- Declaration of the Rights of Man and of the Citizen and a new constitution

Immediate Effects

- End of the Old Regime
- Execution of monarch
- War with other European nations
- Reign of Terror
- Rise of Napoleon

Long-Term Effects

- Conservative reaction
- Decline in French power
- Spread of Enlightenment ideas
- Growth of nationalism
- Revolutions in Latin America

TERMS & NAMES

For each term or name below, briefly explain its connection to the French Revolution or the rise and fall of Napoleon.

1. estate
2. Great Fear
3. guillotine
4. Maximilien Robespierre
5. coup d'état
6. Napoleonic Code
7. Waterloo
8. Congress of Vienna

MAIN IDEAS

The French Revolution Begins Section 1 (pages 217–221)

9. Why were the members of the Third Estate dissatisfied with their way of life under the Old Regime?
10. Why was the fall of the Bastille important to the French people?

Revolution Brings Reform and Terror Section 2 (pages 222–228)

11. What political reforms resulted from the French Revolution?
12. What was the Reign of Terror, and how did it end?

Napoleon Forges an Empire Section 3 (pages 229–233)

13. What reforms did Napoleon introduce?
14. What steps did Napoleon take to create an empire in Europe?

Napoleon's Empire Collapses Section 4 (pages 234–237)

15. What factors led to Napoleon's defeat in Russia?
16. Why were the European allies able to defeat Napoleon in 1814 and again in 1815?

The Congress of Vienna Section 5 (pages 238–241)

17. What were Metternich's three goals at the Congress of Vienna?
18. How did the Congress of Vienna ensure peace in Europe?

CRITICAL THINKING

1. USING YOUR NOTES

Copy the chart of dates and events in Napoleon's career into your notebook. For each event, draw an arrow up or down to show whether Napoleon gained or lost power because of the event.

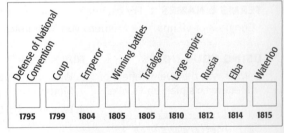

2. COMPARING AND CONTRASTING

ECONOMICS How were the economic conditions in France and the American colonies before their revolutions similar? How were they different?

3. ANALYZING ISSUES

REVOLUTION There is a saying: "Revolutions devour their own children." What evidence from this chapter supports that statement?

4. RECOGNIZING EFFECTS

POWER AND AUTHORITY How did the Congress of Vienna affect power and authority in European countries after Napoleon's defeat? Consider who held power in the countries and the power of the countries themselves.

Use the excerpt—from the South American liberator Simón Bolívar, whose country considered giving refuge to Napoleon after Waterloo—and your knowledge of world history to answer questions 1 and 2.
Additional Test Practice, pp. S1–S33

PRIMARY SOURCE

If South America is struck by the thunderbolt of Bonaparte's arrival, misfortune will ever be ours if our country accords him a friendly reception. His thirst for conquest is insatiable [cannot be satisfied]; he has mowed down the flower of European youth . . . in order to carry out his ambitious projects. The same designs will bring him to the New World.

SIMÓN BOLÍVAR

1. In Bolívar's opinion, if his country gave Napoleon a friendly reception it would
   A. be beset by misfortune.
   B. become a great power in South America.
   C. become a part of the French Empire.
   D. be attacked by the United States.

2. Which of the following gives Bolívar's view of Napoleon?
   A. His desire for power cannot be satisfied.
   B. He is not ambitious.
   C. He cares for the lives of others.
   D. He does not want to come to the New World.

Use the map, which shows Great Britain and the French Empire in 1810, and your knowledge of world history to answer question 3.

3. What geographical barrier helped to protect Britain from an invasion by Napoleon?
   A. Mediterranean Sea   C. Alps
   B. English Channel   D. Pyrenees

INTEGRATED TECHNOLOGY

TEST PRACTICE Go to classzone.com
• Diagnostic tests   • Strategies
• Tutorials   • Additional practice

ALTERNATIVE ASSESSMENT

1. Interact with History

On page 216, you considered how to bring about change in the French government in the late 1700s. Now that you have read the chapter, reevaluate your thoughts on how to change an unjust government. Was violent revolution justified? effective? Would you have advised different actions? Discuss your opinions with a small group.

2. WRITING ABOUT HISTORY

Imagine that you lived in Paris throughout the French Revolution. Write journal entries on several of the major events of the Revolution. Include the following events:
• the storming of the Bastille
• the women's march on Versailles
• the trial of Louis XVI
• the Reign of Terror
• the rise of Napoleon

INTEGRATED TECHNOLOGY

NetExplorations: The French Revolution

Go to NetExplorations at classzone.com to learn more about the French Revolution. Then plan a virtual field trip to sites in France related to the revolution. Be sure to include sites outside Paris. Begin your research by exploring the Web sites recommended at NetExplorations. Include the following in your field trip plan:
• a one-paragraph description of each site and the events that happened there
• specific buildings, statues, or other items to view at each site
• documents and other readings to help visitors prepare for each stop on the field trip
• topics to discuss at each site
• a list of Web sites used to create your virtual field trip

Nationalist Revolutions Sweep the West,
1789–1900

Previewing Main Ideas

REVOLUTION Inspired by Enlightenment ideas, the people of Latin America rebelled against European rule in the early 19th century. Rebels in Europe responded to nationalistic calls for independence.

Geography *Study the time line. What were the first two countries in Latin America and the Caribbean to work toward independence?*

POWER AND AUTHORITY Challenges by nationalist groups created unrest in Europe. Strong leaders united Italian lands and German-speaking lands.

Geography *Based on the map, in which area of Europe did the greatest number of revolts occur?*

CULTURAL INTERACTION Artists and intellectuals created new schools of thought. Romanticism and realism changed the way the world was viewed.

Geography *Which event shown on the time line involves a realistic way to view the world?*

INTEGRATED TECHNOLOGY

eEdition
- Interactive Maps
- Interactive Visuals
- Interactive Primary Sources

VIDEO *Patterns of Interaction: Revolutions in Latin America and South Africa*

INTERNET RESOURCES
Go to **classzone.com** for:
- Research Links
- Internet Activities
- Primary Sources
- Chapter Quiz
- Maps
- Test Practice
- Current Events

LATIN AMERICA AND EUROPE

1804
Haiti wins freedom from France.

1810
Padre Hidalgo calls for Mexican independence. ▶

1837
Louis Daguerre perfects a method for photography.

1800

1825

WORLD

1804
Napoleon crowned Emperor. ▶

1815
Napoleon defeated and exiled.

Revolutions, 1848

Legend:
- —— Boundary of German Confederation
- � Small German states
- ✳ Revolution in 1848–49

NORWAY

SWEDEN

North Sea

DENMARK

RUSSIAN EMPIRE

St. Petersburg

Baltic Sea

UNITED KINGDOM

NETHERLANDS

Hamburg

PRUSSIA

Berlin

Warsaw

London

BELGIUM

Brussels

POLAND

Prague

Paris

LUX.

Stuttgart

AUSTRIAN EMPIRE

ATLANTIC OCEAN

FRANCE

SWITZ.

Vienna

Buda

Milan

ILLYRIAN PROVINCES

ITALY

PORTUGAL

Madrid

PAPAL STATES

OTTOMAN EMPIRE

SPAIN

Rome

Adriatic Sea

Naples

KINGDOM OF THE TWO SICILIES

GREECE

Mediterranean Sea

Scale:
0   200   400 Miles
0   200   400 Kilometers
Conic Projection

Timeline:

1848 Revolts shake Europe.

1861 Russia frees serfs.

1870 Italy unites.

1871 Wilhelm I crowned Kaiser of united Germany.

1850

1875

1900

1863 ◀ Lincoln's Emancipation Proclamation frees enslaved persons in Confederate states.

1869 Suez Canal completed.

1884–1885 Berlin Conference divides Africa among European nations.

What symbolizes your country's values?

You are an artist in a nation that has just freed itself from foreign rule. The new government is asking you to design a symbol that will show what your country stands for. It's up to you to design the symbol that best suits the spirit and values of your people. Look at the symbols below. Will your symbol be peaceful or warlike, dignified or joyful? Or will it be a combination of these and other qualities?

Botswana
Industry and livestock are connected by water, the key to the country's prosperity. *Pula* in the Setswana language means "rain." But to a Setswana speaker, it is also a common greeting meaning luck, life, and prosperity.

Austria
The eagle was the symbol of the old Austrian Empire. The shield goes back to medieval times. The hammer and sickle symbolize agriculture and industry. The broken chains celebrate Austria's liberation from Germany at the end of World War II.

United States
The 13 original colonies are symbolized in the stars, stripes, leaves, and arrows. The Latin phrase *E pluribus unum* means "Out of many, one," expressing unity of the states. The American bald eagle holds an olive branch and arrows to symbolize a desire for peace but a readiness for war.

EXAMINING *the* ISSUES

- **What values and goals of your new country do you want to show?**

- **Will your symbols represent your country's past or future?**

As a class, discuss these questions. During the discussion, think of the role played by symbols in expressing a country's view of itself and the world. As you read about the rise of new nations in Latin America and Europe, think of how artists encourage national pride.

Latin American Peoples Win Independence

MAIN IDEA	WHY IT MATTERS NOW	TERMS & NAMES
REVOLUTION Spurred by discontent and Enlightenment ideas, peoples in Latin America fought colonial rule.	Sixteen of today's Latin American nations gained their independence at this time.	• *peninsulare* • José de San Martín • creole • Miguel Hidalgo • mulatto • José María Morelos • Simón Bolívar

SETTING THE STAGE The successful American Revolution, the French Revolution, and the Enlightenment changed ideas about who should control government. Ideas of liberty, equality, and democratic rule found their way across the seas to European colonies. In Latin America, most of the population resented the domination of European colonial powers. The time seemed right for the people who lived there to sweep away old colonial masters and gain control of the land.

Colonial Society Divided

In Latin American colonial society, class dictated people's place in society and jobs. At the top of Spanish-American society were the ***peninsulares*** (peh•neen•soo•LAH•rehs), people who had been born in Spain, which is on the Iberian peninsula. They formed a tiny percentage of the population. Only *peninsulares* could hold high office in Spanish colonial government. **Creoles**, Spaniards born in Latin America, were below the *peninsulares* in rank. Creoles could not hold high-level political office, but they could rise as officers in

TAKING NOTES

Clarifying Identify details about Latin American independence movements.

Who	Where
When	Why

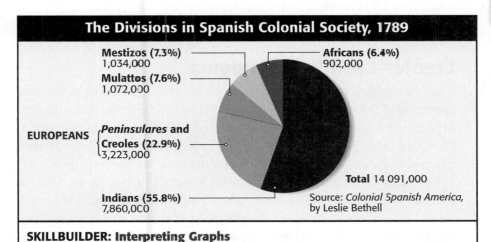

The Divisions in Spanish Colonial Society, 1789

Mestizos (7.3%) 1,034,000
Mulattos (7.6%) 1,072,000
Africans (6.4%) 902,000

EUROPEANS { *Peninsulares* and Creoles (22.9%) 3,223,000

Indians (55.8%) 7,860,000

Total 14,091,000

Source: *Colonial Spanish America,* by Leslie Bethell

SKILLBUILDER: Interpreting Graphs
1. **Clarifying** *Which two groups made up the vast majority of the population in Spanish America?*
2. **Making Inferences** *Of the Europeans, which group—peninsulares or creoles—probably made up a larger percentage?*

Spanish colonial armies. Together these two groups controlled land, wealth, and power in the Spanish colonies.

Below the *peninsulares* and creoles came the mestizos, persons of mixed European and Indian ancestry. Next were the **mulattos**, persons of mixed European and African ancestry, and enslaved Africans. Indians were at the bottom of the social ladder.

Revolutions in the Americas

By the late 1700s, colonists in Latin America, already aware of Enlightenment ideas, were electrified by the news of the American and French Revolutions. The success of the American Revolution encouraged them to try to gain freedom from their European masters.

Revolution in Haiti The French colony called Saint Domingue was the first Latin American territory to free itself from European rule. The colony, now known as Haiti, occupied the western third of the island of Hispaniola in the Caribbean Sea.

Nearly 500,000 enslaved Africans worked on French plantations, and they outnumbered their masters dramatically. White masters used brutal methods to terrorize them and keep them powerless.

While the French Revolution was taking place, oppressed people in the French colony of Haiti rose up against their French masters. In August 1791, 100,000 enslaved Africans rose in revolt. A leader soon emerged, Toussaint L'Ouverture (too•SAN loo•vair•TOOR). Formerly enslaved, Toussaint was unfamiliar with military and diplomatic matters. Even so, he rose to become a skilled general and diplomat. By 1801, Toussaint had taken control of the entire island and freed all the enslaved Africans.

▼ Toussaint L'Ouverture led enslaved Africans in a revolt against the French that ended slavery and resulted in the new nation of Haiti.

In January 1802, 30,000 French troops landed in Saint Domingue to remove Toussaint from power. In May, Toussaint agreed to halt the revolution if the French would end slavery. Despite the agreement, the French soon accused him of planning another uprising. They seized him and sent him to a prison in the French Alps, where he died in April 1803.

Haiti's Independence Toussaint's lieutenant, Jean-Jacques Dessalines (zhahn•ZHAHK day•sah•LEEN), took up the fight for freedom. On January 1, 1804, General Dessalines declared the colony an independent country. It was the first black colony to free itself from European control. Dessalines called the country Haiti, which in the language of the Arawak natives meant "mountainous land."

Creoles Lead Independence

Even though they could not hold high public office, creoles were the least oppressed of those born in Latin America. They were also the best educated. In fact, many wealthy young creoles traveled to Europe for their education. In Europe, they read about and adopted Enlightenment ideas. When they returned to Latin America, they brought ideas of revolution with them.

Napoleon's conquest of Spain in 1808 triggered revolts in the Spanish colonies. Removing Spain's King Ferdinand VII, Napoleon made his brother Joseph king of Spain. Many creoles might have supported a Spanish king. However, they felt no loyalty to a king imposed by the French. Creoles, recalling Locke's idea of the consent of the governed, argued that when the real king was removed, power shifted to the people. In 1810, rebellion broke out in several parts of Latin America. The drive toward independence had begun. **A**

MAIN IDEA

Recognizing Effects
A How did the French Revolution affect the colonists in the Americas?

Simón Bolívar
1783–1830

Called *Libertador* (Liberator), Bolívar was a brilliant general, a visionary, a writer, and a fighter. He is called the "George Washington of South America." Bolívar planned to unite the Spanish colonies of South America into a single country called Gran Colombia. The area of upper Peru was renamed Bolivia in his honor.

Discouraged by political disputes that tore the new Latin American nations apart, he is reported to have said, "America is ungovernable. Those who have served the revolution have ploughed the sea."

José de San Martín
1778–1850

Unlike the dashing Bolívar, San Martín was a modest man. Though born in Argentina, he spent much of his youth in Spain as a career military officer. He fought with Spanish forces against Napoleon. He returned to Latin America to be a part of its liberation from Spain. Fighting for 10 years, he became the liberator of Argentina, Chile, and Peru.

Discouraged by political infighting, San Martín sailed for Europe. He died, almost forgotten, on French soil in 1850.

The South American wars of independence rested on the achievements of two brilliant creole generals. One was **Simón Bolívar** (see•MAWN boh•LEE•vahr), a wealthy Venezuelan creole. The other great liberator was **José de San Martín** (hoh•SAY day san mahr•TEEN), an Argentinian.

Bolívar's Route to Victory Simón Bolívar's native Venezuela declared its independence from Spain in 1811. But the struggle for independence had only begun. Bolívar's volunteer army of revolutionaries suffered numerous defeats. Twice Bolívar had to go into exile. A turning point came in August 1819. Bolívar led over 2,000 soldiers on a daring march through the Andes into what is now Colombia. (See the 1830 map on page 251.) Coming from this direction, he took the Spanish army in Bogotá completely by surprise and won a decisive victory.

By 1821, Bolívar had won Venezuela's independence. He then marched south into Ecuador. In Ecuador, Bolívar finally met José de San Martín. Together they would decide the future of the Latin American revolutionary movement.

San Martín Leads Southern Liberation Forces San Martín's Argentina had declared its independence in 1816. However, Spanish forces in nearby Chile and Peru still posed a threat. In 1817, San Martín led an army on a grueling march across the Andes to Chile. He was joined there by forces led by Bernardo O'Higgins, son of a former viceroy of Peru. With O'Higgins's help, San Martín finally freed Chile.

In 1821, San Martín planned to drive the remaining Spanish forces out of Lima, Peru. But to do so, he needed a much larger force. San Martín and Bolívar discussed this problem when they met at Guayaquil, Ecuador, in 1822.

No one knows how the two men reached an agreement. But San Martín left his army for Bolívar to command. With unified revolutionary forces, Bolívar's army went on to defeat the Spanish at the Battle of Ayacucho (Peru) on December 9, 1824. In this last major battle of the war for independence, the Spanish colonies in Latin America won their freedom. The future countries of Venezuela, Colombia, Panama, and Ecuador were united into a country called Gran Colombia.

Struggling Toward Democracy

Revolutions are as much a matter of ideas as they are of weapons. Simón Bolívar, the hero of Latin American independence, was both a thinker and a fighter. By 1800, Enlightenment ideas spread widely across the Latin American colonies. Bolívar combined Enlightenment political ideas, ideas from Greece and Rome, and his own original thinking. The result was a system of democratic ideas that would help spark revolutions throughout Latin America.

Enlightenment Ideas Spread to Latin America, 1789–1810
INTERACTIVE

① Bolívar's 1807 return from Europe by way of the United States allowed him to study the American system of government.

② In 1810, Bolívar went to London to seek support for the revolution in Latin America. At the same time, he studied British institutions of government.

After winning South American independence, Simón Bolívar realized his dream of Gran Colombia, a sort of United States of South America.

Patterns of Interaction

Struggling Toward Democracy: Revolutions in Latin America and South Africa

The Latin American independence movement is one example of how the Enlightenment spread democratic ideals throughout the world. Democratic ideals continue to inspire people to struggle for political independence and to overthrow oppressive governments.

Connect *to* Today

1. **Making Inferences** How are Enlightenment thought and the successes of the American and French Revolutions reflected in Bolívar's thinking?

   See Skillbuilder Handbook, page R10.

2. **Comparing** What recent events in today's world are similar to Simón Bolívar's movement for Latin American independence?

Mexico Ends Spanish Rule

In most Latin American countries, creoles led the revolutionary movements. But in Mexico, ethnic and racial groups mixed more freely. There Indians and mestizos played the leading role.

A Cry for Freedom In 1810, Padre **Miguel Hidalgo** (mee•GEHL ee•THAHL•goh), a priest in the small village of Dolores, took the first step toward independence. Hidalgo was a poor but well-educated man. He firmly believed in Enlightenment ideals. On September 16, 1810, he rang the bells of his village church. When the peasants gathered in the church, he issued a call for rebellion against the Spanish. Today, that call is known as the *grito de Dolores* (the cry of Dolores).

The very next day, Hidalgo's Indian and mestizo followers began a march toward Mexico City. This unruly army soon numbered 80,000 men. The uprising of the lower classes alarmed the Spanish army and creoles, who feared the loss of their property, control of the land, and their lives. The army defeated Hidalgo in 1811. The rebels then rallied around another strong leader, Padre **José María Morelos** (moh•RAY•lohs). Morelos led the revolution for four years. However, in 1815, a creole officer, Agustín de Iturbide (ah•goos•TEEN day ee•toor•BEE•day), defeated him.

Mexico's Independence Events in Mexico took yet another turn in 1820 when a revolution in Spain put a liberal group in power there. Mexico's creoles feared the loss of their privileges in the Spanish-controlled colony. So they united in support of Mexico's independence from Spain. Ironically, Agustín de Iturbide—the man who had defeated the rebel Padre Morelos—proclaimed independence in 1821.

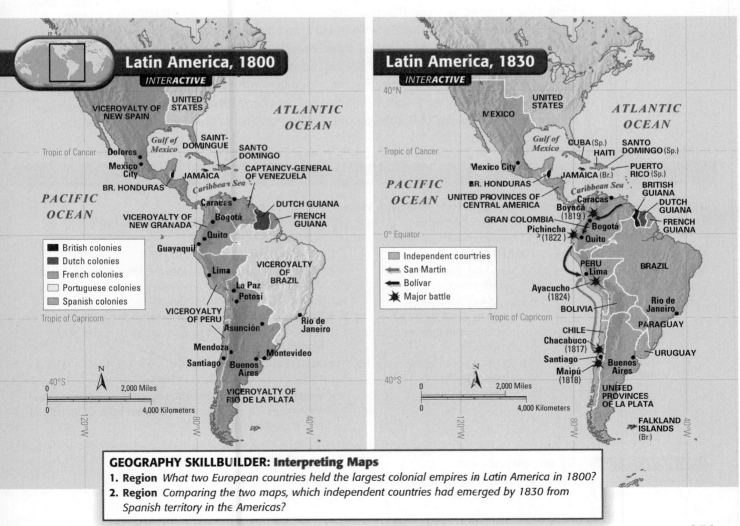

GEOGRAPHY SKILLBUILDER: Interpreting Maps

1. **Region** What two European countries held the largest colonial empires in Latin America in 1800?
2. **Region** Comparing the two maps, which independent countries had emerged by 1830 from Spanish territory in the Americas?

Before the Mexican revolution, Central America was part of the viceroyalty of New Spain. It had been governed by the Spanish from the seat of colonial government in Mexico. In 1821, several Central American states declared their independence from Spain—and from Mexico as well. However, Iturbide (who had declared himself emperor), refused to recognize the declarations of independence. Iturbide was finally overthrown in 1823. Central America then declared its absolute independence from Mexico. It took the name the United Provinces of Central America. The future countries of Nicaragua, Guatemala, Honduras, El Salvador, and Costa Rica would develop in this region.

Brazil's Royal Liberator

Brazil's quest for independence was unique in this period of Latin American history because it occurred without violent upheavals or widespread bloodshed. In fact, a member of the Portuguese royal family actually played a key role in freeing Brazil from Portugal.

In 1807, Napoleon's armies invaded both Spain and Portugal. Napoleon's aim was to close the ports of these countries to British shipping. As French troops approached Lisbon, the Portuguese capital, Prince John (later King John VI) and the royal family boarded ships to escape capture. They took their court and royal treasury to Portugal's largest colony, Brazil. Rio de Janiero became the capital of the Portuguese empire. For 14 years, the Portuguese ran their empire from Brazil. After Napoleon's defeat in 1815, King John and the Portuguese government returned to Portugal six years later. Dom Pedro, King John's son, stayed behind in Brazil.

King John planned to make Brazil a colony again. However, many Brazilians could not accept a return to colonial status. In 1822, creoles demanded Brazil's independence from Portugal. Eight thousand Brazilians signed a petition asking Dom Pedro to rule. He agreed. On September 7, 1822, he officially declared Brazil's independence. Brazil had won its independence in a bloodless revolution. **B**

Meanwhile, the ideas of the French Revolution and the aftermath of the Napoleonic Wars were causing upheaval in Europe, as you will learn in Section 2.

MAIN IDEA

Making Inferences
B In what way did the presence of the royal family in Brazil help Portugal's largest colony?

SECTION 1 ASSESSMENT

TERMS & NAMES 1. For each term or name, write a sentence explaining its significance.
• *peninsulare*   • creole   • mulatto   • Simón Bolívar   • José de San Martín   • Miguel Hidalgo   • José María Morelos

USING YOUR NOTES	**MAIN IDEAS**	**CRITICAL THINKING & WRITING**
2. Which independence movement was led by Toussaint L'Ouverture?	3. How was Spanish colonial society structured? 4. How was the Haitian Revolution different from revolutions in the rest of Latin America? 5. Which groups led the quest for Mexican independence?	6. **COMPARING AND CONTRASTING** Compare and contrast the leadership of the South American revolutions to the leadership of Mexico's revolution. 7. **FORMING AND SUPPORTING OPINIONS** Would creole revolutionaries tend to be democratic or authoritarian leaders? Explain. 8. **ANALYZING CAUSES** How were events in Europe related to the revolutions in Latin America? 9. **WRITING ACTIVITY** REVOLUTION Write a **response** to this statement: "Through its policies, Spain gave up its right to rule in South America."

Who | Where
When | Why

INTEGRATED TECHNOLOGY **INTERNET ACTIVITY**
Use the Internet to find information on the Mexican Indian rebel group, the *Zapatistas*. Create a **multimedia presentation** describing the group and its goals.

INTERNET KEYWORD
Zapatistas

Europe Faces Revolutions

<table>
<tr><th>MAIN IDEA</th><th>WHY IT MATTERS NOW</th><th>TERMS & NAMES</th></tr>
<tr><td>REVOLUTION Liberal and nationalist uprisings challenged the old conservative order of Europe.</td><td>The system of nation-states established in Europe during this period continues today.</td><td>• conservative   • nation-state
• liberal   • the Balkans
• radical   • Louis-Napoleon
• nationalism   • Alexander II</td></tr>
</table>

SETTING THE STAGE As revolutions shook the colonies in Latin America, Europe was also undergoing dramatic changes. Under the leadership of Prince Metternich of Austria, the Congress of Vienna had tried to restore the old monarchies and territorial divisions that had existed before the French Revolution. (See Chapter 7.) On an international level, this attempt to turn back history succeeded. For the next century, European countries seldom turned to war to solve their differences. Within countries, however, the effort failed. Revolutions erupted across Europe between 1815 and 1848.

Clash of Philosophies

In the first half of the 1800s, three schools of political thought struggled for supremacy in European societies. Each believed that its style of government would best serve the people. Each attracted a different set of followers. The list below identifies the philosophies, goals, and followers.

▼ Prince Clemens von Metternich shaped conservative control of Europe for almost 40 years.

- **Conservative**: usually wealthy property owners and nobility. They argued for protecting the traditional monarchies of Europe.
- **Liberal**: mostly middle-class business leaders and merchants. They wanted to give more power to elected parliaments, but only the educated and the landowners would vote.
- **Radical**: favored drastic change to extend democracy to all people. They believed that governments should practice the ideals of the French Revolution—liberty, equality, and brotherhood.

Nationalism Develops

As conservatives, liberals, and radicals debated issues of government, a new movement called nationalism emerged. **Nationalism** is the belief that people's greatest loyalty should not be to a king or an empire but to a nation of people who share a common culture and history. The nationalist movement would blur the lines that separated the three political theories.

When a nation had its own independent government, it became a **nation-state**. A nation-state defends the nation's territory and way of life, and it represents the nation to the rest of the world. In Europe in 1815, only

TAKING NOTES
Summarizing Identify major revolutions in Europe.

Revolts
1821   1830   1848

Nationalism

Nationalism—the belief that people should be loyal to their nation—was not widespread until the 1800s. The rise of modern nationalism is tied to the spread of democratic ideas and the growth of an educated middle class. People wanted to decide how they were governed, instead of having monarchs impose government on them.

Bonds That Create a Nation-State

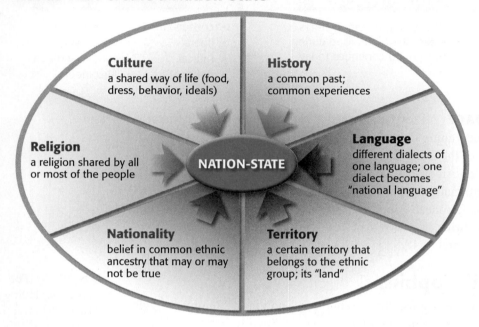

Culture
a shared way of life (food, dress, behavior, ideals)

History
a common past; common experiences

Religion
a religion shared by all or most of the people

NATION-STATE

Language
different dialects of one language; one dialect becomes "national language"

Nationality
belief in common ethnic ancestry that may or may not be true

Territory
a certain territory that belongs to the ethnic group; its "land"

Positive and Negative Results of Nationalism

Nationalism has not always been a positive influence. For example, extremely strong nationalistic feelings sometimes lead a group to turn against outsiders. The chart below lists some positive and negative results of nationalism. Note how some results, such as competition, can be both positive and negative.

Positive Results	Negative Results
• People within a nation overcoming their differences for the common good	• Forced assimilation of minority cultures into a nation's majority culture
• The overthrow of colonial rule	• Ethnic cleansing, such as in Bosnia and Herzegovina in the 1990s
• Democratic governments in nations throughout the world	• The rise of extreme nationalistic movements, such as Nazism
• Competition among nations spurring scientific and technological advances	• Competition between nations leading to warfare

INTEGRATED TECHNOLOGY
RESEARCH LINKS For more on nationalism, go to **classzone.com**

> DATA FILE

IMPACT OF NATIONALISM
• Between 1950 and 1980, 47 African countries overthrew colonial rulers and became independent nations.

• In the 1990s, the republics of Bosnia and Herzegovina, Croatia, Slovenia, and Macedonia broke away from Yugoslavia.

• In 2003, Yugoslavia changed its name to Serbia and Montenegro.

• Europe has 47 countries. (Some of those lie partially in Europe, partially in Asia.) About 50 languages are spoken in the region.

• In most of Latin America, Spanish or Portuguese is the official language. However, many native languages are still spoken. For example, Bolivia has three official languages: Spanish and the Indian languages of Aymara and Quechua.

Connect *to* Today

1. Forming and Supporting Opinions
Do you think nationalism has had more of a positive or negative impact on the world? Support your opinion with evidence.

 See Skillbuilder Handbook, page R20.

2. Comparing and Contrasting
Which of the bonds used to create nation-states are found in the United States?

France, England, and Spain could be called nation-states. But soon that would change as nationalist movements achieved success.

Most of the people who believed in nationalism were either liberals or radicals. In most cases, the liberal middle class—teachers, lawyers, and businesspeople—led the struggle for constitutional government and the formation of nation-states. In Germany, for example, liberals wanted to gather the many different German states into a single nation-state. Other liberals in large empires, such as the Hungarians in the Austrian Empire, wanted to split away and establish self-rule.

Nationalists Challenge Conservative Power

The first people to win self-rule during this period were the Greeks. For centuries, Greece had been part of the Ottoman Empire. The Ottomans controlled most of **the Balkans**. That region includes all or part of present-day Greece, Albania, Bulgaria, Romania, Turkey, and the former Yugoslavia. Greeks, however, had kept alive the memory of their ancient history and culture. Spurred on by the nationalist spirit, they demanded independence and rebelled against the Ottoman Turks in 1821.

Greeks Gain Independence The most powerful European governments opposed revolution. However, the cause of Greek independence was popular with people around the world. Russians, for example, felt a connection to Greek Orthodox Christians, who were ruled by the Muslim Ottomans. Educated Europeans and Americans loved and respected ancient Greek culture.

Eventually, as popular support for Greece grew, the powerful nations of Europe took the side of the Greeks. In 1827, a combined British, French, and Russian fleet destroyed the Ottoman fleet at the Battle of Navarino. In 1830, Britain, France, and Russia signed a treaty guaranteeing an independent kingdom of Greece. **Ⓐ**

MAIN IDEA

Analyzing Motives
Ⓐ Why would Europeans and Americans support the Greek revolutionary movement?

1830s Uprisings Crushed By the 1830s, the old order, carefully arranged at the Congress of Vienna, was breaking down. Revolutionary zeal swept across Europe. Liberals and nationalists throughout Europe were openly revolting against conservative governments.

Nationalist riots broke out against Dutch rule in the Belgian city of Brussels. In October 1830, the Belgians declared their independence from Dutch control. In Italy, nationalists worked to unite the many separate states on the Italian peninsula. Some were independent. Others were ruled by Austria, or by the pope. Eventually, Prince Metternich sent Austrian troops to restore order in Italy. The Poles living under the rule of Russia staged a revolt in Warsaw late in 1830. Russian armies took nearly an entire year to crush the Polish uprising. By the mid-1830s, the old order seemed to have reestablished itself. But the appearance of stability did not last long.

1848 Revolutions Fail to Unite In 1848, ethnic uprisings erupted throughout Europe. (See the map on page 245.) After an unruly mob in Vienna clashed with police, Metternich resigned and liberal uprisings broke out throughout the Austrian empire. In Budapest, nationalist leader Louis Kossuth called for a parliament and self-government

Social History

Nationalistic Music
As the force of nationalism began to rise in Europe, ethnic groups recognized their music as a unique element of their culture. Composers used folk melodies in their works. For example, Czech composer Antonin Dvořák (DVAWR•zhahk), pictured above, and the Norwegian composer Edvard Grieg incorporated popular melodies and legends into their works. These works became a source of pride and further encouraged the sense of nationalism. Richard Wagner created a cycle of four musical dramas called *Der Ring des Nibelungen*. His operas are considered the pinnacle of German nationalism.

▲ In *Combat Before the Hotel de Ville, July 28th, 1830,* Victor Schnetz portrays the riots in Paris that forced Charles X to flee to Great Britain.

for Hungary. Meanwhile in Prague, Czech liberals demanded Bohemian independence.

European politics continued to seesaw. Many liberal gains were lost to conservatives within a year. In one country after another, the revolutionaries failed to unite themselves or their nations. Conservatives regained their nerve and their power. By 1849, Europe had practically returned to the conservatism that had controlled governments before 1848. **B**

MAIN IDEA

Hypothesizing
B Why weren't the revolutions of 1830 and 1848 successful?

Radicals Change France

Radicals participated in many of the 1848 revolts. Only in France, however, was the radical demand for democratic government the main goal of revolution. In 1830, France's King Charles X tried to stage a return to absolute monarchy. The attempt sparked riots that forced Charles to flee to Great Britain. He was replaced by Louis-Philippe, who had long supported liberal reforms in France.

The Third Republic However, in 1848, after a reign of almost 18 years, Louis-Philippe fell from popular favor. Once again, a Paris mob overturned a monarchy and established a republic. The new republican government began to fall apart almost immediately. The radicals split into factions. One side wanted only political reform. The other side also wanted social and economic reform. The differences set off bloody battles in Parisian streets. The violence turned French citizens away from the radicals. As a result, a moderate constitution was drawn up later in 1848. It called for a parliament and a strong president to be elected by the people.

France Accepts a Strong Ruler In December 1848, <u>Louis-Napoleon</u>, the nephew of Napoleon Bonaparte, won the presidential election. Four years later, Louis-Napoleon Bonaparte took the title of Emperor Napoleon III. A majority of French voters accepted this action without complaint. The French were weary of instability. They welcomed a strong ruler who would bring peace to France. **C**

As France's emperor, Louis-Napoleon built railroads, encouraged industrialization, and promoted an ambitious program of public works. Gradually, because of Louis-Napoleon's policies, unemployment decreased in France, and the country experienced real prosperity.

MAIN IDEA

Summarizing
C How would you describe the political swings occurring in France between 1830 and 1852?

Reform in Russia

Unlike France, Russia in the 1800s had yet to leap into the modern industrialized world. Under Russia's feudal system, serfs were bound to the nobles whose land they worked. Nobles enjoyed almost unlimited power over them. By the 1820s, many Russians believed that serfdom must end. In their eyes, the system was morally wrong. It also prevented the empire from advancing economically. The czars, however, were reluctant to free the serfs. Freeing them would anger the landowners, whose support the czars needed to stay in power.

Defeat Brings Change Eventually, Russia's lack of development became obvious to Russians and to the whole world. In 1853, Czar Nicholas I threatened to take over part of the Ottoman Empire in the Crimean War. However, Russia's industries and transportation system failed to provide adequate supplies for the country's troops. As a result, in 1856, Russia lost the war against the combined forces of France, Great Britain, Sardinia, and the Ottoman Empire.

After the war, Nicholas's son, **Alexander II**, decided to move Russia toward modernization and social change. Alexander and his advisers believed that his reforms would allow Russia to compete with western Europe for world power.

Reform and Reaction The first and boldest of Alexander's reforms was a decree freeing the serfs in 1861. The abolition of serfdom, however, went only halfway. Peasant communities—rather than individual peasants—received about half the farmland in the country. Nobles kept the other half. The government paid the nobles for their land. Each peasant community, on the other hand, had 49 years to pay the government for the land it had received. So, while the serfs were legally free, the debt still tied them to the land.

Political and social reforms ground to a halt when terrorists assassinated Alexander II in 1881. His successor, Alexander III, tightened czarist control over the country. Alexander III and his ministers, however, encouraged industrial development to expand Russia's power. A major force behind Russia's drive toward industrial expansion was nationalism. Nationalism also stirred other ethnic groups. During the 1800s, such groups were uniting into nations and building industries to survive among other nation-states. **D**

History *in* Depth

Emancipation

In 1861, on the day before Abraham Lincoln became president of the United States, Czar Alexander II issued the Edict of Emancipation, freeing 20 million serfs. Less than two years later, President Lincoln issued the Emancipation Proclamation, freeing enslaved peoples living under the Confederacy.

The emancipation edicts did not entirely fulfill the hopes of Russian serfs or former slaves in the United States. Russian peasant communities, like the one pictured above, were still tied to the land. And Lincoln did not free enslaved people in the border states.

MAIN IDEA

Analyzing Issues
D Why did czars push for industrialization?

SECTION 2 ASSESSMENT

TERMS & NAMES 1. For each term or name, write a sentence explaining its significance.
• conservative • liberal • radical • nationalism • nation-state • the Balkans • Louis-Napoleon • Alexander II

USING YOUR NOTES	MAIN IDEAS	CRITICAL THINKING & WRITING
2. Why did most of the revolts fail?	3. How were radicals different from liberals? 4. Why did France's Third Republic fail? 5. What was the driving force behind Russia's industrial expansion?	6. **MAKING INFERENCES** Why might liberals and radicals join together in a nationalist cause? 7. **DRAWING CONCLUSIONS** Why did some liberals disapprove of the way Louis-Napoleon ruled France after the uprisings of 1848? 8. **EVALUATING DECISIONS** What consequences did Alexander's reforms have on Russia? 9. **WRITING ACTIVITY** REVOLUTION Imagine you live in Europe in 1848. Write a **letter** to a friend, stating your political position—conservative, liberal, or radical. Express your feelings about the uprisings and the future of Europe.

Revolts
1821   1830
1848

CONNECT TO TODAY WRITING A TV NEWS SCRIPT

Early in the 21st century, hostility between Greeks and Turks on the island of Cyprus was reduced. Prepare a **TV news script** about the current status of governing the island.

3

Nationalism

CASE STUDY: Italy and Germany

MAIN IDEA	WHY IT MATTERS NOW	TERMS & NAMES

POWER AND AUTHORITY Nationalism contributed to the formation of two new nations and a new political order in Europe.	Nationalism is the basis of world politics today and has often caused conflicts and wars.	• Russification • Junker
		• Camillo di • Otto von
		  Cavour Bismarck
		• Giuseppe • realpolitik
		  Garibaldi • kaiser

SETTING THE STAGE Nationalism was the most powerful idea of the 1800s. Its influence stretched throughout Europe and the Americas. It shaped countries by creating new ones or breaking up old ones. In Europe, it also upset the balance of power set up at the Congress of Vienna in 1815, affecting the lives of millions. Empires in Europe were made up of many different groups of people. Nationalism fed the desire of most of those groups to be free of the rule of empires and govern themselves in their traditional lands.

TAKING NOTES

Following Chronological Order List major events in the unification of Italy and of Germany.

1800   1900
├───────┼───────┤

Nationalism: A Force for Unity or Disunity

During the 1800s, nationalism fueled efforts to build nation-states. Nationalists were not loyal to kings, but to their people—to those who shared common bonds. Nationalists believed that people of a single "nationality," or ancestry, should unite under a single government. However, people who wanted to restore the old order from before the French Revolution saw nationalism as a force for disunity.

Gradually, authoritarian rulers began to see that nationalism could also unify masses of people. They soon began to use nationalist feelings for their own purposes. They built nation-states in areas where they remained firmly in control.

Types of Nationalist Movements		
Type	**Characteristics**	**Examples**
Unification	• Mergers of politically divided but culturally similar lands	• 19th century Germany • 19th century Italy
Separation	• Culturally distinct group resists being added to a state or tries to break away	• Greeks in the Ottoman Empire • French-speaking Canadians
State-building	• Culturally distinct groups form into a new state by accepting a single culture	• The United States • Turkey
SKILLBUILDER: Interpreting Charts **1. Categorizing** What types of nationalist movements can evolve in lands with culturally distinct groups? **2. Drawing Conclusions** What must be present for state-building to take place?		

In the chart on page 258, you can see the characteristics and examples of three types of nationalist movements. In today's world, groups still use the spirit of nationalism to unify, separate, or build up nation-states.

Nationalism Shakes Aging Empires

Three aging empires—the Austrian Empire of the Hapsburgs, the Russian Empire of the Romanovs, and the Ottoman Empire of the Turks—contained a mixture of ethnic groups. Control of land and ethnic groups moved back and forth between these empires, depending on victories or defeats in war and on royal marriages. When nationalism emerged in the 19th century, ethnic unrest threatened and eventually toppled these empires.

The Breakup of the Austrian Empire The Austrian Empire brought together Slovenes, Hungarians, Germans, Czechs, Slovaks, Croats, Poles, Serbs, and Italians. In 1866, Prussia defeated Austria in the Austro-Prussian War. With its victory, Prussia gained control of the newly organized North German Confederation, a union of Prussia and 21 smaller German political units. Then, pressured by the Hungarians, Emperor Francis Joseph of Austria split his empire in half, declaring Austria and Hungary independent states, with himself as ruler of both. The empire was now called Austria-Hungary or the Austro-Hungarian Empire. Nationalist disputes continued to weaken the empire for more than 40 years. Finally, after World War I, Austria-Hungary broke into several separate nation-states.

The Russian Empire Crumbles Nationalism also helped break up the 370-year-old empire of the czars in Russia. In addition to the Russians themselves, the czar ruled over 22 million Ukrainians, 8 million Poles, and smaller numbers of Lithuanians, Latvians, Estonians, Finns, Jews, Romanians, Georgians, Armenians, Turks, and others. Each group had its own culture.

The ruling Romanov dynasty of Russia was determined to maintain iron control over this diversity. They instituted a policy of **Russification**, forcing Russian culture on all the ethnic groups in the empire. This policy actually strengthened ethnic nationalist feelings and helped to disunify Russia. The weakened czarist empire finally could not withstand the double shock of World War I and the communist revolution. The last Romanov czar gave up his power in 1917. **A**

The Ottoman Empire Weakens The ruling Turks of the Ottoman Empire controlled Greeks, Slavs, Arabs, Bulgarians, and Armenians. In 1856, under pressure from the British and French, the Ottomans granted equal citizenship to all the people under their rule. That measure angered conservative Turks, who wanted no change in the situation, and caused tensions in the empire. For example, in response to nationalism in

MAIN IDEA

Making Inferences

A Why might a policy like Russification produce results that are opposite those intended?

◄ Driven from their homes, Armenians beg for bread at a refugee center.

Armenia, the Ottomans massacred and deported Armenians from 1894 to 1896 and again in 1915. Like Austria-Hungary, the Ottoman Empire broke apart soon after World War I.

Cavour Unites Italy

While nationalism destroyed empires, it also built nations. Italy was one of the countries to form from the territory of crumbling empires. Between 1815 and 1848, fewer and fewer Italians were content to live under foreign rulers.

Cavour Leads Italian Unification Italian nationalists looked for leadership from the kingdom of Piedmont-Sardinia, the largest and most powerful of the Italian states. The kingdom had adopted a liberal constitution in 1848. So, to the liberal Italian middle classes, unification under Piedmont-Sardinia seemed a good plan.

In 1852, Sardinia's king, Victor Emmanuel II, named Count **Camillo di Cavour** (kuh•VOOR) as his prime minister. Cavour was a cunning statesman who worked tirelessly to expand Piedmont-Sardinia's power. Using skillful diplomacy and well-chosen alliances he set about gaining control of northern Italy for Sardinia.

Cavour realized that the greatest roadblock to annexing northern Italy was Austria. In 1858, the French emperor Napoleon III agreed to help drive Austria out of the northern Italian provinces. Cavour then provoked a war with the Austrians. A combined French-Sardinian army won two quick victories. Sardinia succeeded in taking all of northern Italy, except Venetia.

Garibaldi Brings Unity As Cavour was uniting northern Italy, he secretly started helping nationalist rebels in southern Italy. In May 1860, a small army of Italian nationalists led by a bold and visionary soldier, **Giuseppe Garibaldi** (GAR•uh• BAWL•dee), captured Sicily. In battle, Garibaldi always wore a bright red shirt, as did his followers. As a result, they became known as the Red Shirts.

From Sicily, Garibaldi and his forces crossed to the Italian mainland and marched north. Eventually, Garibaldi agreed to unite the southern areas he had conquered with the kingdom of Piedmont-Sardinia. Cavour arranged for King Victor Emmanuel II to meet Garibaldi in Naples. "The Red One" willingly agreed to step aside and let the Sardinian king rule. **B**

In 1866, the Austrian province of Venetia, which included the city of Venice, became part of Italy. In 1870,

The Unification of Italy, 1858–1870
INTERACTIVE

FRANCE
SWITZERLAND
ALPS
AUSTRIAN EMPIRE
SAVOY
To France, 1860
Milan
Turin LOMBARDY
PIEDMONT
Genoa
NICE
PARMA
MODENA
LUCCA
Pisa
Florence
TUSCANY
CORSICA (Fr.)
Rome
PAPAL STATES
Mediterranean Sea
SARDINIA
Naples
KINGDOM OF THE TWO SICILIES
Palermo
SICILY
Tyrrhenian Sea
Adriatic Sea
OTTOMAN EMPIRE
VENETIA
Venice
Rhône R.
Loire R.
Po R.
Arno R.
Tiber R.
Drava R.
Sava R.
Danube R.
50° N
42° N

- Kingdom of Sardinia, 1858
- Added to Sardinia, 1859–1860
- Added to Italy, 1866
- Added to Italy, 1870
- Papal States

0   200 Miles
0   400 Kilometers
N

GEOGRAPHY SKILLBUILDER: Interpreting Maps
1. **Movement** During what time period was the greatest share of territory unified in Italy?
2. **Region** Which territories did the Italians lose to France during their process of unification?

MAIN IDEA
Hypothesizing
B What reasons might Garibaldi have had to step aside and let the Sardinian king rule?

"Right Leg in the Boot at Last"

In this 1860 British cartoon, the king of Sardinia is receiving control of lands taken by the nationalist Garibaldi. The act was one of the final steps in the unification of Italy.

SKILLBUILDER: Analyzing Political Cartoons

1. **Clarifying** *What symbol does the cartoonist use for the soon-to-be nation of Italy?*
2. **Making Inferences** *How is Garibaldi portrayed?*
3. **Analyzing Bias** *What does the title of the cartoon say about the cartoonist's view of Italian unification?*

 See Skillbuilder Handbook, page R29

Italian forces took over the last part of a territory known as the Papal States. With this victory, the city of Rome came under Italian control. Soon after, Rome became the capital of the united kingdom of Italy. The pope, however, would continue to govern a section of Rome known as Vatican City.

CASE STUDY: GERMANY

Bismarck Unites Germany

Like Italy, Germany also achieved national unity in the mid-1800s. Beginning in 1815, 39 German states formed a loose grouping called the German Confederation. The Austrian Empire dominated the confederation. However, Prussia was ready to unify all the German states.

Prussia Leads German Unification Prussia enjoyed several advantages that would eventually help it forge a strong German state. First of all, unlike the Austro-Hungarian Empire, Prussia had a mainly German population. As a result, nationalism actually unified Prussia. In contrast, ethnic groups in Austria-Hungary tore the empire apart. Moreover, Prussia's army was by far the most powerful in central Europe. In 1848, Berlin rioters forced a constitutional convention to write up a liberal constitution for the kingdom, paving the way for unification.

Bismarck Takes Control In 1861, Wilhelm I succeeded Frederick William to the throne. The liberal parliament refused him money for reforms that would double the strength of the army. Wilhelm saw the parliament's refusal as a major challenge to his authority. He was supported in his view by the **Junkers** (YUNG•kuhrz), strongly conservative members of Prussia's wealthy landowning class. In 1862, Wilhelm chose a conservative Junker named **Otto von Bismarck** as his prime minister. Bismarck was a master of what came to be known as **realpolitik**. This

Otto von Bismarck
1815–1898

To some Germans, Bismarck was the greatest and noblest of Germany's statesmen. They say he almost single-handedly unified the nation and raised it to greatness. To others, he was nothing but a devious politician who abused his powers and led Germany into dictatorship.

His speeches, letters, and memoirs show him to be both crafty and deeply religious. At one moment, he could declare, "It is the destiny of the weak to be devoured by the strong." At another moment he might claim, "We Germans shall never wage aggressive war, ambitious war, a war of conquest."

INTEGRATED TECHNOLOGY

INTERNET ACTIVITY Create an interactive time line of Bismarck's actions to unite Germany. Go to **classzone.com** for your research.

German term means "the politics of reality." The term is used to describe tough power politics with no room for idealism. With realpolitik as his style, Bismarck would become one of the commanding figures of German history.

With the king's approval, Bismarck declared that he would rule without the consent of parliament and without a legal budget. Those actions were in direct violation of the constitution. In his first speech as prime minister, he defiantly told members of the Prussian parliament, "It is not by means of speeches and majority resolutions that the great issues of the day will be decided—that was the great mistake of 1848 and 1849—but by blood and iron." **C**

Prussia Expands In 1864, Bismarck took the first step toward molding an empire. Prussia and Austria formed an alliance and went to war against Denmark to win two border provinces, Schleswig and Holstein.

A quick victory increased national pride among Prussians. It also won new respect from other Germans and lent support for Prussia as head of a unified Germany. After the victory, Prussia governed Schleswig, while Austria controlled Holstein.

Seven Weeks' War Bismarck purposely stirred up border conflicts with Austria over Schleswig and Holstein. The tensions provoked Austria into declaring war on Prussia in 1866. This conflict was known as the Seven Weeks' War. The Prussians used their superior training and equipment to win a devastating victory. They humiliated Austria. The Austrians lost the region of Venetia, which was given to Italy. They had to accept Prussian annexation of more German territory.

With its victory in the Seven Weeks' War, Prussia took control of northern Germany. For the first time, the eastern and western parts of the Prussian kingdom were joined. In 1867, the remaining states of the north joined the North German Confederation, which Prussia dominated completely.

The Franco-Prussian War By 1867, a few southern German states remained independent of Prussian control. The majority of southern Germans were Catholics. Many in the region resisted domination by a Protestant Prussia. However, Bismarck felt he could win the support of southerners if they faced a threat from outside. He reasoned that a war with France would rally the south.

Bismarck was an expert at manufacturing "incidents" to gain his ends. For example, he created the impression that the French ambassador had insulted the Prussian king. The French reacted to Bismarck's deception by declaring war on Prussia on July 19, 1870.

The Prussian army immediately poured into northern France. In September 1870, the Prussian army surrounded the main French force at Sedan. Among the 83,000 French prisoners taken was Napoleon III himself. Parisians withstood a German siege until hunger forced them to surrender.

The Franco-Prussian War was the final stage in German unification. Now the nationalistic fever also seized people in southern Germany. They finally accepted Prussian leadership. On January 18, 1871, at the captured French palace of

MAIN IDEA

Hypothesizing
C Bismarck ignored both the parliament and the constitution. How do you think this action would affect Prussian government?

Versailles, King Wilhelm I of Prussia was crowned **kaiser** (KY•zuhr), or emperor. Germans called their empire the Second Reich. (The Holy Roman Empire was the first.) Bismarck had achieved Prussian dominance over Germany and Europe "by blood and iron."

A Shift in Power

The 1815 Congress of Vienna had established five Great Powers in Europe—Britain, France, Austria, Prussia, and Russia. In 1815, the Great Powers were nearly equal in strength. The wars of the mid-1800s greatly strengthened one of the Great Powers, as Prussia joined with other German states to form Germany.

By 1871, Britain and Germany were clearly the most powerful, both militarily and economically. Austria and Russia lagged far behind. France struggled along somewhere in the middle. The European balance of power had broken down. This shift also found expression in the art of the period. In fact, during that century, artists, composers, and writers pointed to paths that they believed European society should follow.

The Unification of Germany, 1865–1871

INTER*ACTIVE*

Prussia, 1865

Annexed by Prussia, 1866

Joined Prussia in North German Confederation, 1867

South German States (joined Prussia to form German Empire, 1871)

Conquered from France, 1871

— German Empire, 1871

GEOGRAPHY SKILLBUILDER: Interpreting Maps
1. **Location** What was unusual about the territory of Prussia as it existed in 1865?
2. **Movement** After 1865, what year saw the biggest expansion of Prussian territory?

SECTION 3 ASSESSMENT

TERMS & NAMES 1. For each term or name, write a sentence explaining its significance.
• Russification   • Camillo di Cavour   • Giuseppe Garibaldi   • Junker   • Otto von Bismarck   • realpolitik   • kaiser

USING YOUR NOTES
2. Identify an event that made the unification of Italy or Germany possible.

1800   1900

MAIN IDEAS
3. Which aging empires suffered from the forces of nationalism?

4. What role did Garibaldi play in the unification of Italy?

5. What advantages did Prussia have in leading the German states to unify?

CRITICAL THINKING & WRITING
6. **CLARIFYING** How can nationalism be both a unifying and a disunifying force?

7. **FORMING GENERALIZATIONS** Why did the Austrian, Russian, and Ottoman Empires face such great challenges to their control of land?

8. **EVALUATING COURSES OF ACTION** Many liberals wanted government by elected parliaments. How was Bismarck's approach to achieving his goals different?

9. **WRITING ACTIVITY** POWER AND AUTHORITY Write a one paragraph **biographical essay** on either Garibaldi or Cavour.

CONNECT TO TODAY CREATING A MAP AND DATABASE

Study the chart on page 258. Research the names of nations that have emerged in the last ten years. Categorize each nation's nationalist movement using the chart. Then create a **database** and **map** showing the location of the new nations and the category into which each new nation falls.

Revolutions in the Arts

MAIN IDEA	**WHY IT MATTERS NOW**	**TERMS & NAMES**
CULTURAL INTERACTION Artistic and intellectual movements both reflected and fueled changes in Europe during the 1800s.	Romanticism and realism are still found in novels, dramas, and films produced today.	• romanticism • impressionism • realism

SETTING THE STAGE During the first half of the 1800s, artists focused on ideas of freedom, the rights of individuals, and an idealistic view of history. After the great revolutions of 1848, political focus shifted to leaders who practiced realpolitik. Similarly, intellectuals and artists expressed a "realistic" view of the world. In this view, the rich pursued their selfish interests while ordinary people struggled and suffered. Newly invented photography became both a way to detail this struggle and a tool for scientific investigation.

TAKING NOTES

Outlining Organize ideas and details about movements in the arts.

I. The Romantic Movement
A.
B.
II. The Shift to Realism in the Arts

The Romantic Movement

At the end of the 18th century, the Enlightenment idea of reason gradually gave way to another major movement in art and ideas: **romanticism**. This movement reflected deep interest both in nature and in the thoughts and feelings of the individual. In many ways, romantic thinkers and writers reacted against the ideals of the Enlightenment. They turned from reason to emotion, from society to nature. Romantics rejected the rigidly ordered world of the middle class. Nationalism also fired the romantic imagination. For example, George Gordon, Lord Byron, one of the leading romantic poets of the time, fought for Greece's freedom.

The Ideas of Romanticism Emotion, sometimes wild emotion, was a key element of romanticism. However, romanticism went beyond feelings. Romantics expressed a wide range of ideas and attitudes. In general, romantic thinkers and artists shared these beliefs:

- emphasized inner feelings, emotions, and imagination
- focused on the mysterious, the supernatural, and the exotic, grotesque, or horrifying
- loved the beauties of untamed nature
- idealized the past as a simpler and nobler time
- glorified heroes and heroic actions
- cherished folk traditions, music, and stories
- valued the common people and the individual
- promoted radical change and democracy

Romanticism in Literature Poetry, music, and painting were the most influential arts because they were able to capture the emotion of romanticism. To romantics, poetry was the highest

▼ Romantic poet Lord Byron fought with Greek nationalists. He did not live to see their victory.

form of expression. The British romantic poets William Wordsworth and Samuel Taylor Coleridge both honored nature as the source of truth and beauty. Later English romantic poets, such as Lord Byron, Percy Bysshe Shelley, and John Keats, wrote poems celebrating rebellious heroes, passionate love, and the mystery and beauty of nature. Like many romantics, many of these British poets lived stormy lives and died young. Byron, for example, died at the age of 36, while Shelley died at 29.

Germany produced one of the earliest and greatest romantic writers. In 1774, Johann Wolfgang von Goethe (YO•hahn VUHLF•gahng fuhn GER•tuh) published *The Sorrows of Young Werther*. Goethe's novel told of a sensitive young man whose hopeless love for a virtuous married woman drives him to suicide. Also in Germany, the brothers Jakob and Wilhelm Grimm collected German fairy tales and created a dictionary and grammar of the German language. Both the tales and the dictionary celebrated the German spirit.

Victor Hugo led the French romantics. His works also reflect the romantic fascination with history and the individual. His novels *Les Misérables* and *The Hunchback of Notre Dame* show the struggles of individuals against a hostile society.

The Gothic Novel Gothic horror stories became hugely popular. These novels often took place in medieval Gothic castles. They were filled with fearful, violent, sometimes supernatural events. Mary Shelley, wife of the poet Percy Bysshe Shelley, wrote one of the earliest and most successful Gothic horror novels, *Frankenstein*. The novel told the story of a monster created from the body parts of dead human beings.

Composers Emphasize Emotion Emotion dominated the music produced by romantic composers. These composers moved away from the tightly controlled, formal compositions of the Enlightenment period. Instead, they celebrated heroism and national pride with a new power of expression.

As music became part of middle-class life, musicians and composers became popular heroes. Composer and pianist Franz Liszt (lihst), for example, achieved earnings and popularity comparable to those of today's rock stars.

One of the composers leading the way into the Romantic period was also its greatest: Ludwig van Beethoven (LOOD•vihg vahn BAY•toh•vuhn). His work evolved from the classical music of the Enlightenment into romantic compositions. His Ninth Symphony soars, celebrating freedom, dignity, and the triumph of the human spirit.

Later romantic composers also appealed to the hearts and souls of their listeners. Robert Schumann's compositions sparkle with merriment. Like many romantic composers, Felix Mendelssohn drew on literature, such as Shakespeare's A *Midsummer Night's Dream*, as the inspiration for his music. Polish composer and concert pianist Frederic Chopin (SHOH•pan) used Polish dance rhythms in his music. Guiseppe Verdi and Richard Wagner brought European opera to a dramatic and theatrical high point. **A**

MAIN IDEA

Summarizing

A What are some of the themes that are key to romantic literature and art?

History Makers

Ludwig van Beethoven
1770–1827

A genius of European music, Beethoven suffered the most tragic disability a composer can endure. At the age of 30, he began to go deaf. His deafness grew worse for 19 years. By 1819, it was total.

At first, Beethoven's handicap barely affected his career. By 1802, however, he knew that his hearing would only worsen. He suffered from bouts of depression. The depression would bring him to the brink of suicide. Nonetheless, he would rebound:

It seemed unthinkable for me to leave the world forever before I had produced all that I felt called upon to produce.

INTEGRATED / TECHNOLOGY

RESEARCH LINKS For more on Ludwig van Beethoven, go to **classzone.com**

The Shift to Realism in the Arts

By the middle of the 19th century, rapid industrialization deeply affected everyday life in Europe. The growing class of industrial workers lived grim lives in dirty, crowded cities. Industrialization began to make the dreams of the romantics seem pointless. In literature and the visual arts, **realism** tried to show life as it was, not as it should be. Realist painting reflected the increasing political importance of the working class in the 1850s. Along with paintings, novels proved especially suitable for describing workers' suffering.

Photographers Capture Reality As realist painters and writers detailed the lives of actual people, photographers could record an instant in time with scientific precision. The first practical photographs were called daguerreotypes (duh•GEHR•uh•TYPS). They were named after their French inventor, Louis Daguerre. The images in his daguerreotypes were startlingly real and won him worldwide fame.

British inventor William Talbot invented a light-sensitive paper that he used to produce photographic negatives. The advantage of paper was that many prints could be made from one negative. The Talbot process also allowed photos to be reproduced in books and newspapers. Mass distribution gained a wide audience for the realism of photography. With its scientific, mechanical, and mass-produced features, photography was the art of the new industrial age.

Writers Study Society Realism in literature flourished in France with writers such as Honoré de Balzac and Émile Zola. Balzac wrote a massive series of almost 100 novels entitled *The Human Comedy*. They describe in detail the brutal struggle for wealth and power among all levels of French society. Zola's novels exposed the

> Analyzing Photographs

Motion Studies

Eadweard Muybridge had a varied career as a photographer. He devoted part of his career to motion studies. These photographic studies froze the motion of an object at an instant in time. They allowed scientists to study motion and to better understand time. The equipment he built helped lead to the development of motion pictures.

This series of photographs taken in 1878, titled "The Horse in Motion," was designed to discover if all of a running horse's legs ever left the ground at the same time.

SKILLBUILDER: Interpreting Visual Sources

1. **Drawing Conclusions** *What do the series of photographs reveal about the question of whether all the legs of a horse ever left the ground at the same time?*

2. **Developing Historical Perspective** *What reaction do you think these pictures would have generated among the general public?*

See Skillbuilder Handbook, page R23.

MAIN IDEA

Forming Opinions

 Which do you th nk would be more effective in spurring reforms—photographs or a realist novel? Explain.

miseries of French workers in small shops, factories, and coal mines. His revelations shocked readers and spurred reforms of labor laws and working conditions in France. The famous English realist novelist Charles Dickens created unforgettable characters and scenes of London's working poor. Many of the scenes were humorous, but others showed the despair of London's poor. In his book *Little Dorrit*, Dickens described the life of a working-class person as sheer monotony set in a gloomy neighborhood. **B**

Impressionists React Against Realism

Beginning in the 1860s, a group of painters in Paris reacted against the realist style. Instead of showing life "as it really was," they tried to show their impression of a subject or a moment in time. For this reason, their style of art came to be known as **impressionism**. Fascinated by light, impressionist artists used pure, shimmering colors to capture a moment seen at a glance.

Life in the Moment Unlike the realists, impressionists showed a more positive view of the new urban society in western Europe. Instead of abused workers, they showed shop clerks and dock workers enjoying themselves in dance halls and cafés. They painted performers in theaters and circuses. And they glorified the delights of the life of the rising middle class. Claude Monet (moh•NAY), Edgar Degas (duh•GAH), and Pierre-Auguste Renoir (ruhn•WHAR) were leaders in the movement that became very popular.

Composers also created impressions of mood and atmosphere. By using different combinations of instruments, tone patterns, and music structures, they were able to create mental pictures of such things as flashing lights, the feel of a warm summer day, or the sight of the sea. French composers Maurice Ravel and Claude Debussy are the most notable members of the impressionist music movement.

Changes in political, social, artistic, and intellectual movements during the 19th century signaled important changes in daily life. One of the most significant causes of change was industrialization, which you will learn about in Chapter 9.

SECTION 4 ASSESSMENT

TERMS & NAMES 1. For each term or name, write a sentence explaining its significance.
• romanticism   • realism   • impressionism

USING YOUR NOTES

2. What was the goal of realist writers?

I. The Romantic Movement
   A.
   B.
II. The Shift to Realism in the Arts

MAIN IDEAS

3. What was the key element of romanticism?

4. What characteristics did photography have that made it the art of the industrial age?

5. What was the goal of impressionist painters?

CRITICAL THINKING & WRITING

6. **COMPARING AND CONTRASTING** How are the movements of romanticism and realism alike and different?

7. **ANALYZING CAUSES** How might a realist novel bring about changes in society? Describe the ways by which this might happen.

8. **SUMMARIZING** How did nationalism influence the artistic movements you read about?

9. **WRITING ACTIVITY** CULTURAL INTERACTION Listen to a piece of music by Beethoven, and then listen to a piece of contemporary music that you like. Write a **comparison-and-contrast essay** on the two pieces of music.

CONNECT TO TODAY Creating an Arts Chart

Look at newspaper listings for films being shown today. Make a **chart** showing which of them might be categorized as romantic and which might be categorized as realistic. Present reasons why each film fell into the designated category.

Revolutions in Painting

European painting underwent revolutionary changes during the 1800s. In the early years, romanticism—which stressed emotion above all else—was the dominant style. As revolutions swept Europe in the 1840s, some artists rejected romanticism in favor of realism. They portrayed common people and everyday life in a realistic manner. Toward the end of the century, art underwent another revolution, influenced by scientific discoveries about vision. Impressionist painters experimented with light and color to capture their impressions of a passing moment.

INTEGRATED / TECHNOLOGY

RESEARCH LINKS For more on 19th-century painting go to **classzone.com**

▼ Romanticism

In their eagerness to explore emotion, romantic artists had certain favorite subjects: nature, love, religion, and nationalism. This painting, *The Lion Hunt* by Eugène Delacroix, shows that violence and exotic cultures were also popular themes. The swirling capes, snarling lions, and bold reds and yellows help convey the ferocity of the hunt.

▲ Realism

The Stone Breakers by Gustave Courbet shows that realist artists tried to portray everyday life just as it was, without making it pretty or trying to tell a moralistic story. Notice how the workers' clothes are torn and shabby. The boy rests the heavy basket of stones on his knee to ease his burden, while the man bends to his task. The colors are dull and gritty, just as the job itself is.

▼ Impressionism

The impressionists wanted to record the perceptions of the human eye rather than physical reality. To do this, they tried to portray the effect of light on landscapes and buildings. They combined short strokes of many colors to create a shimmering effect. They also used brighter, lighter colors than the artists before them had used. As the painting *Ducal Palace, Venice* by Claude Monet shows, the impressionists often painted water because of its reflective nature.

Connect *to* Today

1. **Developing Historical Perspective** If you were a political revolutionary of the 1800s, which of these artistic styles would you use for your propaganda posters? Why?
   See Skillbuilder Handbook, page R12.

2. **Drawing Conclusions** Impressionism remains extremely popular more than a century after it was first developed. What do you think accounts for its popularity today?

269

TERMS & NAMES

Briefly explain the importance of each of the following to the revolutions in Latin America or Europe.

1. conservative
2. liberal
3. nationalism
4. nation-state
5. realpolitik
6. romanticism
7. realism
8. impressionism

MAIN IDEAS

Latin American Peoples Win Independence
Section 1 (pages 247–252)

9. What caused the creoles in South America to rebel against Spain?
10. What role did Agustín de Iturbide play in the independence of Mexico?
11. Who was Dom Pedro, and what role did he play in Brazil's move to independence?

Europe Faces Revolutions Section 2 (pages 253–257)

12. How is a liberal different from a conservative?
13. How successful were the revolts of 1848? Explain.
14. Why did the French accept Louis-Napoleon as an emperor?

Case Study: Nationalism Section 3 (pages 258–263)

15. How did nationalism in the 1800s work as a force for both disunity and unity?
16. What approaches did Camillo di Cavour use to acquire more territory for Piedmont-Sardinia?
17. What strategy did Otto von Bismarck use to make Prussia the leader of a united Germany?

Revolutions in the Arts Section 4 (pages 264–269)

18. What are five elements of romanticism?
19. What are two ideas or attitudes of the romantic movement that reflect the ideals of nationalism?
20. What new conditions caused a change in the arts from romanticism to realism?

CRITICAL THINKING

1. USING YOUR NOTES

Using a chart, describe the nationalist movement in each of the countries listed and the results of each movement.

Country	Nationalism and Its Results
Mexico	
Greece	
Italy	
Germany	

2. EVALUATING DECISIONS

POWER AND AUTHORITY Why do you think Giuseppe Garibaldi stepped aside to let Victor Emmanuel II rule areas that Garibaldi had conquered in southern Italy?

3. ANALYZING MOTIVES

REVOLUTION How do you think nationalism might help revolutionaries overcome the disadvantages of old weapons and poor supplies to win a war for national independence? Explain.

4. MAKING INFERENCES

Do you believe the Latin American revolutions would have occurred without a push from European events? Explain.

5. SYNTHESIZING

CULTURAL INTERACTION How did artistic and intellectual movements reflect and fuel changes in Europe in the 1800s?

VISUAL SUMMARY

Nationalist Revolutions Sweep the West

NATIONALISM

Latin America	1830 & 1848 Revolutions	Unification Movements	The Arts
• Enlightenment ideas • Haiti: slave-led • South America: creole-led, especially Bolívar and San Martín • Brazil: royalty-led	• Reactions against conservatives • A few reforms • Most failed	• Garibaldi begins in Italy. • Prime Minister Cavour completes the task. • Prime Minister Bismarck leads the way in Germany.	• Romantics inspired by emotion • Dedication to common people or the group • Realists see flaws and set new goals for nation. • Impressionists capture the moment.

Use the quotation and your knowledge of world history to answer questions 1 and 2.
Additional Test Practice, pp. S1–S33

PRIMARY SOURCE

When I say that we must strive continually to be ready for all emergencies, I advance the proposition that, on account of our geographical position, we must make greater efforts than other powers would be obliged to make in view of the same ends. We lie in the middle of Europe. We have at least three fronts on which we can be attacked. France has only an eastern boundary; Russia only its western, exposed to assault. . . . So we are spurred forward on both sides to endeavors which perhaps we would not make otherwise.

OTTO VON BISMARCK, *speech to the German parliament on February 6, 1888*

1. According to Bismarck, what key factor makes Germany a potential target for invasion?

   A. dangerous neighbors

   B. three borders to protect

   C. location in the middle of Europe

   D. massive supplies of coal and iron

2. Based on his remarks above, what actions might Bismarck take?

   A. form alliances with other nations in Europe

   B. make peace with France

   C. make peace with England

   D. expand industry

Use this 20th-century mural titled *Grito de Dolores* painted by Juan O'Gorman and your knowledge of world history to answer question 3.

3. Look at the people portrayed in the mural. What does the artist suggest about the Mexican revolt against the Spanish?

   A. It was condemned by the Catholic Church.

   B. Only the poor fought against Spanish rule.

   C. People of all classes fought against Spanish rule.

   D. Only Indians fought Spanish rule.

INTEGRATED TECHNOLOGY

TEST PRACTICE Go to **classzone.com**

• Diagnostic tests   • Strategies

• Tutorials   • Additional practice

ALTERNATIVE ASSESSMENT

1. Interact *with* History

On page 246, you were asked to create a symbol for your newly independent country. Show your symbol to the class. Explain the elements of your design and what they are intended to express. With your classmates' comments in mind, what might you change in your design?

2. WRITING ABOUT HISTORY

Write a **speech** that might have been delivered somewhere in Europe at a rally for Greek independence. Urge the country's leaders to help the Greeks in their struggle for independence from the Ottoman Empire. Consider the following:

• the connections of Greece to Europeans

• reasons to support Greek revolutionaries

• the cause of democracy

INTEGRATED TECHNOLOGY

Creating a Web Page

Use the Internet, newspapers, magazines, and your own experience to make a list of movies that portray social and political conditions. Then create a Web page that classifies each portrayal as either romantic or realistic. Remember to focus on the meanings of the terms romantic and realistic as they apply to the two movements in art and literature. You may want to include on your Web page:

• descriptions of movie plots or character portrayals

• still shots from movies that support your conclusions

• romantic or realistic quotations from movies

Revolutions Across Time

Revolution—which is a sudden or significant change in the old ways of doing things—can occur in many areas, such as government, technology, or art. In Unit 2, you studied political revolutions in Europe and the Americas, in which people rebelled against unjust rulers to gain more rights. Each revolution led to major changes in governmental, social, and economic structures. In these six pages, you will gain a better understanding of those revolutions by examining their similarities and differences.

English Civil War and Glorious Revolution ▶

In 1642, civil war broke out between those who supported Parliament and those who supported the king. Parliament won and set up a commonwealth, led by Oliver Cromwell. In time, he became a dictator. After his death, the monarchy returned, but tensions built anew. In 1688, Parliament ousted King James II, shown at right, in the Glorious Revolution and invited William and Mary to rule.

1642   **1776**   **1789**

◀ American Revolution

After 1763, Americans began to resent British rule. Clashes such as the Boston Massacre, shown at left, took place. The colonies declared their independence **in 1776**. War ensued, and the United States won its freedom by defeating Britain.

▼ French Revolution

Beginning in 1789, the French people rose up to overthrow their king. The uprisings included the march by hungry women shown below. Differing goals soon split the revolutionaries. Several years of terror followed. Napoleon restored order and eventually made himself emperor of France.

1791

▲ **Latin American Revolutions**

From 1791 to 1824, revolutions took place in Haiti, Mexico, and the huge Spanish empire that spread across Central and South America. By the end of that period, nearly all of Latin America had gained its independence from European control. One of South America's great liberators was José de San Martín, shown in the painting above.

Model of a Revolution

From his study of the French Revolution, historian Crane Brinton developed a model of the stages that revolutions often go through. The model below is based on his work. Compare it with the revolutions you learned about in this unit.

STAGE 1 **Fall of the Old Order**

Revolutions usually cannot occur until a ruler becomes weak. Often this weakness results in problems such as starvation and unfair taxes. Anger builds until the ruler is overthrown.

STAGE 2 **Rule by Moderates**

The people relax because they think they have achieved their goal. A moderate group rules. But simply overthrowing the old order rarely solves the problems that led to the revolution.

STAGE 3 **The Terror**

When people realize that the old problems still exist, they look for someone to blame. Radicals take control, push for more extreme changes, and execute "enemies of the revolution."

STAGE 4 **Turn from Radical Rule**

In time, the violence sickens people, and the use of terror ends. The former radicals adopt a more gradual plan for effecting change.

STAGE 5 **Military Rule**

The terror often kills most of a country's leaders. Then the turn from radicalism makes people doubt revolutionary ideals. A military leader steps into the gap and becomes dictator.

STAGE 6 **Restoration**

When the dictatorship ends, through death or overthrow, a power vacuum results. The order that existed before the revolution is restored.

Comparing & Contrasting

1. Which of the revolutions on the time line, besides the French Revolution, is most like the model? Explain.

2. Which revolution is least like the model? Explain.

Causes of the Revolutions

Each of the revolutions you studied in this unit had political, economic, and social causes, as shown in the chart below. Some of the causes mentioned on the chart are the subjects of the primary sources located on the next page. Use the chart and the primary sources together to understand the causes of revolution more fully.

	England	North America	France	Latin America
Political	• King claimed divine right. • King dissolved Parliament. • Parliament sought guarantee of freedoms.	• Colonists accused British leaders of tyranny. • Colonists demanded the same rights as English citizens.	• Third Estate wanted greater representation. • Louis XVI was a weak ruler; his wife was unpopular. • American Revolution inspired political ideas.	• French Revolution inspired political ideas. • Royal officials committed injustices and repression. • Napoleon's conquest of Spain triggered revolts.
Economic	• King wanted money for wars. • King levied taxes and fines without Parliament's approval.	• Britain imposed mercantilism. • Britain expected colonies to pay for defense. • Colonists opposed taxation without representation.	• Wars and royal extravagance created debt. • Inflation and famine caused problems. • Peasants made little money but paid high taxes.	• Peninsulares and creoles controlled wealth. • Lower classes toiled as peasants with little income or as slaves.
Social	• Early Stuart kings refused to make Puritan reforms. • Parliament feared James II would restore Catholicism.	• Colonists began to identify as Americans. • Colonists were used to some independence. • Enlightenment ideas of equality and liberty spread.	• Third Estate resented the First and Second estates' privileges. • Enlightenment ideas of equality and liberty spread.	• Only peninsulares and creoles had power. • Mestizos, mulattos, Africans, and Indians had little status. • Educated creoles spread Enlightenment ideas.

SKILLBUILDER: Interpreting Charts

1. Analyzing Causes *What was the most frequent political cause of revolution? economic cause? social cause?*

2. Contrasting *How did the causes of the revolutions in Latin America differ from those of the other three revolutions?*

◄ In the 1780s, many French peasants could not afford bread to feed their families. At the same time, Marie Antoinette spent so much money on clothes that her enemies called her Madame Deficit. The harsh contrast between starvation and luxury sparked the anger that led to the Revolution.

Political Cartoon, 1789

This French political cartoon portrayed the way the privileges of the First and Second estates affected the Third Estate.

DOCUMENT-BASED QUESTION
Do you think a member of the First, Second, or Third Estate created this cartoon? Interpret the cartoon and explain who was most likely to hold the viewpoint conveyed.

INTER**ACTIVE**

The English Bill of Rights, 1689

This excerpt from the English Bill of Rights attempted to justify the Glorious Revolution by describing the injustices King James II committed.

The late King James the Second, by the assistance of diverse evil counselors, judges and ministers employed by him, did endeavor to subvert and extirpate [destroy] the Protestant religion and the laws and liberties of this kingdom;

By assuming and exercising a power of dispensing with and suspending of laws and the execution of laws without consent of Parliament; . . .

By levying money for and to the use of the Crown by pretense of prerogative [privilege] for other time and in other manner than the same was granted by Parliament;

By raising and keeping a standing army within this kingdom in time of peace without consent of Parliament; . . .

By violating the freedom of election of members to serve in Parliament; . . .

And excessive bail hath been required of persons committed in criminal cases to elude the benefit of the laws made for the liberty of the subjects;

And excessive fines have been imposed;

And illegal and cruel punishments inflicted.

DOCUMENT-BASED QUESTION
According to this document, how did King James II take away power from Parliament? How did he violate the rights of citizens?

Political Cartoon, 1765

This political cartoon expressed an opinion about the Stamp Act. The act was a British law that required all legal and commercial documents in the American colonies to carry a stamp showing that a tax had been paid.

DOCUMENT-BASED QUESTION
What opinion does this cartoon express about the effect of the Stamp Act on the American economy?

Comparing & Contrasting

1. How are the opinions expressed by the three primary sources similar?
2. Reread the excerpt from the English Bill of Rights. Based on this document, what causes could you add to the chart on page 274?

Effects of Revolutions

The chart below shows political, economic, and social effects of the various revolutions. The primary sources on these two pages describe the political outcomes that three different revolutionaries expected to achieve. Use the chart and the primary sources together to understand the effects of revolution more fully.

	England	North America	France	Latin America
Political	• A constitutional monarchy was established. • The Bill of Rights increased Parliament's power and guaranteed certain rights. • The overthrow of a monarch helped inspire American revolutionaries.	• The United States gained independence. • The Constitution set up a republican government. • Revolutionary ideals continued to inspire groups seeking political equality. • The American Revolution inspired later revolutions.	• The Revolution led to a succession of governments: a republic, a dictatorship, a restored monarchy. • It created expectations for equality and freedom that sparked later uprisings in France. • It inspired later revolutions.	• Nearly all colonial rule in Latin America ended. • New countries were established. • Representative government was slow to develop. The military or the wealthy controlled much of the region until the late 1900s.
Economic	• Because it was answerable to taxpayers, Parliament encouraged trade.	• The removal of Britain's mercantilist policies allowed free enterprise to develop.	• The Revolution and ensuing wars with Europe devastated France's economy.	• Upper classes kept control of wealth. • Many places kept the plantation system.
Social	• England remained Protestant.	• The ideals of the Revolution continued to inspire groups seeking social equality.	• The French feudal system was abolished.	• Much of Latin America continued to have a strong class system.

SKILLBUILDER: Interpreting Charts
1. **Contrasting** *Which revolutions had positive economic effects, and which had negative? Explain.*
2. **Recognizing Effects** *What common political effect did the revolutions in North America and Latin America achieve?*

PRIMARY SOURCE

INTERACTIVE

Thomas Paine

In this excerpt from the pamphlet *Common Sense,* Thomas Paine described the ideal government he wanted to see set up after the American Revolution.

But where, say some, is the king of America? I'll tell you, friend, he reigns above, and doth not make havoc of mankind like the Royal Brute of Great Britain. . . . Let a day be solemnly set apart for proclaiming the charter [constitution]; let it be brought forth placed on the divine law, the Word of God; let a crown be placed thereon, by which the world may know, that so far as we approve of monarchy, that in America THE LAW IS KING. For as in absolute governments the king is law, so in free countries the law *ought* to BE king, and there ought to be no other.

DOCUMENT-BASED QUESTION
What did Paine believe should be the highest power in a new American government?

INTER**ACTIVE**

Simón Bolívar

"The Jamaica Letter" is one of Simón Bolívar's most important political documents. In this excerpt, he discussed his political goals for South America after the revolution—and his fear that South Americans were not ready to achieve those goals.

The role of the inhabitants of the American hemisphere has for centuries been purely passive. Politically they were non-existent. . . . We have been harassed by a conduct which has not only deprived us of our rights but has kept us in a sort of permanent infancy with regard to public affairs. . . . Americans today, and perhaps to a greater extent than ever before, who live within the Spanish system occupy a position in society no better than that of serfs destined for labor. . . . Although I seek perfection for the government of my country, I cannot persuade myself that the New World can, at the moment, be organized as a great republic.

DOCUMENT-BASED QUESTION
Why did Bolívar believe that South Americans were not ready for a republican form of government?

INTER**ACTIVE**

Maximilien Robespierre

In a speech given on February 5, 1794, Robespierre described his goals for the French Revolution. In this excerpt, he explained his reasons for using terror.

It is necessary to annihilate both the internal and external enemies of the republic or perish with its fall. Now, in this situation your first political maxim should be that one guides the people by reason, and the enemies of the people by terror.

If the driving force of popular government in peacetime is virtue, that of popular government during a revolution is both virtue and terror: virtue, without which terror is destructive; terror, without which virtue is impotent. Terror is only justice that is prompt, severe, and inflexible; it is thus an emanation of virtue; it is less a distinct principle than a consequence of the general principle of democracy applied to the most pressing needs of the patrie [nation].

DOCUMENT-BASED QUESTION
Why did Robespierre believe the use of terror against his enemies was necessary?

Comparing & Contrasting

1. Judging from the information on the chart, which revolutions resulted in the establishment of representative government, and which resulted in a return to tyrannical rule?

2. How do the political goals of the revolutionary leaders quoted here differ?

3. Compare the types of government set up in the United States, France, and Latin America after their revolutions. Did Paine, Robespierre, and Bolívar achieve the political goals quoted? Explain.

EXTENSION ACTIVITY
Revolutionary activity continued after the period covered by this unit. Two major 20th-century revolutions were the Russian Revolution (see Chapter 14) and the Chinese revolution and civil war (see Chapter 14 and Chapter 17). Read about one of these revolutions either in this textbook or in an encyclopedia. Then create a chart comparing that revolution with either the American Revolution or the French Revolution.

3

Industrialism and the Race for Empire
1700–1914

Although this painting shows Canton, China, the flags flying over the fenced-in areas near the shore are those of Spain, the United States, Great Britain, and the Netherlands. Canton was one of only two Chinese ports open to Westerners until 1842.

Comparing & Contrasting

Scientific and Technological Changes
In Unit 3, you will learn about scientific and technological changes that led to the Industrial Revolution and helped Western nations establish colonies around the world. At the end of the unit, you will have a chance to compare and contrast those changes. (See pages 396–401.)

The Industrial Revolution, 1700–1900

Previewing Main Ideas

SCIENCE AND TECHNOLOGY From the spinning jenny to the locomotive train, there was an explosion of inventions and technological advances. These improvements paved the way for the Industrial Revolution.

Geography *What other European countries besides England had coal, iron, and textile industries in the 1800s?*

EMPIRE BUILDING The global power balance shifted after the Industrial Revolution. This shift occurred because industrialized nations dominated the rest of the world.

Geography *Study the map. Which country appears to be the most industrialized?*

ECONOMICS The Industrial Revolution transformed economic systems. In part, this was because nations dramatically changed the way they produced and distributed goods.

Geography *What geographic factors might have encouraged the development of industry in certain places?*

INTEGRATED TECHNOLOGY

eEdition
- Interactive Maps
- Interactive Visuals
- Interactive Primary Sources

VIDEO *Patterns of Interaction: The Industrial and Electronic Revolutions*

INTERNET RESOURCES
Go to **classzone.com** for:
- Research Links   • Maps
- Internet Activities • Test Practice
- Primary Sources   • Current Events
- Chapter Quiz

EUROPE AND UNITED STATES

1701
Jethro Tull invents seed drill. ▶

1765
James Watt builds steam engine.

1700

1750

WORLD

1736
Qian-long begins his reign as emperor of China.
(Imperial Palace compound at Beijing) ▶

Industry in Europe, 1870

Industrialization 1870
- • City population greater than 250,000
- — Major railroads constructed by 1870

Industry
- Ironworking
- Textile industry
- Coal mining

NORWAY

SWEDEN

North Sea

DENMARK

Baltic Sea

UNITED KINGDOM

Glasgow

Liverpool
Leeds
Manchester

NETHERLANDS

Birmingham

London

BELGIUM

Amsterdam

Brussels

Berlin

Warsaw

GERMANY

LUX.

ATLANTIC OCEAN

Paris

FRANCE

SWITZERLAND

Lyon

Milan

Vienna

AUSTRIA-HUNGARY

45°N

Marseille

ITALY

SERBIA

Adriatic Sea

PORTUGAL

Madrid

SPAIN

Corsica

Sardinia

Naples

GREECE

Sicily

Mediterranean Sea

0   200   400 Miles
0   200   400 Kilometers
Conic Projection

1793
Eli Whitney invents cotton gin. ▶

1848
Marx and Engels publish *The Communist Manifesto.* ▶

1875
British unions win right to strike.

1800

1850

1900

1804
Haiti wins freedom from France.

1867
Meiji era begins a period of modernization in Japan.

1869
Suez Canal opens in Africa.

What are fair working conditions?

You are a 15-year-old living in England where the Industrial Revolution has spurred the growth of thousands of factories. Cheap labor is in great demand. Like millions of other teenagers, you do not go to school. Instead, you work in a factory 6 days a week, 14 hours a day. The small pay you receive is needed to help support your family. You trudge to work before dawn every day and work until after sundown. Inside the workplace the air is hot and foul, and after sunset it is so dark it is hard to see. Minding the machines is exhausting, dirty, and dangerous.

1 Long hours: The sun may be shining through the windows as this child's day begins, but it will have disappeared by the time his day ends.

2 Dangerous machines: Children usually worked in bare feet with no safety equipment among machines with many moving parts.

3 Hot temperatures and dust-filled air: Dust particles from thousands of bobbins cling to the clothing and hang in air heated by the machinery.

EXAMINING *the* ISSUES

- **Would you attempt to change your working conditions in the factory?**

- **Would you join a union, go to school, or run away?**

In small groups, discuss these questions. Share your conclusions with your class. In your discussions, think about how children lived in preindustrial and industrial societies all over the world. As you read about the changes caused by industrialization, note how reform movements eventually improved conditions for most laborers.

The Beginnings of Industrialization

MAIN IDEA	WHY IT MATTERS NOW	TERMS & NAMES
SCIENCE AND TECHNOLOGY The Industrial Revolution started in England and soon spread to other countries.	The changes that began in Britain paved the way for modern industrial societies.	• Industrial Revolution • enclosure • crop rotation • industrialization • factors of production • factory • entrepreneur

SETTING THE STAGE In the United States, France, and Latin America, political revolutions brought in new governments. A different type of revolution now transformed the way people worked. The **Industrial Revolution** refers to the greatly increased output of machine-made goods that began in England in the middle 1700s. Before the Industrial Revolution, people wove textiles by hand. Then, machines began to do this and other jobs. Soon the Industrial Revolution spread from England to Continental Europe and North America.

Industrial Revolution Begins in Britain

In 1700, small farms covered England's landscape. Wealthy landowners, however, began buying up much of the land that village farmers had once worked. The large landowners dramatically improved farming methods. These innovations amounted to an agricultural revolution.

The Agricultural Revolution Paves the Way After buying up the land of village farmers, wealthy landowners enclosed their land with fences or hedges. The increase in their landholdings enabled them to cultivate larger fields. Within these larger fields, called **enclosures**, landowners experimented with more productive seeding and harvesting methods to boost crop yields. The enclosure movement had two important results. First, landowners tried new agricultural methods. Second, large landowners forced small farmers to become tenant farmers or to give up farming and move to the cities.

Jethro Tull was one of the first of these scientific farmers. He saw that the usual way of sowing seed by scattering it across the ground was wasteful. Many seeds failed to take root. He solved this problem with an invention called the seed drill in about 1701. It allowed farmers to sow seeds in well-spaced rows at specific depths. A larger share of the seeds took root, boosting crop yields.

Rotating Crops The process of **crop rotation** proved to be one of the best developments by the scientific farmers. The process improved upon older methods of crop rotation, such as the medieval three-field system. One year, for example, a farmer might plant a field with wheat, which exhausted soil nutrients. The next year he planted a root crop, such as turnips, to restore nutrients. This might be followed in turn by barley and then clover.

TAKING NOTES
Following Chronological Order On a time line, note important events in Britain's industrialization.

1700   1830

▶ An English
farmer plants his
fields in the early
1700s using a
seed drill.

Livestock breeders improved their methods too. In the 1700s, for example, Robert Bakewell increased his mutton (sheep meat) output by allowing only his best sheep to breed. Other farmers followed Bakewell's lead. Between 1700 and 1786, the average weight for lambs climbed from 18 to 50 pounds. As food supplies increased and living conditions improved, England's population mushroomed. An increasing population boosted the demand for food and goods such as cloth. As farmers lost their land to large enclosed farms, many became factory workers. **A**

Why the Industrial Revolution Began in England In addition to a large population of workers, the small island country had extensive natural resources. **Industrialization**, which is the process of developing machine production of goods, required such resources. These natural resources included
- water power and coal to fuel the new machines
- iron ore to construct machines, tools, and buildings
- rivers for inland transportation
- harbors from which merchant ships set sail

In addition to its natural resources, Britain had an expanding economy to support industrialization. Businesspeople invested in the manufacture of new inventions. Britain's highly developed banking system also contributed to the country's industrialization. People were encouraged by the availability of bank loans to invest in new machinery and expand their operations. Growing overseas trade, economic prosperity, and a climate of progress led to the increased demand for goods.

Britain's political stability gave the country a tremendous advantage over its neighbors. Though Britain took part in many wars during the 1700s, none occurred on British soil. Their military successes gave the British a positive attitude. Parliament also passed laws to help encourage and protect business ventures. Other countries had some of these advantages. But Britain had all the **factors of production**, the resources needed to produce goods and services that the Industrial Revolution required. They included land, labor, and capital (or wealth).

Inventions Spur Industrialization

In an explosion of creativity, inventions now revolutionized industry. Britain's textile industry clothed the world in wool, linen, and cotton. This industry was the first to be transformed. Cloth merchants boosted their profits by speeding up the process by which spinners and weavers made cloth.

Changes in the Textile Industry As you will learn in the feature on textile technology on page 285, by 1800, several major inventions had modernized the cotton industry. One invention led to another. In 1733, a machinist named John Kay made a shuttle that sped back and forth on wheels. This flying shuttle, a boat-shaped piece

MAIN IDEA

Recognizing Effects

A How did population growth spur the Industrial Revolution?

284 Chapter 9

Textiles Industrialize First

The Industrial Revolution that began in Britain was spurred by a revolution in technology. It started in the textile industry, where inventions in the late 1700s transformed the manufacture of cloth. The demand for clothing in Britain had greatly increased as a result of the population boom caused by the agricultural revolution. These developments, in turn, had an impact worldwide. For example, the consumption of cotton rose dramatically in Britain (see graph at right). This cotton came from plantations in the American South, where cotton production skyrocketed from 1820 to 1860 in response to demand from English textile mills.

British Cotton Consumption, 1800–1900

Cotton Consumption (in thousands of metric tons)

1000
900
800
700
600
500
400
300
200
100
0

1800 1810 1820 1830 1840 1850 1860 1870 1880 1890 1900

Source: *European Historical Statistics, 1750–1975*

▶ John Kay's flying shuttle (below) speedily carried threads of yarn back and forth when the weaver pulled a handle on the loom. The flying shuttle greatly increased the productivity of weavers.

▲ Flying shuttle

Patterns of Interaction

Technology Transforms an Age: The Industrial and Electronic Revolutions

Inventions in the textile industry started in Britain and brought about the Industrial Revolution. This revolution soon spread to other countries. The process of industrialization is still spreading around the world, especially in developing countries. A similar technological revolution is occurring in electronics today, transforming the distribution of information around the world.

Connect *to* Today

1. **Synthesizing** How might the technological innovation and industrialization that took place in the textile industry during the Industrial Revolution have provided a model for other industries?

   See Skillbuilder Handbook, Page R21.

2. **Recognizing Effects** Research the textile industry today to learn how it has been affected by new technology, including computerization. Prepare a two-paragraph summary on the effects of the new technology.

285

Inventions in America

In the United States, American inventors worked at making railroad travel more comfortable, inventing adjustable upholstered seats. They also revolutionized agriculture, manufacturing, and communications:

1831 Cyrus McCormick's reaper boosted American wheat production.

1837 Samuel F. B. Morse, a New England painter, first sent electrical signals over a telegraph.

1851 I. M. Singer improved the sewing machine by inventing a foot treadle (see photograph).

1876 Scottish-born inventor Alexander Graham Bell patented the telephone.

INTEGRATED TECHNOLOGY

INTERNET ACTIVITY Create a photo exhibit on American inventions of the 19th century. Include the name of the inventor and the date with each photograph. Go to **classzone.com** for your research.

---

of wood to which yarn was attached, doubled the work a weaver could do in a day. Because spinners could not keep up with these speedy weavers, a cash prize attracted contestants to produce a better spinning machine. Around 1764, a textile worker named James Hargreaves invented a spinning wheel he named after his daughter. His spinning jenny allowed one spinner to work eight threads at a time.

At first, textile workers operated the flying shuttle and the spinning jenny by hand. Then, Richard Arkwright invented the water frame in 1769. This machine used the waterpower from rapid streams to drive spinning wheels. In 1779, Samuel Crompton combined features of the spinning jenny and the water frame to produce the spinning mule. The spinning mule made thread that was stronger, finer, and more consistent than earlier spinning machines. Run by waterpower, Edmund Cartwright's power loom sped up weaving after its invention in 1787. **B**

The water frame, the spinning mule, and the power loom were bulky and expensive machines. They took the work of spinning and weaving out of the house. Wealthy textile merchants set up the machines in large buildings called **factories**. Factories needed waterpower, so the first ones were built near rivers and streams:

MAIN IDEA

Summarizing
B What inventions transformed the textile industry?

PRIMARY SOURCE

A great number of streams . . . furnish water-power adequate to turn many hundred mills: they afford the element of water, indispensable for scouring, bleaching, printing, dyeing, and other processes of manufacture: and when collected in their larger channels, or employed to feed canals, they supply a superior inland navigation, so important for the transit of raw materials and merchandise.

EDWARD BAINS, *The History of Cotton Manufacture in Great Britain* (1835)

England's cotton came from plantations in the American South in the 1790s. Removing seeds from the raw cotton by hand was hard work. In 1793, an American inventor named Eli Whitney invented a machine to speed the chore. His cotton gin multiplied the amount of cotton that could be cleaned. American cotton production skyrocketed from 1.5 million pounds in 1790 to 85 million pounds in 1810.

Improvements in Transportation

Progress in the textile industry spurred other industrial improvements. The first such development, the steam engine, stemmed from the search for a cheap, convenient source of power. As early as 1705, coal miners were using steam-powered pumps to remove water from deep mine shafts. But this early model of a steam engine gobbled great quantities of fuel, making it expensive to run.

Watt's Steam Engine James Watt, a mathematical instrument maker at the University of Glasgow in Scotland, thought about the problem for two years. In 1765, Watt figured out a way to make the steam engine work faster and more efficiently while burning less fuel. In 1774, Watt joined with a businessman named Matthew Boulton. Boulton was an **entrepreneur** (AHN•truh•pruh•NUR), a person who organizes, manages, and takes on the risks of a business. He paid Watt a salary and encouraged him to build better engines.

Water Transportation Steam could also propel boats. An American inventor named Robert Fulton ordered a steam engine from Boulton and Watt. He built a steamboat called the *Clermont*, which made its first successful trip in 1807. The *Clermont* later ferried passengers up and down New York's Hudson River.

In England, water transportation improved with the creation of a network of canals, or human-made waterways. By the mid-1800s, 4,250 miles of inland channels slashed the cost of transporting both raw materials and finished goods.

Road Transportation British roads improved, too, thanks largely to the efforts of John McAdam, a Scottish engineer. Working in the early 1800s, McAdam equipped road beds with a layer of large stones for drainage. On top, he placed a carefully smoothed layer of crushed rock. Even in rainy weather heavy wagons could travel over the new "macadam" roads without sinking in mud.

Private investors formed companies that built roads and then operated them for profit. People called the new roads turnpikes because travelers had to stop at toll-gates (turnstiles or turnpikes) to pay tolls before traveling farther.

The Railway Age Begins

Steam-driven machinery powered English factories in the late 1700s. A steam engine on wheels—the railroad locomotive—drove English industry after 1820.

Steam-Driven Locomotives In 1804, an English engineer named Richard Trevithick won a bet of several thousand dollars. He did this by hauling ten tons of iron over nearly ten miles of track in a steam-driven locomotive. Other British engineers soon built improved versions of Trevithick's locomotive. One of these early

▼ First-class passengers on the Liverpool-Manchester Railway in the 1830s rode in covered cars; all others, in open cars.

▲ George
Stephenson's
Rocket

railroad engineers was George Stephenson. He had gained a solid reputation by building some 20 engines for mine operators in northern England. In 1821, Stephenson began work on the world's first railroad line. It was to run 27 miles from the Yorkshire coal fields to the port of Stockton on the North Sea. In 1825, the railroad opened. It used four locomotives that Stephenson had designed and built.

The Liverpool-Manchester Railroad News of this success quickly spread throughout Britain. The entrepreneurs of northern England wanted a railroad line to connect the port of Liverpool with the inland city of Manchester. The track was laid. In 1829, trials were held to choose the best locomotive for use on the new line. Five engines entered the competition. None could compare with the *Rocket*, designed by Stephenson and his son.

Smoke poured from the *Rocket*'s tall smokestack, and its two pistons pumped to and fro as they drove the front wheels. The locomotive hauled a 13-ton load at an unheard-of speed—more than 24 miles per hour. The Liverpool-Manchester Railway opened officially in 1830. It was an immediate success.

Railroads Revolutionize Life in Britain The invention and perfection of the locomotive had at least four major effects. First, railroads spurred industrial growth by giving manufacturers a cheap way to transport materials and finished products. Second, the railroad boom created hundreds of thousands of new jobs for both railroad workers and miners. These miners provided iron for the tracks and coal for the steam engines. Third, the railroads boosted England's agricultural and fishing industries, which could transport their products to distant cities.

Finally, by making travel easier, railroads encouraged country people to take distant city jobs. Also, railroads lured city dwellers to resorts in the countryside. Like a locomotive racing across the country, the Industrial Revolution brought rapid and unsettling changes to people's lives. **C**

MAIN IDEA

Synthesizing
C How did improvements in transportation promote industrialization in Britain?

SECTION **1** **ASSESSMENT**

TERMS & NAMES 1. For each term or name, write a sentence explaining its significance.
• Industrial Revolution   • enclosure   • crop rotation   • industrialization   • factors of production   • factory   • entrepreneur

USING YOUR NOTES
2. Which of the events listed do you think was the most important? Explain.

1700   1830

MAIN IDEAS
3. What were four factors that contributed to industrialization in Britain?

4. How did rising population help the Industrial Revolution?

5. What American invention aided the British textile industry?

CRITICAL THINKING & WRITING
6. **EVALUATING** Was the revolution in agriculture necessary to the Industrial Revolution? Explain.

7. **MAKING INFERENCES** What effect did entrepreneurs have upon the Industrial Revolution?

8. **FORMING AND SUPPORTING OPINIONS** Do you agree or disagree with the statement that the steam engine was the greatest invention of the Industrial Revolution? Why?

9. **WRITING ACTIVITY** SCIENCE AND TECHNOLOGY Write a **letter**, as a British government official during the Industrial Revolution, to an official in a nonindustrial nation explaining how the railroad has changed Britain.

CONNECT TO TODAY CREATING AN ILLUSTRATED NEWS ARTICLE
Find information on a recent agricultural or technological invention or improvement. Write a two-paragraph **news article** about its economic effects and include an illustration, if possible.

Industrialization
CASE STUDY: Manchester

ECONOMICS The factory system changed the way people lived and worked, introducing a variety of problems.

Many less-developed countries are undergoing the difficult process of industrialization today.

• urbanization
• middle class

SETTING THE STAGE The Industrial Revolution affected every part of life in Great Britain, but proved to be a mixed blessing. Eventually, industrialization led to a better quality of life for most people. But the change to machine production initially caused human suffering. Rapid industrialization brought plentiful jobs, but it also caused unhealthy working conditions, air and water pollution, and the ills of child labor. It also led to rising class tensions, especially between the working class and the middle class.

Industrialization Changes Life

The pace of industrialization accelerated rapidly in Britain. By the 1800s, people could earn higher wages in factories than on farms. With this money, more people could afford to heat their homes with coal from Wales and dine on Scottish beef. They wore better clothing, too, woven on power looms in England's industrial cities. Cities swelled with waves of job seekers.

Industrial Cities Rise For centuries, most Europeans had lived in rural areas. After 1800, the balance shifted toward cities. This shift was caused by the growth of the factory system, where the manufacturing of goods was concentrated in a central location. Between 1800 and 1850, the number of European cities boasting more than 100,000 inhabitants rose from 22 to 47. Most of Europe's urban areas at least doubled in population; some even quadrupled. This period was one of **urbanization**—city building and the movement of people to cities.

TAKING NOTES
Outlining Organize main ideas and details.

I. Industrialization
   Changes Life
   A.
   B.
II. Class Tensions
    Grow

◄ As cities grew, people crowded into tenements and row houses such as these in London.

The Day of a Child Laborer, William Cooper

William Cooper began working in a textile factory at the age of ten. He had a sister who worked upstairs in the same factory. In 1832, Cooper was called to testify before a parliamentary committee about the conditions among child laborers in the textile industry. The following sketch of his day is based upon his testimony.

5 A.M. The workday began. Cooper and his sister rose as early as 4:00 or 4:30 in order to get to the factory by 5:00. Children usually ate their breakfast on the run.

12 NOON The children were given a 40-minute break for lunch. This was the only break they received all day.

Factories developed in clusters because entrepreneurs built them near sources of energy, such as water and coal. Major new industrial centers sprang up between the coal-rich area of southern Wales and the Clyde River valley in Scotland. But the biggest of these centers developed in England. (See map on page 281.)

Britain's capital, London, was the country's most important city. It had a population of about one million people by 1800. During the 1800s, its population exploded, providing a vast labor pool and market for new industry. London became Europe's largest city, with twice as many people as its closest rival (Paris). Newer cities challenged London's industrial leadership. Birmingham and Sheffield became iron-smelting centers. Leeds and Manchester dominated textile manufacturing. Along with the port of Liverpool, Manchester formed the center of Britain's bustling cotton industry. During the 1800s, Manchester experienced rapid growth from around 45,000 in 1760 to 300,000 by 1850.

Living Conditions Because England's cities grew rapidly, they had no development plans, sanitary codes, or building codes. Moreover, they lacked adequate housing, education, and police protection for the people who poured in from the countryside to seek jobs. Most of the unpaved streets had no drains, and garbage collected in heaps on them. Workers lived in dark, dirty shelters, with whole families crowding into one bedroom. Sickness was widespread. Epidemics of the deadly disease cholera regularly swept through the slums of Great Britain's industrial cities. In 1842, a British government study showed an average life span to be 17 years for working-class people in one large city, compared with 38 years in a nearby rural area.

Elizabeth Gaskell's *Mary Barton* (1848) is a work of fiction. But it presents a startlingly accurate portrayal of urban life experienced by many at the time. Gaskell provides a realistic description of the dank cellar dwelling of one family in a Manchester slum:

▼ Elizabeth Gaskell (1810–1865) was a British writer whose novels show a sympathy for the working class.

PRIMARY SOURCE Ⓐ

You went down one step even from the foul area into the cellar in which a family of human beings lived. It was very dark inside. The window-panes many of them were broken and stuffed with rags . . . . the smell was so fetid [foul] as almost to knock the two men down. . . . they began to penetrate the thick darkness of the place, and to see three or four little children rolling on the damp, nay wet brick floor, through which the stagnant, filthy moisture of the street oozed up.

ELIZABETH GASKELL, *Mary Barton*

MAIN IDEA

Analyzing Primary Sources

Ⓐ How does Gaskell indicate her sympathy for the working class in this passage?

But not everyone in urban areas lived miserably. Well-to-do merchants and factory owners often built luxurious homes in the suburbs.

3 P.M. The children often became drowsy during the afternoon or evening hours. In order to keep them awake, adult overseers sometimes whipped the children.

6 P.M. There was no break allowed for an evening meal. Children again ate on the run.

9 P.M. William Cooper's day ended after an exhausting 16-hour shift at work.

11 P.M. Cooper's sister worked another two hours even though she had to be back at work at 5:00 the next morning.

Working Conditions To increase production, factory owners wanted to keep their machines running as many hours as possible. As a result, the average worker spent 14 hours a day at the job, 6 days a week. Work did not change with the seasons, as it did on the farm. Instead, work remained the same week after week, year after year.

Industry also posed new dangers for workers. Factories were seldom well lit or clean. Machines injured workers. A boiler might explode or a drive belt might catch an arm. And there was no government program to provide aid in case of injury. The most dangerous conditions of all were found in coal mines. Frequent accidents, damp conditions, and the constant breathing of coal dust made the average miner's life span ten years shorter than that of other workers. Many women and children were employed in the mining industry because they were the cheapest source of labor.

Class Tensions Grow

Though poverty gripped Britain's working classes, the Industrial Revolution created enormous amounts of wealth in the nation. Most of this new money belonged to factory owners, shippers, and merchants. These people were part of a growing **middle class**, a social class made up of skilled workers, professionals, businesspeople, and wealthy farmers.

The Middle Class The new middle class transformed the social structure of Great Britain. In the past, landowners and aristocrats had occupied the top position in British society. With most of the wealth, they wielded the social and political power. Now some factory owners, merchants, and bankers grew wealthier than the landowners and aristocrats. Yet important social distinctions divided the two wealthy classes. Landowners looked down on those who had made their fortunes in the "vulgar" business world. Not until late in the 1800s were rich entrepreneurs considered the social equals of the lords of the countryside.

Gradually, a larger middle class—neither rich nor poor—emerged. The upper middle class consisted of government employees, doctors, lawyers, and managers of factories, mines, and shops. The lower middle class included factory overseers and such skilled workers as toolmakers, mechanical drafters, and printers. These people enjoyed a comfortable standard of living. **B**

MAIN IDEA

Summarizing
B Describe the social classes in Britain.

The Working Class During the years 1800 to 1850, however, laborers, or the working class, saw little improvement in their living and working conditions. They watched their livelihoods disappear as machines replaced them. In frustration, some smashed the machines they thought were putting them out of work.

One group of such workers was called the Luddites. They were named after Ned Ludd. Ludd, probably a mythical English laborer, was said to have destroyed weaving machinery around 1779. The Luddites attacked whole factories in northern England beginning in 1811, destroying laborsaving machinery. Outside the factories, mobs of workers rioted, mainly because of poor living and working conditions.

Positive Effects of the Industrial Revolution

Despite the problems that followed industrialization, the Industrial Revolution had a number of positive effects. It created jobs for workers. It contributed to the wealth of the nation. It fostered technological progress and invention. It greatly increased the production of goods and raised the standard of living. Perhaps most important, it provided the hope of improvement in people's lives.

The Industrial Revolution produced a number of other benefits as well. These included healthier diets, better housing, and cheaper, mass-produced clothing. Because the Industrial Revolution created a demand for engineers as well as clerical and professional workers, it expanded educational opportunities.

The middle and upper classes prospered immediately from the Industrial Revolution. For the workers it took longer, but their lives gradually improved during the 1800s. Laborers eventually won higher wages, shorter hours, and better working conditions after they joined together to form labor unions.

Long-Term Effects The long-term effects of the Industrial Revolution are still evident. Most people today in industrialized countries can afford consumer goods that would have been considered luxuries 50 or 60 years ago. In addition, their living and working conditions are much improved over those of workers in the 19th century. Also, profits derived from industrialization produced tax revenues. These funds have allowed local, state, and federal governments to invest in urban improvements and raise the standard of living of most city dwellers.

The economic successes of the Industrial Revolution, and also the problems created by it, were clearly evident in one of Britain's new industrial cities in the 1800s—Manchester.

CASE STUDY: Manchester

The Mills of Manchester

Manchester's unique advantages made it a leading example of the new industrial city. This northern English town had ready access to waterpower. It also had available labor from the nearby countryside and an outlet to the sea at Liverpool.

"From this filthy sewer pure gold flows," wrote Alexis de Tocqueville (ah•lehk•SEE duh TOHK•vihl), the French writer, after he visited Manchester in 1835. Indeed, the industrial giant showed the best and worst of the Industrial Revolution. Manchester's rapid, unplanned growth made it an unhealthy place for the poor people who lived and worked there. But wealth flowed from its factories. It went first to the mill owners and the new middle class. Eventually, although not immediately, the working class saw their standard of living rise as well.

Manchester's business owners took pride in mastering each detail of the manufacturing process. They worked many hours and risked their own money. For their efforts, they were rewarded with high profits. Many erected gracious homes on the outskirts of town.

To provide the mill owners with high profits, workers labored under terrible conditions. Children as young as six joined their parents in the factories. There, for six days a week, they toiled from 6 A.M. to 7 or 8 P.M., with only half an hour for

Industrialization

Industrialization is the process of developing industries that use machines to produce goods. This process not only revolutionizes a country's economy, it also transforms social conditions and class structures.

Effects of Industrialization

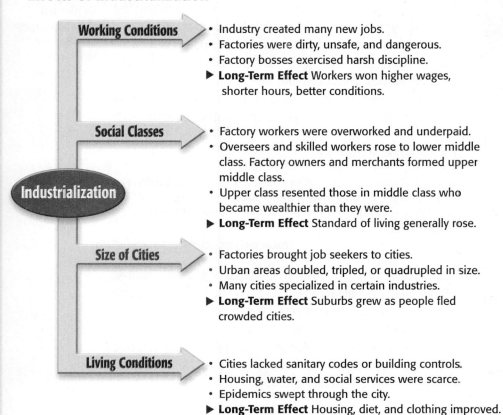

Working Conditions
- Industry created many new jobs.
- Factories were dirty, unsafe, and dangerous.
- Factory bosses exercised harsh discipline.
- ▶ **Long-Term Effect** Workers won higher wages, shorter hours, better conditions.

Social Classes
- Factory workers were overworked and underpaid.
- Overseers and skilled workers rose to lower middle class. Factory owners and merchants formed upper middle class.
- Upper class resented those in middle class who became wealthier than they were.
- ▶ **Long-Term Effect** Standard of living generally rose.

Size of Cities
- Factories brought job seekers to cities.
- Urban areas doubled, tripled, or quadrupled in size.
- Many cities specialized in certain industries.
- ▶ **Long-Term Effect** Suburbs grew as people fled crowded cities.

Living Conditions
- Cities lacked sanitary codes or building controls.
- Housing, water, and social services were scarce.
- Epidemics swept through the city.
- ▶ **Long-Term Effect** Housing, diet, and clothing improved.

▼ This engraving shows urban growth and industrial pollution in Manchester.

INTEGRATED TECHNOLOGY

RESEARCH LINKS For more on industrialization, go to **classzone.com**

> DATA FILE

GROWTH OF CITIES

MANCHESTER

Population (in thousands)

1800	1870
90	351

BIRMINGHAM

Population (in thousands)

1800	1870
74	344

GLASGOW

Population (in thousands)

1800	1870
77	522

LONDON

Population (in thousands)

1800	1870
1,117	3,890

Source: European Historical Statistics, 1750–1975

Connect *to* Today

1. **Recognizing Effects** What were some advantages and disadvantages of industrialization?

   See Skillbuilder Handbook, page R6.

2. **Making Inferences** Many nations around the world today are trying to industrialize. What do you think they hope to gain from that process?

Connect to Today

Child Labor Today

To save on labor costs in the 1990s and 2000s, many corporations moved their manufacturing operations overseas to developing countries. There, in sweatshops, young children work long hours under wretched conditions. They are unprotected by child labor laws. For mere pennies per hour, children weave carpets, sort vegetables, or assemble expensive athletic shoes.

Several organizations are working to end child labor, including the Child Welfare League of America and the International Labor Rights Fund.

lunch and an hour for dinner. To keep the children awake, mill supervisors beat them. Tiny hands repaired broken threads in Manchester's spinning machines, replaced thread in the bobbins, or swept up cotton fluff. The dangerous machinery injured many children. The fluff filled their lungs and made them cough.

Until the first Factory Act passed in 1819, the British government exerted little control over child labor in Manchester and other factory cities. The act restricted working age and hours. For years after the act passed, young children still did heavy, dangerous work in Manchester's factories. **C**

Putting so much industry into one place polluted the natural environment. The coal that powered factories and warmed houses blackened the air. Textile dyes and other wastes poisoned Manchester's Irwell River. An eyewitness observer wrote the following description of the river in 1862:

PRIMARY SOURCE
Steam boilers discharge into it their seething contents, and drains and sewers their fetid impurities; till at length it rolls on— here between tall dingy walls, there under precipices of red sandstone—considerably less a river than a flood of liquid manure.

HUGH MILLER, *"Old Red Sandstone"*

Like other new industrial cities of the 19th century, Manchester produced consumer goods and created wealth on a grand scale. Yet, it also stood as a reminder of the ills of rapid and unplanned industrialization.

As you will learn in Section 3, the industrialization that began in Great Britain spread to the United States and to continental Europe in the 1800s.

MAIN IDEA

Drawing Conclusions
C Whose interests did child labor serve?

SECTION 2 ASSESSMENT

TERMS & NAMES 1. For each term or name, write a sentence explaining its significance.
• urbanization   • middle class

USING YOUR NOTES	**MAIN IDEAS**	**CRITICAL THINKING & WRITING**
2. Which change brought about by industrialization had the greatest impact? I. *Industrialization Changes Life* A. B. II. *Class Tensions Grow*	3. Why did people flock to British cities and towns during the Industrial Revolution? 4. What social class expanded as a result of industrialization? 5. What were some of the negative effects of the rapid growth of Manchester?	6. **SUMMARIZING** How did industrialization contribute to city growth? 7. **EVALUATING** How were class tensions affected by the Industrial Revolution? 8. **FORMING AND SUPPORTING OPINIONS** The Industrial Revolution has been described as a mixed blessing. Do you agree or disagree? Support your answer with text references. 9. **WRITING ACTIVITY** ECONOMICS As a factory owner during the Industrial Revolution, write a **letter** to a newspaper justifying working conditions in your factory.

CONNECT TO TODAY **CREATING A COMPARISON CHART**
Make a **comparison chart** listing information on child labor in three developing nations—one each from Asia, Africa, and Latin America—and compare with data from the United States.

Industrialization Spreads

MAIN IDEA	WHY IT MATTERS NOW	TERMS & NAMES
EMPIRE BUILDING The industrialization that began in Great Britain spread to other parts of the world.	The Industrial Revolution set the stage for the growth of modern cities and a global economy.	• stock • corporation

SETTING THE STAGE Great Britain's favorable geography and its financial systems, political stability, and natural resources sparked industrialization. British merchants built the world's first factories. When these factories prospered, more laborsaving machines and factories were built. Eventually, the Industrial Revolution that had begun in Britain spread both to the United States and to continental Europe. Countries that had conditions similar to those in Britain were ripe for industrialization.

Industrial Development in the United States

The United States possessed the same resources that allowed Britain to mechanize its industries. America had fast-flowing rivers, rich deposits of coal and iron ore, and a supply of laborers made up of farm workers and immigrants. During the War of 1812, Britain blockaded the United States, trying to keep it from engaging in international trade. This blockade forced the young country to use its own resources to develop independent industries. Those industries would manufacture the goods the United States could no longer import.

Industrialization in the United States As in Britain, industrialization in the United States began in the textile industry. Eager to keep the secrets of industrialization to itself, Britain had forbidden engineers, mechanics, and toolmakers to leave the country. In 1789, however, a young British mill worker named Samuel Slater emigrated to the United States. There, Slater built a spinning machine from memory and a partial design. The following year, Moses Brown opened the first factory in the United States to house Slater's machines in Pawtucket, Rhode Island. But the Pawtucket factory mass-produced only one part of finished cloth, the thread.

In 1813, Francis Cabot Lowell of Boston and four other investors revolutionized the American textile industry. They mechanized every stage in the manufacture of cloth. Their weaving factory in Waltham, Massachusetts, earned them enough money to fund a larger

▼ Teenage mill girls at a Georgia cotton mill

TAKING NOTES
Comparing Use a Venn diagram to compare industrialization in the United States and in Europe.

United States / both / Europe

The Growth of Railroads in the United States

Railroad System, 1840

The United States
Railroad tracks

0   500 Miles
0   1,000 Kilometers

Total trackage: 2,818 miles

Railroad System, 1890

Total trackage: 208,152 miles

GEOGRAPHY SKILLBUILDER: Interpreting Maps

1. **Region** *In what part of the country were the first railroads built? By 1890, what other part of the country was densely covered by railroad tracks?*
2. **Movement** *In what direction did the railroads help people move across the country?*

operation in another Massachusetts town. When Lowell died, the remaining partners named the town after him. By the late 1820s, Lowell, Massachusetts, had become a booming manufacturing center and a model for other such towns.

Thousands of young single women flocked from their rural homes to work as mill girls in factory towns. There, they could make higher wages and have some independence. However, to ensure proper behavior, they were watched closely inside and outside the factory by their employers. The mill girls toiled more than 12 hours a day, 6 days a week, for decent wages. For some, the mill job was an alternative to being a servant and was often the only other job open to them:

PRIMARY SOURCE

Country girls were naturally independent, and the feeling that at this new work the few hours they had of everyday leisure were entirely their own was a satisfaction to them. They preferred it to going out as "hired help." It was like a young man's pleasure in entering upon business for himself. Girls had never tried that experiment before, and they liked it.

LUCY LARCOM, *A New England Girlhood*

MAIN IDEA

Analyzing Primary Sources

A Why did Lucy Larcom think mill work benefited young women?

Textiles led the way, but clothing manufacture and shoemaking also underwent mechanization. Especially in the Northeast, skilled workers and farmers had formerly worked at home. Now they labored in factories in towns and cities such as Waltham, Lowell, and Lawrence, Massachusetts.

Later Expansion of U.S. Industry The Northeast experienced much industrial growth in the early 1800s. Nonetheless, the United States remained primarily agricultural until the Civil War ended in 1865. During the last third of the 1800s, the country experienced a technological boom. As in Britain, a number of causes contributed to this boom. These included a wealth of natural resources, among them oil, coal, and iron; a burst of inventions, such as the electric light bulb and the telephone; and a swelling urban population that consumed the new manufactured goods.

Also, as in Britain, railroads played a major role in America's industrialization. Cities like Chicago and Minneapolis expanded rapidly during the late 1800s. This was due to their location along the nation's expanding railroad lines. Chicago's stockyards and Minneapolis's grain industries prospered by selling products to the rest of the country. Indeed, the railroads themselves proved to be a profitable business. By the end of the 1800s, a limited number of large, powerful companies controlled more than two-thirds of the nation's railroad tracks. Businesses of all kinds began to merge as the railroads had. Smaller companies joined together to form a larger one.

The Rise of Corporations Building large businesses like railroads required a great deal of money. To raise the money, entrepreneurs sold shares of **stock**, or certain rights of ownership. Thus people who bought stock became part owners of these businesses, which were called corporations. A **corporation** is a business owned by stockholders who share in its profits but are not personally responsible for its debts. Corporations were able to raise the large amounts of capital needed to invest in industrial equipment.

In the late 1800s, large corporations such as Standard Oil (founded by John D. Rockefeller) and the Carnegie Steel Company (founded by Andrew Carnegie) sprang up. They sought to control every aspect of their own industries in order to make big profits. Big business—the giant corporations that controlled entire industries—also made big profits by reducing the cost of producing goods. In the United States as elsewhere, workers earned low wages for laboring long hours, while stockholders earned high profits and corporate leaders made fortunes.

Continental Europe Industrializes

European businesses yearned to adopt the "British miracle," the result of Britain's profitable new methods of manufacturing goods. But the troubles sparked by the French Revolution and the Napoleonic wars between 1789 and 1815 had halted trade, interrupted communication, and caused inflation in some parts of the continent. European countries watched the gap widen between themselves and Britain. Even so, industrialization eventually reached continental Europe.

▼ Danish workers labor in a steel mill in this 1885 painting by Peter Severin Kroyer.

Beginnings in Belgium Belgium led Europe in adopting Britain's new technology. It had rich deposits of iron ore and coal as well as fine waterways for transportation. As in the United States, British skilled workers played a key role in industrializing Belgium.

Samuel Slater had smuggled the design of a spinning machine to the United States. Much like him, a Lancashire carpenter named William Cockerill illegally made his way to Belgium in 1799. He carried secret plans for building spinning machinery. His son John eventually built an enormous industrial enterprise in eastern Belgium. It produced a variety of mechanical equipment, including steam engines and railway locomotives. Carrying the latest British advances, more British workers came to work with Cockerill. Several then founded their own companies in Europe.

Germany Industrializes Germany was politically divided in the early 1800s. Economic isolation and scattered resources hampered countrywide industrialization. Instead, pockets of industrialization appeared, as in the coal-rich Ruhr Valley of west central Germany. Beginning around 1835, Germany began to copy the British model. Germany imported British equipment and engineers. German manufacturers also sent their children to England to learn industrial management. **B**

Most important, Germany built railroads that linked its growing manufacturing cities, such as Frankfurt, with the Ruhr Valley's coal and iron ore deposits. In 1858, a German economist wrote, "Railroads and machine shops, coal mines and iron foundries, spinneries and rolling mills seem to spring up out of the ground, and smokestacks sprout from the earth like mushrooms." Germany's economic strength spurred its ability to develop as a military power. By the late 1800s, a unified, imperial Germany had become both an industrial and a military giant.

MAIN IDEA

Analyzing Causes

B What factors slowed industrialization in Germany?

Expansion Elsewhere in Europe In the rest of Europe, as in Germany, industrialization during the early 1800s proceeded by region rather than by country. Even in countries where agriculture dominated, pockets of industrialization arose. For example, Bohemia developed a spinning industry. Spain's Catalonia processed more cotton than Belgium. Northern Italy mechanized its textile production, specializing in silk spinning. Serf labor ran factories in regions around Moscow and St. Petersburg.

In France, sustained industrial growth occurred after 1830. French industrialization was more measured and controlled than in other countries because the agricultural economy remained strong. As a result, France avoided the great social and economic problems caused by industrialization. A thriving national market for new French products was created after 1850, when the government began railroad construction.

For a variety of reasons, many European countries did not industrialize. In some nations, the social structure delayed the adoption of new methods of production. The accidents of geography held back others. In Austria-Hungary and Spain, transportation posed great obstacles. Austria-Hungary's mountains defeated railroad builders. Spain lacked both good roads and waterways for canals.

The Impact of Industrialization

The Industrial Revolution shifted the world balance of power. It increased competition between industrialized nations and poverty in less-developed nations.

Rise of Global Inequality Industrialization widened the wealth gap between industrialized and nonindustrialized countries, even while it strengthened their economic ties. To keep factories running and workers fed, industrialized countries required a steady supply of raw materials from less-developed lands. In turn, industrialized countries viewed poor countries as markets for their manufactured products.

Britain led in exploiting its overseas colonies for resources and markets. Soon other European countries, the United States, Russia, and Japan followed Britain's lead, seizing colonies for their economic resources. Imperialism, the policy of extending one country's rule over many other lands, gave even more power and wealth to these already wealthy nations. Imperialism was born out of the cycle of industrialization, the need for resources to supply the factories of Europe, and the development of new markets around the world. (See Chapter 11.) **C**

▲ The Crystal Palace Exposition in London in 1851 (shown above) celebrated the "works of industry of all nations."

MAIN IDEA

Clarifying
C Why did imperialism grow out of industrialization?

Transformation of Society Between 1700 and 1900, revolutions in agriculture, production, transportation, and communication changed the lives of people in Western Europe and the United States. Industrialization gave Europe tremendous economic power. In contrast, the economies of Asia and Africa were still based on agriculture and small workshops. Industrialization revolutionized every aspect of society, from daily life to life expectancy. Despite the hardships early urban workers suffered, population, health, and wealth eventually rose dramatically in all industrialized countries. The development of a middle class created great opportunities for education and democratic participation. Greater democratic participation, in turn, fueled a powerful movement for social reform.

SECTION 3 ASSESSMENT

TERMS & NAMES 1. For each term or name, write a sentence explaining its significance.
• stock • corporation

USING YOUR NOTES

2. Which development had the most impact in the United States? in continental Europe?

United States

both

Europe

MAIN IDEAS

3. What early industries mechanized in the United States?

4. Why did Belgium lead Europe in adopting industrialization?

5. How did the Industrial Revolution shift the world balance of power?

CRITICAL THINKING & WRITING

6. **RECOGNIZING BIAS** Go back to the quote from Lucy Larcom on page 296. Do you think her feelings about working in the mill are typical? Why or why not?

7. **MAKING INFERENCES** Why was Britain unable to keep industrial secrets away from other nations?

8. **FORMING AND SUPPORTING OPINIONS** What was the most significant effect of the Industrial Revolution?

9. **WRITING ACTIVITY** [EMPIRE BUILDING] Draw a **political cartoon** that could have been used by the British government to show their sense of their own superiority over nonindustrialized nations that they planned to colonize.

INTEGRATED TECHNOLOGY **INTERNET ACTIVITY**

Use the Internet to research the economy of a less-developed nation in either Asia, Africa, or South America. Create a **database** of economic statistics for that country.

INTERNET KEYWORD
country profiles

Reforming the Industrial World

MAIN IDEA	WHY IT MATTERS NOW	TERMS & NAMES
ECONOMICS The Industrial Revolution led to economic, social, and political reforms.	Many modern social welfare programs developed during this period of reform.	• laissez faire • Karl Marx • Adam Smith • communism • capitalism • union • utilitarianism • strike • socialism

SETTING THE STAGE In industrialized countries in the 19th century, the Industrial Revolution opened a wide gap between the rich and the poor. Business leaders believed that governments should stay out of business and economic affairs. Reformers, however, felt that governments needed to play an active role to improve conditions for the poor. Workers also demanded more rights and protection. They formed labor unions to increase their influence.

TAKING NOTES
Summarizing Use a chart to summarize the characteristics of capitalism and socialism.

Capitalism	Socialism
1.	1.
2.	2.
3.	3.

The Philosophers of Industrialization

The term **laissez faire** (LEHS•ay•FAIR) refers to the economic policy of letting owners of industry and business set working conditions without interference. This policy favors a free market unregulated by the government. The term is French for "let do," and by extension, "let people do as they please."

Laissez-faire Economics Laissez-faire economics stemmed from French economic philosophers of the Enlightenment. They criticized the idea that nations grow wealthy by placing heavy tariffs on foreign goods. In fact, they argued, government regulations only interfered with the production of wealth. These philosophers believed that if government allowed free trade—the flow of commerce in the world market without government regulation—the economy would prosper.

Adam Smith, a professor at the University of Glasgow, Scotland, defended the idea of a free economy, or free markets, in his 1776 book *The Wealth of Nations*. According to Smith, economic liberty guaranteed economic progress. As a result, government should not interfere. Smith's arguments rested on what he called the three natural laws of economics:

- the law of self-interest—People work for their own good.
- the law of competition—Competition forces people to make a better product.
- the law of supply and demand—Enough goods would be produced at the lowest possible price to meet demand in a market economy.

The Economists of Capitalism Smith's basic ideas were supported by British economists Thomas Malthus and David Ricardo. Like Smith, they believed that natural laws governed economic life. Their important ideas were the foundation of laissez-faire capitalism. **Capitalism** is an economic system in which the factors of production are privately owned and money is invested in business ventures to make a profit. These ideas also helped bring about the Industrial Revolution.

In *An Essay on the Principle of Population*, written in 1798, Thomas Malthus argued that population tended to increase more rapidly than the food supply. Without wars and epidemics to kill off the extra people, most were destined to be poor and miserable. The predictions of Malthus seemed to be coming true in the 1840s.

David Ricardo, a wealthy stockbroker, took Malthus's theory one step further in his book, *Principles of Political Economy and Taxation* (1817). Like Malthus, Ricardo believed that a permanent underclass would always be poor. In a market system, if there are many workers and abundant resources, then labor and resources are cheap. If there are few workers and scarce resources, then they are expensive. Ricardo believed that wages would be forced down as population increased.

MAIN IDEA

Summarizing

A What did Malthus and Ricardo say about the effects of population growth?

Laissez-faire thinkers such as Smith, Malthus, and Ricardo opposed government efforts to help poor workers. They thought that creating minimum wage laws and better working conditions would upset the free market system, lower profits, and undermine the production of wealth in society. **A**

The Rise of Socialism

In contrast to laissez-faire philosophy, which advised governments to leave business alone, other theorists believed that governments should intervene. These thinkers believed that wealthy people or the government must take action to improve people's lives. The French writer Alexis de Tocqueville gave a warning:

History Makers

Adam Smith
1723–1790

In his book *The Wealth of Nations*, Smith argued that if individuals freely followed their own self-interest, the world would be an orderly and progressive place. Social harmony would result without any government direction, "as if by an invisible hand."

Smith applied an invisible hand of his own. After his death, people discovered that he had secretly donated large sums of his income to charities.

INTEGRATED / TECHNOLOGY

RESEARCH LINKS For more on Adam Smith, go to **classzone.com**

PRIMARY SOURCE
Consider what is happening among the working classes. . . . Do you not see spreading among them, little by little, opinions and ideas that aim not to overturn such and such a ministry, or such laws, or such a government, but society itself, to shake it to the foundations upon which it now rests?

ALEXIS DE TOCQUEVILLE, 1848 speech

Utilitarianism English philosopher Jeremy Bentham modified the ideas of Adam Smith. In the late 1700s, Bentham introduced the philosoophy of **utilitarianism**. Bentham wrote his most influential works in the late 1700s. According to Bentham's theory, people should judge ideas, institutions, and actions on the basis of their utility, or usefulness. He argued that the government should try to promote the greatest good for the greatest number of people. A government policy was only useful if it promoted this goal. Bentham believed that in general the individual should be free to pursue his or her own advantage without interference from the state.

John Stuart Mill, a philosopher and economist, led the utilitarian movement in the 1800s. Mill came to question unregulated capitalism. He believed it was wrong that workers should lead deprived lives that sometimes bordered on starvation. Mill wished to help ordinary working people with policies that would lead to a more equal division of profits. He also favored a cooperative system of agriculture and women's rights, including the right to vote. Mill called for the government to do away with great differences in wealth. Utilitarians also pushed for reforms in the legal and prison systems and in education. **B**

MAIN IDEA

Clarifying

B How did Mill want to change the economic system?

Utopian Ideas Other reformers took an even more active approach. Shocked by the misery and poverty of the working class, a British factory owner named Robert Owen improved working conditions for his employees. Near his cotton mill in New Lanark, Scotland, Owen built houses, which he rented at low rates. He prohibited children under ten from working in the mills and provided free schooling.

Then, in 1824, he traveled to the United States. He founded a cooperative community called New Harmony in Indiana, in 1825. He intended this community to be a utopia, or perfect living place. New Harmony lasted only three years but inspired the founding of other communities.

Socialism French reformers such as Charles Fourier (FUR•ee•AY), Saint-Simon (san see•MOHN), and others sought to offset the ill effects of industrialization with a new economic system called socialism. In **socialism**, the factors of production are owned by the public and operate for the welfare of all.

Socialism grew out of an optimistic view of human nature, a belief in progress, and a concern for social justice. Socialists argued that the government should plan the economy rather than depend on free-market capitalism to do the job. They argued that government control of factories, mines, railroads, and other key industries would end poverty and promote equality. Public ownership, they believed, would help workers, who were at the mercy of their employers. Some socialists—such as Louis Blanc—advocated change through extension of the right to vote.

History Makers

Karl Marx
1818–1883

Karl Marx studied philosophy at the University of Berlin before he turned to journalism and economics. In 1849, Marx joined the flood of radicals who fled continental Europe for England. He had declared in *The Communist Manifesto* that "the working men have no country."

Marx's theories of socialism and the inevitable revolt of the working class made him little money. He earned a meager living as a journalist. His wealthy coauthor and fellow German, Friedrich Engels, gave Marx financial aid.

INTEGRATED / TECHNOLOGY

RESEARCH LINKS For more on Karl Marx, go to **classzone.com**

Marxism: Radical Socialism

The writings of a German journalist named **Karl Marx** introduced the world to a radical type of socialism called Marxism. Marx and Friedrich Engels, a German whose father owned a textile mill in Manchester, outlined their ideas in a 23-page pamphlet called *The Communist Manifesto*.

The Communist Manifesto In their manifesto, Marx and Engels argued that human societies have always been divided into warring classes. In their own time, these were the middle class "haves" or employers, called the bourgeoisie (BUR•zhwah•ZEE), and the "have-nots" or workers, called the proletariat (PROH•lih•TAIR•ee•iht). While the wealthy controlled the means of producing goods, the poor performed backbreaking labor under terrible conditions. This situation resulted in conflict:

PRIMARY SOURCE
Freeman and slave, patrician and plebeian, lord and serf, guild-master and journeyman, in a word, oppressor and oppressed, stood in constant opposition to one another, carried on an uninterrupted, now hidden, now open fight, a fight that each time ended, either in a revolutionary reconstitution of society at large, or in the common ruin of the contending classes.
KARL MARX and **FRIEDRICH ENGELS**, *The Communist Manifesto* (1848)

According to Marx and Engels, the Industrial Revolution had enriched the wealthy and impoverished the poor. The two writers predicted that the workers would overthrow the owners: "The proletarians have nothing to lose but their chains. They have a world to win. Workingmen of all countries, unite." **C**

MAIN IDEA

Summarizing
C What were the ideas of Marx and Engels concerning relations between the owners and the working class?

Capitalism vs. Socialism

The economic system called capitalism developed gradually over centuries, beginning in the late Middle Ages. Because of the ways industrialization changed society, some people began to think that capitalism led to certain problems, such as the abuse of workers. They responded by developing a new system of economic ideas called socialism.

Capitalism	Socialism
• Individuals and businesses own property and the means of production.	• The community or the state should own property and the means of production.
• Progress results when individuals follow their own self-interest.	• Progress results when a community of producers cooperate for the good of all.
• Businesses follow their own self-interest by competing for the consumer's money. Each business tries to produce goods or services that are better and less expensive than those of competitors.	• Socialists believe that capitalist employers take advantage of workers. The community or state must act to protect workers.
• Consumers compete to buy the best goods at the lowest prices. This competition shapes the market by affecting what businesses are able to sell.	• Capitalism creates unequal distribution of wealth and material goods. A better system is to distribute goods according to each person's need.
• Government should not interfere in the economy because competition creates efficiency in business.	• An unequal distribution of wealth and material goods is unfair. A better system is to distribute goods according to each person's need.

SKILLBUILDER: Interpreting Charts
1. **Developing Historical Perspective** *Consider the following people from 19th-century Britain: factory worker, shop owner, factory owner, unemployed artisan. Which of them would be most likely to prefer capitalism and which would prefer socialism? Why?*
2. **Forming and Supporting Opinions** *Which system of economic ideas seems most widespread today? Support your opinion.*

The Future According to Marx Marx believed that the capitalist system, which produced the Industrial Revolution, would eventually destroy itself in the following way. Factories would drive small artisans out of business, leaving a small number of manufacturers to control all the wealth. The large proletariat would revolt, seize the factories and mills from the capitalists, and produce what society needed. Workers, sharing in the profits, would bring about economic equality for all people. The workers would control the government in a "dictatorship of the proletariat." After a period of cooperative living and education, the state or government would wither away as a classless society developed.

Marx called this final phase pure communism. Marx described **communism** as a form of complete socialism in which the means of production—all land, mines, factories, railroads, and businesses—would be owned by the people. Private property would in effect cease to exist. All goods and services would be shared equally.

Published in 1848, *The Communist Manifesto* produced few short-term results. Though widespread revolts shook Europe during 1848 and 1849, Europe's leaders eventually put down the uprisings. Only after the turn of the century did the fiery Marxist pamphlet produce explosive results. In the 1900s, Marxism inspired revolutionaries such as Russia's Lenin, China's Mao Zedong, and Cuba's Fidel Castro. These leaders adapted Marx's beliefs to their own specific situations and needs.

Communism Today

Communism expanded to all parts
of the world during the Cold War that
followed the end of World War II.
(See map on page 529.) At the peak
of Communist expansion in the
1980s, about 20 nations were
Communist-controlled, including two
of the world's largest—China and the
Soviet Union. However, dissatisfaction
with the theories of Karl Marx had
been developing.

Eventually, most Communist
governments were replaced. Today,
there are only five Communist
countries—China, North Korea,
Vietnam, and Laos in Asia and Cuba
in the Caribbean. (See map above.)

In *The Communist Manifesto*, Marx and Engels stated their belief that economic forces alone dominated society. Time has shown, however, that religion, nationalism, ethnic loyalties, and a desire for democratic reforms may be as strong influences on history as economic forces. In addition, the gap between the rich and the poor within the industrialized countries failed to widen in the way that Marx and Engels predicted, mostly because of the various reforms enacted by governments.

Labor Unions and Reform Laws

Factory workers faced long hours, dirty and dangerous working conditions, and the threat of being laid off. By the 1800s, working people became more active in politics. To press for reforms, workers joined together in voluntary labor associations called **unions**.

Unionization A union spoke for all the workers in a particular trade. Unions engaged in collective bargaining, negotiations between workers and their employers. They bargained for better working conditions and higher pay. If factory owners refused these demands, union members could **strike**, or refuse to work.

Skilled workers led the way in forming unions because their special skills gave them extra bargaining power. Management would have trouble replacing such skilled workers as carpenters, printers, and spinners. Thus, the earliest unions helped the lower middle class more than they helped the poorest workers.

The union movement underwent slow, painful growth in both Great Britain and the United States. For years, the British government denied workers the right to form unions. The government saw unions as a threat to social order and stability. Indeed, the Combination Acts of 1799 and 1800 outlawed unions and strikes. Ignoring the threat of jail or job loss, factory workers joined unions anyway. Parliament finally repealed the Combination Acts in 1824. After 1825, the British government unhappily tolerated unions.

British unions had shared goals of raising wages for their members and improving working conditions. By 1875, British trade unions had won the right to strike and picket peacefully. They had also built up a membership of about 1 million people.

In the United States, skilled workers had belonged to unions since the early 1800s. In 1886, several unions joined together to form the organization that would become the American Federation of Labor (AFL). A series of successful strikes won AFL members higher wages and shorter hours.

Reform Laws Eventually, reformers and unions forced political leaders to look into the abuses caused by industrialization. In both Great Britain and the United States, new laws reformed some of the worst abuses of industrialization. In the 1820s and 1830s, for example, Parliament began investigating child labor and working conditions in factories and mines. As a result of its findings, Parliament passed the Factory Act of 1833. The new law made it illegal to hire children under 9 years old. Children from the ages of 9 to 12 could not work more than 8 hours a day. Young people from 13 to 17 could not work more than 12 hours. In 1842, the Mines Act prevented women and children from working underground.

MAIN IDEA

D Summarizing
What were some of the important reform bills passed in Britain during this period?

In 1847, the Parliament passed a bill that helped working women as well as their children. The Ten Hours Act of 1847 limited the workday to ten hours for women and children who worked in factories. **D**

Reformers in the United States also passed laws to protect child workers. In 1904, a group of progressive reformers organized the National Child Labor Committee to end child labor. Arguing that child labor lowered wages for all workers, union members joined the reformers. Together they pressured national and state politicians to ban child labor and set maximum working hours.

In 1919, the U.S. Supreme Court objected to a federal child labor law, ruling that it interfered with states' rights to regulate labor. However, individual states were allowed to limit the working hours of women and, later, of men.

▲ Hungarian workers meet to plan their strategy before a strike.

The Reform Movement Spreads

Almost from the beginning, reform movements rose in response to the negative impact of industrialization. These reforms included improving the workplace and extending the right to vote to working-class men. The same impulse toward reform, along with the ideals of the French Revolution, also helped to end slavery and promote new rights for women and children.

The Abolition of Slavery William Wilberforce, a highly religious man, was a member of Parliament who led the fight for abolition—the end of the slave trade and slavery in the British Empire. Parliament passed a bill to end the slave trade in the British West Indies in 1807. After he retired from Parliament in 1825, Wilberforce continued his fight to free the slaves. Britain finally abolished slavery in its empire in 1833.

British antislavery activists had mixed motives. Some, such as the abolitionist Wilberforce, were morally against slavery. Others viewed slave labor as an economic threat. Furthermore, a new class of industrialists developed who supported cheap labor rather than slave labor. They soon gained power in Parliament.

In the United States the movement to fulfill the promise of the Declaration of Independence by ending slavery grew in the early 1800s. The enslavement of African people finally ended in the United States when the Union won the Civil War in 1865. Then, enslavement persisted in the Americas only in Puerto Rico, Cuba, and Brazil. In Puerto Rico, slavery was ended in 1873. Spain finally abolished slavery in its Cuban colony in 1886. Not until 1888 did Brazil's huge enslaved population win freedom.

The Fight for Women's Rights The Industrial Revolution proved a mixed blessing for women. On the one hand, factory work offered higher wages than work done at home. Women spinners in Manchester, for example, earned much more money than women who stayed home to spin cotton thread. On the other hand, women factory workers usually made only one-third as much money as men did.

Women led reform movements to address this and other pressing social issues. During the mid-1800s, for example, women formed unions in the trades where they dominated. In Britain, some women served as safety inspectors in factories where other women worked. In the United States, college-educated women like Jane Addams ran settlement houses. These community centers served the poor residents of slum neighborhoods.

Jane Addams
1860–1935

After graduating from college, Jane Addams wondered what to do with her life.

I gradually became convinced that it would be a good thing to rent a house in a part of the city where many primitive and actual needs are found, in which young women who had been given over too exclusively to study, might . . . learn of life from life itself.

Addams and her friend Ellen Starr set up Hull House in a working-class district in Chicago. Eventually the facilities included a nursery, a gym, a kitchen, and a boarding house for working women. Hull House not only served the immigrant population of the neighborhood, it also trained social workers.

In both the United States and Britain, women who had rallied for the abolition of slavery began to wonder why their own rights should be denied on the basis of gender. The movement for women's rights began in the United States as early as 1848. Women activists around the world joined to found the International Council for Women in 1888. Delegates and observers from 27 countries attended the council's 1899 meeting. **E**

Reforms Spread to Many Areas of Life In the United States and Western Europe, reformers tried to correct the problems troubling the newly industrialized nations. Public education and prison reform ranked high on the reformers' lists.

One of the most prominent U.S. reformers, Horace Mann of Massachusetts, favored free public education for all children. Mann, who spent his own childhood working at hard labor, warned, "If we do not prepare children to become good citizens . . . if we do not enrich their minds with knowledge, then our republic must go down to destruction." By the 1850s, many states were starting public school systems. In Western Europe, free public schooling became available in the late 1800s.

In 1831, French writer Alexis de Tocqueville had contrasted the brutal conditions in American prisons to the "extended liberty" of American society. Those who sought to reform prisons emphasized the goal of providing prisoners with the means to lead to useful lives upon release.

During the 1800s, democracy grew in industrialized countries even as foreign expansion increased. The industrialized democracies faced new challenges both at home and abroad. You will learn about these challenges in Chapter 10.

MAIN IDEA
E) Making Inferences
Why might women abolitionists have headed the movement for women's rights?

SECTION 4 ASSESSMENT

TERMS & NAMES 1. For each term or name, write a sentence explaining its significance.
• laissez faire • Adam Smith • capitalism • utilitarianism • socialism • Karl Marx • communism • union • strike

USING YOUR NOTES
2. What characteristics do capitalism and socialism share?

Capitalism	Socialism
1.	1.
2.	2.
3.	3.

MAIN IDEAS
3. What were Adam Smith's three natural laws of economics?
4. What kind of society did early socialists want?
5. Why did workers join together in unions?

CRITICAL THINKING & WRITING
6. **IDENTIFYING PROBLEMS** What were the main problems faced by the unions during the 1800s and how did they overcome them?
7. **DRAWING CONCLUSIONS** Why do you think that Marx's "dictatorship of the proletariat" did not happen?
8. **MAKING INFERENCES** Why did the labor reform movement spread to other areas of life?
9. **WRITING ACTIVITY** ECONOMICS Write a two-paragraph **persuasive essay** on how important economic forces are in society. Support your opinion using evidence from this and previous chapters.

CONNECT TO TODAY PREPARING AN ECONOMIC REPORT
Research a present-day corporation. Prepare an **economic report** that includes the corporation's structure, products or services, number of employees, and any other relevant economic information you are able to find.

INTERACTIVE

Industrialization

Industrialization eventually raised the standard of living for many people in Europe and North America in the 1800s. Yet the process also brought suffering to countless workers who crowded into filthy cities to toil for starvation wages. The following excerpts reveal a variety of perspectives on this major historical event.

A PRIMARY SOURCE

Mary Paul

Mary Paul worked in a textile factory in Lowell, Massachusetts. In an 1846 letter to her father in New Hampshire, the 16-year-old expressed her satisfaction with her situation at Lowell.

—

I am at work in a spinning room tending four sides of warp which is one girl's work. The overseer tells me that he never had a girl get along better than I do. . . . I have a very good boarding place, have enough to eat. . . . The girls are all kind and obliging. . . . I think that the factory is the best place for me and if any girl wants employment, I advise them to come to Lowell.

B PRIMARY SOURCE

Andrew Carnegie

In his autobiography, published in 1920, the multimillionaire industrialist views with optimism the growth of American industry.

—

One great advantage which America will have in competing in the markets of the world is that her manufacturers will have the best home market. Upon this they can depend for a return upon capital, and the surplus product can be exported with advantage, even when the prices received for it do no more than cover actual cost, provided the exports be charged with their proportion of all expenses. The nation that has the best home market, especially if products are standardized, as ours are, can soon outsell the foreign producer.

C PRIMARY SOURCE

Friedrich Engels

Friedrich Engels, who coauthored *The Communist Manifesto* and also managed a textile factory in Manchester, England, spent his nights wandering the city's slums.

—

Nobody troubles about the poor as they struggle helplessly in the whirlpool of modern industrial life. The working man may be lucky enough to find employment, if by his labor he can enrich some member of the middle classes. But his wages are so low that they hardly keep body and soul together. If he cannot find work, he can steal, unless he is afraid of the police; or he can go hungry and then the police will see to it that he will die of hunger in such a way as not to disturb the equanimity of the middle classes.

D PRIMARY SOURCE

Walter Crane

This political cartoon was published in *Cartoons for the Cause* in Britain in 1886. It shows the vampire bat of Capitalism attacking a laborer. Socialism is pictured as an angel who is coming to the rescue.

Document-Based QUESTIONS

1. Why would Andrew Carnegie (Source B) and Friedrich Engels (Source C) disagree about the effects of industrialization?

2. What might be reasons for 16-year-old Mary Paul's (Source A) satisfaction with her job and life in Lowell?

3. Why might the political cartoon by Walter Crane (Source D) be useful in getting workers to rally to the cause of socialism?

VISUAL SUMMARY

The Industrial Revolution

Economic Effects

- New inventions and development of factories
- Rapidly growing industry in the 1800s
- Increased production and higher demand for raw materials
- Growth of worldwide trade
- Population explosion and expanding labor force
- Exploitation of mineral resources
- Highly developed banking and investment system
- Advances in transportation, agriculture, and communication

Social Effects

- Increase in population of cities
- Lack of city planning
- Loss of family stability
- Expansion of middle class
- Harsh conditions for laborers, including children
- Workers' progress versus laissez-faire economic attitudes
- Improved standard of living
- Creation of new jobs
- Encouragement of technological progress

Political Effects

- Child labor laws to end abuses
- Reformers urging equal distribution of wealth
- Trade unions formed
- Social reform movements, such as utilitarianism, utopianism, socialism, and Marxism
- Reform bills in Parliament and Congress

TERMS & NAMES

For each term or name below, briefly explain its connection to the Industrial Revolution.

1. Industrial Revolution
2. enclosure
3. factory
4. urbanization
5. middle class
6. corporation
7. laissez faire
8. socialism
9. Karl Marx
10. union

MAIN IDEAS

The Beginnings of Industrialization Section 1 (pages 283–288)

11. What were the four natural resources needed for British industrialization?
12. How did the enclosure movement change agriculture in England?
13. What were two important inventions created during the Industrial Revolution? Describe their impact.

Case Study: Industrialization Section 2 (pages 289–294)

14. What were the living conditions like in Britain during industrialization?
15. How did the new middle class transform the social structure of Great Britain during industrialization?
16. How did industrialization affect Manchester's natural environment?

Industrialization Spreads Section 3 (pages 295–299)

17. Why were other European countries slower to industrialize than Britain?
18. What might explain the rise of global inequality during the Industrial Revolution?

Reforming the Industrial World Section 4 (pages 300–307)

19. What were the two warring classes that Marx and Engels outlined in *The Communist Manifesto*?
20. How did women fight for change during the Industrial Revolution?

CRITICAL THINKING

1. USING YOUR NOTES

In a chart, list some of the major technological advances and their effects on society.

Technological Advance	Effect(s)

2. EVALUATING

SCIENCE AND TECHNOLOGY How significant were the changes that the Industrial Revolution brought to the world? Explain your conclusion.

3. ANALYZING CAUSES AND RECOGNIZING EFFECTS

ECONOMICS How important were labor unions in increasing the power of workers? Give reasons for your opinion.

4. DRAWING CONCLUSIONS

How did the Industrial Revolution help to increase Germany's military power? Support your answer with information from the chapter.

5. DEVELOPING HISTORICAL PERSPECTIVE

EMPIRE BUILDING Would a nonindustrialized or an industrialized nation more likely be an empire builder? Why?

Use the quotation about industrialization and your knowledge of world history to answer questions 1 and 2. Additional Test Practice, pp. S1–S33

PRIMARY SOURCE

It was a town of red brick, or of brick that would have been red if the smoke and ashes had allowed it. . . . It was a town of machinery and tall chimneys, out of which interminable [endless] serpents of smoke trailed themselves for ever and ever. . . . It contained several large streets all very like one another, and many small streets still more like one another, inhabited by people equally like one another, who went in and out at the same hours, with the same sound upon the same pavements, to do the same work, and to whom every day was the same as yesterday and tomorrow, and every year the counterpart of the last and the next.

CHARLES DICKENS, *Hard Times*

1. In this passage, the writer is trying to describe how
   A. people came from the countryside to the city to work in industry.
   B. entrepreneurs built factories.
   C. capitalism works.
   D. difficult life is for workers in industrial cities.

2. What is Dickens's view of industrialization?
   A. that it is good for factory owners
   B. that it brings progress to a nation
   C. that it pollutes the air and exploits the workers
   D. that it causes population growth

Use the graph below and your knowledge of world history to answer question 3.

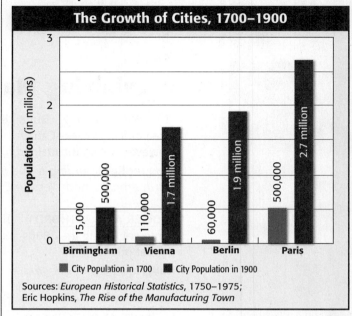

The Growth of Cities, 1700–1900

City Population in 1700 ■ City Population in 1900 ■

Sources: *European Historical Statistics*, 1750–1975; Eric Hopkins, *The Rise of the Manufacturing Town*

3. The graph above shows population growth in four European cities from 1700 to 1900, that is, before and after the Industrial Revolution. Which statement best describes the information in the chart?
   A. All of the cities grew at the same rate.
   B. The increase in population for each city was less than 2 million people.
   C. Paris was the most populous city both before and after the Industrial Revolution.
   D. Berlin's population in 1900 was four times its size in 1700.

INTEGRATED TECHNOLOGY

TEST PRACTICE Go to **classzone.com**
• Diagnostic tests   • Strategies
• Tutorials   • Additional practice

ALTERNATIVE ASSESSMENT

1. Interact *with* History

On page 282, you looked at working conditions in an English factory in the 19th century. Now that you have read the chapter about the Industrial Revolution, rethink your decision about what you would do to change your situation. What working conditions would you like to see change? What benefits might a union bring? What disadvantages might result if workers organize? Discuss your opinions with a small group.

2. WRITING ABOUT HISTORY

The Industrial Revolution's impact varied according to social class. Write a three-paragraph **expository essay** indicating how these people would view the changes in industry: an inventor, an entrepreneur, a skilled worker, and a hand weaver.

INTEGRATED TECHNOLOGY

Using Graphics Software

Make a list of five major inventions or innovations of the Industrial Revolution. Research each to learn about the scientific, economic, and social changes that contributed to its development and the effects that it caused. Use the Internet, books, and other resources to conduct your research. Then use graphics software to create a chart, graph, or diagram depicting the relationship between the inventions and innovations, the changes, and the effects.
You may include some of the following:
• the plow   • the cotton gin
• the power loom   • the telegraph
• the sewing machine

An Age of Democracy and Progress, 1815–1914

Previewing Main Ideas

EMPIRE BUILDING During the 1800s, Great Britain gradually allowed three of its colonies—Canada, Australia, and New Zealand—greater self-rule. However, Britain maintained tight control over Ireland.

Geography *According to the map, what Western democracies existed in North America and Western Europe in 1900?*

POWER AND AUTHORITY The United States expanded across the continent during the 1800s and added new states to its territory to become a great power.

Geography *What geographical factors might have helped to make the United States a great power?*

SCIENCE AND TECHNOLOGY The transcontinental railroad helped to link the United States from the Atlantic Ocean to the Pacific Ocean. It was a triumph of 19th-century technology.

Geography *How might a technological achievement such as the transcontinental railroad have contributed to American prosperity?*

INTEGRATED TECHNOLOGY

eEdition
- Interactive Maps
- Interactive Visuals
- Interactive Primary Sources

INTERNET RESOURCES

Go to **classzone.com** for:
- Research Links
- Internet Activities
- Primary Sources
- Chapter Quiz
- Maps
- Test Practice
- Current Events

EUROPE

1837
◄ Queen Victoria comes to power in Great Britain.

1845
Ireland is struck by famine.

1859
Darwin publishes theory of evolution.

1815

1850

WORLD

1821
Mexico wins independence from Spain.

1857
◄ Sepoy Mutiny challenges British rule in India. (native troops in Britain's East India Company)

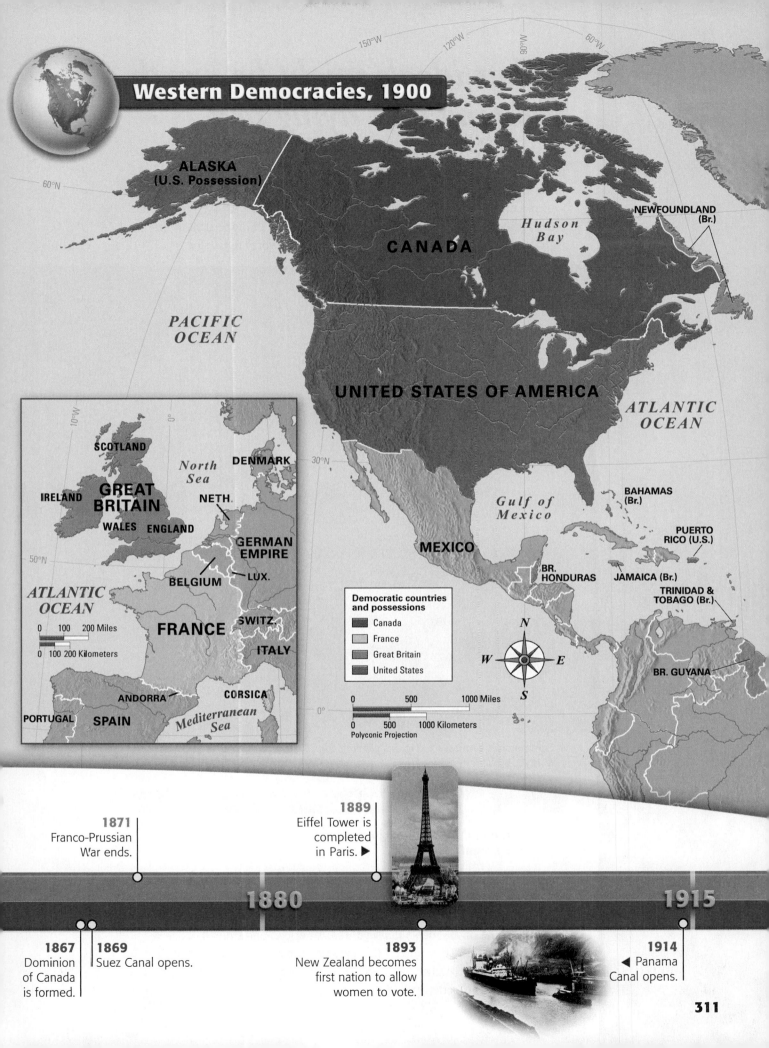

Western Democracies, 1900

ALASKA
(U.S. Possession)

CANADA

*Hudson
Bay*

NEWFOUNDLAND
(Br.)

*PACIFIC
OCEAN*

UNITED STATES OF AMERICA

*ATLANTIC
OCEAN*

*Gulf of
Mexico*

BAHAMAS
(Br.)

PUERTO
RICO (U.S.)

MEXICO

BR.
HONDURAS

JAMAICA (Br.)

TRINIDAD &
TOBAGO (Br.)

BR. GUYANA

Inset map (Europe):

SCOTLAND

*North
Sea*

DENMARK

IRELAND

GREAT
BRITAIN

NETH.

WALES   ENGLAND

GERMAN
EMPIRE

BELGIUM   LUX.

*ATLANTIC
OCEAN*

0   100   200 Miles

0   100   200 Kilometers

FRANCE

SWITZ.

ITALY

ANDORRA

CORSICA

PORTUGAL   SPAIN

*Mediterranean
Sea*

**Democratic countries
and possessions**

- Canada
- France
- Great Britain
- United States

N
W   E
S

0   500   1000 Miles

0   500   1000 Kilometers
Polyconic Projection

Timeline:

1871
Franco-Prussian
War ends.

1889
Eiffel Tower is
completed
in Paris. ▶

1880

1915

1867
Dominion
of Canada
is formed.

1869
Suez Canal opens.

1893
New Zealand becomes
first nation to allow
women to vote.

1914
◀ Panama
Canal opens.

311

Interact *with* History

What ideals might be worth fighting and dying for?

You are living in Paris in 1871. France is in a state of political upheaval following the Franco-Prussian War. When workers in Paris set up their own government, called the Paris Commune, French soldiers quickly stamp out the movement. Most of the Communards (the supporters of the Commune) are either killed or imprisoned. When your good friend Philippe dies in the fighting, you wonder whether self-government is worth dying for.

▲ Communards lie massacred in this painting titled *A Street in Paris in May 1871,* by Maximilien Luce.

EXAMINING *the* ISSUES

- **What might lead you to join a group seeking self-government?**

- **What ideals would you choose to help shape a new government?**

As a class, discuss these questions. During the discussion, think about some of the ideals that inspired American and French revolutionaries. As you read this chapter, consider the ideals that moved people to action. Also consider how people tried to change government to better reflect their ideals.

Democratic Reform and Activism

MAIN IDEA	WHY IT MATTERS NOW	TERMS & NAMES
POWER AND AUTHORITY Spurred by the demands of the people, Great Britain and France underwent democratic reforms.	During this period, Britain and France were transformed into the democracies they are today.	• suffrage • Chartist movement • Queen Victoria	• Third Republic • Dreyfus affair • anti-Semitism • Zionism

SETTING THE STAGE Urbanization and industrialization brought sweeping changes to Western nations. People looking for solutions to the problems created by these developments began to demand reforms. They wanted to improve conditions for workers and the poor. Many people also began to call for political reforms. They demanded that more people be given a greater voice in government. Many different groups, including the middle class, workers, and women, argued that the right to vote be extended to groups that were excluded.

Britain Enacts Reforms

As Chapter 5 explained, Britain became a constitutional monarchy in the late 1600s. Under this system of government, the monarch serves as the head of state, but Parliament holds the real power. The British Parliament consists of a House of Lords and a House of Commons. Traditionally, members of the House of Lords either inherited their seats or were appointed. However, this changed in 1999, when legislation was passed that abolished the right of hereditary peers to inherit a seat in the House of Lords. Members of the House of Commons are elected by the British people.

In the early 1800s, the method of selecting the British government was not a true democracy. Only about five percent of the population had the right to elect the members of the House of Commons. Voting was limited to men who owned a substantial amount of land. Women could not vote at all. As a result, the upper classes ran the government.

The Reform Bill of 1832 The first group to demand a greater voice in politics was the wealthy middle class—factory owners, bankers, and merchants. Beginning in 1830, protests took place around England in favor of a bill in Parliament that would extend **suffrage**, or the right to vote. The Revolution of 1830 in France frightened parliamentary leaders. They feared that revolutionary violence would spread to Britain. Thus, Parliament passed the Reform Bill of 1832. This law eased the property requirements so that well-to-do men in the middle class could vote. The Reform Bill also modernized the districts for electing members of Parliament and gave the thriving new industrial cities more representation.

Chartist Movement Although the Reform Bill increased the number of British voters, only a small percentage of men were eligible to vote. A popular movement

TAKING NOTES

Evaluating Courses of Action Use a chart to list and evaluate events in this section according to whether they expanded (+) or impeded (-) democracy.

Event	Evaluation

Expansion of Suffrage in Britain

Before 1832	1832	1867, 1884	1918

Before 1832
- 5%
- 95%

Percentage of population over age 20
- ■ had right to vote
- ■ gained right to vote
- ■ could not vote

1832
- 2%
- 5%
- 93%

Reform Bill granted vote to middle-class men.

1867, 1884
- 7%
- 21%
- 72%

Reforms granted vote to working-class men in 1867 and to rural men in 1884.

1918
- 26%
- 28%
- 46%

Reforms granted vote to women over 30.

Source: R. L. Leonard, *Elections in Britain*

SKILLBUILDER: Interpreting Graphs
1. **Clarifying** *What percentage of the adults in Britain could vote in 1832?*
2. **Comparing** *By how much did the percentage of voters increase after the reforms of 1867 and 1884?*

arose among the workers and other groups who still could not vote to press for more rights. It was called the **Chartist movement** because the group first presented its demands to Parliament in a petition called The People's Charter of 1838.

The People's Charter called for suffrage for all men and annual Parliamentary elections. It also proposed to reform Parliament in other ways. In Britain at the time, eligible men voted openly. Since their vote was not secret, they could feel pressure to vote in a certain way. Members of Parliament had to own land and received no salary, so they needed to be wealthy. The Chartists wanted to make Parliament responsive to the lower classes. To do this, they demanded a secret ballot, an end to property requirements for serving in Parliament, and pay for members of Parliament.

Parliament rejected the Chartists' demands. However, their protests convinced many people that the workers had valid complaints. Over the years, workers continued to press for political reform, and Parliament responded. It gave the vote to working-class men in 1867 and to male rural workers in 1884. After 1884, most adult males in Britain had the right to vote. By the early 1900s, all the demands of the Chartists, except for annual elections, became law. **A**

The Victorian Age The figure who presided over all this historic change was **Queen Victoria**. Victoria came to the throne in 1837 at the age of 18. She was queen for nearly 64 years. During the Victorian Age, the British Empire reached the height of its wealth and power. Victoria was popular with her subjects, and she performed her duties capably. However, she was forced to accept a less powerful role for the monarchy.

The kings who preceded Victoria in the 1700s and 1800s had exercised great influence over Parliament. The spread of democracy in the 1800s shifted political power almost completely to Parliament, and especially to the elected House of Commons. Now the government was completely run by the prime minister and the cabinet.

History Makers

Queen Victoria and Prince Albert

About two years after her coronation, Queen Victoria (1819–1901) fell in love with her cousin Albert (1819–1861), a German prince. She proposed to him and they were married in 1840. Together they had nine children. Prince Albert established a tone of politeness and correct behavior at court, and the royal couple presented a picture of loving family life that became a British ideal.

After Albert died in 1861, the queen wore black silk for the rest of her life in mourning. She once said of Albert, "Without him everything loses its interest."

MAIN IDEA

Making Inferences
A Why do you think the Chartists demanded a secret ballot rather than public voting?

Women Get the Vote

By 1890, several industrial countries had universal male suffrage (the right of all men to vote). No country, however, allowed women to vote. As more men gained suffrage, more women demanded the same.

Organization and Resistance During the 1800s, women in both Great Britain and the United States worked to gain the right to vote. British women organized reform societies and protested unfair laws and customs. As women became more vocal, however, resistance to their demands grew. Many people, both men and women, thought that woman suffrage was too radical a break with tradition. Some claimed that women lacked the ability to take part in politics.

Militant Protests After decades of peaceful efforts to win the right to vote, some women took more drastic steps. In Britain, Emmeline Pankhurst formed the Women's Social and Political Union (WSPU) in 1903. The WSPU became the most militant organization for women's rights. Its goal was to draw attention to the cause of woman suffrage. When asked about why her group chose militant means to gain women's rights, Pankhurst replied:

PRIMARY SOURCE

I want to say here and now that the only justification for violence, the only justification for damage to property, the only justification for risk to the comfort of other human beings is the fact that you have tried all other available means and have failed to secure justice.

EMMELINE PANKHURST, *Why We Are Militant*

MAIN IDEA

Analyzing Motives
B Was the use of militant action effective in achieving the goal of woman suffrage? Explain.

Emmeline Pankhurst, her daughters Christabel and Sylvia, and other WSPU members were arrested and imprisoned many times. When they were jailed, the Pankhursts led hunger strikes to keep their cause in the public eye. British officials force-fed Sylvia and other activists to keep them alive.

Though the woman suffrage movement gained attention between 1880 and 1914, its successes were gradual. Women did not gain the right to vote in national elections in Great Britain and the United States until after World War I. **B**

France and Democracy

While Great Britain moved toward greater democracy in the late 1800s, democracy finally took hold in France.

The Third Republic In the aftermath of the Franco-Prussian War, France went through a series of crises. Between 1871 and 1914, France averaged a change of government almost yearly. A dozen political parties competed for power. Not until 1875 could the National Assembly agree on a new government. Eventually, the members voted to set up a republic. The **Third Republic** lasted over 60 years. However, France remained divided.

The Dreyfus Affair During the 1880s and 1890s, the Third Republic was threatened by monarchists, aristocrats, clergy, and army leaders. These groups wanted a monarchy or military rule. A controversy known as the **Dreyfus affair** became a battleground for these opposing forces. Widespread feelings of **anti-Semitism**, or prejudice against Jews, also played a role in this scandal.

Global Impact

The Women's Movement

By the 1880s, women were working internationally to win more rights. In 1888, women activists from the United States, Canada, and Europe met in Washington, D.C., for the International Council of Women. In 1893, delegates and observers from many countries attended a large congress of women in Chicago. They came from lands as far apart as New Zealand, Argentina, Iceland, Persia, and China.

The first countries to grant suffrage to women were New Zealand (1893) and Australia (1902). Only in two European countries—Finland (1906, then part of the Russian Empire) and Norway (1913)—did women gain voting rights before World War I. In the United States, the territory of Wyoming allowed women to vote in 1869. Several other Western states followed suit.

▲ *Zola Under Attack,* painted in 1898 by Henry de Groux, shows Émile Zola surrounded by an anti-Semitic mob.

In 1894, Captain Alfred Dreyfus, one of the few Jewish officers in the French army, was accused of selling military secrets to Germany. A court found him guilty, based on false evidence, and sentenced him to life in prison. In a few years, new evidence showed that Dreyfus had been framed by other army officers.

Public opinion was sharply divided over the scandal. Many army leaders, nationalists, leaders in the clergy, and anti-Jewish groups refused to let the case be reopened. They feared sudden action would cast doubt on the honor of the army. Dreyfus's defenders insisted that justice was more important. In 1898, the writer Émile Zola published an open letter titled *J'accuse!* (I accuse) in a popular French newspaper. In the letter, Zola denounced the army for covering up a scandal. Zola was sentenced to a year in prison for his views, but his letter gave strength to Dreyfus's cause. Eventually, the French government declared his innocence.

The Rise of Zionism The Dreyfus case showed the strength of anti-Semitism in France and other parts of Western Europe. However, persecution of Jews was even more severe in Eastern Europe. Russian officials permitted pogroms (puh•GRAHMS), organized campaigns of violence against Jews. From the late 1880s on, thousands of Jews fled Eastern Europe. Many headed for the United States.

For many Jews, the long history of exile and persecution convinced them to work for a homeland in Palestine. In the 1890s, a movement known as **Zionism** developed to pursue this goal. Its leader was Theodor Herzl (HEHRT•suhl), a writer in Vienna. It took many years, however, before the state of Israel was established.

SECTION 1 ASSESSMENT

TERMS & NAMES 1. For each term or name, write a sentence explaining its significance.
• suffrage   • Chartist movement   • Queen Victoria   • Third Republic   • Dreyfus affair   • anti-Semitism   • Zionism

USING YOUR NOTES
2. Which of these events most expanded democracy, and why?

Event	Evaluation

MAIN IDEAS
3. What were some effects of the Reform Bill of 1832?
4. What was the goal of the WSPU in Britain?
5. What was the Dreyfus affair?

CRITICAL THINKING & WRITING
6. **COMPARING** Why was the road to democracy more difficult for France than for England?
7. **SYNTHESIZING** Look again at the primary source on page 315. What is Pankhurst demanding?
8. **RECOGNIZING EFFECTS** What was the connection between anti-Semitism and Zionism?
9. **WRITING ACTIVITY** POWER AND AUTHORITY Among the Chartists' demands was pay for members of Parliament. Write a **letter to the editor** that supports or criticizes a pay raise for your legislators.

CONNECT TO TODAY CREATING A POSTER
Find information on issues in today's world that involve a call for social justice. Then make a **poster** in which you illustrate what you regard as the most compelling example of a current social injustice.

2

Self-Rule for British Colonies

MAIN IDEA	WHY IT MATTERS NOW	TERMS & NAMES
EMPIRE BUILDING Britain allowed self-rule in Canada, Australia, and New Zealand but delayed it for Ireland.	Canada, Australia, and New Zealand are strong democracies today, while Ireland is divided.	• dominion • Maori • Aborigine • penal colony • home rule • Irish Republican Army

SETTING THE STAGE By 1800, Great Britain had colonies around the world. These included outposts in Africa and Asia. In these areas, the British managed trade with the local peoples, but they had little influence over the population at large. In the colonies of Canada, Australia, and New Zealand, on the other hand, European colonists dominated the native populations. As Britain industrialized and prospered in the 1800s, so did these colonies. Some were becoming strong enough to stand on their own.

Canada Struggles for Self-Rule

Canada was originally home to many Native American peoples. The first European country to colonize Canada was France. The earliest French colonists, in the 1600s and 1700s, had included many fur trappers and missionaries. They tended to live among the Native Americans. Some French intermarried with Native Americans.

Great Britain took possession of the country in 1763 after it defeated France in the French and Indian War. The French who remained lived mostly in the lower St. Lawrence Valley. Many English-speaking colonists arrived in Canada after it came under British rule. Some came from Great Britain, and others were Americans who had stayed loyal to Britain after the American Revolution. They settled separately from the French along the Atlantic seaboard and the Great Lakes.

French and English Canada Religious and cultural differences between the mostly Roman Catholic French and the mainly Protestant English-speaking colonists caused conflict in Canada. Both groups pressed Britain for a greater voice in governing their own affairs. In 1791 the British Parliament tried to resolve both issues by creating two new Canadian provinces. Upper Canada (now Ontario) had an English-speaking majority. Lower Canada (now Quebec) had a French-speaking majority. Each province had its own elected assembly.

The Durham Report The division of Upper and Lower Canada temporarily eased tensions. In both colonies, the royal governor and a small group of wealthy British held most of the power. But during the early 1800s, middle-class professionals in both colonies began to demand political and economic reforms. In Lower Canada, these demands were also fueled by French resentment toward British rule. In the late 1830s, rebellions broke out in both Upper and Lower

Comparing Use a chart to compare progress toward self-rule by recording significant events.

Country	Political Events
Canada	
Australia	
New Zealand	
Ireland	

CANADA   Acadia

500 Miles

1,000 Kilometers

Acadians to Cajuns

Colonists from France founded the colony of Acadia on the eastern coast of what is now Canada in 1604. Tensions flared between these settlers and later arrivals from England and Scotland.

In 1713, the British gained control of Acadia and renamed it Nova Scotia (New Scotland). They expelled thousands of descendants of the original Acadians. Many eventually settled in southern Louisiana. Today, their culture still thrives in the Mississippi Delta area, where the people are called Cajuns (an alteration of Acadian).

Canada. The British Parliament sent a reform-minded statesman, Lord Durham, to investigate.

In 1839, Durham sent a report to Parliament that urged two major reforms. First, Upper and Lower Canada should be reunited as the Province of Canada, and British immigration should be encouraged. In this way, the French would slowly become part of the dominant English culture. Second, colonists in the provinces of Canada should be allowed to govern themselves in domestic matters. **A**

The Dominion of Canada By the mid-1800s, many Canadians believed that Canada needed a central government. A central government would be better able to protect the interests of Canadians against the United States, whose territory now extended from the Atlantic to the Pacific oceans. In 1867, Nova Scotia and New Brunswick joined the Province of Canada to form the Dominion of Canada. As a **dominion**, Canada was self-governing in domestic affairs but remained part of the British Empire.

Canada's Westward Expansion Canada's first prime minister, John MacDonald, expanded Canada westward by purchasing lands and persuading frontier territories to join the union. Canada stretched to the Pacific Ocean by 1871. MacDonald began the construction of a transcontinental railroad, completed in 1885.

MAIN IDEA
Recognizing Effects
A How do you think Durham's report affected French-speaking Canadians?

Australia and New Zealand

The British sea captain James Cook claimed New Zealand in 1769 and part of Australia in 1770 for Great Britain. Both lands were already inhabited. In New Zealand, Cook was greeted by the **Maori**, a Polynesian people who had settled in New Zealand around A.D. 800. Maori culture was based on farming, hunting, and fishing.

When Cook reached Australia, he considered the land uninhabited. In fact, Australia was sparsely populated by **Aborigines**, as Europeans later called the native peoples. Aborigines are the longest ongoing culture in the world. These nomadic peoples fished, hunted, and gathered food.

Britain's Penal Colony Britain began colonizing Australia in 1788 with convicted criminals. The prisons in England were severely overcrowded. To solve this problem, the British government established a penal colony in Australia. A **penal colony** was a place where convicts were sent to serve their sentences. Many European nations used penal colonies as a way to prevent overcrowding of prisons. After their release, the newly freed prisoners could buy land and settle.

Free Settlers Arrive Free British settlers eventually joined the former convicts in both Australia and New Zealand. In the early 1800s, an Australian settler experimented with breeds of sheep until he found one that produced high quality wool and thrived in the country's warm, dry weather. Although sheep are not native to Australia, the raising and exporting of wool became its biggest business.

To encourage immigration, the government offered settlers cheap land. The population grew steadily in the early 1800s and then skyrocketed after a gold rush in 1851. The scattered settlements on Australia's east coast grew into separate colonies. Meanwhile, a few pioneers pushed westward across the vast dry interior and established outposts in western Australia.

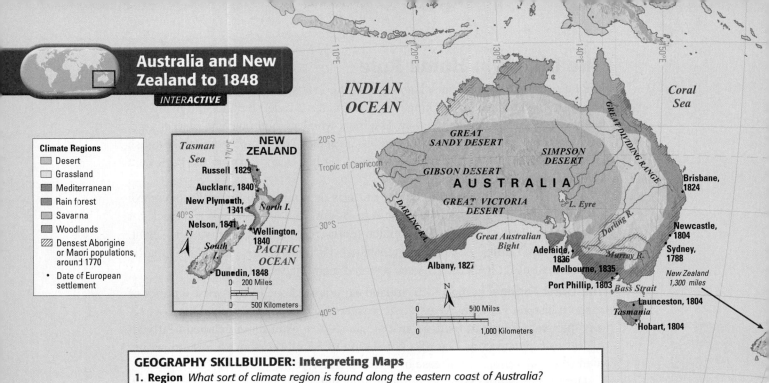

Australia and New Zealand to 1848

INTER**ACTIVE**

INDIAN OCEAN

Coral Sea

Climate Regions
- ☐ Desert
- ☐ Grassland
- ■ Mediterranean
- ■ Rain forest
- ☐ Savanna
- ■ Woodlands
- ▨ Densest Aborigine or Maori populations, around 1770
- • Date of European settlement

NEW ZEALAND

Tasman Sea

Russell 1829
Auckland, 1840
New Plymouth, 1341
Nelson, 1841
Wellington, 1840
Dunedin, 1848

North I.
South I.

PACIFIC OCEAN

0   200 Miles
0   500 Kilometers

GREAT SANDY DESERT
GIBSON DESERT
GREAT VICTORIA DESERT
SIMPSON DESERT

AUSTRALIA

DARLING R.
Great Australian Bight
Albany, 1827
Adelaide, 1836
Melbourne, 1835
Port Phillip, 1803

GREAT DIVIDING RANGE
L. Eyre
Murray R.
Darling R.

Brisbane, 1824
Newcastle, 1804
Sydney, 1788

New Zealand 1,300 miles

Bass Strait
Launceston, 1804
Tasmania
Hobart, 1804

Tropic of Capricorn
20°S
30°S
40°S

0   500 Miles
0   1,000 Kilometers

GEOGRAPHY SKILLBUILDER: Interpreting Maps
1. **Region** *What sort of climate region is found along the eastern coast of Australia?*
2. **Region** *What regions of Australia and New Zealand were most densely inhabited by native peoples?*

Settling New Zealand European settlement of New Zealand grew more slowly. This was because Britain did not claim ownership of New Zealand, as it did Australia. Rather, it recognized the land rights of the Maori. In 1814, missionary groups began arriving from Australia seeking to convert the Maori to Christianity.

The arrival of more foreigners stirred conflicts between the Maori and the European settlers over land. Responding to the settlers' pleas, the British decided to annex New Zealand in 1839 and appointed a governor to negotiate with the Maori. In a treaty signed in 1840, the Maori accepted British rule in exchange for recognition of their land rights.

Self-Government Like Canadians, the colonists of Australia and New Zealand wanted to rule themselves yet remain in the British Empire. During the 1850s, the colonies in both Australia and New Zealand became self-governing and created parliamentary forms of government. In 1901, the Australian colonies were united under a federal constitution as the Commonwealth of Australia. During the early 1900s, both Australia and New Zealand became dominions.

The people of Australia and New Zealand pioneered a number of political reforms. For example, the secret ballot, sometimes called the Australian ballot, was first used in Australia in the 1850s. In 1893, New Zealand became the first nation in the world to give full voting rights to women. However, only white women gained these rights.

Status of Native Peoples Native peoples and other non-Europeans were excluded from democracy and prosperity. Diseases brought by the Europeans killed Aborigines and Maori. As Australian settlement grew, the colonists displaced or killed many Aborigines.

In New Zealand, tensions between settlers and Maori continued to grow after it became a British colony. Between 1845 and 1872, the colonial government fought the Maori in a series of wars. Reduced by disease and outgunned by British weapons, the Maori were finally driven into a remote part of the country. **B**

▼ This photograph shows a Maori warrior with traditional dress and face markings.

MAIN IDEA

Contrasting
B How did the colonial settlement of Australia and New Zealand differ?

An Age of Democracy and Progress **319**

The Irish Win Home Rule

English expansion into Ireland had begun in the 1100s, when the pope granted control of Ireland to the English king. English knights invaded Ireland, and many settled there to form a new aristocracy. The Irish, who had their own ancestry, culture, and language, bitterly resented the English presence. Laws imposed by the English in the 1500s and 1600s limited the rights of Catholics and favored the Protestant religion and the English language.

Over the years, the British government was determined to maintain its control over Ireland. It formally joined Ireland to Britain in 1801. Though a setback for Irish nationalism, this move gave Ireland representation in the British Parliament. Irish leader Daniel O'Connell persuaded Parliament to pass the Catholic Emancipation Act in 1829. This law restored many rights to Catholics.

The Great Famine In the 1840s, Ireland experienced one of the worst famines of modern history. For many years, Irish peasants had depended on potatoes as virtually their sole source of food. From 1845 to 1848, a plant fungus ruined nearly all of Ireland's potato crop. Out of a population of 8 million, about a million people died from starvation and disease over the next few years.

During the famine years, about a million and a half people fled from Ireland. Most went to the United States; others went to Britain, Canada, and Australia. At home, in Ireland, the British government enforced the demands of the English landowners that the Irish peasants pay their rent. Many Irish lost their land and fell hopelessly in debt, while large landowners profited from higher food prices.

Demands for Home Rule During the second half of the 1800s, opposition to British rule over Ireland took two forms. Some Irish wanted independence for Ireland. A greater number of Irish preferred **home rule**, local control over internal

---

> Analyzing Primary Sources

Starvation in Ireland

A traveler described what he saw on a journey through Ireland in 1847:

PRIMARY SOURCE

We entered a cabin. Stretched in one dark corner, scarcely visible, from the smoke and rags that covered them, were three children huddled together, lying there because they were too weak to rise, pale and ghastly, their little limbs—on removing a portion of the filthy covering—perfectly emaciated, eyes sunk, voice gone, and evidently in the last stage of actual starvation.

WILLIAM BENNETT, quoted in *Narrative of a Recent Journey of Six Weeks in Ireland*

DOCUMENT-BASED QUESTIONS

1. **Determining Main Ideas** *What was the effect of the destruction of Ireland's potato crop on the population of Ireland?*
2. **Clarifying** *How did 18 percent of the population deal with the famine?*
3. **Comparing** *Which country received the most Irish emigrants?*

The Great Famine, 1845–1851

Fate of the Irish during the famine:

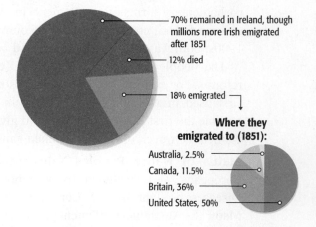

- 70% remained in Ireland, though millions more Irish emigrated after 1851
- 12% died
- 18% emigrated

Where they emigrated to (1851):

- Australia, 2.5%
- Canada, 11.5%
- Britain, 36%
- United States, 50%

Sources: R. F. Foster, *Modern Ireland, 1600–1972;* D. Fitzpatrick, *Irish Emigration, 1804–1921* matters only. The British, fearful of Irish moves toward independence, refused to consider either option.

One reason for Britain's opposition to home rule was concern for Ireland's Protestants. They feared being a minority in a country dominated by Catholics. Most Protestants lived in the northern part of Ireland, known as Ulster. Finally, in 1914, Parliament enacted a home rule bill for southern Ireland. Just one month before the plan was to take effect, World War I broke out in Europe. Irish home rule was put on hold.

Rebellion and Division Frustrated over the delay in gaining independence, a small group of Irish nationalists rebelled in Dublin during Easter week, 1916. British troops put down the Easter Rising and executed its leaders. Their fate, however, aroused wider popular support for the nationalist movement.

After World War I, the Irish nationalists won a victory in the elections for the British Parliament. To protest delays in home rule, the nationalist members decided not to attend Parliament. Instead, they formed an underground Irish government and declared themselves independent. The **Irish Republican Army** (IRA), an unofficial military force seeking independence for Ireland, staged a series of attacks against British officials in Ireland. The attacks sparked war between the nationalists and the British government.

In 1921, Britain divided Ireland and granted home rule to southern Ireland. Ulster, or Northern Ireland, remained a part of Great Britain. The south became a dominion called the Irish Free State. However, many Irish nationalists, led by Eamon De Valera, continued to seek total independence from Britain. In 1949, the Irish Free State declared itself the independent Republic of Ireland. **C**

MAIN IDEA

Evaluating Decisions

C Was Britain's policy in dividing Ireland successful? Why or why not?

Connect *to* Today

Northern Ireland Today

When Northern Ireland decided to stay united with Great Britain, many Catholics there refused to accept the partition, or division. In the late 1960s, Catholic groups began to demonstrate for more civil rights.

Their protests touched off fighting between Catholics and Protestants. Militant groups on both sides engaged in terrorism. This violent period, called the "troubles," continued into the 1990s.

In 1999, with a peace accord, Catholics and Protestants began sharing power in a new home-rule government. Nonetheless, tensions between the two sides remain.

INTEGRATED TECHNOLOGY

INTERNET ACTIVITY Design a Web page about the peace process in Northern Ireland today. Include Gerry Adams and David Trimble. Go to **classzone.com** for your research.

SECTION 2 ASSESSMENT

TERMS & NAMES 1. For each term or name, write a sentence explaining its significance.
• dominion   • Maori   • Aborigine   • penal colony   • home rule   • Irish Republican Army

USING YOUR NOTES

2. In what ways was Ireland different from the other three colonies?

Country	Political Events
Canada	
Australia	
New Zealand	

MAIN IDEAS

3. What were the two major reforms urged by the Durham report?

4. What was unusual about the first European settlers in Australia?

5. What are the main countries to which the Irish emigrated during the famine?

CRITICAL THINKING & WRITING

6. **COMPARING** How was Britain's policy toward Canada beginning in the late 1700s similar to its policy toward Ireland in the 1900s?

7. **DRAWING CONCLUSIONS** What impact did the Great Famine have on the population of Ireland?

8. **CLARIFYING** Why did Britain create Upper Canada and Lower Canada, and who lived in each colony?

9. **WRITING ACTIVITY** EMPIRE BUILDING Britain encouraged emigration to each of the colonies covered in this section. What effects did this policy have on these areas? Write a **paragraph** in which you provide an explanation.

INTEGRATED TECHNOLOGY **INTERNET ACTIVITY**
Use the Internet to find information on Irish emigration to the United States. Create a **bar graph** showing the years when the largest numbers of Irish came to the United States.

INTERNET KEYWORD
Irish immigration

Life in Early Australia

European explorers located Australia long after they had begun colonizing other lands. Dutch explorers were probably the first Europeans to reach Australia around 1605. Australia was not claimed by a European power, however, until the British did so in 1770.

Early Australia had many groups of people with diverse interests, including a native population that had lived on the island for at least 40,000 years. On these pages you will discover the occupations, motivations, and interests of some Australians in the 17th and 18th centuries.

INTEGRATED/TECHNOLOGY

RESEARCH LINKS For more on early Australia, go to **classzone.com**

▼ Gold Miners

In 1851, lured by the potential of striking it rich, thousands of people began prospecting for gold in Australia. Sometimes whole families moved to the gold fields, but life in the gold camps was hard and very few people struck it rich. Searching for gold was hard and dirty work, as this painting illustrates.

▼ Original Australians

Aboriginal society developed in close harmony with nature. There were between 200 and 300 Aboriginal languages, and most people were bilingual or multilingual. By 1900, half of Australia's original inhabitants had died fighting the British or from disease. The engraving below depicts an Aboriginal man with ceremonial face paint and scars. The other image below is an ancient Aboriginal rock painting.

▲ Farmers and Ranchers

Free settlers made the journey to Australia willingly. Many went into farming and ranching. Farms provided much-needed food, and sheep ranching provided wool as a valuable export. Convicts were hired out to farmers and ranchers as cheap labor. Sheep ranching, shown in the picture above, remains an important part of Australia's economy.

▼ Convicts

Beginning in 1788, England sent both male and female prisoners to Australia—sometimes with their children. Convicts built public buildings, roads, and bridges. England stopped sending convicts to Australia in 1868. The prison ship shown here housed prisoners before they went to Australia.

Australia Today
- Australia still mines gold, but it also produces 95 percent of the world's precious opals and 99 percent of black opals.
- Australia has 24 million head of cattle and is the world's largest exporter of beef.
- Australians had 8.6 million cell phones in 2000.

Australia's Population
- In 2001, there was an average of 6.5 people per square mile in Australia. That same year in the United States there were 77.8 people per square mile.
- In Australia's 2001 census, 410,003 people identified themselves as being of indigenous origin.

Australia's Population

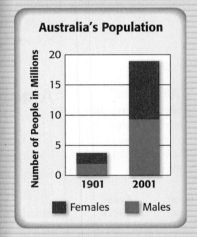

Number of People in Millions

20
15
10
5
0

1901   2001

■ Females   ■ Males

Connect *to* Today

1. Forming and Supporting Opinions Of the groups represented on this page, which do you believe had highest quality of living? Why?

See Skillbuilder Handbook, page R20.

2. Comparing and Contrasting Use the Internet to research the issues that Australian Aborigines and Native Americans in the United States face today and compare them. How are they similar? How are they different?

War and Expansion in the United States

MAIN IDEA	WHY IT MATTERS NOW	TERMS & NAMES
POWER AND AUTHORITY The United States expanded across North America and fought a civil war.	The 20th-century movements to ensure civil rights for African Americans and others are a legacy of this period.	• manifest destiny • Abraham Lincoln • secede • U.S. Civil War • Emancipation Proclamation • segregation

SETTING THE STAGE The United States won its independence from Britain in 1783. At the end of the Revolutionary War, the Mississippi River marked the western boundary of the new republic. As the original United States filled with settlers, land-hungry newcomers pushed beyond the Mississippi. The government helped them by acquiring new territory for settlement. Meanwhile, tensions between northern and southern states over the issues of states' rights and slavery continued to grow and threatened to reach a boiling point.

TAKING NOTES

Following Chronological Order Create a time line to record major events of the United States in the 19th century.

Americans Move West

In 1803, President Thomas Jefferson bought the Louisiana Territory from France. The Louisiana Purchase doubled the size of the new republic and extended its boundary to the Rocky Mountains. In 1819, Spain gave up Florida to the United States. In 1846, a treaty with Great Britain gave the United States part of the Oregon Territory. The nation now stretched from the Atlantic to the Pacific oceans.

Manifest Destiny Many Americans believed in **manifest destiny**, the idea that the United States had the right and duty to rule North America from the Atlantic Ocean to the Pacific Ocean. Government leaders used manifest destiny to justify evicting Native Americans from their tribal lands.

The Indian Removal Act of 1830 made such actions official policy. This law enabled the federal government to force Native Americans living in the East to move to the West. Georgia's Cherokee tribe challenged the law before the Supreme Court. The Court, however, ruled that the suit was not valid. The Cherokees had to move. Most of them traveled 800 miles to Oklahoma, mainly on foot, on a journey later called the Trail of Tears. About a quarter of the Cherokees died on the trip. A survivor recalled how the journey began:

PRIMARY SOURCE

The day was bright and beautiful, but a gloomy thoughtfulness was depicted in the lineaments of every face. . . . At this very moment a low sound of distant thunder fell on my ear . . . and sent forth a murmur, I almost thought a voice of divine indignation for the wrong of my poor and unhappy countrymen, driven by brutal power from all they loved and cherished in the land of their fathers.

WILLIAM SHOREY COODEY, quoted in *The Trail of Tears*

When the Cherokees reached their destination, they ended up on land inferior to that which they had left. As white settlers moved west during the 19th century, the government continued to push Native Americans off their land.

Texas Joins the United States When Mexico had gained its independence from Spain in 1821, its territory included the lands west of the Louisiana Purchase. With Mexico's permission, American settlers moved into the Mexican territory of Texas. However, settlers were unhappy with Mexico's rule.

In 1836, Texans revolted against Mexican rule and won their independence. Then, in 1845, the United States annexed Texas. Since Mexico still claimed Texas, it viewed this annexation as an act of war.

War with Mexico Between May 1846 and February 1848, war raged between the two countries. Finally, Mexico surrendered. As part of the settlement of the Mexican-American War, Mexico ceded territory to the United States. The

U.S. Expansion, 1783–1853
INTER*ACTIVE*

- U.S. in 1783
- Louisiana Purchase, 1803
- Florida Cession, 1819
- By treaty with Great Britain, 1818 and 1842
- Texas Annexation, 1845
- Oregon, 1846
- Mexican Cession, 1848
- Gadsden Purchase, 1853

GEOGRAPHY SKILLBUILDER: Interpreting Maps
1. **Movement** What was the first territory to be added to the United States after 1783?
2. **Region** What present-day states were part of the Mexican Cession?

Mexican Cession included California and a huge area in the Southwest. In 1853, the Gadsden Purchase from Mexico brought the lower continental United States to its present boundaries.

Civil War Tests Democracy

America's westward expansion raised questions about what laws and customs should be followed in the West. Since the nation's early days, the northern and southern parts of the United States had followed different ways of life. Each section wanted to extend its own way of life to the new territories and states in the West.

North and South The North had a diversified economy, with both farms and industry. For both its factories and farms, the North depended on free workers. The South's economy, on the other hand, was based on just a few cash crops, mainly cotton. Southern planters relied on slave labor. **A**

The economic differences between the two regions led to a conflict over slavery. Many Northerners considered slavery morally wrong. They wanted to outlaw slavery in the new western states. Most white Southerners believed slavery was necessary for their economy. They wanted laws to protect slavery in the West so that they could continue to raise cotton on the fertile soil there.

The disagreement over slavery fueled a debate about the rights of the individual states against those of the federal government. Southern politicians argued that the states had freely joined the Union, and so they could freely leave. Most Northerners felt that the Constitution had established the Union once and for all.

Civil War Breaks Out Conflict between the North and South reached a climax in 1860, when **Abraham Lincoln** was elected president. Southerners fiercely

MAIN IDEA

Contrasting
A What were the main economic differences between the Northern and Southern states?

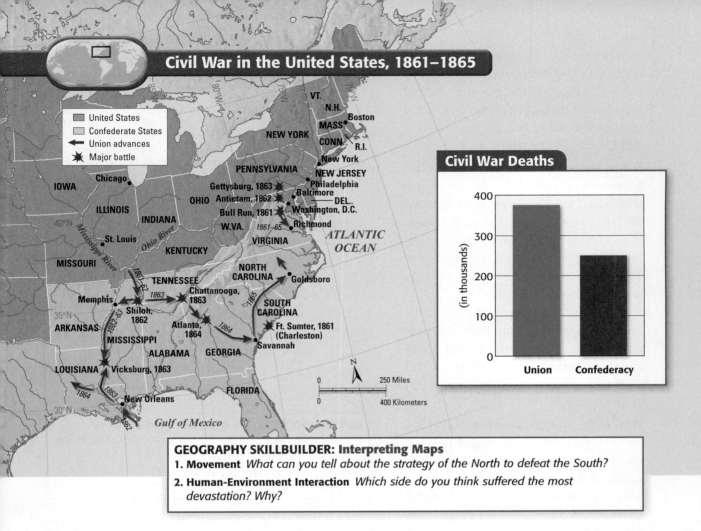

Civil War in the United States, 1861–1865

Legend:
- United States
- Confederate States
- ← Union advances
- ✷ Major battle

Civil War Deaths (in thousands)
- Union: ~380
- Confederacy: ~250

GEOGRAPHY SKILLBUILDER: Interpreting Maps
1. **Movement** *What can you tell about the strategy of the North to defeat the South?*
2. **Human-Environment Interaction** *Which side do you think suffered the most devastation? Why?*

opposed Lincoln, who had promised to stop the spread of slavery. One by one, Southern states began to **secede**, or withdraw, from the Union. These states came together as the Confederate States of America.

On April 12, 1861, Confederate forces fired on Fort Sumter, a federal fort in Charleston, South Carolina. Lincoln ordered the army to bring the rebel states back into the Union. The **U.S. Civil War** had begun. Four years of fighting followed, most of it in the South. Although the South had superior military leadership, the North had a larger population, better transportation, greater resources, and more factories. These advantages proved too much, and in April 1865, the South surrendered.

Abolition of Slavery Lincoln declared that the war was being fought to save the Union and not to end slavery. He eventually decided that ending slavery would help to save the Union. Early in 1863, he issued the **Emancipation Proclamation**, declaring that all slaves in the Confederate states were free. **B**

At first, the proclamation freed no slaves, because the Confederate states did not accept it as law. As Union armies advanced into the South, however, they freed slaves in the areas they conquered. The Emancipation Proclamation also showed European nations that the war was being fought against slavery. As a result, these nations did not send the money and supplies that the South had hoped they would.

In the aftermath of the war, the U.S. Congress passed the Thirteenth Amendment to the Constitution, which abolished slavery in the United States. The Fourteenth and Fifteenth Amendments extended the rights of citizenship to all Americans and guaranteed former slaves the right to vote.

Reconstruction From 1865 to 1877, Union troops occupied the South and enforced the constitutional protections. This period is called Reconstruction. After federal troops left the South, white Southerners passed laws that limited African

MAIN IDEA

Analyzing Issues
B Did the Emancipation Proclamation reflect a change in Lincoln's main goal for the war?

Americans' rights and made it difficult for them to vote. Such laws also encouraged **segregation**, or separation, of blacks and whites in the South. African Americans continued to face discrimination in the North as well.

The Postwar Economy

The need for mass production and distribution of goods during the Civil War speeded industrialization. After the war, the United States experienced industrial expansion unmatched in history. By 1914, it was a leading industrial power.

Immigration Industrialization could not have occurred so rapidly without immigrants. During the 1870s, immigrants arrived at a rate of nearly 2,000 a day. By 1914, more than 20 million people had moved to the United States from Europe and Asia. Many settled in the cities of the Northeast and Midwest. Others settled in the open spaces of the West.

The Railroads As settlers moved west, so did the nation's rail system. In 1862, Congress had authorized money to build a transcontinental railroad. For seven years, immigrants and other workers dug tunnels, built bridges, and laid track. When the railroad was completed in 1869, railroads linked California with the eastern United States. **C**

By 1900, nearly 200,000 miles of track crossed the nation. This system linked farm to city and boosted trade and industry. The railroads bought huge quantities of steel. Also, trains brought materials such as coal and iron ore to factories and moved the finished goods to market. They carried corn, wheat, and cattle from the Great Plains to processing plants in St. Louis, Chicago, and Minneapolis. These developments helped to make the United States a world leader.

MAIN IDEA

Recognizing Effects

C How did railroads affect the growth of the United States?

History Makers

Abraham Lincoln
1809–1865

Lincoln passionately believed in preserving the Union. His upbringing might help explain why. The son of rural, illiterate parents, he educated himself. After working as rail splitter, boatman, storekeeper, and surveyor, he taught himself to be a lawyer. This career path led eventually to the White House.

In Europe, people stayed at the level of society into which they had been born. Yet the United States had been founded on the belief that all men were created equal. Small wonder that Lincoln fought to preserve the democracy he described as the "last best hope of earth."

SECTION 3 ASSESSMENT

TERMS & NAMES 1. For each term or name, write a sentence explaining its significance.
• manifest destiny   • Abraham Lincoln   • secede   • U.S. Civil War   • Emancipation Proclamation   • segregation

USING YOUR NOTES	MAIN IDEAS	CRITICAL THINKING & WRITING

USING YOUR NOTES

2. Which events contributed to U.S. expansion?

```
Event        Event
one          three
|-----|-----|-----|
      Event        Event
      two          four
```

MAIN IDEAS

3. What territory did the Mexican-American War open up to American settlers?

4. What were some of the economic differences between the North and the South before the Civil War?

5. How did the Civil War speed up America's industrialization?

CRITICAL THINKING & WRITING

6. **DISTINGUISHING FACT FROM OPINION** Reread the quotation from William Shorey Coodey on page 324. What facts are conveyed in his statement? What opinions does he express about the Trail of Tears?

7. **COMPARING** What were the relative resources of the North and South in the U.S. Civil War?

8. **MAKING INFERENCES** How might the Mexican Cession (see map, page 325) have consequences today?

9. **WRITING ACTIVITY** POWER AND AUTHORITY Imagine that you are making the westward journey by wagon train. Write a number of **journal entries** describing your experience.

CONNECT TO TODAY MAKING A TABLE

Find information on countries today that are experiencing civil wars or conflicts. Make a **table** that includes the name of each country, the continent it is located on, and the dates of the conflict.

Nineteenth-Century Progress

4

MAIN IDEA	WHY IT MATTERS NOW	TERMS & NAMES
SCIENCE AND TECHNOLOGY Breakthroughs in science and technology transformed daily life and entertainment.	Electric lights, telephones, cars, and many other conveniences of modern life were invented during this period.	• assembly line • Charles Darwin • theory of evolution • radioactivity • psychology • mass culture

SETTING THE STAGE The Industrial Revolution happened because of inventions such as the spinning jenny and the steam engine. By the late 1800s, advances in both industry and technology were occurring faster than ever before. In turn, the demands of growing industries spurred even greater advances in technology. A surge of scientific discovery pushed the frontiers of knowledge forward. At the same time, in industrialized countries, economic growth produced many social changes.

TAKING NOTES

Summarizing Use a web diagram to connect people with their ideas and inventions.

People and Progress

Inventions Make Life Easier

In the early 1800s, coal and steam drove the machines of industry. By the late 1800s, new kinds of energy were coming into use. One was gasoline (made from oil), which powered the internal combustion engine. This engine would make the automobile possible. Another kind of energy was electricity. In the 1870s, the electric generator was developed, which produced a current that could power machines.

Edison the Inventor During his career, Thomas Edison patented more than 1,000 inventions, including the light bulb and the phonograph. Early in his career, Edison started a research laboratory in Menlo Park, New Jersey. Most of his important inventions were developed there, with help from the researchers he employed, such as Lewis H. Latimer, an African-American inventor. Indeed, the idea of a research laboratory may have been Edison's most important invention.

Bell and Marconi Revolutionize Communication Other inventors helped harness electricity to transmit sounds over great distances. Alexander Graham Bell was a teacher of deaf students who invented the telephone in his spare time. He displayed his device at the Philadelphia Centennial Exposition of 1876.

The Italian inventor Guglielmo Marconi used theoretical discoveries about electromagnetic waves to create the first radio in 1895. This device was important because it sent messages (using Morse Code) through the air, without the use of wires. Primitive radios soon became standard equipment for ships at sea.

Ford Sparks the Automobile Industry In the 1880s, German inventors used a gasoline engine to power a vehicle—the automobile. Automobile technology developed quickly, but since early cars were built by hand, they were expensive.

An American mechanic named Henry Ford decided to make cars that were affordable for most people. Ford used standardized, interchangeable parts. He

Edison's Inventions

Thomas Alva Edison was one of the greatest inventors in history. He held thousands of patents for his inventions in over 30 countries. The United States Patent Office alone issued Edison 1,093 patents. Among his inventions was an electric light bulb, the phonograph, and motion pictures, all shown on this page.

Some scientists and historians, however, believe that Edison's greatest achievement was his development of the research laboratory. Edison worked with a team of different specialists to produce his creations. His precise manner is illustrated by his famous quote: "Genius is 1 percent inspiration and 99 percent perspiration."

▲ Thomas Edison in his West Orange, New Jersey, laboratory, 1915

INTEGRATED / TECHNOLOGY

RESEARCH LINKS For more on Thomas Alva Edison, go to **classzone.com**

▼ Phonograph Commonplace today, a device for recording sound did not exist until Thomas Edison invented it. He first demonstrated his phonograph in 1877.

▼ Motion pictures The idea of "moving pictures" was not Edison's, but his "Kinetoscope," shown below, made movies practical.

▲ **Light bulb** Edison and his team are working on an electric light bulb in this painting. Edison's inventions often developed from existing technologies. Many people were working on an electric light bulb, but Edison made it practical.

Connect *to* Today

1. **Clarifying** What did Edison mean when he said, "Genius is 1 percent inspiration and 99 percent perspiration"?

   See Skillbuilder Handbook, page R4.

2. **Forming and Supporting Opinions** Which of Edison's inventions shown on this page do you think has had the most influence?

▲ **Telephone**
Alexander Graham Bell demonstrated the first telephone in 1876. It quickly became an essential of modern life. By 1900, there were 1.4 million telephones in the United States. By 1912, there were 8.7 million.

▲ **Airplane**
Through trial and error, the Wright brothers designed wings that provided lift and balance in flight. Their design is based on principles that are still used in every aircraft.

◄ **Automobile Assembly Line**
Ford's major innovation was to improve efficiency in his factory. By introducing the assembly line, he reduced the time it took to build a car from 12.5 to 1.5 worker-hours.

also built them on an **assembly line**, a line of workers who each put a single piece on unfinished cars as they passed on a moving belt.

Assembly line workers could put together an entire Model T Ford in less than two hours. When Ford introduced this plain, black, reliable car in 1908, it sold for $850. As his production costs fell, Ford lowered the price. Eventually it dropped to less than $300. Other factories adopted Ford's ideas. By 1916, more than 3.5 million cars were traveling around on America's roads. **Ⓐ**

The Wright Brothers Fly Two bicycle mechanics from Dayton, Ohio, named Wilbur and Orville Wright, solved the age-old riddle of flight. On December 17, 1903, they flew a gasoline-powered flying machine at Kitty Hawk, North Carolina. The longest flight lasted only 59 seconds, but it started the aircraft industry.

New Ideas in Medicine

As you learned in Chapter 6, earlier centuries had established the scientific method. Now this method brought new insights into nature as well as practical results.

The Germ Theory of Disease An important breakthrough in the history of medicine was the germ theory of disease. It was developed by French chemist Louis Pasteur in the mid-1800s. While examining the fermentation process of alcohol, Pasteur discovered that it was caused by microscopic organisms he called bacteria. He also learned that heat killed bacteria. This led him to develop the process of pasteurization to kill germs in liquids such as milk. Soon, it became clear to Pasteur and others that bacteria also caused diseases.

Joseph Lister, a British surgeon, read about Pasteur's work. He thought germs might explain why half of surgical patients died of infections. In 1865, he ordered that his surgical wards be kept spotlessly clean. He insisted that wounds be washed in antiseptics, or germ-killing liquids. As a result, 85 percent of Lister's patients survived. Other hospitals adopted Lister's methods.

Public officials, too, began to understand that cleanliness helped prevent the spread of disease. Cities built plumbing and sewer systems and took other steps to improve public health. Meanwhile, medical researchers developed vaccines or cures for such deadly diseases as typhus, typhoid fever, diphtheria, and yellow fever. These advances helped people live longer, healthier lives.

MAIN IDEA

Making Inferences
Ⓐ Why do you think Ford reduced the price of the Model T?

New Ideas in Science

No scientific idea of modern times aroused more controversy than the work of English naturalist **Charles Darwin**. The cause of the controversy was Darwin's answer to the question that faced biologists: How can we explain the tremendous variety of plants and animals on earth? A widely accepted answer in the 1800s was the idea of special creation—every kind of plant and animal had been created by God at the beginning of the world and had remained the same since then.

Darwin's Theory of Evolution Darwin challenged the idea of special creation. Based on his research as a naturalist on the voyage of the *H.M.S. Beagle,* he developed a theory that all forms of life, including human beings, evolved from earlier living forms that had existed millions of years ago.

In 1859, Darwin published his thinking in a book titled *On the Origin of Species by Means of Natural Selection.* According to the idea of natural selection, populations tend to grow faster than the food supply and so must compete for food. The members of a species that survive are those that are fittest, or best adapted to their environment. These surviving members of a species produce offspring that share their advantages. Gradually, over many generations, the species may change. In this way, new species evolve. Darwin's idea of change through natural selection came to be called the **theory of evolution**. **B**

MAIN IDEA

Clarifying

B According to Darwin, how does natural selection affect evolution?

Mendel and Genetics Although Darwin said that living things passed on their variations from one generation to the next, he did not know how they did so. In the 1850s and 1860s, an Austrian monk named Gregor Mendel discovered that there is a pattern to the way that certain traits are inherited. Although his work was not widely known until 1900, Mendel's work began the science of genetics.

Advances in Chemistry and Physics In 1803, the British chemist John Dalton theorized that all matter is made of tiny particles called atoms. Dalton showed that elements contain only one kind of atom, which has a specific weight. Compounds, on the other hand, contain more than one kind of atom.

In 1869, Dmitri Mendeleev (MEHN•duh•LAY•uhf), a Russian chemist, organized a chart on which all the known elements were arranged in order of weight, from lightest to heaviest. He left gaps where he predicted that new elements would be discovered. Later, his predictions proved correct. Mendeleev's chart, the Periodic Table, is still used today.

A husband and wife team working in Paris, Marie and Pierre Curie, discovered two of the missing elements, which they named radium and polonium. The elements were found in a mineral called pitchblende that released a powerful form of energy. In 1898, Marie Curie gave this energy the name **radioactivity**. In 1903, the Curies shared the Nobel Prize for physics for their work on radioactivity. In 1911, Marie Curie won the Nobel Prize for chemistry for the discovery of radium and polonium.

Physicists around 1900 continued to unravel the secrets of the atom. Earlier scientists believed that the atom was the smallest particle that existed. A British physicist named

History Makers

Marie Curie
1867–1934

Marie Curie's original name was Marya Sklodowska. Born in Warsaw, Poland, she emigrated to Paris to study, where she changed her name to Marie.

She achieved a number of firsts in her career. She was the first woman to teach in the Sorbonne, a world-famous college that was part of the University of Paris. She was the first woman to win a Nobel Prize—two, in fact.

In 1911, she won the Nobel prize for chemistry. In 1921, she made a journey to the U.S. In 1934, she died from leukemia caused by the radiation she had been exposed to in her work.

INTEGRATED TECHNOLOGY

RESEARCH LINKS For more on Marie Curie, go to **classzone.com**.

Social Darwinism

Charles Darwin (above) was a naturalist, but a number of 19th-century thinkers tried to apply his ideas to economics and politics. The leader in this movement was Herbert Spencer, an English philosopher.

Free economic competition, Spencer argued, was natural selection in action. The best companies make profits, while inefficient ones go bankrupt. Spencer applied the same rules to individuals. Those who were fittest for survival enjoyed wealth and success, while the poor remained poor because they were unfit. This idea became known as Social Darwinism. It also provided a rationalization for imperialism and colonialism.

Ernest Rutherford suggested that atoms were made up of yet smaller particles. Each atom, he said, had a nucleus surrounded by one or more particles called electrons. Soon other physicists such as Max Planck, Neils Bohr, and Albert Einstein were studying the structure and energy of atoms.

Social Sciences Explore Behavior

The scientific theories of the 1800s prompted scholars to study human society and behavior in a scientific way. Interest in these fields grew enormously during that century, as global expeditions produced a flood of new discoveries about ancient civilizations and world cultures. This led to the development of modern social sciences such as archaeology, anthropology, and sociology.

An important new social science was **psychology**, the study of the human mind and behavior. The Russian physiologist Ivan Pavlov believed that human actions were often unconscious reactions to experiences and could be changed by training.

Another pioneer in psychology, the Austrian doctor Sigmund Freud, also believed that the unconscious mind drives how people think and act. In Freud's view, unconscious forces such as suppressed memories, desires, and impulses shape behavior. He founded a type of therapy called psychoanalysis to deal with psychological conflicts created by these forces.

Freud's theories became very influential. However, his idea that the mind was beyond conscious control also shocked many people. The theories of Freud and Pavlov challenged the fundamental idea of the Enlightenment—that reason was supreme. The new ideas about psychology began to shake the 19th-century faith that humans could perfect themselves and society through reason. **C**

MAIN IDEA

Clarifying
C Why was the work of Pavlov and Freud groundbreaking?

The Rise of Mass Culture

In earlier periods, art, music, and theater were enjoyed by the wealthy. This group had the money, leisure time, and education to appreciate high culture. It was not until about 1900 that people could speak of **mass culture**—the appeal of art, writing, music, and other forms of entertainment to a larger audience.

Changes Produce Mass Culture There were several causes for the rise of mass culture. Their effects changed life in Europe and North America. Notice in the chart on the next page how working class people's lives were changed by mass culture. The demand for leisure activities resulted in a variety of new pursuits for people to enjoy. People went to music performances, movies, and sporting events.

Music Halls, Vaudeville, and Movies A popular leisure activity was a trip to the local music hall. On a typical evening, a music hall might offer a dozen or more different acts. It might feature singers, dancers, comedians, jugglers, magicians, and acrobats. In the United States, musical variety shows were called vaudeville. Vaudeville acts traveled from town to town, appearing at theaters.

During the 1880s, several inventors worked at trying to project moving images. One successful design came from France. Another came from Thomas Edison's laboratory. The earliest motion pictures were black and white and lasted less than a minute.

Rise of Mass Culture		
Cause	**Effect/Cause**	**Effect**
• Public education	• Increase in literacy	• Mass market for books and newspapers
• Improvement in communications	• Publications cheaper and more accessible	• Mass market for books and newspapers
• Invention of phono-graph and records	• More music directly in people's homes	• Greater demand for musical entertainment
• Shorter workday— 10 hours shorter workweek— 5-1/2 days	• More leisure time	• Greater demand for mass entertainment activities

SKILLBUILDER: Interpreting Charts
1. **Analyzing Causes** *What was the immediate cause for the increased demand for mass entertainment activities?*
2. **Recognizing Effects** *What was the ultimate effect of public education and improved communications?*

By the early 1900s, filmmakers were producing the first feature films. Movies quickly became big business. By 1910, five million Americans attended some 10,000 theaters each day. The European movie industry experienced similar growth.

Sports Entertain Millions With time at their disposal, more people began to enjoy sports and outdoor activities. Spectator sports now became entertainment. In the United States, football and baseball soared in popularity. In Europe, the first professional soccer clubs formed and drew big crowds. Favorite English sports such as cricket spread to the British colonies of Australia, India, and South Africa.

As a result of the growing interest in sports, the International Olympic Games began in 1896. They revived the ancient Greek tradition of holding an athletic competition every four years. Fittingly, the first modern Olympics took place in Athens, Greece, the country where the games had originated.

SECTION 4 ASSESSMENT

TERMS & NAMES 1. For each term or name, write a sentence explaining its significance.
• assembly line   • Charles Darwin   • theory of evolution   • radioactivity   • psychology   • mass culture

USING YOUR NOTES
2. Which breakthrough helped people the most? Why?

 People and Progress

MAIN IDEAS
3. What effect did the assembly line have on production costs?
4. How did Joseph Lister improve the survival rate of his patients?
5. What effect did the spread of public education have on culture?

CRITICAL THINKING & WRITING
6. **COMPARING AND CONTRASTING** How is the mass culture that rose at the end of the 19th century similar to mass culture today? How is it different? Explain your response.
7. **RECOGNIZING EFFECTS** How did the germ theory change living conditions in Europe and the United States?
8. **ANALYZING CAUSES** What changes led to the rise of mass culture around 1900?
9. **WRITING ACTIVITY** SCIENCE AND TECHNOLOGY Write a two-paragraph **expository essay** in which you discuss whether advances in science and technology have had a largely positive or negative impact on society.

CONNECT TO TODAY MAKING A POSTER
Find information on the current state of medicines such as antibiotics and problems with their use and overuse. Create a **poster** that shows examples of current antibiotics, their benefits, and their potential negative long-term impact.

TERMS & NAMES

For each term or name below, briefly explain its connection to the reforms, crises, or advances of Western nations from 1815 to 1914.

1. suffrage
2. anti-Semitism
3. dominion
4. home rule
5. manifest destiny
6. Emancipation Proclamation
7. assembly line
8. theory of evolution

MAIN IDEAS

Democratic Reform and Activism Section 1
(pages 313–316)

9. What political reforms expanded democracy for men in Britain?
10. Why did the woman suffrage movement in Great Britain become more militant?

Self-Rule for British Colonies Section 2 (pages 317–323)

11. What cultural conflict caused problems for Canada?
12. How did Australia's early history differ from that of other British colonies?
13. Why did the British pass a home rule bill for southern Ireland only?

War and Expansion in the United States
Section 3 (pages 324–327)

14. In what ways did the United States gain territory in the 1800s?
15. Why was the issue of slavery in the United States so divisive?

Nineteenth-Century Progress Section 4 (pages 328–333)

16. What was Darwin's principle of natural selection?
17. What prompted the growth of the social sciences?
18. What were some of the effects of increased leisure time?

CRITICAL THINKING

1. USING YOUR NOTES
Create a web diagram of the major political, economic, social and cultural, and scientific and technological changes of the 1800s and early 1900s.

2. RECOGNIZING EFFECTS
SCIENCE AND TECHNOLOGY For a worker, what might be the advantages and disadvantages of an assembly line?

3. ANALYZING MOTIVES
POWER AND AUTHORITY What effect did the call for home rule in British colonies have on Ireland's desire for independence?

4. HYPOTHESIZING
Imagine that circumstances had forced the North to surrender to the South in the Civil War, causing two countries to share the region now occupied by the United States. What economic effects might this have had on the North? the South? the region as a whole?

5. DRAWING CONCLUSIONS
How did manifest destiny help shape the U.S. government's policies of land acquisition?

VISUAL SUMMARY

An Age of Democracy and Progress

PROGRESS

- **1850s** Mendel experiments with genetics
- **1859** Darwin's *Origin of Species*
- **1860s** Medical advances of Lister
- **1869** Transcontinental railroad completed in U.S.; Mendeleev's Periodic Table of Elements
- **1876** Bell patents telephone
- **1879** Edison develops light bulb
- **1880s** Internal combustion engine perfected
- **1895** Marconi sends first radio signals
- **1896** First modern Olympic Games
- **1903** First airplane flight by Wright brothers;
- **1908** Ford introduces the Model T

1830 — 1850 — 1870 — 1890 — 1910

DEMOCRACY

- **1832** First Reform Bill in Britain
- **1861** Outbreak of U.S. Civil War
- **1863** Emancipation Proclamation
- **1867** Suffrage extended to working-class men in Britain; Dominion of Canada formed
- **1871** Paris Commune
- **1875** Third Republic in France
- **1884** Suffrage extended to male rural workers in Britain
- **1893** Women gain voting rights in New Zealand
- **1894** Dreyfus affair begins
- **1903** WSPU founded

Use the declaration from the Seneca Falls convention (held in New York) and your knowledge of world history to answer questions 1 and 2.
Additional Test Practice, pp. S1–S33

PRIMARY SOURCE

The history of mankind is a history of repeated injuries and usurpations on the part of man toward woman, having in direct object the establishment of an absolute tyranny over her. To prove this, let facts be submitted to a candid world.

He has never permitted her to exercise her inalienable right to the elective franchise.

He has compelled her to submit to laws, in the formation of which she had no voice.

THE SENECA FALLS CONVENTION, *"Declaration of Sentiments"*

1. The purpose of the Seneca Falls convention was to
   A. call for an end to slavery.
   B. call for the South to secede from the Union.
   C. call for women's rights.
   D. call for the release of Emmeline Pankhurst.

2. The style of this primary source is based on
   A. the U.S. Constitution.
   B. the U.S. Declaration of Independence.
   C. the Reform Bill of 1832.
   D. Émile Zola's *J'accuse!*

Use this cartoon (*A Court for King Cholera*) and your knowledge of world history to answer question 3.

3. Cholera is an infectious disease that has claimed many lives. What details does the artist show about what causes epidemic disease?
   A. open windows and signs for travelers
   B. children playing with a rat and a woman digging in trash
   C. clothing hanging over the street
   D. crowded street scene

INTEGRATED TECHNOLOGY

TEST PRACTICE Go to **classzone.com**
• Diagnostic tests   • Strategies
• Tutorials   • Additional practice

ALTERNATIVE ASSESSMENT

1. Interact *with* History

On page 312, you considered what political ideals might be worth fighting and possibly even dying for. Now that you have read the chapter, reexamine your conclusions both in terms of the content of the chapter and your knowledge of events in the world today. Discuss your opinions with a small group. Consider:

• political ideals
• religious ideals
• family values

2. ✍ WRITING ABOUT HISTORY

EMPIRE BUILDING Write an **editorial** that might have appeared in a newspaper in 19th-century New Zealand. In the editorial, address the issue of British settlers' taking land from the Maori, and the Maori response.

Consider the following:

• the original inhabitants of New Zealand
• means for negotiating land disputes
• balancing the rights of native peoples and new settlers

INTEGRATED TECHNOLOGY

Net Explorations: Mass Entertainment

Go to *NetExplorations* at **classzone.com** to learn more about the rise of mass culture and mass entertainment. Then use the Internet and the material at *NetExplorations* to research and write a newspaper article about spectators at one of the new forms of mass entertainment. Include in your article quotes from fictional visitors and their reactions to actual events and spectacles. You may want to mention one or more of the following:

• the Boston Pilgrims' victory over the Pittsburgh Pirates in baseball's first World Series
• the "Luna" ride at Coney Island
• a late 19th-century European appearance of Barnum & Bailey's circus
• a visit to the Palace of Electricity at the 1904 World's Fair in St. Louis

The Age of Imperialism, 1850–1914

Previewing Main Ideas

EMPIRE BUILDING During the 19th and early 20th centuries, Western powers divided Africa and colonized large areas of Asia.

Geography *Study the map and time line. How many countries colonized Africa? Which country controlled India? the Philippines?*

POWER AND AUTHORITY At the Berlin Conference in 1884–1885, European nations established rules for the division of Africa with little concern about how their actions would affect the African people.

Geography *Which two countries claimed most of Africa?*

ECONOMICS Industrialization increased the need for raw materials and new markets. Western imperialists were driven by this need as they looked for colonies to acquire.

Geography *Compare the size of the Western countries with the areas they colonized. Why were these Western powers interested in lands in Africa and Asia?*

INTEGRATED TECHNOLOGY

eEdition
- Interactive Maps
- Interactive Visuals
- Interactive Primary Sources

INTERNET RESOURCES
Go to **classzone.com** for:
- Research Links   • Maps
- Internet Activities   • Test Practice
- Primary Sources   • Current Events
- Chapter Quiz

AFRICA AND ASIA

1850
European trading with Africa becomes well established. (Asante brass sculpture) ▶

1869
Suez Canal opens.

1884–1885
Berlin Conference sets rules for African colonization.

1850   **1875**

WORLD

1852
Napoleon III proclaims himself emperor of France. ▶

1871
Bismarck completes unification of German Empire.

Colonial Claims, 1900

RUSSIAN EMPIRE

EUROPE

ASIA

CHINA

OTTOMAN EMPIRE

PERSIA

AFGHANISTAN

Arabian Peninsula

INDIA

AFRICA

Tropic of Cancer

PHILIPPINES

PACIFIC OCEAN

0° Equator

INDIAN OCEAN

DUTCH EAST INDIES

N
W   E
S

Tropic of Capricorn

30°S

AUSTRALIA

Territory controlled by:

Belgium	The Netherlands
France	Portugal
German Empire	Spain
Great Britain	United States
Italy	Independent states in Africa and Asia

0   1000   2000 Miles
0   1000   2000 Kilometers
Winkel II Projection

ATLANTIC OCEAN

1898
United States acquires Philippines, annexes Hawaii.

1899
Boer War begins in South Africa. ▶

1914
Most of Africa is under European control.

1900

1925

1898
United States wins Spanish-American War.

1910
◀ Mexican Revolution begins.

1914
World War I begins.

1918
World War I ends.

How would you react to the colonizers?

You are a young South African living in the 1880s. Gold and diamonds have recently been discovered in your country. The European colonizers need laborers to work the mines, such as the one shown below in an 1888 photograph. Along with thousands of other South Africans, you've left your farm and rural village to work for the colonizers. Separated from your family and living in a city for the first time, you don't know what to expect.

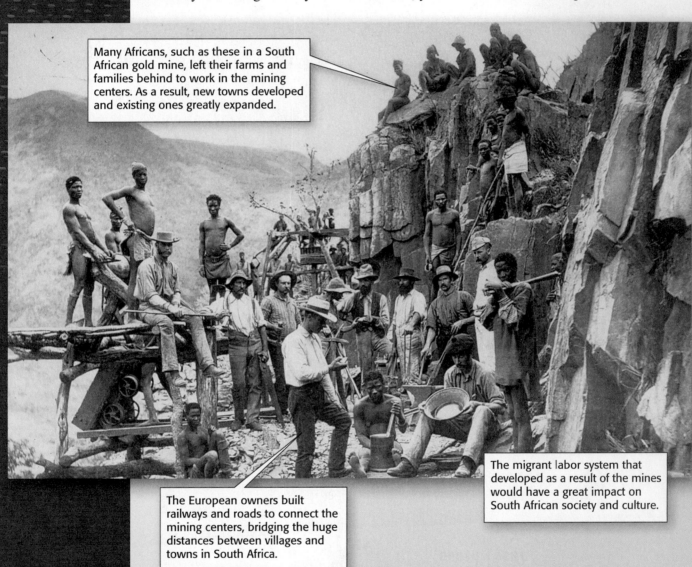

Many Africans, such as these in a South African gold mine, left their farms and families behind to work in the mining centers. As a result, new towns developed and existing ones greatly expanded.

The migrant labor system that developed as a result of the mines would have a great impact on South African society and culture.

The European owners built railways and roads to connect the mining centers, bridging the huge distances between villages and towns in South Africa.

EXAMINING *the* ISSUES

- **What advantages and disadvantages might colonizers bring?**
- **What does the photograph suggest about colonization?**

Discuss these questions with your classmates. In your discussion, remember what you have already learned about conquests and cultural interaction. As you read about imperialism in this chapter, look for its effects on both the colonizers and the colonized.

The Scramble for Africa

MAIN IDEA	WHY IT MATTERS NOW	TERMS & NAMES
EMPIRE BUILDING Ignoring the claims of African ethnic groups, kingdoms, and city-states, Europeans established colonies.	African nations continue to feel the effects of the colonial presence more than 100 years later.	• imperialism • Shaka • racism • Boer • Social Darwinism • Boer War • Berlin Conference

SETTING THE STAGE Industrialization stirred ambitions in many European nations. They wanted more resources to fuel their industrial production. They competed for new markets for their goods. Many nations looked to Africa as a source of raw materials and as a market for industrial products. As a result, colonial powers seized vast areas of Africa during the 19th and early 20th centuries. This seizure of a country or territory by a stronger country is called **imperialism**. As occurred throughout most of Africa, stronger countries dominated the political, economic, and social life of the weaker countries.

Africa Before European Domination

In the mid-1800s, on the eve of the European domination of Africa, African peoples were divided into hundreds of ethnic and linguistic groups. Most continued to follow traditional beliefs, while others converted to Islam or Christianity. These groups spoke more than 1,000 different languages. Politically, they ranged from large empires that united many ethnic groups to independent villages.

Europeans had established contacts with sub-Saharan Africans as early as the 1450s. However, powerful African armies were able to keep the Europeans out of most of Africa for 400 years. In fact, as late as 1880, Europeans controlled only 10 percent of the continent's land, mainly on the coast.

Furthermore, European travel into the interior on a large-scale basis was virtually impossible. Europeans could not navigate African rivers, which had many rapids, cataracts, and changing flows. The introduction of steam-powered riverboats in the early 1800s allowed Europeans to conduct major expeditions into the interior of Africa. Disease also discouraged European exploration.

Finally, Africans controlled their own trade networks and provided the trade items. These networks were specialized. The Chokwe, for example, devoted themselves to collecting ivory and beeswax in the Angolan highlands.

Nations Compete for Overseas Empires Those Europeans who did penetrate the interior of Africa were explorers, missionaries, or humanitarians who opposed the European and American slave trade. Europeans and Americans learned about Africa through travel books and newspapers. These publications competed for readers by hiring reporters to search the globe for stories of adventure, mystery, or excitement.

TAKING NOTES

Outlining Use an outline to list the forces and events surrounding imperialism in Africa.

The Scramble for Africa
I. Africa Before European Domination
   A.
   B.
II. Forces Driving Imperialism

▲ This stamp celebrates the centenary (100th) anniversary of Stanley and Livingstone's meeting in 1871.

The Congo Sparks Interest In the late 1860s, David Livingstone, a missionary from Scotland, traveled with a group of Africans deep into central Africa to promote Christianity. When several years passed with no word from him or his party, many people feared he was dead. An American newspaper hired reporter Henry Stanley to find Livingstone. In 1871, he found Dr. Livingstone on the shores of Lake Tanganyika. Stanley's famous greeting—"Dr. Livingstone, I presume?"— made headlines around the world.

Stanley set out to explore Africa himself and trace the course of the Congo River. His explorations sparked the interest of King Leopold II of Belgium, who commissioned Stanley to help him obtain land in the Congo. Between 1879 and 1882, Stanley signed treaties with local chiefs of the Congo River valley. The treaties gave King Leopold II of Belgium control of these lands.

Leopold claimed that his primary motive in establishing the colony was to abolish the slave trade and promote Christianity. However, he licensed companies that brutally exploited Africans by forcing them to collect sap from rubber plants. At least 10 million Congolese died due to the abuses inflicted during Leopold's rule. As a result of his cruelty, humanitarians around the world demanded changes. In 1908, the Belgian government took control of the colony away from Leopold. The Belgian Congo, as the colony later became known, was 80 times larger than Belgium. The Belgian government's seizure of the Congo alarmed France. Earlier, in 1882, the French had approved a treaty that gave France the north bank of the Congo River. Soon Britain, Germany, Italy, Portugal, and Spain were also claiming parts of Africa.

Forces Driving Imperialism

The motives that drove colonization in Africa were also at work in other lands. Similar economic, political, and social forces accelerated the drive to take over land in all parts of the globe. The Industrial Revolution in particular provided European countries with a reason to add lands to their control. As European nations industrialized, they searched for new markets and raw materials to improve their economies.

Belief in European Superiority The race for colonies also grew out of a strong sense of national pride. Europeans viewed an empire as a measure of national greatness. As the competition for colonies intensified, each country was determined to plant its flag on as much of the world as possible.

Many Europeans believed that they were better than other peoples. The belief that one race is superior to others is called **racism**. The attitude was a reflection of **Social Darwinism**, a social theory of the time. In this theory, Charles Darwin's ideas about evolution and natural selection were applied to human society. Those who were fittest for survival enjoyed wealth and success and were considered superior to others. According to the theory, non-Europeans were considered to be on a lower scale of cultural and physical development because they had not made the scientific and technological progress that Europeans had. Europeans believed that they had the right and the duty to bring the results of their progress to other countries. Cecil Rhodes, a successful businessman and a major supporter of British expansion, clearly stated this position:

Analyzing Primary Sources

A What attitude about the British does Rhodes's statement display?

PRIMARY SOURCE A

I contend that we [Britons] are the first race in the world, and the more of the world we inhabit, the better it is for the human race. . . . It is our duty to seize every opportunity of acquiring more territory and we should keep this one idea steadily before our eyes that more territory simply means more of the Anglo-Saxon race, more of the best, the most human, most honourable race the world possesses.

CECIL RHODES, *Confession of Faith*, 1877

The push for expansion also came from missionaries who worked to convert the peoples of Asia, Africa, and the Pacific Islands to Christianity. Many missionaries believed that European rule was the best way to end evil practices such as the slave trade. They also wanted to "civilize," that is, to "Westernize," the peoples of the foreign land.

▲ Rhodes's De Beers Consolidated Mines is the biggest diamond company in the world today.

Factors Promoting Imperialism in Africa Several factors contributed to the Europeans' conquest of Africa. One overwhelming advantage was the Europeans' technological superiority. The Maxim gun, invented in 1884, was the world's first automatic machine gun. European countries quickly acquired the Maxim, while the resisting Africans were forced to rely on outdated weapons.

European countries also had the means to control their empire. The invention of the steam engine allowed Europeans to easily travel on rivers to establish bases of control deep in the African continent. Railroads, cables, and steamships allowed close communications within a colony and between the colony and its controlling nation.

Even with superior arms and steam engines to transport them, another factor might have kept Europeans confined to the coast. They were highly susceptible to malaria, a disease carried by the dense swarms of mosquitoes in Africa's interior. The perfection of the drug quinine in 1829 eventually protected Europeans from becoming infected with this disease.

Factors within Africa also made the continent easier for Europeans to colonize. Africans' huge variety of languages and cultures discouraged unity among them. Wars fought between ethnic groups over land, water, and trade rights also prevented a unified stand. Europeans soon learned to play rival groups against each other.

The Division of Africa

Vocabulary

scramble: a frantic struggle to obtain something. The word is frequently used to describe the competition for African land.

The scramble for African territory had begun in earnest about 1880. At that time, the French began to expand from the West African coast toward western Sudan. The discoveries of diamonds in 1867 and gold in 1886 in South Africa increased European interest in colonizing the continent. No European power wanted to be left out of the race.

Berlin Conference Divides Africa The competition was so fierce that European countries feared war among themselves. To prevent conflict, 14 European nations met at the **Berlin Conference** in 1884–85 to lay down rules for the division of Africa. They agreed that any European country could claim land in Africa by notifying other nations of its claims and showing it could control the area. The European nations divided the continent with little thought about how African ethnic or linguistic groups were distributed. No African ruler was invited to attend these meetings, yet the conference sealed Africa's fate. By 1914, only Liberia and Ethiopia remained free from European control. **B**

MAIN IDEA

Clarifying

B What was the purpose of the Berlin Conference?

Demand for Raw Materials Shapes Colonies When European countries began colonizing, many believed that Africans would soon be buying European goods in great quantities. They were wrong; few Africans bought European goods. However, European businesses still needed raw materials from Africa. The major source of great wealth in Africa proved to be the continent's rich mineral resources. The Belgian Congo contained untold wealth in copper and tin. Even these riches seemed small compared with the gold and diamonds in South Africa.

Businesses eventually developed cash-crop plantations to grow peanuts, palm oil, cocoa, and rubber. These products displaced the food crops grown by farmers to feed their families.

Three Groups Clash over South Africa

South Africa demonstrated the impact that Europeans had on African peoples. The history of South Africa is a history of Africans, Dutch, and British clashing over land and resources. Although the African lands seemed empty to the Europeans, various ethnic groups had competing claims over huge areas. The local control of these lands, especially in the east, had been in dispute for about 100 years.

▼ Reinstated as ruler over part of his former nation, King Cetshwayo was soon driven away and died in exile in 1884.

Zulus Fight the British From the late 1700s to the late 1800s, a series of local wars shook southern Africa. Around 1816, a Zulu chief, **Shaka**, used highly disciplined warriors and good military organization to create a large centralized state.

Shaka's successors, however, were unable to keep the kingdom together against the superior arms of the British invaders. In 1879, after Zulu king Cetshwayo refused to dismiss his army and accept British rule, the British invaded the Zulu nation. Although the Zulus used spears and shields against British guns, they nearly defeated the great European army. In July 1879, however, the Zulus lost the Battle of Ulundi and their kingdom. The Zulu nation fell to British control in 1887.

Boers and British Settle in the Cape The first Europeans to settle in South Africa had been the Dutch. The Dutch came to the Cape of Good Hope in 1652 to establish a way station for their ships sailing between the Dutch East Indies and the Netherlands. Dutch settlers known as **Boers** (Dutch for "farmers") gradually took Africans' land and established large farms. (The Boers are also known as Afrikaners.) When the British took over the Cape Colony permanently in the early 1800s, they and the Boers clashed over British policy regarding land and slaves.

Imperialism in Africa, 1913

INTERACTIVE

EUROPE

PORTUGAL
SPAIN
ITALY
OTTOMAN
EMPIRE

40°N

Str. of Gibraltar
SPANISH MOROCCO
Algiers
TUNISIA
Mediterranean Sea
Tripoli
Suez Canal
ARABIA

MADEIRA (Port.)
MOROCCO
IFNI (Sp.)
Agadir
Cairo
Nile R.

CANARY ISLANDS (Sp.)
ALGERIA
LIBYA
EGYPT

RIO DE ORO

Tropic of Cancer

FRENCH WEST AFRICA
Niger R.
L. Chad
ANGLO-EGYPTIAN SUDAN
Red Sea
ERITREA
FRENCH SOMALILAND

Dakar
GAMBIA
PORTUGUESE GUINEA
NIGERIA
Fashoda
Addis Ababa
BRITISH SOMALILAND

SIERRA LEONE
LIBERIA
TOGO
GOLD COAST
Lagos
FRENCH EQUATORIAL AFRICA
ETHIOPIA
ITALIAN SOMALILAND

CAMEROONS
FERNANDO PO (Sp.)
RIO MUNI (Sp.)
PRINCIPE
SÃO TOMÉ (Port.)
FRENCH EQUATORIAL AFRICA
Congo R.
BELGIAN CONGO
UGANDA
BRITISH EAST AFRICA

0° Equator

ATLANTIC OCEAN
CABINDA
L. Victoria
Mombasa
GERMAN EAST AFRICA
ZANZIBAR (Br.)

ANGOLA
L. Tanganyika
COMORO IS. (Fr.)

NORTHERN RHODESIA
NYASALAND

Imperialism in Africa, 1878

Ceuta
Melilla
TUNISIA
ALGERIA
TRIPOLI
EGYPT
GERMAN SOUTHWEST AFRICA
SOUTHERN RHODESIA
MOZAMBIQUE
MADAGASCAR

INDIAN OCEAN

Tropic of Cancer
SENEGAL
GAMBIA
PORTUGUESE GUINEA
SIERRA LEONE
LAGOS
IVORY COAST
GOLD COAST
Fernando Po
Principe
São Tomé
GABON
ETHIOPIA

WALVIS BAY (Br.)
BECHUANALAND
Pretoria
Johannesburg
SWAZILAND
Tropic of Capricorn

0° Equator

ATLANTIC OCEAN
ANGOLA

UNION OF SOUTH AFRICA
BASUTOLAND

Cape Town

Tropic of Capricorn
TRANSVAAL
MOZAMBIQUE
ORANGE FREE STATE
CAPE COLONY
NATAL
INDIAN OCEAN

N

0   1,500 Miles
0   3,000 Kilometers

Traditional Ethnic Boundaries of Africa

— Ethnic group
▨ Borders of Africa, 1913

N

0   1,000 Miles
0   2,000 Kilometers

N

0   1,000 Miles
0   2,000 Kilometers

Legend:
- ■ Belgian
- □ Boer
- ■ British
- ■ French
- ■ German
- ■ Italian
- ■ Ottoman
- ■ Portuguese
- ■ Spanish
- ■ Independent states

GEOGRAPHY SKILLBUILDER: Interpreting Maps

1. **Region** How does imperialism in Africa in 1878 compare with that in 1913?
2. **Region** What does the map of ethnic boundaries suggest about the number of ethnic groups in Africa in 1913?

343

Winston Churchill and the Boer War

Winston Churchill, who served as the British prime minister during World War II, first came to public attention during the Boer War.

A war correspondent, Churchill was traveling with British soldiers when their train was ambushed by the Boers. Churchill pulled some of the wounded men to safety. When he returned to help the others, however, he was arrested by a Boer soldier. (The soldier, Louis Botha, would later become the prime minister of the Union of South Africa and Churchill's close friend.)

Churchill managed to escape from the South African prison. When he returned to Britain, Churchill was hailed as a national hero at the age of 26.

In the 1830s, to escape the British, several thousand Boers began to move north. This movement has become known as the Great Trek. The Boers soon found themselves fighting fiercely with Zulu and other African groups whose land they were taking.

The Boer War Diamonds and gold were discovered in southern Africa in the 1860s and 1880s. Suddenly, adventurers from all parts of the world rushed in to make their fortunes. The Boers tried to keep these "outsiders" from gaining political rights. An attempt to start a rebellion against the Boers failed. The Boers blamed the British and, in 1899, took up arms against them.

In many ways, the **Boer War** (also known as the South African War) between the British and the Boers was the first modern "total" war. The Boers launched commando raids and used guerrilla tactics against the British. The British countered by burning Boer farms and imprisoning women and children in disease-ridden concentration camps.

Black South Africans were also involved in the war. Some fought; others served as scouts, guards, drivers, and workers. Many black South Africans were captured by the British and placed in concentration camps, where over 14,000 died.

Britain finally won the war. In 1910, the Boer republics were joined into a self-governing Union of South Africa, which was controlled by the British. **C**

The establishing of colonies signaled a change in the way of life of the Africans. The Europeans made efforts to change the political, social, and economic lives of the peoples they conquered. You will learn about these changes in Section 2.

MAIN IDEA

Contrasting
C How was the struggle for land in the Boer War different from other takeovers in Africa?

SECTION 1 ASSESSMENT

TERMS & NAMES 1. For each term or name, write a sentence explaining its significance.
• imperialism • racism • Social Darwinism • Berlin Conference • Shaka • Boer • Boer War

USING YOUR NOTES

2. How did Europeans use Social Darwinism to justify empire building?

The Scramble
for Africa
   I. Africa Before
   European
   Domination
      A.
      B.
   II. Forces Driving
   Imperialism

MAIN IDEAS

3. Why did the Europeans control such a small portion of Africa in the 1800s?

4. What were some of the internal factors that contributed to imperialism in Africa?

5. Why did the Boers and the British fight over southern Africa?

CRITICAL THINKING & WRITING

6. **MAKING INFERENCES** What can you infer about the Europeans' attitude toward Africans from the Berlin Conference?

7. **FORMING OPINIONS** Why do you think Africans weren't interested in buying European products?

8. **DEVELOPING HISTORICAL PERSPECTIVE** What sort of problems might result from combining or splitting groups of people without regard for ethnic or linguistic traditions?

9. **WRITING ACTIVITY** [EMPIRE BUILDING] Write an **expository essay** explaining which European motive behind imperialism in Africa was the most powerful.

INTEGRATED / TECHNOLOGY **INTERNET ACTIVITY**
Use the Internet to find out about the population and status of Afrikaners, or Boers, in South Africa today. Present your findings in an **oral report**.

INTERNET KEYWORD
Afrikaners in South Africa

2

Imperialism

Case Study: Nigeria

MAIN IDEA	WHY IT MATTERS NOW	TERMS & NAMES
POWER AND AUTHORITY Europeans embarked on a new phase of empire building that affected both Africa and the rest of the world.	Many former colonies have political problems that are the result of colonial rule.	• paternalism • assimilation • Menelik II

SETTING THE STAGE The Berlin Conference of 1884–85 was a European conference. And, although black South Africans participated in it, the Boer War was largely a European war. Europeans argued and fought among themselves over the lands of Africa. In carving up the continent, the European countries paid little or no attention to historical political divisions or to the many ethnic and language groupings in Africa. Uppermost in the minds of the Europeans was the ability to control Africa's land, its people, and its resources.

A New Period of Imperialism

The imperialism of the 18th and 19th centuries was conducted differently from the explorations of the 15th and 16th centuries. In the earlier period, imperial powers often did not penetrate far into the conquered areas in Asia and Africa. Nor did they always have a substantial influence on the lives of the people. During this new period of imperialism, the Europeans demanded more influence over the economic, political, and social lives of the people. They were determined to shape the economies of the lands to benefit European economies. They also wanted the people to adopt European customs.

Forms of Control Each European nation had certain policies and goals for establishing colonies. To establish control of an area, Europeans used different techniques. Over time, four forms of colonial control emerged: colony, protectorate, sphere of influence, and economic imperialism. These terms are defined and discussed in the chart on page 346. In practice, gaining control of an area might involve the use of several of these forms.

Methods of Management European rulers also developed methods of day-to-day management of the colony. Two basic methods emerged. Britain and other nations—such as the United States in its Pacific Island colonies—preferred indirect control. France and most other European nations wielded a more direct control. Later, when colonies gained independence, the management method used had an influence on the type of government chosen in the new nation.

Indirect Control Indirect control relied on existing political rulers. In some areas, the British asked a local ruler to accept British authority to rule. These local officials handled much of the daily management of the colony. In addition,

TAKING NOTES

Summarizing Use a web to record the forms and methods of European imperialism in Africa, the resistance it met with, and its impact.

Imperialism

Imperialism is a policy in which one country seeks to extend its authority by conquering other countries or by establishing economic and political dominance over other countries. The first chart below discusses the four forms of imperialist authority. The second chart shows the two management methods that can be used to control an area.

Forms of Imperialism

Form	Definition	Example
Colony	A country or a territory governed internally by a foreign power	Somaliland in East Africa was a French colony.
Protectorate	A country or a territory with its own internal government but under the control of an outside power	Britain established a protectorate over the Niger River delta.
Sphere of Influence	An area in which an outside power claims exclusive investment or trading privileges	Liberia was under the sphere of influence of the United States.
Economic Imperialism	An independent but less-developed country controlled by private business interests rather than other governments	The Dole Fruit company controlled pineapple trade in Hawaii.

Imperial Management Methods

Indirect Control	Direct Control
• Local government officials used	• Foreign officials brought in to rule
• Limited self-rule	• No self-rule
• Goal: to develop future leaders	• Goal: assimilation
• Government institutions are based on European styles but may have local rules.	• Government institutions are based only on European styles.
Examples:	Examples:
• British colonies such as Nigeria, India, Burma	• French colonies such as Somaliland, Vietnam
• U.S. colonies on Pacific Islands	• German colonies such as German East Africa
	• Portuguese colonies such as Angola

INTEGRATED TECHNOLOGY

RESEARCH LINKS For more on imperialism, go to **classzone.com**

> **DATA FILE**

In 1905, the British Empire
• was the largest and most powerful in the world's history.
• covered about 11 million square miles.
• had about 400 million inhabitants.

Today, the United Kingdom has 13 small dependent territories and is the head of a voluntary association of 54 independent states.

African Colonization and Independence
• In 1884, Western leaders met to divide Africa into colonial holdings.
• By 1914, nearly all of Africa had been distributed among European powers.
• European imperial powers set national borders in Africa without regard for local ethnic or political divisions. This continues to be a problem for African nations today.

Independent African Countries

		50
	4	
	1945	2003

Connect *to* Today

1. **Forming and Supporting Opinions** Which form of managing imperial interests do you think would be most effective and why?

    See Skillbuilder Handbook, page R20.

2. **Recognizing Effects** Use the Internet or library resources to research the problems many African nations are facing today as a result of imperialism. Report your findings to the class.

each colony had a legislative council that included colonial officials as well as local merchants and professionals nominated by the colonial governor.

The assumption was that the councils would train local leaders in the British method of government and that a time would come when the local population would govern itself. This had happened earlier in the British colonies of Australia and Canada. In the 1890s, the United States began to colonize. It chose the indirect method of control for the Philippines.

Direct Control The French and other European powers preferred more direct control of their colonies. They viewed the Africans as unable to handle the complex business of running a country. Based on this attitude, the Europeans developed a policy called **paternalism**. Using that policy, Europeans governed people in a parental way by providing for their needs but not giving them rights. To accomplish this, the Europeans brought in their own bureaucrats and did not train local people in European methods of governing.

The French also supported a policy of **assimilation**. That policy was based on the idea that in time, the local populations would adopt French culture and become like the French. To aid in the transition, all local schools, courts, and businesses were patterned after French institutions. In practice, the French abandoned the ideal of assimilation for all but a few places and settled for a policy of "association," which was similar to indirect control. They recognized African institutions and culture but regarded them as inferior to French culture.

CASE STUDY: Nigeria

A British Colony

A close look at Britain's rule of Nigeria illustrates the forms of imperialism used by European powers to gain control of an area. It also shows management methods used to continue the control of the economic and political life of the area.

Gaining Control Britain gained control of southern Nigeria through both diplomatic and military means. Some local rulers agreed to sign treaties of protection with Britain and accepted British residents. However, others opposed the foreign intervention and rebelled against it. The British used force to put down and defeat these rebellions.

British conquest of northern Nigeria was accomplished by the Royal Niger Company. The company gained control of the palm-oil trade along the Niger River after the Berlin Conference gave Britain a protectorate over the Niger River delta. In 1914, the British claimed the entire area of Nigeria as a colony.

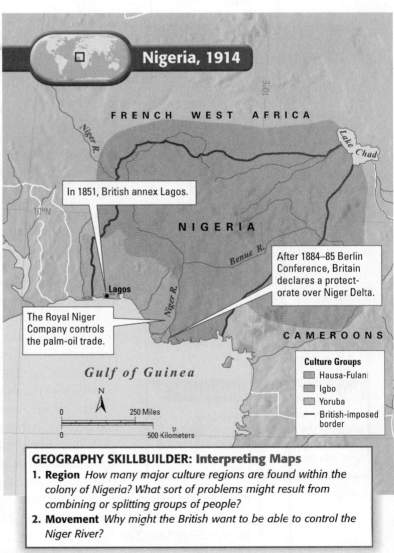

Nigeria, 1914

FRENCH WEST AFRICA

In 1851, British annex Lagos.

NIGERIA

After 1884–85 Berlin Conference, Britain declares a protectorate over Niger Delta.

The Royal Niger Company controls the palm-oil trade.

CAMEROONS

Gulf of Guinea

Culture Groups
- Hausa-Fulani
- Igbo
- Yoruba
- British-imposed border

GEOGRAPHY SKILLBUILDER: Interpreting Maps
1. **Region** How many major culture regions are found within the colony of Nigeria? What sort of problems might result from combining or splitting groups of people?
2. **Movement** Why might the British want to be able to control the Niger River?

Managing the Colony In this new age of imperialism, it was necessary not only to claim a territory but also to govern the people living there. However, managing Nigeria would not prove to be easy. It was one of the most culturally diverse areas in Africa. **A**

About 250 different ethnic groups lived there. The three largest groups were the Hausa-Fulani in the north, the Yoruba in the southwest, and the Igbo in the southeast. These groups were different from one another in many ways, including language, culture, and religion. The Hausa-Fulani people were Muslim and had a strong central government. The Igbo and Yoruba peoples followed traditional religions and relied on local chiefs for control.

Britain did not have enough troops to govern such a complex area. As a result, the British turned to indirect rule of the land. Ruling indirectly through local officials worked well with the Hausa-Fulani. However, this management method did not work as well with the Igbo and Yoruba peoples. Their local chiefs resented having their power limited by the British.

MAIN IDEA

Summarizing
A Which forms of imperialistic control did Britain use in Nigeria?

African Resistance

As in Nigeria, Africans across the continent resisted European attempts to colonize their lands. However, the contest between African states and European powers was never equal because of the Europeans' superior arms. Africans resisted the Europeans with whatever forces they could raise and often surprised the Europeans with their military ability. With the single exception of Ethiopia, though, all these attempts at resistance ultimately failed. Edward Morel, a British journalist who lived for a time in the Congo, made an observation about the Africans' dilemma:

PRIMARY SOURCE
Nor is violent physical opposition to abuse and injustice henceforth possible for the African in any part of Africa. His chances of effective resistance have been steadily dwindling with the increasing perfectibility in the killing power of modern armament.

Thus the African is really helpless against the material gods of the white man, as embodied in the trinity of imperialism, capitalistic exploitation, and militarism.

EDWARD MOREL, *The Black Man's Burden*

Unsuccessful Movements The unsuccessful resistance attempts included active military resistance and resistance through religious movements. Algeria's almost 50-year resistance to French rule was one outstanding example of active resistance. The resistance movement led by Samori Touré in West Africa against the French is another example. After modernizing his army, Touré fought the French for 16 years.

Africans in German East Africa put their faith in a spiritual defense. African villagers resisted the Germans' insistence that they plant cotton, a cash crop for export, rather than attend to their own food crops. In 1905, the belief suddenly arose that a magic water (*maji-maji*) sprinkled on their bodies would turn the Germans' bullets into water. The uprising became known as the Maji Maji rebellion. Over 20 different ethnic groups united to fight for their freedom. The fighters believed that their war had been ordained by God and that their ancestors would return to life and assist their struggle.

History Makers

Samori Touré
about 1830–1900

Samori Touré is a hero of the Mandingo people. His empire is often compared to the great Mali Empire of the 1300s.

Touré was a nationalist who built a powerful Mandingo kingdom by conquering neighboring states. His kingdom became the third largest empire in West Africa.

For 16 years, Touré opposed the French imperialists in West Africa. The well-armed Mandingo were France's greatest foe in West Africa, and the two armies clashed several times. The Mandingo Empire was finally brought down, not in battle, but by a famine.

INTEGRATED TECHNOLOGY

INTERNET ACTIVITY Draw a map showing the extent of the Mandingo Empire. Go to **classzone.com** for your research.

However, when resistance fighters armed with spears and protected by the magic water attacked a German machine-gun post, they were mowed down by the thousands. Officially, Germans recorded 75,000 resisters dead. But more than twice that number perished in the famine that followed. The Germans were shaken by the rebellion and its outcome. As a result, they made some government reforms in an effort to make colonialism more acceptable to the Africans.

Ethiopia: A Successful Resistance Ethiopia was the only African nation that successfully resisted the Europeans. Its victory was due to one man—<u>**Menelik II**</u>. He became emperor of Ethiopia in 1889. He successfully played Italians, French, and British against each other, all of whom were striving to bring Ethiopia into their spheres of influence. In the meantime, he built up a large arsenal of modern weapons purchased from France and Russia. In 1889, shortly after Menelik had signed a treaty with Italy, he discovered differences between the wording of the treaty in the Ethiopian language and in Italian. Menelik believed he was giving up a tiny portion of Ethiopia. However, the Italians claimed all of Ethiopia as a protectorate. Meanwhile, Italian forces were advancing into northern Ethiopia. Menelik declared war. In 1896, in one of the greatest battles in the history of Africa—the Battle of Adowa—Ethiopian forces successfully defeated the Italians and kept their nation independent. After the battle, Menelik continued to stockpile rifles and other modern weapons in case another foreign power challenged Ethiopia's liberty.

▼ After defeating Italy, Menelik II modernized Ethiopia by constructing a railroad and weakening the power of the nobility.

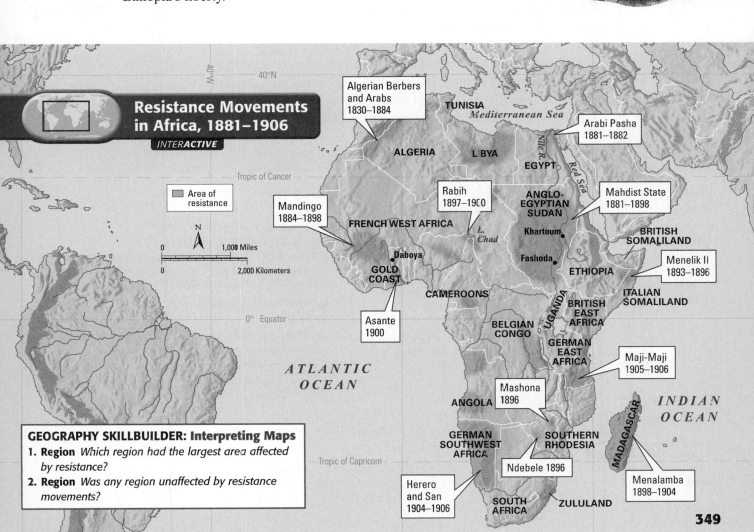

Resistance Movements in Africa, 1881–1906
INTER**ACTIVE**

Algerian Berbers and Arabs 1830–1884

TUNISIA
Mediterranean Sea

Arabi Pasha 1881–1882

ALGERIA   LIBYA
EGYPT

Rabih 1897–1900

ANGLO-EGYPTIAN SUDAN

Mahdist State 1881–1898

Tropic of Cancer

☐ Area of resistance

Mandingo 1884–1898

FRENCH WEST AFRICA

L. Chad

Khartoum

BRITISH SOMALILAND

N

0   1,000 Miles

0   2,000 Kilometers

Daboya
GOLD COAST

Fashoda

ETHIOPIA

Menelik II 1893–1896

CAMEROONS

ITALIAN SOMALILAND

Asante 1900

UGANDA
BELGIAN CONGO

BRITISH EAST AFRICA

0° Equator

ATLANTIC OCEAN

GERMAN EAST AFRICA

Maji-Maji 1905–1906

Mashona 1896

ANGOLA

INDIAN OCEAN

MADAGASCAR

GERMAN SOUTHWEST AFRICA

SOUTHERN RHODESIA

Tropic of Capricorn

Ndebele 1896

Menalamba 1898–1904

Herero and San 1904–1906

SOUTH AFRICA   ZULULAND

GEOGRAPHY SKILLBUILDER: Interpreting Maps
1. **Region** Which region had the largest area affected by resistance?
2. **Region** Was any region unaffected by resistance movements?

349

The Legacy of Colonial Rule

European colonial rule forever altered Africans' lives. In some cases, the Europeans brought benefits, but for the most part, the effects were negative.

Negative Effects On the negative side, Africans lost control of their land and their independence. Many died of new diseases such as smallpox. They also lost thousands of their people in resisting the Europeans. Famines resulted from the change to cash crops in place of subsistence agriculture.

Africans also suffered from a breakdown of their traditional cultures. Traditional authority figures were replaced. Homes and property were transferred with little regard to their importance to the people. Men were forced to leave villages to find ways to support themselves and their families. Contempt for the traditional culture and admiration of European life undermined stable societies and caused identity problems for Africans.

The most harmful political legacy from the colonial period was the division of the African continent. Long-term rival chiefdoms were sometimes united, while at other times, kinship groups were split between colonies. The artificial boundaries combined or unnaturally divided groups, creating problems that plagued African colonies during European occupation. These boundaries continue to create problems for the nations that evolved from the former colonies.

Positive Effects On the positive side, colonialism reduced local warfare. Humanitarian efforts in some colonies improved sanitation and provided hospitals and schools. As a result, lifespans increased and literacy rates improved. Also positive was the economic expansion. African products came to be valued on the international market. To aid the economic growth, railroads, dams, and telephone and telegraph lines were built in African colonies. But for the most part, these benefited only European business interests, not Africans' lives.

The patterns of behavior of imperialist powers were similar, no matter where their colonies were located. Dealing with local traditions and peoples continued to cause problems in other areas of the world dominated by Europeans. Resistance to the European imperialists also continued, as you will see in Section 3. **B**

MAIN IDEA

Drawing Conclusions
B Why might the problems caused by artificial boundaries continue after the Europeans left?

SECTION 2 ASSESSMENT

TERMS & NAMES 1. For each term or name, write a sentence explaining its significance.
- paternalism
- assimilation
- Menelik II

USING YOUR NOTES	**MAIN IDEAS**	**CRITICAL THINKING & WRITING**
2. Do you think the positive effects of imperialism outweighed the negative impact? Why or why not?	3. What idea is the policy of assimilation based on? 4. Why were African resistance movements usually unsuccessful? 5. How did colonial rule cause a breakdown in traditional African culture?	6. **FORMING OPINIONS** Do you think Europeans could have conquered Africa if the Industrial Revolution had never occurred? Explain your answer. 7. **COMPARING** How was the policy of paternalism like Social Darwinism? 8. **ANALYZING CAUSES** Why would the French and Russians sell arms to Ethiopia? 9. **WRITING ACTIVITY** POWER AND AUTHORITY Write a **speech** that you might deliver to colonial rulers, expressing your views on European imperialism in Africa.

CONNECT TO TODAY CREATING A POSTER

After gaining its independence from Portugal in 1975, Angola was plagued by civil war for 27 years. Research to learn what role the legacy of colonialism played in Angola's conflict. Summarize your findings on a **poster** using text, pictures, maps, and charts.

INTERACTIVE

Views of Imperialism

European imperialism extended to the continents beyond Africa. As imperialism spread, the colonizer and the colonized viewed the experience of imperialism in very different ways. Some Europeans were outspoken about the superiority they felt toward the peoples they conquered. Others thought imperialism was very wrong. Even the conquered had mixed feelings about their encounter with the Europeans.

A PRIMARY SOURCE

J. A. Hobson

Hobson's 1902 book, *Imperialism,* made a great impression on his fellow Britons.

——

For Europe to rule Asia by force for purposes of gain, and to justify that rule by the pretence that she is civilizing Asia and raising her to a higher level of spiritual life, will be adjudged by history, perhaps, to be the crowning wrong and folly of Imperialism. What Asia has to give, her priceless stores of wisdom garnered from her experience of ages, we refuse to take; the much or little which we could give we spoil by the brutal manner of our giving. This is what Imperialism has done, and is doing, for Asia.

B PRIMARY SOURCE

Dadabhai Naoroji

Dadabhai Naoroji was the first Indian elected to the British Parliament. In 1871, he delivered a speech about the impact of Great Britain on India.

——

To sum up the whole, the British rule has been—morally, a great blessing; politically peace and order on one hand, blunders on the other, materially, impoverishment. . . . The natives call the British system "Sakar ki Churi," the knife of sugar. That is to say there is no oppression, it is all smooth and sweet, but it is the knife, notwithstanding. I mention this that you should know these feelings. Our great misfortune is that you do not know our wants. When you will know our real wishes, I have not the least doubt that you would do justice. The genius and spirit of the British people is fair play and justice.

C PRIMARY SOURCE

Jules Ferry

The following is from a speech Ferry delivered before the French National Assembly on July 28, 1883.

——

Nations are great in our times only by means of the activities which they develop; it is not simply 'by the peaceful shining forth of institutions . . .' that they are great at this hour. . . . Something else is needed for France: . . . that she must also be a great country exercising all of her rightful influence over the destiny of Europe, that she ought to propagate this influence throughout the world and carry everywhere that she can her language, her customs, her flag, her arms, and her genius.

D PRIMARY SOURCE

This 1882 American political cartoon, titled "The Devilfish in Egyptian Waters," depicts England as an octopus. Notice that Egypt is not yet one of the areas controlled by the British.

THE DEVILFISH IN EGYPTIAN WATERS.

Document-Based QUESTIONS

1. According to Hobson (Source A), what mistake did European imperialists make in Asia?

2. What position on imperialism does Jules Ferry take in Source C?

3. In Source D, what does the representation of England suggest about the cartoonist's view of British imperialism?

4. In what way does the view of imperialism in Source B contrast with that in Source D?

Europeans Claim Muslim Lands

3

MAIN IDEA	WHY IT MATTERS NOW	TERMS & NAMES
EMPIRE BUILDING European nations expanded their empires by seizing territories from Muslim states.	Political events in this vital resource area are still influenced by actions from the imperialistic period.	• geopolitics • Crimean War • Suez Canal

SETTING THE STAGE The European powers who carved up Africa also looked elsewhere for other lands to control. The Muslim lands that rimmed the Mediterranean had largely been claimed as a result of Arab and Ottoman conquests. As you learned in Chapter 2, the Ottoman Empire at its peak stretched from Hungary in the north, around the Black Sea, and across Egypt all the way west to the borders of Morocco. (See map opposite.) But during the empire's last 300 years, it had steadily declined in power. Europeans competed with each other to gain control of this strategically important area.

TAKING NOTES

Determining Main Ideas
Use a diagram to fill in three details that support the main idea.

> Muslim states failed to keep European imperialists out of their lands.
>
> | detail | detail | detail |

Ottoman Empire Loses Power

The declining Ottoman Empire had difficulties trying to fit into the modern world. However, the Ottomans made attempts to change before they finally were unable to hold back the European imperialist powers.

Reforms Fail When Suleyman I, the last great Ottoman sultan, died in 1566, he was followed by a succession of weak sultans. The palace government broke up into a number of quarreling, often corrupt factions. Weakening power brought other problems. Corruption and theft had caused financial losses. Coinage was devalued, causing inflation. Once the Ottoman Empire had embraced modern technologies, but now it fell further and further behind Europe.

When Selim III came into power in 1789, he attempted to modernize the army. However, the older janissary corps resisted his efforts. Selim III was overthrown, and reform movements were temporarily abandoned. Meanwhile, nationalist feelings began to stir among the Ottomans' subject peoples. In 1830, Greece gained its independence, and Serbia gained self-rule. The Ottomans' weakness was becoming apparent to European powers, who were expanding their territories. They began to look for ways to take the lands away from the Ottomans.

Europeans Grab Territory

<u>Geopolitics</u>, an interest in or taking of land for its strategic location or products, played an important role in the fate of the Ottoman Empire. World powers were attracted to its strategic location. The Ottomans controlled access to the Mediterranean and the Atlantic sea trade. Merchants in landlocked countries

that lay beyond the Black Sea had to go through Ottoman lands. Russia, for example, desperately wanted passage for its grain exports across the Black Sea and into the Mediterranean Sea. This desire strongly influenced Russia's relations with the Ottoman Empire. Russia attempted to win Ottoman favor, formed alliances with Ottoman enemies, and finally waged war against the Ottomans. Discovery of oil in Persia around 1900 and in the Arabian Peninsula after World War I focused even more attention on the area.

Russia and the Crimean War Each generation of Russian czars launched a war on the Ottomans to try to gain land on the Black Sea. The purpose was to give Russia a warm-weather port. In 1853, war broke out between the Russians and the Ottomans. The war was called the **Crimean War**, after a peninsula in the Black Sea where most of the war was fought. Britain and France wanted to prevent the Russians from gaining control of additional Ottoman lands. So they entered the war on the side of the Ottoman Empire. The combined forces of the Ottoman Empire, Britain, and France defeated Russia. The Crimean War was the first war in which women, led by Florence Nightingale, established their position as army nurses. It was also the first war to be covered by newspaper correspondents.

MAIN IDEA

Making Inferences

A How did the Crimean War help lead to the decline of the Ottoman Empire?

The Crimean War revealed the Ottoman Empire's military weakness. Despite the help of Britain and France, the Ottoman Empire continued to lose lands. The Russians came to the aid of Slavic people in the Balkans who rebelled against the Ottomans. The Ottomans lost control of Romania, Montenegro, Cyprus, Bosnia, Herzegovina, and an area that became Bulgaria. The Ottomans lost land in Africa too. By the beginning of World War I, the Ottoman Empire was reduced in size and in deep decline. **A**

Ottoman Empire, 1699–1914

- ▨ Ottoman Empire at its greatest extent in 1699
- ▨ Ottoman Empire in 1914
- → Territory becomes part of

GEOGRAPHY SKILLBUILDER: Interpreting Maps
1. **Region** Approximately how much of the Ottoman Empire was lost by 1914?
2. **Region** How many European nations claimed parts of the Ottoman Empire? Which areas became independent?

The Great Game For much of the 19th century, Great Britain and Russia engaged in yet another geopolitical struggle, this time over Muslim lands in Central Asia. Known as the "Great Game," the war was waged over India, one of Britain's most profitable colonies. Russia sought to extend its empire and gain access to India's riches. Britain defended its colony and also attempted to spread its empire beyond India's borders. Afghanistan, which lay between the Russian and British empires, became the center of their struggle. (See the map on page 337.)

In the 1800s, Afghanistan was an independent Muslim kingdom. Its dry, mountainous terrain and determined people continually frustrated the invading imperial powers. After decades of fighting, Great Britain finally withdrew from Afghanistan in 1881. In 1921, Britain formally agreed that its empire would not extend beyond the Khyber Pass, which borders eastern Afghanistan. The newly formed Soviet Union, meanwhile, signed a nonaggression pact with Afghanistan. That agreement was honored until 1979, when the Soviet Union invaded Afghanistan.

Egypt Initiates Reforms

Observing the slow decline of the Ottoman Empire, some Muslim leaders decided that their countries would either have to adjust to the modern world or be consumed by it. Egypt initiated political and social reforms, in part to block European domination of its land.

Military and Economic Reforms Modernization came to Egypt as a result of the interest in the area created by the French occupation. Egypt's strategic location at the head of the Red Sea appeared valuable to France and Britain. After Napoleon failed to win Egypt, a new leader emerged: Muhammad Ali. The Ottomans sent him as part of an expeditionary force to govern Egypt, but he soon broke away from Ottoman control. Beginning in 1831, he fought a series of battles in which he gained control of Syria and Arabia. Through the combined efforts of European powers, Muhammad Ali and his heirs were recognized as the hereditary rulers of Egypt.

Muhammad Ali began a series of reforms in the military and in the economy. Without foreign assistance, he personally directed a shift of Egyptian agriculture to a plantation cash crop—cotton. This brought Egypt into the international marketplace but at a cost to the peasants. They lost the use of lands they traditionally farmed and were forced to grow cash crops in place of food crops. **B**

The Suez Canal Muhammad Ali's efforts to modernize Egypt were continued by his grandson, Isma'il. Isma'il supported the construction of the **Suez Canal**. The canal was a human-made waterway that cut

▼ Muhammad Ali was a common soldier who rose to leadership as a result of his military skill and political shrewdness.

MAIN IDEA

Recognizing Effects

B What two effects did raising cotton have on Egyptian agriculture?

Suez Canal

The Suez Canal was viewed as the "Lifeline of the Empire" because it allowed Britain quicker access to its colonies in Asia and Africa. In a speech to Parliament, Joseph Chamberlain explained that he believed Britain should continue its occupation of Egypt because of "the necessity for using every legitimate opportunity to extend our influence and control in that great African continent which is now being opened up to civilization and to commerce."

This painting represents the opening celebration of the canal on November 17, 1869.

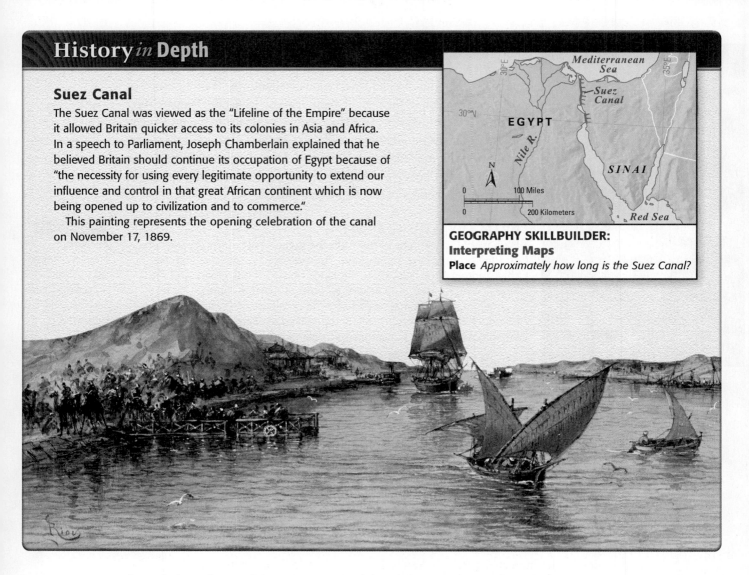

GEOGRAPHY SKILLBUILDER:
Interpreting Maps
Place *Approximately how long is the Suez Canal?*

through the Isthmus of Suez. It connected the Red Sea to the Mediterranean. It was built mainly with French money from private interest groups, using Egyptian labor. The Suez Canal opened in 1869 with a huge international celebration. However, Isma'il's modernization efforts, such as irrigation projects and communication networks, were enormously expensive. Egypt soon found that it could not pay its European bankers even the interest on its $450 million debt. The British insisted on overseeing financial control of the canal, and in 1882 the British occupied Egypt.

Persia Pressured to Change

Elsewhere in southwest Asia, Russia and Britain competed to exploit Persia commercially and to bring that country under their own spheres of influence. (See map on page 353.) Russia was especially interested in gaining access to the Persian Gulf and the Indian Ocean. Twice Persia gave up territories to Russia, after military defeats in 1813 and 1828. Britain was interested in using Afghanistan as a buffer between India and Russia. In 1857, Persia resisted British demands but was forced to give up all claims to Afghanistan. Britain's interest in Persia increased greatly after the discovery of oil there in 1908.

Persia lacked the capital to develop its own resources. To raise money and to gain economic prestige, the Persian ruler began granting concessions to Western businesses. These concessions allowed businesses to buy the right to operate in a certain area or develop a certain product. For example, a British corporation, the Anglo-Persian Oil Company, began to develop Persia's rich oil fields in the early 1900s.

Battle over Tobacco Tension arose between the often corrupt rulers, who wanted to sell concessions to Europeans, and the people. The people were often backed by religious leaders who feared change or disliked Western influence in their nation. In 1890, Persian ruler Nasir al-Din sold a concession to a British company to export Persian tobacco. This action outraged Jamal al-Din al-Afghani, a leader who supported the modernization of Persia. He helped set up a tobacco boycott by the heavy-smoking Persians. In the following quote, he expresses his contempt for the Persian ruler:

PRIMARY SOURCE ⓒ
He has sold to the foes of our Faith the greater part of the Persian lands and the profits derived from them, for example . . . tobacco, with the chief centers of its cultivation, the lands on which it is grown and the warehouses, carriers, and sellers, wherever these are found. . . .
In short, this criminal has offered the provinces of Persia to auction among the Powers, and is selling the realms of Islam and the abodes of Muhammad and his household to foreigners.
JAMAL AL-DIN AL-AFGHANI, in a letter to Hasan Shirazi, April 1891

MAIN IDEA

Analyzing Primary Sources
ⓒ Why did al-Afghani condemn the actions of the Persian ruler?

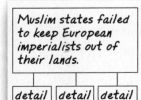

▲ Nasir al-Din was killed by one of al-Afghani's followers a few years after the boycott.

The tobacco boycott worked. Riots broke out, and the ruler was forced to cancel the concession. As unrest continued in Persia, however, the government was unable to control the situation. In 1906, a group of revolutionaries forced the ruler to establish a constitution. In 1907, Russia and Britain took over the country and divided it into spheres of influence. They exercised economic control over Persia.

In the Muslim lands, many European imperialists gained control by using economic imperialism and creating spheres of influence. Although some governments made attempts to modernize their nations, in most cases it was too little too late. In other areas of the globe, imperialists provided the modernization. India, for example, became a colony that experienced enormous change as a result of the occupation of the imperialist British. You will learn about India in Section 4.

SECTION 3 ASSESSMENT

TERMS & NAMES 1. For each term or name, write a sentence explaining its significance.
• geopolitics   • Crimean War   • Suez Canal

USING YOUR NOTES
2. What imperialistic forms of control did the Europeans use to govern these lands?

Muslim states failed to keep European imperialists out of their lands.

detail | detail | detail

MAIN IDEAS
3. What is geopolitics?
4. Why did Great Britain want to control the Suez Canal?
5. Why did the Persian people oppose their ruler's policy of selling business concessions to Europeans?

CRITICAL THINKING & WRITING
6. **COMPARING AND CONTRASTING** How were the reactions of African and Muslim rulers to imperialism similar? How were they different?
7. **MAKING PREDICTIONS** What do you think happened as a result of Muhammad Ali's agriculture reform?
8. **ANALYZING BIAS** What does the quotation in the History in Depth on page 355 suggest about Joseph Chamberlain's view of British imperialism in Africa?
9. **WRITING ACTIVITY** ⌈EMPIRE BUILDING⌋ Write a **cause-and-effect paragraph** about reform efforts undertaken in Muslim lands.

CONNECT TO TODAY CREATING A TIME LINE
Iran (formerly Persia) has undergone many changes since the late 1800s. Create a **time line** of important events in Iran's modern history. Include photographs that illustrate the events.

British Imperialism in India

MAIN IDEA	WHY IT MATTERS NOW	TERMS & NAMES
EMPIRE BUILDING As the Mughal Empire declined, Britain seized Indian territory and soon controlled almost the whole subcontinent.	India, the second most populated nation in the world, adopted some of its modern political institutions from the British.	• sepoy • "jewel in the crown"	• Sepoy Mutiny • Raj

SETTING THE STAGE British economic interest in India began in the 1600s, when the British East India Company set up trading posts at Bombay, Madras, and Calcutta. At first, India's ruling Mughal Dynasty kept European traders under control. By 1707, however, the Mughal Empire was collapsing. Dozens of small states, each headed by a ruler or maharajah, broke away from Mughal control. In 1757, Robert Clive led East India Company troops in a decisive victory over Indian forces allied with the French at the Battle of Plassey. From that time until 1858, the East India Company was the leading power in India.

British Expand Control over India

The area controlled by the East India Company grew over time. Eventually, it governed directly or indirectly an area that included modern Bangladesh, most of southern India, and nearly all the territory along the Ganges River in the north.

East India Company Dominates Officially, the British government regulated the East India Company's efforts both in London and in India. Until the beginning of the 19th century, the company ruled India with little interference from the British government. The company even had its own army, led by British officers and staffed by **sepoys**, or Indian soldiers. The governor of Bombay, Mountstuart Elphinstone, referred to the sepoy army as "a delicate and dangerous machine, which a little mismanagement may easily turn against us."

Britain's "Jewel in the Crown" At first, the British treasured India more for its potential than its actual profit. The Industrial Revolution had turned Britain into the world's workshop, and India was a major supplier of raw materials for that workshop. Its 300 million people were also a large potential market for British-made goods. It is not surprising, then, that the British considered India the brightest **"jewel in the crown,"** the most valuable of all of Britain's colonies.

The British set up restrictions that prevented the Indian economy from operating on its own. British policies called for India to produce raw materials for British manufacturing and to buy British goods. In addition, Indian competition with British goods was prohibited. For example, India's own handloom textile industry was almost put out of business by imported British textiles. Cheap cloth from England flooded the Indian market and undercut local producers.

▼ A sepoy in uniform

TAKING NOTES

Recognizing Effects Use a diagram to identify the effects of the three causes listed.

Cause	Effect
1. Decline of the Mughal Empire	
2. Colonial policies	
3. Sepoy Mutiny	

British Transport Trade Goods India became increasingly valuable to the British after they established a railroad network there. Railroads transported raw products from the interior to the ports and manufactured goods back again. Most of the raw materials were agricultural products produced on plantations. Plantation crops included tea, indigo, coffee, cotton, and jute. Another crop was opium. The British shipped opium to China and exchanged it for tea, which they then sold in England.

Vocabulary
jute: a fiber used for sacks and cord

Trade in these crops was closely tied to international events. For example, the Crimean War in the 1850s cut off the supply of Russian jute to Scottish jute mills. This boosted the export of raw jute from Bengal, a province in India. Likewise, cotton production in India increased when the Civil War in the United States cut off supplies of cotton for British textile mills. **A**

MAIN IDEA

Summarizing
A On which continents were Indian goods being traded?

Impact of Colonialism India both benefited from and was harmed by British colonialism. On the negative side, the British held much of the political and economic power. The British restricted Indian-owned industries such as cotton textiles. The emphasis on cash crops resulted in a loss of self-sufficiency for many villagers. The conversion to cash crops reduced food production, causing famines in the late 1800s. The British officially adopted a hands-off policy regarding Indian religious and social customs. Even so, the increased presence of missionaries and the racist attitude of most British officials threatened traditional Indian life.

On the positive side, the laying of the world's third largest railroad network was a major British achievement. When completed, the railroads enabled India to develop a modern economy and brought unity to the connected regions. Along with the railroads, a modern road network, telephone and telegraph lines, dams, bridges, and irrigation canals enabled India to modernize. Sanitation and public health improved. Schools and colleges were founded, and literacy increased. Also, British troops cleared central India of bandits and put an end to local warfare among competing local rulers.

Western-Held Territories in Asia, 1910

Legend:
- France
- Germany
- Great Britain
- The Netherlands
- United States

GEOGRAPHY SKILLBUILDER: Interpreting Maps
1. **Region** Which nation in 1910 held the most land in colonies?
2. **Location** How is the location of India a great advantage for trade?

Social Class in India

In the photograph at right, a British officer is waited on by Indian servants. This reflects the class system in India.

British Army

Social class determined the way of life for the British Army in India. Upper-class men served as officers. Lower-class British served at lesser rank and did not advance past the rank of sergeant. Only men with the rank of sergeant and above were allowed to bring their wives to India.

Each English officer's wife attempted to re-create England in the home setting. Like a general, she directed an army of 20 to 30 servants.

Indian Servants

Caste determined Indian occupations. Castes were divided into four broad categories called varna. Indian civil servants were of the third varna. House and personal servants were of the fourth varna.

Even within the varna, jobs were strictly regulated, which is why such large servant staffs were required. For example, in the picture here, both servants were of the same varna. Although the two servants were from the same varna, they had different jobs..

The Sepoy Mutiny

By 1850, the British controlled most of the Indian subcontinent. However, there were many pockets of discontent. Many Indians believed that in addition to controlling their land, the British were trying to convert them to Christianity. The Indian people also resented the constant racism that the British expressed toward them.

Indians Rebel As economic problems increased for Indians, so did their feelings of resentment and nationalism. In 1857, gossip spread among the sepoys, the Indian soldiers, that the cartridges of their new Enfield rifles were greased with beef and pork fat. To use the cartridges, soldiers had to bite off the ends. Both Hindus, who consider the cow sacred, and Muslims, who do not eat pork, were outraged by the news.

A garrison commander was shocked when 85 of the 90 sepoys refused to accept the cartridges. The British handled the crisis badly. The soldiers who had disobeyed were jailed. The next day, on May 10, 1857, the sepoys rebelled. They marched to Delhi, where they were joined by Indian soldiers stationed there. They captured the city of Delhi. From Delhi, the rebellion spread to northern and central India.

Some historians have called this outbreak the <u>**Sepoy Mutiny**</u>. The uprising spread over much of northern India. Fierce fighting took place. Both British and sepoys tried to slaughter each other's armies. The East India Company took more than a year to regain control of the country. The British government sent troops to help them. **B**

The Indians could not unite against the British due to weak leadership and serious splits between Hindus and Muslims. Hindus did not want the Muslim Mughal Empire restored. Indeed, many Hindus preferred British rule to Muslim rule. Most of the princes and maharajahs who had made alliances with the East India

MAIN IDEA

Recognizing Effects

B Look back at Elphinstone's comment on page 357. Did the Sepoy Mutiny prove him correct?

Company did not take part in the rebellion. The Sikhs, a religious group that had been hostile to the Mughals, also remained loyal to the British. Indeed, from then on, the bearded and turbaned Sikhs became the mainstay of Britain's army in India.

Turning Point The mutiny marked a turning point in Indian history. As a result of the mutiny, in 1858 the British government took direct command of India. The term **Raj** referred to British rule after India came under the British crown during the reign of Queen Victoria. A cabinet minister in London directed policy, and a British governor-general in India carried out the government's orders. After 1877, this official held the title of viceroy.

To reward the many princes who had remained loyal to Britain, the British promised to respect all treaties the East India Company had made with them. They also promised that the Indian states that were still free would remain independent. Unofficially, however, Britain won greater and greater control of those states.

The Sepoy Mutiny fueled the racist attitudes of the British. The British attitude is illustrated in the following quote by Lord Kitchener, British commander in chief of the army in India:

PRIMARY SOURCE

It is this consciousness of the inherent superiority of the European which has won for us India. However well educated and clever a native may be, and however brave he may prove himself, I believe that no rank we can bestow on him would cause him to be considered an equal of the British officer.

LORD KITCHENER, quoted in K. M. Panikkar, *Asia and Western Dominance*

MAIN IDEA

Recognizing Effects

C In what ways did the Sepoy Mutiny change the political climate of India?

The mutiny increased distrust between the British and the Indians. A political pamphlet suggested that both Hindus and Muslims "are being ruined under the tyranny and oppression of the . . . treacherous English." **C**

▼ This engraving shows sepoys attacking the British infantry at the Battle of Cawnpore in 1857.

Nationalism Surfaces in India

In the early 1800s, some Indians began demanding more modernization and a greater role in governing themselves. Ram Mohun Roy, a modern-thinking, well-educated Indian, began a campaign to move India away from traditional practices and ideas. Ram Mohun Roy saw arranged child marriages and the rigid caste separation as parts of Indian life that needed to be changed. He believed that if the practices were not changed, India would continue to be controlled by outsiders. Roy's writings inspired other Indian reformers to call for adoption of Western ways. Roy also founded a social reform movement that worked for change in India.

Besides modernization and Westernization, nationalist feelings started to surface in India. Indians hated a system that made them second-class citizens in their own country. They were barred from top posts in the Indian Civil Service. Those who managed to get middle-level jobs were paid less than Europeans. A British engineer on the East India Railway, for example, made nearly 20 times as much money as an Indian engineer.

Nationalist Groups Form This growing nationalism led to the founding of two nationalist groups, the Indian National Congress in 1885 and the Muslim League in 1906. At first, such groups concentrated on specific concerns for Indians. By the early 1900s, however, they were calling for self-government.

The nationalists were further inflamed in 1905 by the partition of Bengal. The province was too large for administrative purposes, so the British divided it into a Hindu section and a Muslim section. Keeping the two religious groups apart made it difficult for them to unite in calling for independence. In 1911, yielding to pressure, the British took back the order and divided the province in a different way. **D**

Conflict over the control of India continued to develop between the Indians and the British in the following years. Elsewhere in Southeast Asia, the same struggles for control of land took place between local groups and the major European powers that dominated them. You will learn about them in Section 5.

MAIN IDEA

Analyzing Motives
D Why would the British think that dividing the Hindus and Muslims into separate sections would be good?

SECTION 4 ASSESSMENT

TERMS & NAMES 1. For each term or name, write a sentence explaining its significance.
• sepoy   • "jewel in the crown"   • Sepoy Mutiny   • Raj

USING YOUR NOTES	MAIN IDEAS	CRITICAL THINKING & WRITING
2. Which of the effects you listed later became causes?	3. Why did Britain consider India its "jewel in the crown"?	6. **MAKING INFERENCES** How did economic imperialism lead to India's becoming a British colony?
	4. Why didn't Indians unite against the British in the Sepoy Mutiny?	7. **EVALUATING DECISIONS** What might the decision to grease the sepoys' cartridges with beef and pork fat reveal about the British attitude toward Indians?
	5. What form did British rule take under the Raj?	8. **SYNTHESIZING** How did imperialism contribute to unity and to the growth of nationalism in India?
		9. **WRITING ACTIVITY** EMPIRE BUILDING Write an **editorial** to an underground Indian newspaper, detailing grievances against the British and calling for self-government.

Cause	Effect
1. Decline of the Mughal Empire	
2. Colonial policies	
3. Sepoy Mutiny	

CONNECT TO TODAY CREATING A POLITICAL CARTOON

In 1947, India was divided into two countries: mostly Hindu India and mostly Muslim Pakistan. However, the two countries maintain a tense relationship today. Research to learn about the cause of this tension and illustrate it in a **political cartoon.**

Imperialism in Southeast Asia

MAIN IDEA	WHY IT MATTERS NOW	TERMS & NAMES
ECONOMICS Demand for Asian products drove Western imperialists to seek possession of Southeast Asian lands.	Southeast Asian independence struggles in the 20th century have their roots in this period of imperialism.	• Pacific Rim • King Mongkut • Emilio Aguinaldo • annexation • Queen Liliuokalani

SETTING THE STAGE Just as the European powers rushed to divide Africa, they also competed to carve up the lands of Southeast Asia. These lands form part of the **Pacific Rim**, the countries that border the Pacific Ocean. Western nations desired the Pacific Rim lands for their strategic location along the sea route to China. Westerners also recognized the value of the Pacific colonies as sources of tropical agriculture, minerals, and oil. As the European powers began to appreciate the value of the area, they challenged each other for their own parts of the prize.

TAKING NOTES

Clarifying Use a spider map to identify a Western power and the areas it controlled.

Western powers in Southeast Asia

European Powers Invade the Pacific Rim

Early in the 18th century, the Dutch East India Company established control over most of the 3,000-mile-long chain of Indonesian islands. The British established a major trading port at Singapore. The French took over Indochina on the Southeast Asian mainland. The Germans claimed the Marshall Islands and parts of New Guinea and the Solomon islands.

The lands of Southeast Asia were perfect for plantation agriculture. The major focus was on sugar cane, coffee, cocoa, rubber, coconuts, bananas, and pineapple. As these products became more important in the world trade markets, European powers raced each other to claim lands.

Dutch Expand Control The Dutch East India Company, chartered in 1602, actively sought lands in Southeast Asia. It seized Malacca from the Portuguese and fought the British and Javanese for control of Java. The discovery of oil and tin on the islands and the desire for more rubber plantations prompted the Dutch to gradually expand their control over Sumatra, part of Borneo, Celebes, the Moluccas, and Bali. Finally the Dutch ruled the whole island chain of Indonesia, then called the Dutch East Indies. (See map opposite.)

Management of plantations and trade brought a large Dutch population to the islands. In contrast to the British, who lived temporarily in India but retired in Britain, the Dutch thought of Indonesia as their home. They moved to Indonesia and created a rigid social class system there. The Dutch were on top, wealthy and educated Indonesians came next, and plantation workers were at the bottom. The Dutch also forced farmers to plant one-fifth of their land in specified export crops.

British Take the Malayan Peninsula To compete with the Dutch, the British sought a trading base that would serve as a stop for their ships that traveled the India-China sea routes. They found a large, sheltered harbor on Singapore, an island just off the tip of the Malay Peninsula. The opening of the Suez Canal and the increased demand for tin and rubber combined to make Singapore one of the world's busiest ports.

Britain also gained colonies in Malaysia and in Burma (modern Myanmar). Malaysia had large deposits of tin and became the world's leading rubber exporter. Needing workers to mine the tin and tap the rubber trees, Britain encouraged Chinese to immigrate to Malaysia. Chinese flocked to the area. As a result of such immigration, the Malays soon became a minority in their own country. Conflict between the resident Chinese and the native Malays remains unresolved today. **A**

French Control Indochina The French had been active in Southeast Asia since the 17th century. They even helped the Nguyen (nuh•WIN) dynasty rise to power in Vietnam. In the 1840s, during the rule of an anti-Christian Vietnamese emperor, seven French missionaries were killed. Church leaders and capitalists who wanted a larger share of the overseas market demanded military intervention. Emperor Napoleon III ordered the French army to invade southern Vietnam. Later, the French added Laos, Cambodia, and northern Vietnam to the territory. The combined states would eventually be called French Indochina.

Using direct colonial management, the French themselves filled all important positions in the government bureaucracy. They did not encourage local industry. Four times as much land was devoted to rice production. However, the peasants' consumption of rice decreased because much of the rice was exported. Anger over this reduction set the stage for Vietnamese resistance against the French.

Colonial Impact In Southeast Asia, colonization brought mixed results. Economies grew based on cash crops or goods that could be sold on the world market. Roads, harbors, and rail systems improved communication and transportation but mostly benefited European business. However, education, health, and sanitation did improve.

Unlike other colonial areas, millions of people from other areas of Asia and the world migrated to work on plantations and in the mines in Southeast Asia. The region became a melting pot of Hindus, Muslims, Christians, and Buddhists. The resulting cultural changes often led to racial and religious clashes that are still seen today.

Siam Remains Independent

While its neighbors on all sides fell under the control of imperialists, Siam (present-day Thailand) maintained its independence throughout the colonial period. Siam lay between British-controlled Burma and French Indochina. (See map above.) France and Britain each aimed to prevent the other from gaining control of Siam. Knowing this, Siamese kings skillfully promoted Siam as a neutral zone between the two powers.

MAIN IDEA

Analyzing Motives
A Why do you think so many Chinese moved to Malaysia?

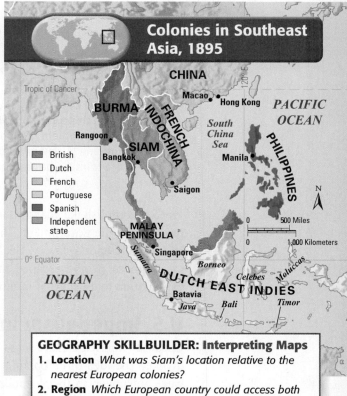

Colonies in Southeast Asia, 1895

British
Dutch
French
Portuguese
Spanish
Independent state

CHINA
Tropic of Cancer
Macao
Hong Kong
PACIFIC OCEAN
BURMA
FRENCH INDOCHINA
Rangoon
South China Sea
SIAM
Bangkok
Manila
PHILIPPINES
Saigon
MALAY PENINSULA
0° Equator
Singapore
INDIAN OCEAN
Sumatra
Borneo
Celebes
Moluccas
DUTCH EAST INDIES
Batavia
Java
Bali
Timor
0   500 Miles
0   1,000 Kilometers
N

GEOGRAPHY SKILLBUILDER: Interpreting Maps
1. **Location** What was Siam's location relative to the nearest European colonies?
2. **Region** Which European country could access both the Indian and the Pacific oceans from its colony?

Siam modernized itself under the guidance of **King Mongkut** and his son Chulalongkorn. In a royal proclamation, King Chulalongkorn showed his understanding of the importance of progress:

PRIMARY SOURCE
As the times and the course of things in our country have changed, it is essential to promote the advancement of all our academic and technical knowledge and to prevent it from succumbing [giving in] to competition from the outside. In order to achieve this, it is imperative to make haste in education so that knowledge and ability will increase.

KING CHULALONGKORN, "Royal Proclamation in Education"

To accomplish the changes, Siam started schools, reformed the legal system, and reorganized the government. The government built its own railroads and telegraph systems and ended slavery. Because the changes came from their own government, the Siamese people escaped the social turmoil, racist treatment, and economic exploitation that occurred in other countries controlled by foreigners.

U.S. Imperialism in the Pacific Islands

Because Americans had fought for their independence from Britain, most of them disliked the idea of colonizing other nations. However, two groups of Americans were outspoken in their support of imperialism. One group of ambitious empire builders felt the United States should fulfill its destiny as a world power, colonizing like the Europeans. The other group, composed of business interests, welcomed the opening of new markets and trade possibilities.

The Philippines Change Hands The United States acquired the Philippine Islands, Puerto Rico, and Guam as a result of the Spanish-American War in 1898. Gaining the Philippines touched off a debate in the United States over imperialism. President McKinley's views swayed many to his side. He told a group of Methodist ministers his intention to "educate Filipinos, and uplift and Christianize them."

Vocabulary
Filipino: an inhabitant of the Philippine Islands

Filipino nationalists were not happy to trade one colonizer—the Spanish—for another, the Americans. **Emilio Aguinaldo** (eh•MEE•lyoh AH•gee•NAHL•doh), leader of the Filipino nationalists, claimed that the United States had promised immediate independence after the Spanish-American War ended. The nationalists declared independence and established the Philippine Republic.

▼ This photograph shows American soldiers fighting the Filipino nationalists in the early years of the war.

The United States plunged into a fierce struggle with the Filipino nationalists in 1899 and defeated them in 1902. The United States promised the Philippine people that it would prepare them for self-rule. To achieve this goal, the United States built roads, railroads, and hospitals, and set up school systems. However, as with other Southeast Asian areas, businessmen encouraged growing cash crops such as sugar at the expense of basic food crops. This led to food shortages for the Filipinos.

Hawaii Becomes a Republic U.S. interest in Hawaii began around the 1790s when Hawaii was a port on the way to China and East India. Beginning about the 1820s, sugar trade began to change the Hawaiian economy. Americans established sugar-cane plantations and became highly successful. By the mid-19th century, American sugar plantations accounted for 75 percent of Hawaii's wealth. At the same time, American sugar planters also gained great political power in Hawaii.

Then in 1890, the McKinley Tariff Act passed by the U.S. government set off a crisis in the islands. The act eliminated the tariffs on all sugar entering the United States. Now, sugar from Hawaii was no longer cheaper than sugar produced elsewhere. That change cut into the sugar producers' profits. Some U.S. business leaders pushed for **annexation** of Hawaii, or the adding of the territory to the United States. Making Hawaii a part of the United States meant that Hawaiian sugar could be sold for greater profits because American producers got an extra two cents a pound from the U.S. government.

About the same time, the new Hawaiian ruler, **Queen Liliuokalani** (luh•LEE•uh•oh•kuh•LAH•nee), took the throne. In 1893, she called for a new constitution that would increase her power. It would also restore the political power of Hawaiians at the expense of wealthy planters. To prevent this from happening, a group of American businessmen hatched a plot to overthrow the Hawaiian monarchy. In 1893, Queen Liliuokalani was removed from power.

In 1894, Sanford B. Dole, a wealthy plantation owner and politician, was named president of the new Republic of Hawaii. The president of the new republic asked the United States to annex it. At first, President Cleveland refused. In 1898, however, the Republic of Hawaii was annexed by the United States.

The period of imperialism was a time of great power and domination of others by mostly European powers. As the 19th century closed, the lands of the world were all claimed. The European powers now faced each other with competing claims. Their battles would become the focus of the 20th century.

History Makers

**Queen Liliuokalani
1838–1917**

Liliuokalani was Hawaii's only queen and the last monarch of Hawaii. She bitterly regretted her brother's loss of power to American planters and worked to regain power for the Hawaiian monarchy. As queen, she refused to renew a treaty signed by her brother that would have given commercial privileges to foreign businessmen. It was a decision that would cost her the crown.

INTEGRATED/TECHNOLOGY

RESEARCH LINKS For more on Queen Liliuokalani, go to **classzone.com**

SECTION 5 ASSESSMENT

TERMS & NAMES 1. For each term or name, write a sentence explaining its significance.
• Pacific Rim   • King Mongkut   • Emilio Aguinaldo   • annexation   • Queen Liliuokalani

USING YOUR NOTES

2. Which Western power do you think had the most negative impact on its colonies?

Western powers in Southeast Asia

MAIN IDEAS

3. How were the Dutch East India Trading Company and the British East India Company similar?

4. What changes took place in Southeast Asia as a result of colonial control?

5. Why did some groups believe that the United States should colonize like the Europeans?

CRITICAL THINKING & WRITING

6. **DRAWING CONCLUSIONS** How did the reforms of the Siamese kings help Siam remain independent?

7. **ANALYZING BIAS** What does President McKinley's desire to "uplift and Christianize" the Filipinos suggest about his perception of the people?

8. **ANALYZING MOTIVES** Why do you think Sanford Dole wanted the United States to annex Hawaii?

9. **WRITING ACTIVITY** ECONOMICS Compose a **letter to the editor** expressing a Hawaiian's view on the U.S. businessmen who pushed for the annexation of Hawaii for economic gain.

CONNECT TO TODAY DRAWING A BAR GRAPH

Research to find out about the economic situation of Southeast Asian countries today. Rank the economies and present your findings in a **bar graph.**

TERMS & NAMES

For each term or name below, briefly explain its connection to the imperialism of 1850–1914.

1. imperialism
2. racism
3. Berlin Conference
4. Menelik II
5. geopolitics
6. Suez Canal
7. Raj
8. Queen Liliuokalani

MAIN IDEAS

The Scramble for Africa Section 1 (pages 339–344)

9. What motivated the nations of Europe to engage in imperialist activities?
10. What effect did the Boer War have on Africans?

Case Study: Imperialism Section 2 (pages 345–351)

11. What are the forms of imperial rule?
12. How did Ethiopia successfully resist European rule?

Europeans Claim Muslim Lands Section 3 (pages 352–356)

13. Why were the European nations interested in controlling the Muslim lands?
14. What methods did the Muslim leaders use to try to prevent European imperialism?

British Imperialism in India Section 4 (pages 357–361)

15. How was the economy of India transformed by the British?
16. What caused the Sepoy Mutiny?

Imperialism in Southeast Asia Section 5 (pages 362–365)

17. How did Siam manage to remain independent while other countries in the area were being colonized?
18. Describe American attitudes toward colonizing other lands.

CRITICAL THINKING

1. USING YOUR NOTES

In a chart, tell how the local people resisted the demands of the Europeans.

Africa	Muslim lands	India	Southeast Asia

2. RECOGNIZING EFFECTS

ECONOMICS What effects did imperialism have on the economic life of the lands and people colonized by the European imperialists?

3. DRAWING CONCLUSIONS

Why do you think the British viewed the Suez Canal as the lifeline of their empire?

4. SYNTHESIZING

What positive and negative impact did inventions such as the railroad and the steamship have on the land and people conquered by the imperialists?

5. DEVELOPING HISTORICAL PERSPECTIVE

EMPIRE BUILDING What economic, political, and social conditions encouraged the growth of imperialism in Africa and Asia?

VISUAL SUMMARY

The New Imperialism, 1850–1914

Causes

- **Nationalism**
  To gain power, European nations compete for colonies and trade.

- **Economic Competition**
  Demand for raw materials and new markets spurs a search for colonies.

- **Missionary Spirit**
  Europeans believe they must spread their Christian teachings to the world.

IMPERIALISM
Europeans exert influence over the economic, political, and social lives of people they colonize.

Effects

- **Colonization**
  Europeans control land and people in areas of Africa, Asia, and Latin America.

- **Colonial Economics**
  Europeans control trade in the colonies and set up dependent cash-crop economies.

- **Christianization**
  Christianity spreads to Africa, India, and Asia.

Use the quotation from the king of the Asante people and your knowledge of world history to answer questions 1 and 2.
Additional Test Practice, pp. S1–S33

PRIMARY SOURCE

The suggestion that Ashanti [Asante] in its present state should come and enjoy the protection of Her Majesty the Queen and Empress of India, I may say this is a matter of serious consideration, and which I am happy to say we have arrived at the conclusion, that my kingdom of Ashanti will never commit itself to any such conclusion, that Ashanti must remain independent as of old, at the same time to remain friendly with all white men. I do not write this with a boastful spirit, but in the clear sense of its meaning. Ashanti is an independent kingdom.

KWAKU DUA III to Frederic M. Hodgson, December 27, 1889

1. What is Kwaku Dua III's answer to the queen?

A. He would enjoy the protection of the queen.

B. He cannot commit himself at this time.

C. He is offended by her offer.

D. He refuses her offer.

2. Why do you think Kwaku Dua III responded that he wanted to remain friendly to white men?

A. He wanted his country to be placed under the protection of white men.

B. He was trying to be diplomatic.

C. He wanted to adopt white men's culture.

D. He wanted the assistance of white men.

Use the map of the British Empire and your knowledge of world history to answer question 3.

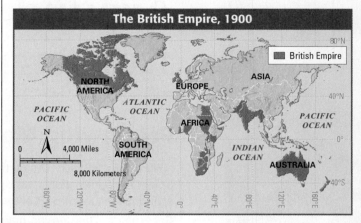

The British Empire, 1900

3. "The sun never sets on the British Empire" was a saying about the British Empire at the peak of its power. What do you think this saying meant?

A. The British Empire had colonies in every part of the world.

B. The British felt that the sun revolved around them.

C. The British Empire represented sunlight and hope to the rest of the world.

D. The British were hard working and never slept.

INTEGRATED TECHNOLOGY

TEST PRACTICE Go to **classzone.com**

- Diagnostic tests
- Tutorials
- Strategies
- Additional practice

ALTERNATIVE ASSESSMENT

1. Interact with History

On page 338, you considered the advantages and disadvantages of colonialism. Now, make a chart showing the advantages and disadvantages to a local person living in a place that became a European colony. Next, make a similar chart for a European living in a foreign place. How do they compare? Discuss with members of your class a way to decide whether the advantages outweigh the disadvantages for each group.

2. WRITING ABOUT HISTORY

POWER AND AUTHORITY Write a **news article** about the effects of colonization. Be sure to address the following points:

- Provide some background on the country you're writing about.
- Tell where the colonizers have come from.
- Describe how the colonizers treat the colonized people.
- Include quotations from both the colonizers and the colonized.
- Draw conclusions about each side's opinion of the other.

INTEGRATED TECHNOLOGY

Creating an Interactive Time Line

Use the Internet and your textbook to create a time line of the events covered in Chapter 11. The time line on pages 336–337 can serve as a guide. Use graphics software to add maps and pictures that illustrate the events. Be sure to include the following on your time line:

- important events in the colonization of Africa and Asia
- efforts on the part of the colonies to resist the imperialist powers
- people who played important roles in the events
- places where key events occurred
- visuals that illustrate the events

Transformations Around the Globe,

1800–1914

Previewing Main Ideas

EMPIRE BUILDING During the 19th and early 20th centuries, Great Britain, other European nations, the United States, and Japan sought political and economic influence over other countries.
Geography *What foreign powers were involved in China in the late 1800s?*

CULTURAL INTERACTION Imperialism brought new religions, philosophies, and technological innovations to East Asia and Latin America. People in these areas resisted some Western ideas and adopted or adapted others.
Geography *What geographic factors might explain why certain parts of China were under Japanese, Russian, and French influence?*

REVOLUTION Both China and Japan struggled to deal with foreign influence and to modernize. Mexico underwent a revolution that brought political and economic reforms.
Geography *Japan built up its navy as a step toward modernization. Why do you think Japan wanted a strong navy?*

INTEGRATED TECHNOLOGY

eEdition
• Interactive Maps
• Interactive Visuals
• Interactive Primary Sources

INTERNET RESOURCES
Go to **classzone.com** for:
• Research Links   • Maps
• Internet Activities • Test Practice
• Primary Sources   • Current Events
• Chapter Quiz

EAST ASIA AND LATIN AMERICA

1823
Monroe Doctrine reflects special U.S. interest in Americas.

1839
China and Britain clash in Opium War.

1853
◄ Commodore Perry enters Tokyo harbor.

1800   **1825**   **1850**

WORLD

1815
Congress of Vienna creates a new balance of power in Europe.

1858
Great Britain establishes direct control of India.

Colonial Powers Carve Up China, 1850–1910

INTER**ACTIVE**

Sea of
Okhotsk

RUSSIA

to Russia
1858

MANCHURIA
1900–05 Russian,
After 1905 Japanese

MONGOLIA
autonomous 1912

Sakhalin

to Russia
1864

Vladivostok

Huang He

Beijing

KOREA
to Japan 1910

Sea of
Japan

Seoul

JAPAN

Tokyo

CHINA

Pusan

Yokohama

Yellow
Sea

TIBET
autonomous
1912

Nanjing

Shanghai

East
China
Sea

30°N

PACIFIC
OCEAN

NEPAL

BHUTAN

Chang Jiang

Pescadores
Islands

INDIA

Hong Kong
(Br.)

BURMA

Guangzhou

TAIWAN
to Japan 1895

Hainan

Bay of
Bengal

N

W   E

S

SIAM

FRENCH
INDOCHINA

Philippine
Sea

INDIAN
OCEAN

South
China
Sea

PHILIPPINES
to U.S. 1898

Colonial possessions	Spheres of influence
British	British
French	French
German	German
Japanese	Japanese
Russian	Russian
Cing Empire, 1850	

BRUNEI

0   300   600 Miles

MALAYA

SARAWAK

BRITISH
NORTH
BORNEO

0   300   600 Kilometers
Polyconic Projection

SINGAPORE

0°Equator

120°E

90°E

1898
◄ United States wins
Spanish-American War.
(Teddy Roosevelt)

1910
Mexican
Revolution
begins.

1914
Panama Canal
opens. ▶

1875

1900

1925

1869
Suez Canal
opens.

1901
◄ Australia becomes an
independent nation. (British flag
showing countries of the Empire)

1905
Russian soldiers open fire
on protesting workers in
St. Petersburg.

Why might you seek out or resist foreign influence?

You are a local government official in 19th-century China. You are proud of your country, which produces everything that its people need. Like other Chinese officials, you discourage contact with foreigners. Nevertheless, people from the West are eager to trade with China.

Most foreign products are inferior to Chinese goods. However, a few foreign products are not available in China. You are curious about these items. At the same time, you wonder why foreigners are so eager to trade with China and what they hope to gain.

▲ Finely made lanterns were among the Chinese goods favored by Western merchants.

EXAMINING *the* ISSUES

- **How might foreign products affect the quality of life in China both positively and negatively?**

- **What demands might foreigners make on countries they trade with?**

As a class, discuss these questions. Recall what happened in other parts of the world when different cultures came into contact for the first time. As you read this chapter, compare the decisions various governments made about foreign trade and the reasons they made those decisions.

China Resists Outside Influence

MAIN IDEA	WHY IT MATTERS NOW	TERMS & NAMES
CULTURAL INTERACTION Western economic pressure forced China to open to foreign trade and influence.	China has become an increasingly important member of the global community.	• Opium War • extraterritorial rights • Taiping Rebellion • sphere of influence • Open Door Policy • Boxer Rebellion

SETTING THE STAGE Out of pride in their ancient culture, the Chinese looked down on all foreigners. In 1793, however, the Qing emperor agreed to receive an ambassador from England. The Englishman brought gifts of the West's most advanced technology—clocks, globes, musical instruments, and even a hot-air balloon. The emperor was not impressed. In a letter to England's King George III, he stated that the Chinese already had everything they needed. They were not interested in the "strange objects" and gadgets that the West was offering them.

China and the West

China was able to reject these offers from the West because it was largely self-sufficient. The basis of this self-sufficiency was China's healthy agricultural economy. During the 11th century, China had acquired a quick-growing strain of rice from Southeast Asia. By the time of the Qing Dynasty, the rice was being grown throughout the southern part of the country. Around the same time, the 17th and 18th centuries, Spanish and Portuguese traders brought maize, sweet potatoes, and peanuts from the Americas. These crops helped China increase the productivity of its land and more effectively feed its huge population.

China also had extensive mining and manufacturing industries. Rich salt, tin, silver, and iron mines produced great quantities of ore. The mines provided work for tens of thousands of people. The Chinese also produced beautiful silks, high-quality cottons, and fine porcelain.

The Tea-Opium Connection Because of their self-sufficiency, the Chinese had little interest in trading with the West. For decades, the only place they would allow foreigners to do business was at the southern port of Guangzhou (gwahng•joh). And the balance of trade at Guangzhou was clearly in China's favor. This means that China earned much more for its exports than it spent on imports.

European merchants were determined to find a product the Chinese would buy in large quantities. Eventually they found one—opium. Opium is a habit-forming narcotic made from the poppy plant. Chinese doctors had been using it to relieve pain for hundreds of years. In the late 18th century, however, British merchants smuggled opium into China for nonmedical use. It took a few decades for opium smoking to catch on, but by 1835, as many as 12 million Chinese people were addicted to the drug.

TAKING NOTES

Identifying Problems
Use a chart to identify the internal and external problems faced by China in the 1800s and early 1900s.

China's Problems	
Internal	External

War Breaks Out This growing supply of opium caused great problems for China. The Qing emperor was angry about the situation. In 1839, one of his highest advisers wrote a letter to England's Queen Victoria about the problem:

PRIMARY SOURCE
By what right do they [British merchants] . . . use the poisonous drug to injure the Chinese people? . . . I have heard that the smoking of opium is very strictly forbidden by your country; that is because the harm caused by opium is clearly understood. Since it is not permitted to do harm to your own country, then even less should you let it be passed on to the harm of other countries.

LIN ZEXU, quoted in *China's Response to the West*

The pleas went unanswered, and Britain refused to stop trading opium. The result was an open clash between the British and the Chinese—the **Opium War** of 1839. The battles took place mostly at sea. China's outdated ships were no match for Britain's steam-powered gunboats. As a result, the Chinese suffered a humiliating defeat. In 1842, they signed a peace treaty, the Treaty of Nanjing. **A**

This treaty gave Britain the island of Hong Kong. After signing another treaty in 1844, U.S. and other foreign citizens also gained **extraterritorial rights**. Under these rights, foreigners were not subject to Chinese law at Guangzhou and four other Chinese ports. Many Chinese greatly resented the foreigners and the bustling trade in opium they conducted.

MAIN IDEA

Analyzing Issues
A What conflicting British and Chinese positions led to the Opium War?

Growing Internal Problems

Foreigners were not the greatest of China's problems in the mid-19th century, however. The country's own population provided an overwhelming challenge. The number of Chinese grew to 430 million by 1850, a 30 percent gain in only 60 years. Yet, in the same period of time, food production barely increased. As a result, hunger was widespread, even in good years. Many people became discouraged, and opium addiction rose steadily. As their problems mounted, the Chinese began to rebel against the Qing Dynasty.

Connect *to* Today

Special Economic Zones

Today, as in the late 1800s, the Chinese government limits foreign economic activity to particular areas of the country. Most of these areas, called special economic zones (SEZs), are located on the coast and waterways of southeastern China. Established in the late 1970s, the SEZs are designed to attract, but also control, foreign investment.

One of the most successful SEZs is Shanghai (pictured at right). By the late 1990s, dozens of foreign companies—including IBM of the United States, Hitachi of Japan, Siemens of Germany, and Unilever of Great Britain—had invested about $21 billion in the building and operating of factories, stores, and other businesses. This investment had a huge impact on the economy of Shanghai. Throughout the 1990s, it grew by more than 10 percent each year.

The Taiping Rebellion During the late 1830s, Hong Xiuquan (hung shee•oo•choo•ahn), a young man from Guangdong province in southern China, began recruiting followers to help him build a "Heavenly Kingdom of Great Peace." In this kingdom, all Chinese people would share China's vast wealth and no one would live in poverty. Hong's movement was called the **Taiping Rebellion**, from the Chinese word *taiping,* meaning "great peace."

By the 1850s, Hong had organized a massive peasant army of some one million people. Over time, the Taiping army took control of large areas of southeastern China. Then, in 1853, Hong captured the city of Nanjing and declared it his capital. Hong soon withdrew from everyday life and left family members and his trusted lieutenants in charge of the government of his kingdom.

The leaders of the Taiping government, however, constantly feuded among themselves. Also, Qing imperial troops and British and French forces all launched attacks against the Taiping. By 1864, this combination of internal fighting and outside assaults had brought down the Taiping government. But China paid a terrible price. At least 20 million—and possibly twice that many—people died in the rebellion. **B**

MAIN IDEA
Recognizing Effects
B What were the results of the Taiping Rebellion?

▲ A Taiping force surrounds and destroys an enemy village.

Foreign Influence Grows

The Taiping Rebellion and several other smaller uprisings put tremendous internal pressure on the Chinese government. And, despite the Treaty of Nanjing, external pressure from foreign powers was increasing. At the Qing court, stormy debates raged about how best to deal with these issues. Some government leaders called for reforms patterned on Western ways. Others, however, clung to traditional ways and accepted change very reluctantly.

Vocabulary
A *dowager* is a widow who holds a title or property from her deceased husband.

Resistance to Change During the last half of the 19th century, one person was in command at the Qing imperial palace. The Dowager Empress Cixi (tsoo•shee) held the reins of power in China from 1862 until 1908 with only one brief gap. Although she was committed to traditional values, the Dowager Empress did support certain reforms. In the 1860s, for example, she backed the self-strengthening movement. This program aimed to update China's educational system, diplomatic service, and military. Under this program, China set up factories to manufacture steam-powered gunboats, rifles, and ammunition. The self-strengthening movement had mixed results, however.

Other Nations Step In Other countries were well aware of China's continuing problems. Throughout the late 19th century, many foreign nations took advantage of the situation and attacked China. Treaty negotiations after each conflict gave these nations increasing control over China's economy. Many of Europe's major powers and Japan gained a strong foothold in China. This foothold, or **sphere of influence**, was an area in which the foreign nation controlled trade and investment. (See the map on page 374.)

The United States was a long-time trading partner with China. Americans worried that other nations would soon divide China into formal colonies and shut out American traders. To prevent this occurrence, in 1899 the United States declared

China: Spheres of Influence and Treaty Ports, c. 1900

Spheres of Influence
- British
- French
- German
- Japanese
- Russian

Treaty Ports
- • Original port opened by Treaty of Nanjing (1842)
- • Treaty port opened by 1900
- • Major city

GEOGRAPHY SKILLBUILDER: Interpreting Maps
1. **Human-Environment Interaction** Which countries had spheres of influence in China?
2. **Location** What foreign power shown on the map had access to inland China? What geographic feature made this possible?

the **Open Door Policy**. This proposed that China's "doors" be open to merchants of all nations. Britain and the other European nations agreed. The policy thus protected both U.S. trading rights in China, and China's freedom from colonization. But the country was still at the mercy of foreign powers.

An Upsurge in Chinese Nationalism

Humiliated by their loss of power, many Chinese pressed for strong reforms. Among those demanding change was China's young emperor, Guangxu (gwahng•shoo). In June 1898, Guangxu introduced measures to modernize China. These measures called for reorganizing China's educational system, strengthening the economy, modernizing the military, and streamlining the government.

Most Qing officials saw these innovations as threats to their power. They reacted with alarm, calling the Dowager Empress back to the imperial court. On her return, she acted with great speed. She placed Guangxu under arrest and took control of the government. She then reversed his reforms. Guangxu's efforts brought about no change whatsoever. The Chinese people's frustration with their situation continued to grow.

The Boxer Rebellion This widespread frustration finally erupted into violence. Poor peasants and workers resented the special privileges granted to foreigners. They also resented Chinese Christians, who had adopted a foreign faith. To demonstrate their discontent, they formed a secret organization called the Society of Righteous and Harmonious Fists. They soon came to be known as the Boxers. Their campaign against the Dowager Empress's rule and foreigner privilege was called the **Boxer Rebellion**.

In the spring of 1900, the Boxers descended on Beijing. Shouting "Death to the foreign devils," the Boxers surrounded the European section of the city. They kept it under siege for several months. The Dowager Empress expressed support for the Boxers but did not back her words with military aid. In August, a multinational force of 19,000 troops marched on Beijing and quickly defeated the Boxers. **C**

MAIN IDEA

Analyzing Causes

C Why did the Boxer Rebellion fail?

Despite the failure of the Boxer Rebellion, a strong sense of nationalism had emerged in China. The Chinese people realized that their country must resist more foreign intervention. Even more important, they felt that the government must become responsive to their needs.

▲ A gang of Boxers attacks Chinese Christians.

The Beginnings of Reform At this point, even the Qing court realized that China needed to make profound changes to survive. In 1905, the Dowager Empress sent a select group of Chinese officials on a world tour to study the operation of different governments. The group traveled to Japan, the United States, Britain, France, Germany, Russia, and Italy. On their return in the spring of 1906, the officials recommended that China restructure its government. They based their suggestions on the constitutional monarchy of Japan. The empress accepted this recommendation and began making reforms. Although she convened a national assembly within a year, change was slow. In 1908, the court announced that it would establish a full constitutional government by 1917.

However, the turmoil in China did not end with these progressive steps. China experienced unrest for the next four decades as it continued to face internal and external threats. China's neighbor Japan also faced pressure from the West during this time. But it responded to this influence in a much different way.

SECTION 1 ASSESSMENT

TERMS & NAMES 1. For each term or name, write a sentence explaining its significance.
• Opium War   • extraterritorial rights   • Taiping Rebellion   • sphere of influence   • Open Door Policy   • Boxer Rebellion

USING YOUR NOTES

2. Which created the most trouble for China, internal problems or external problems? Why?

China's Problems	
Internal	External

MAIN IDEAS

3. Why did the Chinese have little interest in trading with the West?

4. What internal problems did China face prior to the Taiping Rebellion?

5. Why did Emperor Guangxu's efforts at reform and modernization fail?

CRITICAL THINKING & WRITING

6. **ANALYZING MOTIVES** Why do you think European powers established spheres of influence in China rather than colonies, as they did in Africa and other parts of Asia?

7. **MAKING INFERENCES** What importance did spheres of influence have for China?

8. **COMPARING AND CONTRASTING** What were the similarities and differences between the Taiping Rebellion and the Boxer Rebellion?

9. **WRITING ACTIVITY** CULTURAL INTERACTION Write a **dialogue** between two of Dowager Empress Cixi's advisers—one arguing for continued isolation, the other for openness to foreign influence and trade.

INTEGRATED TECHNOLOGY INTERNET ACTIVITY

Use the Internet to find information on special economic zones in China. Use your findings to create an **annotated map** showing the location of these zones.

INTERNET KEYWORDS
special economic zones, SEZs

Modernization in Japan

MAIN IDEA	WHY IT MATTERS NOW	TERMS & NAMES
CULTURAL INTERACTION Japan followed the model of Western powers by industrializing and expanding its foreign influence.	Japan's continued development of its own way of life has made it a leading world power.	• Treaty of Kanagawa • Meiji era • Russo-Japanese War • annexation

SETTING THE STAGE In the early 17th century, Japan had shut itself off from almost all contact with other nations. Under the rule of the Tokugawa shoguns, Japanese society was very tightly ordered. The shogun parceled out land to the daimyo, or lords. The peasants worked for and lived under the protection of their daimyo and his small army of samurai, or warriors. This rigid feudal system managed to keep the country free of civil war. Peace and relative prosperity reigned in Japan for two centuries.

TAKING NOTES
Analyzing Causes List the steps that Japan took toward modernization and the events that contributed to its growth as an imperialistic power.

Modernization
Imperialism

Japan Ends Its Isolation

The Japanese had almost no contact with the industrialized world during this time of isolation. They continued, however, to trade with China and with Dutch merchants from Indonesia. They also had diplomatic contact with Korea. However, trade was growing in importance, both inside and outside Japan.

The Demand for Foreign Trade Beginning in the early 19th century, Westerners tried to convince the Japanese to open their ports to trade. British, French, Russian, and American officials occasionally anchored off the Japanese coast. Like China, however, Japan repeatedly refused to receive them. Then, in 1853, U.S. Commodore Matthew Perry took four ships into what is now Tokyo Harbor. These massive black wooden ships powered by steam astounded the Japanese. The ships' cannons also shocked them. The Tokugawa shogun realized he had no choice but to receive Perry and the letter Perry had brought from U.S. president Millard Fillmore.

Fillmore's letter politely asked the shogun to allow free trade between the United States and Japan. Perry delivered it with a threat, however. He would come back with a larger fleet in a year to receive Japan's reply. That reply was the **Treaty of Kanagawa** of 1854. Under its terms, Japan opened two ports at which U.S. ships could take on supplies. After the United States had pushed open the door, other Western powers soon followed. By 1860, Japan, like China, had granted foreigners permission to trade at several treaty ports. It had also extended extraterritorial rights to many foreign nations.

Meiji Reform and Modernization The Japanese were angry that the shogun had given in to the foreigners' demands. They turned to Japan's young emperor, Mutsuhito (moot•soo•HEE•toh), who seemed to symbolize the country's sense of pride and nationalism. In 1867, the Tokugawa shogun stepped down, ending the military dictatorships that had lasted since the 12th century. Mutsuhito took control of the government. He chose the name *Meiji* for his reign, which means "enlightened rule." Mutsuhito's reign, which lasted 45 years, is known as the **Meiji era**.

The Meiji emperor realized that the best way to counter Western influence was to modernize. He sent diplomats to Europe and North America to study Western ways. The Japanese then chose what they believed to be the best that Western civilization had to offer and adapted it to their own country. They admired Germany's strong centralized government, for example. And they used its constitution as a model for their own. The Japanese also admired the discipline of the German army and the skill of the British navy. They attempted to imitate these European powers as they modernized their military. Japan adopted the American system of universal public education and required that all Japanese children attend school. Their teachers often included foreign experts. Students could go abroad to study as well.

The emperor also energetically supported following the Western path of industrialization. By the early 20th century, the Japanese economy had become as modern as any in the world. The country built its first railroad line in 1872. The track connected Tokyo, the nation's capital, with the port of Yokohama, 20 miles to the south. By 1914, Japan had more than 7,000 miles of railroad. Coal production grew from half a million tons in 1875 to more than 21 million tons in 1913. Meanwhile, large, state-supported companies built thousands of factories. Traditional Japanese industries, such as tea processing and silk production, expanded to give the country unique products to trade. Developing modern industries, such as shipbuilding, made Japan competitive with the West.

Imperial Japan

Japan's race to modernize paid off. By 1890, the country had several dozen warships and 500,000 well-trained, well-armed soldiers. It had become the strongest military power in Asia.

Japan had gained military, political, and economic strength. It then sought to eliminate the extraterritorial rights of foreigners. The Japanese foreign minister assured foreigners that they could rely on fair treatment in Japan. This was because its constitution and legal codes were similar to those of European nations, he explained. His reasoning was convincing, and in 1894, foreign powers accepted the

China and Japan Confront the West

▲ The Dowager Empress Cixi (1862–1908)

China
- Remains committed to traditional values
- Loses numerous territorial conflicts
- Grants other nations spheres of influence within China
- Finally accepts necessity for reform

Both
- Have well-established traditional values
- Initially resist change
- Oppose Western imperialism

Japan
- Considers modernization to be necessary
- Borrows and adapts Western ways
- Strengthens its economic and military power
- Becomes an empire builder

▲ The Meiji Emperor Mutsuhito (1867–1912)

SKILLBUILDER: Interpreting Charts

1. **Contrasting** *According to the diagram, in what ways did China and Japan deal differently with Western influence?*

2. **Comparing** *What similar responses did each country share despite the different paths they followed?*

377

abolition of extraterritorial rights for their citizens living in Japan. Japan's feeling of strength and equality with the Western nations rose.

As Japan's sense of power grew, the nation also became more imperialistic. As in Europe, national pride played a large part in Japan's imperial plans. The Japanese were determined to show the world that they were a powerful nation. **A**

Japan Attacks China The Japanese first turned their sights to their neighbor, Korea. In 1876, Japan forced Korea to open three ports to Japanese trade. But China also considered Korea to be important both as a trading partner and a military outpost. Recognizing their similar interests in Korea, Japan and China signed a hands-off agreement. In 1885, both countries pledged that they would not send their armies into Korea.

In June 1894, however, China broke that agreement. Rebellions had broken out against Korea's king. He asked China for military help in putting them down. Chinese troops marched into Korea. Japan protested and sent its troops to Korea to fight the Chinese. This Sino-Japanese War lasted just a few months. In that time, Japan drove the Chinese out of Korea, destroyed the Chinese navy, and gained a foothold in Manchuria. In 1895, China and Japan signed a peace treaty. This treaty gave Japan its first colonies, Taiwan and the neighboring Pescadores Islands. (See the map on page 369.)

Russo-Japanese War Japan's victory over China changed the world's balance of power. Russia and Japan emerged as the major powers—and enemies—in East Asia. The two countries soon went to war over Manchuria. In 1903, Japan offered to recognize Russia's rights in Manchuria if the Russians would agree to stay out of Korea. But the Russians refused.

In February 1904, Japan launched a surprise attack on Russian ships anchored off the coast of Manchuria. In the resulting **Russo-Japanese War**, Japan drove

MAIN IDEA

Making Inferences

A Why did Japan become imperialistic?

Vocabulary
Sino: a prefix meaning "Chinese"

> Analyzing Political Cartoons

Warlike Japan

Cartoonists often use symbols to identify the countries, individuals, or even ideas featured in their cartoons. Russia has long been symbolized as a bear by cartoonists. Here, the cartoonist uses a polar bear.

Prior to the Meiji era, cartoonists usually pictured Japan as a fierce samurai. Later, however, Japan often was symbolized by a caricature of Emperor Mutsuhito. Here, the cartoonist has exaggerated the emperor's physical features to make him look like a bird of prey.

SKILLBUILDER:
Interpreting Political Cartoons
1. **Clarifying** *How does the cartoonist signify that Japan is warlike?*
2. **Making Inferences** *In their fight, Russia and Japan appear to be crushing someone. Who do you think this might be?*

Russian troops out of Korea and captured most of Russia's Pacific fleet. It also destroyed Russia's Baltic fleet, which had sailed all the way around Africa to participate in the war.

In 1905, Japan and Russia began peace negotiations. U.S. president Theodore Roosevelt helped draft the treaty, which the two nations signed on a ship off Portsmouth, New Hampshire. This agreement, the Treaty of Portsmouth, gave Japan the captured territories. It also forced Russia to withdraw from Manchuria and to stay out of Korea.

Japanese Occupation of Korea After defeating Russia, Japan attacked Korea with a vengeance. In 1905, it made Korea a protectorate. Japan sent in "advisers," who grabbed more and more power from the Korean government. The Korean king was unable to rally international support for his regime. In 1907, he gave up control of the country. Within two years the Korean Imperial Army was disbanded. In 1910, Japan officially imposed **annexation** on Korea, or brought that country under Japan's control.

The Japanese were harsh rulers. They shut down Korean newspapers and took over Korean schools. There they replaced the study of Korean language and history with Japanese subjects. They took land away from Korean farmers and gave it to Japanese settlers. They encouraged Japanese businessmen to start industries in Korea, but forbade Koreans from going into business. Resentment of Japan's repressive rule grew, helping to create a strong Korean nationalist movement. **B**

The rest of the world clearly saw the brutal results of Japan's imperialism. Nevertheless, the United States and other European countries largely ignored what was happening in Korea. They were too busy with their own imperialistic aims, as you will learn in Section 3.

Vocabulary
protectorate: a country under the partial control and protection of another nation

MAIN IDEA
Clarifying
B How did Japan treat the Koreans after it annexed the country?

Global Impact

Western Views of the East

The Japanese victory over the Russians in 1905 exploded a strong Western myth. Many Westerners believed that white people were a superior race. The overwhelming success of European colonialism and imperialism in the Americas, Africa, and Asia had reinforced this belief. But the Japanese had shown Europeans that people of other races were their equals in modern warfare.

Unfortunately, Japan's military victory led to a different form of Western racism. Influenced by the ideas of Germany's Emperor Wilhelm II, the West imagined the Japanese uniting with the Chinese and conquering Europe. The resulting racist Western fear of what was called the *yellow peril* influenced world politics for many decades.

SECTION **2** **ASSESSMENT**

TERMS & NAMES 1. For each term or name, write a sentence explaining its significance.
• Treaty of Kanagawa • Meiji era • Russo-Japanese War • annexation

USING YOUR NOTES
2. Do you think that Japan could have become an imperialistic power if it had not modernized? Why or why not?

| Modernization |
| Imperialism |

MAIN IDEAS
3. How was the Treaty of Kanagawa similar to the treaties that China signed with various European powers?

4. What steps did the Meiji emperor take to modernize Japan?

5. How did Japan begin its quest to build an empire?

CRITICAL THINKING & WRITING
6. **ANALYZING CAUSES** What influences do you think were most important in motivating Japan to build its empire?

7. **FORMING AND SUPPORTING OPINIONS** In your view, was Japan's aggressive imperialism justified? Support your answer with information from the text.

8. **ANALYZING BIAS** How did Japan's victory in the Russo-Japanese War both explode and create stereotypes?

9. **WRITING ACTIVITY** [EMPIRE BUILDING] In the role of a Japanese official, write a **letter** to the government of a Western power explaining why you think it is necessary for your country to build an empire.

CONNECT TO TODAY **CREATING A SYMBOL**

Conduct research to discover the name that Akihito, the present emperor of Japan, chose for his reign. Then create a **symbol** that expresses the meaning of this name.

Japanese Woodblock Printing

Woodblock printing in Japan evolved from black-and-white prints created by Buddhists in the 700s. By the late 1700s, artists learned how to create multicolor prints.

Woodblock prints could be produced quickly and in large quantities, so they were cheaper than paintings. In the mid-1800s, a Japanese person could buy a woodblock print for about the same price as a bowl of noodles. As a result, woodblock prints like those shown here became a widespread art form. The most popular subjects included actors, beautiful women, urban life, and landscapes.

INTEGRATED / TECHNOLOGY

RESEARCH LINKS For more on Japanese woodblock printing, go to **classzone.com**

▲ Naniwaya Okita

The artist Kitagawa Utamaro created many prints of attractive women. This print shows Naniwaya Okita, a famous beauty of the late 1700s. Her long face, elaborate hairstyle, and many-colored robes were all considered part of her beauty.

▲ Carving the Block

These photographs show a modern artist carving a block for the black ink. (The artist must carve a separate block for each color that will be in the final print.)

Carving the raised image requires precision and patience. For example, David Bull, the artist in the photographs, makes five cuts to create each strand of hair. One slip of the knife, and the block will be ruined.

▲ Under the Wave off Kanagawa

Katsushika Hokusai was one of the most famous of all Japanese printmakers. This scene is taken from his well-known series *Thirty-Six Views of Mount Fuji*. Mount Fuji, which many Japanese considered sacred, is the small peak in the background of this scene.

▲ Printing

After the carved block is inked, the artist presses paper on it, printing a partial image. He or she repeats this stage for each new color. The artist must ensure that every color ends up in exactly the right place, so that no blocks of color extend beyond the outlines or fall short of them.

Connect *to* Today

1. **Making Inferences** What personal qualities and skills would an artist need to be good at making woodblock prints?

   📖 See Skillbuilder Handbook, page R10.

2. **Forming and Supporting Opinions** Hokusai's print of the wave, shown above, remains very popular today. Why do you think this image appeals to modern people?

U.S. Economic Imperialism

MAIN IDEA	WHY IT MATTERS NOW	TERMS & NAMES
EMPIRE BUILDING The United States put increasing economic and political pressure on Latin America during the 19th century.	This policy set the stage for 20th-century relations between Latin America and the United States.	• caudillo • Monroe Doctrine • José Martí • Spanish-American War	• Panama Canal • Roosevelt Corollary

SETTING THE STAGE Latin America's long struggle to gain independence from colonial domination between the late 18th and the mid-19th centuries left the new nations in shambles. Farm fields had been neglected and were overrun with weeds. Buildings in many cities bore the scars of battle. Some cities had been left in ruins. The new nations of Latin America faced a struggle for economic and political recovery that was every bit as difficult as their struggle for independence had been.

TAKING NOTES

Following Chronological Order Use a time line to list the major events in U.S. involvement in Latin America.

1823	1898	1903	1914

Latin America After Independence

Political independence meant little for most citizens of the new Latin American nations. The majority remained poor laborers caught up in a cycle of poverty.

Colonial Legacy Both before and after independence, most Latin Americans worked for large landowners. The employers paid their workers with vouchers that could be used only at their own supply stores. Since wages were low and prices were high, workers went into debt. Their debt accumulated and passed from one generation to the next. In this system known as peonage, "free" workers were little better than slaves.

Landowners, on the other hand, only got wealthier after independence. Many new Latin American governments took over the lands owned by native peoples and by the Catholic Church. Then they put those lands up for sale. Wealthy landowners were the only people who could afford to buy them, and they snapped them up. But as one Argentinean newspaper reported, "Their greed for land does not equal their ability to use it intelligently." The unequal distribution of land and the landowners' inability to use it effectively combined to prevent social and economic development in Latin America.

Political Instability Political instability was another widespread problem in 19th-century Latin America. Many Latin American army leaders had gained fame and power during their long struggle for independence. They often continued to assert their power. They controlled the new nations as military dictators, or **caudillos** (kaw•DEEL•yohz). They were able to hold on to power because they were backed by the military. By the mid-1800s, nearly all the countries of Latin America were ruled by caudillos. One typical caudillo was Juan Vicente Gómez.

He was a ruthless man who ruled Venezuela for nearly 30 years after seizing power in 1908. "All Venezuela is my cattle ranch," he once boasted.

There were some exceptions, however. Reform-minded presidents, such as Argentina's Domingo Sarmiento, made strong commitments to improving education. During Sarmiento's presidency, between 1868 and 1874, the number of students in Argentina doubled. But such reformers usually did not stay in office long. More often than not, a caudillo, supported by the army, seized control of the government.

The caudillos faced little opposition. The wealthy landowners usually supported them because they opposed giving power to the lower classes. In addition, Latin Americans had gained little experience with democracy under European colonial rule. So, the dictatorship of a caudillo did not seem unusual to them. But even when caudillos were not in power, most Latin Americans still lacked a voice in the government. Voting rights—and with them, political power—were restricted to the relatively few members of the upper and middle classes who owned property or could read. **Ⓐ**

MAIN IDEA

Identifying Problems

Ⓐ What difficulties did lower-class Latin Americans continue to face after independence?

▲ Argentine reformer Domingo Sarmiento

Economies Grow Under Foreign Influence

When colonial rule ended in Latin America in the early 1800s, the new nations were no longer restricted to trading with colonial powers. Britain and, later, the United States became Latin America's main trading partners.

Old Products and New Markets Latin America's economies continued to depend on exports, no matter whom they were trading with. As during the colonial era, each country concentrated on one or two products. With advances in technology, however, Latin America's exports grew. The development of the steamship and the building of railroads in the 19th century, for example, greatly increased Latin American trade. Toward the end of the century, the invention of refrigeration helped increase Latin America's exports. The sale of beef, fruits and vegetables, and other perishable goods soared.

But foreign nations benefited far more from the increased trade than Latin America did. In exchange for their exports, Latin Americans imported European and North American manufactured goods. As a result, they had little reason to develop their own manufacturing industries. And as long as Latin America remained unindustrialized, it could not play a leading role on the world economic stage.

▼ Workers unload coffee beans at a plantation in Brazil. Until recently, Brazil's economy depended heavily on the export of coffee.

Outside Investment and Interference Furthermore, Latin American countries used little of their export income to build roads, schools, or hospitals. Nor did they fund programs that would help them become self-sufficient. Instead, they often borrowed money at high interest rates to develop facilities for their export industries. Countries such as Britain, France, the United States, and Germany were willing lenders. The Latin American countries often were unable to pay back their loans, however. In response, foreign lenders sometimes threatened to collect the debt by force. At other times, they threatened to take over the facilities they had funded. In this way, foreign companies gained control of many Latin American industries. This began a new age of economic colonialism in Latin America.

History Makers

José Martí
1853–1895

José Martí was only 15 in 1868 when he first began speaking out for Cuban independence. In 1871, the Spanish colonial government punished Martí's open opposition with exile. Except for a brief return to his homeland in 1878, Martí remained in exile for about 20 years. For most of this time, he lived in New York City. There he continued his career as a writer and a revolutionary. "Life on earth is a hand-to-hand combat . . . between the law of love and the law of hate," he proclaimed.

While in New York, Martí helped raise an army to fight for Cuban independence. He died on the battlefield only a month after the war began. But Martí's cry for freedom echoes in his essays and poems and in folk songs about him that are still sung throughout the world.

INTEGRATED / TECHNOLOGY

RESEARCH LINKS For more on José Martí, go to **classzone.com**

A Latin American Empire

Long before the United States had any economic interest in Latin American countries, it realized that it had strong links with its southern neighbors. Leaders of the United States were well aware that their country's security depended on the security of Latin America.

The Monroe Doctrine Most Latin American colonies had gained their independence by the early 1800s. But their position was not secure. Many Latin Americans feared that European countries would try to reconquer the new republics. The United States, a young nation itself, feared this too. So, in 1823, President James Monroe issued what came to be called the **Monroe Doctrine**. This document stated that "the American continents . . . are henceforth not to be considered as subjects for future colonization by any European powers." Until 1898, though, the United States did little to enforce the Monroe Doctrine. Cuba provided a real testing ground.

Cuba Declares Independence The Caribbean island of Cuba was one of Spain's last colonies in the Americas. In 1868, Cuba declared its independence and fought a ten-year war against Spain. In 1878, with the island in ruins, the Cubans gave up the fight. But some Cubans continued to seek independence from Spain. In 1895, **José Martí**, a writer who had been exiled from Cuba by the Spanish, returned to launch a second war for Cuban independence. Martí was killed early in the fighting, but the Cubans battled on.

By the mid-1890s, the United States had developed substantial business holdings in Cuba. Therefore it had an economic stake in the fate of the country. In addition, the Spanish had forced many Cuban civilians into concentration camps. Americans objected to the Spanish brutality. In 1898, the United States joined the Cuban war for independence. This conflict, which became known as the **Spanish-American War**, lasted about four months. U.S. forces launched their first attack not on Cuba but on the Philippine Islands, a Spanish colony thousands of miles away in the Pacific. Unprepared for a war on two fronts, the Spanish military quickly collapsed. (See the maps on the opposite page.) **B**

MAIN IDEA

Analyzing Motives
B Why did the United States join the Cuban war for independence?

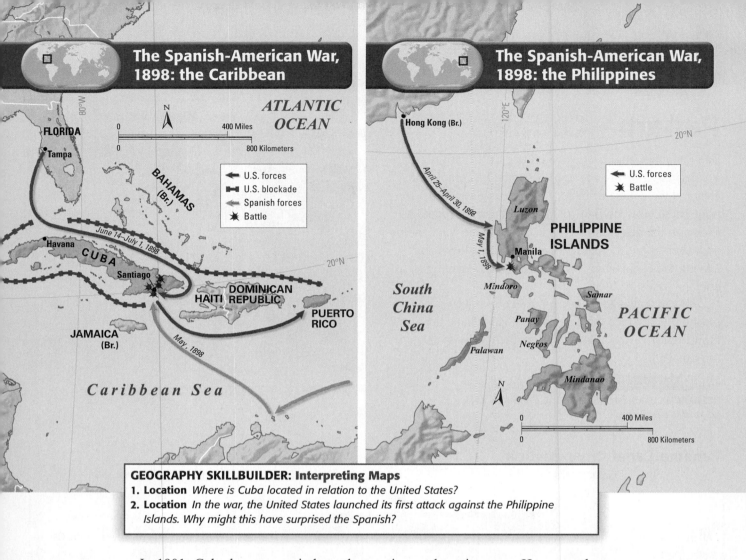

The Spanish-American War, 1898: the Caribbean

ATLANTIC OCEAN

0 400 Miles
0 800 Kilometers

FLORIDA
Tampa

BAHAMAS (Br.)

← U.S. forces
■—■ U.S. blockade
← Spanish forces
✳ Battle

June 14–July 1, 1898

Havana
CUBA
Santiago

20°N

DOMINICAN REPUBLIC
HAITI

PUERTO RICO

JAMAICA (Br.)

May, 1898

Caribbean Sea

The Spanish-American War, 1898: the Philippines

Hong Kong (Br.)

120°E

20°N

April 25–April 30, 1898

Luzon

PHILIPPINE ISLANDS

May 1, 1898

Manila

← U.S. forces
✳ Battle

South China Sea

Mindoro

Samar

Panay

PACIFIC OCEAN

Palawan

Negros

Mindanao

0 400 Miles
0 800 Kilometers

GEOGRAPHY SKILLBUILDER: Interpreting Maps
1. **Location** *Where is Cuba located in relation to the United States?*
2. **Location** *In the war, the United States launched its first attack against the Philippine Islands. Why might this have surprised the Spanish?*

In 1901, Cuba became an independent nation, at least in name. However, the United States installed a military government and continued to exert control over Cuban affairs. This caused tremendous resentment among many Cubans, who had assumed that the United States' aim in intervening was to help Cuba become truly independent. The split that developed between the United States and Cuba at this time continues to keep these close neighbors miles apart more than a century later.

After its defeat in the Spanish-American War, Spain turned over the last of its colonies. Puerto Rico, Guam, and the Philippines became U.S. territories. Having become the dominant imperial power in Latin America, the United States next set its sights on Panama.

Vocabulary
A *colossus* is a huge statue that towers over the surrounding area.

Connecting the Oceans Latin Americans were beginning to regard the United States as the political and economic "Colossus of the North." The United States was a colossus in geographic terms too. By the 1870s, the transcontinental railroad connected its east and west coasts. But land travel still was time-consuming and difficult. And sea travel between the coasts involved a trip of about 13,000 miles around the tip of South America. If a canal could be dug across a narrow section of Central America, however, the coast-to-coast journey would be cut in half.

The United States had been thinking about such a project since the early 19th century. In the 1880s, a French company tried—but failed—to build a canal across Panama. Despite this failure, Americans remained enthusiastic about the canal. And no one was more enthusiastic than President Theodore Roosevelt, who led the nation from 1901 to 1909. In 1903, Panama was a province of Colombia. Roosevelt offered that country $10 million plus a yearly payment for the right to build a canal. When the Colombian government demanded more money, the United States

Transformations Around the Globe **385**

Panama Canal

The Panama Canal is considered one of the world's greatest engineering accomplishments. Its completion changed the course of history by opening a worldwide trade route between the Atlantic and Pacific oceans. As shown in the diagram below, on entering the canal, ships are raised about 85 feet in a series of three locks. On leaving the canal, ships are lowered to sea level by another series of three locks.

The canal also had a lasting effect on other technologies. Since the early 1900s, ships have been built to dimensions that will allow them to pass through the canal's locks.

INTEGRATED TECHNOLOGY
RESEARCH LINKS For more on the Panama Canal, go to **classzone.com**

▲ Ships passing through the Pedro Miguel Locks

Panama Canal Cross-section

Gatún Locks
Gaillard Cut
Pedro Miguel Locks
Gatún Lake
Miraflores Lake
Miraflores Locks
85'
Atlantic Ocean
Pacific Ocean
85'
Sea level

←————— 51 miles —————→

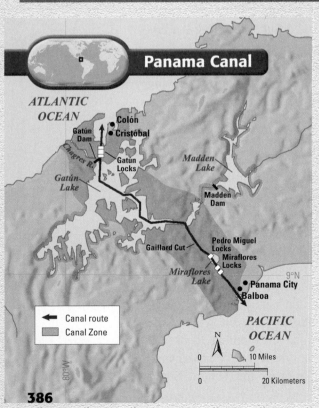

Panama Canal

ATLANTIC OCEAN
Colón
Cristóbal
Gatún Dam
Chagres R.
Gatún Locks
Madden Lake
Gatún Lake
Madden Dam
Gaillard Cut
Pedro Miguel Locks
Miraflores Locks
Miraflores Lake
9°N
Panama City
Balboa
PACIFIC OCEAN

←— Canal route
▢ Canal Zone

N

0   10 Miles
0   20 Kilometers

▲ This cross-section shows the different elevations and locks that a ship moves through on the trip through the canal.

Canal Facts

• The canal took ten years to build (1904–1914) and cost $380 million.

• During the construction of the canal, workers dug up more than 200 million cubic yards of earth.

• Thousands of workers died from diseases while building the canal.

• The trip from San Francisco to New York City via the Panama Canal is about 9,000 miles shorter than the trip around South America.

• The 51-mile trip through the canal takes 8 to 10 hours.

• The canal now handles more than 13,000 ships a year from around 70 nations carrying 192 million short tons of cargo.

• Panama took control of the canal on December 31, 1999.

Connect *to* Today

1. **Identifying Problems** What difficulties did workers face in constructing the canal?

   See Skillbuilder Handbook, page R5.

2. **Evaluating Decisions** In the more than 90 years since it was built, do you think that the benefits of the Panama Canal to world trade have outweighed the costs in time, money, and human life? Explain your answer.

responded by encouraging a revolution in Panama. The Panamanians had been trying to break away from Colombia for almost a century. In 1903, with help from the United States Navy, they won their country's independence. In gratitude, Panama gave the United States a ten-mile-wide zone in which to build a canal.

For the next decade, American engineers contended with floods and withering heat to build the massive waterway. However, their greatest challenge was the disease-carrying insects that infested the area. The United States began a campaign to destroy the mosquitoes that carried yellow fever and malaria, and the rats that carried bubonic plague. The effort to control these diseases was eventually successful. Even so, thousands of workers died during construction of the canal. The **Panama Canal** finally opened in 1914. Ships from around the world soon began to use it. Latin America had become a crossroads of world trade. And the United States controlled the tollgate. **C**

MAIN IDEA

Analyzing Motives
C Why was the United States so interested in building the Panama Canal?

▼ This cartoon suggests that the Roosevelt Corollary turned the Caribbean into a U.S. wading pool.

The Roosevelt Corollary The building of the Panama Canal was only one way that the United States expanded its influence in Latin America in the early 20th century. Its presence in Cuba and its large investments in many Central and South American countries strengthened its foothold. To protect those economic interests, in 1904, President Roosevelt issued a corollary, or extension, to the Monroe Doctrine. The **Roosevelt Corollary** gave the United States the right to be "an international police power" in the Western Hemisphere.

The United States used the Roosevelt Corollary many times in the following years to justify U.S. intervention in Latin America. U.S. troops occupied some countries for decades. Many Latin Americans protested this intervention, but they were powerless to stop their giant neighbor to the north. The U.S. government simply turned a deaf ear to their protests. It could not ignore the rumblings of revolution just over its border with Mexico, however. You will learn about this revolution in Section 4.

SECTION 3 ASSESSMENT

TERMS & NAMES 1. For each term or name, write a sentence explaining its significance.
• caudillo   • Monroe Doctrine   • José Martí   • Spanish-American War   • Panama Canal   • Roosevelt Corollary

USING YOUR NOTES	**MAIN IDEAS**	**CRITICAL THINKING & WRITING**
2. Which event do you think was most beneficial to Latin America? Why?	3. Why did the gap between rich and poor in Latin America grow after independence? 4. What economic gains and setbacks did Latin American countries experience after independence? 5. Why was the United States so interested in the security of Latin America?	6. **ANALYZING MOTIVES** Why do you think upper-class Latin Americans favored governments run by caudillos? 7. **FORMING OPINIONS** Do you think that U.S. imperialism was more beneficial or harmful to Latin American people? Explain. 8. **CONTRASTING** How was the principle of the Roosevelt Corollary different from that of the Monroe Doctrine? 9. **WRITING ACTIVITY** REVOLUTION Assume the role of a Cuban fighting for independence from Spain. Design a political **poster** that shows your feelings about the United States joining the struggle for independence.

CONNECT TO TODAY CREATING A DATAFILE
Conduct research to find statistics on the ships and cargo that travel through the Panama Canal. Use your findings to create a **datafile** for usage of the canal in a recent year.

Turmoil and Change in Mexico

MAIN IDEA	WHY IT MATTERS NOW	TERMS & NAMES
REVOLUTION Political, economic, and social inequalities in Mexico triggered a period of revolution and reform.	Mexico has moved toward political democracy and is a strong economic force in the Americas.	• Antonio López de Santa Anna • Benito Juárez • *La Reforma* • Porfirio Díaz • Francisco Madero • "Pancho" Villa • Emiliano Zapata

SETTING THE STAGE The legacy of Spanish colonialism and long-term political instability that plagued the newly emerging South American nations caused problems for Mexico as well. Mexico, however, had a further issue to contend with—a shared border with the United States. The "Colossus of the North," as the United States was known in Latin America, wanted to extend its territory all the way west to the Pacific Ocean. But most of the lands in the American Southwest belonged to Mexico.

TAKING NOTES

Comparing Use a chart to compare the major accomplishments of the Mexican leaders discussed in this section.

Leader	Major Accomplishment

Santa Anna and the Mexican War

During the early 19th century, no one dominated Mexican political life more than **Antonio López de Santa Anna**. Santa Anna played a leading role in Mexico's fight for independence from Spain in 1821. In 1829, he fought against Spain again as the European power tried to regain control of Mexico. Then, in 1833, Santa Anna became Mexico's president.

One of Latin America's most powerful caudillos, Santa Anna was a clever politician. He would support a measure one year and oppose it the next if he thought that would keep him in power. His policy seemed to work. Between 1833 and 1855, Santa Anna was Mexico's president four times. He gave up the presidency twice, however, to serve Mexico in a more urgent cause—leading the Mexican army in an effort to retain the territory of Texas.

▼ Mexican leader Santa Anna

The Texas Revolt In the 1820s, Mexico encouraged American citizens to move to the Mexican territory of Texas to help populate the country. Thousands of English-speaking colonists, or Anglos, answered the call. In return for inexpensive land, they pledged to follow the laws of Mexico. As the Anglo population grew, though, tensions developed between the colonists and Mexico over several issues, including slavery and religion. As a result, many Texas colonists wanted greater self-government. But when Mexico refused to grant this, Stephen Austin, a leading Anglo, encouraged a revolt against Mexico in 1835.

◄ Santa Anna's army met with strong resistance from the defenders of the Alamo.

Santa Anna led Mexican forces north to try to hold on to the rebellious territory. He won a few early battles, including a bitter fight at the Alamo, a mission in San Antonio. However, his fortunes changed at the Battle of San Jacinto. His troops were defeated and he was captured. Texan leader Sam Houston released Santa Anna after he promised to respect the independence of Texas. When Santa Anna returned to Mexico in 1836, he was quickly ousted from power.

War and the Fall of Santa Anna Santa Anna regained power, though, and fought against the United States again. In 1845, the United States annexed Texas. Outraged Mexicans considered this an act of aggression. In a dispute over the border, the United States invaded Mexico. Santa Anna's army fought valiantly, but U.S. troops defeated them after two years of war. In 1848, the two nations signed the Treaty of Guadalupe Hidalgo. The United States received the northern third of what was then Mexico, including California and the American Southwest. Santa Anna went into exile. He returned as dictator one final time, however, in 1853. After his final fall, in 1855, he remained in exile for almost 20 years. When he returned to Mexico in 1874, he was poor, blind, powerless, and essentially forgotten.

Juárez and *La Reforma*

During the mid-19th century, as Santa Anna's power rose and fell, a liberal reformer, **Benito Juárez** (HWAHR•ehz), strongly influenced the politics of Mexico. Juárez was Santa Anna's complete opposite in background as well as in goals. Santa Anna came from a well-off Creole family. Juárez was a poor Zapotec Indian who was orphaned at the age of three. While Santa Anna put his own personal power first, Juárez worked primarily to serve his country. **Ⓐ**

Juárez Rises to Power Ancestry and racial background were important elements of political power and economic success in 19th-century Mexico. For that reason, the rise of Benito Juárez was clearly due to his personal leadership qualities. Juárez was raised on a small farm in the Mexican state of Oaxaca. When he was 12, he moved to the city of Oaxaca. He started going to school at age 15, and in 1829, he entered a newly opened state-run university. He received a law degree in 1831.

MAIN IDEA

Contrasting

Ⓐ In what ways did Benito Juárez differ from Santa Anna?

Juárez: Symbol of Mexican Independence

In 1948, more than 75 years after Benito Juárez's death, Mexican mural painter José Clemente Orozco celebrated him in the fresco *Juárez, the Church and the Imperialists*. A portrait of Juárez, which accentuates his Indian features, dominates the work. The supporters of Emperor Maximilian, carrying his body, are shown below Juárez. To either side of Juárez, the soldiers of Mexican independence prepare to attack these representatives of imperialism. By constructing the fresco in this way, Orozco seemed to suggest that Juárez was both a symbol of hope and a rallying cry for Mexican independence.

SKILLBUILDER: Interpreting Visual Sources
1. **Contrasting** *How is Orozco's portrayal of the imperialists different from his portrayal of the forces of independence?*
2. **Drawing Conclusions** *Based on this fresco, how do you think Orozco felt about Benito Juárez?*

He then returned to the city of Oaxaca, where he opened a law office. Most of his clients were poor people who could not otherwise have afforded legal assistance. Juárez gained a reputation for honesty, integrity, hard work, and good judgment. He was elected to the city legislature and then rose steadily in power. Beginning in 1847, he served as governor of the state of Oaxaca.

Juárez Works for Reform Throughout the late 1840s and early 1850s, Juárez worked to start a liberal reform movement. He called this movement ***La Reforma***. Its major goals were redistribution of land, separation of church and state, and increased educational opportunities for the poor. In 1853, however, Santa Anna sent Juárez and other leaders of *La Reforma* into exile.

Just two years later, a rebellion against Santa Anna brought down his government. Juárez and other exiled liberal leaders returned to Mexico to deal with their country's tremendous problems. As in other Latin American nations, rich landowners kept most other Mexicans in a cycle of debt and poverty. Liberal leader Ponciano Arriaga described how these circumstances led to great problems for both poor farmers and the government:

PRIMARY SOURCE B
There are Mexican landowners who occupy . . . an extent of land greater than the areas of some of our sovereign states, greater even than that of one of several European states. In this vast area, much of which lies idle, deserted, abandoned . . . live four or five million Mexicans who know no other industry than agriculture, yet are without land or the means to work it, and who cannot emigrate in the hope of bettering their fortunes. . . . How can a hungry, naked, miserable people practice popular government? How can we proclaim the equal rights of men and leave the majority of the nation in [this condition]?

PONCIANO ARRIAGA, speech to the Constitutional Convention, 1856–1857

MAIN IDEA

Analyzing Primary Sources
B What does Ponciano Arriaga think is Mexico's greatest problem?

Not surprisingly, Arriaga's ideas and those of the other liberals in government threatened most conservative upper-class Mexicans. Many conservatives responded by launching a rebellion against the liberal government in 1858. They enjoyed some early successes in battle and seized control of Mexico City. The liberals kept up the fight from their headquarters in the city of Veracruz. Eventually the liberals gained the upper hand and, after three years of bitter civil war, they defeated the rebels. Juárez became president of the reunited country after his election in 1861.

The French Invade Mexico The end of the civil war did not bring an end to Mexico's troubles, though. Exiled conservatives plotted with some Europeans to reconquer Mexico. In 1862, French ruler Napoleon III responded by sending a large army to Mexico. Within 18 months, France had taken over the country. Napoleon appointed Austrian Archduke Maximilian to rule Mexico as emperor. Juárez and other Mexicans fought against French rule. After five years under siege, the French decided that the struggle was too costly. In 1867, Napoleon ordered the army to withdraw from Mexico. Maximilian was captured and executed.

Juárez was reelected president of Mexico in 1867. He returned to the reforms he had proposed more than ten years earlier. He began rebuilding the country, which had been shattered during years of war. He promoted trade with foreign countries, the opening of new roads, the building of railroads, and the establishment of a telegraph service. He set up a national education system separate from that run by the Catholic Church. In 1872, Juárez died of a heart attack. But after half a century of civil strife and chaos, he left his country a legacy of relative peace, progress, and reform.

Porfirio Díaz and "Order and Progress"

Juárez's era of reform did not last long, however. In the mid-1870s, a new caudillo, **Porfirio Díaz**, came to power. Like Juárez, Díaz was an Indian from Oaxaca. He rose through the army and became a noted general in the civil war and the fight against the French. Díaz expected to be rewarded with a government position for the part he played in the French defeat. Juárez refused his request, however. After this, Díaz opposed Juárez. In 1876, Díaz took control of Mexico by ousting the president. He had the support of the military, whose power had been reduced during and after the Juárez years. Indians and small landholders also supported him, because they thought he would work for more radical land reform.

During the Díaz years, elections became meaningless. Díaz offered land, power, or political favors to anyone who supported him. He terrorized many who refused to support him, ordering them to be beaten or put in jail. Using such strong-arm methods, Díaz managed to remain in power until 1911. Over the years, Díaz used a political slogan adapted from a rallying cry of the Juárez era. Juárez had called for "Liberty, Order, and Progress." Díaz, however, wanted merely "Order and Progress."

Díaz's use of dictatorial powers ensured that there was order in Mexico. But the country saw progress under Díaz too. Railroads expanded, banks were built, the currency stabilized, and foreign investment grew. Mexico seemed to be a stable, prospering country. Appearances were deceiving,

History Makers

Porfirio Díaz
1830–1915

To control all the various groups in Mexican society, Porfirio Díaz adopted an approach called *pan o palo*— "bread or the club." The "bread" he provided took many forms. To potential political opponents, he offered positions in his government. To business leaders, he gave huge subsidies or the chance to operate as monopolies in Mexico. And he won the support of the Church and wealthy landowners simply by promising not to meddle in their affairs. Those who turned down the offer of bread and continued to oppose Díaz soon felt the blow of the club. Thousands were killed, beaten, or thrown into jail.

His use of the club, Díaz admitted, was harsh and cruel—but also necessary if Mexico was to have peace. That peace, Díaz argued, enabled the country to progress economically. "If there was cruelty," he said, "results have justified it."

however. The wealthy acquired more and more land, which they did not put to good use. As a result, food costs rose steadily. Most Mexicans remained poor farmers and workers, and they continued to grow poorer. **C**

MAIN IDEA

Recognizing Effects
C What effects did Díaz's rule have on Mexico?

Revolution and Civil War

In the early 1900s, Mexicans from many walks of life began to protest Díaz's harsh rule. Idealistic liberals hungered for liberty. Farm laborers hungered for land. Workers hungered for fairer wages and better working conditions. Even some of Díaz's handpicked political allies spoke out for reform. A variety of political parties opposed to Díaz began to form. Among the most powerful was a party led by Francisco Madero.

Madero Begins the Revolution Born into one of Mexico's ten richest families, **Francisco Madero** was educated in the United States and France. He believed in democracy and wanted to strengthen its hold in Mexico. Madero announced his candidacy for president of Mexico early in 1910. Soon afterward, Díaz had him arrested. From exile in the United States, Madero called for an armed revolution against Díaz.

The Mexican Revolution began slowly. Leaders arose in different parts of Mexico and gathered their own armies. In the north, Francisco **"Pancho" Villa** became immensely popular. He had a bold Robin Hood policy of taking money from the rich and giving it to the poor. South of Mexico City, another strong, popular leader, **Emiliano Zapata**, raised a powerful revolutionary army. Like Villa, Zapata came from a poor family. He was determined to see that land was returned to peasants and small farmers. He wanted the laws reformed to protect their rights. *"Tierra y Libertad"* ("Land and Liberty") was his battle cry. Villa, Zapata, and other armed revolutionaries won important victories against Díaz's army. By the spring of 1911, Díaz agreed to step down. He called for new elections.

Mexican Leaders Struggle for Power Madero was elected president in November 1911. However, his policies were seen as too liberal by some and not revolutionary enough by others. Some of those who had supported Madero, including Villa and Zapata, took up arms against him. In 1913, realizing that he could not hold on to power, Madero resigned. The military leader General Victoriano Huerta then took over the presidency. Shortly after, Madero was assassinated, probably on Huerta's orders.

Huerta was unpopular with many people, including Villa and Zapata. These revolutionary leaders allied themselves with Venustiano Carranza, another politician who wanted to overthrow Huerta. Their three armies advanced, seizing the Mexican countryside from Huerta's forces and approaching the capital, Mexico City. They overthrew Huerta only 15 months after he took power.

Carranza took control of the government and then turned his army on his former revolutionary allies. Both Villa and Zapata continued to fight. In 1919, however, Carranza lured

History Makers

Emiliano Zapata 1879–1919

Shortly after Francisco Madero took office, he met with Emiliano Zapata, one of his leading supporters. Madero's reluctance to quickly enact real land reform angered Zapata. He left the meeting convinced that Madero was not the man to carry through the Mexican Revolution.

A few days later, Zapata issued the Plan of Ayala. This called for the removal of Madero and the appointment of a new president. The plan also demanded that the large landowners give up a third of their land for redistribution to the peasants. Zapata's rallying cry, "Land and Liberty," grew out of the Plan of Ayala.

When Venustiano Carranza ordered Zapata's assassination, he expected Zapata's revolutionary ideas on land reform to die with him. However, they lived on and were enacted by Alvaro Obregón, a follower of Zapata, who seized power from Carranza in 1920.

INTEGRATED TECHNOLOGY

INTERNET ACTIVITY Create a short biographical dictionary of leaders of the Mexican Revolution. Go to **classzone.com** for your research.

Reforms of Mexican Constitution of 1917			
Land	**Religion**	**Labor**	**Social Issues**
• Breakup of large estates • Restrictions on foreign ownership of land • Government control of resources (oil)	• State takeover of land owned by the Church	• Minimum wage for workers • Right to strike • Institution of labor unions	• Equal pay for equal work • Limited legal rights for women (spending money and bringing lawsuits)

SKILLBUILDER: Interpreting Charts
1. **Making Inferences** *Which reforms do you think landowners resented?*
2. **Recognizing Effects** *Which reforms benefited workers?*

Zapata into a trap and murdered him. With Zapata's death, the civil war also came to an end. More than a million Mexicans had lost their lives.

The New Mexican Constitution Carranza began a revision of Mexico's constitution. It was adopted in 1917. A revolutionary document, that constitution is still in effect today. As shown in the chart above, it promoted education, land reforms, and workers' rights. Carranza did not support the final version of the constitution, however, and in 1920, he was overthrown by one of his generals, Alvaro Obregón.

Although Obregón seized power violently, he did not remain a dictator. Instead, he supported the reforms the constitution called for, particularly land reform. He also promoted public education. Mexican public schools taught a common language—Spanish—and stressed nationalism. In this way, his policies helped unite the various regions and peoples of the country. Nevertheless, Obregón was assassinated in 1928. **D**

The next year, a new political party, the Institutional Revolutionary Party (PRI), arose. Although the PRI did not tolerate opposition, it initiated an ongoing period of peace and political stability in Mexico. While Mexico was struggling toward peace, however, the rest of the world was on the brink of war.

MAIN IDEA

Summarizing
D What were Obregón's accomplishments?

SECTION 4 ASSESSMENT

TERMS & NAMES 1. For each term or name, write a sentence explaining its significance.
• Antonio López de Santa Anna • Benito Juárez • *La Reforma* • Porfirio Díaz • Francisco Madero • "Pancho" Villa • Emiliano Zapata

USING YOUR NOTES

2. Which leader do you think benefited Mexico most? Why?

Leader	Major Accomplishment

MAIN IDEAS

3. In what ways was Santa Anna a typical caudillo?

4. How did Porfirio Díaz change the direction of government in Mexico?

5. How were "Pancho" Villa and Emiliano Zapata different from other Mexican revolutionary leaders?

CRITICAL THINKING & WRITING

6. **MAKING INFERENCES** Why might Benito Juárez's rise to power be considered surprising?

7. **ANALYZING CAUSES** Why did Villa and Zapata turn against Madero?

8. **SUPPORTING OPINIONS** The revision of Mexico's constitution is considered revolutionary. Do you agree with this characterization? Why or why not?

9. **WRITING ACTIVITY** REVOLUTION Juárez's motto was "Liberty, Order, and Progress." Díaz's slogan was "Order and Progress." Write an **expository essay** explaining what this difference in goals meant for the people of Mexico.

CONNECT TO TODAY **DESIGNING A CAMPAIGN POSTER**

Conduct research on the Institutional Revolutionary Party (PRI) today, particularly its political platform. Use your findings to design a **campaign poster** for the PRI in an upcoming election.

Chapter 12 Assessment

TERMS & NAMES

For each term or name below, briefly explain its connection to the changes in global power between 1800 and 1914.

1. Opium War
2. Boxer Rebellion
3. Meiji era
4. Russo-Japanese War
5. Monroe Doctrine
6. Spanish-American War
7. Benito Juárez
8. Porfirio Díaz

MAIN IDEAS

China Resists Outside Influence Section 1 (pages 371–375)

9. Why was China traditionally not interested in trading with the West?

10. Although Guangxu's effort at reform failed, what changes did it finally set in motion?

Modernization in Japan Section 2 (pages 376–381)

11. What events caused Japan to end its isolation and begin to westernize?

12. What were the results of Japan's growing imperialism at the end of the 19th century?

U.S. Economic Imperialism Section 3 (pages 382–387)

13. How were Latin American caudillos able to achieve power and hold on to it?

14. What effects did the Monroe Doctrine and the Roosevelt Corollary have on Latin America?

Turmoil and Change in Mexico Section 4 (pages 388–393)

15. What were the major causes of tension between the Mexicans and the American colonists who settled in Texas?

16. What roles did Francisco "Pancho" Villa and Emiliano Zapata play in the Mexican Revolution?

CRITICAL THINKING

1. USING YOUR NOTES

On a time line, indicate the major events of Santa Anna's military and political career in Mexico. Why do you think he was able to remain in power for so long?

Fights for independence from Spain

1820s

2. MAKING INFERENCES

Do you think that Emperor Guangxu would have been able to put his reforms into practice if the Dowager Empress Cixi had not intervened? Why or why not?

3. COMPARING

CULTURAL INTERACTION How do Japan's efforts at westernization in the late 1800s compare with Japan's cultural borrowing of earlier times?

4. EVALUATING COURSES OF ACTION

REVOLUTION Consider what you have learned in this and other chapters about Latin American colonial history and about how countries undergo change. What are the pros and cons of using both military strategies and peaceful political means to improve a country's economic, social, and political conditions?

VISUAL SUMMARY

Transformations Around the Globe

FOREIGN INFLUENCE

China

- Fails to prevent Britain from pursuing illegal opium trade
- Deals with internal unrest during almost two decades of Taiping Rebellion
- Attempts to build self-sufficiency during 1860s in self-strengthening movement
- Violently opposes foreigners in 1900 Boxer Rebellion
- Begins to establish constitutional government in 1908

Japan

- Signs 1854 Treaty of Kanagawa, opening Japanese ports to foreign trade
- Modernizes based on Western models during Meiji era (1867–1912)
- Fights 1894 Sino-Japanese War to control Korea
- Wages 1904 Russo-Japanese War to control Manchuria
- Annexes Korea in 1910

Latin America

- Depends on exports to fuel economy
- Receives much foreign investment
- Gains U.S. military support in 1898 Spanish-American War
- Becomes crossroads of world trade when U.S. completes Panama Canal in 1914

Mexico

- Fights to hold Texas territory from U.S. colonialism (1835–1845)
- Tries to establish a national identity in the early 1850s under Benito Juárez's *La Reforma*
- Overcomes French occupation in 1867
- Stages the Mexican Revolution in 1910

Use the excerpt—which deals with changes made during the Meiji era in Japan—and your knowledge of world history to answer questions 1 and 2.
Additional Test Practice, pp. S1–S33

PRIMARY SOURCE

In the second and third years of Meiji, the demand for foreign goods remarkably increased. Those who formerly looked upon them with contempt changed their minds and even dressed in foreign clothes. Our males adopted the European style. They put on fine tall hats instead of wearing large [queues] on their heads, and took to carrying sticks after discarding their swords. They dressed in coats of the English fashion and trousers of the American. They would only eat from tables and nothing would satisfy them but French cookery.

Tokyo Times, 1877

1. According to the excerpt, what happened in the second and third years of Meiji?

   A. The Japanese ate only English food.

   B. The Japanese wore only Japanese clothes.

   C. The demand for foreign goods increased.

   D. The demand for Japanese goods decreased.

2. Which statement best sums up the way the writer feels about the Japanese adoption of foreign ways?

   A. The writer expresses no opinion of the matter.

   B. The writer chooses to reserve judgment until a later date.

   C. The writer feels that it is a good thing for Japan.

   D. The writer feels that it is a bad thing for Japan.

Use the graph and your knowledge of world history to answer question 3.

Tolls Collected on the Panama Canal, 1916–1920

*Canal closed for about seven months because of rock slides.

Source: *Historical Statistics of the United States*

Tolls Collected

3. In which year did tolls collected on the Panama Canal first exceed $6 million?

   A. 1917   **C.** 1919

   B. 1918   **D.** 1920

INTEGRATED TECHNOLOGY

TEST PRACTICE Go to **classzone.com**

- Diagnostic tests   • Strategies
- Tutorials   • Additional practice

ALTERNATIVE ASSESSMENT

1. Interact *with* History

On page 370, you considered whether you would seek out or resist foreign influence. Now that you have learned how several countries dealt with foreign influence and what the results were, would you change your recommendation? Discuss your ideas in a small group.

2. WRITING ABOUT HISTORY

EMPIRE BUILDING Write a **dialogue** that might have taken place between a conservative member of the Dowager Empress Cixi's court and an official in Emperor Mutsuhito's Meiji government. In the dialogue, have the characters discuss

- the kinds of foreign intervention their countries faced
- the actions their leaders took to deal with this foreign intervention

---

INTEGRATED TECHNOLOGY

Planning a Television News Special

On May 5, 1862, badly outnumbered Mexican forces defeated the French at the Battle of Puebla. Mexicans still celebrate their country's triumph on the holiday Cinco de Mayo. Working in a group with two other students, plan a television news special on how Cinco de Mayo is celebrated by Mexicans today. Focus on celebrations in Mexico or in Mexican communities in cities in the United States. Consider including

- information on the Battle of Puebla
- an explanation of how and why Cinco de Mayo became a national holiday
- images of any special activities or traditions that have become part of the celebration
- interviews with participants discussing how they feel about Cinco de Mayo

A Period of Change

The period from 1700 to 1914 was a time of tremendous scientific and technological change. The great number of discoveries and inventions in Europe and the United States promoted economic, social, and cultural changes. Use the information on these six pages to study the impact of scientific and technological changes.

▲ Spinning Jenny
Using James Hargreaves's invention, a spinner could turn several spindles with one wheel and produce many threads. Machine-made thread was weak, so it was used only for the horizontal threads of fabric.

Theory of Atoms
John Dalton theorized that atoms are the basic parts of elements and that each type of atom has a specific weight. He was one of the founders of atomic chemistry.

▲ Steamboat
Robert Fulton held the first commercially successful steamboat run. One advan-tage of a steamboat was that it could travel against a river's current. These boats soon began to travel rivers around the world.

| 1733 | 1764 | 1785 | 1803 | 1807 | 1830 |

Flying Shuttle
A shuttle is a holder that carries horizontal threads back and forth between the vertical threads in weaving. John Kay's mechanical flying shuttle enabled one weaver to do the work of two.

Power Loom
Edmund Cartwright created the first water-powered loom. Others later improved on the speed and efficiency of looms and the quality of the fabrics.

▼ Steam Locomotive
In 1830, the first steam locomotive was put into operation in the United States. Besides passengers, locomotives could rapidly transport tons of raw materials from mines to factories, and manufactured goods from factories to consumers and ports.

Panama Canal

The Panama Canal shortened trips between the Atlantic and Pacific oceans by thousands of miles since ships no longer had to go around South America.

◄ Radioactivity

Marie Curie won the Nobel prize in chemistry for her (and her late husband's) discovery of the elements polonium and radium. Their work paved the way for later discoveries in nuclear physics and chemistry.

Antiseptics

Joseph Lister pioneered the use of carbolic acid to kill bacteria in operating rooms and later directly in wounds. The rate of death by infection after surgery dropped from about 50 to 15 percent.

Radio

Guglielmo Marconi's radio sent Morse code messages by electromagnetic waves that traveled through the air. It enabled rapid communication between distant places.

| 1865 | 1876 | 1879 | 1895 | 1903 | 1908 | 1911 | 1914 |

▼ Telephone

Alexander Graham Bell produced the first instrument that successfully carried the sounds of speech over electric wires. The telephone's design underwent a number of changes in its early years.

Airplane

The Wright brothers built the first machine-powered aircraft, which burned gasoline. The edge of the wing was adjusted during flight to steer.

Model T Ford

By using a moving assembly line, Henry Ford produced an automobile that working people could afford to buy.

Light Bulb

The light bulb that Thomas A. Edison and his staff made was first used in businesses and public buildings that installed small lighting plants. Cities slowly built the electrical systems needed to power lights.

Comparing & Contrasting

1. How were the steamboat and the locomotive similar in their impact?
2. How did the scientific theory of John Dalton differ from Joseph Lister's discovery in terms of its impact on daily life?

Impact of Technological Change

Use the charts below, and the documents and photograph on the next page, to learn about some of the great changes technology produced.

Technological Change

Industrialization

Economic Change	Social Change	Culture Change
• Productivity increased, which led to an economic boom. • Cheaper goods became available. • A middle class emerged. • Industries searched for overseas resources and markets, encouraging imperialism. • Colonial economies were shaped to benefit Europe.	• Cities grew at a rapid pace. • Poor working and living conditions led to social unrest. • Diseases spread in slums. • Unions formed to protect workers. • Laws were passed to improve working conditions. • Immigration to North America increased.	• Businesses needed engineers, professionals, and clerical workers, so education was emphasized. • The spread of public education increased literacy. • The publishing industry grew; book and magazine sales boomed. • Reform movements arose in response to unfair conditions.

Inventions/Progress

Economic Change	Social Change	Culture Change
• Large machines led to the development of factories. • Steamboats, canals, paved roads, and railroads opened travel to the interior of continents and reduced transportation costs. • Investors formed corporations to undertake large projects. • Superior arms and transport helped Europeans colonize. • Inventions such as the telephone and electric light helped business grow.	• Steamboats and railroads made travel cheaper and easier. • The telegraph, telephone, and radio aided communication. • Convenience products like canned food and ready-made clothes made daily life easier. • The assembly line made products like cars affordable for many. • Fewer workers were needed to produce the same amount of goods. Some workers lost jobs.	• People placed increasing emphasis on making homes more comfortable and convenient. • Improvements in one aspect of agriculture and manufacturing promoted the creation of new inventions to improve other aspects. • Mass culture grew through the availability of phonographs and movies, and an increase in leisure time.

SKILLBUILDER: Interpreting Charts

1. **Synthesizing** *How might limiting working hours for children promote literacy?*
2. **Analyzing Motives** *Why would Europeans build transportation and communication networks in their colonies?*

Child Workers in Textile Factory

Many jobs did not require skilled workers, so children were hired to do them because they could be paid lower wages than adults. Some industries also hired children because their small fingers could fit between the machinery or handle fine parts more easily than adult fingers could.

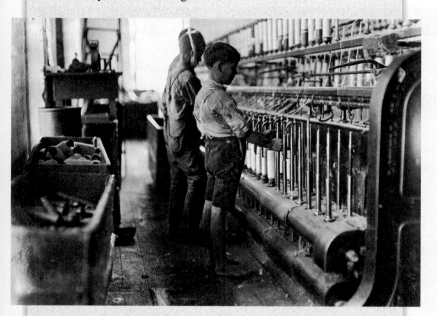

DOCUMENT-BASED QUESTION
Judging by the children's appearance, how generous were the wages they received? Explain your answer.

INTER**ACTIVE**

Impact of the Telephone

In this excerpt from "Thirty Years of the Telephone," published in September 1906, John Vaughn discussed how Bell's invention affected life in the United States.

Various industries, unknown thirty years ago, but now sources of employment to many thousands of workers, depend entirely on the telephone for support. . . . The Bell Companies employ over 87,000 persons, and it may be added, pay them well. . . . These figures may be supplemented by the number of telephones in use (5,698,000), by the number of miles of wire (6,043,000) in the Bell lines, and by the number of conversations (4,479,500,000) electrically conveyed in 1905. The network of wire connects more than 33,000 cities, towns, villages, and hamlets.

DOCUMENT-BASED QUESTION
What were some of the effects of the invention of the telephone?

INTER**ACTIVE**

How Technology Aided Imperialism

In this excerpt from the book *Guns, Germs, and Steel*, Jared Diamond related an incident to show how technology helped Europeans conquer other lands.

In 1808 a British sailor named Charlie Savage equipped with muskets and excellent aim arrived in the Fiji Islands. [He] proceeded single-handedly to upset Fiji's balance of power. Among his many exploits, he paddled his canoe up a river to the Fijian village of Kasavu, halted less than a pistol shot's length from the village fence, and fired away at the undefended inhabitants. His victims were so numerous that . . . the stream beside the village was red with blood. Such examples of the power of guns against native peoples lacking guns could be multiplied indefinitely.

DOCUMENT-BASED QUESTION
How did guns give Europeans an advantage over native peoples?

Comparing & Contrasting

1. Reread the passage by John Vaughn and then compare it with the information on the chart. What could you add to the chart based on this passage?

2. Does the photograph of factory workers confirm or contradict the information on the chart? Explain.

Impact of Scientific Change

Many scientific discoveries resulted in practical applications that affected daily life. Other discoveries increased our understanding of the way the universe works. Use the information on these two pages to explore the impact of scientific change.

Scientific Change

Economic Change

- Discovery of quinine as a malaria treatment helped people colonize tropical areas.
- Control of diseases like yellow fever and bubonic plague enabled the Panama Canal to be built.
- More accurate clocks and new astronomical discoveries led to safer navigation, which improved shipping.
- Study of electricity and magnetism led to the invention of the dynamo and motor, which aided industry.

Social Change

- Vulcanized rubber was used for raincoats and car tires.
- Discoveries about air, gases, and temperature resulted in better weather forecasting.
- Vaccines and treatments were found for illnesses like diphtheria and heart disease; X-rays and other new medical techniques were developed.
- Plumbing and sewers improved sanitation and public health.
- Psychiatry improved the treatment of mental illness.

Culture Change

- Many scientific and technical schools were founded; governments began funding scientific research.
- Psychological discoveries began to be applied to the social sciences, such as sociology and anthropology.
- Some painters and writers created work that reflected the new psychological ideas.
- Social Darwinism, the idea that some people were more "fit" than others, was used to justify racism.

SKILLBUILDER: Interpreting Charts

1. **Drawing Conclusions** *How do you think such advances in public health as vaccinations and sanitation services affected the lives of ordinary people?*
2. **Analyzing Bias** *Who would be more likely to accept the idea of social Darwinism— a European colonizer or an African in a colony? Why?*

PRIMARY SOURCE

Chloroform Machine

The person with the mask is receiving the anesthetic chloroform. By removing pain, anesthetics enabled doctors to perform procedures—such as surgery—that would have been difficult for the patient to endure.

DOCUMENT-BASED QUESTION
How did practical inventions, like the chloroform machine, contribute to medicine and other sciences?

Smallpox Vaccination

This newspaper engraving shows a Board of Health doctor administering the smallpox vaccine to poor people at a police station in New York City.

DOCUMENT-BASED QUESTION
Why would public health officials especially want to carry out vaccination programs in poor neighborhoods?

INTERACTIVE

Impact of Scientific Research

This passage from *The Birth of the Modern* by Paul Johnson discusses the far-reaching results of Michael Faraday's experiments with electromagnetism in the 1820s.

[By 1831, Faraday] had not only the first electric motor, but, in essence, the first dynamo: He could generate power. . . . What was remarkable about his work between 1820 and 1831 was that by showing exactly how mechanical could be transformed into electrical power, he made the jump between theoretical research and its practical application a comparatively narrow one. The electrical industry was the direct result of his work, and its first product, the electric telegraph, was soon in use. The idea of cause and effect was of great importance, for both industry and governments now began to appreciate the value of fundamental research and to finance it.

DOCUMENT-BASED QUESTION
How did Faraday's work affect society in the long term?

Comparing & Contrasting

1. In your opinion, was there more economic progress or social progress during the period 1700 to 1914? Use information from the charts on pages 398 and 400 to support your answer.

2. Consider the impact of medical advances and the idea of Social Darwinism on imperialism. How were their impacts alike?

EXTENSION ACTIVITY
Research a more recent scientific or technological change, such as the development of computer chips, plastics, the Internet, or space travel. Make a chart like the one shown on page 400 listing the economic, social, and cultural changes that have resulted.

The World at War
1900–1945

World War I was characterized by long, bloody battles. This painting by François Flameng shows one such engagement. French soldiers attempt to cross the River Yser in Belgium on pontoon bridges.

Comparing & Contrasting

The Changing Nature of Warfare
In Unit 4, you will learn about the changing nature of warfare in the 20th century. At the end of the unit, you will have a chance to compare and contrast different aspects of the wars you studied. (See pages 520–525.)

The Great War, 1914–1918

Previewing Main Ideas

SCIENCE AND TECHNOLOGY Advances in weaponry, from improvements to the machine gun and airplane, to the invention of the tank, led to mass devastation during World War I.

Geography *Which Allied nation could the Central Powers invade only by airplane?*

ECONOMICS The war affected many European economies. Desperate for resources, the warring governments converted many industries to munitions factories. They also took greater control of the production of goods.

Geography *According to the map, why might Russia have struggled to obtain resources from its allies?*

POWER AND AUTHORITY The quest among European nations for greater power played a role in causing World War I. By the turn of the 20th century, relations among these countries had grown increasingly tense.

Geography *Which alliance may have had the greater challenge, given the geography of the conflict? Why?*

INTEGRATED TECHNOLOGY

eEdition
• Interactive Maps
• Interactive Visuals
• Interactive Primary Sources

INTERNET RESOURCES
Go to **classzone.com** for:
• Research Links   • Maps
• Internet Activities • Test Practice
• Primary Sources   • Current Events
• Chapter Quiz

EUROPE

1914
World War I begins as Austria declares war on Serbia.

1915
◀ A World War I soldier readies for battle on the Western Front.

1914

1915

WORLD

1914
U.S.-built Panama Canal opens for operation.

May 1915
◀ German forces sink the British ship *Lusitania.*

Europe, 1914

Central Powers
Allied Powers
Nations neutral or not yet aligned

NORWAY

SWEDEN

Petrograd (St. Petersburg)

North Sea

DENMARK

Baltic Sea

RUSSIA

UNITED KINGDOM

Ireland

Great Britain

London

NETHERLANDS

Amsterdam

Berlin

Warsaw

GERMANY

ATLANTIC OCEAN

Brussels

BELGIUM

LUXEMBOURG

Elbe R.

Vistula R.

Somme R.

Marne R.

Verdun

Versailles

Paris

Meuse R.

Rhine R.

Danube R.

Limanowa

Vienna

FRANCE

SWITZ.

AUSTRIA-HUNGARY

45°N

15°W

PORTUGAL

Lisbon

Madrid

SPAIN

Rome

ITALY

Adriatic Sea

Bosnia and Herzegovina

Sarajevo

MONTENEGRO

ALBANIA

SERBIA

ROMANIA

Bucharest

BULGARIA

Black Sea

Constantinople

Gallipoli

Dardanelles

GREECE

Athens

OTTOMAN EMPIRE

15°E

Mediterranean Sea

0   200   400 Miles
0   200   400 Kilometers
Conic Projection

1916
French and Germans engage in battle at Verdun.

1917
U.S. war poster encourages enlistment as America enters war.

I WANT YOU FOR U.S. ARMY
NEAREST RECRUITING STATION

1918
Armistice signed as Allies defeat Central Powers.

1916

1917

1918

1916
U.S. President Woodrow Wilson wins reelection. ▶

1917
Communists seize power in Russian Revolution.

1918
◀ U.S. worker guards against deadly flu that kills millions worldwide.

Should you always support an ally?

World War I has begun. You are the leader of a European country and must decide what to do. Your nation is one of several that have agreed to support each other in the event of war. Some of your allies already have joined the fight. You oppose the thought of war and fear that joining will lead to even more lives lost. Yet, you believe in being loyal to your allies. You also worry that your rivals want to conquer all of Europe—and if you don't join the war now, your country may end up having to defend itself.

▲ A World War I poster urges nations to come to the aid of Serbia.

EXAMINING *the* ISSUES

- **Should you always support a friend, no matter what he or she does?**

- **What might be the long-term consequences of refusing to help an ally?**

As a class, discuss these questions. In your discussion, consider the various reasons countries go to war. As you read about World War I in this chapter, see what factors influenced the decisions of each nation.

Marching Toward War

MAIN IDEA	WHY IT MATTERS NOW	TERMS & NAMES
POWER AND AUTHORITY In Europe, military buildup, nationalistic feelings, and rival alliances set the stage for a continental war.	Ethnic conflict in the Balkan region, which helped start the war, continued to erupt in that area in the 1990s.	• militarism • Triple Alliance • Kaiser Wilhelm II • Triple Entente

SETTING THE STAGE At the turn of the 20th century, the nations of Europe had been largely at peace with one another for nearly 30 years. This was no accident. Efforts to outlaw war and achieve a permanent peace had been gaining momentum in Europe since the middle of the 19th century. By 1900, hundreds of peace organizations were active. In addition, peace congresses convened regularly between 1843 and 1907. Some Europeans believed that progress had made war a thing of the past. Yet in a little more than a decade, a massive war would engulf Europe and spread across the globe.

Rising Tensions in Europe

While peace and harmony characterized much of Europe at the beginning of the 1900s, there were less visible—and darker—forces at work as well. Below the surface of peace and goodwill, Europe witnessed several gradual developments that would ultimately help propel the continent into war.

The Rise of Nationalism One such development was the growth of nationalism, or a deep devotion to one's nation. Nationalism can serve as a unifying force within a country. However, it also can cause intense competition among nations, with each seeking to overpower the other. By the turn of the 20th century, a fierce rivalry indeed had developed among Europe's Great Powers. Those nations were Germany, Austria-Hungary, Great Britain, Russia, Italy, and France.

This increasing rivalry among European nations stemmed from several sources. Competition for materials and markets was one. Territorial disputes were another. France, for example, had never gotten over the loss of Alsace-Lorraine to Germany in the Franco-Prussian War (1870). Austria-Hungary and Russia both tried to dominate in the Balkans, a region in southeast Europe. Within the Balkans, the intense nationalism of Serbs, Bulgarians, Romanians, and other ethnic groups led to demands for independence.

Imperialism and Militarism Another force that helped set the stage for war in Europe was imperialism. As Chapter 11 explained, the nations of Europe competed fiercely for colonies in Africa and Asia. The quest for colonies sometimes pushed European nations to the brink of war. As European countries continued to compete for overseas empires, their sense of rivalry and mistrust of one another deepened.

TAKING NOTES

Summarizing Create a time line of major events that led to the start of World War I.

event one	event three
event two	event four

Yet another troubling development throughout the early years of the 20th century was the rise of a dangerous European arms race. The nations of Europe believed that to be truly great, they needed to have a powerful military. By 1914, all the Great Powers except Britain had large standing armies. In addition, military experts stressed the importance of being able to quickly mobilize, or organize and move troops in case of a war. Generals in each country developed highly detailed plans for such a mobilization.

The policy of glorifying military power and keeping an army prepared for war was known as **militarism**. Having a large and strong standing army made citizens feel patriotic. However, it also frightened some people. As early as 1895, Frédéric Passy, a prominent peace activist, expressed a concern that many shared:

PRIMARY SOURCE

The entire able-bodied population are preparing to massacre one another; though no one, it is true, wants to attack, and everybody protests his love of peace and determination to maintain it, yet the whole world feels that it only requires some unforeseen incident, some unpreventable accident, for the spark to fall in a flash . . . and blow all Europe sky-high.

FRÉDÉRIC PASSY, quoted in *Nobel: The Man and His Prizes*

History Makers

Kaiser Wilhelm II
1859–1941

Wilhelm II was related to the leaders of two nations he eventually would engage in war. Wilhelm, George V of Great Britain, and Nicholas II of Russia were all cousins.

The kaiser thought a great deal of himself and his place in history. Once, when a doctor told him he had a small cold, Wilhelm reportedly responded, "No, it is a big cold. Everything about me must be big."

He also could be sly and deceitful. After forcing the popular Bismarck to resign, Wilhelm pretended to be upset. Most people, however, including Bismarck, were not fooled.

INTEGRATED / TECHNOLOGY

RESEARCH LINKS For more on Wilhelm II, go to **classzone.com**

Tangled Alliances

Growing rivalries and mutual mistrust had led to the creation of several military alliances among the Great Powers as early as the 1870s. This alliance system had been designed to keep peace in Europe. But it would instead help push the continent into war.

Bismarck Forges Early Pacts Between 1864 and 1871, Prussia's blood-and-iron chancellor, Otto von Bismarck, freely used war to unify Germany. After 1871, however, Bismarck declared Germany to be a "satisfied power." He then turned his energies to maintaining peace in Europe.

Bismarck saw France as the greatest threat to peace. He believed that France still wanted revenge for its defeat in the Franco-Prussian War. Bismarck's first goal, therefore, was to isolate France. "As long as it is without allies," Bismarck stressed, "France poses no danger to us." In 1879, Bismarck formed the Dual Alliance between Germany and Austria-Hungary. Three years later, Italy joined the two countries, forming the **Triple Alliance**. In 1881, Bismarck took yet another possible ally away from France by making a treaty with Russia.

Shifting Alliances Threaten Peace In 1890, Germany's foreign policy changed dramatically. That year, **Kaiser Wilhelm II**—who two years earlier had become ruler of Germany—forced Bismarck to resign. A proud and stubborn man, Wilhelm II did not wish to share power with anyone. Besides wanting to assert his own power, the new kaiser was eager to show the world just how mighty Germany had become. The army was his greatest pride. "I and the army were born for one another," Wilhelm declared shortly after taking power.

Wilhelm let his nation's treaty with Russia lapse in 1890. Russia responded by forming a defensive military alliance with France in 1892 and 1894. Such an alliance had been Bismarck's fear. War with either Russia or France would make Germany the enemy of both. Germany would then be forced to fight a two-front war, or a war on both its eastern and western borders.

Next, Wilhelm began a tremendous shipbuilding program in an effort to make the German navy equal to that of the mighty British fleet. Alarmed, Great Britain formed an entente, or alliance, with France. In 1907, Britain made another entente, this time with both France and Russia. The **Triple Entente**, as it was called, did not bind Britain to fight with France and Russia. However, it did almost certainly ensure that Britain would not fight against them.

By 1907, two rival camps existed in Europe. On one side was the Triple Alliance—Germany, Austria-Hungary, and Italy. On the other side was the Triple Entente—Great Britain, France, and Russia. A dispute between two rival powers could draw all the nations of Europe into war.

Crisis in the Balkans

Nowhere was that dispute more likely to occur than on the Balkan Peninsula. This mountainous peninsula in the southeastern corner of Europe was home to an assortment of ethnic groups. With a long history of nationalist uprisings and ethnic clashes, the Balkans was known as the "powder keg" of Europe.

A Restless Region By the early 1900s, the Ottoman Empire, which included the Balkan region, was in rapid decline. While some Balkan groups struggled to free themselves from the Ottoman Turks, others already had succeeded in breaking away from their Turkish rulers. These peoples had formed new nations, including Bulgaria, Greece, Montenegro, Romania, and Serbia.

Nationalism was a powerful force in these countries. Each group longed to extend its borders. Serbia, for example, had a large Slavic population. It hoped to absorb all the Slavs on the Balkan Peninsula. Russia, itself a mostly Slavic nation, supported Serbian nationalism. However, Serbia's powerful northern neighbor, Austria-Hungary, opposed such an effort. Austria feared that efforts to create a Slavic state would stir rebellion among its Slavic population.

In 1908, Austria annexed, or took over, Bosnia and Herzegovina. These were two Balkan areas with large Slavic populations. Serbian leaders, who had sought to rule these provinces, were outraged. In the years that followed, tensions between Serbia and Austria steadily rose. The Serbs continually vowed to take Bosnia and Herzegovina away from Austria. In response, Austria-Hungary vowed to crush any Serbian effort to undermine its authority in the Balkans. Ⓐ

MAIN IDEA

Analyzing Issues
Ⓐ What were the reasons for the hostility between Austria-Hungary and Serbia?

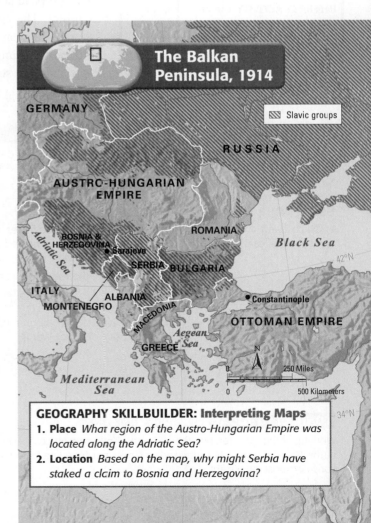

The Balkan Peninsula, 1914

Slavic groups

GERMANY

RUSSIA

AUSTRO-HUNGARIAN EMPIRE

BOSNIA & HERZEGOVINA
• Sarajevo

ROMANIA

Black Sea

42°N

Adriatic Sea

SERBIA
BULGARIA

ITALY
MONTENEGRO
ALBANIA
MACEDONIA

• Constantinople

OTTOMAN EMPIRE

Aegean Sea
GREECE

Mediterranean Sea

0   250 Miles

0   500 Kilometers

34°N

GEOGRAPHY SKILLBUILDER: Interpreting Maps
1. **Place** What region of the Austro-Hungarian Empire was located along the Adriatic Sea?
2. **Location** Based on the map, why might Serbia have staked a claim to Bosnia and Herzegovina?

History *in* Depth

The Armenian Massacre

One group in southeastern Europe that suffered greatly for its independence efforts was the Armenians. By the 1880s, the roughly 2.5 million Armenians in the Ottoman Empire had begun to demand their freedom. As a result, relations between the group and its Turkish rulers grew strained.

Throughout the 1890s, Turkish troops killed tens of thousands of Armenians. When World War I erupted in 1914, the Armenians pledged their support to the Turks' enemies. In response, the Turkish government deported nearly 2 million Armenians. Along the way, more than 600,000 died of starvation or were killed by Turkish soldiers.

INTEGRATED / TECHNOLOGY

INTERNET ACTIVITY Create a chart or graphic about any aspect of modern Armenian culture. Go to **classzone.com** for your research.

A Shot Rings Throughout Europe Into this poisoned atmosphere of mutual dislike and mistrust stepped the heir to the Austro-Hungarian throne, Archduke Franz Ferdinand, and his wife, Sophie. On June 28, 1914, the couple paid a state visit to Sarajevo, the capital of Bosnia. It would be their last. The royal pair was shot at point-blank range as they rode through the streets of Sarajevo in an open car. The killer was Gavrilo Princip, a 19-year-old Serbian and member of the Black Hand. The Black Hand was a secret society committed to ridding Bosnia of Austrian rule.

Because the assassin was a Serbian, Austria decided to use the murders as an excuse to punish Serbia. On July 23, Austria presented Serbia with an ultimatum containing numerous demands. Serbia knew that refusing the ultimatum would lead to war against the more powerful Austria. Therefore, Serbian leaders agreed to most of Austria's demands. They offered to have several others settled by an international conference.

Austria, however, was in no mood to negotiate. The nation's leaders, it seemed, had already settled on war. On July 28, Austria rejected Serbia's offer and declared war. That same day, Russia, an ally of Serbia with its largely Slavic population, took action. Russian leaders ordered the mobilization of troops toward the Austrian border.

Leaders all over Europe suddenly took notice. The fragile European stability seemed ready to collapse into armed conflict. The British foreign minister, the Italian government, and even Kaiser Wilhelm himself urged Austria and Russia to negotiate. But it was too late. The machinery of war had been set in motion.

Vocabulary
An *ultimatum* is a list of demands that, if not met, will lead to serious consequences.

SECTION 1 ASSESSMENT

TERMS & NAMES **1.** For each term or name, write a sentence explaining its significance.
- militarism
- Triple Alliance
- Kaiser Wilhelm II
- Triple Entente

USING YOUR NOTES

2. Which event do you consider most significant? Why?

MAIN IDEAS

3. What were the three forces at work in Europe that helped set the stage for war?

4. Who were the members of the Triple Alliance? the Triple Entente?

5. What single event set in motion the start of World War I?

CRITICAL THINKING & WRITING

6. ANALYZING CAUSES Which of the forces at work in Europe played the greatest role in helping to prompt the outbreak of war?

7. ANALYZING ISSUES Was the description of the Balkans as the "powder keg" of Europe justified? Explain.

8. FORMING AND SUPPORTING OPINIONS Do you think World War I was avoidable? Use information from the text to support your answer.

9. WRITING ACTIVITY [POWER AND AUTHORITY] Write a brief **letter to the editor** of a European newspaper expressing what your views might have been about the coming war.

CONNECT TO TODAY **CREATING A TIME LINE**

Working with a partner, use the library and other resources to create a **time line** of key events in the Balkans from 1914 until today. Limit your time line to the six to eight events you consider most significant.

2

Europe Plunges into War

MAIN IDEA	WHY IT MATTERS NOW	TERMS & NAMES
SCIENCE AND TECHNOLOGY One European nation after another was drawn into a large and industrialized war that resulted in many casualties.	Much of the technology of modern warfare, such as fighter planes and tanks, was introduced in World War I.	• Central Powers • Allies • Western Front • Schlieffen Plan • trench warfare • Eastern Front

SETTING THE STAGE By 1914, Europe was divided into two rival camps. One alliance, the Triple Entente, included Great Britain, France, and Russia. The other, known as the Triple Alliance, included Germany, Austria-Hungary, and Italy. Austria-Hungary's declaration of war against Serbia set off a chain reaction within the alliance system. The countries of Europe followed through on their pledges to support one another. As a result, nearly all of Europe soon joined what would be the largest, most destructive war the world had yet seen.

The Great War Begins

In response to Austria's declaration of war, Russia, Serbia's ally, began moving its army toward the Russian-Austrian border. Expecting Germany to join Austria, Russia also mobilized along the German border. To Germany, Russia's mobilization amounted to a declaration of war. On August 1, the German government declared war on Russia.

Russia looked to its ally France for help. Germany, however, did not even wait for France to react. Two days after declaring war on Russia, Germany also declared war on France. Soon afterward, Great Britain declared war on Germany. Much of Europe was now locked in battle.

Nations Take Sides By mid-August 1914, the battle lines were clearly drawn. On one side were Germany and Austria-Hungary. They were known as the **Central Powers** because of their location in the heart of Europe. Bulgaria and the Ottoman Empire would later join the Central Powers in the hopes of regaining lost territories.

On the other side were Great Britain, France, and Russia. Together, they were known as the Allied Powers or the **Allies**. Japan joined the Allies within weeks. Italy joined later. Italy had been a member of the Triple Alliance with Germany and Austria-Hungary. However, the Italians joined the other side after accusing their former partners of unjustly starting the war.

In the late summer of 1914, millions of soldiers marched happily off to battle, convinced that the war would be short. Only a few people foresaw the horror ahead. One of them was Britain's foreign minister, Sir Edward Grey. Staring out over London at nightfall, Grey said sadly to a friend, "The lamps are going out all over Europe. We shall not see them lit again in our lifetime."

TAKING NOTES

Outlining Use an outline to organize main ideas and details.

> I. The Great War
>   Begins
>   A.
>   B.
> II. A Bloody Stalemate

Legend:
- Allied countries
- Central Powers
- Neutral countries
- ⇐ Central Powers advance
- ← Allied advance
- Farthest Central Powers advance
- Farthest Allied advance
- ✳ Central Powers victory
- ✷ Allied victory
- Armistice Line, Nov. 1918

Map labels: SWEDEN, DENMARK, GREAT BRITAIN, London, North Sea, Baltic Sea, RUSSIA, Treaty of Brest-Litovsk March, 1918, Dec. 1917, Masurian Lakes, Sep. 1914, EAST PRUSSIA, Tannenberg, Aug. 1914, NETH., Berlin, GERMANY, Ypres, Nov. 1914, Somme, July 1916, BELGIUM, Rhine R., Lodz, Nov. 1914, Amiens, Aug. 1918, LUX., Paris, Kovel, June 1916, 1st Marne, Sept. 1914, 2nd Marne, July 1918, Verdun, Feb. 1916, Limanowa, Dec. 1914, Kerensky Offensive, July 1917, ATLANTIC OCEAN, Loire R., Galicia, May 1915, FRANCE, SWITZ., 1916, Vienna, AUSTRIA-HUNGARY, Czernowitz, June 1916, Milan, Caporetto, Oct. 1917, Po R., 1917, 1916, Madrid, ITALY, Rome, MONTENEGRO, SERBIA, ROMANIA, Danube R., BULGARIA, Black Sea, 1918, 1916, SPAIN, ALBANIA, GREECE, Gallipoli, Feb. 1915, Jan. 1916, OTTOMAN EMPIRE

Scale: 0 – 400 Miles / 0 – 800 Kilometers

GEOGRAPHY SKILLBUILDER: Interpreting Maps
1. **Location** *In which country was almost all of the war in the West fought?*
2. **Location** *What geographic disadvantage did Germany and Austria-Hungary face in fighting the war? How might this have affected their war strategy?*

A Bloody Stalemate

It did not take long for Sir Edward Grey's prediction to ring true. As the summer of 1914 turned to fall, the war turned into a long and bloody stalemate, or deadlock, along the battlefields of France. This deadlocked region in northern France became known as the **Western Front**.

The Conflict Grinds Along Facing a war on two fronts, Germany had developed a battle strategy known as the **Schlieffen Plan**, named after its designer, General Alfred Graf von Schlieffen (SHLEE•fuhn). The plan called for attacking and defeating France in the west and then rushing east to fight Russia. The Germans felt they could carry out such a plan because Russia lagged behind the rest of Europe in its railroad system and thus would take longer to supply its front lines. Nonetheless, speed was vital to the Schlieffen Plan. German leaders knew they needed to win a quick victory over France.

Early on, it appeared that Germany would do just that. By early September, German forces had swept into France and reached the outskirts of Paris. A major German victory appeared just days away. On September 5, however, the Allies regrouped and attacked the Germans northeast of Paris, in the valley of the Marne River. Every available soldier was hurled into the struggle. When reinforcements were needed, more than 600 taxicabs rushed soldiers from Paris to the front. After four days of fighting, the German generals gave the order to retreat.

Although it was only the first major clash on the Western Front, the First Battle of the Marne was perhaps the single most important event of the war. The defeat of the Germans left the Schlieffen Plan in ruins. A quick victory in the west no longer seemed possible. In the east, Russian forces had already invaded Germany. Germany was going to have to fight a long war on two fronts. Realizing this, the German high command sent thousands of troops from France to aid its forces in the east. Meanwhile, the war on the Western Front settled into a stalemate. **A**

War in the Trenches By early 1915, opposing armies on the Western Front had dug miles of parallel trenches to protect themselves from enemy fire. This set the stage for what became known as **trench warfare**. In this type of warfare, soldiers fought each other from trenches. And armies traded huge losses of human life for pitifully small land gains.

Life in the trenches was pure misery. "The men slept in mud, washed in mud, ate mud, and dreamed mud," wrote one soldier. The trenches swarmed with rats. Fresh food was nonexistent. Sleep was nearly impossible.

The space between the opposing trenches won the grim name "no man's land." When the officers ordered an attack, their men went over the top of their trenches into this bombed-out landscape. There, they usually met murderous rounds of machine-gun fire. Staying put, however, did not ensure one's safety. Artillery fire brought death right into the trenches. "Shells of all calibers kept raining on our sector," wrote one French soldier. "The trenches disappeared, filled with earth . . . the air was unbreathable. Our blinded, wounded, crawling, and shouting soldiers kept falling on top of us and died splashing us with blood. It was living hell."

The Western Front had become a "terrain of death." It stretched nearly 500 miles from the North Sea to the Swiss border. A British officer described it in a letter:

PRIMARY SOURCE
Imagine a broad belt, ten miles or so in width, stretching from the Channel to the German frontier near Basle, which is positively littered with the bodies of men and scarified with their rude graves; in which farms, villages and cottages are shapeless heaps of blackened masonry; in which fields, roads and trees are pitted and torn and twisted by shells and disfigured by dead horses, cattle, sheep and goats, scattered in every attitude of repulsive distortion and dismemberment.

VALENTINE FLEMING, quoted in *The First World War*

▼ Allied troops crawl through a trench along the Western Front.

413

The New Weapons of War

Poison Gas

Soldiers wore masks like those shown at left to protect themselves from poison gas. Gas was introduced by the Germans but used by both sides. Some gases caused blindness or severe blisters, others death by choking.

Machine Gun

The machine gun, which fires ammunition automatically, was much improved by the time of World War I. The gun, shown to the left, could wipe out waves of attackers and thus made it difficult for forces to advance.

Tank

The tank, shown to the left, was an armored combat vehicle that moved on chain tracks—and thus could cross many types of terrain. It was introduced by the British in 1916 at the Battle of the Somme.

Submarine

In 1914, the Germans introduced the submarine as an effective warship. The submarine's primary weapon against ships was the torpedo, an underwater missile.

Military strategists were at a loss. New tools of war—machine guns, poison gas, armored tanks, larger artillery—had not delivered the fast-moving war they had expected. All this new technology did was kill greater numbers of people more effectively.

The slaughter reached a peak in 1916. In February, the Germans launched a massive attack against the French near Verdun. Each side lost more than 300,000 men. In July, the British army tried to relieve the pressure on the French. British forces attacked the Germans northwest of Verdun, in the valley of the Somme River. In the first day of battle alone, more than 20,000 British soldiers were killed. By the time the Battle of the Somme ended in November, each side had suffered more than half a million casualties.

What did the warring sides gain? Near Verdun, the Germans advanced about four miles. In the Somme valley, the British gained about five miles.

Vocabulary
In war, a *casualty* is anyone killed, injured, captured, or considered missing in action.

The Battle on the Eastern Front

Even as the war on the Western Front claimed thousands of lives, both sides were sending millions more men to fight on the **Eastern Front**. This area was a stretch of battlefield along the German and Russian border. Here, Russians and Serbs battled Germans and Austro-Hungarians. The war in the east was a more mobile war than that in the west. Here too, however, slaughter and stalemate were common.

Early Fighting At the beginning of the war, Russian forces had launched an attack into both Austria and Germany. At the end of August, Germany counterattacked near the town of Tannenberg. During the four-day battle, the Germans crushed the invading Russian army and drove it into full retreat. More than 30,000 Russian soldiers were killed.

Russia fared somewhat better against the Austrians. Russian forces defeated the Austrians twice in September 1914, driving deep into their country. Not until December of that year did the Austrian army manage to turn the tide. Austria defeated the Russians and eventually pushed them out of Austria-Hungary.

Russia Struggles By 1916, Russia's war effort was near collapse. Unlike the nations of western Europe, Russia had yet to become industrialized. As a result, the Russian army was continually short on food, guns, ammunition, clothes, boots, and blankets. Moreover, the Allied supply shipments to Russia were sharply limited by German control of the Baltic Sea, combined with Germany's relentless submarine campaign in the North Sea and beyond. In the south, the Ottomans still controlled the straits leading from the Mediterranean to the Black Sea.

The Russian army had only one asset—its numbers. Throughout the war the Russian army suffered a staggering number of battlefield losses. Yet the army continually rebuilt its ranks from the country's enormous population. For more than three years, the battered Russian army managed to tie up hundreds of thousands of German troops in the east. As a result, Germany could not hurl its full fighting force at the west. **B**

Germany and her allies, however, were concerned with more than just the Eastern or Western Front. As the war raged on, fighting spread beyond Europe to Africa, as well as to Southwest and Southeast Asia. In the years after it began, the massive European conflict indeed became a world war.

MAIN IDEA

Synthesizing
B Why was Russia's involvement in the war so important to the other Allies?

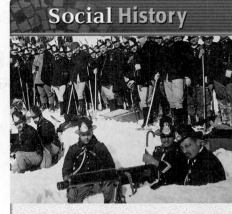

Social History

The Frozen Front
For soldiers on the Eastern Front, like those shown above, the overall misery of warfare was compounded by deadly winters. "Every day hundreds froze to death," noted one Austro-Hungarian officer during a particularly brutal spell.

Russian troops suffered too, mainly due to their lack of food and clothing. "I am at my post all the time—frozen [and] soaked . . . ," lamented one soldier. "We walk barefoot or in rope-soled shoes. It's incredible that soldiers of the Russian army are in rope-soled shoes!"

SECTION 2 ASSESSMENT

TERMS & NAMES 1. For each term or name, write a sentence explaining its significance.
• Central Powers   • Allies   • Western Front   • Schlieffen Plan   • trench warfare   • Eastern Front

USING YOUR NOTES
2. What were some of the conditions that soldiers on the front lines had to face?

    I. The Great War
        Begins
        A.
        B.
    II. A Bloody Stalemate

MAIN IDEAS
3. Which countries comprised the Central Powers? Which countries comprised the Allies?

4. What were the characteristics of trench warfare?

5. What factors contributed to Russia's war difficulties?

CRITICAL THINKING & WRITING
6. **COMPARING AND CONTRASTING** How was war on the Western and Eastern Fronts different? How was it the same?

7. **ANALYZING CAUSES** Why did the Schlieffen Plan ultimately collapse? Cite specific details from the text.

8. **MAKING INFERENCES** Why might it be fair to say that neither side won the battles of the Somme or Verdun?

9. **WRITING ACTIVITY** SCIENCE AND TECHNOLOGY In an **explanatory essay**, describe the effects of the new technology on warfare. Use examples from your reading.

CONNECT TO TODAY PRESENTING AN ORAL REPORT

Find an image of a World War I monument from any one of the combatant countries. In an **oral report**, present the image to the class and provide details about its origin and purpose.

Military Aviation

World War I introduced airplane warfare—and by doing so, ushered in an era of tremendous progress in the field of military aviation. Although the plane itself was relatively new and untested by 1914, the warring nations quickly recognized its potential as a powerful weapon. Throughout the conflict, countries on both sides built faster and stronger aircraft, and designed them to drop bombs and shoot at one another in the sky. Between the beginning and end of the war, the total number of planes in use by the major combatants soared from around 850 to nearly 10,000. After the war, countries continued to maintain a strong and advanced airforce, as they realized that supremacy of the air was a key to military victory.

INTEGRATED / TECHNOLOGY

RESEARCH LINKS For more on military aviation go to **classzone.com**

▲ A World War I pilot shows off an early air-to-ground communication device.

1 Designers kept nearly all weight in the center, giving the planes tremendous maneuverability.

2 A timing device enabled machine guns to fire through the propeller.

3 Engines were continuously strengthened for greater speed and carrying capability.

Two Top Fighter Planes: A Comparison		
	Fokker D VII (German)	**Sopwith F1 Camel** (British)
Length	23 feet	18 feet 8 inches
Wingspan	29 feet 3 inches	28 feet
Maximum Speed	116 mph	122 mph
Maximum Height	22,900 feet	24,000 feet
Maximum Flight Time	1.5 hours	2.5 hours

Connect *to* Today

1. Drawing Conclusions Why would communication with someone outside the plane be important for pilots of World War I and today?

See Skillbuilder Handbook, Page R11.

2. Comparing Using the Internet and other resources, find out more about a recent innovation with regard to fighter planes and explain its significance.

3
A Global Conflict

MAIN IDEA	WHY IT MATTERS NOW	TERMS & NAMES
ECONOMICS World War I spread to several continents and required the full resources of many governments.	The war propelled the United States to a new position of international power, which it holds today.	• unrestricted submarine warfare • total war • rationing • propaganda • armistice

SETTING THE STAGE World War I was much more than a European conflict. Australia and Japan, for example, entered the war on the Allies' side, while India supplied troops to fight alongside their British rulers. Meanwhile, the Ottoman Turks and later Bulgaria allied themselves with Germany and the Central Powers. As the war promised to be a grim, drawn-out affair, all the Great Powers looked for other allies around the globe to tip the balance. They also sought new war fronts on which to achieve victory.

War Affects the World

As the war dragged on, the main combatants looked beyond Europe for a way to end the stalemate. However, none of the alliances they formed or new battle-fronts they opened did much to end the slow and grinding conflict.

The Gallipoli Campaign A promising strategy for the Allies seemed to be to attack a region in the Ottoman Empire known as the Dardanelles. This narrow sea strait was the gateway to the Ottoman capital, Constantinople. By securing the Dardanelles, the Allies believed that they could take Constantinople, defeat the Turks, and establish a supply line to Russia.

Gallipoli Campaign

Black Sea

Bosporus

Constantinople

Gallipoli Peninsula

GREECE

OTTOMAN EMPIRE

Sea of Marmara

Dardanelles

N

Aegean Sea

0   100 Miles

0   200 Kilometers

The effort to take the Dardanelles strait began in February 1915. It was known as the Gallipoli campaign. British, Australian, New Zealand, and French troops made repeated assaults on the Gallipoli Peninsula on the western side of the strait. Turkish troops, some commanded by German officers, vigorously defended the region. By May, Gallipoli had turned into another bloody stalemate. Both sides dug trenches, from which they battled for the rest of the year. In December, the Allies gave up the campaign and began to evacuate. They had suffered about 250,000 casualties.

Battles in Africa and Asia In various parts of Asia and Africa, Germany's colonial possessions came under assault. The Japanese quickly overran German outposts in

TAKING NOTES
Recognizing Effects Use a web diagram to show the effects of World War I.

Effects of WWI

The World at War, 1914–1918
INTERACTIVE

War rages in Southwest Asia as Arab nationalists battle their Turkish rulers.

Japan declares war on Germany in 1914; seizes German colonies in China and the Pacific.

Main fighting of the war occurs on Western and Eastern Fronts.

The United States enters the war on the side of the Allies in 1917.

Brazil is the only South American country to enter the war. It supports the Allies with warships and personnel.

The European colonies throughout Africa become a battlefield as the warring parties strike at one another's colonial possessions.

India provides about 1.3 million men to fight and labor alongside their British rulers throughout Europe.

Both countries fight on the side of the Allies and contribute many troops to the 1915 Gallipoli campaign in Southwest Asia.

GEOGRAPHY SKILLBUILDER: Interpreting Maps
1. **Region** *Which countries were aligned with the European Allies?*
2. **Location** *Outside of Europe, where was World War I fought?*

China. They also captured Germany's Pacific island colonies. English and French troops attacked Germany's four African possessions. They seized control of three.

Elsewhere in Asia and Africa, the British and French recruited subjects in their colonies for the struggle. Fighting troops as well as laborers came from India, South Africa, Senegal, Egypt, Algeria, and Indochina. Many fought and died on the battlefield. Others worked to keep the front lines supplied. To be sure, some colonial subjects wanted nothing to do with their European rulers' conflicts. Others volunteered in the hope that service would lead to their independence. This was the view of Indian political leader Mohandas Gandhi, who supported Indian participation in the war. "If we would improve our status through the help and cooperation of the British," he wrote, "it was our duty to win their help by standing by them in their hour of need."

America Joins the Fight In 1917, the focus of the war shifted to the high seas. That year, the Germans intensified the submarine warfare that had raged in the Atlantic Ocean since shortly after the war began. In January 1917, the Germans announced that their submarines would sink without warning any ship in the waters around Britain. This policy was called **unrestricted submarine warfare**.

The Germans had tried this policy before. On May 7, 1915, a German submarine, or U-boat, had sunk the British passenger ship *Lusitania*. The attack left 1,198 people dead, including 128 U.S. citizens. Germany claimed that the ship had been carrying ammunition, which turned out to be true. Nevertheless, the American public was outraged. President Woodrow Wilson sent a strong protest to Germany. After two further attacks, the Germans finally agreed to stop attacking neutral and passenger ships.

Desperate for an advantage over the Allies, however, the Germans returned to unrestricted submarine warfare in 1917. They knew it might lead to war with the United States. They gambled that their naval blockade would starve Britain into defeat before the United States could mobilize. Ignoring warnings by President Wilson, German U-boats sank three American ships.

In February 1917, another German action pushed the United States closer to war. Officials intercepted a telegram written by Germany's foreign secretary, Arthur Zimmermann, stating that Germany would help Mexico "reconquer" the land it had lost to the United States if Mexico would ally itself with Germany.

The Zimmermann note simply proved to be the last straw. A large part of the American population already favored the Allies. In particular, America felt a bond with England. The two nations shared a common ancestry and language, as well as similar democratic institutions and legal systems. More important, America's economic ties with the Allies were far stronger than those with the Central Powers. On April 2, 1917, President Wilson asked Congress to declare war on Germany. The United States entered the war on the side of the Allies.

War Affects the Home Front

By the time the United States joined the Allies, the war had been raging for nearly three years. In those three years, Europe had lost more men in battle than in all the wars of the previous three centuries. The war had claimed the lives of millions and had changed countless lives forever. The Great War, as the conflict came to be known, affected everyone. It touched not only the soldiers in the trenches, but civilians as well.

Governments Wage Total War World War I soon became a **total war**. This meant that countries devoted all their resources to the war effort. In Britain, Germany, Austria, Russia, and France, the entire force of government was dedicated to winning the conflict. In each country, the wartime government took control of the economy. Governments told factories what to produce and how much.

Global Impact

The Influenza Epidemic

In the spring of 1918, a powerful new enemy emerged, threatening nations on each side of World War I. This "enemy" was a deadly strain of influenza. The Spanish flu, as it was popularly known, hit England and India in May. By the fall, it had spread through Europe, Russia, Asia, and to the United States.

The influenza epidemic killed soldiers and civilians alike. In India, at least 12 million people died of influenza. In Berlin, on a single day in October, 1,500 people died. In the end, this global epidemic was more destructive than the war itself, killing 20 million people worldwide.

▶ City officials and street cleaners in Chicago guard against the Spanish flu.

Numerous facilities were converted to munitions factories. Nearly every able-bodied civilian was put to work. Unemployment in many European countries all but disappeared.

So many goods were in short supply that governments turned to **rationing**. Under this system, people could buy only small amounts of those items that were also needed for the war effort. Eventually, rationing covered a wide range of goods, from butter to shoe leather.

Governments also suppressed antiwar activity, sometimes forcibly. In addition, they censored news about the war. Many leaders feared that honest reporting of the war would turn people against it. Governments also used **propaganda**, one-sided information designed to persuade, to keep up morale and support for the war. **A**

Women and the War Total war meant that governments turned to help from women as never before. Thousands of women replaced men in factories, offices, and shops. Women built tanks and munitions, plowed fields, paved streets, and ran hospitals. They also kept troops supplied with food, clothing, and weapons. Although most women left the work force when the war ended, they changed many people's views of what women were capable of doing.

Women also saw the horrors of war firsthand, working on or near the front lines as nurses. Here, American nurse Shirley Millard describes her experience with a soldier who had lost both eyes and feet:

▲ A woman relief worker writes a letter home for a wounded soldier.

MAIN IDEA
Summarizing
A How did the governments of the warring nations fight a total war?

A PRIMARY SOURCE
He moaned through the bandages that his head was splitting with pain. I gave him morphine. Suddenly aware of the fact that he had [numerous] wounds, he asked: "Sa-ay! What's the matter with my legs?" Reaching down to feel his legs before I could stop him, he uttered a heartbreaking scream. I held his hands firmly until the drug I had given him took effect.

SHIRLEY MILLARD, *I Saw Them Die*

The Allies Win the War

With the United States finally in the war, the balance, it seemed, was about to tip in the Allies' favor. Before that happened, however, events in Russia gave Germany a victory on the Eastern Front, and new hope for winning the conflict.

Russia Withdraws In March 1917, civil unrest in Russia—due in large part to war-related shortages of food and fuel—forced Czar Nicholas to step down. In his place a provisional government was established. The new government pledged to continue fighting the war. However, by 1917, nearly 5.5 million Russian soldiers had been wounded, killed, or taken prisoner. As a result, the war-weary Russian army refused to fight any longer.

Eight months after the new government took over, a revolution shook Russia (see Chapter 14). In November 1917, Communist leader Vladimir Ilyich Lenin seized power. Lenin insisted on ending his country's involvement in the war. One of his first acts was to offer Germany a truce. In March 1918, Germany and Russia signed the Treaty of Brest-Litovsk, which ended the war between them.

Allied View of Armistice

News of the armistice affected the Allied and Central powers differently. Here, a U.S. soldier named Harry Truman, who would go on to become president, recalls the day the fighting stopped.

PRIMARY SOURCE

Every single one of them [the French soldiers] had to march by my bed and salute and yell, "Vive President Wilson, Vive le capitaine d'artillerie américaine!" No sleep all night. The infantry fired Very pistols, sent up all the flares they could lay their hands on, fired rifles, pistols, whatever else would make noise, all night long.

HARRY TRUMAN, quoted in *The First World War*

German Reaction to Armistice

On the other side of the fighting line, German officer Herbert Sulzbach struggled to inform his troops of the war's end.

PRIMARY SOURCE

"Hostilities will cease as from 12 noon today." This was the order which I had to read out to my men. The war is over. . . . How we looked forward to *this* moment; how we used to picture it as the most splendid event of our lives; and here we are now, humbled, our souls torn and bleeding, and know that we've surrendered. Germany has surrendered to the Entente!

HERBERT SULZBACH, *With the German Guns*

DOCUMENT-BASED QUESTIONS

1. **Summarizing** *What is the main difference between these two excerpts?*
2. **Drawing Conclusions** *How did Herbert Sulzbach's vision of the armistice differ from what actually occurred?*

The Central Powers Collapse Russia's withdrawal from the war at last allowed Germany to send nearly all its forces to the Western Front. In March 1918, the Germans mounted one final, massive attack on the Allies in France. As in the opening weeks of the war, the German forces crushed everything in their path. By late May 1918, the Germans had again reached the Marne River. Paris was less than 40 miles away. Victory seemed within reach.

By this time, however, the German military had weakened. The effort to reach the Marne had exhausted men and supplies alike. Sensing this weakness, the Allies—with the aid of nearly 140,000 fresh U.S. troops—launched a counterattack. In July 1918, the Allies and Germans clashed at the Second Battle of the Marne. Leading the Allied attack were some 350 tanks that rumbled slowly forward, smashing through the German lines. With the arrival of 2 million more American troops, the Allied forces began to advance steadily toward Germany. **B**

Soon, the Central Powers began to crumble. First the Bulgarians and then the Ottoman Turks surrendered. In October, revolution swept through Austria-Hungary. In Germany, soldiers mutinied, and the public turned on the kaiser.

On November 9, 1918, Kaiser Wilhelm II stepped down. Germany declared itself a republic. A representative of the new German government met with French Commander Marshal Foch in a railway car near Paris. The two signed an **armistice**, or an agreement to stop fighting. On November 11, World War I came to an end.

MAIN IDEA

Comparing

B How was the Second Battle of the Marne similar to the first?

The Legacy of the War

World War I was, in many ways, a new kind of war. It involved the use of new technologies. It ushered in the notion of war on a grand and global scale. It also left behind a landscape of death and destruction such as was never before seen.

Both sides in World War I paid a tremendous price in terms of human life. About 8.5 million soldiers died as a result of the war. Another 21 million were wounded. In addition, the war led to the death of countless civilians by way of

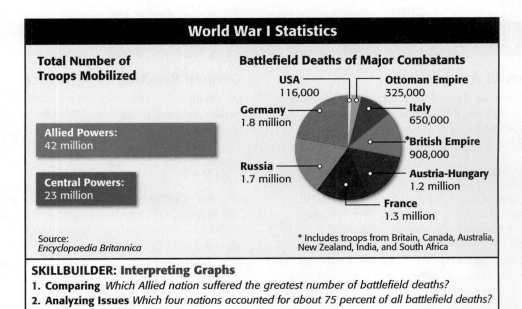

World War I Statistics

Total Number of Troops Mobilized

Allied Powers:
42 million

Central Powers:
23 million

Source:
Encyclopaedia Britannica

Battlefield Deaths of Major Combatants

- USA 116,000
- Ottoman Empire 325,000
- Germany 1.8 million
- Italy 650,000
- *British Empire 908,000
- Russia 1.7 million
- Austria-Hungary 1.2 million
- France 1.3 million

* Includes troops from Britain, Canada, Australia, New Zealand, India, and South Africa

SKILLBUILDER: Interpreting Graphs
1. **Comparing** *Which Allied nation suffered the greatest number of battlefield deaths?*
2. **Analyzing Issues** *Which four nations accounted for about 75 percent of all battlefield deaths?*

starvation, disease, and slaughter. Taken together, these figures spelled tragedy—an entire generation of Europeans wiped out.

The war also had a devastating economic impact on Europe. The great conflict drained the treasuries of European countries. One account put the total cost of the war at $338 billion, a staggering amount for that time. The war also destroyed acres of farmland, as well as homes, villages, and towns.

The enormous suffering that resulted from the Great War left a deep mark on Western society as well. A sense of disillusionment settled over the survivors. The insecurity and despair that many people experienced are reflected in the art and literature of the time.

Another significant legacy of the war lay in its peace agreement. As you will read in the next section, the treaties to end World War I were forged after great debate and compromise. And while they sought to bring a new sense of security and peace to the world, they prompted mainly anger and resentment.

SECTION 3 ASSESSMENT

TERMS & NAMES 1. For each term or name, write a sentence explaining its significance.
- unrestricted submarine warfare
- total war
- rationing
- propaganda
- armistice

USING YOUR NOTES

2. Which effect do you think was most significant? Why?

Effects of WWI

MAIN IDEAS

3. What factors helped prompt the United States to join the war for the Allies?

4. What role did women play in the war?

5. What was the significance of the Second Battle of the Marne?

CRITICAL THINKING & WRITING

6. **ANALYZING ISSUES** In what ways was World War I truly a global conflict?

7. **FORMING OPINIONS** Do you think governments are justified in censoring war news? Why or why not?

8. **DRAWING CONCLUSIONS** Which of the non-European countries had the greatest impact on the war effort? Explain.

9. **WRITING ACTIVITY** ECONOMICS Write a **paragraph** explaining how the concept of total war affected the warring nations' economies.

CONNECT TO TODAY CREATING A GRAPHIC

Using the library and other resources, compare the role of women in combat today in any two countries. Display your comparison in a **chart** or other type of **graphic**.

INTERACTIVE

Views of War

When World War I broke out, Europe had not experienced a war involving all the major powers for nearly a century, since Napoleon's defeat in 1815. As a result, people had an unrealistic view of warfare. Many expected the war to be short and romantic. Many men enlisted in the army because of patriotism or out of a desire to defend certain institutions. What the soldiers experienced changed their view of war forever.

Ⓐ PRIMARY SOURCE

Woodrow Wilson

On April 2, 1917, President Wilson asked Congress to declare war so that the United States could enter World War I. This excerpt from his speech gives some of his reasons.

———

The world must be made safe for democracy. Its peace must be planted upon the tested foundations of political liberty. We have no selfish ends to serve. We desire no conquest, no dominion. We seek no indemnities for ourselves, no material compensation for the sacrifice we shall freely make. We are but one of the champions of the rights of mankind. We shall be satisfied when those rights have been made as secure as the faith and the freedom of nations can make them.

Ⓑ FICTION

Erich Maria Remarque

In the German novel *All Quiet on the Western Front*, Erich Maria Remarque draws upon his own wartime experience of trench warfare.

———

No one would believe that in this howling waste there could still be men; but steel helmets now appear on all sides of the trench, and fifty yards from us a machine-gun is already in position and barking.

The wire entanglements are torn to pieces. Yet they offer some obstacle. We see the storm-troops coming. Our artillery opens fire. . . .

I see [a French soldier], his face upturned, fall into a wire cradle. His body collapses, his hands remain suspended as though he were praying. Then his body drops clean away and only his hands with the stumps of his arms, shot off, now hang in the wire.

Ⓒ POETRY

Wilfred Owen

The English poet Wilfred Owen was killed in the trenches just one week before World War I ended. This excerpt from his poem "Dulce et Decorum Est" describes a gas attack.

———

Gas! GAS! Quick, boys!—An ecstasy of
　fumbling,
Fitting the clumsy helmets just in time;
But someone still was yelling out and
　stumbling,
And flound'ring like a man in fire or
　lime . . .
Dim, through the misty panes and
　thick green light,
As under a green sea, I saw him
　drowning.

In all my dreams, before my helpless
　sight,
He plunges at me, guttering, choking,
　drowning.

Ⓓ PRIMARY SOURCE

Maurice Neumont

France, 1918
This French poster is titled, "They Shall Not Pass, 1914–1918." Translated into English, the text at the bottom reads, "Twice I have stood fast and conquered on the Marne, my brother civilian. A deceptive 'peace offensive' will attack you in your turn; like me you must stand firm and conquer. Be strong and shrewd—beware of Boche [German] hypocrisy."

Document-Based
QUESTIONS

1. What reasons does Woodrow Wilson (Source A) give for entering the war?

2. What emotions does the French poster (Source D) try to arouse?

3. Judging from Sources B and C, what was it like for the average soldier in the trenches? Explain how you think such experiences affected the average soldier's view of war.

4

A Flawed Peace

MAIN IDEA	WHY IT MATTERS NOW	TERMS & NAMES
POWER AND AUTHORITY After winning the war, the Allies dictated a harsh peace settlement that left many nations feeling betrayed.	Hard feelings left by the peace settlement helped cause World War II.	• Woodrow Wilson • Georges Clemenceau • Fourteen Points	• self-determination • Treaty of Versailles • League of Nations

SETTING THE STAGE World War I was over. The killing had stopped. The terms of peace, however, still had to be worked out. On January 18, 1919, a conference to establish those terms began at the Palace of Versailles, outside Paris. Attending the talks, known as the Paris Peace Conference, were delegates representing 32 countries. For one year, this conference would be the scene of vigorous, often bitter debate. The Allied powers struggled to solve their conflicting aims in various peace treaties.

TAKING NOTES

Clarifying Use a chart to record the reaction by various groups to the Treaty of Versailles.

Reaction to Treaty	
Germany	
Africans & Asians	
Italy & Japan	

The Allies Meet and Debate

Despite representatives from numerous countries, the meeting's major decisions were hammered out by a group known as the Big Four: **Woodrow Wilson** of the United States, **Georges Clemenceau** of France, David Lloyd George of Great Britain, and Vittorio Orlando of Italy. Russia, in the grip of civil war, was not represented. Neither were Germany and its allies.

Wilson's Plan for Peace In January 1918, while the war was still raging, President Wilson had drawn up a series of peace proposals. Known as the **Fourteen Points**, they outlined a plan for achieving a just and lasting peace.

The first four points included an end to secret treaties, freedom of the seas, free trade, and reduced national armies and navies. The fifth goal was the adjustment of colonial claims with fairness toward colonial peoples. The sixth through thirteenth points were specific suggestions for changing borders and creating new nations. The guiding idea behind these points was **self-determination**. This meant allowing people to decide for themselves under what government they wished to live.

Finally, the fourteenth point proposed a "general association of nations" that would protect "great and small states alike." This reflected Wilson's hope for an organization that could peacefully negotiate solutions to world conflicts.

The Versailles Treaty As the Paris Peace Conference opened, Britain and France showed little sign of agreeing to Wilson's vision of peace. Both nations were concerned with national security. They also wanted to strip Germany of its war-making power.

The differences in French, British, and U.S. aims led to heated arguments among the nations' leaders. Finally a compromise was reached. The **Treaty of Versailles** between Germany and the Allied powers was signed on June 28, 1919, five years to the day after Franz Ferdinand's assassination in Sarajevo. Adopting Wilson's fourteenth point, the treaty created a **League of Nations**. The league was to be an international association whose goal would be to keep peace among nations.

The treaty also punished Germany. The defeated nation lost substantial territory and had severe restrictions placed on its military operations. As tough as these provisions were, the harshest was Article 231. It was also known as the "war guilt" clause. It placed sole responsibility for the war on Germany's shoulders. As a result, Germany had to pay reparations to the Allies.

All of Germany's territories in Africa and the Pacific were declared mandates, or territories to be administered by the League of Nations. Under the peace agreement, the Allies would govern the mandates until they were judged ready for independence.

Vocabulary
Reparations is money paid by a defeated nation to compensate for damage or injury during a war.

A Troubled Treaty

The Versailles treaty was just one of five treaties negotiated by the Allies. In the end, these agreements created feelings of bitterness and betrayal—among the victors and the defeated.

The Creation of New Nations The Western powers signed separate peace treaties in 1919 and 1920 with each of the other defeated nations: Austria-Hungary, Bulgaria, and the Ottoman Empire. These treaties, too, led to huge land losses for the Central Powers. Several new countries were created out of the Austro-Hungarian Empire. Austria, Hungary, Czechoslovakia, and Yugoslavia were all recognized as independent nations.

The Ottoman Turks were forced to give up almost all of their former empire. They retained only the territory that is today the country of Turkey. The Allies carved up the lands that the Ottomans lost in Southwest Asia into mandates rather than independent nations. Palestine, Iraq, and Transjordan came under British control; Syria and Lebanon went to France.

Russia, which had left the war early, suffered land losses as well. Romania and Poland both gained Russian territory. Finland, Estonia, Latvia, and Lithuania, formerly part of Russia, became independent nations.

"A Peace Built on Quicksand" In the end, the Treaty of Versailles did little to build a lasting peace. For one thing, the United States—considered after the war to be the dominant nation in the world—ultimately rejected the treaty. Many Americans objected to the settlement and especially to President Wilson's League of Nations. Americans believed that the United States' best hope for peace was to stay out of European affairs. The United States worked out a separate treaty with Germany and its allies several years later.

History Makers

Woodrow Wilson
1856–1924
Wilson was tall and thin and often in poor health. He suffered from terrible indigestion and sometimes had to use a stomach pump on himself. A scholarly man, Wilson once served as president of Princeton University in New Jersey.
Passionate about international peace, he took on the U.S. Senate after it vowed to reject the Treaty of Versailles. During the political battle, he suffered a stroke that disabled him for the rest of his term.

Georges Clemenceau
1841–1929
The near opposite of Wilson, Clemenceau had a compact physique and a combative style that earned him the nickname "Tiger." He had worked as a physician and journalist before entering the political arena.
Determined to punish Germany, Clemenceau rarely agreed with Wilson and his larger quest for world peace. He once remarked of Wilson, "He thinks he is another Jesus Christ come upon earth to reform men."

INTEGRATED/TECHNOLOGY

RESEARCH LINKS For more on Woodrow Wilson and Georges Clemenceau, go to **classzone.com**

NORWAY
Oslo
Stockholm
SWEDEN
St. Petersburg
DENMARK
Copenhagen
North Sea
Baltic Sea
RUSSIA
GREAT BRITAIN
London
NETH.
Amsterdam
Berlin
Brussels
BELGIUM
GERMANY
LUX.
Paris
ATLANTIC OCEAN
Vienna
Bern
FRANCE
SWITZ.
AUSTRIA-HUNGARY
ROMANIA
Bucharest
Black Sea
PORTUGAL
Madrid
ANDORRA
ITALY
Belgrade
SERBIA
Sofia
SPAIN
MONTENEGRO
Rome
BULGARIA
Constantinople (Istanbul)
Tirane
ALBANIA
OTTOMAN EMPIRE
Mediterranean Sea
GREECE
Athens

N

0   400 Miles
0   800 Kilometers

Europe Post-World War I

FINLAND
Helsinki
NORWAY
Oslo
SWEDEN
Stockholm
Tallinn
ESTONIA
Riga
LATVIA
Moscow
North Sea
DENMARK
Copenhagen
Baltic Sea
LITHUANIA
Kaunas
IRELAND
Dublin
GREAT BRITAIN
DANZIG
E. PRUSSIA (Germany)
SOVIET UNION
London
NETH.
Amsterdam
Berlin
Warsaw
Brussels
BELGIUM
GERMANY
POLAND
LUX.
Paris
SAAR
Prague
ATLANTIC OCEAN
CZECHOSLOVAKIA
Vienna
Budapest
Bern
FRANCE
SWITZ.
AUSTRIA
HUNGARY
ROMANIA
Bucharest
PORTUGAL
Madrid
ANDORRA
ITALY
YUGOSLAVIA
Belgrade
Black Sea
BULGARIA
Sofia
Rome
Tirane
ALBANIA
Ankara
Mediterranean Sea
GREECE
Athens
TURKEY

N

0   400 Miles
0   800 Kilometers

GEOGRAPHY SKILLBUILDER: Interpreting Maps
1. **Region** *Which Central Powers nation appears to have lost the most territory?*
2. **Location** *On which nation's former lands were most of the new countries created?*

The Treaty of Versailles: Major Provisions

League of Nations	Territorial Losses	Military Restrictions	War Guilt
• International peace organization; enemy and neutral nations initially excluded • Germany and Russia excluded	• Germany returns Alsace-Lorraine to France; French border extended to west bank of Rhine River • Germany surrenders all of its overseas colonies in Africa and the Pacific	• Limits set on the size of the German army • Germany prohibited from importing or manufacturing weapons or war material • Germany forbidden to build or buy submarines or have an air force	• Sole responsibility for the war placed on Germany's shoulders • Germany forced to pay the Allies $33 billion in reparations over 30 years

SKILLBUILDER: Interpreting Charts
1. **Analyzing Issues** *In what ways did the treaty punish Germany?*
2. **Clarifying** *What two provinces were returned to France as a result of the treaty?*

In addition, the treaty with Germany, in particular the war-guilt clause, left a legacy of bitterness and hatred in the hearts of the German people. Other countries felt cheated and betrayed by the peace settlements as well. Throughout Africa and Asia, people in the mandated territories were angry at the way the Allies disregarded their desire for independence. The European powers, it seemed to them, merely talked about the principle of national self-determination. European colonialism, disguised as the mandate system, continued in Asia and Africa. **A**

Some Allied powers, too, were embittered by the outcome. Both Japan and Italy, which had entered the war to gain territory, had gained less than they wanted. Lacking the support of the United States, and later other world powers, the League of Nations was in no position to take action on these and other complaints. The settlements at Versailles represented, as one observer noted, "a peace built on quicksand." Indeed, that quicksand eventually would give way. In a little more than two decades, the treaties' legacy of bitterness would help plunge the world into another catastrophic war.

MAIN IDEA

Analyzing Issues
A What complaints did various mandated countries voice about the Treaty of Versailles?

SECTION 4 ASSESSMENT

TERMS & NAMES 1. For each term or name, write a sentence explaining its significance.
• Woodrow Wilson • Georges Clemenceau • Fourteen Points • self-determination • Treaty of Versailles • League of Nations

USING YOUR NOTES

2. Which group was most justified in its reaction to the treaty? Why?

Reaction to Treaty	
Germany	
Africans & Asians	
Italy & Japan	

MAIN IDEAS

3. What was the goal of Woodrow Wilson's Fourteen Points?

4. What was the "war guilt" clause in the Treaty of Versailles?

5. Why did the United States reject the Treaty of Versailles?

CRITICAL THINKING & WRITING

6. **FORMING OPINIONS** Were the Versailles treaties fair? Consider all the nations affected.

7. **ANALYZING MOTIVES** Why might the European Allies have been more interested in punishing Germany than in creating a lasting peace?

8. **EVALUATING DECISIONS** Was the United States right to reject the Treaty of Versailles? Why or why not?

9. **WRITING ACTIVITY** POWER AND AUTHORITY Create a list of five **interview questions** a reporter might ask Wilson or Clemenceau about the Paris Peace Conference. Then write the possible **answers** to those questions.

INTEGRATED TECHNOLOGY **INTERNET ACTIVITY**
Use the Internet to explore a recent achievement or activity by the United Nations, the modern-day equivalent of the League of Nations. Present your findings in a brief **oral report** to the class.

INTERNET KEYWORD
United Nations

VISUAL SUMMARY

The Great War

Long-Term Causes

- Nationalism spurs competition among European nations.
- Imperialism deepens national rivalries.
- Militarism leads to large standing armies.
- The alliance system divides Europe into two rival camps.

Immediate Causes

- The assassination of Archduke Franz Ferdinand in June 1914 prompts Austria to declare war on Serbia.
- The alliance system requires nations to support their allies.

WORLD WAR I

Immediate Effects

- A generation of Europeans is killed or wounded.
- Dynasties fall in Germany, Austria-Hungary, and Russia.
- New countries are created.
- The League of Nations is established to help promote peace.

Long-Term Effects

- Many nations feel bitter and betrayed by the peace settlements.
- Forces that helped cause the war—nationalism, competition—remain.

TERMS & NAMES

For each term below, briefly explain its connection to World War I.

1. Triple Alliance
2. Triple Entente
3. Central Powers
4. Allies
5. total war
6. armistice
7. Fourteen Points
8. Treaty of Versailles

MAIN IDEAS

Marching Toward War Section 1 (pages 407–410)

9. How did nationalism, imperialism, and militarism help set the stage for World War I?
10. Why was the Balkans known as "the powder keg of Europe"?

Europe Plunges into War Section 2 (pages 411–416)

11. Why was the first Battle of the Marne considered so significant?
12. Where was the Western Front? the Eastern Front?
13. What were the characteristics of trench warfare?

A Global Conflict Section 3 (pages 417–423)

14. What was the purpose of the Gallipoli campaign?
15. What factors prompted the United States to enter the war?
16. In what ways was World War I a total war?

A Flawed Peace Section 4 (pages 424–427)

17. What was the purpose of the League of Nations?
18. What was the mandate system, and why did it leave many groups feeling betrayed?

CRITICAL THINKING

1. USING YOUR NOTES

Trace the formation of the two major alliance systems that dominated Europe on the eve of World War I by providing the event that corresponds with each date on the chart.

2. EVALUATING DECISIONS

POWER AND AUTHORITY How did the Treaty of Versailles reflect the different personalities and agendas of the men in power at the end of World War I?

3. CLARIFYING

ECONOMICS How did the war have both a positive and negative impact on the economies of Europe?

4. ANALYZING ISSUES

One British official commented that the Allied victory in World War I had been "bought so dear [high in price] as to be indistinguishable from defeat." What did he mean by this statement? Use examples from the text to support your answer.

Use the quotation about Germany's sinking of the British passenger ship *Lusitania* and your knowledge of world history to answer questions 1 and 2.
Additional Test Practice, pp. S1–S33.

PRIMARY SOURCE

The responsibility for the death of so many American citizens, which is deeply regretted by everyone in Germany, in a large measure falls upon the American government. It could not admit that Americans were being used as shields for English contraband [smuggled goods]. In this regard America had permitted herself to be misused in a disgraceful manner by England. And now, instead of calling England to account, she sends a note to the German government.

from *Vossische Zeitung*, May 18, 1915

1. Which of the following statements best describes the sentiments of the writer?

A. The sinking of the *Lusitania* was a tragic mistake.

B. America was right to blame Germany for the attack.

C. The American government failed to protect its citizens.

D. England should keep its vessels off the Atlantic Ocean.

2. The sinking of the *Lusitania* ultimately played a role in prompting Germany to

A. abandon the Schlieffen Plan.

B. halt unrestricted submarine warfare.

C. declare war on the United States.

D. begin a widespread rationing program.

Use this anti-German (Hun) World War I poster and your knowledge of world history to answer question 3.

HALT the HUN!

BUY U.S. GOVERNMENT BONDS
THIRD LIBERTY LOAN

3. Which of the following best describes the depiction of the German soldier in this poster?

A. noble and courageous

B. weak and disorganized

C. cruel and barbaric

D. dangerous and cunning

INTEGRATED TECHNOLOGY

TEST PRACTICE Go to **classzone.com**

• Diagnostic tests   • Strategies
• Tutorials   • Additional practice

ALTERNATIVE ASSESSMENT

1. Interact *with* History

On page 406, you examined whether it is always right to support an ally or friend. Now that you have read the chapter, reevaluate your decision. If you chose to follow your ally into World War I, do you still feel it was the right thing to do? Why or why not? If you decided to stay out of war, what are your feelings now? Discuss your opinions with a small group.

2. WRITING ABOUT HISTORY

SCIENCE AND TECHNOLOGY Explain in several **paragraphs** which one of the new or enhanced weapons of World War I you think had the greatest impact on the war and why. Consider the following:

• which weapon might have had the widest use

• which weapon might have inflicted the greatest damage on the enemy

INTEGRATED TECHNOLOGY

Conducting Internet Research

While World War I was extremely costly, staying prepared for the possibility of war today is also expensive. Work in groups of three or four to research the defense budgets of several of the world's nations. Have each group member be responsible for one country. Go to the *Web Research Guide* at **classzone.com** to learn about conducting research on the Internet. Use your research to

• examine how much money each country spends on defense, as well as what percentage of the overall budget such spending represents.

• create a large comparison chart of the countries' budgets.

• discuss with your classmates whether the amounts spent for military and defense are justified.

Present your research to the class. Include a list of your Web resources.

Revolution and Nationalism, 1900–1939

Previewing Main Ideas

REVOLUTION Widespread social unrest troubled China and Russia during the late 1800s and early 1900s. Eventually revolutions erupted.

Geography *Study the time line. In what years did revolutions take place in China and in Russia?*

POWER AND AUTHORITY New nations appeared during the 1920s and 1930s in the former Ottoman Empire in Southwest Asia. These nations adopted a variety of government styles—from a republic to a monarchy.

Geography *According to the map, which new nations in Southwest Asia emerged from the former Ottoman Empire?*

EMPIRE BUILDING Nationalist movements in Southwest Asia, India, and China successfully challenged the British, Ottoman, and Chinese Empires.

Geography *According to the map, which European nations still control large areas of Southwest Asia?*

INTEGRATED TECHNOLOGY

eEdition
- Interactive Maps
- Interactive Visuals
- Interactive Primary Sources

INTERNET RESOURCES
Go to **classzone.com** for:
- Research Links
- Maps
- Internet Activities
- Test Practice
- Primary Sources
- Current Events
- Chapter Quiz

EUROPE AND ASIA

1905
Russian workers protest for better conditions.

1911
◄Chinese Nationalists oust the last Qing emperor. (Emperor P'u-i)

1917
Russian Bolsheviks rebel in October Revolution.

1900

1910

WORLD

1910
◄ Mexican Revolution begins.

1914–1918
World War I

Southwest Asia, 1926

Black Sea

USSR

Baku

Constantinople

40°N

GREECE

Ankara

TURKEY

USSR

Caspian
Sea

Mediterranean Sea

N
W E
S

CYPRUS
(Br.)

LEBANON

Tripoli

SYRIA

Beirut

Damascus

Baghdad

PERSIA

PALESTINE

Jerusalem

Amman

IRAQ

Cairo

TRANSJORDAN

Persian Gulf

KUWAIT

LIBYA

EGYPT

Hejaz

Riyadh

Tropic of Cancer

Red Sea

Mecca

SAUDI
ARABIA

TRUCIAL
STATES

MUSCAT
AND
OMAN

*Arabian
Sea*

ANGLO-
EGYPTIAN
SUDAN

YEMEN

ADEN
PROTECTORATE

ERITREA

FRENCH
SOMALILAND

Aden

Gulf of Aden

ETHIOPIA

BRITISH
SOMALILAND

ITALIAN
SOMALILAND

British mandate
French mandate
Borders, 1926
Ottoman Empire, 1914

0   250   500 Miles
0   250   500 Kilometers
Gall Projection

1920
Gandhi leads
Indian campaign of
civil disobedience.

1923
Mustafa Kemal
transforms Turkey
into a republic.

1929
Stalin becomes
dictator of
Soviet Union.

1934
Mao Zedong
heads Long
March.

1920

1930

1940

1922
Mussolini comes to
power in Italy.

1929
U.S. stock
market crashes.

1933
Hitler is named
chancellor of
Germany. ▶

How do you resist oppressive rule–with violent or nonviolent action?

You believe that the policies of your government are unjust and oppressive. The policies favor a small, wealthy class—but the vast majority of people are poor with few rights. The government has failed to tackle economic, social, and political problems. Many of your friends are joining revolutionary groups that plan to overthrow the government by force. Others support nonviolent methods of change, such as peaceful strikes, protests, and refusal to obey unjust laws. You wonder which course of action to choose.

▼ **Mao Zedong**, Communist leader, believed revolution would solve China's problems.

▼ **Mohandas K. Gandhi** became the leader of the independence movement to free India of British rule.

"Political power grows out of the barrel of a gun."

"Victory attained by violence is tantamount to a defeat, for it is momentary."

EXAMINING *the* ISSUES

- How might armed and powerful opponents respond to groups committed to nonviolent action?

- Which strategy might prove more successful and bring more long-lasting consequences? Why?

As a class, discuss these questions. In your discussion, consider what you have learned about the strategies revolutionaries use to accomplish change. As you read about the revolutions and independence movements, see which strategy was successful.

Revolutions in Russia

MAIN IDEA	WHY IT MATTERS NOW	TERMS & NAMES
REVOLUTION Long-term social unrest in Russia exploded in revolution, and ushered in the first Communist government.	The Communist Party controlled the Soviet Union until the country's breakup in 1991.	• proletariat • provisional government • Bolsheviks • soviet • Lenin • Communist Party • Rasputin • Joseph Stalin

SETTING THE STAGE The Russian Revolution was like a firecracker with a very long fuse. The explosion came in 1917, yet the fuse had been burning for nearly a century. The cruel, oppressive rule of most 19th-century czars caused widespread social unrest for decades. Army officers revolted in 1825. Secret revolutionary groups plotted to overthrow the government. In 1881, revolutionaries angry over the slow pace of political change assassinated the reform-minded czar, Alexander II. Russia was heading toward a full-scale revolution.

Czars Resist Change

In 1881, Alexander III succeeded his father, Alexander II, and halted all reforms in Russia. Like his grandfather Nicholas I, Alexander III clung to the principles of autocracy, a form of government in which he had total power. Anyone who questioned the absolute authority of the czar, worshiped outside the Russian Orthodox Church, or spoke a language other than Russian was labeled dangerous.

Czars Continue Autocratic Rule To wipe out revolutionaries, Alexander III used harsh measures. He imposed strict censorship codes on published materials and written documents, including private letters. His secret police carefully watched both secondary schools and universities. Teachers had to send detailed reports on every student. Political prisoners were sent to Siberia, a remote region of eastern Russia.

To establish a uniform Russian culture, Alexander III oppressed other national groups within Russia. He made Russian the official language of the empire and forbade the use of minority languages, such as Polish, in schools. Alexander made Jews the target of persecution. A wave of pogroms—organized violence against Jews—broke out in many parts of Russia. Police and soldiers stood by and watched Russian citizens loot and destroy Jewish homes, stores, and synagogues.

When Nicholas II became czar in 1894, he continued the tradition of Russian autocracy. Unfortunately, it blinded him to the changing conditions of his times.

▼ Alexander III turned Russia into a police state, teeming with spies and informers.

TAKING NOTES

Following Chronological Order Create a time line to show major events in the changing of Russian government.

```
1894                    1922
|-----------|-----------|
```

Russia Industrializes

Rapid industrialization changed the face of the Russian economy. The number of factories more than doubled between 1863 and 1900. Still, Russia lagged behind the industrial nations of western Europe. In the 1890s, Nicholas's most capable minister launched a program to move the country forward. To finance the buildup of Russian industries, the government sought foreign investors and raised taxes. These steps boosted the growth of heavy industry, particularly steel. By around 1900, Russia had become the world's fourth-ranking producer of steel. Only the United States, Germany, and Great Britain produced more steel.

Vocabulary
minister: person in charge of an area of government, such as finance

With the help of British and French investors, work began on the world's longest continuous rail line—the Trans-Siberian Railway. Begun in 1891, the railway was not completed until 1916. It connected European Russia in the west with Russian ports on the Pacific Ocean in the east.

The Revolutionary Movement Grows Rapid industrialization stirred discontent among the people of Russia. The growth of factories brought new problems, such as grueling working conditions, miserably low wages, and child labor. The government outlawed trade unions. To try to improve their lives, workers unhappy with their low standard of living and lack of political power organized strikes. **A**

MAIN IDEA

Analyzing Causes
A Why did industrialization in Russia lead to unrest?

As a result of all of these factors, several revolutionary movements began to grow and compete for power. A group that followed the views of Karl Marx successfully established a following in Russia. The Marxist revolutionaries believed that the industrial class of workers would overthrow the czar. These workers would then form "a dictatorship of the proletariat." This meant that the **proletariat**—the workers—would rule the country.

In 1903, Russian Marxists split into two groups over revolutionary tactics. The more moderate Mensheviks (MEHN•shuh•vihks) wanted a broad base of popular support for the revolution. The more radical **Bolsheviks** (BOHL•shuh•vihks) supported a small number of committed revolutionaries willing to sacrifice everything for change.

The major leader of the Bolsheviks was Vladimir Ilyich Ulyanov (ool•YAH•nuhf). He adopted the name of **Lenin**. He had an engaging personality and was an excellent organizer. He was also ruthless. These traits would ultimately help him gain command of the Bolsheviks. In the early 1900s, Lenin fled to western Europe to avoid arrest by the czarist regime. From there he maintained contact with other Bolsheviks. Lenin then waited until he could safely return to Russia.

Crises at Home and Abroad

The revolutionaries would not have to wait long to realize their visions. Between 1904 and 1917, Russia faced a series of crises. These events showed the czar's weakness and paved the way for revolution.

The Russo-Japanese War In the late 1800s, Russia and Japan competed for control of Korea and Manchuria. The two nations signed a series of agreements over the territories,

History Makers

V. I. Lenin
1870–1924

In 1887, when he was 17, Lenin's brother, Alexander, was hanged for plotting to kill the czar. Legend has it that this event turned Lenin into a revolutionary.

Though Alexander's execution influenced Lenin, he already harbored ill feelings against the government. By the early 1900s, he planned to overthrow the czar. After the revolution in 1917, Russians revered him as the "Father of the Revolution."

Following Lenin's death in 1924, the government placed his tomb in Red Square in Moscow. His preserved body, encased in a bulletproof, glass-topped coffin, is still on display. Many Russians today, though, favor moving Lenin's corpse away from public view.

INTEGRATED / TECHNOLOGY

RESEARCH LINKS For more on V. I. Lenin, go to **classzone.com**

but Russia broke them. Japan retaliated by attacking the Russians at Port Arthur, Manchuria, in February 1904. News of repeated Russian losses sparked unrest at home and led to a revolt in the midst of the war.

Bloody Sunday: The Revolution of 1905 On January 22, 1905, about 200,000 workers and their families approached the czar's Winter Palace in St. Petersburg. They carried a petition asking for better working conditions, more personal freedom, and an elected national legislature. Nicholas II's generals ordered soldiers to fire on the crowd. More than 1,000 were wounded and several hundred were killed. Russians quickly named the event "Bloody Sunday."

▲ Soldiers fired on unarmed workers demonstrating at the czar's Winter Palace on "Bloody

Bloody Sunday provoked a wave of strikes and violence that spread across the country. In October 1905, Nicholas reluctantly promised more freedom. He approved the creation of the Duma (DOO•muh)—Russia's first parliament. The first Duma met in May 1906. Its leaders were moderates who wanted Russia to become a constitutional monarchy similar to Britain. But because he was hesitant to share his power, the czar dissolved the Duma after ten weeks.

World War I: The Final Blow In 1914, Nicholas II made the fateful decision to drag Russia into World War I. Russia was unprepared to handle the military and economic costs. Its weak generals and poorly equipped troops were no match for the German army. German machine guns mowed down advancing Russians by the thousands. Defeat followed defeat. Before a year had passed, more than 4 million Russian soldiers had been killed, wounded, or taken prisoner. As in the Russo-Japanese War, Russia's involvement in World War I revealed the weaknesses of czarist rule and military leadership.

In 1915, Nicholas moved his headquarters to the war front. From there, he hoped to rally his discouraged troops to victory. His wife, Czarina Alexandra, ran the government while he was away. She ignored the czar's chief advisers. Instead, she fell under the influence of the mysterious **Rasputin** (ras•PYOO•tihn). A self-described "holy man," he claimed to have magical healing powers.

Nicholas and Alexandra's son, Alexis, suffered from hemophilia, a life-threatening disease. Rasputin seemed to ease the boy's symptoms. To show her gratitude, Alexandra allowed Rasputin to make key political decisions. He opposed reform measures and obtained powerful positions for his friends. In 1916, a group of nobles murdered Rasputin. They feared his increasing role in government affairs.

Meanwhile, on the war front Russian soldiers mutinied, deserted, or ignored orders. On the home front, food and fuel supplies were dwindling. Prices were wildly inflated. People from all classes were clamoring for change and an end to the war. Neither Nicholas nor Alexandra proved capable of tackling these enormous problems.

The March Revolution

In March 1917, women textile workers in Petrograd led a citywide strike. In the next five days, riots flared up over shortages of bread and fuel. Nearly 200,000 workers swarmed the streets shouting, "Down with the autocracy!" and "Down with the war!" At first the soldiers obeyed orders to shoot the rioters but later sided with them.

The Czar Steps Down The local protest exploded into a general uprising—the March Revolution. It forced Czar Nicholas II to abdicate his throne. A year later revolutionaries executed Nicholas and his family. The three-century czarist rule of the Romanovs finally collapsed. The March Revolution succeeded in bringing down the czar. Yet it failed to set up a strong government to replace his regime.

Leaders of the Duma established a **provisional government**, or temporary government. Alexander Kerensky headed it. His decision to continue fighting in World War I cost him the support of both soldiers and civilians. As the war dragged on, conditions inside Russia worsened. Angry peasants demanded land. City workers grew more radical. Socialist revolutionaries, competing for power, formed soviets. **Soviets** were local councils consisting of workers, peasants, and soldiers. In many cities, the soviets had more influence than the provisional government. **B**

Lenin Returns to Russia The Germans believed that Lenin and his Bolshevik supporters would stir unrest in Russia and hurt the Russian war effort against Germany. They arranged Lenin's return to Russia after many years of exile. Traveling in a sealed railway boxcar, Lenin reached Petrograd in April 1917.

MAIN IDEA

Making Inferences

B Why did Kerensky's decision to continue fighting the war cost him the support of the Russian people?

The Bolshevik Revolution

Lenin and the Bolsheviks soon gained control of the Petrograd soviet, as well as the soviets in other major Russian cities. By the fall of 1917, people in the cities were rallying to the call, "All power to the soviets." Lenin's slogan—"Peace, Land, and Bread"—gained widespread appeal. Lenin decided to take action.

The Provisional Government Topples In November 1917, without warning, armed factory workers stormed the Winter Palace in Petrograd. Calling themselves

Russian Revolution and Civil War, 1905–1922
INTER**ACTIVE**

Legend:
- Bolshevik territory, Oct. 1919
- Territories lost (Treaty of Brest-Litovsk, 1918)
- ★ Bolshevik uprisings, 1917–1918
- ✳ Major civil war battle areas, 1918–1920
- ⇐ White Russian and Allied attacks, 1918–1920
- ◄ Bolshevik counterattacks, 1918–1920
- — Western boundaries of Russia, 1905–1917
- — Boundaries of Russia, 1922
- ⊦⊦⊦ Trans-Siberian Railroad

GEOGRAPHY SKILLBUILDER: Interpreting Maps

1. **Region** What was the extent (north to south, east to west) of the Bolshevik territory in 1919?
2. **Region** Which European countries had territory that was no longer within Russian boundaries because of the Brest-Litovsk treaty?

the Bolshevik Red Guards, they took over government offices and arrested the leaders of the provisional government. Kerensky and his colleagues disappeared almost as quickly as the czarist regime they had replaced.

Bolsheviks in Power Within days after the Bolshevik takeover, Lenin ordered that all farmland be distributed among the peasants. Lenin and the Bolsheviks gave control of factories to the workers. The Bolshevik government also signed a truce with Germany to stop all fighting and began peace talks.

In March 1918, Russia and Germany signed the Treaty of Brest-Litovsk. Russia surrendered a large part of its territory to Germany and its allies. The humiliating terms of this treaty triggered widespread anger among many Russians. They objected to the Bolsheviks and their policies and to the murder of the royal family.

▲ Red Army forces were victorious in the two-year civil war against the White Army.

Civil War Rages in Russia The Bolsheviks now faced a new challenge—stamping out their enemies at home. Their opponents formed the White Army. The White Army was made up of very different groups. There were those groups who supported the return to rule by the czar, others who wanted democratic government, and even socialists who opposed Lenin's style of socialism. Only the desire to defeat the Bolsheviks united the White Army. The groups barely cooperated with each other. At one point there were three White Armies fighting against the Bolsheviks' Red Army.

The revolutionary leader, Leon Trotsky, expertly commanded the Bolshevik Red Army. From 1918 to 1920, civil war raged in Russia. Several Western nations, including the United States, sent military aid and forces to Russia to help the White Army. However, they were of little help.

Causes and Effects of Two Russian Revolutions, 1917

Causes: Czarist Russia	Effects/Causes: March Revolution	Effects: Bolshevik Revolution
• Czar's leadership was weak.	• Czar abdicates.	• Provisional government is overthrown.
• Revolutionary agitation challenges the government.	• Provisional government takes over. • Lenin and soviets gain power.	• Bolsheviks take over.
• Widespread discontent found among all classes.	• Russia stays in World War I.	• Bolsheviks sign peace treaty with Germany and leave World War I. • Civil war begins in Russia.

SKILLBUILDER: Interpreting Charts
1. **Analyzing Causes** *What role did World War I play in the two revolutions?*
2. **Recognizing Effects** *Why were the effects of the March Revolution also causes of the Bolshevik Revolution?*

Russia's civil war proved far more deadly than the earlier revolutions. Around 14 million Russians died in the three-year struggle and in the famine that followed. The destruction and loss of life from fighting, hunger, and a worldwide flu epidemic left Russia in chaos. In the end, the Red Army crushed all opposition. The victory showed that the Bolsheviks were able both to seize power and to maintain it. **C**

Comparing World Revolutions In its immediate and long-term effects, the Russian Revolution was more like the French Revolution than the American Revolution. The American Revolution expanded English political ideas into a constitutional government that built on many existing structures. In contrast, both the French and Russian revolutions attempted to destroy existing social and political structures. Revolutionaries in France and Russia used violence and terror to control people. France became a constitutional monarchy for a time, but the Russian Revolution established a state-controlled society that lasted for decades.

MAIN IDEA

Identifying Problems
C What problems did Lenin and the Bolsheviks face after the revolution?

Lenin Restores Order

War and revolution destroyed the Russian economy. Trade was at a standstill. Industrial production dropped, and many skilled workers fled to other countries. Lenin turned to reviving the economy and restructuring the government.

New Economic Policy In March 1921, Lenin temporarily put aside his plan for a state-controlled economy. Instead, he resorted to a small-scale version of capitalism called the New Economic Policy (NEP). The reforms under the NEP allowed peasants to sell their surplus crops instead of turning them over to the government. The government kept control of major industries, banks, and means of communication, but it let some small factories, businesses, and farms operate under private ownership. The government also encouraged foreign investment.

> Analyzing Key Concepts

Communism

Communism is a political and economic system of organization. In theory, property is owned by the community and all citizens share in the common wealth according to their need. In practice, this was difficult to achieve.

German philosopher Karl Marx saw communism as the end result of an essential historical process. Russian revolutionary Vladimir Lenin built on Marx's theories and sought ways of applying those theories. Ultimately, however, Lenin's communist state—the Union of Soviet Socialist Republics (USSR)—became a one-party, totalitarian system. This chart compares how Marx and Lenin viewed communism.

SKILLBUILDER: Interpreting Charts
Comparing and Contrasting *How did Lenin's ideas about communism differ from those of Marx?*

Evolution of Communist Thought

Marx	Lenin
• History was the story of class struggle.	• History was the story of class struggle.
• The struggle Marx saw was between capitalists and the proletariat, or the workers.	• The struggle Lenin saw was capitalists against the proletariat and the peasants.
• The proletariat's numbers would become so great and their condition so poor that a spontaneous revolution would occur.	• The proletariat and the peasants were not capable of leading a revolution and needed the guidance of professional revolutionaries.
• The revolution would end with a "dictatorship of the proletariat"—the communal ownership of wealth.	• After the revolution, the state needed to be run by a single party with disciplined, centrally directed administrators in order to ensure its goals.

Thanks partly to the new policies and to the peace that followed the civil war, the country slowly recovered. By 1928, Russia's farms and factories were producing as much as they had before World War I.

Political Reforms Bolshevik leaders saw nationalism as a threat to unity and party loyalty. To keep nationalism in check, Lenin organized Russia into several self-governing republics under the central government. In 1922, the country was named the Union of Soviet Socialist Republics (USSR), in honor of the councils that helped launch the Bolshevik Revolution. **D**

MAIN IDEA

Summarizing
D How did the Communist government prevent nationalism from threatening the new state created by the revolution?

The Bolsheviks renamed their party the **Communist Party**. The name came from the writings of Karl Marx. He used the word *communism* to describe the classless society that would exist after workers had seized power. In 1924, the Communists created a constitution based on socialist and democratic principles. In reality, the Communist Party held all the power. Lenin had established a dictatorship of the Communist Party, not "a dictatorship of the proletariat," as Marx had promoted.

Stalin Becomes Dictator

Lenin suffered a stroke in 1922. He survived, but the incident set in motion competition for heading up the Communist Party. Two of the most notable men were Leon Trotsky and **Joseph Stalin**. Stalin was cold, hard, and impersonal. During his early days as a Bolshevik, he changed his name to Stalin, which means "man of steel" in Russian. The name fit well.

Stalin began his ruthless climb to the head of the government between 1922 and 1927. In 1922, as general secretary of the Communist Party, he worked behind the scenes to move his supporters into positions of power. Lenin believed that Stalin was a dangerous man. Shortly before he died in 1924, Lenin wrote, "Comrade Stalin . . . has concentrated enormous power in his hands, and I am not sure that he always knows how to use that power with sufficient caution." By 1928, Stalin was in total command of the Communist Party. Trotsky, forced into exile in 1929, was no longer a threat. Stalin now stood poised to wield absolute power as a dictator.

SECTION **1** **ASSESSMENT**

TERMS & NAMES **1.** For each term or name, write a sentence explaining its significance.
• proletariat • Bolsheviks • Lenin • Rasputin • provisional government • soviet • Communist Party • Joseph Stalin

USING YOUR NOTES	MAIN IDEAS	CRITICAL THINKING & WRITING
2. Which event on your time line caused the deaths of 14 million Russians?	**3.** How did World War I help to bring about the Russian Revolution? **4.** What groups made up the Red Army and the White Army? **5.** Why did the Bolsheviks rename their party the Communist Party?	**6. DRAWING CONCLUSIONS** How did the czar's autocratic policies toward the people lead to social unrest? **7. EVALUATING DECISIONS** What do you think were Czar Nicholas II's worst errors in judgment during his rule? **8. FORMING OPINIONS** Which of the events during the last phase of czarist rule do you think was most responsible for the fall of the czar? **9. WRITING ACTIVITY** REVOLUTION Write a paragraph **analysis** of Lenin's leadership in the success of the Bolshevik Revolution.

1894   *1922*

INTEGRATED TECHNOLOGY **INTERNET ACTIVITY**
Use the Internet to visit Lenin's Tomb in Red Square in Moscow. Write an **evaluation** of the Web site.

INTERNET KEYWORD
Lenin's mausoleum

Totalitarianism

CASE STUDY: Stalinist Russia

MAIN IDEA	WHY IT MATTERS NOW	TERMS & NAMES
POWER AND AUTHORITY After Lenin died, Stalin seized power and transformed the Soviet Union into a totalitarian state.	More recent dictators have used Stalin's tactics for seizing total control over individuals and the state.	• totalitarianism • Five-Year Plan • Great Purge • collective farm • command economy

SETTING THE STAGE Stalin, Lenin's successor, dramatically transformed the government of the Soviet Union. Stalin was determined that the Soviet Union should find its place both politically and economically among the most powerful of nations in the world. Using tactics designed to rid himself of opposition, Stalin worked to establish total control of all aspects of life in the Soviet Union. He controlled not only the government, but also the economy and many aspects of citizens' private lives.

TAKING NOTES

Categorizing Create a chart listing examples of methods of control used in the Soviet Union.

Methods of control	Example
1.	
2.	
3.	
4.	

A Government of Total Control

The term **totalitarianism** describes a government that takes total, centralized, state control over every aspect of public and private life. Totalitarian leaders appear to provide a sense of security and to give a direction for the future. In the 20th century, the widespread use of mass communication made it possible to reach into all aspects of citizens' lives.

A dynamic leader who can build support for his policies and justify his actions heads most totalitarian governments. Often the leader utilizes secret police to crush opposition and create a sense of fear among the people. No one is exempt from suspicion or accusations that he or she is an enemy of the state.

Totalitarianism challenges the highest values prized by Western democracies—reason, freedom, human dignity, and the worth of the individual. As the chart on the next page shows, all totalitarian states share basic characteristics.

To dominate an entire nation, totalitarian leaders devised methods of control and persuasion. These included the use of terror, indoctrination, propaganda, censorship, and religious or ethnic persecution.

Police Terror Dictators of totalitarian states use terror and violence to force obedience and to crush opposition. Normally, the police are expected to respond to criminal activity and protect the citizens. In a totalitarian state, the police serve to enforce the central government's policies. They may do this by spying on the citizens or by intimidating them. Sometimes they use brutal force and even murder to achieve their goals.

Indoctrination Totalitarian states rely on indoctrination—instruction in the government's beliefs—to mold people's minds. Control of education is absolutely essential to glorify the leader and his policies and to convince all citizens that their

Totalitarianism

Totalitarianism is a form of government in which the national government takes control of all aspects of both public and private life. Thus, totalitarianism seeks to erase the line between government and society. It has an ideology, or set of beliefs, that all citizens are expected to approve. It is often led by a dynamic leader and a single political party.

Mass communication technology helps a totalitarian government spread its aims and support its policies. Also, surveillance technology makes it possible to keep track of the activities of many people. Finally, violence, such as police terror, discourages those who disagree with the goals of the government.

Key Traits of Totalitarianism

Diagram showing TOTALITARIANISM in center with traits: Ideology (sets goals of the state, glorifies aims of the state, justifies government actions); State Control of Individuals (demands loyalty, denies basic liberties, expects personal sacrifice for the good of the state); Methods of Enforcement (police terror, indoctrination, censorship, persecution); Modern Technology (mass communication to spread propaganda, advanced military weapons); State Control of Society (business, labor, housing, education, religion, the arts, personal life, youth groups); Dictatorship and One-Party Rule (exercises absolute authority, dominates the government); Dynamic Leader (unites people, symbolizes government, encourages popular support through force of will)

Fear of Totalitarianism

George Orwell illustrated the horrors of a totalitarian government in his novel, *1984*. The novel depicts a world in which personal freedom and privacy have vanished. It is a world made possible through modern technology. Even citizens' homes have television cameras that constantly survey their behavior.

INTEGRATED TECHNOLOGY

RESEARCH LINKS For more on totalitarianism, go to **classzone.com**

> DATA FILE

Totalitarian leaders in the 20th century

- Adolf Hitler (Germany) 1933–1945
- Benito Mussolini (Italy) 1925–1943
- Joseph Stalin (Soviet Union) 1929–1953
- Kim IL Sung (North Korea) 1948–1994
- Saddam Hussein (Iraq) 1979–2003

State Terror

- The two most infamous examples of state terror in the 20th century were in Nazi Germany and Stalinist Russia.
- An estimated 12.5–20 million people were killed in Nazi Germany.
- An estimated 8–20 million people were killed in Stalinist Russia.

Totalitarianism Today

- There are many authoritarian regimes in the world, but there are very few actual totalitarian governments. In 2000, one monitoring agency identified five totalitarian regimes—Afghanistan, Cuba, North Korea, Laos, and Vietnam.

Connect *to* Today

1. **Synthesizing** How does a totalitarian state attempt to make citizens obey its rules?
   See Skillbuilder Handbook, page R21.

2. **Hypothesizing** How would your life change if you lived in a totalitarian state?

441

▲ Members of a Russian youth group called Young Communists line up for a parade. Notice the picture of Stalin in the background.

unconditional loyalty and support are required. Indoctrination begins with very young children, is encouraged by youth groups, and is strongly enforced by schools.

Propaganda and Censorship Totalitarian states spread propaganda, biased or incomplete information used to sway people to accept certain beliefs or actions. Control of all mass media allows this to happen. No publication, film, art, or music is allowed to exist without the permission of the state. Citizens are surrounded with false information that appears to be true. Suggesting that the information is incorrect is considered an act of treason and severely punished. Individuals who dissent must retract their work or they are imprisoned or killed.

Religious or Ethnic Persecution Totalitarian leaders often create "enemies of the state" to blame for things that go wrong. Frequently these enemies are members of religious or ethnic groups. Often these groups are easily identified and are subjected to campaigns of terror and violence. They may be forced to live in certain areas or are subjected to rules that apply only to them. **A**

MAIN IDEA

Evaluating Courses of Action
A Of the weapons of totalitarianism, which allows the most long-term control?

CASE STUDY: Stalinist Russia

Stalin Builds a Totalitarian State

Stalin aimed to create a perfect Communist state in Russia. To realize his vision, Stalin planned to transform the Soviet Union into a totalitarian state. He began building his totalitarian state by destroying his enemies—real and imagined.

Police State Stalin built a police state to maintain his power. Stalin's secret police used tanks and armored cars to stop riots. They monitored telephone lines, read mail, and planted informers everywhere. Even children told authorities about disloyal remarks they heard at home. Every family came to fear the knock on the door in the early morning hours, which usually meant the arrest of a family member. The secret police arrested and executed millions of so-called traitors.

In 1934, Stalin turned against members of the Communist Party. In 1937, he launched the **Great Purge**, a campaign of terror directed at eliminating anyone who threatened his power. Thousands of old Bolsheviks who helped stage the Revolution in 1917 stood trial. They were executed or sent to labor camps for "crimes against the Soviet state." When the Great Purge ended in 1938, Stalin had gained total control of the Soviet government and the Communist Party. Historians estimate that during this time he was responsible for 8 million to 13 million deaths. **B**

MAIN IDEA

Recognizing Effects
B How would the actions of the Great Purge increase Stalin's power?

Russian Propaganda and Censorship Stalin's government controlled all newspapers, motion pictures, radio, and other sources of information. Many Soviet writers, composers, and other artists also fell victim to official censorship. Stalin would not tolerate individual creativity that did not conform to the views of the state. Soviet newspapers and radio broadcasts glorified the achievements of communism, Stalin, and his economic programs.

Under Stalin, the arts also were used for propaganda. In 1930, an editorial in the Communist Party newspaper *Pravda* explained the purpose of art: "Literature, the cinema, the arts are levers in the hands of the proletariat which must be used to show the masses positive models of initiative and heroic labor."

Education and Indoctrination Under Stalin, the government controlled all education from nursery schools through the universities. Schoolchildren learned the virtues of the Communist Party. College professors and students who questioned the Communist Party's interpretations of history or science risked losing their jobs or faced imprisonment. Party leaders in the Soviet Union lectured workers and peasants on the ideals of communism. They also stressed the importance of sacrifice and hard work to build the Communist state. State-supported youth groups trained future party members.

Religious Persecution Communists aimed to replace religious teachings with the ideals of communism. Under Stalin, the government and the League of the Militant Godless, an officially sponsored group of atheists, spread propaganda attacking religion. "Museums of atheism" displayed exhibits to show that religious beliefs were mere superstitions. Yet many people in the Soviet Union still clung to their faiths.

The Russian Orthodox Church was the main target of persecution. Other religious groups also suffered greatly. The police destroyed magnificent churches and synagogues, and many religious leaders were killed or sent to labor camps.

Achieving the perfect Communist state came at a tremendous cost to Soviet citizens. Stalin's total control of society eliminated personal rights and freedoms in favor of the power of the state.

Stalin Seizes Control of the Economy

As Stalin began to gain complete control of society, he was setting plans in motion to overhaul the economy. He announced, "We are fifty or a hundred years behind the advanced countries. We must make good this distance in ten years." In 1928 Stalin's plans called for a **command economy**, a system in which the government made all economic decisions. Under this system, political leaders identify the country's economic needs and determine how to fulfill them.

An Industrial Revolution Stalin outlined the first of several **Five-Year Plans** for the development of the Soviet Union's economy. The Five-Year Plans set impossibly high quotas, or numerical goals, to increase the output of steel, coal, oil, and electricity. To reach these targets, the government limited production of consumer goods. As a result, people faced severe shortages of housing, food, clothing, and other necessary goods.

Stalin's tough methods produced impressive economic results. Although most of the targets of the first Five-Year Plan fell short, the Soviets made substantial gains. (See the graphs on page 444 for coal and steel production.) A second plan, launched in 1933, proved equally successful. From 1928 to 1937, industrial production of steel increased more than 25 percent.

History Makers

Joseph Stalin
1879–1953

Stalin was born in bitter poverty in Georgia, a region in southern Russia. Unlike the well-educated and cultured Lenin, Stalin was rough and crude.

Stalin tried to create a myth that he was the country's father and savior. Stalin glorified himself as the symbol of the nation. He encouraged people to think of him as "The Greatest Genius of All Times and Peoples."

Many towns, factories, and streets in the Soviet Union were named for Stalin. A new metal was called Stalinite. An orchid was named Stalinchid. Children standing before their desks every morning said, "Thank Comrade Stalin for this happy life."

INTEGRATED TECHNOLOGY

INTERNET ACTIVITY Create a Web page on Joseph Stalin. Include pictures and a time line of his rule in the USSR. Go to **classzone.com** for your research.

An Agricultural Revolution In 1928, the government began to seize over 25 million privately owned farms in the USSR. It combined them into large, government-owned farms, called **collective farms**. Hundreds of families worked on these farms, called collectives, producing food for the state. The government expected that the modern machinery on the collective farms would boost food production and reduce the number of workers. Resistance was especially strong among kulaks, a class of wealthy peasants. The Soviet government decided to eliminate them.

Peasants actively fought the government's attempt to take their land. Many killed livestock and destroyed crops in protest. Soviet secret police herded peasants onto collective farms at the point of a bayonet. Between 5 million and 10 million peasants died as a direct result of Stalin's agricultural revolution. By 1938, more than 90 percent of all peasants lived on collective farms. As you see in the charts below, agricultural production was on the upswing. That year the country produced almost twice the wheat than it had in 1928 before collective farming. **C**

In areas where farming was more difficult, the government set up state farms. These state farms operated like factories. The workers received wages instead of a share of the profits. These farms were much larger than collectives and mostly produced wheat.

MAIN IDEA

Clarifying
C What methods did Stalin use to bring agriculture under state control?

Daily Life Under Stalin

Stalin's totalitarian rule revolutionized Soviet society. Women's roles greatly expanded. People became better educated and mastered new technical skills. The dramatic changes in people's lives, came at great cost. Soviet citizens found their personal freedoms limited, consumer goods in short supply, and dissent prohibited.

Stalin's economic plans created a high demand for many skilled workers. University and technical training became the key to a better life. As one young man explained, "If a person does not want to become a collective farmer or just a cleaning woman, the only means you have to get something is through education."

Women Gain Rights The Bolshevik Revolution of 1917 declared men and women equal. Laws were passed to grant women equal rights. After Stalin became dictator, women helped the state-controlled economy prosper. Under his Five-Year

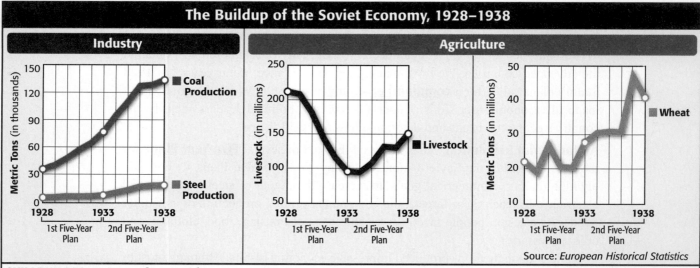

The Buildup of the Soviet Economy, 1928–1938

Source: *European Historical Statistics*

SKILLBUILDER: Interpreting Graphs
1. **Clarifying** *How many more metric tons of coal were produced in 1938 than in 1928?*
2. **Drawing Conclusions** *What do the graphs show about the contrast between the progress of industry and agriculture production under Stalin's first Five-Year Plan?*

Plans, they had no choice but to join the labor force. The state provided child care for all working mothers. Some young women performed the same jobs as men. Millions of women worked in factories and in construction. However, men continued to hold the best jobs.

Given new educational opportunities, women prepared for careers in engineering and science. Medicine, in particular, attracted many women. By 1950, they made up 75 percent of Soviet doctors.

MAIN IDEA

Summarizing

D How did daily life under Stalin's rule change the lives of women in the Soviet Union?

Soviet women paid a heavy price for their rising status in society. Besides having full-time jobs, they were responsible for housework and child care. Motherhood is considered a patriotic duty in totalitarian regimes. Soviet women were expected to provide the state with future generations of loyal, obedient citizens. **D**

Total Control Achieved

By the mid-1930s, Stalin had forcibly transformed the Soviet Union into a totalitarian regime and an industrial and political power. He stood unopposed as dictator and maintained his authority over the Communist Party. Stalin would not tolerate individual creativity. He saw it as a threat to the conformity and obedience required of citizens in a totalitarian state. He ushered in a period of total social control and rule by terror, rather than constitutional government.

Like Russia, China would fall under the influence of Karl Marx's theories and Communist beliefs. The dynamic leader Mao Zedong would pave the way for transforming China into a totalitarian Communist state, as you will read in Section 3.

Social History

Ukrainian Kulaks

The kulaks in Ukraine (shown above) fiercely resisted collectivization. They murdered officials, torched the property of the collectives, and burned their own crops and grain in protest.

Recognizing the threat kulaks posed to his policies, Stalin declared that they should "liquidate kulaks as a class." The state took control of kulak land and equipment, and confiscated stores of food and grain. More than 3 million Ukrainians were shot, exiled, or imprisoned. Some 6 million people died in the government-engineered famine that resulted from the destruction of crops and animals. By 1935, the kulaks had been eliminated.

SECTION **2** **ASSESSMENT**

TERMS & NAMES **1.** For each term or name, write a sentence explaining its significance.
• totalitarianism • Great Purge • command economy • Five-Year Plans • collective farm

USING YOUR NOTES

2. Which of the methods of control do you think was most influential in maintaining Stalin's power? Why?

Methods of control	Example
1.	
2.	
3.	
4.	

MAIN IDEAS

3. What are the key traits of a totalitarian state?

4. What are some ways totalitarian rulers keep their power?

5. How did the Soviet economy change under the direction of Stalin?

CRITICAL THINKING & WRITING

6. CONTRASTING How do totalitarian states and constitutional governments differ?

7. SUMMARIZING Summarize Joseph Stalin's rise to power and how his control expanded.

8. EVALUATING COURSES OF ACTION Were the Five-Year plans the best way to move the Soviet economy forward? Explain.

9. WRITING ACTIVITY POWER AND AUTHORITY As an industrial worker, a female doctor, a Russian Orthodox priest, or a Communist Party member, write a **journal entry** about your life under Stalin.

CONNECT TO TODAY Graphing Russia's Economy

Research Russia's industrial and agricultural production in the last 10 years.
Create a series of **graphs** similar to those found on page 444.

Propaganda

You have read how a totalitarian government can use propaganda to support its goals. These pages show three examples of visual propaganda from the Soviet Union—low-cost posters, traditional painting, and altered photographs.

Posters were mass produced and placed in very visible areas. They were constant reminders of Communist policy and guides for proper thought. Artists were required to paint scenes that supported and glorified the Communist Party. Even photographs were altered if they contained individuals who had fallen out of favor with the party leadership.

INTEGRATED / TECHNOLOGY

RESEARCH LINKS For more on propaganda, go to **classzone.com**

◀ **Factory Poster**
"Help build the gigantic factories." This poster advertises a state loan for the building of large factories. Developing heavy industry was an important goal in the early days of the Soviet Union.

▼ **Painting**
In this painting the central figure, Communist leader Joseph Stalin, is greeted enthusiastically. The expressions of the diverse and happy crowd imply not only that Stalin has broad support, but that he is worshiped as well.

Woman Worker Poster ▲
A translation of this poster says, "What the October Revolution has given to working and peasant women." The woman is pointing to buildings such as a library, a worker's club, and a school for adults.

▼ Altered Photographs

Stalin attempted to enhance his legacy and erase his rivals from history by extensively altering photographs as this series shows.

1 The original photograph was taken in 1926 and showed, from left to right, Nikolai Antipov, Stalin, Sergei Kirov, and Nikolai Shvernik.

2 This altered image appeared in a 1949 biography of Stalin. Why Shvernik was removed is unclear—he was head of the Central Committee of the Communist Party until Stalin's death in 1954. Antipov, however, was arrested during Stalin's purge and executed in 1941.

3 This heroic oil painting by Isaak Brodsky is based on the original photograph, but only Stalin is left. Kirov was assassinated in 1934 by a student, but the official investigation report has never been released. Stalin did fear Kirov's popularity and considered him a threat to his leadership.

Connect *to* Today

1. Forming and Supporting Opinions Of the examples on this page, which do you think would have been most effective as propaganda? Why?

See Skillbuilder Handbook, page R20.

2. Comparing and Contrasting What are the similarities and differences between propaganda and modern advertising campaigns? Support your answer with examples.

447

Imperial China Collapses

MAIN IDEA	WHY IT MATTERS NOW	TERMS & NAMES
REVOLUTION After the fall of the Qing dynasty, nationalist and Communist movements struggled for power.	The seeds of China's late-20th-century political thought, communism, were planted at this time.	• Kuomintang • Mao Zedong • Sun Yixian • Jiang Jieshi • May Fourth • Long March Movement

SETTING THE STAGE In the early 1900s, China was ripe for revolution. China had faced years of humiliation at the hands of outsiders. Foreign countries controlled its trade and economic resources. Many Chinese believed that modernization and nationalism held the country's keys for survival. They wanted to build up the army and navy, to construct modern factories, and to reform education. Yet others feared change. They believed that China's greatness lay in its traditional ways.

TAKING NOTES

Comparing and Contrasting Make a chart to compare and contrast the actions of Jiang Jieshi and Mao Zedong in controlling China.

Jiang	Mao
1.	1.
2.	2.
3.	3.

Nationalists Overthrow Qing Dynasty

Among the groups pushing for modernization and nationalization was the **Kuomintang** (KWOH•mihn•TANG), or the Nationalist Party. Its first great leader was **Sun Yixian** (soon yee•shyahn). In 1911, the Revolutionary Alliance, a forerunner of the Kuomintang, succeeded in overthrowing the last emperor of the Qing dynasty. The Qing had ruled China since 1644.

▼ Sun Yixian led the overthrow of the last Chinese emperor.

Shaky Start for the New Republic In 1912, Sun became president of the new Republic of China. Sun hoped to establish a modern government based on the "Three Principles of the People": (1) nationalism—an end to foreign control, (2) people's rights—democracy, and (3) people's livelihood—economic security for all Chinese. Sun Yixian considered nationalism vital. He said, "The Chinese people . . . do not have national spirit. Therefore even though we have four hundred million people gathered together in one China, in reality, they are just a heap of loose sand." Despite his lasting influence as a revolutionary leader, Sun lacked the authority and military support to secure national unity.

Sun turned over the presidency to a powerful general, Yuan Shikai, who quickly betrayed the democratic ideals of the revolution. His actions sparked local revolts. After the general died in 1916, civil war broke out. Real authority fell into the hands of provincial warlords or powerful military leaders. They ruled territories as large as their armies could conquer.

World War I Spells More Problems In 1917, the government in Beijing, hoping for an Allied victory, declared war against Germany. Some leaders mistakenly believed that for China's participation the thankful Allies would return control of Chinese territories that had previously belonged to Germany. However, under the Treaty of Versailles, the Allied leaders gave Japan those territories.

When news of the Treaty of Versailles reached China, outrage swept the country. On May 4, 1919, over 3,000 angry students gathered in the center of Beijing. The demonstrations spread to other cities and exploded into a national movement. It was called the **May Fourth Movement**. Workers, shopkeepers, and professionals joined the cause. Though not officially a revolution, these demonstrations showed the Chinese people's commitment to the goal of establishing a strong, modern nation. Sun Yixian and members of the Kuomintang also shared the aims of the movement. But they could not strengthen central rule on their own. Many young Chinese intellectuals turned against Sun Yixian's belief in Western democracy in favor of Lenin's brand of Soviet communism. **A**

MAIN IDEA

Identifying Problems

A What problems did the new Republic of China face?

The Communist Party in China

In 1921, a group met in Shanghai to organize the Chinese Communist Party. **Mao Zedong** (MOW dzuh•dahng), an assistant librarian at Beijing University, was among its founders. Later he would become China's greatest revolutionary leader.

Mao Zedong had already begun to develop his own brand of communism. Lenin had based his Marxist revolution on his organization in Russia's cities. Mao envisioned a different setting. He believed he could bring revolution to a rural country

Connect to Today

Tiananmen Square

In Tiananmen Square, the Gate of Heavenly Peace was the site of many political activities during the 20th century. Early in the century, May 4, 1919, thousands of students gathered there to protest the terms of the Versailles Treaty. (upper right). The May Fourth Movement was born that day. The movement marks the beginning of Chinese nationalism.

Seventy years later, in 1989, students once again gathered at the square to demand political reforms. Shortly after the anniversary of the May 4 event, thousands—and perhaps a million people—gathered at the square. On June 3, 1989, the Chinese army was ordered to clear the square of all protesters. Thousands were killed or injured.

where the peasants could be the true revolutionaries. He argued his point passionately in 1927:

PRIMARY SOURCE B

The force of the peasantry is like that of the raging winds and driving rain. It is rapidly increasing in violence. No force can stand in its way. The peasantry will tear apart all nets which bind it and hasten along the road to liberation. They will bury beneath them all forces of imperialism, militarism, corrupt officialdom, village bosses and evil gentry.

MAO ZEDONG, quoted in *Chinese Communism and the Rise of Mao*

MAIN IDEA

Analyzing Primary Sources
B What forces does Mao identify as those that the peasants will overcome?

Lenin Befriends China While the Chinese Communist Party was forming, Sun Yixian and his Nationalist Party set up a government in south China. Like the Communists, Sun became disillusioned with the Western democracies that refused to support his struggling government. Sun decided to ally the Kuomintang with the newly formed Communist Party. He hoped to unite all the revolutionary groups for common action.

Lenin seized the opportunity to help China's Nationalist government. In 1923, he sent military advisers and equipment to the Nationalists in return for allowing the Chinese Communists to join the Kuomintang.

Peasants Align with the Communists After Sun Yixian died in 1925, <u>Jiang Jieshi</u> (jee•ahng jee•shee), formerly called Chiang Kai-shek, headed the Kuomintang. Jiang was the son of a middle-class merchant. Many of Jiang's followers were bankers and businesspeople. Like Jiang, they feared the Communists' goal of creating a socialist economy modeled after the Soviet Union's.

Jiang had promised democracy and political rights to all Chinese. Yet his government became steadily less democratic and more corrupt. Most peasants believed that Jiang was doing little to improve their lives. As a result, many peasants threw their support to the Chinese Communist Party. To enlist the support of the peasants, Mao divided land that the Communists won among the local farmers.

Nationalists and Communists Clash At first, Jiang put aside his differences with the Communists. Together Jiang's Nationalist forces and the Communists successfully fought the warlords. Soon afterward, though, he turned against the Communists.

In April 1927, Nationalist troops and armed gangs moved into Shanghai. They killed many Communist leaders and trade union members in the city streets. Similar killings took place in other cities. The Nationalists nearly wiped out the Chinese Communist Party.

In 1928, Jiang became president of the Nationalist Republic of China. Great Britain and the United States both formally recognized the new government. Because of the slaughter of Communists at Shanghai, the Soviet Union did not. Jiang's treachery also had long-term effects. The Communists' deep-seated rage over the massacre erupted in a civil war that would last until 1949.

▲ Jiang Jieshi and the Nationalist forces united China under one government in 1928.

Civil War Rages in China

By 1930, Nationalists and Communists were fighting a bloody civil war. Mao and other Communist leaders established themselves in the hills of south-central China. Mao referred to this tactic of taking his revolution to the countryside as "swimming in the peasant sea." He recruited the peasants to join his Red Army. He then trained them in guerrilla warfare. Nationalists attacked the Communists repeatedly but failed to drive them out.

The Long March In 1933, Jiang gathered an army of at least 700,000 men. Jiang's army then surrounded the Communists' mountain stronghold. Outnumbered, the

The Long March

The Long March of the Chinese Communists from the south of China to the caves of Shaanxi [shahn•shee] in the north is a remarkable story. The march covered 6,000 miles, about the distance from New York to San Francisco and back again. They crossed miles of swampland. They slept sitting up, leaning back-to-back in pairs, to keep from sinking into the mud and drowning. In total, the Communists crossed 18 mountain ranges and 24 rivers in their yearlong flight from the Nationalist forces.

The Long March, 1934–1935

- ➜ Route of march
- Communist base 1934
- Communist base 1935
- Mountains
- Pass

Beijing

3 Yan'au

Huang He

Songpan Plateau

2 Snowy Mts. (Jiajin Shan)

Tatu R.—

Luding

Chang Jiang

Shanghai

1 Loushan Pass

Ruijin (Juichin)

Taiwan

Tropic of Cancer

South China Sea

Hainan

0 400 Miles
0 600 Kilometers

GEOGRAPHY SKILLBUILDER: Interpreting Maps

1. **Movement** *What was the course of the Long March, in terms of direction, beginning in Ruijin and ending near Yan'an?*
2. **Movement** *Why didn't Mao's forces move west or south?*

▼ In one of the more daring and difficult acts of the march, the Red Army crossed a bridge of iron chains whose planks had been removed.

▼ The Red Army had to cross the Snowy Mountains, some of the highest in the world. Every man carried enough food and fuel to last for ten days. They marched six to seven hours a day.

◄ After finally arriving at the caves in Shaanxi, Mao declared, "If we can survive all this, we can survive everything. This is but the first stage of our Long March. The final stage leads to Peking [Beijing]!"

▲ A Japanese landing party approaches the Chinese mainland. The invasion forced Mao and Jiang to join forces to fight the Japanese.

Communist Party leaders realized that they faced defeat. In a daring move, 100,000 Communist forces fled. They began a hazardous, 6,000-mile-long journey called the **Long March**. Between 1934 and 1935, the Communists kept only a step ahead of Jiang's forces. Thousands died from hunger, cold, exposure, and battle wounds.

Finally, after a little more than a year, Mao and the seven or eight thousand Communist survivors settled in caves in northwestern China. There they gained new followers. Meanwhile, as civil war between Nationalists and Communists raged, Japan invaded China. **C**

MAIN IDEA

Recognizing Effects

C What were the results of the Long March?

Civil War Suspended In 1931, as Chinese fought Chinese, the Japanese watched the power struggles with rising interest. Japanese forces took advantage of China's weakening situation. They invaded Manchuria, an industrialized province in the northeast part of China.

In 1937, the Japanese launched an all-out invasion of China. Massive bombings of villages and cities killed thousands of Chinese. The destruction of farms caused many more to die of starvation. By 1938, Japan held control of a large part of China.

The Japanese threat forced an uneasy truce between Jiang's and Mao's forces. The civil war gradually ground to a halt as Nationalists and Communists temporarily united to fight the Japanese. The National Assembly further agreed to promote changes outlined in Sun Yixian's "Three Principles of the People"—nationalism, democracy, and people's livelihood. As you will learn in Section 4, similar principles were also serving as a guiding force in India and Southwest Asia.

SECTION 3 ASSESSMENT

TERMS & NAMES 1. For each term or name, write a sentence explaining its significance.
• Kuomintang • Sun Yixian • May Fourth Movement • Mao Zedong • Jiang Jieshi • Long March

USING YOUR NOTES

2. Whose reforms had a greater appeal to the peasants? Why?

Jiang	Mao
1.	1.
2.	2.
3.	3.

MAIN IDEAS

3. How did the Treaty of Versailles trigger the May Fourth Movement?

4. How was Mao's vision of communism different from that of Lenin?

5. What started the civil war in China?

CRITICAL THINKING & WRITING

6. **RECOGNIZING EFFECTS** What influence did foreign nations have on China from 1912 to 1938?

7. **ANALYZING CAUSES** What caused the Communist revolutionary movement in China to gain strength?

8. **HYPOTHESIZING** If the Long March had failed, do you think the Nationalist party would have been successful in uniting the Chinese? Why or why not?

9. **WRITING ACTIVITY** REVOLUTION Write a series of **interview questions** you would pose to Sun Yixian, Mao Zedong, and Jiang Jieshi.

CONNECT TO TODAY REPORTING ON CURRENT EVENTS

Research the selection of the newest Communist Party leader of China. Write a brief **report** identifying that person and explaining how this new leader got into office.

4

Nationalism in India and Southwest Asia

MAIN IDEA	WHY IT MATTERS NOW	TERMS & NAMES
EMPIRE BUILDING Nationalism triggered independence movements to overthrow colonial powers.	These independent nations—India, Turkey, Iran, and Saudi Arabia—are key players on the world stage today.	• Rowlatt Acts • Amritsar Massacre • Mohandas K. Gandhi • civil disobedience • Salt March • Mustafa Kemal

SETTING THE STAGE As you learned in Chapter 13, the end of World War I broke up the Ottoman Empire. The British Empire, which controlled India, began to show signs of cracking. The weakening of these empires stirred nationalist activity in India, Turkey, and some Southwest Asian countries. Indian nationalism had been growing since the mid-1800s. Many upper-class Indians who attended British schools learned European views of nationalism and democracy. They began to apply these political ideas to their own country.

Indian Nationalism Grows

Two groups formed to rid India of foreign rule: the primarily Hindu Indian National Congress, or Congress Party, in 1885, and the Muslim League in 1906. Though deep divisions existed between Hindus and Muslims, they found common ground. They shared the heritage of British rule and an understanding of democratic ideals. These two groups both worked toward the goal of independence from the British.

▼ Ali Jinnah, leader of the Muslim League of India, fought for Indian independence from Great Britain.

World War I Increases Nationalist Activity Until World War I, the vast majority of Indians had little interest in nationalism. The situation changed as over a million Indians enlisted in the British army. In return for their service, the British government promised reforms that would eventually lead to self-government.

In 1918, Indian troops returned home from the war. They expected Britain to fulfill its promise. Instead, they were once again treated as second-class citizens. Radical nationalists carried out acts of violence to show their hatred of British rule. To curb dissent, in 1919 the British passed the **Rowlatt Acts**. These laws allowed the government to jail protesters without trial for as long as two years. To Western-educated Indians, denial of a trial by jury violated their individual rights.

Amritsar Massacre To protest the Rowlatt Acts, around 10,000 Hindus and Muslims flocked to Amritsar, a major city in the Punjab, in the spring of 1919. At a huge festival in an enclosed square, they intended to fast and pray and to listen to political

TAKING NOTES

Categorizing Create a web diagram identifying the styles of government adopted by nations in this section.

speeches. The demonstration, viewed as a nationalist outburst, alarmed the British. They were especially concerned about the alliance of Hindus and Muslims.

Most people at the gathering were unaware that the British government had banned public meetings. However, the British commander at Amritsar believed they were openly defying the ban. He ordered his troops to fire on the crowd without warning. The shooting in the enclosed courtyard continued for ten minutes. Official reports showed nearly 400 Indians died and about 1,200 were wounded. Others estimate the numbers were higher.

News of the slaughter, called the **Amritsar Massacre**, sparked an explosion of anger across India. Almost overnight, millions of Indians changed from loyal British subjects into nationalists. These Indians demanded independence. **A**

MAIN IDEA
Recognizing Effects
A What changes resulted from the Amritsar massacre?

Gandhi's Tactics of Nonviolence

The massacre at Amritsar set the stage for **Mohandas K. Gandhi** (GAHN•dee) to emerge as the leader of the independence movement. Gandhi's strategy for battling injustice evolved from his deeply religious approach to political activity. His teachings blended ideas from all of the major world religions, including Hinduism, Jainism, Buddhism, Islam, and Christianity. Gandhi attracted millions of followers. Soon they began calling him the Mahatma (muh•HAHT•muh), meaning "great soul."

Noncooperation When the British failed to punish the officers responsible for the Amritsar massacre, Gandhi urged the Indian National Congress to follow a policy of noncooperation with the British government. In 1920, the Congress Party endorsed **civil disobedience**, the deliberate and public refusal to obey an unjust law, and nonviolence as the means to achieve independence. Gandhi then launched his campaign of

> Analyzing Primary Sources

Satyagraha

A central element of Gandhi's philosophy of nonviolence was called *satyagraha*, often translated as "soul-force" or "truth-force."

PRIMARY SOURCE

Passive resistance is a method of securing rights by personal suffering; it is the reverse of resistance by arms. When I refuse to do a thing that is repugnant to my conscience, I use soul-force. For instance, the government of the day has passed a law which is applicable to me: I do not like it, if, by using violence, I force the government to repeal the law, I am employing what may be termed body-force. If I do not obey the law and accept the penalty for its breach, I use soul-force. It involves sacrifice of self.

GANDHI Chapter XVII, *Hind Swaraj*

Nonviolence

In *The Origin of Nonviolence*, Gandhi offered a warning to those who were contemplating joining the struggle for independence.

PRIMARY SOURCE

[I]t is not at all impossible that we might have to endure every hardship that we can imagine, and wisdom lies in pledging ourselves on the understanding that we shall have to suffer all that and worse. If some one asks me when and how the struggle may end, I may say that if the entire community manfully stands the test, the end will be near. If many of us fall back under storm and stress, the struggle will be prolonged. But I can boldly declare, and with certainty, that so long as there is even a handful of men true to their pledge, there can only be one end to the struggle, and that is victory.

GANDHI *The Origin of Nonviolence*

DOCUMENT-BASED QUESTIONS
1. **Comparing** *How is soul-force different from body-force?*
2. **Making Inferences** *What do Gandhi's writings suggest about his view of suffering? Give examples from each document.*

of civil disobedience to weaken the British government's authority and economic power over India.

Boycotts Gandhi called on Indians to refuse to buy British goods, attend government schools, pay British taxes, or vote in elections. Gandhi staged a successful boycott of British cloth, a source of wealth for the British. He urged all Indians to weave their own cloth. Gandhi himself devoted two hours each day to spinning his own yarn on a simple handwheel. He wore only homespun cloth and encouraged Indians to follow his example. As a result of the boycott, the sale of British cloth in India dropped sharply.

Strikes and Demonstrations Gandhi's weapon of civil disobedience took an economic toll on the British. They struggled to keep trains running, factories operating, and overcrowded jails from bursting. Throughout 1920, the British arrested thousands of Indians who had participated in strikes and demonstrations. But despite Gandhi's pleas for nonviolence, protests often led to riots.

The Salt March In 1930, Gandhi organized a demonstration to defy the hated Salt Acts. According to these British laws, Indians could buy salt from no other source but the government. They also had to pay sales tax on salt. To show their opposition, Gandhi and his followers walked about 240 miles to the seacoast. There they began to make their own salt by collecting seawater and letting it evaporate. This peaceful protest was called the **Salt March**.

Soon afterward, some demonstrators planned a march to a site where the British government processed salt. They intended to shut this saltworks down. Police officers with steel-tipped clubs attacked the demonstrators. An American journalist was an eyewitness to the event. He described the "sickening whacks of clubs on unprotected skulls" and people "writhing in pain with fractured skulls or broken shoulders." Still the people continued to march peacefully, refusing to defend themselves against their attackers. Newspapers across the globe carried the journalist's story, which won worldwide support for Gandhi's independence movement.

More demonstrations against the salt tax took place throughout India. Eventually, about 60,000 people, including Gandhi, were arrested. **B**

▲ Gandhi adopted the spinning wheel as a symbol of Indian resistance to British rule. The wheel was featured on the Indian National Congress flag, a forerunner of India's national flag.

MAIN IDEA

Making Inferences

B How did the Salt March represent Gandhi's methods for change?

Britain Grants Limited Self-Rule

Gandhi and his followers gradually reaped the rewards of their civil disobedience campaigns and gained greater political power for the Indian people. In 1935, the British Parliament passed the Government of India Act. It provided local self-government and limited democratic elections, but not total independence.

However, the Government of India Act also fueled mounting tensions between Muslims and Hindus. These two groups had conflicting visions of India's future as an independent nation. Indian Muslims, outnumbered by Hindus, feared that Hindus would control India if it won independence. In Chapter 18, you will read about the outcome of India's bid for independence.

Mustafa Kemal
1881–1938

As president of Turkey, Mustafa Kemal campaigned vigorously to mold the new republic into a modern nation. His models were the United States and other European countries.

Kemal believed that even the clothing of the Turks should be changed to reflect a civilized, international dress. To reach this goal, Kemal set rules for clothing. He required government workers to wear Western-style business suits and banned the fez, a brimless red felt hat that was part of traditional Turkish clothing.

Nationalism in Southwest Asia

The breakup of the Ottoman Empire and growing Western political and economic interest in Southwest Asia spurred the rise of nationalism in this region. Just as the people of India fought to have their own nation after World War I, the people of Southwest Asia also launched independence movements to rid themselves of imperial rulers.

Turkey Becomes a Republic At the end of World War I, the Ottoman Empire was forced to give up all its territories except Turkey. Turkish lands included the old Turkish homeland of Anatolia and a small strip of land around Istanbul.

In 1919, Greek soldiers invaded Turkey and threatened to conquer it. The Turkish sultan was powerless to stop the Greeks. However, in 1922, a brilliant commander, **Mustafa Kemal** (keh•MAHL), successfully led Turkish nationalists in fighting back the Greeks and their British backers. After winning a peace, the nationalists overthrew the last Ottoman sultan.

In 1923, Kemal became the president of the new Republic of Turkey, the first republic in Southwest Asia. To achieve his goal of transforming Turkey into a modern nation, he ushered in these sweeping reforms:

- separated the laws of Islam from the laws of the nation
- abolished religious courts and created a new legal system based on European law
- granted women the right to vote and to hold public office
- launched government-funded programs to industrialize Turkey and to spur economic growth

Kemal died in 1938. From his leadership, Turkey gained a new sense of its national identity. His influence was so strong that the Turkish people gave him the name Ataturk—"father of the Turks."

Persia Becomes Iran Before World War I, both Great Britain and Russia had established spheres of influence in the ancient country of Persia. After the war, when Russia was still reeling from the Bolshevik Revolution, the British tried to take over all of Persia. This maneuver triggered a nationalist revolt in Persia. In 1921, a Persian army officer seized power. In 1925 he deposed the ruling shah.

Persia's new leader, Reza Shah Pahlavi (PAL•uh•vee), like Kemal in Turkey, set out to modernize his country. He established public schools, built roads and railroads, promoted industrial growth, and extended women's rights. Unlike Kemal, Reza Shah Pahlavi kept all power in his own hands. In 1935, he changed the name of the country from the Greek name Persia to the traditional name Iran. **C**

Saudi Arabia Keeps Islamic Traditions While Turkey broke with many Islamic traditions, another new country held strictly to Islamic law. In 1902, Abd al-Aziz Ibn Saud (sah•OOD), a member of a once-powerful Arabian family, began a successful campaign to unify Arabia. In 1932, he renamed the new kingdom Saudi Arabia after his family.

Ibn Saud carried on Arab and Islamic traditions. Loyalty to the Saudi government was based on custom, religion, and family ties. Like Kemal and Reza Shah, Ibn Saud brought some modern technology, such as telephones and radios, to his

MAIN IDEA

Comparing
C How were Kemal's leadership and Reza Shah Pahlavi's leadership similar?

country. However, modernization in Saudi Arabia was limited to religiously acceptable areas. There also were no efforts to begin to practice democracy.

Oil Drives Development While nationalism steadily emerged as a major force in Southwest Asia, the region's economy was also taking a new direction. The rising demand for petroleum products in industrialized countries brought new oil explorations to Southwest Asia. During the 1920s and 1930s, European and American companies discovered enormous oil deposits in Iran, Iraq, Saudi Arabia, and Kuwait. Foreign businesses invested huge sums of money to develop these oil fields. For example, the Anglo-Persian Oil Company, a British company, started developing the oil fields of Iran. Geologists later learned that the land around the Persian Gulf has nearly two-thirds of the world's known supply of oil.

This important resource led to rapid and dramatic economic changes and development. Because oil brought huge profits, Western nations tried to dominate this region. Meanwhile, these same Western nations were about to face a more immediate crisis as power-hungry leaders seized control in Italy and Germany.

Oil Fields, 1938

| ⚒ | Oil fields |
| 1908 | Date of first oil discovery |

USSR
TURKEY
CYPRUS (Br.)
SYRIA
LEBANON
IRAQ 1927
IRAN 1908
PALESTINE
TRANS-JORDAN
KUWAIT 1938
EGYPT
BAHRAIN 1932
QATAR 1938
TRUCIAL STATES
SAUDI ARABIA 1936
OMAN
ADEN PROTECTORATE
YEMEN
Caspian Sea
Persian Gulf
Red Sea
Arabian Sea

GEOGRAPHY SKILLBUILDER: Interpreting Maps
1. **Location** Along what geographical feature are most of the oil-producing regions located?
2. **Movement** How will water transportation routes be changed by the discovery of oil in the region?

SECTION 4 **ASSESSMENT**

TERMS & NAMES 1. For each term or name, write a sentence explaining its significance.
• Rowlatt Acts   • Amritsar Massacre   • Mohandas K. Gandhi   • civil disobedience   • Salt March   • Mustafa Kemal

USING YOUR NOTES
2. Why do you think the nations in this section adopted different styles of government?

Iran   Turkey
styles of government
India   Saudi Arabia

MAIN IDEAS
3. How did Gandhi's tactics of civil disobedience affect the British?
4. How did Southwest Asia change as a result of nationalism?
5. How did newly found petroleum supplies change the new nations in Southwest Asia?

CRITICAL THINKING & WRITING
6. **HYPOTHESIZING** What do you think a nation might gain and lose by modernizing?
7. **RECOGNIZING EFFECTS** How did World War I create an atmosphere for political change in both India and Southwest Asia?
8. **COMPARING AND CONTRASTING** Compare and contrast the different forms of government adopted by the four nations in this section.
9. **WRITING ACTIVITY** POWER AND AUTHORITY Write a **persuasive essay** supporting the use of nonviolent resistance.

CONNECT TO TODAY GRAPHING OIL EXPORTS
Do research to find out how many barrels of oil have been exported each year for the last ten years from Iran, Iraq, and Saudi Arabia. Create a **graph** showing your results.

TERMS & NAMES

Briefly explain the importance of each of the following in Russia, China, or India.

1. Bolsheviks
2. Lenin
3. soviet
4. Joseph Stalin
5. totalitarianism
6. Mao Zedong
7. Mohandas K. Gandhi
8. civil disobedience

MAIN IDEAS

Revolutions in Russia Section 1 (pages 433–439)

9. How did World War I lead to the downfall of Czar Nicholas II?
10. Why did the provisional government fail?
11. Explain the causes of Russia's civil war and its outcome.

Case Study: Totalitarianism Section 2 (pages 440–447)

12. What are the key traits of totalitarianism?
13. What individual freedoms are denied in a totalitarian state?
14. How did Joseph Stalin create a totalitarian state in the Soviet Union?

Imperial China Collapses Section 3 (pages 448–452)

15. Why did the peasants align themselves with the Chinese Communists?
16. Why did Mao Zedong undertake the Long March?

Nationalism in India and Southwest Asia
Section 4 (pages 453–457)

17. What are some examples of civil disobedience led by Mohandas Gandhi?
18. What steps did Kemal take to modernize Turkey?

CRITICAL THINKING

1. USING YOUR NOTES

In a diagram show the causes of changes in government in the countries listed.

China   Russia
Causes of Government Changes
Turkey   India

2. FORMING AND SUPPORTING OPINIONS

Which of the weapons of totalitarian governments do you think is most effective in maintaining control of a country? Explain.

3. ANALYZING CAUSES

REVOLUTION What role did World War I play in the revolutions and nationalistic uprisings discussed in this chapter?

4. HYPOTHESIZING

EMPIRE BUILDING Why were the empires discussed in this chapter unable to remain in control of all of their lands?

5. RECOGNIZING EFFECTS

POWER AND AUTHORITY How did women's roles change under Stalin in Russia and Kemal in Turkey?

VISUAL SUMMARY

Revolutionary Leaders: 1900–1939

	Lenin	Stalin	Sun Yixian	Mao Zedong	Gandhi	Kemal
Country	Russia	Russia	China	China	India	Turkey
Career	late 1890s–1924	early 1900s–1953	late 1890s–1925	early 1900s–1976	late 1800s–1948	early 1900s–1938
Key Role	Bolshevik revolutionary and first ruler of Communist Russia	Dictator	First president of the new Republic of China	Leader of the Chinese Communist Party	Leader of the Indian independence movement	First president of the new Republic of Turkey
Popular Name	"Father of the Revolution"	"Man of Steel"	"Father of Modern China"	"The Great Helmsman"	"Great Soul"	"Father of the Turks"
Goal	Promote a worldwide Communist revolution led by workers	Perfect a Communist state in Russia through totalitarian rule	Establish a modern government based on nationalism, democracy, and economic security	Stage a Communist revolution in China led by peasants	Achieve Indian self-rule through campaigns of civil disobedience	Transform Turkey into a modern nation

Use the quotation and your knowledge of world history to answers questions 1 and 2
Additional Test Practice, pp. S1–S33

PRIMARY SOURCE

India does not need to be industrialized in the modern sense of the term. It has 7,500,000 villages scattered over a vast area 1,900 miles long, 1,500 broad. The people are rooted to the soil, and the vast majority are living a hand-to-mouth life. . . . Agriculture does not need revolutionary changes. The Indian peasant requires a supplementary industry. The most natural is the introduction of the spinning-wheel.

MOHANDAS K. GANDHI, Letter to Sir Daniel Hamilton

1. What picture does Gandhi present of India and its people?

   A. India is adequately industrialized.

   B. India is dominated by the British.

   C. India is primarily an agricultural nation.

   D. Indians are well-off and do not need additional industries.

2. What did Gandhi believe about the spinning wheel?

   A. Gandhi believed that the spinning wheel would make Indians less dependent on the British economy.

   B. Gandhi believed that the spinning wheel was a threat to the Indian economy.

   C. Gandhi believed the main economic industry in India should be spinning cloth.

   D. Gandhi believed the spinning wheel was not necessary to the Indian economy.

Use the graph and your knowledge of world history to answer question 3.

Oil Output, 1910–1940

Source: *International Historical Statistics*

3. Between which years did Iran show a dramatic increase in oil production?

   A. 1910–1920

   B. 1920–1925

   C. 1930–1935

INTEGRATED TECHNOLOGY

TEST PRACTICE Go to **classzone.com**

- Diagnostic tests
- Strategies
- Tutorials
- Additional practice

ALTERNATIVE ASSESSMENT

1. **Interact *with* History**

   On page 432, you played the role of a citizen whose country was brimming with revolutionary activity. You evaluated two tactics for change—violence and nonviolence. Now that you have read the chapter, how would you assess the pros and cons of Mao's and Gandhi's strategies? What role did violence play in the Russian and Chinese revolutions? How successful were Gandhi's nonviolent methods in India? Discuss your opinions in a small group.

2. **WRITING ABOUT HISTORY**

   Write a **science fiction story** about a totalitarian state that uses modern technology to spread propaganda and control people. Refer to the case study on totalitarianism for ideas. Consider the following:

   - the need to control information
   - methods to control the actions of people
   - reasons people oppose totalitarian control of a country

INTEGRATED TECHNOLOGY

Writing a Documentary Film Script

Write a documentary film script profiling a country where nationalistic revolutionary movements are currently active. Consider the following:

- What type of government is currently in power? (constitutional monarchy, single-party dictatorship, theocracy, republic) How long has it been in power?
- Who are the top political leaders, and how are they viewed inside and outside the country?
- Do citizens have complaints about their government? What are they?
- What nationalist revolutionary groups are active? What are their goals and strategies?

The script should also include narration, locations, sound, and visuals.

Years of Crisis, 1919–1939

Previewing Main Ideas

SCIENCE AND TECHNOLOGY In the 1920s, new scientific ideas changed the way people looked at the world. New inventions improved transportation and communication.

Geography *Innovations in transportation allowed pilot Charles Lindbergh to fly solo from North America across the Atlantic Ocean. Toward what continent did Lindbergh fly?*

ECONOMICS The collapse of the American economy in 1929 triggered a depression that threatened the economic and political systems of countries throughout the world.

Geography *Study the map and time line. What events occurred after the economic crisis that changed the balance of world power?*

POWER AND AUTHORITY In the 1930s, several countries—including Japan, Germany, and Italy—adopted aggressive, militaristic policies.

Geography *What land did Germany invade in 1939?*

INTEGRATED TECHNOLOGY

eEdition
• Interactive Maps
• Interactive Visuals
• Interactive Primary Sources

INTERNET RESOURCES
Go to **classzone.com** for:
• Research Links   • Maps
• Internet Activities • Test Practice
• Primary Sources   • Current Events
• Chapter Quiz

1919
Weimar Republic is established in Germany.

1921
Albert Einstein receives the Nobel Prize. ▶

1928
Kellogg-Briand peace pact is signed by almost every country in the world.

EUROPE

1920   **1925**

WORLD

1927
◀ American pilot Charles Lindbergh crosses Atlantic.

1929
U.S. stock market crashes; Great Depression begins.

Expansion in Europe, 1931–1939

SWEDEN

DENMARK

North Sea

Baltic Sea

LATVIA

MEMEL TERR. March 1939

LITHUANIA

EAST PRUSSIA (Ger.)

GREAT BRITAIN

NETHERLANDS

GERMANY

Germany invades Poland, Sept. 1939

BELGIUM

POLAND

LUXEMBOURG

RHINELAND (Remilitarized by Germany, 1936)

SUDETENLAND October 1938

CZECHOSLOVAKIA

March 1939

FRANCE

SWITZ.

AUSTRIA March 1938

HUNGARY

45°N

ROMANIA

Adriatic Sea

YUGOSLAVIA

ITALY

CORSICA

BULGARIA

SPAIN

SARDINIA

ALBANIA April 1939

Mediterranean Sea

15°E

GREECE

Germany, 1935
German annexations
Italy, 1935
Italian annexation

N E S W

0   125   250 Miles
0   125   250 Kilometers
Conic Projection

1933
Hitler is named German chancellor.

1936
◄ Spanish Civil War begins.

1939
Germany and Soviet Union sign nonaggression pact.

1930

1935

1940

1931
Hirohito's Japan seizes Manchuria. ▶

1935
Ethiopia is invaded by Italian forces.

Which candidate will you choose?

On a spring evening in the early 1930s during the Great Depression, you are one of thousands of Germans gathered at an outdoor stadium in Munich. You are unemployed; your country is suffering. Like everyone else, you have come to this mass meeting to hear two politicians campaigning for office. Huge speakers blare out patriotic music, while you and the rest of the crowd wait impatiently for the speeches to begin.

Before long you will have to cast your ballot.

First candidate's platform

- Remember Germany's long and glorious past
- Replace our present indecisive leadership with a strong, effective leader
- Rebuild the army to protect against enemies
- Regain the lands taken unfairly from us
- Make sacrifices to return to economic health
- Put the welfare of the state above all, and our country will be a great power again

Second candidate's platform

- Realize that there are no simple or quick solutions to problems
- Put people back to work, but economic recovery will be slow
- Provide for the poor, elderly, and sick
- Avoid reckless military spending
- Act responsibly to safeguard democracy
- Be a good neighbor country; honor our debts and treaty commitments

EXAMINING *the* ISSUES

- **What strategy does each candidate have for solving the nation's problems?**
- **Which candidate makes the stronger appeal to the listener's emotions?**

As a class, discuss these questions. In your discussion, remember what you have read about the defeated nations' bitterness toward the Versailles Treaty following World War I. As you read this chapter, notice that dictators were voted into power as people lost faith in democratic government in the 1920s and 1930s.

Postwar Uncertainty

MAIN IDEA	WHY IT MATTERS NOW	TERMS & NAMES
SCIENCE AND TECHNOLOGY The postwar period was one of loss and uncertainty but also one of invention, creativity, and new ideas.	Postwar trends in physics, psychiatry, art, literature, communication, music, and transportation still affect our lives.	• Albert Einstein • theory of relativity • Sigmund Freud • existentialism • Friedrich Nietzsche • surrealism • jazz • Charles Lindbergh

SETTING THE STAGE The horrors of World War I shattered the Enlightenment belief that progress would continue and reason would prevail. In the postwar period, people began questioning traditional beliefs. Some found answers in new scientific developments, which challenged the way people looked at the world. Many enjoyed the convenience of technological improvements in transportation and communication. As society became more open, women demanded more rights, and young people adopted new values. Meanwhile, unconventional styles and ideas in literature, philosophy, and music reflected the uncertain times.

A New Revolution in Science

The ideas of Albert Einstein and Sigmund Freud had an enormous impact on the 20th century. These thinkers were part of a scientific revolution as important as that brought about centuries earlier by Copernicus and Galileo.

Impact of Einstein's Theory of Relativity German-born physicist **Albert Einstein** offered startling new ideas on space, time, energy, and matter. Scientists had found that light travels at exactly the same speed no matter what direction it moves in relation to earth. In 1905, Einstein theorized that while the speed of light is constant, other things that seem constant, such as space and time, are not. Space and time can change when measured relative to an object moving near the speed of light—about 186,000 miles per second. Since relative motion is the key to Einstein's idea, it is called the **theory of relativity**. Einstein's ideas had implications not only for science but also for how people viewed the world. Now uncertainty and relativity replaced Isaac Newton's comforting belief of a world operating according to absolute laws of motion and gravity.

Influence of Freudian Psychology The ideas of Austrian physician **Sigmund Freud** were as revolutionary as Einstein's. Freud treated patients with psychological problems. From his experiences, he constructed a theory about the human mind. He believed that much of human behavior is irrational, or beyond reason. He called the irrational part of the mind the unconscious. In the unconscious, a number of drives existed, especially pleasure-seeking drives, of which the conscious mind was unaware. Freud's ideas weakened faith in reason. Even so, by the 1920s, Freud's theories had developed widespread influence.

TAKING NOTES

Summarizing Use a chart to identify two people who contributed to each field.

Field	Contributors
science	
literature and philosophy	
art and music	
technology	

Literature in the 1920s

The brutality of World War I caused philosophers and writers to question accepted ideas about reason and progress. Disillusioned by the war, many people also feared the future and expressed doubts about traditional religious beliefs. Some writers and thinkers expressed their anxieties by creating disturbing visions of the present and the future.

In 1922, T. S. Eliot, an American poet living in England, wrote that Western society had lost its spiritual values. He described the postwar world as a barren "wasteland," drained of hope and faith. In 1921, the Irish poet William Butler Yeats conveyed a sense of dark times ahead in the poem "The Second Coming": "Things fall apart; the centre cannot hold; / Mere anarchy is loosed upon the world."

Writers Reflect Society's Concerns The horror of war made a deep impression on many writers. The Czech-born author Franz Kafka wrote eerie novels such as *The Trial* (1925) and *The Castle* (1926). His books feature people caught in threatening situations they can neither understand nor escape. The books struck a chord among readers in the uneasy postwar years.

Many novels showed the influence of Freud's theories on the unconscious. The Irish-born author James Joyce gained widespread attention with his stream-of-consciousness novel *Ulysses* (1922). This book focuses on a single day in the lives of three people in Dublin, Ireland. Joyce broke with normal sentence structure and vocabulary in a bold attempt to mirror the workings of the human mind.

Thinkers React to Uncertainties In their search for meaning in an uncertain world, some thinkers turned to the philosophy known as **existentialism**. A major leader of this movement was the philosopher Jean Paul Sartre (SAHR•truh) of France. Existentialists believed that there is no universal meaning to life. Each person creates his or her own meaning in life through choices made and actions taken.

Vocabulary
stream of consciousness: a literary technique used to present a character's thoughts and feelings as they develop

---

> Analyzing Primary Sources

Writers of the "Lost Generation"

During the 1920s, many American writers, musicians, and painters left the United States to live in Europe. These expatriates, people who left their native country to live elsewhere, often settled in Paris. American writer Gertrude Stein called them the "Lost Generation." They moved frantically from one European city to another, trying to find meaning in life. Life empty of meaning is the theme of F. Scott Fitzgerald's *The Great Gatsby* (1925).

PRIMARY SOURCE

And as I sat there brooding on the old, unknown world, I thought of Gatsby's wonder when he first picked out the green light at the end of Daisy's dock. He had come a long way to this blue lawn, and his dream must have seemed so close that he could hardly fail to grasp it. He did not know that it was already behind him, somewhere back in that vast obscurity beyond the city, where the dark fields of the republic rolled on under the night.

Gatsby believed in the green light, the . . . future that year by year recedes before us. It eluded us then, but that's no matter—tomorrow we will run faster, stretch out our arms farther. . . . And one fine morning—

So we beat on, boats against the current, borne back ceaselessly into the past.

F. SCOTT FITZGERALD, *The Great Gatsby*

A 1920s photo of F. Scott Fitzgerald

DOCUMENT-BASED QUESTIONS
1. **Making Inferences** *What seems to be the narrator's attitude toward the future?*
2. **Drawing Conclusions** *How would you describe the overall mood of the excerpt?*

The existentialists were influenced by the German philosopher **Friedrich Nietzsche** (NEE•chuh). In the 1880s, Nietzsche wrote that Western ideas such as reason, democracy, and progress had stifled people's creativity and actions. Nietzsche urged a return to the ancient heroic values of pride, assertiveness, and strength. His ideas attracted growing attention in the 20th century and had a great impact on politics in Italy and Germany in the 1920s and 1930s.

Revolution in the Arts

Although many of the new directions in painting and music began in the prewar period, they evolved after the war.

Artists Rebel Against Tradition Artists rebelled against earlier realistic styles of painting. They wanted to depict the inner world of emotion and imagination rather than show realistic representations of objects. Expressionist painters like Paul Klee and Wassily Kandinsky used bold colors and distorted or exaggerated forms.

Inspired by traditional African art, Georges Braque of France and Pablo Picasso of Spain founded Cubism in 1907. Cubism transformed natural shapes into geometric forms. Objects were broken down into different parts with sharp angles and edges. Often several views were depicted at the same time.

Surrealism, an art movement that sought to link the world of dreams with real life, was inspired by Freud's ideas. The term *surreal* means "beyond or above reality." Surrealists tried to call on the unconscious part of their minds. Many of their paintings have an eerie, dreamlike quality and depict objects in unrealistic ways. **A**

MAIN IDEA

Making Inferences

A What was the major trend in postwar art?

Composers Try New Styles In both classical and popular music, composers moved away from traditional styles. In his ballet masterpiece, *The Rite of Spring,* the Russian composer Igor Stravinsky used irregular rhythms and dissonances, or harsh combinations of sound. The Austrian composer Arnold Schoenberg rejected traditional harmonies and musical scales.

A new popular musical style called **jazz** emerged in the United States. It was developed by musicians, mainly African Americans, in New Orleans, Memphis, and Chicago. It swept the United States and Europe. The lively, loose beat of jazz seemed to capture the new freedom of the age.

◄ *The Persistence of Memory* (1931), a surrealist work by Spanish artist Salvador Dali, shows watches melting in a desert.

▲ Women like these marching in a 1912 suffrage parade in New York City helped gain American women's right to vote in 1920.

Society Challenges Convention

World War I had disrupted traditional social patterns. New ideas and ways of life led to a new kind of individual freedom during the 1920s. Young people especially were willing to break with the past and experiment with modern values.

Women's Roles Change The independent spirit of the times showed clearly in the changes women were making in their lives. The war had allowed women to take on new roles. Their work in the war effort was decisive in helping them win the right to vote. After the war, women's suffrage became law in many countries, including the United States, Britain, Germany, Sweden, and Austria.

Women abandoned restrictive clothing and hairstyles. They wore shorter, looser garments and had their hair "bobbed," or cut short. They also wore makeup, drove cars, and drank and smoked in public. Although most women still followed traditional paths of marriage and family, a growing number spoke out for greater freedom in their lives. Margaret Sanger and Emma Goldman risked arrest by speaking in favor of birth control. As women sought new careers, the numbers of women in medicine, education, journalism, and other professions increased. **B**

MAIN IDEA

Summarizing
B How did the changes of the postwar years affect women?

Technological Advances Improve Life

During World War I, scientists developed new drugs and medical treatments that helped millions of people in the postwar years. The war's technological advances were put to use to improve transportation and communication after the war.

The Automobile Alters Society The automobile benefited from a host of wartime innovations and improvements—electric starters, air-filled tires, and more powerful engines. Cars were now sleek and brightly polished, complete with headlights and chrome-plated bumpers. In prewar Britain, autos were owned exclusively by the rich. British factories produced 34,000 autos in 1913. After the war, prices dropped, and the middle class could afford cars. By 1937, the British were producing 511,000 autos a year.

Increased auto use by the average family led to lifestyle changes. More people traveled for pleasure. In Europe and the United States, new businesses opened to serve the mobile tourist. The auto also affected where people lived and worked. People moved to suburbs and commuted to work in the cities.

Airplanes Transform Travel International air travel became an objective after the war. In 1919, two British pilots made the first successful flight across the Atlantic, from Newfoundland to Ireland. In 1927, an American pilot named **Charles Lindbergh** captured world attention with a 33-hour solo flight from New York to Paris. Most of the world's major passenger airlines were established during the 1920s. At first only the rich were able to afford air travel. Still, everyone enjoyed the exploits of the aviation pioneers, including those of Amelia Earhart. She was an American who, in 1932, became the first woman to fly solo across the Atlantic.

Radio and Movies Dominate Popular Entertainment Guglielmo Marconi conducted his first successful experiments with radio in 1895. However, the real push for radio development came during World War I.

MAIN IDEA

Recognizing Effects

C What were the results of the peacetime adaptations of the technology of war?

In 1920, the world's first commercial radio station—KDKA in Pittsburgh, Pennsylvania—began broadcasting. Almost overnight, radio mania swept the United States. Every major city had stations broadcasting news, plays, and even live sporting events. Soon most families owned a radio. **C**

Motion pictures were also a major industry in the 1920s. Many countries, from Cuba to Japan, produced movies. In Europe, film was a serious art form. However, in the Hollywood district of Los Angeles, where 90 percent of all films were made, movies were entertainment.

The king of Hollywood's silent screen was the English-born Charlie Chaplin, a comic genius best known for his portrayal of the lonely little tramp bewildered by life. In the late 1920s, the addition of sound transformed movies.

The advances in transportation and communication that followed the war had brought the world in closer touch. Global prosperity came to depend on the economic well-being of all major nations, especially the United States.

▲ Dressed in a ragged suit and oversize shoes, Charlie Chaplin's little tramp used gentle humor to get himself out of difficult situations.

SECTION 1 ASSESSMENT

TERMS & NAMES 1. For each term or name, write a sentence explaining its significance.
• Albert Einstein • theory of relativity • Sigmund Freud • existentialism • Friedrich Nietzsche • surrealism • jazz • Charles Lindbergh

USING YOUR NOTES	MAIN IDEAS	CRITICAL THINKING & WRITING
2. In your opinion, whose contribution has had the most lasting impact?	3. Why were the ideas of Einstein and Freud revolutionary?	6. **HYPOTHESIZING** Why do you think writers and artists began exploring the unconscious?

USING YOUR NOTES

2. In your opinion, whose contribution has had the most lasting impact?

Field	Contributors
science	
literature and philosophy	

MAIN IDEAS

3. Why were the ideas of Einstein and Freud revolutionary?

4. How did literature in the 1920s reflect the uncertainty of the period?

5. What impact did the increased use of the automobile have on average people?

CRITICAL THINKING & WRITING

6. **HYPOTHESIZING** Why do you think writers and artists began exploring the unconscious?

7. **DEVELOPING HISTORICAL PERSPECTIVE** Why did some women begin demanding more political and social freedom?

8. **MAKING INFERENCES** Why were new medical treatments and inventions developed during World War I?

9. **WRITING ACTIVITY** SCIENCE AND TECHNOLOGY Write an **advertisement** that might have appeared in a 1920s newspaper or magazine for one of the technological innovations discussed in this section.

CONNECT TO TODAY PREPARING AN ORAL REPORT

Movies in the 1920s reflected the era. What do films made today say about our age? Review some recent, representative films and present your ideas in an **oral report**.

Labor-Saving Devices in the United States

Several changes that took place during the 1920s made the use of electrical household appliances more widespread.

- Wiring for electricity became common. In 1917, only 24 percent of U.S. homes had electricity; by 1930, that figure was almost 70 percent.
- Merchants offered the installment plan, which allowed buyers to make payments over time. That way, people could purchase appliances even if they didn't have the whole price.
- The use of advertising grew. Ads praised appliances, claiming that they would shorten tasks and give women more free time.

Ironically, the new labor-saving devices generally did not decrease the amount of time women spent doing housework. Because the tasks became less physically difficult, many families stopped hiring servants to do the work and relied on the wife to do all the jobs herself.

INTEGRATED TECHNOLOGY

RESEARCH LINKS For more on daily life in the 1920s, go to **classzone.com**

▼ Refrigerator

People used to keep perishable food in iceboxes cooled by large chunks of ice that gradually melted and had to be replaced. Electric refrigerators, like the one in this 1929 advertisement, kept the food at a fairly constant temperature, which reduced spoilage. Because food kept longer, housewives could shop less frequently.

▼ Washing Machine

To do laundry manually, women had to carry and heat about 50 gallons of water for each load. They rubbed the clothes on ridged washboards, rinsed them in tubs, and wrung them out by hand.

This early electric washing machine, photographed in 1933, made the job less strenuous. The casters on the legs made it easier to move tubs of water. The two rollers at the top of the machine squeezed water from clothes. That innovation alone saved women's wrists from constant strain.

Some day you'll buy her a Frigidaire

why not for Christmas

Of course, she wants Frigidaire! And some day you'll buy it. So why not make that *some day* now?

Give her a Frigidaire for Christmas.

Give her the convenience of making desserts with the famous Frigidaire "Cold Control." Give her the care-free, healthful refrigeration assured by Frigidaire's surplus power. Give her the advantages of self-sealing freezing trays that permit two widely different temperatures in the same cabinet at the same time.

In other words, give her a *real* Frigidaire . . . one with the Frigidaire name-plate on it. Then you'll be *sure* she'll have a truly *modern* electric refrigerator. She'll have a cabinet of striking beauty in Tu-Tone Porcelain-on-steel. She'll have the incredible quietness of the Frigidaire power unit . . . a unit that is out of sight and away from dust and dirt. And she'll have the convenient arrangement of the Frigidaire shelves . . . shelves placed at a height that makes stooping unnecessary.

And it's *easy* to give her a Frigidaire. Prices are low and terms can be arranged to suit your convenience. So, avoid the usual last minute rush. Call at the nearest Frigidaire display room and have Frigidaire in your home on Christmas morning. Frigidaire Corporation, Subsidiary of General Motors Corporation, Dayton, Ohio.

FRIGIDAIRE
More than a MILLION in use

Stop This!
What an iron fails to supply in heat, a woman must furnish in arm-aching pressure.

Start This!
If your iron KEEPS hot regardless of damp things, you can do nearly all pieces sitting down.

Five women's magazine editors agree that women would sit to iron if they could

▲ Iron

Before electrical appliances, women heated irons on a stove. The irons cooled quickly, and as they did so, women had to push down harder to press out wrinkles. Early electric irons also had inconsistent heat. This 1926 ad offered an electric iron that stayed evenly hot, so women didn't have to put so much force into their ironing. Therefore, they could iron sitting down.

Coffee Pot ▶

The electric coffee pot shown in this 1933 photograph was a vacuum pot. The water in the bottom chamber would come to a boil and bubble up into the top chamber, where the grounds were. The resulting vacuum in the lower chamber pulled the liquid back through the grounds and into the lower chamber.

> DATA FILE

APPLIANCES IN THE HOME

- In 1929, a survey of 100 Ford employees showed that 98 of them had electric irons in their homes.
- The same survey showed that 49 of the 100 had washing machines at home.

Mechanical Washing Machines Shipped

Numbers in Thousands

1500 / 1300 / 1100 / 900 / 700 / 500

1927 · 1931 · 1935 · 1939

Source: *Historical Statistics of the United States*

Persons Employed as Private Laundress

Numbers in Thousands

500 / 400 / 300 / 200 / 100 / 0

1920 · 1930 · 1940 · 1950

Source: *Historical Statistics of the United States*

Twice the cleaning... twice the leisure!

TWICE as many rooms cleaned. Cleaned more easily, with greater thoroughness. Yet twice as much leisure left for you to enjoy. To enjoy more fully, with fresher body.

Clean with double action—and you clean quickly and easily. When a motor-driven brush and strong suction work together, your tasks are soon done. The brush sweeps up threads and dislodges dirt. The suction draws up the dirt. With double action the Premier Duplex cleans all the dirt.

It requires no after-hours' care. Its ball bearings in brush and motor needs no oiling. For years to come Premier Duplex will do double the work and give you double the leisure.

Premier Duplex

VACUUM CLEANER CO., INC.
Cleveland, Ohio.

◀ Vacuum Cleaner

This 1920 ad promised "Twice as many rooms cleaned. . . . twice as much leisure left for you to enjoy." However, women rarely experienced that benefit. Because the new appliances made housework easier, people began to expect homes to be cleaner. As a result, many women vacuumed more often and generally used their newfound "leisure" time to do even more household chores than before.

Connect *to* Today

1. **Analyzing Issues** What benefits did advertisers promise that the new electrical appliances would provide for women? Explain whether women actually received those benefits.

   See Skillbuilder Handbook, page R17.

2. **Comparing and Contrasting** Ask two or three adults about the way that technology has affected their work life and whether modern technologies are "labor-saving devices." How do your findings compare to the effect of electrical appliances in the 1920s?

A Worldwide Depression

MAIN IDEA	WHY IT MATTERS NOW	TERMS & NAMES
ECONOMICS An economic depression in the United States spread throughout the world and lasted for a decade.	Many social and economic programs introduced worldwide to combat the Great Depression are still operating.	• coalition government • Weimar Republic • Great Depression • Franklin D. Roosevelt • New Deal

SETTING THE STAGE By the late 1920s, European nations were rebuilding war-torn economies. They were aided by loans from the more prosperous United States. Only the United States and Japan came out of the war in better financial shape than before. In the United States, Americans seemed confident that the country would continue on the road to even greater economic prosperity. One sign of this was the booming stock market. Yet the American economy had serious weaknesses that were soon to bring about the most severe economic downturn the world had yet known.

TAKING NOTES

Recognizing Effects
Use a diagram to show the effects of the Great Depression in the United States.

The Great Depression

Postwar Europe

In both human suffering and economic terms, the cost of World War I was immense. The Great War left every major European country nearly bankrupt. In addition, Europe's domination in world affairs declined after the war.

Unstable New Democracies War's end saw the sudden rise of new democracies. From 1914 to 1918, Europe's last absolute rulers had been overthrown. The first of the new governments was formed in Russia in 1917. The Provisional Government, as it was called, hoped to establish constitutional and democratic rule. However, within months it had fallen to a Communist dictatorship. Even so, for the first time, most European nations had democratic governments.

Many citizens of the new democracies had little experience with representative government. For generations, kings and emperors had ruled Germany and the new nations formed from Austria-Hungary. Even in France and Italy, whose parliaments had existed before World War I, the large number of political parties made effective government difficult. Some countries had a dozen or more political groups. In these countries, it was almost impossible for one party to win enough support to govern effectively. When no single party won a majority, a **coalition government**, or temporary alliance of several parties, was needed to form a parliamentary majority. Because the parties disagreed on so many policies, coalitions seldom lasted very long.

Frequent changes in government made it hard for democratic countries to develop strong leadership and move toward long-term goals. The weaknesses of a coalition government became a major problem in times of crisis. Voters in several countries were then willing to sacrifice democratic government for strong, authoritarian leadership.

The Weimar Republic

Germany's new democratic government was set up in 1919. Known as the **Weimar** (WY•MAHR) **Republic**, it was named after the city where the national assembly met. The Weimar Republic had serious weaknesses from the start. First, Germany lacked a strong democratic tradition. Furthermore, postwar Germany had several major political parties and many minor ones. Worst of all, millions of Germans blamed the Weimar government, not their wartime leaders, for the country's defeat and postwar humiliation caused by the Versailles Treaty. **A**

MAIN IDEA

Identifying Problems

A What political problems did the Weimar Republic face?

Inflation Causes Crisis in Germany Germany also faced enormous economic problems that had begun during the war. Unlike Britain and France, Germany had not greatly increased its wartime taxes. To pay the expenses of the war, the Germans had simply printed money. After Germany's defeat, this paper money steadily lost its value. Burdened with heavy reparations payments to the Allies and with other economic problems, Germany printed even more money. As a result, the value of the mark, as Germany's currency was called, fell sharply. Severe inflation set in. Germans needed more and more money to buy even the most basic goods. For example, in Berlin a loaf of bread cost less than a mark in 1918, more than 160 marks in 1922, and some 200 billion marks by late 1923. People took wheelbarrows full of money to buy food. As a result, many Germans questioned the value of their new democratic government.

Attempts at Economic Stability Germany recovered from the 1923 inflation thanks largely to the work of an international committee. The committee was headed by Charles Dawes, an American banker. The Dawes Plan provided for a $200 million loan from American banks to stabilize German currency and strengthen its economy. The plan also set a more realistic schedule for Germany's reparations payments.

Put into effect in 1924, the Dawes Plan helped slow inflation. As the German economy began to recover, it attracted more loans and investments from the United States. By 1929, German factories were producing as much as they had before the war.

Efforts at a Lasting Peace As prosperity returned, Germany's foreign minister, Gustav Stresemann (STRAY•zuh•MAHN), and France's foreign minister, Aristide Briand (bree•AHND), tried to improve relations between their countries. In 1925, the two ministers met in Locarno, Switzerland, with officials from Belgium, Italy, and Britain. They signed a treaty promising that France and Germany would never

▼ German children use stacks of money as building blocks during the 1923 inflation.

again make war against each other. Germany also agreed to respect the existing borders of France and Belgium. It then was admitted to the League of Nations.

In 1928, the hopes raised by the "spirit of Locarno" led to the Kellogg-Briand peace pact. Frank Kellogg, the U.S. Secretary of State, arranged this agreement with France's Briand. Almost every country in the world, including the Soviet Union, signed. They pledged "to renounce war as an instrument of national policy."

Unfortunately, the treaty had no means to enforce its provisions. The League of Nations, the obvious choice as enforcer, had no armed forces. The refusal of the United States to join the League also weakened it. Nonetheless, the peace agreements seemed a good start.

Financial Collapse

In the late 1920s, American economic prosperity largely sustained the world economy. If the U.S. economy weakened, the whole world's economic system might collapse. In 1929, it did.

A Flawed U.S. Economy Despite prosperity, several weaknesses in the U.S. economy caused serious problems. These included uneven distribution of wealth, overproduction by business and agriculture, and the fact that many Americans were buying less.

By 1929, American factories were turning out nearly half of the world's industrial goods. The rising productivity led to enormous profits. However, this new wealth was not evenly distributed. The richest 5 percent of the population received 33 percent of all personal income in 1929. Yet 60 percent of all American families earned less than $2,000 a year. Thus, most families were too poor to buy the goods being produced. Unable to sell all their goods, store owners eventually cut back their orders from factories. Factories in turn reduced production and laid off workers. A downward economic spiral began. As more workers lost their jobs, families bought even fewer goods. In turn, factories made further cuts in production and laid off more workers.

During the 1920s, overproduction affected American farmers as well. Scientific farming methods and new farm machinery had dramatically increased crop yields. American farmers were producing more food. Meanwhile, they faced new competition from farmers in Australia, Latin America, and Europe. As a result, a worldwide surplus of agricultural products drove prices and profits down.

Unable to sell their crops at a profit, many farmers could not pay off the bank loans that kept them in business. Their unpaid debts weakened banks and forced some to close. The danger signs of overproduction by factories and farms should have warned people against gambling on the stock market. Yet no one heeded the warning. **B**

The Stock Market Crashes In 1929, New York City's Wall Street was the financial capital of the world. Banks and investment companies lined its sidewalks. At Wall Street's New York Stock Exchange, optimism about the booming U.S. economy showed in soaring prices for stocks. To get in on the boom, many middle-income people began buying

History *in* Depth

Investing in Stocks

Stocks are shares of ownership in a company. Businesses get money to operate by selling "shares" of stock to investors, or buyers. Companies pay interest on the invested money in the form of dividends to the shareholders. Dividends rise or fall depending on a company's profits.

Investors do not buy stocks directly from the company; instead, stockbrokers transact the business of buying and selling.

Investors hope to make more money on stocks than if they put their money elsewhere, such as in a savings account with a fixed rate of interest. However, if the stock price goes down, investors lose money when they sell their stock at a lower price than when they bought it.

Stock Prices, 1925–1933

Source: *Historical Statistics of the United States*

MAIN IDEA

Identifying Problems
B What major weaknesses had appeared in the American economy by 1929?

Life in the Depression

During the Great Depression of 1929 to 1939, millions of people worldwide lost their jobs or their farms. At first the unemployed had to depend on the charity of others for food, clothing, and shelter. Many, like the men in this photo taken in New York City, made their home in makeshift shacks. Local governments and charities opened soup kitchens to provide free food. There were long lines of applicants for what work was available, and these jobs usually paid low wages.

INTEGRATED TECHNOLOGY

INTERNET ACTIVITY Create a photo-essay on the Great Depression in the United States. Go to **classzone.com** for your research.

stocks on margin. This meant that they paid a small percentage of a stock's price as a down payment and borrowed the rest from a stockbroker. The system worked well as long as stock prices were rising. However, if they fell, investors had no money to pay off the loan.

In September 1929, some investors began to think that stock prices were unnaturally high. They started selling their stocks, believing the prices would soon go down. By Thursday, October 24, the gradual lowering of stock prices had become an all-out slide downward. A panic resulted. Everyone wanted to sell stocks, and no one wanted to buy. Prices plunged to a new low on Tuesday, October 29. A record 16 million stocks were sold. Then the market collapsed.

The Great Depression

People could not pay the money they owed on margin purchases. Stocks they had bought at high prices were now worthless. Within months of the crash, unemployment rates began to rise as industrial production, prices, and wages declined. A long business slump, which would come to be called the **Great Depression**, followed. The stock market crash alone did not cause the Great Depression, but it quickened the collapse of the economy and made the Depression more difficult. By 1932, factory production had been cut in half. Thousands of businesses failed, and banks closed. Around 9 million people lost the money in their savings accounts when banks had no money to pay them. Many farmers lost their lands when they could not make mortgage payments. By 1933, one-fourth of all American workers had no jobs.

A Global Depression The collapse of the American economy sent shock waves around the world. Worried American bankers demanded repayment of their overseas loans, and American investors withdrew their money from Europe. The American market for European goods dropped sharply as the U.S. Congress placed high tariffs on imported goods so that American dollars would stay in the United States and pay for American goods. This policy backfired. Conditions worsened for the United

Vocabulary
tariffs: taxes charged by a government on imported or exported goods

Unemployment Rate, 1928–1938

Percent of Work Force

■ Great Britain   ■ Germany   ■ United States

Sources: *European Historical Statistics: 1750–1970; Historical Statistics of the United States: Colonial Times to 1970.*

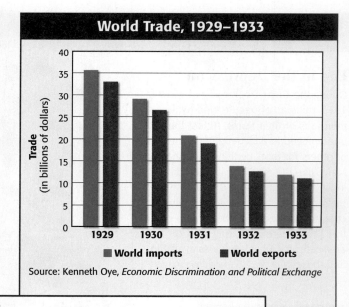

World Trade, 1929–1933

Trade (in billions of dollars)

■ World imports   ■ World exports

Source: Kenneth Oye, *Economic Discrimination and Political Exchange*

SKILLBUILDER: Interpreting Graphs
1. **Comparing** *What nation had the highest rate of unemployment? How high did it reach?*
2. **Clarifying** *Between 1929 and 1933, how much did world exports drop? What about world imports?*

States. Many countries that depended on exporting goods to the United States also suffered. Moreover, when the United States raised tariffs, it set off a chain reaction. Other nations imposed their own higher tariffs. World trade dropped by 65 percent. This contributed further to the economic downturn. Unemployment rates soared.

Effects Throughout the World Because of war debts and dependence on American loans and investments, Germany and Austria were particularly hard hit. In 1931, Austria's largest bank failed. In Asia, both farmers and urban workers suffered as the value of exports fell by half between 1929 and 1931. The crash was felt heavily in Latin America as well. As European and U.S. demand for such Latin American products as sugar, beef, and copper dropped, prices collapsed.

The World Confronts the Crisis

The Depression confronted democracies with a serious challenge to their economic and political systems. Each country met the crisis in its own way.

Britain Takes Steps to Improve Its Economy The Depression hit Britain severely. To meet the emergency, British voters elected a multiparty coalition known as the National Government. It passed high protective tariffs, increased taxes, and regulated the currency. It also lowered interest rates to encourage industrial growth. These measures brought about a slow but steady recovery. By 1937, unemployment had been cut in half, and production had risen above 1929 levels. Britain avoided political extremes and preserved democracy.

France Responds to Economic Crisis Unlike Britain, France had a more self-sufficient economy. In 1930, it was still heavily agricultural and less dependent on foreign trade. Nevertheless, by 1935, one million French workers were unemployed.

The economic crisis contributed to political instability. In 1933, five coalition governments formed and fell. Many political leaders were frightened by the growth of antidemocratic forces both in France and in other parts of Europe. So in 1936, moderates, Socialists, and Communists formed a coalition. The Popular Front, as it was called, passed a series of reforms to help the workers. Unfortunately, price increases quickly offset wage gains. Unemployment remained high. Yet France also preserved democratic government.

Socialist Governments Find Solutions The Socialist governments in the Scandinavian countries of Denmark, Sweden, and Norway also met the challenge of economic crisis successfully. They built their recovery programs on an existing tradition of cooperative community action. In Sweden, the government sponsored massive public works projects that kept people employed and producing. All the Scandinavian countries raised pensions for the elderly and increased unemployment insurance, subsidies for housing, and other welfare benefits. To pay for these benefits, the governments taxed all citizens. Democracy remained intact.

Recovery in the United States In 1932, in the first presidential election after the Depression had begun, U.S. voters elected **Franklin D. Roosevelt**. His confident manner appealed to millions of Americans who felt bewildered by the Depression. On March 4, 1933, the new president sought to restore Americans' faith in their nation.

MAIN IDEA

Analyzing Primary Sources
Ⓒ What effect do you think Roosevelt's speech had on the American people?

PRIMARY SOURCE Ⓒ
This great Nation will endure as it has endured, will revive and will prosper. . . . let me assert my firm belief that the only thing we have to fear is fear itself—nameless, unreasoning, unjustified terror which paralyzes needed efforts to convert retreat into advance.

FRANKLIN ROOSEVELT, First Inaugural Address

Roosevelt immediately began a program of government reform that he called the **New Deal**. Large public works projects helped to provide jobs for the unemployed. New government agencies gave financial help to businesses and farms. Large amounts of public money were spent on welfare and relief programs. Roosevelt and his advisers believed that government spending would create jobs and start a recovery. Regulations were imposed to reform the stock market and the banking system.

The New Deal did eventually reform the American economic system. Roosevelt's leadership preserved the country's faith in its democratic political system. It also established him as a leader of democracy in a world threatened by ruthless dictators, as you will read about in Section 3.

▲ Stricken with polio in 1921, Roosevelt vowed he would not allow bodily disability to defeat his will.

SECTION 2 ASSESSMENT

TERMS & NAMES 1. For each term or name, write a sentence explaining its significance.
• coalition government   • Weimar Republic   • Great Depression   • Franklin D. Roosevelt   • New Deal

USING YOUR NOTES

2. What did President Roosevelt do to try to counter the effects of the Great Depression?

The Great Depression

MAIN IDEAS

3. How did World War I change the balance of economic power in the world?

4. What problems did the collapse of the American economy cause in other countries?

5. How did Europe respond to the economic crisis?

CRITICAL THINKING & WRITING

6. **MAKING PREDICTIONS** What did the weakness of the League of Nations in 1928 suggest about its future effectiveness?

7. **ANALYZING CAUSES** List one cause for each of the following effects: American market for European goods dropped; unemployment rates soared; European banks and businesses closed.

8. **EVALUATING COURSES OF ACTION** Why do you think Roosevelt immediately established the New Deal?

9. **WRITING ACTIVITY** ECONOMICS Write **headlines** on the stock market crash and the world's response to it.

INTEGRATED/TECHNOLOGY **INTERNET ACTIVITY**

Use the Internet to follow the ups and downs of the stock market for a week. Chart the stock market's course in a **line graph**.

INTERNET KEYWORD
stock market

Fascism Rises in Europe

MAIN IDEA	WHY IT MATTERS NOW	TERMS & NAMES
POWER AND AUTHORITY In response to political turmoil and economic crises, Italy and Germany turned to totalitarian dictators.	These dictators changed the course of history, and the world is still recovering from their abuse of power.	• fascism • Benito Mussolini • Adolf Hitler • Nazism • *Mein Kampf* • *lebensraum*

SETTING THE STAGE Many democracies, including the United States, Britain, and France, remained strong despite the economic crisis caused by the Great Depression. However, millions of people lost faith in democratic government. In response, they turned to an extreme system of government called fascism. Fascists promised to revive the economy, punish those responsible for hard times, and restore order and national pride. Their message attracted many people who felt frustrated and angered by the peace treaties that followed World War I and by the Great Depression.

TAKING NOTES

Comparing and Contrasting Use a chart to compare Mussolini's rise to power and his goals with Hitler's.

Hitler	Mussolini
Rise:	Rise:
Goals:	Goals:

Fascism's Rise in Italy

<u>Fascism</u> (FASH•IHZ•uhm) was a new, militant political movement that emphasized loyalty to the state and obedience to its leader. Unlike communism, fascism had no clearly defined theory or program. Nevertheless, most Fascists shared several ideas. They preached an extreme form of nationalism, or loyalty to one's country. Fascists believed that nations must struggle—peaceful states were doomed to be conquered. They pledged loyalty to an authoritarian leader who guided and brought order to the state. In each nation, Fascists wore uniforms of a certain color, used special salutes, and held mass rallies.

In some ways, fascism was similar to communism. Both systems were ruled by dictators who allowed only their own political party (one-party rule). Both denied individual rights. In both, the state was supreme. Neither practiced any kind of democracy. However, unlike Communists, Fascists did not seek a classless society. Rather, they believed that each class had its place and function. In most cases, Fascist parties were made up of aristocrats and industrialists, war veterans, and the lower middle class. Also, Fascists were nationalists, and Communists were internationalists, hoping to unite workers worldwide.

Mussolini Takes Control Fascism's rise in Italy was fueled by bitter disappointment over the failure to win large territorial gains at the 1919 Paris Peace Conference. Rising inflation and unemployment also contributed to widespread social unrest. To growing numbers of Italians, their democratic government seemed helpless to deal with the country's problems. They wanted a leader who would take action.

Fascism

Fascism is a political movement that promotes an extreme form of nationalism and militarism. It also includes a denial of individual rights and dictatorial one-party rule. Nazism was the Fascist movement that developed in Germany in the 1920s and the 1930s; it included a belief in the racial superiority of the German people. The Fascists in Italy were led by Benito Mussolini, shown in the chart at right.

Cultural
- censorship
- indoctrination
- secret police

Social
- supported by middle class, industrialists, and military

Economic
- economic functions controlled by state corporations or state

CHARACTERISTICS OF FASCISM

Chief Examples
- Italy
- Spain
- Germany

Political
- nationalist
- racist (Nazism)
- one-party rule
- supreme leader

Basic Principles
- authoritarianism
- state more important than the individual
- charismatic leader
- action oriented

SKILLBUILDER: Interpreting Charts

1. **Synthesizing** *Which political, cultural, and economic characteristics helped make fascism an authoritarian system?*
2. **Making Inferences** *What characteristics of fascism might make it attractive to people during times of crisis such as the Great Depression?*

A newspaper editor and politician named **Benito Mussolini** boldly promised to rescue Italy by reviving its economy and rebuilding its armed forces. He vowed to give Italy strong leadership. Mussolini had founded the Fascist Party in 1919. As economic conditions worsened, his popularity rapidly increased. Finally, Mussolini publicly criticized Italy's government. Groups of Fascists wearing black shirts attacked Communists and Socialists on the streets. Because Mussolini played on the fear of a workers' revolt, he began to win support from the middle classes, the aristocracy, and industrial leaders.

In October 1922, about 30,000 Fascists marched on Rome. They demanded that King Victor Emmanuel III put Mussolini in charge of the government. The king decided that Mussolini was the best hope for his dynasty to survive. After widespread violence and a threatened uprising, Mussolini took power "legally." **A**

Il Duce's Leadership Mussolini was now Il Duce (ihl DOO•chay), or the leader. He abolished democracy and outlawed all political parties except the Fascists. Secret police jailed his opponents. Government censors forced radio stations and publications to broadcast or publish only Fascist doctrines. Mussolini outlawed strikes. He sought to control the economy by allying the Fascists with the industrialists and large landowners. However, Mussolini never had the total control achieved by Joseph Stalin in the Soviet Union or Adolf Hitler in Germany.

MAIN IDEA

Clarifying

A What promises did Mussolini make to the Italian people?

Hitler Rises to Power in Germany

When Mussolini became dictator of Italy in the mid-1920s, **Adolf Hitler** was a little-known political leader whose early life had been marked by disappointment. When World War I broke out, Hitler found a new beginning. He volunteered for the German army and was twice awarded the Iron Cross, a medal for bravery.

**Benito Mussolini
1883–1945**

Because Mussolini was of modest height, he usually chose a location for his speeches where he towered above the crowds—often a balcony high above a public square. He then roused audiences with his emotional speeches and theatrical gestures and body movements.

Vowing to lead Italy "back to her ways of ancient greatness," Mussolini peppered his speeches with aggressive words such as *war* and *power*.

**Adolf Hitler
1889–1945**

Like Mussolini, Hitler could manipulate huge audiences with his fiery oratory. Making speeches was crucial to Hitler. He believed: "All great world-shaking events have been brought about . . . by the spoken word!"

Because he appeared awkward and unimposing, Hitler rehearsed his speeches. Usually he began a speech in a normal voice. Suddenly, he spoke louder as his anger grew. His voice rose to a screech, and his hands flailed the air. Then he would stop, smooth his hair, and look quite calm.

INTEGRATED / TECHNOLOGY

RESEARCH LINKS For more on Benito Mussolini and Adolf Hitler, go to **classzone.com**

The Rise of the Nazis At the end of the war, Hitler settled in Munich. In 1919, he joined a tiny right-wing political group. This group shared his belief that Germany had to overturn the Treaty of Versailles and combat communism. The group later named itself the National Socialist German Workers' Party, called Nazi for short. Its policies formed the German brand of fascism known as **Nazism**. The party adopted the swastika, or hooked cross, as its symbol. The Nazis also set up a private militia called the storm troopers or Brown Shirts.

Within a short time, Hitler's success as an organizer and speaker led him to be chosen *der Führer* (duhr FYUR•uhr), or the leader, of the Nazi party. Inspired by Mussolini's march on Rome, Hitler and the Nazis plotted to seize power in Munich in 1923. The attempt failed, and Hitler was arrested. He was tried for treason but was sentenced to only five years in prison. He served less than nine months.

While in jail, Hitler wrote **Mein Kampf** (*My Struggle*). This book set forth his beliefs and his goals for Germany. Hitler asserted that the Germans, whom he incorrectly called "Aryans," were a "master race." He declared that non-Aryan "races," such as Jews, Slavs, and Gypsies, were inferior. He called the Versailles Treaty an outrage and vowed to regain German lands. Hitler also declared that Germany was overcrowded and needed more **lebensraum**, or living space. He promised to get that space by conquering eastern Europe and Russia.

After leaving prison in 1924, Hitler revived the Nazi Party. Most Germans ignored him and his angry message until the Great Depression ended the nation's brief postwar recovery. When American loans stopped, the German economy collapsed. Civil unrest broke out. Frightened and confused, Germans now turned to Hitler, hoping for security and firm leadership.

Hitler Becomes Chancellor

The Nazis had become the largest political party by 1932. Conservative leaders mistakenly believed they could control Hitler and use him for their purposes. In January 1933, they advised President Paul von Hindenburg to name Hitler chancellor. Thus Hitler came to power legally. Soon after, General Erich Ludendorff, a former Hitler ally, wrote to Hindenburg:

Vocabulary
chancellor: the prime minister or president in certain countries

PRIMARY SOURCE
By naming Hitler as Reichschancellor, you have delivered up our holy Fatherland to one of the greatest [rabblerousers] of all time. I solemnly [predict] that this accursed man will plunge our Reich into the abyss and bring our nation into inconceivable misery.
ERICH LUDENDORFF, letter to President Hindenburg, February 1, 1933

Once in office, Hitler called for new elections, hoping to win a parliamentary majority. Six days before the election, a fire destroyed the Reichstag building, where the parliament met. The Nazis blamed the Communists. By stirring up fear of the Communists, the Nazis and their allies won by a slim majority.

Hitler used his new power to turn Germany into a totalitarian state. He banned all other political parties and had opponents arrested. Meanwhile, an elite, black-uniformed unit called the SS (*Schutzstaffel,* or protection squad) was created. It was loyal only to Hitler. In 1934, the SS arrested and murdered hundreds of Hitler's enemies. This brutal action and the terror applied by the Gestapo, the Nazi secret police, shocked most Germans into total obedience.

The Nazis quickly took command of the economy. New laws banned strikes, dissolved independent labor unions, and gave the government authority over business and labor. Hitler put millions of Germans to work. They constructed factories, built highways, manufactured weapons, and served in the military. As a result, the number of unemployed dropped from about 6 million to 1.5 million in 1936. **B**

MAIN IDEA

Making Inferences

B Why did Germans at first support Hitler?

The Führer Is Supreme Hitler wanted more than just economic and political power—he wanted control over every aspect of German life. To shape public opinion and to win praise for his leadership, Hitler turned the press, radio, literature, painting, and film into propaganda tools. Books that did not conform to Nazi beliefs were burned in huge bonfires. Churches were forbidden to criticize the Nazis or the government. Schoolchildren had to join the Hitler Youth (for boys) or the League of German Girls. Hitler believed that continuous struggle brought victory to the strong. He twisted the philosophy of Friedrich Nietzsche to support his use of brute force.

Hitler Makes War on the Jews Hatred of Jews, or anti-Semitism, was a key part of Nazi ideology. Although Jews were less than 1 percent of the population, the Nazis used them as scapegoats for all Germany's troubles since the war. This led to a wave of anti-Semitism across Germany. Beginning in 1933, the Nazis passed laws depriving Jews of most of their rights. Violence against Jews mounted. On the

▼ At a 1933 rally in Nuremberg, Germany, storm troopers carried flags bearing the swastika.

Fascism in Argentina

Juan Perón served as Argentina's president from 1946 to 1955 and again in 1973 and 1974. The two years he spent in Europe before World War II greatly influenced his strong-man rule.

A career army officer, Perón went to Italy in 1939 for military training. He then served at the Argentine embassy in Rome. A visit to Berlin gave Perón a chance to see Nazi Germany. The ability of Hitler and Mussolini to manipulate their citizens impressed Perón.

When Perón himself gained power, he patterned his military dictatorship on that of the European Fascists.

night of November 9, 1938, Nazi mobs attacked Jews in their homes and on the streets and destroyed thousands of Jewish-owned buildings. This rampage, called *Kristallnacht* (Night of the Broken Glass), signaled the real start of the process of eliminating the Jews from German life. You'll learn more about this in Chapter 16.

Other Countries Fall to Dictators

While Fascists took power in Italy and Germany, the nations formed in eastern Europe after World War I also were falling to dictators. In Hungary in 1919, after a brief Communist regime, military forces and wealthy landowners joined to make Admiral Miklós Horthy the first European postwar dictator. In Poland, Marshal Jozef Pilsudski (pihl•SOOT•skee) seized power in 1926. In Yugoslavia, Albania, Bulgaria, and Romania, kings turned to strong-man rule. They suspended constitutions and silenced foes. In 1935, only one democracy, Czechoslovakia, remained in eastern Europe.

Only in European nations with strong democratic traditions—Britain, France, and the Scandinavian countries—did democracy survive. With no democratic experience and severe economic problems, many Europeans saw dictatorship as the only way to prevent instability.

By the mid-1930s, the powerful nations of the world were split into two antagonistic camps—democratic and totalitarian. And to gain their ends, the Fascist dictatorships had indicated a willingness to use military aggression. Although all of these dictatorships restricted civil rights, none asserted control with the brutality of the Russian Communists or the Nazis.

SECTION 3 ASSESSMENT

TERMS & NAMES 1. For each term or name, write a sentence explaining its significance.
• fascism   • Benito Mussolini   • Adolf Hitler   • Nazism   • *Mein Kampf*   • *lebensraum*

USING YOUR NOTES

2. Do you think Hitler and Mussolini were more alike or different? Explain why.

Hitler	Mussolini
Rise:	Rise:
Goals:	Goals:

MAIN IDEAS

3. What factors led to the rise of fascism in Italy?

4. How did Hitler maintain power?

5. Why did the leadership of many eastern European nations fall to dictators?

CRITICAL THINKING & WRITING

6. **DRAWING CONCLUSIONS** Why did a movement like fascism and leaders like Mussolini and Hitler come to power during a period of crisis?

7. **ANALYZING MOTIVES** Why do you think Hitler had German children join Nazi organizations?

8. **SYNTHESIZING** What emotions did both Hitler and Mussolini stir in their followers?

9. **WRITING ACTIVITY** POWER AND AUTHORITY Reread the History Makers on Mussolini and Hitler on page 478. Then write a **description** of the techniques the two leaders used to appear powerful to their listeners.

CONNECT TO TODAY PRESENTING AN ORAL REPORT

Some modern rulers have invaded other countries for political and economic gain. Research to learn about a recent invasion and discuss your findings in an **oral report**.

Aggressors Invade Nations

4

MAIN IDEA	WHY IT MATTERS NOW	TERMS & NAMES
POWER AND AUTHORITY As Germany, Italy, and Japan conquered other countries, the rest of the world did nothing to stop them.	Many nations today take a more active and collective role in world affairs, as in the United Nations.	• appeasement • Axis Powers • Francisco Franco	• isolationism • Third Reich • Munich Conference

SETTING THE STAGE By the mid-1930s, Germany and Italy seemed bent on military conquest. The major democracies—Britain, France, and the United States—were distracted by economic problems at home and longed to remain at peace. With the world moving toward war, many nations pinned their hopes for peace on the League of Nations. As fascism spread in Europe, however, a powerful nation in Asia moved toward a similar system. Following a period of reform and progress in the 1920s, Japan fell under military rule.

Japan Seeks an Empire

During the 1920s, the Japanese government became more democratic. In 1922, Japan signed an international treaty agreeing to respect China's borders. In 1928, it signed the Kellogg-Briand Pact renouncing war. Japan's parliamentary system had several weaknesses, however. Its constitution put strict limits on the powers of the prime minister and the cabinet. Most importantly, civilian leaders had little control over the armed forces. Military leaders reported only to the emperor.

Militarists Take Control of Japan As long as Japan remained prosperous, the civilian government kept power. But when the Great Depression struck in 1929, many Japanese blamed the government. Military leaders gained support and soon won control of the country. Unlike the Fascists in Europe, the militarists did not try to establish a new system of government. They wanted to restore traditional control of the government to the military. Instead of a forceful leader like Mussolini or Hitler, the militarists made the emperor the symbol of state power.

Keeping Emperor Hirohito as head of state won popular support for the army leaders who ruled in his name. Like Hitler and Mussolini, Japan's militarists were extreme nationalists. They wanted to solve the country's economic problems through foreign expansion. They planned a Pacific empire that included a conquered China. The empire would provide Japan with raw materials and markets for its goods. It would also give Japan room for its rising population.

Japan Invades Manchuria Japanese businesses had invested heavily in China's northeast province, Manchuria. It was an area rich in iron and coal. In 1931, the Japanese army seized Manchuria, despite objections from the Japanese parliament. The army then set up a puppet government. Japanese engineers and technicians began arriving in large numbers to build mines and factories.

TAKING NOTES
Following Chronological Order Use a time line to trace the movement of Japan from democratic reform to military aggression.

The Japanese attack on Manchuria was the first direct challenge to the League of Nations. In the early 1930s, the League's members included all major democracies except the United States. The League also included the three countries that posed the greatest threat to peace—Germany, Japan, and Italy. When Japan seized Manchuria, many League members vigorously protested. Japan ignored the protests and withdrew from the League in 1933. **A**

MAIN IDEA

Making Inferences
A What was the major weakness of the League of Nations?

Japan Invades China Four years later, a border incident touched off a full-scale war between Japan and China. Japanese forces swept into northern China. Despite having a million soldiers, China's army led by Jiang Jieshi was no match for the better equipped and trained Japanese.

Beijing and other northern cities as well as the capital, Nanjing, fell to the Japanese in 1937. Japanese troops killed tens of thousands of captured soldiers and civilians in Nanjing. Forced to retreat westward, Jiang Jieshi set up a new capital at Chongqing. At the same time, Chinese guerrillas led by China's Communist leader, Mao Zedong, continued to fight the Japanese in the conquered area.

European Aggressors on the March

The League's failure to stop the Japanese encouraged European Fascists to plan aggression of their own. The Italian leader Mussolini dreamed of building a colonial empire in Africa like those of Britain and France.

Mussolini Attacks Ethiopia Ethiopia was one of Africa's three independent nations. The Ethiopians had successfully resisted an Italian attempt at conquest during the 1890s. To avenge that defeat, Mussolini ordered a massive invasion of Ethiopia in October 1935. The spears and swords of the Ethiopians were no match for Italian airplanes, tanks, guns, and poison gas.

The Ethiopian emperor, Haile Selassie, urgently appealed to the League for help. Although the League condemned the attack, its members did nothing. Britain continued to let Italian troops and supplies pass through the British-controlled Suez Canal on their way to Ethiopia. By giving in to Mussolini in Africa, Britain and France hoped to keep peace in Europe.

Hitler Defies Versailles Treaty Hitler had long pledged to undo the Versailles Treaty. Among its provisions, the treaty limited the size of Germany's army. In March 1935, the Führer announced that Germany would not obey these restrictions. The League issued only a mild condemnation.

The League's failure to stop Germany from rearming convinced Hitler to take even greater risks. The treaty had forbidden German troops to enter a 30-mile-wide zone on either side of the Rhine River. Known as the Rhineland, the zone formed

Aggression in Europe, Asia, and Africa, 1931–1939

September 1931
Japan invades Manchuria.

October 1935
Italy attacks Ethiopia.

March 1938
Germany annexes Austria.

September 1938
Germany takes Sudetenland.

March 1936
Germany occupies Rhineland.

July 1937
Japan invades China.

March 1939
Germany seizes Czechoslovakia.

April 1939
Italy conquers Albania.

Aggression in Africa, 1935–1939

- Italy
- Italian colony
- Invaded by Italy

ITALY
ALBANIA (1939)
Mediterranean Sea
LIBYA
EGYPT
ANGLO-EGYPTIAN SUDAN
ERITREA
FRENCH EQUATORIAL AFRICA
ETHIOPIA (1935)
SOMALIA
NIGERIA
KENYA
BELGIAN CONGO
0° Equator
INDIAN OCEAN
ATLANTIC OCEAN
Tropic of Cancer
40°N
40°E
0°
0 1,000 Miles
0 2,000 Kilometers
N

Aggression in Asia, 1931–1937

- Japan and its colonies
- Invaded by Japan

MANCHURIA (1931)
JEHOL (1933)
Japan invades China, July 1937
CHINA
KOREA
Sea of Japan
JAPAN
Yellow Sea
TAIWAN
PACIFIC OCEAN
Tropic of Cancer
40°N
120°E
0 1,000 Miles
0 2,000 Kilometers
N

GEOGRAPHY SKILLBUILDER: Interpreting Maps
1. **Location** *On these maps, which countries are the aggressors?*
2. **Movement** *On what two continents did the aggression occur?*

a buffer between Germany and France. It was also an important industrial area. On March 7, 1936, German troops moved into the Rhineland. Stunned, the French were unwilling to risk war. The British urged **appeasement**, giving in to an aggressor to keep peace.

Hitler later admitted that he would have backed down if the French and British had challenged him. The German reoccupation of the Rhineland marked a turning point in the march toward war. First, it strengthened Hitler's power and prestige within Germany. Second, the balance of power changed in Germany's favor. France and Belgium were now open to attack from German troops. Finally, the weak response by France and Britain encouraged Hitler to speed up his expansion.

Hitler's growing strength convinced Mussolini that he should seek an alliance with Germany. In October 1936, the two dictators reached an agreement that became known as the Rome-Berlin Axis. A month later, Germany also made an agreement with Japan. Germany, Italy, and Japan came to be called the **Axis Powers**.

Civil War Erupts in Spain Hitler and Mussolini again tested the will of the democracies of Europe in the Spanish Civil War. Spain had been a monarchy until 1931, when a republic was declared. The government, run by liberals and Socialists, held office amid many crises. In July 1936, army leaders, favoring a Fascist-style government, joined General **Francisco Franco** in a revolt. Thus began a civil war that dragged on for three years.

Hitler and Mussolini sent troops, tanks, and airplanes to help Franco's forces, which were called the Nationalists. The armed forces of the Republicans, as supporters of Spain's elected government were known, received little help from abroad. The Western democracies remained neutral. Only the Soviet Union sent equipment and advisers. An international brigade of volunteers fought on the Republican side. Early in 1939, Republican resistance collapsed. Franco became Spain's Fascist dictator.

Vocabulary
axis: a straight line around which an object rotates. Hitler and Mussolini expected their alliance to become the axis around which Europe would rotate.

Years of Crisis **483**

Guernica

On April 26, 1937, Franco's German allies bombed the ancient Basque city of Guernica in Spain. The photograph (above) shows the city reduced to rubble by the bombing. However, Spanish artist Pablo Picasso's painting, called *Guernica* (below), captures the human horror of the event.

Using the geometric forms of Cubism, Picasso shows a city and people that have been torn to pieces. Unnatural angles and overlapping images of people, severed limbs, and animals reflect the suffering and chaos caused by the attack. At left, a mother cries over her dead child. In the center, a horse screams and a soldier lies dead. At right, a woman falls from a burning house.

SKILLBUILDER:
Interpreting Visual Sources
1. **Analyzing Motives** *What were Picasso's probable motives for painting* Guernica?
2. **Hypothesizing** *What feelings do you think* Guernica *stirred in the public in the late 1930s?*

Democratic Nations Try to Preserve Peace

Instead of taking a stand against Fascist aggression in the 1930s, Britain and France repeatedly made concessions, hoping to keep peace. Both nations were dealing with serious economic problems as a result of the Great Depression. In addition, the horrors of World War I had created a deep desire to avoid war.

United States Follows an Isolationist Policy Many Americans supported **isolationism**, the belief that political ties to other countries should be avoided. Isolationists argued that entry into World War I had been a costly error. Beginning in 1935, Congress passed three Neutrality Acts. These laws banned loans and the sale of arms to nations at war.

The German Reich Expands On November 5, 1937, Hitler announced to his advisers his plans to absorb Austria and Czechoslovakia into the **Third Reich** (ryk), or German Empire. The Treaty of Versailles prohibited *Anschluss* (AHN•SHLUS), or a union between Austria and Germany. However, many Austrians supported unity with Germany. In March 1938, Hitler sent his army into Austria and annexed it. France and Britain ignored their pledge to protect Austrian independence.

Hitler next turned to Czechoslovakia. About three million German-speaking people lived in the western border regions of Czechoslovakia called the Sudetenland. (See map, page 461.) This heavily fortified area formed the Czechs' main defense against Germany. The Anschluss raised pro-Nazi feelings among Sudeten Germans. In September 1938, Hitler demanded that the Sudetenland be given to Germany. The Czechs refused and asked France for help.

Britain and France Again Choose Appeasement France and Britain were preparing for war when Mussolini proposed a meeting of Germany, France, Britain, and Italy in Munich, Germany. The **Munich Conference** was held on September 29, 1938. The Czechs were not invited. British prime minister Neville Chamberlain believed that he could preserve peace by giving in to Hitler's demand. Britain and France agreed that Hitler could take the Sudetenland. In exchange, Hitler pledged to respect Czechoslovakia's new borders.

When Chamberlain returned to London, he told cheering crowds, "I believe it is peace for our time." Winston Churchill, then a member of the British Parliament, strongly disagreed. He opposed the appeasement policy and gloomily warned of its consequences:

▲ Chamberlain waves the statement he read following the Munich Conference.

MAIN IDEA

Analyzing Primary Sources

 Why did Churchill believe that Chamberlain's policy of appeasement was a defeat for the British?

PRIMARY SOURCE B
We are in the presence of a disaster of the first magnitude. . . . we have sustained a defeat without a war. . . . And do not suppose that this is the end. . . . This is only the first sip, the first foretaste of a bitter cup which will be proffered to us year by year unless, by a supreme recovery of moral health and martial vigor, we arise again and take our stand for freedom as in the olden time.
WINSTON CHURCHILL, speech before the House of Commons, October 5, 1938

Less than six months after the Munich meeting, Hitler took Czechoslovakia. Soon after, Mussolini seized Albania. Then Hitler demanded that Poland return the former German port of Danzig. The Poles refused and turned to Britain and France for aid. But appeasement had convinced Hitler that neither nation would risk war.

Nazis and Soviets Sign Nonaggression Pact Britain and France asked the Soviet Union to join them in stopping Hitler's aggression. As Stalin talked with Britain and France, he also bargained with Hitler. The two dictators reached an agreement. Once bitter enemies, Fascist Germany and Communist Russia now publicly pledged never to attack one another. On August 23, 1939, their leaders signed a nonaggression pact. As the Axis Powers moved unchecked at the end of the decade, war appeared inevitable.

SECTION 4 ASSESSMENT

TERMS & NAMES 1. For each term or name, write a sentence explaining its significance.
• appeasement   • Axis Powers   • Francisco Franco   • isolationism   • Third Reich   • Munich Conference

USING YOUR NOTES
2. What event was the most significant? Why?

MAIN IDEAS
3. Compare the militarists in Japan with the European Fascists.
4. Which countries formed the Axis Powers?
5. What were the effects of isolationism and appeasement?

CRITICAL THINKING & WRITING
6. **SYNTHESIZING** What similar goals did Hitler, Mussolini, and Hirohito share?
7. **FORMING OPINIONS** Do you think the Fascist nations of the Axis Powers could have been stopped? Explain.
8. **EVALUATING DECISIONS** Why weren't the Czechs invited to take part in the Munich Conference?
9. **WRITING ACTIVITY** POWER AND AUTHORITY Write a **letter to the editor** in which you voice your opinion about the U.S. policy of isolationism during the 1930s.

CONNECT TO TODAY STAGING A DEBATE
Established in 1945, the United Nations was intended to be an improvement on the League of Nations. Research to learn about the recent successes and failures of the UN. Then hold a **debate** in which you argue whether the institution should be preserved.

VISUAL SUMMARY

The Great Depression

Long-Term Causes

- World economies are connected.
- Some countries have huge war debts from World War I.
- Europe relies on American loans and investments.
- Prosperity is built on borrowed money.
- Wealth is unequally distributed.

Immediate Causes

- U.S. stock market crashes.
- Banks demand repayment of loans.
- Farms fail and factories close.
- Americans reduce foreign trade to protect economy.
- Americans stop loans to foreign countries.
- American banking system collapses.

WORLDWIDE ECONOMIC DEPRESSION

Immediate Effects

- Millions become unemployed worldwide.
- Businesses go bankrupt.
- Governments take emergency measures to protect economies.
- Citizens lose faith in capitalism and democracy.
- Nations turn toward authoritarian leaders.

Long-Term Effects

- Nazis take control in Germany.
- Fascists come to power in other countries.
- Democracies try social welfare programs.
- Japan expands in East Asia.
- World War II breaks out.

TERMS & NAMES

For each term or name below, briefly explain its connection to world history from 1919 to 1939.

1. Albert Einstein
2. Sigmund Freud
3. Weimar Republic
4. New Deal
5. fascism
6. Benito Mussolini
7. Adolf Hitler
8. appeasement
9. Francisco Franco
10. Munich Conference

MAIN IDEAS

Postwar Uncertainty Section 1 (pages 463–469)

11. What effect did Einstein's theory of relativity and Freud's theory of the unconscious have on the public?
12. What advances were made in transportation and communication in the 1920s and 1930s?

A Worldwide Depression Section 2 (pages 470–475)

13. Why was the Weimar Republic considered weak?
14. What caused the stock market crash of 1929?

Fascism Rises in Europe Section 3 (pages 476–480)

15. For what political and economic reasons did the Italians turn to Mussolini?
16. What beliefs and goals did Hitler express in *Mein Kampf*?

Aggressors Invade Nations Section 4 (pages 481–485)

17. How did Japan plan to solve its economic problems?
18. Why was Germany's reoccupation of the Rhineland a significant turning point toward war?

CRITICAL THINKING

1. **USING YOUR NOTES**

   ECONOMICS Use a sequence graphic to identify the events that led to the stock market collapse.

2. **MAKING INFERENCES**

   POWER AND AUTHORITY What were the advantages and disadvantages of being under Fascist rule?

3. **DRAWING CONCLUSIONS**

   What weaknesses made the League of Nations an ineffective force for peace in the 1920s and 1930s?

4. **SYNTHESIZING**

   SCIENCE AND TECHNOLOGY How did the scientific and technological revolutions of the 1920s help set the stage for transportation in the United States today?

5. **HYPOTHESIZING**

   What might have been the outcome if Great Britain, France, and other European nations had not chosen to appease German, Italian, and Japanese aggression?

Use the quotation from a live radio report during the Munich Conference and your knowledge of world history to answer questions 1 and 2.
Additional Test Practice, pp. S1–S33

PRIMARY SOURCE

> It took the Big Four [France, Britain, Italy, and Germany] just five hours and twenty-five minutes here in Munich today to dispel the clouds of war and come to an agreement over the partition of Czechoslovakia. There is to be no European war. . . the price of that peace is, roughly, the ceding by Czechoslovakia of the Sudeten territory to Herr Hitler's Germany. The German Führer gets what he wanted, only he has to wait a little longer for it.
>
> **WILLIAM SHIRER,** quoted in *The Strenuous Decade*

1. Why did France, Britain, and Italy agree to give the Sudeten territory to Germany?

   A. to provoke war

   B. to avoid war

   C. to make Czechoslovakia happy

   D. to make Czechoslovakia unhappy

2. How were the expectations expressed in the radio report overturned by reality?

   A. Czechoslovakia refused to give the Sudeten territory to Hitler.

   B. Hitler did not get what he wanted.

   C. The Big Four didn't come to an agreement over Czechoslovakia.

   D. Europe was not saved from war.

Use the photograph of Adolf Hitler and your knowledge of world history to answer question 3.

3. Why do you think Hitler had his photograph taken with this little girl?

   A. to demonstrate his power

   B. to frighten his enemies

   C. to make him appear more human

   D. to demonstrate his hatred of Jews

INTEGRATED / TECHNOLOGY

TEST PRACTICE Go to **classzone.com**

- Diagnostic tests
- Strategies
- Tutorials
- Additional practice

ALTERNATIVE ASSESSMENT

1. Interact *with* History

On page 462, you chose a candidate to support in German elections in the early 1930s. Now that you have read the chapter, did what you read confirm your decision? Why or why not? Would the candidate you selected have a good or bad effect on the rest of the world? Discuss your opinions with a small group.

2. WRITING ABOUT HISTORY

Write a **radio script** for a report on a speech given by Hitler or Mussolini. Imagine that you have just seen the dictator deliver the speech and you want to share your impressions with the public in your broadcast. Be sure to

- summarize the main ideas of the speech.
- describe the speaker's gestures and facial expressions.
- provide phrases that demonstrate the emotional power of the speech.
- convey the public's response to the speech.
- offer your opinion of the speech and speaker.

INTEGRATED / TECHNOLOGY

NetExplorations: Life in the 1920s

Go to *NetExplorations* at **classzone.com** to learn more about life in the 1920s. Use your research to create a Web page on films from that era. Consider including

- reviews of the films, including a positive or negative recommendation.
- background information about silent films.
- biographical information about the stars and directors of the films.
- stills and clips from the films.
- a comparison between films of the 1920s and modern films.

World War II, 1939–1945

Previewing Main Ideas

EMPIRE BUILDING Germany, Italy, and Japan tried to build empires. They began their expansion by conquering other nations and dominating them politically and economically.

Geography *What areas did the Axis powers control at the height of their power?*

SCIENCE AND TECHNOLOGY Far-reaching developments in science and technology changed the course of World War II. Improvements in aircraft, tanks, and submarines and the development of radar and the atomic bomb drastically altered the way wars were fought.

Geography *Why might submarines have been a key weapon for the Axis powers in their fight against Great Britain?*

ECONOMICS Fighting the Axis terror weakened the economies of Great Britain, the Soviet Union, and other European countries. In contrast, when the United States entered the war, its economy grew sharply. The strength of the American economy bolstered the Allied war effort.

Geography *In terms of location, why was the American economy able to function at a high level while the European economies struggled?*

INTEGRATED TECHNOLOGY

eEdition
• Interactive Maps
• Interactive Visuals
• Interactive Primary Sources

VIDEO *Patterns of Interaction: Modern and Medieval Weapons*

INTERNET RESOURCES
Go to **classzone.com** for:
• Research Links   • Maps
• Internet Activities • Test Practice
• Primary Sources   • Current Events
• Chapter Quiz

EUROPE AND THE MEDITERRANEAN

Sept. 1939
Germany invades Poland; France and Great Britain declare war on Germany. (political cartoon) ▼

June 1940
France surrenders to Germany; Battle of Britain begins.

June 1941
Germans invade Soviet Union.

1939   **1940**   **1941**

PACIFIC

Dec. 1941
◄ Japan attacks Pearl Harbor.

European and African Battles, 1939–1945

NORWAY
SWEDEN
FINLAND
ESTONIA
LATVIA
LITHUANIA

Leningrad
(Sept. 8, 1941–
Jan. 27, 1944)

UNITED KINGDOM
IRELAND
DENMARK

SOVIET UNION

Battle of Britain
(July, 1940–Oct., 1940)

NETH.

Berlin
(Apr. 16, 1945–
Apr. 30, 1945)

EAST PRUSSIA (Ger.

Warsaw
(Sept. 8, 1939–
Sept. 27, 1939)

GERMANY

BELGIUM

Normandy (D-day)
(June 6, 1944)

Battle of the Bulge
(Dec. 16, 1944–
Jan. 16, 1945)

Dresden
(Feb. 13, 1945–
Apr. 17, 1945)

POLAND

Battle of Stalingrad
(Aug 23, 1942–
Feb. 2, 1943)

ATLANTIC OCEAN

Paris
(Aug. 19, 1944–
Aug. 25, 1944)

LUX.

CZECHOSLOVAKIA

LIECH.

FRANCE

SWITZ.

AUSTRIA

HUNGARY

ROMANIA

Caucasus Mts.

PORTUGAL

SPAIN

YUGOSLAVIA

ITALY

ALBANIA

BULGARIA

Black Sea

TURKEY

GREECE

MOROCCO

ALGERIA

TUNISIA

Sicily
(July 10, 1943–
Aug. 17, 1943)

Mediterranean Sea

Tobruk
(June 20, 1942–
June 21, 1942)

Al-Agheila
(Mar. 24, 1941)

El Alamein
(Oct. 23, 1942–
Nov. 4, 1942)

LIBYA

EGYPT

Legend:
- Allied control
- Axis nation
- Farthest extent of Axis control
- Neutral nation
- ✳ Major Battle

N W E S

0   250   500 Miles
0   250   500 Kilometers
Conic Projection

Nov. 1942
Allies invade North Africa.

Feb. 1943
Germans surrender at Stalingrad.

June 1944
◄ D-Day invasion takes place.

May 1945
Germany surrenders.

1942   1943   1944   1945

June 1942
Allies defeat Japan at Battle of Midway.

Feb. 1943
Allies defeat Japan at Guadalcanal.

Oct. 1944
Japanese suffer devastating defeat at the Battle of Leyte Gulf.

Aug.–Sept. 1945
◄ Allies use atomic bombs; Japan surrenders.

Under what circumstances is war justified?

Every day your newspaper carries stories of the latest bombing raids on London and other British cities. The photographs of the devastation are shocking. As you read the stories and view the photographs, you wonder what the United States should do to help Great Britain, its longtime ally. The editorial pages of the newspapers ask the same question. Should the United States stand aside and let the European nations settle the issues themselves? Should it offer help to Great Britain in the form of arms and other supplies? Or should the United States join Britain in its struggle against the Axis powers?

▲ A German bombing raid on London during the Battle of Britain

EXAMINING *the* ISSUES

- **What circumstances would lead you to support or oppose your country's participation in a war?**

- **How are civilians sometimes as much a part of a war effort as soldiers?**

As a class, discuss these questions. In your discussion, weigh the arguments for and against fighting. As you read about World War II, think about the role that civilians play in a situation of total war. Think also about the hard moral choices that people often face in times of war.

Hitler's Lightning War

MAIN IDEA	WHY IT MATTERS NOW	TERMS & NAMES
EMPIRE BUILDING Using the sudden mass attack called the blitzkrieg, Germany overran much of Europe and North Africa.	Hitler's actions set off World War II. The results of the war still affect the politics and economics of today's world.	• nonaggression pact • Battle of Britain • blitzkrieg • Erwin Rommel • Charles de Gaulle • Atlantic Charter • Winston Churchill

SETTING THE STAGE During the 1930s, Hitler played on the hopes and fears of the Western democracies. Each time the Nazi dictator grabbed new territory, he would declare an end to his demands. Peace seemed guaranteed—until Hitler moved again. After his moves into the Rhineland, Austria, and Czechoslovakia, Hitler turned his eyes to Poland. After World War I, the Allies had cut out the Polish Corridor from German territory to give Poland access to the sea. In 1939, Hitler demanded that the Polish Corridor be returned to Germany.

Germany Sparks a New War in Europe

At this point, as you recall from Chapter 15, Soviet dictator Joseph Stalin signed a ten-year **nonaggression pact** with Hitler. After being excluded from the Munich Conference, Stalin was not eager to join with the West. Also, Hitler had promised him territory. In a secret part of the pact, Germany and the Soviet Union agreed to divide Poland between them. They also agreed that the USSR could take over Finland and the Baltic countries of Lithuania, Latvia, and Estonia.

Germany's Lightning Attack After signing this nonaggression pact, Hitler quickly moved ahead with plans to conquer Poland. His surprise attack took place at dawn on September 1, 1939. German tanks and troop trucks rumbled across the Polish border. At the same time, German aircraft and artillery began a merciless bombing of Poland's capital, Warsaw.

France and Great Britain declared war on Germany on September 3. But Poland fell some time before those nations could make any military response. After his victory, Hitler annexed the western half of Poland. That region had a large German population.

The German invasion of Poland was the first test of Germany's newest military strategy—the **blitzkrieg** (BLIHTS•kreeg), or "lightning war." It involved using fast-moving airplanes and tanks, followed by massive infantry forces, to take enemy defenders by surprise and quickly overwhelm them. In the case of Poland, the strategy worked.

The Soviets Make Their Move On September 17, Stalin sent Soviet troops to occupy the eastern half of Poland. Stalin then moved to annex countries to the north of Poland. Lithuania, Latvia, and Estonia fell without a struggle, but Finland resisted. In November, Stalin sent nearly one million Soviet troops into

TAKING NOTES

Recognizing Effects
Use a chart to identify the effects of some of the early events of World War II.

Cause	Effect
First blitzkrieg	
Allies stranded at Dunkirk	
Lend-Lease Act	

Finland. The Soviets expected to win a quick victory, so they were not prepared for winter fighting. This was a crucial mistake.

The Finns were outnumbered and outgunned, but they fiercely defended their country. In the freezing winter weather, soldiers on skis swiftly attacked Soviet positions. In contrast, the Soviets struggled to make progress through the deep snow. The Soviets suffered heavy losses, but they finally won through sheer force of numbers. By March 1940, Stalin had forced the Finns to accept his surrender terms. **A**

The Phony War After they declared war on Germany, the French and British had mobilized their armies. They stationed their troops along the Maginot (MAZH•uh•NOH) Line, a system of fortifications along France's border with Germany. There they waited for the Germans to attack—but nothing happened. With little to do, the bored Allied soldiers stared eastward toward the enemy. Equally bored, German soldiers stared back from their Siegfried Line a few miles away. Germans jokingly called it the *sitzkrieg,* or "sitting war." Some newspapers referred to it simply as "the phony war."

Suddenly, on April 9, 1940, the calm ended. Hitler launched a surprise invasion of Denmark and Norway. In just four hours after the attack, Denmark fell. Two months later, Norway surrendered as well. The Germans then began to build bases along the Norwegian and Danish coasts from which they could launch strikes on Great Britain.

The Fall of France

In May of 1940, Hitler began a dramatic sweep through the Netherlands, Belgium, and Luxembourg. This was part of a strategy to strike at France. Keeping the Allies' attention on those countries, Hitler then sent an even larger force of tanks

MAIN IDEA

Analyzing Motives
A What were Stalin's goals in Europe at the beginning of World War II?

World War II: German Advances, 1939–1941

INTER**ACTIVE**

Legend:
- Axis nations, 1938
- Axis-controlled, 1941
- Allies
- Neutral nations
- → German advances

SKILLBUILDER:
Interpreting Maps
1. **Region** *Which countries did Germany invade?*
2. **Location** *In what way was Germany's geographic location an advantage when it was on the offensive in the war?*

and troops to slice through the Ardennes (ahr•DEHN). This was a heavily wooded area in northern France, Luxembourg, and Belgium. Moving through the forest, the Germans "squeezed between" the Maginot Line. From there, they moved across France and reached the country's northern coast in ten days.

Rescue at Dunkirk After reaching the French coast, the German forces swung north again and joined with German troops in Belgium. By the end of May 1940, the Germans had trapped the Allied forces around the northern French city of Lille (leel). Outnumbered, outgunned, and pounded from the air, the Allies retreated to the beaches of Dunkirk, a French port city near the Belgian border. They were trapped with their backs to the sea.

In one of the most heroic acts of the war, Great Britain set out to rescue the army. It sent a fleet of about 850 ships across the English Channel to Dunkirk. Along with Royal Navy ships, civilian craft—yachts, lifeboats, motorboats, paddle steamers, and fishing boats—joined the rescue effort. From May 26 to June 4, this amateur armada, under heavy fire from German bombers, sailed back and forth from Britain to Dunkirk. The boats carried some 338,000 battle-weary soldiers to safety.

France Falls Following Dunkirk, resistance in France began to crumble. By June 14, the Germans had taken Paris. Accepting the inevitable, French leaders surrendered on June 22, 1940. The Germans took control of the northern part of the country. They left the southern part to a puppet government headed by Marshal Philippe Pétain (pay•TAN), a French hero from World War I. The headquarters of this government was in the city of Vichy (VEESH•ee).

After France fell, **Charles de Gaulle** (duh GOHL), a French general, set up a government-in-exile in London. He committed all his energy to reconquering France. In a radio broadcast from England, de Gaulle called on the people of France to join him in resisting the Germans:

PRIMARY SOURCE
It is the bounden [obligatory] duty of all Frenchmen who still bear arms to continue the struggle. For them to lay down their arms, to evacuate any position of military importance, or agree to hand over any part of French territory, however small, to enemy control would be a crime against our country.

GENERAL CHARLES DE GAULLE, quoted in
Charles de Gaulle: A Biography

De Gaulle went on to organize the Free French military forces that battled the Nazis until France was liberated in 1944.

The Battle of Britain

With the fall of France, Great Britain stood alone against the Nazis. **Winston Churchill**, the new British prime minister, had already declared that his nation would never give in. In a rousing speech, he proclaimed, "We shall fight on the beaches, we shall fight on the landing grounds, we shall fight in the fields and in the streets . . . we shall never surrender."

Hitler now turned his mind to an invasion of Great Britain. His plan was first to knock out the Royal Air Force (RAF) and then to land more than 250,000 soldiers on England's shores.

History Makers

Winston Churchill
1874–1965

Possibly the most powerful weapon the British had as they stood alone against Hitler's Germany was the nation's prime minister—Winston Churchill. "Big Winnie," Londoners boasted, "was the lad for us."

Although Churchill had a speech defect as a youngster, he grew to become one of the greatest orators of all time. He used all his gifts as a speaker to rally the people behind the effort to crush Germany. In one famous speech he promised that Britain would

. . . wage war, by sea, land and air, with all our might and with all the strength that God can give us . . . against a monstrous tyranny.

INTEGRATED TECHNOLOGY

RESEARCH LINKS For more on Winston Churchill, go to **classzone.com**

▲ A London bus is submerged in a bomb crater after a German air raid.

In the summer of 1940, the Luftwaffe (LOOFT•VAHF•uh), Germany's air force, began bombing Great Britain. At first, the Germans targeted British airfields and aircraft factories. Then, on September 7, 1940, they began focusing on the cities, especially London, to break British morale. Despite the destruction and loss of life, the British did not waver.

Vocabulary
Luftwaffe is the German word for "air weapon."

The RAF, although badly outnumbered, began to hit back hard. Two technological devices helped turn the tide in the RAF's favor. One was an electronic tracking system known as radar. Developed in the late 1930s, radar could tell the number, speed, and direction of incoming warplanes. The other device was a German code-making machine named Enigma. A complete Enigma machine had been smuggled into Great Britain in the late 1930s. Enigma enabled the British to decode German secret messages. With information gathered by these devices, RAF fliers could quickly launch attacks on the enemy.

To avoid the RAF's attacks, the Germans gave up daylight raids in October 1940 in favor of night bombing. At sunset, the wail of sirens filled the air as Londoners flocked to the subways, which served as air-raid shelters. Some rode out the bombing raids at home in smaller air-raid shelters or basements. This **Battle of Britain** continued until May 10, 1941. Stunned by British resistance, Hitler decided to call off his attacks. Instead, he focused on the Mediterranean and Eastern Europe. The Battle of Britain taught the Allies a crucial lesson. Hitler's attacks could be blocked. **B**

MAIN IDEA
Recognizing Effects
B Why was the outcome of the Battle of Britain important for the Allies?

The Mediterranean and the Eastern Front

The stubborn resistance of the British in the Battle of Britain caused a shift in Hitler's strategy in Europe. He decided to deal with Great Britain later. He then turned his attention east to the Mediterranean area and the Balkans—and to the ultimate prize, the Soviet Union.

Axis Forces Attack North Africa Germany's first objective in the Mediterranean region was North Africa, mainly because of Hitler's partner, Mussolini. Despite its alliance with Germany, Italy had remained neutral at the beginning of the war. With Hitler's conquest of France, however, Mussolini knew he had to take action. After declaring war on France and Great Britain, Mussolini moved into France.

Mussolini took his next step in North Africa in September 1940. While the Battle of Britain was raging, he ordered his army to attack British-controlled Egypt. Egypt's Suez Canal was key to reaching the oil fields of the Middle East. Within a week, Italian troops had pushed 60 miles inside Egypt, forcing British units back. Then both sides dug in and waited.

Vocabulary
The *Middle East* includes the countries of Southwest Asia and northeast Africa.

Britain Strikes Back Finally, in December, the British struck back. The result was a disaster for the Italians. By February 1941, the British had swept 500 miles across North Africa and had taken 130,000 Italian prisoners. Hitler had to step in to save his Axis partner. To reinforce the Italians, Hitler sent a crack German tank force, the Afrika Korps, under the command of General **Erwin Rommel**. In late March 1941, Rommel's Afrika Korps attacked. Caught by surprise, British forces retreated east to Tobruk, Libya. (See the map on page 489.)

After fierce fighting for Tobruk, the British began to drive Rommel back. By mid-January 1942, Rommel had retreated to where he had started. By June 1942, the tide of battle turned again. Rommel regrouped, pushed the British back across the desert, and seized Tobruk—a shattering loss for the Allies. Rommel's successes in North Africa earned him the nickname "Desert Fox."

The War in the Balkans While Rommel campaigned in North Africa, other German generals were active in the Balkans. Hitler had begun planning to attack his ally, the USSR, as early as the summer of 1940. The Balkan countries of southeastern Europe were key to Hitler's invasion plan. Hitler wanted to build bases in southeastern Europe for the attack on the Soviet Union. He also wanted to make sure that the British did not interfere.

To prepare for his invasion, Hitler moved to expand his influence in the Balkans. By early 1941, through the threat of force, he had persuaded Bulgaria, Romania, and Hungary to join the Axis powers. Yugoslavia and Greece, which had pro-British governments, resisted. In early April 1941, Hitler invaded both countries. Yugoslavia fell in 11 days. Greece surrendered in 17. In Athens, the Nazis celebrated their victory by raising swastikas on the Acropolis.

Hitler Invades the Soviet Union With the Balkans firmly in control, Hitler could move ahead with Operation Barbarossa, his plan to invade the Soviet Union. Early in the morning of June 22, 1941, the roar of German tanks and aircraft announced the beginning of the invasion. The Soviet Union was not prepared for this attack. Although it had the largest army in the world, its troops were neither well equipped nor well trained.

The invasion rolled on week after week until the Germans had pushed 500 miles inside the Soviet Union. As the Soviet troops retreated, they burned and destroyed everything in the enemy's path. The Russians had used this scorched-earth strategy against Napoleon.

On September 8, German forces put Leningrad under siege. By early November, the city was completely cut off from the rest of the Soviet Union. To force a surrender, Hitler was ready to starve the city's more than 2.5 million inhabitants. German bombs destroyed warehouses where food was stored. Desperately hungry, people began eating cattle and horse feed, as well as cats and dogs and, finally, crows and rats. Nearly one million people died in Leningrad during the winter of 1941–1942. Yet the city refused to fall.

▼ Russian soldiers prepare to attack German lines outside Leningrad.

Impatient with the progress in Leningrad, Hitler looked to Moscow, the capital and heart of the Soviet Union. A Nazi drive on the capital began on October 2, 1941. By December, the Germans had advanced to the outskirts of Moscow. Soviet General Georgi Zhukov (ZHOO•kuhf) counterattacked. As temperatures fell, the Germans, in summer uniforms, retreated. Ignoring Napoleon's winter defeat 130 years before, Hitler sent his generals a stunning order: "No retreat!" German troops dug in about 125 miles west of Moscow. They held the line against the Soviets until March 1943. Hitler's advance on the Soviet Union gained nothing but cost the Germans 500,000 lives. **C**

MAIN IDEA

Making Inferences
C What does the fact that German armies were not prepared for the Russian winter indicate about Hitler's expectations for the Soviet campaign?

The United States Aids Its Allies

Most Americans felt that the United States should not get involved in the war. Between 1935 and 1937, Congress passed a series of Neutrality Acts. The laws made it illegal to sell arms or lend money to nations at war. But President Roosevelt knew that if the Allies fell, the United States would be drawn into the war. In September 1939, he asked Congress to allow the Allies to buy American arms. The Allies would pay cash and then carry the goods on their own ships.

Under the Lend-Lease Act, passed in March 1941, the president could lend or lease arms and other supplies to any country vital to the United States. By the summer of 1941, the U.S. Navy was escorting British ships carrying U.S. arms. In response, Hitler ordered his submarines to sink any cargo ships they met.

Although the United States had not yet entered the war, Roosevelt and Churchill met secretly and issued a joint declaration called the **Atlantic Charter**. It upheld free trade among nations and the right of people to choose their own government. The charter later served as the Allies' peace plan at the end of World War II.

On September 4, a German U-boat fired on a U.S. destroyer in the Atlantic. In response, Roosevelt ordered navy commanders to shoot German submarines on sight. The United States was now involved in an undeclared naval war with Hitler. To almost everyone's surprise, however, the attack that actually drew the United States into the war did not come from Germany. It came from Japan.

SECTION 1 ASSESSMENT

TERMS & NAMES 1. For each term or name, write a sentence explaining its significance.
• nonaggression pact • blitzkrieg • Charles de Gaulle • Winston Churchill • Battle of Britain • Erwin Rommel • Atlantic Charter

USING YOUR NOTES
2. Which of the listed events might be considered a turning point for the Allies? Why?

Cause	Effect
First blitzkrieg	
Allies stranded at Dunkirk	
Lend-Lease Act	

MAIN IDEAS
3. Why were the early months of World War II referred to as the "phony war"?

4. Why was Egypt of strategic importance in World War II?

5. Why did President Franklin Roosevelt want to offer help to the Allies?

CRITICAL THINKING & WRITING
6. **CLARIFYING** What do you think is meant by the statement that Winston Churchill possibly was Britain's most powerful weapon against Hitler's Germany?

7. **MAKING INFERENCES** What factors do you think a country's leaders consider when deciding whether to surrender or fight?

8. **COMPARING** How were Napoleon's invasion of Russia and Hitler's invasion of the Soviet Union similar?

9. **WRITING ACTIVITY** EMPIRE BUILDING Write a **magazine article** on German conquests in Europe through 1942.

CONNECT TO TODAY **PREPARING AN ORAL REPORT**
Conduct research into "stealth" technology, which is designed to evade radar. Use your findings to prepare a brief **oral report** titled "How Stealth Technology Works."

Japan's Pacific Campaign

MAIN IDEA	WHY IT MATTERS NOW	TERMS & NAMES
EMPIRE BUILDING Japan attacked Pearl Harbor in Hawaii and brought the United States into World War II.	World War II established the United States as a leading player in international affairs.	• Isoroku Yamamoto • Pearl Harbor • Battle of Midway • Douglas MacArthur • Battle of Guadalcanal

SETTING THE STAGE Like Hitler, Japan's military leaders also had dreams of empire. Japan's expansion had begun in 1931. That year, Japanese troops took over Manchuria in northeastern China. Six years later, Japanese armies swept into the heartland of China. They expected quick victory. Chinese resistance, however, caused the war to drag on. This placed a strain on Japan's economy. To increase their resources, Japanese leaders looked toward the rich European colonies of Southeast Asia.

Surprise Attack on Pearl Harbor

By October 1940, Americans had cracked one of the codes that the Japanese used in sending secret messages. Therefore, they were well aware of Japanese plans for Southeast Asia. If Japan conquered European colonies there, it could also threaten the American-controlled Philippine Islands and Guam. To stop the Japanese advance, the U.S. government sent aid to strengthen Chinese resistance. And when the Japanese overran French Indochina—Vietnam, Cambodia, and Laos—in July 1941, Roosevelt cut off oil shipments to Japan.

Despite an oil shortage, the Japanese continued their conquests. They hoped to catch the European colonial powers and the United States by surprise. So they planned massive attacks on British and Dutch colonies in Southeast Asia and on American outposts in the Pacific—at the same time. Admiral **Isoroku Yamamoto** (ih•soh•ROO•koo YAH•muh•MOH•toh), Japan's greatest naval strategist, also called for an attack on the U.S. fleet in Hawaii. It was, he said, "a dagger pointed at [Japan's] throat" and must be destroyed.

Day of Infamy Early in the morning of December 7, 1941, American sailors at **Pearl Harbor** in Hawaii awoke to the roar of explosives. A Japanese attack was underway! U.S. military leaders had known from a coded Japanese message that an attack might come. But they did not know when or where it would occur. Within two hours, the Japanese had sunk or damaged 19 ships, including 8 battleships, moored in Pearl Harbor. More than 2,300 Americans were killed—with over 1,100 wounded. News of the attack stunned the American people. The next day, President Roosevelt addressed Congress. December 7, 1941, he declared, was "a date which will live in infamy." Congress quickly accepted his request for a declaration of war on Japan and its allies.

TAKING NOTES

Recognizing Effects
Use a chart to identify the effects of four major events of the war in the Pacific between 1941 and 1943.

Event	Effect

▲ The *U.S.S. West Virginia* is engulfed by flames after taking a direct hit during the Japanese attack on Pearl Harbor.

Almost at the same time of the Pearl Harbor attack, the Japanese launched bombing raids on the British colony of Hong Kong and American-controlled Guam and Wake Island. (See the map on the opposite page.) They also landed an invasion force in Thailand. The Japanese drive for a Pacific empire was under way.

Japanese Victories

Lightly defended, Guam and Wake Island quickly fell to Japanese forces. The Japanese then turned their attention to the Philippines. In January 1942, they marched into the Philippine capital of Manila. American and Filipino forces took up a defensive position on the Bataan (buh•TAN) Peninsula on the northwestern edge of Manila Bay. At the same time, the Philippine government moved to the island of Corregidor just to the south of Bataan. After about three months of tough fighting, the Japanese took the Bataan Peninsula in April. Corregidor fell the following month.

The Japanese also continued their strikes against British possessions in Asia. After seizing Hong Kong, they invaded Malaya from the sea and overland from Thailand. By February 1942, the Japanese had reached Singapore, strategically located at the southern tip of the Malay Peninsula. After a fierce pounding, the colony surrendered. Within a month, the Japanese had conquered the resource-rich Dutch East Indies (now Indonesia), including the islands of Java, Sumatra, Borneo, and Celebes (SEHL•uh•BEEZ). The Japanese also moved westward, taking Burma. From there, they planned to launch a strike against India, the largest of Great Britain's colonies.

By the time Burma fell, Japan had taken control of more than 1 million square miles of Asian land. About 150 million people lived in this vast area. Before these conquests, the Japanese had tried to win the support of Asians with the anticolonialist idea of "East Asia for the Asiatics." After victory, however, the Japanese quickly made it clear that they had come as conquerors. They often treated the people of their new colonies with extreme cruelty.

However, the Japanese reserved the most brutal treatment for Allied prisoners of war. The Japanese considered it dishonorable to surrender, and they had contempt for the prisoners of war in their charge. On the Bataan Death March—a forced march of more than 50 miles up the peninsula—the Japanese subjected their captives to terrible cruelties. One Allied prisoner of war reported:

PRIMARY SOURCE

I was questioned by a Japanese officer, who found out that I had been in a Philippine Scout Battalion. The [Japanese] hated the Scouts. . . . Anyway, they took me outside and I was forced to watch as they buried six of my Scouts alive. They made the men dig their own graves, and then had them kneel down in a pit. The guards hit them over the head with shovels to stun them and piled earth on top.

LIEUTENANT JOHN SPAINHOWER, quoted in *War Diary 1939–1945*

Of the approximately 70,000 prisoners who started the Bataan Death March, only 54,000 survived.

World War II in Asia and the Pacific, 1941–1945
INTERACTIVE

SOVIET UNION

Alaska (U.S.)

MONGOLIA　　MANCHURIA

CHINA

Beijing (Peking)

KOREA　JAPAN
Hiroshima Aug. 1945
Nanking
Shanghai
Nagasaki, Aug. 1945

Sakhalin
Karafuto Is.
Kuril Is.
Hokkaido
Honshu
Tokyo
Shikoku
Kyushu

Aleutian Islands

Attu May 1943

PACIFIC OCEAN

Midway Island June 1942

Tropic of Cancer

INDIA (Br.)

BURMA
THAILAND
FRENCH INDOCHINA

Taiwan
Hong Kong (Br.)
Luzon
PHILIPPINES
Leyte Gulf Oct. 1944
Mindanao

Okinawa Apr.–July 1945
Iwo Jima Feb.–Mar. 1945

Mariana Islands
Saipan June–July 1944
Guam July–Aug. 1944

Wake Island Dec. 1941

Pearl Harbor Dec. 1941
Hawaiian Islands (U.S.)

1945
1945
1945
1945
1944

MALAYA
Singapore
Sumatra
DUTCH EAST INDIES
Java
Borneo
Celebes　Moluccas

Caroline Islands

Marshall Islands

Tarawa Nov. 1943
Gilbert Islands

Ellice Islands

1944
1944
1943
1943

0° Equator

INDIAN OCEAN

N

0　1,000 Miles
0　2,000 Kilometers

NEW GUINEA
1944
1943–1944
1943–1944

Solomon Islands

Coral Sea May 1942
Coral Sea

Guadalcanal Aug. 1942–Feb. 1943

1942

Legend:
- ■ Japanese empire, 1931
- ■ Japanese gains by 1942
- — Extent of Japanese expansion
- ■ Allies
- ■ Neutral nations
- ← Allied advances
- ✷ Battle

AUSTRALIA

Battle of Midway, June 1942

180° W　179° W　178° W　177° W

From Pearl Harbor

Hornet & Enterprise
Yorktown
Enterprise
31° N
Yorktown (sinks June 7)

Hiryu (sinks June 5)
Soryu (sinks June 4)
Akegi (sinks June 5)
Kaga (sinks June 4)
Hiryu

From Japan

Legend:
- → Japanese fleet movements
- → U.S. fleet movements
- ⊣⊢ Japanese air strikes
- ⊣⊢ U.S. air strikes
- ⬥ Japanese aircraft carriers
- ⬥ U.S. aircraft carriers

N

0　50 Miles
0　100 Kilometers

PACIFIC OCEAN

30° N
29° N

Kure Atoll
Midway Islands

Some Japanese search aircraft were late getting into the air. As a result, the Japanese were completely unaware that U.S. ships were nearby.

The Japanese warship *Mikuma* lists and begins to sink after being struck by bombs from American aircraft during the Battle of Midway.

GEOGRAPHY SKILLBUILDER: Interpreting Maps
1. **Location** *Which battle was fought in the most northern region?*
2. **Movement** *From what two general directions did Allied forces move in on Japan?*

The Allies Strike Back

After a string of victories, the Japanese seemed unbeatable. Nonetheless, the Allies—mainly Americans and Australians—were anxious to strike back in the Pacific. The United States in particular wanted revenge for Pearl Harbor. In April 1942, 16 B-25 bombers under the command of Lieutenant Colonel James H. Doolittle bombed Tokyo and several other Japanese cities. The bombs did little damage. The raid, however, made an important psychological point to both Americans and Japanese: Japan was vulnerable to attack.

The Allies Turn the Tide Doolittle's raid on Japan raised American morale and shook the confidence of some in Japan. As one Japanese citizen noted, "We started to doubt that we were invincible." In addition, some Japanese worried that defending and controlling a vast empire had caused them to spread their resources too thin.

Vocabulary
invincible:
unconquerable

Slowly, the Allies began to turn the tide of war. Early in May 1942, an American fleet with Australian support intercepted a Japanese strike force headed for Port Moresby in New Guinea. This city housed a critical Allied air base. Control of the air base would put the Japanese in easy striking distance of Australia.

In the battle that followed—the Battle of the Coral Sea—both sides used a new kind of naval warfare. The opposing ships did not fire a single shot. In fact, they often could not see one another. Instead, airplanes taking off from huge aircraft carriers attacked the ships. The Allies suffered more losses in ships and troops than did the Japanese. However, the Battle of the Coral Sea was something of a victory, for the Allies had stopped Japan's southward advance.

The Battle of Midway Japan next targeted Midway Island, some 1,500 miles west of Hawaii, the location of a key American airfield. Thanks to Allied code breakers, Admiral Chester Nimitz, commander in chief of the U.S. Pacific Fleet, knew that a huge Japanese force was heading toward Midway. Admiral Yamamoto himself was in command of the Japanese fleet. He hoped that the attack on Midway would draw the whole of the U.S. Pacific Fleet from Pearl Harbor to defend the island. Ⓐ

On June 4, with American forces hidden beyond the horizon, Nimitz allowed the Japanese to begin their assault on the island. As the first Japanese planes got into the air, American planes swooped in to attack the Japanese fleet. Many Japanese planes were still on the decks of the aircraft carriers. The strategy was a success. American pilots destroyed 332 Japanese planes, all four aircraft carriers, and one support ship. Yamamoto ordered his crippled fleet to withdraw. By June 7, 1942, the battle was over. The **Battle of Midway** turned the tide of war in the Pacific. (See the inset map on page 499.)

MAIN IDEA
Analyzing Motives
Ⓐ Why might the Americans send their entire Pacific Fleet to defend Midway Island?

An Allied Offensive

With morale high after their victory at Midway, the Allies took the offensive. The war in the Pacific involved vast distances. Japanese troops had dug in on hundreds of islands across the ocean. General **Douglas MacArthur**, the commander of the Allied land forces in the Pacific, developed a plan to handle this problem.

History Makers

**General Douglas MacArthur
1880–1964**

Douglas MacArthur's qualities as a leader and a fighting soldier emerged in France during World War I. Showing incredible dash and courage on the battlefield, he received several decorations for bravery. And he won promotion from the rank of major to brigadier general.

After serving in several positions in the United States, MacArthur received a posting to the Philippines in 1935. He remained there until shortly before the islands fell in 1941. But he left very reluctantly. In a message to the troops who remained behind, he vowed, "I shall return." As you will read later in the chapter, MacArthur kept his promise.

MAIN IDEA

Identifying Problems

 If the vast distances of the Pacific caused problems for the Allies, how might they have also caused problems for the Japanese?

MacArthur believed that storming each island would be a long, costly effort. Instead, he wanted to "island-hop" past Japanese strongholds. He would then seize islands that were not well defended but were closer to Japan. **B**

MacArthur's first target soon presented itself. U.S. military leaders had learned that the Japanese were building a huge air base on the island of Guadalcanal in the Solomon Islands. The Allies had to strike fast before the base was completed and became another Japanese stronghold. At dawn on August 7, 1942, several thousand U.S. Marines, with Australian support, landed on Guadalcanal and the neighboring island of Tulagi.

The marines had little trouble seizing Guadalcanal's airfield. But the battle for control of the island turned into a savage struggle as both sides poured in fresh troops. In February 1943, after six months of fighting on land and at sea, the **Battle of Guadalcanal** finally ended. After losing more than 24,000 of a force of 36,000 soldiers, the Japanese abandoned what they came to call "the Island of Death."

To American war correspondent Ralph Martin and the U.S. soldiers who fought there, Guadalcanal was simply "hell":

▲ U.S. Marines storm ashore at Guadalcanal.

PRIMARY SOURCE

Hell was red furry spiders as big as your fist, . . . enormous rats and bats everywhere, and rivers with waiting crocodiles. Hell was the sour, foul smell of the squishy jungle, humidity that rotted a body within hours. . . . Hell was an enemy . . . so fanatic that it used its own dead as booby traps.

RALPH G. MARTIN, *The GI War*

As Japan worked to establish a new order in Southeast Asia and the Pacific, the Nazis moved ahead with Hitler's design for a new order in Europe. This design included plans for dealing with those Hitler considered unfit for the Third Reich. You will learn about these plans in Section 3.

SECTION 2 ASSESSMENT

TERMS & NAMES 1. For each term or name, write a sentence explaining its significance.
• Isoroku Yamamoto   • Pearl Harbor   • Battle of Midway   • Douglas MacArthur   • Battle of Guadalcanal

USING YOUR NOTES

2. Which event was most important in turning the tide of the war in the Pacific against the Japanese? Why?

Event	Effect

MAIN IDEAS

3. How did the Japanese plan to catch the European colonial powers and the United States by surprise?

4. In what way was the Battle of the Coral Sea a new kind of naval warfare?

5. What was General Douglas MacArthur's island-hopping strategy?

CRITICAL THINKING & WRITING

6. **EVALUATING DECISIONS** Did Admiral Yamamoto make a wise decision in bombing Pearl Harbor? Why or why not?

7. **ANALYZING MOTIVES** Why do you think the Japanese changed their approach from trying to win the support of the colonized peoples to acting as conquerors?

8. **IDENTIFYING PROBLEMS** What problems did Japan face in building an empire in the Pacific?

9. **WRITING ACTIVITY** EMPIRE BUILDING Imagine you are a foreign diplomat living in Asia during World War II. Write **journal entries** describing the Japanese advance across Asia and the Pacific during 1941 and 1942.

INTEGRATED TECHNOLOGY **INTERNET ACTIVITY**

Use the Internet to research the Pearl Harbor Memorial in Hawaii. Create a **Web page** that describes the memorial and provides background information on the attack.

INTERNET KEYWORD
Pearl Harbor

3

The Holocaust

MAIN IDEA	WHY IT MATTERS NOW	TERMS & NAMES
EMPIRE BUILDING During the Holocaust, Hitler's Nazis killed six million Jews and five million other "non-Aryans."	The violence against Jews during the Holocaust led to the founding of Israel after World War II.	• Aryan • *Kristallnacht* • ghetto • "Final Solution" • genocide • Holocaust

SETTING THE STAGE As part of their vision for Europe, the Nazis proposed a new racial order. They proclaimed that the Germanic peoples, or **Aryans**, were a "master race." (This was a misuse of the term *Aryan*. The term actually refers to the Indo-European peoples who began to migrate into the Indian subcontinent around 1500 B.C.) The Nazis claimed that all non-Aryan peoples, particularly Jewish people, were inferior. This racist message would eventually lead to the **Holocaust**, the systematic mass slaughter of Jews and other groups judged inferior by the Nazis.

TAKING NOTES

Analyzing Bias Use a web diagram to identify examples of Nazi persecution.

The Holocaust Begins

To gain support for his racist ideas, Hitler knowingly tapped into a hatred for Jews that had deep roots in European history. For generations, many Germans, along with other Europeans, had targeted Jews as the cause of their failures. Some Germans even blamed Jews for their country's defeat in World War I and for its economic problems after that war.

In time, the Nazis made the targeting of Jews a government policy. The Nuremberg Laws, passed in 1935, deprived Jews of their rights to German citizenship and forbade marriages between Jews and non-Jews. Laws passed later also limited the kinds of work that Jews could do.

"Night of Broken Glass" Worse was yet to come. Early in November 1938, 17-year-old Herschel Grynszpan (GRIHN•shpahn), a Jewish youth from Germany, was visiting an uncle in Paris. While Grynszpan was there, he received a postcard. It said that after living in Germany for 27 years, his father had been deported to Poland. On November 7, wishing to avenge his father's deportation, Grynszpan shot a German diplomat living in Paris.

When Nazi leaders heard the news, they launched a violent attack on the Jewish community. On November 9, Nazi storm troopers attacked Jewish homes, businesses, and synagogues across Germany and murdered close to 100 Jews. An American in Leipzig wrote, "Jewish shop windows by the hundreds were systematically . . . smashed. . . . The main streets of the city were a positive litter of shattered plate glass." It is for this reason that the night of November 9 became known as ***Kristallnacht*** (krih•STAHL•NAHKT), or "Night of Broken Glass." A 14-year-old boy described his memory of that awful night:

PRIMARY SOURCE
All the things for which my parents had worked for eighteen long years were destroyed in less than ten minutes. Piles of valuable glasses, expensive furniture, linens—in short, everything was destroyed. . . . The Nazis left us, yelling, "Don't try to leave this house! We'll soon be back again and take you to a concentration camp to be shot."

M. I. LIBAU, quoted in *Never to Forget: The Jews of the Holocaust*

Kristallnacht marked a major step-up in the Nazi policy of Jewish persecution. The future for Jews in Germany looked truly grim.

A Flood of Refugees After *Kristallnacht*, some Jews realized that violence against them was bound to increase. By the end of 1939, a number of German Jews had fled to other countries. Many however, remained in Germany. Later, Hitler conquered territories in which millions more Jews lived.

At first, Hitler favored emigration as a solution to what he called "the Jewish problem." Getting other countries to continue admitting Germany's Jews became an issue, however. After admitting tens of thousands of Jewish refugees, such countries as France, Britain, and the United States abruptly closed their doors to further immigration. Germany's foreign minister observed, "We all want to get rid of our Jews. The difficulty is that no country wishes to receive them."

Isolating the Jews When Hitler found that he could not get rid of Jews through emigration, he put another plan into effect. He ordered Jews in all countries under his control to be moved to designated cities. In those cities, the Nazis herded the Jews into dismal, overcrowded **ghettos**, or segregated Jewish areas. The Nazis then sealed off the ghettos with barbed wire and stone walls. They hoped that the Jews inside would starve to death or die from disease. **A**

Even under these horrible conditions, the Jews hung on. Some, particularly the Jews in Warsaw, Poland, formed resistance organizations within the ghettos. They also struggled to keep their traditions. Ghetto theaters produced plays and concerts. Teachers taught lessons in secret schools. Scholars kept records so that one day people would find out the truth.

The "Final Solution"

Hitler soon grew impatient waiting for Jews to die from starvation or disease. He decided to take more direct action. His plan was called the "**Final Solution**." It was actually a program of **genocide**, the systematic killing of an entire people.

▲ After 1941, all Jews in German-controlled areas had to wear a yellow Star of David patch.

▼ German soldiers round up Jews in the Warsaw ghetto.

Hitler believed that his plan of conquest depended on the purity of the Aryan race. To protect racial purity, the Nazis had to eliminate other races, nationalities, or groups they viewed as inferior—as "subhumans." They included Roma (gypsies), Poles, Russians, homosexuals, the insane, the disabled, and the incurably ill. But the Nazis focused especially on the Jews. **B**

MAIN IDEA

Analyzing Bias
B How was the "Final Solution" a natural outcome of Nazi racial theory?

The Killings Begin As Nazi troops swept across Eastern Europe and the Soviet Union, the killings began. Units from the SS (Hitler's elite security force) moved from town to town to hunt down Jews. The SS and their collaborators rounded up men, women, children, and even babies and took them to isolated spots. They then shot their prisoners in pits that became the prisoners' graves.

Jews in communities not reached by the killing squads were rounded up and taken to concentration camps, or slave-labor prisons. These camps were located mainly in Germany and Poland. Hitler hoped that the horrible conditions in the camps would speed the total elimination of the Jews.

The prisoners worked seven days a week as slaves for the SS or for German businesses. Guards severely beat or killed their prisoners for not working fast enough. With meals of thin soup, a scrap of bread, and potato peelings, most prisoners lost 50 pounds in the first few months. Hunger was so intense, recalled one survivor, "that if a bit of soup spilled over, prisoners would . . . dig their spoons into the mud and stuff the mess in their mouths."

The Final Stage Hitler's war on the Jews turned toward the "Final Solution" in 1942. The Nazis built extermination camps equipped with huge gas chambers that could kill as many as 6,000 human beings in a day. (See the map on page 519.)

When prisoners arrived at Auschwitz (OUSH•vihts), the largest of the extermination camps, they paraded before a committee of SS doctors. With a wave of the hand, these doctors separated the strong—mostly men—from the weak—mostly women, young children, the elderly, and the sick. Those labeled as weak would die that day. They were told to undress for a shower and then led into a chamber with

History *in* Depth

Jewish Resistance

Even in the extermination camps, Jews rose up and fought against the Nazis. At Treblinka in August 1943, and at Sobibor in October 1943, small groups of Jews revolted. They killed guards, stormed the camp armories and stole guns and grenades, and then broke out. In both uprisings, about 300 prisoners escaped. Most were killed soon after. Of those who survived, many joined up with partisan groups and continued to fight until the end of the war.

Late in 1944, prisoners at Auschwitz revolted, too. Like the escapees at Treblinka and Sobibor, most were caught and killed. Young women like Ella Gartner and Roza Robota made the Auschwitz uprising possible. Gartner smuggled gunpowder into the camp from the munitions factory where she worked. Robota helped organize resistance in the camp. Gartner and Robota were executed on January 6, 1945. Less than a month later, Auschwitz was liberated.

▲ Ella Gartner

▶ Roza Robota

Jews Killed Under Nazi Rule*			
	Original Jewish Population	**Jews Killed**	**Percent Surviving**
Poland	3,300,000	2,800,000	15%
Soviet Union (area occupied by Germans)	2,100,000	1,500,000	29%
Hungary	404,000	200,000	49%
Romania	850,000	425,000	50%
Germany/Austria	270,000	210,000	22%

*Estimates   Source: Hannah Vogt, *The Burden of Guilt*

fake showerheads. After the doors were closed, cyanide gas or carbon dioxide poured from the showerheads or holes in the ceiling. All inside were killed in minutes. Later, the Nazis installed crematoriums, or ovens, to burn the bodies.

The Survivors Some six million European Jews died in these death camps and in Nazi massacres. Fewer than four million survived. Some escaped the horrors of the death camps with help from non-Jewish people. These rescuers, at great risk to their own lives, hid Jews in their homes or helped them escape to neutral countries.

Those who survived the camps were changed forever by what they had experienced. As Elie Wiesel, nearly 15 years old when he entered Auschwitz, noted:

PRIMARY SOURCE
Never shall I forget the little faces of the children, whose bodies I saw turned into wreaths of smoke beneath a silent blue sky. Never shall I forget those flames which consumed my faith forever. . . . Never shall I forget those moments which murdered my God and my soul and turned my dreams to dust. . . . Never.

ELIE WIESEL, quoted in *Night*

SECTION 3 ASSESSMENT

TERMS & NAMES 1. For each term or name, write a sentence explaining its significance.
- Aryan
- Holocaust
- *Kristallnacht*
- ghetto
- "Final Solution"
- genocide

USING YOUR NOTES

2. What Nazi actions were part of the "Final Solution"?

Nazi persecution

MAIN IDEAS

3. What was the new racial order proposed by the Nazis?

4. What Nazi action marked the final stage of the "Final Solution"?

5. How did some non-Jews oppose Hitler's "Final Solution"?

CRITICAL THINKING & WRITING

6. **ANALYZING MOTIVES** Why might people want to blame a minority group for most of their country's problems?

7. **MAKING INFERENCES** Why do you think the German people went along with the Nazi policy of persecution of the Jews?

8. **RECOGNIZING EFFECTS** What impact did the Holocaust have on the Jewish population of Europe?

9. **WRITING ACTIVITY** SCIENCE AND TECHNOLOGY Write a **persuasive essay** discussing how German scientists, engineers, and doctors asked to participate in the Holocaust might have opposed Hitler's policy.

CONNECT TO TODAY CREATING A MAP
Find information on instances of genocide and ethnic cleansing in the last 20 years. Use the information to create an **annotated map** titled "Genocide in the Late 20th Century."

The Allied Victory

MAIN IDEA	WHY IT MATTERS NOW	TERMS & NAMES
EMPIRE BUILDING Led by the United States, Great Britain, and the Soviet Union, the Allies scored key victories and won the war.	The Allies' victory in World War II set up conditions for both the Cold War and today's post-Cold War world.	• Dwight D. Eisenhower • Battle of Stalingrad • D-Day • Battle of the Bulge • kamikaze

SETTING THE STAGE On December 22, 1941, just after Pearl Harbor, Winston Churchill and President Roosevelt met at the White House to develop a joint war policy. Stalin had asked his allies to relieve German pressure on his armies in the east. He wanted them to open a second front in the west. This would split the Germans' strength by forcing them to fight major battles in two regions instead of one. Churchill agreed with Stalin's strategy. The Allies would weaken Germany on two fronts before dealing a deathblow. At first, Roosevelt was torn, but ultimately he agreed.

TAKING NOTES

Recognizing Effects
Use a chart to identify the outcomes of several major World War II battles.

Battle	Outcome
Battle of El Alamein	
Battle of Stalingrad	
D-Day Invasion	

The Tide Turns on Two Fronts

Churchill wanted Britain and the United States to strike first at North Africa and southern Europe. The strategy angered Stalin. He wanted the Allies to open the second front in France. The Soviet Union, therefore, had to hold out on its own against the Germans. All Britain and the United States could offer in the way of help was supplies. Nevertheless, late in 1942, the Allies began to turn the tide of war both in the Mediterranean and on the Eastern Front.

The North African Campaign As you recall from Section 1, General Erwin Rommel took the key Libyan port city of Tobruk in June 1942. With Tobruk's fall, London sent General Bernard Montgomery—"Monty" to his troops—to take control of British forces in North Africa. By the time Montgomery arrived, however, the Germans had advanced to an Egyptian village called El Alamein (AL•uh•MAYN), west of Alexandria. (See the map on page 508.) They were dug in so well that British forces could not go around them. The only way to dislodge them, Montgomery decided, was with a massive frontal attack. The Battle of El Alamein began on the night of October 23. The roar of about 1,000 British guns took the Axis soldiers totally by surprise. They fought back fiercely and held their ground for several days. By November 4, however, Rommel's army had been beaten. He and his forces fell back.

As Rommel retreated west, the Allies launched Operation Torch. On November 8, an Allied force of more than 100,000 troops—mostly Americans—landed in Morocco and Algeria. American general **Dwight D. Eisenhower** led this force. Caught between Montgomery's and Eisenhower's armies, Rommel's Afrika Korps was finally crushed in May 1943.

The Battle for Stalingrad As Rommel suffered defeats in North Africa, German armies also met their match in the Soviet Union. The German advance had stalled at Leningrad and Moscow late in 1941. And the bitter winter made the situation worse. When the summer of 1942 arrived, however, Hitler sent his Sixth Army, under the command of General Friedrich Paulus, to seize the oil fields in the Caucasus Mountains. The army was also to capture Stalingrad (now Volgograd), a major industrial center on the Volga River. (See the map on page 508.)

▲ Soviet troops launch an attack during the battle for Stalingrad.

The **Battle of Stalingrad** began on August 23, 1942. The Luftwaffe went on nightly bombing raids that set much of the city ablaze and reduced the rest to rubble. The situation looked desperate. Nonetheless, Stalin had already told his commanders to defend the city named after him to the death.

By early November 1942, Germans controlled 90 percent of the ruined city. Then another Russian winter set in. On November 19, Soviet troops outside the city launched a counterattack. Closing in around Stalingrad, they trapped the Germans inside and cut off their supplies. General Paulus begged Hitler to order a retreat. But Hitler refused, saying the city was "to be held at all costs." **A**

MAIN IDEA

Making Inferences

A What advantages might a weaker army fighting on its home soil have over a stronger invading army?

On February 2, 1943, some 90,000 frostbitten, half-starved German troops surrendered to the Soviets. These pitiful survivors were all that remained of an army of 330,000. Stalingrad's defense had cost the Soviets over one million soldiers. The city was 99 percent destroyed. However, the Germans were now on the defensive, with the Soviets pushing them steadily westward.

The Invasion of Italy As the Battle of Stalingrad raged, Stalin continued to urge the British and Americans to invade France. However, Roosevelt and Churchill decided to attack Italy first. On July 10, 1943, Allied forces landed on Sicily and captured it from Italian and German troops about a month later.

The conquest of Sicily toppled Mussolini from power. On July 25, King Victor Emmanuel III had the dictator arrested. On September 3, Italy surrendered. But the Germans seized control of northern Italy and put Mussolini back in charge. Finally, the Germans retreated northward, and the victorious Allies entered Rome on June 4, 1944. Fighting in Italy, however, continued until Germany fell in May 1945. On April 27, 1945, Italian resistance fighters ambushed some German trucks near the northern Italian city of Milan. Inside one of the trucks, they found Mussolini disguised as a German soldier. They shot him the next day and later hung his body in downtown Milan for all to see.

The Allied Home Fronts

Wherever Allied forces fought, people on the home fronts rallied to support them. In war-torn countries like the Soviet Union and Great Britain, civilians endured extreme hardships. Many lost their lives. Except for a few of its territories, such as Hawaii, the United States did not suffer invasion or bombing. Nonetheless, Americans at home made a crucial contribution to the Allied war effort. Americans produced the weapons and equipment that would help win the war.

Axis nations, 1938
Axis-controlled, 1942
Allies
Neutral nations
Allied advances
Major Battles

FINLAND

NORWAY

SWEDEN

Leningrad

SOVIET UNION

Moscow

Smolensk

DENMARK

Baltic Sea

North Sea

EAST PRUSSIA

Minsk (1944)

1944

Kursk (1943)

UNITED KINGDOM

IRELAND

NETH.

Berlin (1945)

GERMANY

Warsaw (1944–45)

POLAND

1945

London

1944

Dunkirk

BELG.

1944

Battle of the Bulge (1944–45)

LUX.

1944

Paris

CZECHOSLOVAKIA

1944

Dnieper R.

1943

Volga R.

1942

English Channel

Normandy (1944)

1945

AUSTRIA

HUNGARY

1944

ROMANIA

1943

Stalingrad (1942–43)

FRANCE

SWITZ.

1944

ITALY

YUGOSLAVIA

1943

Caspian Sea

PORTUGAL

SPAIN

Rome

Anzio (1944)

1944

1943

ALBANIA

BULGARIA

Black Sea

GREECE

TURKEY

Crete

1944

IRAN

1942

Algiers (1942)

Sicily (1943)

Oran (1942)

1942

Tunis (1943)

1943

Mediterranean Sea

SYRIA

LEBANON

Casablanca (1942)

TUNISIA (Fr.)

1943

Tobruk

1942

PALESTINE

IRAQ

MOROCCO (Fr.)

ALGERIA (Fr.)

1943

1942

El Alamein (1942)

Alexandria

TRANSJORDAN

LIBYA (It.)

EGYPT

SAUDI ARABIA

Arctic Circle

60° N

40° E

40° N

Tropic of Cancer

N

0   250 Miles

0   500 Kilometers

GEOGRAPHY SKILLBUILDER: Interpreting Maps

1. **Region** Which European countries remained neutral during World War II?
2. **Movement** What seems to be the destination for most of the Allied advances that took place in Europe during 1943–1944?

Mobilizing for War Defeating the Axis powers required mobilizing for total war. In the United States, factories converted their peacetime operations to wartime production and made everything from machine guns to boots. Automobile factories produced tanks. A typewriter company made armor-piercing shells. By 1944, between 17 and 18 million U.S. workers—many of them women—had jobs in war industries.

With factories turning out products for the war, a shortage of consumer goods hit the United States. From meat and sugar to tires and gasoline, from nylon stockings to laundry soap, the American government rationed scarce items. Setting the speed limit at 35 miles per hour also helped to save gasoline and rubber. In European countries directly affected by the war, rationing was even more drastic.

We Are Ready • What About You?

Join the

SCHOOLS AT WAR

Program

▲ American schoolchildren helped the war effort by recycling scrap metal and rubber and by buying war bonds.

To inspire their people to greater efforts, Allied governments conducted highly effective propaganda campaigns. In the Soviet Union, a Moscow youngster collected enough scrap metal to produce 14,000 artillery shells. And a Russian family used its life savings to buy a tank for the Red Army. In the United States, youngsters saved their pennies and bought government war stamps and bonds to help finance the war.

War Limits Civil Rights Government propaganda also had a negative effect. After Pearl Harbor, a wave of prejudice arose in the United States against Japanese Americans. Most lived in Hawaii and on the West Coast. The bombing of Pearl Harbor frightened Americans. This fear, encouraged by government propaganda, was turned against Japanese Americans. They were suddenly seen as "the enemy." On February 19, 1942, President Roosevelt issued an executive order calling for the internment of Japanese Americans because they were considered a threat to the country. **B**

In March, the military began rounding up "aliens" and shipping them to relocation camps. The camps were restricted military areas located far away from the coast. Such locations, it was thought, would prevent these "enemy aliens" from assisting a Japanese invasion. However, two-thirds of those interned were Nisei, native-born American citizens whose parents were Japanese. Many of them volunteered for military service and fought bravely for the United States, even though their families remained in the camps.

Victory in Europe

While the Allies were dealing with issues on the home front, they also were preparing to push toward victory in Europe. In 1943, the Allies began secretly building an invasion force in Great Britain. Their plan was to launch an attack on German-held France across the English Channel.

The D-Day Invasion By May 1944, the invasion force was ready. Thousands of planes, ships, tanks, and landing craft and more than three million troops awaited the order to attack. General Dwight D. Eisenhower, the commander of this enormous force, planned to strike on the coast of Normandy, in northwestern France. The Germans knew that an attack was coming. But they did not know where it would be launched. To keep Hitler guessing, the Allies set up a huge dummy army with its own headquarters and equipment. This make-believe army appeared to be preparing to attack the French seaport of Calais (ka•LAY).

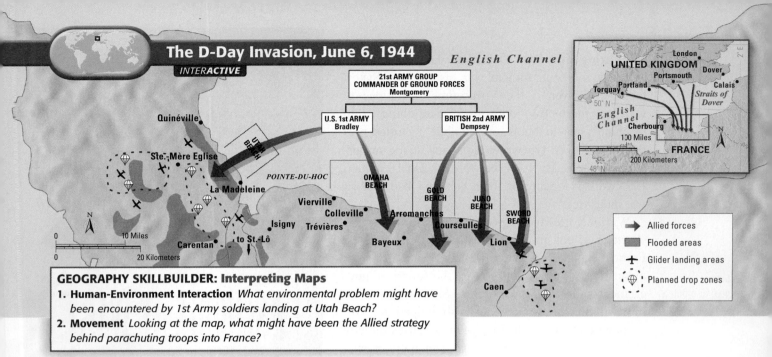

21st ARMY GROUP
COMMANDER OF GROUND FORCES
Montgomery

U.S. 1st ARMY
Bradley

BRITISH 2nd ARMY
Dempsey

UNITED KINGDOM
London
Dover
Portsmouth
Portland
Torquay
Calais
Straits of Dover
50° N
English Channel
Cherbourg
0   100 Miles
0   200 Kilometers
48° N
FRANCE
N

Quinéville
Ste.-Mère Eglise
UTAH BEACH
La Madeleine
POINTE-DU-HOC
OMAHA BEACH
Vierville
Colleville
Arromanches
GOLD BEACH
JUNO BEACH
Courseulles
SWORD BEACH
Isigny
Trévières
Bayeux
Lion
Carentan
to St.-Lô
Caen

N
0   10 Miles
0   20 Kilometers

→ Allied forces
■ Flooded areas
✝ Glider landing areas
⊕ Planned drop zones

GEOGRAPHY SKILLBUILDER: Interpreting Maps

1. **Human-Environment Interaction** *What environmental problem might have been encountered by 1st Army soldiers landing at Utah Beach?*
2. **Movement** *Looking at the map, what might have been the Allied strategy behind parachuting troops into France?*

History Makers

General Dwight D. Eisenhower
1890–1969

In his career, U.S. General Dwight Eisenhower had shown an uncommon ability to work with all kinds of people—even competitive Allies. His chief of staff said of Eisenhower, "The sun rises and sets on him for me." He was also wildly popular with the troops, who affectionately called him "Uncle Ike."

So it was not a surprise when, in December 1943, U.S. Army Chief of Staff George Marshall named Eisenhower as supreme commander of the Allied forces in Europe. The new commander's "people skills" enabled him to join American and British forces together to put a permanent end to Nazi aggression.

INTEGRATED TECHNOLOGY

INTERNET ACTIVITY Create an illustrated report on Eisenhower's military career. Go to **classzone.com** for your research.

Code-named Operation Overlord, the invasion of Normandy was the largest land and sea attack in history. The invasion began on June 6, 1944—known as **D-Day**. At dawn on that day, British, American, French, and Canadian troops fought their way onto a 60-mile stretch of beach in Normandy. (See the map on this page.) The Germans had dug in with machine guns, rocket launchers, and cannons. They sheltered behind concrete walls three feet thick. Not surprisingly, the Allies took heavy casualties. Among the American forces alone, more than 2,700 men died on the beaches that day.

Despite heavy losses, the Allies held the beachheads. Within a month of D-Day, more than one million additional troops had landed. Then, on July 25, the Allies punched a hole in the German defenses near Saint-Lô (san•LOH), and the United States Third Army, led by General George Patton, broke out. A month later, the Allies marched triumphantly into Paris. By September, they had liberated France, Belgium, and Luxembourg. They then set their sights on Germany.

The Battle of the Bulge As Allied forces moved toward Germany from the west, the Soviet army was advancing toward Germany from the east. Hitler now faced a war on two fronts. In a desperate gamble, he decided to counter-attack in the west. Hitler hoped a victory would split American and British forces and break up Allied supply lines. Explaining the reasoning behind his plan, Hitler said, "This battle is to decide whether we shall live or die. . . . All resistance must be broken in a wave of terror."

On December 16, German tanks broke through weak American defenses along a 75-mile front in the Ardennes. The push into Allied lines gave the campaign its name—the **Battle of the Bulge**. Although caught off guard, the Allies eventually pushed the Germans back. The Germans had little choice but to retreat, since there were no reinforcements available.

Vocabulary
beachheads: enemy shoreline captured just before invading forces move inland

Germany's Unconditional Surrender After the Battle of the Bulge, the war in Europe rapidly drew to a close. In late March 1945, the Allies rolled across the Rhine River into Germany. By the middle of April, a noose was closing around Berlin. About three million Allied soldiers approached Berlin from the southwest. Another six million Soviet troops approached from the east. By April 25, 1945, the Soviets had surrounded the capital and were pounding the city with artillery fire.

While Soviet shells burst over Berlin, Hitler prepared for his end in an underground headquarters beneath the crumbling city. On April 29, he married his longtime companion, Eva Braun. The next day, Hitler and Eva Braun committed suicide. Their bodies were then carried outside and burned.

On May 7, 1945, General Eisenhower accepted the unconditional surrender of the Third Reich from the German military. President Roosevelt, however, did not live to witness the long-awaited victory. He had died suddenly on April 12, as Allied armies were advancing toward Berlin. Roosevelt's successor, Harry Truman, received the news of the Nazi surrender. On May 9, the surrender was officially signed in Berlin. The United States and other Allied powers celebrated V-E Day—Victory in Europe Day. After nearly six years of fighting, the war in Europe had ended.

Victory in the Pacific

Although the war in Europe was over, the Allies were still fighting the Japanese in the Pacific. With the Allied victory at Guadalcanal, however, the Japanese advances in the Pacific had been stopped. For the rest of the war, the Japanese retreated before the counterattack of the Allied powers.

The Japanese in Retreat By the fall of 1944, the Allies were moving in on Japan. In October, Allied forces landed on the island of Leyte (LAY•tee) in the Philippines. General Douglas MacArthur, who had been ordered to leave the islands before their surrender in May 1942, waded ashore at Leyte with his troops. On reaching the beach, he declared, "People of the Philippines, I have returned."

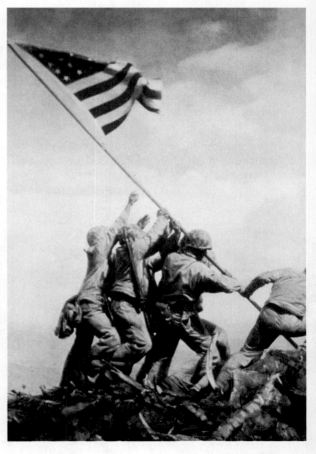

▼ U.S. marines raise the Stars and Stripes after their victory at Iwo Jima.

Actually, the takeover would not be quite that easy. The Japanese had devised a bold plan to halt the Allied advance. They would destroy the American fleet, thus preventing the Allies from resupplying their ground troops. This plan, however, required risking almost the entire Japanese fleet. They took this gamble on October 23, in the Battle of Leyte Gulf. Within four days, the Japanese navy had lost disastrously—eliminating it as a fighting force in the war. Now, only the Japanese army and the feared kamikaze stood between the Allies and Japan. The **kamikazes** were Japanese suicide pilots. They would sink Allied ships by crash-diving their bomb-filled planes into them.

Vocabulary
These pilots took their name from the *kamikaze,* or "divine wind," that saved Japan from a Mongol invasion in 1281.

In March 1945, after a month of bitter fighting and heavy losses, American Marines took Iwo Jima (EE•wuh JEE•muh), an island 760 miles from Tokyo. On April 1, U.S. troops moved onto the island of Okinawa, only about 350 miles from southern Japan. The Japanese put up a desperate fight. Nevertheless, on June 21, one of the bloodiest land battles of the war ended. The Japanese lost over 100,000 troops, and the Americans 12,000.

The Atomic Bomb

On the eve of World War II, scientists in Germany succeeded in splitting the nucleus of a uranium atom, releasing a huge amount of energy. Albert Einstein wrote to President Franklin Roosevelt and warned him that Nazi Germany might be working to develop atomic weapons. Roosevelt responded by giving his approval for an American program, later code-named the Manhattan Project, to develop an atomic bomb. Roosevelt's decision set off a race to ensure that the United States would be the first to develop the bomb.

▼ On the morning of August 6, 1945, the B-29 bomber *Enola Gay*, flown by Colonel Paul W. Tibbets, Jr., took off from Tinian Island in the Mariana Islands.

▶ At precisely 8:16 A.M., the atomic bomb exploded above Hiroshima, a city on the Japanese island of Honshu.

Patterns of Interaction

Arming for War: Modern and Medieval Weapons

Just as in World War I, the conflicts of World War II spurred the development of ever more powerful weapons. Mightier tanks, more elusive submarines, faster fighter planes—all emerged from this period. From ancient times to the present day, the pattern remains the same: Every new weapon causes other countries to develop weapons of similar or greater force. This pattern results in a deadly race for an ultimate weapon: for example, the atomic bomb.

▼ Nagasaki citizens trudge through the still smoldering ruins of their city in this photograph by Yosuke Yamahata.

Hiroshima: Day of Fire

Impact of the Bombing	
Ground temperatures	7,000°F
Hurricane force winds	980 miles per hour
Energy released	20,000 tons of TNT
Buildings destroyed	62,000 buildings
Killed immediately	70,000 people
Dead by the end of 1945	140,000 people
Total deaths related to A-bomb	210,000 people

The overwhelming destructive power of the Hiroshima bomb, and of the bomb dropped on Nagasaki three days later, changed the nature of war forever. Nuclear destruction also led to questions about the ethics of scientists and politicians who chose to develop and use the bomb.

Connect *to* Today

1. **Making Inferences** What advantages did the United States have over Germany in the race to develop the atomic bomb?

   See Skillbuilder Handbook, page R10.

2. **Comparing and Contrasting** If you were to design a memorial to the victims of the Hiroshima and Nagasaki bombings, what symbol would you use? Make a sketch of your memorial.

The Japanese Surrender After Okinawa, the next stop for the Allies had to be Japan. President Truman's advisers had informed him that an invasion of the Japanese homeland might cost the Allies half a million lives. Truman had to make a decision whether to use a powerful new weapon called the atomic bomb, or A-bomb. Most of his advisers felt that using it would bring the war to the quickest possible end. The bomb had been developed by the top-secret Manhattan Project, headed by General Leslie Groves and chief scientist J. Robert Oppenheimer. Truman first learned of the new bomb's existence when he became president.

The first atomic bomb was exploded in a desert in New Mexico on July 16, 1945. President Truman then warned the Japanese. He told them that unless they surrendered, they could expect a "rain of ruin from the air." The Japanese did not reply. So, on August 6, 1945, the United States dropped an atomic bomb on Hiroshima, a Japanese city of nearly 350,000 people. Between 70,000 and 80,000 people died in the attack. Three days later, on August 9, a second bomb was dropped on Nagasaki, a city of 270,000. More than 70,000 people were killed immediately. Radiation fallout from the two explosions killed many more.

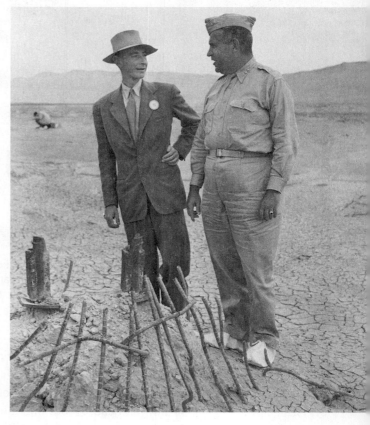

▲ J. Robert Oppenheimer (left) and General Leslie Groves inspect the site of the first atomic bomb test near Alamogordo, New Mexico.

The Japanese finally surrendered to General Douglas MacArthur on September 2. The ceremony took place aboard the United States battleship *Missouri* in Tokyo Bay. With Japan's surrender, the war had ended. Now, countries faced the task of rebuilding a war-torn world.

SECTION 4 ASSESSMENT

TERMS & NAMES 1. For each term or name, write a sentence explaining its significance.
• Dwight D. Eisenhower • Battle of Stalingrad • D-Day • Battle of the Bulge • kamikaze

USING YOUR NOTES
2. Which battle do you think was most important in turning the war in favor of the Allies? Why?

Battle	Outcome
Battle of El Alamein	
Battle of Stalingrad	
D-Day Invasion	

MAIN IDEAS
3. Why did Stalin want the United States and Britain to launch a second front in the west?

4. How did the Allies try to conceal the true location for the D-Day landings?

5. What brought about the Japanese surrender?

CRITICAL THINKING & WRITING
6. **CLARIFYING** How do governments gather support for a war effort on the home front?

7. **ANALYZING ISSUES** Should governments have the power to limit the rights of their citizens during wartime? Explain your answer.

8. **FORMING AND SUPPORTING OPINIONS** Did President Truman make the correct decision in using the atomic bomb? Why or why not?

9. **WRITING ACTIVITY** SCIENCE AND TECHNOLOGY Write a **research report** on the work of the Manhattan Project in developing the atomic bomb.

CONNECT TO TODAY CREATING A POSTER
During World War II, the U.S. government used propaganda posters to encourage citizens to support the war effort. Create a similar kind of **poster** to encourage support for a war on litter in your neighborhood.

Europe and Japan in Ruins

MAIN IDEA	WHY IT MATTERS NOW	TERMS & NAMES
ECONOMICS World War II cost millions of human lives and billions of dollars in damages. It left Europe and Japan in ruins.	The United States survived World War II undamaged, allowing it to become a world leader.	• Nuremberg Trials • demilitarization • democratization

SETTING THE STAGE After six long years of war, the Allies finally were victorious. However, their victory had been achieved at a very high price. World War II had caused more death and destruction than any other conflict in history. It left 60 million dead. About one-third of these deaths occurred in one country, the Soviet Union. Another 50 million people had been uprooted from their homes and wandered the countryside in search of somewhere to live. Property damage ran into billions of U.S. dollars.

TAKING NOTES

Comparing and Contrasting Use a Venn diagram to compare and contrast the aftermath of World War II in Europe and Japan.

Europe only

both

Japan only

Devastation in Europe

By the end of World War II, Europe lay in ruins. Close to 40 million Europeans had died, two-thirds of them civilians. Constant bombing and shelling had reduced hundreds of cities to rubble. The ground war had destroyed much of the countryside. Displaced persons from many nations were left homeless.

A Harvest of Destruction A few of the great cities of Europe—Paris, Rome, and Brussels—remained largely undamaged by war. Many, however, had suffered terrible destruction. The Battle of Britain left huge areas of London little more than blackened ruins. Warsaw, the capital of Poland, was almost completely destroyed. In 1939, Warsaw had a population of nearly 1.3 million. When Soviet soldiers entered the city in January 1945, only 153,000 people remained. Thousands of tons of Allied bombs had demolished 95 percent of the central area of Berlin. One U.S. officer stationed in the German capital reported, "Wherever we looked we saw desolation. It was like a city of the dead."

After the bombings, many civilians stayed where they were and tried to get on with their lives. Some lived in partially destroyed homes or apartments. Others huddled in cellars or caves made from rubble. They had no water, no electricity, and very little food.

A large number of people did not stay where they were. Rather, they took to the roads. These displaced persons included the survivors of concentration camps, prisoners of war, and refugees who found themselves in the wrong country when postwar treaties changed national borders. They wandered across Europe, hoping to find their families or to find a safe place to live.

Simon Weisenthal, a prisoner at Auschwitz, described the search made by Holocaust survivors:

Costs of World War II: Allies and Axis

	Direct War Costs	Military Killed/Missing	Civilians Killed
United States	$288.0 billion*	292,131**	–
Great Britain	$117.0 billion	272,311	60,595
France	$111.3 billion	205,707***	173,260†
USSR	$93.0 billion	13,600,000	7,720,000
Germany	$212.3 billion	3,300,000	2,893,000††
Japan	$41.3 billion	1,140,429	953,000

* In 1994 dollars.
** An additional 115,187 servicemen died from non-battle causes.
*** Before surrender to Nazis.
† Includes 65,000 murdered Jews.
†† Includes about 170,000 murdered Jews and 56,000 foreign civilians in Germany.

SKILLBUILDER: Interpreting Charts
1. **Drawing Conclusions** *Which of the nations listed in the chart suffered the greatest human costs?*
2. **Comparing** *How does U.S. spending on the war compare with the spending of Germany and Japan?*

PRIMARY SOURCE
Across Europe a wild tide of frantic survivors was flowing. . . . Many of them didn't really know where to go. . . . And yet the survivors continued their pilgrimage of despair. . . . "Perhaps someone is still alive. . . ." Someone might tell where to find a wife, a mother, children, a brother—or whether they were dead. . . . The desire to find one's people was stronger than hunger, thirst, fatigue.

SIMON WEISENTHAL, quoted in *Never to Forget: The Jews of the Holocaust*

Misery Continues After the War The misery in Europe continued for years after the war. The fighting had ravaged Europe's countryside, and agriculture had been completely disrupted. Most able-bodied men had served in the military, and the women had worked in war production. Few remained to plant the fields. With the transportation system destroyed, the meager harvests often did not reach the cities. Thousands died as famine and disease spread through the bombed-out cities. The first postwar winter brought more suffering as people went without shoes and coats.

Postwar Governments and Politics

Despairing Europeans often blamed their leaders for the war and its aftermath. Once the Germans had lost, some prewar governments—like those in Belgium, Holland, Denmark, and Norway—returned quickly. In countries like Germany, Italy, and France, however, a return to the old leadership was not desirable. Hitler's Nazi government had brought Germany to ruins. Mussolini had led Italy to defeat. The Vichy government had collaborated with the Nazis. Much of the old leadership was in disgrace. Also, in Italy and France, many resistance fighters were communists. **A**

After the war, the Communist Party promised change, and millions were ready to listen. In both France and Italy, Communist Party membership skyrocketed. The communists made huge gains in the first postwar elections. Anxious to speed up a political takeover, the communists staged a series of violent strikes. Alarmed French and Italians reacted by voting for anticommunist parties. Communist Party membership and influence began to decline. And they declined even more as the economies of France and Italy began to recover.

MAIN IDEA
Identifying Problems
A Why might it have been difficult to find democratic government leaders in post-Nazi Germany?

A New War Crimes Tribunal

In 1993, the UN established the International Criminal Tribunal for the Former Yugoslavia (ICTY) to prosecute war crimes committed in the Balkan conflicts of the 1990s. (See Chapter 19.) This was the first international war crimes court since those held in Nuremberg and Tokyo after World War II.

The ICTY issued its first indictment in 1994 and began trial proceedings in 1996. By mid-2003, more than 30 defendants had been tried and found guilty. They received sentences of 5 to 48 years in jail. Another 25 were on trial or awaiting trial. The most prominent of these defendants was Slobadan Milosevic, the former president of Yugoslavia. He was charged with 66 counts of genocide, crimes against humanity, and other war crimes.

The Nuremberg Trials While nations were struggling to recover politically and economically, they also tried to deal with the issue of war crimes. During 1945 and 1946, an International Military Tribunal representing 23 nations put Nazi war criminals on trial in Nuremberg, Germany. In the first of these **Nuremberg Trials**, 22 Nazi leaders were charged with waging a war of aggression. They were also accused of committing "crimes against humanity"—the murder of 11 million people.

Adolf Hitler, SS chief Heinrich Himmler, and Minister of Propaganda Joseph Goebbels had committed suicide long before the trials began. However, Hermann Göring, the commander of the Luftwaffe; Rudolf Hess, Hitler's former deputy; and other high-ranking Nazi leaders remained to face the charges.

Hess was found guilty and was sentenced to life in prison. Göring received a death sentence, but cheated the executioner by committing suicide. Ten other Nazi leaders were hanged on October 16, 1946. Hans Frank, the "Slayer of Poles," was the only convicted Nazi to express remorse: "A thousand years will pass," he said, "and still this guilt of Germany will not have been erased." The bodies of those executed were burned at the concentration camp of Dachau (DAHK•ow). They were cremated in the same ovens that had burned so many of their victims.

Postwar Japan

The defeat suffered by Japan in World War II left the country in ruins. Two million lives had been lost. The country's major cities, including the capital, Tokyo, had been largely destroyed by bombing raids. The atomic bomb had turned Hiroshima and Nagasaki into blackened wastelands. The Allies had stripped Japan of its colonial empire.

Occupied Japan General Douglas MacArthur, who had accepted the Japanese surrender, took charge of the U.S. occupation of Japan. MacArthur was determined to be fair and not to plant the seeds of a future war. Nevertheless, to ensure that peace would prevail, he began a process of **demilitarization**, or disbanding the Japanese armed forces. He achieved this quickly, leaving the Japanese with only a small police force. MacArthur also began bringing war criminals to trial. Out of 25 surviving defendants, former Premier Hideki Tojo and six others were condemned to hang.

MacArthur then turned his attention to **democratization**, the process of creating a government elected by the people. In February 1946, he and his American political advisers drew up a new constitution. It changed the empire into a constitutional monarchy like that of Great Britain. The Japanese accepted the constitution. It went into effect on May 3, 1947.

MacArthur was not told to revive the Japanese economy. However, he was instructed to broaden land ownership and increase the participation of workers and farmers in the new democracy. To this end, MacArthur put forward a plan that required absentee landlords with huge estates to sell land to the government. The government then sold the land to tenant farmers at reasonable prices. Other reforms pushed by MacArthur gave workers the right to create independent labor unions. **B**

MAIN IDEA

Making Inferences
B How would demilitarization and a revived economy help Japan achieve democracy?

Occupation Brings Deep Changes

The new constitution was the most important achievement of the occupation. It brought deep changes to Japanese society. A long Japanese tradition had viewed the emperor as divine. He was also an absolute ruler whose will was law. The emperor now had to declare that he was not divine. That admission was as shocking to the Japanese as defeat. His power was also dramatically reduced. Like the ruler of Great Britain, the emperor became largely a figurehead—a symbol of Japan. **C**

MAIN IDEA

Analyzing Causes
C Why did the Americans choose the British system of government for the Japanese, instead of the American system?

The new constitution guaranteed that real political power in Japan rested with the people. The people elected a two-house parliament, called the Diet. All citizens over the age of 20, including women, had the right to vote. The government was led by a prime minister chosen by a majority of the Diet. A constitutional bill of rights protected basic freedoms. One more key provision of the constitution—Article 9—stated that the Japanese could no longer make war. They could fight only if attacked.

In September 1951, the United States and 47 other nations signed a formal peace treaty with Japan. The treaty officially ended the war. Some six months later, the U.S. occupation of Japan was over. However, with no armed forces, the Japanese agreed to a continuing U.S. military presence to protect their country. The United States and Japan, once bitter enemies, were now allies.

In the postwar world, enemies not only became allies. Sometimes, allies became enemies. World War II had changed the political landscape of Europe. The Soviet Union and the United States emerged from the war as the world's two major powers. They also ended the war as allies. However, it soon became clear that their postwar goals were very different. This difference stirred up conflicts that would shape the modern world for decades.

▲ Emperor Hirohito and U.S. General Douglas MacArthur look distant and uncomfortable as they pose here.

SECTION 5 ASSESSMENT

TERMS & NAMES 1. For each term or name, write a sentence explaining its significance.
• Nuremberg Trials   • demilitarization   • democratization

USING YOUR NOTES
2. How did the aftermath of the war in Europe differ from the aftermath of the war in Japan?

Europe only

both

Japan only

MAIN IDEAS
3. Why did so many Europeans take to the roads and wander the countryside after the war?

4. How did the Allies deal with the issue of war crimes in Europe?

5. What three programs did General Douglas MacArthur introduce during the U.S. occupation of Japan?

CRITICAL THINKING & WRITING
6. **ANALYZING CAUSES** Why do you think that many Europeans favored communism after World War II?

7. **FORMING AND SUPPORTING OPINIONS** Do you think it was right for the Allies to try only Nazi and Japanese leaders for war crimes? Why or why not?

8. **MAKING INFERENCES** Why was demilitarization such an important part of the postwar program for Japan?

9. **WRITING ACTIVITY** [ECONOMICS] In the role of an observer for the United States government, write a **report** on the economic situation in Europe after World War II. Illustrate your report with appropriate charts and graphs.

CONNECT TO TODAY CREATING A RADIO NEWS REPORT
Conduct research on a recent trial at the International War Crimes Tribunal in The Hague. Use your findings to create a two-minute radio **news report** on the trial.

Chapter 16 Assessment

TERMS & NAMES

For each term or name below, briefly explain its connection to World War II.

1. blitzkrieg
2. Atlantic Charter
3. Battle of Midway
4. Holocaust
5. genocide
6. D-Day
7. Nuremberg Trials
8. demilitarization

MAIN IDEAS

Hitler's Lightning War Section 1 (pages 491–496)

9. What event finally unleashed World War II?
10. Why was capturing Egypt's Suez Canal so important to the Axis powers?

Japan's Pacific Campaign Section 2 (pages 497–501)

11. What was Yamamoto's objective at Pearl Harbor?
12. How did Japan try to win support from other Asian countries?

The Holocaust Section 3 (pages 502–505)

13. Name two tactics that Hitler used to rid Germany of Jews before creating his "Final Solution."
14. What tactics did Hitler use during the "Final Solution"?

The Allied Victory Section 4 (pages 506–513)

15. Why were consumer goods rationed during the war?
16. What was Operation Overlord?

Europe and Japan in Ruins Section 5 (pages 514–517)

17. Why did Europeans leave their homes following the war?
18. What were two of the most important steps that MacArthur took in Japan following the war?

CRITICAL THINKING

1. USING YOUR NOTES

Copy the chart into your notebook and specify for each listed battle or conflict whether the Axis powers or the Allied powers gained an advantage.

Battle/Conflict	Allied or Axis Powers?
Battle of Britain	
War in the Balkans	
Pearl Harbor	
Battle of the Coral Sea	
Battle of Midway	

2. DRAWING CONCLUSIONS

Consider the personalities, tactics, and policies of Hitler, Rommel, MacArthur, and Churchill. What qualities make a good war leader?

3. COMPARING AND CONTRASTING

EMPIRE BUILDING Compare and contrast Japan's and Germany's goals in World War II.

4. EVALUATING COURSES OF ACTION

ECONOMICS Why do you think the governments of the United States and other countries encouraged people on the home front to organize programs for such activities as scrap collection and Victory gardens?

VISUAL SUMMARY

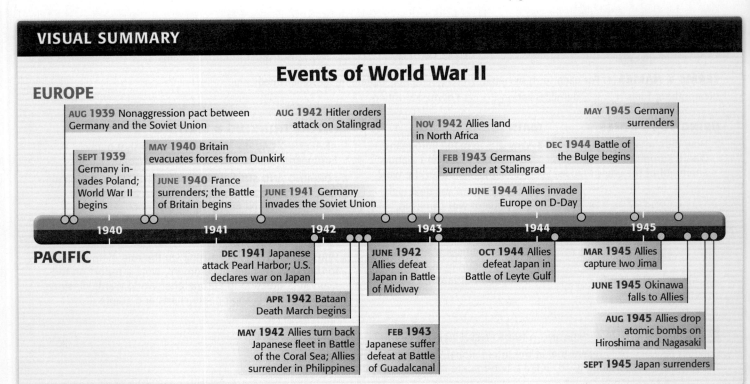

Events of World War II

EUROPE

- **AUG 1939** Nonaggression pact between Germany and the Soviet Union
- **SEPT 1939** Germany invades Poland; World War II begins
- **MAY 1940** Britain evacuates forces from Dunkirk
- **JUNE 1940** France surrenders; the Battle of Britain begins
- **JUNE 1941** Germany invades the Soviet Union
- **AUG 1942** Hitler orders attack on Stalingrad
- **NOV 1942** Allies land in North Africa
- **FEB 1943** Germans surrender at Stalingrad
- **JUNE 1944** Allies invade Europe on D-Day
- **DEC 1944** Battle of the Bulge begins
- **MAY 1945** Germany surrenders

1940 — 1941 — 1942 — 1943 — 1944 — 1945

PACIFIC

- **DEC 1941** Japanese attack Pearl Harbor; U.S. declares war on Japan
- **APR 1942** Bataan Death March begins
- **MAY 1942** Allies turn back Japanese fleet in Battle of the Coral Sea; Allies surrender in Philippines
- **JUNE 1942** Allies defeat Japan in Battle of Midway
- **FEB 1943** Japanese suffer defeat at Battle of Guadalcanal
- **OCT 1944** Allies defeat Japan in Battle of Leyte Gulf
- **MAR 1945** Allies capture Iwo Jima
- **JUNE 1945** Okinawa falls to Allies
- **AUG 1945** Allies drop atomic bombs on Hiroshima and Nagasaki
- **SEPT 1945** Japan surrenders

Use the excerpt and your knowledge of world history to answer question 1.
Additional Test Practice, pp. S1–S33

PRIMARY SOURCE

But there was no military advantage in hurling the bomb upon Japan without warning. The least we might have done was to announce to our foe that we possessed the atomic bomb; that its destructive power was beyond anything known in warfare; and that its terrible effectiveness had been experimentally demonstrated in this country. . . . If she [Japan] doubted the good faith of our representations, it would have been a simple matter to select a demonstration target in the enemy's own country at a place where the loss of human life would be at a minimum. If, despite such warning, Japan had still held out, we would have been in a far less questionable position had we then dropped the bombs on Hiroshima and Nagasaki.

The Christian Century, August 29, 1945

1. According to the writer, what is the least the Allies might have done with reference to using the atomic bomb?

A. tell Japan that they possessed the atomic bomb, a weapon with incredible destructive power

B. demonstrate it on a selected target in Japan where loss of life would be limited

C. invite Japanese leaders to a demonstration explosion of the bomb in the United States

D. drop the bomb on cities in Germany as well as on Japanese cities

Use the map and your knowledge of world history to answer question 2.

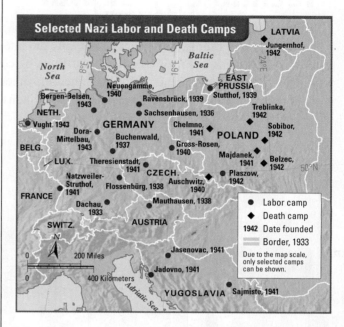

2. In which country were most death camps located?

A. Austria   **C.** Poland

B. Germany   **D.** Yugoslavia

INTEGRATED / TECHNOLOGY

TEST PRACTICE Go to **classzone.com**

• Diagnostic tests   • Strategies

• Tutorials   • Additional practice

ALTERNATIVE ASSESSMENT

1. Interact *with* History

On page 490, you had to decide under what circumstances war is justified. Now that you have read the chapter, do you think that Germany and Japan were justified in waging war? Were the Allies justified in declaring war on Germany and Japan? As you think about these questions, consider the moral issues that confront world leaders when they contemplate war as an option.

2. WRITING ABOUT HISTORY

SCIENCE AND TECHNOLOGY Conduct research on the scientific and technological developments used in the Allied war effort. Use your findings to create several **information cards** for a card series titled "Science and Technology During World War II." Organize the information on your cards in the following categories:

• name of invention or development

• country

• year

• use in the war

• use today

INTEGRATED / TECHNOLOGY

Writing an Internet-based Research Paper

During World War II, many consumer-goods manufacturers switched to the production of military goods. Many of these companies still exist. Working with a partner, use the Internet to research one such company. Find out what products the company made before and during the war, and how the company's wartime role affected its reputation. Go to the Web Research Guide at **classzone.com** to learn about conducting research on the Internet.

Present the results of your research in a well-organized paper. Be sure to

• apply a search strategy when using directories and search engines to locate Web resources.

• judge the usefulness and reliability of each Web site.

• correctly cite your Web sources.

• edit for organization and correct use of language.

Technology of War

In Unit 4, you studied the economic and political upheavals that led to two world wars. For the first time, war involved not only the interested countries, but also their allies near and far and their colonies in far-flung places. In the next six pages, you will analyze the widespread use of machines and other technologies as tools for fighting and the increasingly involved role of civilians in war.

Maxim Machine Gun ▲
Hiram Maxim (above) invented the first portable, automatic machine gun. Machine guns fired hundreds of rounds per minute and were used by all the combatants in World War I.

Tanks ▲
Tanks, like the early British model shown above, enabled armies to travel over uneven ground and barbed wire. Although too slow to be used to full advantage at first, they were devastating against soldiers in trenches.

1884   **1909**   **1915 1916**

▼ First Military Plane
The earliest military planes were used for reconnaissance of enemy positions. A passenger could drop bombs (below) and, in later World War I models, operate a machine gun.

Poison Gas ▼
Poison gases were introduced to help break the stalemate of trench warfare. They caused suffocation, blistered skin, or blindness (below) to those exposed.

Blitzkrieg ▲
The Germans used
blitzkrieg or "lightning
war" to invade Poland.
They employed air
strikes, fast tanks, and
artillery, followed by
soldiers sped into
battle on trucks
(shown above). They
swiftly overwhelmed
Poland and disrupted
its command and
communications.

Atomic Bomb ▶
The United States dropped two atomic bombs on
Japan and became the first nation to use nuclear
weapons. An atomic bomb (right) creates an explosion
that causes massive damage. The radioactive particles
released are carried by winds for weeks.

1939   1944 1945

▼ German Me 262
Military jet planes were first used by
the Germans in 1944. These planes
added speed to fire power. The Me
262 (below) was the only jet to be
used extensively in World War II.

Comparing &
Contrasting

1. How did technology change the
   nature of war in the 20th century?

2. Compared with earlier guns, what
   made machine guns so effective?

3. How did airplanes change the way
   war was carried out?

Expansion of Warfare

World War I and World War II both began as localized wars. As the allies of the opposing combatants became involved in the wars, combat spread to distant parts of the world. Countries attacked each other's colonies, attempted to gain territory for themselves, dedicated massive amounts of physical and human resources, and sometimes sought to kill entire populations.

Total War

A feature of warfare in the 20th century was how entire national economies were directed toward the war effort. As a result, civilians were not only potential victims of combat, but they also became actual targets themselves. Civilians also became active participants, producing arms, food, vehicles, and other goods needed for war. Many factories stopped producing consumer goods and began making products needed by the military.

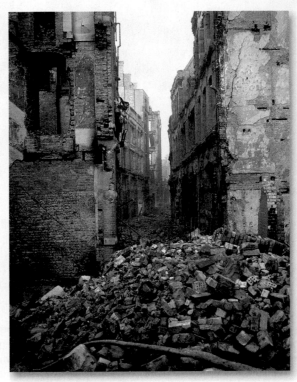

London ►
The photograph shows a section of London destroyed by bombs in the Battle of Britain during World War II.

DOCUMENT-BASED QUESTION
What effect do you think the kind of destruction shown in the photograph had on the residents of London?

The Lost Cunard Steamship Lusitania

◄ Lusitania
This newspaper shows the headline and various articles about the sinking of the British passenger ship *Lusitania* during World War I. Note also the announcement from the German embassy warning civilians not to travel to Great Britain because Germany considered it a war zone.

DOCUMENT-BASED QUESTION
What effect would the headline and photograph have on the American public?

Genocide

Genocide is the calculated and methodical destruction of a national, religious, ethnic, or racial group. The perpetrators consider their victims inferior or wish to take over their lands and property, or both. The mass killing of Armenians by Ottoman Turks beginning in 1915 is considered the first genocide of the 20th century. During the Holocaust, the Nazis killed more than 6 million people. As a result, in 1948 the United Nations approved an international convention to prevent and punish genocide.

INTER*ACTIVE*

Genocide in WWI

The following excerpts are from telegrams sent to the secretary of state by the U.S. embassy in the Ottoman Empire. They concern the situation of Armenians in Turkey. The first passage was written by the American Consul General at Beirut and describes the deportation of villagers from the Zeitoon region, and the second calls attention to the killing of people in eastern Turkey.

July 20, 1915:
Whole villages were deported at an hours notice, with no opportunity to prepare for the journey, not even in some cases to gather together the scattered members of the family, so that little children were left behind. . . .

In many cases the men were (those of military age were nearly all in the army) bound tightly together with ropes or chains. Women with little children in their arms, or in the last days of pregnancy were driven along under the whip like cattle. Three different cases came under my knowledge where the woman was delivered on the road, and because her brutal driver hurried her along she died. . . .

These people are being scattered in small units, three or four families in a place, among a population of different race and religion, and speaking a different language. I speak of them as being composed of families, but four fifths of them are women and children.

July 31, 1915:
[The president of a charitable organization] has information from [a] reliable source that Armenians, mostly women and children, deported from the Erzerum district, have been massacred near Kemakh. . . . Similar reports comes from other sources showing that but few of these unfortunate people will ever reach their stated destination.

DOCUMENT-BASED QUESTION
What would be the result of scattering Armenian villagers in unfamiliar places under such terrible conditions?

INTER*ACTIVE*

Genocide in WWII

Primo Levi describes how prisoners at the Nazi concentration camp of Auschwitz were selected for death.

Each one of us, as he comes naked out of the Tagesraum [common room] into the cold October air, has to run the few steps between the two doors, give the card to the SS man [the Nazi guard] and enter the dormitory door. The SS man, in the fraction of a second between two successive crossings, with a glance at one's back and front, judges everyone's fate, and in turn gives the card to the man on his right or his left, and this is the life or death of each of us. In three or four minutes a hut of 200 men is 'done', as is the whole camp of twelve thousand men in the course of the afternoon.

Jammed in the charnel-house [a place of great suffering] of the Tagesraum, I gradually felt the human pressure around me slacken, and in a short time it was my turn. Like everyone, I passed by with a brisk and elastic step, trying to hold my head high, my chest forward and my muscles contracted and conspicuous. With the corner of my eye I tried to look behind my shoulders, and my card seemed to end on the right.

DOCUMENT-BASED QUESTION
What was the Nazis' attitude toward selecting prisoners to be killed?

Comparing & Contrasting

1. Judging from the examples on these two pages, in what ways did warfare expand to include civilians?

2. If civilians manufacture materials for the war effort, should they be military targets? Why or why not?

3. How did modern weaponry contribute to both the sinking of the *Lusitania* and the bombing of London?

The Human Cost of War

The global nature of World Wars I and II wreaked a level of destruction unknown before. National economies were exhausted; farmland, towns, and villages were destroyed. More soldiers died in World War I than in all the conflicts of the previous three centuries, and millions more died in World War II. Civilians died by the millions as a result of military operations, concentration camps, the bombing of towns and cities, and starvation and disease.

Military Cost

Both sides in the two world wars suffered tremendous military casualties, including dead, wounded, and missing in action. About 8.5 million soldiers died in World War I and 19.4 million in World War II. The excerpts show how weapons and tactics contributed to the large number of casualties.

PRIMARY SOURCE

INTERACTIVE

Trench Warfare

British sergeant major Ernest Shephard remembers the first day of the Battle of the Somme in his diary.

A lovely day, intensely hot. Lots of casualties in my trench. The enemy are enfilading us with heavy shell, dropping straight on us. A complete trench mortar battery of men killed by one shell, scores of dead and badly wounded in trench . . . Every move we make brings intense fire, as trenches so badly battered the enemy can see all our movements. Lot of wounded [from the front] . . . several were hit again and killed in trench. We put as many wounded as possible in best spots in trench and I sent a lot down, but I had so many of my own men killed and wounded that after a time I could not do this. . . .

   [L]iterally we were blown from place to place. Men very badly shaken. As far as possible we cleared trenches of debris and dead. These we piled in heaps, enemy shells pitching on them made matters worse.

DOCUMENT-BASED QUESTION
Judging from the quotation, what was Shephard's attitude toward the battle?

PRIMARY SOURCE

INTERACTIVE

Iwo Jima

Japan lost 21,000 soldiers and the United States 6,800 in the Battle of Iwo Jima. A U.S. Marines correspondent described part of the fighting below.

Behind a rolling artillery barrage and with fixed bayonets, the unit leaped forward in . . . [a] charge and advanced to the very mouths of the fixed [Japanese] defenses. . . . [T]he men flung themselves at the tiny flaming holes, throwing grenades and jabbing with bayonets. Comrades went past, hurdled the defenses and rushed across Airfield no. 2. . . . Men died at every step. That was how we broke their line. . . .
   Across the field we attacked a ridge. The enemy rose up out of holes to hurl our assault back. The squads re-formed and went up again. At the crest they plunged on the [Japanese] with bayonets. . . . The [Japanese] on the ridge were annihilated.

DOCUMENT-BASED QUESTION
What attitude do you think the soldiers on both sides had to adopt to fight in such a bloody conflict as this?

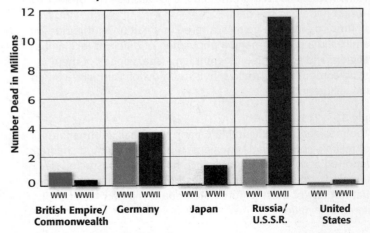

Military Casualties, World War I and World War II

Source: Encyclopaedia Britannica

SKILLBUILDER: Interpreting Graphs
What factors may have contributed to the increased number of deaths in World War II over World War I?

Civilian Cost

Civilians suffered not only as the direct victims of war, but also from the loss of their homes, the workplaces that gave them an income and produced useful goods, and the farms that supplied food. They also experienced the unsanitary conditions that resulted from bombing.

INTER**ACTIVE**

Displaced Persons

Laura de Gozdawa Turczynowicz, an American married to a Polish nobleman, described fleeing the advance of the German army into Suwalki, Poland.

At the [Vilno] station were crowds of Suwalki people. One man of our acquaintance had brought with him only his walking stick! Another man had become separated from his young son, fourteen, and daughter, sixteen, . . . and the poor father was on the verge of losing his reason. . . .

Such a lot of people came for help that my money melted like snow in the sunshine. I took just as many as could be packed in our [hotel] rooms. . . .

The next day dragged wearily along, everybody waiting, living only to hear better news. The city was rapidly filling with refugees. In one place, an old convent, they were given a roof to sleep under, and hot tea.

DOCUMENT-BASED QUESTION
Under what conditions did the Polish refugees flee from the Germans?

Internment Camps

After Pearl Harbor, thousands of Japanese Americans were sent to internment camps mainly located in the western United States.

DOCUMENT-BASED QUESTION
Judging from the photograph, what was the government's attitude toward Japanese Americans?

INTER**ACTIVE**

Atomic Bomb

In this excerpt, Dr. Tatsuichiro Akizuki describes the people who began arriving at his hospital in Nagasaki the day the bomb was dropped.

It was all he could do to keep standing. Yet it didn't occur to me that he had been seriously injured. . . .

As time passed, more and more people in a similar plight came up to the hospital . . . All were of the same appearance, sounded the same. "I'm hurt, *hurt!* I'm burning! Water!" They all moaned the same lament. . . .[T]hey walked with strange, slow steps, groaning from deep inside themselves as if they had travelled from the depths of hell. They looked whitish; their faces were like masks.

DOCUMENT-BASED QUESTION
Why did the doctor not recognize his patients' symptoms?

Comparing & Contrasting

1. Given the conditions described during trench warfare and on Iwo Jima, why would soldiers continue to fight?

2. How were the human costs of war, military and civilian, similar to each other? How were they different?

3. Given what you have read on these pages, if another world war broke out, would you prefer to be in the military or to be a civilian? Why?

EXTENSION ACTIVITY
Look up the numbers of civilian casualties suffered in different countries during World War II in an encyclopedia or other reference source. Use the graph on page 524 as a model. Be sure to include the countries with the most significant figures in different parts of the world. Write a paragraph explaining why these countries had the greatest number of casualties.

Perspectives
On the Present
1945–present

On November 10, 1989, all borders between East and West Germany were opened. Here, people celebrate in front of the Brandenburg Gate, one of the former border crossings between East and West.

Comparing & Contrasting

Nation Building

In Unit 5, you will learn about the emergence or growth of several different nations. At the end of the unit, you will have a chance to compare and contrast the nations you have studied. (See pages 666–671.)

527

Restructuring the Postwar World,

1945–Present

Previewing Main Ideas

ECONOMICS Two conflicting economic systems, capitalism and communism, competed for influence and power after World War II. The superpowers in this struggle were the United States and the Soviet Union.

Geography *Study the map and the key. What does the map show about the state of the world in 1949?*

REVOLUTION In Asia, the Americas, and Eastern Europe, people revolted against repressive governments or rule by foreign powers. These revolutions often became the areas for conflict between the two superpowers.

Geography *Look at the map. Which of the three areas mentioned was not Communist in 1949?*

EMPIRE BUILDING The United States and the Soviet Union used military, economic, and humanitarian aid to extend their control over other countries. Each also tried to prevent the other superpower from gaining influence.

Geography *Why might the clear-cut division shown on this map be misleading?*

INTEGRATED TECHNOLOGY

eEdition
- Interactive Maps
- Interactive Visuals
- Interactive Primary Sources

INTERNET RESOURCES
Go to **classzone.com** for:
- Research Links
- Internet Activities
- Primary Sources
- Chapter Quiz
- Maps
- Test Practice
- Current Events

1945
◄ United Nations formed.

1949
Communists take control of China.

1957
Soviets launch *Sputnik.*

1959
Cuba becomes Communist. (Fidel Castro) ►

WORLD   1945   1965

1947
Independent India partitioned into India and Pakistan.

1957
Ghana achieves independence from Great Britain. ►

Cold War Enemies, 1949

Legend:
- ■ Communist
- ■ Non-Communist

Lambert Azimuthal Equal-Area Projection

**Map labels:**

PACIFIC OCEAN

Tropic of Cancer

140°W · 160°W · 180° · 160°E · 140°E

120°W · 100°W · 0° · 40°W · 20°W

PHILIPPINES
JAPAN
TAIWAN
S. KOREA
N. KOREA
INNER MONGOLIA
FRENCH INDOCHINA (FR.)
CHINA
THAILAND
BURMA
MONGOLIA
BHUTAN · E. PAK.
TIBET
NEPAL

NORTH AMERICA
MEXICO
UNITED STATES
CANADA

ARCTIC OCEAN
+North Pole

SOVIET UNION

ASIA

INDIA

WEST PAKISTAN
AFGHANISTAN

Arctic Circle
ICELAND
FINLAND
NORWAY
SWEDEN

IRAN
INDIAN OCEAN

EUROPE
DEN.
IRELAND
U.K.
NETH.
E. GER.
POL.
BEL.
W. GER.
CZ.
LUX.
AU.
HUN.
ROM.
FRANCE
YUGO.
BUL.
TURKEY
SYRIA
IRAQ
SWITZ.
ITALY
GREECE
LEBANON
ISRAEL
JORDAN
SPAIN
ALBANIA
PORTUGAL

TRUCIAL STATES
OMAN (U.K.)
QATAR (U.K.)
SAUDI ARABIA
ADEN (U.K.)
YEMEN

60°E

ATLANTIC OCEAN

SOUTH AMERICA

AFRICA

Tropic of Cancer

Tropic of Capricorn
40°S · 20°S · 0° · 20°S · 40°S
20°W · 60°E · 40°E

Timeline

1969 U.S. lands astronauts on the moon. ▶

1975 Vietnam War ends.

1990 Communists voted out of power in Nicaragua.

2000 South Korea and North Korea meet to improve relations.

1985

2003

1973 Arab forces attack Israel in the Yom Kippur War.

1989 ◀ Berlin Wall is knocked down in Germany.

1994 First all-race election in South Africa is held. (Nelson Mandela) ▶

If you were president, what policies would you follow to gain allies?

World War II has ended. You are the leader of a great superpower—one of two in the world. To keep the balance of power in your nation's favor, you want to gain as many allies as possible. You are particularly interested in gaining the support of nations in Africa, Asia, and Central and South America who do not yet favor either superpower.

You call your advisers together to develop policies for making uncommitted nations your allies.

Send troops.

Join together in an alliance.

Support anti-government rebels.

Give economic aid.

EXAMINING *the* ISSUES

- How might the actions taken affect your country? the other superpower?

- How might being caught in a struggle between superpowers affect a developing nation?

As a class, discuss how the conflict between the superpowers affects the rest of the world. As you read about how the superpowers tried to gain allies, notice the part weaker countries played in their conflict.

Cold War: Superpowers Face Off

MAIN IDEA	WHY IT MATTERS NOW	TERMS & NAMES
ECONOMICS The opposing economic and political philosophies of the United States and the Soviet Union led to global competition.	The conflicts between the United States and the Soviet Union played a major role in reshaping the modern world.	• United Nations • Cold War • iron curtain • NATO • containment • Warsaw Pact • Truman Doctrine • brinkmanship • Marshall Plan

SETTING THE STAGE During World War II, the United States and the Soviet Union had joined forces to fight against the Germans. The Soviet army marched west; the Americans marched east. When the Allied soldiers met at the Elbe River in Germany in 1945, they embraced each other warmly because they had defeated the Nazis. Their leaders, however, regarded each other much more coolly. This animosity caused by competing political philosophies would lead to a nearly half-century of conflict called the Cold War.

Allies Become Enemies

Even before World War II ended, the U.S. alliance with the Soviet Union had begun to unravel. The United States was upset that Joseph Stalin, the Soviet leader, had signed a nonaggression pact with Germany in 1939. Later, Stalin blamed the Allies for not invading German-occupied Europe earlier than 1944. Driven by these and other disagreements, the two allies began to pursue opposing goals.

Yalta Conference: A Postwar Plan The war was not yet over in February 1945. But the leaders of the United States, Britain, and the Soviet Union met at the Soviet Black Sea resort of Yalta. There, they agreed to divide Germany into zones of occupation controlled by the Allied military forces. Germany also would have

TAKING NOTES

Following Chronological Order Organize important early Cold War events in a time line.

1945   1960

Yalta   U-2
conference   incident

▶ Winston Churchill, Franklin D. Roosevelt, and Joseph Stalin meet at Yalta in 1945.

to pay the Soviet Union to compensate for its loss of life and property. Stalin agreed to join the war against Japan. He also promised that Eastern Europeans would have free elections. A skeptical Winston Churchill predicted that Stalin would keep his pledge only if the Eastern Europeans followed "a policy friendly to Russia."

Creation of the United Nations In June 1945, the United States and the Soviet Union temporarily set aside their differences. They joined 48 other countries in forming the **United Nations** (UN). This international organization was intended to protect the members against aggression. It was to be based in New York.

The charter for the new peacekeeping organization established a large body called the General Assembly. There, each UN member nation could cast its vote on a broad range of issues. An 11-member body called the Security Council had the real power to investigate and settle disputes, though. Its five permanent members were Britain, China, France, the United States, and the Soviet Union. Each could veto any Security Council action. This provision was intended to prevent any members of the Council from voting as a bloc to override the others.

Differing U.S. and Soviet Goals Despite agreement at Yalta and their presence on the Security Council, the United States and the Soviet Union split sharply after the war. The war had affected them very differently. The United States, the world's richest and most powerful country, suffered 400,000 deaths. But its cities and factories remained intact. The Soviet Union had at least 50 times as many fatalities. One in four Soviets was wounded or killed. Also, many Soviet cities were demolished. These contrasting situations, as well as political and economic differences, affected the two countries' postwar goals. (See chart below.) **A**

MAIN IDEA

Summarizing
A Why did the United States and the Soviet Union split after the war?

Superpower Aims in Europe
INTERACTIVE

United States

- Encourage democracy in other countries to help prevent the rise of Communist governments
- Gain access to raw materials and markets to fuel booming industries
- Rebuild European governments to promote stability and create new markets for U.S. goods
- Reunite Germany to stabilize it and increase the security of Europe

Soviet Union

- Encourage communism in other countries as part of a worldwide workers' revolution
- Rebuild its war-ravaged economy using Eastern Europe's industrial equipment and raw materials
- Control Eastern Europe to protect Soviet borders and balance the U.S. influence in Western Europe
- Keep Germany divided to prevent its waging war again

Map legend:
- Communist countries, 1948
- Non-Communist countries, 1948
- Iron curtain

SKILLBUILDER: Interpreting Maps and Charts
1. **Drawing Conclusions** Which countries separated the Soviet Union from Western Europe?
2. **Comparing** Which U.S. and Soviet aims in Europe conflicted?

Eastern Europe's Iron Curtain

A major goal of the Soviet Union was to shield itself from another invasion from the west. Centuries of history had taught the Soviets to fear invasion. Because it lacked natural western borders, Russia fell victim to each of its neighbors in turn. In the 17th century, the Poles captured the Kremlin. During the next century, the Swedes attacked. Napoleon overran Moscow in 1812. The Germans invaded Russia during World Wars I and II.

Soviets Build a Buffer As World War II drew to a close, the Soviet troops pushed the Nazis back across Eastern Europe. At war's end, these troops occupied a strip of countries along the Soviet Union's own western border. Stalin regarded these countries as a necessary buffer, or wall of protection. He ignored the Yalta agreement and installed or secured Communist governments in Albania, Bulgaria, Hungary, Czechoslovakia, Romania, Poland, and Yugoslavia.

The Soviet leader's American partner at Yalta, Franklin D. Roosevelt, had died on April 12, 1945. To Roosevelt's successor, Harry S. Truman, Stalin's reluctance to allow free elections in Eastern European nations was a clear violation of those countries' rights. Truman, Stalin, and Churchill met at Potsdam, Germany, in July 1945. There, Truman pressed Stalin to permit free elections in Eastern Europe. The Soviet leader refused. In a speech in early 1946, Stalin declared that communism and capitalism could not exist in the same world.

An Iron Curtain Divides East and West Europe now lay divided between East and West. Germany had been split into two sections. The Soviets controlled the eastern part, including half of the capital, Berlin. Under a Communist government, East Germany was named the German Democratic Republic. The western zones became the Federal Republic of Germany in 1949. Winston Churchill described the division of Europe:

▲ The Iron Curtain is shown dropping on Czechoslovakia in this 1948 political cartoon.

MAIN IDEA

Analyzing Primary Sources

B Why might Winston Churchill use "iron curtain" to refer to the division between Western and Eastern Europe?

PRIMARY SOURCE **B**

From Stettin in the Baltic to Trieste in the Adriatic, an iron curtain has descended across the continent. Behind that line lie all the capitals of the ancient states of Central and Eastern Europe. . . . All these famous cities and the populations around them lie in the Soviet sphere and all are subject in one form or another, not only to Soviet influence but to a very high and increasing measure of control from Moscow.

WINSTON CHURCHILL, "Iron Curtain" speech, March 5, 1946

Churchill's phrase "**iron curtain**" came to represent Europe's division into mostly democratic Western Europe and Communist Eastern Europe.

United States Tries to Contain Soviets

U.S.-Soviet relations continued to worsen in 1946 and 1947. An increasingly worried United States tried to offset the growing Soviet threat to Eastern Europe. President Truman adopted a foreign policy called **containment**. It was a policy directed at blocking Soviet influence and stopping the expansion of communism. Containment policies included forming alliances and helping weak countries resist Soviet advances.

The Truman Doctrine In a speech asking Congress for foreign aid for Turkey and Greece, Truman contrasted democracy with communism:

PRIMARY SOURCE
One way of life is based upon the will of the majority, and is distinguished by free institutions . . . free elections . . . and freedom from political oppression. The second way of life is based upon the will of a minority forcibly imposed upon the majority. It relies upon terror and oppression . . . fixed elections, and the suppression of personal freedoms. I believe it must be the policy of the United States to support free people . . . resisting attempted subjugation [control] by armed minorities or by outside pressures.
PRESIDENT HARRY S. TRUMAN, speech to Congress, March 12, 1947

Truman's support for countries that rejected communism was called the **Truman Doctrine**. It caused great controversy. Some opponents objected to American interference in other nations' affairs. Others argued that the United States could not afford to carry on a global crusade against communism. Congress, however, immediately authorized more than $400 million in aid to Turkey and Greece.

The Marshall Plan Much of Western Europe lay in ruins after the war. There was also economic turmoil—a scarcity of jobs and food. In 1947, U.S. Secretary of State George Marshall proposed that the United States give aid to needy European countries. This assistance program, called the **Marshall Plan**, would provide food, machinery, and other materials to rebuild Western Europe. (See chart.) As Congress debated the $12.5 billion program in 1948, the Communists seized power in Czechoslovakia. Congress immediately voted approval. The plan was a spectacular success. Even Communist Yugoslavia received aid after it broke away from Soviet domination. **C**

MAIN IDEA
Making Inferences
C What was Truman's major reason for offering aid to other countries?

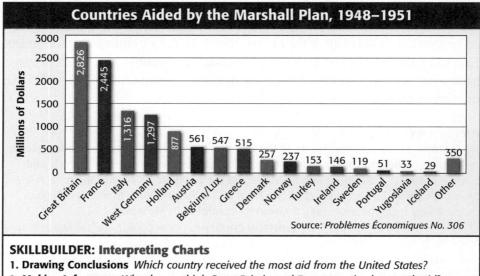

Countries Aided by the Marshall Plan, 1948–1951

Millions of Dollars

Great Britain 2,826
France 2,445
Italy 1,316
West Germany 1,297
Holland 877
Austria 561
Belgium/Lux. 547
Greece 515
Denmark 257
Norway 237
Turkey 153
Ireland 146
Sweden 119
Portugal 51
Yugoslavia 33
Iceland 29
Other 350

Source: *Problèmes Économiques No. 306*

SKILLBUILDER: Interpreting Charts
1. **Drawing Conclusions** *Which country received the most aid from the United States?*
2. **Making Inferences** *Why do you think Great Britain and France received so much aid?*

The Berlin Airlift While Europe began rebuilding, the United States and its allies clashed with the Soviet Union over Germany. The Soviets wanted to keep their former enemy weak and divided. But in 1948, France, Britain, and the United States decided to withdraw their forces from Germany and allow their occupation zones to form one nation. The Soviet Union responded by holding West Berlin hostage.

Although Berlin lay well within the Soviet occupation zone of Germany, it too had been divided into four zones. (See map on next page.) The Soviet Union cut off highway, water, and rail traffic into Berlin's western zones. The city faced starvation. Stalin gambled that the Allies would surrender West Berlin or give up

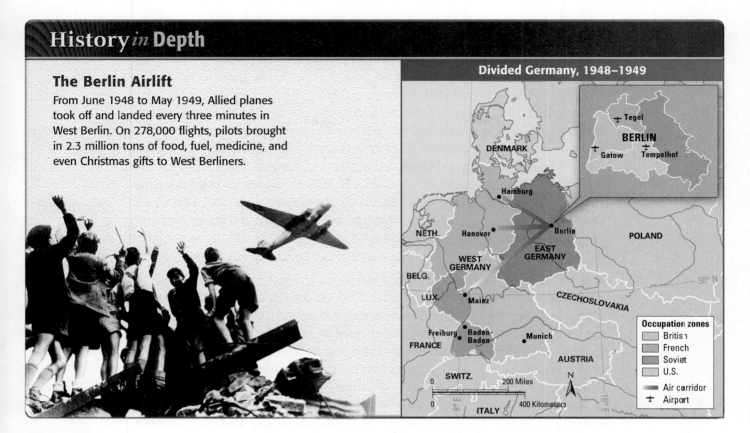

The Berlin Airlift

From June 1948 to May 1949, Allied planes took off and landed every three minutes in West Berlin. On 278,000 flights, pilots brought in 2.3 million tons of food, fuel, medicine, and even Christmas gifts to West Berliners.

Divided Germany, 1948–1949

DENMARK

Hamburg

NETH.   Hanover •   • Berlin

BELG.   WEST   EAST
         GERMANY GERMANY   POLAND

LUX.   • Mainz

CZECHOSLOVAKIA

50° N

Freiburg • Baden-   • Munich
FRANCE   Baden

AUSTRIA

SWITZ.

0   200 Miles
0   400 Kilometers   ITALY

BERLIN
+ Tegel
+   +
Gatow   Tempelhof

Occupation zones
British
French
Soviet
U.S.
▬ Air corridor
+ Airport

MAIN IDEA

Summarizing

D What Soviet actions led to the Berlin airlift?

their idea of reunifying Germany. But American and British officials flew food and supplies into West Berlin for nearly 11 months. In May 1949, the Soviet Union admitted defeat and lifted the blockade. **D**

The Cold War Divides the World

These conflicts marked the start of the **Cold War** between the United States and the Soviet Union. A cold war is a struggle over political differences carried on by means short of military action or war. Beginning in 1949, the superpowers used spying, propaganda, diplomacy, and secret operations in their dealings with each other. Much of the world allied with one side or the other. In fact, until the Soviet Union finally broke up in 1991, the Cold War dictated not only U.S. and Soviet foreign policy, but influenced world alliances as well.

Superpowers Form Rival Alliances The Berlin blockade heightened Western Europe's fears of Soviet aggression. As a result, in 1949, ten western European nations joined with the United States and Canada to form a defensive military alliance. It was called the North Atlantic Treaty Organization (**NATO**). An attack on any NATO member would be met with armed force by all member nations.

The Soviet Union saw NATO as a threat and formed it's own alliance in 1955. It was called the **Warsaw Pact** and included the Soviet Union, East Germany, Czechoslovakia, Poland, Hungary, Romania, Bulgaria, and Albania. In 1961, the East Germans built a wall to separate East and West Berlin. The Berlin Wall symbolized a world divided into rival camps. However, not every country joined the new alliances. Some, like India, chose not to align with either side. And China, the largest Communist country, came to distrust the Soviet Union. It remained nonaligned.

The Threat of Nuclear War As these alliances were forming, the Cold War threatened to heat up enough to destroy the world. The United States already had atomic bombs. In 1949, the Soviet Union exploded its own atomic weapon. President Truman was determined to develop a more deadly weapon before the Soviets did. He authorized work on a thermonuclear weapon in 1950.

The hydrogen or H-bomb would be thousands of times more powerful than the A-bomb. Its power came from the fusion, or joining together, of atoms, rather than the splitting of atoms, as in the A-bomb. In 1952, the United States tested the first H-bomb. The Soviets exploded their own in 1953.

Dwight D. Eisenhower became the U.S. president in 1953. He appointed the firmly anti-Communist John Foster Dulles as his secretary of state. If the Soviet Union or its supporters attacked U.S. interests, Dulles threatened, the United States would "retaliate instantly, by means and at places of our own choosing." This willingness to go to the brink, or edge, of war became known as **brinkmanship**. Brinkmanship required a reliable source of nuclear weapons and airplanes to deliver them. So, the United States strengthened its air force and began producing stockpiles of nuclear weapons. The Soviet Union responded with its own military buildup, beginning an arms race that would go on for four decades. **E**

The Cold War in the Skies The Cold War also affected the science and education programs of the two countries. In August 1957, the Soviets announced the development of a rocket that could travel great distances—an intercontinental ballistic missile, or ICBM. On October 4, the Soviets used an ICBM to push *Sputnik,* the first unmanned satellite, above the earth's atmosphere. Americans felt they had fallen behind in science and technology, and the government poured money into science education. In 1958, the United States launched its own satellite.

In 1960, the skies again provided the arena for a superpower conflict. Five years earlier, Eisenhower had proposed that the United States and the Soviet Union be able to fly over each other's territory to guard against surprise nuclear attacks. The Soviet Union said no. In response, the U.S. Central Intelligence Agency (CIA) started secret high-altitude spy flights over Soviet territory in planes called U-2s. In May 1960, the Soviets shot down a U-2 plane, and its pilot, Francis Gary Powers, was captured. This U-2 incident heightened Cold War tensions.

While Soviet Communists were squaring off against the United States, Communists in China were fighting a civil war for control of that country.

MAIN IDEA

Recognizing Effects
E How did the U.S. policy of brinkmanship contribute to the arms race?

SECTION 1 ASSESSMENT

TERMS & NAMES 1. For each term or name, write a sentence explaining its significance.
• United Nations • iron curtain • containment • Truman Doctrine • Marshall Plan • Cold War • NATO • Warsaw Pact • brinkmanship

USING YOUR NOTES	**MAIN IDEAS**	**CRITICAL THINKING & WRITING**
2. Which effect of the Cold War was the most significant? Explain. 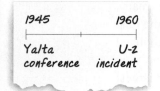	**3.** What was the purpose in forming the United Nations? **4.** What was the goal of the Marshall Plan? **5.** What were the goals of NATO and the Warsaw Pact?	**6. COMPARING AND CONTRASTING** What factors help to explain why the United States and the Soviet Union became rivals instead of allies? **7. ANALYZING MOTIVES** What were Stalin's objectives in supporting Communist governments in Eastern Europe? **8. ANALYZING ISSUES** Why might Berlin be a likely spot for trouble to develop during the Cold War? **9. WRITING ACTIVITY** ECONOMICS Draw a **political cartoon** that shows either capitalism from the Soviet point of view or communism from the U.S. point of view.

INTEGRATED/TECHNOLOGY **INTERNET ACTIVITY**
Use the Internet to research NATO today. Prepare a **chart** listing members today and the date they joined. Then compare it with a list of the founding members.

INTERNET KEYWORD
North Atlantic Treaty Organization

Science & *Technology*

The Space Race

Beginning in the late 1950s, the United States and the Soviet Union competed for influence not only among the nations of the world, but in the skies as well. Once the superpowers had ICBMs (intercontinental ballistic missiles) to deliver nuclear warheads and aircraft for spying missions, they both began to develop technology that could be used to explore—and ultimately control—space. However, after nearly two decades of costly competition, the two superpowers began to cooperate in space exploration.

INTEGRATED TECHNOLOGY

RESEARCH LINKS For more on the space race, go to **classzone.com**

▲ In a major technological triumph, the United States put human beings on the moon on July 20, 1969. Astronaut Buzz Aldrin is shown on the lunar surface with the lunar lander spacecraft.

UNITED STATES

1958 U.S. launches an artificial satellite (*Explorer I*)

1961 First American in space (Alan Shepard)

1962 First American orbits Earth (John Glenn, Jr.); *Mariner 2* flies past Venus

1965 *Mariner 4* space probe flies past Mars

1969 *Apollo 11* first manned moon landing (Neil Armstrong, Buzz Aldrin, Michael Collins)

1973 *Pioneer 7* sent toward Jupiter

1975 U.S. and Soviet Union launch first joint space mission

SOVIET UNION

1957 Soviet Union launches *Sputnik*

1959 *Luna 2* probe reaches the moon

1961 First human orbits Earth (Yuri Gagarin)

1963 First woman in space (Valentina Tereshkova)

1970 *Venera 7* lands on Venus

1971 First manned space station; *Mars 3* drops capsule on Mars

▲ The Soviet Union launched *Sputnik*, the first successful artificial space satellite, on October 4, 1957. As it circled the earth every 96 minutes, Premier Nikita Khrushchev boasted that his country would soon be "turning out long-range missiles like sausages." The United States accelerated its space program. After early failures, a U.S. satellite was launched in 1958.

◄ The joint *Apollo* and *Soyuz* mission ushered in an era of U.S.-Soviet cooperation in space.

Connect *to* Today

1. **Comparing** Which destinations in space did both the United States and the Soviet Union explore?
   See Skillbuilder Handbook, page R7.

2. **Making Inferences** What role might space continue to play in achieving world peace?

537

Communists Take Power in China

MAIN IDEA	WHY IT MATTERS NOW	TERMS & NAMES
REVOLUTION After World War II, Chinese Communists defeated Nationalist forces and two separate Chinas emerged.	China remains a Communist country and a major power in the world.	• Mao Zedong • Red Guards • Jiang Jieshi • Cultural Revolution • commune

SETTING THE STAGE In World War II, China fought on the side of the victorious Allies. But the victory proved to be a hollow one for China. During the war, Japan's armies had occupied and devastated most of China's cities. China's civilian death toll alone was estimated between 10 to 22 million persons. This vast country suffered casualties second only to those of the Soviet Union. However, conflict did not end with the defeat of the Japanese. In 1945, opposing Chinese armies faced one another.

TAKING NOTES

Recognizing Effects
Use a chart to identify the causes and effects of the Communist Revolution in China.

Cause	Effect
1.	1.
2.	2.
3.	3.

Communists vs. Nationalists

As you read in Chapter 14, a bitter civil war was raging between the Nationalists and the Communists when the Japanese invaded China in 1937. During World War II, the political opponents temporarily united to fight the Japanese. But they continued to jockey for position within China.

World War II in China Under their leader, <u>Mao Zedong</u> (MOW dzuh•dahng), the Communists had a stronghold in northwestern China. From there, they mobilized peasants for guerrilla war against the Japanese in the northeast. Thanks to their efforts to promote literacy and improve food production, the Communists won the peasants' loyalty. By 1945, they controlled much of northern China.

Meanwhile, the Nationalist forces under <u>Jiang Jieshi</u> (jee•ahng jee•shee) dominated southwestern China. Protected from the Japanese by rugged mountain ranges, Jiang gathered an army of 2.5 million men. From 1942 to 1945, the United States sent the Nationalists at least $1.5 billion in aid to fight the Japanese. Instead of benefiting the army, however, these supplies and money often ended up in the hands of a few corrupt officers. Jiang's army actually fought few battles against the Japanese. Instead, the Nationalist army saved its strength for the coming battle against Mao's Red Army. After Japan surrendered, the Nationalists and Communists resumed fighting.

Civil War Resumes The renewed civil war lasted from 1946 to 1949. At first, the Nationalists had the advantage. Their army outnumbered the Communists' army by as much as three to one. And the United States continued its support by providing nearly $2 billion in aid. The Nationalist forces, however, did little to win popular support. With China's economy collapsing, thousands of Nationalist soldiers deserted to the Communists. In spring 1949, China's major cities fell to

Nationalists	Chinese Political Opponents, 1945	Communists
Jiang Jieshi	**Leader**	Mao Zedong
Southern China	**Area Ruled**	Northern China
United States	**Foreign Support**	Soviet Union
Defeat of Communists	**Domestic Policy**	National liberation
Weak due to inflation and failing economy	**Public Support**	Strong due to promised land reform for peasants
Ineffective, corrupt leadership and poor morale	**Military Organization**	Experienced, motivated guerrilla army

SKILLBUILDER: Interpreting Charts
1. **Drawing Conclusions** *Which party's domestic policy might appeal more to Chinese peasants?*
2. **Forming and Supporting Opinions** *Which aspect of the Communist approach do you think was most responsible for Mao's victory? Explain.*

the well-trained Red forces. Mao's troops were also enthusiastic about his promise to return land to the peasants. The remnants of Jiang's shattered army fled south. In October 1949, Mao Zedong gained control of the country. He proclaimed it the People's Republic of China. Jiang and other Nationalist leaders retreated to the island of Taiwan, which Westerners called Formosa.

Mao Zedong's victory fueled U.S. anti-Communist feelings. Those feelings only grew after the Chinese and Soviets signed a treaty of friendship in 1950. Many people in the United States viewed the takeover of China as another step in a Communist campaign to conquer the world. **A**

The Two Chinas Affect the Cold War

China had split into two nations. One was the island of Taiwan, or Nationalist China, with an area of 13,000 square miles. The mainland, or People's Republic of China, had an area of more than 3.5 million square miles. The existence of two Chinas, and the conflicting international loyalties they inspired, intensified the Cold War.

The Superpowers React After Jiang Jieshi fled to Taiwan, the United States helped him set up a Nationalist government on that small island. It was called the Republic of China. The Soviets gave financial, military, and technical aid to Communist China. In addition, the Chinese and the Soviets pledged to come to each other's defense if either was attacked. The United States tried to halt Soviet expansion in Asia. For example, when Soviet forces occupied the northern half of Korea after World War II and set up a Communist government, the United States supported a separate state in the south.

China Expands under the Communists In the early years of Mao's reign, Chinese troops expanded into Tibet, India, and southern, or Inner, Mongolia. Northern, or Outer, Mongolia, which bordered the Soviet Union, remained in the Soviet sphere.

In a brutal assault in 1950 and 1951, China took control of Tibet. The Chinese promised autonomy to Tibetans, who followed their religious leader, the Dalai Lama. When China's control over Tibet tightened in the late 1950s, the Dalai Lama fled to India. India welcomed many Tibetan refugees after a failed revolt in Tibet in

MAIN IDEA

Recognizing Effects
A How did the outcome of the Chinese civil war contribute to Cold War tensions?

Mao Zedong
1893–1976

Born into a peasant family, Mao embraced Marxist socialism as a young man. Though he began as an urban labor organizer, Mao quickly realized the revolutionary potential of China's peasants. In 1927, Mao predicted:

The force of the peasantry is like that of the raging winds and driving rain. . . . They will bury beneath them all forces of imperialism, militarism, corrupt officialdom, village bosses and evil gentry.

Mao's first attempt to lead the peasants in revolt failed in 1927. But during the Japanese occupation, Mao and his followers won widespread peasant support by reducing rents and promising to redistribute land.

INTEGRATED/TECHNOLOGY

RESEARCH LINKS For more on Mao Zedong, go to **classzone.com**

1959. As a result, resentment between India and China grew. In 1962, they clashed briefly over the two countries' unclear border. The fighting stopped but resentment continued.

The Communists Transform China

For decades, China had been in turmoil, engaged in civil war or fighting with Japan. So, when the Communists took power, they moved rapidly to strengthen their rule over China's 550 million people. They also aimed to restore China as a powerful nation.

Communists Claim a New "Mandate of Heaven" After taking control of China, the Communists began to tighten their hold. The party's 4.5 million members made up just 1 percent of the population. But they were a disciplined group. Like the Soviets, the Chinese Communists set up two parallel organizations, the Communist party and the national government. Mao headed both until 1959.

Mao's Brand of Marxist Socialism Mao was determined to reshape China's economy based on Marxist socialism. Eighty percent of the people lived in rural areas, but most owned no land. Instead, 10 percent of the rural population controlled 70 percent of the farmland. Under the Agrarian Reform Law of 1950, Mao seized the holdings of these landlords. His forces killed more than a million landlords who resisted. He then divided the land among the peasants. Later, to further Mao's socialist principles, the government forced peasants to join collective farms. Each of these farms was comprised of 200 to 300 households.

Mao's changes also transformed industry and business. Gradually, private companies were nationalized, or brought under government ownership. In 1953, Mao launched a five-year plan that set high production goals for industry. By 1957, China's output of coal, cement, steel, and electricity had increased dramatically. **B**

MAIN IDEA

Analyzing Issues
B What aspects of Marxist socialism did Mao try to bring to China?

"The Great Leap Forward" To expand the success of the first Five-Year Plan, Mao proclaimed the "Great Leap Forward" in early 1958. This plan called for still larger collective farms, or **communes**. By the end of 1958, about 26,000 communes had been created. The average commune sprawled over 15,000 acres and supported over 25,000 people. In the strictly controlled life of the communes, peasants worked the land together. They ate in communal dining rooms, slept in communal dormitories, and raised children in communal nurseries. And they owned nothing. The peasants had no incentive to work hard when only the state profited from their labor.

The Great Leap Forward was a giant step backward. Poor planning and inefficient "backyard," or home, industries hampered growth. The program was ended in 1961 after crop failures caused a famine that killed about 20 million people.

New Policies and Mao's Response China was facing external problems as well as internal ones in the late 1950s. The spirit of cooperation that had bound the Soviet Union and China began to fade. Each sought to lead the worldwide Communist movement. As they also shared the longest border in the world, they faced numerous territorial disputes.

After the failure of the Great Leap Forward and the split with the Soviet Union, Mao reduced his role in government. Other leaders moved away from Mao's strict socialist ideas. For example, farm families could live in their own homes and could sell crops they grew on small private plots. Factory workers could compete for wage increases and promotions.

Mao thought China's new economic policies weakened the Communist goal of social equality. He was determined to revive the revolution. In 1966, he urged China's young people to "learn revolution by making revolution." Millions of high school and college students responded. They left their classrooms and formed militia units called **Red Guards**.

The Cultural Revolution The Red Guards led a major uprising known as the **Cultural Revolution**. Its goal was to establish a society of peasants and workers in which all were equal. The new hero was the peasant who worked with his hands. The life of the mind—intellectual and artistic activity—was considered useless and dangerous. To stamp out this threat, the Red Guards shut down colleges and schools. They targeted anyone who resisted the regime. Intellectuals had to "purify" themselves by doing hard labor in remote villages. Thousands were executed or imprisoned.

Chaos threatened farm production and closed down factories. Civil war seemed possible. By 1968, even Mao admitted that the Cultural Revolution had to stop. The army was ordered to put down the Red Guards. Zhou Enlai (joh ehn•leye), Chinese Communist party founder and premier since 1949, began to restore order. While China was struggling to become stable, the Cold War continued to rage. Two full-scale wars were fought—in Korea and in Vietnam. **C**

MAIN IDEA

Drawing Conclusions

C Why did the Cultural Revolution fail?

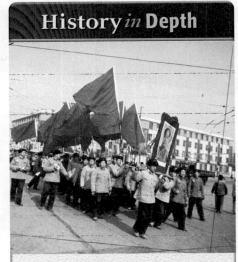

History *in* Depth

The Red Guards

The Red Guards were students, mainly teenagers. They pledged their devotion to Chairman Mao and the Cultural Revolution. From 1966 to 1968, 20 to 30 million Red Guards roamed China's cities and countryside causing widespread chaos. To smash the old, non-Maoist way of life, they destroyed buildings and beat and even killed Mao's alleged enemies. They lashed out at professors, government officials, factory managers, and even parents.

Eventually, even Mao turned on them. Most were exiled to the countryside. Others were arrested and some executed.

SECTION 2 ASSESSMENT

TERMS & NAMES 1. For each term or name, write a sentence explaining its significance.
• Mao Zedong   • Jiang Jieshi   • commune   • Red Guards   • Cultural Revolution

USING YOUR NOTES

2. Which effect of the Communist Revolution in China do you think had the most permanent impact? Explain.

Cause	Effect
1.	1.
2.	2.
3.	3.

MAIN IDEAS

3. How did the Chinese Communists increase their power during World War II?

4. What actions did the Nationalists take during World War II?

5. What was the goal of the Cultural Revolution?

CRITICAL THINKING & WRITING

6. **MAKING INFERENCES** Why did the United States support the Nationalists in the civil war in China?

7. **ANALYZING ISSUES** What policies or actions enabled the Communists to defeat the Nationalists in their long civil war?

8. **IDENTIFYING PROBLEMS** What circumstances prevented Mao's Great Leap Forward from bringing economic prosperity to China?

9. **WRITING ACTIVITY** REVOLUTION Write **summaries** of the reforms Mao Zedong proposed for China that could be placed on a propaganda poster.

CONNECT TO TODAY CREATING A COMPARISON CHART

Find political, economic, and demographic information on the People's Republic of China and Taiwan, and make a **comparison chart**.

Wars in Korea and Vietnam

MAIN IDEA	WHY IT MATTERS NOW	TERMS & NAMES
REVOLUTION In Asia, the Cold War flared into actual wars supported mainly by the superpowers.	Today, Vietnam is a Communist country, and Korea is split into Communist and non-Communist nations.	• 38th parallel • Ngo Dinh Diem • Douglas • Vietcong MacArthur • Vietnamization • Ho Chi Minh • Khmer Rouge • domino theory

SETTING THE STAGE When World War II ended, Korea became a divided nation. North of the **38th parallel**, a line that crosses Korea at 38 degrees north latitude, Japanese troops surrendered to Soviet forces. South of this line, the Japanese surrendered to American troops. As in Germany, two nations developed. (See map on next page.) One was the Communist industrial north, whose government had been set up by the Soviets. The other was the non-Communist rural south, supported by the Western powers.

War in Korea

TAKING NOTES

Comparing and Contrasting Use a diagram to compare and contrast the Korean and Vietnam Wars.

By 1949, both the United States and the Soviet Union had withdrawn most of their troops from Korea. The Soviets gambled that the United States would not defend South Korea. So they supplied North Korea with tanks, airplanes, and money in an attempt to take over the peninsula.

Standoff at the 38th Parallel On June 25, 1950, North Koreans swept across the 38th parallel in a surprise attack on South Korea. Within days, North Korean troops had penetrated deep into the south. President Truman was convinced that the North Korean aggressors were repeating what Hitler, Mussolini, and the Japanese had done in the 1930s. Truman's policy of containment was being put to the test. And Truman resolved to help South Korea resist communism.

South Korea also asked the United Nations to intervene. When the matter came to a vote in the Security Council, the Soviets were absent. They had refused to take part in the Council to protest admission of Nationalist China (Taiwan), rather than

▼ UN forces landing at Inchon in South Korea in 1950

Communist China, into the UN. As a result, the Soviet Union could not veto the UN's plan to send an international force to Korea to stop the invasion. A total of 15 nations, including the United States and Britain, participated under the command of General **Douglas MacArthur**.

Meanwhile, the North Koreans continued to advance. By September 1950, they controlled the entire Korean peninsula except for a tiny area around Pusan in the far southeast. That month, however, MacArthur launched a surprise attack. Troops moving north from Pusan met with forces that had made an amphibious landing at Inchon. Caught in this "pincer action," about half of the North Koreans surrendered. The rest retreated.

The Fighting Continues The UN troops pursued the retreating North Koreans across the 38th parallel into North Korea. They pushed them almost to the Yalu River at the Chinese border. The UN forces were mostly from the United States. The Chinese felt threatened by these troops and by an American fleet off their coast. In October 1950, they sent 300,000 troops into North Korea.

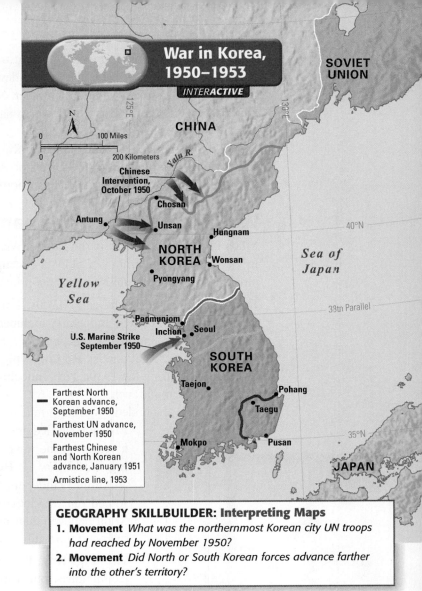

War in Korea, 1950–1953

INTERACTIVE

- Farthest North Korean advance, September 1950
- Farthest UN advance, November 1950
- Farthest Chinese and North Korean advance, January 1951
- Armistice line, 1953

GEOGRAPHY SKILLBUILDER: Interpreting Maps
1. **Movement** What was the northernmost Korean city UN troops had reached by November 1950?
2. **Movement** Did North or South Korean forces advance farther into the other's territory?

The Chinese greatly outnumbered the UN forces. By January 1951, they had pushed UN and South Korean troops out of North Korea. The Chinese then moved into South Korea and captured the capital of Seoul. "We face an entirely new war," declared MacArthur. He called for a nuclear attack against China. Truman viewed MacArthur's proposals as reckless. "We are trying to prevent a world war, not start one," he said. MacArthur tried to go over the President's head by taking his case to Congress and the press. In response, Truman removed him.

Over the next two years, UN forces fought to drive the Chinese and North Koreans back. By 1952, UN troops had regained control of South Korea. Finally, in July 1953, the UN forces and North Korea signed a cease-fire agreement. The border between the two Koreas was set near the 38th parallel, almost where it had been before the war. In the meantime, 4 million soldiers and civilians had died. **A**

Aftermath of the War After the war, Korea remained divided. A demilitarized zone, which still exists, separated the two countries. In North Korea, the Communist dictator Kim Il Sung established collective farms, developed heavy industry, and built up the military. At Kim's death in 1994, his son Kim Jong Il took power. Under his rule, Communist North Korea developed nuclear weapons but had serious economic problems. On the other hand, South Korea prospered, thanks partly to massive aid from the United States and other countries. In the 1960s, South

MAIN IDEA

Recognizing Effects

A What effects did the Korean war have on the Korean people and nation?

Korea concentrated on developing its industry and expanding foreign trade. A succession of dictatorships ruled the rapidly developing country. With the 1987 adoption of a democratic constitution, however, South Korea established free elections. During the 1980s and 1990s, South Korea had one of the highest economic growth rates in the world.

Political differences have kept the two Koreas apart, despite periodic discussions of reuniting the country. North Korea's possession of nuclear weapons is a major obstacle. The United States still keeps troops in South Korea.

War Breaks Out in Vietnam

Much like its involvement in the Korean War, the involvement of the United States in Vietnam stemmed from its Cold War containment policy. After World War II, stopping the spread of communism was the principal goal of U.S. foreign policy.

The Road to War In the early 1900s, France controlled most of resource-rich Southeast Asia. (French Indochina included what are now Vietnam, Laos, and Cambodia.) But nationalist independence movements had begun to develop. A young Vietnamese nationalist, **Ho Chi Minh**, turned to the Communists for help in his struggle. During the 1930s, Ho's Indochinese Communist party led revolts and strikes against the French.

The French responded by jailing Vietnamese protesters. They also sentenced Ho to death. He fled into exile, but returned to Vietnam in 1941, a year after the Japanese seized control of his country during World War II. Ho and other nationalists founded the Vietminh (Independence) League. The Japanese were forced out of Vietnam after their defeat in 1945. Ho Chi Minh believed that independence would follow, but France intended to regain its colony.

The Fighting Begins Vietnamese Nationalists and Communists joined to fight the French armies. The French held most major cities, but the Vietminh had widespread support in the countryside. The Vietminh used hit-and-run tactics to confine the French to the cities. In France the people began to doubt that their colony was worth the lives and money the struggle cost. In 1954, the French suffered a major military defeat at Dien Bien Phu. They surrendered to Ho.

The United States had supported France in Vietnam. With the defeat of the French, the United States saw a rising threat to the rest of Asia. President Eisenhower described this threat in terms of the **domino theory**. The Southeast Asian nations were like a row of dominos, he said. The fall of one to communism would lead to the fall of its neighbors. This theory became a major justification for U.S. foreign policy during the Cold War era. **B**

Vietnam—A Divided Country After France's defeat, an international peace conference met in Geneva to discuss the future of Indochina. Based on these talks, Vietnam was divided at 17° north latitude. North of that line, Ho Chi Minh's Communist forces governed. To the south, the United States and France set up an anti-Communist government under the leadership of **Ngo Dinh Diem** (NOH dihn D'YEM).

History Makers

Ho Chi Minh
1890–1969

When he was young, the poor Vietnamese Nguyen That (uhng•wihn thaht) Thanh worked as a cook on a French steamship. In visiting U.S. cities where the boat docked, he learned about American culture and ideals. He later took a new name—Ho Chi Minh, meaning "He who enlightens." Though a Communist, in proclaiming Vietnam's independence from France in 1945, he declared, "All men are created equal."

His people revered him, calling him Uncle Ho. However, Ho Chi Minh did not put his democratic ideals into practice. He ruled North Vietnam by crushing all opposition.

MAIN IDEA

Making Inferences
B What actions might the United States have justified by the domino theory?

War in Vietnam, 1957–1973

CHINA

NORTH VIETNAM

Dien Bien Phu

Hanoi

Haiphong

Gulf of Tonkin

20°N

LAOS

Hainan

U.S. Seventh Fleet, 1964

Vihn

Mekong R.

Dong Hoi

Demarcation Line, 1954

Ho Chi Mihn Trail

Hue

Da Nang

Chulai

15°N

South China Sea

Kon Tum

SOUTH VIETNAM

CAMBODIA

Cam Rahn Bay

Phnom Penh

Gulf of Thailand

Bien Hoa

Saigon

Mekong Delta

10°N

105°E

110°E

Areas controlled in 1973
- National Liberation Front (Vietcong)
- Saigon government
- Contested areas

N

0   100 Miles
0   200 Kilometers

1965—U.S. bombing of North Vietnam

1968—U.S. Marines at the Battle of Hue

1975—Evacuation of the U.S. embassy in Saigon

GEOGRAPHY SKILLBUILDER: Interpreting Maps
1. **Human-Environment Interaction** *Did the Saigon government or the Vietcong control more of South Vietnam in 1973?*
2. **Movement** *Through what other countries did North Vietnamese troops move to invade South Vietnam?*

Diem ruled the south as a dictator. Opposition to his government grew. Communist guerrillas, called **Vietcong**, began to gain strength in the south. While some of the Vietcong were trained soldiers from North Vietnam, most were South Vietnamese who hated Diem. Gradually, the Vietcong won control of large areas of the countryside. In 1963, a group of South Vietnamese generals had Diem assassinated. But the new leaders were no more popular than he had been. It appeared that a takeover by the Communist Vietcong, backed by North Vietnam, was inevitable.

The United States Gets Involved

Faced with the possibility of a Communist victory, the United States decided to escalate, or increase, its involvement. Some U.S. troops had been serving as advisers to the South Vietnamese since the late 1950s. But their numbers steadily grew, as did the numbers of planes and other military equipment sent to South Vietnam.

U.S. Troops Enter the Fight In August 1964, U.S. President Lyndon Johnson told Congress that North Vietnamese patrol boats had attacked two U.S. destroyers in the Gulf of Tonkin. As a result, Congress authorized the president to send U.S. troops to fight in Vietnam. By late 1965, more than 185,000 U.S. soldiers were in combat on Vietnamese soil. U.S. planes had also begun to bomb North Vietnam. By 1968, more than half a million U.S. soldiers were in combat there.

The United States had the best-equipped, most advanced army in the world. Yet it faced two major difficulties. First, U.S. soldiers were fighting a guerrilla war in unfamiliar jungle terrain. Second, the South Vietnamese government that they were defending was becoming more unpopular. At the same time, support for the Vietcong grew, with help and supplies from Ho Chi Minh, the Soviet Union, and China. Unable to win a decisive victory on the ground, the United States turned to air power. U.S. forces bombed millions of acres of farmland and forest in an attempt to destroy enemy hideouts. This bombing strengthened peasants' opposition to the South Vietnamese government.

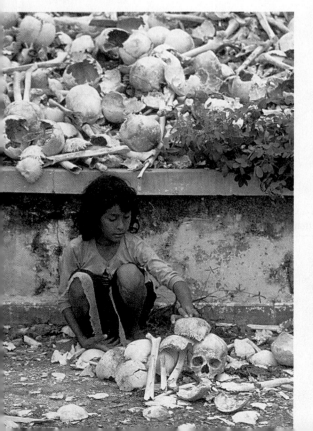

▼ The skulls and bones of Cambodian citizens form a haunting memorial to the brutality of its Communist government in the 1970s.

The United States Withdraws During the late 1960s, the war grew increasingly unpopular in the United States. Dissatisfied young people began to protest the tremendous loss of life in a conflict on the other side of the world. Bowing to intense public pressure, President Richard Nixon began withdrawing U.S. troops from Vietnam in 1969.

Nixon had a plan called **Vietnamization**. It allowed for U.S. troops to gradually pull out, while the South Vietnamese increased their combat role. To pursue Vietnamization while preserving the South Vietnamese government, Nixon authorized a massive bombing campaign against North Vietnamese bases and supply routes. He also authorized bombings in neighboring Laos and Cambodia to destroy Vietcong hiding places.

In response to protests and political pressure at home, Nixon kept withdrawing U.S. troops. The last left in 1973. Two years later, the North Vietnamese overran South Vietnam. The war ended, but more than 1.5 million Vietnamese and 58,000 Americans lost their lives.

Postwar Southeast Asia

War's end did not bring an immediate halt to bloodshed and chaos in Southeast Asia. Cambodia (also known as Kampuchea) was under siege by Communist rebels.

During the war, it had suffered U.S. bombing when it was used as a sanctuary by North Vietnamese and Vietcong troops.

Cambodia in Turmoil In 1975, Communist rebels known as the <u>Khmer Rouge</u> set up a brutal Communist government under the leadership of Pol Pot. In a ruthless attempt to transform Cambodia into a Communist society, Pol Pot's followers slaughtered 2 million people. This was almost one quarter of the nation's population. The Vietnamese invaded in 1978. They overthrew the Khmer Rouge and installed a less repressive government. But fighting continued. The Vietnamese withdrew in 1989. In 1993, under the supervision of UN peacekeepers, Cambodia adopted a democratic constitution and held free elections. **C**

Vietnam after the War After 1975, the victorious North Vietnamese imposed tight controls over the South. Officials sent thousands of people to "reeducation camps" for training in Communist thought. They nationalized industries and strictly controlled businesses. They also renamed Saigon, the South's former capital, Ho Chi Minh City. Communist oppression caused 1.5 million people to flee Vietnam. Most escaped in dangerously overcrowded ships. More than 200,000 "boat people" died at sea. The survivors often spent months in refugee camps in Southeast Asia. About 70,000 eventually settled in the United States or Canada. Although Communists still govern Vietnam, the country now welcomes foreign investment. The United States normalized relations with Vietnam in 1995.

While the superpowers were struggling for advantage during the Korean and Vietnam wars, they also were seeking influence in other parts of the world.

MAIN IDEA

Recognizing
Effects

C What was one of the effects of Pol Pot's efforts to turn Cambodia into a rural society?

Connect *to* Today

Vietnam Today

Vietnam remains a Communist country. But, like China, it has introduced elements of capitalism into its economy. In 1997, a travel magazine claimed that Hanoi, the capital of Vietnam, "jumps with vitality, its streets and shops jammed with locals and handfuls of Western tourists and businesspeople." Above, two executives tour the city.

Along Hanoi's shaded boulevards, billboards advertise U.S. and Japanese copiers, motorcycles, video recorders, and soft drinks. On the streets, enterprising Vietnamese businesspeople offer more traditional services. These include bicycle repair, a haircut, a shave, or a tasty snack.

SECTION 3 ASSESSMENT

TERMS & NAMES 1. For each term or name, write a sentence explaining its significance.
• 38th parallel • Douglas MacArthur • Ho Chi Minh • domino theory • Ngo Dinh Diem • Vietcong • Vietnamization • Khmer Rouge

USING YOUR NOTES
2. In what ways were the causes and effects of the wars in Korea and Vietnam similar?

Korean War
both
Vietnam War

MAIN IDEAS
3. What role did the United Nations play in the Korean War?

4. How did Vietnam become divided?

5. What was the Khmer Rouge's plan for Cambodia?

CRITICAL THINKING & WRITING
6. **ANALYZING MOTIVES** What role did the policy of containment play in the involvement of the United States in wars in Korea and Vietnam?

7. **IDENTIFYING CAUSES** How might imperialism be one of the causes of the Vietnam War?

8. **FORMING OPINIONS** Do you think U.S. involvement in Vietnam was justified? Why or why not?

9. **WRITING ACTIVITY** [EMPIRE BUILDING] Write a two-paragraph **expository essay** for either the United States or the Soviet Union supporting its involvement in Asia.

CONNECT TO TODAY WRITING A BIOGRAPHY
Research the present-day leader of one of the countries discussed in this section.
Then write a three-paragraph **biography**.

The Cold War Divides the World

MAIN IDEA	WHY IT MATTERS NOW	TERMS & NAMES
REVOLUTION The superpowers supported opposing sides in Latin American and Middle Eastern conflicts.	Many of these areas today are troubled by political, economic, and military conflict and crisis.	• Third World • nonaligned nations • Fidel Castro • Anastasio Somoza • Daniel Ortega • Ayatollah Ruholla Khomeini

SETTING THE STAGE Following World War II, the world's nations were grouped politically into three "worlds." The first was the industrialized capitalist nations, including the United States and its allies. The second was the Communist nations led by the Soviet Union. The **Third World** consisted of developing nations, often newly independent, who were not aligned with either superpower. These nonaligned countries provided yet another arena for competition between the Cold War superpowers.

TAKING NOTES

Determining Main Ideas
Use a chart to list main points about Third World confrontations.

Country	Conflict
Cuba	
Nicaragua	
Iran	

Fighting for the Third World

The Third World nations were located in Latin America, Asia, and Africa. They were economically poor and politically unstable. This was largely due to a long history of colonialism. They also suffered from ethnic conflicts and lack of technology and education. Each needed a political and economic system around which to build its society. Soviet-style communism and U.S.-style free-market democracy were the main choices.

Cold War Strategies The United States, the Soviet Union, and, in some cases, China, used a variety of techniques to gain influence in the Third World. (See feature on next page.) They backed wars of revolution, liberation, or counterrevolution. The U.S. and Soviet intelligence agencies—the CIA and the KGB—engaged in various covert, or secret, activities, ranging from spying to assassination attempts. The United States also gave military aid, built schools, set up programs to combat poverty, and sent volunteer workers to many developing nations. The Soviets offered military and technical assistance, mainly to India and Egypt.

Association of Nonaligned Nations Other developing nations also needed assistance. They became important players in the Cold War competition between the United States, the Soviet Union, and later, China. But not all Third World countries wished to play a role in the Cold War. As mentioned earlier India vowed to remain neutral. Indonesia, a populous island nation in Southeast Asia, also struggled to stay uninvolved. In 1955, it hosted many leaders from Asia and Africa at the Bandung Conference. They met to form what they called a "third force" of independent countries, or **nonaligned nations**. Some nations, such as India and Indonesia, were able to maintain their neutrality. But others took sides with the superpowers or played competing sides against each other.

How the Cold War Was Fought

During the Cold War, the United States and the Soviet Union both believed that they needed to stop the other side from extending its power. What differentiated the Cold War from other 20th century conflicts was that the two enemies did not engage in a shooting war. Instead, they pursued their rivalry by using the strategies shown below.

NATO, 1955
Warsaw Pact, 1955
Non-aligned, 1955

Egypt built the Aswan Dam with Soviet aid.

Major Strategies of the Cold War

Foreign Aid	Espionage	Multinational Alliances
The two superpowers tried to win allies by giving financial aid to other nations. For instance, Egypt took aid from the Soviet Union to build the Aswan High Dam (see photograph above).	Fearing the enemy might be gaining the advantage, each side spied on the other. One famous incident was the Soviet downing of a U.S. U-2 spy plane in 1960.	To gain the support of other nations, both the Soviet Union and the United States entered into alliances. Two examples of this were NATO and the Warsaw Pact (shown on map above).
Propaganda	**Brinkmanship**	**Surrogate Wars**
Both superpowers used propaganda to try to win support overseas. For example, Radio Free Europe broadcast radio programs about the rest of the world into Eastern Europe.	The policy of brinkmanship meant going to the brink of war to make the other side back down. One example was the Cuban Missile Crisis.	The word surrogate means substitute. Although the United States and the Soviet Union did not fight each other directly, they fought indirectly by backing opposing sides in many smaller conflicts.

SKILLBUILDER: Interpreting Visuals
1. **Generalizing** *Judging from the map, how would you describe the effect on Europe of multinational alliances?*
2. **Analyzing Motives** *What motive did the two superpowers have for fighting surrogate wars?*

Cold War Hot Spots, 1948–1975
INTERACTIVE

1. The United States helps Greece defeat Communist-led rebels (1946–1949) and gives economic and military aid to Turkey (1947–1950).

2. Communists retain or gain control after bloody wars in Korea (1950–1953) and Vietnam (1957–1975).

3. The Soviets down U.S. U-2 pilot Francis Gary Powers in 1960.

4. The United States and the Soviet Union bring the world to the brink of nuclear war during the Cuban missile crisis in 1962.

5. The Soviet Union aids anticolonial struggles in Congo (1960), Mozambique (1971), and Angola (1974).

6. Britain helps Indonesia repress a Communist uprising in 1965.

7. The United States intervenes in the governments of Guatemala (1954), Bolivia (1956), and Chile (1973).

Legend:
- Communist expansion
- Communist expansion prevented by U.S. and allies

GEOGRAPHY SKILLBUILDER: Interpreting Maps
1. **Location** *On what continents identified on the map did Cold War conflicts not occur?*
2. **Region** *About what fraction of the globe did Communists control by 1975?*

Confrontations in Latin America

After World War II, rapid industrialization, population growth, and a lingering gap between the rich and the poor led Latin American nations to seek aid from both superpowers. At the same time, many of these countries alternated between short-lived democracy and harsh military rule. As described in Chapter 12, U.S. involvement in Latin America began long before World War II. American businesses backed leaders who protected U.S. interests but who also often oppressed their people. After the war, communism and nationalistic feelings inspired revolutionary movements. These found enthusiastic Soviet support. In response, the United States provided military and economic assistance to anti-Communist dictators.

Fidel Castro and the Cuban Revolution In the 1950s, Cuba was ruled by an unpopular dictator, Fulgencio Batista, who had U.S. support. Cuban resentment led to a popular revolution, which overthrew Batista in January 1959. A young lawyer named **Fidel Castro** led that revolution. At first, many people praised Castro for bringing social reforms to Cuba and improving the economy. Yet Castro was a harsh dictator. He suspended elections, jailed or executed his opponents, and tightly controlled the press.

When Castro nationalized the Cuban economy, he took over U.S.-owned sugar mills and refineries. In response, Eisenhower ordered an embargo on all trade with Cuba. Castro then turned to the Soviets for economic and military aid.

In 1960, the CIA began to train anti-Castro Cuban exiles. In April 1961, they invaded Cuba, landing at the Bay of Pigs. However, the United States did not provide the hoped for air support. Castro's forces easily defeated the invaders, humiliating the United States.

Nuclear Face-off: the Cuban Missile Crisis The failed Bay of Pigs invasion convinced Soviet leader Nikita Khrushchev that the United States would not resist Soviet expansion in Latin America. So, in July 1962, Khrushchev secretly began to build 42 missile sites in Cuba. In October, an American spy plane discovered the sites. President John F. Kennedy declared that missiles so close to the U.S. mainland were a threat. He demanded their removal and also announced a naval blockade of Cuba to prevent the Soviets from installing more missiles.

Castro protested his country's being used as a pawn in the Cold War:

> **PRIMARY SOURCE**
> Cuba did not and does not intend to be in the middle of a conflict between the East and the West. Our problem is above all one of national sovereignty. Cuba does not mean to get involved in the Cold War.
>
> **FIDEL CASTRO,** quoted in an interview October 27, 1962

But Castro and Cuba were deeply involved. Kennedy's demand for the removal of Soviet missiles put the United States and the Soviet Union on a collision course. People around the world feared nuclear war. Fortunately, Khrushchev agreed to remove the missiles in return for a U.S. promise not to invade Cuba. **A**

The resolution of the Cuban Missile Crisis left Castro completely dependent on Soviet support. In exchange for this support, Castro backed Communist revolutions in Latin America and Africa. Soviet aid to Cuba, however, ended abruptly with the breakup of the Soviet Union in 1991. This loss dealt a crippling blow to the Cuban economy. Eventually, Castro loosened state control of Cuba's economy and sought better relations with other countries.

Civil War in Nicaragua Just as the United States had supported Batista in Cuba, it had funded the Nicaraguan dictatorship of **Anastasio Somoza** and his family since 1933. In 1979, Communist Sandinista rebels toppled Somoza's son. Both the United States and the Soviet Union initially gave aid to the Sandinistas and their leader, **Daniel Ortega** (awr•TAY•guh). The Sandinistas, however, gave assistance to other Marxist rebels in nearby El Salvador. To help the El Salvadoran government fight those rebels, the United States supported Nicaraguan anti-Communist forces called the Contras or *contrarevolucionarios.* **B**

The civil war in Nicaragua lasted more than a decade and seriously weakened the country's economy. In 1990, President Ortega agreed to hold free elections, the first in the nation's history. Violeta Chamorro, a reform candidate, defeated him. The Sandinistas were also defeated in elections in 1996 and 2001.

MAIN IDEA

Contrasting
A What differing U.S. and Soviet aims led to the Cuban missile crisis?

MAIN IDEA

Analyzing Motives
B Why did the U.S. switch its support from the Sandinistas to the Contras?

History Makers

Fidel Castro
1926–

The son of a wealthy Spanish-Cuban farmer, Fidel Castro became involved in politics at the University of Havana. He first tried to overthrow the Cuban dictator, Batista, in 1953. He was imprisoned, but vowed to continue the struggle for independence:

Personally, I am not interested in power nor do I envisage assuming it at any time. All that I will do is to make sure that the sacrifices of so many compatriots should not be in vain.

Despite this declaration, Castro has ruled Cuba as a dictator for more than 40 years.

INTEGRATED TECHNOLOGY

INTERNET ACTIVITY Create a time line of the important events in Castro's rule of Cuba. Go to **classzone.com** for your research.

Confrontations in the Middle East

As the map on page 550 shows, Cold War confrontations continued to erupt around the globe. The oil-rich Middle East attracted both superpowers.

Religious and Secular Values Clash in Iran Throughout the Middle East, oil industry wealth fueled a growing clash between traditional Islamic values and modern Western materialism. In no country was this cultural conflict more dramatically shown than in Iran (Persia before 1935). After World War II, Iran's leader, Shah Mohammed Reza Pahlavi (pah•luh•vee), embraced Western governments and wealthy Western oil companies. Iranian nationalists resented these foreign alliances and united under Prime Minister Muhammed Mossadeq (moh•sah•DEHK). They nationalized a British-owned oil company and, in 1953, forced the shah to flee. Fearing Iran might turn to the Soviets for support, the United States helped restore the shah to power. **C**

MAIN IDEA

Analyzing Motives
C Why did the United States support the shah of Iran?

The United States Supports Secular Rule With U.S. support, the shah westernized his country. By the end of the 1950s, Iran's capital, Tehran, featured gleaming skyscrapers, foreign banks, and modern factories. Millions of Iranians, however, still lived in extreme poverty. The shah tried to weaken the political influence of Iran's conservative Muslim leaders, known as ayatollahs (eye•uh• TOH•luhz), who opposed Western influences. The leader of this religious opposition, **Ayatollah Ruholla Khomeini** (koh• MAY•nee), was living in exile. Spurred by his tape-recorded messages, Iranians rioted in every major city in late 1978. Faced with overwhelming opposition, the shah fled Iran in 1979. A triumphant Khomeini returned to establish an Islamic state and to export Iran's militant form of Islam.

Khomeini's Anti-U.S. Policies Strict adherence to Islam ruled Khomeini's domestic policies. But hatred of the United States, because of U.S. support for the shah, was at the heart of his foreign policy. In 1979, with the ayatollah's blessing, young Islamic revolutionaries seized the U.S. embassy in Tehran. They took more than 60 Americans hostage and demanded the United States force the shah to face trial. Most hostages remained prisoners for 444 days before being released in 1981.

Khomeini encouraged Muslim radicals elsewhere to overthrow their secular governments. Intended to unify Muslims, this policy heightened tensions between Iran and its neighbor and territorial rival, Iraq. A military leader, Saddam Hussein (hoo•SAYN), governed Iraq as a secular state.

▼ Ayatollah Khomeini (inset) supported the taking of U.S. hostages by Islamic militants in Tehran in 1979.

War broke out between Iran and Iraq in 1980. The United States secretly gave aid to both sides because it did not want the balance of power in the region to change. The Soviet Union, on the other hand, had long been a supporter of Iraq. A million Iranians and Iraqis died in the war before the UN negotiated a ceasefire in 1988.

The Superpowers Face Off in Afghanistan For several years following World War II, Afghanistan maintained its independence from both the neighboring Soviet Union and the United States. In the 1950s, however, Soviet influence in the country began to increase. In the late 1970s, a Muslim revolt threatened to topple Afghanistan's Communist regime. This revolt led to a Soviet invasion in 1979.

The Soviets expected to prop up the Afghan Communists and quickly withdraw. Instead, just like the United States in Vietnam, the Soviets found themselves stuck. And like the Vietcong in Vietnam, rebel forces outmaneuvered a military superpower. Supplied with American weapons, the Afgan rebels, called mujahideen, or holy warriors, fought on. **D**

The United States had armed the rebels because they considered the Soviet invasion a threat to Middle Eastern oil supplies. President Jimmy Carter warned the Soviets against any attempt to gain control of the Persian Gulf. To protest the invasion, he stopped U.S. grain shipments to the Soviet Union and ordered a U.S. boycott of the 1980 Moscow Olympics. In the 1980s, a new Soviet president, Mikhail Gorbachev, acknowledged the war's devastating costs. He withdrew all Soviet troops by 1989. By then, internal unrest and economic problems were tearing apart the Soviet Union itself.

MAIN IDEA

Comparing

D In what ways were U.S. involvement in Vietnam and Soviet involvement in Afghanistan similar?

Connect to Today

The Taliban

Islamic religious students, or taliban, were among the *mujahideen* rebels who fought the Soviet occupation of Afghanistan. Various groups of students loosely organized themselves during a civil war among *mujahideen* factions that followed the Soviet withdrawal in 1989.

In 1996, one of these groups, called the Taliban, seized power and established an Islamic government. At first, they were popular among many Afghans. But they imposed a repressive rule especially harsh on women, and failed to improve the lives of the people. They also gave sanctuary to international Islamic terrorists. In 2001, an anti-terrorist coalition led by the United States drove them from power.

SECTION 4 **ASSESSMENT**

TERMS & NAMES 1. For each term or name, write a sentence explaining its significance.
• Third World • nonaligned nations • Fidel Castro • Anastasio Somoza • Daniel Ortega • Ayatollah Ruholla Khomeini

USING YOUR NOTES	MAIN IDEAS	CRITICAL THINKING & WRITING
2. Which confrontation had the most lasting significance?	3. How was the Cuban Missile Crisis resolved?	6. **MAKING INFERENCES** What advantages and disadvantages might being nonaligned have offered a developing nation during the Cold War?
	4. What was significant about the 1990 elections in Nicaragua?	7. **COMPARING** What similarities do you see among U.S. actions in Nicaragua, Cuba, and Iran?
	5. Why did the Soviet Union invade Afghanistan?	8. **ANALYZING CAUSES** What were the reasons that Islamic fundamentalists took control of Iran?
		9. **WRITING ACTIVITY** REVOLUTION For either Cuba, Nicaragua, or Iran, write an annotated **time line** of events discussed in this section.

USING YOUR NOTES table:

Country	Conflict
Cuba	
Nicaragua	
Iran	

CONNECT TO TODAY WRITING AN OPINION PAPER

Research the effects of the U.S. trade embargo on Cuba. Write a two-paragraph **opinion paper** on whether it would be in the best interests of the United States to lift that embargo.

The Cold War Thaws

MAIN IDEA	WHY IT MATTERS NOW	TERMS & NAMES
EMPIRE BUILDING The Cold War began to thaw as the superpowers entered an era of uneasy diplomacy.	The United States and the countries of the former Soviet Union continue to cooperate and maintain a cautious peace.	• Nikita Khrushchev • détente • Leonid Brezhnev • Richard M. Nixon • John F. Kennedy • SALT • Lyndon Johnson • Ronald Reagan

SETTING THE STAGE In the postwar years, the Soviet Union kept a firm grip on its satellite countries in Eastern Europe. These countries were Poland, Czechoslovakia, Hungary, Romania, Bulgaria, Albania, and East Germany. (Yugoslavia had broken away from Soviet control in 1948, although it remained Communist.) The Soviet Union did not allow them to direct and develop their own economies. Instead, it insisted that they develop industries to meet Soviet needs. These policies greatly hampered Eastern Europe's economic recovery.

TAKING NOTES

Outlining Organize main ideas and details about the Cold War thaw.

```
I. Soviet Policy in
   Eastern Europe
   and China
   A.
   B.
II. From Brinkmanship
    to Détente
```

Soviet Policy in Eastern Europe and China

More moderate Soviet leaders came to power after Stalin's death. They allowed satellite countries somewhat more independence, as long as they remained allied with the Soviet Union. During the 1950s and 1960s, however, growing protest movements in Eastern Europe threatened the Soviet grip on the region. Increasing tensions with China also diverted Soviet attention and forces.

Destalinization and Rumblings of Protest After Stalin died in 1953, **Nikita Khrushchev** became the dominant Soviet leader. In 1956, the shrewd, tough Khrushchev denounced Stalin for jailing and killing loyal Soviet citizens. His speech signaled the start of a policy called destalinization, or purging the country of Stalin's memory. Workers destroyed monuments of the former dictator. Khrushchev called for "peaceful competition" with capitalist states.

But this new Soviet outlook did not change life in satellite countries. Their resentment at times turned to active protest. In October 1956, for example, the Hungarian army joined protesters to overthrow Hungary's Soviet-controlled government. Storming through the capital, Budapest, mobs waved Hungarian flags with the Communist hammer-and-sickle emblem cut out. "From the youngest child to the oldest man," one protester declared, "no one wants communism."

A popular and liberal Hungarian Communist leader named Imre Nagy (IHM•ray nahj) formed a new government. Nagy promised free elections and demanded Soviet troops leave. In response, Soviet tanks and infantry entered Budapest in November. Thousands of Hungarian freedom fighters armed themselves with pistols and bottles, but were overwhelmed. A pro-Soviet government was installed, and Nagy was eventually executed.

History Makers

Imre Nagy (1896–1958)

Imre Nagy was born into a peasant family in Hungary. During World War I, he was captured by the Soviets and recruited into their army. He then became a Communist.

Nagy held several posts in his country's Communist government, but his loyalty remained with the peasants. Because of his independent approach, he fell in and out of favor with the Soviet Union. In October 1956, he led an anti-Soviet revolt. After the Soviets forcefully put down the uprising, they tried and executed him.

In 1989, after Communists lost control of Hungary's government, Nagy was reburied with official honors.

▲ Czech demonstrators fight Soviet tanks in 1968.

Alexander Dubček (1921–1992)

Alexander Dubček was the son of a Czech Communist Party member. He moved rapidly up through its ranks, becoming party leader in 1968.

Responding to the spirit of change in the 1960s, Dubček instituted broad reforms during the so-called Prague Spring of 1968. The Soviet Union reacted by sending tanks into Prague to suppress a feared revolt. The Soviets expelled Dubček from the party. He regained political prominence in 1989, when the Communists agreed to share power in a coalition government. When Czechoslovakia split into two nations in 1992, Dubček became head of the Social Democratic Party in Slovakia.

The Revolt in Czechoslovakia Despite the show of force in Hungary, Khrushchev lost prestige in his country as a result of the Cuban Missile Crisis in 1962. In 1964, party leaders voted to remove him from power. His replacement, **Leonid Brezhnev**, quickly adopted repressive domestic policies. The party enforced laws to limit such basic human rights as freedom of speech and worship. Government censors controlled what writers could publish. Brezhnev clamped down on those who dared to protest his policies. For example, the secret police arrested many dissidents, including Aleksandr Solzhenitsyn, winner of the 1970 Nobel Prize for literature. They then expelled him from the Soviet Union. **A**

Brezhnev made clear that he would not tolerate dissent in Eastern Europe either. His policy was put to the test in early 1968. At that time, Czech Communist leader Alexander Dubček (DOOB•chehk) loosened controls on censorship to offer his country socialism with "a human face." This period of reform, when Czechoslovakia's capital bloomed with new ideas, became known as Prague Spring. However, it did not survive the summer. On August 20, armed forces from the Warsaw Pact nations invaded Czechoslovakia. Brezhnev justified this invasion by claiming the Soviet Union had the right to prevent its satellites from rejecting communism, a policy known as the Brezhnev Doctrine.

The Soviet-Chinese Split While many satellite countries resisted Communist rule, China was committed to communism. In fact, to cement the ties between Communist powers, Mao and Stalin had signed a 30-year treaty of friendship in 1950. Their spirit of cooperation, however, ran out before the treaty did.

The Soviets assumed the Chinese would follow Soviet leadership in world affairs. As the Chinese grew more confident, however, they resented being in Moscow's shadow. They began to spread their own brand of communism in Africa and other

MAIN IDEA

Analyzing Issues

A Why was Nikita Khruschev removed from power in 1964?

Reconstructing the Postwar World **555**

parts of Asia. In 1959, Khrushchev punished the Chinese by refusing to share nuclear secrets. The following year, the Soviets ended technical economic aid. The Soviet-Chinese split grew so wide that fighting broke out along their common border. After repeated incidents, the two neighbors maintained a fragile peace.

From Brinkmanship to Détente

In the 1970s, the United States and the Soviet Union finally backed away from the aggressive policies of brinkmanship that they had followed during the early postwar years. The superpowers slowly moved to lower tensions.

Brinkmanship Breaks Down The brinkmanship policy followed during the presidencies of Eisenhower, Kennedy, and Johnson led to one terrifying crisis after another. Though these crises erupted all over the world, they were united by a common fear. Nuclear war seemed possible.

In 1960, the U-2 incident prevented a meeting between the United States and the Soviet Union to discuss the buildup of arms on both sides. Then, during the administration of **John F. Kennedy** in the early 1960s, the Cuban Missile Crisis made the superpowers' use of nuclear weapons a real possibility. (See page 551.) The crisis ended when Soviet ships turned back to avoid a confrontation at sea. "We're eyeball to eyeball," the relieved U.S. Secretary of State Dean Rusk said, "and I think the other fellow just blinked." But Kennedy's secretary of defense, Robert McNamara, admitted how close the world had come to disaster:

PRIMARY SOURCE Ⓑ
In the face of an air attack [on Cuba] and in the face of the probability of a ground attack, it was certainly possible, and I would say probable, that a Cuban sergeant or Soviet officer in a missile silo, without authority from Moscow, would have launched one or more of those intermediate-range missiles, equipped with a nuclear warhead, against one or more of the cities on the East Coast of the United States.

ROBERT MCNAMARA, quoted in *Inside the Cold War*

MAIN IDEA
Analyzing Primary Sources
Ⓑ Do you think that Robert McNamara's view of the Soviet threat in Cuba was justified? Explain.

Tensions remained high. After the assassination of Kennedy in 1963, **Lyndon Johnson** assumed the presidency. Committed to stopping the spread of communism, President Johnson escalated U.S. involvement in the war in Vietnam.

The United States Turns to Détente Widespread popular protests wracked the United States during the Vietnam War. And the turmoil did not end with U.S. withdrawal. As it tried to heal its internal wounds, the United States backed away from its policy of direct confrontation with the Soviet Union. **Détente**, a policy of lessening Cold War tensions, replaced brinkmanship under **Richard M. Nixon**.

Vocabulary
Détente is a French word meaning "a loosening."

President Nixon's move toward détente grew out of a philosophy known as realpolitik. This term comes from the German word meaning "realistic politics." In practice, realpolitik meant dealing with other nations in a practical and flexible manner. While the United States continued to try to contain the spread of communism, the two superpowers agreed to pursue détente and to reduce tensions.

Nixon Visits Communist Powers Nixon's new policy represented a personal reversal as well as a political shift for the country. His rise in politics in the 1950s was largely due to his strong anti-Communist position. Twenty years later, he became the first U.S. president to visit Communist China. The visit made sense in a world in which three, not just two,

▼ U.S. president Nixon visits China in 1972, accompanied by Chinese premier Zhou Enlai (left).

superpowers eyed each other suspiciously. "We want the Chinese with us when we sit down and negotiate with the Russians," Nixon explained.

Three months after visiting Beijing in February 1972, Nixon visited the Soviet Union. After a series of meetings called the Strategic Arms Limitation Talks (**SALT**), Nixon and Brezhnev signed the SALT I Treaty. This five-year agreement, limited to 1972 levels the number of intercontinental ballistic and submarine-launched missiles each country could have. In 1975, 33 nations joined the United States and the Soviet Union in signing a commitment to détente and cooperation, the Helsinki Accords.

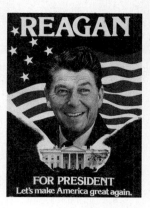

The Collapse of Détente

Under presidents Nixon and Gerald Ford, the United States improved relations with China and the Soviet Union. In the late 1970s, however, President Jimmy Carter was concerned over harsh treatment of protesters in the Soviet Union. This threatened to prevent a second round of SALT negotiations. In 1979, Carter and Brezhnev finally signed the SALT II agreement. When the Soviets invaded Afghanistan later that year, however, the U.S. Congress refused to ratify SALT II. Concerns mounted as more nations, including China and India, began building nuclear arsenals.

▲ Ronald Reagan's 1980 political poster highlights the strong patriotic theme of his campaign.

Reagan Takes an Anti-Communist Stance A fiercely anti-Communist U.S. president, <u>Ronald Reagan</u>, took office in 1981. He continued to move away from détente. He increased defense spending, putting both economic and military pressure on the Soviets. In 1983, Reagan also announced the Strategic Defense Initiative (SDI), a program to protect against enemy missiles. It was not put into effect but remained a symbol of U.S. anti-Communist sentiment. **C**

MAIN IDEA

Contrasting
C In what ways did Nixon's and Reagan's policies toward the Soviet Union differ?

Tensions increased as U.S. activities such as arming Nicaragua's Contras pushed the United States and Soviet Union further from détente. However, a change in Soviet leadership in 1985 brought a new policy toward the United States and the beginnings of a final thaw in the Cold War. Meanwhile, as you will learn in the next chapter, developing countries continued their own struggles for independence.

SECTION 5 ASSESSMENT

TERMS & NAMES 1. For each term or name, write a sentence explaining its significance.
• Nikita Khrushchev • Leonid Brezhnev • John F. Kennedy • Lyndon Johnson • détente • Richard M. Nixon • SALT • Ronald Reagan

USING YOUR NOTES	**MAIN IDEAS**	**CRITICAL THINKING & WRITING**

2. What do you consider the most significant reason for the collapse of détente?
 	
I. Soviet Policy in Eastern Europe and China
  A.
  B.
II. From Brinkmanship to Détente
	3. What effects did destalinization have on Soviet satellite countries?
	
	4. What changes did Alexander Dubček seek to make in Czechoslovakia in 1968, and what happened?
	
	5. Why was the policy of brinkmanship replaced?
		6. **DEVELOPING HISTORICAL PERSPECTIVE** In view of Soviet policies toward Eastern Europe in the postwar era, what reasons did people in Eastern Europe have for resistance?
		
		7. **EVALUATING DECISIONS** Do you think it was a wise political move for Nixon to visit Communist China and the Soviet Union? Why or why not?
		
		8. **RECOGNIZING EFFECTS** What was the result of Reagan's move away from détente?
		
		9. **WRITING ACTIVITY** REVOLUTION Write a short **poem** or **song lyrics** expressing protest against Communist rule by a citizen of a country behind the Iron Curtain.

CONNECT TO TODAY WRITING A SUMMARY
Look through a major newspaper or newsmagazine for articles on Eastern European countries. Then, write a brief **summary** of recent developments there.

Chapter 17 Assessment

TERMS & NAMES

For each term or name below, briefly explain its connection to the restructuring of the postwar world since 1945.

1. containment
2. Cold War
3. Mao Zedong
4. Cultural Revolution
5. 38th parallel
6. Vietnamization
7. Fidel Castro
8. Nikita Khrushchev
9. détente
10. SALT

MAIN IDEAS

Cold War: Superpowers Face Off
Section 1 (pages 531–537)

11. Why did some Americans oppose the Truman Doctrine?
12. How did the Soviet Union respond to the U.S. policy of brinkmanship?

Communists Take Power in China
Section 2 (pages 538–541)

13. Who did the superpowers support in the Chinese civil war?
14. What were the results of Mao Zedong's Great Leap Forward and Cultural Revolution?

Wars in Korea and Vietnam Section 3 (pages 542–547)

15. What effects did the Korean War have on Korea's land and its people?
16. What difficulties did the U.S. Army face fighting the war in Vietnam?

The Cold War Divides the World
Section 4 (pages 548–553)

17. Why did developing nations often align themselves with one or the other superpower?
18. How did the Soviet Union respond to the Bay of Pigs?

The Cold War Thaws Section 5 (pages 554–557)

19. In what ways did Soviet actions hamper Eastern Europe's economic recovery after World War II?
20. What policies characterized realpolitik?

CRITICAL THINKING

1. **USING YOUR NOTES**
Use a diagram to show superpower Cold War tactics.

Cold War Tactics

2. **COMPARING**
EMPIRE BUILDING In what ways were the United States and the Soviet Union more similar than different?

3. **HYPOTHESIZING**
ECONOMICS How might the Cold War have proceeded if the United States had been economically and physically damaged in World War II?

4. **DRAWING CONCLUSIONS**
REVOLUTION Which two Cold War events do you think had the greatest impact on the U.S. decision to pursue détente?

5. **MAKING INFERENCES**
Why do you think the United States and the Soviet Union chose cooperation in space after years of competition?

VISUAL SUMMARY

Cold War, 1946–1980

United States

- **1946** Institutes containment policy
- **1948** Begins Marshall Plan
- **1952** Tests first H-bomb
- **1953** Adopts brinkmanship policy
- **1965** Sends troops to Vietnam

1945 — 1950 — 1955 — 1960 — 1965 — 1970 — 1975 — 1980

- **1948** U.S. and Britain fly airlift to break Soviet blockade of Berlin
- **1950** Communist North Korea attacks South Korea
- **1960** U-2 incident reignites superpower tension
- **1962** U.S. blockades Cuba in response to buildup of Soviet missiles
- **1972** Nixon and Brezhnev sign SALT I treaty
- **1980** U.S. boycotts Moscow Olympics to protest Soviet invasion of Afghanistan

1945 — 1950 — 1955 — 1960 — 1965 — 1970 — 1975 — 1980

- **1950** Signs friendship treaty with China
- **1953** Tests first H-bomb
- **1957** Launches *Sputnik*, starting space race
- **1956** Puts down Hungarian revolt
- **1968** Sends tanks into Prague
- **1979** Invades Afghanistan

Soviet Union

Use the quotation and your knowledge of world history to answer questions 1 and 2.
Additional Test Practice, pp. S1-S33

The following poem by Ho Chi Minh was broadcast over Hanoi Radio on January 1, 1968.

PRIMARY SOURCE

This Spring far outshines the previous Springs,
Of victories throughout the land come happy tidings.
South and North, rushing heroically together, shall
smite the American invaders!
Go Forward!
Total victory shall be ours.

HO CHI MINH, quoted in *America and Vietnam*

1. In Ho's opinion, who was the enemy in the Vietnam War?
   A. the South Vietnamese
   B. the changing seasons
   C. the United States
   D. the French

2. What purpose might the North Vietnamese have had in broadcasting this poem?
   A. to show that their political leader was also a poet
   B. to warn the United States that it would be defeated
   C. to single out the North Vietnamese people for special attention
   D. to be used as propaganda to show that North and South were fighting together

Use the chart and your knowledge of world history to answer question 3.

U.S.	U.S.–Soviet Military Power, 1986–1987	Soviet
1,010	Intercontinental ballistic missiles	1,398
640	Submarine-launched missiles	983
260	Long-range bombers	160
24,700	Nuclear warheads	36,800
0	Antiballistic missile launchers	100
14	Aircraft carriers	5
2,143,955	Armed forces personnel	5,130,000

Sources: *The Military Balance 1986–1987; Nuclear Weapons Databook, Vol. IV, Soviet Nuclear Weapons*

3. The chart clearly shows that
   A. the United States had more troops than the Soviet Union.
   B. the Soviet Union had clear superiority in the number of ballistic missiles.
   C. the United States and the Soviet Union were equal in nuclear warheads.
   D. the Soviet Union had more aircraft carriers.

INTEGRATED TECHNOLOGY

TEST PRACTICE Go to **classzone.com**
• Diagnostic tests   • Strategies
• Tutorials   • Additional practice

ALTERNATIVE ASSESSMENT

1. Interact *with* History

On page 530, you considered what policies a nation might follow to gain allies. Now that you have learned more about the Cold War, would your decision change? Discuss your ideas with a small group.

2. WRITING ABOUT HISTORY

Study the information in the infographic on how the Cold War was fought on page 549. Write a two-paragraph **persuasive essay** on which means was the most successful for the United States and which was most successful for the Soviet Union.

Consider the following:
• who received foreign aid
• whether propaganda was successful
• how strong the military alliances were
• what was gained in surrogate wars

INTEGRATED TECHNOLOGY

Creating an Interactive Time Line

In October 1962, President John F. Kennedy and his advisers had to defuse a potentially devastating nuclear standoff with the Soviet Union. Using books, the Internet, and other resources, create an interactive time line of the crisis. Use graphics software to add maps and photographs. In addition to noting key dates, use the time line to address some of the following:
• Who were members of Kennedy's inner circle during the crisis?
• What did Kennedy say about the events in his first public address to the nation?
• How did Soviet premier Nikita Krushchev approach the crisis in Cuba?
• What details did Americans learn only after the crisis had been resolved?

CHAPTER

18

The Colonies Become New Nations, 1945–Present

Previewing Main Ideas

REVOLUTION Independence movements swept Africa and Asia as World War II ended. Through both nonviolent and violent means, revolutionaries overthrew existing political systems to create their own nations.

Geography *Which continent witnessed the greatest number of its countries gain independence?*

POWER AND AUTHORITY Systems of government shifted for one billion people when colonies in Africa and Asia gained their freedom. New nations struggled to unify their diverse populations. In many cases, authoritarian rule and military dictatorships emerged.

Geography *According to the time line, which southeast Asian country dealt with dictatorship in the years following independence?*

ECONOMICS The emergence of new nations from European- and U.S.-ruled colonies brought a change in ownership of vital resources. In many cases, however, new nations struggled to create thriving economies.

Geography *Which colonial power had enjoyed the resources from the greatest number of regions of the world?*

INTEGRATED TECHNOLOGY

eEdition
- Interactive Maps
- Interactive Visuals
- Interactive Primary Sources

INTERNET RESOURCES
Go to **classzone.com** for:
- Research Links   • Maps
- Internet Activities   • Test Practice
- Primary Sources   • Current Events
- Chapter Quiz

COLONIES

1945
Sukarno proclaims Indonesian independence.

1947
India gains independence from Britain.

1957
Ghana wins independence. (first prime minister Kwame Nkrumah) ▶

1945

1965

WORLD

1948
South Africa establishes apartheid system. ("whites only" sign) ▶

1966
Mao Zedong launches Cultural Revolution in China.

New Nations, 1946–1991

Mediterranean Sea

INDIAN OCEAN

ATLANTIC OCEAN

40°N

0° Equator

Former Belgian colony
Former British colony
Former Dutch colony
Former French colony
Former Portuguese colony
Former Soviet Union bloc
Former Spanish colony
Former U.S. colony

N
W   E
S

0   1000   2000 Miles
0   1000   2000 Kilometers
Gall Projection

0°   40°E   80°E

1986
◀ Election of Corazón Aquino ends Marcos dictatorship in Philippines.

1997
Mobutu dictatorship in Zaire falls.

1985

2003

1975
Communist North Vietnam conquers South Vietnam.

1982
Britain defeats Argentina in war over Falkland Islands.

1991
Soviet Union breaks up into 15 republics.

2003
United States drives Saddam Hussein from power in Iraq.

How would you build a new nation?

As a political leader of a former colony, you watch with pride as your country becomes independent. However, you know that difficult days lay ahead. You want peace and prosperity for your nation. To accomplish this, however, you need to create a sound government and a strong economy. In addition, food and adequate health care are scarce and many people receive little education. These and other challenges await your immediate attention.

▼ Agriculture

▼ Health Care

▲ Education

▲ Employment

▲ Voting Rights

EXAMINING *the* ISSUES

- **What are the first steps you would take? Why?**

- **What might be the most difficult challenge to overcome?**

As a class, discuss these questions. Remember what you have learned about what makes a stable and unified nation. As you read about the emergence of new nations around the world, note what setbacks and achievements they make in their effort to build a promising future.

The Indian Subcontinent Achieves Freedom

MAIN IDEA	WHY IT MATTERS NOW	TERMS & NAMES
POWER AND AUTHORITY New nations emerged from the British colony of India.	India today is the largest democracy in the world.	• Congress Party • Muslim League • Muhammad Ali Jinnah • partition • Jawaharlal Nehru • Indira Gandhi • Benazir Bhutto

SETTING THE STAGE After World War II, dramatic political changes began to take place across the world. This was especially the case with regard to the policy of colonialism. Countries that held colonies began to question the practice. After the world struggle against dictatorship, many leaders argued that no country should control another nation. Others questioned the high cost and commitment of holding colonies. Meanwhile, the people of colonized regions continued to press even harder for their freedom. All of this led to independence for one of the largest and most populous colonies in the world: British-held India.

A Movement Toward Independence

The British had ruled India for almost two centuries. Indian resistance to Britain, which had existed from the beginning, intensified in 1939, when Britain committed India's armed forces to World War II without first consulting the colony's elected representatives. The move left Indian nationalists stunned and humiliated. Indian leader Mohandas Gandhi launched a nonviolent campaign of noncooperation with the British. Officials imprisoned numerous nationalists for this action. In 1942, the British tried to gain the support of the nationalists by promising governmental changes after the war. But the offer did not include Indian independence.

As they intensified their struggle against the British, Indians also struggled with each other. India has long been home to two main religious groups. In the 1940s, India had approximately 350 million Hindus and about 100 million Muslims. The Indian National Congress, or the **Congress Party**, was India's national political party. Most members of the Congress Party were Hindus, but the party at times had many Muslim members.

In competition with the Congress Party was the **Muslim League**, an organization founded in 1906 in India to protect Muslim interests. Members of the league felt that the mainly Hindu Congress Party looked out primarily for Hindu interests. The leader of the Muslim League, **Muhammad Ali Jinnah** (mu•HAM•ihd ah•LEE JINH•uh), insisted that all Muslims resign from the Congress Party. The Muslim League stated that it would never accept Indian independence if it meant rule by the Hindu-dominated Congress Party. Jinnah stated, "The only thing the Muslim has in common with the Hindu is his slavery to the British."

TAKING NOTES

Following Chronological Order Create a time line of prominent Indian prime ministers from independence through the current day.

Freedom Brings Turmoil

When World War II ended, Britain found itself faced with enormous war debts. As a result, British leaders began to rethink the expense of maintaining and governing distant colonies. With India continuing to push for independence, the stage was set for the British to hand over power. However, a key problem emerged: Who should receive the power—Hindus or Muslims?

Partition and Bloodshed Muslims resisted attempts to include them in an Indian government dominated by Hindus. Rioting between the two groups broke out in several Indian cities. In August 1946, four days of clashes in Calcutta left more than 5,000 people dead and more than 15,000 hurt.

British officials soon became convinced that partition, an idea first proposed by India's Muslims, would be the only way to ensure a safe and secure region. <u>Partition</u> was the term given to the division of India into separate Hindu and Muslim nations. The northwest and eastern regions of India, where most Muslims lived, would become the new nation of Pakistan. (Pakistan, as the map shows, comprised two separate states in 1947: West Pakistan and East Pakistan.)

The British House of Commons passed an act on July 16, 1947, that granted two nations, India and Pakistan, independence in one month's time. In that short period, more than 500 independent native princes had to decide which nation they would join. The administration of the courts, the military, the railways, and the police—the whole of the civil service—had to be divided down to the last paper clip. Most difficult of all, millions of Indian citizens—Hindus, Muslims, and yet another significant religious group, the Sikhs—had to decide where to go.

The Indian Subcontinent, 1947

GEOGRAPHY SKILLBUILDER: Interpreting Maps
1. **Location** Which Muslim country, divided into two states, bordered India on the east and the west?
2. **Location** Which Buddhist countries bordered India to the north and the south?

Mostly Buddhist
Mostly Hindu
Mostly Muslim
Mostly Sikhs
Present day boundaries are shown.

During the summer of 1947, 10 million people were on the move in the Indian subcontinent. As people scrambled to relocate, violence among the different religious groups erupted. Muslims killed Sikhs who were moving into India. Hindus and Sikhs killed Muslims who were headed into Pakistan. The following passage is representative of the experiences of people in both the Hindu and Muslim communities.

PRIMARY SOURCE
All passengers were forced into compartments like sheep and goats. Because of which the heat and suffocating atmosphere was intensified and it was very hard to breathe. In the ladies compartment women and children were in a terrible condition. Women tried in vain to calm down and comfort their children. If you looked out the window you could see dead bodies lying in the distance. At many places you could see corpses piled on top of each other and no one seemed to have any concern. . . . These were the scenes that made your heart bleed and everybody loudly repented their sins and recited verses asking God's forgiveness. Every moment seemed to be the most terrifying and agonizing.

ZAHIDA AMJAD ALI, quoted in *Freedom, Trauma, Continuities*

In all, an estimated 1 million died. "What is there to celebrate?" Gandhi mourned. "I see nothing but rivers of blood." Gandhi personally went to the Indian capital of Delhi to plead for fair treatment of Muslim refugees. While there, he himself became a victim of the nation's violence. A Hindu extremist who thought Gandhi too protective of Muslims shot and killed him on January 30, 1948.

The Battle for Kashmir As if partition itself didn't result in enough bloodshed between India's Muslims and Hindus, the two groups quickly squared off over the small region of Kashmir. Kashmir lay at the northern point of India next to Pakistan. Although its ruler was Hindu, Kashmir had a majority Muslim population. Shortly after independence, India and Pakistan began battling each other for control of the region. The fighting continued until the United Nations arranged a cease-fire in 1949. The cease-fire left a third of Kashmir under Pakistani control and the rest under Indian control. The two countries continue to fight over the region today. Ⓐ

MAIN IDEA
Analyzing Causes
Ⓐ What was the cause of the conflict between India and Pakistan over Kashmir?

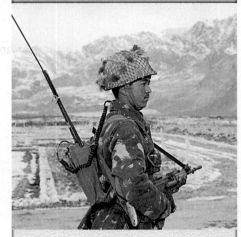

Connect *to* Today

The Coldest War
No part of Kashmir is beyond a fight for India and Pakistan—including the giant Siachen glacier high above the region. The dividing line established by the 1949 cease-fire did not extend to the glacier because officials figured neither side would try to occupy such a barren and frigid strip of land.

They figured wrong. In 1984, both sides sent troops to take the glacier, and they have been dug in ever since. At altitudes nearing 21,000 feet, Indian and Pakistani soldiers shoot at each other from trenches in temperatures that reach 70 degrees below zero. While it is believed that more soldiers have died from the cold than from enemy bullets, neither side will budge.

Modern India

With the granting of its independence on August 15, 1947, India became the world's largest democracy. As the long-awaited hour of India's freedom approached, **Jawaharlal Nehru**, the independent nation's first prime minister, addressed the country's political leaders:

PRIMARY SOURCE
Long years ago, we made a tryst [appointment] with destiny, and now the time comes when we shall redeem our pledge, not wholly or in full measure, but very substantially. At the stroke of the midnight hour, when the world sleeps, India will wake to life and freedom.

JAWAHARLAL NEHRU, speech before the Constituent Assembly, August 14, 1947

Jawaharlal Nehru
1889–1964

Nehru's father was an influential attorney, and so the first prime minister of India grew up amid great wealth. As a young man, he lived and studied in England. "In my likes and dislikes I was perhaps more an Englishman than an Indian," he once remarked.

Upon returning to India, however, he became moved by the horrible state in which many of his fellow Indians lived. "A new picture of India seemed to rise before me," he recalled, "naked, starving, crushed, and utterly miserable." From then on, he devoted his life to improving conditions in his country.

INTEGRATED TECHNOLOGY

RESEARCH LINKS For more on Jawaharlal Nehru, go to **classzone.com**

Nehru Leads India Nehru served as India's leader for its first 17 years of independence. He had been one of Gandhi's most devoted followers. Educated in Britain, Nehru won popularity among all groups in India. He emphasized democracy, unity, and economic modernization.

Nehru used his leadership to move India forward. He led other newly independent nations of the world in forming an alliance of countries that were neutral in the Cold War conflicts between the United States and the Soviet Union. On the home front, Nehru called for a reorganization of the states by language. He also pushed for industrialization and sponsored social reforms. He tried to elevate the status of the lower castes, or those at the bottom of society, and help women gain the rights promised by the constitution.

Troubled Times Nehru died in 1964. His death left the Congress Party with no leader strong enough to hold together the many political factions that had emerged with India's independence. Then, in 1966, Nehru's daughter, **Indira Gandhi**, was chosen prime minister. After a short spell out of office, she was reelected in 1980.

Although she ruled capably, Gandhi faced many challenges, including the growing threat from Sikh extremists who themselves wanted an independent state. The Golden Temple at Amritsar stood as the religious center for the Sikhs. From there, Sikh nationalists ventured out to attack symbols of Indian authority. In June 1984, Indian army troops overran the Golden Temple. They killed about 500 Sikhs and destroyed sacred property. In retaliation, Sikh bodyguards assigned to Indira Gandhi gunned her down. This violent act set off another murderous frenzy, causing the deaths of thousands of Sikhs.

In the wake of the murder of Indira Gandhi, her son, Rajiv (rah•JEEV) Gandhi, took over as prime minister. His party, however, lost its power in 1989 because of accusations of widespread corruption. In 1991, while campaigning again for prime minister near the town of Madras, Rajiv was killed by a bomb. Members of a group opposed to his policies claimed responsibility.

Twenty-First Century Challenges Since winning election as prime minister in 1998, Atal Bihari Vajpayee, leader of the Hindu nationalist party, has ruled over a vibrant but often unstable nation. He faces challenges brought on by an increasing population that is expected to push India past China as the world's most populous nation by 2035. In addition, the country is racked with social inequality and constantly threatened by religious strife.

Even more troubling are India's tense relations with its neighbor Pakistan, and the fact that both have become nuclear powers. In 1974, India exploded a "peaceful" nuclear device. For the next 24 years, the nation quietly worked on building up its nuclear capability. In 1998, Indian officials conducted five underground nuclear tests. Meanwhile, the Pakistanis had been building their own nuclear program. Shortly after India conducted its nuclear tests, Pakistan demonstrated that it, too, had nuclear weapons. The presence of these weapons in the hands of such bitter enemies and neighbors has become a matter of great international concern, especially in light of their continuing struggle over Kashmir:

PRIMARY SOURCE
Now that India and Pakistan have tested nuclear weapons, the dispute over their border region of lush valleys and jagged Himalayan peaks has become a matter of urgent concern. . . . [There is] fear that a remote but savage ethnic and religious conflict could deteriorate into a nuclear exchange with global consequences. India and Pakistan must learn to talk to each other and move toward a more trusting relationship.

The *New York Times,* June 28, 1998

Pakistan Copes with Freedom

The history of Pakistan since independence has been no less turbulent than that of India. Pakistan actually began as two separate and divided states, East Pakistan and West Pakistan. East Pakistan lay to the east of India, West Pakistan to the northwest. These regions were separated by more than 1,000 miles of Indian territory. In culture, language, history, geography, economics, and ethnic background, the two regions were very different. Only the Islamic religion united them.

Civil War From the beginning, the two regions of Pakistan experienced strained relations. While East Pakistan had the larger population, it was often ignored by West Pakistan, home to the central government. In 1970, a giant cyclone and tidal wave struck East Pakistan and killed an estimated 266,000 residents. While international aid poured into Pakistan, the government in West Pakistan did not quickly transfer that aid to East Pakistan. Demonstrations broke out in East Pakistan, and protesters called for an end to all ties with West Pakistan.

On March 26, 1971, East Pakistan declared itself an independent nation called Bangladesh. A civil war followed between Bangladesh and Pakistan. Eventually,

A Turbulent History

Pakistan

1977 Ali Bhutto
Prime Minister Ali Bhutto of Pakistan is deposed in a coup led by General Zia. Bhutto is later hanged for having ordered the assassination of a political opponent.

1988 General Zia
General Zia, president of Pakistan, dies in a mysterious plane crash.

1950   1960   1970   1980   1990

India

1948 Mohandas Gandhi
Gandhi is shot to death by a Hindu extremist. The assassin opposes Gandhi's efforts to achieve equal treatment for all Indians, including Muslims.

1984 Indira Gandhi
Indira Gandhi is gunned down by two of her Sikh bodyguards. Her murder is in retaliation for an attack she ordered on a Sikh temple.

1991 Rajiv Gandhi
Rajiv Gandhi is killed by a bomb while campaigning. The bomb is carried by a woman opposed to Gandhi's policies.

Indian forces stepped in and sided with Bangladesh. About two weeks after the arrival of Indian troops, Pakistan forces surrendered. More than 1 million people died in the war. Pakistan lost about one-seventh of its area and about one-half of its population to Bangladesh. **B**

A Pattern of Instability Pakistan, however, could ill afford to dwell on its lost territory, for there were many problems at home. Muhammad Ali Jinnah, the first governor-general of Pakistan, died shortly after independence. This left the nation without strong leadership. As a result, Pakistan went through a series of military coups, the first in 1958. Ali Bhutto took control of the country following the civil war. A military coup in 1977 led by General Zia removed Bhutto, who was later executed for crimes allegedly committed while in office.

After Zia's death, Bhutto's daughter, **Benazir Bhutto**, was twice elected prime minister. After months of disorder, she was removed from office in 1996. Nawaz Sharif became prime minister after the 1997 elections. In 1999, army leaders ousted Sharif in yet another coup and imposed military rule over Pakistan. The nation continues to struggle with challenges from Muslim militants and ongoing disputes with India, especially over the territory of Kashmir.

Bangladesh and Sri Lanka Struggle

Meanwhile, the newly created nations of Bangladesh and Sri Lanka struggled with enormous problems of their own in the decades following independence.

Bangladesh Faces Many Problems The war with Pakistan had ruined the economy of Bangladesh and fractured its communications system. Rebuilding the shattered country seemed like an overwhelming task. Sheik Mujibur Rahman became the nation's first prime minister. He appeared more interested in strengthening his own power than in rebuilding his nation. He soon took over all authority and declared Bangladesh a one-party state. In August 1975, military leaders assassinated him.

Over the years Bangladesh has attempted with great difficulty to create a more democratic form of government. Charges of election fraud and government corruption are common. In recent years, however, the government has become more stable. The latest elections were held in October of 2001, and Begum Khaleda Zia took over as the nation's prime minister.

In the years following its independence, Bangladesh also has had to cope with crippling natural disasters. Bangladesh is a low-lying nation that is subject to many cyclones and tidal waves. Massive storms regularly flood the land, ruin crops and

MAIN IDEA

Comparing
B How does the history of Pakistan in 1971 parallel the history of India in 1947?

▼ Overcrowded and poor villages are a common sight throughout Bangladesh.

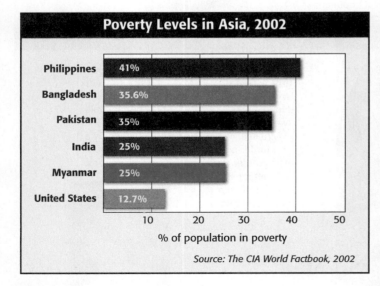

Poverty Levels in Asia, 2002

	% of population in poverty
Philippines	41%
Bangladesh	35.6%
Pakistan	35%
India	25%
Myanmar	25%
United States	12.7%

Source: The CIA World Factbook, 2002

homes, and take lives. A particularly powerful cyclone hit in 1991 and killed approximately 139,000 people. Such catastrophes, along with a rapidly growing population, have put much stress on the country's economy. Bangladesh is one of the poorest nations in the world. The per capita income there is about $360 per year.

Civil Strife Grips Sri Lanka Another newly freed and deeply troubled country on the Indian subcontinent is Sri Lanka, a small, teardrop-shaped island nation just off the southeast coast of India. Formerly known as Ceylon, Sri Lanka gained its independence from Britain in February of 1948. Two main ethnic groups dominate the nation. Three-quarters of the population are Sinhalese, who are Buddhists. A fifth are Tamils, a Hindu people of southern India and northern Sri Lanka.

Sri Lanka's recent history has also been one of turmoil. A militant group of Tamils has long fought an armed struggle for a separate Tamil nation. Since 1981, thousands of lives have been lost. In an effort to end the violence, Rajiv Gandhi and the Sri Lankan president tried to reach an accord in 1987. The agreement called for Indian troops to enter Sri Lanka and help disarm Tamil rebels. This effort was not successful, and the Indian troops left in 1990. A civil war between Tamils and other Sri Lankans continues today.

As difficult as post-independence has been for the countries of the Indian subcontinent, the same can be said for former colonies elsewhere. As you will read in the next section, a number of formerly held territories in Southeast Asia faced challenges as they became independent nations.

▲ This emblem of the separatist group Liberation Tigers of Tamil Eelam represents the struggle for independence of the Tamils.

SECTION 1 ASSESSMENT

TERMS & NAMES 1. For each term or name, write a sentence explaining its significance.
• Congress Party • Muslim League • Muhammad Ali Jinnah • partition • Jawaharlal Nehru • Indira Gandhi • Benazir Bhutto

USING YOUR NOTES

2. What tragic connection did many of the leaders share?

MAIN IDEAS

3. Why did British officials partition India into India and Pakistan?

4. In what way did Pakistan also undergo a partition?

5. What is the main cause today of civil strife in Sri Lanka?

CRITICAL THINKING & WRITING

6. **SYNTHESIZING** Why might India's political and economic success be so crucial to the future of democracy in Asia?

7. **ANALYZING ISSUES** How did religious and cultural differences create problems for newly emerging nations?

8. **DRAWING CONCLUSIONS** Why has the conflict between India and Pakistan over Kashmir become such a concern to the world today?

9. **WRITING ACTIVITY** POWER AND AUTHORITY Write several **paragraphs** detailing the problems shared by leaders of India and Pakistan.

CONNECT TO TODAY CREATING A GRAPHIC

Research the current percentages of religions in India, Pakistan, Bangladesh, or Sri Lanka.
Create a **graphic** of your choosing to illustrate your findings.

Southeast Asian Nations Gain Independence

MAIN IDEA	WHY IT MATTERS NOW	TERMS & NAMES
ECONOMICS Former colonies in Southeast Asia worked to build new governments and economies.	The power and influence of the Pacific Rim nations are likely to expand during the next century.	• Ferdinand Marcos • Corazón Aquino • Aung San Suu Kyi • Sukarno • Suharto

SETTING THE STAGE World War II had a significant impact on the colonized groups of Southeast Asia. During the war, the Japanese seized much of Southeast Asia from the European nations that had controlled the region for many years. The Japanese conquest helped the people of Southeast Asia see that the Europeans were far from invincible. When the war ended, and the Japanese themselves had been forced out, many Southeast Asians refused to live again under European rule. They called for and won their independence, and a series of new nations emerged.

TAKING NOTES

Summarizing Use a chart to summarize the major challenges that Southeast Asian countries faced after independence.

Nation	Challenges Following Independence
The Philippines	
Burma	
Indonesia	

The Philippines Achieves Independence

The Philippines became the first of the world's colonies to achieve independence following World War II. The United States granted the Philippines independence in 1946, on the anniversary of its own Declaration of Independence, the Fourth of July.

The United States and the Philippines The Filipinos' immediate goals were to rebuild the economy and to restore the capital of Manila. The city had been badly damaged in World War II. The United States had promised the Philippines $620 million in war damages. However, the U.S. government insisted that Filipinos approve the Bell Act in order to get the money. This act would establish free trade between the United States and the Philippines for eight years, to be followed by gradually increasing tariffs. Filipinos were worried that American businesses would exploit the resources and environment of the Philippines. In spite of this concern, Filipinos approved the Bell Act and received their money.

The United States also wanted to maintain its military presence in the Philippines. With the onset of the Cold War (see Chapter 17), the United States needed to protect its interests in Asia. Both China and the Soviet Union were rivals of the United States at the time. Both were Pacific powers with bases close to allies of the United States and to resources vital to U.S. interests. Therefore, the United States demanded a 99-year lease on its military and naval bases in the Philippines. The bases, Clark Air Force Base and Subic Bay Naval Base near Manila, proved to be critical to the United States later in the staging of the Korean and Vietnam wars.

CHINA

INDIA

BANGLADESH

BURMA
1948

LAOS
1954
Vientiane

NORTH
VIETNAM
1954

Hanoi

Rangoon

THAILAND

South
China
Sea

PHILIPPINES
1946

Bangkok

CAMBODIA
1954
Phnom
Penh

SOUTH
VIETNAM
1954

Saigon

Manila

INDIAN
OCEAN

MALAYSIA
1957

BRUNEI
(Br.)

Kuala Lumpur

PACIFIC
OCEAN

Singapore
1965

BORNEO

0° Equator

I N D O N E S I A
1949

Jakarta

EAST TIMOR
(Port.)

Former British colony
Former Dutch colony
Former French colony
Former U.S. colony
Continuously independent
1945 Date of independence

N

0   1,000 Miles
0   2,000 Kilometers

GEOGRAPHY SKILLBUILDER: Interpreting Maps
1. **Location** *Which former Dutch colony is made up of a series of islands spread out from the Indian Ocean to the Pacific Ocean?*
2. **Region** *From what European country did the most colonies shown above gain their independence?*

MAIN IDEA

Making Inferences

A Why might the United States have been interested in maintaining military bases in the Philippines?

These military bases also became the single greatest source of conflict between the United States and the Philippines. Many Filipinos regarded the bases as proof of American imperialism. Later agreements shortened the terms of the lease, and the United States gave up both bases in 1992. **A**

After World War II, the Philippine government was still almost completely dependent on the United States economically and politically. The Philippine government looked for ways to lessen this dependency. It welcomed Japanese investments. It also broadened its contacts with Southeast Asian neighbors and with nonaligned nations.

From Marcos to Ramos <u>Ferdinand Marcos</u> was elected president of the Philippines in 1965. The country suffered under his rule from 1966 to 1986. Marcos imposed an authoritarian regime and stole millions of dollars from the public treasury. Although the constitution limited Marcos to eight years in office, he got around this restriction by imposing martial law from 1972 to 1981. Two years later, his chief opponent, Benigno Aquino, Jr., was assassinated as he returned from the United States to the Philippines, lured by the promise of coming elections.

In the elections of 1986, Aquino's widow, **Corazón Aquino**, challenged Marcos. Aquino won decisively, but Marcos refused to acknowledge her victory. When he declared himself the official winner, a public outcry resulted. He was forced into exile in Hawaii, where he later died. In 1995, the Philippines succeeded in recovering $475 million Marcos had stolen from his country and deposited in Swiss banks.

The Colonies Become New Nations **571**

As she took the oath of office, Aquino promised to usher in a more open and democratic form of government.

PRIMARY SOURCE
I pledge a government dedicated to upholding truth and justice, morality and decency in government, freedom and democracy. I ask our people not to relax, but to maintain more vigilance in this, our moment of triumph. The Motherland can't thank them enough, yet we all realize that more is required of each of us to achieve a truly just society for our people. This is just the beginning.

CORAZÓN AQUINO, inaugural speech, Feb. 24, 1986

During Aquino's presidency, the Philippine government ratified a new constitution. It also negotiated successfully with the United States to end the lease on the U.S. military bases. In 1992, Fidel V. Ramos succeeded Aquino as president. Ramos was restricted by the constitution to a single six-year term. The single-term limit is intended to prevent the abuse of power that occurred during Marcos's 20-year rule.

The Government Battles Rebels Since gaining its independence, the Philippines has had to battle its own separatist group. For centuries, the southern part of the country has been a stronghold of Muslims known as the Moros. In the early 1970s, a group of Moros formed the Moro National Liberation Front (MNLF). They began an armed struggle for independence from Philippine rule.

In 1996, the government and rebels agreed to a cease-fire, and the Moros were granted an autonomous region in the southern Philippines. The agreement, however, did not satisfy a splinter group of the MNLF called Abu Sayyaf. These rebels have continued fighting the government, often using terror tactics to try to achieve their goals. In 2000, they kidnapped 21 people including foreign tourists. While the group eventually was freed, subsequent kidnappings by Abu Sayyaf have resulted in the death of several hostages. The current Philippines president, Gloria Macapagal Arroyo, has launched an all-out military response to this group. The United States has provided military assistance to the government's efforts.

British Colonies Gain Independence

Britain's timetable for granting independence to its Southeast Asian colonies depended on local circumstances. Burma had been pressing for independence from Britain for decades. It became a sovereign republic in 1948. In 1989, Burma was officially named Myanmar (myahn•MAH), its name in the Burmese language.

Burma Experiences Turmoil After gaining freedom, Burma suffered one political upheaval after another. Its people struggled between repressive military governments and pro-democracy forces. Conflict among Communists and ethnic minorities also disrupted the nation. In 1962, General Ne Win set up a military government, with the goal of making Burma a socialist state. Although Ne Win stepped down in 1988, the military continued to rule repressively.

In 1988, __Aung San Suu Kyi__ (owng sahn soo chee) returned to Burma after many years abroad. She is the

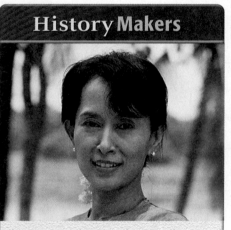

History Makers

Aung San Suu Kyi
1945–

Aung San Suu Kyi won the Nobel Peace Prize in 1991 for her efforts to establish democracy in Myanmar. She could not accept the award in person, however, because she was still under house arrest.

The Nobel Prize committee said that in awarding her the peace prize, it intended:

to show its support for the many people throughout the world who are striving to attain democracy, human rights, and ethnic conciliation by peaceful means. Suu Kyi's struggle is one of the most extraordinary examples of civil courage in Asia in recent decades.

daughter of Aung San, a leader of the Burmese nationalists' army killed years before by political rivals. Aung San Suu Kyi became active in the newly formed National League for Democracy. For her pro-democracy activities, she was placed under house arrest for six years by the government. In the 1990 election—the country's first multiparty election in 30 years—the National League for Democracy won 80 percent of the seats. The military government refused to recognize the election, and it kept Aung San Suu Kyi under house arrest. She was finally released in 1995, only to be placed under house arrest again in 2000. Freed in 2002, she was detained again in 2003, leaving many residents to doubt whether Burma will embrace democracy anytime soon.

Vocabulary
House arrest is confinement to one's quarters, or house, rather than to prison.

Malaysia and Singapore During World War II, the Japanese conquered the Malay Peninsula, formerly ruled by the British. The British returned to the peninsula after the Japanese defeat in 1945. They tried, unsuccessfully, to organize the different peoples of Malaya into one state. They also struggled to put down a Communist uprising. Ethnic groups resisted British efforts to unite their colonies on the peninsula and in the northern part of the island of Borneo. Malays were a slight majority on the peninsula, while Chinese were the largest group on the southern tip, the island of Singapore.

In 1957, officials created the Federation of Malaya from Singapore, Malaya, Sarawak, and Sabah. The two regions—on the Malay Peninsula and on northern Borneo—were separated by 400 miles of ocean. In 1965, Singapore separated from the federation and became an independent city-state. The federation, consisting of Malaya, Sarawak, and Sabah, became known as Malaysia. A coalition of many ethnic groups maintained steady economic progress in Malaysia.

MAIN IDEA

Making Inferences
B What do the top economies listed by the Geneva World Economic Forum have in common?

Singapore, which has one of the busiest ports in the world, has become an extremely prosperous nation. Lee Kuan Yew ruled Singapore as prime minister from 1959 to 1990. Under his guidance, Singapore emerged as a banking center as well as a center of trade. It had a standard of living far higher than any of its Southeast Asian neighbors. In 1997, the Geneva World Economic Forum listed the world's strongest economies. Singapore topped the list. It was followed, in order, by Hong Kong, the United States, Canada, New Zealand, Switzerland, and Great Britain. **B**

▼ A glittering skyline rises above the bustling harbor of Singapore.

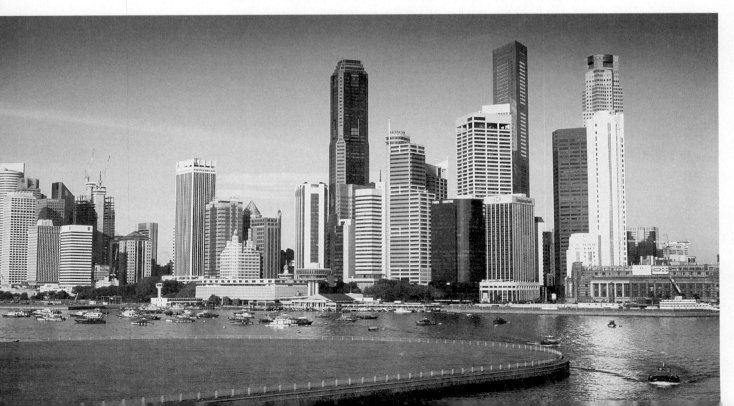

Indonesia Gains Independence from the Dutch

Like members of other European nations, the Dutch, who ruled the area of Southeast Asia known as Indonesia, saw their colonial empire crumble with the onset of World War II. The Japanese conquered the region and destroyed the Dutch colonial order. When the war ended and the defeated Japanese were forced to leave, the people of Indonesia moved to establish a free nation.

Sukarno Leads the Independence Movement Leading the effort to establish an independent Indonesia was **Sukarno** (soo•KAHR•noh), known only by his one name. In August 1945, two days after the Japanese surrendered, Sukarno proclaimed Indonesia's independence and named himself president. A guerrilla army backed him. The Dutch, supported initially by Britain and the United States, attempted to regain control of Indonesia. But after losing the support of the United Nations and the United States, the Dutch agreed to grant Indonesia its independence in 1949.

The new Indonesia became the world's fourth most populous nation. It consisted of more than 13,600 islands, with 300 different ethnic groups, 250 languages, and most of the world's major religions. It contained the world's largest Islamic population. Sukarno, who took the official title of "life-time president," attempted to guide this diverse nation in a parliamentary democracy.

Instability and Turmoil Sukarno's efforts to build a stable democratic nation were unsuccessful. He was not able to manage Indonesia's economy, and the country slid downhill rapidly. Foreign banks refused to lend money to Indonesia and inflation occasionally soared as high as one thousand percent. In 1965, a group of junior army officers attempted a coup. A general named **Suharto** (suh•HAHR•toh) put down the rebellion. He then seized power for himself and began a bloodbath in which 500,000 to 1 million Indonesians were killed.

Suharto, officially named president in 1967, turned Indonesia into a police state and imposed frequent periods of martial law. Outside observers heavily criticized him for his annexation of nearby East Timor in 1976 and for human rights violations there. (See the map on page 571.) Suharto's government also showed little tolerance for religious freedoms.

Bribery and corruption became commonplace. The economy improved under Suharto for a while but from 1997 through 1998 the nation suffered one of the worst financial crises in its history. Growing unrest over both government repression and a crippling economic crisis prompted Suharto to step down in 1998. While turmoil continued to grip the country, it moved slowly toward democracy. The daughter of Sukarno, Megawati Sukarnoputri, was elected to the presidency in 2001.

Upon taking office, the new president hailed the virtues of democracy and urged her fellow Indonesians to do what they could to maintain such a form of government:

Vocabulary
A *coup* is the sudden overthrow of a government by a small group of people.

PRIMARY SOURCE ⓒ
Democracy requires sincerity and respect for the rules of the game. Beginning my duty, I urge all groups to sincerely and openly accept the outcome of the democratic process . . . . In my opinion, respect for the people's voice, sincerity in accepting it, and respect for the rules of game are the main pillars of democracy which we will further develop. I urge all Indonesians to look forward to the future and unite to improve the life and our dignity as a nation.

MEGAWATI SUKARNOPUTRI, July 23, 2001

MAIN IDEA

Analyzing Primary Sources
ⓒ What are the cornerstones of democracy, according to Sukarnoputri?

Sukarnoputri faces enormous challenges, including a still-fragile economy, ethnic strife, security problems, and a government still hobbled by corruption.

East Timor Wins Independence As Indonesia worked to overcome its numerous obstacles, it lost control of East Timor. Indonesian forces had ruled the land with brutal force since Suharto seized it in the 1970s. The East Timorese, however, never stopped pushing to regain their freedom. Jose Ramos Horta, an East Timorese independence campaigner, won the 1996 Nobel Peace Prize (along with East Timor's Roman Catholic bishop) for his efforts to gain independence for the region without violence.

In a United Nations-sponsored referendum held in August 1999, the East Timorese voted overwhelmingly for independence. The election angered pro-Indonesian forces in the region. They ignored the referendum results and went on a bloody rampage. They killed hundreds and forced thousands into refugee camps in West Timor, which is a part of Indonesia. UN intervention forces eventually brought peace to the area. In 2002 East Timor celebrated independence.

As on the Indian subcontinent, violence and struggle were part of the transition in Southeast Asia from colonies to free nations. The same would be true in Africa, where numerous former colonies shed European rule and created independent countries in the wake of World War II.

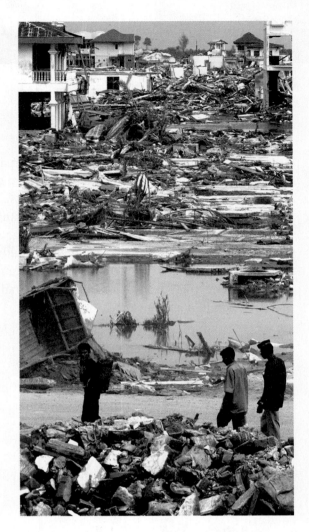

▲ An earthquake off the coast of Indonesia on December 26, 2004, triggered a devastating tsunami. The tidal waves and floods killed more than 150,000 people.

SECTION 2 ASSESSMENT

TERMS & NAMES 1. For each term or name, write a sentence explaining its significance.
• Ferdinand Marcos   • Corazón Aquino   • Aung San Suu Kyi   • Sukarno   • Suharto

USING YOUR NOTES
2. Which nation faced the greatest challenges? Why?

Nation	Challenges Following Independence
The Philippines	
Burma	
Indonesia	

MAIN IDEAS
3. Why did the retention of U.S. military bases in the Philippines so anger Filipinos?

4. What was the outcome of the 1990 Myanmar election? How did the government respond?

5. How did Suharto come to power in Indonesia?

CRITICAL THINKING & WRITING
6. **CLARIFYING** How did World War II play a role in the eventual decolonization of Southeast Asia?

7. **MAKING INFERENCES** Why do you think that the United States demanded a 99-year lease on military and naval bases in the Philippines?

8. **COMPARING AND CONTRASTING** What was similar and different about the elections that brought defeat to the ruling governments in the Philippines and in Burma?

9. **WRITING ACTIVITY** ECONOMICS Write a two-paragraph **expository essay** contrasting Singapore's economy with others in Southeast Asia.

CONNECT TO TODAY CREATING A TELEVISION NEWS SCRIPT

Locate several of the most recent news articles about one of the countries discussed in this section. Combine the stories into a brief television **news script** and present it to the class.

Changing Times in Southeast Asia

As you have read, many countries in Southeast Asia have undergone revolutionary changes in their political and social organization. The region continues to struggle with its past and to face new challenges, but democratic reforms are becoming more common.

The past and present exist side by side throughout much of Southeast Asia. For an increasing number of Southeast Asians, housing, transportation, even purchasing food are a mixture of old and new. These images explore the differences between traditional and modern, rich and poor, past and present.

INTEGRATED / TECHNOLOGY

RESEARCH LINKS For more on life in Southeast Asia, go to **classzone.com**

▲▼ Transportation
The water buffalo-drawn cart (shown above) is a common sight in rural Thailand. It is a mode of transport that reaches deep into the past.

In Bangkok, Thailand (shown below)—with its cars, motorcycles, and public buses—transportation is a very different thing. These distinctly past and present modes of transportation symbolize the changes many Southeast Asian countries are facing.

◄ Housing
The luxury apartment building (background) in Jakarta, Indonesia, towers over the shabby and polluted slum of Muarabaru (foreground). Indonesia declared its independence in 1945, but was not recognized by the United Nations until 1950. Since independence, Indonesians have enjoyed relative economic prosperity, but bridging the gap between rich and poor is an issue that faces Indonesia and much of Southeast Asia.

> DATA FILE

SOUTHEAST ASIA

Geography
- Eleven countries are generally referred to as Southeast Asia: Brunei, Cambodia, East Timor, Indonesia, Laos, Malaysia, Myanmar, the Philippines, Singapore, Thailand, and Vietnam.

Population
- About 8 percent of the world's population lives in Southeast Asia.
- Indonesia is the world's fourth most populous country, behind China, India, and the United States.

Economics
- Ten Southeast Asian nations— Indonesia, Malaysia, the Philippines, Singapore, Brunei, Cambodia, Laos, Vietnam, Myanmar, and Thailand—make up a trading alliance known as the Association of South-East Asian Nations (ASEAN)

▲▼ Markets

As the post-colonial economies of Southeast Asia grow, traditional markets, like the floating market in Thailand (shown below), give way to the modern convenience of stores with prepackaged foods, like this street-side store (above) in Vietnam.

ASEAN Exports, 1990–2001

Billions of Dollars

Year	Exports
1990	144.20
1995	320.88
2000	427.48
2001	385.27

Source: World Trade Organization

Connect *to* Today

1. Drawing Conclusions Why might some countries in Southeast Asia have more successful economies than others?

📁 See Skillbuilder Handbook, page R10.

2. Forming and Supporting Opinions Are the issues facing Southeast Asians discussed here also a concern for Americans? Why or why not?

New Nations in Africa

MAIN IDEA	WHY IT MATTERS NOW	TERMS & NAMES

REVOLUTION After World War II, African leaders threw off colonial rule and created independent countries.

Today, many of those independent countries are engaged in building political and economic stability.

- Negritude movement
- Kwame Nkrumah
- Jomo Kenyatta
- Ahmed Ben Bella
- Mobutu Sese Seko

SETTING THE STAGE Throughout the first half of the 20th century, Africa resembled little more than a European outpost. As you recall, the nations of Europe had marched in during the late 1800s and colonized much of the continent. Like the diverse groups living in Asia, however, the many different peoples of Africa were unwilling to return to colonial domination after World War II. And so, in the decades following the great global conflict, they, too, won their independence from foreign rule and went to work building new nations.

TAKING NOTES

Clarifying Use a chart to list an idea, an event, or a leader important to that country's history.

Ghana	
Kenya	
Zaire	
Algeria	
Angola	

Achieving Independence

The African push for independence actually began in the decades before World War II. French-speaking Africans and West Indians began to express their growing sense of black consciousness and pride in traditional Africa. They formed the **Negritude movement**, a movement to celebrate African culture, heritage, and values.

When World War II erupted, African soldiers fought alongside Europeans to "defend freedom." This experience made them unwilling to accept colonial domination when they returned home. The war had changed the thinking of Europeans too. Many began to question the cost, as well as the morality, of maintaining colonies abroad. These and other factors helped African colonies gain their freedom throughout the 1950s and 1960s.

The ways in which African nations achieved independence, however, differed across the continent. In Chapter 11, you learned that European nations employed two basic styles of government in colonial Africa—direct and indirect. Under indirect rule, local officials did much of the governing and colonists enjoyed limited self-rule. As a result, these colonies generally experienced an easier transition to independence. For colonies under direct rule, in which foreigners governed at all levels and no self-rule existed, independence came with more difficulty. Some colonies even had to fight wars of liberation, as European settlers refused to surrender power to African nationalist groups.

No matter how they gained their freedom, however, most new African nations found the road to a strong and stable nation to be difficult. They had to deal with everything from creating a new government to establishing a postcolonial economy. Many new countries were also plagued by great ethnic strife. In colonizing Africa, the Europeans had created artificial borders that had little to do with the areas where ethnic groups actually lived. While national borders separated people with similar cultures, they also enclosed traditional enemies who began fighting each other soon after the Europeans left. For many African nations, all of this led to instability, violence, and an overall struggle to deal with their newly gained independence.

Ghana Leads the Way

The British colony of the Gold Coast became the first African colony south of the Sahara to achieve independence. Following World War II, the British in the Gold Coast began making preparations. For example, they allowed more Africans to be nominated to the Legislative Council. However, the Africans wanted full freedom. The leader of their largely nonviolent movement was **Kwame Nkrumah** (KWAH•mee uhn•KROO•muh). Starting in 1947, he worked to liberate the Gold Coast from the British. Nkrumah organized strikes and boycotts and was often imprisoned by the British government. Ultimately, his efforts were successful.

On receiving its independence in 1957, the Gold Coast took the name Ghana. This name honored a famous West African kingdom of the past. Nkrumah became Ghana's first prime minister and later its president-for-life. Nkrumah pushed through new roads, new schools, and expanded health facilities. These costly projects soon crippled the country. His programs for industrialization, health and welfare, and expanded educational facilities showed good intentions. However, the expense of the programs undermined the economy and strengthened his opposition.

Vocabulary
Pan-African refers to a vision of strengthening all of Africa, not just a single country.

In addition, Nkrumah was often criticized for spending too much time on Pan-African efforts and neglecting economic problems in his own country. He dreamed of a "United States of Africa." In 1966, while Nkrumah was in China, the army and police in Ghana seized power. Since then, the country has shifted back and forth between civilian and military rule and has struggled for economic stability. In 2000, Ghana held its first open elections.

Fighting for Freedom

In contrast to Ghana, nations such as Kenya and Algeria had to take up arms against their European rulers in order to ultimately win their freedom.

Kenya Claims Independence The British ruled Kenya, and many British settlers resisted Kenyan independence—especially those who had taken over prize farmland in the northern highlands of the country. They were forced to accept African self-government as a result of two developments. One was the strong leadership of Kenyan nationalist **Jomo Kenyatta**. The second was the rise of a group known as the Mau Mau (MOW mow). This was a secret society made up mostly of native Kenyan farmers forced out of the highlands by the British. Ⓐ

Using guerrilla war tactics, the Mau Mau sought to push the white farmers into leaving the highlands. Kenyatta claimed to have no connection to the Mau Mau. However, he refused to condemn the organization. As a result, the

MAIN IDEA

Contrasting
Ⓐ How did the granting of independence to the British colonies of Ghana and Kenya differ?

Jomo Kenyatta
1891–1978
A man willing to spend years in jail for his beliefs, Kenyatta viewed independence as the only option for Africans.

The African can only advance to a "higher level" if he is free to express himself, to organize economically, politically and socially, and to take part in the government of his own country.

On the official day that freedom finally came to Kenya, December 12, 1963, Kenyatta recalls watching with overwhelming delight as the British flag came down and the new flag of Kenya rose up. He called it "the greatest day in Kenya's history and the happiest day in my life."

INTEGRATED / TECHNOLOGY

RESEARCH LINKS For more on Jomo Kenyatta, go to **classzone.com**

Africa, 1955
INTER**ACTIVE**

SPANISH MOROCCO
TUNISIA
Mediterranean Sea
MOROCCO
ALGERIA
LIBYA 1951
EGYPT 1922
SPANISH SAHARA
FRENCH WEST AFRICA
FRENCH SOMALILAND
BRITISH SOMALILAND
SUDAN
GAMBIA
PORTUGUESE GUINEA
GOLD COAST
NIGERIA
ETHIOPIA
SIERRA LEONE
LIBERIA
CAMEROONS
FRENCH EQUATORIAL AFRICA
SOMALIA
TOGO
DAHOMEY
RIO MUNI
UGANDA
KENYA
BELGIAN CONGO
RUANDA-URUNDI
CABINDA
TANGANYIKA
NYASALAND
COMOROS
ANGOLA
NORTHERN RHODESIA
SOUTH-WEST AFRICA
SOUTHERN RHODESIA
MOZAMBIQUE
MADAGASCAR
BECHUANALAND
SWAZILAND
UNION OF SOUTH AFRICA 1910
BASUTOLAND

Tropic of Cancer
0° Equator
Tropic of Capricorn
40° W
ATLANTIC OCEAN
INDIAN OCEAN
40° E
80° E

Legend:
- Colonies
- Independent countries
- 1951 Date of independence

N
0   1,000 Miles
0   2,000 Kilometers

Africa, 1975
INTER**ACTIVE**

TUNISIA 1956
Mediterranean Sea
MOROCCO 1956
ALGERIA 1962
LIBYA
EGYPT
SPANISH SAHARA
MAURITANIA 1960
MALI 1960
NIGER 1960
CHAD 1960
SUDAN 1956
AFARS AND ISSAS TERR. (FR.)
SENEGAL 1960
GAMBIA 1965
GUINEA-BISSAU 1974
GUINEA 1958
UPPER VOLTA 1960
NIGERIA 1960
CENTRAL AFRICAN REP. 1960
ETHIOPIA
SIERRA LEONE 1961
IVORY COAST 1960
CAMEROON 1960
SOMALIA 1960
LIBERIA
GHANA 1957
TOGO 1960
DAHOMEY 1960
CONGO 1960
ZÄIRE 1960
UGANDA 1962
KENYA 1963
SÃO TOMÉ AND PRÍNCIPE 1975
EQ. GUINEA 1968
RWANDA 1962
GABON 1960
BURUNDI 1962
TANZANIA 1961
MALAWI 1964
COMOROS 1975
ANGOLA 1975
ZAMBIA 1964
MOZAMBIQUE 1975
MAURITIUS 1968
RHODESIA (BR.)
MALAGASY REPUBLIC 1960
SOUTH-WEST AFRICA (NAMIBIA)
BOTSWANA 1966
SWAZILAND 1968
SOUTH AFRICA
LESOTHO 1966

Tropic of Cancer
40° W
0° Equator
ATLANTIC OCEAN
INDIAN OCEAN
40° E
80° E

N
0   1,000 Miles
0   2,000 Kilometers

GEOGRAPHY SKILLBUILDER: Interpreting Maps

1. **Place** *Which countries in Africa were already independent in 1955?*
2. **Location** *In what decade did most of the African nations gain their independence?*

British imprisoned him for nearly a decade. By the time the British granted Kenya independence in 1963, more than 10,000 Africans and 100 settlers had been killed.

Kenyatta became president of the new nation. He worked hard to unite the country's various ethnic and language groups. Kenyatta died in 1978. His successor, Daniel arap Moi, was less successful in governing the country. Moi faced increasing opposition to his one-party rule. Adding to the nation's woes were corruption in Moi's government and ethnic conflicts that killed hundreds and left thousands homeless. Moi stepped down in 2002, and a new party gained power through free elections.

Algeria Struggles with Independence France's principal overseas colony, Algeria, had a population of one million French colonists and nine million Arabs and Berber Muslims. After World War II, the French colonists refused to share political power with the native Algerians. In 1954, the Algerian National Liberation Front, or FLN, announced its intention to fight for independence. The French sent about half a million troops into Algeria to fight the FLN. Both sides committed atrocities. The FLN prevailed, and Algeria gained its independence in July 1962.

The leader of the FLN, **Ahmed Ben Bella**, became first president of the newly independent Algeria. He attempted to make Algeria a socialist state, but was overthrown in 1965 by his army commander. From 1965 until 1988, Algerians tried unsuccessfully to modernize and industrialize the nation. Unemployment and dissatisfaction with the government contributed to the rise of religious fundamentalists who wanted to make Algeria an Islamic state. The chief Islamic party, the Islamic Salvation Front (FIS), won local and parliamentary elections in 1990 and 1991. However, the ruling government and army refused to accept the election results. As a result, a civil war broke out between Islamic militants and the government. The war continues, on and off, to this day.

Civil War in Congo and Angola

Civil war also plagued the new nations of Congo and Angola. Congo's problems lay in its corrupt dictatorship and hostile ethnic groups. Meanwhile, Angola's difficulties stemmed from intense political differences.

Freedom and Turmoil for Congo Of all the European possessions in Africa, one of the most exploited was the Belgian Congo. Belgium had ruthlessly plundered the colony's rich resources of rubber and copper. In addition, Belgian officials ruled with a harsh hand and provided the population with no social services. They also had made no attempt to prepare the people for independence. Not surprisingly, Belgium's granting of independence in 1960 to the Congo (known as Zaire from 1971 to 1997) resulted in upheaval. **B**

MAIN IDEA

Recognizing Effects

B Why was the Congo vulnerable to turmoil after independence?

After years of civil war, an army officer, Colonel Joseph Mobutu, later known as **Mobutu Sese Seko** (moh•BOO•too SAY•say SAY•koh), seized power in 1965. For 32 years, Mobutu ruled the country that he renamed Zaire. He maintained control though a combination of force, one-party rule, and gifts to supporters. Mobutu successfully withstood several armed rebellions. He was finally overthrown in 1997 by rebel leader Laurent Kabila after months of civil war. Shortly thereafter, the country was renamed the Democratic Republic of the Congo.

▲ Mobuto Sese Seko

On becoming president, Kabila promised a transition to democracy and free elections by April 1999. Such elections never came. By 2000 the nation endured another round of civil war, as three separate rebel groups sought to overthrow Kabila's autocratic rule. In January 2001, a bodyguard assassinated Kabila.

Genocide in Rwanda

Of all the African nations that have struggled with ethnic violence, perhaps none has seen more blood spilled than Rwanda. The tiny nation in East Africa gained its independence in 1962. Over the next 30 years, its main ethnic groups, Hutus and Tutsis, often clashed.

In the spring of 1994, the Rwandan president, a Hutu, died in a suspicious plane crash. In the months that followed, Hutus slaughtered about 1 million Tutsis before Tutsi rebels put an end to the killings. The United Nations set up a tribunal to punish those responsible for the worst acts of genocide.

His son, Joseph Kabila, took power and began a quest for peace. In July of 2002, some of the rebel forces agreed to a cease-fire, offering hope that a larger peace might one day become a reality.

War Tears at Angola To the southwest of Congo lies Angola, a country that not only had to fight to gain its freedom but to hold itself together after independence. The Portuguese had long ruled Angola and had no desire to stop. When an independence movement broke out in the colony, Portugal sent in 50,000 troops. The cost of the conflict amounted to almost half of Portugal's national budget. The heavy cost of fighting, as well as growing opposition at home to the war, prompted the Portuguese to withdraw from Angola in 1975.

Almost immediately, the Communist-leaning MPLA (Popular Movement for the Liberation of Angola) declared itself the new nation's rightful government. This led to a prolonged civil war, as various rebel groups fought the government and each other for power. Each group received help from outside sources. The MPLA was assisted by some 50,000 Cuban troops and by the Soviet Union. The major opposition to the MPLA was UNITA (National Union for the Total Independence of Angola), to which South Africa and the United States lent support. For decades, the two sides agreed to and then abandoned various cease-fire agreements. In 2002, the warring sides agreed to a peace accord, and the long civil war came to an end.

As the colonies of Africa worked to become stable nations, the new nation of Israel was emerging in the Middle East. Its growth, as you will read in the next section, upset many in the surrounding Arab world and prompted one of the longest-running conflicts in modern history.

SECTION 3 ASSESSMENT

TERMS & NAMES 1. For each term or name, write a sentence explaining its significance.
• Negritude movement   • Kwame Nkrumah   • Jomo Kenyatta   • Ahmed Ben Bella   • Mobutu Sese Seko

USING YOUR NOTES	**MAIN IDEAS**	**CRITICAL THINKING & WRITING**
2. Which item had the greatest impact on its country? Why?	3. Who were the Mau Mau of Kenya? What was their goal?	6. **DRAWING CONCLUSIONS** How did the way in which European colonialists carved up Africa in the 1800s lead to civil strife in many new African nations?
	4. What sparked the present-day civil struggle in Algeria?	7. **ANALYZING MOTIVES** Why do you think the United States and the Soviet Union participated in Angola's civil war?
	5. What prompted Portugal to eventually grant Angola its freedom?	8. **ANALYZING ISSUES** Why do you think revolution swept so many African nations following their independence from European rule?
		9. **WRITING ACTIVITY** REVOLUTION Imagine you are a reporter covering a revolution in one of the African nations. Write a **headline** and **article** describing it.

Table (Using Your Notes):

Ghana	
Kenya	
Zaire	
Algeria	
Angola	

INTEGRATED TECHNOLOGY **INTERNET ACTIVITY**

Use the Internet to examine the current status of two countries discussed in this section. Choose from various economic, governmental, and social statistics and display your information in a **comparison chart.**

INTERNET KEYWORD
country profiles

4

Conflicts in the Middle East

MAIN IDEA	WHY IT MATTERS NOW	TERMS & NAMES
POWER AND AUTHORITY Division of Palestine after World War II made the Middle East a hotbed of competing nationalist movements.	The conflict in the Middle East threatens the stability of the world today.	• Anwar Sadat • Camp David • Golda Meir Accords • PLO • intifada • Yasir Arafat • Oslo Peace Accords

SETTING THE STAGE In the years following World War II, the Jewish people won what for so long had eluded them: their own state. The gaining of their homeland along the eastern coast of the Mediterranean Sea, however, came at a heavy price. A Jewish state was unwelcome in this mostly Arab region, and the resulting hostility led to a series of wars. Perhaps no Arab people, however, have been more opposed to a Jewish state than the Palestinians, who claim that much of the Jewish land belongs to them. These two groups have waged a bloody battle that goes on today.

Israel Becomes a State

The land now called Palestine consists of Israel, the West Bank, and the Gaza Strip. To Jews, their claim to the land dates back 3,000 years, when Jewish kings ruled the region from Jerusalem. To Palestinians, the land has belonged to them since most, but not all, Jews were driven out around A.D. 135. Islam spread in the 7th century and quickly became the dominant religion.

  The Jews who were forced out of Palestine during the second century, were not able to establish their own state. They settled in different countries throughout the world. The global dispersal of the Jews is known as the Diaspora. During the late 19th and early 20th centuries, a group of Jews began returning to the region their ancestors had fled so long ago. They were known as Zionists, people who favored a Jewish national homeland in Palestine. At this time, Palestine was still part of the Ottoman Empire, ruled by Islamic Turks. After the defeat of the Ottomans in World War I, the League of Nations asked Britain to oversee Palestine until it was ready for independence.

  By this time, the Jews had become a growing presence in Palestine, and were already pressing for their own nation in the territory. The Palestinians living in the region strongly opposed such a move. In a 1917 letter to Zionist leaders, British Foreign Secretary Sir Arthur Balfour promoted the idea of creating a Jewish homeland in Palestine while protecting the "rights of existing non-Jewish communities." Despite the Balfour Declaration, however, efforts to create a Jewish state failed—and hostility between Palestinians and Jews continued to grow.

TAKING NOTES

Following Chronological Order Use a graphic to fill in some important political and military events that occurred following the Suez Crisis.

Suez Crisis

The Colonies Become New Nations **583**

At the end of World War II, the United Nations took up the matter. In 1947, the UN General Assembly voted for a partition of Palestine into a Palestinian state and a Jewish state. Jerusalem was to be an international city owned by neither side. The terms of the partition gave Jews 55 percent of the area even though they made up only 34 percent of the population. In the wake of the war and the Holocaust, the United States and many European nations felt great sympathy for the Jews.

All of the Islamic countries voted against partition, and the Palestinians rejected it outright. They argued that the UN did not have the right to partition a country without considering the wishes of the majority of its people. Finally, the date was set for Israel's formation. On May 14, 1948, David Ben Gurion, long-time leader of the Jews residing in Palestine, announced the creation of an independent Israel. **A**

MAIN IDEA

Summarizing

A What recommendations did the UN make for Palestine?

Israel and Arab States in Conflict

The new nation of Israel got a hostile greeting from its neighbors. The day after it proclaimed itself a state, six Islamic states—Egypt, Iraq, Jordan, Lebanon, Saudi Arabia, and Syria—invaded Israel. The first of many Arab-Israeli wars, this one ended within months in a victory for Israel. Full-scale war broke out again in 1956, 1967, and 1973. Because of Arab-Israeli tensions, several hundred thousand Jews living in Arab lands moved to Israel.

Largely as a result of this fighting, the state that the UN had set aside for Palestinians never came into being. Israel seized half the land in the 1948–1949 fighting. While the fighting raged, at least 600,000 Palestinians fled, migrating from the areas under Israeli control. They settled in UN-sponsored refugee camps that ringed the borders of their former homeland. Meanwhile, various Arab nations seized other Palestinian lands. Egypt took control of the Gaza Strip, while Jordan annexed the West Bank of the Jordan River. (See the map at left.)

The 1956 Suez Crisis The second Arab-Israeli war followed in 1956. That year, Egypt seized control of the Suez Canal, which ran along Egypt's eastern border between the Gulf of Suez and the Mediterranean Sea. Egyptian president Gamal Abdel Nasser sent in troops to take the canal, which was controlled by British interests. The military action was prompted in large part by Nasser's anger over the loss of U.S. and British financial support for the building of Egypt's Aswan Dam.

Outraged, the British made an agreement with France and Israel to retake the canal. With air support provided by their European allies, the Israelis marched on the Suez Canal and quickly defeated the Egyptians. However, pressure from

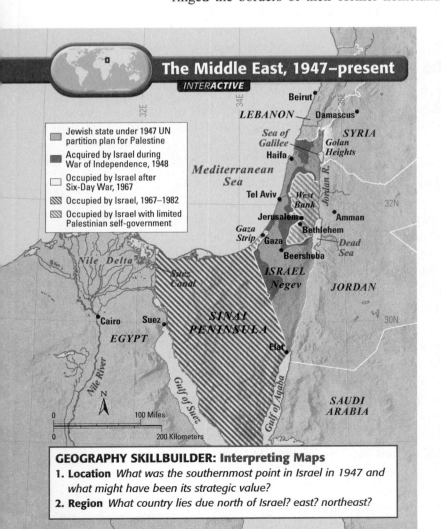

The Middle East, 1947–present

INTERACTIVE

- Jewish state under 1947 UN partition plan for Palestine
- Acquired by Israel during War of Independence, 1948
- Occupied by Israel after Six-Day War, 1967
- Occupied by Israel, 1967–1982
- Occupied by Israel with limited Palestinian self-government

Beirut
LEBANON — Damascus
Sea of Galilee
Golan Heights
Haifa
SYRIA
Mediterranean Sea
Tel Aviv
West Bank
Jordan R.
32N
Jerusalem
Amman
Gaza Strip
Bethlehem
Gaza
Dead Sea
Beersheba
ISRAEL
Negev
JORDAN
Nile Delta
Suez Canal
30N
Cairo   Suez
SINAI PENINSULA
EGYPT
Elat
Nile River
Gulf of Suez
Gulf of Aqaba
SAUDI ARABIA

0   100 Miles
0   200 Kilometers

GEOGRAPHY SKILLBUILDER: Interpreting Maps
1. **Location** What was the southernmost point in Israel in 1947 and what might have been its strategic value?
2. **Region** What country lies due north of Israel? east? northeast?

the world community, including the United States and the Soviet Union, forced Israel and the Europeans to withdraw from Egypt. This left Egypt in charge of the canal and thus ended the Suez Crisis.

Arab-Israeli Wars Continue Tensions between Israel and the Arab states began to build again in the years following the resolution of the Suez Crisis. By early 1967, Nasser and his Arab allies, equipped with Soviet tanks and aircraft, felt ready to confront Israel. "We are eager for battle in order to force the enemy to awake from his dreams," Nasser announced, "and meet Arab reality face to face." He moved to close off the Gulf of Aqaba, Israel's outlet to the Red Sea.

Convinced that the Arabs were about to attack, the Israelis struck airfields in Egypt, Iraq, Jordan, and Syria. Safe from air attack, Israeli ground forces struck like lightning on three fronts. Israel defeated the Arab states in what became known as the Six-Day War, because it was over in six days. Israel lost 800 troops in the fighting, while Arab losses exceeded 15,000.

As a consequence of the Six-Day War, Israel gained control of the old city of Jerusalem, the Sinai Peninsula, the Golan Heights, and the West Bank. Israelis saw these new holdings along their southern, eastern, and western borders as a key buffer zone against further Arab attacks. Palestinians who lived in Jerusalem were given the choice of Israeli or Jordanian citizenship. Most chose the latter. Palestinians who lived in the other areas were not offered Israeli citizenship and simply came under Jewish control.

A fourth Arab-Israeli conflict erupted in October 1973. Nasser's successor, Egyptian president **Anwar Sadat** (AHN•wahr suh•DAT), planned a joint Arab attack on the date of Yom Kippur, the holiest of Jewish holidays. This time the Israelis were caught by surprise. Arab forces inflicted heavy casualties and recaptured some of the territory lost in 1967. The Israelis, under their prime minister, **Golda Meir** (MY•uhr), launched a counterattack and

MAIN IDEA

Recognizing Effects

B What were some of the effects of the Arab-Israeli conflicts?

regained most of the lost territory. Both sides agreed to a truce after several weeks of fighting, and the Yom Kippur war came to an end. **B**

The Palestine Liberation Organization As Israel and its Arab neighbors battled each other, the Palestinians struggled for recognition. While the United Nations had granted the Palestinians their own homeland, the Israelis had seized much of that land, including the West Bank and Gaza Strip, during various wars. Israel insisted that such a move was vital to its national security.

In 1964, Palestinian officials formed the Palestine Liberation Organization (**PLO**) to push for the formation of a Palestinian state. Originally, the PLO was an umbrella organization made up of different groups—laborers, teachers, lawyers, and guerrilla fighters. Soon, guerrilla groups came to dominate the organization and insisted that the only way to achieve their goal was through armed struggle. In 1969 **Yasir Arafat** (YAH•sur AR•uh•FAT) became chairman of the PLO. Throughout the 1960s and 1970s the group carried out numerous attacks against Israel. Some of Israel's Arab neighbors supported the organization's goals by allowing the PLO to operate from their lands.

The Palestinian View

Writer Fawaz Turki articulates the view held by many of his fellow Palestinians—that the Israelis are illegal occupiers of Palestinian land.

PRIMARY SOURCE

These people have walked off with our home and homeland, with our movable and immovable property, with our land, our farms, our shops, our public buildings, our paved roads, our cars, our theaters, our clubs, our parks, our furniture, our tricycles. They hounded us out of ancestral patrimony [land] and shoved us in refugee camps. . . . Now they were astride the whole of historic Palestine and then some, jubilant at the new role as latter day colonial overlords.

FAWAZ TURKI, quoted in *The Arab-Israeli Conflict*

The Israeli View

Many Israelis, including former Israeli General Abraham Tamir, feel that controlling Palestinian lands is vital to their security.

PRIMARY SOURCE

Since the establishment of the State of Israel, its national security policy has been designed to defend its existence, integrity and security, and not for expansionist territorial aspirations. Hence, if Arab confrontation states did not initiate wars against Israel or pose threats to its existence, then Israel would not start a war . . . to extend its territories . . . Our national security policy created from its very beginning the linkage between Israel's political willingness for peace and Israel's military capability to repel aggression of any kind and scale.

ABRAHAM TAMIR, quoted in *From War to Peace*

DOCUMENT-BASED QUESTIONS
1. **Analyzing Issues** *Why does Fawaz Turki refer to the Israelis as colonizers?*
2. **Drawing Conclusions** *What might be the best way for the Palestinians to regain control of their land, according to Abraham Tamir?*

Efforts at Peace

In November 1977, just four years after the Yom Kippur war, Anwar Sadat stunned the world by extending a hand to Israel. No Arab country up to this point had recognized Israel's right to exist. In a dramatic gesture, Sadat went before the Knesset, the Israeli parliament, and invited his one-time enemies to join him in a quest for peace.

PRIMARY SOURCE

Today, through my visit to you, I ask you why don't we stretch our hands with faith and sincerity and so that together we might . . . remove all suspicion of fear, betrayal, and bad intention? Why don't we stand together with the courage of men and the boldness of heroes who dedicate themselves to a sublime [supreme] aim? Why don't we stand together with the same courage and daring to erect a huge edifice [building] of peace? An edifice that . . . serves as a beacon for generations to come with the human message for construction, development, and the dignity of man.

ANWAR SADAT, Knesset speech, November 20, 1977

Sadat emphasized that in exchange for peace Israel would have to recognize the rights of Palestinians. Furthermore, it would have to withdraw from territory seized in 1967 from Egypt, Jordan, and Syria.

U.S. president Jimmy Carter recognized that Sadat had created a historic opportunity for peace. In 1978, Carter invited Sadat and Israeli prime minister Menachem Begin (mehn•AHK•hehm BAY•gihn) to Camp David, the presidential retreat in rural Maryland. Isolated from the press and from domestic political pressures, Sadat and Begin worked to reach an agreement. After 13 days of negotiations, Carter triumphantly announced that Egypt recognized Israel as a legitimate state. In exchange, Israel agreed to return the Sinai Peninsula to Egypt. Signed in 1979, the **Camp David Accords** ended 30 years of hostilities between Egypt and Israel and became the first signed agreement between Israel and an Arab country.

While world leaders praised Sadat, his peace initiative enraged many Arab countries. In 1981, a group of Muslim extremists assassinated him. However, Egypt's new leader, Hosni Mubarak (HAHS•nee moo•BAHR•uhk), has worked to maintain peace with Israel. **C**

Israeli-Palestinian Tensions Increase One Arab group that continued to clash with the Israelis was the Palestinians, a large number of whom lived in the West Bank and Gaza Strip—lands occupied by Israel. During the 1970s and 1980s, the military wing of the PLO intensified its armed struggle against Israel. Israel responded forcefully, bombing suspected rebel bases in Palestinian towns. In 1982, the Israeli army went as far as invading the neighboring country of Lebanon in an attempt to destroy Palestinian strongholds. The Israelis soon became involved in Lebanon's civil war and were forced to withdraw.

In 1987, Palestinians began to express their frustrations in a widespread campaign of civil disobedience called the **intifada**, or "uprising." The intifada took the form of boycotts, demonstrations, attacks on Israeli soldiers, and rock throwing by unarmed teenagers. The intifada continued into the 1990s, with little progress made toward a solution. However, the civil disobedience affected world opinion, which, in turn, put pressure on Israel to seek negotiations with the Palestinians. Finally, in October 1991, Israeli and Palestinian delegates met for a series of peace talks.

The Oslo Peace Accords Negotiations between the two sides made little progress, as the status of the Palestinian territories occupied by Israel proved to be a bitterly divisive issue. In 1993, however, secret talks held in Oslo, Norway, produced a surprise agreement: a document called the Declaration of Principles, also known as the **Oslo Peace Accords**. Israel, under the leadership of Prime Minister Yitzhak Rabin (YIHTS•hahk rah•BEEN), agreed to grant the Palestinians self-rule in the Gaza Strip and the West Bank, beginning with the town of Jericho. Rabin and Arafat signed the agreement on September 13, 1993.

The difficulty of making the agreement work was demonstrated by the assassination of Rabin in 1995. He was killed by a right-wing Jewish extremist who opposed concessions to the Palestinians. Rabin was succeeded as prime minister by Benjamin Netanyahu (neh•tan•YAH•hoo), who had opposed the Oslo Accords. Still, Netanyahu made efforts to keep to the agreement. In January 1997, Netanyahu met with Arafat to work out plans for a partial Israeli withdrawal from the West Bank.

The Israeli–Palestinian Struggle

1947 UN votes to partition Palestine into Jewish and Palestinian states.

1987 Palestinians intensify their resistance with start of intifada movement (see below).

1993 Israel agrees to withdraw from several Palestinian regions in historic Oslo Peace Accords.

1950 1960 1970 1980 1990 2000

1949 Israel repels attack by Arab states and takes more land than originally assigned.

1967 Israel wins Six-Day War and seizes more Palestinian land for what it calls security purposes.

2000 Visit by Israeli leader Ariel Sharon to holy Arab site launches second intifada and years of violence.

Signs of Hope

Amid the cycle of violence and disagreement in the Middle East, there are small but inspiring efforts to bring together Israelis and Palestinians. One is Seeds of Peace, a summer camp that hosts teenagers from opposing sides of world conflicts in the hopes of creating lasting friendships. Another is the West-Eastern Divan, an orchestra made up of Jewish and Arab musicians—the creation of famous Jewish conductor Daniel Barenboim and prominent Palestinian writer Edward Said.

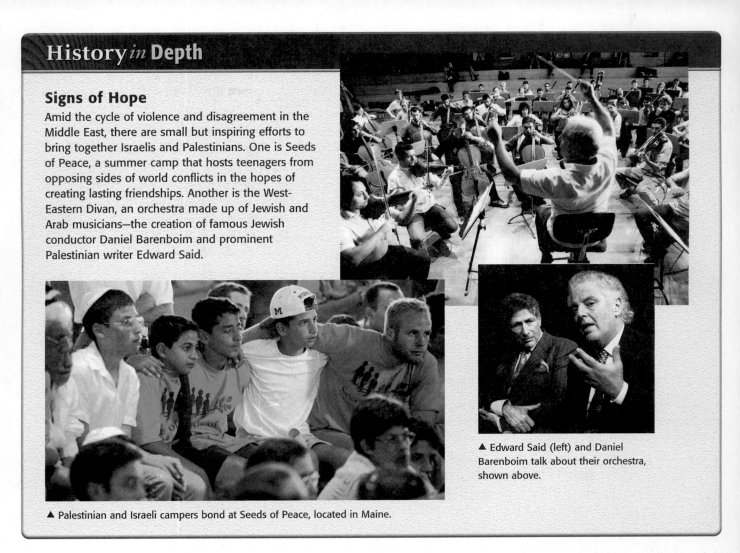

▲ Edward Said (left) and Daniel Barenboim talk about their orchestra, shown above.

▲ Palestinian and Israeli campers bond at Seeds of Peace, located in Maine.

Peace Slips Away

In 1999, the slow and difficult peace negotiations between Israel and the Palestinians seemed to get a boost. Ehud Barak won election as Israeli prime minister. Many observers viewed him as a much stronger supporter of the peace plan than Netanyahu had been. The world community, led by the United States, was determined to take advantage of such a development.

In July of 2000, U.S. president Bill Clinton hosted a 15-day summit meeting at Camp David between Ehud Barak and Yasir Arafat. The two men, however, could not reach a compromise, and the peace plan once again stalled. Just two months later an Israeli political leader, Ariel Sharon, visited a Jewish holy place, the Temple Mount in Jerusalem. The Temple Mount is also the location of one of the most holy places for Muslims, The Dome of the Rock. Sharon's visit to the vicinity of such a revered Muslim site outraged Palestinians. A day later, riots broke out and a second intifada was launched.

The Conflict Intensifies The second intifada began much like the first with demonstrations, attacks on Israeli soldiers, and rock throwing by unarmed teenagers. But this time the Palestinian militant groups increasingly used—suicide bombers. Their attacks on Jewish settlements in occupied territories and on civilian locations throughout Israel significantly raised the level of bloodshed. In the first 17 months of the uprising, one Israeli died for every three Palestinians, a rate much higher than during the first intifada.

In response to the uprising, Israeli forces moved into Palestinian refugee camps and clamped down on militants. Troops destroyed buildings in which they suspected extremists were hiding and bulldozed entire areas of Palestinian towns and camps. The Israeli army even bombed Arafat's headquarters, trapping him inside his compound for many days.

In recent years, peace between these two bitter enemies has seemed farther away than ever. In 2001, Ariel Sharon was elected Israeli prime minister. A former military leader, Sharon refused to negotiate with the Palestinians until attacks on Israelis stopped. Meanwhile, relations between Yasir Arafat and Israeli leaders grew so strained that Israeli officials declared they no longer would meet with the long-time leader of the PLO.

Working Toward a Solution Despite all this, peace efforts continue. Under intense pressure from the world community, Arafat agreed to take a less prominent role in peace talks with Israel. In early 2003, Palestinian leaders appointed their first-ever prime minister, high-ranking PLO official, Mahmoud Abbas. In his new position, Abbas became the main negotiator for the Palestinian side. Shortly afterward, U.S. president George W. Bush brought together Sharon and Abbas to begin working on a new peace plan known as the "road map."

The two men appeared committed to reaching an agreement. Abbas declared, "Our goal is two states, Israel and Palestine, living side by side in peace and security." Meanwhile, Sharon expressed his desire to see Palestinians "govern themselves in their own state." To be sure, many divisive issues remain between the two groups. With leaders from both sides willing to work together, however, hope remains that harmony will one day come to this region.

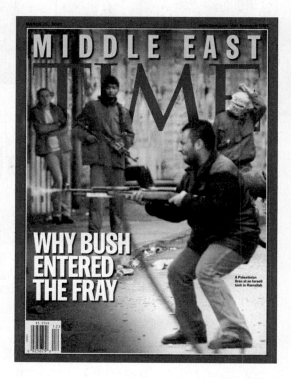

MIDDLE EAST
TIME
WHY BUSH ENTERED THE FRAY

▲ A U.S. magazine cover highlights America's involvement in the Middle East crisis.

SECTION 4 **ASSESSMENT**

TERMS & NAMES 1. For each term or name, write a sentence explaining its significance.
• Anwar Sadat   • Golda Meir   • PLO   • Yasir Arafat   • Camp David Accords   • intifada   • Oslo Peace Accords

USING NOTES

2. Which event was most important? Why?

Suez Crisis

MAIN IDEAS

3. What historic claim do both Palestinians and Jews make to the land of Palestine?

4. What land did Israel gain from the wars against its Arab neighbors?

5. What were the terms of the Oslo Accords?

CRITICAL THINKING & WRITING

6. **COMPARING** How was the creation of Israel similar to the establishment of an independent India?

7. **DRAWING CONCLUSIONS** Why do you think all the Israeli-Palestinian accords ultimately have failed?

8. **ANALYZING ISSUES** Some have said that the Palestinian-Israeli conflict represents the struggle of right against right. Explain why you agree or disagree.

9. **WRITING ACTIVITY** POWER AND AUTHORITY In groups of three or four, create a list of ten **interview questions** for Gamal Abdel Nasser, Anwar Sadat, Yasir Arafat, Yitzhak Rabin, or a current leader of either Israel or Palestine.

CONNECT TO TODAY

DRAWING A POLITICAL CARTOON

Draw a **political cartoon** or other type of image that conveys your thoughts about the stalled peace effort today between Palestinians and Israelis.

Central Asia Struggles

MAIN IDEA	WHY IT MATTERS NOW	TERMS & NAMES
POWER AND AUTHORITY Lands controlled or influenced by the Soviet Union struggle with the challenges of establishing new nations.	The security issues in these nations pose a threat to world peace and security.	• Transcaucasian Republics • Central Asian Republics • mujahideen • Taliban

SETTING THE STAGE For thousands of years, the different peoples of Central Asia suffered invasions and domination by powerful groups such as the Mongols, Byzantines, Ottomans, and finally the Communist rulers of the Soviet Union. While such occupation brought many changes to this region, its various ethnic groups worked to keep alive much of their culture. They also longed to create nations of their own, a dream they realized in the early 1990s with the collapse of the Soviet Union. In the decade since then, however, these groups have come to know the challenges of building strong and stable independent nations.

TAKING NOTES

Outlining Use an outline to organize main ideas and details.

Freedom Brings New Challenges
   A.
   B.

Afghanistan and the World
   A.
   B.

Freedom Brings New Challenges

In 1991 the Soviet Union collapsed, and the republics that it had conquered emerged as 15 independent nations. Among them were those that had made up the Soviet empire's southern borders. Geographers often group these new nations into two geographic areas.

Armenia, Azerbaijan, and Georgia make up the **Transcaucasian Republics**. These three nations lie in the Caucasus Mountains between the Black and Caspian seas. East of the Caspian Sea and extending to the Tian Shan and Pamir mountains lie the five nations known as the **Central Asian Republics**. They are Uzbekistan, Turkmenistan, Tajikistan, Kazakhstan, and Kyrgyzstan.

Economic Struggles Since gaining independence, these nations have struggled economically and are today some of the poorest countries in the world. Much of the problem stems from their heavy reliance on the Soviet Union for economic help. As a result, they have had a difficult time standing on their own. Economic practices during the Soviet era have created additional problems. The Soviets, for example, converted much of the available farmland in the Central Asian Republics to grow "white gold"—cotton. Dependence on a single crop has hurt the development of a balanced economy in these nations.

Azerbaijan, which is located among the oil fields of the Caspian Sea, has the best chance to build a solid economy based on the income from oil and oil products. Meanwhile, Kazakhstan and Turkmenistan are working hard to tap their large reserves of oil and natural gas.

Ethnic and Religious Strife Fighting among various ethnic and religious groups has created another obstacle to stability for many of the newly independent countries of Central Asia. The region is home to a number of different peoples, including some with long histories of hostility toward each other. With their iron-fisted rule, the Soviets kept a lid on these hostilities and largely prevented any serious ethnic clashes. After the breakup of the Soviet Union, however, long-simmering ethnic rivalries erupted into fighting. Some even became small regional wars.

Such was the case in Azerbaijan. Within this mostly Muslim country lies Nagorno-Karabakh, a small region of mainly Armenian Christians. In the wake of the Soviet Union's collapse, the people of this area declared their independence. Azerbaijan had no intention of letting go of this land, and fighting quickly broke out. Neighboring Armenia rushed to aid the Armenian people in the district. The war raged from 1991 through 1994, when the two sides agreed to a cease-fire. The status of Nagorno-Karabakh remains unresolved. **A**

MAIN IDEA

Clarifying

A Why was there little ethnic or religious strife in Central Asia during Soviet rule?

Afghanistan and the World

Just to the south of the Central Asian Republics lies one of the region's more prominent nations. Afghanistan is a small nation with both mountainous and desert terrain. It is one of the least-developed countries in the world, as most of its inhabitants are farmers or herders. And yet, over the past several decades, this mostly Muslim nation has grabbed the world's attention with two high-profile wars—one against the Soviet Union and the other against the United States.

Struggle for Freedom Afghanistan has endured a long history of struggle. During the 1800s, both Russia and Britain competed for control of its land. Russia wanted access to the Indian Ocean through Afghanistan, while Britain wanted control of the land in order to protect the northern borders of its Indian Empire. Britain fought three separate wars with the Afghanis before eventually leaving in 1919.

▼ The terrain of Central Asia varies widely, from mountains to plains.

Central Asia

GEOGRAPHY SKILLBUILDER: Interpreting Maps

1. **Location** Which Transcaucasian Republic nation extends the farthest east?

2. **Place** Which is the only Central Asian Republic that neither contains nor has access to a sea or lake?

That year, Afghanistan declared itself an independent nation and established a monarchy. The government implemented various reforms and tried to modernize the country. In 1964, the country devised a constitution that sought to establish a more democratic style of government. However, officials could not agree on a reform program and most people showed little interest in the effort to transform the government. As a result, a democratic system failed to develop.

Pushing Back the Soviets Nonetheless, Afghanistan had grown stable enough to establish good relations with many Western European nations and to hold its own on the world stage. When the Cold War conflict between the United States and Soviet Union broke out, Afghanistan chose to remain neutral. However, over the years, it received aid from both of the opposing superpowers.

Situated so close to the Soviet Union, however, Afghanistan could not hold out against the force of communism forever. In 1973, military leaders overthrew the government. Five years later, in 1978, a rival group with strong ties to the Soviet Union seized control of the country. Much of the population opposed the group and its strong association with communism. Many Afghanis felt that Communist policies conflicted with the teachings of Islam.

The opposition forces banded together to form a group known as the **mujahideen** (moo•JAH•heh•DEEN), or holy warriors. These rebels took up arms and fought fiercely against the Soviet-supported government. The rebellion soon prompted the Soviet Union to step in. In 1979 and 1980, Soviet troops rolled into Afghanistan to conquer the country and add it to their Communist empire.

With the Soviets' superior military force and advanced weaponry, the war had all the makings of a quick and lopsided affair. But the Afghan rebels used the land and guerrilla tactics to their advantage. In addition, the United States provided financial and military assistance. After nearly 10 years of bloody and fruitless fighting, the Soviet Union withdrew its troops. The Afghanis had taken on the world's Communist superpower and won. **B**

Rise and Fall of the Taliban With the Soviets gone, various Afghan rebel groups began battling each other for control of the country. A conservative Islamic group known as the **Taliban** emerged as the victor. By 1998, it controlled 90 percent of the country. Another rebel group, the Northern Alliance, held the northwest corner of the country. Observers initially viewed the Taliban as a positive force, as it brought order to the war-torn nation, rooted out corruption, and promoted the growth of business.

However, the group followed an extreme interpretation of Islamic law and applied it to nearly every aspect of Afghan society. Taliban leaders restricted women's lives by forbidding them to go to school or hold jobs. They banned everything from television and movies to modern music. Punishment for violating the rules included severe beatings, amputation, and even execution.

Even more troubling to the world community was the Taliban's role in the growing problem of world terrorism, which you will read more about in Chapter 20. Western

History *in* Depth

Destroying the Past

Among the Taliban's extreme policies that stemmed from their interpretation of Islam, one in particular shocked and angered historians around the world. In the years after gaining power, Taliban leaders destroyed some of Afghanistan's most prized artifacts—two centuries-old Buddhas carved out of cliffs.

The Taliban deemed the giant statues offensive to Islam. Ignoring pleas from scholars and museums, they demolished the ancient figures with dynamite and bombs. One of the two statues was thought to have dated back to the third century A.D.

INTEGRATED / TECHNOLOGY

INTERNET ACTIVITY Choose a country and highlight its top archaeological treasures. Go to **classzone.com** for your research.

MAIN IDEA

Drawing Conclusions
B Why do you think the Soviets finally decided to leave Afghanistan?

leaders accused the Taliban of allowing terrorist groups to train in Afghanistan. The Taliban also provided refuge for terrorist leaders, including Osama bin Laden, whose al-Qaeda organization is thought to be responsible for numerous attacks on the West—including the attacks on the World Trade Center in New York and the Pentagon in Washington, D.C., on September 11, 2001.

In the wake of the September 11 attacks, the U.S. government demanded that the Taliban turn over bin Laden. After its leaders refused, the United States took military action. In October 2001, U.S. forces began bombing Taliban air defense, airfields, and command centers, as well as al-Qaeda training camps. On the ground, the United States provided assistance to anti-Taliban forces, such as the Northern Alliance. By December, the United States had driven the Taliban from power.

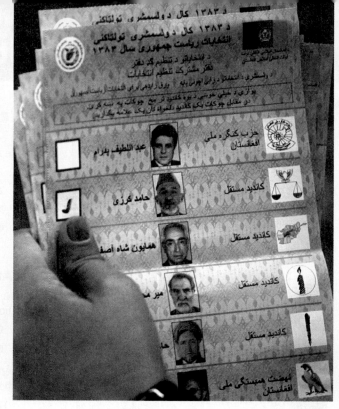

▲ In the Afghanistan elections, the ballot included photographs of the candidates and symbols for each party to help voters who could not read.

Challenges Ahead With the Taliban defeated, Afghan officials selected a new government under the leadership of Hamid Karzai. Later, in 2004, he was elected president for a five-year term. His government faces the task of rebuilding a country that has endured more than two decades of warfare. What's more, Afghanistan remains a country of roughly a dozen ethnic groups with distinct language and cultural patterns, all of which makes the job of creating a unified nation a difficult one.

The challenge before Afghanistan, however, is neither unique nor new. As you will read in the next chapter, over the past 50 years countries around the world have attempted to shed their old and often repressive forms of rule and implement a more democratic style of government.

SECTION 5 ASSESSMENT

TERMS & NAMES 1. For each term or name, write a sentence explaining its significance.
• Transcaucasian Republics   • Central Asian Republics   • mujahideen   • Taliban

USING YOUR NOTES

2. Which challenge for the Central Asian nations is most difficult to overcome?

Freedom Brings New Challenges
   A.
   B.
Afghanistan and the World
   A.
   B.

MAIN IDEA

3. What countries make up the Transcaucasian Republics? the Central Asian Republics?

4. Why did Afghanis oppose the notion of Communist rule?

5. Why did the United States take military action against the Taliban?

CRITICAL THINKING & WRITING

6. **MAKING INFERENCES** Some historians call the Soviet-Afghan war the Soviet Union's "Vietnam." What do they mean by this reference? Do you agree with it?

7. **DRAWING CONCLUSIONS** Why might Afghanis have been willing to accept Taliban rule by 1998?

8. **IDENTIFYING PROBLEMS** Why did the new nations of Central Asia experience such economic difficulties?

9. **WRITING ACTIVITY** POWER AND AUTHORITY Imagine you are a speechwriter for Hamid Karzai. Write what you feel would be an appropriate **first paragraph** for his initial speech upon taking power.

CONNECT TO TODAY CREATING A TIME LINE

Choose one of the countries discussed in this section and create a **time line** of the eight to ten most significant events in its history over the last 50 years.

VISUAL SUMMARY

The Struggle for Independence

The time line shows the dates on which various countries in Asia and Africa achieved their independence after World War II. It also shows (in parentheses) the countries from which they achieved independence.

1946 the Philippines (United States)

1947 India, Pakistan (Great Britain)

1948 Israel (Great Britain)

1949 Indonesia (The Netherlands)

1957 Ghana (Great Britain)

1962 Algeria (France)

1963 Kenya (Great Britain)

1965 Singapore (Great Britain, Malaysia)

1971 Congo (Belgium)

1971 Bangladesh (Pakistan)

1975 Angola (Portugal)

TERMS & NAMES

For each term or name below, briefly explain its connection to colonial independence around the world after World War II.

1. partition
2. Jawaharlal Nehru
3. Indira Gandhi
4. Corazón Aquino
5. Jomo Kenyatta
6. Anwar Sadat
7. PLO
8. mujahideen

MAIN IDEAS

The Indian Subcontinent Achieves Freedom
Section 1 (pages 563–569)

9. What two nations emerged from the British colony of India in 1947?
10. Briefly explain the reason for the civil disorder in Sri Lanka.

Southeast Asian Nations Gain Independence
Section 2 (pages 570–577)

11. What were some concerns the Filipinos had regarding the Bell Act?
12. Who was Sukarno?

New Nations in Africa Section 3 (pages 578–582)

13. Why were Kwame Nkrumah's politics criticized?
14. Why did Zaire face such difficulty upon gaining independence?

Conflicts in the Middle East Section 4 (pages 583–589)

15. What was the Suez Crisis?
16. What were the Camp David Accords?

Central Asia Struggles Section 5 (pages 590–593)

17. Which nations comprise the Transcaucasian Republics?
18. What was the Taliban?

CRITICAL THINKING

1. USING YOUR NOTES

Use a web diagram to show some of the challenges that newly independent nations have faced.

Challenges for Newly Independent Nations

2. FORMING AND SUPPORTING OPINIONS

REVOLUTION Do you think there should be a limit to the methods revolutionaries use? Explain your opinion.

3. ANALYZING ISSUES

ECONOMICS Why have so many of the new nations that emerged over the past half-century struggled economically?

4. DRAWING CONCLUSIONS

In your view, was religion a unifying or destructive force as colonies around the world became new nations? Support your answer with specific examples from the text.

Use the following excerpt from the Balfour Declaration and your knowledge of world history to answer questions 1 and 2.
Additional Test Practice, pp. S1–S33

PRIMARY SOURCE

His Majesty's Government view with favour the establishment in Palestine of a national home for the Jewish people, and will use their best endeavours to facilitate the achievement of this object, it being clearly understood that nothing shall be done which may prejudice the civil and religious rights of existing non-Jewish communities in Palestine, or the rights and political status enjoyed by Jews in any other country.

ARTHUR JAMES BALFOUR, in a letter to Lord Rothschild, November 2, 1917

1. The intent of the British government was to

  A. give all of Palestine to the Jewish people.

  B. leave Palestine in the hands of the Arabs.

  C. divide Palestine between Jews and Arabs.

  D. ensure justice for Jews around the world.

2. The group most likely to have opposed the Balfour Declaration was the

  A. Arabs.

  B. Jews.

  C. French.

  D. Americans.

Use the political cartoon about Corazón Aquino's election victory and your knowledge of world history to answer question 3.

3. Aquino was expected by many to "clean up" the Philippines by ending years of

  A. slavery.

  B. dictatorship.

  C. business corruption.

  D. unchecked pollution.

INTEGRATED TECHNOLOGY

TEST PRACTICE Go to **classzone.com**

• Diagnostic tests

• Tutorials

• Strategies

• Additional practice

ALTERNATIVE ASSESSMENT

1. Interact *with* History

On page 562, you discussed the most important areas to address in building a new nation. Now that you have read about the efforts by so many former colonies to forge new countries, do you think that you focused on the right areas? Work as a class to identify the main factors that determine whether a new nation struggles or thrives. Be sure to cite specific examples from the text.

2. WRITING ABOUT HISTORY

POWER AND AUTHORITY   Select one of the leaders discussed in this chapter. Review the decisions the leader made while in power. Write an evaluation of the leader's decisions and his or her impact on the country. Consider the following

• the leader's views on government and democracy

• the leader's handling of the economy

• the leader's accomplishments and failures

INTEGRATED TECHNOLOGY

Creating a Database

Use the Internet, library, and other reference materials to create a database showing the economic growth of any four countries discussed in this chapter. Create one table for each country, with column headings for each measure of economic growth you chose to record and row headings for each 10-year period. Then insert the most current data you can find. Consider the following questions to get started.

• What statistics will be most useful in making comparisons between nations?

• Which nations have capitalist economies? What other types of economies did you discover?

• Which nations have "one crop" economies?

CHAPTER

19

Struggles for Democracy, 1945–Present

Previewing Main Ideas

ECONOMICS Many nations, such as Brazil, Poland, Russia, and China, discovered that economic stability is important for democratic progress.
Geography *Which type of government seems to predominate in the Western Hemisphere?*

REVOLUTION In 1989, revolutions overthrew Communist governments in the Soviet Union and Central and Eastern Europe. In China, the Communist government and the army put down a student protest calling for democracy.
Geography *Which two countries in the Eastern Hemisphere are still Communist?*

CULTURAL INTERACTION Chinese students imported democratic ideas from the West. Democratic reforms spread across Central and Eastern Europe, causing Communist governments to fall.
Geography *Which type of government predominates in the labeled countries of Europe?*

INTEGRATED TECHNOLOGY

eEdition
- Interactive Maps
- Interactive Visuals
- Interactive Primary Sources

INTERNET RESOURCES
Go to **classzone.com** for:
- Research Links   • Maps
- Internet Activities   • Test Practice
- Primary Sources   • Current Events
- Chapter Quiz

WORLD

1945

1948
South Africa imposes apartheid policy of racial discrimination.

1959
◄ Fidel Castro seizes power in Cuba.

1967
Nigerian civil war begins.

1965

USA

1948
Harry Truman wins second term as president. ►

1964
Congress authorizes President Johnson to send troops to Vietnam.

1969
Neil Armstrong on the moon i lunar landing.

Types of Government, 2003

RUSSIA

CANADA

UNITED STATES

MEXICO   CUBA

0°Equator

BRAZIL

40°S

ARGENTINA

NORTH KOREA

CHINA

NIGERIA

SOUTH AFRICA

N
W   E
S

0   1000   2000 Miles
0   1000   2000 Kilometers
Eckert IV Projection

Communist State
The government controls public and private life and most means of production, and limits private property and individual rights.

Federation
Power is loosely divided between a central authority and a number of individual states.

Parliamentary Democracy
Power resides in a body of representatives (the parliament) that makes laws for the nation.

Republic/Federal Republic
Power is in the hands of representatives, and leaders are elected by the people; in the federal version, power is divided between a central government and individual states.

Map shows types of government for selected countries.

GERMANY POLAND
CZECH REPUBLIC SLOVAKIA HUNGARY
MACEDONIA

40°N

1978
Deng Xiaoping begins economic reforms in China. ▶

1989
Berlin Wall comes down.

1994
South Africa holds its first multiracial election.

1985

2005

1980
◀ Ronald Reagan elected president.

1988
George Bush elected president.

1992
Bill Clinton elected president.

2000
George W. Bush elected president.

Why do so many people want democracy?

Your grandparents came to the United States because they wanted to live in a democracy. Although that was more than 50 years ago, you know that people in many parts of the world still seek democracy today. On the news, you watch stories about protesters, such as those in Venezuela, who are demanding more democracy and freedom. Their demonstrations are often led by students and sometimes help to bring about democratic reform.

One evening you and a friend are watching a news story about a leader who has promised his people greater democracy. What might you answer when your friend asks why so many people want democracy?

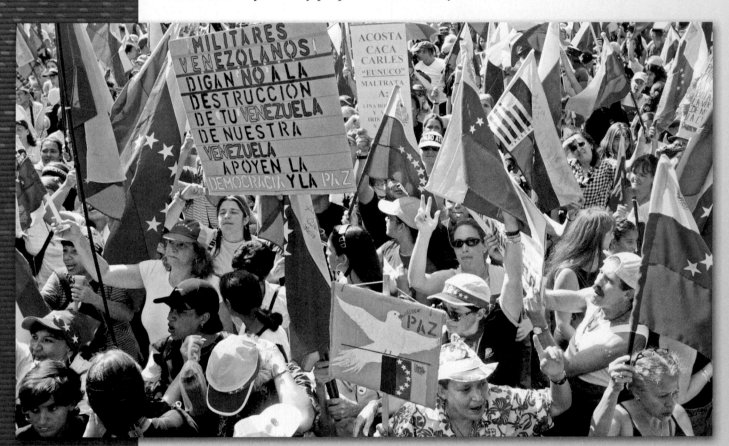

Protesters march in Caracas, Venezuela, in opposition to the policies of President Hugo Chávez.

EXAMINING *the* ISSUES

- **What rights and institutions are necessary for a government to be democratic?**

- **How do citizens participate in a democracy? How can participation be encouraged?**

Discuss these questions in class and list important points on the board. For your discussion, consider what you know about democracy in ancient Greece and in the United States. As you read this chapter, think about the challenges many countries face in trying to develop democratic systems.

Democracy

CASE STUDY: Latin American Democracies

MAIN IDEA	WHY IT MATTERS NOW	TERMS & NAMES
ECONOMICS In Latin America, economic problems and authoritarian rule delayed democracy.	By the mid-1990s, almost all Latin American nations had democratic governments.	• Brasília • land reform • standard of living • recession • PRI

SETTING THE STAGE By definition, democracy is government by the people. Direct democracy, in which all citizens meet to pass laws, is not practical for nations. Therefore, democratic nations developed indirect democracies, or republics, in which citizens elect representatives to make laws for them. For example, the United States is a republic. But democracy is more than a form of government. It is also a way of life and an ideal goal. A democratic way of life includes practices such as free and open elections.

Democracy As a Goal

The chart below lists four practices in a democracy, together with conditions that help these democratic practices succeed. Many nations follow these practices to a large degree. However, establishing democracy is a process that takes years.

Even in the United States, the establishment of democracy has taken time. Although the principle of equality is part of the Constitution, many Americans have struggled for equal rights. To cite one example, women did not receive the right to vote until 1920. Democracy is always a "work in progress."

TAKING NOTES

Summarizing Use a chart to sum up the steps Brazil, Mexico, and Argentina have taken toward democracy.

Nation	Steps toward democracy
Brazil	
Mexico	
Argentina	

Making Democracy Work	
Common Practices	**Conditions That Foster Those Practices**
• Free elections	• Having more than one political party • Universal suffrage—all adult citizens can vote
• Citizen participation	• High levels of education and literacy • Economic security • Freedoms of speech, press, and assembly
• Majority rule, minority rights	• All citizens equal before the law • Shared national identity • Protection of such individual rights as freedom of religion • Representatives elected by citizens to carry out their will
• Constitutional government	• Clear body of traditions and laws on which government is based • Widespread education about how government works • National acceptance of majority decisions • Shared belief that no one is above the law

Democratic institutions may not ensure stable, civilian government if other conditions are not present. The participation of a nation's citizens in government is essential to democracy. Education and literacy—the ability to read and write—give citizens the tools they need to make political decisions. Also, a stable economy with a strong middle class and opportunities for advancement helps democracy. It does so by giving citizens a stake in the future of their nation. **A**

Other conditions advance democracy. First, a firm belief in the rights of the individual promotes the fair and equal treatment of citizens. Second, rule by law helps prevent leaders from abusing power without fear of punishment. Third, a sense of national identity helps encourage citizens to work together for the good of the nation.

The struggle to establish democracy continued into the 21st century as many nations abandoned authoritarian rule for democratic institutions. However, a United Nations study released in July 2002 warned that the spread of democracy around the world could be derailed if free elections in poor countries are not followed by economic growth. The UN Development Program's annual report warned particularly about Latin America.

MAIN IDEA

Making Inferences
A Why would democracy suffer if citizens didn't participate?

CASE STUDY: Brazil

Dictators and Democracy

Many Latin American nations won their independence from Spain and Portugal in the early 1800s. However, three centuries of colonial rule left many problems. These included powerful militaries, economies that were too dependent on a single crop, and large gaps between rich and poor. These patterns persisted in the modern era.

After gaining independence from Portugal in 1822, Brazil became a monarchy. This lasted until 1889, when Brazilians established a republican government, which a wealthy elite controlled. Then, in the 1930s, Getulio Vargas became dictator. Vargas suppressed political opposition. At the same time, however, he promoted economic growth and helped turn Brazil into a modern industrial nation.

Kubitschek's Ambitious Program After Vargas, three popularly elected presidents tried to steer Brazil toward democracy. Juscelino Kubitschek (zhoo•suh•LEE•nuh KOO•bih•chehk), who governed from 1956 to 1961, continued to develop Brazil's economy. Kubitschek encouraged foreign investment to help pay for development projects. He built a new capital city, **Brasília** (bruh•ZIHL•yuh), in the country's interior. Kubitschek's dream proved expensive. The nation's foreign debt soared and inflation shot up.

Kubitschek's successors proposed reforms to ease economic and social problems. Conservatives resisted this strongly. They especially opposed the plan for **land reform**—breaking up large estates and distributing that land to peasants. In 1964, with the blessing of wealthy Brazilians, the army seized power in a military coup. **B**

Military Dictators For two decades military dictators ruled Brazil. Emphasizing economic growth, the generals fostered foreign investment. They began huge development projects in the Amazon jungle. The economy boomed.

The boom had a downside, though. The government froze wages and cut back on social programs. This caused a decline in the **standard of living**, or level of material comfort, which is judged by the amount of goods people have. When Brazilians protested, the government imposed censorship. It also jailed, tortured, and sometimes killed government critics. Nevertheless, opposition to military rule continued to grow.

The Road to Democracy By the early 1980s, a **recession**, or slowdown in the economy, gripped Brazil. At that point, the generals decided to open up the political system. They allowed direct elections of local, state, and national officials.

MAIN IDEA

Analyzing Motives
B Why might the wealthy have preferred military rule to land reform?

UNITED STATES

Rio Grande

Gulf of Mexico

Tropic of Cancer

MEXICO

•Mexico City

BAHAMAS

W E S T

CUBA

I N D I E S

HAITI

DOMINICAN REPUBLIC

BELIZE

GUATEMALA

HONDURAS

EL SALVADOR

NICARAGUA

JAMAICA

Caribbean Sea

ATLANTIC OCEAN

COSTA RICA

PANAMA

VENEZUELA

Orinoco R.

GUYANA

SURINAME

FRENCH GUIANA

COLOMBIA

0° Equator

ECUADOR

Amazon River

A N D E S

PACIFIC OCEAN

BRAZIL

•Brasília

PERU

M O U N T A I N S

BOLIVIA

N

0   1,000 Miles

0   2,000 Kilometers

Paraná River

Tropic of Capricorn

PARAGUAY

CHILE

URUGUAY

Buenos Aires•

ARGENTINA

40°S

FALKLAND IS. (Br.)

GEOGRAPHY SKILLBUILDER: Interpreting Maps

1. **Location** *Which country—Argentina, Brazil, or Mexico—spans the equator?*
2. **Region** *Which one of the three countries has a coast on the Caribbean Sea?*

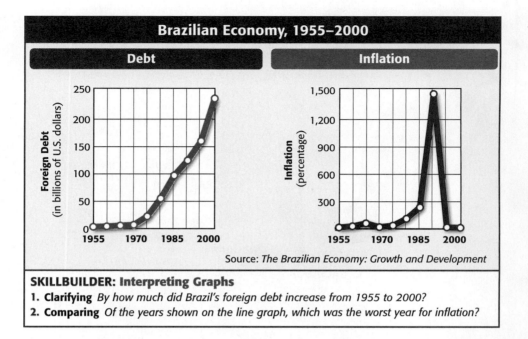

Brazilian Economy, 1955–2000

Debt

Foreign Debt (in billions of U.S. dollars)

250
200
150
100
50
0

1955   1970   1985   2000

Inflation

Inflation (percentage)

1,500
1,200
900
600
300

1955   1970   1985   2000

Source: *The Brazilian Economy: Growth and Development*

SKILLBUILDER: Interpreting Graphs
1. **Clarifying** *By how much did Brazil's foreign debt increase from 1955 to 2000?*
2. **Comparing** *Of the years shown on the line graph, which was the worst year for inflation?*

In 1985, a new civilian president, José Sarney (zhoh•ZAY SAHR•nay), took office. Sarney inherited a country in crisis because of foreign debt and inflation. He proved unable to solve the country's problems and lost support. The next elected president fared even worse. He resigned because of corruption charges. **C**

In 1994 and again in 1998, Brazilians elected Fernando Henrique Cardoso, who achieved some success in tackling the nation's economic and political problems. Although trained as a Marxist scholar, Cardoso became a strong advocate of free markets. One of his main concerns was the widening income gap in Brazil. He embarked on a program to promote economic reform.

The 2002 Presidential Election In the presidential election of October 2002, Cardoso's handpicked successor to lead his centrist coalition was José Serra. Serra faced two candidates who proposed a sharp break with Cardoso's pro-business policies. These candidates included Luiz Inácio Lula da Silva, a candidate of the leftist Workers Party.

An economic crisis hit many countries in South America, including Brazil, in 2002. Because of stalled economic growth, rising unemployment, and poverty, there was a backlash against free-market economic policies. This made the election of 2002 a close contest. Da Silva, the leftist candidate, won the hotly disputed election, defeating the ruling party candidate, Serra. Da Silva has proved a more moderate president than his supporters and opponents had expected. Although Brazil faces many challenges, it continues on the path of democracy.

MAIN IDEA

Analyzing Issues
C In your opinion, which of the problems faced by Sarney was worse? Explain.

CASE STUDY: Mexico

One-Party Rule

Unlike Brazil, Mexico enjoyed relative political stability for most of the 20th century. Following the Mexican Revolution, the government passed the Constitution of 1917. The new constitution outlined a democracy and promised reforms.

Beginnings of One-Party Domination From 1920 to 1934, Mexico elected several generals as president. However, these men did not rule as military dictators. They did create a ruling party—the National Revolutionary Party, which dominated Mexico under various names for the rest of the 20th century.

From 1934 to 1940, President Lázaro Cárdenas (KAHR•day•nahs) tried to improve life for peasants and workers. He carried out land reform and promoted labor rights. He nationalized the Mexican oil industry, kicking out foreign oil companies and creating a state-run oil industry. After Cárdenas, however, a series of more conservative presidents turned away from reform.

The Party Becomes the PRI In 1946, the main political party changed its name to the Institutional Revolutionary Party, or **PRI**. In the half-century that followed, the PRI became the main force for political stability in Mexico.

Although stable, the government was an imperfect democracy. The PRI controlled the congress and won every presidential election. The government allowed opposition parties to compete, but fraud and corruption tainted the elections.

Even as the Mexican economy rapidly developed, Mexico continued to suffer severe economic problems. Lacking land and jobs, millions of Mexicans struggled for survival. In addition, a huge foreign debt forced the government to spend money on interest payments. Two episodes highlighted Mexico's growing difficulties. In the late 1960s, students and workers began calling for economic and political change. On October 2, 1968, protesters gathered at the site of an ancient Aztec market in Mexico City. Soldiers hidden in the ruins opened fire on the protesters. The massacre claimed several hundred lives.

MAIN IDEA

Recognizing Effects

D Why does over-reliance on one product weaken an economy?

A second critical episode occurred during the early 1980s. By that time, huge new oil and natural gas reserves had been discovered in Mexico. The economy had become dependent on oil and gas exports. In 1981, world oil prices fell, cutting Mexico's oil and gas revenues in half. Mexico went into an economic decline. **D**

Economic and Political Crises The 1980s and 1990s saw Mexico facing various crises. In 1988, opposition parties challenged the PRI in national elections. The PRI candidate, Carlos Salinas, won the presidency. Even so, opposition parties won seats in the congress and began to force a gradual opening of the political system.

> Analyzing Political Cartoons

Military Rule and Democracy
Throughout the 20th century, many Latin American countries were ruled by military dictators or political bosses. Most typically, the dictator's support came from the wealthy and the military. But sometimes the dictator's support came from the people.

SKILLBUILDER:
Interpreting Visual Sources
1. **Drawing Conclusions** Do dictators typically take into account the opinions of the people they rule?
2. **Making Inferences** What does this cartoon suggest about the dictator's attitude toward the opinion of the people he rules?

"*My goodness, if I'd known how badly you wanted democracy I'd have given it to you ages ago.*"

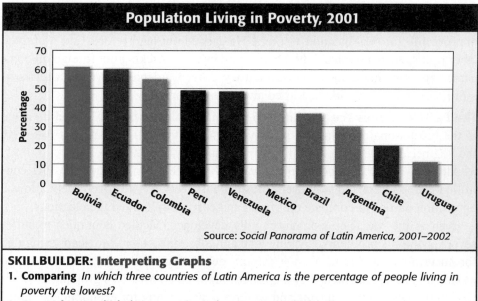

Population Living in Poverty, 2001

Source: *Social Panorama of Latin America, 2001–2002*

SKILLBUILDER: Interpreting Graphs

1. **Comparing** *In which three countries of Latin America is the percentage of people living in poverty the lowest?*
2. **Comparing** *In which three countries is the poverty rate highest?*

During his presidency, Salinas signed NAFTA, the North American Free Trade Agreement. NAFTA removed trade barriers between Mexico, the United States, and Canada. In early 1994, peasant rebels in the southern Mexican state of Chiapas (chee•AH•pahs) staged a major uprising. Shortly afterward, a gunman assassinated Luis Donaldo Colosio, the PRI presidential candidate for the upcoming election.

The PRI Loses Control After these events, Mexicans grew increasingly concerned about the prospects for democratic stability. Nevertheless, the elections of 1994 went ahead. The new PRI candidate, Ernesto Zedillo (zuh•DEE•yoh), won. Opposition parties continued to challenge the PRI.

In 1997, two opposition parties each won a large number of congressional seats, denying the PRI control of congress. Then, in 2000, Mexican voters ended 71 years of PRI rule by electing center-right candidate Vicente Fox as president.

New Policies and Programs Fox's agenda was very ambitious. He advocated reforming the police, rooting out political corruption, ending the rebellion in Chiapas, and opening up Mexico's economy to free-market forces.

Fox also argued that the United States should legalize the status of millions of illegal Mexican immigrant workers. Fox hoped that a negotiated agreement between the United States and Mexico would provide amnesty for these undocumented Mexican workers in the United States. In the wake of the terrorist attacks of September 11, 2001, any such agreement appeared remote. However, in 2002, Fox created a cabinet-level agency to lobby for the interests of Mexico's 22 million citizens who lived abroad, a great many of whom lived in the United States. In the meantime, Mexico's democracy continued to strengthen.

▲ President Vicente Fox of Mexico

CASE STUDY: Argentina

Political and Economic Disorder

Mexico and Brazil were not the only Latin American countries where democracy had made progress. By the late 1990s, most of Latin America was under democratic rule.

Perón Rules Argentina Argentina had struggled to establish democracy. It was a major exporter of grain and beef. It was also an industrial nation with a large working class. In 1946, Argentine workers supported an army officer, Juan Perón, who won the presidency and then established a dictatorship.

Vocabulary

welfare state: a government that tries to provide for all its citizens' needs—including health, education, and employment

Perón did not rule alone. He received critical support from his wife, Eva—known as Evita to the millions of Argentines who idolized her. Together, the Peróns created a welfare state. The state offered social programs with broad popular appeal but limited freedoms. After Eva's death in 1952, Perón's popularity declined and his enemies—the military and the Catholic Church—moved against him. In 1955, the military ousted Perón and drove him into exile.

Repression in Argentina For many years, the military essentially controlled Argentine politics. Perón returned to power once more, in 1973, but ruled for only a year before dying in office. By the mid-1970s, Argentina was in chaos.

In 1976, the generals seized power again. They established a brutal dictatorship and hunted down political opponents. For several years, torture and murder were everyday events. By the early 1980s, several thousand Argentines had simply disappeared, kidnapped by their own government.

▲ Eva Perón

MAIN IDEA

Analyzing Causes

Ⓔ What finally caused military rule to end in Argentina?

Democracy and the Economy In 1982, the military government went to war with Britain over the nearby Falkland Islands and suffered a defeat. Disgraced, the generals agreed to step down. In 1983, Argentines elected Raúl Alfonsín (ahl•fohn•SEEN) president in the country's first free election in 37 years. Ⓔ

During the 1980s, Alfonsín worked to rebuild democracy and the economy. Carlos Menem gained the presidency in 1989 and continued the process. He attempted to stabilize the currency and privatize industry. By the late 1990s, however, economic problems intensified as the country lived beyond its means.

A Growing Crisis In December 2001, the International Monetary Fund (IMF) refused to provide financial aid to Argentina. Then President Fernando de la Rua resigned in the face of protests over the economy. He was succeeded by Eduardo Duhalde, who tried to deal with the economic and social crisis. In 2002, Argentina had an unemployment rate of about 24 percent. The country defaulted on $132 billion in debt, the largest debt default in history, and devalued its currency. In 2003, Argentina struggled to regain its political and economic footing. In elections that year, Nestor Kirchner became the new president of Argentina.

SECTION 1 ASSESSMENT

TERMS & NAMES 1. For each term or name, write a sentence explaining its significance.
• Brasília   • land reform   • standard of living   • recession   • PRI

USING YOUR NOTES
2. Which country do you think has made the most progress? Explain.

Nation	Steps toward democracy
Brazil	
Mexico	
Argentina	

MAIN IDEAS
3. What role did the military play in shaping the economy of Brazil?

4. What were some of the positive benefits of one-party rule in Mexico?

5. What effect did the Falklands war have on the military government in Argentina?

CRITICAL THINKING & WRITING
6. **COMPARING AND CONTRASTING** Compare and contrast the roles of the military in the governments of Brazil, Mexico, and Argentina.

7. **SYNTHESIZING** What have been some of the obstacles to democracy in Latin America?

8. **DEVELOPING HISTORICAL PERSPECTIVE** What are some of the attributes of democracy?

9. **WRITING ACTIVITY** [ECONOMICS] What might be the effect of a welfare state (such as that created in Argentina by the Peróns) on a nation's economy? Support your opinions in a two-paragraph **essay.**

CONNECT TO TODAY MAKING A GRAPH
Research the economies of Mexico, Brazil, and Argentina to determine which is doing the best. Present your findings in a **graph.**

The Challenge of Democracy in Africa

MAIN IDEA	WHY IT MATTERS NOW	TERMS & NAMES
REVOLUTION As the recent histories of Nigeria and South Africa show, ethnic and racial conflicts can hinder democracy.	In 1996, as Nigeria struggled with democracy, South Africa adopted a bill of rights that promotes racial equality.	• federal system • martial law • dissident • apartheid • Nelson Mandela

SETTING THE STAGE Beginning in the late 1950s, dozens of European colonies in Africa gained their independence and became nations. As in Latin America, the establishment of democracy in Africa proved difficult. In many cases, the newly independent nations faced a host of problems that slowed their progress toward democracy. The main reason for Africa's difficulties was the negative impact of colonial rule. European powers had done little to prepare their African colonies for independence.

TAKING NOTES

Comparing Use a Venn diagram to compare political events in Nigeria and South Africa.

Nigeria
both
South Africa

Colonial Rule Limits Democracy

The lingering effects of colonialism undermined efforts to build stable, democratic economies and states. This can be seen throughout Africa.

European Policies Cause Problems When the Europeans established colonial boundaries, they ignored existing ethnic or cultural divisions. New borders divided peoples of the same background or threw different—often rival—groups together. Because of this, a sense of national identity was difficult to develop. After independence, the old colonial boundaries became the borders of the newly independent states. As a result, ethnic and cultural conflicts remained.

Other problems had an economic basis. European powers had viewed colonies as sources of wealth for the home country. The colonial powers encouraged the export of one or two cash crops, such as coffee or rubber, rather than the production of a range of products to serve local needs. Europeans developed plantations and mines but few factories. Manufactured goods were imported from European countries. These policies left new African nations with unbalanced economies and a small middle class. Such economic problems lessened their chances to create democratic stability.

European rule also disrupted African family and community life. In some cases, colonial powers moved Africans far from their families and villages to work in mines or on plantations. In addition, most newly independent nations still lacked a skilled, literate work force that could take on the task of building a new nation.

Short-Lived Democracies When Britain and France gave up their colonies, they left fragile democratic governments in place. Soon problems threatened those governments. Rival ethnic groups often fought for power. Strong militaries became tools for ambitious leaders. In many cases, a military dictatorship replaced democracy.

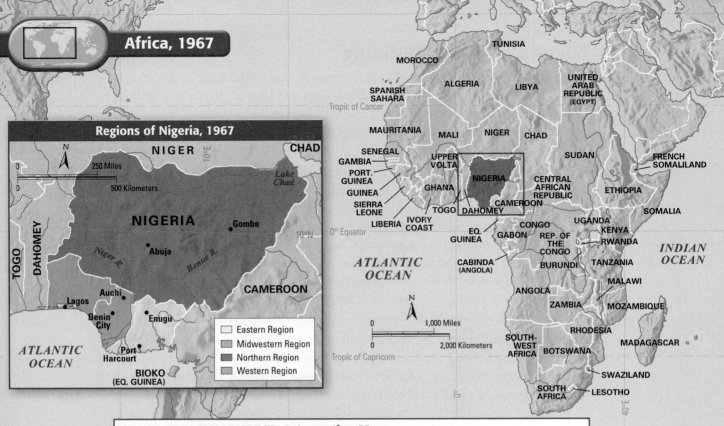

Africa, 1967

Regions of Nigeria, 1967

250 Miles
500 Kilometers

NIGER

CHAD

NIGERIA

Gombe

Abuja

Niger R.

Benue R.

Auchi

Lagos

Benin City

Enugu

CAMEROON

Port Harcourt

ATLANTIC OCEAN

TOGO

DAHOMEY

BIOKO (EQ. GUINEA)

Eastern Region
Midwestern Region
Northern Region
Western Region

TUNISIA

MOROCCO

ALGERIA   LIBYA   UNITED ARAB REPUBLIC (EGYPT)

SPANISH SAHARA

Tropic of Cancer

MAURITANIA   MALI   NIGER   CHAD

SENEGAL

GAMBIA   UPPER VOLTA   SUDAN   FRENCH SOMALILAND

PORT. GUINEA

GHANA   NIGERIA   CENTRAL AFRICAN REPUBLIC   ETHIOPIA

GUINEA

SIERRA LEONE   TOGO   DAHOMEY   CAMEROON   SOMALIA

LIBERIA   IVORY COAST

0° Equator

EQ. GUINEA   CONGO   UGANDA   KENYA

GABON   REP. OF THE CONGO   RWANDA

INDIAN OCEAN

ATLANTIC OCEAN

CABINDA (ANGOLA)   BURUNDI   TANZANIA

MALAWI

ANGOLA   ZAMBIA   MOZAMBIQUE

1,000 Miles
2,000 Kilometers

Tropic of Capricorn

RHODESIA

SOUTH-WEST AFRICA   BOTSWANA   MADAGASCAR

SWAZILAND

SOUTH AFRICA   LESOTHO

GEOGRAPHY SKILLBUILDER: Interpreting Maps
1. **Region** Describe the Eastern Region, which seceded as Biafra. Describe its size and location compared to the rest of Nigeria.
2. **Location** In which region is Lagos, Nigeria's capital in 1967?

Civil War in Nigeria

Nigeria, a former British colony, won its independence peacefully in 1960. Nigeria is Africa's most populous country and one of its richest. However, the country was ethnically divided. This soon created problems that led to war.

A Land of Many Peoples Three major ethnic groups live within Nigeria's borders. In the north are the Hausa-Fulani, who are mostly Muslim. In the south are the Yoruba and the Igbo (also called Ibo), who are mostly Christians, Muslims, or animists, who believe that spirits are present in animals, plants, and natural objects. The Yoruba, a farming people with a tradition of kings, live to the west. The Igbo, a farming people who have a democratic tradition, live to the east.

After independence, Nigeria adopted a **federal system**. In a federal system, power is shared between state governments and a central authority. The Nigerians set up three states, one for each region and ethnic group, with a political party in each.

War with Biafra Although one group dominated each state, the states also had ethnic minorities. In the Western Region, non-Yoruba minorities began to resent Yoruba control. In 1963, they tried to break away and form their own region. This led to fighting. In January 1966, a group of army officers, most of them Igbo, seized power in the capital city of Lagos. These officers abolished the regional governments and declared **martial law**, or temporary military rule.

The Hausa-Fulani, who did not trust the Igbo, launched an attack from the north. They persecuted and killed many Igbo. The survivors fled east. In 1967, the Eastern Region seceded from Nigeria, declaring itself the new nation of Biafra (bee•AF•ruh).

The Nigerian government then went to war to reunite the country. The Igbo were badly outnumbered and outgunned. In 1970, Biafra surrendered. Nigeria was reunited, but perhaps more than a million Igbo died, most from starvation. **A**

MAIN IDEA

Recognizing Effects
A What was the effect of the war on the Igbo?

Struggles for Democracy **607**

Nigeria's Nation-Building

After the war, Nigerians returned to the process of nation-building. "When the war ended," noted one officer, "it was like a referee blowing a whistle in a football game. People just put down their guns and went back to the business of living." The Nigerian government did not punish the Igbo. It used federal money to rebuild the Igbo region.

Federal Government Restored The military governed Nigeria for most of the 1970s. During this time, Nigerian leaders tried to create a more stable federal system, with a strong central government and a number of regional units. The government also tried to build a more modern economy, based on oil income.

In 1979, the military handed power back to civilian rulers. Nigerians were cheered by the return to democracy. Some people, however, remained concerned about ethnic divisions in the nation. Nigerian democracy was short-lived. In 1983, the military overthrew the civilian government, charging it with corruption. A new military regime, dominated by the Hausa-Fulani, took charge.

A Return to Civilian Rule In the years that followed, the military governed Nigeria, while promising to bring back civilian rule. The army held elections in 1993, which resulted in the victory of popular leader Moshood Abiola. However, officers declared the results invalid, and a dictator, General Sani Abacha, took control.

General Abacha banned political activity and jailed **dissidents**, or government opponents. Upon Abacha's death in 1998, General Abdulsalami Abubakar seized power and promised to end military rule. He kept his word. In 1999, Nigerians elected their first civilian president, Olusegun Obasanjo, in nearly 20 years. In 2003, Obasanjo was reelected.

> Analyzing Primary Sources

Ken Saro-Wiwa

On November 10, 1995, Nigeria hanged nine political prisoners—all critics of the military government. Many around the world believed the nine were convicted on false charges to silence them. One of the nine was Ken Saro-Wiwa, a noted writer and activist. Shortly before his death, Saro-Wiwa smuggled several manuscripts out of prison.

DOCUMENT-BASED QUESTIONS

1. **Drawing Conclusions** What do Saro-Wiwa's imprisonment and execution suggest about the government of the military dictator, General Sani Abacha?
2. **Making Inferences** What seems to be Saro-Wiwa's attitude toward his persecutors?

PRIMARY SOURCE

Injustice stalks the land like a tiger on the prowl. To be at the mercy of buffoons [fools] is the ultimate insult. To find the instruments of state power reducing you to dust is the injury. . . .

It is also very important that we have chosen the path of non-violent struggle. Our opponents are given to violence and we cannot meet them on their turf, even if we wanted to. Non-violent struggle offers weak people the strength which they otherwise would not have. The spirit becomes important, and no gun can silence that. I am aware, though, that non-violent struggle occasions more death than armed struggle. And that remains a cause for worry at all times. Whether the Ogoni people will be able to withstand the rigors of the struggle is yet to be seen. Again, their ability to do so will point the way of peaceful struggle to other peoples on the African continent. It is therefore not to be underrated.

KEN SARO-WIWA, *A Month and a Day: A Detention Diary*

President Obasanjo Obasanjo was an ethnic Yoruba from southwest Nigeria. As a critic of Nigerian military regimes, he had spent three years in jail (1995–1998) under Sani Abacha. As a former general, Obasanjo had the support of the military.

Obasanjo worked for a strong, unified Nigeria. He made some progress in his battle against corruption. He also attempted to draw the attention of the world to the need for debt relief for Nigeria. In May 2001, he called on President George W. Bush to support the canceling of Nigeria's $30 billion debt to the international community. Obasanjo saw debt relief as essential to the relief of hunger and the future of democracy in Nigeria and the rest of Africa.

Despite Obasanjo's efforts, Nigeria was still beset by a variety of problems. These included war, violence, corruption, poverty, and hunger. Nonetheless, Nigeria was increasing its oil exports and experiencing economic growth.

South Africa Under Apartheid

In South Africa, racial conflict was the result of colonial rule. From its beginnings under Dutch and British control, South Africa was racially divided. A small white minority ruled a large black majority. In 1910, South Africa gained self-rule as a dominion of the British Empire. In 1931, it became an independent member of the British Commonwealth. Although South Africa had a constitutional government, the constitution gave whites power and denied the black majority its rights.

Apartheid Segregates Society In 1948, the National Party came to power in South Africa. This party promoted Afrikaner, or Dutch South African, nationalism. It also instituted a policy of **apartheid**, complete separation of the races. The minority government banned social contacts between whites and blacks. It established segregated schools, hospitals, and neighborhoods.

MAIN IDEA

Making Inferences
B How did the policy of apartheid strengthen whites' hold on power?

In 1959, the minority government set up reserves, called homelands, for the country's major black groups. Blacks were forbidden to live in white areas unless they worked as servants or laborers for whites. The homelands policy was totally unbalanced. Although blacks made up about 75 percent of the population, the government set aside only 13 percent of the land for them. Whites kept the best land. **B**

Blacks Protest The blacks of South Africa resisted the controls imposed by the white minority. In 1912, they formed the African National Congress (ANC) to fight for their rights. The ANC organized strikes and boycotts to protest racist policies. The government banned the ANC and imprisoned many of its members. One was ANC leader **Nelson Mandela** (man•DEHL•uh).

The troubles continued. In 1976, riots over school policies broke out in the black township of Soweto, leaving about 600 students dead. In 1977, police beat popular protest leader Stephen Biko to death while he was in custody. As protests mounted, the government declared a nationwide state of emergency in 1986.

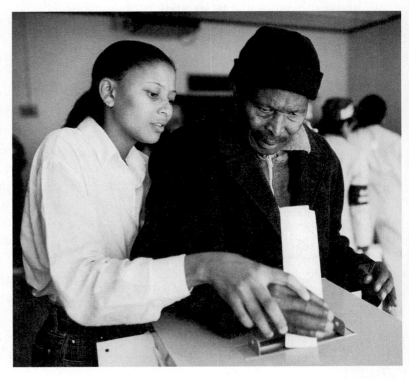

▼ A young South African poll worker helps an elderly man to vote in the first election open to citizens of all races.

Struggle for Democracy

By the late 1980s, South Africa was under great pressure to change. For years, a black South African bishop, Desmond Tutu, had led an economic campaign against apartheid. He asked foreign nations not to do business with South Africa. In response, many nations imposed trade restrictions. They also isolated South Africa in other ways, for example, by banning South Africa from the Olympic Games. (In 1984, Tutu won the Nobel Peace Prize for his nonviolent methods.) **C**

MAIN IDEA

Recognizing Effects

C How did Desmond Tutu help force South Africa to end apartheid?

The First Steps In 1989, white South Africans elected a new president, F. W. de Klerk. His goal was to transform South Africa and end its isolation. In February 1990, he legalized the ANC and also released Nelson Mandela from prison.

These dramatic actions marked the beginning of a new era in South Africa. Over the next 18 months, the South African parliament repealed apartheid laws that had segregated public facilities and restricted land ownership by blacks. World leaders welcomed these changes and began to ease restrictions on South Africa.

Although some legal barriers had fallen, others would remain until a new constitution was in place. First, the country needed to form a multiracial government. After lengthy negotiations, President de Klerk agreed to hold South Africa's first universal elections, in which people of all races could vote, in April 1994.

Majority Rule Among the candidates for president were F. W. de Klerk and Nelson Mandela. During the campaign, the Inkatha Freedom Party—a rival party to the ANC—threatened to disrupt the process. Nevertheless, the vote went smoothly. South Africans of all races peacefully waited at the polls in long lines. To no one's surprise, the ANC won 63 percent of the vote. They won 252 of 400 seats in the National Assembly (the larger of the two houses in Parliament). Mandela was elected president. Mandela stepped down in 1999, but the nation's democratic government continued.

A New Constitution In 1996, after much debate, South African lawmakers passed a new, more democratic constitution. It guaranteed equal rights for all citizens. The constitution included a bill of rights modeled on the U.S. Bill of Rights. The political changes that South Africa had achieved gave other peoples around the world great hope for the future of democracy.

South Africa Today In 1999, ANC official Thabo Mbeki won election as president in a peaceful transition of power. As Mbeki assumed office, he faced a number of serious challenges. These included high crime rates—South Africa's

History Makers

Nelson Mandela
1918–

Nelson Mandela has said that he first grew interested in politics when he heard elders in his village describe how freely his people lived before whites came. Inspired to help his people regain that freedom, Mandela trained as a lawyer and became a top official in the ANC. Convinced that apartheid would never end peacefully, he joined the armed struggle against white rule. For this, he was imprisoned for 27 years.

After his presidential victory, Mandela continued to work to heal his country.

F. W. de Klerk
1936–

Like Mandela, Frederik W. de Klerk also trained as a lawyer. Born to an Afrikaner family with close links to the National Party, de Klerk was elected to Parliament in 1972.

A firm party loyalist, de Klerk backed apartheid but was also open to reform. Friends say that his flexibility on racial issues stemmed from his relatively liberal religious background.

In 1993, de Klerk and Mandela were jointly awarded the Nobel Peace Prize for their efforts to bring democracy to South Africa.

INTEGRATED / TECHNOLOGY

RESEARCH LINKS For more on Nelson Mandela and F. W. de Klerk, go to **classzone.com**

South Africa, 1948–2000

1948 National Party comes to power, passes apartheid laws

1959 Black homelands established

1960 Sharpeville Massacre, 69 protesters killed

1962 Nelson Mandela jailed

1976 600 black students killed during Soweto protest

1977 Stephen Biko killed in police custody

1989 F. W. de Klerk elected president

1990 ANC legalized and Mandela released

1994 ANC wins 63% of the vote; Mandela elected president

1996 New constitution adopted

1999 ANC candidate Thabo Mbeki elected president

▲ This was South Africa's flag from 1927 to 1994.

rape and murder rates were among the highest in the world. Unemployment stood at about 40 percent among South Africa's blacks, and about 60 percent lived below the poverty level. In addition, an economic downturn discouraged foreign investment.

Mbeki promoted a free-market economic policy to repair South Africa's infra-structure and to encourage foreign investors. In 2002, South Africa was engaged in negotiations to establish free-trade agreements with a number of countries around the world, including those of the European Union as well as Japan, Canada, and the United States. This was an attempt at opening the South African economy to for-eign competition and investment, and promoting growth and employment.

One of the biggest problems facing South Africa was the AIDS epidemic. Some estimates concluded that 6 million South Africans were likely to die of AIDS by 2010. Mbeki disputed that AIDS was caused by HIV (human immunodeficiency virus). His opinion put South Africa at odds with the scientific consensus through-out the world. The *New York Times* stated that Mbeki was in danger of undermin-ing "all his good work with his stance on AIDS."

In Section 3, you will read how democratic ideas changed another part of the world, the Communist Soviet Union.

▲ South Africa adopted this flag in 1994.

SECTION 2 ASSESSMENT

TERMS & NAMES 1. For each term or name, write a sentence explaining its significance.
• federal system • martial law • dissident • apartheid • Nelson Mandela

USING YOUR NOTES

2. Which country is more democratic? Explain.

MAIN IDEAS

3. What effect did old colonial boundaries have on newly independent African states?

4. What was the outcome of the war between Nigeria and Biafra?

5. What were the homelands in South Africa?

CRITICAL THINKING & WRITING

6. **IDENTIFYING PROBLEMS** What do you think is the main problem that Nigeria must overcome before it can establish a democratic government?

7. **ANALYZING ISSUES** What are some of the important issues facing South Africa today?

8. **RECOGNIZING EFFECTS** What were the main negative effects of the economic policies of European colonizers?

9. **WRITING ACTIVITY** REVOLUTION Working in small teams, write **biographies** of South African leaders who were instrumental in the revolutionary overturn of apartheid. Include pictures if possible.

CONNECT TO TODAY MAKING AN ORAL REPORT

Do research on the current policy of Thabo Mbeki and the South African government on HIV and AIDS in South Africa. Report your findings in an **oral report** to the class.

The Collapse of the Soviet Union

MAIN IDEA	WHY IT MATTERS NOW	TERMS & NAMES
REVOLUTION Democratic reforms brought important changes to the Soviet Union.	Russia continues to struggle to establish democracy.	• Politburo • Mikhail Gorbachev • glasnost • perestroika	• Boris Yeltsin • CIS • "shock therapy"

SETTING THE STAGE After World War II, the Soviet Union and the United States engaged in a Cold War, which you read about in Chapter 17. Each tried to increase its worldwide influence. The Soviet Union extended its power over much of Eastern Europe. By the 1960s, it appeared that communism was permanently established in the region. During the 1960s and 1970s, the Soviet Union's Communist leadership kept tight control over the Soviet people. But big changes, including democratic reforms, were on the horizon.

TAKING NOTES

Following Chronological Order Use a time line to record significant events in the Soviet Union and Russia.

1985   2002

Gorbachev Moves Toward Democracy

Soviet premier Leonid Brezhnev and the **Politburo**—the ruling committee of the Communist Party—crushed all political disagreement. Censors decided what writers could publish. The Communist Party also restricted freedom of speech and worship. After Brezhnev's death in 1982, the aging leadership of the Soviet Union tried to hold on to power. However, each of Brezhnev's two successors died after only about a year in office. Who would succeed them?

A Younger Leader To answer that question, the Politburo debated between two men. One was **Mikhail Gorbachev** (mih•KYL GAWR•buh•chawf). Gorbachev's supporters praised his youth, energy, and political skills. With their backing, Gorbachev became the party's new general secretary. In choosing him, Politburo members did not realize they were unleashing another Russian Revolution.

The Soviet people welcomed Gorbachev's election. At 54, he was the youngest Soviet leader since Stalin. Gorbachev was only a child during Stalin's ruthless purge of independent-minded party members. Unlike other Soviet leaders, Gorbachev decided to pursue new ideas.

Glasnost Promotes Openness Past Soviet leaders had created a totalitarian state. It rewarded silence and discouraged individuals from acting on their own. As a result, Soviet society rarely changed, and the Soviet economy stagnated. Gorbachev realized that economic and social reforms could not occur without a free flow of ideas and information. In 1985, he announced a policy known as **glasnost** (GLAHS•nuhst), or openness.

Glasnost brought remarkable changes. The government allowed churches to open. It released dissidents from prison and allowed the publication of books by previously banned authors. Reporters investigated problems and criticized officials.

Glasnost

Mikhail Gorbachev's policies of glasnost and perestroika shook up the traditional way of doing things in the Soviet economy and in the society at large.

JEFF STAHLER
Courtesy Cincinnati Post

SKILLBUILDER:
Interpreting Visual Sources

1. **Making Inferences** *One arrow points down the road toward stagnation. Where is the other arrow, pointing in the opposite direction, likely to lead?*
2. **Drawing Conclusions** *Why might the Soviet Union look different to the figure in the cartoon?*

Reforming the Economy and Politics

The new openness allowed Soviet citizens to complain about economic problems. Consumers protested that they had to stand in lines to buy food and other basics.

Economic Restructuring Gorbachev blamed these problems on the Soviet Union's inefficient system of central planning. Under central planning, party officials told farm and factory managers how much to produce. They also told them what wages to pay and what prices to charge. Because individuals could not increase their pay by producing more, they had little motive to improve efficiency. **Ⓐ**

In 1985, Gorbachev introduced the idea of **perestroika** (PEHR•ih•STROY•kuh), or economic restructuring. In 1986, he made changes to revive the Soviet economy. Local managers gained greater authority over their farms and factories, and people were allowed to open small private businesses. Gorbachev's goal was not to throw out communism, but to make the economic system more efficient and productive.

Democratization Opens the Political System Gorbachev also knew that for the economy to improve, the Communist Party would have to loosen its grip on Soviet society and politics. In 1987, he unveiled a third new policy, called democratization. This would be a gradual opening of the political system.

The plan called for the election of a new legislative body. In the past, voters had merely approved candidates who were handpicked by the Communist Party. Now, voters could choose from a list of candidates for each office. The election produced many surprises. In several places, voters chose lesser-known candidates and reformers over powerful party bosses.

Foreign Policy Soviet foreign policy also changed. To compete militarily with the Soviet Union, President Ronald Reagan had begun the most expensive military buildup in peacetime history, costing more than $2 trillion. Under pressure from U.S. military spending, Gorbachev realized that the Soviet economy could not afford the costly arms race. Arms control became one of Gorbachev's top priorities. In December 1987, he and Reagan signed the Intermediate-Range Nuclear Forces (INF) Treaty. This treaty banned nuclear missiles with ranges of 300 to 3,400 miles.

MAIN IDEA

Making Inferences

Ⓐ Why would it be inefficient for the central government to decide what should be produced all over the country?

The Soviet Union Faces Turmoil

Gorbachev's new thinking led him to support movements for change in both the economic and political systems within the Soviet Union. Powerful forces for democracy were building in the country, and Gorbachev decided not to oppose reform. Glasnost, perestroika, and democratization were all means to reform the system. However, the move to reform the Soviet Union ultimately led to its breakup.

Various nationalities in the Soviet Union began to call for their freedom. More than 100 ethnic groups lived in the Soviet Union. Russians were the largest, most powerful group. However, non-Russians formed a majority in the 14 Soviet republics other than Russia.

Ethnic tensions brewed beneath the surface of Soviet society. As reforms loosened central controls, unrest spread across the country. Nationalist groups in Georgia, Ukraine, and Moldavia (now Moldova) demanded self-rule. The Muslim peoples of Soviet Central Asia called for religious freedom.

Lithuania Defies Gorbachev The first challenge came from the Baltic nations of Lithuania, Estonia, and Latvia. These republics had been independent states between the two world wars, until the Soviets annexed them in 1940. Fifty years later, in March 1990, Lithuania declared its independence. To try to force it back into the Soviet Union, Gorbachev ordered an economic blockade of the republic.

Although Gorbachev was reluctant to use stronger measures, he feared that Lithuania's example might encourage other republics to secede. In January 1991, Soviet troops attacked unarmed civilians in Lithuania's capital. The army killed 14 and wounded hundreds.

Yeltsin Denounces Gorbachev The assault in Lithuania and the lack of economic progress damaged Gorbachev's popularity. People looked for leadership to **Boris Yeltsin**. He was a member of parliament and former mayor of Moscow. Yeltsin criticized the crackdown in Lithuania and the slow pace of reforms. In June 1991, voters chose Yeltsin to become the Russian Federation's first directly elected president.

In spite of their rivalry, Yeltsin and Gorbachev faced a common enemy in the old guard of Communist officials. Hard-liners—conservatives who opposed reform—were furious that Gorbachev had given up the Soviet Union's role as the dominant force in Eastern Europe. They also feared losing their power and privileges. These officials vowed to overthrow Gorbachev and undo his reforms.

History Makers

Mikhail Gorbachev
1931–

Mikhail Gorbachev's background shaped the role he would play in history. Both of his grandfathers were arrested during Stalin's purges. Both were eventually freed. However, Gorbachev never forgot his grandfathers' stories.

After working on a state farm, Gorbachev studied law in Moscow and joined the Communist Party. As an official in a farming region, Gorbachev learned much about the Soviet system and its problems.

He advanced quickly in the party. When he became general secretary in 1985, he was the youngest Politburo member and a man who wanted to bring change. He succeeded. Although he pursued reform to save the Soviet Union, ultimately he triggered its breakup.

Boris Yeltsin
1931–

Boris Yeltsin was raised in poverty. For 10 years, his family lived in a single room.

As a youth, Yeltsin earned good grades but behaved badly. Mikhail Gorbachev named him party boss and mayor of Moscow in 1985. Yeltsin's outspokenness got him into trouble. At one meeting, he launched into a bitter speech criticizing conservatives for working against perestroika. Gorbachev fired him for the sake of party unity.

Yeltsin made a dramatic comeback and won a seat in parliament in 1989. Parliament elected him president of Russia in 1990, and voters reelected him in 1991. Due at least in part to his failing health (heart problems), Yeltsin resigned in 1999.

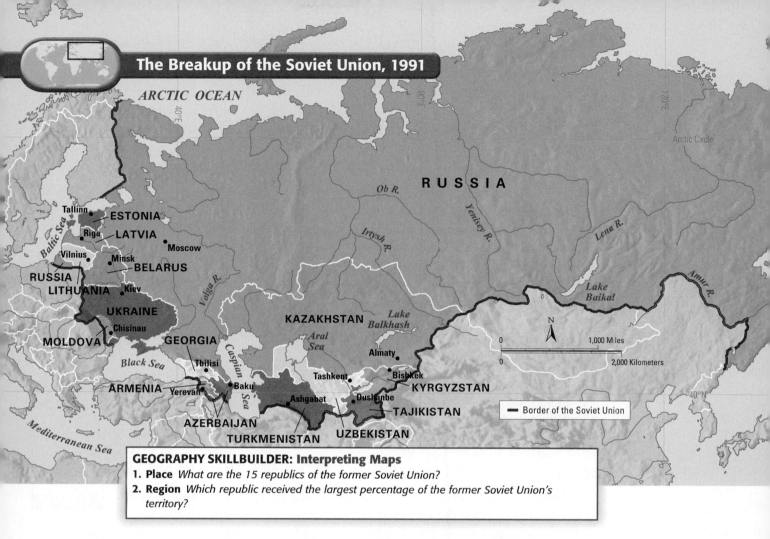

The Breakup of the Soviet Union, 1991

GEOGRAPHY SKILLBUILDER: Interpreting Maps
1. **Place** *What are the 15 republics of the former Soviet Union?*
2. **Region** *Which republic received the largest percentage of the former Soviet Union's territory?*

The August Coup On August 18, 1991, the hardliners detained Gorbachev at his vacation home on the Black Sea. They demanded his resignation as Soviet president. Early the next day, hundreds of tanks and armored vehicles rolled into Moscow. However, the Soviet people had lost their fear of the party. They were willing to defend their freedoms. Protesters gathered at the Russian parliament building, where Yeltsin had his office.

Around midday, Yeltsin emerged and climbed atop one of the tanks. As his supporters cheered, Yeltsin declared, "We proclaim all decisions and decrees of this committee to be illegal. . . . We appeal to the citizens of Russia to . . . demand a return of the country to normal constitutional developments."

MAIN IDEA

Analyzing Motives
B Why do you think the Soviet troops refused the order to attack the parliament building?

On August 20, the hardliners ordered troops to attack the parliament building, but they refused. Their refusal turned the tide. On August 21, the military withdrew its forces from Moscow. That night, Gorbachev returned to Moscow. **B**

End of the Soviet Union The coup attempt sparked anger against the Communist Party. Gorbachev resigned as general secretary of the party. The Soviet parliament voted to stop all party activities. Having first seized power in 1917 in a coup that succeeded, the Communist Party now collapsed because of a coup that failed.

The coup also played a decisive role in accelerating the breakup of the Soviet Union. Estonia and Latvia quickly declared their independence. Other republics soon followed. Although Gorbachev pleaded for unity, no one was listening. By early December, all 15 republics had declared independence.

Yeltsin met with the leaders of other republics to chart a new course. They agreed to form the Commonwealth of Independent States, or **CIS**, a loose federation of former Soviet territories. Only the Baltic republics and Georgia declined to join. The formation of the CIS meant the death of the Soviet Union. On Christmas Day 1991, Gorbachev announced his resignation as president of the Soviet Union, a country that ceased to exist.

Russia Under Boris Yeltsin

As president of the large Russian Federation, Boris Yeltsin was now the most powerful figure in the CIS. He would face many problems, including an ailing economy, tough political opposition, and an unpopular war.

Yeltsin Faces Problems One of Yeltsin's goals was to reform the Russian economy. He adopted a bold plan known as **"shock therapy,"** an abrupt shift to free-market economics. Yeltsin lowered trade barriers, removed price controls, and ended subsidies to state-owned industries.

Vocabulary
subsidies: government funds given in support of industries

Initially, the plan produced more shock than therapy. Prices soared; from 1992 to 1994, the inflation rate averaged 800 percent. Many factories dependent on government money had to cut production or shut down entirely. This forced thousands of people out of work. By 1993, most Russians were suffering economic hardship:

PRIMARY SOURCE
A visitor to Moscow cannot escape the feeling of a society in collapse. Child beggars accost foreigners on the street. . . . Children ask why they should stay in school when educated professionals do not make enough money to survive. . . . A garment worker complains that now her wages do not cover even the food bills, while fear of growing crime makes her dread leaving home.

DAVID M. KOTZ, "The Cure That Could Kill"

Economic problems fueled a political crisis. In October 1993, legislators opposed to Yeltsin's policies shut themselves inside the parliament building. Yeltsin ordered troops to bombard the building, forcing hundreds of rebel legislators to surrender. Many were killed. Opponents accused Yeltsin of acting like a dictator. **C**

Chechnya Rebels Yeltsin's troubles included war in Chechnya (CHEHCH•nee•uh), a largely Muslim area in southwestern Russia. In 1991, Chechnya declared its independence, but Yeltsin denied the region's right to secede. In 1994, he ordered 40,000 Russian troops into the breakaway republic. Russian forces reduced the capital city of Grozny (GROHZ•nee) to rubble. News of the death and destruction sparked anger throughout Russia.

▼ A Russian soldier throws away a spent shell case near the Chechnyan capital of Grozny.

With an election coming, Yeltsin sought to end the war. In August 1996, the two sides signed a cease-fire. That year, Yeltsin won reelection. War soon broke out again between Russia and Chechnya, however. In 1999, as the fighting raged, Yeltsin resigned and named Vladimir Putin as acting president.

MAIN IDEA

Evaluating Decisions
C Compare Yeltsin's action here to his actions during the August Coup. Which were more supportive of democracy?

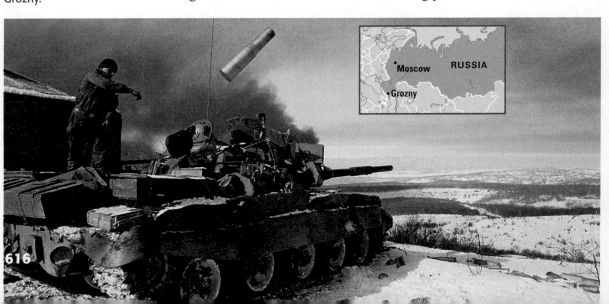

Russia Under Vladimir Putin

Putin forcefully dealt with the rebellion in Chechnya—a popular move that helped him win the presidential election in 2000. Nonetheless, the fighting in the region dragged on for years.

Troubles Continue in Chechnya In 2002, Russia said that the war in Chechnya was nearing an end. In July 2002, the Kremlin said it would begin pulling some of its 80,000 troops out of Chechnya, but Russia had made and broken such a promise before. Then, in October 2002, Chechen rebels seized a theater in Moscow, and more than 150 people died in the rescue attempt by Russian forces.

Economic, Political, and Social Problems The nation's economic problems continued, and some observers wondered whether Russian democracy could survive. A decade of change and reform between 1992 and 2002 caused enormous social upheaval in Russia. Experts estimated that there were between 30,000 and 50,000 homeless children on the streets of Moscow. About half of these children were younger than 13. Other indications of a society experiencing severe stress included high rates of domestic violence and unemployment, a steep population decline, and declines in the standard of living and the average life expectancy.

Nonetheless, there were some signs of improvement under Putin. He stated that he favored a market economy, but one adapted to Russia's special circumstances. Unrest in the Soviet Union had an enormous impact on Central and Eastern Europe, as you will read in the next section.

History Makers

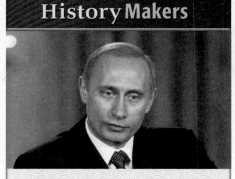

Vladimir Putin
1952–

Vladimir Putin worked for 15 years as an intelligence officer in the KGB (Committee for State Security). Six of those years were spent in East Germany. In 1990, at the age of 38, he retired from the KGB with the rank of lieutenant colonel.

Putin became first deputy mayor of Leningrad. In 1996, he moved to Moscow, where he joined the presidential staff. Eventually, Boris Yeltsin appointed Putin prime minister. When Yeltsin resigned at the end of 1999, he appointed Putin acting president. In March 2000, Putin won election as president.

INTEGRATED TECHNOLOGY

RESEARCH LINKS For more on Vladimir Putin, go to **classzone.com**

SECTION 3 ASSESSMENT

TERMS & NAMES 1. For each term or name, write a sentence explaining its significance.
• Politburo • Mikhail Gorbachev • glasnost • perestroika • Boris Yeltsin • CIS • "shock therapy"

USING YOUR NOTES

2. In what year did the Soviet Union break apart?

1985   2002

MAIN IDEAS

3. What are some of the changes that Gorbachev made to the Soviet economy?

4. After the breakup of the Soviet Union, what problems did Yeltsin face as the president of the Russian Federation?

5. How did Putin deal with Chechnya?

CRITICAL THINKING & WRITING

6. SYNTHESIZING How did Gorbachev's reforms help to move the Soviet Union toward democracy?

7. ANALYZING ISSUES What are some of the problems that faced President Vladimir Putin in Russia?

8. COMPARING In what ways were the policies of Gorbachev, Yeltsin, and Putin similar?

9. WRITING ACTIVITY REVOLUTION It has been said that Gorbachev's reforms led to another Russian Revolution. In your opinion, what did this revolution overthrow? Support your opinion in a two-paragraph **essay.**

INTEGRATED TECHNOLOGY **INTERNET ACTIVITY**

Use the Internet to research the situation in Chechnya today. Make a **poster** that includes a time line of the conflict, the leaders of the two sides, and war images.

INTERNET KEYWORD
Chechnya

Changes in Central and Eastern Europe

MAIN IDEA	WHY IT MATTERS NOW	TERMS & NAMES
CULTURAL INTERACTION Changes in the Soviet Union led to changes throughout Central and Eastern Europe.	Many Eastern European nations that overthrew Communist governments are still struggling with reform.	• Solidarity • Lech Walesa • reunification • ethnic cleansing

SETTING THE STAGE The Soviet reforms of the late 1980s brought high hopes to the people of Central and Eastern Europe. For the first time in decades, they were free to make choices about the economic and political systems governing their lives. However, they soon discovered that increased freedom sometimes challenges the social order. Mikhail Gorbachev's new thinking in the Soviet Union led him to urge Central and Eastern European leaders to open up their economic and political systems.

TAKING NOTES

Analyzing Causes Use a chart to record reasons that nations in Central and Eastern Europe broke apart.

Former nations	Reasons for breakup
Yugoslavia	
Czecho-slovakia	

Poland and Hungary Reform

The aging Communist rulers of Europe resisted reform. However, powerful forces for democracy were building in their countries. In the past, the threat of Soviet intervention had kept such forces in check. Now, Gorbachev was saying that the Soviet Union would not oppose reform.

Poland and Hungary were among the first countries in Eastern Europe to embrace the spirit of change. In 1980, Polish workers at the Gdansk shipyard went on strike, demanding government recognition of their union, **Solidarity**. When millions of Poles supported the action, the government gave in to the union's demands. Union leader **Lech Walesa** (lehk vah•WEHN•sah) became a national hero.

Solidarity Defeats Communists The next year, however, the Polish government banned Solidarity again and declared martial law. The Communist Party discovered that military rule could not revive Poland's failing economy. In the 1980s, industrial production declined, while foreign debt rose to more than $40 billion.

Public discontent deepened as the economic crisis worsened. In August 1988, defiant workers walked off their jobs. They demanded raises and the legalization of Solidarity. The military leader, General Jaruzelski (YAH•roo•ZEHL•skee), agreed to hold talks with Solidarity leaders. In April 1989, Jaruzelski legalized Solidarity and agreed to hold Poland's first free election since the Communists took power.

In elections during 1989 and 1990, Polish voters voted against Communists and overwhelmingly chose Solidarity candidates. They elected Lech Walesa president.

Poland Votes Out Walesa After becoming president in 1990, Lech Walesa tried to revive Poland's bankrupt economy. Like Boris Yeltsin, he adopted a strategy of shock therapy to move Poland toward a free-market economy. As in Russia, inflation and unemployment shot up. By the mid-1990s, the economy was improving.

Nevertheless, many Poles remained unhappy with the pace of economic progress. In the elections of 1995, they turned Walesa out of office in favor of a former Communist, Aleksander Kwasniewski (kfahs•N'YEHF•skee).

Poland Under Kwasniewski President Kwasniewski led Poland in its drive to become part of a broader European community. In 1999, Poland became a full member of NATO. As a NATO member, Poland provided strong support in the war against terrorism after the attack on the World Trade Center in New York on September 11, 2001. In appreciation of Poland's support, President Bush invited Kwasniewski to Washington for a formal state visit in July 2002.

Kwasniewski continued the efforts of previous leaders to establish a strong market economy in Poland. Although unemployment and poverty continued to be deep-rooted problems, Kwasniewski pushed for democracy and free markets.

Hungarian Communists Disband Inspired by the changes in Poland, Hungarian leaders launched a sweeping reform program. To stimulate economic growth, reformers encouraged private enterprise and allowed a small stock market to operate. A new constitution permitted a multiparty system with free elections.

Vocabulary
deposed: removed from power

The pace of change grew faster when radical reformers took over a Communist Party congress in October 1989. The radicals deposed the party's leaders and then dissolved the party itself. Here was another first: a European Communist Party had voted itself out of existence. A year later, in national elections, the nation's voters put a non-Communist government in power.

In 1994, a socialist party—largely made up of former Communists—won a majority of seats in Hungary's parliament. The socialist party and a democratic party formed a coalition, or alliance, to rule.

In parliamentary elections in 1998, a liberal party won the most seats in the National Assembly. In 1999, Hungary joined the North Atlantic Treaty Organization as a full member. In the year 2001, there was a general economic downtown in Hungary. This was due to weak exports, decline in foreign investment, and excessive spending on state pensions and increased minimum wages.

▼ The fall of the Berlin Wall, November 10, 1989

Germany Reunifies

While Poland and Hungary were moving toward reform, East Germany's 77-year-old party boss, Erich Honecker, dismissed reforms as unnecessary. Then, in 1989, Hungary allowed vacationing East German tourists to cross the border into Austria. From there they could travel to West Germany. Thousands of East Germans took this new escape route to the west. **A**

Fall of the Berlin Wall In response, the East German government closed its borders entirely. By October 1989, huge demonstrations had broken out

MAIN IDEA

Analyzing Causes
A How did the fall of communism in Hungary contribute to turmoil in East Germany?

in cities across East Germany. The protesters demanded the right to travel freely, and later added the demand for free elections. Honecker lost his authority with the party and resigned on October 18.

In June 1987, President Reagan had stood before the Berlin Wall and demanded: "Mr. Gorbachev, tear down this wall!" Two years later, the wall was indeed about to come down. The new East German leader, Egon Krenz, boldly gambled that he could restore stability by allowing people to leave East Germany. On November 9, 1989, he opened the Berlin Wall. The long-divided city of Berlin erupted in joyous celebration. Krenz's dramatic gamble to save communism did not work. By the end of 1989, the East German Communist Party had ceased to exist.

Reunification With the fall of Communism in East Germany, many Germans began to speak of **reunification**—the merging of the two Germanys. However, the movement for reunification worried many people, who feared a united Germany.

The West German chancellor, Helmut Kohl, assured world leaders that Germans had learned from the past. They were now committed to democracy and human rights. Kohl's assurances helped persuade other European nations to accept German reunification. Germany was officially reunited on October 3, 1990. **B**

MAIN IDEA

Clarifying
B Why would Europeans fear the reunification of Germany?

Germany's Challenges The newly united Germany faced serious problems. More than 40 years of Communist rule had left eastern Germany in ruins. Its railroads, highways, and telephone system had not been modernized since World War II. East German industries produced goods that could not compete in the global market.

Rebuilding eastern Germany's bankrupt economy was going to be a difficult, costly process. To pay these costs, Kohl raised taxes. As taxpayers tightened their belts, workers in eastern Germany faced a second problem—unemployment. Inefficient factories closed, depriving millions of workers of their jobs.

Major Industries of Germany, 2003

- ⊛ National capital
- • Other city
- ⬤ Major business center
- — Major highway
- ⚗ Chemicals
- Electronics
- ☼ Engineering
- Optics
- Research & development
- Shipbuilding
- Vehicle assembly
- Wine

0 200 Miles
0 400 Kilometers

GEOGRAPHY SKILLBUILDER: Interpreting Maps
1. **Location** *What is the relative location of business centers? Give possible reasons.*
2. **Movement** *Why might Hamburg and Kiel be shipbuilding centers, and what does this suggest about the movement of goods?*

A New Chancellor In 1998, voters turned Kohl out of office and elected a new chancellor, Gerhard Schroeder, of the Socialist Democratic Party. Schroeder started out as a market reformer, but the slow growth of the German economy made the task of reform difficult. Although Germany had the world's third largest economy, it was the slowest-growing economy in Europe in the early years of the 21st century. Germany's unemployment rate was among the highest in Europe, and rising inflation was also a continuing problem. Nonetheless, Schroeder won re-election in 2002.

Reunification forced Germany to rethink its role in international affairs. As Central Europe's largest country, Germany gained global responsibilities. Schroeder and his foreign minister took an active role in European affairs.

Democracy Spreads in Czechoslovakia

Changes in East Germany affected other European countries, including Czechoslovakia and Romania.

Czechoslovakia Reforms While huge crowds were demanding democracy in East Germany, neighboring Czechoslovakia remained quiet. A conservative government led by Milos Jakes resisted all change. In 1989, the police arrested several dissidents. Among these was the Czech playwright Václav Havel (VAH•tslahv HAH•vehl), a popular critic of the government.

On October 28, 1989, about 10,000 people gathered in Wenceslas Square in the center of Prague. They demanded democracy and freedom. Hundreds were arrested. Three weeks later, about 25,000 students inspired by the fall of the Berlin Wall gathered in Prague to demand reform. Following orders from the government, the police brutally attacked the demonstrators and injured hundreds.

The government crackdown angered the Czech people. Huge crowds gathered in Wenceslas Square. They demanded an end to Communist rule. On November 25, about 500,000 protesters crowded into downtown Prague. Within hours, Milos Jakes and his entire Politburo resigned. One month later, a new parliament elected Václav Havel president of Czechoslovakia.

Czechoslovakia Breaks Up In Czechoslovakia, reformers also launched an economic program based on "shock therapy." The program caused a sharp rise in unemployment. It especially hurt Slovakia, the republic occupying the eastern third of Czechoslovakia.

Unable to agree on economic policy, the country's two parts—Slovakia and the Czech Republic—drifted apart. In spite of President Václav Havel's pleas for unity, a movement to split the nation gained support among the people. Havel resigned because of this. Czechoslovakia split into two countries on January 1, 1993.

Havel was elected president of the Czech Republic. He won reelection in 1998. Then, in 2003, Havel stepped down as president, in part because of ill health. The Czech parliament chose Václav Klaus, a right-wing economist and former prime minister, to succeed him. The economy of the Czech Republic slowly improved in the face of some serious problems. The Czech Republic pushed to become a full member of the European Union (EU) by 2004.

Slovakia, too, proceeded on a reformist, pro-Western path. It experienced one of the highest economic growth rates in the region in 2002. It hoped to join both NATO and the EU in the near future.

Overthrow in Romania

By late 1989, only Romania seemed unmoved by the calls for reform. Romania's ruthless Communist dictator Nicolae Ceausescu (chow•SHES•koo) maintained a firm grip on power. His secret police enforced his orders brutally. Nevertheless, Romanians were aware of the reforms in other countries. They began a protest movement of their own.

A Popular Uprising In December, Ceausescu ordered the army to fire on demonstrators in the city of Timisoara

Social History

The Romanian Language

The Romanians are the only people in Eastern Europe whose ancestry and language go back to the ancient Romans. Romanian is the only Eastern European language that developed from Latin. For this reason, Romanian is very different from the other languages spoken in the region.

Today's Romanians are descended from the Dacians (the original people in the region), the Romans, and tribes that arrived later, such as the Goths, Huns, and Slavs.

Romanian remains the official language today. Minority groups within Romania (such as Hungarians, Germans, Gypsies, Jews, Turks, and Ukrainians) sometimes speak their own ethnic languages among themselves. Nonetheless, almost all the people speak Romanian as well.

INTEGRATED TECHNOLOGY

INTERNET ACTIVITY Create a poster on all the Romance languages, which developed from Latin. Go to **classzone.com** for your research.

(tee•mee•SHWAH•rah). The army killed and wounded hundreds of people. The massacre in Timisoara ignited a popular uprising against Ceausescu. Within days, the army joined the people. Shocked by the collapse of his power, Ceausescu and his wife attempted to flee. They were captured, however, and then tried and executed on Christmas Day, 1989. Romania held general elections in 1990, 1992, and 1996. In the 2000 elections, Ion Iliescu was elected to a third term as president. **C**

MAIN IDEA

Contrasting
C Contrast the democratic revolutions in Czechoslovakia and Romania.

The Romanian Economy Throughout the 1990s, Romania struggled with corruption and crime as it tried to salvage its economy. In 2001, overall production was still only 75 percent of what it had been in 1989, the year of Ceausescu's overthrow. In the first years of the 21st century, two-thirds of the economy was still state owned.

However, the government made economic reforms to introduce elements of capitalism. The government also began to reduce the layers of bureaucracy in order to encourage foreign investors. Furthermore, in order to achieve membership in the European Union, the Romanian government began to move away from a state-controlled economy.

The Breakup of Yugoslavia

Ethnic conflict plagued Yugoslavia. This country, formed after World War I, had eight major ethnic groups—Serbs, Croats, Muslims, Slovenes, Macedonians, Albanians, Hungarians, and Montenegrins. Ethnic and religious differences dating back centuries caused these groups to view one another with suspicion. After World War II, Yugoslavia became a federation of six republics. Each republic had a mixed population.

A Bloody Breakup Josip Tito, who led Yugoslavia from 1945 to 1980, held the country together. After Tito's death, ethnic resentments boiled over. Serbian leader Slobodan Milosevic (mee•LOH•sheh•vihch) asserted leadership over Yugoslavia. Many Serbs opposed Milosevic and his policies and fled the country.

Two republics, Slovenia and Croatia, declared independence. In June 1991, the Serbian-led Yugoslav army invaded both republics. After months of bloody fighting, both republics freed themselves from Serbian rule. Early in 1992, Bosnia-Herzegovina joined Slovenia and Croatia in declaring independence. (In April, Serbia and Montenegro formed a new Yugoslavia.) Bosnia's population included Muslims (44 percent), Serbs (31 percent), and Croats (17 percent). While Bosnia's Muslims and Croats backed independence, Bosnian Serbs strongly opposed it. Supported by Serbia, the Bosnian Serbs launched a war in March 1992.

During the war, Serbian military forces used violence and forced emigration against Bosnian Muslims living in Serb-held lands. Called **ethnic cleansing**, this policy was intended to rid Bosnia of its Muslim population. By 1995, the Serbian military controlled 70 percent of Bosnia. In December of that year, leaders of the three factions involved in the war signed a UN- and U.S.-brokered peace treaty. In September 1996, Bosnians elected a three-person presidency, one leader from each ethnic group. By 2001, Bosnia and

▼ A view of downtown Sarajevo through a bullet-shattered window

Ethnic Groups in the Former Yugoslavia

Many ethnic and religious groups lived within Yugoslavia, which was a federation of six republics. The map shows how the ethnic groups were distributed. Some of those groups held ancient grudges against one another. The chart summarizes some of the cultural differences among the groups.

Ethnic Groups in the Former Yugoslavia, 1992

Legend:
- Albanian
- Croat
- Hungarian
- Macedonian
- Montenegrin
- Muslim
- Serb
- Slovene
- No majority present
- Former Yugoslavia
- **Borders of 1992**
- Republic boundaries
- Provincial boundaries

Differences Among the Ethnic Groups

Group	Language (slavic unless noted)	Religion
Albanians	Albanian (not Slavic)	mostly Muslim
Croats	dialect of Serbo-Croatian*	mostly Roman Catholic
Hungarians	Magyar (not Slavic)	many types of Christians
Macedonians	Macedonian	mostly Eastern Orthodox
Montenegrins	dialect of Serbo-Croatian*	mostly Eastern Orthodox
Muslims	dialect of Serbo-Croatian*	Muslim (converted under Ottoman rule)
Serbs	dialect of Serbo-Croatian*	mostly Eastern Orthodox
Slovenes	Slovenian	mostly Roman Catholic

SKILLBUILDER: Interpreting Visuals

1. **Analyzing Issues** *Use the chart to find out information about the various groups that lived in Bosnia and Herzegovina (as shown on the map). What were some of the differences among those groups?*
2. **Contrasting** *Kosovo was a province within Serbia. What group was in the majority there, and how did it differ from Serbs?*

* Since Yugoslavia broke apart, many residents of the former republics have started to refer to their dialects as separate languages: Croatian for Croats, Bosnian for Muslims, Serbian for Serbs and Montenegrins.

Herzegovina began to stand on its own without as much need for supervision by the international community. **D**

MAIN IDEA

Identifying Problems
D Why did Bosnia's mixed population cause a problem after Bosnia declared independence?

Rebellion in Kosovo The Balkan region descended into violence and bloodshed again in 1998, this time in Kosovo, a province in southern Serbia made up almost entirely of ethnic Albanians. As an independence movement in Kosovo grew increasingly violent, Serbian military forces invaded the province and fought back with a harsh hand. In response to growing reports of atrocities—and the failure of diplomacy to bring peace—NATO began a bombing campaign against Yugoslavia in the spring of 1999. After enduring more than two months of sustained bombing, Yugoslav leaders finally withdrew their troops from Kosovo.

The Region Faces Its Problems In the early years of the 21st century, there were conflicting signs in Yugoslavia. Slobodan Milosevic was extradited to stand trial for war crimes. A large portion of the country's foreign debt was erased. Despite an independence movement in Kosovo, parliamentary elections under UN supervision took place in November 2001 without violence.

And in Montenegro (which together with Serbia made up Yugoslavia), an independence movement seemed to lack support from the people as well as from the international community. Nonetheless, in February 2003, Yugoslavia's parliament voted to replace what remained of the federation with a loose union of Serbia and Montenegro. Outright independence for each could come as early as 2006. However, problems remained, as indicated by the assassination of the Serbian prime minister, Zoran Djindjic, in March 2003.

The nations of Central and Eastern Europe made many gains in the early years of the 21st century. Even so, they continued to face serious obstacles to democracy. Resolving ethnic conflicts remained crucial, as did economic progress. If the nations of Central and Eastern Europe and the former Soviet Union can improve their standard of living, democracy may have a better chance to grow. Meanwhile, economic reforms in Communist China sparked demands for political reforms, as you will read in the next section.

SECTION 4 ASSESSMENT

TERMS & NAMES 1. For each term or name, write a sentence explaining its significance.
• Solidarity   • Lech Walesa   • reunification   • ethnic cleansing

USING YOUR NOTES

2. Which nation seems to have done best since the breakup? Explain.

Former nations	Reasons for breakup
Yugoslavia	
Czecho- slovakia	

MAIN IDEAS

3. How did Solidarity affect Communist rule in Poland?

4. What effect did reunification have on Germany's international role?

5. What was the main cause of the breakup of Czechoslovakia?

CRITICAL THINKING & WRITING

6. **ANALYZING CAUSES** Why did ethnic tension become such a severe problem in the Soviet Union and Yugoslavia?

7. **DRAWING CONCLUSIONS** What are some of the problems faced in Central and Eastern Europe in the 21st century?

8. **RECOGNIZING EFFECTS** What effect did economic reform have on Slovakia?

9. **WRITING ACTIVITY** CULTURAL INTERACTION With a partner, create a **cause-and-effect diagram** to show how democratic reform spread through Central and Eastern Europe. The diagram should show the order in which reform happened and which countries influenced others.

CONNECT TO TODAY **MAKING A PIE GRAPH**

Research the size of the populations of Central and Eastern Europe countries mentioned in this section. Construct a **pie graph** showing the comparative sizes of the populations.

5

China: Reform and Reaction

MAIN IDEA	WHY IT MATTERS NOW	TERMS & NAMES
CULTURAL INTERACTION In response to contact with the West, China's government has experimented with capitalism but has rejected calls for democracy.	After the 1997 death of Chinese leader Deng Xiaoping, President Jiang Zemin seemed to be continuing Deng's policies.	• Zhou Enlai • Deng Xiaoping • Four Modernizations • Tiananmen Square • Hong Kong

SETTING THE STAGE The trend toward democracy around the world also affected China to a limited degree. A political reform movement arose in the late 1980s. It built on economic reforms begun earlier in the decade. However, although the leadership of the Communist Party in China generally supported economic reform, it opposed political reform. China's Communist government clamped down on the political reformers. At the same time, it maintained a firm grip on power in the country.

The Legacy of Mao

After the Communists came to power in China in 1949, Mao Zedong set out to transform China. Mao believed that peasant equality, revolutionary spirit, and hard work were all that was needed to improve the Chinese economy.

However, lack of modern technology damaged Chinese efforts to increase agricultural and industrial output. In addition, Mao's policies stifled economic growth. He eliminated incentives for higher production. He tried to replace family life with life in the communes. These policies took away the peasants' motive to work for the good of themselves and their families.

Facing economic disaster, some Chinese Communists talked of modernizing the economy. Accusing them of "taking the capitalist road," Mao began the Cultural Revolution in 1966 to cleanse China of antirevolutionary influences.

TAKING NOTES

Following Chronological Order Use a diagram to show events leading up to the demonstration in Tiananmen Square.

Mao's Attempts to Change China	
Mao's Programs	**Program Results**
First Five-Year Plan 1953–1957	• Industry grew 15 percent a year. • Agricultural output grew very slowly.
Great Leap Forward 1958–1961	• China suffered economic disaster—industrial declines and food shortages. • Mao lost influence.
Cultural Revolution 1966–1976	• Mao regained influence by backing radicals. • Purges and conflicts among leaders created economic, social, and political chaos.

▲ Zhou Enlai, a translator, Mao Zedong, President Nixon, and Henry Kissinger meet in Beijing in 1972.

Instead of saving radical communism, however, the Cultural Revolution turned many people against it. In the early 1970s, China entered another moderate period under **Zhou Enlai** (joh ehn•ly). Zhou had been premier since 1949. During the Cultural Revolution, he had tried to restrain the radicals. **A**

MAIN IDEA
Recognizing Effects
A What was the ultimate result of Mao's radical Communist policies?

China and the West

Throughout the Cultural Revolution, China played almost no role in world affairs. In the early 1960s, China had split with the Soviet Union over the leadership of world communism. In addition, China displayed hostility toward the United States because of U.S. support for the government on Taiwan.

China Opened Its Doors China's isolation worried Zhou. He began to send out signals that he was willing to form ties to the West. In 1971, Zhou startled the world by inviting an American table-tennis team to tour China. It was the first visit by an American group to China since 1949.

The visit began a new era in Chinese-American relations. In 1971, the United States reversed its policy and endorsed UN membership for the People's Republic of China. The next year, President Nixon made a state visit to China. He met with Mao and Zhou. The three leaders agreed to begin cultural exchanges and a limited amount of trade. In 1979, the United States and China established diplomatic relations.

Economic Reform Both Mao and Zhou died in 1976. Shortly afterward, moderates took control of the Communist Party. They jailed several of the radicals who had led the Cultural Revolution. By 1980, **Deng Xiaoping** (duhng show•pihng) had emerged as the most powerful leader in China. He was the last of the "old revolutionaries" who had ruled China since 1949.

Although a lifelong Communist, Deng boldly supported moderate economic policies. Unlike Mao, he was willing to use capitalist ideas to help China's economy. He embraced a set of goals known as the **Four Modernizations**. These called for progress in agriculture, industry, defense, and science and technology. Deng launched an ambitious program of economic reforms.

First, Deng eliminated Mao's communes and leased the land to individual farmers. The farmers paid rent by delivering a fixed quota of food to the government. They could then grow crops and sell them for a profit. Under this system, food production increased by 50 percent in the years 1978 to 1984.

Deng extended his program to industry. The government permitted private businesses to operate. It gave the managers of state-owned industries more freedom to set production goals. Deng also welcomed foreign technology and investment.

Deng's economic policies produced striking changes in Chinese life. As incomes increased, people began to buy appliances and televisions. Chinese youths now wore stylish clothes and listened to Western music. Gleaming hotels filled with foreign tourists symbolized China's new policy of openness.

Massacre in Tiananmen Square

Deng's economic reforms produced a number of unexpected problems. As living standards improved, the gap between the rich and poor widened. Increasingly, the public believed that party officials profited from their positions.

MAIN IDEA

Analyzing Causes
B How did economic reform introduce new political ideas to China?

Furthermore, the new policies admitted not only Western investments and tourists but also Western political ideas. Increasing numbers of Chinese students studied abroad and learned about the West. In Deng's view, the benefits of opening the economy exceeded the risks. Nevertheless, as Chinese students learned more about democracy, they began to question China's lack of political freedom. **B**

Students Demand Democracy In 1989, students sparked a popular uprising that stunned China's leaders. Beginning in April of that year, more than 100,000 students occupied **Tiananmen** (tyahn•ahn•mehn) **Square**, a huge public space in the heart of Beijing. The students mounted a protest for democracy. (See photograph on page 630.)

The student protest won widespread popular support. When thousands of students began a hunger strike to highlight their cause, people poured into Tiananmen Square to support them. Many students called for Deng Xiaoping to resign.

Deng Orders a Crackdown Instead of considering political reform, Deng declared martial law. He ordered about 100,000 troops to surround Beijing. Although many students left the square after martial law was declared, about 5,000 chose to remain and continue their protest. The students revived their spirits by defiantly erecting a 33-foot statue that they named the "Goddess of Democracy."

On June 4, 1989, the standoff came to an end. Thousands of heavily armed soldiers stormed Tiananmen Square. Tanks smashed through barricades and crushed the Goddess of Democracy. Soldiers sprayed gunfire into crowds of frightened students. They also attacked protesters elsewhere in Beijing. The assault killed hundreds and wounded thousands.

> Analyzing Primary Sources

Training the Chinese Army

After the massacre in Tiananmen Square, Xiao Ye (a former Chinese soldier living in the United States) explained how Chinese soldiers are trained to obey orders without complaint.

PRIMARY SOURCE

We usually developed bleeding blisters on our feet after a few days of . . . hiking. Our feet were a mass of soggy peeling flesh and blood, and the pain was almost unbearable. . . . We considered the physical challenge a means of tempering [hardening] ourselves for the sake of the Party. . . . No one wanted to look bad. . . .

And during the days in Tiananmen, once again the soldiers did not complain. They obediently drove forward, aimed, and opened fire on command. In light of their training, how could it have been otherwise?

XIAO YE, "Tiananmen Square: A Soldier's Story"

DOCUMENT-BASED QUESTIONS
1. **Making Inferences** For whom did the soldiers seem to believe they were making their physical sacrifices?
2. **Drawing Conclusions** What attitude toward obeying orders did their training seem to encourage in the soldiers?

The attack on Tiananmen Square marked the beginning of a massive government campaign to stamp out protest. Police arrested thousands of people. The state used the media to announce that reports of a massacre were untrue. Officials claimed that a small group of criminals had plotted against the government. Television news, however, had already broadcast the truth to the world.

China Enters the New Millennium

The brutal repression of the prodemocracy movement left Deng firmly in control of China. During the final years of his life, Deng continued his program of economic reforms.

Although Deng moved out of the limelight in 1995, he remained China's leader. In February 1997, after a long illness, Deng died. Communist Party General Secretary Jiang Zemin (jee•ahng zeh•meen) assumed the presidency.

China Under Jiang Many questions arose after Deng's death. What kind of leader would Jiang be? Would he be able to hold on to power and ensure political stability? A highly intelligent and educated man, Jiang had served as mayor of Shanghai. He was considered skilled, flexible, and practical. However, he had no military experience. Therefore, Jiang had few allies among the generals. He also faced challenges from rivals, including hard-line officials who favored a shift away from Deng's economic policies.

Other questions following Deng's death had to do with China's poor human rights record, its occupation of Tibet, and relations with the United States. During the 1990s, the United States pressured China to release political prisoners and ensure basic rights for political opponents. China remained hostile to such pressure. Its government continued to repress the prodemocracy movement. Nevertheless, the desire for freedom still ran through Chinese society. If China remained economically open but politically closed, tensions seemed bound to surface.

In late 1997, Jiang paid a state visit to the United States. During his visit, U.S. protesters demanded more democracy in China. Jiang admitted that China had made some mistakes but refused to promise that China's policies would change.

President Jiang Zemin and Premier Zhu Rongji announced their retirement in late 2002. Jiang's successor was Hu Jintao. However, Jiang was expected to wield influence over his successor behind the scenes. Hu became president of the country and general secretary of the Communist Party. Jiang remained political leader of the military. Both supported China's move to a market economy.

Transfer of Hong Kong Another major issue for China was the status of **Hong Kong**. Hong Kong was a thriving business center and British colony on the southeastern coast of China. On July 1, 1997, Great Britain handed Hong Kong over to China, ending 155 years of colonial rule. As part of the transfer, China promised to respect Hong Kong's economic system and political liberties for 50 years.

Many of Hong Kong's citizens worried about Chinese rule and feared the loss of their freedoms. Others, however, saw the transfer as a way to reconnect with their Chinese

History Makers

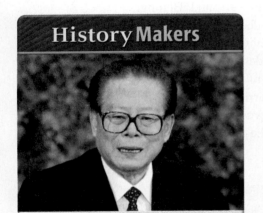

Jiang Zemin
1926–

Jiang Zemin was trained as an engineer. After working as an engineer, heading several technological institutes, and serving as minister of the electronics industry, he moved up in politics.

In 1982, he joined the Central Committee of the Communist Party in China. He became mayor of Shanghai in 1985, in which post he proved to be an effective administrator. In 1989, he became general secretary of the Chinese Communist Party. This promotion was largely due to his support for the government's putdown of the prodemocracy demonstrations in that year. In 1993, he became president. In 2003, he stepped down and was replaced by Hu Jintao; however, Jiang retained power behind the scenes.

heritage. In the first four or five years after the transfer, the control of mainland China over Hong Kong tightened.

China Beyond 2000

The case of China demonstrates that the creation of democracy can be a slow, fitful, and incomplete process. Liberal reforms in one area, such as the economy, may not lead immediately to political reforms.

Economics and Politics In China, there has been a dramatic reduction in poverty. Some experts argue that China managed to reform its economy and reduce poverty because it adopted a gradual approach to selling off state industries and privatizing the economy rather than a more abrupt approach. At any rate, as the global economy slowed in the early years of the 21st century, China managed to maintain economic growth.

▲ People celebrate in Tiananmen Square after Beijing won the bid for the 2008 Olympic Games.

People in China and around the world have a desire for more political freedom. As economic and social conditions improve—for example, as the middle class expands and educational opportunities grow—the prospects for democracy also may improve. In addition, as countries are increasingly linked through technology and trade, they will have more opportunity to influence each other politically. In 2000, for example, the U.S. Congress voted to normalize trade with China. Supporters of such a move argue that the best way to prompt political change in China is through greater engagement rather than isolation. Another sign of China's increasing engagement with the world is its successful campaign to host the 2008 Summer Olympics in Beijing.

SECTION 5 ASSESSMENT

TERMS & NAMES 1. For each term or name, write a sentence explaining its significance.
• Zhou Enlai   • Deng Xiaoping   • Four Modernizations   • Tiananmen Square   • Hong Kong

USING YOUR NOTES
2. Other than the demonstration in Tiananmen Square, which of these events was most important? Explain.

MAIN IDEAS
3. What effect did Mao's policies have on economic growth?

4. What were some of Deng Xiaoping's economic reforms?

5. How would you describe China's record on human rights?

CRITICAL THINKING & WRITING
6. **SUPPORTING OPINIONS** Judging from what you have read about the Chinese government, do you think Hong Kong will keep its freedoms under Chinese rule? Explain.

7. **FOLLOWING CHRONOLOGICAL ORDER** What were some of the events that followed the demonstration in Tiananmen Square?

8. **COMPARING AND CONTRASTING** Has there been greater progress in political or economic reform in China?

9. **WRITING ACTIVITY** CULTURAL INTERACTION Imagine that you are a Chinese student visiting the West. Write a **letter** home in which you explain what you have seen abroad.

CONNECT TO TODAY MAKING A POSTER

China will be hosting the 2008 Summer Olympics in Beijing. Research the efforts that China is making to prepare the city for the festivities and present your findings in a **poster**.

Photojournalism

From the earliest days of photography, magazines and newspapers have used photographs to convey the news. Photojournalists must respond quickly to recognize a history-making moment and to record that moment before it passes. As the photographs on this page demonstrate, photojournalists have captured many of the democratic struggles that have occurred in the last few decades. In some cases, news photographs have helped protesters or oppressed people gain the support of the world.

INTEGRATED/TECHNOLOGY

RESEARCH LINKS For more on photojournalism, go to **classzone.com**

Flight from Srebrenica ▶
During the conflicts in Bosnia and Herzegovina, the United Nations declared the city of Srebrenica a safe area. Even so, the Bosnian Serb army invaded in July 1995 and expelled more than 20,000 Muslims—nearly all of them women, children, or elderly people. In addition, the soldiers held more than 7,000 men and boys prisoner and over a five-day period massacred them.

▼ Man Defying Tanks
A single Chinese man blocked tanks on their way to crush prodemocracy protests in Tiananmen Square in June 1989. No one knows for sure what happened to the man afterward—or even who he was. Even so, this image has become one of the enduring photographs of the 20th century; it has come to stand for one man's courage in defying tyranny.

Fall of the Wall ▼

When the East German government opened the Berlin Wall in November 1989, a huge celebration broke out. Some people began to use pickaxes to demolish the wall entirely. Others danced on top of the wall. (See also the image on page 619.)

Abuelas de Plaza de Mayo ▲

From 1976 to 1983, the military government of Argentina tortured and killed thousands of political dissidents and sometimes stole their children. In this demonstration in December 1979, the *Abuelas de Plaza de Mayo* (Grandmothers of the Plaza de Mayo) demanded to know the fate of their relatives. The banner they carried reads "Disappeared Children."

Voting Line

When South Africa held its first all-race election in April 1994, people were so eager to vote that they stood in lines that sometimes stretched nearly a kilometer (0.62 mile).

Connect *to* Today

1. **Forming and Supporting Opinions**
   Which of these photographs do you think has the greatest impact on the viewer? Explain why.

   See Skillbuilder Handbook, page R20.

2. **Forming and Supporting Opinions**
   Using Internet or library resources, find a news photograph that you think effectively shows a recent historic event. Bring a copy of the photograph to class, and explain orally or in writing what it conveys about the event.

631

TERMS & NAMES

For each term or name below, briefly explain its connection to the democratic movements that took place from 1945 to the present.

1. PRI
2. apartheid
3. Nelson Mandela
4. Mikhail Gorbachev
5. glasnost
6. Lech Walesa
7. Deng Xiaoping
8. Tiananmen Square

MAIN IDEAS

Case Study: Latin American Democracies Section 1
(pages 599–605)

9. What are four common democratic practices?
10. What group held up democratic progress in both Brazil and Argentina until the 1980s?

The Challenge of Democracy in Africa Section 2
(pages 606–611)

11. What brought about the civil war in Nigeria?
12. What were three significant steps toward democracy taken by South Africa in the 1990s?

The Collapse of the Soviet Union Section 3
(pages 612–617)

13. What were the main reforms promoted by Soviet leader Mikhail Gorbachev?
14. What was the August Coup and how did it end?

Changes in Central and Eastern Europe Section 4
(pages 618–624)

15. Which nations overthrew Communist governments in 1989?
16. What led to the breakup of Yugoslavia?

China: Reform and Reaction Section 5 (pages 625–631)

17. What changes took place in China during the 1970s?
18. How did the Chinese government react to demands for democratic reform?

CRITICAL THINKING

1. USING YOUR NOTES

List several leaders who helped their nations make democratic progress. For each, cite one positive action.

Leader	Nation	Positive Action

2. ANALYZING ISSUES

CULTURAL INTERACTION What are some examples from this chapter in which the negative impact of one culture on another blocked democratic progress?

3. SYNTHESIZING

Consider what conditions helped democratic movements succeed and what conditions caused difficulties for them. What do you think were their hardest challenges?

4. DRAWING CONCLUSIONS

ECONOMICS How does a nation's economy affect its democratic progress?

5. SUMMARIZING

What were Deng Xiaoping's economic reforms for China?

VISUAL SUMMARY

18 Years of Democratic Struggles

PROGRESS TOWARD DEMOCRACY

1989
Poland Legalizes Solidarity trade union; agrees to free elections
Germany Opens Berlin Wall and starts reunification process
Hungary Disbands Communist Party
Czechoslovakia Holds free elections
Romania Overthrows a dictator

1985 Brazil Elects civilian government

1986 Soviet Union Begins economic reforms

1983 Argentina Holds first free election in 37 years

1991 Soviet Union Breaks up peacefully into 15 republics

1996 South Africa Adopts new constitution

2000 Mexico Ends 71 years of PRI rule

1999 Nigeria Holds free elections

1980 · 1985 · 1990 · 1995 · 2000

1983 Nigeria Military overthrows civilian rule

1989 China Government massacres protesters calling for democracy

1991 Yugoslavia Ethnic conflicts lead to breakup of country; years of war follow

1993 Russia Yeltsin orders troops to attack opponents in parliament building

1990 · 1995 · 2000

SETBACKS TO DEMOCRACY

Use the quotation and your knowledge of world history to answer questions 1 and 2.
Additional Test Practice, pp. S1–S33

PRIMARY SOURCE

> Whatever else you can say about the new Hong Kong, it will be more Chinese. Liu Heung-shing, the editor of the new Hong Kong magazine *The Chinese,* says that "for any meaningful art and culture to take off here, Hong Kong must find somewhere to anchor itself. To find that anchor, people will have to go north [to mainland China]." . . . Increasing numbers of Hong Kong's Cantonese speakers are studying mainland Mandarin. . . . At the same time that [Hong Kong] must resist China to retain Britain's legacy of rule of law, it knows that the most logical place for it to turn for commerce and culture is China.
>
> **ORVILLE SCHELL, "The Coming of Mao Zedong Chic"**

1. What is the main change that is taking place in Hong Kong's culture?

A. China is looking to Hong Kong for cultural inspiration.

B. Hong Kong is turning to China for cultural inspiration.

C. Hong Kong is turning to the West for cultural inspiration.

D. Hong Kong is turning inward.

2. What point of view might a Hong Kong politician have about this change?

A. may fear China will restrict the city's freedoms

B. may welcome tighter controls from China

C. may threaten military action against China

D. may vow never to cooperate with mainland China

Use this political cartoon and your knowledge of world history to answer question 3.

3. What is the cartoon saying about the state of communism in Poland, China, and the Soviet Union?

A. Communism is thriving.

B. Communism is helping nations gain economic health.

C. Communism is failing around the world.

D. Communism is sick but will recover.

INTEGRATED TECHNOLOGY

TEST PRACTICE Go to **classzone.com**

• Diagnostic tests
• Tutorials
• Strategies
• Additional practice

ALTERNATIVE ASSESSMENT

1. Interact *with* History

REVOLUTION On page 598, you considered why so many people want democracy. Now that you've read the chapter, have your explanations changed? Would you add anything to what you said before? Would you change anything you said before?

2. WRITING ABOUT HISTORY

A government official has asked you for suggestions on how to move a Communist economy to a free-market economy. Go through the chapter and compile a "Things to Do" **report** based on actions that other governments have taken. Consider the following issues:

• unemployment
• inflation
• political effects
• social upheaval

INTEGRATED TECHNOLOGY

Creating a Virtual Field Trip

With two other classmates, plan a two-week virtual field trip to explore the sights in China, including the Forbidden City and the sites of the 2008 Summer Olympics. After selecting and researching the sites you'd like to visit, use maps to determine your itinerary. Consider visiting these places and enjoying these excursions:

• Sites of the 2008 Summer Olympic games
• Sites around Beijing
• Great Wall
• A cruise along the Chang Jiang or Huang He rivers
• Three Gorges Dam
• Shanghai

For each place or excursion, give one reason why it is an important destination on a field trip to China. Include pictures and sound in your presentation.

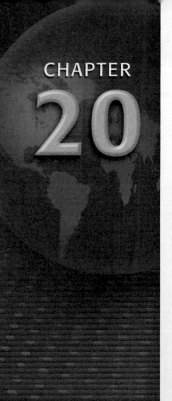

Global Interdependence,
1960–Present

Previewing Main Ideas

SCIENCE AND TECHNOLOGY Advances in science and technology have changed the lives of people around the globe. Improved communications and transportation have allowed goods, services, and ideas to move rapidly.

Geography *How does this map illustrate the idea of global interdependence?*

CULTURAL INTERACTION Inventions and innovations have brought the nations of the world closer and exposed people to other cultures. Cultures are now blending ideas and customs much faster than before.

Geography *Which countries in the Western Hemisphere are major destinations for immigrants?*

ECONOMICS Since World War II, nations have worked to expand trade and commerce in world markets. Changes in technology have blurred national boundaries and created a global market.

Geography *What do most countries with a net migration rate above 3.0 have in common economically?*

POWER AND AUTHORITY Since the end of World War II, nations have adopted collective efforts to ensure their security. One of the greatest challenges in maintaining global security is international terrorism.

Geography *What do most countries with a net migration rate above 3 have in common politically?*

INTEGRATED / TECHNOLOGY

eEdition
• Interactive Maps
• Interactive Visuals
• Interactive Primary Sources

VIDEO *Patterns of Interaction: The United States and the World*

INTERNET RESOURCES
Go to **classzone.com** for:
• Research Links   • Maps
• Internet Activities   • Test Practice
• Primary Sources   • Current Events
• Chapter Quiz

1968
◄ Many nations sign the Nuclear Non-Proliferation Treaty. (atomic energy symbol)

1975
Helsinki Accords support human rights.

WORLD   1960   1970

1972
U.S. and Soviet Union agree to joint space venture. Terrorists carry out attack at the Summer Olympic games in Munich. (masked terrorist in Munich) ▶

World Migration, 2002

GREENLAND

ICELAND

UNITED KINGDOM

IRELAND

GERMANY

POLAND

UKRAINE

RUSSIA

CANADA

FRANCE

SPAIN

ITALY

BULGARIA

SERBIA & MONT.

JORDAN

KAZAKHSTAN

MONGOLIA

AFGHANISTAN

TAJIKISTAN

ATLANTIC OCEAN

MOROCCO

ALGERIA

LIBYA

EGYPT

IRAQ

IRAN

PAKISTAN

KUWAIT

QATAR

INDIA

CHINA

SOUTH KOREA

JAPAN

UNITED STATES

MEXICO

JAMAICA

DOMINICAN REP.

GUATEMALA

EL SALVADOR

HONDURAS

PANAMA

NICARAGUA

VENEZUELA

COSTA RICA

COLOMBIA

ECUADOR

PERU

GUYANA

SURINAME

FR. GUIANA

SENEGAL

SIERRA LEONE

LIBERIA

MALI

NIGER

NIGERIA

SUDAN

ERITREA

ETHIOPIA

SAUDI ARABIA

U.A.E.

OMAN

THAILAND

VIETNAM

MALAYSIA

SINGAPORE

BRUNEI

TAIWAN

PHILIPPINES

INDONESIA

PACIFIC OCEAN

Tropic of Cancer

0° Equator

BRAZIL

BOLIVIA

DEM. REP. OF THE CONGO

TANZANIA

SOMALIA

INDIAN OCEAN

PAPUA NEW GUINEA

PACIFIC OCEAN

PARAGUAY

CHILE

URUGUAY

ARGENTINA

ZAMBIA

ZIMBABWE

SOUTH AFRICA

Tropic of Capricorn

AUSTRALIA

NEW ZEALAND

40°N

80°N

40°S

N W E S

0   2000   4000 Miles
0   4000   8000 Kilometers

Gall Projection

SOUTHERN OCEAN

Net Migration Rate*
- 3.01 and greater
- 0.01 to 3.0
- 0
- -0.01 to -3.0
- -3.01 and greater

Source: CIA World Factbook, 2002

*The difference between the number of persons entering and leaving a country during the year per 1,000 population.

1983
French research scientists isolate the AIDS virus.

1986
Accident takes place at Soviet nuclear power plant in Chernobyl.

1995
World Trade Organization is set up.

1998
Construction of the International Space Station begins.

1980

1990

2000

1981
U.S. carries out first space shuttle flight. ▶

2001
UN issues the Declaration of Commitment on HIV/AIDS. Terrorists launch attacks in New York and Washington, D.C.

2003
Human Genome Project is completed.

How do global events affect your daily life?

You have just seen a television program recapping some recent news events. You are surprised at the number of stories that involve the United States and other countries. You begin to think about how events in such distant places as China and Iraq can affect life in your own country.

▼ War in Iraq, 2003

▼ Mapping the Human Genome

▲ Homeland Security Alert

▲ Severe Acute Respiratory Syndrome in China

EXAMINING *the* ISSUES

- **How do the events shown in the photographs illustrate the political interdependence of different nations?**

- **What do these events tell you about scientific and cultural interdependence among nations?**

As a class, discuss these questions. Remember what you have learned about the recent history of nations in different regions of the world. Try to think of reasons that nations are becoming increasingly dependent on one another. As you read this chapter, look for examples of economic, political, and cultural interdependence among the nations of the world.

The Impact of Science and Technology

MAIN IDEA	WHY IT MATTERS NOW	TERMS & NAMES
SCIENCE AND TECHNOLOGY Advances in technology after World War II led to increased global interaction and improved quality of life.	Advances in science and technology affect the lives of people around the world.	• International Space Station • Internet • genetic engineering • cloning • green revolution

SETTING THE STAGE Beginning in the late 1950s, the United States and the Soviet Union competed in the exploration of space. The Soviets launched Earth's first artificial satellite and put the first human in orbit around the planet. By the late 1960s, however, the United States had surpassed the Soviets. U.S. astronauts landed on the moon in 1969. The heavy emphasis on science and technology that the space race required led to the development of products that changed life for people across the globe.

Exploring the Solar System and Beyond

In its early years, competition between the United States and the Soviet Union in the space race was intense. Eventually, however, space exploration became one of the world's first and most successful arenas for cooperation between U.S. and Soviet scientists.

Cooperation in Space In 1972, years before the end of the Cold War, the United States and Soviet space programs began work on a cooperative project—the docking of U.S. and Soviet spacecraft in orbit. This goal was achieved on July 17, 1975, when spacecraft from the two countries docked some 140 miles above Earth. Television viewers across the globe watched as the hatch between the space vehicles opened and crews from Earth's fiercest rival countries greeted each other.

This first cooperative venture in space between the United States and the Soviet Union was an isolated event. People from different countries, however, continued to work together to explore space. The Soviets were the first to send an international crew into space. The crew of *Soyuz 28,* which orbited Earth in 1978, included a Czech cosmonaut. Since the mid-1980s, crews on United States space shuttle flights have included astronauts from Saudi Arabia, France, Germany, Canada, Italy, Japan, Israel, and Mexico. (Space shuttles are larger than other spacecraft and are reusable.) Shuttle missions put crews in orbit around Earth to accomplish a variety of scientific and technological tasks.

The space shuttle is being used in the most ambitious cooperative space venture. The project, sponsored by the United States, Russia, and 14 other nations, involves the building of the **International Space Station** (ISS). Since 1998, U.S. shuttles and Russian spacecraft have transported sections of the ISS to be assembled in space. By the time it is completed, the ISS will cover an area the size

TAKING NOTES
Recognizing Effects Use a chart to list the effects of scientific and technological developments.

Developments	Effects
Communications	
Health and Medicine	
Green Revolution	

▲ This view of the ISS was taken from the space shuttle *Endeavor.*

of a football field and house a crew of six. Since October 2000, smaller crews have been working aboard the ISS. By early 2003, they had conducted more than 100 experiments. However, the suspension of the shuttle program after the crash of the shuttle *Columbia* in February 2003 put the future of the ISS in question.

Exploring the Universe Unmanned space probes have been used to study the farther reaches of the solar system. The Soviet *Venera* spacecraft in the 1970s and the U.S. probe *Magellan* in 1990 provided in-depth information about Venus. On a 12-year journey that began in 1977, the U.S. *Voyager 2* sent dazzling pictures of Jupiter, Saturn, Uranus, and Neptune back to Earth. Both the United States and the Soviet Union have shown particular interest in the planet Mars. The United States probe *Pathfinder,* which landed on Mars in 1997, provided spectacular results.

In 1990, the U.S. space agency, NASA, and the European space agency, ESA, worked together to develop and launch the Hubble Space Telescope. This orbiting telescope continues to observe and send back images of objects in the most remote regions of the universe. **A**

MAIN IDEA

Hypothesizing
A Why might rival nations cooperate in space activities but not on Earth?

Expanding Global Communications

Since the 1960s, artificial satellites launched into orbit around Earth have aided worldwide communications. With satellite communication, the world has been gradually transformed into a global village. Today, political and cultural events occurring in one part of the world often are witnessed live by people thousands of miles away. This linking of the globe through worldwide communications is made possible by the miniaturization of the computer.

Smaller, More Powerful Computers In the 1940s, when computers first came into use, they took up a huge room. The computer required fans or an elaborate air-conditioning system to cool the vacuum tubes that powered its operations. In the years since then, however, the circuitry that runs the computer has been miniaturized and made more powerful. This change is due, in part, to the space program,

▼ Some computers are so small that they can be held in the hand.

for which equipment had to be downsized to fit into tiny space capsules. Silicon chips replaced the bulky vacuum tubes used earlier. Smaller than contact lenses, silicon chips hold millions of microscopic circuits.

Following this development, industries began to use computers and silicon chips to run assembly lines. Today a variety of consumer products such as microwave ovens, telephones, keyboard instruments, and cars use computers and chips. Computers have become essential in most offices, and millions of people around the globe have computers in their homes.

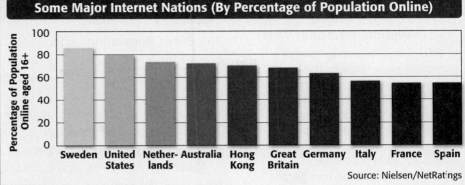

Access to the Internet, 2002

Internet Users Worldwide	
Africa	6.31 million
Asia and the Pacific	187.24 million
Europe	190.91 million
Middle East	5.12 million
Canada and U.S.	182.67 million
Latin America	33.35 million
Worldwide	**605.60 million**

Source: Nua Internet Surveys

Some Major Internet Nations (By Percentage of Population Online)

Source: Nielsen/NetRatings

SKILLBUILDER: Interpreting Charts and Graphs
1. **Comparing** *In which world region do most Internet users live?*
2. **Drawing Conclusions** *How would you describe most of the nations with large percentages of their populations online?*

Communications Networks Starting in the 1990s, businesses and individuals began using the <u>Internet</u>. The Internet is the voluntary linkage of computer networks around the world. It began in the late 1960s as a method of linking scientists so they could exchange information about research. Through telephone-line links, business and personal computers can be hooked up with computer networks. These networks allow users to communicate with people across the nation and around the world. Between 1995 and late 2002, the number of worldwide Internet users soared from 26 million to more than 600 million.

Conducting business on the Internet has become a way of life for many. The Internet, along with fax machines, transmits information electronically to remote locations. Both paved the way for home offices and telecommuting—working at home using a computer connected to a business network. Once again, as it has many times in the past, technology has changed how and where people work. **B**

MAIN IDEA

Summarizing
B What types of technology have recently changed the workplace?

Transforming Human Life

Advances with computers and communications networks have transformed not only the ways people work but lifestyles as well. Technological progress in the sciences, medicine, and agriculture has improved the quality of the lives of millions of people.

Health and Medicine Before World War II, surgeons seldom performed operations on sensitive areas such as the eye or the brain. However, in the 1960s and 1970s, new technologies, such as more powerful microscopes, the laser, and ultrasound, were developed. Many of these technologies advanced surgical techniques.

Advances in medical imaging also helped to improve health care. Using data provided by CAT scans and MRI techniques, doctors can build three-dimensional images of different organs or regions of the body. Doctors use these images to diagnose injuries, detect tumors, or collect other medical information.

In the 1980s, genetics, the study of heredity through research on genes, became a fast-growing field of science. Found in the cells of all organisms, genes are hereditary units that cause specific traits, such as eye color, in every living organism. Technology allowed scientists to isolate and examine individual genes that are responsible for different traits. Through <u>genetic engineering</u>, scientists were able to introduce new genes into an organism to give that organism new traits.

Another aspect of genetic engineering is <u>cloning</u>. This is the creation of identical copies of DNA, the chemical chains of genes that determine heredity. Cloning actually allows scientists to reproduce both plants and animals that are identical to existing plants and animals. The application of genetics research to everyday life has led to many breakthroughs, especially in agriculture.

The Green Revolution In the 1960s, agricultural scientists around the world started a campaign known as the **green revolution**. It was an attempt to increase food production worldwide. Scientists promoted the use of fertilizers, pesticides, and high-yield, disease-resistant strains of a variety of crops. The green revolution helped avert famine and increase crop yields in many parts of the world.

However, the green revolution had its negative side. Fertilizers and pesticides often contain dangerous chemicals that may cause cancer and pollute the environment. Also, the cost of the chemicals and the equipment to harvest more crops was far too expensive for an average peasant farmer. Consequently, owners of small farms received little benefit from the advances in agriculture. In some cases, farmers were forced off the land by larger agricultural businesses.

Advances in genetics research seem to be helping to fulfill some of the goals of the green revolution. In this new "gene revolution," resistance to pests is bred into plant strains, reducing the need for pesticides. Plants being bred to tolerate poor soil conditions also reduce the need for fertilizers. The gene revolution involves some risks, including the accidental creation of disease-causing organisms. However, the revolution holds great promise for increasing food production in a world with an expanding population. **C**

Science and technology have changed the lives of millions of people. What people produce and even their jobs have changed. These changes have altered the economies of nations. Not only have nations become linked through communications networks but they are also linked in a global economic network, as you will see in Section 2.

MAIN IDEA

Recognizing Effects

C What are some of the positive and negative effects of genetic engineering?

SECTION 1 ASSESSMENT

TERMS & NAMES 1. For each term or name, write a sentence explaining its significance.
- International Space Station
- Internet
- genetic engineering
- cloning
- green revolution

USING YOUR NOTES

2. Which of the three developments do you think has had the greatest global effect? Why?

Developments	Effects
Communications	
Health and Medicine	
Green Revolution	

MAIN IDEAS

3. How does the development of the International Space Station show that space exploration has become a cooperative endeavor?

4. How has the development of the computer and the Internet changed the way people work?

5. What areas of medicine have benefited from scientific and technological developments?

CRITICAL THINKING & WRITING

6. **MAKING INFERENCES** Why do you think that space exploration became an arena for cooperation between the Soviet Union and the United States?

7. **HYPOTHESIZING** How do you think the Internet will affect the world of work in the future?

8. **FORMING AND SUPPORTING OPINIONS** Is there a limit to how far cloning should go? Why or why not?

9. **WRITING ACTIVITY** SCIENCE AND TECHNOLOGY Use encyclopedia yearbooks and science magazines to identify a technological advance made in the last year. Write a brief **report** on the impact this advance has had on daily life.

CONNECT TO TODAY CREATING A GRAPH

Conduct research into how people use the Internet. Use your findings to construct a **graph** showing the most common Internet activities.

Global Economic Development

MAIN IDEA	WHY IT MATTERS NOW	TERMS & NAMES
ECONOMICS The economies of the world's nations are so tightly linked that the actions of one nation affect others.	Every individual is affected by the global economy and the environment.	• developed nation • emerging nation • global economy • free trade • ozone layer • sustainable growth

SETTING THE STAGE At the end of World War II, much of Europe and Asia lay in ruins, with many of the major cities leveled by bombing. The devastation of the war was immense. However, with aid from the United States, the economies of Western European nations and Japan began expanding rapidly within a decade. Their growth continued for half a century, long after the United States ceased supplying aid. Advances in science and technology contributed significantly to this ongoing economic growth.

Technology Revolutionizes the World's Economy

In both Asia and the Western world, an explosion in scientific knowledge prompted great progress that quickly led to new industries. A prime example was plastics. In the 1950s, a process to develop plastics from petroleum at low pressures and low temperatures was perfected. Within a few years, industries made a host of products easily and cheaply out of plastics. Other technological advances have also changed industrial processes, lowered costs, and increased the quality or the speed of production. For example, robotic arms on automobile assembly lines made possible the fast and safe manufacture of high-quality cars.

Information Industries Change Economies Technological advances in manufacturing reduced the need for factory workers. But in other areas of the economy, new demands were emerging. Computerization and communications advances changed the processing of information. By the 1980s, people could transmit information quickly and cheaply. Information industries such as financial services, insurance, market research, and communications services boomed. Those industries depended on "knowledge workers," or people whose jobs focus on working with information.

The Effects of New Economies In the postwar era, the expansion of the world's economies led to an increase in the production of goods and services so that many nations benefited. The economic base of some nations shifted. Manufacturing jobs began to move out of **developed nations**, those nations with the industrialization, transportation, and business facilities for advanced production of manufactured goods. The jobs moved to **emerging nations**, those in the process of becoming industrialized. Emerging nations became prime locations for new manufacturing operations. Some economists believe these areas were chosen because

Forces that shape a global economy

they had many eager workers whose skills fit manufacturing-type jobs. Also, these workers would work for less money than those in developed nations. On the other hand, information industries that required better-educated workers multiplied in the economies of developed nations. Thus the changes brought by technology then changed the workplace of both developed and emerging nations.

Economic Globalization

Economies in different parts of the world have been linked for centuries through trade and through national policies, such as colonialism. However, a true global economy did not begin to take shape until well into the second half of the 1800s. The **global economy** includes all the financial interactions—among people, businesses, and governments—that cross international borders. In recent decades, several factors hastened the process of globalization. Huge cargo ships could inexpensively carry enormous supplies of fuels and other goods from one part of the world to another. Telephone and computer linkages made global financial transactions quick and easy. In addition, multinational corporations developed around the world. **A**

MAIN IDEA

Analyzing Causes
A What elements helped to accelerate the process of globalization?

Multinational Corporations Companies that operate in a number of different countries are called multinational or transnational corporations. U.S. companies such as Exxon Mobil, General Motors, and Ford; European companies such as BP, DaimlerChrysler, and Royal Dutch/Shell; and Japanese companies such as Toyota, Mitsubishi, and Mitsui all became multinational giants.

All of these companies have established manufacturing plants, offices, or stores in many countries. For their manufacturing plants, they select spots where the raw materials or labor are cheapest. This enables them to produce components of their products on different continents. They ship the various components to another location to be assembled. This level of economic integration allows such companies to view the whole world as the market for their goods. Goods or services are distributed throughout the world as if there were no national boundaries.

Expanding Free Trade Opening up the world's markets to trade is a key aspect of globalization. In fact, a major goal of globalization is **free trade**, or the elimination of trade barriers, such as tariffs, among nations. This movement toward free trade is not new. As early as 1947, nations began discussing ways to open trade. The result of these discussions was the General Agreement on Tariffs and Trade (GATT). Over the years, several meetings among the nations that signed the GATT have brought about a general lowering of protective tariffs and considerable expansion of free trade. Since 1995, the World Trade Organization (WTO) has overseen the GATT to ensure that trade among nations flows as smoothly and freely as possible.

Vocabulary
tariff: a tax on goods imported from another country

Regional Trade Blocs A European organization set up in 1951 promoted tariff-free trade among member countries. This experiment in economic cooperation was so successful that six years later, a new organization, the European Economic Community (EEC), was formed. Over time,

Multinational Corporations, 2002

Based on a comparison of revenues with GDP, some of the top multinationals have economies bigger than those of several countries.

MULTINATIONAL'S REVENUE (in billions)		COUNTRY'S GDP (in billions)
Exxon Mobil $205	200	Austria $203
	190	Norway $189
General Motors $187		Poland $188
BP and Shell $179	180	Turkey $183
	170	Denmark $175
Ford $162	160	
	150	
DaimlerChrysler $141	140	
Toyota $132	130	Greece $133
		Finland $131
	120	Portugal $121
Mitsubishi and Mitsui $109	110	
	100	South Africa $104

Source: *Forbes Magazine*/World Bank

SKILLBUILDER: Interpreting Graphs
1. **Comparing** Which has the larger economy, Poland or Ford?
2. **Clarifying** Which multinationals have an economy greater than that of South Africa but smaller than that of Portugal?

Legend:
- Andean Community (CAN)
- Asia-Pacific Economic Cooperation (APEC)
- Association of Southeast Asian Nations (ASEAN)
- Central American Common Market (CACM)
- Caribbean Community and Common Market (CARICOM)
- Commonwealth of Independent States (CIS)
- Council of Arab Economic Unity (CAEU)
- European Free Trade Association (EFTA)
- European Union (EU)
- Group of Eight (G8)
- Monetary and Economic Community of Central Africa (CEMAC)
- North American Free Trade Agreement (NAFTA)
- Organization of the Petroleum Exporting Countries (OPEC)
- Southern Common Market (MERCOSUR)
- Southern African Development Community (SADC)

GEOGRAPHY SKILLBUILDER: Interpreting Maps
1. **Location** *Which countries in OPEC are located outside of Southwest Asia?*
2. **Location** *To which world trade organizations does the United States belong?*

most of the other Western European countries joined the organization, which has been known as the European Union (EU) since 1992. Several of the former Communist nations of Eastern Europe also have applied to become EU members.

Through this economic unification, Europe began to exert a major force in the world economy. The economic success of the EU inspired countries in other regions to make trade agreements with each other. The North American Free Trade Agreement (NAFTA), put into effect in 1994, called for the gradual elimination of tariffs and trade restrictions among Canada, the United States, and Mexico. Organizations in Asia, Africa, Latin America, and the South Pacific have also created regional trade policies.

Globalization—For and Against In recent years, there has been considerable debate on the impact of globalization. Supporters suggest that open, competitive markets and the free flow of goods, services, technology, and investments benefit all nations. Globalization, they argue, has resulted in a dramatic increase in the standard of living across the world. Even some opponents agree that practically all nations have seen some benefit from globalization. However, they note that the developed nations have benefited the most. Other opponents charge that globalization has been a disaster for the poorest countries. They suggest that many poor countries are worse off today than they were in the past. They argue that investment practices, trade agreements, and aid packages must be designed to protect the interests of the poorest nations.

Globalization

Globalization can be described in broad terms as a process that makes something worldwide in its reach or operation. Currently, globalization is most often used in reference to the spread and diffusion of economic or cultural influences. The graphics below focus on economic globalization. The first shows a global corporation. The second lists some arguments for and against economic globalization.

Global Corporation

SUPPLIES
Italy, South Korea, Russia, Colombia

CORPORATE HEADQUARTERS

RAW MATERIALS
U.S., Egypt, South Africa, Canada

Manufacturing and Production Centers

| U.S. | Japan | U.K. | France | Germany | Mexico |

Products and Services

| Pharmaceuticals | Communications Equipment | Television Networks | Fertilizers |
| Cell Phones | Defense Contractors | Film Companies | Laboratory Equipment |

Sales

| Africa | Asia | Australia |
| Europe | North America | South America |

Arguments for and Against Economic Globalization

For	Against
• promotes peace through trade	• creates conflict because of an inherently unfair system
• raises the standard of living around the world	• benefits developed nations disproportionately
• creates jobs in emerging countries	• takes jobs from high-paid laborers in developed countries
• promotes investment in less developed countries	• benefits those who already have money
• creates a sense of world community	• erodes local cultures

INTEGRATED TECHNOLOGY

RESEARCH LINKS For more on globalization, go to **classzone.com**

> **DATA FILE**

INTERNATIONAL REGULATION
Many countries have joined international organizations to help regulate and stimulate the global economy. Such groups face the same criticisms against globalization in general.

World Trade Organization (WTO)
• Stated goal: "Help trade flow smoothly, freely, fairly, and predictably"
• 146 member nations; around 30 nations negotiating for admission (193 countries in the world)
• WTO members account for over 97 percent of world trade.

International Monetary Fund (IMF)
• Stated goal: "Promote international monetary cooperation; to foster economic growth and high levels of employment; and to provide temporary financial assistance to countries"
• 184 member countries
• In March 2003, IMF total resources were around $300 billion.

The World Bank Group
• Stated goal: "A world free of poverty"
• 184 member countries
• In 2002, this group provided $19.5 billion to emerging countries.

Connect *to* Today

1. **Making Inferences** How are money and culture related to each other when discussing globalization?
   See Skillbuilder Handbook, page R10.

2. **Making Predictions** Will globalization continue or will another process replace it? Why or why not?

Impact of Global Development

The development of the global economy has had a notable impact on the use of energy and other resources. Worldwide demand for these resources has led to both political and environmental problems.

Political Impacts Manufacturing requires the processing of raw materials. Trade requires the transport of finished goods. These activities, essential for development, require the use of much energy. For the past 50 years, one of the main sources of energy used by developed and emerging nations has been oil. For nations with little of this resource available in their own land, disruption of the distribution of oil causes economic and political problems.

On the other hand, nations possessing oil reserves have the power to affect economic and political situations in countries all over the world. For example, in the 1970s the Organization of Petroleum Exporting Countries (OPEC) declared an oil embargo—a restriction of trade. This contributed to a significant economic decline in many developed nations during that decade.

In 1990, Iraq invaded Kuwait and seized the Kuwaiti oil fields. Fears began to mount that Iraq would also invade Saudi Arabia, another major source of oil. This would have put most of the world's petroleum supplies under Iraqi control. Economic sanctions imposed by the UN failed to persuade Iraq to withdraw from Kuwait. Then, in early 1991, a coalition of some 39 nations declared war on Iraq. After several weeks of fighting, the Iraqis left Kuwait and accepted a cease-fire. This Persian Gulf War showed the extent to which the economies of nations are globally linked.

Environmental Impacts Economic development has had a major impact on the environment. The burning of coal and oil as an energy source releases carbon dioxide into the atmosphere, causing health-damaging air pollution and acid rain. Some scientists believe that the buildup of carbon dioxide in the atmosphere also has contributed to global warming.

The release of chemicals called chlorofluorocarbons (CFCs), used in refrigerators, air conditioners, and manufacturing processes, has destroyed ozone in Earth's upper atmosphere. The **ozone layer** is our main protection against the Sun's damaging ultraviolet rays. With the increase in ultraviolet radiation reaching Earth's surface, the incidence of skin cancer continues to rise in many parts of the world. Increased ultraviolet radiation also may result in damage to populations of plants and plankton at the bases of the food chains, which sustain all life on Earth.

▼ During the 1991 Persian Gulf War, the Iraqis set hundreds of Kuwaiti oil wells ablaze. Smoke from these fires clouded the skies more than 250 miles away.

Ozone Levels

A large area of the ozone layer has become much thinner in recent years.

1979

2000

less ozone   more ozone

Economic development has also led to problems with the land. Large-scale soil erosion is a worldwide problem due to damaging farming techniques. The habitat destruction that comes from land development has also led to shrinking numbers of wildlife around the world. At present, the extinction rate of plants and animals is about a thousand times greater than it would naturally be, and appears to be increasing. This high extinction rate means that certain species can no longer serve as an economic resource. The resulting loss of wildlife could endanger complex and life-sustaining processes that keep Earth in balance.

"Sustainable Growth" Working together, economists and scientists are looking for ways to reduce the negative effect that development has on the environment. Their goal is to manage development so that growth can occur, but without destroying air, water, and land resources. The concept is sometimes called "green growth." Many people feel that the negative impact of economic growth on the environment will not be completely removed.

But "greener growth," also known as **sustainable growth**, is possible. This involves two goals: meeting current economic needs, while ensuring the preservation of the environment and the conservation of resources for future generations. Making such plans and putting them into practice have proved to be difficult. But many scientists believe that meeting both goals is essential for the health of the planet in the future. Because the economies of nations are tied to their political climates, such development plans will depend on the efforts of nations in both economic and political areas. **B**

MAIN IDEA

Clarifying
B What is meant by the term *sustainable growth*?

SECTION **2** **ASSESSMENT**

TERMS & NAMES 1. For each term or name, write a sentence explaining its significance.
• developed nation   • emerging nation   • global economy   • free trade   • ozone layer   • sustainable growth

USING YOUR NOTES

2. Which of these forces do you think has had the greatest impact on the development of a global economy?

Forces that shape a global economy

MAIN IDEAS

3. Why are "knowledge workers" becoming more important in the developed nations?

4. What impact did the economic success of the EU have on other regions of the world?

5. How has global economic development affected the environment?

CRITICAL THINKING & WRITING

6. **RECOGNIZING EFFECTS** In what ways has technology changed the workplace of people across the world?

7. **ANALYZING MOTIVES** Why might some nations favor imposing tariffs on the imports of certain products?

8. **SUPPORTING OPINIONS** Do you think that sustainable growth is possible? Why or why not?

9. **WRITING ACTIVITY** [ECONOMICS] Make a survey of the labels on class members' clothing and shoes. List the countries in which these items were produced. Write a short **explanation** of how the list illustrates the global economy.

CONNECT TO TODAY CREATING A POSTER

Recycling is an important aspect of sustainable growth. Create a **poster** encouraging local businesses to recycle cans, paper products, and plastics.

Economics and the Environment

Economists, politicians, and environmentalists came up with the concept of "sustainable growth"—both economic development and environmental protection are considered when producing a development plan for a nation. Some people see the relationship between economics and the environment as strained and getting worse. Others view policies protecting the environment as harmful to economies and ultimately harmful to the environment. The selections below examine these different perspectives.

A) PRIMARY SOURCE

Lester R. Brown

Lester R. Brown is president of the Earth Policy Institute, which researches how to attain an environmentally sustainable economy and assesses current economic programs around the world.

———

Most decisions taken in economic policy are made by economic advisors. You can see this in the World Bank's annual development reports where they see the environment as a sub-sector of the economy. However, if you look at it as a natural scientist or ecologist, you have to conclude that the economy is a subset of the earth's ecosystem. . . .

Many of the problems that we face are the result of the incompatibility of the economy with the ecosystem. The relationship between the global economy, which has expanded sixfold over the last half century, and the earth's ecosystem is a very stressed one. The manifestations of this stress are collapsing fisheries, falling water tables, shrinking forests, expanding deserts, rising carbon dioxide levels, rising temperatures, melting ice, dying coral reefs, and so forth. Not only is this a stressed relationship but a deteriorating one.

B) PRIMARY SOURCE

The Liberty Institute

The Liberty Institute is based in India and seeks to strengthen individual rights, rule of law, limited government, and free markets.

———

The market is the natural ally of the environment. Environmental resources, like other economic resources can be most efficiently allocated if these are brought under the discipline of the marketplace. It is ironic . . . [that] rather than creating a market for environmental resources, new restrictions are being imposed on the economy in the name of protecting the environment.

Environmental quality is like a value-added product that becomes economically affordable and technologically viable with economic growth. It is no paradox therefore that the environment is much cleaner and safer in industrially developed countries that adopted a more market-friendly approach. . . .

The market allows the consumer to register his price preference for a particular quality of product, including environmental quality.

C) POLITICAL CARTOON

Chris Madden

Educating through humor, cartoonist Chris Madden illustrates the close connection between the environment and economics. A "ship of fools" is a metaphor for human weakness.

The ship of fools and the rocks of short-term economic planning

Document-Based
QUESTIONS

1. Compare Sources A and B. Which perspective do you support? Why?

2. In your own words, describe the meaning of the cartoon in Source C.

3. Research an environmental issue facing your community and how economics is a part of the debate. Present your findings to the class.

647

3

Global Security Issues

POWER AND AUTHORITY Since 1945, nations have used collective security efforts to solve problems.

Personal security of the people of the world is tied to security within and between nations.

- proliferation
- Universal Declaration of Human Rights
- political dissent
- gender inequality
- AIDS
- refugee

SETTING THE STAGE World War II was one of history's most devastating conflicts. More than 55 million people died as a result of bombings, the Holocaust, combat, starvation, and disease. Near the end of the war, one of humankind's most destructive weapons, the atomic bomb, killed more than 100,000 people in Hiroshima and Nagasaki in a matter of minutes. Perhaps because of these horrors, world leaders look for ways to make the earth a safer, more secure place to live.

TAKING NOTES

Categorizing Use a chart to list collective methods employed by the world's nations to increase global security.

Method	Examples
Form military alliances	NATO, SEATO, Warsaw Pact

Issues of War and Peace

In the years after the end of World War II, the Cold War created new divisions and tensions among the world's nations. This uneasy situation potentially threatened the economic, environmental, and personal security of people across the world. So, nations began to work together to pursue collective security.

Nations Unite and Take Action Many nations consider that having a strong military is important to their security. After World War II, nations banded together to create military alliances. They formed the North Atlantic Treaty Organization (NATO), the Southeast Asia Treaty Organization (SEATO), the Warsaw Pact, and others. The member nations of each of these alliances generally pledged military aid for their common defense.

In addition to military alliances to increase their security, world leaders also took steps to reduce the threat of war. The United Nations (UN) works in a variety of ways toward increasing collective global security.

Peacekeeping Activities One of the major aims of the UN is to promote world peace. The UN provides a public forum, private meeting places, and skilled mediators to help nations try to resolve conflicts at any stage of their development. At the invitation of the warring parties, the UN also provides peacekeeping forces. These forces are made up of soldiers from different nations. They work to carry out peace agreements, monitor cease-fires, or put an end to fighting to allow peace negotiations to go forward.

As of the end of 2002, the UN had close to 40,000 soldiers and police in 13 peacekeeping forces around the world. Some forces, such as those in India and Pakistan, have been in place for decades. Others, such as those in East Timor, achieved their goals in only a few months.

Weapons of Mass Destruction

Nations have not only worked to prevent and contain conflicts, they also have forged treaties to limit the manufacturing, testing, and trade of weapons. The weapons of most concern are those that cause mass destruction. These include nuclear, chemical, and biological weapons that can kill thousands, even millions of people.

In 1968, many nations signed a Nuclear Non-Proliferation Treaty to help prevent the **proliferation**, or spread, of nuclear weapons to other nations. In the 1970s, the United States and the Soviet Union signed the Strategic Arms Limitation Treaties. In the 1980s, both countries talked about deactivating some of their nuclear weapons. Many nations also signed treaties promising not to produce biological or chemical weapons.

▲ In central Baghdad, a U.S. Marine watches as a statue of Saddam Hussein is pulled down.

Disarming Iraq Other nations, however, have tried to develop weapons of mass destruction. Iraq, for example, used chemical weapons in conflicts during the 1980s. Many people suspected that the Iraqi leader, Saddam Hussein, had plans to develop biological and nuclear weapons too. As part of the cease-fire arrangements in the Persian Gulf War, Iraq agreed to destroy its weapons of mass destruction. UN inspectors were sent to monitor this disarmament process. However, in 1998, the Iraqis ordered the inspectors to leave.

In 2002, Saddam Hussein once again came under suspicion of developing weapons of mass destruction. The UN Security Council issued a resolution threatening Iraq with "severe consequences" unless the weapons inspectors were allowed to return. Iraq complied, but some UN members suspected that the Iraqis were not fully cooperating with the inspectors. So, in March 2003, a coalition led by the United States and Great Britain sent troops to disarm Iraq by force. After four weeks of fighting, Saddam Hussein's government fell.

Ethnic and Religious Conflicts Conflicts among people of different racial, national, religious, linguistic, or cultural groups are not new. Some struggles have roots that reach back for decades and, in some cases, for centuries. Such conflicts include those between Protestants and Catholics in Ireland, between Palestinians and Israelis in the Middle East, and among Serbs, Bosnians, and Croats in the former Yugoslavia.

Ethnic and religious conflicts have often led to terrible violence. People caught in these conflicts sometimes suffered torture, or massacres of their whole towns or villages. The Kurds of southwest Asia have been the victims of such violence. For decades, Kurds have wanted their own separate country. But their traditional lands cross the borders of three nations—Turkey, Iran, and Iraq. In the past, the Turks responded to Kurdish nationalism by forbidding Kurds to speak their native language. The Iranians also persecuted the Kurds, attacking them over religious issues. In the late 1980s, the Iraqis dropped poison gas on the Kurds, killing 5,000. Several international organizations, including the UN, are working to end the human rights abuses inflicted upon the Kurds.

Human Rights Issues

In 1948, the UN issued the <u>Universal Declaration of Human Rights</u>, which set human rights standards for all nations. It stated that "All human beings are born free and equal in dignity and rights. . . . Everyone has the right to life, liberty, and security of person." The declaration further listed specific rights that all human beings should have. Later, in the Helsinki Accords of 1975, the UN addressed the issues of freedom of movement and freedom to publish and exchange information.

Both the declaration and the accords are nonbinding. However, the sentiments in these documents inspired many people around the world. They made a commitment to ensuring that basic human rights are respected. The UN and other international agencies, such as Amnesty International, identify and publicize human rights violations. They also encourage people to work toward a world in which liberty and justice are guaranteed for all.

Vocabulary
A *nonbinding* agreement means that a nation does not suffer a penalty if it does not meet the terms of the declaration.

Continuing Rights Violations Despite the best efforts of various human rights organizations, protecting human rights remains an uphill battle. Serious violations of fundamental rights continue to occur around the world.

One type of violation occurs when governments try to stamp out **political dissent**, or the difference of opinion over political issues. In many countries around the world, from Cuba to Iran to Myanmar, individuals and groups have been persecuted for holding political views that differ from those of the people in power. In some countries, ethnic or racial hatreds lead to human rights abuses. In Rwanda, for example, fighting between Hutus and Tutsis—the two main ethnic groups—led to horrendous rights violations. In 1994, Hutus massacred about 500,000 Tutsis in one of the worst cases of genocide. **A**

Women's Status Improves In the past, when women in Western nations entered the work force, they often faced discrimination in employment and salary. In non-Western countries, many women not only faced discrimination in jobs, they were denied access to education. In regions torn by war or ethnic conflict, they were often victims of violence and abuse. As women suffered, so too did their family members, especially children.

However, in the 1970s, a heightened awareness of human rights encouraged women in many countries to work to improve their lives. They pushed for new laws and government policies that gave them greater equality. In 1975, the UN held the first of several international conferences on women's status in the world. The fourth conference was held in Beijing, China, in 1995. It addressed such issues as preventing violence against women and empowering women to take leadership roles in politics and in business.

In 2000, the UN reviewed the status of women. Its report, titled *Progress of the World's Women 2000,* found that women had made notable gains during the 1990s, especially in the areas of education and work. Even so, the report concluded that **gender inequality**—the difference between men and women in terms of wealth and status—still very much existed.

MAIN IDEA

Analyzing Issues
A What responsibilities do nations have for protecting human rights in other countries?

History Makers

Mother Teresa 1910–1997
Mother Teresa was one of the great champions of human rights for all people. Born Agnes Gonxha Bojaxhiu in what today is Macedonia, Mother Teresa joined a convent in Ireland at the age of 18. A short time later, she headed to India to teach at a girls' school. Over time, she noticed many sick and homeless people in the streets. She soon vowed to devote her life to helping India's poor.

In 1948, she established the Order of the Missionaries of Charity in Calcutta, which committed itself to serving the sick, needy, and unfortunate. In recognition of her commitment to the downtrodden, Mother Teresa received the Nobel Peace Prize in 1979.

INTEGRATED / TECHNOLOGY

RESEARCH LINKS For more on Mother Teresa, go to **classzone.com**

World AIDS Situation, 2002

EASTERN EUROPE & CENTRAL ASIA

NORTH AMERICA

WESTERN EUROPE

NORTH AFRICA & MIDDLE EAST

REST OF ASIA & PACIFIC

CARIBBEAN

SUB-SAHARAN AFRICA

LATIN AMERICA

= 500,000 people living with HIV/AIDS

= 50,000 people newly infected with HIV in 2002

= 30,000 deaths from AIDS in 2002

Source: UNAIDS/WHO, 2002

GEOGRAPHY SKILLBUILDER: Interpreting Maps
1. **Region** *Which region is confronted by the greatest challenge from the AIDS epidemic?*
2. **Region** *Which region had the greatest number of new HIV infections in 2002, Latin America or Eastern Europe and Central Asia?*

Health Issues

In recent decades, the enjoyment of a decent standard of health has become recognized as a basic human right. However, for many people across the world, poor health is still the norm. World health faced a major threat in 2003, with the outbreak of severe acute respiratory syndrome (SARS). This pneumonia-like disease emerged in China and rapidly spread to other Asian countries, Europe, and North America. Afraid of infection, many people canceled travel to Asia. The resulting loss of business hurt the economies of several Asian countries.

The AIDS Epidemic Perhaps the greatest global health issue is a disease known as **AIDS**, or acquired immune deficiency syndrome. It attacks the immune system, leaving sufferers open to deadly infections. The disease was first detected in the early 1980s. Since that time, AIDS has claimed the lives of nearly 25 million people worldwide. By the end of 2002, there were 42 million people across the world living with HIV (the virus that causes AIDS) or AIDS. And in 2002, 5 million people were newly infected with HIV.

While AIDS is a worldwide problem, Sub-Saharan Africa has suffered most from the epidemic. About 70 percent of the world's HIV and AIDS sufferers live in this region. And in 2002, on average more than 6,500 people died of AIDS each day. Most of the people dying are between the ages of 15 and 49—the years when people are at their most productive economically. AIDS, therefore, is reducing the number of people available as workers, managers, and entrepreneurs. As a result, economic growth is slowing in many countries in the region.

In response to the devastating impact of the disease, the UN issued the Declaration of Commitment on HIV/AIDS in 2001. This document set targets for halting the spread of AIDS and provided guidelines on how countries could pool their efforts.

Population Movement

The global movement of people has increased dramatically in recent years. This migration has taken place for both negative and positive reasons.

Push-Pull Factors People often move because they feel pushed out of their homelands. Lack of food due to drought, natural disasters, and political oppression are examples of push factors of migration. In 2005, the number of **refugees**—people who leave their country to move to another to find safety—stood at 19.2 million.

Not only negative events push people to migrate. Most people have strong connections to their home countries and do not leave unless strong positive attractions pull them away. They hope for a better life for themselves and for their children, and thus migrate to developed nations. For example, hundreds of thousands of people migrate from Africa to Europe and from Latin America to the United States every year. **B**

Effects of Migration Everyone has the right to leave his or her country. However, the country to which a migrant wants to move may not accept that person. The receiving country might have one policy about accepting refugees from political situations, and another about migrants coming for economic reasons. Because of the huge volume of people migrating from war-torn, famine-stricken, and politically unstable regions, millions of immigrants have no place to go. Crowded into refugee camps, often under squalid conditions, these migrants face a very uncertain future.

On the positive side, immigrants often are a valuable addition to their new country. They help offset labor shortages in a variety of industries. They bring experiences and knowledge that can spur the economy. In addition, they contribute to the sharing, shaping, and blending of a newly enriched culture.

▲ Two Afghan girls quietly wait for food at a refugee camp on the Afghanistan-Iran border.

MAIN IDEA

Analyzing Causes
B What push and pull factors cause people to migrate?

SECTION 3 ASSESSMENT

TERMS & NAMES 1. For each term or name, write a sentence explaining its significance.
- proliferation
- Universal Declaration of Human Rights
- political dissent
- gender inequality
- AIDS
- refugee

USING YOUR NOTES
2. What methods have resulted in the greatest contribution to global security? Why?

Method	Examples
Form military alliances	NATO, SEATO, Warsaw Pact

MAIN IDEAS
3. What steps have nations taken to control the proliferation of weapons of mass destruction?
4. How has AIDS affected the economy of Sub-Saharan Africa?
5. What positive effects does immigration have?

CRITICAL THINKING & WRITING
6. **MAKING INFERENCES** Why might nations want to retain or develop an arsenal of nuclear, biological, and chemical weapons?
7. **IDENTIFYING PROBLEMS** How are ethnic and religious conflicts related to problems of global security?
8. **RECOGNIZING EFFECTS** How can individuals affect social conditions around the world? Consider the example of Mother Teresa when writing your answer.
9. **WRITING ACTIVITY** SCIENCE AND TECHNOLOGY Write a **paragraph** explaining how advances in science and technology have increased threats to global security.

CONNECT TO TODAY CREATING A DATABASE

Locate recent information on refugees around the world. Use your findings to create a **database** of charts and graphs titled "The Global Refugee Situation."

4

Terrorism

CASE STUDY: September 11, 2001

MAIN IDEA	WHY IT MATTERS NOW	TERMS & NAMES
POWER AND AUTHORITY Terrorism threatens the safety of people all over the world.	People and nations must work together against the dangers posed by terrorism.	• terrorism • cyberterrorism • Department of Homeland Security • USA Patriot Act

SETTING THE STAGE Wars are not the only threat to international peace and security. **Terrorism**, the use of violence against people or property to force changes in societies or governments, strikes fear in the hearts of people everywhere. Recently, terrorist incidents have increased dramatically around the world. Because terrorists often cross national borders to commit their acts or to escape to countries friendly to their cause, most people consider terrorism an international problem.

What Is Terrorism?

Terrorism is not new. Throughout history, individuals, small groups, and governments have used terror tactics to try to achieve political or social goals, whether to bring down a government, eliminate opponents, or promote a cause. In recent times, however, terrorism has changed.

Modern Terrorism Since the late 1960s, more than 14,000 terrorist attacks have occurred worldwide. International terrorist groups have carried out increasingly destructive, high-profile attacks to call attention to their goals and to gain major media coverage. Many countries also face domestic terrorists who oppose their governments' policies or have special interests to promote.

The reasons for modern terrorism are many. The traditional motives, such as gaining independence, expelling foreigners, or changing society, still drive various terrorist groups. These groups use violence to force concessions from their enemies, usually the governments in power. But other kinds of terrorists, driven by radical religious and cultural motives, began to emerge in the late 20th century.

The goal of these terrorists is the destruction of what they consider the forces of evil. This evil might be located in their own countries or in other parts of the world. These terrorists are ready to use any kind of weapon to kill their enemies. They are even willing to die to ensure the success of their attacks.

Terrorist Methods Terrorist acts involve violence. The weapons most frequently used by terrorists are the bomb and the bullet. The targets of terrorist attacks often are crowded places where people normally feel safe—subway stations, bus stops, restaurants, or shopping malls, for example. Or terrorists might target something that symbolizes what they are against, such as a government building

TAKING NOTES

Categorizing Use a chart to note information about the September 11 terrorist attacks and other terrorist incidents around the world.

World Terrorist Incidents
September 11 Attacks

▲ The sarin gas attack in the Tokyo subway in 1995 is the most notorious act of biochemical terrorism.

or a religious site. Such targets are carefully chosen in order to gain the most attention and to achieve the highest level of intimidation. **A**

Recently, some terrorist groups have used biological and chemical agents in their attacks. These actions involved the release of bacteria or poisonous gases into the atmosphere. While both biological and chemical attacks can inflict terrible casualties, they are equally powerful in generating great fear among the public. This development in terrorism is particularly worrisome, because biochemical agents are relatively easy to acquire. Laboratories all over the world use bacteria and viruses in the development of new drugs. And the raw materials needed to make some deadly chemical agents can be purchased in many stores.

Cyberterrorism is another recent development. This involves politically motivated attacks on information systems, such as hacking into computer networks or spreading computer viruses. Experts suggest that as more governments and businesses switch to computers to store data and run operations, the threat of cyberterrorism will increase.

MAIN IDEA

Analyzing Motives
A Of what value would gaining public attention be to a terrorist group?

Responding to Terrorism Governments take various steps to stamp out terrorism. Most adopt a very aggressive approach in tracking down and punishing terrorist groups. This approach includes infiltrating the groups to gather information on membership and future plans. It also includes striking back harshly after a terrorist attack, even to the point of assassinating known terrorist leaders.

Another approach governments use is to make it more difficult for terrorists to act. This involves eliminating extremists' sources of funds and persuading governments not to protect or support terrorist groups. It also involves tightening security measures so as to reduce the targets vulnerable to attack.

Terrorism Around the World

The problem of modern international terrorism first came to world attention in a shocking way during the 1972 Summer Olympic Games in Munich, Germany (then West Germany). Members of a Palestinian terrorist group killed two Israeli athletes and took nine others hostage. Five of the terrorists, all the hostages, and a police officer were later killed in a bloody gun battle. Since then, few regions of the world have been spared from terrorist attacks.

The Middle East Many terrorist organizations have roots in the Israeli-Palestinian conflict over land in the Middle East. Groups such as the Palestine Islamic Jihad, Hamas, and Hizballah have sought to prevent a peace settlement between Israel and the Palestinians. They want a homeland for the Palestinians on their own terms, with the most extreme among them denying Israel's right to exist. In a continual cycle of violence, the Israelis retaliate after most terrorist attacks, and the terrorists strike again. Moderates in the region believe that the only long-term solution is a compromise between Israel and the Palestinians over the issue of land. However, the violence has continued with only an occasional break.

Europe Many countries in Europe have been targets of domestic terrorists who oppose government policies. For example, for decades the mostly Catholic Irish Republican Army (IRA) engaged in terrorist attacks against Britain because it opposed British control of Northern Ireland. Since 1998, however, the British, the IRA, and representatives of Northern Ireland's Protestants have been negotiating a peaceful solution to the situation. An agreement was reached in 2005.

Asia Afghanistan, in Southwest Asia, became a haven for international terrorists after the Taliban came to power in 1996. (See Chapter 18.) In that year, Osama bin Laden, a Saudi Arabian millionaire involved in terrorist activities, moved to Afghanistan. There he began using mountain hideouts as a base of operations for his global network of Muslim terrorists known as al-Qaeda.

Terrorist groups have arisen in East Asia, as well. One, known as Aum Shinrikyo ("Supreme Truth"), is a religious cult that wants to control Japan. In 1995, cult members released sarin, a deadly nerve gas, in subway stations in Tokyo. Twelve people were killed and more than 5,700 injured. This attack brought global attention to the threat of biological and chemical agents as terrorist weapons.

Africa Civil unrest and regional wars were the root causes of most terrorist activity in Africa at the end of the 20th century. But al-Qaeda cells operated in many African countries, and several major attacks against U.S. personnel and facilities in Africa were linked to al-Qaeda. In 1998, for example, bombings at the U.S. embassies in Kenya and Tanzania left over 200 dead and more than 5,000 people injured. The United States responded to these attacks with missile strikes on suspected terrorist facilities in Afghanistan and in Sudan, where bin Laden was based from 1991 to 1996.

Latin America Narcoterrorism, or terrorism linked to drug trafficking, is a major problem in Latin America, particularly in Colombia. The powerful groups that control that country's narcotics trade have frequently turned to violence. The Revolutionary Armed Forces of Colombia (FARC) is a left-wing guerrilla group that has links with these drug traffickers. The FARC has attacked Colombian political, military, and economic targets, as well as those with American ties. **B**

MAIN IDEA

Analyzing Causes
B What are some reasons for terrorism in various regions of the world?

International Terrorist Attacks

Total Attacks, 1982–2002

International Casualties of Terrorism, 1997–2002

	Africa	Asia	Eurasia	Latin America	Middle East	North America	Western Europe
1997	28	344	27	11	480	7	17
1998	5,379	635	12	195	68	0	405
1999	185	690	8	10	31	0	16
2000	102	904	103	20	78	0	4
2001	150	651	0	6	513	4,091	20
2002	12	1281	615	52	772	0	6
Total	5,856	4,505	765	294	1,942	4,098	468

Source: U.S. Department of State

SKILLBUILDER: Interpreting Charts and Graphs
1. **Comparing** *Which three areas suffered the greatest numbers of casualties of terrorism?*
2. **Drawing Conclusions** *How would you describe the overall trend in worldwide terrorist attacks since the mid-1980s?*

Attack on the United States

On the morning of September 11, 2001, 19 Arab terrorists hijacked four airliners heading from East Coast airports to California. In a series of coordinated strikes, the hijackers crashed two of the jets into the twin towers of the World Trade Center in New York City and a third into the Pentagon outside Washington, D.C. The fourth plane crashed in an empty field in Pennsylvania. **C**

The Destruction The planes, loaded with fuel, became destructive missiles when they crashed into the World Trade Center and the Pentagon. The explosions and fires so weakened the damaged skyscrapers that they crumbled to the ground less than two hours after impact. The fire and raining debris caused nearby buildings to collapse as well. The damage at the Pentagon, though extensive, was confined to one section of the building.

The toll in human lives was great. About 3,000 people died in the attacks. All passengers on the four planes were killed, as well as workers and visitors in the World Trade Center and the Pentagon. The dead included more than 340 New York City firefighters and 60 police officers who rushed to the scene to help and were buried in the rubble when the skyscrapers collapsed.

The Impact of the Attack September 11 had a devastating impact on the way Americans looked at life. Many reported feeling that everything had changed— that life would never be the same. Before, Americans had viewed terrorism as something that happened in other countries. Now they felt vulnerable and afraid.

This sense of vulnerability was underscored just a few days after September 11, when terrorism struck the United States again. Letters containing spores of a bacterium that causes the disease anthrax were sent to people in the news media and to members of Congress in Washington, D.C. Anthrax bacteria, when inhaled, can

MAIN IDEA

Making Inferences

C Why were the specific targets of the September 11 attacks selected by the terrorists?

Destruction in New York City and the Pentagon

▲ The strike on the Pentagon left a charred, gaping hole in the southwest side of the building.

◄ Stunned bystanders look on as smoke billows from the twin towers of the World Trade Center.

▲ A hazardous materials team prepares to enter a congressional building during the anthrax scare.

damage the lungs and cause death. Five people who came in contact with spores from the tainted letters died of inhalation anthrax. Two were postal workers.

Investigators did not find a link between the September 11 attacks and the anthrax letters. Some of them believed that the letters might be the work of a lone terrorist rather than an organized group. Regardless of who was responsible for the anthrax scare, it caused incredible psychological damage. Many Americans were now fearful of an everyday part of life—the mail.

The United States Responds

Immediately after September 11, the United States called for an international effort to combat terrorist groups. President George W. Bush declared, "This battle will take time and resolve. But make no mistake about it: we will win."

As a first step in this battle, the U.S. government organized a massive effort to identify those responsible for the attacks. Officials concluded that Osama bin Laden directed the terrorists. The effort to bring him to justice led the United States to begin military action against Afghanistan in October, as you read in Chapter 18.

Antiterrorism Measures The federal government warned Americans that additional terrorist attacks were likely. It then took action to prevent such attacks. The **Department of Homeland Security** was created in 2002 to coordinate national efforts against terrorism. Antiterrorism measures included a search for terrorists in the United States and the passage of antiterrorism laws.

The al-Qaeda network was able to carry out its terrorist attacks partly through the use of "sleepers." These are agents who move to a country, blend into a community, and then, when directed, secretly prepare for and carry out terrorist acts. A search to find any al-Qaeda terrorists who remained in the United States was begun. Officials began detaining and questioning Arabs and other Muslims whose behavior was considered suspicious or who had violated immigration regulations.

Some critics charged that detaining these men was unfair to the innocent and violated their civil rights. However, the government held that the actions were justified because the hijackers had been Arabs. The government further argued that it was not unusual to curtail civil liberties during wartime in order to protect national security. This argument was also used to justify a proposal to try some terrorist suspects in military tribunals rather than in criminal courts. On October 26, 2001,

Gates D1–D10   Passengers Only

Security
Position Closed

▲ Passengers wait to go through a security check at La Guardia Airport in New York.

President Bush signed an antiterrorism bill into law. The law, known as the **USA Patriot Act**, allowed the government to

- detain foreigners suspected of terrorism for seven days without charging them with a crime
- tap all phones used by suspects and monitor their e-mail and Internet use
- make search warrants valid across states
- order U.S. banks to investigate sources of large foreign accounts
- prosecute terrorist crimes without any time restrictions or limitations.

Again, critics warned that these measures allowed the government to infringe on people's civil rights.

Aviation Security The federal government also increased its involvement in aviation security. The Federal Aviation Administration (FAA) ordered airlines to install bars on cockpit doors to prevent passengers from gaining control of planes, as the hijackers had done. Sky marshals—trained security officers—were assigned to fly on planes, and National Guard troops began patrolling airports.

The Aviation and Transportation Security Act, which became law in November 2001, made airport security the responsibility of the federal government. Previously, individual airports had been responsible. The law provided for a federal security force that would inspect passengers and carry-on bags. It also required the screening of checked baggage.

Airline and government officials debated these and other measures for making air travel more secure. Major concerns were long delays at airports and respect for passengers' privacy. It has also become clear that public debate over security measures will continue as long as the United States fights terrorism and tries to balance national security with civil rights.

SECTION 4 ASSESSMENT

TERMS & NAMES 1. For each term or name, write a sentence explaining its significance.
- terrorism
- cyberterrorism
- Department of Homeland Security
- USA Patriot Act

USING YOUR NOTES

2. How were the September 11 terrorist attacks unique? How were they similar to other terrorist incidents?

World Terrorist Incidents

September II Attacks

MAIN IDEAS

3. How has terrorism changed in recent years?

4. What methods do terrorists use?

5. What steps did the United States take in response to the terrorist attacks of September 11, 2001?

CRITICAL THINKING & WRITING

6. **ANALYZING MOTIVES** What might cause individuals to use terror tactics to bring about change?

7. **FORMING AND SUPPORTING OPINIONS** Is it important for the U.S. government to respect peoples' civil rights as it wages a war against terrorism? Why or why not?

8. **DRAWING CONCLUSIONS** What do you think has been the greatest impact of terrorism on American life?

9. **WRITING ACTIVITY** SCIENCE AND TECHNOLOGY Conduct research to find information on how science and technology are used to combat terrorism. Then write an **illustrated report** titled "Science and Counterterrorism."

INTEGRATED / TECHNOLOGY **INTERNET ACTIVITY**
Use the Internet to research terrorist incidents since the end of 2001. Use your findings to create a **time line** titled "Recent Major Terrorist Attacks."

INTERNET KEYWORD
terrorism

Cultures Blend in a Global Age

MAIN IDEA	WHY IT MATTERS NOW	TERMS & NAMES
CULTURAL INTERACTION Technology has increased contact among the world's people, changing their cultures.	Globalization of culture has changed the ways people live, their perceptions, and their interactions.	• popular culture • materialism

SETTING THE STAGE Since the beginnings of civilization, people have blended ideas and ways of doing things from other cultures into their own culture. The same kind of cultural sharing and blending continues today. But, because of advances in technology, it occurs at a much more rapid pace and over much greater distances. Twenty-first-century technologies allow people from all over the world to have increasing interaction with one another. Such contacts promote widespread sharing of cultures.

Cultural Exchange Accelerates

Cultural elements that reflect a group's common background and changing interests are called **popular culture**. Popular culture involves music, sports, movies, clothing fashions, foods, and hobbies or leisure activities. Popular culture around the world incorporates features from many different lands. Of all the technologies that contribute to such cultural sharing, television, movies, and other mass media have been the most powerful.

Mass Media More people in the United States have televisions than telephones. In fact, 98 percent of American households have at least one television set. Eighty-six percent of the homes have videocassette recorders (VCRs). In Western Europe, too, most households have one or more televisions. Access to television is not so widespread in the emerging nations, but it is growing. Recent estimates suggest that about half the population of the emerging world—some 2.5 billion people—have regular access to a television set.

Television provides a window to the world through daily newscasts and documentaries. The speed at which television can present information helps create an up-to-the-minute shared experience of global events. For example, in 2003, millions of television viewers across the world watched the war in Iraq. Wars, natural disasters, and political drama in faraway places have become a part of everyday life.

Television and other mass media, including radio and movies, are among the world's most popular forms of entertainment. Popular programs not only entertain but also show how people in other parts of the world live and what they value. Mass media is the major way popular culture spreads to all parts of the globe.

International Elements of Popular Culture The entertainment field, especially television, has a massive influence on popular culture. People from around

TAKING NOTES

Categorizing Use a web diagram to identify areas of popular culture that have become international in scope.

International popular culture

International Baseball

The sport of baseball is an example of global popular culture. When American missionaries and teachers arrived in Japan in the 1870s, they introduced the game of baseball. Over the years the game gained popularity there. Today, some Major League teams have Japanese players and several American players play in the Japanese league.

Baseball spread to Mexico, Cuba, Puerto Rico, Panama, and the Dominican Republic in the late 19th and early 20th centuries. Today baseball is a popular game in these and other Latin American countries. And more than 25 percent of the players in Major League Baseball come from Latin America.

INTEGRATED / TECHNOLOGY

INTERNET ACTIVITY Create a scrapbook of foreign players in Major League Baseball. Go to **classzone.com** for your research.

---

the world are avid viewers of American TV programs. For example, in Bhutan, a tiny country high in the Himalaya, ESPN, HBO, Cartoon Network, and CNN are among the most-watched channels. CNN truly is a global channel, since it reaches more than 200 million households in over 200 countries.

Television broadcasts of sporting events provide a front-row seat for sports fans all over the globe. Basketball and soccer are among the most popular televised sports. National Basketball Association (NBA) games are televised in over 200 countries. In China, for example, broadcasts of NBA games of the week regularly attract an audience in the millions. One of the most-watched international sporting events is the soccer World Cup. Nearly 63 million viewers worldwide watched the 2002 World Cup Final.

Music is another aspect of popular culture that has become international. As the equipment for listening to music has become more portable, there are only a few places in the world that do not have access to music from other cultures. People from around the world dance to reggae bands from the Caribbean, chant rap lyrics from the United States, play air guitar to rowdy European bands, and enjoy the fast drumming of Afropop tunes. And the performers who create this music often gain international fame. **A**

MAIN IDEA

Recognizing Effects

A What effects have television and mass media had on popular culture?

Rock 'n' Roll

In the middle of the 1950s, a new style of music emerged on the American scene. It was called rock 'n' roll. The music explored social and political themes. Rock music, which seemed to adults to reflect a youth rebellion, soon became the dominant popular music for young people across the world. As the influence of rock music spread, international artists added their own traditions, instruments, and musical styles to the mix called rock.

"The King" ▶

"Rock and roll music, if you like it and you feel it, you just can't help but move to it. That's what happens to me, I can't help it."—Elvis Presley, called the "King of rock 'n' roll" by many.

U2 ▶

U2, led by singer Bono (right), is one of the world's most popular and influential rock bands. Over a career spanning more than 20 years, this Irish band has kept its music vibrant and fresh by absorbing and reworking all manner of musical styles. The band has drawn on the blues, gospel, 1950s rock 'n' roll, 1960s protest songs, and hip-hop to create a very distinctive kind of music.

World Culture Blends Many Influences

Greater access to the ideas and customs of different cultures often results in cultural blending. As cultural ideas move with people among cultures, some beliefs and habits seem to have a greater effect than others. In the 20th century, ideas from the West have been very dominant in shaping cultures in many parts of the globe.

Westernizing Influences on Different Cultures Western domination of the worldwide mass media helps explain the huge influence the West has on many different cultures today. However, heavy Western influence on the rest of the world's cultures is actually rooted in the 19th century. Western domination of areas all over the globe left behind a legacy of Western customs and ideas. Western languages are spoken throughout the world, mainly because of Europe's history of colonization in the Americas, Asia, and Africa.

Over the past 50 years, English has emerged as the premier international language. English is spoken by about 500 million people as their first or second language. Although more people speak Mandarin Chinese than English, English speakers are more widely distributed. English is the most common language used on the Internet and at international conferences. The language is used by scientists, diplomats, doctors, and businesspeople around the world. The widespread use of English is responsible, in part, for the emergence of a dynamic global culture.

Western influence can be seen in other aspects of popular culture. For example, blue jeans are the clothes of choice of most of the world's youth. Western business suits are standard uniforms among many people. American-style hamburgers and soft drinks can be purchased in many countries of the world. Mickey Mouse and other Disney characters are almost universally recognized. Western influence also has an effect on ways of thinking in other parts of the world. For example, people

▲ "World Pop"
Youssou N'Dour, a singer from the West African country of Senegal, blends traditional African styles with American rock to create a new form that has been called "world-pop fusion."

Patterns of Interaction

Cultural Crossroads: The United States and the World

The spread of American culture, including sports, fashion, and fast food, has created an international culture recognizable in all corners of the globe. In some cases American culture is simply a powerful influence, as other societies blend American culture with local customs. Cultural blending is evident even in America's past. Symbols of American culture like baseball and hot dogs are themselves the result of cross-cultural influences.

Connect *to* Today

1. **Making Inferences** How have improvements in technology and global communications aided in the blending of musical styles?

   See Skillbuilder Handbook, page R10.

2. **Creating Oral Presentations** Find out the global origins of such aspects of American culture as rock 'n' roll and baseball. Report your findings to the class in an oral presentation.

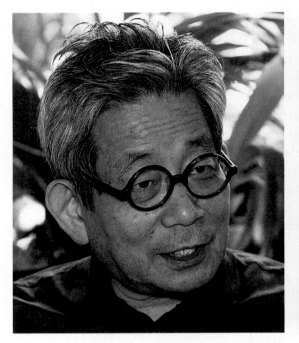

▲ Kenzaburo Oe of Japan was awarded the Nobel literature prize in 1994. Oe studied Western literature in college, and he has used Western literary styles to tell stories about his personal life and the myths and history of his country.

▲ South African writer Nadine Gordimer won the Nobel Prize for Literature in 1991. Many of her novels and stories published prior to 1991 focused on the evils of the apartheid system. As a result, much of her work was censored or banned by the South African government.

from many different cultures have adopted **materialism**, the Western mindset of placing a high value on acquiring material possessions.

Non-Western Influences Cultural ideas are not confined to moving only from the West to other lands. Non-Western cultures also influence people in Europe and the United States. From music and clothing styles to ideas about art and architecture, to religious and ethical systems, non-Western ideas are incorporated into Western life. And cultural blending of Western and non-Western elements opens communications channels for the further exchange of ideas throughout the globe.

The Arts Become International Modern art, like popular culture, has become increasingly international. Advances in transportation and technology have facilitated the sharing of ideas about art and the sharing of actual works of art. Shows and museums throughout the world exhibit art of different styles and from different places. It became possible to see art from other cultures that had not previously been available to the public.

Literature, too, has become internationally appreciated. Well-known writers routinely have their works translated into dozens of languages, resulting in truly international audiences. The list of Nobel Prize winners in literature over the last 20 years reflects a broad variety of nationalities, including Nigerian, Egyptian, Mexican, South African, West Indian, Japanese, Polish, Chinese, and Hungarian. **B**

MAIN IDEA
Summarizing
B Name three advances that allow a greater sharing of the arts.

Future Challenges and Hopes

Many people view with alarm the development of a global popular culture heavily influenced by Western, and particularly American, ways of life. They fear that this will result in the loss of their unique identity as a people or nation. As a result, many countries have adopted policies that reserve television broadcast time for national programming. For example, France requires that 40 percent of broadcast time be set aside for French-produced programs. And in South Korea, the government limits foreign programming to just 20 percent of broadcast time.

Some countries take a different approach to protecting cultural diversity in the media. Television programmers take American shows and rework them according to their own culture and traditions. As an Indian media researcher noted, "We really want to see things our own way." Other countries take more drastic steps to protect their cultural identity. They strictly censor the mass media to keep unwanted ideas from entering their nation.

Sometimes people respond to perceived threats to their culture by trying to return to traditional ways. Cultural practices and rites of passage may receive even more emphasis as a group tries to preserve its identity. In some countries, native groups take an active role in preserving the traditional ways of life. For example, the Maori in New Zealand have revived ancestral customs rather than face cultural extinction. Many Maori cultural activities are conducted in a way that preserves Maori ways of thinking and behaving. In 1987, the New Zealand government recognized the importance of this trend by making the Maori language one of the country's official languages. **C**

MAIN IDEA

Recognizing Effects

C How do people react against greater global interdependence?

Global Interdependence Despite the fear and uncertainty accompanying global interdependence, economic, political, and environmental issues do bring all nations closer together. Nations have begun to recognize that they are dependent on other nations and deeply affected by the actions of others far away. As elements of everyday life and expressions of culture become more international in scope, people across the world gain a sense of connectedness with people in other areas of the world. For example, the response to the events of September 11, 2001, was international in scope. People from around the world expressed their concern and support for the United States. It was as if this act of terrorism had struck their own countries.

Throughout history, human beings have faced challenges to survive and to live better. In the 21st century, these challenges will be faced by people who are in increasing contact with one another. They have a greater stake in learning to live in harmony together and with the physical planet. As Martin Luther King, Jr., stated, "Our loyalties must transcend our race, our tribe, our class, and our nation; and this means we must develop a world perspective."

SECTION 5 ASSESSMENT

TERMS & NAMES 1. For each term or name, write a sentence explaining its significance.
• popular culture   • materialism

USING YOUR NOTES

2. Which of the international popular culture aspects has the greatest effect on your life? Why?

International popular culture

MAIN IDEAS

3. How do the mass media spread popular culture across the world?

4. Why do Western cultures tend to dominate other cultures?

5. What steps have governments and people taken to protect cultural diversity?

CRITICAL THINKING & WRITING

6. **CLARIFYING** Why are the mass media such an effective means of transmitting culture?

7. **RECOGNIZING EFFECTS** Do you think that limiting the amount of foreign television programming is an effective way to protect cultural diversity? Why or why not?

8. **FORMING AND SUPPORTING OPINIONS** "Ethnocentrism— the belief in the superiority of one's own ethnic group—has taken hold in the world." Do you agree or disagree? Explain.

9. **WRITING ACTIVITY** CULTURAL INTERACTION Write a **letter** to a friend in another country describing the elements of American popular culture they might appreciate.

CONNECT TO TODAY CREATING A SCRAPBOOK

Study current newspapers and magazines to find pictures that show cultural blending. Create a **scrapbook** of these pictures. Write captions explaining how each picture illustrates cultural blending.

TERMS & NAMES

For each term or name below, briefly explain its connection to global interdependence from 1960 to the present.

1. Internet
2. genetic engineering
3. global economy
4. free trade
5. political dissent
6. refugee
7. terrorism
8. USA Patriot Act
9. popular culture
10. materialism

MAIN IDEAS

The Impact of Science and Technology Section 1
(pages 637–640)

11. In what ways have science and technology changed the lives of people today?
12. What was the goal of the green revolution?

Global Economic Development Section 2
(pages 641–647)

13. How are a developed nation and an emerging nation different?
14. What is the function of the World Trade Organization?

Global Security Issues Section 3 (pages 648–652)

15. What methods has the world community used to resolve conflicts since World War II?
16. What efforts have been made to guarantee basic human rights?

Case Study: Terrorism Section 4 (pages 653–658)

17. What methods do terrorists employ?
18. How did the United States respond to the terrorist attacks of September 11, 2001?

Cultures Blend in a Global Age Section 5 (pages 659–663)

19. Which technologies have had the most powerful impact on cultural sharing?
20. Why have Western influences had a major impact all over the world?

CRITICAL THINKING

1. USING YOUR NOTES

SCIENCE AND TECHNOLOGY Use the diagram to show how advances in science and technology have changed lifestyles.

Cause	Effect
Miniaturization of computer parts	→
Expanded global communication	→
Genetic research	→

2. EVALUATING COURSES OF ACTION

POWER AND AUTHORITY How is the UN working to address the unresolved problems of the world?

3. IDENTIFYING SOLUTIONS

CULTURAL INTERACTION Imagine you are the culture minister of a small country. What steps would you take to ensure that your country's cultural identity is protected? Explain why you think these steps would be effective.

4. RECOGNIZING EFFECTS

ECONOMICS How are individuals affected by the global economy?

VISUAL SUMMARY

Global Interdependence

Economics	Culture	Science and Technology	Politics
• Service industries grow in developed nations. • Free trade expands world markets. • Environmental challenges continue.	• Mass media spreads many cultures. • Popular culture becomes more international. • Global interdependence awareness develops.	• Space cooperation stretches horizons. • Advanced communications allow wider contact. • Inventions improve life and health.	• Terrorism and weapons of mass destruction threaten global security. • Nations take collective security actions. • Human rights improve worldwide. • Immigrants change cultures.

Use the passage, which was written by a German journalist, and your knowledge of world history to answer questions 1 and 2.
Additional Test Practice, pp. S1–S33

PRIMARY SOURCE

Imagine a roomful of 14-year-olds—from Germany, Japan, Israel, Russia and Argentina. Obviously, they would all be wearing Levi's and baseball caps. But how would they relate to one another? They would communicate in English, though haltingly and with heavy accents. About what? . . . They would debate the merits of Nike versus Converse, of Chameleon versus Netscape. Sure, they would not discuss Herman Melville or George Gershwin, but neither would they compare notes on Dante or Thomas Mann. The point is that they would talk about icons and images "made in the U.S.A."

JOSEF JOFFE, from "America the Inescapable"

1. Which statement best describes the main idea of the excerpt?

   A. Many teenagers have little understanding of world literature.

   B. American popular culture plays a major role in teenagers' lives.

   C. All teenagers communicate in English.

   D. Most teenagers wear American-made clothes.

2. Which is the most likely way that teenagers in other countries learn about American popular culture?

   A. through the mass media

   B. through discussions with their parents

   C. through school textbooks

   D. through Internet bulletin boards

Use the graph and your knowledge of world history to answer question 3.

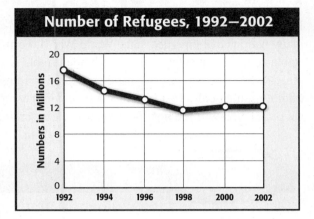

Number of Refugees, 1992–2002

3. Which statement best describes the overall trend shown in this graph?

   A. There has been a steady rise in the number of refugees.

   B. The number of refugees has risen dramatically.

   C. There has been a steady fall in the number of refugees.

   D. The number of refugees has fallen dramatically.

INTEGRATED TECHNOLOGY

TEST PRACTICE Go to **classzone.com**

• Diagnostic tests
• Strategies
• Tutorials
• Additional practice

ALTERNATIVE ASSESSMENT

1. Interact *with* History

After reading Chapter 20, do you believe events in other nations affect your life? Which kinds of events are more likely to affect you in a very personal way? Create a survey about global interdependence to ask students in your class or school. Consider organizing your questions in four broad categories: science and technology, economics, security, and culture.

2. WRITING ABOUT HISTORY

Use the Internet and library resources to find information on SARS. Use your findings to write a brief **report.** Your report should cover the following topics:

• where and when the disease emerged.

• possible causes and methods of prevention.

• statistics on the disease.

INTEGRATED TECHNOLOGY

NetExplorations: The Environment

Go to *NetExplorations* at **classzone.com** to learn more about the environment and the dangers it faces. Working in a team with three other students, find information on a recent discovery concerning changes in the environment. Use your findings to create the script for a 10-minute television news segment on the discovery and its implications for everyday life. The script should include

• a description and explanation of the discovery

• interviews on the subject with scientists, government officials, and representatives of non-governmental organizations

• references to locations, sound, and visuals

• a concluding statement on the overall significance of the discovery and what, if anything, needs to be done about it

Five Developing Nations

Nation building is the creation of a state with a national identity. In Unit 5, you studied many nations that emerged since World War II. Forming a politically and economically stable country that safeguards basic human rights is a formidable task, especially in places where the people have different ethnic or religious backgrounds and different traditions and goals. To succeed, a new nation must forge a national identity. In the next six pages, you will see how five countries are working to become developed nations.

Israel   1945   1955   1965   1975

Six-Day War 1967
When the Egyptian military moved to strike Israel, Israeli forces attacked, destroying airfields in Syria, Jordan, Egypt, and Iraq. Israel won the war in six days.

India   1945   1975

Pakistan-India split 1947 ▲
After riots in 1946 killed thousands of Hindus and Muslims, the British agreed to partition India. About one million people were killed trying to move to one country or the other.

Mexico   1945   1955   1965   1975

The new party 1946
In 1946, the Mexican Revolutionary Party became the Institutional Revolutionary Party (PRI), which ruled for the next fifty years. Although the PRI promoted stability, it was politically corrupt.

Nigeria   1945   1965   1975

Independence 1960 ▲
Britain granted independence to Nigeria without military struggle.

War over Biafra 1967
The Ibos ethnic group tried to secede and form a new nation called Biafra. A bloody war ensued and the Ibos were defeated.

Philippines   1945   1955   1965   1975

Independence 1946
On July 4, the United States granted independence to the Philippines.

Marcos elected 1965
After being elected president, Ferdinand Marcos became an authoritarian ruler and stole money from the government. In 1972, he imposed martial law.

1985	1995	present

Camp David Accords 1979
Egypt and Israel signed the first treaty between Arabs and Israelis.

First intifada 1987 ►
The intifada was a widespread campaign of civil disobedience. Palestinians all over Israel participated in boycotts, demonstrations, rock throwing, and attacks on Israeli soldiers.

1985	1995	present

Indira Gandhi killed 1984
In October, prime minister Indira Gandhi was shot by two of her Sikh bodyguards in retaliation for an attack on a Sikh temple where terrorists were hiding.

Leadership changes 1998
The Congress Party had been in power in India since the country's creation in 1947, but in 1998 the Hindu nationalist party gained control.

1985	1995	present

Political opening 1988
In 1988, opposition parties were able to seriously challenge the ruling party for the first time.

Zapatista Uprising 1994 ►
Rebels seized control of several towns in the state of Chiapas, demanding more democracy and a better life for the native people.

1985	1995	present

Free election 1999
Nigeria held its first free election after almost 20 years of military dictators.

1985	1995	present

Fall of Marcos rule 1986 ▲
Marcos was forced into exile when he attempted to falsify the results of the 1986 election. Corazón Aquino became president.

Comparing & Contrasting

1. What are some problems that can arise in developing nations as a result of ethnic, religious, and economic problems?

2. How do Israel's religious problems differ from those of the other countries on the time line?

National Characteristics

Many developing nations are trying to bring together a patchwork of ethnic groups that historically competed or were hostile to each other. To complicate matters more, the groups often speak different languages. Choosing one group's language as the official language could earn government leaders the ill-will of the other groups. Moreover, the traditions of one group might be objectionable to another for moral or religious reasons. The chart below describes the current situation in the five sample countries.

	Political		Cultural	
	Government	**Flag**	**Language**	**Religion**
Israel	• Parliamentary democracy • Unicameral Knesset (parliament) • President elected for seven-year term by Knesset • Prime minister heads the largest party in the Knesset • Supreme Court appointed for life by president		• Hebrew (official) • Arabic (official for minority Arabs) • English (used commonly)	• Jewish, 80.1% • Muslim, 14.6% • Christian, 2.1%
India	• Federal Republic • Bicameral legislature elected by people and state assemblies • President chosen by electoral college; five-year term • Prime minister chosen by ruling party • Supreme Court appointed by president to serve until age 65		• Hindi (official and most common) • Over 200 languages spoken • English (used in education and government)	• Hindu, 81.3% • Muslim, 12% • Christian, 2.3% • Sikh, 1.9% • Buddhist, Jain, Parsi in small numbers
Mexico	• Federal Republic • Bicameral legislature, elected by popular vote or by party vote • President elected by popular vote for six-year term • Supreme Court appointed by president with consent of the Senate		• Spanish • Mayan, Nahuatl and other indigenous languages	• Roman Catholic, 89% • Protestant, 6%
Nigeria	• Republic • Bicameral legislature elected by popular vote • President elected by popular vote for one or two four-year terms • Supreme Court appointed by president		• English (official) • Hausa, Yoruba, Igbo, Fulani	• Muslim, 50% • Christian, 40% • Indigenous faiths, 10%
Philippines	• Republic • Bicameral legislature elected by popular vote • President elected by popular vote for six-year term • Supreme Court appointed by president to serve until age 70		• Filipino (official) • English (official) • Eight major dialects	• Roman Catholic, 83% • Protestant, 9% • Muslim, 5%

Economic	
Trading	**Main Export**
• Imports: crude oil, grains, military equipment, raw materials • Exports: fruits, vegetables, cut diamonds, high-technology equipment.	• cut diamonds
• Imports: crude oil, machinery, fertilizer, chemicals, gems • Exports: software services, engineering products, gems, jewelry, textiles, chemicals, leather goods	• textiles and clothing
• Imports: metalworking and agricultural machinery, electrical equipment, car parts for assembly and repair • Exports: petroleum products, silver, manufactured goods, cotton, coffee, fruits, and vegetables	• manufactured goods
• Imports: machinery, chemicals, manufactured goods, food • Exports: petroleum and petroleum products, cocoa, rubber	• petroleum
• Imports: fuels, consumer goods, raw materials, capital goods • Exports: coconut products, clothing, electronic products, machinery, and transport equipment	• electronics

"How can [a people] think of themselves as a national people if they don't even have a single language unifying them? Language is one of the most important instruments of nation-building, a potentially powerful unifying force."

David Lamb, from *The Africans*

Comparing & Contrasting

1. What similarities are there among the governments of the countries listed on the chart?

2. Why does David Lamb think language is such an important part of nation building?

Important Trends

In their inaugural speeches, the following leaders outlined the principal problems they wished to address during their terms in office. Below are some highlights of what they said. Note that the problems they discuss are shared by many of the developing nations you studied in Unit 5.

PRIMARY SOURCE

INTER**ACTIVE**

Israel

Prime Minister Ariel Sharon discusses the Israeli national identity.

I believe wholeheartedly that the State of Israel has no greater resource than themselves, the Jewish people. We shall strengthen the bond and connection with the Jews of the Diaspora and the Zionist education of our education system. We will work towards bringing masses of Jewish immigrants to Israel and their absorption in the country. We must educate our children towards values: to respect for others, to equality between people, to national pride and love of country.

DOCUMENT-BASED QUESTION
In Sharon's view, what should be the continuing objectives of Israel?

PRIMARY SOURCE

INTER**ACTIVE**

India

President Abdul Kalam stresses the importance of keeping religion separate from government.

I wish to emphasize my unflinching commitment to the principle of secularism, which is the cornerstone of our nationhood and which is the key feature of our civilization strength. During the last one year I met a number of spiritual leaders of all religions. They all echoed one message, that is, unity of minds and hearts of our people will happen and we will see the golden age of our country, very soon. I would like to endeavor to work for bringing about unity of minds among the divergent traditions of our country.

DOCUMENT-BASED QUESTION
Why does Kalam think India needs a secular government?

PRIMARY SOURCE

INTER**ACTIVE**

Mexico

Equal rights and economic opportunities are what the poor need in the view of President Vicente Fox.

I emphatically maintain that social justice is part of an efficient economy, not its adversary. It is time we recognized that everything cannot be solved by the State, nor can everything be solved by the market. I believe that the vote for democracy is inseparable from the vote for social equity.
   Quality education, employment and regional development are the levers to remove, once and for all, the signs of poverty, which are inequity, injustice, discrimination and exclusion.

DOCUMENT-BASED QUESTION
According to Fox, what does Mexico have to provide its poor so they can obtain social equity?

Nigeria

President Olusegun Obasanjo explains his plan to curb the military.

The incursion of the military into government has been a disaster for our country and for the military over the last thirty years. . . . [P]rofessionalism has been lost. Youths go into the military not to pursue a noble career but with the sole intention of taking part in coups and to be appointed as military administrators of states and chairmen of task forces. . . . A great deal of reorientation has to be undertaken and a re-definition of roles, re-training and re-education will have to be done to ensure that the military submits to civil authority and regains its pride, professionalism and traditions. We shall restore military cooperation and exchanges with our traditional friends.

DOCUMENT-BASED QUESTION

How does President Obasanjo propose to change the military culture in Nigeria?

Philippines

President Gloria Macapagal Arroyo discusses the importance of the rule of law.

Politics and political power as traditionally practiced and used in the Philippines are among the roots of the social and economic inequities that characterize our national problems. Thus, to achieve true reforms, we need to outgrow our traditional brand of politics based on patronage and personality. Traditional politics is the politics of the status quo. It is a structural part of our problem.

We need to promote a new politics of true party programs and platforms, of an institutional process of dialogue with our citizenry. This new politics is the politics of genuine reform. It is a structural part of the solution.

DOCUMENT-BASED QUESTION

According to Macapagal Arroyo, how does traditional politics promote poverty and how does party politics promote social equity?

Comparing & Contrasting

1. How does Kalam's view of religion in national self-identity and government contrast with Sharon's?

2. How might party politics as described by Macapagal Arroyo help to achieve the solutions Fox considers essential?

EXTENSION ACTIVITY

Choose one of the countries studied in Unit 5 that became independent after World War II. Research on the Internet how that country has fared in recent times. Use the Web sites of major newspapers, magazines, and other news organizations to find information on how ethnic, religious, economic, and other relevant concerns are being handled. Organize this information into an oral presentation to explain how the country is or is not changing.

Unresolved Problems of the Modern World

Previewing Main Ideas

SCIENCE AND TECHNOLOGY As humankind enters the 21st century, advances in electronics and computers have dramatically altered how millions work and live and have brought people together in ways that once seemed unimaginable.

INTERACTION WITH ENVIRONMENT At the dawn of a new millennium, humans face a host of environmental challenges as they try to strike a balance between economic and industrial growth and conservation of the earth's natural resources.

POWER AND AUTHORITY Leaders of the world community have faced pressing problems in recent years. They include how to feed the earth's growing population, how to keep the world safe against the increasing threat of terrorism, and how to ensure human rights for all.

ECONOMICS As less-developed countries seek a greater share of the world's wealth and prosperity, they face numerous challenges in building strong and independent economies.

◄ The Red Cross offers relief in Rwanda, Africa

◄ Coalition troops
battle in Iraq

◄ Burning of the
Brazilian Amazon
Rain Forest

es of the missing in
rch for justice

► Victims of the Khumer
Rouge regime in Cambodia

What can you do to make a difference?

In this age of multimedia—from radio and magazines to television and the Internet—it is easier than ever to become informed about today's major issues and challenges. As you learn about these challenges, you wonder what you can do in your community to address them. Although you are not yet a voter or in the working world, you are interested in joining a local organization or activity to help make a difference in your part of the world.

▲ College students build a home for an underprivileged family in Mississippi.

EXAMINING *the* ISSUES

- What are some environmental, economic, and social concerns of your country or community?

- What things might you do locally to address these concerns?

As a class, discuss these questions. As you consider how to address the major challenges facing your country and community, talk about why you think it is important to get involved.

Technology Transforms Life

MAIN IDEA	WHY IT MATTERS NOW	TERMS & NAMES
SCIENCE AND TECHNOLOGY The rapid emergence of new technologies holds promises as well as challenges for people around the world.	New technology touches nearly every aspect of life for many people.	• mass media

SETTING THE STAGE For centuries, people have used science to find new ways to do things. But the pace of technological change has increased dramatically since the second half of the 20th century. The development of the silicon chip and other electronic circuits has paved the way for revolutions in electronics and computers. These technological revolutions have dramatically impacted numerous aspects of daily life, from how people live and work to the ways in which they communicate.

A Revolution in Electronics

New forms of electronic circuits have made possible the production of powerful new machines, such as computers. Computers, along with advances in telecommunications, have greatly changed the way people handle information. They have done so by vastly increasing the speed at which information can be carried.

The Influence of Computers The earliest and most basic use of computers was computing—figuring out complex math problems. As electronic circuits have grown faster, computers have been able to solve problems even more quickly. Powerful computers can make billions of computations every second.

The ability to compute quickly makes computers very helpful. They are used to guide rockets and satellites into space. Air traffic controllers use them to track airline traffic. Many automobiles use computers to control fuel gauges, engines, and even brakes. Banks and other businesses use computers to keep track of accounts and inventory. In 1997, an IBM-built computer named Deep Blue defeated world chess champion Garry Kasparov in a six-game chess match. Some people feared that computers might some day control humans. David Gelernter, a Yale University computer science professor, offered a different opinion:

PRIMARY SOURCE
Deep Blue is just a machine. It doesn't have a mind any more than a flowerpot has a mind. . . . Machines will continue to make life easier, healthier, richer, and more puzzling. And humans will continue to care . . . about the same things they always have: about themselves, about one another and, many of them, about God. On those terms, machines have never made a difference. And they never will.

DAVID GELERNTER, *Time*

TAKING NOTES
Summarizing Use a chart to list various technological innovations and what effect each has had on daily life.

Innovation	Effect

A Continuous Revolution

Electronic and computer technologies, it seems, are advancing at a breakneck pace. Every day, people are working to improve the latest equipment and devices or to create something entirely new. The result is an ongoing revolution in the way we do everything from travel to communicate. Perhaps nowhere is the pace of change faster than in the fields of computers and electronics—where what was once considered science fiction has become a reality.

▲ Iris Identification

A woman looks through the Iris Access system, which scans the iris, or colored ring around the eye's pupil. Like fingerprints, the iris is unique to each person.

▲ Human Transporter

A police officer travels his beat on the Segway Human Transporter, an electric-powered machine that one drives simply by leaning forward. The Segway travels at a top speed of about 12 miles per hour.

◄ Miniature Music Player

A music lover shows off his MP3 music player-wristwatch, which enables him to download and listen to his favorite songs from pay-for-use Internet sites.

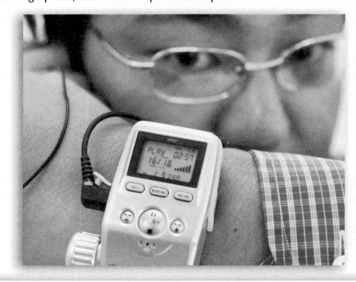

DOCUMENT-BASED QUESTIONS

1. **Comparing and Contrasting** *What advantages and disadvantages does the Human Transporter have to a bicycle or automobile?*
2. **Forming and Supporting Opinions** *Which of these inventions do you consider to be the most important? Why?*

Information Spreads in New Ways Electronic technology also has had a great impact on how people communicate. People are increasing their use of cellular phones, fax machines, and computers—including the Internet—to move information instantly across the planet. As a result, people can very easily conduct business, or just chat from great distances. These technologies have helped draw the world closer together.

The Internet has become one of the most exciting ways for people to communicate. People can use the Internet to find ever-increasing amounts of information. More and more businesses advertise and sell their goods on the Internet. Governments use the Internet to provide their citizens with more information than ever before. In addition, people around the world can use chat rooms and electronic mail, or e-mail, to send messages to one another. **A**

MAIN IDEA

Hypothesizing
A How do you think the Internet will affect businesses in the 21st century?

A Connected World

The Internet and other new technologies have made the world a much smaller place, as these advances have enabled the flow of information, ideas, and entertainment across cities and nations, and across the globe.

A Changing Workforce Rapid communications and data transmission have helped to transform workplaces around the world. Many white-collar workers now "telecommute," or do their jobs by computer from home. Investors can conduct business in any market in the world, from almost anywhere, by using telephones, fax machines, and computers. Television, radio, and the Internet can instantly give investors the news and information they need to conduct business. As a result, some professionals no longer need to live near business offices. In addition, modern telecommunications allow trading, banking, and financial transactions to be done electronically.

As you read in Chapter 20, technological changes such as these have had both positive and negative effects on businesses and workers. In manufacturing, robots perform more and more jobs that were once done by people. As a result, many companies have cut their workforces. In more technologically advanced economies, employment is shifting from blue-collar industries to high-tech industries. Many workers are being forced to improve their skills in order to keep their jobs because high-tech industries need workers with more technical skills.

Furthermore, high-tech workplaces are found mainly in industrialized countries, such as the United States, Japan, and the countries of western Europe. This technological imbalance has given rise to a new kind of economic imperialism in which the industrialized nations dominate less-developed countries.

Cultures Converge The **mass media**—which include television, radio, movies, the music industry, and the popular press—are expanding their influence with the growth of technology. Television has spread to the extent that billions of people around the planet now watch sporting events such as the Olympics and the World Cup soccer championships. In addition, some 2 billion people worldwide viewed the funeral of Princess Diana of England on live television in 1997.

Global Impact

"Chat Room Savior" Sean Redden

On the afternoon of April 14, 1997, Sean Redden, a seventh-grader in Denton, Texas, received a startling message through the Internet: "Help me. I'm having trouble breathing." At first, Sean thought the message was a joke. When the pleas continued, though, Sean realized that the emergency was real.

In fact, the writer—Tarja Laitinen, a 20-year-old student in Finland, 7,000 miles away—was having a seizure. Sean's mother phoned 911, and after a series of phone calls, Finnish rescue workers found Tarja and rushed her to the hospital. Thanks to Sean and the Internet, Tarja's life was saved.

▲ A traveler talks by cell phone in rural Israel.

Because the media now reach around the world, they are able to spread images, ideas, and fashions from one country to another. Many of these ideas or trends travel from the developed world outward. But the mass media also bring cultural offerings from Africa, Asia, and Latin America to wealthier nations. The increased familiarity in Europe and the United States with African music, Asian philosophy, and Latin American literature demonstrates the power of the mass media to promote a greater awareness of and mixing of different cultures. For instance, the English translation of *Como Agua Para Chocolate* (Like Water for Chocolate), the popular novel by Laura Esquivel, sold over two million copies in the United States. **B**

Old Ways Abandoned As mass media spread new images and ideas, however, they may cause deep changes in traditional cultures. Old ways may be lost. In some cases, people experience a loss of identity and culture. Or they may find themselves in conflict over competing values. In addition, some observers, such as author and columnist Thomas Friedman, worry that so much technology is weakening the old and more personal ways of interacting:

MAIN IDEA

Recognizing Effects

B How have new technologies affected your own life?

PRIMARY SOURCE
Yes, globalization and the Internet can bring people together who have never connected before—like my mom and her French Internet bridge partners. But rather than creating new kinds of communities, this technology often creates a false sense of connection and intimacy. It's like two beepers communicating with each other. Can we really connect with each other through E-mail or Internet bridge or chat rooms? Or is all this standardizing technology just empowering us to reach farther into the world while exempting us from the real work required to build relationships and community with the folks next door?

THOMAS FRIEDMAN, *The Lexus and the Olive Tree*

Sometimes the challenge posed by new ideas and technology can stimulate the desire to preserve traditions. Technology may even play a positive role in this process. In the Amazon region of Brazil, for example, some native Brazilians are using video cameras to document and preserve traditional ways of life.

SECTION 1 ASSESSMENT

TERMS & NAMES 1. For the following term, write a sentence explaining its significance.
• mass media

USING YOUR NOTES
2. Which innovation has had the greatest impact? Why?

Innovation	Effect

MAIN IDEAS
3. What are three modern communications devices?

4. How has technology led to the emergence of telecommuting?

5. What has been the main effect of the growth of mass media?

CRITICAL THINKING & WRITING
6. **IDENTIFYING PROBLEMS** What challenges has technology created for some in the workforce?

7. **RECOGNIZING EFFECTS** What are the benefits and drawbacks of the spread of mass media?

8. **ANALYZING ISSUES** What problems, if any, do you see arising from the growth of the Internet?

9. **WRITING ACTIVITY** SCIENCE AND TECHNOLOGY With a partner, use the library or the Internet to review the past year's issues of a leading science journal. Write a **report** on an important technological advance that was made during the year.

CONNECT TO TODAY **CREATING A CHART**
Create a two-column **chart** that lists the top three or four technological devices you use and briefly explains the benefits of using each one.

Environmental Challenges

2

MAIN IDEA	WHY IT MATTERS NOW	TERMS & NAMES
INTERACTION WITH ENVIRONMENT Technology and industrialization have created environmental challenges that affect the entire world.	Failure to solve environmental problems will threaten the health of the planet.	• greenhouse effect • sustainable development

SETTING THE STAGE Technology and industrialization have helped to raise standards of living for many people. But they have also affected the global environment. For two centuries, industrialization has increased the demands for energy and natural resources. In addition, industry and technology have increased the amount of pollution on the planet. Pollution and the potential shortage of natural resources have prompted everyone from world leaders to ordinary citizens to look for ways to better protect our natural surroundings.

World Concern over the Environment

Two major areas of concern are the effects of industrial pollution on the earth's atmosphere and on its climate. As you read in Chapter 20, environmentalists are especially concerned that various human-made chemicals are destroying the ozone layer, which protects earth from the sun's damaging rays. Scientists also are worried about global warming, also known as the **greenhouse effect**.

The Greenhouse Effect Scientists use the term *greenhouse effect* to describe problems caused by industrial pollution. Much of this pollution comes in the form of gases, such as carbon dioxide. These gases—sometimes called greenhouse gases—are the exhaust from factories and automobiles. The gases create a kind of ceiling, like the roof of a greenhouse, that traps heat near the earth's surface. This buildup of heat near the earth's surface causes a gradual warming of the earth's atmosphere.

Not all scientists agree with the theory of the greenhouse effect. But tests do indicate that the earth's climate is slowly warming. If this trend continues, deserts will expand and crops will fail. The polar icecaps will melt and oceans will rise.

To combat this problem, the industrialized nations have called for limits on the release of greenhouse gases. In the past, developed nations were the worst polluters. But future limits would have the greatest effect on those countries that are trying to industrialize. So far, developing countries have resisted strict limits. They argue that they are being asked to carry too much of the burden for reducing greenhouse gases.

Air Pollution Varies In addition to its possible warming effects, air pollution can be a serious health hazard. In recent years, many cities in Europe and the United States have taken steps to clean up the air. But air pollution is still severe

TAKING NOTES

Determining Main Ideas
Use a web chart to take notes on the environmental problems that the world faces.

Atmosphere

Environmental Problems

Energy

Natural Resources

in many parts of the world, especially Asia. The World Health Organization has pointed out that 13 of the world's 15 most-polluted cities are in Asia.

Meanwhile, South Korea, China, and Japan have begun talks to reduce the effects of pollution caused by China's rapid industrialization. And some Chinese cities are trying to reduce air pollution locally. For example, Shanghai has reportedly banned leaded gasoline and diesel fuel, which cause heavy pollution.

Depletion of Natural Resources

While air pollution and global warming are indeed a growing concern, so too is the growing strain on natural resources. Due largely to industrialization and increasing population, vital resources such as clean water, forests, and energy supplies all run the risk of becoming scarce.

Scarcity of Clean Water In the developing world, water pollution and scarcity of clean water are serious problems. One-fourth of the world's population has no access to clean water. Eighty percent of all illnesses in developing nations can be traced to inadequate supplies of fresh water.

In some parts of the world, nations share the water supplies in lakes and rivers. In southwest Asia, for example, Israel and Jordan share the Jordan River—an essential source of water for farming. Any nation that pollutes shared water or stops water from flowing into a neighboring country runs the risk of starting an international conflict. Many nations try to cooperate to make sure water supplies remain clean.

In the United States, California has complex water issues. The state's large population and agricultural industry have put severe pressure on water resources. The problems worsened during a drought that lasted from 1987 to 1992. However, the state limited the negative effects of the drought by developing new ways to conserve and use water.

Destruction of Rain Forests Another critical resource issue is the destruction of tropical rain forests in such countries as Malaysia and Brazil. By 1990, the world

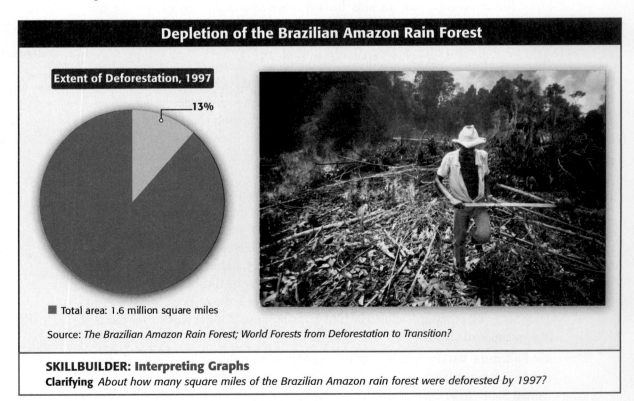

Depletion of the Brazilian Amazon Rain Forest

Extent of Deforestation, 1997

13%

■ Total area: 1.6 million square miles

Source: *The Brazilian Amazon Rain Forest; World Forests from Deforestation to Transition?*

SKILLBUILDER: Interpreting Graphs
Clarifying *About how many square miles of the Brazilian Amazon rain forest were deforested by 1997?*

Economics

Deforestation is an issue that often pits economic and environmental interests against one another. Here, William Wade Keye, chairman of the Northern California Society of American Foresters, criticizes the efforts of environmentalists.

PRIMARY SOURCE

It used to be about protecting spotted owls, saving old-growth forests or putting an end to clear-cutting. That was 1990. . . . Now the demand is for absolute purity. To many environmentalists in 2001, nothing less than "zero-cut" is acceptable—no commercial timber harvesting from America's vast network of publicly owned national forests. Not one stick. . . . In a region blessed with some of the planet's most fertile and sustainable temperate forest ecosystems, struggling sawmill communities are subsisting on raw logs imported from hundreds—sometimes even thousands—of miles away.

WILLIAM WADE KEYE, from *Southern Loggin' Times*

Environmentalism

Edward O. Wilson, a research professor emeritus at Harvard University, makes it clear that environmental concerns should outweigh all else when considering America's forests.

PRIMARY SOURCE

If we have learned anything from the scientific studies of forests, it is that each such environment is a unique combination of thousands of kinds of plants, animals, and microorganisms. . . . It is this biological diversity that creates a healthy ecosystem—a self-assembled powerhouse generating clean water, productive soil and fresh air, all without human intervention and completely free of charge. . . . America's national forests are the common property of its citizens. They are a public trust of incalculable value. They should be freed from commercial logging altogether and cut only very locally and in extreme cases.

EDWARD O. WILSON, from *The Washington Post*

DOCUMENT-BASED QUESTIONS

1. **Recognizing Effects** *What effect have environmental regulations had on the logging industry, according to Keye?*
2. **Analyzing Issues** *What reason does Wilson give for arguing that forests should be maintained and protected?*

had lost more than half its rain forests to logging or farming operations. Experts estimated that another 20 percent had been lost by the year 2000.

This loss could affect all people on the planet. The rain forests help to maintain water quality, recycle rainfall and oxygen into the atmosphere, and protect the soil. These forests also are home to as many as half of the world's species of plants and animals.

In recent years, nations like Brazil have made efforts to slow the destruction of the rain forests. Success has been limited, however, by Brazil's desire to develop economically. As one American diplomat put it, "Environmental concerns are a luxury of the rich, and this is not a rich country. Brazilians are not going to just preserve the Amazon. They are going to develop it. The question is, how."

Many other developing nations face the same problem as Brazil. They need to achieve **sustainable development**, the process of creating economic growth while preserving the environment.

A Growing Appetite for Energy

Sustainable development depends on using energy sources wisely. All sources of energy can be defined as renewable or nonrenewable. Renewable energy sources, such as wind, water, and solar power, can be replenished. Nonrenewable energy sources, such as oil and coal, cannot. Although nonrenewable sources are generally cheaper to use, supplies are limited. Also, their use can cause environmental damage.

Energy Use and its Challenges Eighty percent of the earth's energy supply now comes from nonrenewable sources. Developed countries consume most of this

Alternative Fuel Cars

Automobiles, which run on oil-based gasoline, use a great deal of the world's nonrenewable energy. But perhaps not for long. Automakers have begun creating cars fueled by alternative power, such as hydrogen—one of the most abundant natural elements on earth.

While it may be a while before such cars catch on, the trend toward environmentally safer vehicles is growing. California, for example, recently required the production of millions of low-emission vehicles—which use a combination of gas and electric power—over the next two decades.

energy. Although these nations account for just 25 percent of the world's population, they use 75 percent of the energy consumed worldwide.

Using nonrenewable energy has many environmental effects. The burning of coal emits greenhouse gases. Cutting down trees leads to soil erosion and the expansion of deserts in some areas. Nuclear power plants produce radioactive wastes that can remain hazardous for many years. **A**

The Exxon Valdez Oil Spill Oil spills are another example of energy-related pollution. Every year, several serious oil spills take place around the world. They foul water and shorelines and kill sea life. Although oil companies take precautions to prevent spills, spills appear to be an inevitable result of oil use.

The largest oil spill in U.S. history occurred in March 1989. The giant oil tanker Exxon Valdez hit a reef in Prince William Sound, off the coast of Alaska. The ship spilled 11 million gallons of crude oil into the sea. The environmental consequences were horrendous. But the federal government responded forcefully. It ordered a cleanup and forced Exxon to pay more than $5 billion in damages.

Solutions for the 21st Century Government action and stronger regulations may provide solutions to the world's environmental problems in the 21st century. In the long run, however, improved technology might stand as the best hope for a cleaner environment. More inexpensive ways to use renewable energy sources, such as wind and solar power, may reduce air pollution and the greenhouse effect. In any event, the nations of the world will need to agree on how to achieve sustainable development in this new millennium.

MAIN IDEA

Identifying Problems

A What are some problems associated with the use of nonrenewable energy?

SECTION **2** ASSESSMENT

TERMS & NAMES 1. For each term, write a sentence explaining its significance.
• greenhouse effect   • sustainable development

USING YOUR NOTES

2. Which set of problems do you consider to be the most serious? Why?

- Atmosphere
- Environmental Problems
- Energy
- Natural Resources

MAIN IDEAS

3. What are the main greenhouse gases?

4. What natural resources does the world community fear are becoming scarce?

5. What is the difference between renewable and nonrenewable energy?

CRITICAL THINKING & WRITING

6. **HYPOTHESIZING** Why do you think the environmental problems of the earth have become more dangerous?

7. **FORMING AND SUPPORTING OPINIONS** Should developing nations have to meet the same environmental standards as developed nations? Why or why not?

8. **ANALYZING ISSUES** Should developed nations take any responsibility for preventing the destruction of the rain forests? Explain.

9. **WRITING ACTIVITY** INTERACTION WITH ENVIRONMENT Write one or two **slogans** that might encourage your community to better protect the environment.

CONNECT TO TODAY CREATING A VISUAL

Examine your local newspaper to determine an environmental problem in your community.
Then create a **poster, cartoon,** or other **graphic** that depicts that problem.

Feeding a Growing Population

MAIN IDEA	WHY IT MATTERS NOW	TERMS & NAMES
POWER AND AUTHORITY Population growth has put great pressure on the earth's resources, including the food supply.	Nations must find ways to support their growing human populations or else face famines.	• overpopulation • biorevolution

SETTING THE STAGE As humanity moves further into the 21st century, another issue of growing concern is world hunger. Potential causes of famine are overpopulation, forces of nature, and war. **Overpopulation** occurs when there are too many people for the natural resources of an area to support. In some cases, it is war or natural catastrophes that push groups into starvation. Across the globe, nations are working to implement both temporary and more long lasting measures aimed at reducing starvation and hunger.

Causes of World Hunger

Since 1950, the world's population has more than doubled, to about 6 billion people. More growth is predicted. According to researchers, the world's population will increase to nearly 10 billion by 2050. Rapid population growth directly affects the quality of life on the planet. As more people try to live on a limited supply of natural resources, poverty rates rise—and so too does the risk of widespread hunger.

The Role of Nature In some areas of the world, changes in the climate have played a major role in creating famine. In Africa, for example, rainfall was plentiful during the 1950s and 1960s. The rain helped produce good crops and steady economic growth for many African nations. In 1968, however, drought began to weaken African agriculture. In the 1970s and 1980s, rainfall returned to typically low levels. In many areas, food supplies ran short. Ethiopia, for example, confronted severe famines in the 1980s and 1990s because of drought. Tens of thousands of Ethiopians died. Many others suffered malnutrition and disease.

The situation is just as grim in other African nations. Traveling through Zimbabwe in late 2002, U.S. government official Tony P. Hall recalled witnessing the devastating effects of hunger:

TAKING NOTES

Comparing and Contrasting Use a chart to compare and contrast the advantages and disadvantages of the green revolution and the biorevolution.

Green Revolution	Bio-revolution

PRIMARY SOURCE

I . . . met children in school, some of whom had not eaten at all that day. Others had a cup of tea for breakfast and nothing for lunch. Some were showing clear signs of malnutrition—with their hair turning orange and their limbs like twigs. The headmaster said that about 40 percent of the kids have dropped out of school. A few kids had their eyes glazed over and showed little ability to learn the lessons in front of them.

TONY P. HALL, statement in Harare, Zimbabwe, October 11, 2002

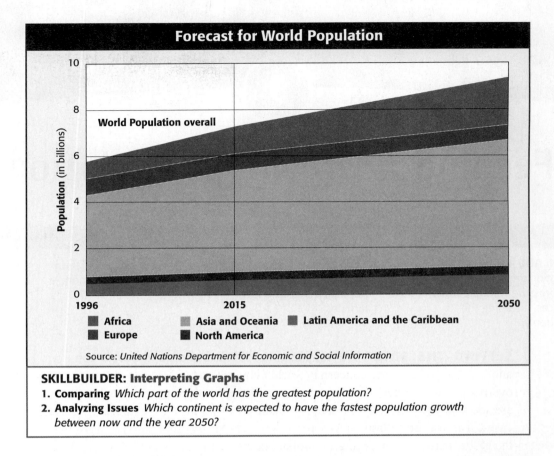

Forecast for World Population

Population (in billions)

World Population overall

1996   2015   2050

- Africa
- Europe
- Asia and Oceania
- North America
- Latin America and the Caribbean

Source: *United Nations Department for Economic and Social Information*

SKILLBUILDER: Interpreting Graphs
1. **Comparing** *Which part of the world has the greatest population?*
2. **Analyzing Issues** *Which continent is expected to have the fastest population growth between now and the year 2050?*

Government-Produced Famine In addition to droughts, wars have contributed to famine. The drought that hit Ethiopia in the early 1990s hit Somalia as well. But Somalia was also engaged in a civil war that disrupted food production and delivery by outside relief agencies. As a result, thousands of Somalis died of starvation, and more than a million refugees fled the nation.

The reduction in food supply caused by drought and war created deep problems for many African nations. While agriculture declined, the prices for major African exports also fell. High African birth rates made these problems even worse. Food supplies were getting smaller while populations were getting larger. **A**

Revolutions in Food Production

One response to the problem of rapid population growth, and the potential for hunger and starvation it brings, has been to boost food production. As you read in Chapter 20, agricultural scientists around the world embarked on what became known as the green revolution—a successful effort to increase food production through the use of fertilizers, pesticides and high-yield strains of crops.

Unfortunately, the techniques of the green revolution often call for much irrigation, or watering, of crops. Because many African nations have limited water supplies, they have not been able to make full use of the new seeds. This severely limits the usefulness of these methods in much of Africa, where there is little water.

Moreover, the new hybrid varieties of plants require chemicals, such as fertilizers, herbicides, and pesticides, to help them grow. This requirement has caused a number of problems. First, the chemicals are expensive. Peasant farmers usually cannot afford them. Second, the use of such chemicals often clashes with age-old methods of farming. Third, these chemicals pose a threat to the environment.

In addition to the methods of the green revolution, genetic research has played a growing role in agricultural science in recent years. In this approach, scientists

MAIN IDEA

Recognizing Effects
A How have droughts and wars affected African food supplies?

Vocabulary
A *pesticide* is a chemical used to kill insects; a *herbicide* is one used to destroy plants, especially weeds.

alter plant genes to produce new plants that are more productive and more resistant to pests and disease.

This **biorevolution**, or gene revolution, has led to some important developments. For example, one U.S. company has developed a genetically altered tomato that ripens more slowly than other tomatoes. This means that the altered tomatoes keep much of their flavor and freshness longer. Similar tests are being conducted with other kinds of produce. **B**

But the biorevolution has raised some troubling issues. Critics fear that altering genes may accidentally create new disease-causing organisms. Another fear is that plants produced by altering genes may become diseased more easily. As with the green revolution, science offers great opportunities in the search for more food, but the results may also have negative consequences.

MAIN IDEA

Clarifying

B How has the biorevolution helped increase food production?

Other Solutions to Population Problems

Various approaches to curbing overpopulation have been proposed over the years. Three main strategies are to improve the economies of less-developed countries, to limit population growth, and to improve the status of women.

Improving Economies Many experts believe that the best way to tackle overpopulation is through economic development. When a country's economy improves, birth rates fall. They do so for two reasons. First, women become pregnant less frequently because more newborn children survive. More children survive because stronger economies provide better health care, nutrition, and child-care education for mothers. Second, when economies are strong, families do not need as many children to work to support the family and parents in their old age. The result is slower population growth and less risk of widespread hunger.

Limiting Population Growth A second major strategy is to lower the rate at which the population is growing. In 1994, in Cairo, Egypt, the International Conference on Population and Development met for the third time. Delegates

History *in* Depth

Red Cross and UNICEF

Two organizations that have played a crucial role in supplying food and other forms of aid to needy populations are UNICEF and the Red Cross. UNICEF, the United Nations Children's Fund, was founded in 1946 to help children in Europe after World War II. Now, it provides food, medicine, and education funds to children in developing countries.

The Red Cross was first established in the 1800s to help war victims. Later it branched into peacetime service, including emergency food relief. The work of both of these organizations has been instrumental in helping to combat starvation, disease, and hardship in many lands.

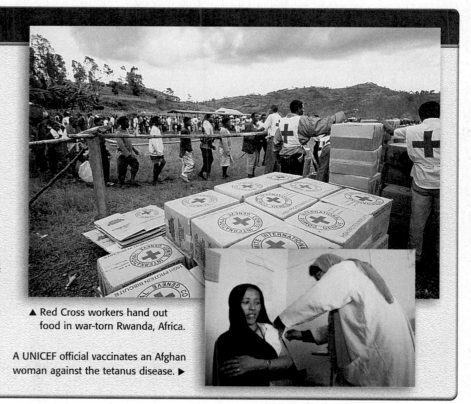

▲ Red Cross workers hand out food in war-torn Rwanda, Africa.

A UNICEF official vaccinates an Afghan woman against the tetanus disease. ▶

agreed on a plan to keep population growth to a minimum through the year 2050. It called for greater use of family planning, reductions in child mortality, and increased women's rights. Some delegates did not support the entire plan, but it passed nonetheless.

Some critics have pointed out problems in limiting population growth when it is carried out in extreme ways. A strict policy may reduce birth rates at the expense of personal freedom, or it may target specific groups that cannot defend their rights. For example, church leaders and some politicians in Peru have charged that a government program has forced poor Indian women to undergo sterilization, making them unable to have children. The critics have said that poor, uneducated women are lured into having the sterilization procedure by health workers who promise gifts for the families.

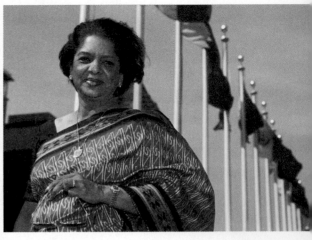

▲ Dr. Nafis Sadik stands outside United Nations headquarters in New York City.

Improving Women's Status Most experts believe that protecting the rights of women is essential to reducing birth rates. For example, the birth rate for uneducated Peruvian women in recent years was 6.2. By contrast, the rate for Peruvian women with some college education was only 1.7. According to population experts like Dr. Nafis Sadik of the United Nations Population Fund, there is a close link between women's status in society and population growth. The greater the status of women, the lower the birth rates.

Improving conditions for women will be a crucial part of any effort to solve the world's population problem. However, other actions will also need to be taken to reduce the threat of famine and food shortages. New technologies may provide a key to increasing food supplies. In addition, creating and protecting political stability around the world can help to ensure that people have access to food. The best way to conquer starvation, however, may be to improve the economies of developing nations.

SECTION 3 ASSESSMENT

TERMS & NAMES 1. For each term, write a sentence explaining its significance.
• overpopulation   • biorevolution

USING YOUR NOTES
2. Which of these campaigns combats hunger more effectively? Why?

Green Revolution	Bio-revolution

MAIN IDEAS
3. What are the main causes of famine in the world?

4. Why have some countries been unable to benefit from the green revolution?

5. What are the three main strategies for controlling overpopulation?

CRITICAL THINKING & WRITING
6. **MAKING INFERENCES** How will improving women's rights have an impact on population problems?

7. **ANALYZING ISSUES** Do the benefits of new agricultural techniques outweigh the drawbacks? Explain.

8. **FORMING AND SUPPORTING OPINIONS** Should governments establish policies to reduce population growth? Why or why not?

9. **WRITING ACTIVITY** POWER AND AUTHORITY Write an **expository essay** identifying and explaining the different positions governments have taken on the issue of population growth.

CONNECT TO TODAY CREATING A CHART

Choose a country and track its population figures over the past century on a **chart**. Display your chart to the class and discuss possible reasons for the trends you found.

Economic Issues in the Developing World

MAIN IDEA	WHY IT MATTERS NOW	TERMS & NAMES
ECONOMICS Developing nations face a set of economic challenges that must be resolved.	Sustainable economic development enables more people to lead productive lives and makes the world more stable.	• less-developed countries (LDCs) • investment capital • World Bank • International Monetary Fund (IMF) • grassroots development

SETTING THE STAGE The economies of the industrialized nations grew rapidly after World War II. Such has not been the case, however, for many **less-developed countries (LDCs)**, or countries not fully industrialized. Among other things, the LDCs have lacked financial resources and a strong infrastructure—roads, airports, plumbing, and electrical systems—necessary for economic growth. Nevertheless, the industrialized nations have remained interested in the LDCs as sources of raw materiais and as potential markets for goods. Indeed, the industrialized nations would like the economies of the LDCs to become strong and stable.

Providing International Aid

Most economists cite the following factors as necessary for economic development:
- **investment capital**, funds to pay for the construction of industries and infrastructure, such as roads and bridges
- technology to help companies and workers be as productive as possible
- healthy and well-trained workers to help reduce waste and inefficiency
- qualified managers to make sure that workers and materials are used efficiently

Roots of the Difficulties A serious problem that LDCs face is how to acquire these factors. Many people believe that imperialism and colonialism are the reasons that the LDCs have not industrialized. The imperial nations limited the economic growth of their colonies. In addition, the colonial governments robbed the colonized people of the chance to govern themselves. When most colonized regions gained their independence after World War II, they had underdeveloped economies and weak political traditions. These problems made it difficult for the LDCs to achieve stable economic growth. In recent years, however, more and more LDCs have been developing stable democratic governments and making greater strides toward a stronger economy.

Industrialized nations have tried to work with the LDCs by providing aid through international organizations, such as the **World Bank** and the **International Monetary Fund (IMF)**. The World Bank provides loans for large-scale development projects, such as dams. The IMF offers emergency loans to countries in financial crisis.

TAKING NOTES

Identifying Solutions
Create a web diagram showing the various solutions to creating economic growth.

Solutions to Economic Growth

Tense Relations International agencies can play an important role in development, but they also have drawbacks. The World Bank, for example, might fund a project that it considers worthy, such as a large dam. But the project may do little to help the people of a country. The IMF, as well, has been criticized for setting harsh financial conditions upon countries receiving IMF loans. For instance, the IMF might require a country to cut its government spending drastically.

Latin American nations have had troubled relationships with international lenders. For instance, Brazil repeatedly clashed with the IMF since the 1980s over economic policy and repayment schedules. By 1997, Brazil had worked out a repayment plan, but its debt level remained very high—$200 billion by the middle of 1999.

Different Economic Approaches

Today, many LDCs use two main approaches to spur economic growth—investment by multinational corporations and smaller, more localized efforts known collectively as grassroots development.

Multinational Corporations As you learned in Chapter 20, multinational corporations are companies that do business in many countries. These giant companies build factories in countries where the costs of labor and materials are low in order to increase their profits. Multinational companies often bring jobs, investment capital, and technology to nations that need them. Yet some of these companies have been criticized for exploiting workers and harming the environment in their host countries.

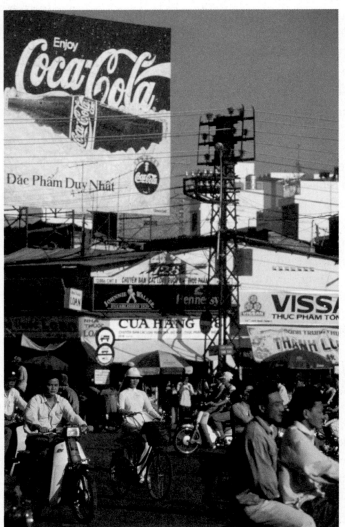

▼ Residents of Ho Chi Minh City, Vietnam, travel beneath advertisements for various international companies.

Most LDCs want multinational companies to invest in them because the multinationals do create jobs. Some LDCs offer multinational corporations favorable tax rates and work regulations. For instance, Nicaragua offers a package of benefits to multinational clothing firms that operate *maquilas,* or factories, in Nicaragua. The package exempts the companies from having to pay income taxes for ten years and allows them to pay a minimum wage of 41 cents an hour.

On the whole, Nicaraguan *maquilas* are a mixed blessing for the country. The unemployment rate is high, and the *maquilas* provide jobs. But maquilas do little to contribute technology, capital, or infrastructure to the country.

Grassroots Development Another approach to economic development is **grassroots development**. Grassroots development calls for small-scale, community-based projects to help poor people lift themselves from poverty. Grassroots programs usually focus on helping individuals and communities to improve their lives. Grassroots development responds to community needs and can help raise standards of living while preserving local customs.

An example of a grassroots development program is microcredit. Microcredit programs give small loans—often less than $100—to individuals as seed money to enable them to begin small-scale businesses and lift themselves from poverty. Many organizations, including the World Bank and multinational corporations, run microcredit programs.

Julia Sairitupac, a single mother living in Sarita Colonia, Peru, was one person who benefitted from the microcredit program. She received between $100 and $200 for kitchen tools and other equipment to help her struggling business selling fruit juice and *salchipapas* (hot dogs and french fries.) "I feel like I have begun, for the first time, to leave poverty," she said. "Although my work requires many sacrifices, I want to continue progressing and install my business in my own home, which, with the help of my children, we are already building bit by bit."

No matter what approach is used, however, the development process is slow. And the gap between rich and poor nations remains large. Although the economic output of Asia and Africa grew during the 1980s, these regions still lag far behind the richer, more productive nations.

Free Trade or Protectionism Another key issue that developing countries face is whether to follow policies of protectionism or free trade. Free trade, as you learned in Chapter 20, is the reduction of trade barriers among nations. This includes eliminating tariffs, or taxes on imported goods. Supporters of free trade believe that doing away with tariffs stimulates commerce by increasing trade among nations. Protectionists are those who oppose free trade. They support tariffs as a way to protect local products and industries from international competition.

Since the 1980s, many LDCs have embraced free trade under the terms established by the General Agreement on Tariffs and Trade (GATT) and the North American Free Trade Agreement (NAFTA), both of which were detailed in Chapter 20. Regional trading blocs are now forming in Latin America, Africa, and Asia. These blocs may provide many LDCs with the support they need to strengthen their economies. The success of these trading blocs appears to be crucial to the economic growth and long-term stability of developing countries. **A**

MAIN IDEA

Forming and Supporting Opinions

A Do you support free trade or protectionism? Why?

SECTION 4 ASSESSMENT

TERMS & NAMES 1. For each term or name, write a sentence explaining its significance.
• less-developed countries (LDCs) • investment capital • World Bank • International Monetary Fund (IMF) • grassroots development

USING YOUR NOTES	MAIN IDEAS	CRITICAL THINKING & WRITING
2. Which solution do you think most LDCs will choose?	3. What are the main factors needed for economic development? 4. What are the two main approaches to economic development in LDCs? 5. How do supporters of free trade and protectionism differ in their view of tariffs?	6. **ANALYZING ISSUES** What are the advantages and disadvantages to grassroots development? 7. **CLARIFYING** What factors must LDCs consider in making plans to develop their economies? 8. **FORMING AND SUPPORTING OPINIONS** Do organizations providing economic aid have the right to place restrictions on their aid? Why or why not? 9. **WRITING ACTIVITY** [ECONOMICS] Imagine you are an editorial writer for a newspaper in a developing nation. Write a brief **editorial** expressing your view on free trade versus protectionism.

CONNECT TO TODAY CREATE A TIME LINE

Choose a developing country in Latin America, Africa, or Asia and create a **time line** of significant economic events in its history over the past 50 years.

Seeking Global Security

MAIN IDEA	WHY IT MATTERS NOW	TERMS & NAMES
POWER AND AUTHORITY War, terrorism, and weapons of mass destruction threaten the safety of people all over the world.	People can work against the dangers posed by war, terrorism, and weapons of mass destruction.	• conventional arms • bioweapons

SETTING THE STAGE Among the most pressing issues facing the world community today are warfare and terrorism. So long as nations continue to use the threat of military force as a tool of foreign policy, armed conflicts will erupt. In addition, the threat of terrorism—the use of violence against people or property to force changes in societies or governments—strikes fear in the hearts of many people. Nevertheless, many nations and organizations have been working together to reduce the threats of such violence and bloodshed.

TAKING NOTES
Summarizing Create a diagram to illustrate the sources of threats to international peace and security.

Threats to International Peace and Security

Worldwide Arms Trade

Many people hoped that the end of the Cold War would reduce the risk of armed conflict around the world. However, developments following the Cold War have introduced new threats. First, the collapse of the Soviet empire led to political instability and violence in parts of the world the Soviets once controlled. Second, a bustling international arms trade has emerged to ensure that few conflicts around the world suffer from a shortage of weapons.

The Market for Weapons During the Cold War, the main suppliers of **conventional arms**—tanks, planes, rifles, and all other non-nuclear weapons—were the United States, Western Europe, and the Soviet Union. These nations sold most of their weapons to developing nations. This government-sponsored trade has declined considerably since the mid-1980s, but it has not ceased.

What has grown, however, is the illegal market for weapons. Many of the weapons bought on the illegal market find their way to trouble spots around the world. These illegal weapons have frequently contributed to armed conflict in regions with political, ethnic, or religious tensions.

Protests against Weapons Sales Some people are beginning to take action against international arms dealers. In Belgium, the Flemish Forum voor Vredesaktie (Forum for Peace Action) has organized nonviolent protests against the Armed Forces Communication and Electronics Association (AFCEA), which held its annual arms fair in Brussels, Belgium, in 1997. Protesters convinced Belgian customs officers to seize all of the military equipment at the fair that year because the equipment was not properly licensed.

Demonstrations such as those in Belgium have a long way to go before they stop international arms deals. But opponents of the arms trade are determined not to abandon their fight.

Weapons of Mass Destruction

Weapons of mass destruction, which you read about in Chapter 20, pose a different kind of threat to peace. Such weapons, which include nuclear armaments and biological and chemical weapons, have the potential to kill or injure large numbers of people at one time. Many of these tools of war are the products of sophisticated technologies. Even so, some are frighteningly easy to make and use.

The Threat of Nuclear Weapons The existence of nuclear weapons poses a significant threat to world peace—and even to human survival. In the years since World War II, a number of nations have developed nuclear weapons while other countries continue working toward that goal. Opponents of nuclear weapons have tried to prevent the proliferation, or spread, of such weapons.

A major step toward stopping nuclear proliferation was the Treaty on the Non-Proliferation of Nuclear Weapons (NPT). This treaty was passed by the United Nations General Assembly in 1968. It went into force in 1970 for 25 years. In 1995, 170 nations signed on to renew the NPT forever. Only India and Pakistan have continued to test nuclear arms. However, there is growing concern that hostile nations, such as North Korea, are on the verge of developing nuclear weapons. Such a dilemma highlights the continuing threat of nuclear war.

Biological and Chemical Weapons The possible proliferation of biological and chemical weapons is also a growing concern to many nations. These weapons are

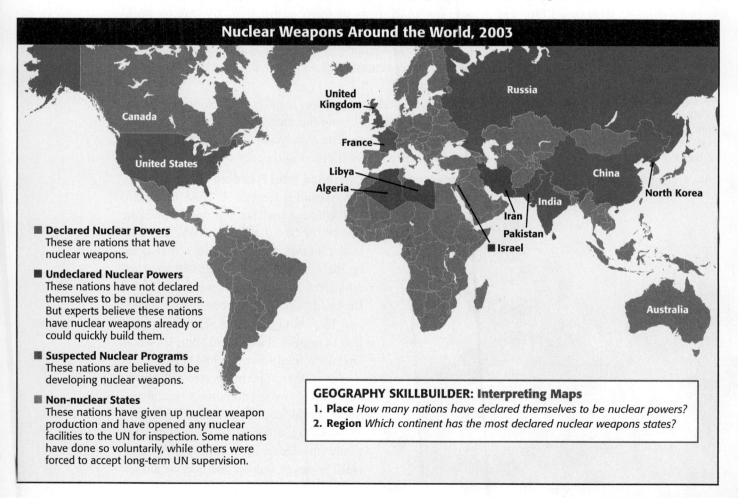

Nuclear Weapons Around the World, 2003

- ■ **Declared Nuclear Powers**
  These are nations that have nuclear weapons.

- ■ **Undeclared Nuclear Powers**
  These nations have not declared themselves to be nuclear powers. But experts believe these nations have nuclear weapons already or could quickly build them.

- ■ **Suspected Nuclear Programs**
  These nations are believed to be developing nuclear weapons.

- ■ **Non-nuclear States**
  These nations have given up nuclear weapon production and have opened any nuclear facilities to the UN for inspection. Some nations have done so voluntarily, while others were forced to accept long-term UN supervision.

GEOGRAPHY SKILLBUILDER: Interpreting Maps
1. **Place** *How many nations have declared themselves to be nuclear powers?*
2. **Region** *Which continent has the most declared nuclear weapons states?*

relatively easy to produce and distribute, making them much more available than nuclear weapons to terrorists and less-developed countries. Author Richard Preston feels that biological weapons, or **bioweapons**, can be the most deadly:

PRIMARY SOURCE Ⓐ

Bioweapons are microorganisms, bacteria or viruses, that invade the body, multiply inside it, and destroy it. Bioweapons can be used as strategic weapons. That is, they are incredibly powerful and dangerous. They can kill huge numbers of people if they are used properly, and their effects are not limited to one place or a small target. Chemical weapons, on the other hand, can be used only tactically. It is virtually impossible to put enough of a chemical in the air in a high enough concentration to wipe out a large number of people over a large territory. And chemicals aren't alive and can't spread through an infectious process.

RICHARD PRESTON, "The Bioweaponeers," *The New Yorker*

MAIN IDEA

Analyzing Primary Sources
Ⓐ Why are biological weapons more destructive than chemical weapons?

The War in Iraq

In the spring of 2003, amid growing worries about terrorism and the development of deadly weapons that resulted from the terrorist attacks of September 11, 2001, the United States confronted the leader of Iraq, Saddam Hussein. The longtime dictator had concerned the world community for years. During the 1980s, Hussein had used chemical weapons to put down a rebellion in Iraq. In 1990, he had invaded Kuwait, only to be pushed back by a U.S.-led military effort. In light of such history, many viewed Hussein as a threat to peace and stability in the world. As a result, the United States led an effort to remove the Iraqi leader from power.

The Path to War Throughout much of 2002, the United States and other nations accused Hussein of developing weapons of mass destruction. Bowing to world pressure, Hussein allowed inspectors from the United Nations to search Iraq for such outlawed weapons. Some investigators, however, insisted that the Iraqis were not fully cooperating with the inspections. U.S. and British officials soon threatened to use force to disarm Iraq.

The UN Security Council debated what action to take next. Some countries, such as France and Germany, called for letting the inspectors continue searching for weapons. British prime minister Tony Blair, however, accused the Iraqis of "deception and evasion" and insisted inspections would never work.

▼ With war reporters looking on, coalition troops battle enemy soldiers outside the town of Basra in Iraq.

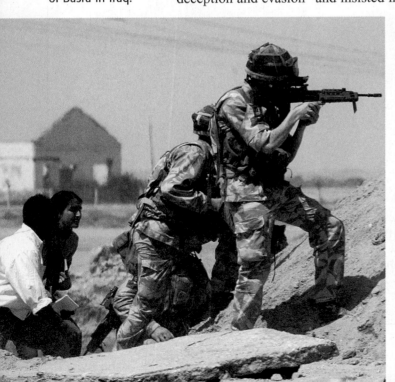

Operation Iraqi Freedom In March 2003, U.S. president George W. Bush demanded that Hussein and his top aides leave the country or face a military strike. The Iraqi leader refused. Within days, a coalition led by the United States and Britain launched air strikes in and around the Iraqi capital, Baghdad. Coalition forces then marched into Iraq through Kuwait. The invasion of Iraq to remove Saddam Hussein, known as Operation Iraqi Freedom, had begun.

The military operation met with strong opposition from numerous countries. Some world leaders criticized the policy of attacking a nation to prevent it from future misdeeds. U.S. and British officials, however, argued that they would not wait for Hussein to strike first.

As coalition forces marched north to Baghdad, troops parachuted into northern Iraq and began moving south toward the capital city. By early April, Baghdad had fallen and the regime of Saddam Hussein had collapsed. After less than four weeks of fighting, the coalition had won the war.

The Struggle Continues Despite the coalition victory, much work remained in Iraq. With the help of U.S. officials, Iraqis began rebuilding their nation. They established an interim government several months after the war. The new governing body went to work creating a constitution and planning democratic elections, which were held in February 2005. A party heavily supported by Shiite Muslims won the most votes.

Meanwhile, numerous U.S. troops remained behind to help maintain order in Iraq and battle pockets of fighters loyal to Hussein. Violence also increased due to growing opposition to the coalition's presence. As for the defeated dictator, Hussein was finally captured on December 13, 2003. Finally, the United States and Britain came under increasing fire for failing to find any weapons of mass destruction in the months after the conflict ended. U.S. and British officials insisted that it would be only a matter of time before they found Hussein's deadly arsenal. Yet by mid-August 2005, none had been found. **B**

Despite the unresolved issues, coalition leaders declared the defeat of Saddam Hussein to be a victory for global security. "The war on terror is not over, yet it is not endless," declared President Bush shortly after the fighting. "We do not know the day of final victory, but we have seen the turning of the tide. No act of the terrorists will change our purpose, or weaken our resolve, or alter their fate. Their cause is lost. Free nations will press on to victory."

MAIN IDEA

Identifying Problems

B What challenges remained in Iraq after the conflict ended?

▲ President George W. Bush (right) and Prime Minister Tony Blair stood together throughout the war.

SECTION 5 ASSESSMENT

TERMS & NAMES 1. For each term, write a sentence explaining its significance.
• conventional arms   • bioweapons

USING YOUR NOTES	**MAIN IDEAS**	**CRITICAL THINKING & WRITING**
2. Which of the threats to peace and security is the most dangerous? Why? Threats to International Peace and Security	3. Why is the growth of the illegal arms market a threat to world peace? 4. What are the types of weapons of mass destruction? 5. What was the result of Operation Iraqi Freedom?	6. **SUMMARIZING** List ways in which people and nations of the world have attempted to control threats to the world's peace and security. 7. **ANALYZING ISSUES** What reasons might nations have to retain or maintain a nuclear or bioweapons arsenal? 8. **EVALUATING DECISIONS** Do you think the United States was justified in invading Iraq? Why or why not? 9. **WRITING ACTIVITY** POWER AND AUTHORITY Imagine you are a speechwriter for President Bush. Write the introductory **paragraph** of a speech to coalition forces after their victory in Iraq.

INTEGRATED/TECHNOLOGY INTERNET ACTIVITY

Use the Internet to research an armed conflict somewhere in the world. Use your findings to deliver a brief **oral report** about the origins and impact of the conflict.

INTERNET KEYWORD
global conflict

Defending Human Rights and Freedoms

MAIN IDEA	WHY IT MATTERS NOW	TERMS & NAMES
POWER AND AUTHORITY Human rights and freedoms have become a major international concern.	Protecting fundamental rights for all people is an important way to improve life in the 21st century.	• Universal Declaration of Human Rights

SETTING THE STAGE Since the end of World War II, the international community, working through the United Nations and other organizations, has made human rights a primary concern in international affairs. Human rights are the basic rights and freedoms that all people are entitled to enjoy. The UN has passed several declarations setting standards for such rights and freedoms. Around the world, however, repressive governments continue to deny people these rights. Thus, numerous political and organization leaders remain committed to bringing human rights to all people who inhabit the earth.

TAKING NOTES

Clarifying Use a chart to list the steps being taken to improve human rights for particular groups.

Group	Improvements
Children	
Women	

The Struggle for Human Rights

The **Universal Declaration of Human Rights** was adopted by the United Nations in 1948. This declaration defines human rights goals for the world community. The preamble of the declaration lists several reasons why the declaration is necessary, including the need to promote friendly relations between nations.

Article 1 of the declaration states, "All human beings are born free and equal in dignity and rights. They are endowed with reason and conscience and should act towards one another in a spirit of brotherhood." The declaration goes on to spell out the rights that all nations should seek to guarantee for their citizens.

With regard to people's basic rights, the declaration states, "The will of the people shall be the basis of the authority of government" and that "everyone has the right to take part in the government of his country." The declaration also calls for free and fair elections. Finally, it calls for basic civil liberties such as freedom of speech and religion as well as freedom from political terror.

Various organizations, including UN agencies and independent groups such as Amnesty International and Americas Watch, observe whether countries are meeting human rights standards. These groups perform a valuable service by helping to improve conditions and even save lives.

Despite the best efforts of human rights organizations, protecting human rights remains an uphill battle. Serious violations of fundamental rights continue to occur around the world. The violations result from a number of causes, including political dissent, racial or ethnic hatreds, and religious differences.

Political Dissent Opposition to political dissent—the difference of opinion over political issues—is one of the most common causes of human rights violations.

In many countries around the world, from El Salvador to Iran to the former Soviet Union, individuals and groups have been persecuted for holding political views that differ from those of the people in power.

There are many examples of political rights violations in the world. One nation that has been criticized for abuses is Nigeria. General Sani Abacha of Nigeria earned a reputation as a ruthless military dictator. Despite repeated statements that he intended to open up the Nigerian government and hold free elections, Abacha imprisoned his political opponents. Abacha took power in 1993 during the chaos that erupted after results of the presidential election held that year were wiped out. Abacha refused to make public the results of that election. Among his prisoners was Moshood Abiola, a wealthy businessman who many believe won the 1993 election. Abacha died in June 1998. In a hopeful sign for the future, his successor has instituted democratic civilian rule. **A**

Ethnic and Racial Conflicts In some countries, ethnic or racial hatreds lead to human rights abuses. For example, human rights groups have charged the fundamentalist Muslim military regime in Sudan of committing genocide against the Nuba, an agricultural people in southern Sudan. In addition, Christian groups have accused the Sudanese regime of persecuting Christians, many of whom live in the southern region of Sudan.

In Rwanda, fighting between Hutus and Tutsis—the two main ethnic groups— has led to horrendous rights violations. In 1994, Hutus massacred up to 500,000 Tutsis in the worst case of genocide since the 1970s Khmer Rouge reign of terror in Cambodia.

Religious Persecution Human rights violations based on religious differences have also occurred. Such violations often have ethnic and political overtones. For example, Tibetans—under Chinese rule since 1950—have been persecuted by the Chinese for their Buddhist religion, their traditional culture, and their desire for political independence. [Many Tibetan leaders were imprisoned in China in the 1990s.] And the Dalai Lama, the most important Tibetan religious leader, remained in exile.

MAIN IDEA

Making Inferences
A Why do you think some government leaders try to repress political dissent?

The Struggle for Human Rights

South Africa
South Africa institutionalizes racism by separating blacks and whites in 1948. Known as apartheid, the policy was repealed in the early 1990s.

Chile
Families of missing relatives march against former Chilean leader Augusto Pinochet in the early 1990s. Thousands of alleged dissidents disappeared during Pinochet's rule in 1970s and 1980s.

| 1940 | | 1950 | 1960 | 1970 | 1980 | 1990 | 2000 |

Nazi Germany
Prisoners stare out from behind the barbed-wire fence at Buchenwald Concentration Camp during World War II. Millions were put to death at camps like this in what became known as the Holocaust.

Cambodia
One million Cambodians die in the 1970s at the hands of the Khmer Rouge, a rebel group that sought to remake society.

Iraq
Officials in 2003 locate mass graves containing thousands of people suspected of opposing the former regime of Saddam Hussein.

Children at Risk

Children are the most vulnerable of the world's citizens. They are among those who run the highest risk of suffering human rights abuses. The abuses children suffer are mainly social and economic, and they occur primarily in less-developed countries. A lack of food, education, and health care is foremost among these abuses.

In addition, children in many parts of the world are forced to work long hours, often in dangerous conditions, for little or no pay. During the early 1990s Iqbal Masih, a child activist from Pakistan, helped bring attention to the plight of child labor. To help pay off a debt owed by his family, Masih was forced at age four to work for a local carpet maker. He often worked 12-hour days, and frequently was chained to his work station. At age 10, he escaped and worked with various international organizations to highlight the problem of child workers and free thousands of children from forced labor. In 1995, he was shot and killed shortly after returning to Pakistan.

▲ Former child laborer Iqbal Masih became an outspoken critic of the practice.

Meanwhile, the United Nations has played a leading role in trying to improve conditions for children around the world. In 1989, the UN adopted a document called the Convention on the Rights of the Child. Known as the Magna Carta for Children, this document established a framework for children's rights. It covers basic rights, such as health care and education, and calls for protection against the exploitation, abuse, and neglect of children. Similar goals were advanced in 1990 at the World Summit for Children, where world leaders adopted a 25-point program in favor of children's welfare.

Signs of Hope

The work of the international community is a positive sign in the struggle to advance human rights. Despite great obstacles, efforts to make human rights a priority are achieving some successes around the world.

Human Rights Successes The greatest human rights successes have come in the area of political rights and freedoms. In Europe, most countries that were once part of the Soviet bloc have opened up their political systems to allow for democratic elections and the free expression of ideas. There have been similar successes in South Africa, where the apartheid system of racial separation came to an end. Free elections were held in South Africa in 1994, bringing a multiracial government to power.

Women's Rights Addressed The past few decades have also seen major efforts to advance human rights for women. Throughout the world, women tend to be poorer than men and attain less access to social benefits such as education and health care. Conditions for women are especially poor in the less-developed countries. But even in the richer nations, women often have second-class status.

Beginning in the 1970s, international organizations began to address women's rights issues. In 1979, the UN adopted a measure called the Convention for the Elimination of All Forms of Discrimination Against Women. The convention was eventually signed by nearly 100 nations. In 1995, the UN sponsored the Fourth Conference on Women, held in Beijing, China. Issues of women's leadership, property ownership, education, health, and population control were top priorities at the conference.

Human Rights in the 21st Century Progress in all areas of human rights is encouraging—but it is only a beginning. Much work must still be done before people in all countries of the world have the democratic rights and freedoms set forth in the Universal Declaration of Human Rights.

However, important trends in the world provide reasons to hope for continued progress on human rights. Rising levels of education are providing people with the skills to exercise their political rights and improve their lives. Modern communications networks are helping human rights organizations like Amnesty International to investigate and report on human rights abuses. In addition, today's mass media can make people instantly aware of abuses in the world.

But perhaps the greatest reason for optimism regarding human rights arises from world history since 1989. In early 1989, millions of people in the Soviet Union, Eastern Europe, and South Africa lived under repressive governments that denied basic political rights, such as the right to vote in a multi-party election. Then, beginning with Poland later in 1989, one country after another threw off its old regime and turned to a democratic form of government. The Soviet Union came to an end in 1991. In that same year, the republic of Russia had its first free presidential election. And in 1994, South Africa held its first universal elections, in which people of all races could vote.

These historic events transformed the world by extending human rights and democratic institutions to millions of people. They continue to inspire optimism that millions more can win their human and political rights while the new century is still young. **B**

MAIN IDEA

Forming and Supporting Opinions

B What responsibilities do nations have for protecting human rights in foreign countries?

SECTION 6 ASSESSMENT

TERMS & NAMES 1. For the following term, write a sentence explaining its significance.
• Universal Declaration of Human Rights

USING YOUR NOTES	MAIN IDEAS	CRITICAL THINKING & WRITING
2. Which group do you think has made the greatest progress? Explain.	3. What are two examples of human rights?	6. **MAKING INFERENCES** What role can the mass media play in helping people understand human rights problems?
	4. What are the three main causes of human rights violations?	7. **IDENTIFYING PROBLEMS** What problems might arise when a government takes an official role in protecting human rights at home and abroad?
	5. What trends have raised hopes that progress will be made in protecting human rights?	8. **ANALYZING ISSUES** Which group in society do you think needs the most help in obtaining human rights? Why?
		9. **WRITING ACTIVITY** POWER AND AUTHORITY Write an **expository paragraph** explaining which human right discussed in this section you consider the most important and why.

Group	Improvements
Children	
Women	

CONNECT TO TODAY DELIVERING AN ORAL REPORT

Choose a country and investigate its record with regard to human rights. Present your findings in an **oral report** to the class.

Epilogue Assessment

TERMS & NAMES

Briefly explain the importance of each of the following terms and names to the unresolved problems the world faces in the 21st century.

1. mass media
2. greenhouse effect
3. sustainable development
4. overpopulation
5. less-developed countries
6. investment capital
7. World Bank
8. grassroots development
9. bioweapons
10. Universal Declaration of Human Rights

MAIN IDEAS

Technology Transforms Life Section 1 (pages 675–678)

11. Describe two ways in which the revolution in electronics has changed the world.
12. Name two ways in which technology has transformed the workplace.

Environmental Challenges Section 2 (pages 679–682)

13. Discuss three effects of air pollution on the environment.
14. How do rain forests benefit the environment?

Feeding a Growing Population Section 3 (pages 683–686)

15. What factors have contributed to famine in Africa?

Economic Issues in the Developing World Section 4 (pages 687–689)

16. What are the IMF and the World Bank?
17. What is microcredit?

Seeking Global Security Section 5 (pages 690–693)

18. What challenges remained in Iraq after Operation Iraqi Freedom?
19. What makes terrorism frightening to so many people?

Defending Human Rights and Freedoms Section 6 (pages 694–697)

20. How has the UN attempted to protect the rights of children?

CRITICAL THINKING

1. USING YOUR NOTES

SCIENCE AND TECHNOLOGY Use a problem-solution chart to show how technology can help solve two of the unresolved problems of the modern world.

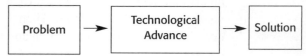

2. ANALYZING ISSUES

Which unresolved problem of the modern world do you think poses the most serious threat to humanity? Explain.

3. FORMING AND SUPPORTING OPINIONS

ECONOMICS Which of the four factors necessary for economic development discussed on page 687 do you consider to be the most vital? Explain.

VISUAL SUMMARY

Unresolved Problems of the Modern World

Technology	Environment	Population	Economics	Terrorism	Human Rights
• The electronic revolution improves communications. • Technological advances change businesses and workplaces. • Mass media change culture.	• Air pollution threatens the atmosphere. • Industry and population growth threaten natural resources. • Energy use creates pollution and depletes resources.	• World population will grow in the next century. • Wars and droughts can cause famines. • Efforts are underway to increase food supplies and reduce population growth.	• Investment capital, technology, good workers, and qualified managers are necessary for economic growth. • Free trade and protectionist policies offer different opportunities for economic development.	• International arms sales can contribute to instability. • Weapons of mass destruction and terrorism threaten international peace.	• Human rights violations arise from political, ethnic, racial, and religious differences. • Progress is made in the 1990s to expand democracy and human rights.

Use the chart and your knowledge of world history to answer questions 1 and 2.
Additional Test Practice, pp. S1–S33

Country	Infant Mortality Rate, 2002 (per 1,000 live births)	Life Expectancy at Birth, 2002 (years)	Per Capita GDP, 2000 (U.S. Dollars)
India	62	63 (male) 64 (female)	2,200
Ethiopia	99	43 (male) 45 (female)	600
France	4	75 (male) 83 (female)	24,400
United States	7	75 (male) 80 (female)	36,200

Source: *The World Almanac,* and *Book of Facts 2003*

1. In which nation does a newborn have the best chance of surviving?

A. India

B. Ethiopia

C. France

D. United States

2. Which of the following can be said about prosperous nations?

A. They have a largely illiterate population.

B. They have a low infant mortality rate.

C. Their residents have a short life expectancy.

D. They have a population that is mostly female.

Use this passage about concerns over North Korea and its possible nuclear capabilities to answer question 3.

PRIMARY SOURCE

It is hard to exaggerate the danger in North Korea's finger-on-trigger taunts to America and the world that it already has a few nuclear bombs, is busily producing the stuff to build more, and will make use of them in whatever way it chooses... More weapons means enough spares to be able, say, to test one to intimidate the neighbors; or to auction one off to the highest bidder (an Iran, a Libya, or perhaps even [terrorist leader] Osama bin Laden).

THE ECONOMIST, May 3, 2003

3. A major concern expressed by the authors is that North Korea could supply nuclear weapons to

A. terrorists.

B. corporations.

C. its neighbors.

D. the United States.

INTEGRATED TECHNOLOGY

TEST PRACTICE Go to **classzone.com**

• Diagnostic tests   • Strategies

• Tutorials   • Additional practice

ALTERNATIVE ASSESSMENT

1. Interact *with* History

On page 674, you considered various social, economic, and environmental problems that exist in your country and community and discussed ways to address these problems. Now that you have read the chapter, what do you think are the most pressing challenges the world faces today? Do you agree with all the actions being taken to meet these challenges? What are some ways that you and others might address these challenges on a local level? Discuss your ideas in small groups.

2. WRITING ABOUT HISTORY

POWER AND AUTHORITY   Using the library or the Internet, research a problem that exists in your community. After you have collected your information, write a letter to your congressional representative about what might be done to solve the problem you have chosen.

Consider the following:

• How did the problem start?

• What effect does it have on the community?

• What is the best way to address the problem?

INTEGRATED TECHNOLOGY

Create a Multimedia Presentation

All of the unresolved problems discussed in the Epilogue have long histories. With a group of students, choose one of the six problems and create a multimedia presentation that explains the history of the problem you have chosen. Use the Internet, periodicals, and other library sources to research your presentation.

• Find historical, literary, musical, and visual materials that relate to your topic and collect them for a class presentation.

• Give your presentation to the rest of the class. Explain the history of the problem you chose, ending with the current situation.

A Global View

Religion is defined as an organized system of beliefs, ceremonies, practices, and worship that centers on one or more gods. As many chapters in this book explain, religion has had a significant impact on world history. Throughout the centuries, religion has guided the beliefs and actions of millions around the globe. It has brought people together. But it has also torn them apart.

Religion continues to be a dominant force throughout the world, affecting everything from what people wear to how they behave. There are thousands of religions in the world. The following pages concentrate on five major religions and on Confucianism, an ethical system. They examine some of the characteristics and rituals that make these religions and systems similar as well as unique. They also present some of each religion's sects and denominations.

2%
2%
12%
84%

North America

3%
9%
88%

Latin America

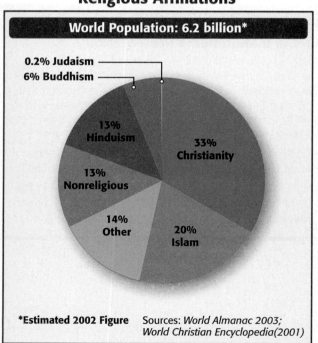

World Population's Religious Affiliations

World Population: 6.2 billion*

0.2% Judaism
6% Buddhism
13% Hinduism
33% Christianity
13% Nonreligious
14% Other
20% Islam

*****Estimated 2002 Figure**   Sources: *World Almanac 2003;*
World Christian Encyclopedia(2001)

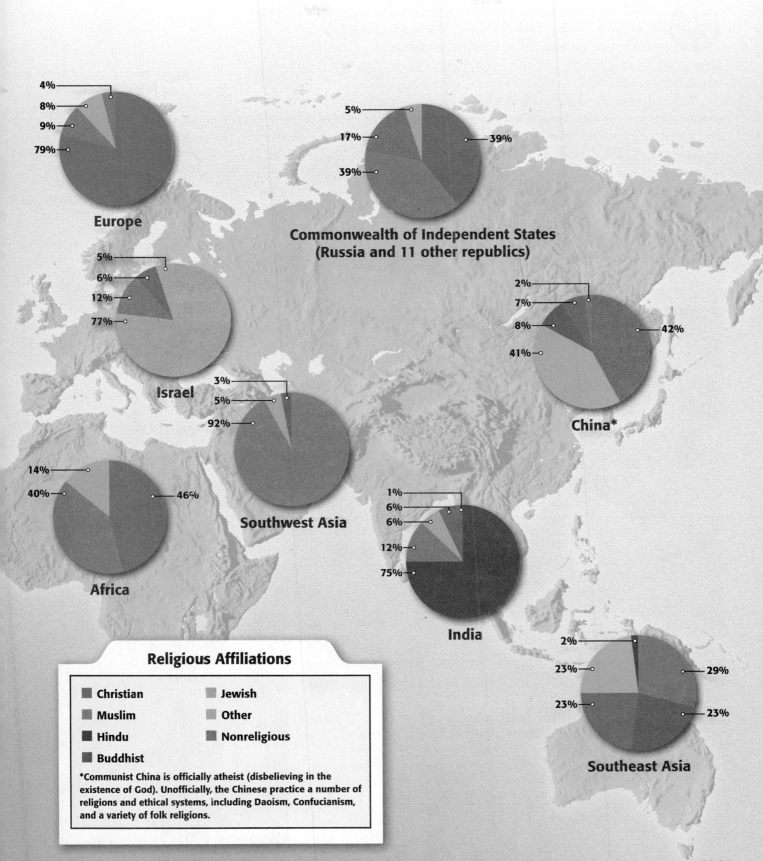

4%
8%
9%
79%

Europe

5%
17%
39%
39%

Commonwealth of Independent States
(Russia and 11 other republics)

5%
6%
12%
77%

Israel

2%
7%
8%
42%
41%

China*

3%
5%
92%

Southwest Asia

14%
40%
46%

Africa

1%
6%
6%
12%
75%

India

2%
23%
29%
23%
23%

Southeast Asia

Religious Affiliations

- ■ Christian
- ■ Muslim
- ■ Hindu
- ■ Buddhist
- ■ Jewish
- ■ Other
- ■ Nonreligious

*Communist China is officially atheist (disbelieving in the existence of God). Unofficially, the Chinese practice a number of religions and ethical systems, including Daoism, Confucianism, and a variety of folk religions.

Buddhism

Buddhism has influenced Asian religion, society, and culture for over 2,500 years. Today, most Buddhists live in Sri Lanka, East and Southeast Asia, and Japan. Buddhism consists of several different sects. A religious sect is a group within a religion that distinguishes itself by one or more unique beliefs.

Buddhists are united in their belief in the Buddha's teachings, known as the dharma. Because the Buddha is said to have "set in motion the wheel of the dharma" during his first sermon, his teaching is often symbolized by a wheel, as shown above. The Buddha taught that the key to happiness was detachment from all worldly goods and desires. This was achieved by following the Noble Eightfold Path, or the Middle Way, a life between earthly desires and extreme forms of self-denial.

INTEGRATED / TECHNOLOGY

RESEARCH LINKS For more on Buddhism, go to **classzone.com**

Ritual ►

Women in Rangoon, Myanmar, sweep the ground so that monks can avoid stepping on and killing any insects. Many Buddhists believe in rebirth, the idea that living beings, after death, are reborn and continue to exist. Buddhists believe that all living beings possess the potential for spiritual growth—and the possibility of rebirth as humans.

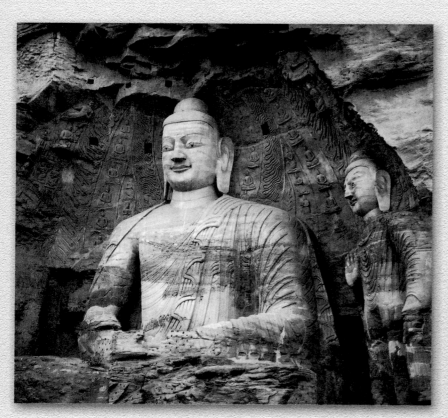

▼ Leadership

Those who dedicate their entire life to the teachings of the Buddha are known as Buddhist monks and nuns. In many Buddhist sects, monks are expected to lead a life of poverty, meditation, and study. Here, Buddhist monks file past shrines in Thailand. To learn humility, monks must beg for food and money.

▲ Worship Practices

Statues of the Buddha, such as this one in China, appear in shrines throughout Asia. Buddhists strive to follow the Buddha's teachings through meditation, a form of religious contemplation. They also make offerings at shrines, temples, and monasteries.

Learn More About Buddhism

Major Buddhist Sects

Theravada   **Mahayana**

Buddhism

Mantrayana

The Three Cardinal Faults

This image depicts what Buddhists consider the three cardinal faults of humanity: greed (the pig); hatred (the snake); and delusion (the rooster).

Dhammapada

PRIMARY SOURCE

One of the most well-known Buddhist scriptures is the *Dhammapada*, or *Verses of Righteousness*. The book is a collection of sayings on Buddhist practices. In this verse, Buddhists are instructed to avoid envying others:

Let him not despise what he has received, nor should he live envying the gains of others. The disciple who envies the gains of others does not attain concentration.

Dhammapada 365

Christianity

Christianity is the largest religion in the world, with about 2 billion followers. It is based on the life and teachings of Jesus Christ. Most Christians are members of one of three major groups: Roman Catholic, Protestant, or Eastern Orthodox. Christianity teaches the existence of only one God. Christians regard Jesus as the son of God. They believe that Jesus entered the world and died to save humanity from sin. The cross shown above, a symbol of the crucifixion of Jesus Christ, represents Jesus' love for humanity by dying for its sins. Christians believe that they reach salvation by following the teachings of Jesus Christ.

INTEGRATED / TECHNOLOGY

RESEARCH LINKS For more on Christianity, go to **classzone.com**

Ritual ▶

Each year, hundreds of thousands of Christians from all over the world visit the Basilica of Guadalupe in northern Mexico City. The church is considered the holiest in Mexico. It is near the site where the Virgin Mary, the mother of Jesus Christ, is said to have appeared twice in 1531. Out of deep respect for Mary, some pilgrims approach the holy cathedral on their knees.

Worship Practices ▶

Worshiping as a group is an important part of Christian life. Most Protestant services include praying, singing, and a sermon. Some services include baptism and communion, in which bread and wine are consumed in remembrance of Jesus' death.

Communion celebrates the last meal Jesus took with his disciples, as illustrated here in the *Last Supper* by Leonardo da Vinci.

▲ Leadership

In some Christian churches, the person who performs services in the local church is known as a priest. Shown here is a priest of the Ethiopian Orthodox Church. These priests, like the ministers and clergy in other Christian sects, conduct worship services and preside over marriages and funerals. Monks and nuns also provide leadership and guidance in the Christian church.

Learn More About Christianity

Major Christian Sects

Eastern Orthodox — Christianity — Roman Catholic

AME** — Protestant* — Baptist

Lutheran — Methodist

Episcopal — Pentecostal

Mormon — Church of God

Presbyterian

*In the United States alone, there are 30 Protestant denominations with over 400,000 members in each.
**African Methodist Episcopal

Fish Symbol

The fish is an early symbol of Christianity. There are many theories about the origin of the symbol, but some Christians believe that it derives from the fact that Jesus called his disciples, or followers, "fishers of men."

The Bible

PRIMARY SOURCE

The Bible is the most sacred book of the Christian religion. It is divided into two major parts: the Old Testament, which focuses on Jewish history, and the New Testament, which describes the teachings of Jesus Christ. The following verse from the New Testament reveals the fundamental teaching of Jesus:

"Men, what must I do to be saved?" And they said, "Believe in the Lord Jesus, and you will be saved, you and your household."

Acts 16:30–31

Hinduism

Hinduism, one of the world's oldest surviving religions, is the major religion of India. It also has followers in Indonesia, as well as in parts of Africa, Europe, and the Western Hemisphere. Hinduism is a collection of religious beliefs that developed over thousands of years. Hindus worship several gods, which represent different forms of Brahman. Brahman is the most divine spirit in the Hindu religion. Hinduism, like Buddhism, stresses that persons reach true enlightenment and happiness only after they free themselves from their earthly desires. Followers of Hinduism achieve this goal through worship, the attainment of knowledge, and a lifetime of virtuous acts. The sound "Om," or "Aum," shown above, is the most sacred syllable for Hindus. It often is used in prayers.

INTEGRATED / TECHNOLOGY

RESEARCH LINKS For more on Hinduism, go to **classzone.com**

▼ Ritual

Each year, thousands of Hindus make a pilgrimage to India's Ganges River. The Ganges is considered a sacred site in the Hindu religion. Most Hindus come to bathe in the water, an act they believe will cleanse and purify them. The sick and disabled come in the belief that the holy water might cure their ailments.

▲ Leadership

Gurus, or spiritual teachers, play a major role in spreading Hindu beliefs. These holy men are believed to have had the gods' words revealed to them. Brahmin priests, like the one shown here, are also religious leaders. They take care of the divine images in the temples and read from the sacred books.

▲ Celebration

Each spring, Hindus in India celebrate the festival of Holi. Originally a harvest festival, Holi also symbolizes the triumph of good over evil. The festival recalls the story of Prince Prahlada, who faced death rather than cease worshiping Vishnu. During this joyous celebration, people dance in the streets and shower each other with colored powder and dyed water.

Learn More About Hinduism

Major Hindu Sects

Shaktism   Reform Hinduism

Hinduism

Vaishnavites   Shaivites

Three Main Gods

This statue represents Brahma, creator of the universe. Brahma, Vishnu, and Shiva are the three main gods of Hinduism. Vishnu is the preserver of the universe, while Shiva is its destroyer.

Rig Veda

PRIMARY SOURCE

The Vedas are the oldest Hindu scriptures—and they are older than the sacred writings of any other major religion. The following is a verse from the Rig Veda, the oldest of the four Vedas:

He who gives liberally goes straight to the gods; on the high ridge of heaven he stands exalted.

Rig Veda 1.125.5

Islam

Islam is a religion based on the teachings of the prophet Muhammad. Followers of Islam, known as Muslims, believe that God revealed these teachings to Muhammad through the angel Gabriel. Muslims are concentrated from southwest to central Asia and parts of Africa. Islam also has many followers in Southeast Asia. Sunni Muslims believe that their leaders should follow Muhammad's example. Shi'a Muslims believe that their leaders should be Muhammad's descendants.

Islam teaches the existence of only one God, called Allah in the Arabic language. Muslims believe in all prophets of Judaism and Christianity. They show their devotion by performing lifelong acts of worship known as the Five Pillars of Islam. These include faith, prayer, almsgiving (charity), fasting, and a pilgrimage to Mecca. The crescent moon (shown above) has become a familiar symbol for Islam. It may be related to the new moon that begins each month in the Islamic lunar calendar, which orders religious life for Muslims. The five points of the star may represent the Five Pillars of Islam.

INTEGRATED/TECHNOLOGY

RESEARCH LINKS For more on Islam, go to **classzone.com**

▼ Ritual

At least once in their lifetime, all Muslims who are physically and financially able go on hajj, or pilgrimage, to the holy city of Mecca in Saudi Arabia. There, pilgrims perform several rites, or acts of worship. One rite, shown here, is walking seven times around the Ka'aba—the house of worship that Muslims face in prayer.

▲ Celebration

During the sacred month known as Ramadan, Muslims fast, or abstain from food and drink, from dawn to sunset. The family shown here is ending their fast. The most important night of Ramadan is called the Night of Power. This is believed to be the night the angel Gabriel first spoke to Muhammad.

▲ Worship Practices

Five times a day Muslims throughout the world face Mecca and pray to Allah. Pictured here are Muslims praying at a mosque in Turkey.

There are no priests or other clergy in Islam. However, a Muslim community leader known as the imam conducts the prayers in a mosque. Islam also has a scholar class called the ulama, which includes religious teachers.

Learn More About Islam

Major Islamic Sects

Sunni

Islam

Shi'a

Prayer Rug

Muslims often pray by kneeling on a rug. The design of the rug includes a pointed or arch-shaped pattern. The rug must be placed so that the arch points toward Mecca.

The Qur'an

PRIMARY SOURCE

The Qur'an, the sacred book of Muslims, consists of verses grouped into 114 chapters, or suras. The book is the spiritual guide on matters of Muslim faith. It also contains teachings for Muslim daily life. In the following verse, Muslims are instructed to appreciate the world's physical and spiritual riches:

> *Do you not see that God has subjected to your use all things in the heavens and on earth, and has made His bounties flow to you in exceeding measure, both seen and unseen?*

> Qur'an, sura 31:20

Judaism

Judaism is the religion of the more than 14 million Jews throughout the world. Judaism was the first major religion to teach the existence of only one god. The basic laws and teachings of Judaism come from the Torah, the first five books of the Hebrew Bible. Judaism teaches that a person serves God by studying the Torah and living by its teachings. Orthodox Jews obey the Torah without question. Conservative and Reform Jews interpret the Torah to make its teachings relevant to today's world. The Star of David (shown above), also called the Shield of David, is the universal symbol of Judaism. The emblem refers to King David, who ruled the kingdom of Israel from about 1000–962 B.C.

INTEGRATED/TECHNOLOGY

RESEARCH LINKS For more on Judaism, go to **classzone.com**

Ritual ►

Major events in a Jew's life are marked by special rites and ceremonies. When Jewish children reach the age of 13, for example, they enter the adult religious community. The event is marked in the synagogue with a ceremony called a bar mitzvah for a boy and a bat mitzvah for a girl, shown here.

▲ Worship Practices

The synagogue is the Jewish house of worship and the center of Jewish community life. Services in the synagogue are usually conducted by a rabbi, the congregation's spiritual leader. Many Jews make the pilgrimage to the Western Wall, shown here. The sacred structure, built in the second century B.C., formed the western wall of the courtyard of the Second Temple of Jerusalem. The Romans destroyed the temple in A.D. 70.

▼ Celebration

Jews celebrate a number of holidays that honor their history as well as their God. Pictured here are Jews celebrating the holiday of Purim. Purim is a festival honoring the survival of the Jews who, in the fifth century B.C., were marked for death by their Persian rulers.

Jews celebrate Purim by sending food and gifts. They also dress in costumes and hold carnivals and dances.

Major Jewish Sects

Reform   Orthodox

Judaism

Conservative

Yarmulke

Out of respect for God, Jewish men are not supposed to leave their head uncovered. Therefore, many Orthodox and Conservative Jews wear a skullcap known as a yarmulke, or kippah.

The Torah

PRIMARY SOURCE

During a synagogue service, the Torah scroll is lifted, while the congregation declares: "This is the Law which Moses set before the children of Israel." The following verse from the Torah makes clear Moses' law regarding belief in one God:

Hear O Israel: the Lord our God, the Lord is One.

Deuteronomy 6:4

Confucianism

With no clergy and with no gods to worship, Confucianism is not a religion in the traditional sense. Rather, it is an ethical system that provides direction for personal behavior and good government. However, this ancient philosophy guides the actions and beliefs of millions of Chinese and other peoples of the East. Thus, many view it as a religion.

Confucianism is a way of life based on the teachings of the Chinese scholar Confucius. It stresses social and civic responsibility. Over the centuries, however, Confucianism has greatly influenced people's spiritual beliefs as well. While East Asians declare themselves to follow any one of a number of religions, many also claim to be Confucian. The yin and yang symbol shown above represents opposite forces in the world working together. It symbolizes the social order and harmony that Confucianism stresses.

INTEGRATED / TECHNOLOGY

RESEARCH LINKS For more on Confucianism, go to **classzone.com**

▼ Celebration

While scholars remain uncertain of Confucius's date of birth, people throughout East Asia celebrate it on September 28. In Taiwan, it is an official holiday, known as Teachers' Day. The holiday also pays tribute to teachers. Confucius himself was a teacher, and he believed that education was an important part of a fulfilled life. Here, dancers take part in a ceremony honoring Confucius.

Leadership ▶

Confucius was born at a time of crisis and violence in China. He hoped his ideas and teachings would restore the order of earlier times to his society. But although he was active in politics, he never had enough political power to put his ideas into practice. Nonetheless, his ideas would become the foundation of Chinese thought for more than 2,000 years.

Learn More About Confucianism

The Five Relationships

Confucius believed society should be organized around five basic relationships between the following:

1. ruler ⟷ subject
2. father ⟷ son
3. husband ⟷ wife
4. older brother ⟷ younger brother
5. friend ⟷ friend

Confucius's Golden Rule

"Do not do unto others what you would not want others to do unto you."

The *Analects*

PRIMARY SOURCE

The earliest and most authentic record of Confucius's ideas was collected by his students. Around 400 B.C., they compiled Confucius's thoughts in a book called the *Analects*. In the following selection from the *Analects*, Confucius (the Master) advises people to avoid judging others:

The Master said: "Don't worry if people don't recognize your merits; worry that you may not recognize theirs."

Analects 1.16

▲ Ritual

A key aspect of Confucianism is filial piety, the respect children owe their parents. Traditionally, filial piety meant complete obedience to one's parents during their lifetime. It also required the performance of certain rituals after their death. In this 12th-century Chinese painting, a sage instructs a pupil on the virtue of filial piety.

World Religions *and* Ethical Systems

A Comparison

	Buddhism	Christianity	Hinduism	Islam	Judaism	Confucianism
Followers Worldwide (estimated 2001 figures)	362 million	2 billion	820 million	1.2 billion	14.5 million	6.3 million
Name of Deity	The Buddha did not teach a personal deity.	God	Three main gods: Brahma, Vishnu, Shiva	God (Allah)	God (Yahweh)	Confucius (viewed by many as a god)
Founder	The Buddha	Jesus Christ	No one founder	Muhammad	Abraham	Confucius
Holy Book	No one book—sacred texts, including the *Dhammapada*	Bible	No one book—sacred texts, including the Vedas, the Puranas	Qur'an	Hebrew Bible, including the Torah	the *Analects*, the Five Classics
Leadership	Buddhist monks and nuns	Priests, ministers, monks, and nuns	Guru, holy man, Brahmin priest	No clergy but a scholar class called the ulama and the imam, who may lead prayers	Rabbis	No clergy
Basic Beliefs	• Persons achieve complete peace and happiness (nirvana) by eliminating their attachment to worldly things. • Nirvana is reached by following the Noble Eightfold Path: Right views; Right resolve; Right speech; Right conduct; Right livelihood; Right effort; Right mindfulness; Right concentration.	• There is only one God, who watches over and cares for his people. • Jesus Christ was the son of God. He died to save humanity from sin. His death and resurrection made eternal life possible for others.	• The soul never dies, but is continually reborn. • Persons achieve happiness and enlightenment after they free themselves from their earthly desires. • Freedom from earthly desires comes from a lifetime of worship, knowledge, and virtuous acts.	• Persons achieve salvation by following the Five Pillars of Islam and living a just life. These pillars are: faith; prayer; almsgiving, or charity to the poor; fasting, which Muslims perform during Ramadan; pilgrimage to Mecca.	• There is only one God, who watches over and cares for his people. • God loves and protects his people, but also holds people accountable for their sins and shortcomings. • Persons serve God by studying the Torah and living by its teachings.	• Social order, harmony, and good government should be based on strong family relationships. • Respect for parents and elders is important to a well-ordered society. • Education is important both to the welfare of the individual and to society.

Assessment

MAIN IDEAS

Buddhism (pages 702–703)

1. According to the Buddha, how does one achieve happiness and fulfillment?

2. Why do Buddhists take special care to avoid killing any living being?

Christianity (pages 704–705)

3. Why is Jesus Christ central to the Christian religion?

4. What do Christians hope to achieve by following the teachings of Jesus Christ?

Hinduism (pages 706–707)

5. What is the importance of the Ganges River in Hinduism?

6. Who are the three main gods of Hinduism?

Islam (pages 708–709)

7. What is the most important night of Ramadan? Why?

8. What are the Five Pillars of Islam?

Judaism (pages 710–711)

9. Why do Jews consider the Western Wall to be sacred?

10. What is the role of the rabbi in the Jewish tradition?

Confucianism (pages 712–713)

11. Around what five relationships did Confucius believe society should be organized?

12. According to tradition, what does filial piety require of children?

CRITICAL THINKING

1. COMPARING AND CONTRASTING

Using information from the text and chart at left, choose two religions and identify their similarities and differences in a Venn diagram.

Religion 1

similarities

Religion 2

2. SYNTHESIZING

What basic principles do all of the religions have in common?

3. DRAWING CONCLUSIONS

What role does religion play in people's everyday lives?

4. MAKING INFERENCES

Why do you think ritual and celebrations are an important part of all religions?

5. FORMING OPINIONS

What do you think people hope to gain from their religion?

Use the quotation and your knowledge of world history to answer questions 1 and 2.
Additional Test Practice, pp. S1–S33

PRIMARY SOURCE

Human beings are spiritual animals. Indeed, there is a case for arguing that *Homo sapiens* is also *Homo religiosus*. Men and women started to worship gods as soon as they became recognizably human; they created religions at the same time they created works of art. . . . These early faiths expressed the wonder and mystery that seem always to have been an essential component of the human experience of this beautiful yet terrifying world. Like art, religion has been an attempt to find meaning and value in life, despite the suffering that flesh is heir to.

KAREN ARMSTRONG, *History of God*

1. With which of the following opinions would Armstrong probably agree?

   A. People are naturally religious.

   B. People have no need of religion.

   C. People only believe in what they can see.

   D. People created religion out of fear.

2. According to Armstrong, what is the main similarity between art and religion?

   A. They both express the suffering human beings must endure.

   B. They first appeared at around the same time.

   C. They both place value on beauty.

   D. They are both used to find life's meaning.

INTEGRATED / TECHNOLOGY

TEST PRACTICE Go to **classzone.com**

- Diagnostic tests
- Tutorials
- Strategies
- Additional practice

ALTERNATIVE ASSESSMENT

1. Interact *with* History

Imagine that you could meet one of the founders listed in the chart on page 714. What questions would you ask about his life and beliefs? What views of your own would you share? Take turns role-playing your conversation with a partner.

2. WRITING ABOUT HISTORY

Research to learn more about one of the celebrations you read about in this section. Then write a three-paragraph **essay** about its origins. Discuss the celebration's history, symbolism, and meaning.

McDougal Littell

MODERN WORLD HISTORY

PATTERNS OF INTERACTION

Skillbuilder Handbook

Refer to the Skillbuilder Handbook when you need help in answering Main Idea questions or questions in Section Assessments and Chapter Assessments. In addition, the handbook will help you answer questions about maps, charts, and graphs.

1.1 Determining Main Ideas

The **MAIN IDEA** is a statement that sums up the most important point of a paragraph, a passage, an article, or a speech. Determining the main idea will increase your understanding as you read about historic events, people, and places. Main ideas are supported by details and examples.

Understanding the Skill

STRATEGY: IDENTIFY THE TOPIC. To find the main idea of a passage, first identify the topic. Then, as you read, define the central idea about the topic that the many details explain or support. The following passage contains information about the Renaissance. The diagram organizes the information to help you determine the main idea.

1 **Identify the topic by first looking at the title or subtitle.** This title suggests a quick way to identify the topic by looking for the name of the Renaissance woman, Isabella d'Este.

2 **Look at the beginning and ending sentences of each paragraph for possible clues to the main idea.**

3 **Read the entire passage.** Look for details about the topic. What central idea do they explain or support?

> **1** A Renaissance Woman
>
> Isabella d'Este was a woman who lived during the Renaissance. This historic period produced the ideal, or "universal," man—one who excelled in many fields. The concept of universal excellence applied almost exclusively to men. **2** Yet a few women managed to succeed in exercising power.
>
> **2** Isabella d'Este was one such woman. Born into the ruling family of the city-state of Ferrara, she married the ruler of Mantua, another city-state. Isabella brought many Renaissance artists to her court and acquired an art collection that was famous throughout Europe. She was also skilled in politics. When her husband was taken captive in war, Isabella defended Mantua and won his release. **3**

STRATEGY: MAKE A DIAGRAM. State the topic and list the supporting details in a chart. Use the information you record to help you state the main idea.

Think how each detail supports the main idea.

Applying the Skill

MAKE YOUR OWN DIAGRAM. Turn to Chapter 3, page 96. Read "Technology Makes Exploration Possible." Make a diagram, like the one above, to identify the topic, the most important details, and the main idea of the passage.

1.2 Following Chronological Order

CHRONOLOGICAL ORDER is the order in which events happen in time. Historians need to figure out the order in which things happened to get an accurate sense of the relationships among events. As you read history, figure out the sequence, or time order, of events.

Understanding the Skill

STRATEGY: LOOK FOR TIME CLUES. The following paragraph is about the rulers of England after the death of Henry VIII. Notice how the time line that follows puts the events in chronological order.

1 **Look for clue words about time.** These are words like *first, initial, next, then, before, after, followed, finally,* and *by that time.*

2 **Use specific dates provided in the text.**

3 **Watch for references to previous historical events that are included in the background.**

> ### Henry's Children Rule England
>
> **1** After the death of Henry VIII in **2** 1547, each of his three children eventually ruled. This created religious turmoil. Edward VI became king at age nine and ruled only six years. During his reign, the Protestants gained power. Edward's half-sister Mary **1** followed him to the throne. She was a Catholic who returned the English Church to the rule of the pope. Mary had many Protestants killed. England's **1** next ruler was Anne Boleyn's daughter, Elizabeth. After inheriting the throne in 1558, Elizabeth I returned her kingdom to Protestantism. In **2** 1559 Parliament followed Elizabeth's **3** request and set up a national church much like the one under Henry VIII.

STRATEGY: MAKE A TIME LINE.

If the events are complex, make a time line of them. Write the dates below the line and the events above the line.

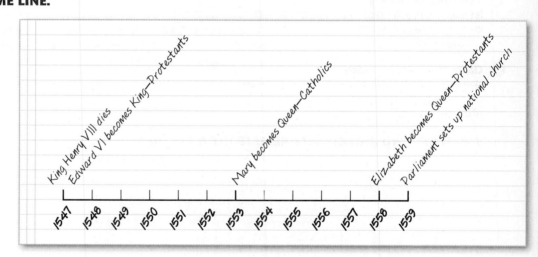

Applying the Skill

MAKE YOUR OWN TIME LINE. Skim Chapter 19, Section 4, "Changes in Central and Eastern Europe," to find out about the spread of democracy in parts of Europe controlled by the former Soviet Union. List the important dates and events. Start with the demonstrations in East Germany in October 1989, include events in Czechoslovakia and Romania, and end with reunification of Germany in October of 1990. Decide on a scale for your time line. Show the important dates below the line and write what happened on each date above the line.

1.3 Clarifying; Summarizing

CLARIFYING means making clear and fully understanding what you read. One way to do this is by asking yourself questions about the material. In your answers, restate in your own words what you have read.

SUMMARIZING means condensing what you read into fewer words. You state only the main ideas and the most important details. In your own words, reduce the paragraph or section into a brief report of its general ideas.

Understanding the Skill

STRATEGY: UNDERSTAND AND CONDENSE THE TEXT. The passage below tells about trade in West Africa between 300 and 1600. Following the description is a summary that condenses and also clarifies the key information.

1 **Summarize: Look for topic sentences stating the main idea.** These are often at the beginning of a section or paragraph. Restate each main idea briefly.

2 **Clarify: Look up words or concepts you don't know.**

3 **Summarize: Include key facts and statistics.** Watch for numbers, dates, quantities, percentages, and facts.

4 **Clarify: Make sure you understand.** Ask yourself questions and answer them. For example, who's carrying what?

> **West African Trade**
>
> **1** The wealth of the savanna empires was based on trade in two precious commodities, gold and salt. The gold came from a forest region south of the **2** savanna between the Niger and Senegal rivers. Working in utmost secrecy, miners dug gold from shafts as much as 100 feet deep or sifted it from fast-moving streams. **3** Until about 1350, at least two thirds of the world's supply of gold came from West Africa.
>
> Although rich in gold, the savanna and forest areas lacked salt, a material essential to human life. In contrast, the **3** Sahara contained abundant deposits of salt. Arab traders, eager to obtain West African gold, carried salt across the Sahara by camel caravan. After a long journey, they reached the market towns of the savanna. **4** Meanwhile, the other traders brought gold north from the forest region. The two sets of merchants met in trading centers such as Timbuktu. Royal officials made sure that all traders weighed goods fairly and did business according to law.

STRATEGY: FIND AND CLEARLY RESTATE THE MAIN IDEA.

> <u>MAIN IDEA</u>
> Gold and salt were traded in West Africa.

STRATEGY: WRITE A SUMMARY.

Clarify and Summarize: Write a summary to clarify your understanding of the main ideas.

> Summary
> Trade in West Africa was based on gold from the south and salt from the north. Gold was mined in the forest regions. Two thirds of all the world's gold supply came from West Africa. Salt came from the desert. Arab traders met with African traders at trade centers such as Timbuktu.

Applying the Skill

CLARIFY AND WRITE YOUR OWN SUMMARY. Turn to Chapter 14, pages 440–442, and read "A Government of Total Control." Note the main ideas. Look up any words you don't recognize. Then write a summary of the section. Condense the section in your own words.

1.4 Identifying Problems and Solutions

IDENTIFYING PROBLEMS means finding and understanding the difficulties faced by a particular group of people at a certain time. Noticing how the people solved their problems is **IDENTIFYING SOLUTIONS.** Checking further to see how well those solutions worked is identifying outcomes.

Understanding the Skill

STRATEGY: LOOK FOR PROBLEMS AND SOLUTIONS. The passage below summarizes some economic problems facing Latin American nations during the early 20th century.

1 **Look for implied problems.** Problems may be suggested indirectly. This sentence suggests that a serious problem in Latin America was the uneven division of wealth.

2 **Look for problems people face.**

3 **Look for solutions people tried to deal with each problem.**

4 **Check outcomes to the solutions.** See how well the solutions worked. Sometimes the solution to one problem caused another problem.

Land Reform In Latin America

In Latin America, concentration of productive land in the hands of a **1** few created extremes of wealth and poverty. Poor peasants had no choice but to work large estates owned by a few wealthy families. Landlords had no reason to invest in expensive farm machinery when labor was so cheap. **2** Farming methods were inefficient and economic development was slow.

As Latin American nations began to modernize in the 20th century, land ownership became a political issue. In response, a handful of countries began land reform programs. These programs **3** divided large estates into smaller plots. Small plots of land were in turn distributed to farm families or granted to villages for communal farming. However, just turning over the land to the landless was not enough. **4** Peasant farmers needed instruction, seeds, equipment, and credit. If the land and the people were to be productive, governments would have to provide assistance to the peasants.

Skillbuilder Handbook

STRATEGY: MAKE A CHART.

Summarize the problems and solutions in a chart. Identify the problem or problems and the steps taken to solve them. Look for the short- and long-term effects of the solutions.

Problems	Solutions	Outcomes
A few wealthy people owned most of the land.	Land reform programs divided large estates into smaller plots.	Peasants were given land, and communal farms were set up.
Inefficient farming resulted in slow economic development.		
Peasants lacked equipment, resources, skills.	Governments would have to assist with loans and instruction.	Not stated.

Applying the Skill

MAKE YOUR OWN CHART. Turn to Chapter 15 and read "Postwar Europe" on page 470. Make a chart that lists the problems Germany faced after World War I. List the solutions that were tried and whatever outcomes are mentioned.

1.5 Analyzing Causes and Recognizing Effects

CAUSES are the events, conditions, and other reasons that lead to an event. Causes happen before the event in time; they explain why it happened. **EFFECTS** are the results or consequences of the event. One effect often becomes the cause of other effects, resulting in a chain of events. Causes and effects can be both short-term and long-term. Examining **CAUSE-AND-EFFECT RELATIONSHIPS** helps historians see how events are related and why they took place.

Understanding the Skill

STRATEGY: KEEP TRACK OF CAUSES AND EFFECTS AS YOU READ. The passage below describes events leading to the rise of feudalism in Japan. The diagram that follows summarizes the chain of causes and effects.

1 **Causes: Look for clue words that show cause.** These include *because, due to, since,* and *therefore.*

2 **Look for multiple causes and multiple effects.** The weakness of the central government caused the three effects (a,b,c) shown here.

3 **Effects: Look for results or consequences.** Sometimes these are indicated by clue words such as *brought about, led to, as a result,* and *consequently.*

4 **Notice that an effect may be the cause of another event.** This begins a chain of causes and effects.

Feudalism Comes to Japan

For most of the Heian period, the rich Fujiwara family held the real power in Japan. Members of this family held many influential posts. By about the middle of the 11th century, the power of the central government and the Fujiwaras began to slip. This was **1** due in part to court families' greater interest in luxury and artistic pursuits than in governing.

2 Since the central government was weak, **(a)** large landowners living away from the capital set up private armies. **3** As a result, **(b)** the countryside became lawless and dangerous. Armed soldiers on horseback preyed on farmers and travelers, while pirates took control of the seas. **(c)** For safety, farmers and small landowners traded parts of their land to strong warlords in exchange for protection. **4** Because the lords had more land, the lords gained more power. This marked the beginning of a feudal system of localized rule like that of ancient China and medieval Europe.

STRATEGY: MAKE A CAUSE-AND-EFFECT DIAGRAM.

Summarize cause-and-effect relationships in a diagram. Starting with the first cause in a series, fill in the boxes until you reach the end result.

Cause ⟶	Effect/Cause ⟶	Effect/Cause ⟶	Effect
Ruling families had little interest in governing.	Weak central government was unable to control the land.	• Landowners set up private armies. • Countryside became dangerous. • Farmers traded land for safety under warlords.	Feudalism was established in Japan.

Applying the Skill

MAKE YOUR OWN CAUSE-AND-EFFECT DIAGRAM. Turn to Chapter 12, pages 389–391. Read "Juárez and *La Reforma*" and make notes about the causes and effects of Juárez's reform movement in Mexico. Make a diagram, like the one shown above, to summarize the information you find.

Skillbuilder Handbook

1.6 Comparing and Contrasting

Historians compare and contrast events, personalities, ideas, behaviors, beliefs, and institutions in order to understand them thoroughly. **COMPARING** involves finding both similarities and differences between two or more things. **CONTRASTING** means examining only the differences between them.

Understanding the Skill

STRATEGY: LOOK FOR SIMILARITIES AND DIFFERENCES. The following passage describes life in the ancient Greek city-states of Sparta and Athens. The Venn diagram below shows some of the similarities and differences between the two city-states.

❶ **Compare: Look for features that two subjects have in common.** Here you learn that both Athens and Sparta started out as farming communities.

❷ **Compare: Look for clue words indicating that two things are alike.** Clue words include *all, both, like, as, likewise,* and *similarly.*

❸ **Contrast: Look for clue words that show how two things differ.** Clue words include *unlike, by contrast, however, except, different,* and *on the other hand.*

Sparta and Athens

The Greek city-states developed separately but shared certain characteristics, ❶ including language and religion. Economically, all began as farming economies, and all except Sparta eventually moved to trade. Politically, ❷ all city-states, except for Sparta, evolved into early forms of democracies.

The leader in the movement to democracy was Athens. After a series of reforms, every Athenian citizen was considered equal before the law. However, as in the other Greek city-states, only about one fifth of the population were citizens. Slaves did much of the work, so Athenian citizens were free to create works of art, architecture, and literature, including drama.

❸ By contrast, Sparta lived in constant fear of revolts by *helots,* people who were held in slave-like conditions to work the land. The city was set up as a military dictatorship, and Spartan men dedicated their lives to the military. ❹ In Sparta, duty, strength, and discipline were valued over beauty, individuality, and creativity. As a result, Spartans created little art, architecture, or literature.

❹ **Contrast: Look for ways in which two things are different.** Here you learn that Athens and Sparta had different values.

STRATEGY: MAKE A VENN DIAGRAM.

Compare and Contrast: Summarize similarities and differences in a Venn diagram. In the overlapping area, list characteristics shared by both subjects. Then, in one oval list the characteristics of one subject not shared by the other. In the other oval, list unshared characteristics of the second subject.

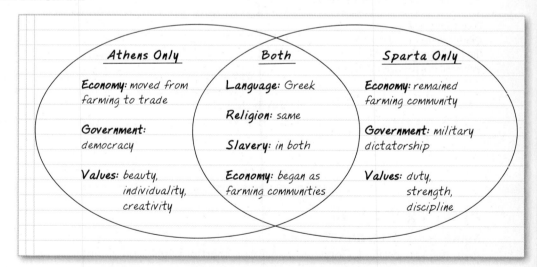

Athens Only

Economy: *moved from farming to trade*

Government: *democracy*

Values: *beauty, individuality, creativity*

Both

Language: *Greek*

Religion: *same*

Slavery: *in both*

Economy: *began as farming communities*

Sparta Only

Economy: *remained farming community*

Government: *military dictatorship*

Values: *duty, strength, discipline*

Applying the Skill

MAKE YOUR OWN VENN DIAGRAM. Turn to Chapter 4, pages 130–131, and read the section called "Native Americans Respond." Make a Venn diagram comparing and contrasting Dutch and English colonists' relations with Native Americans.

Skillbuilder Handbook

1.7 Distinguishing Fact from Opinion

FACTS are events, dates, statistics, or statements that can be proved to be true. Facts can be checked for accuracy. **OPINIONS** are judgments, beliefs, and feelings of the writer or speaker.

Understanding the Skill

STRATEGY: FIND CLUES IN THE TEXT. The following excerpt tells about the uprising of Jews in the Warsaw ghetto in 1943. The chart summarizes the facts and opinions.

❶ Facts: Look for specific names, dates, statistics, and statements that can be proved. The first two paragraphs provide a factual account of the event.

❷ Opinion: Look for assertions, claims, hypotheses, and judgments. Here Goebbels expresses his opinion of the uprising and of the Jews.

❸ Opinion: Look for judgment words that the writer uses to describe the people and events. Judgment words are often adjectives that are used to arouse a reader's emotions.

> **The Warsaw Ghetto Uprising**
>
> With orders from Himmler to crush the Jews, ❶ the Nazis attacked on April 19, 1943, at the start of the holiday of Passover. ❶ Two thousand armed SS troops entered the ghetto, marching with tanks, rifles, machine guns, and trailers full of ammunition. The Jewish fighters were in position—in bunkers, in windows, on rooftops. ❶ They had rifles and handguns, hand grenades and bombs that they had made. And they let fly. . . .
>
> Unbelievably, the Jews won the battle that day. The Germans were forced to retreat. . . . ❶ The Germans brought in more troops, and the fighting intensified. German pilots dropped bombs on the ghetto. . . .
>
> ❷ On May 1, Goebbels [Nazi propaganda minister] wrote in his diary: "Of course this jest will probably not last long." He added a complaint. "But it shows what one can expect of the Jews if they have guns."
>
> Goebbels' tone was mocking. But his forecast was inevitable—and correct. . . . Goebbels did not record in his diary, when the uprising was over, that the ❸ starving Jews of the ghetto, with their ❸ pathetic supply of arms, had held out against the German army for forty days, longer than Poland or France had held out.
>
> Source: *A Nightmare in History,* by Miriam Chaikin. (New York: Clarion Books, 1987) pp. 77–78

STRATEGY: MAKE A CHART.

Divide facts and opinions in a chart. Summarize and separate the facts from the opinions expressed in a passage.

FACTS	OPINIONS
On April 19, 1943, 2,000 armed SS troops attacked the Warsaw ghetto. Jewish fighters held out for 40 days.	**Goebbels:** The uprising was a jest, but showed the danger of letting Jews get hold of guns. **Author:** It is difficult to believe that Warsaw Jews with their pathetic supply of arms were able to defeat the powerful Nazis.

Applying the Skill

MAKE YOUR OWN CHART. Turn to Chapter 10, page 335. Find the Primary Source from the Seneca Falls Convention. Make a chart in which you summarize the facts in your own words, and list the opinions and judgments stated. Look carefully at the language used in order to separate one from the other.

2.1 Categorizing

CATEGORIZING means organizing similar kinds of information into groups. Historians categorize information to help them identify and understand historical patterns.

Understanding the Skill

STRATEGY: DECIDE WHAT INFORMATION NEEDS TO BE CATEGORIZED. The following passage describes India's Taj Mahal, a memorial built by a Mughal ruler. As you read, look for facts and details that are closely related. Then choose appropriate categories.

1 Look at topic sentences for clues to defining categories.

2 Look at the type of information each paragraph contains. A paragraph often contains similar kinds of information.

> **Building the Taj Mahal**
>
> **1** Some 20,000 workers labored for 22 years to build the famous tomb. It is made of white marble brought from 250 miles away. The minaret towers are about 130 feet high. The building itself is 186 feet square.
>
> **1** The design of the building is a blend of Hindu and Muslim styles. The pointed **2** arches are of Muslim design, and the perforated marble **2** windows and **2** doors are typical of a style found in Hindu temples.
>
> The inside of the building is a glittering garden **2** of thousands of carved marble flowers inlaid with tiny precious stones. One tiny flower, one inch square, had 60 different inlays.

STRATEGY: MAKE A CHART.

3 Add a title.

4 Sort information into the categories you have chosen.

5 Make one column for each category.

3 THE TAJ MAHAL

4 Labor	Dimensions	Design features
• 20,000 workers • 22 years to complete	• Minaret towers: 130 feet high • Building: 186 feet	• Made of white marble • Pointed arches (Muslim influence) • Perforated marble windows and doors (Hindu influence) • Interior: thousands of carved marble flowers inlaid with precious stones
5	**5**	**5**

Applying the Skill

MAKE YOUR OWN CHART. Turn to Chapter 6, page 203. Read "New Artistic Styles." Decide what categories you will use to organize the information. Then make a chart, like the one above, that organizes the information in the passage into the categories you have chosen.

Skillbuilder Handbook

2.2 Making Inferences

Inferences are ideas and meanings not stated in the material. **MAKING INFERENCES** means reading between the lines to extend the information provided. Your inferences are based on careful study of what is stated in the passage as well as your own common sense and previous knowledge.

Understanding the Skill

STRATEGY: DEVELOP INFERENCES FROM THE FACTS. This passage describes the Nok culture of West Africa. Following the passage is a diagram that organizes the facts and ideas that lead to inferences.

1 **Read the stated facts and ideas.**

2 **Use your knowledge, logic, and common sense to draw conclusions.** You could infer from these statements that the Nok were a settled people with advanced technology and a rich culture.

3 **Consider what you already know that could apply.** Your knowledge of history might lead you to infer the kinds of improvements in life brought about by better farming tools.

4 **Recognize inferences that are already made.** Phrases like "the evidence suggests" or "historians believe" indicate inferences and conclusions experts have made from historical records.

The Nok Culture

1 The earliest known culture of West Africa was that of the Nok people. They lived in what is now Nigeria between 900 B.C. and A.D. 200. Their name came from the village where the first artifacts from their culture were discovered by archaeologists. The **2** Nok were farmers. They were also **2** the first West African people known to smelt iron. The Nok began making iron around 500 B.C., using it to make tools for farming and weapons for hunting. **3** These iron implements lasted longer than wood or stone and vastly improved the lives of the Nok.

Nok artifacts have been found in an area stretching for 300 miles between the Niger and Benue rivers. **2** Many are sculptures made of terra cotta, a reddish-brown clay. Carved in great artistic detail, some depict the heads of animals such as elephants and others depict human heads. The features of some of the heads reveal a great deal about their history. One of the human heads, for example, shows an elaborate hairdo arranged in six buns, a style that is still worn by some people in Nigeria today. **4** This similarity suggests that the Nok may have been the ancestors of modern-day Africans.

STRATEGY: MAKE A CHART.

Summarize the facts and inferences you make in a chart.

Stated Facts and Ideas	Inferences
• iron farming tools • iron harder than wood • tools improved life	iron tools improved agriculture and contributed to cultural development
• Nok artifacts found in 300-mile radius	Nok culture spread across this area
• heads carved in great artistic detail	Nok were skilled potters and sculptors
• sculptures included elephant heads	elephants played a role in people's lives

Applying the Skill

MAKE YOUR OWN CHART. Read the poem by Vittoria Colonna in Chapter 1, page 43. Using a chart like the one above, make inferences from the poem about its author, its subject, and the culture it comes from.

2.3 Drawing Conclusions

DRAWING CONCLUSIONS means analyzing what you have read and forming an opinion about its meaning. To draw conclusions, you look closely at the facts, combine them with inferences you make, and then use your own common sense and experience to decide what the facts mean.

Understanding the Skill

STRATEGY: COMBINE INFORMATION TO DRAW CONCLUSIONS. The passage below presents information about the reunification of East and West Germany in 1990. The diagram that follows shows how to organize the information to draw conclusions.

1 **Read carefully to understand all the facts.** Fact: Reunification brought social and political freedoms to East Germans.

2 **Read between the lines to make inferences.** Inference: After a market economy was introduced, many industries in eastern Germany failed, which put people out of work.

3 **Use the facts to make an inference.** Inference: Reunification put a strain on government resources.

4 **Ask questions of the material.** What are the long-term economic prospects for eastern Germany? Conclusion: Although it faced challenges, it seemed to have a greater chance for success than other former Communist countries.

Germany is Reunified

On October 3, 1990, Germany once again became a single nation. **1** After more than 40 years of Communist rule, most East Germans celebrated their new political freedoms. Families that had been separated for years could now visit whenever they chose.

Economically, the newly united Germany faced serious problems. More than 40 years of Communist rule had left East Germany in ruins. Its transportation and telephone systems had not been modernized since World War II. State-run industries in East Germany had to be turned over to private control and operate under free-market rules. **2** However, many produced shoddy goods that could not compete in the global market.

Rebuilding eastern Germany's bankrupt economy was going to be a difficult, costly process. **3** Some experts estimated the price tag for reunification could reach $200 billion. In the short-term, the government had to provide **2** unemployment benefits to some 1.4 million workers from the east who found themselves out of work.

4 In spite of these problems, Germans had reasons to be optimistic. Unlike other Eastern European countries, who had to transform their Communist economies by their own means, East Germany had the help of a strong West Germany. Many Germans may have shared the outlook expressed by one worker: "Maybe things won't be rosy at first, but the future will be better."

Skillbuilder Handbook

STRATEGY: MAKE A DIAGRAM.

Summarize the facts, inferences, and your conclusion in a diagram.

Facts →	Inferences →	Conclusion About Passage
East Germans gained freedoms.	East Germans welcomed the end of Communist rule.	Although eastern Germany was in bad shape at the time of reunification, it had the advantage of the strength of western Germany as it made the transition to democracy and capitalism.
Transportation and telephone systems were outmoded.	Rebuilding took time.	
State-run industries produced shoddy goods.	Industries couldn't compete in free-market economy.	
Unemployment skyrocketed.	Reunification put a great financial burden on Germany.	
Cost for reunification could be $200 billion.		

Applying the Skill

MAKE A DIAGRAM. Look at Chapter 5, Section 1, pages 158–159, on the decline of the Spanish empire. As you read, draw conclusions based on the facts. Use the diagram above as a model for organizing facts, inferences, and conclusions about the passage.

2.4 Developing Historical Perspective

DEVELOPING HISTORICAL PERSPECTIVE means understanding events and people in the context of their times. It means not judging the past by current values, but by taking into account the beliefs of the time.

Understanding the Skill

STRATEGY: LOOK FOR VALUES OF THE PAST. The following passage was written by Bartolomé de Las Casas, a Spanish missionary who defended the rights of Native Americans. It challenges an argument presented by a scholar named Sepúlveda, who held that the Spaniards had the right to enslave the Native Americans. Following the passage is a chart that summarizes the information from a historical perspective.

1 **Identify the historical figure, the occasion, and the date.**

2 **Look for clues to the attitudes, customs, and values of people living at the time.** As a Spanish missionary, Las Casas assumes that Europeans are more civilized than Native Americans and that Native Americans need to be converted to Catholicism.

3 **Explain how people's actions and words reflected the attitudes, values, and passions of the era.** Las Casas challenges prejudices about Native Americans that were widely held in Europe. His language emphasizes a favorable comparison between Native American and European societies.

4 **Notice words, phrases, and settings that reflect the period.** Las Casas speaks from a time when Europeans looked to classical Greece as a benchmark for civilization.

> **1** In Defense of the Indians (1550)
> Bartolomé de Las Casas
>
> Now if we shall have shown that among our Indians of the western and southern shores **2** (granting that we call them barbarians and that they are barbarians) there are important kingdoms, large numbers of people who live settled lives in a society, great cities, kings, judges and laws, persons who engage in commerce, buying, selling, lending, and the other contracts of the law of nations, will it not stand proved that the Reverend Doctor Sepúlveda has spoken wrongly and viciously against peoples like these?. . . From the fact that the Indians are barbarians it does not necessarily follow that they are incapable of government and have to be ruled by others, **2** except to be taught about the Catholic faith and to be admitted to the holy sacraments. **3** They are not ignorant, inhuman, or bestial. Rather, long before they had heard the word Spaniard they had **3** properly organized states, wisely ordered by excellent laws, religion, and custom. They cultivated friendship and, bound together in common fellowship, lived in populous cities in which they wisely administered the affairs of both peace and war justly and equitably, truly governed by laws that at very many points surpass ours, and could have won **4** the admiration of the sages of Athens. . . .

STRATEGY: WRITE A SUMMARY.

Use historical perspective to understand Las Casas's attitudes. In a chart, list key words, phrases, and details from the passage. In a short paragraph, summarize the basic values and attitudes of Las Casas.

Key Phrases	Las Casas's In Defense of the Indians
• barbarians • Catholic faith • not inhuman, ignorant, or bestial • properly organized states, wisely ordered • sages of Athens	Las Casas argues that Native Americans are not inhuman and do not deserve cruelty and slavery. Rather, they are fully capable of "coming up" to the level of Spanish civilization. Although he makes the statement that Native Americans are barbarians, his language and comparisons seem to suggest that he believes them to be highly civilized in many respects. At the same time, he believes in the importance of converting them to Catholicism.

Applying the Skill

WRITE YOUR OWN SUMMARY. Turn to Chapter 2, page 75, and read the excerpt from the *Life of Mehmed the Conqueror*. Read the passage using historical perspective. Then summarize your ideas in a chart like the one above.

2.5 Formulating Historical Questions

FORMULATING HISTORICAL QUESTIONS is important as you examine primary sources—firsthand accounts, documents, letters, and other records of the past. As you analyze a source, ask questions about what it means and why it is significant. Then, when you are doing research, write questions that you want your research to answer. This step will help to guide your research and organize the information you collect.

Understanding the Skill

STRATEGY: QUESTION WHAT YOU READ. The Muslim scholar Ibn Battuta published an account of his journeys in Asia and Africa in the 1300s. The following passage is part of his description of China. After the passage is a web diagram that organizes historical questions about it.

1 **Ask about the historical record itself.** Who produced it? When was it produced?

2 **Ask about the facts presented.** Who were the main people? What did they do? What were they like?

3 **Ask about the person who created the record.** What judgments or opinions does the author express?

4 **Ask about the significance of the record.** How would you interpret the information presented? How does it fit in with the history of this time and place? What more do you need to know to answer these questions?

> **1** Ibn Battuta in China, Around 1345
>
> **2** The Chinese themselves are infidels, who worship idols and burn their dead like the Hindus. . . . In every Chinese city there is a quarter for Muslims in which they live by themselves, and in which they have mosques both for the Friday services and for other religious purposes. The Muslims are honored and respected. **3** The Chinese infidels eat the flesh of swine and dogs, and sell it in their markets. **2** They are wealthy folk and well-to-do, but they make no display either in their food or their clothes. You will see one of their principal merchants, a man so rich that his wealth cannot be counted, wearing a coarse cotton tunic. But there is one thing that the Chinese take a pride in, that is gold and silver plate. Every one of them carries a stick, on which they lean in walking, and which they call "the third leg." **4** Silk is very plentiful among them, because the silk-worm attaches itself to fruits and feeds on them without requiring much care. For that reason, it is so common as to be worn by even the very poorest there. Were it not for the merchants it would have no value at all, for a single piece of cotton cloth is sold in their country for the price of many pieces of silk.

STRATEGY: MAKE A WEB DIAGRAM.

Investigate a topic in more depth by asking questions. Ask a large question and then ask smaller questions that explore and develop from the larger question.

Applying the Skill

MAKE YOUR OWN WEB DIAGRAM. Turn to the quotation by Olaudah Equiano in Chapter 4, page 135. Use a web diagram to write historical questions about the passage.

Skillbuilder Handbook

2.6 Making Predictions

MAKING PREDICTIONS means projecting the outcome of a situation that leaders or groups face or have faced in the past. Historians use their knowledge of past events and the decisions that led up to them to predict the outcome of current situations. Examining decisions and their alternatives will help you understand how events in the past shaped the future.

Understanding the Skill

STRATEGY: IDENTIFY DECISIONS. The following passage describes relations between Cuba and the United States following Fidel Castro's successful attempt to overthrow former Cuban dictator Fulgencio Batista. The chart lists decisions that affected U.S./Cuban relations, along with alternative decisions and predictions of their possible outcomes.

1 To help you identify decisions, look for words such as *decide, decision,* and *chose.*

2 Notice how one political decision often leads to another.

3 Notice both positive and negative decisions.

> **U.S./Cuban Relations under Castro**
>
> During the 1950s, Cuban dictator Fidel Castro **1** chose to nationalize the Cuban economy, which resulted in the takeover of U.S.-owned sugar mills and refineries. **2** U.S. President Eisenhower responded by ordering an embargo on all trade with Cuba. As relations between the two countries deteriorated, Cuba became more dependent on the USSR for economic and military aid. In 1960, the CIA trained anti-Castro Cuban exiles to invade Cuba. **3** Although they landed at Cuba's Bay of Pigs, the United States **1** decided not to provide them with air support. Castro's forces defeated the exiles, which humiliated the United States.

STRATEGY: MAKE A CHART.

4 Use a chart to record decisions.

5 Suggest alternative decisions.

6 Predict a possible outcome for each alternative decision.

4 Decisions	**5** Alternative Decisions	**6** Prediction of Outcome
Castro nationalized Cuban economy.	Castro did not nationalize Cuban economy.	There was no United States embargo of trade with Cuba.
The United States placed an embargo on trade with Cuba.	The United States continued to trade with Cuba.	Cuba continued to depend on the United States economically.
CIA trained Cuban exiles, who invaded Cuba.	The CIA did not train exiles to invade Cuba.	There was no invasion of Cuba.
The United States did not provide air support for the invasion.	The United States provided air support to the invaders.	The United States successfully invaded Cuba.

APPLYING THE SKILL

MAKE A CHART like the one above. Turn to Chapter 5, page 181, and read the first four paragraphs of the section "English Civil War." Identify three decisions of England's King Charles I. Record them on your chart, along with an alternative decision for each. Then predict a possible outcome for each alternative decision.

2.7 Hypothesizing

HYPOTHESIZING means developing a possible explanation for historical events. A hypothesis is an educated guess about what happened in the past or a prediction about what might happen in the future. A hypothesis takes available information, links it to previous experience and knowledge, and comes up with a possible explanation, conclusion, or prediction.

Understanding the Skill

STRATEGY: FIND CLUES IN THE READING. In studying the Indus Valley civilization, historians do not yet know exactly what caused that culture to decline. They have, however, developed hypotheses about what happened to it. Read this passage and look at the steps that are shown for building a hypothesis. Following the passage is a chart that organizes the information.

1 **Identify the event, pattern, or trend you want to explain.**

2 **Determine the facts you have about the situation.** These facts support various hypotheses about what happened to the Indus Valley civilization.

3 **Develop a hypothesis that might explain the event.** Historians hypothesize that a combination of ecological change and sudden catastrophe caused the Indus Valley civilization to collapse.

4 **Determine what additional information you need to test the hypothesis.** You might refer to a book about India, for example, to learn more about the impact of the Aryan invasions.

1 Mysterious End to Indus Valley Culture

2 Around 1750 B.C., the quality of building in the Indus Valley cities declined. Gradually, the great cities fell into decay. What happened? Some historians think that the Indus River changed course, as it tended to do, so that its floods no longer fertilized the fields near the cities. Other scholars suggest that people wore out the valley's land. They overgrazed it, overfarmed it, and overcut its trees, brush, and grass.

As the Indus Valley civilization neared its end, around 1500 B.C., a sudden catastrophe may have had a hand in the cities' downfall. **2** Archaeologists have found a half-dozen groups of skeletons in the ruins of Mohenjo-Daro, seemingly never buried. **3** Their presence suggests that the city, already weakened by its slow decline, may have been abandoned after a natural disaster or a devastating attack from human enemies. The Aryans, a nomadic people from north of the Hindu Kush mountains, swept into the Indus Valley at about this time. **4** Whether they caused the collapse of the Indus Valley civilization or followed in its wake is not known.

STRATEGY: MAKE A CHART.

Use a chart to summarize your hypothesis about events. Write down your hypothesis and the facts that support it. Then you can see what additional information you need to help prove or disprove it.

Hypothesis	Facts that support the hypothesis	Additional information needed
A combination of ecological change and sudden catastrophe caused the Indus Valley civilization to collapse	• Building quality declined • Indus River tended to change course • Unburied skeletons were found at Mohenjo-Daro • Aryan invasions occurred around same time	• What was Indus Valley culture like? • What were the geographical characteristics of the region? • How did overfarming tend to affect the environment? • What factors affected the decline of other ancient civilizations?

Applying the Skill

MAKE YOUR OWN CHART. Turn to Chapter 3, page 111, and read the Primary Source. Predict what impact the introduction of firearms might have had on Japan. Then read the surrounding text material. List facts that support your hypothesis and what additional information you might gather to help prove or disprove it.

2.8 Analyzing Motives

ANALYZING MOTIVES means examining the reasons why a person, group, or government takes a particular action. To understand those reasons, consider the needs, emotions, prior experiences, and goals of the person or group.

Understanding the Skill

STRATEGY: LOOK FOR REASONS WHY. On June 28, 1914, Serb terrorists assassinated Austria-Hungary's Archduke Franz Ferdinand and his wife when they visited Sarajevo, the capital of Bosnia. In the following passage, Borijove Jevtic, a Serb terrorist, explains why the assassination occurred. Before this passage, he explains that the terrorists had received a telegram stating that the Archduke would be visiting Sarajevo on June 28. The diagram that follows summarizes the motives of the terrorists for murdering the Archduke.

1 Look for motives based on basic needs and human emotions. Needs include food, shelter, safety, freedom. Emotions include fear, anger, pride, desire for revenge, and patriotism, for example.

2 Look for motives based on past events or inspiring individuals.

3 Notice both positive and negative motives.

> **The Assassination of the Archduke**
>
> How dared Franz Ferdinand, not only the representative of the oppressor but in his own person an **1** arrogant tyrant, enter Sarajevo on that day? Such an entry was a **1** studied insult.
>
> **2** 28 June is a date engraved deeply in the heart of every Serb, so that the day has a name of its own. It is called the vidovnan. It is the day on which the old Serbian kingdom was conquered by the Turks at the battle of Amselfelde in 1389. It is also the day on which in the second Balkan War the Serbian arms took glorious revenge on the Turk for his old victory and for the years of enslavement.
>
> **3** That was no day for Franz Ferdinand, the new oppressor, to venture to the very doors of Serbia for a display of the force of arms which kept us beneath his heel.
>
> Our decision was taken almost immediately. Death to the tyrant!

STRATEGY: MAKE A DIAGRAM.

Make a diagram that summarizes motives and actions. List the important action in the middle of the diagram. Then list motives in different categories around the action.

Applying the Skill

MAKE YOUR OWN DIAGRAM. Turn to Chapter 11, Section 1, "The Scramble for Africa." Read the section and look for motives of European nations in acquiring lands in other parts of the world. Make a diagram, like the one above, showing the European nations' motives for taking the land.

2.9 Analyzing Issues

An issue is a matter of public concern or debate. Issues in history are usually economic, social, political, or moral. Historical issues are often more complicated than they first appear. **ANALYZING AN ISSUE** means taking a controversy apart to find and describe the different points of view about the issue.

Understanding the Skill

STRATEGY: LOOK FOR DIFFERENT SIDES OF THE ISSUE. The following passage describes working conditions in English factories in the early 1800s. The cluster diagram that follows the passage helps you to analyze the issue of child labor.

1 **Look for a central problem with its causes and effects.**

2 **Look for facts and statistics.** Factual information helps you understand the issue and evaluate the different sides or arguments.

3 **Look for different sides to the issue.** You need to consider all sides of an issue before deciding your position.

Children at Work

1 Child labor was one of the most serious problems of the early Industrial Revolution. Children as young as 6 years worked exhausting jobs in factories and mines. Because wages were very low, many families in cities could not survive unless all their members, including children, worked.

2 In most factories, regular work hours were 6 in the morning to 6 in the evening, often with two "over-hours" until 8. It was common for 40 or more children to work together in one room—a room with little light or air. Those who lagged behind in their work were often beaten. Because safety was a low concern for many factory owners, accidents were common.

In 1831, Parliament set up a committee to investigate abuses of child labor. **2** Medical experts reported that long hours of factory work caused young children to become crippled or stunted in their growth. They recommended that children younger than age 14 should work no more than 8 hours. **3** Factory owners responded that they needed children to work longer hours in order to be profitable. As one owner testified, reduced working hours for children would "much reduce the value of my mill and machinery, and consequently of . . . my manufacture." As a result of the committee's findings, Parliament passed the Factory Act of 1833. The act made it illegal to hire children under 9 years old, and it limited the working hours of older children.

STRATEGY: MAKE A CLUSTER DIAGRAM.

If an issue is complex, make a cluster diagram. A cluster diagram can help you analyze an issue.

Issue: *Should Parliament restrict child labor?*

Facts:
- *Children as young as 6 years worked.*
- *Working hours were typically 12 hours a day, often with 2 hours overtime.*
- *Working conditions were dangerous, unhealthy, and inhumane.*
- *Factory work caused deformities in young children.*

In favor of child labor:
Who: *factory owners, some parents*
Reasons: *Shorter hours would reduce profits. Children's income essential for families.*

Against child labor:
Who: *medical examiners*
Reasons: *Children working in factories suffered permanent deformities.*

Applying the Skill

MAKE YOUR OWN CLUSTER DIAGRAM. Chapter 18, page 564, describes the partition of India. Make a cluster diagram to analyze the issue and the positions of the people involved.

2.10 Analyzing Bias

BIAS is a prejudiced point of view. Historical accounts that are biased tend to be one-sided and reflect the personal prejudices of the historian.

Understanding the Skill

STRATEGY: THINK ABOUT THE WRITER AS YOU READ. The European explorer Amerigo Vespucci reached the coast of Brazil in 1502, on his second voyage to the Americas. Below are his impressions of the people he met.

❶ Identify the author and information about him or her. Does the author belong to a special-interest group, social class, political party, or movement that might promote a one-sided or slanted viewpoint on the subject?

❷ Search for clues. Are there words, phrases, statements, or images that might convey a positive or negative slant? What might these clues reveal about the author's bias?

❸ Examine the evidence. Is the information that the author presents consistent with other accounts? Is the behavior described consistent with human nature as you have observed it?

❶ Amerigo Vespucci Reports on the People of Brazil

For twenty-seven days I ate and slept among them, and what I learned about them is as follows.

Having no laws and no religious faith, they live according to nature. **❷** They understand nothing of the immortality of the soul. There is no possession of private property among them, for everything is in common. They have no boundaries of kingdom or province. They have no king, nor do they obey anyone. Each one is his own master. **❸** There is no administration of justice, which is unnecessary to them, because in their code no one rules…

They are also **❷** a warlike people and very cruel to their own kind… That which made me… astonished at their wars and cruelty was that I could not understand from them why they made war upon each other, considering that they held no private property or sovereignty of empire and kingdoms and **❸** did not know any such thing as lust for possession, that is pillaging or a desire to rule, which appear to me to be the causes of wars and every disorderly act. When we requested them to state the cause, they did not know how to give any other cause than that this curse upon them began in ancient times and they sought to avenge the deaths of their forefathers.

STRATEGY: MAKE A CHART.

Make a chart of your analysis. For each of the heads listed on the left side of the chart, summarize information presented in the passage.

Vespucci's impressions of the native peoples of Brazil	
author, date	Amerigo Vespucci, 1502
occasion	exploration of coast of Brazil on second voyage to Americas
tone	judging, negative, superior
bias	Since the native people do not live in organized states and have no private property, they have no system of authority, laws, or moral principles. They have no apparent religious beliefs. They are warlike and cruel and seem to make war on one another for no reason. The author's comments about the soul seem to show a bias towards his own religious beliefs. He also reveals a prejudice that European customs and practices are superior to all others.

Applying the Skill

MAKE YOUR OWN CHART. Look at the quotation by the Qing emperor Kangxi in the Primary Source in Chapter 3, page 115. Summarize the underlying assumptions and biases using a chart like the one shown.

2.11 Evaluating Decisions and Courses of Action

EVALUATING DECISIONS means making judgments about the decisions that historical figures made. Historians evaluate decisions on the basis of their moral implications and their costs and benefits from different points of view.

EVALUATING VARIOUS COURSES OF ACTION means carefully judging the choices that historical figures had to make. By doing this, you can better understand why they made some of the decisions they did.

Understanding the Skill

STRATEGY: LOOK FOR CHOICES AND REASONS. The following passage describes the decisions U.S. President John Kennedy had to make when he learned of Soviet missile bases in Cuba. As you read it, think of the alternative responses he could have made at each turn of events. Following the passage is a chart that organizes information about the Cuban missile crisis.

1 **Look at decisions made by individuals or by groups.** Notice the decisions Kennedy made in response to Soviet actions.

2 **Look at the outcome of the decisions.**

3 **Analyze a decision in terms of the choices that were possible.** Both Kennedy and Khrushchev faced the same choice. Either could carry out the threat, or either could back down quietly and negotiate.

The Cuban Missile Crisis

During the summer of 1962, the flow of Soviet weapons into Cuba—including nuclear missiles—greatly increased. **1** President Kennedy responded cautiously at first, issuing a warning that the United States would not tolerate the presence of offensive nuclear weapons in Cuba. Then, on October 16, photographs taken by American U-2 planes showed the president that the Soviets were secretly building missile bases on Cuba. Some of the missiles, armed and ready to fire, could reach U.S. cities in minutes.

1 On the evening of October 22, the president made public the evidence of missiles and stated his ultimatum: any missile attack from Cuba would trigger an all-out attack on the Soviet Union. Soviet ships continued to head toward the island, while the U.S. navy prepared to stop them and U.S. invasion troops massed in Florida. To avoid confrontation, the Soviet ships suddenly halted. **2** Soviet Premier Nikita Khrushchev offered to remove the missiles from Cuba in exchange for a pledge not to invade the island. Kennedy agreed, and the crisis ended.

3 Some people criticized Kennedy for practicing brinkmanship, when private talks might have resolved the crisis without the threat of nuclear war. Others believed he had been too soft and had passed up a chance to invade Cuba and oust its Communist leader, Fidel Castro.

STRATEGY: MAKE A CHART.

Make a simple chart of your analysis. The problem was that Soviet nuclear missiles were being shipped to Cuba. The decision to be made was how the United States should respond.

Kennedy's Choices	Pros	Cons	My Evaluation
Publicly confront Khrushchev with navy and prepare for war.	Show Khrushchev and world the power and strong will of the U.S.; force him to back off.	Nuclear war could occur.	In your opinion, which was the better choice? Why?
Say nothing to U.S. public and negotiate quietly.	Avoid frightening U.S. citizens and avoid threat of nuclear war.	The U.S. would look weak publicly; Khrushchev could carry out plan.	

Applying the Skill

MAKE A CHART. Chapter 15, page 485, describes the decisions British and French leaders made when Hitler took over the Sudetenland in Czechoslovakia just before World War II. Make a chart, like the one shown, to summarize the pros and cons of their choice of appeasement and evaluate their decision yourself.

2.12 Forming and Supporting Opinions

Historians do more than reconstruct facts about the past. They also **FORM OPINIONS** about the information they encounter. Historians form opinions as they interpret the past and judge the significance of historical events and people. They **SUPPORT THEIR OPINIONS** with logical thinking, facts, examples, quotes, and references to events.

Understanding the Skill

STRATEGY: FIND ARGUMENTS TO SUPPORT YOUR OPINION. In the following passage, journalist Paul Gray summarizes differing opinions about the significance and impact of Columbus's voyages. As you read, develop your own opinion about the issue.

❶ Decide what you think about a subject after reading all the information available to you. After reading this passage, you might decide that Columbus's legacy was primarily one of genocide, cruelty, and slavery. On the other hand, you might believe that, despite the negatives, his voyages produced many long-term benefits.

❷ Consider the opinions and interpretations of historians and other experts. Weigh their arguments as you form your own opinion.

❸ Support your opinion with facts, quotes, and examples, including references to similar events from other historical eras.

How Should History View the Legacy of Columbus?

In one version of the story, Columbus and the Europeans who followed him ❶ brought civilization to two immense, sparsely populated continents, in the process fundamentally enriching and altering the Old World from which they had themselves come.

Among other things, Columbus' journey was the first step in a long process that eventually produced the United States of America, ❷ a daring experiment in democracy that in turn became a symbol and a haven of individual liberty for people throughout the world. But the revolution that began with his voyages was far greater than that. It altered science, geography, philosophy, agriculture, law, religion, ethics, government—the sum, in other words, of what passed at the time as Western culture.

Increasingly, however, there is a counterchorus, an opposing rendition of the same events that deems Columbus' first footfall in the New World to be fatal to the world he invaded, and even to the rest of the globe. The indigenous peoples and their cultures were doomed by European ❸ arrogance, ❸ brutality, and ❸ infectious diseases. Columbus' gift was ❸ slavery to those who greeted him; ❶ his arrival set in motion the ruthless destruction, continuing at this very moment, of the natural world he entered. Genocide, ecocide, exploitation… are deemed to be a form of Eurocentric theft of history from [the Native Americans].

STRATEGY: MAKE A CHART.

Summarize your opinion and supporting information in a chart. Write an opinion and then list facts, examples, interpretations, or other information that support it.

Opinion: Voyages of Columbus brought more bad than good to the Americas

Facts:	*Historical interpretations:*
• Europeans replaced existing cultures with their own.	• Europeans were arrogant and brutal.
• European diseases killed many Native Americans.	• Columbus's arrival set in motion ruthless destruction of environment.
• Columbus enslaved Native Americans.	• Through conquest and exploitation, Europeans "stole" Native Americans' history and culture.

Applying the Skill

MAKE YOUR OWN CHART. Look at the Different Perspectives on Economics and the Environment in Chapter 20, page 647. Read the selections and form your own opinion about the concept of sustainable development. Summarize your supporting data in a chart like the one shown above.

2.13 Synthesizing

SYNTHESIZING is the skill historians use in developing interpretations of the past. Like detective work, synthesizing involves putting together clues, information, and ideas to form an overall picture of a historical event. A synthesis is often stated as a generalization, or broad summary statement.

Understanding the Skill

STRATEGY: BUILD AN INTERPRETATION AS YOU READ. The passage below describes the first settlement of the Americas. The highlighting indicates the different kinds of information that lead to a synthesis—an overall picture of Native American life.

1 **Read carefully to understand the facts.** Facts such as these enable you to base your interpretations on physical evidence.

2 **Look for explanations that link the facts together.** This statement is based on the evidence provided by baskets, bows and arrows, and nets, which are mentioned in the sentences that follow.

3 **Consider what you already know that could apply.** Your general knowledge will probably lead you to accept this statement as reasonable.

4 **Bring together the information you have about a subject.** This interpretation brings together different kinds of information to arrive at a new understanding of the subject.

The First Americans

1 From the discovery of chiseled arrowheads and charred bones at ancient sites, it appears that the earliest Americans lived as big game hunters. The woolly mammoth, their largest prey, provided them with food, clothing, and bones for constructing tools and shelters. **2** People gradually shifted to hunting small game and gathering available plants. They created baskets to collect nuts, wild rice, chokeberries, gooseberries, and currants. Later they invented bows and arrows to hunt small game such as jackrabbits and deer. They wove nets to fish the streams and lakes.

Between 10,000 and 15,000 years ago, a revolution took place in what is now central Mexico. People began to raise plants as food. Maize may have been the first domesticated plant, with pumpkins, peppers, beans, and potatoes following. Agriculture spread to other regions.

3 The rise of agriculture brought about tremendous changes to the Americas. Agriculture made it possible for people to remain in one place. It also enabled them to accumulate and store surplus food. As their surplus increased, people had the time to develop skills and more complex ideas about the world. **4** From this agricultural base rose larger, more stable societies and increasingly complex societies.

STRATEGY: MAKE A CLUSTER DIAGRAM.

Summarize your synthesis in a cluster diagram. Use a cluster diagram to organize the facts, opinions, examples, and interpretations that you have brought together to form a synthesis.

Applying the Skill

MAKE YOUR OWN CLUSTER DIAGRAM. In Chapter 1 on pages 54–55, the beginnings of the Protestant Reformation are discussed. Read the passage and look for information to support a synthesis about its fundamental causes. Summarize your synthesis in a cluster diagram.

3.1 Analyzing Primary and Secondary Sources

PRIMARY SOURCES are written or created by people who lived during a historical event. The writers might have been participants or observers. Primary sources include letters, diaries, journals, speeches, newspaper articles, magazine articles, eyewitness accounts, and autobiographies.

SECONDARY SOURCES are derived from primary sources by people who were not present at the original event. They are written after the event. They often combine information from a number of different accounts. Secondary sources include history books, historical essays, and biographies.

Understanding the Skill

STRATEGY: EVALUATE THE INFORMATION IN EACH TYPE OF SOURCE. This passage describes political reforms made by Pericles, who led Athens from 461 to 429 B.C. It is mainly a secondary source, but it includes a primary source in the form of a speech.

1 **Secondary Source: Look for information collected from several sources.** Here the writer presents an overall picture of the reforms made by Pericles and the reasons for them.

2 **Secondary Source: Look for analysis and interpretation.** A secondary source provides details and perspective that are missing in a primary source. It also provides context for the primary source.

3 **Primary Source: Identify the author and evaluate his or her credentials.** How is the speaker connected to the event? Here, this speaker is Pericles himself.

4 **Primary Source: Analyze the source using historical perspective.** Read the source for factual information while also noting the speaker's opinions, biases, assumptions, and point of view.

Stronger Democracy in Athens

1 To strengthen democracy, Pericles increased the number of public officials who were paid salaries. Before, only wealthier citizens could afford to hold public office because most positions were unpaid. Now even the poorest could serve if elected or chosen by lot. **2** This reform made Athens one of the most democratic governments in history. However, political rights were still limited to those with citizenship status—a minority of Athens' total population.

The introduction of direct democracy was an important legacy of Periclean Athens. Few other city-states practiced this style of government. In Athens, male citizens who served in the assembly established all the important policies that affected the polis. In a famous "Funeral Oration" for soldiers killed in the Peloponnesian War, **3** Pericles expressed his great pride in Athenian democracy:

4 *Our constitution is called a democracy because power is in the hands not of a minority but of the whole people. When it is a question of settling private disputes, everyone is equal before the law; when it is a question of putting one person before another in positions of public responsibility, what counts is not membership of a particular class, but the actual ability which the man possesses. No one, as long as he has it in him to be of service to the state, is kept in political obscurity because of poverty.*

STRATEGY: MAKE A CHART.

Summarize information from primary and secondary sources on a chart.

Primary Source	Secondary Source
Author: Pericles	**Author**: world history textbook
Qualifications: main figure in the events described	**Qualifications**: had access to multiple accounts of event
Information: describes his view of Athenian democracy—power in the hands of "the whole people"	**Information**: puts events in historical perspective—Athens one of most democratic governments in history but limited rights to citizens

Applying the Skill

MAKE YOUR OWN CHART. Read the passage "Mehmed II Conquers Constantinople" in Chapter 2, pages 74–75, which includes a quote from the Greek historian Kritovoulos. Make a chart in which you summarize information from the primary and secondary sources.

3.2 Visual, Audio, and Multimedia Sources

In addition to written accounts, historians use many kinds of **VISUAL SOURCES.** These include paintings, photographs, political cartoons, and advertisements. Visual sources are rich with historical details and sometimes reflect the mood and trends of an era better than words can.

Spoken language has always been a primary means of passing on human history. **AUDIO SOURCES,** such as recorded speeches, interviews, press conferences, and radio programs, continue the oral tradition today.

Movies, CD-ROMs, television, and computer software are the newest kind of historical sources, called **MULTIMEDIA SOURCES.**

Understanding the Skill

STRATEGY: EXAMINE THE SOURCE CAREFULLY. Below are two portraits from the late 1700s, one of Marie Antoinette, the queen of France, and one of a woman who sells vegetables at the market. The chart that follows summarizes historical information gained from interpreting and comparing the two paintings.

1 Identify the subject and source.

2 Identify important visual details. Look at the faces, poses, clothing, hairstyles, and other elements.

3 Make inferences from the visual details. Marie Antoinette's rich clothing and her hand on the globe symbolize her wealth and power. The contrast between the common woman's ordinary clothing and her defiant pose suggests a different attitude about power.

Use comparisons, information from other sources, and your own knowledge to give support to your interpretation. Royalty usually had their portraits painted in heroic poses. Ordinary people were not usually the subjects of such portraits. David's choice of subject and pose suggests that he sees the common people as the true heroes of France.

A Woman of the Revolution [La maraîchère] (1795), Jacques Louis David **1**

Marie Antoinette, Jacques Gautier d'Agoty **1**

STRATEGY: MAKE A CHART.

Summarize your interpretation in a simple chart.

Subject	Visual Details	Inferences	Message
Common woman	Face is worn and clothing is plain, but her head is held high and she wears the red scarf of revolution	Has worked hard for little in life, but strong, proud, and defiant	Although the details are strikingly different, the two paintings convey similar characteristics about their subjects.
Marie Antoinette	Richly dressed and made up; strikes an imperial pose	Lives life of comfort and power; proud, strong, and defiant	

Applying the Skill

MAKE YOUR OWN CHART. Turn to the painting *School of Athens* by Raphael in Chapter 1, page 45. Use a chart, like the one above, to analyze and interpret the painting.

Skillbuilder Handbook

3.3 Using the Internet

The **INTERNET** is a network of computers associated with universities, libraries, news organizations, government agencies, businesses, and private individuals worldwide. Each location on the Internet has a **HOME PAGE** with its own address, or **URL.**

With a computer connected to the Internet, you can reach the home pages of many organizations and services. You might view your library's home page to find the call number of a book or visit an online magazine to read an article. On some sites you can view documents, photographs, and even moving pictures with sound.

The international collection of home pages, known as the **WORLD WIDE WEB,** is a good source of up-to-the-minute information about current events as well as in-depth research on historical subjects. This textbook contains many suggestions for navigating the World Wide Web. Begin by entering **CLASSZONE.COM** to access the home page for McDougal Littell World History.

Understanding the Skill

STRATEGY: EXPLORE THE ELEMENTS ON THE SCREEN. The computer screen below shows the home page of the history area at PBS, the national public television service based in Washington, D.C.

1 **Go directly to a Web page.** If you know the address of a particular Web page, type the address in the box at the top of the screen and press ENTER (or RETURN). After a few seconds, the Web page will appear on your screen.

2 **Explore the links.** Click on any one of the images or topics to find out more about a specific subject. These links take you to another page at this Web site. Some pages include links to related information that can be found at other places on the Internet.

3 **Learn more about the page.** Scan the page to learn the types of information contained at this site. This site has information about PBS history programs as well as other historical information and special features.

4 **Explore the features of the page.** This page has a feature that lets you compare life today with life in the 1700s.

PBS History screen shot courtesy of PBS ONLINE®.

Applying the Skill

DO YOUR OWN INTERNET RESEARCH. Explore the web sites for Chapter 18 located at classzone.com. **PATH: CLASSZONE.COM** → Social Studies → World History → Chapter 18 → Research Links.

3.4 Interpreting Maps

MAPS are representations of features on the earth's surface. Historians use maps to locate historical events, to show how geography has influenced history, and to illustrate human interaction with the environment.

Different kinds of maps are used for specific purposes.

POLITICAL MAPS show political units, from countries, states, and provinces, to counties, districts, and towns. Each area is shaded a different color.

PHYSICAL MAPS show mountains, hills, plains, rivers, lakes, and oceans. They may use contour lines to indicate elevations on land and depths under water.

HISTORICAL MAPS illustrate such things as economic activity, political alliances, land claims, battles, population density, and changes over time.

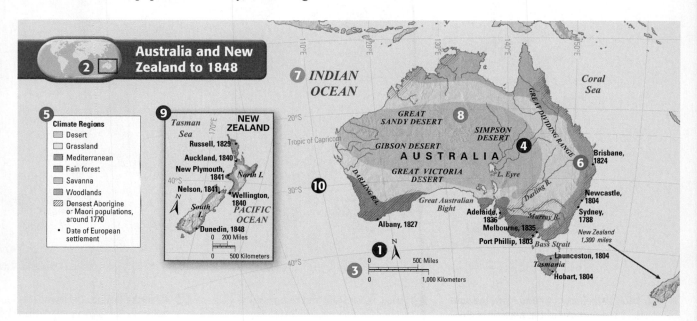

Skillbuilder Handbook

❶ Compass Rose The compass rose is a feature indicating the map's orientation on the globe. It may show all four cardinal directions (N, S, E, W) or just indicate north.

❷ Locator A locator map shows which part of the world the map subject area covers.

❸ Scale The scale shows the ratio between a unit of length on the map and a unit of distance on the earth. The maps in this book usually show the scale in miles and kilometers.

❹ Lines Lines indicate rivers and other waterways, political boundaries, roads, and routes of exploration or migration.

❺ Legend or Key The legend or key explains the symbols, lines, and special colors that appear on the map.

❻ Symbols Locations of cities and towns often appear as dots. A capital city is often shown as a star or as a dot with a circle around it. Picture symbols might be used to indicate an area's products, resources, and special features.

❼ Labels Key places such as cities, bodies of water, and landforms are labeled. Key dates, such as those for the founding of cities, may also be labeled.

❽ Colors Maps use colors and shading for various purposes. On physical maps, color may be used to indicate different physical regions or altitudes. On political maps, color can distinguish different political units. On specialty maps, color can show variable features such as population density, languages, or cultural areas.

❾ Inset An inset is a small map that appears within a larger map. It often shows an area of the larger map in greater detail. Inset maps may also show a different area that is in some way related to the area shown on the larger map.

❿ Lines of Latitude and Longitude Lines of latitude and longitude appear on maps to indicate the absolute location of the area shown.

• Lines of latitude show distance measured in degrees north or south of the equator.

• Lines of longitude show distance measured in degrees east or west of the prime meridian, which runs through Greenwich, England.

3.4 *(Continued)*

Understanding the Skill

STRATEGY: READ ALL THE ELEMENTS OF THE MAP. The historical maps below show European landholdings in North America in 1754 and after 1763. Together they show changes over time.

1 **Look at the map's title to learn the subject and purpose of the map.** What area does the map cover? What does the map tell you about the area? Here the maps show North America in 1754 and after 1763 with the purpose of comparing European claims at two different times.

2 **Look at the scale and compass.** The scale shows you how many miles or kilometers are represented. Here the scale is 500 actual miles to approximately 5/8 inch on the map. The compass shows you which direction on the map is north.

3 **Read the legend.** The legend tells you what the symbols and colors on the map mean.

4 **Find where the map area is located on the earth.** These maps show a large area from the Arctic Circle to below latitude 20°N and 40° to 140°W.

STRATEGY: MAKE A CHART. Study the maps and pose questions about how the geographic patterns and distributions changed. Use the answers to create a chart.

Relate the map to the five geography themes by making a chart. The five themes are described on pages xxxii–xxxiii. Ask questions about the themes and record your answers on the chart.

What Was the Location? Large area from Arctic Circle to below 20° N, and 40° to 140° W

What Was the Place? North American continent

What Was the Region? Western Hemisphere

Was There Any Movement? Between 1754 and 1763, land claimed by France was taken over by the other two colonial powers. Spain expanded its territories northward, while Britain expanded westward.

How Did Humans Interact with the Environment? Europeans carved out political units in the continent, which already had inhabitants. They claimed vast areas, with waterways and large mountain ranges to cross.

Applying the Skill

MAKE YOUR OWN CHART. Turn to Chapter 3, page 100, and study the map titled "Europeans in the East, 1487–1700." Make a chart, like the one shown above, in which you summarize what the map tells you according to the five geography themes.

3.5 Interpreting Charts

CHARTS are visual presentations of materials. Historians use charts to organize, simplify, and summarize information in a way that makes it more meaningful or easier to remember. Several kinds of charts are commonly used.

SIMPLE CHARTS are used to summarize information or to make comparisons.

TABLES are used to organize statistics and other types of information into columns and rows for easy reference.

DIAGRAMS provide visual clues to the meaning of the information they contain. Venn diagrams are used for comparisons. Web diagrams are used to organize supporting information around a central topic. Illustrated diagrams or diagrams that combine different levels of information are sometimes called **INFOGRAPHICS.**

Understanding the Skill

STRATEGY: STUDY ALL THE ELEMENTS OF THE CHART. The infographic below conveys a great deal of information about the three estates, or classes, that existed in 18th-century France. The infographic visually combines a political cartoon, a bulleted chart, a pie graph, and a bar graph.

Read the title.

Identify the symbols and colors and what they represent. Here, three colors are used consistently in the infographic to represent the three estates.

Study each of the elements of the infographic. The political cartoon visually represents the power of the First and Second Estates over the Third Estate. The bulleted chart gives details about the estates. The two graphs give statistics.

Look for the main idea. Make connections among the types of information presented. What was the relationship among the three estates?

The Three Estates

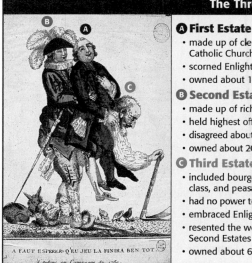

A FAUT ESPERER-Q'EU JEU LA FINIRA BEN TOT.

Ⓐ First Estate
- made up of clergy of Roman Catholic Church
- scorned Enlightenment ideas
- owned about 15% of the land

Ⓑ Second Estate
- made up of rich nobles
- held highest offices in government
- disagreed about Enlightenment ideas
- owned about 20% of the land

Ⓒ Third Estate
- included bourgeoisie, urban lower class, and peasant farmers
- had no power to influence government
- embraced Enlightenment ideas
- resented the wealthy First and Second Estates
- owned about 65% of the land

Population of France, 1787

97% (Third Estate)

less than 1% (First Estate)

2% (Second Estate)

Percent of Income Paid in Taxes

2% (First Estate)

0% (Second Estate)

50% (Third Estate)

0%   20%   40%   60%   80%   100%

Look for geographic patterns and distributions. Pose questions about the way land is distributed among the three estates. Include your answers in your summary paragraph.

STRATEGY: WRITE A SUMMARY.

Write a paragraph to summarize what you learned from the chart.

> In 1787, French society was unevenly divided into three estates. Ninety-seven percent of the people belonged to the Third Estate. They had no political power, paid high taxes, and owned only 65 percent of the land. The First Estate, made up of the clergy, and the Second Estate, made up of rich nobles, held the power, the wealth, and more than their share of the land. Both opposed change and took advantage of the Third Estate.

Applying the Skill

WRITE YOUR OWN SUMMARY. Turn to Chapter 9, page 293, and look at the chart titled "Industrialization." Study the chart and write a paragraph in which you summarize what you learn from it.

3.6 Interpreting Graphs

GRAPHS show statistical information in a visual manner. Historians use graphs to show comparative amounts, ratios, economic trends, and changes over time.

LINE GRAPHS can show changes over time, or trends. Usually, the horizontal axis shows a unit of time, such as years, and the vertical axis shows quantities.

PIE GRAPHS are useful for showing relative proportions. The circle represents the whole, such as the entire population, and the slices represent the different groups that make up the whole.

BAR GRAPHS compare numbers or sets of numbers. The length of each bar indicates a quantity. With bar graphs, it is easy to see at a glance how different categories compare.

Understanding the Skill

STRATEGY: STUDY ALL THE ELEMENTS OF THE GRAPH. The line graphs below show average global temperatures and world population figures over a period of 25,000 years. Pose questions about geographic patterns and distributions shown on this graph; for example, when did worldwide temperature start to rise?

1 **Read the title to identify the main idea of the graph.** When two subjects are shown, look for a relationship between them. This set of graphs shows that the agricultural revolution had links to both global temperature and population.

2 **Read the vertical axis.** The temperature graph shows degrees Fahrenheit. The other shows population in millions, so that 125 indicates 125,000,000.

3 **Note any information that is high-lighted in a box.**

4 **Read the horizontal axis.** Both graphs cover a period of time from 25,000 years ago to 0 (today).

5 **Look at the legend to understand what colors and certain marks stand for.**

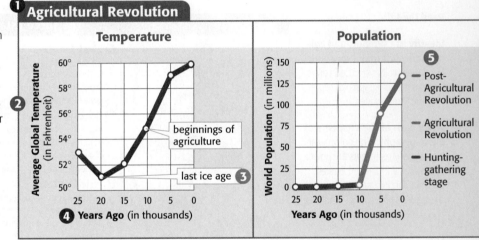

Summarize the information shown in each part of the graph. What trends or changes are shown in each line graph?

STRATEGY: WRITE A SUMMARY.

Use the answers to your questions about geographic patterns and distributions to write your summary paragraph.

Write a paragraph to summarize what you learned from the graphs.

> *Some 20,000 years ago, after the last Ice Age, temperatures started to rise worldwide. This steady rise in average temperature from 51° to 55° made possible the beginnings of agriculture. As a result of the agricultural revolution, world population grew from about 2 million to about 130 million over a period of 10,000 years.*

Applying the Skill

WRITE YOUR OWN SUMMARY. Turn to Chapter 15, page 474, and look at the graph "World Trade, 1929–1933." Study the graph and write a paragraph in which you summarize what you learn from it.

3.7 Analyzing Political Cartoons

POLITICAL CARTOONS are drawings that express the artist's point of view about a local, national, or international situation or event. They may criticize, show approval, or draw attention to a particular issue, and may be either serious or humorous. Political cartoonists often use symbols as well as other visual clues to communicate their message.

Understanding the Skill

STRATEGY: EXAMINE THE CARTOON CAREFULLY. The cartoon below was drawn during the period of détente—a lessening of Cold War tensions between the United States and the Soviet Union.

1 Look at the cartoon as a whole to determine the subject.

2 Look for symbols, which are especially effective in communicating ideas visually. In this cartoon, Szabo uses symbols that stand for two nations. The stars and stripes stand for the United States. The hammer and sickle stand for the Soviet Union.

3 Analyze the visual details, which help express the artist's point of view. The lit fuse suggests that the world is in immediate danger. The United States and the Soviet Union are cooperating to reduce the danger by cutting the fuse.

STRATEGY: MAKE A CHART.

Summarize your analysis in a chart. Look for details and analyze their significance. Then decide on the message of the cartoon.

Symbols and Visual Details	Significance	Message
• Stars and stripes • Hammer and sickle • Lit fuse • Both nations hold the scissors	• United States • Soviet Union • Danger • Cooperation	The United States and the Soviet Union are trying to prevent their differences from destroying the world.

Applying the Skill

MAKE YOUR OWN CHART. Turn to the political cartoon in Chapter 7, page 218. Read the information provided in the chart and graphs to help you understand the basis for the cartoon. Note the clothing and apparent attitudes of the figures in the drawing, as well as how they relate to one another. Then make a chart like the one above.

Skillbuilder Handbook

4.1 Writing for Social Studies

WRITING FOR SOCIAL STUDIES requires you to describe an idea, a situation, or an event. Often, you will be asked to take a stand on a particular issue or to make a specific point. To successfully describe an event or make a point, your writing needs to be clear, concise, and accurate. When you write reports or term papers, you will also need to create a bibliography of your sources; and you need to evaluate how reliable those sources are.

Understanding the Skill

STRATEGY: ORGANIZE INFORMATION AND WRITE CLEARLY. The following passage describes the rise and fall of Napoleon Bonaparte. Notice how the strategies below helped the writer explain the historical importance of Napoleon's power.

❶ Focus on your topic. Be sure that you clearly state the main idea of your piece so that your readers know what you intend to say.

❷ Collect and organize your facts. Collect accurate information about your topic to support the main idea you are trying to make. Use your information to build a logical case to prove your point

To express your ideas clearly, use standard grammar, spelling, sentence structure, and punctuation when writing for social studies. Proofread your work to make sure it is well organized and grammatically correct.

> **❶ The Rise and Fall of Napoleon, 1799–1814**
>
> The power that Napoleon used to bring order to France after the Revolution ultimately proved to be his undoing. Under his command, the troops drove out members of the legislature in 1799 and helped Napoleon seize control of France. **❷** As emperor of France, he stabilized the country's economy. He even created a code of laws. However, Napoleon wanted to control all of Europe. But he made mistakes that cost him his empire. He established a blockade in 1806 to prevent trade between Great Britain and other Europeans nations. But smugglers, aided by the British, managed to get cargo through. He angered Spain by replacing the country's king with his own brother. In 1812, Napoleon also invaded Russia by using many troops who were not French and who felt little loyalty to him. Eventually, all the main powers of Europe joined forces and defeated Napoleon in the spring of 1814.

STRATEGY: USE STANDARD FORMATS WHEN MAKING CITATIONS. Use standard formats when citing books, magazines, newspapers, electronic media, and other sources. The following examples will help you to interpret and create bibliographies.

❸ Video

❹ Newspaper

❺ Magazine

❻ Online database

❼ Book

> ❸ <u>Fire and Ice.</u> Prod. HistoryAlive Videocassette. BBC Video, 1998.
>
> ❹ Gutierrez, Andrew R. "Memorial for Scott at Antarctic." <u>Los Angeles Times</u> 8 January 2001: 14A.
>
> ❺ Hansen, Ron. "The Race for the South Pole." <u>Smithsonian Institute</u> 28 June 1999: 112.
>
> ❻ "Scott's Run for the South Pole." <u>Facts on File.</u> Online. Internet. 28 February 2000.
>
> ❼ Solomon, Susan. <u>The Coldest March: Scott's Fatal Antarctic Expedition.</u> New Haven, CT: Yale UP, 2001.

Applying the Skill

WRITE YOUR OWN RESPONSE. Turn to Chapter 7, Section 4, "Napoleon's Empire Collapses." Read the section and use the strategies above to write your answer to question 6 on page 237.

Find three or four different sources on the Internet or in the library relating to Napoleon's fall. Create a short bibliography and use standard formats for each type of source. Be sure to interpret, or evaluate, how reliable your sources are.

4.2 Creating a Map

CREATING A MAP can help you understand routes, regions, landforms, political boundaries, or other geographical information.

Understanding the Skill

STRATEGY: CREATE A MAP to clarify information and help you visualize what you read. Creating a map is similar to taking notes, except that you draw much of the information. After reading the passage below, a student sketched the map shown.

The French Explore North America

A number of Frenchmen were among the early explorers of North America. In 1534, Jacques Cartier sailed up a broad river that he named the St. Lawrence. When he came to a large island dominated by a mountain, he called the island Mont Real, which eventually became known as Montreal. In 1608, another French explorer, Samuel de Champlain, sailed further up the St. Lawrence and laid claim to a region he called Quebec. In 1673, Jacques Marquette and Louis Joliet explored the Great Lakes and the upper Mississippi River. Nearly 10 years later, Sieur de La Salle explored the lower Mississippi and claimed the entire river valley for France.

1 Create a title that shows the purpose of the map.

2 Consider the purpose of the map as you decide which features to include. Because the main purpose of this sketch map is to show the routes of early explorers, it includes a scale of distance.

3 Find one or more maps to use as a guide. For this sketch map, the student consulted a historical map and a physical map.

4 Create a legend to explain any colors or symbols used.

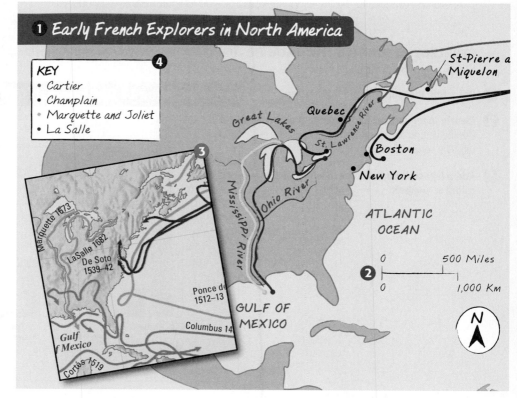

1 Early French Explorers in North America

KEY
- Cartier
- Champlain
- Marquette and Joliet
- La Salle

Great Lakes
Quebec
St. Lawrence River
St-Pierre a Miquelon
Boston
New York
Mississippi River
Ohio River
ATLANTIC OCEAN

Marquette 1673
LaSalle 1682
De Soto 1539–42
Ponce de 1512–13
Gulf f Mexico
Columbus 14
Cortés 1519

GULF OF MEXICO

0   500 Miles
0   1,000 Km

N

Applying the Skill

MAKE YOUR OWN SKETCH MAP. Turn to Chapter 4, page 122, and read the first three paragraphs of the section "Spanish Conquests in Peru." Create a sketch map showing the cities where Pizarro conquered the Inca. Use either a modern map of Peru or an historic map of the Incan Empire as a guide. (The conquered cities of the empire also belong to the modern nation of Peru.) Include a scale of miles to show the distance traveled by the Spanish to make their conquests. Add a legend to indicate which conquest involved a battle and which did not.

4.3 Creating Charts and Graphs

CHARTS and **GRAPHS** are visual representations of information. (See Skillbuilders 3.5, Interpreting Charts, and 3.6, Interpreting Graphs.) Three types of graphs are **BAR GRAPHS, LINE GRAPHS,** and **PIE GRAPHS.** Use a line graph to show changes over time, or trends. Use a pie graph to show relative proportions. Use a bar graph to display and compare information about quantities. Use a **CHART** to organize, simplify, and summarize information.

Understanding the Skill

STRATEGY: CREATE A BAR GRAPH. Choose the information that you wish to compare. After reading the following paragraph, a student created the bar graph below to compare population shifts in three European cities.

> **Population Shifts**
>
> The decline of the Roman Empire led to major population shifts. As Roman centers of trade and government collapsed, nobles retreated to the rural areas. Roman cities were left without strong leadership. The population of Rome dropped from 350,000 in A.D. 100 to 50,000 in A.D. 900. During the same period, other cities in the empire experienced similar declines. For example, the population of Trier, Germany, dropped from 100,000 to around 13,000. The population of Lyon, France, experienced an even greater decline, dropping from 100,000 to approximately 12,000.

STRATEGY: ORGANIZE THE DATA. Be consistent in how you present similar kinds of information.

1 Use a title that sums up the information.

2 Clearly label vertical and horizontal axes. Use the vertical axis to show increasing quantities. Label the horizontal axis with what is being compared.

3 Add a legend to indicate the meaning of any colors or symbols.

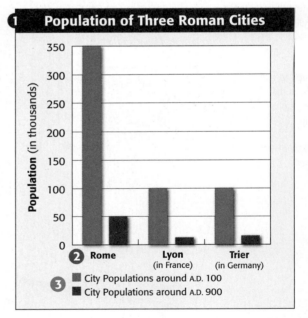

1 Population of Three Roman Cities

Population (in thousands) — 0, 50, 100, 150, 200, 250, 300, 350

2 Rome — Lyon (in France) — Trier (in Germany)

3 ■ City Populations around A.D. 100
■ City Populations around A.D. 900

Applying the Skill

CREATE A BAR GRAPH. Turn to Chapter 7, page 236. Study the map "Napoleon's Russian Campaign, 1812." Use the information to create a bar graph showing the number of soldiers in Napoleon's army from June 1812 to December 6, 1812. Label the vertical axis Soldiers (in thousands) and show the grid in increments of 100, beginning with 0 and ending with 500. Provide a bar for each of the following dates: June 1812, September 7, 1812, November 1812, and December 6, 1812. Label each bar with the number of soldiers. Add a title. Be sure to read carefully the information in the boxes on the chart for each date you include in your graph.

4.4 Creating and Using a Database

A **DATABASE** is a collection of data, or information, that is organized so that you can find and retrieve information on a specific topic quickly and easily. Once a computerized database is set up, you can search it to find specific information without going through the entire database. The database will provide a list of all information in the database related to your topic. Learning how to use a database will help you learn how to create one.

Understanding the Skill

STRATEGY: CREATE THE DATABASE. First, identify the topic of the database. Both words in this title, "Five Empires," are important. These words were used to begin the research for this database.

1 **Determine the order of presentation of information.** For example, will you list items from largest to smallest? from oldest to newest? The five empires are listed in order of date, from earliest empire to latest.

2 **Identify the entries included under each heading.** Here, five empires from the text were chosen as topics for research.

3 **Ask yourself what kind of data to include.** For example, what geographic patterns and distributions will be shown? Your choice of data will provide the column headings. The key words *Dates, Greatest Territory,* and *Greatest Population* were chosen to focus the research.

Five Empires			
	1 **Dates**	**Greatest Territory*** **3**	**Greatest Population****
2 **Persian**	550 B.C.–330 B.C.	2.0	14.0
Roman	27 B.C.–A.D. 476	3.4	54.8
Byzantine	A.D. 395–A.D. 1453	1.4	30.0
Mongol	A.D. 1206–A.D. 1380	11.7	125.0
Aztec	A.D. 1325–A.D. 1521	0.2	6.0

4 * Estimated in millions of square miles
** Estimated in millions of people

4 **Add labels or footnotes as necessary to clarify the nature of the data presented.** Are the figures shown in thousands? hundred of thousands? millions? Users of the database need to know what the figures represent.

STRATEGY: USE THE DATABASE. Use the database to help you find information quickly. For example, in this database you could search for "empires with populations of more than 10 million" and compile a list including the Persian, Roman, Byzantine, and Mongol empires.

Applying the Skill

CREATE A DATABASE for World War II that shows the dates and locations of important battles, estimated casualty figures, and the significance of the outcome for each battle. Use information presented in Chapter 16 to find the data. Follow a chart format similar to the one above for your database. Then use the database to list the three battles that resulted in the highest number of casualties.

4.5 Creating a Model

WHEN YOU CREATE A MODEL, you use information and ideas to show an event or a situation in a visual way. A model might be a poster or a diagram drawn to explain how something happened. Or, it might be a three-dimensional model, such as a diorama, that depicts an important scene or situation.

Understanding the Skill

STRATEGY: CREATE A MODEL. The poster below shows the hardships and dangers that children faced while working in the textile factories in the early 1800s. Use the strategies listed below to help you create your own model.

1 **Gather the information you need to understand the situation or event.** In this case, you need to be able to show the hardships and dangers of child labor.

2 **Visualize and sketch an idea for your model.** Once you have created a picture in your mind, make an actual sketch to plan how it might look.

3 **Think of symbols you may want to use.** Since the model should give information in a visual way, think about ways you can use color, pictures, or other visuals to tell the story.

Gather the supplies you will need and create the model. For example, you may need crayons and markers.

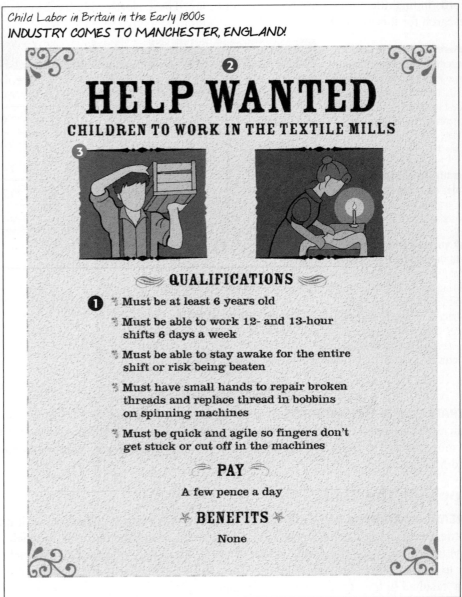

Child Labor in Britain in the Early 1800s
INDUSTRY COMES TO MANCHESTER, ENGLAND!

2 **HELP WANTED**
CHILDREN TO WORK IN THE TEXTILE MILLS

3

QUALIFICATIONS

1 ❧ Must be at least 6 years old

❧ Must be able to work 12- and 13-hour shifts 6 days a week

❧ Must be able to stay awake for the entire shift or risk being beaten

❧ Must have small hands to repair broken threads and replace thread in bobbins on spinning machines

❧ Must be quick and agile so fingers don't get stuck or cut off in the machines

PAY

A few pence a day

❋ BENEFITS ❋

None

Applying the Skill

CREATE YOUR OWN MODEL. Read the Interact with History feature on page 282. Create a poster that shows how working conditions might be made more fair in England during the Industrial Revolution.

4.6 Creating/Interpreting a Research Outline

When you **CREATE A RESEARCH OUTLINE,** you arrange information you have gathered into an organized format. When you **INTERPRET A RESEARCH OUTLINE,** you use the outline's structure to guide you in writing a research report or paper that is clear and focused.

Understanding the Skill

STRATEGY: DECIDE HOW IDEAS ARE CONNECTED, THEN CREATE AN OUTLINE. As you research a topic, you are likely to gather names, dates, facts, and ideas. All of this information needs to be organized to show how the ideas connect to one another. To decide how the ideas connect, think about your purpose for writing the research report.

For example, suppose you are writing a report about Napoleon's retreat from Moscow. You might choose to create an outline using the sequence of events or using the causes and effects that led to the destruction of the Grand Army. Your outline would reflect your purpose.

1 An outline begins with a statement of purpose.

2 An outline is divided into two or more major sections, introduced by Roman numerals (I, II).

3 Each major section is divided into two or more subsections introduced by capital letters (A, B).

4 The subsections may be divided into sub-subsections introduced by Arabic numerals (1, 2).

Chronological outline

1 Purpose: Describe the events that led to Napoleon's defeat in Russia.
2 I. Napoleon's defeat in Russia
   A. June 1812
      1. march into Russia
      2. scorched-earth policy
   B. September 7, 1812
      1. Battle of Borodino
      2. narrow victory for the French
   C. September 14, 1812
      1. arrival in Moscow
      2. city in flames
2 II. Napoleon's defeat in Russia
   A. mid-October 1812
      1. waiting for offer of peace
      2. too late to advance
      3. begins retreat from Moscow
   B. early November 1812
      1. retreat in snow storm
      2. attack by Russians

Cause-and-effect outline

Purpose: Describe the reasons for Napoleon's defeat in Russia.
 I. Napoleon's mistakes
3 A. troops not loyal to Napoleon
   B. waited too long to retreat
4 1. starvation
   2. winter snows
II. Russian tactics
   A. scorched-earth policy
   B. no offer of peace from the czar
   C. attacks on the retreating army

STRATEGY: INTERPRET THE OUTLINE TO WRITE A RESEARCH REPORT.

Use the organization of the outline to choose signal words that match your purpose for writing.

Signal words to show time-order	Signal words to show cause and effect
dates: September 14, 1812	because
time frames: for five weeks	so
order: first, next, then, last	as a result

Applying the Skill

CREATE YOUR OWN OUTLINE. Read Chapter 13, "The Great War, 1914–1918." Create an outline that shows a sequence of events leading up to World War I or that shows the series of causes and effects that resulted in the war. Choose appropriate signal words to write a rough draft from your outline.

4.7 Creating Oral Presentations

When you **CREATE AN ORAL PRESENTATION,** you prepare a speech or a talk to give before an audience. The object of an oral presentation is to provide information about a particular topic or to persuade an audience to think or act in a particular way.

Understanding the Skill

STRATEGY: CHOOSE A TOPIC. The following is an excerpt from a student's speech in support of recycling.

1 State your theme or point of view.

2 Include facts or arguments to support your theme.

3 Choose words and images that reflect the theme. The comparison to Disneyland is a visual image that helps to communicate the amount of waste in the Fresh Kills Landfill.

1 To help preserve the earth's dwindling natural resources, Americans need to get serious about recycling. At the moment, our track record is not very good. **2** Although people in the United States account for less than 5% of the world's population, they use 40% of the world's resources, and generate a huge amount of waste. The Fresh Kills Landfill, which serves New York City, is a prime example. It contains so much garbage that Fresh Kills Landfill is **3** four times the size of Disneyland. And that's just New York's garbage.

With so many people throwing so much away, is there any point in trying to change things? The answer is yes! Recyling one glass bottle saves enough energy to light a 100-watt light bulb for four hours. Twenty-five million trees could be saved every year by recycling just 10% of our newspapers. Making new aluminum products from recycled aluminum, rather than from bauxite, uses 95% less energy. By increasing the recycling of our bottles, jars, cans, and paper, we could dramatically reduce our demand for trees, fossil fuels, and other precious resources.

STRATEGY: USE THESE TIPS FOR SUCCESSFUL ORAL PRESENTATIONS.

- Maintain eye contact with your audience.
- Use gestures and body language to emphasize main points.
- Pace yourself. Speak slowly and distinctly.
- Vary your tone to help bring out the message you wish to make.

STRATEGY: PRACTICE THE PRESENTATION in front of a mirror or ask a friend or family member to listen to your presentation and give you feedback.

Applying the Skill

CREATE YOUR OWN ORAL PRESENTATION. Turn to Chapter 6. Choose a topic from the "New" section of one of the "Changing Idea" boxes on pages 192, 195, 204, or 208. Create an oral presentation in which you explain how the idea was new and why it was important. Use information from the chapter to support your chosen idea.

4.8 Creating Written Presentations

CREATING A WRITTEN PRESENTATION means writing an in-depth report on a topic in history. Your objective may be to inform or to support a particular point of view. To succeed, your writing must be clear and well organized. For additional information on creating a historical research paper, see Skillbuilder 4.1, Writing for Social Studies.

Understanding the Skill

STRATEGY: CREATE AN OUTLINE such as the one below. Use it as a guide to write your presentation.

1 State the main idea.

2 Organize the information by category.

3 Add supporting facts and details.

---

1 The Incan Empire

I. The Inca created a large and highly developed empire.

2 A. A Theocracy
   1. Members of only 11 families could rule
   2. Rulers believed to be descendants of the sun god
   3. Religion supported the state; worship of the sun god, Inti, amounted to worship of the king

B. Expansion
   1. Rulers conquered new territories to acquire wealth
   2. Pachacuti created the largest empire in the Americas
   3. Size by 1500: 2,500 miles along western coast, 16 million people

C. Unifying strategies
   3 1. Rulers practiced diplomacy
   2. Rulers imposed a single official language, Quechua
   3. Schools taught conquered peoples the Incan ways
   4. Extensive system of roads led to Cuzco, the capital

D. Early socialism
   1. Supported aged and disabled
   2. Rewarded citizens' labor with food and beer

E. Culturally advanced
   1. Elaborate calendar system
   2. Artisans created works in gold and silver
   3. Exception: no writing system, but oral tradition

4.8 *(Continued)*

STRATEGY: EDIT AND REVISE YOUR PRESENTATION.

❶ Use punctuation marks for their correct purposes. A comma follows a prepositional phrase at the beginning of a sentence.

❷ Capitalize all proper nouns. Three lines under a letter means to capitalize.

❸ Check spelling with both an electronic spell checker and a dictionary.

❹ Use consistent verb tense. Use past tense for events in the past.

❺ Check for common agreement errors. Subjects and verbs must agree in person and number.

❻ Use correct sentence structure. Every sentence must have a subject and a verb.

The Incan Empire

The Inca created the largest empire ever seen in the Americas. Despite its size ❶ the Incan Empire was highly unified. Its government was diplomatic, bureaucratic, and socialist in nature, and its ruler was believed to be a god-king.

The Incan ruler was selected from one of 11 noble families, who were believed to have descended from ❷ inti, the sun god. Religion therefore supported the state, for worship of the sun god amounted to worship of the king. Thus, the empire was a theocracy, which is a state believed to be ruled directly by divine guidance.

The empire's expansion was largely the result of an important tradition: dead rulers retained the wealth they ❸ acumulated during their lives. To acquire wealth of their own, succeeding rulers often attempted to conquer new territories. One such ruler, Pachacuti, conquered all of Peru and many neighboring lands as well. By 1500, the Incan Empire extended 2,500 miles along the coast of western South America and included an estimated 16 million people.

Incan rulers used a number of strategies to achieve unification. They practiced diplomacy by allowing conquered peoples to retain their own customs as long as they were loyal to the state. The Inca imposed a single official language, Quechua, to be used throughout the empire. They founded schools to teach Incan ways. They ❹ built 14,000 miles of roads and bridges, which connected cities in conquered areas with Cuzco, the Incan capital.

The government's concern for the welfare of its citizens suggests an early form of socialism. Citizens worked for the state and, in turn, were taken care of. At public feasts, food and beer ❺ were was distributed as a reward for labor. In addition, the aged and disabled often received state support.

Among the many cultural achievements of the Inca were the development of an elaborate calendar system and the creation of beautiful works in gold and silver. Surprisingly, ❻ the Inca had no system of writing. They preserved their history and literature by means of an oral tradition.

Applying the Skill

CREATE A TWO-PAGE WRITTEN PRESENTATION on a topic of historical importance that interests you.

Primary Source Handbook

CONTENTS

Primary Source Handbook

from the **Rig Veda**

SETTING THE STAGE The Rig Veda is one of the sacred scriptures of the Aryans, who invaded India around 1500 B.C. The oldest of four Vedas, or books of wisdom, it contains 1,028 hymns to Aryan gods. The "Creation Hymn" speculates about how the world was created.

PRIMARY SOURCE

There was neither non-existence nor existence then; there was neither the realm of space nor the sky which is beyond. What stirred? Where? In whose protection? Was there water, bottomlessly deep?

There was neither death nor immortality then. There was no distinguishing sign of night nor of day. That one breathed, windless, by its own impulse. Other than that there was nothing beyond.

Darkness was hidden by darkness in the beginning; with no distinguishing sign, all this was water. The life force that was covered with emptiness, that one arose through the power of heat.

Desire came upon that one in the beginning; that was the first seed of mind. Poets seeking in their heart with wisdom found the bond of existence in non-existence.

Their cord was extended across. Was there below? Was there above? There were seed-placers; there were powers. There was impulse beneath; there was giving-forth above.

Who really knows? Who will here proclaim it? Whence was it produced? Whence is this creation? The gods came afterwards, with the creation of this universe. Who then knows whence it has arisen?

Whence this creation has arisen—perhaps it formed itself, or perhaps it did not—the one who looks down on it, in the highest heaven, only he knows— or perhaps he does not know.

▲ Indra, the Aryan god of war, seated on an elephant

DOCUMENT-BASED QUESTIONS

1. *What is the basic two-part structure of the "Creation Hymn"?*
2. *Who knows how the universe was created, according to the "Creation Hymn"?*
3. *What questions does the hymn raise about how the universe was created? What answers does it give?*
4. *What are you told about "that one" who is mentioned in the hymn?*
5. *What might the following words mean: "The gods came afterwards, with the creation of this universe"?*

from the King James Bible, Psalm 23

SETTING THE STAGE The Book of Psalms is the hymnal of ancient Israel. Most of the psalms were written to be used during worship in the temple. Many have been traditionally attributed to King David, who ruled over Israel around 1000 B.C. The Book of Psalms contains 150 songs on a variety of topics. Psalm 23 focuses on the relationship between God and the individual.

PRIMARY SOURCE

The Lord is my shepherd;
    I shall not want.
    He maketh me to lie down in green pastures;
    he leadeth me beside the still waters;

he restoreth my soul.
    He leadeth me in the paths of righteousness
    for his name's sake.

Yea, though I walk through the valley
    of the shadow of death,

I will fear no evil: for thou art with me;
    thy rod and thy staff they comfort me.

Thou preparest a table before me
    in the presence of mine enemies:

Thou anointest my head with oil; my cup runneth over.

Surely goodness and mercy shall follow me
    all the days of my life,

and I will dwell in the house of the Lord forever.

▲ David, the young shepherd, plays his pipe and a bell.

DOCUMENT-BASED QUESTIONS

1. *The rod and the staff are two tools of the shepherd. What does this suggest about the role of the Lord, "my shepherd"?*
2. *What kind of relationship does the person speaking have with the Lord?*
3. *In this psalm, the Lord is also presented as a generous host. What are some examples of this?*
4. *Why does the speaker expect goodness and mercy to follow him all the days of his life?*

from the Analects of Confucius

SETTING THE STAGE The *Analects (analect* means "a selection") is a short collection of about 500 sayings, dialogues, and brief stories, that was put together over a period of many years following Confucius' death. The *Analects* presents Confucius' teachings on how people should live to create an orderly and just society. Over time, Confucian thought became the basis for the Chinese system of government and remained a part of Chinese life into the 20th century.

PRIMARY SOURCE

The Master [Confucius] said: "Don't worry if people don't recognize your merits; worry that you may not recognize theirs." (1.16)

The Master said: "To study without thinking is futile [useless]. To think without studying is dangerous." (2.15)

Lord Ji Kang asked: "What should I do in order to make the people respectful, loyal, and zealous?" The Master said: "Approach them with dignity and they will be respectful. Be yourself a good son and a kind father, and they will be loyal. Raise the good and train the incompetent, and they will be zealous." (2.20)

The Master said: "Authority without generosity, ceremony without reverence, mourning without grief—these, I cannot bear to contemplate." (3.26)

The Master said: "Don't worry if you are without a position; worry lest you do not deserve a position. Do not worry if you are not famous; worry lest you do not deserve to be famous." (4.14)

The Master said: "Without ritual, courtesy is tiresome; without ritual, prudence is timid; without ritual, bravery is quarrelsome; without ritual, frankness is hurtful. When gentlemen treat their kin generously, common people are attracted to goodness; when old ties are not forgotten, common people are not fickle." (8.2)

Zingong asked: "Is there any single word that could guide one's entire life?" The master said: "Should it not be *reciprocity*? What you do not wish for yourself, do not do to others." (15.24)

▲ Confucius

DOCUMENT-BASED QUESTIONS

1. *What kinds of behavior does Confucius talk about in the* Analects?
2. *Do you think Confucius views human nature in an optimistic or a pessimistic way? Explain your opinion.*
3. *What does Confucius mean by* reciprocity?
4. *What kind of person does Confucius seem to be?*
5. *Are the teachings in the* Analects *surprising in any way? Explain.*
6. *Does Confucius seem more concerned with individual behavior or with behavior toward others?*

from History of the Peloponnesian War

by Thucydides

SETTING THE STAGE Thucydides was a Greek historian who wrote about the bitter 27-year-long Peloponnesian War between Athens and Sparta. As one of the ten military leaders of Athens, Thucydides was probably in attendance when Pericles, the greatest Athenian statesman of his time, gave a funeral oration. This speech honored the Athenian warriors who had been killed during the first year of the war. In the following excerpt, Pericles speaks of the distinctive qualities of Athens.

PRIMARY SOURCE

Our love of what is beautiful does not lead to extravagance; our love of the mind does not make us soft. We regard wealth as something to be properly used, rather than as something to boast about. As for poverty, no one need be ashamed to admit it: the real shame is in not taking practical measures to escape from it. Here each individual is interested not only in his own affairs but in the affairs of state as well: even those who are mostly occupied with their own business are extremely well-informed on general politics—this is a peculiarity of ours: we do not say that a man who takes no interest in politics is a man who minds his own business; we say that he has no business here at all. We Athenians, in our own persons, take our decisions on policy or submit them to proper discussions: for we do not think that there is an incompatibility between words and deeds; the worst thing is to rush into action before the consequences have been properly debated. And this is another point where we differ from other people. We are capable at the same time of taking risks and of estimating them beforehand. Others are brave out of ignorance; and, when they stop to think, they begin to fear. But the man who can most truly be accounted brave is he who best knows the meaning of what is sweet in life and of what is terrible, and then goes out undeterred to meet what is to come.

▲ Bust of Pericles; Roman copy of the Greek original

DOCUMENT-BASED QUESTIONS

1. *Why is it important to Pericles that all citizens participate in public life?*

2. *What seems to be the Athenians' attitude toward politics?*

3. *Why do the Athenians view public discussion as useful before taking action?*

4. *In what ways do Athenians lead a balanced life, according to Pericles?*

5. *What is Pericles's definition of courage?*

6. *According to Pericles, who has political power in Athens?*

from the Apology

by Plato

SETTING THE STAGE Socrates and Plato were two of the most important philosophers in history. Plato studied under Socrates in Athens. Though Socrates was popular with the young, some Athenians viewed him as a threat to Athenian traditions and ideals. In 399 B.C., a group of citizens came together to prosecute him, charging him with neglecting the gods of Athens and corrupting its youth. Socrates was brought to trial. A jury of 500 citizens heard the charges against him; then Socrates presented his own defense. By a majority of votes, Socrates was sentenced to death. Plato attended Socrates' trial and later based the *Apology* on his memory of what he had heard. In the following excerpt, Socrates addresses the jury.

PRIMARY SOURCE

Well, gentlemen, for the sake of a very small gain in time you are going to earn the reputation—and the blame from those who wish to disparage [belittle] our city—of having put Socrates to death, "that wise man"—because they will say I am wise even if I am not, these people who want to find fault with you. If you had waited just a little while, you would have had your way in the course of nature. You can see that I am well on in life and near to death. . . .

No doubt you think, gentlemen, that I have been condemned for lack of the arguments which I could have used if I had thought it right to leave nothing unsaid or undone to secure my acquittal. But that is very far from the truth. It is not a lack of arguments that has caused my condemnation, but a lack of effrontery [rude boldness] and impudence, and the fact that I have refused to address you in the way which would give you most pleasure. You would have liked to hear me weep and wail, doing and saying all sorts of things which I regard as unworthy of myself, but which you are used to hearing from other people. But I did not think then that I ought to stoop to servility [disgracefully humble behavior] because I was in danger, and I do not regret now the way in which I pleaded my case. I would much rather die as the result of this defense than live as the result of the other sort. In a court of law, just as in warfare, neither I nor any other ought to use his wits to escape death by any means. In battle it is often obvious that you could escape being killed by giving up your arms and throwing yourself upon the mercy of your pursuers, and in every kind of danger there are plenty of devices for avoiding death if you are unscrupulous enough to stick at nothing. But I suggest, gentlemen, that the difficulty is not so much to escape death; the real difficulty is to escape from doing wrong, which is far more fleet of foot.

▲ Roman fresco painting of Socrates

DOCUMENT-BASED QUESTIONS

1. Socrates says that if his accusers would have waited, they could have had what they wanted. What do they want?

2. Socrates insists that he would rather die than have to defend himself in a different way. What would be so wrong if Socrates had defended himself in a different way?

3. What does Socrates mean when he says that evil is more of a threat to people than death?

4. Why doesn't Socrates tell the jury what it wants to hear?

5. What values do you think are most important to Socrates?

from the Annals

by Tacitus

SETTING THE STAGE Tacitus was one of the greatest historians of ancient Rome. He lived in troubled times (A.D. 56–120) when plague and fire frequently ravaged Rome. The *Annals* deals with events from the death of Augustus in A.D. 14 to the death of Nero in A.D. 68. In the following excerpt, Tacitus tells about a terrible fire that swept through Rome in A.D. 64. The fire began near the Circus Maximus, an arena in which chariot races were held, and raged out of control for several days. At the time, Nero was emperor. Many Romans believed that Nero himself had set fire to the city in order to rebuild it according to his own designs.

PRIMARY SOURCE

Now started the most terrible and destructive fire which Rome had ever experienced. It began in the Circus, where it adjoins the . . . hills. Breaking out in shops selling inflammable goods, and fanned by the wind, the conflagration [large fire] instantly grew and swept the whole length of the Circus. There were no walled mansions or temples, or any other obstructions which could arrest it. First, the fire swept violently over the level spaces. Then it climbed the hills—but returned to ravage the lower ground again. It outstripped every countermeasure. The ancient city's narrow winding streets and irregular blocks encouraged its progress.

Terrified, shrieking women, helpless old and young, people intent on their own safety, people unselfishly supporting invalids or waiting for them, fugitives and lingerers alike—all heightened the confusion. When people looked back, menacing flames sprang up before them or outflanked them. When they escaped to a neighboring quarter, the fire followed—even districts believed remote proved to be involved. Finally, with no idea where or what to flee, they crowded on to the country roads, or lay in the fields. Some who had lost everything—even their food for the day—could have escaped, but preferred to die. So did others, who had failed to rescue their loved ones. Nobody dared fight the flames. Attempts to do so were prevented by menacing gangs. Torches, too, were openly thrown in, by men crying that they acted under orders. Perhaps they had received orders. Or they may just have wanted to plunder unhampered.

Nero was at Antium. He only returned to the city when the fire was approaching the mansion he had built to link the Gardens of Maecenas to the Palatine. The flames could not be prevented from overwhelming the whole of the Palatine, including his palace. Nevertheless, for the relief of the homeless, fugitive masses he threw open the Field of Mars, including Agrippa's public buildings, and even his own gardens. Nero also constructed emergency accommodation for the destitute [poor] multitude. Food was brought from Ostia and neighboring towns, and the price of corn was cut. . . . Yet these measures, for all their popular character, earned no gratitude. For a rumor had spread that, while the city was burning, Nero had gone to his private stage and, comparing modern calamities with ancient, had sung of the destruction of Troy. . . .

[P]eople believed that Nero was ambitious to found a new city to be called after himself.

DOCUMENT-BASED QUESTIONS

1. *Who might have ordered the menacing gangs to keep the fire burning?*

2. *What might have been Nero's motive if he indeed caused the fire to be started?*

3. *What actions of Nero suggest that he may not have ordered the burning of Rome?*

4. *What effect might a public calamity such as a fire or an earthquake have on political stability?*

5. *What different interpretations might the people of the time have given to such an event?*

6. *What might you have done to save yourself in the burning of Rome?*

from the Qur'an

SETTING THE STAGE In about A.D. 610, when the prophet Muhammad was 40 years old, he is said to have received his first visit from the archangel Gabriel. According to tradition, during this visit Gabriel revealed the Word of God to Muhammad. This revelation, or act of revealing, was the first of many experienced by Muhammad throughout his life. Together, these revelations formed the basis of the faith called Islam, which literally means "surrender to the will of Allah" (God). At first Muhammad reported God's revelations orally, and his followers memorized them and recited them in ritual prayers. Later the revelations were written down in a book called the Qur'an, which means "recitation."

PRIMARY SOURCE

The Exordium
In the Name of God, the Compassionate, the Merciful
Praise be to God, Lord of the Universe,
The Compassionate, the Merciful,
Sovereign of the Day of Judgment!
You alone we worship, and to You alone we turn for help.
Guide us to the straight path,
The path of those whom You have favored,
Not of those who have incurred Your wrath,
Nor of those who have gone astray.

▲ Qur'an with colored inscriptions and decorative medallions from the 12th or 13th century

Faith in God
In the Name of God, the Compassionate, the Merciful
All that is in the heavens and the earth gives glory to God. He is the Mighty, the Wise One.

It is He that has sovereignty over the heavens and the earth. He ordains life and death, and has power over all things.

He is the First and the Last, the Visible and the Unseen. He has knowledge of all things.

It was He who created the heavens and the earth in six days, and then mounted the throne. He knows all that goes into the earth and all that emerges from it, all that comes down from heaven and all that ascends to it. He is with you wherever you are. God is cognizant [aware] of all your actions.

He has sovereignty over the heavens and the earth. To God shall all things return. He causes the night to pass into the day, and causes the day to pass into the night. He has knowledge of the inmost thoughts of men.

Have faith in God and His Apostle and give in alms of that which He has made your inheritance; for whoever of you believes and gives in alms shall be richly rewarded.

And what cause have you not to believe in God, when the Apostle calls on you to have faith in your Lord, who has made a covenant [agreement] with you, if you are true believers?

DOCUMENT-BASED QUESTIONS

1. Exordium *means a beginning or introduction. What qualities of God are emphasized in "The Exordium"?*
2. *What might be the purpose of the first five paragraphs in "Faith in God"?*
3. *What are some of the qualities and actions that make a person righteous?*
4. *How do these excerpts support the idea of "God, the Compassionate, the Merciful"?*
5. *How might the words of the Qur'an be applied to governments or social groups?*
6. *What kind of rules or guidelines for behavior do you think a person should follow in life? How do these compare with those in the Qur'an?*

from **The Pillow Book**

by Sei Shōnagon

SETTING THE STAGE Sei Shōnagon served as a lady in waiting to Empress Sadako during the last decade of the 900s. During this period, Shōnagon kept a diary recording many aspects of court life. This diary was published as *The Pillow Book,* a collection of character sketches, lists, anecdotes, and poems that provides a vivid glimpse into the lives of the Japanese nobility during the Heian period (794–1185). During this period, the capital was moved to Heian, the present-day city of Kyoto, and a highly refined court society arose among the upper class. The book reveals Shōnagon as an intelligent woman who enjoyed conversing and matching wits with men as equals. Scholar and translator Arthur Waley has called the collection of observations and anecdotes of Heian court life "the most important document of the period that we possess."

PRIMARY SOURCE

from "Hateful Things"

One is in a hurry to leave, but one's visitor keeps chattering away. If it is someone of no importance, one can get rid of him by saying, "You must tell me all about it next time"; but, should it be the sort of visitor whose presence commands one's best behavior, the situation is hateful indeed. . . .

A man who has nothing in particular to recommend him discusses all sorts of subjects at random as though he knew everything. . . .

To envy others and to complain about one's own lot; to speak badly about people; to be inquisitive about the most trivial matters and to resent and abuse people for not telling one, or, if one does manage to worm out some facts, to inform everyone in the most detailed fashion as if one had known all from the beginning—oh, how hateful!

One is just about to be told some interesting piece of news when a baby starts crying.

A flight of crows circle about with loud caws.

An admirer has come on a clandestine [secret] visit, but a dog catches sight of him and starts barking. One feels like killing the beast. . . .

One has gone to bed and is about to doze off when a mosquito appears, announcing himself in a reedy voice. One can actually feel the wind made by his wings and, slight though it is, one finds it hateful in the extreme.

A carriage passes with a nasty, creaking noise. Annoying to think that the passengers may not even be aware of this! If I am traveling in someone's carriage and I hear it creaking, I dislike not only the noise but also the owner of the carriage.

One is in the middle of a story when someone butts in and tries to show that he is the only clever person in the room. Such a person is hateful, and so, indeed, is anyone, child or adult, who tries to push himself forward.

One is telling a story about old times when someone breaks in with a little detail that he happens to know, implying that one's own version is inaccurate—disgusting behavior! . . .

A newcomer pushes ahead of the other members in a group; with a knowing look, this person starts laying down the law and forcing advice upon everyone—most hateful.

DOCUMENT-BASED QUESTIONS

1. *What sort of listing does this excerpt provide?*
2. *How would you describe the author, based on the things she finds hateful?*
3. *Murasaki Shikibu, a contemporary, described Shōnagon as self-satisfied. Do you agree or disagree?*
4. *What might Shōnagon's list of hateful things suggest about Heian court life?*
5. *Which item in Shōnagon's list do you find most hateful?*

from the **Magna Carta**

SETTING THE STAGE King John ruled England from 1199 to 1216. When he raised taxes to finance his wars, his nobles revolted. On June 15, 1215, they forced King John to agree to the Magna Carta (Great Charter). This document, drawn up by English nobles and reluctantly approved by the king, guaranteed certain basic political rights.

PRIMARY SOURCE

1. In the first place [I, John,] have granted to God and by this for our present Charter have confirmed, for us and our heirs . . . , that the English church shall be free, and shall have its rights undiminished and its liberties unimpaired. . . . We have also granted to all the free men of our realm for ourselves and our heirs for ever, all the liberties written below, to have and hold, them and their heirs from us and our heirs. . . .

12. No scutage [tax] or aid is to be levied in our realm except by the common counsel of our realm, unless it is for the ransom of our person, the knighting of our eldest son or the first marriage of our eldest daughter; and for these only a reasonable aid is to be levied. Aids from the city of London are to be treated likewise.

13. And the city of London is to have all its ancient liberties and free customs both by land and water. Furthermore, we will and grant that all other cities, boroughs, towns and ports shall have all their liberties and free customs.

20. A free man shall not be amerced [fined] for a trivial offense; and for a serious offense he shall be amerced according to its gravity, saving his livelihood; and a merchant likewise, saving his merchandise; in the same way a villein [serf] shall be amerced saving his wainage [farming tools]; if they fall into our mercy. And none of the aforesaid amercements shall be imposed except by the testimony of reputable men of the neighborhood.

▲ King John signs the Magna Carta.

21. Earls and barons shall not be amerced [fined] except by their peers and only in accordance with the nature of the offense. . . .

38. Henceforth no bailiff shall put anyone on trial by his own unsupported allegation, without bringing credible witnesses to the charge.

39. No free man shall be taken or imprisoned or disseised [dispossessed] or outlawed or exiled or in any way ruined, nor will we go or send against him, except by the lawful judgment of his peers or by the law of the land.

40. To no one will we sell, to no one will we deny or delay right or justice.

DOCUMENT-BASED QUESTIONS

1. *According to Article 1, to whom does the king grant the rights enumerated in the Magna Carta?*

2. *What are some of the liberties granted by the king to his subjects?*

3. *What do Articles 38 and 39 suggest about the fairness of arrests and trials in King John's England?*

4. *What does Article 40 suggest about the king's use of power?*

5. *What impact might the Magna Carta have had on developing ideas of representative government?*

from the Popol Vuh

SETTING THE STAGE The selection you are about to read is an excerpt from an important Maya work—the *Popol Vuh.* The *Popol Vuh,* or "Book of the Community," contains the Maya story of the creation of the world. It was written not long after the Spanish conquest by an anonymous Maya noble, who may have been trying to keep the work from becoming lost as a result of his people's defeat.

PRIMARY SOURCE

This is the beginning of the Ancient Word, here in this place called Quiché. Here we shall inscribe, we shall implant the Ancient Word, the potential and source for everything done in the citadel of Quiché, in the nation of Quiché people. . . .

This is the account, here it is:
Now it still ripples, now it still murmurs, ripples, it still sighs, still hums, and it is empty under the sky.

Here follow the first words, the first eloquence:

There is not yet one person, one animal, bird, fish, crab, tree, rock, hollow, canyon, meadow, forest. Only the sky alone is there; the face of the earth is not clear. Only the sea alone is pooled under all the sky; there is nothing whatever gathered together. It is at rest; not a single thing stirs. It is held back, kept at rest under the sky.

Whatever there is that might be is simply not there: only the pooled water, only the calm sea, only it alone is pooled.

Whatever might be is simply not there: only murmurs, ripples, in the dark, in the night. Only the Maker, Modeler alone, Sovereign Plumed Serpent, the Bearers, Begetters are in the water, a glittering light. They are there, they are enclosed in quetzal feathers, in blue-green.

Thus the name, "Plumed Serpent." They are great knowers, great thinkers in their very being.

And of course there is the sky, and there is also the Heart of Sky. This is the name of the god, as it is spoken.

And then came his word, he came here to the Sovereign Plumed Serpent, here in the blackness, in the early dawn. He spoke with the Sovereign Plumed Serpent, and they talked, then they thought, then they worried. They agreed with each other, they joined their words, their thoughts. Then it was clear, then they reached accord in the light, and then humanity was clear, when they conceived the growth, the generation of trees, of bushes, and the growth of life, of humankind, in the blackness, in the early dawn, all because of the Heart of Sky, named Hurricane. Thunderbolt Hurricane comes first, the second is Newborn Thunderbolt, and the third is Sudden Thunderbolt. So there were three of them, as Heart of Sky, who came to the Sovereign Plumed Serpent, when the dawn of life was conceived: "How should the sowing be, and the dawning? Who is to be the provider, nurturer?"

"Let it be this way, think about this: this water should be removed, emptied out for the formation of the earth's own plate and platform, then should come the sowing, the dawning of the sky-earth. But there will be no high days and no bright praise for our work, our design, until the rise of the human work, the human design," they said.

DOCUMENT-BASED QUESTIONS

1. *What are some of the names of the gods in this excerpt?*

2. *What are the gods thinking and talking about in this excerpt?*

3. *How do the gods seem to feel about their creation?*

4. *Why do the gods seem to think that humans are necessary to their creation?*

5. *What does this seem to imply about the relationship between gods and humans?*

6. *What surprised you most as you read this excerpt from the* Popol Vuh?

from **The Prince**

by Niccolò Machiavelli

SETTING THE STAGE Niccolò Machiavelli wrote a political guidebook for Renaissance rulers titled *The Prince* (1513). Machiavelli wrote the book to encourage Lorenzo de' Medici to expand his power in Florence. The book argues for a practical, realistic view of human nature and politics.

PRIMARY SOURCE

A prince should make himself feared in such a way that if he does not gain love, he at any rate avoids hatred; for fear and the absence of hatred may well go together, and will be always attained by one who abstains from interfering with the property of his citizens and subjects or with their women. And when he is obliged to take the life of any one, let him do so when there is a proper justification and manifest reason for it; but above all he must abstain from taking the property of others, for men forget more easily the death of their father than the loss of their patrimony. Then also pretexts for seizing property are never wanting, and one who begins to live by rapine will always find some reason for taking the goods of others, whereas causes for taking life are rarer and more fleeting.

But when the prince is with his army and has a large number of soldiers under his control, then it is extremely necessary that he should not mind being thought cruel; for without this reputation he could not keep an army united or disposed to any duty. Among the noteworthy actions of Hannibal is numbered this, that although he had an enormous army, composed of men of all nations and fighting in foreign countries, there never arose any dissension [disagreement] either among them or against the prince, either in good fortune or in bad. This could not be due to anything but his inhuman cruelty, which together with his infinite other virtues, made him always venerated and terrible in the sight of his soldiers, and without it his other virtues would not have sufficed to produce that effect. Thoughtless writers admire on the one hand his actions, and on the other blame the principal cause of them.

And that it is true that his other virtues would not have sufficed may be seen from the case of Scipio [a famous Roman general and opponent of Hannibal] . . . , whose armies rebelled against him in Spain, which arose from nothing but his excessive kindness, which allowed more license to the soldiers than was consonant with military discipline.

▲ Niccolò Machiavelli

DOCUMENT-BASED QUESTIONS

1. *What does Machiavelli believe is the relationship for a ruler and his people between fear on the one hand and love and hatred on the other?*

2. *Why does Machiavelli say that a ruler must show himself to be capable of cruelty to his army?*

3. *What does Machiavelli cite Hannibal as an example of? Explain.*

4. *How was the Roman general Scipio different from Hannibal?*

5. *Why does Machiavelli consider cruelty a virtue in a leader?*

6. *Are Machiavelli's thoughts on rulers still relevant today? Why or why not?*

from **Utopia**

by Sir Thomas More

SETTING THE STAGE Sir Thomas More's *Utopia* is a work of fiction devoted to the exploration of ideas. In 1516, when *Utopia* was published, English society was marked by great extremes in wealth, education, and status. In his book, More criticizes the evils of poverty and wealth that he sees in England. More describes a faraway land called Utopia that does not have the inequalities and injustices of England. Utopian society is governed according to principles of reason. As a result, everyone has work and everyone is educated. Since private property has been abolished there, the citizens have no need for money. Instead, all that is produced is shared equally.

PRIMARY SOURCE

Agriculture is the one pursuit which is common to all, both men and women, without exception. They are all instructed in it from childhood, partly by principles taught in school, partly by field trips to the farms closer to the city as if for recreation. Here they do not merely look on, but, as opportunity arises for bodily exercise, they do the actual work.

Besides agriculture (which is, as I said, common to all), each is taught one particular craft as his own. This is generally either wool-working or linen-making or masonry or metal-working or carpentry. There is no other pursuit which occupies any number worth mentioning. As for clothes, these are of one and the same pattern throughout the island and down the centuries, though there is a distinction between the sexes and between the single and the married. The garments are comely [pleasing] to the eye, convenient for bodily movement, and fit for wear in heat and cold. Each family, I say, does its own tailoring.

Of the other crafts, one is learned by each person, and not the men only, but the women too. The latter as the [women] have the lighter occupations and generally work wool and flax. To the men are committed the remaining more laborious crafts. For the most part, each is brought up in his father's craft, for which most have a natural inclination. But if anyone is attracted to another occupation, he is transferred by adoption to a family pursuing that craft for which he has a liking. Care is taken not only by his father but by the authorities, too, that he will be assigned to a [serious] and honorable householder. Moreover, if anyone after being thoroughly taught one craft desires another also, the same permission is given. Having acquired both, he practices his choice unless the city has more need of the one than of the other.

▲ Title page of a French edition of *Utopia*

Primary Source Handbook

DOCUMENT-BASED QUESTIONS

1. *How many occupations does each Utopian have? What are they?*

2. *Why might Utopians all wear clothes cut from the same pattern?*

3. *Most Utopian men learn their father's craft, and most workers follow the same schedules. What are the benefits and drawbacks of such a system?*

4. *What might be some of the advantages of living in Utopia?*

5. *What might be some of the disadvantages of living in Utopia?*

6. *What present-day societies do you think are most like Utopia? Explain.*

from **The Federalist, "Number 51"**

by James Madison

SETTING THE STAGE James Madison wrote 29 of the essays in *The Federalist* papers to argue in favor of ratifying the Constitution of the United States. In *The Federalist, "Number 51,"* Madison explains how the government set up by the Constitution will protect the rights of the people by weakening the power of any interest, or group, to dominate the government.

PRIMARY SOURCE

It is of great importance in a republic not only to guard against the oppression of its rulers, but to guard one part of the society against the injustice of the other part. Different interests necessarily exist in different classes of citizens. If a majority be united by a common interest, the rights of the minority will be insecure. There are but two methods of providing against this evil: the one by creating a will in the community independent of the majority—that is, of the society itself; the other, by comprehending in the society so many separate descriptions of citizens as will render an unjust combination of a majority of the whole very improbable, if not impracticable. . . .

Whilst all authority in it will be derived from and dependent on the society, the society itself will be broken into so many parts, interests and classes of citizens, that the rights of individuals, or of the minority, will be in little danger from interested combinations of the majority. In a free government the security for civil rights must be the same as that for religious rights. It consists in the one case in the multiplicity of interests, and in the other in the multiplicity of sects. . . .

In the extended republic of the United States, and among the great variety of interests, parties, and sects which it embraces, a coalition of a majority of the whole society could seldom take place on any other principles than those of justice and the general good. . . .

It is no less certain that it is important . . . that the larger the society, provided it lie within a practicable sphere, the more duly capable it will be of self-government. And happily for the republican cause, the practicable sphere may be carried to a very great extent by a judicious modification and mixture of the *federal principle.*

▲ James Madison

DOCUMENT-BASED QUESTIONS

1. *Madison argues that society must be protected from abuses by rulers and by whom else?*
2. *What two methods does Madison suggest a society can use to protect minority rights?*
3. *Does Madison regard special interests in a society as a good thing or a bad? Explain.*

4. *Why does Madison believe that a large republic is likely to protect justice?*
5. *Why does Madison believe that a society broken into many parts will not endanger minority rights?*
6. *Does Madison think most people work for the common good or their own interests? Explain.*

from **A Vindication of the Rights of Woman**

by Mary Wollstonecraft

SETTING THE STAGE Although a number of 18th-century British writers discussed the role of women in society, none became as celebrated for her feminist views as Mary Wollstonecraft (1759–1797). Early in her life, Wollstonecraft learned the value of independence and became openly critical of a society that treated females as inferior creatures who were socially, financially, and legally dependent on men. In 1792, Wollstonecraft published *A Vindication of the Rights of Woman,* in which she called for an end to the prevailing injustices against females. Although her opinions on women's rights may seem conservative by modern standards, they were radical in 18th-century Britain.

PRIMARY SOURCE

My own sex, I hope, will excuse me if I treat them like rational creatures, instead of flattering their *fascinating* graces, and viewing them as if they were in a state of perpetual childhood, unable to stand alone. I earnestly wish to point out in what true dignity and human happiness consists—I wish to persuade women to endeavor to acquire strength, both of mind and body, and to convince them that the soft phrases, susceptibility of heart, delicacy of sentiment, and refinement of taste, are almost synonymous with epithets [terms] of weakness, and that those beings who are only the objects of pity and that kind of love, which has been termed its sister, will soon become objects of contempt. . . .

The education of women has, of late, been more attended to than formerly; yet they are still reckoned a frivolous sex, and ridiculed or pitied by the writers who endeavor by satire or instruction to improve them. It is acknowledged that they spend many of the first years of their lives in acquiring a smattering of accomplishments; meanwhile strength of body and mind are sacrificed to libertine [indecent] notions of beauty, to the desire of establishing themselves—the only way women can rise in the world—by marriage. And this desire making mere animals of them, when they marry they act as such children may be expected to act: they dress, they paint, and nickname God's creatures. Surely these weak beings are only fit for a seraglio [harem]! Can they be expected to govern a family with judgment, or take care of the poor babes whom they bring into the world?

▲ Mary Wollstonecraft

DOCUMENT-BASED QUESTIONS

1. *What is the subject and purpose of Wollstonecraft's essay?*

2. *According to Wollstonecraft, why isn't the system of marriage beneficial to women?*

3. *Would you like to hear Wollstonecraft speak on women's rights? Why or why not?*

4. *How does a woman's lack of education affect her husband and children?*

5. *Do you think that Wollstonecraft believes in the complete equality of men and women?*

6. *In your opinion, what social issues would concern Wollstonecraft today? Would she still feel a need to defend women's rights?*

from the Memoirs of Madame Vigée-Lebrun

by Élisabeth Vigée-Lebrun

SETTING THE STAGE Élisabeth Vigée-Lebrun was a gifted artist who painted portraits of the French nobility. In her memoirs she recalls events of her own life amidst the turmoil of the French Revolution, which began in 1789. She frequently painted Marie Antoinette, queen of France. Vigée-Lebrun became frightened by the increasingly aggressive harassment of the nobility by the revolutionaries and resolved to leave France. She and her daughter escaped at night by stagecoach.

PRIMARY SOURCE

I had my carriage loaded, and my passport ready, so that I might leave next day with my daughter and her governess, when a crowd of national guardsmen burst into my room with their muskets. Most of them were drunk and shabby, and had terrible faces. A few of them came up to me and told me in the coarsest language that I must not go, but that I must remain. I answered that since everybody had been called upon to enjoy his liberty, I intended to make use of mine. They would barely listen to me, and kept on repeating, "You will not go, citizeness; you will not go!" Finally they went away. I was plunged into a state of cruel anxiety when I saw two of them return. But they did not frighten me, although they belonged to the gang, so quickly did I recognize that they wished me no harm. "Madame," said one of them, "we are your neighbors, and we have come to advise you to leave, and as soon as possible. You cannot live here; you are changed so much that we feel sorry for you. But do not go in your carriage: go in the stage-coach; it is much safer." . . .

Opposite me in the coach was a very filthy man, who stunk like the plague, and told me quite simply that he had stolen watches and other things. . . . Not satisfied with relating his fine exploits to us, the thief talked incessantly of stringing up such and such people on lamp-posts, naming a number of my own acquaintances. My daughter thought this man very wicked. He frightened her, and this gave me the courage to say, "I beg you, sir, not to talk of killing before this child."

▲ *Self-Portrait in a Straw Hat* by Élisabeth Vigée-Lebrun

DOCUMENT-BASED QUESTIONS

1. *What does Vigée-Lebrun do to escape the Reign of Terror in France?*

2. *What details does Vigée-Lebrun use to create a vivid picture of the national guardsmen? What impression of them does the author convey?*

3. *What concerns does Vigée-Lebrun reveal in her account of her escape from Paris?*

4. *As you read, how did you feel about the situation Vigée-Lebrun finds herself in?*

5. *What seem to be Vigée-Lebrun's feelings about the French Revolution?*

6. *Do you find Vigée-Lebrun a sympathetic person? Why or why not?*

from the Report on Child Labor

by the Sadler Committee

SETTING THE STAGE In 1831 a parliamentary committee headed by Michael Thomas Sadler investigated child labor in British factories. The following testimony by Elizabeth Bentley, who worked as a child in a textile mill, is drawn from the records of the Sadler Committee. Michael Thomas Sadler is asking the questions.

PRIMARY SOURCE

What age are you?—Twenty-three. . . .

What time did you begin to work at a factory?—When I was six years old. . . .

What kind of mill is it?—Flax mill. . . .

What was your business in that mill?—I was a little doffer [cleaner of textile machines].

What were your hours of labor in that mill?—From 5 in the morning till 9 at night, when they were thronged [busy].

For how long a time together have you worked that excessive length of time?—For about half a year.

What were your usual hours of labor when you were not so thronged?—From 6 in the morning till 7 at night.

What time was allowed for your meals?—Forty minutes at noon.

Had you any time to get your breakfast or drinking?—No, we got it as we could.

And when your work was bad, you had hardly any time to eat it at all?—No; we were obliged to leave it or take it home, and when we did not take it, the overlooker [foreman] took it, and gave it to his pigs.

Do you consider doffing a laborious employment?—Yes.

Explain what it is you had to do.—When the frames are full, they have to stop the frames, and take the flyers off, and take the full bobbins off, and carry them to the roller; and then put empty ones on, and set the frames on again.

Does that keep you constantly on your feet?—Yes, there are so many frames and they run so quick.

Your labor is very excessive?—Yes; you have not time for any thing.

Suppose you flagged a little, or were too late, what would they do?—Strap [beat] us.

Are they in the habit of strapping those who are last in doffing?—Yes.

Constantly?—Yes.

Girls as well as boys?—Yes.

Have you ever been strapped?—Yes.

Severely?—Yes.

Could you eat your food well in that factory?—No, indeed, I had not much to eat, and the little I had I could not eat it, my appetite was so poor, and being covered with dust; and it was no use to take it home, I could not eat it, and the overlooker took it, and gave it to the pigs. . .

DOCUMENT-BASED QUESTIONS

1. *From the employers' and parents' point of view, what might have been some of the reasons for child labor?*

2. *What were some of the difficult working conditions faced by children in the factories?*

3. *How many hours per day did Elizabeth Bentley work when the factory was really busy, and when it was not so busy?*

4. *Do children work this hard today in factories in this country? What about in other parts of the world?*

from the Second Inaugural Address
by Abraham Lincoln

SETTING THE STAGE President Lincoln delivered his Second Inaugural Address on March 4, 1865, just before the end of the American Civil War. In this excerpt, he recalls the major cause of the war and vows to fight for the restoration of peace and unity.

PRIMARY SOURCE

One-eighth of the whole population were colored slaves. . . . These slaves constituted a peculiar and powerful interest. All knew that this interest was somehow the cause of the war. To strengthen, perpetuate, and extend this interest was the object for which the insurgents [rebels] would rend the Union even by war, while the Government claimed no right to do more than to restrict the territorial enlargement of it. Neither party expected for the war the magnitude or the duration which it has already attained. Neither anticipated that the cause of the conflict might cease with or even before the conflict itself should cease. Each looked for an easier triumph, and a result less fundamental and astounding. Both read the same Bible and pray to the same God, and each invokes His aid against the other. . . . Fondly do we hope, fervently do we pray, that this mighty scourge of war may speedily pass away. Yet, if God wills that it continue until all the wealth piled by the bondsman's [slave's] two hundred and fifty years of unrequited [unpaid for] toil shall be sunk, and until every drop of blood drawn with the lash shall be paid by another drawn with the sword, as was said three thousand years ago, so still it must be said "the judgments of the Lord are true and righteous altogether."

With malice toward none, with charity for all, with firmness in the right as God gives us to see the right, let us strive on to finish the work we are in, to bind up the nation's wounds, to care for him who shall have borne the battle and for his widow and his orphan, to do all which may achieve and cherish a just and lasting peace among ourselves and with all nations.

▲ Abraham Lincoln

DOCUMENT-BASED QUESTIONS

1. According to Lincoln's Second Inaugural Address, why did the Confederacy go to war?

2. Why might Southerners have feared that prohibiting slavery in new territories would threaten slavery where it already existed?

3. Why do you think Lincoln believes it would be wiser for Americans not to blame one another?

4. In 1865, if the South had asked to rejoin the Union without ending slavery, do you think Lincoln would have agreed?

5. Reread the last sentence of Lincoln's speech. Do you think Americans are still working to reach the goals set by Lincoln?

from The Natural Rights of Civilized Women
by Elizabeth Cady Stanton

SETTING THE STAGE Elizabeth Cady Stanton (1815–1902) led the fight for women's equality. Her first memory was the birth of a sister when she was four. So many people said, "What a pity it is she's a girl!" that Stanton felt sorry for the new baby. She later wrote, "I did not understand at that time that girls were considered an inferior order of beings." Stanton was determined to prove that girls were just as important as boys. The following excerpt comes from an address that Stanton gave to the New York state legislature in 1860 on a bill for woman suffrage that was before the state senate.

PRIMARY SOURCE

Now do not think, gentlemen, we wish you to do a great many troublesome things for us. We do not ask our legislators to spend a whole session in fixing up a code of laws to satisfy a class of most unreasonable women. We ask no more than the poor devils in the Scripture asked, "Let us alone." In mercy, let us take care of ourselves, our property, our children, and our homes. True, we are not so strong, so wise, so crafty as you are, but if any kind friend leaves us a little money, or we can by great industry earn fifty cents a day, we would rather buy bread and clothes for our children than cigars and champagne for our legal protectors.

There has been a great deal written and said about protection. We as a class are tired of one kind of protection, that which leaves us everything to do, to dare, and to suffer, and strips us of all means for its accomplishment. We would not tax man to take care of us. No, the Great Father has endowed all His creatures with necessary powers for self-support, self-defense, and protection. We do not ask man to represent us, it is hard enough in times like these to represent himself. So long as the mass of men spend most of their time on the fence, not knowing which way to jump, they are surely in no condition to tell us where we had better stand. In pity for man, we would no longer hang like a millstone round his neck. Undo what man did for us in the Dark Ages and strike out all special legislation for us; strike the words "white male" from all your constitutions and then, with fair sailing, let us sink or swim, live or die, survive or perish together.

▲ Elizabeth Cady Stanton

DOCUMENT-BASED QUESTIONS

1. What basic right is Stanton asking for?
2. What sorts of special considerations and laws does Stanton think women are entitled to?
3. What group does Stanton think benefits unfairly from current laws and legislation?
4. According to Stanton, do women want special protection under the law? Explain.
5. What does Stanton mean by the "Dark Ages"?
6. What social issues do you think Stanton would address in today's world?

...urteen Points

The...drow Wilson

...ING THE STAGE Nine months after the United States entered World War I, President ...ilson delivered to Congress a statement of war aims. This statement became known as the "Fourteen Points." In the speech, Wilson set forth 14 proposals for reducing the risk of war in the future. Numbers have been inserted to help identify the main points, as well as those omitted.

PRIMARY SOURCE

All the peoples of the world are in effect partners . . . , and for our own part we see very clearly that unless justice be done to others it will not be done to us. The program of the world's peace, therefore, is our program; and that program, . . . as we see it, is this:

[1] Open covenants [agreements] of peace, openly arrived at, after which there shall be no private international understandings of any kind but diplomacy shall proceed frankly and in the public view.

[2] Absolute freedom of navigation upon the seas . . . in peace and war. . . .

[3] The removal, so far as possible, of all economic barriers and the establishment of an equality of trade conditions among all the nations. . . .

[4] Adequate guarantees given and taken that national armaments [weapons and war supplies] will be reduced. . . .

[5] A free, open-minded, and absolutely impartial adjustment of all colonial claims, based upon . . . the principle that . . . the interests of the populations concerned must have equal weight with the . . . claims of the government whose title is to be determined.

[6–13: These eight points deal with specific boundary changes.]

[14] A general association of nations must be formed under specific covenants for the purpose of affording mutual guarantees of political independence and territorial integrity to great and small states alike.

▲ British Prime Minister David Lloyd George, French Premier Georges Clemenceau, and President Woodrow Wilson walk in Paris during negotiations for the Treaty of Versailles.

DOCUMENT-BASED QUESTIONS

1. *Why should diplomacy avoid private dealings and proceed in public view?*

2. *How might agreements arrived at in public prevent another world war?*

3. *How might equality of trade be important to keeping the peace?*

4. *What must nations join together to guarantee?*

5. *What might be unusual about a leader such as Wilson calling for an impartial adjustment of colonial claims?*

6. *How successful do you think Wilson's ideas have been in the 20th and 21st centuries?*

from **Night**

by Elie Wiesel

SETTING THE STAGE Elie Wiesel (EHL•ee vee•ZEHL) was a Jewish boy from Romania. In 1944, when Wiesel was just 15, the Nazis sent the Jews of his town to Auschwitz in Poland. Wiesel's mother and one of his sisters died there. Wiesel and his father were sent to the Buchenwald concentration camp, where Wiesel's father died just a few months before the camp was liberated. In this excerpt from *Night,* Wiesel describes the terror he experienced on his way to Auschwitz.

PRIMARY SOURCE

The train stopped at Kaschau, a little town on the Czechoslovak frontier. We realized then that we were not going to stay in Hungary. Our eyes were opened, but too late.

The door of the car slid open. A German officer, accompanied by a Hungarian lieutenant-interpreter, came up and introduced himself.

"From this moment, you come under the authority of the German army. Those of you who still have gold, silver, or watches in your possession must give them up now. Anyone who is later found to have kept anything will be shot on the spot. Secondly, anyone who feels ill may go to the hospital car. That's all."

The Hungarian lieutenant went among us with a basket and collected the last possessions from those who no longer wished to taste the bitterness of terror. "There are eighty of you in this wagon," added the German officer. "If anyone is missing, you'll all be shot, like dogs. . . ."

They disappeared. The doors were closed. We were caught in a trap, right up to our necks. The doors were nailed up; the way back was finally cut off. The world was a cattle wagon hermetically [completely] sealed.

▲ Elie Wiesel

DOCUMENT-BASED QUESTIONS

1. *What does the narrator mean when he says, "Our eyes were opened, but too late"?*

2. *What might be the effect on people of uprooting them from their homes?*

3. *What does the narrator mean when he describes "those who no longer wished to taste the bitterness of terror"?*

4. *What might be the effect of sealing people up in railway cars?*

5. *This excerpt is from a book called* Night. *What might be the meaning of the title?*

6. *What elements in this excerpt show the Germans treating the Jews as less than human?*

from Farewell to Manzanar

by Jeanne Wakatsuki Houston and James D. Houston

SETTING THE STAGE When Japan's attack on Pearl Harbor drew the United States into World War II, people on the west coast of the United States began to fear that those of Japanese descent living in their communities might secretly aid Japan. Despite the fact that there was no evidence of Japanese-American espionage or sabotage, President Franklin D. Roosevelt signed an order that cleared the way for the removal of Japanese people from their homes. Jeanne Wakatsuki was seven years old when her family was relocated. As this excerpt from her memoir opens, her family is living in Los Angeles after having been forced to move twice by the government, and is about to be moved a third time to Manzanar.

PRIMARY SOURCE

The American Friends Service helped us find a small house in Boyle Heights, another minority ghetto, in downtown Los Angeles, now inhabited briefly by a few hundred Terminal Island refugees. Executive Order 9066 had been signed by President Roosevelt, giving the War Department authority to define military areas in the western states and to exclude from them anyone who might threaten the war effort. There was a lot of talk about internment, or moving inland, or something like that in store for all Japanese Americans. I remember my brothers sitting around the table talking very intently about what we were going to do, how we would keep the family together. They had seen how quickly Papa was removed, and they knew now that he would not be back for quite a while. Just before leaving Terminal Island, Mama had received her first letter, from Bismarck, North Dakota. He had been imprisoned at Fort Lincoln, in an all-male camp for enemy aliens. . . .

The name Manzanar meant nothing to us when we left Boyle Heights. We didn't know where it was or what it was. We went because the government ordered us to. And in the case of my older brothers and sisters, we went with a certain amount of relief. They had all heard stories of Japanese homes being attacked, of beatings in the streets of California towns. . . .

The simple truth is the camp was no more ready for us when we got there than we were ready for it. We had only the dimmest ideas of what to expect. Most of the families, like us, had moved out from southern California with as much luggage as each person could carry. Some old men left Los Angeles wearing Hawaiian shirts and Panama hats and stepped off the bus at an altitude of 4,000 feet, with nothing available but sagebrush and tarpaper to stop the April winds pouring down off the back side of the Sierras.

▲ Camp boundary sign in California, 1943

DOCUMENT-BASED QUESTIONS

1. *In the foreword to* Farewell to Manzanar, *Jeanne Wakatsuki Houston says, "It has taken me 25 years to reach the point where I could talk openly about Manzanar." Why do you think it took so long for her to be able to talk about her experience?*

2. *Do you think that a forced internment, like that experienced by the Wakatsuki family, could happen in America today? Why or why not?*

3. *What is your impression of the Wakatsuki family?*

4. *How do you think you would have reacted if you had been brought to Manzanar?*

from the **Inaugural Address**

by Nelson Mandela

SETTING THE STAGE The son of a tribal chief, Nelson Mandela became a leader in the African National Congress (ANC), a political party that called for racial equality. In 1964, Mandela, who had advocated acts of sabotage against the government, was sentenced to life in prison, where he became an international symbol of South Africa's struggle against apartheid. After his release, Mandela agreed to work peacefully for racial justice. In 1993, Mandela was awarded a Nobel Prize, and the next year he became president of South Africa. The selection below comes from a speech he gave in 1994 when he was inaugurated as president of South Africa.

PRIMARY SOURCE

We are both humbled and elevated by the honor and privilege that you, the people of South Africa, have bestowed on us, as the first President of a united, democratic, nonracial, and nonsexist South Africa, to lead our country out of the valley of darkness.

We understand it still that there is no easy road to freedom.

We know it well that none of us acting alone can achieve success.

We must therefore act together as a united people, for national reconciliation, for nation building, for the birth of a new world.

Let there be justice for all.

Let there be peace for all.

Let there be work, bread, water and salt for all.

Let each know that for each the body, the mind, and the soul have been freed to fulfill themselves.

Never, never and never again shall it be that this beautiful land will again experience the oppression of one by another and suffer the indignity of being the skunk of the world.

Let freedom reign.

The sun shall never set on so glorious a human achievement!

God bless Africa!

▲ Nelson Mandela

DOCUMENT-BASED QUESTIONS

1. *What challenges do you think Mandela expects as the first black president of South Africa?*

2. *Do you think Mandela was speaking only to the audience gathered before him? Explain.*

3. *What does Mandela mean when he says that South Africa must never again be thought of as the "skunk of the world"?*

4. *What are some examples of Mandela's use of repetition in his speech?*

from **I Have a Dream**

by Martin Luther King, Jr.

SETTING THE STAGE On August 28, 1963, Martin Luther King, Jr., gave his most famous speech at the March on Washington. In it, he shared his dream of equality for all.

PRIMARY SOURCE

I say to you today, my friends, that even though we face the difficulties of today and tomorrow, I still have a dream. It is a dream deeply rooted in the American dream.

I have a dream that one day this nation will rise up and live out the true meaning of its creed—we hold these truths to be self-evident that all men are created equal.

I have a dream that my four little children will one day live in a nation where they will not be judged by the color of their skin but by the content of their character.

I have a dream today!

This is our hope. This is the faith that I will go back to the South with. . . . With this faith we will be able to work together, to pray together, to struggle together, to go to jail together, to stand up for freedom together, knowing that we will be free one day. This will be the day, this will be the day when all of God's children will be able to sing with new meaning "My country 'tis of thee, sweet land of liberty, of thee I sing. Land where my fathers died, land of the Pilgrim's pride, from every mountainside, let freedom ring!" And if America is to be a great nation, this must become true.

And when this happens, when we allow freedom to ring, when we let it ring from every tenement and every hamlet, from every state and every city, we will be able to speed up that day when all of God's children, black men and white men, Jews and Gentiles, Protestants and Catholics, will be able to join hands and sing in the words of the old Negro spiritual, "Free at last, free at last. Thank God Almighty, we are free at last."

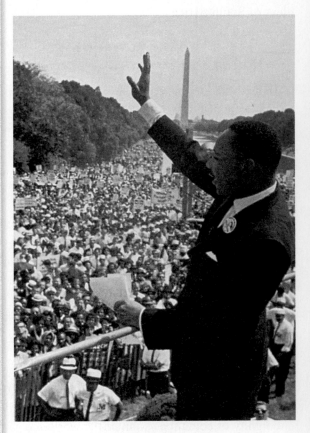

▲ Martin Luther King, Jr., Washington, D.C., August 28, 1963

DOCUMENT-BASED QUESTIONS

1. *How do civil rights fit into the American dream?*
2. *Why do you think civil rights workers were willing to go to jail?*
3. *Why does King declare that the United States is not living up to its creed?*
4. *What does King say must happen before America can be considered a truly great nation?*

An Open Letter

by Cesar Chavez

SETTING THE STAGE In 1969, Cesar Chavez wrote a letter in which he denied accusations that he had used violence to win decent wages and better benefits for farm workers.

Today . . . we remember the life and sacrifice of Martin Luther King, Jr., who gave himself totally to the nonviolent struggle for peace and justice. In his letter from Birmingham jail, Dr. King describes better than I could our hopes for the strike and boycott: "Injustice must be exposed, with all the tension its exposure creates, to the light of human conscience and the air of public opinion before it can be cured." For our part, I admit that we have seized upon every tactic and strategy consistent with the morality of our cause to expose that injustice and thus to heighten the sensitivity of the American conscience so that farmworkers will have without bloodshed their own union and the dignity of bargaining with the agribusiness [large-scale farming] employers. . . .

Our strikers here in Delano and those who represent us throughout the world are well trained for this struggle. . . . They have been taught not to lie down and die or to flee in shame, but to resist with every ounce of human endurance and spirit. To resist not with retaliation in kind but to overcome with love and compassion, with ingenuity and creativity, with hard work and longer hours, with stamina and patient tenacity, with truth and public appeal, with friends and allies, with mobility and discipline, with politics and law, and with prayer and fasting. They were not trained in a month or even a year; after all, this new harvest season will mark our fourth full year of strike and even now we continue to plan and prepare for the years to come. . . .

We shall overcome and change if not by retaliation or bloodshed but by a determined nonviolent struggle carried on by those masses of farmworkers who intend to be free and human.

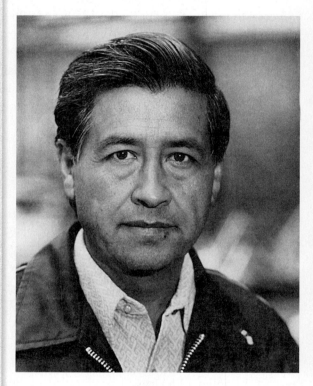

▲ Cesar Chavez, 1974

DOCUMENT-BASED QUESTIONS

1. *Why do you think farm workers wanted to organize a union?*

2. *Why might it be necessary to train for nonviolent protest?*

3. *Why do you think Chavez refers to Martin Luther King, Jr., in his speech?*

4. *In what ways were the problems faced by King and Chavez similar and different?*

Economics Handbook

NOTE: *Boldfaced words are terms that appear in this handbook.*

BOYCOTT

A refusal to have economic dealings with a person, a business, an organization, or a country.

The purpose of a boycott is to show disapproval of particular actions or to force changes in those actions. A boycott often involves an economic act, such as refusing to buy a company's goods or services.

Civil rights campaigners in the United States used boycotts to great effect during the 1950s and 1960s. For example, African Americans in Montgomery, Alabama, organized a bus boycott in 1955 to fight segregation on city buses. The boycotters kept many buses nearly empty for 381 days. The boycott ended when the Supreme Court outlawed bus segregation.

During the 1960s, groups in many countries launched boycotts against South African businesses to protest the policy of apartheid, or complete separation of the races. In the picture above, demonstrators march to protest a tour of Great Britain by the South African rugby team in 1969. Worldwide boycotts helped to bring about the end of apartheid in the 1990s. For information on the dismantling of the apartheid system, read page 610.

In many countries, labor unions have used boycotts to win concessions for their members. Consumer groups, too, have organized boycotts to win changes in business practices.

BUSINESS CYCLE

A pattern of increases and decreases in economic activity.

A business cycle generally consists of four distinct phases—expansion, peak, contraction, and trough—as shown in the graph in the next column. An expansion is marked by increased business

activity. The **unemployment rate** falls, businesses produce more, and consumers buy more goods and services. A peak is a transition period in which expansion slows. A contraction, or **recession,** occurs when business activity decreases. The unemployment rate rises, while both production and consumer spending fall. A deep and long-lasting contraction is called a **depression.** Business activity reaches its lowest point during a trough. After time, business activity starts to increase and a new cycle begins.

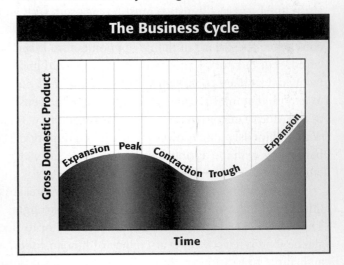

CAPITALISM

An economic system in which there is private ownership of natural resources and capital goods.

The basic idea of capitalism is that producers are driven by the desire to make a profit, the money left over after costs have been subtracted from revenues. This desire for profit motivates producers to provide consumers with the goods and services they desire. Prices and wages are determined by **supply and demand.**

Along with the opportunity to earn a profit there is a risk. Businesses tend to fail if they do not produce goods people want at prices they are willing to pay. Because anyone is free to start a business or enterprise, a capitalist system is also known as a **free enterprise** system.

Capitalism contrasts with **socialism,** an economic system in which the government owns and controls capital and sets prices and production levels. Critics of the capitalist system argue that it allows decisions that ought to be made democratically to be made instead by powerful business owners and that it allows too-great disparities in wealth and well-being between the poor and the rich. For a comparison of capitalism and socialism, read the Analyzing Key Concepts on page 303.

COMMUNISM

An economic system based on one-party rule, government ownership of the means of production, and decision making by centralized authorities.

Under communism there is little or no private ownership of property and little or no political freedom. Government planners make economic decisions, such as which and how many goods and services should be produced. Individuals have little say in a communist economy. Such a system, Communists believe, would end inequality. For more information on the ideas on which communism is based, read Chapter 9, Section 4.

During the 20th century, most communist economies failed to achieve their goals. Economic decisions frequently were made to benefit only Communist Party officials. Also, government economic planning was inefficient, often creating shortages of goods. Those goods that were available were often of poor quality.

People became discontented with the lack of prosperity and political freedom and began to call for change. These demands led in the late 1980s and early 1990s to the collapse of communist governments in the Soviet Union and Eastern Europe.

Even governments that clung to communism—China, for example—have introduced elements of **free enterprise.** The picture above shows people lining up at automated teller machines (ATMs) in Shanghai, one of China's largest free-enterprise zones. (For information on free enterprise in Shanghai, read the Connect to Today on page 372.) While China has allowed greater

economic freedom for its citizens, it has not given them more political freedom.

CONSUMER PRICE INDEX (CPI)

A measure of the change in cost of the goods and services most commonly bought by consumers. In some countries, the CPI is called the retail price index.

The CPI is calculated by surveying the prices of a "basket" of goods and services bought by typical consumers. In Germany, the CPI follows the prices of more than 750 goods and services bought by average consumers on a regular basis. Items on which consumers spend a good deal of their income, such as food, are given more weight in the CPI than items on which consumers spend less.

Price changes are calculated by comparing current prices with prices at a set time in the past. In 2003, for example, the German CPI used the year 2000 as this base. Prices for this year are given a base value of 100. The prices for subsequent years are expressed as percentages of the base. Therefore, a CPI of 103 means that prices have risen by 3 percent since 2000. The graph below illustrates changes in the German CPI from 1992 to 2002.

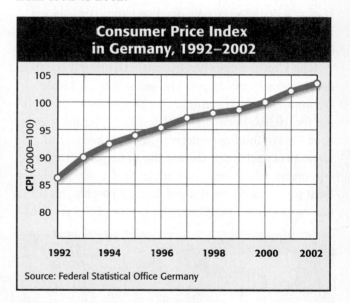

Consumer Price Index in Germany, 1992–2002

Source: Federal Statistical Office Germany

CORPORATION

A company owned by stockholders who have ownership rights to the company's profits.

Stockholders are issued stock, or shares of ownership in the corporation. A corporation sells stock to raise money to do business. Stockholders buy stock in the hope that the corporation will turn a profit. When a corporation does make a profit, stockholders often receive a dividend, a share of the corporation's income after taxes.

The corporation is a legal entity in itself and, therefore, is separate from its owners. As a result, business losses and debts are the responsibility of the corporation alone. Creditors cannot seek payment from the owners, whose liability is limited to the value of the stock they own.

DEFICIT SPENDING

A situation in which a government spends more money than it receives in revenues.

For the most part, the government engages in deficit spending when the economy is in a contraction phase of the **business cycle.** The government borrows or issues money to finance deficit spending.

In theory, the extra funds should stimulate business activity, pushing the economy into an expansion phase. As the economy recovers, revenues should increase, providing the government with a budget surplus. The government then can use the surplus to pay back the money it borrowed.

DEPRESSION

A very severe and prolonged contraction in economic activity.

During a depression, consumer spending, production levels, wages, prices, and profits fall sharply. Many businesses fail, and many workers lose their jobs.

The United States has experienced several economic depressions in its history. The worst was the Great Depression, which started in 1929 and lasted throughout the 1930s. Between 1929 and 1932, business activity in the United States decreased by an average of 10 percent each year. During the same period, some 40 percent of the country's banks failed, and prices for farm products dropped more than 50 percent. By 1933, the worst year of the Great Depression, 25 percent of

American workers were unemployed. Americans in the thousands took to the roads and rail in search of gainful employment. The best job some could find was selling apples on street corners.

The situation in other countries was equally bad. In Great Britain, the unemployment rate averaged 14 percent throughout the Great Depression and hit a peak of 25 percent in early 1931. Unemployment was particularly problematic in such traditional industries as coal mining, shipbuilding, and textiles. The picture at the bottom of the previous column shows unemployed miners' families at a soup kitchen. For information about the global impact of the Great Depression and how the world responded to this economic crisis, read pages 473–475.

DEVELOPED NATION

A nation that has achieved industrialization, a market economy, widespread ownership of private property, and a relatively high standard of living.

Developed nations include the United States, Canada, most European countries, Japan, South Korea, Australia, and New Zealand. Although developed nations account for only one-quarter of the world's population, they produce more than three-quarters of the world's **gross domestic product (GDP).** Economists frequently use per capita GDP (GDP divided by the population) to establish a nation's level of economic development. Most developed nations have per capita GDPs in excess of $20,000.

E-COMMERCE

All forms of buying and selling goods and services electronically.

Short for "electronic commerce," e-commerce refers to business activity on the Internet and on private computer networks. There are two main types of e-commerce: business-to-consumer and business-to-business.

Consumer-related e-commerce includes sales to the public over the computer, usually through a seller's Web site. Many business transactions can be completed wholly electronically, such as sales of computer software, which can be paid for with a credit card number and delivered over the Internet directly to the buyer's computer. A growing proportion of financial transactions are also moving online, such as electronic banking and **stock market** trading, or e-trading. The convenience of online shopping has turned it into a booming enterprise. Between 1998 and 2002, for instance, U.S. consumer spending online grew from about $7.7 billion to more than $45 billion.

Business-to-business e-commerce is growing at an even greater rate, reaching around $700 billion in 2002. Much of that business includes Web-site design and servicing and online advertising. Businesses also use networked computers to purchase supplies and merchandise and to access information from subscription services.

For many businesses, e-commerce is not only convenient but also cost-effective. On average, corporations spend $100 on paperwork alone each time they make a purchase. Moving those transactions online could save companies millions of dollars annually.

EMBARGO

A government ban on trade with another nation, sometimes backed by military force.

In a civil embargo, the nation imposing an embargo prevents exports to or imports from the country against which it has declared the embargo. A hostile embargo involves seizing the goods of another nation.

The major purpose of an embargo is to show disapproval of a nation's actions. For example, in 1980 the United States imposed a civil embargo on grain sales to the Soviet Union to protest the December 1979 Soviet invasion of Afghanistan.

EMERGING NATION

A nation that has lower levels of agricultural and industrial production, lower savings and investment, fewer resources, and lower per capita gross domestic product (GDP) than developed nations.

Emerging nations are sometimes called *developing nations* or *less-developed countries (LDCs)*. Most countries in Africa, Asia, and Latin America and the Caribbean are considered emerging nations. Some three-quarters of the world's population lives in emerging nations, yet these nations produce less than one-quarter of the world's GDP. Therefore, emerging

nations have low per capita GDPs; many have a per capita GDP of less than $1,000.

FREE ENTERPRISE

An economic system based on the private ownership of the means of production, free markets, and the right of individuals to make most economic decisions.

The free enterprise system is also called the free market system or **capitalism.** The United States has a free enterprise economic system. The diagram below illustrates how a free enterprise economy works.

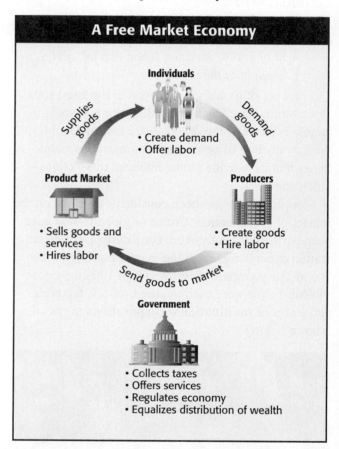

A Free Market Economy

Individuals
- Create demand
- Offer labor

Supplies goods

Demand goods

Product Market
- Sells goods and services
- Hires labor

Producers
- Create goods
- Hire labor

Send goods to market

Government
- Collects taxes
- Offers services
- Regulates economy
- Equalizes distribution of wealth

In a free enterprise system, producers and consumers are motivated by self-interest. To maximize their profits, producers try to make goods and services that consumers want. Producers also engage in competition through lowering prices, advertising their products, and improving product quality, to encourage consumers to buy their goods. Consumers serve their self-interest by purchasing the best goods and services for the lowest price.

Government plays a limited, but important, role in most free enterprise economies:

- It regulates economic activity to ensure there is fair competition, such as by preventing and prosecuting fraud and barring **monopolies.**

- It produces certain necessary goods and services that private producers consider unprofitable, such as roadways.

- It protects the public health and safety, such as through building codes, environmental protection laws, and labor laws.

- It provides economic stability, such as by regulating banks, coining money, and supervising unemployment insurance programs.

GLOBALIZATION

The process of rapid economic integration among countries. This integration involves the increased movement of goods, services, labor, capital, and technology throughout the world.

The process of globalization began in the late 1800s. However, its pace has increased in recent years largely because of the drive toward free trade and the introduction of new telecommunications technologies that have made global financial transactions quick and easy.

Recently, there has been considerable debate on the impact of globalization. Critics of globalization have been particularly outspoken. For example, antiglobalization demonstrations at the Seattle meeting of the World Trade Organization (WTO) in 1999 turned violent. Police were used to guard offices, factories, and stores of **multinational corporations** in the city (shown below).

For a review of the arguments for and against globalization, read the Analyzing Key Concepts on page 644.

GOLD STANDARD

A monetary system in which a country's basic unit of currency is valued at, and can be exchanged for, a fixed amount of gold.

The gold standard tends to curb **inflation,** since a government cannot put more currency into circulation than it can back with its gold supplies. This gives people confidence in the currency.

This advantage is also a weakness of the gold standard. During times of **recession,** a government may want to increase the amount of money in circulation to encourage economic growth. Economic disruption during the Great Depression of the 1930s caused most nations to abandon the gold standard. The United States moved to a modified gold standard in 1934 and abandoned the gold standard completely in 1971.

GROSS DOMESTIC PRODUCT (GDP)

The market value of all the goods and services produced in a nation within a specific time period, such as a quarter (three months) or a year.

Gross domestic product is the standard measure of how a nation's economy is performing. If GDP is growing, the economy is probably in an expansion phase. If GDP is not increasing or is declining, the economy is probably in a contraction phase.

GDP is calculated by adding four components: spending by individual consumers on goods and services; investment in such items as new factories, new factory machinery, and houses; government spending on goods and services; and net exports—the value of exports less the value of imports. (See the diagram below.) GDP figures are presented in two ways. Nominal GDP is reported in current dollars. Real GDP is reported in constant dollars, or dollars adjusted for **inflation.**

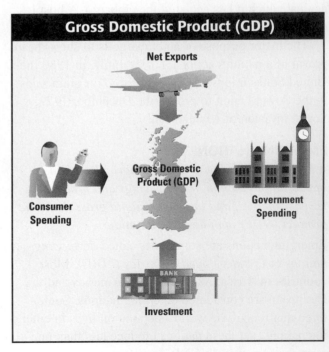

Gross Domestic Product (GDP)

Net Exports

Gross Domestic Product (GDP)

Consumer Spending

Government Spending

Investment

INFLATION

A sustained rise in the average level of prices.

Since more money is required to make purchases when prices rise, inflation is sometimes defined as a decrease in the purchasing value of money. Economists measure price changes with various price indexes. The most widely used index in the United States is the **consumer price index (CPI).**

Inflation may result if the demand for goods increases without an increase in the production of goods. Inflation may also take place if the cost of producing goods increases. Producers pass on increased costs, such as higher wages and more expensive raw materials, by charging consumers higher prices.

INTEREST RATE

The cost of borrowing money.

Interest is calculated as a yearly percentage, or rate, of the money borrowed. A 10 percent interest rate, therefore, would require a borrower to pay $10 per year for every $100 borrowed.

When interest rates are low, people will borrow more, because the cost of borrowing is lower. However, they will save and invest less, because the return on their savings or investment is lower. With high interest rates, people save and invest more but borrow less. Because interest rates affect the economy, governments take steps to control them. The United States government does this through the Federal Reserve System, the nation's central banking system. The graph below shows the relationship between the rate of **inflation** and interest rates in the American economy over time.

Inflation and Interest Rates, 1980–2000

Legend:
- Inflation Rate
- Prime Interest Rate

Y-axis: Percent (0, 2, 4, 6, 8, 10, 12, 14, 16)
X-axis: 1980, 1984, 1988, 1992, 1996, 2000

Source: Bureau of Labor Statistics; Federal Reserve System

KEYNESIAN ECONOMICS

The use of government spending to encourage economic activity by increasing the demand for goods.

This economic approach is based on the ideas of British economist John Maynard Keynes (shown below). In a 1936 study, Keynes pointed out that during economic downturns, more people are unemployed and have less income to spend. As a result, businesses cut production and lay off more workers.

Keynes's answer to this problem was for government to increase spending and reduce taxes. This would stimulate demand for goods and services by replacing the decline in consumer demand. Government would want goods and services for its new programs. More people would be working and earning an income and, therefore, would want to buy more goods and services. Businesses would increase production to meet this new demand. As a result, the economy would soon recover.

Critics maintain, however, that Keynesian economics has led to the growth of government and to high taxes, inflation, high unemployment, and greatly reduced economic growth.

MINIMUM WAGE

The minimum amount of money that employers may legally pay their employees for a set period of time worked.

Legislation sets the minimum wage at a fixed hourly, weekly, or monthly rate. In some countries, the minimum wage applies to all workers. In others, it applies only to workers in particular industries. Also, some countries set a different minimum wage for men, women, and young workers. The first country to pass minimum wage laws was New Zealand in 1894. Since that time, most industrialized countries have adopted such legislation. The graph on the next page shows estimates of minimum monthly wage rates in selected countries.

The first federal minimum wage law in the United States, the Fair Labor Standards Act of 1938, set the base wage at 25 cents an hour. Since then, amendments to the act have raised this hourly rate to $5.15, effective in 1997. The Fair Labor Standards Act applies to workers in most businesses involved in interstate commerce.

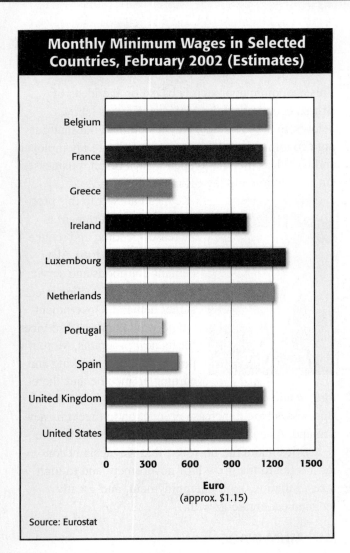

Monthly Minimum Wages in Selected Countries, February 2002 (Estimates)

Euro
(approx. $1.15)

Source: Eurostat

The original intent of minimum wage laws was to ensure that all workers earned enough to survive. However, some economists maintain that these laws may have reduced the chances for unskilled workers to get jobs. They argue that the minimum wage raises the **unemployment rate** because it increases labor costs for business.

MONOPOLY

A situation in which only one seller controls the production, supply, or pricing of a product for which there are no close substitutes.

In the United States, basic public services such as electrical power distributors and cable television suppliers operate as local monopolies. This way of providing utilities is economically more efficient than having several competing companies running electricity or cable lines in the same area.

Monopolies, however, can be harmful to the economy. Since it has no competition, a monopoly does not need to respond to the wants of consumers by improving product quality or by charging fair prices. The government counters the threat of monopoly either by breaking up or regulating the monopoly.

MULTINATIONAL CORPORATION

*A **corporation** that operates in more than one country.*

ExxonMobil (United States), DaimlerChrysler (Germany), Royal Dutch/Shell (Netherlands), BP (Great Britain), and Toyota (Japan) are examples of multinational corporations. A multinational corporation's foreign operations, including factories, offices, and stores, are usually wholly owned subsidiaries run by managers from the home country. Some multinationals, however, enter foreign markets by establishing joint ventures with foreign businesses. Others gain access to foreign markets by buying large amounts of stock in foreign companies.

Such tactics have allowed some multinationals to grow into economic giants with a truly global reach. For more information on the size of some top multinationals, see the graph on page 1076.

NATIONAL DEBT

The money owed by a national government.

During wartime, economic recession, or at other times, the government may employ **deficit spending.** However, the government may not pay back all the money it has borrowed to fund this policy. Each year's government budget deficit adds to the country's national debt. By August 2005, the national debt of the United States stood at $7.93 trillion, or about $26,900 for each citizen.

The rapid growth of the U.S. national debt since 1980 has prompted many Americans to call for changes in government economic policies. Some suggest that the government raise taxes and cut spending to reduce the debt. Others recommend the passage of a constitutional amendment that would require the government to have a balanced budget, spending only as much as it takes in.

POVERTY

The lack of adequate income to maintain a minimum standard of living.

In the United States, this adequate income is referred to as the poverty threshold. The poverty threshold for a family of four in 2004 was $19,307. That year, the poverty rate stood at 12.7 percent. Americans living in poverty numbered 37 million, an increase of 1.1 million from 2003. The graph on the next page shows the changes in the poverty rate in the United States between 1981 and 2001.

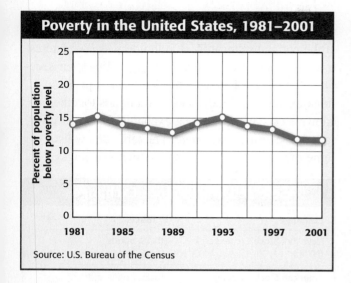

Poverty in the United States, 1981–2001

Percent of population below poverty level

Source: U.S. Bureau of the Census

Because the factors used to determine poverty vary so much from country to country, world poverty figures are difficult to calculate. As a result, such international organizations as the World Bank and the United Nations view poverty differently. These organizations track extreme poverty, the threshold for which is less than $1 a day. In 2001, more than one billion people worldwide lived below this level. And according to World Bank estimates, another 2.7 billion lived on less than $2 a day.

PRODUCTIVITY

The relationship between the output of goods and services and the input of resources.

Productivity is the amount of goods or services that a person can produce at a given time. It is closely linked to economic growth, which is defined as an increase in a nation's real **gross domestic product (GDP)** from one year to the next. A substantial rise in productivity means the average worker is producing more, a key factor in spurring economic expansion. Between 1995 and the early 2000s, for example, worker productivity in the United States increased about 2.5 percent each year. This increase, along with other economic factors, helped the nation's real GDP grow an average of about 3.5 percent during those years.

A number of elements affect productivity, including available supplies of labor and raw materials, education and training, attitudes toward work, and technological innovations. Computer technology, for instance, is believed to have played a significant role in bolstering productivity during the 1990s by allowing workers to do their jobs more quickly and efficiently. Computer-operated robot arms (above, right) have greatly increased production in the automobile industry.

Conversely, a lack of adequate training and fewer technological innovations were thought to be behind the meager productivity growth rates of the 1970s and 1980s—when productivity rose at an annual rate of less than 1 percent.

RECESSION

A period of declining economic activity.

In economic terms, a recession takes place when the **gross domestic product (GDP)** falls for two quarters, or six months, in a row. The United States has experienced several of these **business-cycle** contractions in its history. On average, they have lasted about a year. If a recession persists and economic activity plunges, it is called a **depression.**

SOCIALISM

An economic system in which the government owns most of the means of production and distribution.

Like **communism,** the goal of socialism is to use the power of government to reduce inequality and meet people's needs. Under socialism, however, the government usually owns only major industries, such as coal, steel, and transportation. Other industries are privately owned but regulated by the government. Government and individuals, therefore, share economic decision-making. Also, under socialism, the government may provide such services as reasonably priced health care. The diagram on the next page shows the level of government involvement in various types of economic systems.

Economics Handbook

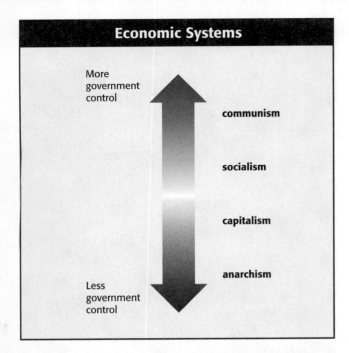

Economic Systems

More government control

- communism
- socialism
- capitalism
- anarchism

Less government control

Some countries, such as Sweden, are called democratic socialist countries. In these nations there is less government ownership of property than in communist nations. These nations also have democratically elected governments.

Critics of socialism maintain that this system leads to less efficiency and higher taxes than does the **capitalist,** or **free enterprise,** system. For a comparison of socialism and capitalism, read the Analyzing Key Concepts on page 303.

STANDARD OF LIVING

The overall economic situation in which people live.

Economists differ on how best to measure the standard of living. Some suggest average personal income, while others propose per capita **gross domestic product**—the GDP divided by the population. Another possible measure is the value of the goods and services bought by consumers during a year. In general terms, the nation's standard of living rises as these measures rise. Some people argue that measuring the quality of life also requires consideration of noneconomic factors such as pollution, health, work hours, and even political freedom.

STOCK MARKET *or* STOCK EXCHANGE

A place where stocks and bonds are bought and sold.

Large companies often need extra money to fund expansion and to help cover operating costs. To raise money, they sell stocks, or shares of ownership, in their companies. They also may borrow by issuing bonds, or certificates of debt, promising to repay the money borrowed, plus interest.

Individuals invest in stocks and bonds to make a profit. Most stockholders receive dividends, or a share of the company's profits. Bondholders receive interest. Investors may also make a profit by selling their securities. This sale of stocks and bonds takes place on stock exchanges. Since stocks and bonds together are known as securities, a stock exchange is sometimes called a securities exchange. The table below lists some of the world's most active stock exchanges.

Selected World Stock Exchanges

Exchange	Products
New York Stock Exchange (NYSE)	stocks, bonds
American Stock Exchange (AMEX) (New York)	stocks, bonds, options
National Association of Securities Dealers Automated Quotations (NASDAQ)	over-the-counter stocks
London Stock Exchange	stocks
Tokyo Stock Exchange	stocks, bonds, futures, options
Hong Kong Exchanges	stocks, bonds, futures, options
German Stock Exchange (Frankfurt) (pictured below)	stocks

The largest and most important exchange in the United States is the New York Stock Exchange. Activity on this and other exchanges often signals how well the economy is doing. A bull market, when stock prices rise, usually indicates economic expansion. A bear market, when stock prices fall, usually indicates economic contraction.

A rapid fall in stock prices is called a crash. The worst stock market crash in the United States came in October 1929. To help protect against another drastic stock market crash, the federal government set up the Securities and Exchange Commission (SEC), which regulates the trading of securities. For more information on stocks and the stock market, read the History in Depth on page 472.

STRIKE

A work stoppage by employees to gain higher wages, better working conditions, or other benefits.

Strikes are also sometimes used as political protests. A strike is usually preceded by a failure in collective bargaining—the negotiation of contracts between labor unions and employers. Union members may decide to call a strike if they believe negotiations with the employer are deadlocked. In the United States, collective bargaining and strikes are regulated by the NLRA, or Wagner Act, of 1935, which is administered by the National Labor Relations Board (NLRB). There are also wildcat strikes, which are not authorized by unions.

Strikes often have a huge impact on everyday life, as the picture below illustrates. Commuters jam the platform of a subway station in Paris, France, during a one-day strike by transport workers in 2003. The strike, over pay and working conditions, shut down about half of the Paris subway network and severely disrupted traffic on the rest.

When strikes do occur, union representatives and employers try to negotiate a settlement. An outside party is sometimes asked to help work out an agreement.

SUPPLY AND DEMAND

The forces that determine prices of goods and services in a market economy.

Supply is the amount of a good or service that producers are willing and able to produce at a given price. Demand is the amount of a good or service consumers are willing and able to buy at a given price. In general, producers are willing to produce more of a good or service when prices are high; conversely, consumers are willing to buy more of a good or service when prices are low.

The table and graph below show supply and demand for a certain product. The line *S* shows the amount of the good that producers would be willing to make at various prices. The line *D* shows the amount that consumers would be willing to buy at various prices. Point *E*, where the two lines intersect, is called the equilibrium price. It is the price at which the amount produced and the amount demanded would be the same.

When the equilibrium price is the market price, the market operates efficiently. At prices above the equilibrium price, consumers will demand less than producers supply. Producers, therefore, will have to lower their prices to sell the surplus, or excess, products. At prices below equilibrium, consumers will demand more. Producers will be able to raise their prices because the product is scarce, or in short supply.

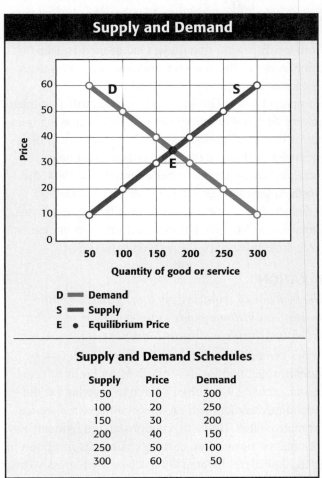

Supply and Demand Schedules

Supply	Price	Demand
50	10	300
100	20	250
150	30	200
200	40	150
250	50	100
300	60	50

SUPPLY-SIDE ECONOMICS

Government policies designed to stimulate the production of goods and services, or the supply side of the economy.

Supply-side economists developed these policies in opposition to **Keynesian economics.** Supply-side policies call for low tax rates particularly in income from investments. Lower taxes mean that people keep more of what they earn. Therefore, supply-side economists argue, people will work harder in order to earn more. They will then use their extra income to save and invest. This investment will fund the development of new businesses and, as a result, create more jobs.

TARIFF

A fee charged for goods brought into a state or country from another state or country.

Governments have collected tariffs since ancient times. Initially, tariffs were used to raise revenue. As time went on, however, governments used them as a way to control imports. In the United States, for example, Congress created tariffs in 1789 to raise revenue and to protect American products from foreign competition. Soon, however, special interest groups used tariffs to protect specific industries and increase profits.

After World War II, many governments moved away from tariffs toward free trade. One of the first steps came in the 1950s, with the creation of the European Economic Community (EEC), now known as the European Union. The EEC encouraged tariff-free trade among its members. In recent decades, a growing number of U.S. economists have favored free trade policies because they believe that such policies will help increase U.S. exports to other countries. In 1994, the North American Free Trade Agreement (NAFTA) established a free-trade zone among the United States, Canada, and Mexico. For more information on regional trade agreements, see the map on page 643.

TAXATION

The practice of requiring persons, groups, or businesses to contribute funds to the government under which they reside or transact business.

In the United States, all levels of government—federal, state, and local—collect many kinds of taxes. Income taxes are the chief source of revenue for the federal government and an important revenue source for many states. Both corporations and individuals pay income tax, or taxes on earnings. Since its inception in 1913, the federal income tax has been a progressive tax,

one that is graduated, or scaled, such that those with greater incomes are taxed at a greater rate. Sales taxes are another important source of income for state governments.

Property taxes are the main source of funds for local governments. Property tax is calculated as a percentage of the assessed value of real estate—land and improvements such as buildings.

TRADE

The exchange of goods and services between countries.

Almost all nations produce goods that other countries need, and they sell (export) those goods to buyers in other countries. At the same time, they buy (import) goods from other countries as well. For example, Americans sell goods such as wheat to people in Japan and buy Japanese goods such as automobiles in return.

The relationship between the value of a country's imports and the value of its exports is called the *balance of trade.* If a country exports more than it imports, it has a trade surplus. However, if the value of a country's imports exceeds the value of its exports, the country has a trade deficit. As the graph below shows, Japan maintained a trade surplus throughout the 1990s.

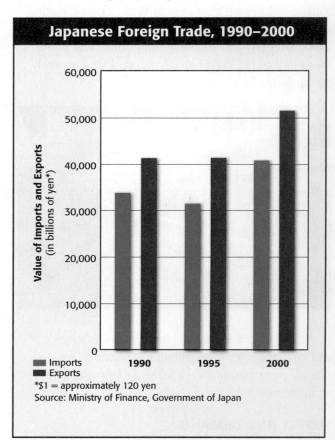

Japanese Foreign Trade, 1990–2000

■ Imports
■ Exports

*$1 = approximately 120 yen

Source: Ministry of Finance, Government of Japan

Economics Handbook

Nations that trade with one another often become dependent on one another's products. Sometimes this brings nations closer together, as it did the United States, Great Britain, and France before World War I. At other times it causes tension among nations, such as that between the United States and Arab oil-producing countries in the 1970s. For an example of how trade influences foreign policy, see page 645.

UNEMPLOYMENT RATE

The percentage of the labor force that is unemployed but actively looking for work.

The labor force consists of all civilians of working age, normally 15 to 16 years of age and older, who are employed or who are unemployed but actively looking and available for work. In the United States, the size of the labor force and the unemployment rate are determined by surveys conducted by the U.S. Bureau of the Census.

The unemployment rate provides an indicator of economic health. Rising unemployment rates signal a contraction in the economy, while falling rates indicate an economic expansion. The graphs below show two different methods of portraying unemployment in Canada.

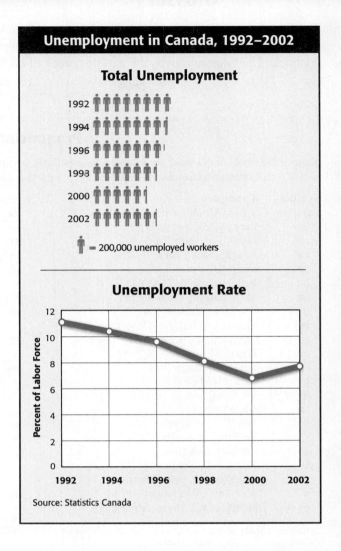

Glossary

The Glossary is an alphabetical listing of many of the key terms from the chapters, along with their meanings. The definitions listed in the Glossary are the ones that apply to the way the words are used in this textbook. The Glossary gives the part of speech of each word. The following abbreviations are used:

adj. adjective   *n.* noun   *v.* verb

Pronunciation Key

Some of the words in this book are followed by respellings that show how the words are pronounced. The following key will help you understand what sounds are represented by the letters used in the respellings.

Symbol	Examples	Symbol	Examples
a	apple [AP•uhl], catch [kach]	oh	road, [rohd], know [noh]
ah	barn [bahrn], pot [paht]	oo	school [skool], glue [gloo]
air	bear [bair], dare [dair]	ow	out [owt], cow [kow]
aw	bought [bawt], horse [hawrs]	oy	coin [koyn], boys [boyz]
ay	ape [ayp], mail [mayl]	p	pig [pihg], top [tahp]
b	bell [behl], table [TAY•buhl]	r	rose [rohz], star [stahr]
ch	chain [chayn], ditch [dihch]	s	soap [sohp], icy [EYE•see]
d	dog [dawg], rained [raynd]	sh	share [shair], nation [NAY•shuhn]
ee	even [EE•vuhn], meal [meel]	t	tired [tyrd], boat [boht]
eh	egg [ehg], ten [tehn]	th	thin [thihn], mother [MUH•thuhr]
eye	iron [EYE•uhrn]	u	pull [pul], look [luk]
f	fall [fawl], laugh [laf]	uh	bump [buhmp], awake [uh•WAYK],
g	gold [gohld], big [bihg]		happen [HAP•uhn], pencil [PEHN•suhl],
h	hot [haht], exhale [ehks•HAYL]		pilot [PY•luht]
hw	white [hwyt]	ur	earth [urth], bird [burd], worm [wurm]
ih	into [IHN•too], sick [sihk]	v	vase [vays], love [luhv]
j	jar [jahr], badge [baj]	w	web [wehb], twin [twihn]
k	cat [kat], luck [luhk]	y	As a consonant: yard [yahrd], mule [myool]
l	load [lohd], ball [bawl]		As a vowel: ice [ys], tried [tryd], sigh [sy]
m	make [mayk], gem [jehm]	z	zone [zohn], reason [REE•zuhn]
n	night [nyt], win [wihn]	zh	treasure [TREHZH•uhr], garage [guh•RAHZH]
ng	song [sawng], anger [ANG•guhr]		

Syllables that are stressed when the words are spoken appear in CAPITAL LETTERS in the respellings. For example, the respelling of *patterns* (PAT•uhrnz) shows that the first syllable of the word is stressed.

Syllables that appear in SMALL CAPITAL LETTERS are also stressed, but not as strongly as those that appear in capital letters. For example, the respelling of *interaction* (IHN•tuhr•AK•shuhn) shows that the third syllable receives the main stress and the first syllable receives a secondary stress.

A

Aborigine [AB•uh•RIHJ•uh•nee] *n.* a member of any of the native peoples of Australia. (p. 318)

absolute monarch [MAHN•uhrk] *n.* a king or queen who has unlimited power and seeks to control all aspects of society. (p. 160)

Allies [uh•LYZ] *n.* in World War I, the nations of Great Britain, France, and Russia, along with the other nations that fought on their side; also, the group of nations—including Great Britain, the Soviet Union, and the United States—that opposed the Axis Powers in World War II. (p. 411)

Amritsar Massacre *n.* killing by British troops of nearly 400 Indians gathered at Amritsar to protest the Rowlatt Acts. (p. 454)

Anabaptist [AN•uh•BAP•tihst] *n.* in the Reformation, a member of a Protestant group that believed in baptizing only those persons who were old enough to decide to be Christian and believed in the separation of church and state. (p. 62)

Anglican [ANG•glih•kuhn] *adj.* relating to the Church of England. (p. 60)

annexation [AN•ihk•SAY•shuhn] *n.* the adding of a region to the territory of an existing political unit. (pp. 365, 379)

annul [uh•NUHL] *v.* to cancel or set aside. (p. 58)

anti-Semitism [AN•tee•SEHM•ih•TIHZ•uhm] *n.* prejudice against Jews. (p. 315)

apartheid [uh•PAHRT•HYT] *n.* a South African policy of complete legal separation of the races, including the banning of all social contacts between blacks and whites. (p. 609)

appeasement *n.* the making of concessions to an aggressor in order to avoid war. (p. 483)

armistice [AHR•mih•stihs] *n.* an agreement to stop fighting. (p. 421)

Aryans [AIR•ee•uhnz] *n.* to the Nazis, the Germanic peoples who formed a "master race." (p. 502)

assembly line *n.* in a factory, an arrangement in which a product is moved from worker to worker, with each person performing a single task in its manufacture. (p. 330)

assimilation [uh•SIHM•uh•LAY•shuhn] *n.* a policy in which a nation forces or encourages a subject people to adopt its institutions and customs. (p. 347)

Atlantic Charter *n.* a declaration of principles issued in August 1941 by British prime minister Winston Churchill and U.S. president Franklin Roosevelt, on which the Allied peace plan at the end of World War II was based. (p. 496)

Atlantic slave trade *n.* the buying, transporting, and selling of Africans for work in the Americas. (p. 133)

Axis Powers *n.* in World War II, the nations of Germany, Italy, and Japan, which had formed an alliance in 1936. (p. 483)

balance of power *n.* a political situation in which no one nation is powerful enough to pose a threat to others. (p. 238)

The Balkans [BAWL•kuhnz] *n.* the region of southeastern Europe now occupied by Greece, Albania, Bulgaria, Romania, the European part of Turkey, and the former republics of Yugoslavia. (p. 255)

baroque [buh•ROHK] *adj.* relating to a grand, ornate style that characterized European painting, music, and architecture in the 1600s and early 1700s. (p. 203)

Battle of Britain *n.* a series of battles between German and British air forces, fought over Britain in 1940–1941. (p. 494)

Battle of Guadalcanal [GWAHD•uhl•kuh•NAL] *n.* a 1942–1943 battle of World War II, in which Allied troops drove Japanese forces from the Pacific island of Guadalcanal. (p. 501)

Battle of Midway *n.* a 1942 sea and air battle of World War II, in which American forces defeated Japanese forces in the central Pacific. (p. 500)

Battle of Stalingrad [STAH•lihn•GRAD] *n.* a 1942–1943 battle of World War II, in which German forces were defeated in their attempt to capture the city of Stalingrad in the Soviet Union. (p. 507)

Battle of the Bulge *n.* a 1944–1945 battle in which Allied forces turned back the last major German offensive of World War II. (p. 510)

Battle of Trafalgar [truh•FAL•guhr] *n.* an 1805 naval battle in which Napoleon's forces were defeated by a British fleet under the command of Horatio Nelson. (p. 233)

Berlin Conference *n.* a meeting (1884–1885) at which representatives of European nations agreed upon rules for the European colonization of Africa. (p. 342)

Bill of Rights *n.* the first ten amendments to the U.S. Constitution, which protect citizens' basic rights and freedoms. (p. 211)

blitzkrieg [BLIHTS•KREEG] *n.* "lightning war"—a form of warfare in which surprise attacks with fast-moving airplanes are followed by massive attacks with infantry forces. (p. 491)

blockade [blah•KAYD] *n.* the use of troops or ships to prevent commercial traffic from entering or leaving a city or region. (p. 234)

Boer [bohr] *n.* a Dutch colonist in South Africa. (p. 342)

Boer War *n.* a conflict, lasting from 1899 to 1902, in which the Boers and the British fought for control of territory in South Africa. (p. 344)

Bolsheviks [BOHL•shuh•VIHKS] *n.* a group of revolutionary Russian Marxists who took control of Russia's government in November 1917. (p. 434)

Boxer Rebellion *n.* a 1900 revolt in China, aimed at ending foreign influence in the country. (p. 374)

boyar [boh•YAHR] *n.* a landowning noble of Russia. (p. 174)

brinkmanship *n.* a policy of threatening to go to war in response to any enemy aggression. (p. 536)

cabinet *n.* a group of advisers or ministers chosen by the head of a country to help make government decisions. (p. 183)

Calvinism [KAL•vih•NIHZ•uhm] *n.* a body of religious teachings based on the ideas of the reformer John Calvin. (p. 61)

Camp David Accords *n.* the first signed agreement between Israel and an Arab country, in which Egyptian president Anwar Sadat recognized Israel as a legitimate state and Israeli prime minister Menachem Begin agreed to return the Sinai Peninsula to Egypt. (p. 586)

capitalism *n.* an economic system based on private ownership and on the investment of money in business ventures in order to make a profit. (pp. 139, 300)

Catholic Reformation [REHF•uhr•MAY•shuhn] *n.* a 16th-century movement in which the Roman Catholic Church sought to make changes in response to the Protestant Reformation. (p. 64)

caudillo [kaw•DEEL•yoh] *n.* a military dictator of a Latin American country. (p. 382)

Central Powers *n.* in World War I, the nations of Germany and Austria-Hungary, along with the other nations that fought on their side. (p. 411)

Chartist movement *n.* in 19th-century Britain, members of the working class demanded reforms in Parliament and in elections, including suffrage for all men. (p. 314)

checks and balances *n.* measures designed to prevent any one branch of government from dominating the others. (p. 211)

CIS *n.* the Commonwealth of Independent States—a loose association of former Soviet republics that was formed after the breakup of the Soviet Union. (p. 615)

civil disobedience *n.* a deliberate and public refusal to obey a law considered unjust. (p. 454)

cloning [KLOH•nihng] *n.* the creation of plants or animals that are genetically identical to an existing plant or animal. (p. 639)

coalition [KOH•uh•LIHSH•uhn] **government** *n.* a government controlled by a temporary alliance of several political parties. (p. 470)

Cold War *n.* the state of diplomatic hostility between the United States and the Soviet Union in the decades following World War II. (p. 535)

collective farm *n.* a large government-controlled farm formed by combining many small farms. (p. 444)

colony *n.* a land controlled by another nation. (p. 120)

Columbian Exchange *n.* the global transfer of plants, animals, and diseases that occurred during the European colonization of the Americas. (p. 137)

command economy *n.* an economic system in which the government makes all economic decisions. (p. 443)

commune [KAHM•YOON] *n.* in Communist China, a collective farm on which a great number of people work and live together. (p. 540)

Communist Party *n.* a political party practicing the ideas of Karl Marx and V.I. Lenin; originally the Russian Bolshevik Party. (p. 439)

communism *n.* an economic system in which all means of production—land, mines, factories, railroads, and businesses—are owned by the people, private property does not exist, and all goods and services are shared equally. (p. 303)

Concert [KAHN•SURT] **of Europe** *n.* a series of alliances among European nations in the 19th century, devised by Prince Klemens von Metternich to prevent the outbreak of revolutions. (p. 240)

concordat [kuhn•KAWR•DAT] *n.* a formal agreement—especially one between the pope and a government, dealing with the control of Church affairs. (p. 230)

Congress of Vienna [vee•EHN•uh] *n.* a series of meetings in 1814–1815, during which the European leaders sought to establish long-lasting peace and security after the defeat of Napoleon. (p. 238)

Congress Party *n.* a major national political party in India—also known as the Indian National Congress. (p. 563)

conquistadors [kahng•KEE•stuh•DAWRZ] *n.* the Spanish soldiers, explorers, and fortune hunters who took part in the conquest of the Americas in the 16th century. (p. 120)

conservative *n.* in the first half of the 19th century, a European—mainly wealthy landowners and nobles—who wanted to preserve the traditional monarchies of Europe. (p. 253)

constitutional monarchy [MAHN•uhr•kee] *n.* a system of governing in which the ruler's power is limited by law. (p. 183)

containment *n.* a U.S. foreign policy adopted by President Harry Truman in the late 1940s, in which the United States tried to stop the spread of communism by creating alliances and helping weak countries to resist Soviet advances. (p. 533)

Continental System *n.* Napoleon's policy of preventing trade between Great Britain and continental Europe, intended to destroy Great Britain's economy. (p. 234)

corporation *n.* a business owned by stockholders who share in its profits but are not personally responsible for its debts. (p. 297)

Council of Trent *n.* a meeting of Roman Catholic leaders, called by Pope Paul III to rule on doctrines criticized by the Protestant reformers. (p. 65)

coup d'état [KOO day•TAH] *n.* a sudden seizure of political power in a nation. (p. 230)

creole [KREE•OHL] *n.* in Spanish colonial society, a colonist who was born in Latin America to Spanish parents. (p. 247)

Crimean [kry•MEE•uhn] **War** *n.* a conflict, lasting from 1853 to 1856, in which the Ottoman Empire, with the aid of Britain and France, halted Russian expansion in the region of the Black Sea. (p. 353)

crop rotation *n.* the system of growing a different crop in a field each year to preserve the fertility of the land. (p. 283)

Cultural Revolution *n.* a 1966–1976 uprising in China led by the Red Guards, with the goal of establishing a society of peasants and workers in which all were equal. (p. 541)

cyberterrorism *n.* politically motivated attacks on information systems. (p. 654)

D

daimyo [DY•mee•OH] *n.* a Japanese feudal lord who commanded a private army of samurai. (p. 108)

D-Day *n.* June 6, 1944—the day on which the Allies began their invasion of the European mainland during World War II. (p. 510)

Declaration of Independence *n.* a statement of the reasons for the American colonies' break with Britain, approved by the Second Continental Congress in 1776. (p. 207)

demilitarization [dee•MIHL•ih•tuhr•ih•ZAY•shuhn] *n.* a reduction in a country's ability to wage war, achieved by disbanding its armed forces and prohibiting it from acquiring weapons. (p. 516)

democratization *n.* the process of creating a government elected by the people. (p. 516)

Department of Homeland Security *n.* U.S. federal agency created in 2002 to coordinate national efforts against terrorism. (p. 657)

détente [day•TAHNT] *n.* a policy of reducing Cold War tensions that was adopted by the United States during the presidency of Richard Nixon. (p. 556)

developed nation *n.* a nation with all the facilities needed for the advanced production of manufactured goods. (p. 641)

devshirme [dehv•SHEER•meh] *n.* in the Ottoman Empire, the policy of taking boys from conquered Christian peoples to be trained as Muslim soldiers. (p. 76)

dissident [DIHS•ih•duhnt] *n.* an opponent of a government's policies or actions. (p. 608)

divine right *n.* the idea that monarchs are God's representatives on earth and are therefore answerable only to God. (p. 160)

dominion *n.* in the British Empire, a nation (such as Canada) allowed to govern its own domestic affairs. (p. 318)

domino theory *n.* the idea that if a nation falls under Communist control, nearby nations will also fall under Communist control. (p. 544)

Dreyfus [DRY•fuhs] **affair** *n.* a controversy in France in the 1890s, centering on the trial and imprisonment of a Jewish army officer, Captain Alfred Dreyfus, who had been falsely accused of selling military secrets to Germany. (p. 315)

Dutch East India Company *n.* a company founded by the Dutch in the early 17th century to establish and direct trade throughout Asia. (p. 100)

E

Eastern Front *n.* in World War I, the region along the German-Russian border where Russians and Serbs battled Germans, Austrians, and Turks. (p. 414)

Edict of Nantes [EE•DIHKT uhv NAHNT] *n.* a 1598 declaration in which the French king Henry IV promised that Protestants could live in peace in France and could set up houses of worship in some French cities. (p. 162)

Emancipation Proclamation [ih•MAN•suh•PAY•shuhn PRAHK•luh•MAY•shuhn] *n.* a declaration issued by U.S. president Abraham Lincoln in 1863, stating that all slaves in the Confederate states were free. (p. 326)

emerging nation *n.* a nation in which the process of industrialization is not yet complete. (p. 641)

émigré [EHM•ih•GRAY] *n.* a person who leaves his native country for political reasons, like the nobles and others who fled France during the peasant uprisings of the French Revolution. (p. 224)

enclosure *n.* one of the fenced-in or hedged-in fields created by wealthy British landowners on land that was formerly worked by village farmers. (p. 283)

encomienda [ehng•kaw•MYEHN•dah] *n.* a grant of land made by Spain to a settler in the Americas, including the right to use Native Americans as laborers on it. (p. 123)

English Civil War *n.* a conflict, lasting from 1642 to 1649, in which Puritan supporters of Parliament battled supporters of England's monarchy. (p. 181)

enlightened despot [DEHS•puht] *n.* one of the 18th-century European monarchs who was inspired by Enlightenment ideas to rule justly and respect the rights of subjects. (p. 204)

Enlightenment *n.* an 18th-century European movement in which thinkers attempted to apply the principles of reason and the scientific method to all aspects of society. (p. 195)

entrepreneur [AHN•truh•pruh•NUR] *n.* a person who organizes, manages, and takes on the risks of a business. (p. 287)

estate [ih•STAYT] *n.* one of the three social classes in France before the French Revolution—the First Estate consisting of the clergy; the Second Estate, of the nobility; and the Third Estate, of the rest of the population. (p. 217)

Estates-General [ih•STAYTS•JEHN•uhr•uhl] *n.* an assembly of representatives from all three of the estates, or social classes, in France. (p. 219)

ethnic cleansing *n.* a policy of murder and other acts of brutality by which Serbs hoped to eliminate Bosnia's Muslim population after the breakup of Yugoslavia. (p. 622)

existentialism [EHG•zih•STEHN•shuh•LIHZ•uhm] *n.* a philosophy based on the idea that people give meaning to their lives through their choices and actions. (p. 464)

extraterritorial [EHK•struh•TEHR•ih•TAWR•ee•uhl] **rights** *n.* an exemption of foreign residents from the laws of a country. (p. 372)

F

factors of production *n.* the resources—including land, labor, and capital—that are needed to produce goods and services. (p. 284)

factory *n.* a large building in which machinery is used to manufacture goods. (p. 286)

fascism [FASH•IHZ•uhm] *n.* a political movement that promotes an extreme form of nationalism, a denial of individual rights, and a dictatorial one-party rule. (p. 476)

favorable balance of trade *n.* an economic situation in which a country sells more goods abroad than it buys from abroad. (p. 141)

federal system *n.* a system of government in which power is divided between a central authority and a number of individual states. (pp. 211, 607)

"Final Solution" *n.* Hitler's program of systematically killing the entire Jewish people. (p. 503)

Five-Year Plans *n.* plans outlined by Joseph Stalin in 1928 for the development of the Soviet Union's economy. (p. 443)

Four Modernizations *n.* a set of goals adopted by the Chinese leader Deng Xiaoping in the late 20th century, involving progress in agriculture, industry, defense, and science and technology. (p. 626)

Fourteen Points *n.* a series of proposals in which U.S. president Woodrow Wilson outlined a plan for achieving a lasting peace after World War I. (p. 424)

free trade *n.* commerce between nations without economic restrictions or barriers (such as tariffs). (p. 642)

French and Indian War *n.* a conflict between Britain and France for control of territory in North America, lasting from 1754 to 1763. (p. 130)

gender inequality *n.* the difference between men and women in terms of wealth and status. (p. 650)

genetic [juh•NEHT•ihk] **engineering** *n.* the transferring of genes from one living thing to another in order to produce an organism with new traits. (p. 639)

genocide [JEHN•uh•SYD] *n.* the systematic killing of an entire people. (p. 503)

geocentric theory *n.* in the Middle Ages, the earth-centered view of the universe in which scholars believed that the earth was an immovable object located at the center of the universe. (p. 189)

geopolitics [JEE•oh•PAHL•ih•tihks] *n.* a foreign policy based on a consideration of the strategic locations or products of other lands. (p. 352)

ghazi [GAH•zee] *n.* a warrior for Islam. (p. 73)

ghettos [GEHT•ohz] *n.* city neighborhoods in which European Jews were forced to live. (p. 503)

glasnost [GLAHS•nuhst] *n.* a Soviet policy of openness to the free flow of ideas and information, introduced in 1985 by Mikhail Gorbachev. (p. 612)

global economy *n.* all the financial interactions—involving people, businesses, and governments—that cross international boundaries. (p. 642)

Glorious Revolution *n.* the bloodless overthrow of the English king James II and his replacement by William and Mary. (p. 182)

Great Depression *n.* the severe economic slump that followed the collapse of the U.S. stock market in 1929. (p. 473)

Great Fear *n.* a wave of senseless panic that spread through the French countryside after the storming of the Bastille in 1789. (p. 221)

Great Purge *n.* a campaign of terror in the Soviet Union during the 1930s, in which Joseph Stalin sought to eliminate all Communist Party members and other citizens who threatened his power. (p. 442)

green revolution *n.* a 20th-century attempt to increase food resources worldwide, involving the use of fertilizers and pesticides and the development of disease-resistant crops. (p. 640)

guerrilla [guh•RIHL•uh] *n.* a member of a loosely organized fighting force that makes surprise attacks on enemy troops occupying his or her country. (p. 235)

guillotine [GIHL•uh•TEEN] *n.* a machine for beheading people, used as a means of execution during the French Revolution. (p. 226)

habeas corpus [HAY•bee•uhs KAWR•puhs] *n.* a document requiring that a prisoner be brought before a court or judge so that it can be decided whether his or her imprisonment is legal. (p. 182)

haiku [HY•koo] *n.* a Japanese form of poetry, consisting of three unrhymed lines of five, seven, and five syllables. (p. 110)

heliocentric [HEE•lee•oh•SEHN•trihk] **theory** *n.* the idea that the earth and the other planets revolve around the sun. (p. 190)

Holocaust [HAHL•uh•KAWST] *n.* a mass slaughter of Jews and other civilians, carried out by the Nazi government of Germany before and during World War II. (p. 502)

Holy Alliance *n.* a league of European nations formed by the leaders of Russia, Austria, and Prussia after the Congress of Vienna. (p. 240)

home rule *n.* a control over internal matters granted to the residents of a region by a ruling government. (p. 320)

humanism [HYOO•muh•NIHZ•uhm] *n.* a Renaissance intellectual movement in which thinkers studied classical texts and focused on human potential and achievements. (p. 38)

Hundred Days *n.* the brief period during 1815 when Napoleon made his last bid for power, deposing the French king and again becoming emperor of France. (p. 237)

imperialism [ihm•PEER•ee•uh•LIHZ•uhm] *n.* a policy in which a strong nation seeks to dominate other countries politically, economically, or socially. (p. 339)

impressionism [ihm•PREHSH•uh•NIHZ•uhm] *n.* a movement in 19th-century painting, in which artists reacted against realism by seeking to convey their impressions of subjects or moments in time. (p. 267)

indulgence [ihn•DUHL•juhns] *n.* a pardon releasing a person from punishments due for a sin. (p. 55)

industrialization [ihn•DUHS•tree•uh•lih•ZAY•shuhn] *n.* the development of industries for the machine production of goods. (p. 284)

Industrial Revolution *n.* the shift, beginning in England during the 18th century, from making goods by hand to making them by machine. (p. 283)

intendant [ihn•TEHN•duhnt] *n.* a French government official appointed by the monarch to collect taxes and administer justice. (p. 164)

International Space Station *n.* cooperative venture sponsored by the United States, Russia, and 14 other nations to establish and maintain a working laboratory for scientific experimentation in space. (p. 637)

Internet *n.* a linkage of computer networks that enables people around the world to exchange information and communicate with one another. (p. 639)

intifada *n.* Palestinian campaign of civil disobedience against Israeli occupation of the West Bank and Gaza Strip, which continued into the 1990s. (p. 587)

Irish Republican Army (IRA) *n.* an unofficial nationalist military force seeking independence for Ireland from Great Britain. (p. 321)

iron curtain *n.* during the Cold War, the boundary separating the Communist nations of Eastern Europe from the mostly democratic nations of Western Europe. (p. 533)

isolationism *n.* a policy of avoiding political or military involvement with other countries. (p. 484)

janissary [JAN•ih•SEHR•ee] *n.* a member of an elite force of soldiers in the Ottoman Empire. (p. 76)

jazz *n.* a 20th-century style of popular music developed mainly by African-American musicians. (p. 465)

Jesuits [JEHZH•oo•ihts] *n.* members of the Society of Jesus, a Roman Catholic religious order founded by Ignatius of Loyola. (p. 65)

"jewel in the crown" *n.* the British colony of India—so called because of its importance in the British Empire, both as a supplier of raw materials and as a market for British trade goods. (p. 357)

joint-stock company *n.* a business in which investors pool their wealth for a common purpose, then share the profits. (p. 139)

kabuki [kuh•BOO•kee] *n.* a type of Japanese drama in which music, dance, and mime are used to present stories. (p. 110)

kaiser [KY•zuhr] *n.* a German emperor (from the Roman title *Caesar*). (p. 263)

kamikaze [KAH•mih•KAH•zee] *n.* during World War II, Japanese suicide pilots trained to sink Allied ships by crashing bomb-filled planes into them. (p. 511)

Khmer Rouge [roozh] *n.* a group of Communist rebels who seized power in Cambodia in 1975. (p. 547)

Kristallnacht [krih•STAHL•NAHKT] *n.* "Night of Broken Glass"—the night of November 9, 1938, on which Nazi storm troopers attacked Jewish homes, businesses, and synagogues throughout Germany. (p. 502)

Kuomintang [KWOH•mihn•TANG] *n.* the Chinese Nationalist Party, formed after the fall of the Qing Dynasty in 1912. (p. 448)

laissez faire [LEHS•ay FAIR] *n.* the idea that government should not interfere with or regulate industries and businesses. (p. 300)

land reform *n.* a redistribution of farmland by breaking up large estates and giving the resulting smaller farms to peasants. (p. 600)

La Reforma [lah reh•FAWR•mah] *n.* a liberal reform movement in 19th-century Mexico, led by Benito Juárez. (p. 390)

League of Nations *n.* an international association formed after World War I with the goal of keeping peace among nations. (p. 425)

lebensraum [LAY•buhns•ROWM] *n.* "living space"—the additional territory that, according to Adolf Hitler, Germany needed because it was overcrowded. (p. 478)

Legislative [LEHJ•ih•SLAY•tihv] **Assembly** *n.* a French congress with the power to create laws and approve declarations of war, established by the Constitution of 1791. (p. 223)

legitimacy [luh•JIHT•uh•muh•see] *n.* the hereditary right of a monarch to rule. (p. 239)

liberal *n.* in the first half of the 19th century, a European—mainly middle-class business leaders and merchants—who wanted to give more political power to elected parliaments. (p. 253)

Long March *n.* a 6,000-mile journey made in 1934–1935 by Chinese Communists fleeing from Jiang Jieshi's Nationalist forces. (p. 452)

Lutheran [LOO•thuhr•uhn] *n.* a member of a Protestant church founded on the teachings of Martin Luther. (p. 56)

lycée [lee•SAY] *n.* a government-run public school in France. (p. 230)

Manchus [MAN•chooz] *n.* a people, native to Manchuria, who ruled China during the Qing Dynasty (1644–1912). (p. 105)

manifest destiny *n.* the idea, popular among mid-19th-century Americans, that it was the right and the duty of the United States to rule North America from the Atlantic Ocean to the Pacific Ocean. (p. 324)

Maori [MOW•ree] *n.* a member of a Polynesian people who settled in New Zealand around A.D. 800. (p. 318)

Marshall Plan *n.* a U.S. program of economic aid to European countries to help them rebuild after World War II. (p. 534)

martial [MAHR•shuhl] **law** *n.* a temporary rule by military authorities over a civilian population, usually imposed in times of war or civil unrest. (p. 607)

mass culture *n.* the production of works of art and entertainment designed to appeal to a large audience. (p. 332)

materialism *n.* a placing of high value on acquiring material possessions. (p. 662)

May Fourth Movement *n.* a national protest in China in 1919, in which people demonstrated against the Treaty of Versailles and foreign interference. (p. 449)

Meiji [MAY•JEE] **era** *n.* the period of Japanese history from 1867 to 1912, during which the country was ruled by Emperor Mutsuhito. (p. 377)

Mein Kampf [MYN KAHMPF] *n.* "My Struggle"—a book written by Adolf Hitler during his imprisonment in 1923–1924, in which he set forth his beliefs and his goals for Germany. (p. 478)

mercantilism [MUR•kuhn•tee•LIHZ•uhm] *n.* an economic policy under which nations sought to increase their wealth and power by obtaining large amounts of gold and silver and by selling more goods than they bought. (p. 140)

mestizo [mehs•TEE•zoh] *n.* a person of mixed Spanish and Native American ancestry. (p. 123)

middle class *n.* a social class made up of skilled workers, professionals, businesspeople, and wealthy farmers. (p. 291)

middle passage *n.* the voyage that brought captured Africans to the West Indies, and later to North and South America, to be sold as slaves—so called because it was considered the middle leg of the triangular trade. (p. 135)

militarism [MIHL•ih•tuh•RIHZ•uhm] *n.* a policy of glorifying military power and keeping a standing army always prepared for war. (p. 408)

Ming Dynasty *n.* a Chinese dynasty that ruled from 1368 to 1644. (p. 102)

Monroe Doctrine *n.* a U.S. policy of opposition to European interference in Latin America, announced by President James Monroe in 1823. (p. 384)

Mughal [MOO•guhl] *n.* one of the nomads who invaded the Indian subcontinent in the 16th century and established a powerful empire there. (p. 82)

mujahideen [moo•JAH•heh•DEEN] *n.* in Afghanistan, holy warriors who banded together to fight the Soviet-supported government in the late 1970s. (p. 592)

mulattos [mu•LAT•ohz] *n.* persons of mixed European and African ancestry. (p. 248)

Munich [MYOO•nihk] **Conference** *n.* a 1938 meeting of representatives from Britain, France, Italy, and Germany, at which Britain and France agreed to allow Nazi Germany to annex part of Czechoslovakia in return for Adolf Hitler's pledge to respect Czechoslovakia's new borders. (p. 485)

Muslim League *n.* an organization formed in 1906 to protect the interests of India's Muslims, which later proposed that India be divided into separate Muslim and Hindu nations. (p. 563)

N

Napoleonic [nuh•POH•lee•AHN•ihk] **Code** *n.* a comprehensive and uniform system of laws established for France by Napoleon. (p. 230)

National Assembly *n.* a French congress established by representatives of the Third Estate on June 17, 1789, to enact laws and reforms in the name of the French people. (p. 220)

nationalism *n.* the belief that people should be loyal mainly to their nation—that is, to the people with whom they share a culture and history—rather than to a king or empire. (p. 253)

nation-state *n.* an independent geopolitical unit of people having a common culture and identity. (p. 253)

NATO [NAY•toh] *n.* the North Atlantic Treaty Organization—a defensive military alliance formed in 1949 by ten Western European nations, the United States, and Canada. (p. 535)

Nazism [NAHT•SIHZ•uhm] *n.* the fascist policies of the National Socialist German Workers' party, based on totalitarianism, a belief in racial superiority, and state control of industry. (p. 478)

Negritude [NEE•grih•TOOD] **movement** *n.* a movement in which French-speaking Africans and West Indians celebrated their heritage of traditional African culture and values. (p. 578)

neoclassical [NEE•oh•KLAS•ih•kuhl] *adj.* relating to a simple, elegant style (based on ideas and themes from ancient Greece and Rome) that characterized the arts in Europe during the late 1700s. (p. 203)

New Deal *n.* U.S. president Franklin Roosevelt's economic reform program designed to solve the problems created by the Great Depression. (p. 475)

nonaggression [NAHN•uh•GRESHS•uhn] **pact** *n.* an agreement in which nations promise not to attack one another. (p. 491)

nonaligned nations *n.* the independent countries that remained neutral in the Cold War competition between the United States and the Soviet Union. (p. 548)

Nuremberg [NUR•uhm•BURG] **Trials** *n.* a series of court proceedings held in Nuremberg, Germany, after World War II, in which Nazi leaders were tried for aggression, violations of the rules of war, and crimes against humanity. (p. 516)

O

Old Regime [ray•ZHEEM] *n.* the political and social system that existed in France before the French Revolution. (p. 217)

Open Door Policy *n.* a policy, proposed by the United States in 1899, under which all nations would have equal opportunities to trade in China. (p. 374)

Opium War *n.* a conflict between Britain and China, lasting from 1839 to 1842, over Britain's opium trade in China. (p. 372)

Oslo Peace Accords *n.* an agreement in 1993 in which Israeli prime minister Rabin granted Palestinian self-rule in the Gaza Strip and the West Bank. (p. 587)

ozone layer *n.* a layer of Earth's upper atmosphere, which protects living things from the sun's damaging ultraviolet rays. (p. 645)

P

Pacific Rim *n.* the lands surrounding the Pacific Ocean—especially those in Asia. (p. 362)

Panama Canal *n.* a human-made waterway connecting the Atlantic and Pacific oceans, built in Panama by the United States and opened in 1914. (p. 387)

partition *n.* a division into parts, like the 1947 division of the British colony of India into the two nations of India and Pakistan. (p. 564)

paternalism [puh•TUR•nuh•LIHZ•uhm] *n.* a policy of treating subject people as if they were children, providing for their needs but not giving them rights. (p. 347)

patron [PAY•truhn] *n.* a person who supports artists, especially financially. (p. 38)

Peace of Augsburg [AWGZ•BURG] *n.* a 1555 agreement declaring that the religion of each German state would be decided by its ruler. (p. 58)

penal [PEE•nuhl] **colony** *n.* a colony to which convicts are sent as an alternative to prison. (p. 318)

peninsulares [peh•neen•soo•LAH•rehs] *n.* in Spanish colonial society, colonists who were born in Spain. (p. 247)

Peninsular [puh•NIHN•syuh•luhr] **War** *n.* a conflict, lasting from 1808 to 1813, in which Spanish rebels, with the aid of British forces, fought to drive Napoleon's French troops out of Spain. (p. 235)

perestroika [PEHR•ih•STROY•kuh] *n.* a restructuring of the Soviet economy to permit more local decision making, begun by Mikhail Gorbachev in 1985. (p. 613)

perspective [puhr•SPEHK•tihv] *n.* an artistic technique that creates the appearance of three dimensions on a flat surface. (p. 40)

philosophe [FIHL•uh•SAHF] *n.* one of a group of social thinkers in France during the Enlightenment. (p. 196)

Pilgrims *n.* a group of people who, in 1620, founded the colony of Plymouth in Massachusetts to escape religious persecution in England. (p. 128)

plebiscite [PLEHB•ih•SYT] *n.* a direct vote in which a country's people have the opportunity to approve or reject a proposal. (p. 230)

PLO *n.* the Palestine Liberation Organization—an organization dedicated to the establishment of an independent state for Palestinians in the Middle East. (p. 585)

Politburo [PAHL•iht•BYOOR•oh] *n.* the ruling committee of the Communist Party in the Soviet Union. (p. 612)

political dissent *n.* the difference of opinion over political issues. (p. 650)

popular culture *n.* the cultural elements—sports, music, movies, clothing, and so forth—that reflect a group's common background and changing interests. (p. 659)

predestination [pree•DEHS•tuh•NAY•shuhn] *n.* the doctrine that God has decided all things beforehand, including which people will be eternally saved. (p. 61)

Presbyterian [PREHZ•bih•TEER•ee•uhn] *n.* a member of a Protestant church governed by presbyters (elders) and founded on the teachings of John Knox. (p. 62)

PRI *n.* the Institutional Revolutionary Party—the main political party of Mexico. (p. 603)

proletariat [PROH•lih•TAIR•ee•iht] *n.* in Marxist theory, the group of workers who would overthrow the czar and come to rule Russia. (p. 434)

proliferation [pruh•LIHF•uh•RAY•shuhn] *n.* a growth or spread—especially the spread of nuclear weapons to nations that do not currently have them. (p. 649)

propaganda [PRAHP•uh•GAN•duh] *n.* information or material spread to advance a cause or to damage an opponent's cause. (p. 420)

Protestant [PRAHT•ih•stuhnt] *n.* a member of a Christian church founded on the principles of the Reformation. (p. 56)

provisional government *n.* a temporary government. (p. 436)

psychology [sy•KAHL•uh•jee] *n.* the study of the human mind and human behavior. (p. 332)

Puritans *n.* a group of people who sought freedom from religious persecution in England by founding a colony at Massachusetts Bay in the early 1600s. (p. 128)

Q

Qing [chihng] **Dynasty** *n.* China's last dynasty, which ruled from 1644 to 1912. (p. 105)

R

racism [RAY•sIHZ•uhm] *n.* the belief that one race is superior to others. (p. 341)

radicals *n.* in the first half of the 19th century, those Europeans who favored drastic change to extend democracy to all people. (p. 253)

radioactivity *n.* a form of energy released as atoms decay. (p. 331)

Raj [rahj] *n.* British rule after India came under the British crown during the reign of Queen Victoria. (p. 360)

rationing [RASH•uh•nihng] *n.* the limiting of the amounts of goods people can buy—often imposed by governments during wartime, when goods are in short supply. (p. 420)

realism *n.* a 19th-century artistic movement in which writers and painters sought to show life as it is rather than life as it should be. (p. 266)

realpolitik [ray•AHL•POH•lih•TEEK] *n.* "the politics of reality"—the practice of tough power politics without room for idealism. (p. 261)

recession *n.* a slowdown in a nation's economy. (p. 600)

Red Guards *n.* militia units formed by young Chinese people in 1966 in response to Mao Zedong's call for a social and cultural revolution. (p. 541)

Reformation [REHF•uhr•MAY•shuhn] *n.* a 16th-century movement for religious reform, leading to the founding of Christian churches that rejected the pope's authority. (p. 55)

refugee *n.* a person who leaves his or her country to move to another to find safety. (p. 652)

Reign [rayn] **of Terror** *n.* the period, from mid-1793 to mid-1794, when Maximilien Robespierre ruled France nearly as a dictator and thousands of political figures and ordinary citizens were executed. (p. 226)

Renaissance [REHN•ih•SAHNS] *n.* a period of European history, lasting from about 1300 to 1600, during which renewed interest in classical culture led to far-reaching changes in art, learning, and views of the world. (p. 37)

Restoration [REHS•tuh•RAY•shuhn] *n.* the period of Charles II's rule over England, after the collapse of Oliver Cromwell's government. (p. 182)

reunification [ree•YOO•nuh•fih•KAY•shuhn] *n.* a bringing together again of things that have been separated, like the reuniting of East Germany and West Germany in 1990. (p. 620)

romanticism [roh•MAN•tih•SIHZ•uhm] *n.* an early-19th-century movement in art and thought, which focused on emotion and nature rather than reason and society. (p. 264)

Roosevelt Corollary [ROH•zuh•VEHLT KAWR•uh•lehr•ee] *n.* President Theodore Roosevelt's 1904 extension of the Monroe Doctrine, in which he declared that the United States had the right to exercise "police power" throughout the Western Hemisphere. (p. 387)

Rowlatt Acts *n.* laws passed in 1919 that allowed the British government in India to jail anti-British protesters without trial for as long as two years. (p. 453)

Russification [RUHS•uh•fih•KAY•shuhn] *n.* the process of forcing Russian culture on all ethnic groups in the Russian Empire. (p. 259)

Russo-Japanese War *n.* a 1904–1905 conflict between Russia and Japan, sparked by the two countries' efforts to dominate Manchuria and Korea. (p. 378)

Safavid [suh•FAH•VIHD] *n.* a member of a Shi'a Muslim dynasty that built an empire in Persia in the 16th–18th centuries. (p. 78)

salon [suh•LAHN] *n.* a social gathering of intellectuals and artists, like those held in the homes of wealthy women in Paris and other European cities during the Enlightenment. (p. 202)

SALT *n.* the Strategic Arms Limitation Talks—a series of meetings in the 1970s, in which leaders of the United States and the Soviet Union agreed to limit their nations' stocks of nuclear weapons. (p. 557)

Salt March *n.* a peaceful protest against the Salt Acts in 1930 in India in which Mohandas Gandhi led his followers on a 240-mile walk to the sea, where they made their own salt from evaporated seawater. (p. 455)

sans-culottes [SANS•kyoo•LAHTS] *n.* in the French Revolution, a radical group made up of Parisian wage-earners and small shopkeepers who wanted a greater voice in government, lower prices, and an end to food shortages. (p. 224)

Schlieffen [SHLEE•fuhn] **Plan** *n.* Germany's military plan at the outbreak of World War I, according to which German troops would rapidly defeat France and then move east to attack Russia. (p. 412)

scientific method *n.* a logical procedure for gathering information about the natural world, in which experimentation and observation are used to test hypotheses. (p. 191)

Scientific Revolution *n.* a major change in European thought, starting in the mid-1500s, in which the study of the natural world began to be characterized by careful observation and the questioning of accepted beliefs. (p. 189)

scorched-earth policy *n.* the practice of burning crops and killing livestock during wartime so that the enemy cannot live off the land. (p. 235)

secede [sih•SEED] *v.* to withdraw formally from an association or alliance. (p. 326)

secular [SEHK•yuh•luhr] *adj.* concerned with worldly rather than spiritual matters. (p. 38)

segregation [SEHG•rih•GAY•shuhn] *n.* the legal or social separation of people of different races. (p. 327)

self-determination [SEHLF•dih•TUR•muh•NAY•shuhn] *n.* the freedom of a people to decide under what form of government they wish to live. (p. 424)

sepoy [SEE•POY] *n.* an Indian soldier serving under British command. (p. 357)

Sepoy Mutiny [MYOOT•uh•nee] *n.* an 1857 rebellion of Hindu and Muslim soldiers against the British in India. (p. 359)

Seven Years' War *n.* a conflict in Europe, North America, and India, lasting from 1756 to 1763, in which the forces of Britain and Prussia battled those of Austria, France, Russia, and other countries. (p. 173)

shah [shah] *n.* hereditary monarch of Iran. (p. 80)

"shock therapy" *n.* an economic program implemented in Russia by Boris Yeltsin in the 1990s, involving an abrupt shift from a command economy to a free-market economy. (p. 616)

Sikh [seek] *n.* a member of a nonviolent religious group whose beliefs blend elements of Buddhism, Hinduism, and Sufism. (p. 85)

skepticism [SKEHP•tih•SIHZ•uhm] *n.* a philosophy based on the idea that nothing can be known for certain. (p. 163)

social contract *n.* the agreement by which people define and limit their individual rights, thus creating an organized society or government. (p. 195)

Social Darwinism [DAHR•wih•NIHZ•uhm] *n.* the application of Charles Darwin's ideas about evolution and "survival of the fittest" to human societies—particularly as justification for imperialist expansion. (p. 341)

socialism *n.* an economic system in which the factors of production are owned by the public and operate for the welfare of all. (p. 302)

Solidarity [SAHL•ih•DAR•ih•tee] *n.* a Polish labor union that during the 1980s became the main force of opposition to Communist rule in Poland. (p. 618)

soviet [SOH•vee•EHT] *n.* one of the local representative councils formed in Russia after the downfall of Czar Nicholas II. (p. 436)

Spanish-American War *n.* an 1898 conflict between the United States and Spain, in which the United States supported Cubans' fight for independence. (p. 384)

sphere of influence *n.* a foreign region in which a nation has control over trade and other economic activities. (p. 373)

standard of living *n.* the quality of life of a person or a population, as indicated by the goods, services, and luxuries available to the person or people. (p. 600)

strike *v.* to refuse to work in order to force an employer to meet certain demands. (p. 304)

Suez [soo•EHZ] **Canal** *n.* a human-made waterway, which was opened in 1869, connecting the Red Sea and the Mediterranean Sea. (p. 354)

suffrage [SUHF•rihj] *n.* the right to vote. (p. 313)

sultan *n.* "overlord," or "one with power"; title for Ottoman rulers during the rise of the Ottoman Empire. (p. 73)

surrealism [suh•REE•uh•LIHZ•uhm] *n.* a 20th-century artistic movement that focuses on the workings of the unconscious mind. (p. 465)

sustainable growth *n.* economic development that meets people's needs but preserves the environment and conserves resources for future generations. (p. 646)

Taiping [ty•pihng] **Rebellion** *n.* a mid-19th century rebellion against the Qing Dynasty in China, led by Hong Xiuquan. (p. 373)

Taj Mahal [TAHZH muh•HAHL] *n.* a beautiful tomb in Agra, India, built by the Mughal emperor Shah Jahan for his wife Mumtaz Mahal. (p. 85)

Taliban *n.* conservative Islamic group that took control of Afghanistan after the Soviet Union withdrew its troops; driven from power by U.S. forces in December, 2001, because of its harboring of suspected terrorists. (p. 592)

Tennis Court Oath *n.* a pledge made by the members of France's National Assembly in 1789, in which they vowed to continue meeting until they had drawn up a new constitution. (p. 220)

terrorism *n.* the use of force or threats to frighten people or governments to change their policies. (p. 653)

theocracy [thee•AHK•ruh•see] *n.* a government controlled by religious leaders. (p. 62)

theory of evolution *n.* the idea, proposed by Charles Darwin in 1859, that species of plants and animals arise by means of a process of natural selection. (p. 331)

theory of relativity [REHL•uh•TIHV•ih•tee] *n.* Albert Einstein's ideas about the interrelationships between time and space and between energy and matter. (p. 463)

Third Reich [ryk] *n.* the Third German Empire, established by Adolf Hitler in the 1930s. (p. 484)

Third Republic *n.* the republic that was established in France after the downfall of Napoleon III and ended with the German occupation of France during World War II. (p. 315)

Third World *n.* during the Cold War, the developing nations not allied with either the United States or the Soviet Union. (p. 548)

Thirty Years' War *n.* a European conflict over religion and territory and for power among ruling families, lasting from 1618 to 1648. (p. 169)

Tiananmen [tyahn•ahn•mehn] **Square** *n.* a huge public space in Beijing, China; in 1989, the site of a student uprising in support of democratic reforms. (p. 627)

Tokugawa Shogunate [TOH•koo•GAH•wah SHOH•guh•niht] *n.* a dynasty of shoguns that ruled a unified Japan from 1603 to 1867. (p. 110)

totalitarianism [toh•TAL•ih•TAIR•ee•uh•NIHZ•uhm] *n.* government control over every aspect of public and private life. (p. 440)

total war *n.* a conflict in which the participating countries devote all their resources to the war effort. (p. 419)

Treaty of Kanagawa [kah•NAH•gah•wah] *n.* an 1854 agreement between the United States and Japan, which opened two Japanese ports to U.S. ships and allowed the United States to set up an embassy in Japan. (p. 376)

Treaty of Tordesillas [TAWR•day•SEEL•yahs] *n.* a 1494 agreement between Portugal and Spain, declaring that newly discovered lands to the west of an imaginary line in the Atlantic Ocean would belong to Spain and newly discovered lands to the east of the line would belong to Portugal. (p. 99)

Treaty of Versailles [vuhr•SY] *n.* the peace treaty signed by Germany and the Allied powers after World War I. (p. 424)

trench warfare *n.* a form of warfare in which opposing armies fight each other from trenches dug in the battlefield. (p. 413)

triangular trade *n.* the transatlantic trading network along which slaves and other goods were carried between Africa, England, Europe, the West Indies, and the colonies in the Americas. (p. 134)

Triple Alliance *n.* a military alliance between Germany, Austria-Hungary, and Italy in the years preceding World War I. (p. 408)

Triple Entente [ahn•TAHNT] *n.* a military alliance between Great Britain, France, and Russia in the years preceding World War I. (p. 409)

Truman Doctrine *n.* announced by President Harry Truman in 1947, a U.S. policy of giving economic and military aid to free nations threatened by internal or external opponents. (p. 534)

UV

union *n.* an association of workers, formed to bargain for better working conditions and higher wages. (p. 304)

United Nations *n.* an international peacekeeping organization founded in 1945 to provide security to the nations of the world. (p. 532)

Universal Declaration of Human Rights *n.* a 1948 statement in which the United Nations declared that all human beings have rights to life, liberty, and security. (p. 650)

unrestricted submarine warfare *n.* the use of submarines to sink without warning any ship (including neutral ships and unarmed passenger liners) found in an enemy's waters. (p. 418)

urbanization [UR•buh•nih•ZAY•shuhn] *n.* the growth of cities and the migration of people into them. (p. 289)

U.S.A. Patriot Act *n.* an antiterrorism bill of 2001 that strengthened governmental rights to detain foreigners suspected of terrorism and prosecute terrorist crimes. (p. 658)

U.S. Civil War *n.* a conflict between Northern and Southern states of the United States over the issue of slavery, lasting from 1861 to 1865. (p. 326)

utilitarianism [yoo•TIHL•ih•TAIR•ee•uh•NIHZ•uhm] *n.* the theory, proposed by Jeremy Bentham in the late 1700s, that government actions are useful only if they promote the greatest good for the greatest number of people. (p. 301)

utopia [yoo•TOH•pee•uh] *n.* an imaginary land described by Thomas More in his book *Utopia*—hence, an ideal place. (p. 48)

vernacular [vuhr•NAK•yuh•luhr] *n.* the everyday language of people in a region or country. (p. 41)

Vietcong [vee•EHT•KAHNG] *n.* a group of Communist guerrillas who, with the help of North Vietnam, fought against the South Vietnamese government in the Vietnam War. (p. 546)

Vietnamization [vee•EHT•nuh•mih•ZAY•shuhn] *n.* President Richard Nixon's strategy for ending U.S. involvement in the Vietnam War, involving a gradual withdrawal of American troops and replacement of them with South Vietnamese forces. (p. 546)

W

War of the Spanish Succession *n.* a conflict, lasting from 1701 to 1713, in which a number of European states fought to prevent the Bourbon family from controlling Spain as well as France. (p. 167)

Warsaw Pact *n.* a military alliance formed in 1955 by the Soviet Union and seven Eastern European countries. (p. 535)

Weimar [WY•MAHR] **Republic** *n.* the republic that was established in Germany in 1919 and ended in 1933. (p. 471)

Western Front *n.* in World War I, the region of northern France where the forces of the Allies and the Central Powers battled each other. (p. 412)

westernization *n.* an adoption of the social, political, or economic institutions of Western—especially European or American—countries. (p. 176)

XYZ

Zionism [ZY•uh•NIHZ•uhm] *n.* a movement founded in the 1890s to promote the establishment of a Jewish homeland in Palestine. (p. 316)

Spanish Glossary

A

Aborigine [aborigen] *s.* miembro de cualquiera de los pueblos nativos de Australia. (pág. 318)

absolute monarch [monarca absoluto] *s.* rey o reina que tiene poder ilimitado y que procura controlar todos los aspectos de la sociedad. (pág. 160)

Allies [Aliados] *s.* durante la I Guerra Mundial, las naciones de Gran Bretaña, Francia y Rusia, junto con otras que lucharon a su lado; también, el grupo de naciones —entre ellas Gran Bretaña, la Unión Soviética y Estados Unidos— opuestas a las Potencias del Eje en la II Guerra Mundial. (pág. 411)

Amritsar Massacre [Masacre de Amritsar] *s.* matanza por tropas británicas de casi 400 indios, reunidos en Amritsar para protestar contra las Leyes Rowlatt. (pág. 454)

Anabaptist [anabaptista] *s.* en la Reforma, miembro de un grupo protestante que enseñaba que sólo los adultos podían ser bautizados, y que la Iglesia y el Estado debían estar separados. (pág. 62)

Anglican [anglicano] *adj.* relacionado con la Iglesia de Inglaterra. (pág. 60)

annexation [anexión] *s.* añadir una región al territorio de una unidad política existente. (págs. 365, 379)

annul [anular] *v.* cancelar o suspender. (pág. 58)

anti-Semitism [antisemitismo] *s.* prejuicio contra los judíos. (pág. 315)

apartheid *s.* política de Sudáfrica de separación total y legalizada de las razas; prohibía todo contacto social entre negros y blancos. (pág. 609)

appeasement [apaciguamiento] *s.* otorgar concesiones a un agresor a fin de evitar la guerra. (pág. 483)

armistice [armisticio] *s.* acuerdo de suspender combates. (pág. 421)

Aryans [arios] *s.* para los nazis, los pueblos germanos que formaban una "raza maestra". (pág. 502)

assembly line [línea de montaje] *s.* en una fábrica, correa que lleva un producto de un trabajador a otro, cada uno de los cuales desempeña una sola tarea. (pág. 330)

assimilation [asimilación] *s.* política de una nación de obligar o alentar a un pueblo subyugado a adoptar sus instituciones y costumbres. (pág. 347)

Atlantic Charter [Carta del Atlántico] *s.* declaración de principios emitida en agosto de 1941 por el primer ministro británico Winston Churchill y el presidente de E.U.A. Franklin Roosevelt, en la cual se basó el plan de paz de los Aliados al final de la II Guerra Mundial. (pág. 496)

Atlantic slave trade [trata de esclavos del Atlántico] *s.* compra, transporte y venta de africanos para trabajar en las Américas. (pág. 133)

Axis Powers [Potencias del Eje] *s.* en la II Guerra Mundial, las naciones de Alemania, Italia y Japón, que formaron una alianza en 1936. (pág. 483)

B

balance of power [equilibrio de poder] *s.* situación política en que ninguna nación tiene suficiente poder para ser una amenaza para las demás. (pág. 238)

The Balkans [Balcanes] *s.* región del sureste de Europa ocupada actualmente por Grecia, Albania, Bulgaria, Rumania, la parte europea de Turquía y las antiguas repúblicas de Yugoslavia. (pág. 255)

baroque [barroco] *s.* estilo grandioso y ornamentado del arte, la música y la arquitectura a fines del siglo 17 y principios del 18. (pág. 203)

Battle of Britain [Batalla Británica] *s.* batallas entre las fuerzas aéreas de Alemania y Gran Bretaña que se libraron sobre el territorio británico entre 1940–1941. (pág. 494)

Battle of Guadalcanal [Batalla de Guadalcanal] *s.* batalla de la II Guerra Mundial ocurrida en 1942–1943 en que las fuerzas aliadas expulsaron a las fuerzas japonesas de la isla de Guadalcanal en el Pacífico. (pág. 501)

Battle of Midway [Batalla del Midway] *s.* batalla aérea y naval de la II Guerra Mundial librada en 1941 en que las fuerzas estadounidenses derrotaron a las japonesas en el Pacífico central. (pág. 500)

Battle of Stalingrad [Batalla de Stalingrado] *s.* batalla de la II Guerra Mundial ocurrida en 1942–1943 en que las fuerzas alemanas perdieron y no lograron capturar la ciudad de Stalingrado en la Unión Soviética. (pág. 507)

Battle of the Bulge [Batalla del Bolsón] *s.* batalla de 1944–45 en que las fuerzas aliadas repulsaron la última ofensiva alemana de envergadura en la II Guerra Mundial. (pág. 510)

Battle of Trafalgar [Batalla de Trafalgar] *s.* batalla naval de 1805 en que las fuerzas de Napoleón fueron derrotadas por una flota inglesa al mando de Horacio Nelson. (pág. 233)

Berlin Conference [Conferencia de Berlín de 1884–1885] *s.* reunión en la cual representantes de las naciones europeas acordaron reglas para la colonización europea de África. (pág. 342)

Bill of Rights [Carta de Derechos] *s.* primeras diez enmiendas a la Constitución de E.U.A., que protegen los derechos y libertades básicos de los ciudadanos. (pág. 211)

blitzkrieg *s.* "guerra relámpago"; táctica bélica de ataque sorpresa con aviones rápidos, seguidos de numerosas fuerzas de infantería. (pág. 491)

blockade [bloqueo] *s.* desplazamiento de tropas o barcos para impedir para evitar la entrada o salida de todo tráfico comercial a una ciudad o región. (pág. 234)

Boer [bóer] *s.* colono holandés que se estableció en Sudáfrica. (pág. 342)

Boer War [Guerra de los Bóers] *s.* conflicto de 1899 a 1902 entre los bóers y los británicos por el control de territorio en Sudáfrica. (pág. 344)

Bolsheviks [bolcheviques] *s.* grupo de marxistas revolucionarios rusos que tomó el control del gobierno ruso en noviembre de 1917. (pág. 434)

Boxer Rebellion [Rebelión de los Bóxers] *s.* rebelión de 1900 en China contra la influencia extranjera en el país. (pág. 374)

boyar [boyardo] *s.* el noble terrateniente de Rusia. (pág. 174)

brinkmanship [política arriesgada] *s.* política de amenazar con lanzarse a la guerra en respuesta a una agresión enemiga. (pág. 536)

cabinet [gabinete] *s.* grupo de asesores o ministros escogidos por el jefe de gobierno de un país para que participen en la toma de decisiones del gobierno. (pág. 183)

Calvinism [calvinismo] *s.* conjunto de enseñanzas religiosas basadas en las ideas del reformador Juan Calvino. (pág. 61)

Camp David Accords [Acuerdos de Camp David] *s.* primer tratado firmado entre Israel y un país árabe, en que el presidente Anwar Sadat de Egipto reconoció el derecho a existir de Israel y el primer ministro israelí Menachem Begin acordó devolver la península del Sinaí a Egipto. (pág. 586)

capitalism [capitalismo] *s.* sistema económico basado en la propiedad privada y en la inversión de dinero en empresas comerciales con el objetivo de obtener ganancias. (págs. 573, 734)

Catholic Reformation [Contrarreforma] *s.* movimiento del siglo 16 en el que la Iglesia Católica intentó reformarse en respuesta a la Reforma protestante. (pág. 64)

caudillo *s.* dictador militar de un país latinoamericano. (pág. 382)

Central Powers [Potencias Centrales] *s.* en la I Guerra Mundial, las naciones de Alemania y Austro-Hungría, y las demás que lucharon a su lado. (pág. 411)

Chartist movement [movimiento cartista] *s.* movimiento de reforma inglés del siglo 19 en que miembros de la clase trabajadora pidieron reformas en el Parlamento y en las elecciones, como el voto para todos los hombres. (pág. 314)

checks and balances [control y compensación de poderes] *s.* medidas para evitar que una rama del gobierno domine sobre las otras. (pág. 211)

CIS [CEI] *s.* Comunidad de Estados Independientes: asociación de los antiguos territorios soviéticos formada cuando la Unión Soviética se desmembró. (pág. 615)

civil disobedience [desobediencia civil] *s.* negativa pública y deliberada a obedecer una ley considerada injusta. (pág. 454)

cloning [clonación] *s.* creación de plantas o animales genéticamente idénticos a plantas o animales existentes. (pág. 639)

coalition government [gobierno de coalición] *s.* gobierno controlado por una alianza temporal de varios partidos políticos. (pág. 470)

Cold War [Guerra Fría] *s.* estado de hostilidad diplomática entre Estados Unidos y la Unión Soviética en las décadas siguientes a la II Guerra Mundial. (pág. 535)

collective farm [granja colectiva] *s.* granja controlada por el gobierno, formada mediante la unión de muchas pequeñas granjas. (pág. 444)

colony [colonia] *s.* tierra controlada por una nación distante. (pág. 120)

Columbian Exchange [trasferencia colombina] *s.* transferencia mundial de plantas, animales y enfermedades durante la colonización europea de América. (pág. 137)

command economy [economía de mando] *s.* sistema económico en el que el gobierno toma todas las decisiones económicas. (pág. 443)

commune [comuna] *s.* en la China comunista, granja colectiva en la que mucha gente trabaja y vive junta. (pág. 540)

communism [comunismo] *s.* sistema económico en el que todos los medios de producción —tierras, minas, fábricas, ferrocarriles y negocios— son propiedad del pueblo, en que no existe la propiedad privada, y en que todos los productos y servicios se comparten por igual. (pág. 303)

Communist Party [Partido Comunista] *s.* partido político basado en las ideas de Karl Marx y V. I. Lenin; originalmente el Partido Bolchevique ruso. (pág. 439)

Concert of Europe [Concierto de Europa] *s.* serie de alianzas entre naciones europeas en el siglo 19, ideadas por el príncipe Klemens von Metternich para impedir revoluciones. (pág. 240)

concordat [concordato] *s.* acuerdo firmado entre Napoleón y el Papa para establecer una nueva relación entre la Iglesia y el Estado. (pág. 230)

Congress of Vienna [Congreso de Viena] *s.* serie de reuniones en 1814 y 1815 en las cuales los dirigentes europeos trataron de establecer una paz y seguridad duraderas tras la derrota de Napoleón. (pág. 238)

Congress Party [Partido del Congreso] *s.* importante partido político nacional de India; también se llama Congreso Nacional de India. (pág. 563)

conquistadors [conquistadores] *s.* soldados, exploradores y aventureros españoles que participaron en la conquista de América en el siglo 16. (pág. 120)

conservative [conservador] *s.* en la primera mitad del siglo 19, el europeo —principalmente los terratenientes y nobles acaudalados— que querían preservar las monarquías tradicionales. (pág. 253)

constitutional monarchy [monarquía constitucional] *s.* monarquía en que el poder del gobernante está limitado por la ley. (pág. 183)

containment [contención] *s.* política exterior estadounidense adoptada por el presidente Harry Truman a fines de la década de 1940 para impedir la expansión del comunismo creando alianzas con países débiles y ayudándolos a contener los avances soviéticos. (pág. 533)

Continental System [Sistema Continental] *s.* política de Napoleón de impedir el comercio de Gran Bretaña con la Europa continental para destruir la economía británica. (pág. 234)

corporation [corporación] *s.* empresa de accionistas que comparten las ganancias pero que no son personalmente responsables de sus deudas. (pág. 297)

Council of Trent [Concilio de Trento] *s.* reunión de líderes de la Iglesia Católica Romana, convocada por el papa Pablo III, para fallar sobre varias doctrinas criticadas por los reformadores protestantes. (pág. 65)

coup d'etat [golpe de Estado] *s.* toma repentina del poder político de una nación. (pág. 230)

creole [criollo] *s.* en la sociedad española colonial, el colono nacido en Latinoamérica de padres españoles. (pág. 247)

Crimean War [Guerra de Crimea] *s.* conflicto de 1853 a 1856, en el cual el imperio otomano, con ayuda de Gran Bretaña y Francia, frenó la expansión rusa en la región del mar Negro. (pág. 353)

crop rotation [rotación de cultivos] *s.* sistema que cultiva distintos productos en un campo cada año para conservar la fertilidad de la tierra. (pág. 283)

Cultural Revolution [Revolución Cultural] *s.* levantamiento de 1966–1976 en China, encabezado por los Guardias Rojos de Mao Tsetung, con el propósito de establecer una sociedad de campesinos y trabajadores donde todos fue-ran iguales. (pág. 541)

cyberterrorism [terrorismo cibernético] *s.* ataques por motivos políticos contra sistemas de tecnología informática. (pág. 654)

D

daimyo *s.* señor feudal de Japón que comandaba un ejército privado de samurais. (pág. 108)

D-Day [Día D] *s.* 6 de junio de 1944; día elegido para la invasión aliada de Europa continental durante la II Guerra Mundial. (pág. 510)

Declaration of Independence [Declaración de Independencia] *s.* declaración de las razones de la ruptura de las colonias americanas con Gran Bretaña, aprobada por el Segundo Congreso Continental. (pág. 207)

demilitarization [desmilitarización] *s.* reducción de la capacidad bélica de un país que se logra desbandando sus fuerzas armadas y prohibiéndole que adquiera armas. (pág. 516)

democratization [democratización] *s.* proceso de crear un gobierno elegido por el pueblo. (pág. 516)

Department of Homeland Security [Departamento de la Seguridad del Territorio Nacional] *s.* agencia federal estadounidense creada en 2002 para coordinar una estrategia nacional integral contra el terrorismo. (pág. 657)

détente *s.* política de reducir las tensiones de la Guerra Fría, adoptada por Estados Unidos durante la presidencia de Richard Nixon. (pág. 556)

developed nation [país desarrollado] *s.* nación con las instalaciones necesarias para la producción avanzada de productos manufacturados. (pág. 641)

devshirme *s.* en el imperio otomano, política de llevarse a los niños de los pueblos cristianos conquistados para entrenarlos como soldados musulmanes. (pág. 76)

dissident [disidente] *s.* opositor a la política oficial de un gobierno. (pág. 608)

divine right [derecho divino] *s.* noción de que los monarcas son representantes de Dios en la Tierra y, por lo tanto, sólo le deben responder a él. (pág. 160)

dominion [dominio] *s.* en el imperio británico, una nación (como Canadá) a la que se permitía gobernar sus asuntos internos. (pág. 318)

domino theory [teoría del dominó] *s.* noción de que si una nación cae bajo control comunista, los países vecinos también lo harán. (pág. 544)

Dreyfus affair [caso Dreyfus] *s.* controversia surgida en Francia en la década de 1890 por el juicio y encarcelamiento del capitán Alfred Dreyfus, oficial judío falsamente acusado de vender secretos militares a Alemania. (pág. 315)

Dutch East India Company [Compañía Holandesa de las Indias Orientales] *s.* empresa fundada por holandeses a principios del siglo 17 para establecer y dirigir comercio por todo Asia. (pág. 100)

E

Eastern Front [Frente Oriental] *s.* en la I Guerra Mundial, región a lo largo de la frontera ruso-alemana donde rusos y servios pelearon contra alemanes, austriacos y turcos. (pág. 414)

Edict of Nantes [Edicto de Nantes] *s.* declaración en que el rey francés Enrique IV prometió que los protestantes podían vivir en paz en Francia y tener centros de veneración en algunas ciudades. (pág. 162)

Emancipation Proclamation [Proclama de Emancipación] *s.* declaración emitida por el presidente Abraham Lincoln en 1862, asentando la libertad de todos los esclavos de los estados confederados. (pág. 326)

emerging nation [nación emergente] *s.* nación en proceso de industrialización cuyo desarrollo no ha terminado todavía. (pág. 641)

émigré *s.* quien abandona su país de origen por razones políticas, como los nobles y otros que huyeron de Francia durante los levantamientos campesinos de la Revolución Francesa. (pág. 224)

enclosure [cercado] *s.* uno de los campos rodeados de cercas o de arbustos que crearon terratenientes británicos ricos en tierras que antes trabajaban los campesinos. (pág. 283)

encomienda *s.* tierras otorgadas por España a un colonizador de América, con el derecho de hacer trabajar a los amerindios que vivían en ellas. (pág. 123)

English Civil War [Guerra Civil Inglesa] *s.* conflicto de 1642 a 1649 en que los seguidores puritanos del Parlamento lucharon contra los defensores de la monarquía de Inglaterra. (pág. 181)

enlightened despot [déspota ilustrado] *s.* uno de los monarcas europeos del siglo 18 inspirados por las ideas de la Ilustración a gobernar con justicia y respeto a los derechos de sus súbditos. (pág. 204)

Enlightenment [Ilustración] *s.* movimiento del siglo 18 en Europa que trató de aplicar los principios de la razón y el método científico a todos los aspectos de la sociedad. (pág. 195)

entrepreneur [empresario] *s.* persona que organiza, administra y asume los riesgos de un negocio. (pág. 287)

estate [estado] *s.* una de las tres clases sociales existentes en Francia antes de la Revolución Francesa; el primer estado era el de la clerecía; el segundo era el de la nobleza; y el tercero era del resto de la población. (pág. 217)

Estates-General [Estados Generales] *s.* asamblea de representantes de los tres estados, o clases sociales, de Francia. (pág. 219)

ethnic cleansing [limpia étnica] *s.* política de asesinatos y otros actos de brutalidad con que los servios quisieron eliminar la población musulmana de Bosnia después de la división de Yugoslavia. (pág. 622)

existentialism [existencialismo] *s.* filosofía basada en la idea de que el ser humano da significado a su vida con sus decisiones y acciones. (pág. 464)

extraterritorial rights [derechos extraterritoriales] *s.* exención a los extranjeros de las leyes de un país. (pág. 372)

factors of production [factores de producción] *s.* recursos —como tierra, mano de obra y capital— necesarios para producir bienes y servicios. (pág. 284)

factory [fábrica] *s.* construcción amplia en que se manufacturan productos con maquinaria. (pág. 286)

fascism [fascismo] *s.* movimiento político que postula una forma extrema de nacionalismo, la supresión de los derechos individuales y un régimen dictatorial de un solo partido. (pág. 476)

favorable balance of trade [balanza comercial favorable] *s.* situación económica en la cual un país exporta más de lo que importa, es decir, que vende más productos de los que compra en el extranjero. (pág. 141)

federal system [sistema federal] *s.* sistema de gobierno en el que el poder se divide entre una autoridad central y varios estados. (págs. 211, 607)

"Final Solution" [solución final] *s.* programa de Hitler de asesinar sistemáticamente a todo el pueblo judío. (pág. 503)

Five-Year Plans [Planes de Cinco Años] *s.* planes delineados por José Stalin en 1928 para desarrollar la economía de la Unión Soviética. (pág. 443)

Four Modernizations [cuatro modernizaciones] *s.* serie de objetivos adoptados por el líder chino Deng Xiaoping a finales del siglo 20 con miras al progreso en agricultura, industria, defensa, y ciencia y tecnología. (pág. 626)

Fourteen Points [los catorce puntos] *s.* serie de propuestas en que el presidente estadounidense Woodrow Wilson esbozó un plan para alcanzar una paz duradera después de la I Guerra Mundial. (pág. 424)

free trade [libre comercio] *s.* comercio entre naciones sin restricciones o barreras económicas (tales como aranceles). (pág. 642)

French and Indian War [Guerra contra Franceses e Indígenas] *s.* conflicto entre Gran Bretaña y Francia por control de territorio en Norteamérica, de 1754 a 1763. (pág. 130)

gender inequality [desigualdad de género] *s.* diferencia entre hombres y mujeres con respecto a riqueza y posición social. (pág. 650)

genetic engineering [ingeniería genética] *s.* transferencia de genes de un organismo a otro para producir un organismo con nuevos rasgos. (pág. 639)

genocide [genocidio] *s* .matanza sistemática de todo un pueblo. (pág. 503)

geocentric theory [teoría geocéntrica] *s.* teoría de la Edad Media en la que los eruditos creían que la Tierra era objeto fijo, localizado en el centro del universo. (pág. 189)

geopolitics [geopolítica] *s* .política exterior basada en una consideración de la ubicación estratégica o de los productos de otras tierras. (pág. 352)

ghazi *s.* guerrero del islam. (pág. 73)

ghettos *s.* barrios en que tenían que vivir los judíos europeos. (pág. 503)

glasnost *s.* política soviética de "apertura" a la libre circulación de ideas e información introducida en 1985 por Mijail Gorbachev. (pág 1046)

global economy [economía global] *s.* todas las interacciones financieras —entre individuos, empresas y gobiernos— que rebasan fronteras internacionales. (pág. 642)

Glorious Revolution [Revolución Gloriosa] *s.* derrocamiento incruento del rey Jacobo II de Inglaterra, quien fue reemplazado por Guillermo y María. (pág. 182)

Great Depression [Gran Depresión] *s.* crisis económica aguda que siguió a la caída del mercado de valores en 1929. (pág. 473)

Great Fear [Gran Miedo] *s.* ola de temor insensato que se extendió por las provincias francesas después de la toma de la Bastilla en 1789. (pág. 221)

Great Purge [Gran Purga] *s.* campaña de terror en la Unión Soviética durante la década de 1930, en la cual José Stalin trató de eliminar a todos los miembros del Partido Comunista y ciudadanos que amenazaban su poder. (pág. 442)

green revolution [revolución verde] *s.* esfuerzo en el siglo 20 de aumentar los alimentos en el mundo entero, a través del uso de fertilizantes y pesticidas, y de la creación de cultivos resistentes a enfermedades. (pág. 640)

guerrilla [guerrillero] *s.* miembro de una unidad de combate informal que ataca por sorpresa las tropas enemigas que ocupan su país. (pág. 235)

guillotine [guillotina] *s.* máquina para decapitar con que se hicieron ejecuciones durante la Revolución Francesa. (pág. 226)

habeas corpus *s.* documento que requiere que un detenido comparezca ante un tribunal o juez para que se determine si su detención es legal. (pág. 182)

haiku *s.* poema japonés que tiene tres versos no rimados de cinco, siete y cinco sílabas. (pág. 110)

heliocentric theory [teoría heliocéntrica] *s.* idea de que la Tierra y los otros planetas giran en torno al Sol. (pág. 190)

Holocaust [Holocausto] *s.* matanza en masa de judíos y otros civiles, ejecutada por el gobierno de la Alemania nazi, antes y durante la II Guerra Mundial. (pág. 502)

Holy Alliance [Alianza Sagrada] *s.* liga de naciones europeas formada por los dirigentes de Rusia, Austria y Prusia después del Congreso de Viena. (pág. 240)

home rule [autogobierno] *s.* control sobre asuntos internos que da el gobierno a los residentes de una región. (pág. 320)

humanism [humanismo] *s.* movimiento intelectual del Renacimiento que estudió los textos clásicos y se enfocó en el potencial y los logros humanos. (pág. 38)

Hundred Days [Cien Días] *s.* corto período de 1815 en que Napoleón hizo su último intento de recuperar el poder, depuso al rey francés y de nuevo se proclamó emperador de Francia. (pág. 237)

imperialism [imperialismo] *s.* política en que una nación fuerte buscar dominar la vida política, económica y social de otros países. (pág. 339)

impressionism [impresionismo] *s.* movimiento de la pintura del siglo 19 en reacción al realismo, que buscaba dar impresiones personales de sujetos o momentos. (pág. 267)

indulgence [indulgencia] *s.* perdón que libera al pecador de la penitencia por un pecado. (pág. 55)

industrialization [industrialización] *s.* desarrollo de industrias para la producción con máquinas. (pág. 284)

Industrial Revolution [Revolución Industrial] *s.* cambio, que comenzó en Inglaterra durante el siglo 18, de la producción manual a la producción con máquinas. (pág. 283)

intendant [intendente] *s.* funcionario del gobierno francés nombrado por el monarca para recaudar impuestos e impartir justicia. (pág. 164)

International Space Station [Estación Espacial Internacional] *s.* colaboración patrocinada por Estados Unidos, Rusia y otras 14 naciones para establecer y mantener un laboratorio activo para realizar experimentos científicos en el espacio. (pág. 637)

Internet *s.* vinculación de redes de computadora que permite a gente de todo el mundo comunicarse e intercambiar información. (pág. 639)

intifada [intifada] *s.* campaña palestina de desobediencia civil contra la ocupación israelí de Cisjordania y la Franja de Gaza, que continuó en la década de 1990. (pág. 587)

Irish Republican Army (IRA) [Ejército Republicano Irlandés (el IRA)] *s.* fuerza paramilitar nacionalista que lucha porque Gran Bretaña dé la independencia la Irlanda del Norte. (pág. 321)

iron curtain [cortina de hierro] *s.* durante la Guerra Fría, división que separaba las naciones comunistas de Europa oriental de las naciones democráticas de Europa occidental. (pág. 533)

isolationism [aislacionismo] *s.* política de evitar lazos políticos o militares con otros países. (pág. 484)

janissary [janísero] *s.* miembro de una fuerza élite de soldados del imperio otomano. (pág. 76)

jazz *s.* estilo de música popular del siglo 20 concebido principalmente por músicos afroamericanos. (pág. 465)

Jesuits [jesuitas] *s.* miembros de la Sociedad de Jesús, orden católica romana fundada por Ignacio de Loyola. (pág. 65)

"jewel in the crown" ["joya de la corona"] *s.* colonia británica de India, así llamada por su importancia para el imperio británico, tanto como proveedor de materia prima como mercado para sus productos. (pág. 357)

joint-stock company [sociedad de capitales] *s.* negocio en el que los inversionistas reúnen capital para un propósito común y después comparten las ganancias. (pág. 139)

kabuki *s.* forma de teatro japonés en que se representa una historia con música, danza y mímica. (pág. 110)

kaiser *s.* emperador alemán (del título romano Caesar). (pág. 263)

kamikaze *s.* durante la II Guerra Mundial, pilotos suicidas japoneses entrenados para hundir barcos de los Aliados lanzándose sobre ellos con aviones llenos de bombas. (pág. 511)

Khmer Rouge *s.* grupo de rebeldes comunistas que tomaron el poder en Camboya en 1975. (pág. 547)

Kristallnacht *s.* "Noche de cristales rotos": noche del 9 de noviembre de 1938, en que milicianos nazis atacaron hogares, negocios y sinagogas judíos en toda Alemania. (pág. 502)

Kuomintang *s.* Partido Nacionalista de China, formado después de la caída de la dinastía Qing en 1912. (pág. 448)

laissez faire *s.* idea de que el gobierno no debe regular ni interferir en las industrias y empresas. (pág. 300)

land reform [reforma agraria] *s.* redistribución de tierras agrícolas con división de grandes latifundios y reparto de fincas a campesinos. (pág. 600)

La Reforma *s.* movimiento de reforma liberal en el siglo 19 en México fundado por Benito Juárez. (pág. 390)

League of Nations [Liga de las Naciones] *s.* organización internacional formada después de la I Guerra Mundial cuyo propósito era mantener la paz entre las naciones. (pág. 425)

lebensraum *s.* "espacio vital": territorio adicional que, según Adolfo Hitler, Alemania necesitaba porque estaba sobrepoblada. (pág. 478)

Legislative Assembly [Asamblea Legislativa] *s.* congreso creado por la Constitución francesa de 1791, con poder para emitir leyes y aprobar declaraciones de guerra. (pág. 223)

legitimacy [legitimidad] *s.* derecho hereditario de un monarca a gobernar. (pág. 239)

liberal [liberale] *s.* en la primera mitad del siglo 19, europeo —principalmente empresarios y comerciantes de clase media— que deseaba darle más poder político a los parlamentos elegidos. (pág. 253)

Long March [Larga Marcha] *s.* viaje de 6,000 millas que realizaron en 1934–35 las fuerzas comunistas de China para escapar de las fuerzas nacionalistas de Jiang Jieshi. (pág. 452)

Lutheran [luterano] *s.* miembro de una iglesia protestante basada en las enseñanzas de Martín Lutero. (pág. 56)

lycée [liceo] *s.* escuela pública en Francia. (pág. 230)

M

Manchus [manchú] *s.* pueblo originario de Manchuria que gobernó en China durante la dinastía Qing (1644–1912). (pág. 105)

manifest destiny [destino manifiesto] *s.* idea popular en el siglo 19 en Estados Unidos de que era su derecho y obligación regir Norteamérica, desde el océano Atlántico hasta el Pacífico. (pág. 324)

Maori [maorí] *s.* miembro de un pueblo polinesio establecido en Nueva Zelanda hacia 800 d.C. (pág. 318)

Marshall Plan [Plan Marshall] programa estadounidense de ayuda económica a países europeos para su reconstrucción después de la II Guerra Mundial. (pág. 534)

martial law [ley marcial] *s.* gobierno militar temporal impuesto a la población civil, normalmente en época de guerra o de trastornos civiles. (pág. 607)

mass culture [cultura de masas] *s.* producción de obras de arte y diversión concebidas con el fin de atraer a un amplio público. (pág. 332)

materialism [materialismo] *s.* alto interés en la adquisición de posesiones materiales. (pág. 662)

May Fourth Movement [Movimiento del 4 de Mayo] *s.* protesta nacional china en 1919 con manifestaciones contra el Tratado de Versalles y la interferencia extranjera. (pág. 449)

Meiji era [era Meiji] *s.* período de la historia japonesa entre 1867 y 1912, cuando gobernó el emperador Mutshito. (pág. 377)

Mein Kampf *[Mi lucha] s.* libro escrito por Adolfo Hitler en prisión (1923–1924), en el cual expone sus creencias y sus ideales para Alemania. (pág. 478)

mercantilism [mercantilismo] *s.* política económica de aumentar la riqueza y poder de una nación obteniendo grandes cantidades de oro y plata, y vendiendo más bienes de los que se compran. (pág. 140)

mestizo *s.* mezcla de español y amerindio. (pág. 123)

middle class [clase media] *s.* clase social formada por trabajadores especializados, profesionales, comerciantes y granjeros acaudalados. (pág. 291)

middle passage [travesía intermedia] *s.* viaje que trajo a africanos capturados al Caribe y, posteriormente, a América del Norte y del Sur, para venderlos como esclavos; recibió este nombre porque era considerada la porción media del triángulo comercial trasatlántico. (pág. 135)

militarism [militarismo] *s.* política de glorificar el poder militar y de mantener un ejército permanente, siempre preparado para luchar. (pág. 408)

Ming Dynasty [dinastía Ming] *s.* dinastía que reinó en China desde 1368 hasta 1644. (pág. 102)

Monroe Doctrine [doctrina Monroe] *s.* política estadounidense de oposición a la interferencia europea en Latinoamérica, anunciada por el presidente James Monroe en 1823. (pág. 384)

Mughal [mogol] *s.* uno de los nómadas que invadieron el subcontinente de India en el siglo 16 y establecieron un poderoso imperio. (pág. 82)

mujahideen [muyahidin] *s.* guerreros religiosos afganos que se unieron para luchar contra el gobierno apoyado por los soviéticos a fines de la década de 1970. (pág. 592)

mulattos [mulatos] *s.* personas de ascendencia europea y africana. (pág. 248)

Munich Conference [Conferencia de Munich] *s.* reunión en 1938 de Inglaterra, Francia, Italia y Alemania, en la cual Gran Bretaña y Francia aceptaron que la Alemania nazi anexara parte de Checoslovaquia, a cambio de la promesa de Adolfo Hitler de respetar las nuevas fronteras checas. (pág. 485)

Muslim League [Liga Musulmana] *s.* organización formada en 1906 para proteger los intereses de los musulmanes de India; después propuso la división del país en dos naciones: una musulmana y una hindú. (pág. 563)

N

Napoleonic Code [código napoleónico] *s.* sistema extenso y uniforme de leyes establecido para Francia por Napoleón. (pág. 230)

National Assembly [Asamblea Nacional] *s.* congreso francés establecido el 17 de junio de 1789 por representantes del Tercer Estado para promulgar leyes y reformas en nombre del pueblo. (pág. 220)

nationalism [nacionalismo] *s.* creencia de que la principal lealtad del pueblo debe ser a su nación —es decir, a la gente con quien comparte historia y cultura— y no al rey o al imperio. (pág. 253)

nation-state [nación Estado] *s.* nación independiente de gente que tiene una cultura e identidad común. (pág. 253)

NATO [OTAN] *s.* Organización del Tratado del Atlántico Norte: alianza militar defensiva formada en 1949 por diez naciones de Europa occidental, Estados Unidos y Canadá. (pág. 535)

Nazism [nazismo] *s.* políticas fascistas del Partido Nacional socialista de los Trabajadores de Alemania, basadas en el totalitarismo, la creencia en superioridad racial y el control estatal de la industria. (pág. 478)

Negritude movement [movimiento de negritud] *s.* movimiento de africanos de lengua francesa que celebra el legado de la cultura tradicional africana y sus valores. (pág. 578)

neoclassical [neoclásico] *adj.* relacionado con un estilo sencillo y elegante (inspirado en ideas y temas de la antigua Grecia y Roma) que caracterizó las artes en Europa a fines del siglo 18. (pág. 203)

New Deal *s.* programa de reformas económicas del presidente Franklin D. Roosevelt ideado para solucionar los problemas creados por la Gran Depresión. (pág. 475)

nonaggression pact [pacto de no agresión] *s.* acuerdo en que dos o más naciones prometen no atacarse. (pág. 491)

nonaligned nations [países no alineados] *s.* naciones independientes que permanecieron neutrales durante la Guerra Fría entre Estados Unidos y la Unión Soviética. (pág. 548)

Nuremberg Trials [juicios de Nuremberg] *s.* serie de juicios realizados en Nuremberg, Alemania, tras la II Guerra Mundial a líderes nazis por agresión, violación a las leyes de guerra y crímenes contra la humanidad. (pág. 516)

Old Regime [antiguo régimen] *s.* sistema político y social que existía en Francia antes de la Revolución Francesa. (pág. 217)

Open Door Policy [política de puertas abiertas] *s.* política propuesta por E.U.A. en 1899, que postulaba que todas las naciones tuvieran las mismas oportunidades de comerciar con China. (pág. 374)

Opium War [Guerra del Opio] *s.* conflicto entre Inglaterra y China, de 1839 a 1842, por el comercio inglés de opio en China. (pág. 372)

Oslo Peace Accords [Acuerdos de Paz de Oslo] *s.* acuerdos de 1993 cuando el primer ministro israelí, Rabin, otorgó autonomía a Palestina en la Franja de Gaza y Cisjordania. (pág. 587)

ozone layer [capa de ozono] *s.* capa de la atmósfera superior de la Tierra que protege a los seres vivos de los rayos ultravioleta de la luz solar. (pág. 645)

Pacific Rim [Cuenca del Pacífico] *s.* tierras que bordean el océano Pacífico, especialmente las de Asia. (pág. 362)

Panama Canal [canal de Panamá] *s.* vía marítima que une al océano Atlántico con el Pacífico, construida en Panamá por Estados Unidos y terminada en 1914. (pág. 387)

partition [partición] *s.* división en partes, como la división en 1947 de la colonia británica de India en dos naciones: India y Paquistán. (pág. 564)

paternalism [paternalismo] *s.* política de tratar a los gobernados como si fueran niños, atendiendo a sus necesidades pero sin darles derechos. (pág. 347)

patron [mecenas] *s.* persona que apoya a los artistas, especialmente, en el aspecto financiero. (pág. 38)

Peace of Augsburg [Paz de Augsburgo] *s.* acuerdo realizado en 1555 que declaró que la religión de cada Estado alemán sería decidida por su gobernante. (pág. 58)

penal colony [colonia penal] *s.* colonia a donde se mandan convictos como alternativa a una prisión. (pág. 318)

peninsulares s. en la sociedad española colonial, colonos nacidos en España. (pág. 247)

Peninsular War [Guerra Peninsular] *s.* conflicto de 1808–1813 en que los rebeldes españoles lucharon con la ayuda de Gran Bretaña para expulsar de España las tropas de Napoleón. (pág. 235)

perestroika *s.* reestructuración de la economía soviética para permitir mayor poder de decisión local, iniciada por Mijail Gorbachev en 1985. (pág. 613)

perspective [perspectiva] *s.* técnica artística que crea la apariencia de tres dimensiones en una superficie plana. (pág. 40)

philosophe *s.* miembro de un grupo de pensadores sociales de la Ilustración en Francia. (pág. 196)

Pilgrims [peregrinos] *s.* grupo que en 1620 fundó la colonia de Plymouth en Massachusetts para escapar de persecución religiosa en Inglaterra. (pág. 128)

plebiscite [plebiscito] *s.* voto directo mediante el cual la población de un país tiene la oportunidad de aceptar o rechazar una propuesta. (pág. 230)

PLO [OLP] *s.* Organización de Liberación Palestina: organización dedicada a establecer un Estado independiente para los palestinos en el Medio Oriente. (pág. 585)

Politburo [Politburó] *s.* comité dirigente del Partido Comunista en la Unión Soviética. (pág. 612)

political dissent [disidencia política] *s.* diferencia de opiniones sobre asuntos políticos. (pág. 650)

popular culture [cultura popular] *s.* elementos culturales—deportes, música, cine, ropa, etc.—que muestran los antecedentes comunes de un grupo y sus intereses cambiantes. (pág. 659)

predestination [predestinación] *s.* doctrina que postula que Dios ha decidido todo de antemano, incluso quiénes obtendrán la salvación eterna. (pág. 61)

Presbyterian [presbiteriano] *s.* miembro de una iglesia protestante gobernada por presbíteros conforme a las enseñanzas de John Knox. (pág. 62)

PRI *s.* Partido Revolucionario Institucional: principal partido político en México. (pág. 603)

proletariat [proletariado] *s.* según la teoría marxista, el grupo de trabajadores que derrocaría al zar y gobernaría a Rusia. (pág. 434)

proliferation [proliferación] *s.* crecimiento o expansión, especialmente la expansión de armas nucleares a naciones que actualmente no las tienen. (pág. 649)

propaganda *s.* información o material distribuido para apoyar una causa o socavar una causa opuesta. (pág. 420)

Protestant [protestante] *s.* miembro de una iglesia cristiana fundada de acuerdo a los principios de la Reforma. (pág. 56)

provisional government [gobierno provisional] *s.* gobierno temporal. (pág. 436)

psychology [psicología] *s.* estudio de la mente y la conducta humanas. (pág. 332)

Puritans [puritanos] *s.* grupo que, para liberarse de la persecución religiosa en Inglaterra, fundó una colonia en la bahía de Massachusetts a principios del siglo 17. (pág. 128)

Qing Dynasty [dinastía Qing] *s.* última dinastía china; reinó de 1644 a 1912. (pág. 105)

R

racism [racismo] *s.* creencia de que una raza es superior a otras. (pág. 341)

radical [radicale] *s.* en la primera mitad del siglo 19, el europeo a favor de cambios drásticos para extender la democracia a toda la población. (pág. 253)

radioactivity [radioactividad] *s.* forma de energía liberada mediante la descomposición de átomos. (pág. 331)

Raj *s.* porciones de India controladas por Gran Bretaña de 1757 a 1947. (pág. 360)

rationing [racionamiento] *s.* limitación de la cantidad de bienes que la población puede comprar, generalmente impuesta por un gobierno durante una guerra debido a escasez. (pág. 420)

realism [realismo] *s.* movimiento artístico del siglo 19 en que los escritores y pintores trataron de mostrar la vida como es, no como debiera ser. (pág. 266)

realpolitik *s.* "política de la realidad"; posición política dura que no da lugar al idealismo. (pág. 261)

recession [recesión] *s.* descenso de la economía de una nación. (pág. 600)

Red Guards [Guardias Rojos] *s.* unidades de milicianos formadas por jóvenes chinos en 1966 en respuesta al llamado de Mao Zedong a llevar a cabo una revolución social y cultural. (pág. 541)

Reformation [Reforma] *s.* movimiento del siglo 16 para realizar cambios religiosos que llevó a la fundación de iglesias cristianas que rechazaron la autoridad del Papa. (pág. 55)

refugee [refugiado] *s.* persona que sale de su país a otro país para buscar seguridad. (pág. 652)

Reign of Terror [Régimen del Terror] *s.* período entre 1793–1794 en que Maximilien Robespierre gobernó a Francia casi como dictador, durante el cual fueron ejecutados miles de personajes políticos y de ciudadanos comunes. (pág. 226)

Renaissance [Renacimiento] *s.* período de la historia europea de aproximadamente 1300 a 1600, durante el cual renació un interés en la cultura clásica que generó importantes cambios en el arte, la educación y la visión del mundo. (pág. 37)

Restoration [Restauración] *s.* en Inglaterra, período del reinado de Carlos II, después del colapso del gobierno de Oliver Cromwell. (pág. 182)

reunification [reunificación] *s.* proceso de unir dos elementos que estaban separados, como la reunificación de Alemania oriental y Alemania occidental en 1990. (pág. 620)

romanticism [romanticismo] *s.* movimiento de principios del siglo 19 en el arte y las ideas que recalca la emoción y la naturaleza, más que la razón y la sociedad. (pág. 264)

Roosevelt Corollary [corolario Roosevelt] *s.* ampliación de la doctrina Monroe, emitida por el presidente Theodore Roosevelt en 1904, en que declaró que Estados Unidos tenía el derecho de ejercer "poderes policiales" en el hemisferio occidental. (pág. 387)

Rowlatt Acts [Leyes Rowlatt] *s.* leyes, ratificadas en 1919, que los permitían al gobierno británico en India encarcelar a manifestantes por dos años sin juicio. (pág. 453)

Russification [rusificación] *s.* proceso que obliga a todos los grupos étnicos a adoptar la cultura rusa en el imperio ruso. (pág. 259)

Russo-Japanese War [Guerra Ruso-Japonesa] *s.* conflicto de 1904–1905 entre Rusia y Japón, causada por el interés de los dos países de dominar Manchuria y Corea. (pág. 378)

S

Safavid [safávido] *s.* miembro de una dinastía musulmana shi'a que construyó un imperio en Persia del siglo 16 al 18. (pág. 78)

salon [salón] *s.* reunión social de intelectuales y artistas, como las que celebraban en sus hogares señoras acaudaladas de París y otras ciudades europeas durante la Ilustración. (pág. 202)

SALT *s.* Conversaciones para la Limitación de Armas Estratégicas: serie de reuniones durante la década de 1970 en que líderes de Estados Unidos y la Unión Soviética acordaron limitar el número de armas nucleares de sus países. (pág. 557)

Salt March [Marcha de la Sal] *s.* manifestación pacífica en 1930 en India ocasionada por las Leyes de la Sal; Mohandas Gandhi condujo a sus seguidores, caminando 240 millas al mar, donde hicieron su propia sal del agua de mar evaporada. (pág. 455)

sans-culottes *s.* en la Revolución Francesa, grupo político radical de parisienses asalariados y pequeños comerciantes que anhelaban más voz en el gobierno, bajas de precios y fin a la escasez de alimentos. (pág. 224)

Schlieffen Plan [Plan Schlieffen] *s.* plan militar alemán al comienzo de la I Guerra Mundial, que preveía que Alemania derrotaría rápidamente a Francia y después atacaría a Rusia en el este. (pág. 412)

scientific method [método científico] *s.* procedimiento lógico para reunir información sobre el mundo natural, en que se usa experimentación y observación para poner a prueba hipótesis. (pág. 191)

Scientific Revolution [Revolución Científica] *s.* profundo cambio en el pensamiento europeo que comenzó a mediados del siglo 16, en que el estudio del mundo natural se caracterizó por cuidadosa observación y cuestionamiento de teorías aceptadas. (pág. 189)

scorched-earth policy [política de arrasamiento de campos] *s.* práctica de quemar campos de cultivo y de matar ganado durante la guerra para que el enemigo no pueda vivir de las tierras. (pág. 235)

secede [seceder] *v.* retirarse formalmente de una asociación o alianza. (pág. 326)

secular *adj.* relacionado con lo mundano más que con los asuntos espirituales. (pág. 38)

segregation [segregación] *s.* separación legal o social de gente de diferentes razas. (pág. 327)

self-determination [autodeterminación] *s.* libertad de un pueblo para decidir libremente la forma de gobierno que desea. (pág. 424)

sepoy [cipayo] *s.* soldado hindú bajo el mando británico. (pág. 357)

Sepoy Mutiny [Motín de Cipayos] *s.* rebelión de 1857 de soldados hindúes y musulmanes contra los británicos en India. (pág. 359)

Seven Years' War [Guerra de los Siete Años] *s.* conflicto en Europa, Norteamérica e India de 1756 a 1763, en que las fuerzas de Inglaterra y Prusia lucharon con las de Austria, Francia, Rusia y otros países. (pág. 173)

shah [sha] *s.* monarca hereditario de Irán. (pág. 80)

"shock therapy" [terapia de shock] *s.* programa económico implementado en Rusia por Boris Yeltsin en la década de 1990, que implicó un cambio abrupto de una economía de mando a una economía de mercado libre. (pág. 616)

Sikh [sikh] *s.* miembro de un grupo religioso no violento cuyas creencias combinaban elementos del budismo, el hinduismo y el sufismo. (pág. 85)

skepticism [escepticismo] *s.* filosofía basada en la noción de que nada puede saberse con certeza. (pág. 163)

social contract [contrato social] *s.* acuerdo mediante el cual el pueblo define y limita sus derechos individuales, creando así una sociedad o gobierno organizados. (pág. 195)

Social Darwinism [darvinismo social] *s.* aplicación de las teorías de Charles Darwin sobre la evolución y la "sobrevivencia del más apto" a las sociedades humanas, particularmente como justificación para la expansión imperialista. (pág. 341)

socialism [socialismo] *s.* sistema económico en el cual los factores de producción son propiedad del pueblo y se administran para el bienestar de todos. (pág. 302)

Solidarity [Solidaridad] *s.* sindicato polaco de trabajadores que presentó la principal fuerza de oposición al gobierno comunista en Polonia en la década de 1980. (pág. 618)

soviet *s.* consejo local de representantes formado en Rusia después de la caída del zar Nicolás II. (pág. 436)

Spanish-American War [Guerra Hispano-Americana] *s.* conflicto de 1898 entre Estados Unidos y España, en que Estados Unidos apoyó la lucha de independencia cubana. (pág. 384)

sphere of influence [esfera de influencia] *s.* región extranjera en que una nación controla el comercio y otras actividades económicas. (pág. 373)

standard of living [nivel de vida] *s.* calidad de la vida de una persona o población que se mide conforme a los bienes, servicios y lujos que tiene a su disposición. (pág. 600)

strike [huelga] *s.* paro de trabajo para obligar al patrón a acceder a ciertas demandas. (pág. 304)

Suez Canal [canal de Suez] *s.* canal marítimo que une al mar Rojo y al golfo de Suez con el mar Mediterráneo, cuya construcción terminó en 1869. (pág. 354)

suffrage [sufragio] *s.* derecho al voto. (pág. 313)

sultan [sultán] *s.* "jefe supremo" o "el que tiene poder"; título de los gobernantes otomanos durante el auge del imperio otomano. (pág. 73)

surrealism [surrealismo] *s.* movimiento artístico del siglo 20 que se concentra en el inconsciente. (pág. 465)

sustainable growth [crecimiento sostenido] *s.* desarrollo económico que satisface las necesidades de la población pero preserva el entorno y conserva recursos para futuras generaciones. (pág. 646)

Taiping Rebellion [Rebelión Taiping] *s.* rebelión a mediados del siglo 19 contra la dinastía Qing en China, encabezada por Hong Xiuquan. (pág. 373)

Taj Mahal *s.* bella tumba en Agra, India, construida por el emperador mogol Shah Jahan para su esposa Mumtaz Mahal. (pág. 85)

Taliban [Talibán] *s.* grupo musulmán conservador que tomó el poder en Afganistán después de que la Unión Soviética retiró sus tropas; expulsado por el ejército estadounidense en diciembre de 2001 por darles amparo a sospechosos de terrorismo. (pág. 592)

Tennis Court Oath [Juramento de la Cancha de Tenis] *s.* promesa hecha por los miembros de la Asamblea Nacional de Francia en 1789 de permanecer reunidos hasta que elaboraran una nueva constitución. (pág. 220)

terrorism [terrorismo] *s.* uso de la fuerza o de amenazas para presionar a personas o gobiernos a que cambien sus políticas. (pág. 653)

theocracy [teocracia] *s.* gobierno controlado por líderes religiosos. (pág. 62)

theory of evolution [teoría de la evolución] *s.* concepto propuesto por Charles Darwin en 1859 de que las especies de plantas y animales surgen debido a un proceso de selección natural. (pág. 331)

theory of relativity [teoría de la relatividad] *s.* ideas de Albert Einstein acerca de la interrelación entre el tiempo y el espacio, y entre la energía y la materia. (pág. 463)

Third Reich [Tercer Reich] *s.* Tercer Imperio Alemán establecido por Adolfo Hitler en la década de 1930. (pág. 484)

Third Republic [Tercera República] *s.* república establecida en Francia después de la caída de Napoleón III; acabó con la ocupación alemana de Francia durante la II Guerra Mundial. (pág. 315)

Third World [Tercer Mundo] *s.* durante la Guerra Fría, naciones que no se aliaron ni con Estados Unidos ni con la Unión Soviética. (pág. 548).

Thirty Years' War [Guerra de los Treinta Años] *s.* conflicto europeo de 1618 a 1648 por cuestiones religiosas, territoriales y de poder entre familias reinantes. (pág. 169)

Tiananmen Square [Plaza Tiananmen] *s.* plaza pública en Beijing, China; sede en 1989 de un enorme levantamiento estudiantil en favor de reformas democráticas. (pág. 627)

Tokugawa Shogunate [shogunato Tokugawa] *s.* dinastía de shogúns que gobernó un Japón unificado de 1603 a 1867. (pág. 110)

totalitarianism [totalitarismo] *s.* gobierno que controla todo aspecto de la vida pública y privada. (pág. 440)

total war [guerra total] *s.* conflicto en el que los países participantes dedican todos sus recursos a la guerra. (pág. 419)

Treaty of Kanagawa [Tratado de Kanagawa] *s.* acuerdo de 1854 entre Estados Unidos y Japón, que abrió dos puertos japoneses a los barcos de Estados Unidos y le permitió abrir una embajada en Japón. (pág. 376)

Treaty of Tordesillas [Tratado de Tordesillas] *s.* acuerdo de 1494 entre Portugal y España que estableció que las tierras descubiertas al oeste de una línea imaginaria en el océano Atlántico pertenecerían a España y las tierras al este pertenecerían a Portugal. (pág. 99)

Treaty of Versailles [Tratado de Versalles] *s.* acuerdo de paz firmado por Alemania y los Aliados después de la I Guerra Mundial. (pág. 424)

trench warfare [guerra de trincheras] *s.* forma de guerra en la que dos ejércitos contrincantes luchan detrás de trincheras cavadas en el campo de batalla. (pág. 413)

triangular trade [triángulo comercial] *s.* red comercial trasatlántica que transportaba esclavos y productos entre África, Inglaterra, Europa continental, el Caribe y las colonias de Norteamérica. (pág. 134)

Triple Alliance [Triple Alianza] *s.* alianza militar establecida entre Alemania, Austro-Hungría e Italia antes de la I Guerra Mundial. (pág. 408)

Triple Entente [Triple Entente] *s.* alianza militar entre Gran Bretaña, Francia y Rusia establecida antes de la I Guerra Mundial. (pág. 409)

Truman Doctrine [Doctrina Truman] *s.* política estadounidense de dar ayuda económica y militar a las naciones libres amenazadas por oponentes internos o externos, anunciada por el presidente Harry Truman en 1947. (pág. 534)

UV

union [sindicato] *s.* asociación de trabajadores formada para negociar mejores salarios y condiciones de trabajo. (pág. 304)

United Nations [Organización de las Naciones Unidas (ONU)] *s.* organización internacional fundada en 1945 con el propósito de ofrecer seguridad a las naciones del mundo. (pág. 532)

Universal Declaration of Human Rights [Declaración Universal de Derechos Humanos] *s.* declaración en que la ONU proclamó en 1948 que todos los seres humanos tienen derecho a la vida, la libertad y la seguridad. (pág. 650)

unrestricted submarine warfare [guerra submarina irrestricta] *s.* uso de submarinos para hundir sin alerta previa cualquier barco (incluso barcos neutrales y de pasajeros sin armamento) que se encuentre en aguas enemigas. (pág. 418)

urbanization [urbanización] *s.* crecimiento de ciudades y migración hacia ellas. (pág. 289)

U.S.A. Patriot Act [Ley Patriota de E.U.A.] *s.* proyecto de ley antiterrorista de 2001 que hizo más fuerte los derechos gubernamentales para detener a extranjeros sospechosos de terrorismo y para procesar crímenes terroristas. (pág. 658)

U.S. Civil War [Guerra Civil de E.U.A.] *s.* conflicto entre los estados del Norte y el Sur de Estados Unidos desde 1861 a 1865, sobre el asunto de la esclavitud. (pág. 326)

utilitarianism [utilitarismo] *s.* teoría, propuesta por Jeremy Bentham a fines del siglo 18, de que las acciones del gobierno sólo son útiles si promueven el mayor bien para el mayor número de personas. (pág. 301)

utopia [Utopía] *s.* tierra imaginaria descrita por Tomás Moro en su libro del mismo nombre; lugar ideal. (pág. 48)

vernacular *s.* lenguaje común y corriente de la gente de una región o país. (pág. 41)

Vietcong *s.* grupo de guerrilleros comunistas que, con la ayuda de Vietnam del Norte, pelearon contra el gobierno de Vietnam del Sur durante la Guerra de Vietnam. (pág. 546)

Vietnamization [vietnamización] *s.* estrategia del presidente de E.U.A. Richard Nixon para terminar con la participación en la Guerra de Vietnam, mediante el retiro gradual de tropas estadounidenses y su reemplazo con fuerzas survietnamitas. (pág. 546)

W

War of the Spanish Succession [Guerra de Sucesión Española] *s.* conflicto de 1701 a 1713 en que varios Estados europeos lucharon para impedir que la familia Borbón controlara a España, como a Francia. (pág. 167)

Warsaw Pact [Pacto de Varsovia] *s.* alianza militar formada en 1955 por la Unión Soviética y siete países de Europa oriental. (pág. 535)

Weimar Republic [República de Weimar] *s.* república establecida en Alemania en 1919 que acabó en 1933. (pág. 471)

Western Front [Frente Occidental] *s.* en la I Guerra Mundial, región del norte de Francia donde peleaban las fuerzas de los Aliados y de las Potencias Centrales. (pág. 412)

westernization [occidentalización] *s.* adopción de las instituciones sociales, políticas o económicas del Occidente, especialmente de Europa o Estados Unidos. (pág. 176)

XYZ

Zionism [sionismo] *s.* movimiento fundado en la década de 1890 para promover el establecimiento de una patria judía en Palestina. (pág. 316)

Index

An *i* preceding an italic page reference indicates that there is an illustration, and usually text information as well, on that page. An *m* or a *c* preceding an italic page reference indicates a map or chart, as well as text information on that page.

Index

proliferation, 649
propaganda
Allied, *i423*, *i429*, 509, *i509*
totalitarian, *c441*, 442, *i487*
in World War I, 420, *i429*
in World War II, 509
prophets, 13
protectionism, 689
protectorate, 345, *c346*
Protestantism, 16–17, *c57*
Calvin's influence on, 61–62
in Spanish Netherlands, 158–159
Protestants, 56, 162
Protestant Union, 169
provisional government, 436
Prussia
alliances of, 173
during the Enlightenment, 204
rise of, 172, 262
psychology
Freud, Sigmund, 332, 463, 464, 465
Pavlov, Ivan, 332
public works projects
during the Depression, 475
purge, 442
Puritans, 21–22
in English Civil War, 181
in "New England," 128–129
victory over Metacom, 131
Putin, Vladimir, 616–617, *i617*

Q

al-Qaeda, 655
Qian-long, 105–106
Qing dynasty, 105, 371, 448
queens. *See* individual names.
Qur'an, 15, *i15*

R

Rabin, Yitzhak, 587
racism
in India, 358, 360
and Social Darwinism, *i332*, 341
Western, 379
radar, 494
Radicals, 223, 253
radio, 328, *c397*
KDKA, 467
Nazi, 479
radioactivity, 331, *c397*
railroads
in England, 287–288, *i287–288*
and Indian economy, 358
in United States, 296–297, *i296*, 327
rain forests, 680–681, *i680*
Raj, 360
Raphael, *i40*, 41
Rasputin, 435
rationing, 420, 509
Reagan, Ronald, *i557*
INF (Intermediate-Range Nuclear
Forces) treaty, 613
Berlin Wall speech, 620
Strategic Defense Initiative, 557
realism, 266–267

realpolitik, 261–262, 556
recession, 600
reconquista, 123
Reconstruction, 326–327
Red Army, 437–438, *c437*
Red Cross, *i685*
Red Guards, 437, 541, *i541*
Red Shirts, 260
Reformation, the, 16–17, 54–67
and absolute monarchy, 59
Catholic, 64–65
causes of, 16, 54–55, *c54*
characteristics of, 55
effects of, 17, 56–60, 66
indulgences, 55
Luther, Martin, 16, 55–56
Peasants' Revolt, *i17*, 56
values in, 17, 55
women in, 60, 62, 64
Reformation Parliament, 58–59
refugees, 652
number of, 1992–2002, *c665*
regional trading blocs, 689
Reign of Terror, 28, *i28*, 226–227
relativity, theory of, 463
religion. *See also* Buddhism; Christianity;
Hinduism; Islam; Judaism.
effect of printing press on, 51
in Europe (1560), *m63*
and nationalism, *c254*
reformers, 55–56
world, 700–714
religious affiliations, world's, *c700–701*
religious beliefs. *See also* religion.
effects of science on, 191
religious conflict, 649
religious persecution. *See also*
Christianity; Holocaust; Inquisition.
of Christians, 15, 695
in Japan, 112
of Muslims, 622
in Spanish colonies, 125
in Sudan, 695
of Tibetans, 695
under Chinese rule, 695
under Stalin, 443
religious symbolism, *i705, c714*
religious tolerance, 15
in Austria, 204
in Edict of Nantes, 162
and French Revolution, 222
in Mughal Empire, 83
in Netherlands, 159
in Ottoman Empire, 76
Rembrandt (van Rijn), 159, *i159, i194*
Renaissance 16–17, 24. *See also* Northern
Renaissance.
art, *i36*, 40, *i40, i44–45*, 47
British, 49
causes of, 37
characteristics of, 38–39, 41
Chinese, *i43*
da Vinci, Leonardo 41, *i41, i44–45*
effects of, 51
European, 37–54
Flanders, 46–47
humanism, 38, 48

Italian, 37–43
literature, 41–43, 48–49
Michelangelo, 41, *i41, i44*
Northern, 46–51
Petrarch, 41–42
Raphael, *i40*, 41, *i45*
themes of, 38
values of, 37–39, 46
women in, 39, *i39*, 43
"Renaissance men," 39, *i39*
"Renaissance women," 39, *i39*
representative government, 27
republic
China, 448
France, 256
Roman, 10–11
United States, 210–211
Republic, The (Plato), 8
Restoration, 22, 182
reunification, 620
revolution(s)
1848, *m245*
American, *i22*, 25–26, 206–211, *c272*
biorevolution, 685
Bolshevik, 436–437, *c437*
causes of, *c274*
Chinese, 448
Cuban, 550
Cultural (Chinese), 541, 625–626
democratic (1989), *i29*
effects of, *c276*
English, 181–182, *c272*
and Enlightenment, 24–29, 207–208,
218, *m250*
failed, 255–256
French, 27–28, *i210*, 217–227, *c272*
gene, 685
Glorious, 22–23, 25, 182, *c272*
Green, 640, 684
in Haiti, 248
ideas and, 247, 250
Latin American, 248–252, *c273*
leaders of, *c458*
Mexican, 251–252, 392–393
model of, *c273*
nationalist, 248–252
role of Enlightenment in, 207–208, 218
Russian, 435–438
in Saint Domingue, 231, 248
Scientific, 24, 189–194, *c192–193*
Southwest Asian, 456
in Soviet Union, 436–437, *c437*
time line of, *c272–273*
Rhodes, Cecil, 341, *i341*
Ricardo, David, 300–301
Ricci, Matteo, 103, 105
Richardson, Samuel, 203
Richard the Lion-Hearted (English
king), 19
Richelieu, Cardinal, 163, *i163*, 170
Rig Veda, *i707*
rights and responsibilities. *See also* Bill
of Rights; constitution.
in Declaration of the Rights of Man, 28,
222
of *habeas corpus*, 22, 182
Locke's treatise on, 25, 196

compared to Congress of Vienna, 241
Convention for the Elimination of All Forms of Discrimination Against Women, 696
Convention on the Rights of the Child, 696
creation of, 532
and human rights, 650, 694, 696–697
inspectors in Iraq, 692
peacekeepers, 648
promotion of democracy, 28–29, 694, 697
Security Council, 692
studies on population growth, 686
UNICEF (United Nations Children's Fund), i685
weapons inspectors, 692
United States. *See also* Native Americans; North America.
Atlantic Charter, 496
Bill of Rights, 183, 211, i211
boycott of 1980 Olympics, 553
civil rights in World War II, 509
Civil War, 325–326, m326
during Cold War, 533–536, 539, 544, 548–553, 556–557
colonies of, 25–26, 206–208, 364–365
Constitution, 26–27, i26, c209, 210–211, 213
and Cuba, 384–385, 550–551
Cuban Missile Crisis, 551, 556
culture, 661–663
democracy in, 26–27, 183, c209
the Depression in, 472–473, 475
détente, 556–557
domino theory, 544
expansion (1783–1853), m325
government, 27, c209, 210–211
immigrants to, 327
imperialism, 364–365, 384–387
industrialization, 295–297, 327
infant mortality rate, c699
isolationism in, 484
in Korean War, 542–543
land acquisition in, 324–325
Lend-Lease Act, 496
life expectancy at birth, c699
Marshall Plan, 534, c534
and Middle East, 552–553, 586, 588–589
Native Americans in, 324–325
occupation of Japan, 516–517
Pearl Harbor, 497–498, i498
per capita GDP, c699
and Philippines, 364, 498, 570–571
settlers in, 128–130
space race, 536–537
as superpower, c532, 535, c559
U-2 incident, 536, 556
war in Vietnam, 544–547, m545, i545
war with Iraq, 692–693, i692
water shortages in, 680
in World War I, 418–420
in World War II, 496, 506–513
Universal Declaration of Human Rights, 1, 29, 650, 694, 697

unrestricted submarine warfare, 418
urban centers. *See* cities.
urbanization, 289
Urdu, 84
USA Patriot Act, 658
USSR (Union of Soviet Socialist Republics), 439. *See also* Russia; Soviet Union.
utilitarianism, 301
utopia, 48, 302
Utopia **(More),** 48
U-2 incident, 536, 556

Vajpayee, Atal Bihari, 566
values
during Enlightenment, 196–198, 201
in Renaissance, 38–39, 46
return to traditional, 663
of Western culture, 662
van Eyck, Jan, i36, 47
Velázquez, Diego, 157, i157
Venezuela, 249, 383, i598
Verdun, 414
Vermeer, Jan, 159
vernacular, 41
Verrazzano, Giovanni da, 127
Versailles
Palace of, 165, i166
Treaty of, 424–427, c427
Vesalius, Andreas, 193–194
Vespucci, Amerigo, 120
Victor Emmanuel III (Italian king), 260, 477, 507
Victoria (British queen), 314, i314
Victorian Age, 314–315
Vietcong, 546
Vietnam
"boat people," 547
capitalism in, i547
divided country, 544
domino theory, 544
and France, 363, 544
Ho Chi Minh, 544, i544, 559
Ngo Dinh Diem, 544, 546
and United States, 544–547
Vietnam War, 544–547, i545, m545
Vietnamization, 546
Villa, Francisco "Pancho," 392
Voltaire, 196, i196
voting. *See also* suffrage.
in ancient Rome, 10–11
in Britain, 313–314, c314
in United States, c209
world voter turnout, 1999–2002, c31

Walesa, Lech, 618–619
war. *See also* civil war(s); empire(s); technology; war against terrorism.
of 1812, 295
American Revolutionary, 206–211
Arab-Israeli, 584–585
of the Austrian Succession, 173

Boer, 344
in Bosnia, 622, i630
Chechnyan, 616–617
Cold, 533–536
Crimean, 353
English Civil, 181, m182
French and Indian, 130, 207
Franco-Prussian, 262
Korean, 542–543
Mexican-American, 325
in Nicaragua, 551
Opium, 372
Peninsular, 235
Persian Gulf, 645, i645
Russo-Japanese, 378–379, 434–435
Seven Weeks', 262
Seven Years', 25, 173
Sino-Japanese, 378
Six-Day, 585
slave trade in, 132
Spanish-American, 384–385, m385
of the Spanish Succession, 167
technology of, 108, i414, i520–521
Thirty Years', 169–170
total, 419, 522
in Vietnam, 544–547, m545
war against terrorism
in Afghanistan, i553, 593, 657
Bush administration and, 657
in Iraq, i636
warriors, feudal, 108
Warsaw Pact, 535, 648
Waterloo, 237
watermills, 286
water resources
in Industrial Revolution, 286
scarcity of, 680
Watt, James, 287
weapons. *See also* technology.
biological, 692
chemical, 691–692
of Cold War, 535–536
conventional, 690
in mail, 656–657
of mass destruction, i520, 649, 654, 691–693
Maxim gun, 341, i520
nuclear, 691, m691
poison gas, i520
protests against sale of, 690–691
tank, i520
of terrorism, 653–654
of totalitarianism, 440
trade in, 690–691
of World War I, 414, i414, i520
of World War II, 513, i521, 525
Weimar Republic, 471
welfare state, 605
Western civilization
effect of Enlightenment on, 199–200
influence on global culture, 661–662
and Russia, 176–177
Western Front
in World War I, 412–414
westernization, 176, 341
Whigs, 182

Acknowledgments

Text Acknowledgments

Chapter 2, page 75: Excerpt from *The Islamic World* by William H. McNeill and M.R. Waldham. Copyright © 1973 by The University of Chicago Press. Reprinted by permission of The University of Chicago Press.

Chapter 3, page 110: Haiku poem, from *Matsuo Basho,* translated by Makoto Veda. By permission of Makoto Veda.

Chapter 4, page 126: Excerpt from "I Won't Be Celebrating Columbus Day," by Suzan Shown Harjo. Copyright © 1991 by Suzan Shown Harjo. Reprinted by permission of Suzan Shown Harjo.

Chapter 13, page 423: Excerpt from *All Quiet on the Western Front* by Erich Maria Remarque. Copyright 1929, 1930 by Little, Brown and Company. Copyright renewed © 1957, 1958 by Erich Maria Remarque. "Im Westen Nichts Neues" by Erich Maria Remarque. Copyright 1928 by Ullstein A. G. Copyright renewed © 1956 by Erich Maria Remarque. All rights reserved. Used by permission of Pryor, Cashman, Sherman & Flynn on behalf of the Estate of Erich Maria Remarque.

Excerpt from "Dulce et Decorum Est," from *The Collected Poems of Wilfred Owen* by Wilfred Owen. Copyright © 1963 by Chatto & Windus, Ltd. Used by permission of New Directions Publishing Corp.

Chapter 14, page 454: Excerpt from *The Origin of Nonviolence* by M. K. Gandhi. Published by Cambridge University Press. Reprinted with the permission of Cambridge University Press.

Chapter 15, page 464: Excerpt from *The Great Gatsby* by F. Scott Fitzgerald. Copyright © 1925 by Charles Scribner's Sons. Copyright renewed 1953 by Frances Scott Fitzgerald Lanahan. Used by permission of Scribner, an imprint of Simon & Schuster Adult Publishing Group.

Chapter 19, page 627: Excerpt from "Tienanmen Square: A Soldier's Story," by Xiao Ye from *Teenage Soldiers, Adult Wars.* Reprinted by permission of the Rosen Publishing Group.

page 1067: Excerpts from "The Coming of Mao Zedong Chic," from *Newsweek,* May 19, 1997, Newsweek, Inc. All rights reserved. Reprinted by permission.

Chapter 20, page 647: Excerpt from "The Market is Green," by the Liberty Institute, New Delhi. Copyright © May 1999. Reprinted by permission of the Liberty Institute, New Delhi, India.

Excerpt from "Eco-Economy: Building an Economy for the Earth," by Lester Brown. Speech, Colloquium on Global Partnerships for Sustainable Development: Harnessing Action for the 21st Century; 24 March 2002 <http://www.earth-policy.org/Transcripts/TERI-4-02.htm>. Reprinted by permission of the Earth Policy Institute.

COMPARING & CONTRASTING FEATURES

Unit 2, Page 276: Excerpt from *The French Revolution,* edited by Paul H. Beik. Copyright © 1971 by Paul H. Beik. Reprinted by permission of HarperCollins Publishers Inc.

Unit 3, Page 401: Excerpt from *The Birth of the Modern: World Society 1815–1830* by Paul Johnson. Copyright © 1991 by Paul Johnson. Reprinted by permission of HarperCollins Publishers Inc.

Unit 4, Page 523: Excerpt from *If This is a Man (Survival in Auschwitz)* by Primo Levi, translated by Stuart Woolf. Copyright © 1960 by Orion Press, Inc. Copyright © 1958 by Giulio Einaudi editore S.P.A. Reprinted by permission of Penguin Putnam, Inc., a division of Penguin Group (USA) Inc.

PRIMARY SOURCE HANDBOOK

Page R40: "Creation Hymn," from *The Rig Veda,* translated by Wendy Doniger O'Flaherty (Penguin Classics, 1981). Copyright © 1981 by Wendy Doniger O'Flaherty. Reproduced by permission of Penguin Books Ltd.

Page R42: Excerpt from *The Analects of Confucius,* translated by Simon Leys. Copyright © 1997 by Pierre Ryckmans. Reprinted by permission of W. W. Norton & Company, Inc.

Page R43: Excerpt from "Pericles' Funeral Oration," from *History of the Peloponnesian War* by Thucydides, translated by Rex Warner (Penguin Classics, 1954). Copyright © 1954 by Rex Warner. Reproduced by permission of Penguin Books Ltd.

Page R44: Excerpt from the *Apology* by Plato, translated by Hugh Tredennick, from *The Collected Dialogues of Plato,* edited by Edith Hamilton and Huntington Cairns. Copyright © 1961 by Princeton University Press. Reprinted by permission of Princeton University Press.

Page R45: Excerpt from "The Burning of Rome," from *The Annals of Imperial Rome* by Tacitus, translated by Michael Grant (Penguin Classics, 1956; sixth revised edition, 1989). Copyright © 1956, 1959, 1971, 1973, 1975, 1977, 1989, 1996 by Michael Grant Publications. Reprinted by permission of Penguin Books Ltd.

Page R46: Excerpt from *The Koran,* translated by N. J. Dawood (Penguin Classics, 1956; fifth revised edition, 1990). Copyright © 1956, 1959, 1966, 1968, 1974, 1990, 1995 by N. J. Dawood. Reprinted by permission of Penguin Books Ltd.

Page R47: Excerpt from *The Pillow Book of Sei Shōnagon,* translated and edited by Ivan Morris. Copyright © 1967 by Ivan Morris. Reprinted by permission of Columbia University Press.

Page R48: Excerpt from the *Magna Carta* by J. C. Holt. Copyright © 1965 by Cambridge University Press. Reprinted with permission of Cambridge University Press.

Page R49: Excerpt from *Popol Vuh: The Definitive Edition of the Mayan Book of The Dawn of Life and The Glories of Gods and Kings,* translated by Dennis Tedlock. Copyright © 1985 by Dennis Tedlock, 1996 (revised and additional material) by Dennis Tedlock. Reprinted with the permission of Simon & Schuster Adult Publishing Group.

Page R51: Excerpt from *Utopia* by St. Thomas More, edited by Edward Surtz, S.J. Copyright © 1964 by Yale University. Reproduced by permission of Yale University Press.

Page R59: Excerpt from *Night* by Elie Wiesel, translated by Stella Rodway. Copyright © 1960 by MacGibbon & Kee. Copyright renewed 1988 by the Collins Publishing Group. Reprinted by permission of Hill and Wang, a division of Farrar, Straus & Giroux, Inc.

Page R60: Excerpt from *Farewell to Manzanar* by James D. Houston and Jeanne Wakatsuki Houston. Copyright © 1973 by James D. Houston. Reprinted by permission of Houghton Mifflin Company. All rights reserved.

Page R61: Excerpt from "Glory and Hope" by Nelson Mandela, from *Vital Speeches of the Day,* Vol. LX, No. 16 (1 June 1994), page 486. Reprinted by permission of City News Publishing Company, Inc.

Page R62: Excerpt from "I Have A Dream" by Dr. Martin Luther King Jr. Copyright © 1963 by Dr. Martin Luther King Jr., copyright renewed 1991 by Coretta Scott King. Reprinted by arrangement with the Estate of Martin Luther King Jr., c/o Writers House as agent for the proprietor, New York, N.Y.

Page R63: Excerpt from "An Open Letter" by Cesar Chavez. Copyright © Cesar E. Chavez Foundation. Reprinted by permission of the Cesar E. Chavez Foundation.

McDougal Littell Inc. has made every effort to locate the copyright holders for selections used in this book and to make full acknowledgment for their use. Omissions brought to our attention will be corrected in a subsequent edition.

Art and Photography Credits

Maps supplied by Mapping Specialists

COVER

Sydney Opera House © Jerry Driend/Getty Images; sky © Rob Matheson/Corbis; Napoleon © Bettmann/Corbis; Queen Victoria (late 19th century). Victoria and Albert Museum, London. Photo © Victoria and Albert Museum, London/Art Resource, New York; *Simon Bolivar* (pre-20th century), unknown artist. Archives Charmet, Paris. Photo © The Bridgeman Art Library; Aung San Suu Kyi © Tom Wagner/Corbis SABA; Ghandi © Getty Images.

FRONT MATTER

Sydney Opera House © Jerry Driend/Getty Images; sky © Rob Matheson/Corbis; Napoleon © Bettmann/Corbis; Queen Victoria (late 19th century). Victoria and Albert Museum, London. Photo © Victoria and Albert Museum, London/Art Resource, New York; *Simon Bolivar* (pre-20th century), unknown artist. Archives Charmet, Paris. Photo © The Bridgeman Art Library; Aung San Suu Kyi © Tom Wagner/Corbis SABA; Ghandi © Getty Images.

Introduction

viii *top left* Greek engraving from red-figure vase. Bibliothèque des Arts Décoratifs, Paris. Photo © Dagli Orti/The Art Archive; *top right* © Corbis; *center left* Page from the Koran (ninth century), Islamic School. Bibliothèque Nationale, Tunis, Tunisia. Photo © Lauros/Giraudon/Bridgeman Art Library ; *center* Athena (A.D. 490). Kunsthistorisches Museum, Vienna, Austria. Photo © Erich Lessing/Art Resource, New York; *bottom, The Signing of the Constitution.* Howard Chandler Christy. Private Collection. Photo © Art Resource, New York ; **ix** *left* © Explorer, Paris/SuperStock; *right (top to bottom)* © Tim Hursley/SuperStock; Elizabeth I (1588), George Gower. Courtesy of The National Portrait Gallery, London; Shah Tahmasp I receiving the Moghul Emperor Humayun. Period of Abbas II. Photo © Giraudon/Art Resource, New York; Globe by Martin Behaim (about 1492). Bibliothèque Nationale, Paris. Photo © Giraudon/Art Resource, New York; **x** *left (top to bottom)* Detail of *Marriage of Louis XIV, King of France and Marie Therese of Austria* (17th century), unknown artist. Musée de Tesse, Le Mans, France. Photo © Dagli Orti/The Art Archive; *Louis XIV, King of France* (1701), Hyacinthe Rigaud. Louvre, Paris. Photo © Erich Lessing/Art Resource, New York; Isaac Newton's reflecting telescope (1672). Photo by Eileen Tweedy/Royal Society/The Art Archive; *Combat Before the Hotel de Ville, July 28th, 1830,* Victor Schnetz. Musée du Petit Palais, Paris. Photo by Bulloz © Réunion des Musées Nationaux/Art Resource, New York; *right* © Todd A. Gipstein/Corbis; **xi** *left* Aboriginal bark painting of abstract picture of body, Lipunja. Milingibi, Australia. Photo © Dagli Orti/Musée des Arts Africains et Oceaniens/The Art Archive; *right (top to bottom) The Battle of Isandhlwana* (1879), Charles Fripp. National Army Museum, London. Photo © The Art Archive; © Bettmann/Corbis; The Granger Collection, New York; The Granger Collection, New York; **xii** *left (top to bottom)* © Getty Images; Popperfoto; © Bettmann/Corbis; © UPI/Bettmann/Corbis; *right* © KJ Historical/Corbis; **xiii** *left* © Steve Vidler/SuperStock; *right (top to bottom)* © SuperStock; Imperial War Museum. Photo © The Art Archive; © David Turnley/Corbis; © Corbis Sygma; **xiv** *top left* © Will & Deni McIntyre/Corbis; *top right* © Mario Tama/Getty Images; *bottom left* © Reuters NewMedia Inc./Corbis; *bottom right* © Reuters New Media Inc./Corbis; **xxx** *top left, Alexander the Great,* Relief by Landolin Ohnmacht. Photo by AKG London; *bottom right Combat Before the Hotel de Ville, July 28th 1830,* Victor Schnetz. Musée du Petit Palais, Paris. Photo by Bulloz © Réunion des Musées Nationaux/Art Resource, New York; **xxxi** *top* © Chad Ehlers/Getty Images; *bottom* © Bettmann/Corbis; **xxxii–xxxiii** © Pacific Stock/Orion Press; **xxxiii** Travel Pix; **xxxvi** Stephen Alvarez/National Geographic Image Collection; **xxxvii** *top* © Kenneth Garrett; *center* Flying man, Leonardo da Vinci. Sketch from *Codex Atlanticus.* Biblioteca Ambrosiana, Milan, Italy/Art Resource, New York; *bottom* © Warren Morgan/Corbis.

Prologue

0–1 © Reuters NewMedia Inc./Corbis; **0** © AFP/Corbis; **2** *left* © David Lees/Corbis; *right* © Scala/Art Resource, New York; **3** *top* © Bettmann/Corbis; *bottom* National Archives; **4** © AFP/Corbis; **5** *top left* Young girl winning chariot race, Greek engraving from red-figure vase. Bibliothèque des Arts Décoratifs, Paris. Photo © Dagli Orti/The Art Archive; *top right* © Corbis; **7** Bust of Solon (630–560 A.D.). Greek. Photo © Scala/Art Resource, New York; **9** *top right, bottom left, bottom right* American School of Classical Studies at Athens, Agora Excavations; *center* Goddess Athena, (A.D. 490). Kunsthistorisches Museum, Vienna, Austria. Photo © Erich Lessing/Art Resource, New York; **10** Emperor Justinian (ninth century A.D.). Byzantine Mosaic. Musée de Chartres, France. Photo © SuperStock; **11** Bibliotheque Nationale de France; **12** *top left* © Richard T. Nowitz/Corbis; *top right* Detail of zodiac mosaic (fourth century). Tiberias, Israel. Photo © Garo Nalbandian/Israelimages.com; **13** © Bettmann/Corbis; **15** Page from the Koran (ninth century), Islamic School. Bibliothèque Nationale, Tunis, Tunisia. Photo © Lauros/Giraudon/Bridgeman Art Library; **16** © Bettmann/Corbis; **17** The Granger

Art and Photography Credits (Cont.)

Collection; **18** *top left* © Corbis; *top right* © Archivo Iconografico, S.A./Corbis; *bottom* The Granger Collection; **19** National Archives; **20** *The House of Commons in Session* (1710), Peter Tillemans. Houses of Parliament, Westminster, London. Photo © Bridgeman Art Library; **21** © Christie's Images/Corbis; **23** *top right King William II* (18th century), English school. Photo © National Trust Photographic Library/Derrick E. Witty/ Bridgeman Art Library; *top left Queen Mary II* (18th century) English school. Photo © National Trust Photographic Library/Derrick E. Witty/Bridgeman Art Library ; **24** *top left* Copernican Solar System (1661). From *Harmonia Macronici.* Andreae Cellarius. Page 30. Victoria and Albert Museum, London. Photo © Art Resource, New York; *top right* © Bettmann/Corbis; **25** © Archivo Iconografico, S.A./Corbis; **26** *The Signing of the Constitution* Howard Chandler Christy. Private Collection. Photo © Art Resource, New York; **27** *James Madison* Gilbert Stuart. Photo © SuperStock; **28** The Granger Collection;

UNIT ONE

32–33 *La Salle's Louisiana expedition in 1684,* J. A. Theodore Gudin. Photo © Réunion des Musées Nationaux/Art Resource, New York.

Chapter 1

34 *top* Bust of Lorenzo de Medici (15th or 16th century). Museo di Andrea del Castagno, Uffizi, Florence, Italy. Photo © Scala/Art Resource, New York; *bottom* Jar with dragon (1425–1435), Ming dynasty, reign of Xuande. Porcelain painted in underglaze blue. 19" high (48.3 cm). Gift of Robert E. Tod, 1937, The Metropolitan Museum of Art, New York. Photo © 2003 The Metropolitan Museum of Art; **35** *left* Gutenberg Bible (about 1455). Volume II, f. 45v-46. PML 818 ch1 ff1. The Pierpont Morgan Library, New York. Photo © The Pierpont Morgan Library/Art Resource, New York; *right* Detail of nobles entertained in garden by musicians and dancers (about 1590), Mughal. Photo © British Library/The Art Archive; **36** *The Madonna of Chancellor Rolin* (about 1434), Jan van Eyck. Louvre, Paris. Photo © Scala/Art Resource, New York; **37** *top left* © Photodisc/Getty Images; *top right* © Ulf E. Wallin/Getty Images; **38** Detail of *Lorenzo de Medici and the Arts in Florence* (about 1634–1636), Giovanni da Sangiovanni. Palazzo Pitti, Florence, Italy. Photo © Dagli Orti/The Art Archive; **39** *left Portrait of Baldassare Castilione* (date unknown), Raphael. Louvre, Paris. © Scala/Art Resource, New York; *right* The Granger Collection, New York; **40** *Marriage of the Virgin* (1504), Raphael. Brera, Milan, Italy. Photo © Scala/Art Resource, New York; **41** *top* © Stephano Bianchetti/Corbis; *bottom* The Granger Collection, New York; **42** *Portrait of Niccolo Machiavelli,* Santi di Tito. Palazzo Vecchio, Florence, Italy. Photo © Scala/Art Resource, New York; **43** The Granger Collection, New York; **44–45** © SuperStock, Inc.; **44** *Mona Lisa* (1503–1506), Leonardo da Vinci. Louvre, Paris. Photo by R.G. Ojeda © Réunion des Musées Nationaux/Art Resource, New York; **45** *The School of Athens* (15th century), Raphael. Stanza della Segnatura, Vatican Palace, Vatican State. Photo © Scala/Art Resource, New York; *bottom* © Bettmann/Corbis; **46** *top left* © Photodisc/Getty Images; *top right* © Ulf E. Wallin/Getty Images; **47** *Peasant Wedding* (1568), Peter Brueghel the Elder. Kunsthistorisches Museum, Vienna, Austria. Photo © Saskia Ltd./Art Resource, New York; **48** *left* Christine de Pizan teaches her son (about 1430). Harley MS 4431, f. 26 ff. The British Library, London. Photo by AKG London/British Library; *right Thomas More, Lord Chancellor* (late 15th century) Private Collection. Photo © The Stapleton Collection/The Bridgeman Art Library; **49** *left, Othello* movie still. Castle Rock/Dakota Films/The Kobal Collection; *center, 10 Things I Hate About You* movie still. Touchstone/The Kobal Collection; *top right, Romeo & Juliet* movie still. Merrick Morton/20th Century Fox/The Kobal Collection; *bottom right, Ran* movie still. Herald Ace/Nippon Herald/Greenwich/The Kobal Collection; **50** Illustration by Peter Dennis/Linda Rogers Associates; **52–53** MS Sloane 2596, f. 52. British Library. Photo by AKG London/British Library; **52** *top* Koninklijk Museum voor Schone Kunsten, Antwerpen, Belgium; *center left* By permission of the Folger Shakespeare Library, Washington, D.C.; *center* Musée de la parfumerie Fragonard, Paris. Photo © Dagli Orti/The Art Archive; **53** The Shakespeare Birthplace Trust; **54** *top left* © Photodisc/Getty Images; *top right* © Ulf E. Wallin/Getty Images; **55** *Portrait of Martin Luther* (1529), Lucas Cranach the Elder. Museo Poldi Pezzoli, Milan, Italy. Photo © The Bridgeman Art Library; **58** *left Portrait of Henry VIII, King of England* (1540), Hans Holbein the Younger. Galleria Nazionale d'Arte Antica, Rome. Photo © Scala/Art Resource, New York; *right* Courtesy of the National Portrait Gallery, London; **59** *top left* © Stapleton Collection/Corbis; *bottom left Mary I Tudor, Queen of England* (1554), Antonis Moro or Mor. Museo del Prado Madrid. Photo © Dagli Orti/The Art Archive; *right Elizabeth I, Queen of England,* Federico Zuccari. Pinacoteca Nazionale di Siena. Photo © Dagli Orti/The Art Archive; **60** *s*(1588), George Gower. Courtesy of the National Portrait Gallery, London; **61** *left* © Photodisc/Getty Images; *right* © Ulf E. Wallin/Getty Images; **62** *John Calvin as a Young Man.* Flemish School. Bibliothèque Publique et Universitaire, Geneva, Switzerland. Photo © Erich Lessing/Art Resource, New York; **64** *Marguerite d'Angouleme, Queen of Navarre* (16th century). Musée Condé, Chantilly, France. Photo © Bridgeman-Giraudon/Art Resource, New York; **65** *Pope Paul III Farnese at the Council of Trent* (1560–1566), Taddeo and Federico Zuccari. Farnese Palace Caprarola. Photo © Dagli Orti/The Art Archive; **66** © Richard T. Nowitz/Corbis; **67** Martin Luther, German priest and Protestant reformer, caricature as seven-headed monster. The British Library. Photo © British Library/The Art Archive; **68** *top to bottom* © SuperStock, Inc.; Illustration by Peter Dennis/Linda Rogers Associates; *Portrait of Martin Luther* (1529) Lucas Cranach the Elder. Museo Poldi Pezzoli, Milan, Italy. Photo © The Bridgeman Art Library; Detail of *Pope Paul III Farnese at the Council of Trent* (1560–1566), Taddeo and Federico Zuccari. Farnese Palace Caprarola. Photo © Dagli Orti/The Art Archive; **69** © Bettmann/Corbis.

Chapter 2

70 *top* Topkapi Palace Museum, Istanbul, Turkey. Photo © Laura Lushington/Sonia Halliday Photographs; *bottom left* Pectoral ornament in the form of a double-headed serpent. Aztec. The British Museum, London. Photo © Werner Forman/Art Resource, New York; *bottom right* By permission of the British Library; **71** © Burstein Collection/Corbis; **72** Shah Tahmasp I receiving the Moghul Emperor Humayun (1660s). Period of Abbas II. Chihil Sutun, Isfahan, Iran. Photo © Giraudon/Art Resource, New York; **73** *top left* James L. Stanfield/National Geographic Image Collection; *top right* © SuperStock, Inc.; **75** Taking of Constantinople by the Turks, MS Fr. 9087 f. 207. Voyage d'Outremer de Bertrand de la Broquiere, Bibliothèque Nationale, Paris. Photo © Sonia Halliday Photographs; **76** *Suleiman the Magnificent.* Galleria degli Uffizi, Florence, Italy. Photo © Dagli Orti/The Art Archive; **77** Sonia Halliday Photographs; **79** Chihil Sutun, Isfahan, Iran. Photo © SEF/Art Resource, New York; **81** Dome of south Iwan (1611–1638). Safavid dynasty. Majid-i Shah, Isfahan, Iran. Photo © SEF/Art Resource, New York; **83** *top left* James L. Stanfield/National Geographic Image Collection; *top right* © SuperStock, Inc.;

84 *Portrait of Akbar and Prince Salim* (19th century). India, Mughal. Gift of Sally Sample Aal, 1997. The Newark Museum, Newark, New Jersey. Photo © The Newark Museum/Art Resource, New York; **85** *left* © Bettmann/Corbis; *left center* © Wally McNamee/Corbis; *right center, right* AP/Wide World Photos ; **86** © Brian A. Vikander/Corbis; **88** *top* Dagger handle in the form of a horse's head. Mughal. India. Victoria and Albert Museum, London. Photo © Victoria and Albert Museum, London/The Bridgeman Art Library; *bottom* © Abbie Enock/Travel Ink/Corbis; **89** *top* Tent hanging (early 18th century). Mughal dynasty. Victoria and Albert Museum, London. Photo © Victoria and Albert Museum, London/Art Resource, New York; *left* Akbar on the elephant Hawai pursuing the elephant rau Bagha (about 1590). Double page miniature from the Akbarnama. Mughal. Victoria and Albert Museum, London. Photo © Victoria and Albert Museum, London/Art Resource, New York.

Chapter 3

92 *left* Helmet (about 1500), Turkish. Victoria and Albert Museum, London. Photo © Victoria and Albert Museum, London/Art Resource, New York; *right* Detail of St. Vincent Polyptych (15th century), Nuno Goncalves. Museu Nacional de Arte Antiga, Lisbon, Portugal. Photo © Scala/Art Resource, New York; **93** *left* © The Flag Institute; *right Washington Crossing the Delaware,* Eastman Johnson. Copy after the Emmanuel Leutze painting in the Metropolitan Museum of Art, New York. Private Collection. Photo © Art Resource, New York; **94** India Orientalis (1606), Gerard Mercator and Jodocus Hondius. Atlas sive cosmographicae Meditationes. Courtesy Sotheby's, London; **95** *top left* © Culver Pictures, Inc./SuperStock, Inc.; *top right* K'ossu (about 1600), Late Ming dynasty. China. Victoria and Albert Museum, London. Photo © Sally Chappell/The Art Archive; *bottom* Globe by Martin Behaim (about 1492). Bibliothèque Nationale, Paris. Photo © Giraudon/Art Resource, New York; **96** Detail of St. Vincent Polyptych (15th century), Nuno Goncalves. Museu Nacional de Arte Antiga, Lisbon, Portugal. Photo © Scala/Art Resource, New York; **97** *background* © Bettmann/Corbis; *top right* Courtesy of Bibliothèque Nationale, Paris; *bottom left* Compass with sextant and dial (1617), Elias Allen. Victoria and Albert Museum, London. Photo © Victoria and Albert Museum, London/Art Resource, New York; *bottom center* © Dorling Kindersley; **98** © Bettmann/Corbis; **99** © Stapleton Collection/Corbis; **101** Corbis; **102** *top left* © Culver Pictures, Inc./SuperStock, Inc.; *top right* K'ossu (about 1600) Late Ming dynasty. China. Victoria and Albert Museum, London, UK. Photo © Sally Chappell/The Art Archive; *bottom right* Ming vase. Chinese School. Musée des Arts Asiatiques-Guimet, Paris. Photo © The Bridgeman Art Library; **104** *top right* © John T. Young/Corbis; *center right* © Brian A. Vikander/Corbis; *bottom right* © Harvey Lloyd/Getty Images; **105** Palace Museum, Beijing, China; **106** Marriage ceremony (19th century). China. Victoria and Albert Museum, London. Photo by Eileen Tweedy/The Art Archive; **107** The Granger Collection, New York; **108** *top left* © Culver Pictures, Inc./SuperStock, Inc.; *top right* K'ossu (about 1600), Late Ming dynasty. China. Victoria and Albert Museum, London, UK. Photo © Sally Chappell/The Art Archive; *bottom* Rijksmuseum, Amsterdam, The Netherlands; **109** © B.S.P.I./Corbis; **110** © Asian Art & Archeology/Corbis **111** © Asian Art & Archaeology/Corbis; *inset* © Michael S. Yamashita/Corbis; **112** © 1995 Christie's Images, Ltd; **113** Monk Tokiyori. Musée des Arts Asiatiques-Guimet, Paris. Photo by Richard Lambert © Réunion des Musées Nationaux/Art Resource, New York; **114** Dutch Merchant ship plate (1756), Qing dynasty. China. Musée des Arts Asiatiques-Guimet, Paris. Photo © Réunion des Musées Nationaux/Art Resource, New York; **115** The Granger Collection, New York.

Chapter 4

116 *top* © Archivo Iconografico, S.A./Corbis; *bottom Portrait of Tokugawa Ieyasu* (17th century). Japanese. Private Collection. Photo © The Bridgeman Art Library; **117** *left* The Granger Collection, New York; *right The Taking of the Bastilie, 14 July 1789* (18th century), French School. Musée de la Ville de Paris, Musée Carnevalet, Paris. Photo © The Bridgeman Art Library; **118** Battle for Tenochtitlan between Cortés and Spaniards and Aztecs (16th century). Antochiw Collection, Mexico. Photo © Mireille Vautier/The Art Archive; **119** *top left* © Bettmann/Corbis; *top right* Detail of letter from Christopher Columbus to his son Diego (5 February 1505). General Archive of the Indies, Seville, Spain. Photo © Dagli Orti/The Art Archive; **120** *Christopher Columbus* (15th century), Sebastiano del Piombo. Metropolitan Museum of Art, New York. Photo © The Bridgeman Art Library; **123** *left* The Granger Collection, New York; **right** South American Pictures; **124** The Granger Collection, New York; **126** The Granger Collection, New York; **127** *top left* Detail of letter from Christopher Columbus to his son Diego (5 February 1505). General Archive of the Indies, Seville, Spain. Photo © Dagli Orti/The Art Archive; *top right* © Bettmann/Corbis; **128** The Granger Collection, New York; **129** North Carolina Collection, University of North Carolina, Chapel Hill; **132** *top left* © Bettmann/Corbis; *top right* Detail of letter from Christopher Columbus to his son Diego (5 February 1505). General Archive of the Indies, Seville, Spain. Photo © Dagli Orti/The Art Archive; **133** The Granger Collection, New York; **135** *center* The Granger Collection, New York; *right* The Newberry Library, Chicago; **137** *top left* Detail of letter from Christopher Columbus to his son Diego (5 February 1505). General Archive of the Indies, Seville, Spain. Photo © Dagli Orti/The Art Archive; *top right* © Bettmann/Corbis; **139** The Granger Collection, New York; **143** The Granger Collection, New York; **144** Portrait of the last Inca Chief, Atahualpa. Private Collection. Photo © The Bridgeman Art Library; **145** *top left Cosimo de'Medici, the Elder,* Agnolo Bronzino. Museo Mediceo, Florence, Italy. Photo © Scala/Art Resource, New York; *top right* © Sakamoto Photo Research Laboratory/Corbis; *bottom* © Bettmann/Corbis; **147** *top* © Araldo de Luca/Corbis; *bottom left* Nautilus pitcher (about 1570). Francesco de Medici Collection. Museo degli Argenti, Florence, Italy. Photo © Erich Lessing/Art Resource, New York; *bottom right* John Bigelow Taylor/American Museum of Natural History, No. 4959(2); **148** *top* © Yann Arthus-Bertrand/Corbis; *bottom* © Steve Vidler/SuperStock, Inc.; **149** © Archivo Iconografico, S.A./Corbis.

UNIT TWO

150–151 The Taking of the Bastille, July 14, 1789, unknown artist. Musée National du Chateau, Versailles, France. Photo © Erich Lessing/Art Resource, New York.

Chapter 5

152 *top Philip II, King of Spain and Portugal* (16th century), Alonso Sanchez Coello. Museo del Prado, Madrid, Spain. Photo © Erich Lessing/Art Resource, New York; *bottom Francisco Pizarro* (1835), Amable-Paul Coutan. Chateaux de Versailles et de Trianon, Versailles, France. Photo by Franck Raux © Réunion des Musées Nationaux/Art Resource, New York; **153** *top* The Granger Collection, New York; *bottom* © Pallava Bagla/Corbis; **154** *Louis XIV, King of France* (1701), Hyacinthe Rigaud. Louvre, Paris. Photo © Erich Lessing/Art Resource, New York; **155** *top left* Detail of *Marriage of Louis XIV, King of*

Art and Photography Credits (Cont.)

France and Marie Therese of Austria (17th century), unknown artist. Musée de Tesse, Le Mans, France. Photo © Dagli Orti/The Art Archive; *top right* © Todd A. Gipstein/Corbis; **156** The Granger Collection, New York; **157** *Las Meninas or The Family of Philip IV,* (about 1656), Diego Rodriguez de Silva y Velasquez. Prado, Madrid, Spain. Photo © The Bridgeman Art Library; **158** Tulipa gesaeriana no. 1908 (late 16th–early 17th century), Jacopo Ligozzi. Gabinetto dei Disegni e delle Stampe. Ufizzi, Florence, Italy. Photo © Scala/Art Resource, New York; **159** The Granger Collection, New York; **162** *top left* Detail of *Marriage of Louis XIV, King of France and Marie Therese of Austria* (17th century), unknown artist. Musée de Tesse, Le Mans, France. Photo © Dagli Orti/The Art Archive; *top right* © Todd A. Gipstein/Corbis; **163** *Cardinal Richelieu* (1636), Phillippe de Champaigne. Musée Condé, Chantilly, France. Photo © Giraudon/Art Resource, New York; **164** Detail of *Colbert Presenting Louis XIV the Members of the Royal Academy of Sciences in 1667,* Henri Tetstelin. Photo © Gerard Blot/Réunion Musées Nationaux; **165** *Louis de Rouvroy, Duke of Saint-Simon* (1887), Viger du Vigneau. Chateaux de Versailles et de Trianon, Versailles, France. Photo © Réunion des Musées Nationaux/Art Resource, New York; **166** © Archivio Iconografico, S.A./Corbis; *left inset* © Archivio Iconografico, S.A./Corbis; *center inset* © Adam Woolfitt/Corbis; *right inset* © Ben Mangor/SuperStock, Inc.; **167** *Battle of Denain, 24th July 1712* (1839), Jean Alaux. Chateau de Versailles et de Trianon, France. Photo © Giraudon/The Bridgeman Art Library; **169** *top left* Detail of *Marriage of Louis XIV, King of France and Marie Therese of Austria* (17th century), unknown artist. Musée de Tesse, Le Mans, France. Photo © Dagli Orti/The Art Archive; *top right* © Todd A. Gipstein/Corbis; **171** Flag of the Imperial Hapsburg dynasty (about 1700). Heeresgeschichtliches Museum, Vienna, Austria. © The Bridgeman Art Library; **172** *top* Detail of *Empress Maria Theresa of Austria.* Museum der Stadt Wien. Photo © Dagli Orti/The Art Archive; *center* Schloss Charlottenburg, Berlin/Bildarchiv Preussischer Kulturbesitz, Berlin; **174** *top left* Detail of *Marriage of Louis XIV, King of France and Marie Therese of Austria* (17th century), unknown artist. Musée de Tesse, Le Mans, France. Photo © Dagli Orti/The Art Archive; *top right* © Todd A. Gipstein/Corbis; **175** The Granger Collection, New York; **178** *top right* © Dorling Kindersley; *center left* Costumes of Crimean tribes (1888), A. Racinet. From Historical Costumes vol, V. Musée des Arts Décoratifs, Paris. Photo © Dagli Orti/The Art Archive; *bottom* © Historical Picture Archive/Corbis; **179** *top Shrovetide* (1919), Boris Kustidiev. The I. Brodsky Museum, St. Petersburg, Russia. Photo courtesy of the Smithsonian Institution Traveling Exhibition Service; *bottom* © Scheufler Collection/Corbis; **180** *top left* Detail of *Marriage of Louis XIV, King of France and Marie Therese of Austria* (17th century), unknown artist. Musée de Tesse, Le Mans, France. Photo © Dagli Orti/The Art Archive; *top right* © Todd A. Gipstein/Corbis; **181** The Granger Collection, New York.

Chapter 6

186 *left Portrait of a Princess Holding a Wine Cup* (17th–18th century). Mughal. India. The Newark Museum, Newark, New Jersey. Photo © The Newark Museum/Art Resource, New York; *right* Isaac Newton's reflecting telescope (1672), Royal Society. Photo by Eileen Tweedy/The Art Archive; **187** *left* Statuette of a Lohan. Ching dynasty. Musée des Arts Asiatiques-Guimet, Paris. Photo © Giraudon/Art Resource, New York; *right* © Leif Skoogfors/Corbis; **188** *A Philosopher Gives a Lecture on the Orrery* (1766), Joseph Wright. Canvas. Derby Museum and Art Gallery, Derby, Great Britain. Photo © Erich Lessing/Art Resource, New York; **189** *top left* Copernican Solar System (1661). From Harmonia Macronici, Andreae Cellarius. Page 30. Photo © Victoria and Albert Museum, London/Art Resource, New York; *top right* © Bettmann/Corbis; **191** *Galileo Before the Holy Office of the Vatican,* John Nicolas Robert-Fleury. Oil on canvas. Louvre, Paris. Photo by Gerard Blot © Réunion des Musées Nationaux /Art Resource, New York; **192** *left* © Bettmann/Corbis; *right* Isaac Newton's reflecting telescope (1672). Royal Society. Photo by Eileen Tweed/The Art Archive; **193** © Bettmann/Corbis; **194** *The Anatomy Lesson of Dr. Tulp,* Rembrandt van Rijn. Mauritshuis, The Hague, The Netherlands. Photo © Scala/Art Resource, New York; **195** *top left* Copernican Solar System (1661). From Harmonia Macronici, Andreae Cellarius. Page 30. Photo © Victoria and Albert Museum, London/Art Resource, New York; *top right* © Bettmann/Corbis; **196** The Granger Collection; **197** *left* The Granger Collection, New York; *right* The Granger Collection, New York; **199** Mary Evans Picture Library; **201** The Granger Collection, New York; **202** *top left* Copernican Solar System (1661). From Harmonia Macronici, Andreae Cellarius. Page 30. Photo © Victoria and Albert Museum, London/Art Resource, New York; *top right* © Bettmann/Corbis; **203** © Kevin Fleming/Corbis; **204** *Joseph II, Emperor of Austria and of the Holy Roman Empire, King of Hungary and Bohemia* (18th century). Musée du Château de Versailles. Photo © Dagli Orti/The Art Archive; **205** © Anatoly Sapronenkov/Tomsk Regional Arts Museum/SuperStock, Inc.; **206** *top left* Copernican Solar System (1661). From Harmonia Macronici, Andreae Cellarius. Page 30. Photo © Victoria and Albert Museum, London/Art Resource, New York; *top right* © Bettmann/Corbis; *bottom* Snuff box. French.The Metropolitan Museum of Art, gift of William H. Huntington, 1883 (83.2.228); **207** Detail of *Thomas Jefferson* (about 1805), Rembrandt Peale. Oil on canvas. Photo © Collection of the New-York Historical Society; **210** © Corbis; **211** © Jon Feingersh/Stock Boston, Inc./PictureQuest **213** *El sueño de la razón produce monstruos* [The sleep of reason produces monsters] from *Los Caprichos* (1799), Francisco José de Goya y Lucientes. Etching and burnished aquatint, 21.5cm. x 15 cm. Bequest of William P. Babcock. Courtesy of Museum of Fine Arts, Boston.

Chapter 7

214 *right* Reduced model of a guillotine. Musée de la Ville de Paris, Musée Carnavalet, Paris. Photo © Giraudon/Art Resource, New York; *left George Washington,* George Healy. Musée du Château de Versailles. Photo © Dagli Orti/The Art Archive; **215** *top* Detail of *Napoleon Bonaparte, Emperor of France.* Musée du Château de Versailles. Photo © Dagli Orti/The Art Archive; *bottom* The Granger Collection, New York; **216** *The Conquerors of the Bastille Before the Hotel de Ville* (1839), Paul Delaroche. Musée du Petit Palais, Paris. Photo © Erich Lessing/Art Resource, New York; **217** *top left* © SuperStock, Inc.; *top right* © Christie's Images/Corbis; **218** Detail of *Caricature of the three estates: Il faut esperer que le jeu finira bientôt.* Color engraving, 18th century. Musée de la Ville de Paris, Musée Carnavalet, Paris. Photo by Bulloz © Réunion des Musées Nationaux /Art Resource, New York; **219** *left Louis XVI, King of France.* Musée de Château de Versailles. Photo © Dagli Orti/The Art Archive; *right Marie Antoinette, Queen of France.* Replica of work painted in 1778. Musée du Château de Versailles. Photo © Dagli Orti/The Art Archive; **220** *The Storming of the Bastille, Paris, France, July 14, 1789.* Gouache. Musée Carnavalet, Paris. Photo © Dagli Orti/The Art Archive; **222** *left* © SuperStock, Inc.; *right* © Christie's Images/Corbis; **223** *Arrest of Louis XVI, King of France and his family attempting to flee the country at Varennes, France June 21–22, 1791.* Musée Carnavalet, Paris. Photo © Dagli Orti/The Art Archive; **224** Musées Royaux des Beaux-Arts, Brussels, Belgium. Photo © Giraudon/Art Resource, New York; **225** Illustration by Patrick Whelan; **226** *Portrait of*

Robespierre, Louis L. Boilly. Musée des Beaux-Arts, Lille, France. Photo R.G. Ojeda © Réunion des Musées Nationaux/Art Resource, New York; **227** *Portrait of Danton* (18th century) Musée de la Ville de Paris, Musée Carnavalet, Paris. Photo © Giraudon/Art Resource, New York; **228** © Bettmann/Corbis; **229** *top left* © SuperStock, Inc.; *top right* © Christie's Images/Corbis; *230 Portrait of Bonaparte, premier consul* (1803), Francois Gerard. Oil on canvas. Musée Condé, Chantilly, France. Photo by Harry Brejat © Réunion des Musées Nationaux/Art Resource, New York; **231** *Napoleon Bonaparte,* Jacques-Louis David. Chateau de Malmaison, Rueil-Malmaison, France. Photo © Giraudon/Art Resource, New York; **234** *top left* © SuperStock, Inc.; *top right* © Christie's Images/Corbis; *bottom* Fotomas Index; **235** © Archivo Iconografico, S.A./Corbis; **237** © Public Record Office/Topham-HIP/The Image Works; **238** *top left* © SuperStock, Inc.; *top right* © Christie's Images/Corbis; **239** © Christel Gerstenberg/Corbis; **242** *left Parisian sans culotte* (18th century), unknown artist. Musée de la Ville de Paris, Musée Carnavalet, Paris. Photo © Giraudon/Art Resource, New York; *right* Reduced model of a guillotine. Musée de la Ville de Paris, Musée Carnavalet, Paris. Photo © Giraudon/Art Resource, New York.

Chapter 8

244 *left Napoleon in His Study at the Tuileries* (1812). Jacques-Louis David. Collection of Prince and Princess Napoleon, Paris. Photo © Giraudon/Art Resource, New York; *right Miguel Hidalgo y Costilla* (1895). From Mexican publication Patria e Independencia, folleto ilustrado. Antiochiw Collection, Mexico. Photo © Mireille Vautier/The Art Archive; **245** *left* © Hulton-Deutsch Collection/Corbis; *right* © Francis G. Mayer/Corbis; **246** Courtesy of the Flag Institute; **247** *left* © Michael S. Lewis/Corbis; *right* © Archivo Iconografico, S.A./Corbis; **248** *Portrait of Francois-Dominique Toussaint, known as Toussaint L'Ouverture,* unknown artist. Musée des Arts d'Oceanie, Paris. Photo J.G. Berizzi © Réunion des Musées Nationaux/Art Resource, New York; **249** *left* © Christie's Images/Corbis; *right* The Granger Collection, New York; **250** © Bettmann/Corbis; **253** *top left* © Michael S. Lewis/Corbis; *top right* © Archivo Iconografico, S.A./Corbis; *bottom Klemens Metternich, Austrian prince and statesman.* Museo Glauco, Lombardi, Parma, Italy. Photo © Dagli Orti/The Art Archive; **255** © Archivo Iconografico, S.A./Corbis; **256** *Combat Before the Hotel de Ville, July 28th, 1830,* Victor Schnetz. Musée du Petit Palais, Paris. Photo by Bulloz © Réunion des Musées Nationaux/Art Resource, New York; **257** © Corbis; **261** The Granger Collection, New York; **262** © Bettmann/Corbis; **264** *top left* © Michael S. Lewis/Corbis; *top right* © Archivo Iconografico, S.A./Corbis; *bottom* © Bettmann/Corbis; **265** *Portrait of Ludwig von Beethoven,* unknown artist. Beethoven House, Bonn, Germany. Photo © Snark/Art Resource, New York; **266** © Hulton-Deutsch Collection/Corbis; **268** *Lion Hunt* (about 1860), Eugène Delacroix, French 1798–1863. Potter Palmer Collection, 1922.404, Reproduction. The Art Institute of Chicago, Chicago, Illinois; **269** *top The Stone Breakers* (1849), Gustave Courbet. Gemäldegalerie, Dresden, Germany. Photo © The Bridgeman Art Library; *bottom* © Francis G. Mayer/Corbis; **271** The Granger Collection, New York; **272–273** *bottom* The Granger Collection, New York; **272** *left* The Bloody Massacre perpetrated in...Boston on March 5th, 1770. Paul Revere. Colored engraving. The Gilder Lehrman Collection on deposit at The Pierpont Morgan Library. GLC 1868. Photo by Joseph Zehavi © The Pierpont Morgan Library/Art Resource, New York; *right Portrait of James II* (about 1685), Benedetto Gennari the Younger. Historical Portraits Ltd, London. Photo © The Bridgeman Art Library; **273** The Granger Collection, New York; **274** *left* Detail of *Marie-Antoinette Standing in her Court Robe with a Rose in her Hand* (1779), Louise Elizabeth Vigée-LeBrun. Châteaux de Versailles et de Trianon, Versailles, France. Photo © Réunion des Musées Nationaux/Art Resource, New York; *bottom right* © Photodisc/Getty Images; **275** *top Il faut esperer que le jeu finira bientot* [Peasant carrying a nobleman and a cleric] (1789). Musée de la Ville de Paris, Musée Carnavalet, Paris. Photo © Giraudon/Art Resource, New York; *bottom* The Granger Collection, New York; **276** The Granger Collection, New York; **277** *top* The Granger Collection, New York; *center Maximilien Robespierre.* Musée Carnavalet, Paris. Photo © Dagli Orti/The Art Archive.

UNIT THREE

278–279 Martyn Gregory Gallery, London.

Chapter 9

280 *top* The Granger Collection, New York; *bottom* © Brian A. Vikander/Corbis; **281** *left* © Bettmann/Corbis; *right* Cover of *The Communist Manifesto* by Karl Marx and Friedrich Engels, edited by Martin Malia, © 1998 by Martin Malia. Used by permission of Signet, an imprint of Penguin Group USA; **282** © Corbis; **283** *top left* © Collin Garratt/Milepost 92 1/2/Corbis; *top right* © H. David Seawell/Corbis; **284** © Getty Images; **285** *center* Blind man using a loom (1817), Dr. Sebastien Guillie. Plate 17 from Essai su l'Instruction des Aveugles. Colored engraving. Bibliothèque de l'Institut d'Ophtalmologie, Paris/Archives Charmet. Photo © The Bridgeman Art Library. *left* © Michael St. Maur Sheil/Corbis; *bottom* Sheffield Galleries & Museum Trust; **286** © Bettmann/Corbis; **287** Liverpool and Manchester passenger train (about 1830). National Railway Museum, York, North Yorkshire, UK. Photo © The Bridgeman Art Library; **288** © Getty Images; **289** The Granger Collection, New York; **293** The Granger Collection, New York; **294** © Steve Raymer/Corbis; **295** *top left* © Collin Garratt/Milepost 92 1/2/Corbis; *top right* © H. David Seawell/Corbis; *bottom* © Corbis; **297** *The Steel Workers at Biermeister and Wain* (1885), Peter Severin Kroyer. Statens Museum for Kunst, Copenhagen, Denmark. Photo © Snark/Art Resource, New York; **299** Mary Evans Picture Library; **300** *top left* © Collin Garratt/Milepost 92 1/2/Corbis; *top right* © H. David Seawell/Corbis; **301** © Bettmann/Corbis; **302** © Archivo Iconografico, S.A./Corbis; **305** *Strike* (1895), Mihaly Munkacsy. Magyar Nemzeti Galeria, Budapest, Hungary. Photo © The Bridgeman Art Library; **306** Jane Addams (about 1920), George de Forest Brush. National Portrait Gallery, Smithsonian Institution, Washington, D.C. Photo © National Portrait Gallery, Smithsonian Institution/Art Resource, New York; **307** Woodcut, from Cartoons for the Cause (1886), Walter Crane.

Chapter 10

310 *top* Queen Victoria (late 19th century). Victoria and Albert Museum, London. Photo © Victoria and Albert Museum, London/Art Resource, New York; *bottom* © The Stapleton Collection/Bridgeman Art Library; **311** *top* The Granger Collection, New York; *bottom* © Corbis; **312** *Une rue de Paris en mai 1871, ou La Commune* [A Paris street in May 1871, or The commune] (1903–1905), Maximilien Luce. Oil on canvas. Musée D'Orsay, Paris. Photo © Erich Lessing/Art Resource, New York; **313** *top left* © Hulton-Deutsch Collection/Corbis; *top right* © Bettmann/Corbis; **314** © Bettmann/Corbis; **316**

Art and Photography Credits (Cont.)

Zola Under Attack (1898), Henry de Groux. Photo by Musée Emile Zola, Médan, France; **317** *top left* © Hulton-Deutsch Collection/Corbis; *top right* © Bettmann/Corbis; **319** © Sean Sexton Collection/Corbis; **322** *center* Nouvelle-Hollande. Cour-Rou-Bari-Gal., Plate XVIII from Atlas historique: du Voyage de decouvertes aux terres australes, by Charles Alexandre Leseur and Nicolas-Martin Petit. State Library of South Australia; *center right* © Charles & Josette Lenars/Corbis; *bottom Australian Gold Diggings* (about 1855), Edwin Stocqueler. National Library of Australia, Canberra; **323** *top* © Graham Monro/photolibrary/PictureQuest; *bottom* The Granger Collection, New York; **324** *top left* © Hulton-Deutsch Collection/Corbis; *top right* © Bettmann/Corbis; **327** Library of Congress; **328** *top left* © Hulton-Deutsch Collection/Corbis; *top right* © Bettmann/Corbis; **329** *top right* The Granger Collection, New York; *center left* Institute of Experimental Physics/University of Innsbruck, Austria; *center right* Library of Congress; *bottom* The Granger Collection, New York; **330** *left* © Bettmann/Corbis; *center* © Bettmann/Corbis; *right* The Granger Collection, New York; **331** The Granger Collection, New York; **332** © Bettmann/Corbis; **335** By permission of the British Library.

Chapter 11

336 *top* © Werner Forman/Art Resource, New York; *bottom* The Bowes Museum, County Durham, Great Britain; **337** *top* © Bettmann/Corbis; *bottom* © Bettmann/Corbis; **338** © Getty Images; **339** *top left* Aboriginal Bark painting of abstract picture of body (19th–20th century), Lipunja. Musée des Arts Africains et Océaniens. Photo © Dagli Orti/The Art Archive; *top right The Battle of Isandhlwana* (19th century), Charles Fripp. National Army Museum, London. Photo © The Art Archive; **340** The Granger Collection, New York; **341** The Granger Collection, New York; **342** *Cetshwayo, King of the Zulus,* Carl Rudolph Sohn. The Royal Collection (England). Photo © 2003 Her Majesty Queen Elizabeth II; **344** © Hulton-Deutsch Collection/Corbis; **349** © Culver Pictures; **351** The Granger Collection, New York; **352** *top left* Aboriginal Bark painting of abstract picture of body, Lipunja. Musée des Arts Africains et Océaniens. Photo © Dagli Orti/The Art Archive; *top right The Battle of Isandhlwana* (19th century), Charles Fripp. National Army Museum, London. Photo © The Art Archive; **354** *Mehemet Ali, Viceroy of Egypt* (19th century), Louis Charles Auguste Couder. Chateau de Versailles, France. Photo © Lauros-Giraudon/The Bridgeman Art Library; **355** *Shipping on the Suez Canal* (1869), Edouard Riou. Chateau de Compiègne, Oise, France. Photo © Lauros-Giraudon/The Bridgeman Art Library; **356** *Portrait of Nasir Al-Din Shah* (19th century), unknown artist. Louvre, Paris. Photo © Réunion des Musées Nationaux/Art Resource, New York; **357** *top left* Aboriginal Bark painting of abstract picture of body, Lipunja. Musée des Arts Africains et Océaniens. Photo © Dagli Orti/The Art Archive; *top right The Battle of Isandhlwana* (19th century), Charles Fripp. National Army Museum, London. Photo © The Art Archive; *bottom A Sepoy (an Indian Soldier in the French Battalion) at Pondicherry* (19th century), Racinet. Photo © The Stapleton Collection/The Bridgeman Art Library; **359** © Getty Images; **360** The Granger Collection, New York; **362** *top left* Aboriginal Bark painting of abstract picture of body, Lipunja. Milingibi, Australia. Musée des Arts Africains et Océaniens. Photo © Dagli Orti/The Art Archive; *top right The Battle of Isandhlwana* (19th century), Charles Fripp. National Army Museum, London. Photo © The Art Archive; **364** © Corbis; **365** The Granger Collection, New York.

Chapter 12

368 © Bettmann/Corbis; **369** *top left* © Corbis; *bottom left* Union Flag with portrait of Queen Victoria and British Colonies. The Bodleian Library, Oxford, England, John Johnson Collection (Printed Fabrics 1). Photo © The Bodleian Library/The Art Archive; *top right* © Corbis; **370** © Historical Picture Archive/Corbis; **371** *top left View of Landscape* (18th–19th century), Katsushika Hokusai. Oriental Art Museum, Genoa, Italy. Photo © Dagli Orti/The Art Archive; *top right* © Archivo Iconografico, S.A./Corbis; **372** © David Lawrence/Corbis; **373** The Granger Collection, New York; **375** © SuperStock, Inc.; **376** *top left View of Landscape* (18th–19th century), Katsushika Hokusai. Oriental Art Museum, Genoa, Italy. Photo © Dagli Orti/The Art Archive; *top right* © Archivo Iconografico, S.A./Corbis; **377** *left* The Granger Collection, New York; *right* © Bettmann/Corbis; **378** Mary Evans Picture Library; **380** *left* © Sakamoto Photo Research Laboratory/Corbis; *top right* Photo by Fumi Bull. Courtesy David Bull; *center right* Photo by Fumi Bull. Courtesy David Bull; *bottom right* Photo by Fumi Bull. Courtesy David Bull; **381** *top* © Historical Picture Archive/Corbis; *bottom* Photo by Fumi Bull. Courtesy David Bull; **382** *top left View of Landscape* (18th–19th century), Katsushika Hokusai. Oriental Art Museum, Genoa, Italy. Photo © Dagli Orti/The Art Archive; *top right* © Archivo Iconografico, S.A./Corbis; **383** *top* © Bettmann/Corbis; **bottom** © Underwood & Underwood/Corbis; **384** The Granger Collection, New York; **386** © Danny Lehman/Corbis; **387** The Granger Collection, New York; **388** *top left View of Landscape* (18th–19th century), Katsushika Hokusai. Oriental Art Museum, Genoa, Italy. Photo © Dagli Orti/The Art Archive; *top right* © Archivo Iconografico, S.A./Corbis; *bottom right* The Granger Collection, New York; **389** © Bettmann/Corbis; **390** The Granger Collection, New York; **391** *Portrait of Porfirio Diaz.* Antochiw Collection, Mexico. Photo © Mireille Vautier/The Art Archive; **392** *Emiliano Zapata* (19th–20th century), unknown artist. National History Museum, Mexico City. Photo © Dagli Orti/The Art Archive; **396** *top left, right* The Granger Collection, New York; *bottom* © Bettmann/Corbis; **397** *top, bottom* © Bettmann/Corbis; **399** © Corbis; **400** © Bettmann/Corbis; **401** The Granger Collection, New York.

UNIT FOUR

402–403 French troops crossing over pontoon bridges on the River Yser, Belgium, August, 1917. Musée de L'Armée, Paris. Photo © Dagli Orti/Art Archive.

Chapter 13

404 *top* © The Image Bank/Getty Images; **bottom** © Bettmann/Corbis; **405** *left* Mary Evans Picture Library; *center* © Bettmann/Corbis; *right* © Bettmann/Corbis; **406** Library of Congress; **407** *top left* © Bettmann/Corbis; *top right For King and Country* (20th century), E. F. Skinner. Royal Collection, United Kingdom. Photo by Eileen Tweedy/The Art Archive; **408** Mary Evans/Weimar Archive; **411** *top left* © Bettmann/Corbis; *top right For King and Country* (20th century), E. F. Skinner. Royal Collection, United Kingdom. Photo by Eileen Tweedy/The Art Archive; **413** © Corbis; **414** *top* © Popperfoto; *bottom* © Getty Images; **415** © Hulton-Deutsch Collection/Corbis; **416** *top* © Hulton-Deutsch Collection/Corbis; *bottom* © Fraser May; **417** *top left* © Bettmann/Corbis; *top right For King and Country* (20th century), E. F. Skinner. Royal Collection,

United Kingdom. Photo by Eileen Tweedy/The Art Archive; **419** © Bettmann/Corbis; **420** © Corbis; **423** Library of Congress; **424** *top left* © Bettmann/Corbis; *top right For King and Country* (20th century), E. F. Skinner. Royal Collection, United Kingdom. Photo by Eileen Tweedy/The Art Archive; **425** *top Thomas Woodrow Wilson* (1921), Edmund Charles Tarbell. National Portrait Gallery, Smithsonian Institution. Photo © National Portrait Gallery, Smithsonian Institution/Art Resource, New York; *bottom Portrait of George Clemenceau* (1879–1880), Edouard Manet. Musée d'Orsay, Paris. Photo © Erich Lessing/Art Resource, New York; **429** Library of Congress.

Chapter 14

430 *top* © Bettmann/Corbis; **bottom** © The Flag Institute; **431** *left* © Elliott & Fry/Getty Images; *center* © Getty Images; *right* © AFP/Corbis; **432** *left* © Getty Images; *right* © Bettmann/Corbis; **433** *bottom* © Archivo Iconografico, S.A./Corbis; **434** © Bettmann/Corbis; **435** © 2003 Tass/Sovfoto; **436** Mapping Specialists; **437** Itar-Tass/Sovfoto; **438** *left* © Archivo Iconografico, S.A./Corbis; *right* © Bettmann/Corbis; **440** *top left* © Swim Ink/Corbis; *top right* © Patrick Field/Eye Ubiquitous/Corbis; **442** © Bettmann/Corbis; **443** David King Collection, London; **445** Itar-Tass/Sovfoto; **446** *top left, top right* Collection of the International Institute of Social History, Amsterdam, Netherlands; *bottom* CTK/Eastfoto; **441** David King Collection, London; **448** *top left* © Swim Ink/Corbis; *top right* © Patrick Field/Eye Ubiquitous/Corbis; *bottom* © Getty Images; **449** *inset* Photo by Sidney D. Gamble; *bottom* © Peter Turnley/Corbis; **450** © Corbis; **451** *top right* From Chinese Communist Sketches and Autobiographies of the Old Guard: Red Dust by Nym Wales. June 1972. Greenwood Publishing Group; *bottom left* AP/Wide World Photos; *bottom right* © Rene Burri/Magnum Photos; **452** © Getty Images; **453** *top left* © Swim Ink/Corbis; *top left* © Patrick Field/Eye Ubiquitous/Corbis; *bottom* © Bettmann/Corbis; **455** *top* Photo by Margaret Bourke-White ©Time Life Pictures/Getty Images; *inset* © The Flag Institute; **456** © Hulton-Deutsch Collection/Corbis; **458** *left to right* © Bettmann/Corbis; David King Collection, London; © Getty Images; © Getty Images; © Bettmann/Corbis; © Hulton-Deutsch Collection/Corbis.

Chapter 15

460 *top* © Getty Images; *bottom* Library of Congress; **461** *left* Roger-Viollet; *right* © Hulton-Deutsch Collection/Corbis; **462** © 1995 Chicago Historical Society; **463** *top left* Chicago Historical Society; *top right* Life cover (July 1, 1926) Fred Cooper; **464** AP/Wide World Photos; **465** *The Persistence of Memory* (1931), Salvador Dali. Oil on canvas, 9 1/2" x 13" (162.1934). The Museum of Modern Art, New York. Given anonymously. © 2003 Salvador Dali, Gala-Salvador Dali Foundation/Artists Rights Society (ARS), New York. Digital Image © The Museum of Modern Art/Licensed by Scala/Art Resource, New York; **466** The Granger Collection, New York; **467** © Bettmann/Corbis; **468** *left* The Granger Collection, New York; *right* © Schenectady Museum/Hall of Electrical History Foundation/Corbis; **469** *top* The Granger Collection, New York; *center* © Schenectady Museum/Hall of Electrical History Foundation/Corbis; **bottom** The Granger Collection, New York; **470** *top left* Chicago Historical Society; *top right* Life cover (July 1, 1926) Fred Cooper; **471** © Getty Images; **473** © Museum of the City of New York; **475** The Granger Collection, New York; **476** *top left* Chicago Historical Society; **top right** Life cover (July 1, 1926) Fred Cooper; **477** © Getty Images; **478** *top* © Getty Images; *bottom* © Getty Images; **479** © Getty Images; **480** © Bettmann/Corbis; **481** *top left* Chicago Historical Society; *top right* Life cover (July 1, 1926) Fred Cooper; **484** *top* © Corbis; *bottom* The Granger Collection, New York; **485** © Getty Images; **487** © Bettmann/Corbis.

Chapter 16

488 *left* The Granger Collection, New York; *right* © Museum of Flight/Corbis; **489** *top* © Bettmann/Corbis; *bottom* U.S. Air Force; **490** German planes bombing London, England (1940). La Domenica del Corriere. Photo © Dagli Orti/Art Archive; **491** *top left* © Getty Images; *top right* © KJ Historical/Corbis; **493** The Granger Collection, New York; **494** © William Vandivert/Getty Images; **495** Photo © The Art Archive; **497** *top left* © Getty Images; *top right* © KJ Historical/Corbis; **498** © UPI/Bettmann/Corbis; **499** The Granger Collection, New York; **500** © Bettmann/Corbis; **501** AP/Wide World Photos; **502** *top left* © Getty Images; *top right* © KJ Historical/Corbis; **503** *top* Courtesy of the Spertus Museum, Chicago; *bottom* © Hulton-Deutsch Collection/Corbis; **504** Courtesy of the United States Holocaust Memorial Museum Photo Archives; **506** *top left* © Getty Images; *top right* © KJ Historical/Corbis; **507** © Getty Images; **509** The Advertising Archive Ltd; **510** © Bettmann/Corbis; **511** © Getty Images; **512** *top left* © UPI/Bettmann/Corbis; *top right* U.S. Air Force; *bottom* Photo of aftermath of bombing of Nagasaki, August 10, 1945, by Yosuke Yamahata. Photo restoration by TX Unlimited, San Francisco; **513** © Bettmann/Corbis; **514** *top left* © Getty Images; *right* © KJ Historical/Corbis; **516** © AFP/Corbis; **517** AP/Wide World Photos. **520** *top left* © Bettmann/Corbis; *top right, bottom right* © Getty Images; *bottom left* © Corbis; **521** *top* © Corbis; *bottom* National Air and Space Museum/Smithsonian Institution; **522** *top* © Williams Vandivert/Getty News Images; *bottom* © Bettman/Corbis; **525** © Hulton-Deutsch Collection/Corbis.

UNIT FIVE

526–527 © Jacques Langevin/Corbis Sygma.

Chapter 17

528 *top* © Wally McNamee/Corbis; *bottom* © The Flag Institute; **529** *left* NASA; *center* © Peter Turnley/Corbis; *right* © David Turnley/Corbis; **530** *left* © Bettmann/Corbis; *right* © Geoffrey Clements/Corbis; **531** *top left* © Peter Turnley/Corbis; *top right* NASA; *bottom* Imperial War Museum. Photo © Art Archive; **533** Tom Little/Nashville Tennessean; **535** © UPI/Bettmann/Corbis; **537** *top, bottom center* NASA; *bottom left* Tass/Sovfoto; **538** *top left* © Peter Turnley/Corbis; *top right* NASA **539** *left* © Corbis; *right* © Roman Soumar/Corbis; **540** © Getty Images; **541** © Bettmann/Corbis; **542** *top left* © Peter Turnley/Corbis; *top right* NASA; *bottom* © Getty Images; **544** © Getty Images; **545** *top* USAF/TRH Pictures; *center* © Bettmann/Corbis; *bottom* © Nik Wheeler/Black Star; **546** © Les Stone/Corbis Sygma; **547** © Catherine Karnow/Corbis; **548** *top left* © Peter Turnley/Corbis; *top right* NASA; **549** © Bettmann/Corbis; **551** © Wally McNamee/Corbis; **552** *right, left* © Alain Mingam/Getty News Services; **553** AP/Wide World Photos; **554** *top left* © Peter Turnley/Corbis; *top right* NASA; **555** *left* © 1994 Sovfoto/PictureQuest; *center* AP/Wide World Photos; *right* © Peter Turnley/Corbis; **556** © Wally McNamee/Corbis; **557** Collection of David J. and Janice L. Frent.

Art and Photography Credits (Cont.)

Chapter 18

560 *left* AP/Wide World Photos; *right* © Black Star; **561** AP/Wide World Photos; **562** *top left, bottom left, bottom right* AP/Wide World Photos; *bottom right* © Liba Taylor/Corbis; *center* © Liz Gilbert /Corbis Sygma; **563** *top left* © SuperStock, Inc.; *top right* © Steve Vidler/SuperStock, Inc.; **565** © AFP/Corbis; **566** © Hulton-Deutsch Collection/Corbis; **567** *top left* © 1979 Romano Cagnoni/Black Star; *top right* © Gamma; *bottom* Photo by Margaret Bourke-White ©Time Life Pictures/Getty Images.; *bottom center* © 1968 Fred Mayer/Magnum Photos; *bottom right* © Gamma; **568** © Nik Wheeler/Corbis; **569** © Nokelsberg/Getty News Images; **570** *top left* © SuperStock, Inc.; *top right* © Steve Vidler/SuperStock, Inc.; **572** © Alison Wright/Corbis; **573** © Paul Russell/Corbis; **574** © AFP/Corbis; **575** AP/Wide World Photos; **576** *top* © Jack Fields/Corbis; *bottom left* AP/Wide World Photos; *bottom right* © Jose Fuste Raga/Corbis; **577** *top* © Steve Raymer/Corbis; *bottom* © ML Sinibaldi/Corbis; **578** *top left* © SuperStock, Inc.; *top right* © Steve Vidler/SuperStock, Inc.; **579** AP/Wide World Photos; **581, 582** © Reuters NewMedia Inc./Corbis; **583** *top left* © SuperStock, Inc.; *top right* © Steve Vidler/SuperStock, Inc.; **585–586** © Wally McNamee/Corbis; **587** *left* © Peter Turnley/Corbis; *right* AP/Wide World Photos; **588** AP/Wide World Photos; **589** © Time Inc./Time Life Pictures/Getty Images; **590** *top left* © SuperStock, Inc.; *top right* © Steve Vidler/SuperStock, Inc.; **591** *top* © Dean Conger/Corbis; *bottom* © Tiziana and Gianni Baldizzone/Corbis; **592** © Reuters NewMedia Inc./Corbis; **593** © AFP/Corbis; **595** By permission of Bob Gorrell and Creators Syndicate, Inc.

Chapter 19

596 *top* © Bettmann/Corbis; *bottom* © Getty Images; **597** *left* © Wally McNamee/Corbis; *right* © Bettmann/Corbis; **598** AP/Wide World Photos; **599** *top left* © Owen Franken/Corbis; *top right* AP/Wide World Photos; **603** © 2001 The New Yorker Collection from cartoonbank.com. All Rights Reserved; **604** AP/Wide World Photos; **605** © Bettmann/Corbis; **606** *top left* © Owen Franken/Corbis; *top right* AP/Wide World Photos; **608** © Greenpeace/Corbis Sygma; **609** © David Turnley/Corbis; **610** *top* © David Turnley/Corbis; *bottom* AP/Wide World Photos; **612** *top left* © Owen Franken/Corbis; *top right* AP/Wide World Photos; **613** Jeff Stahler. Reprinted by permission of Newspaper Enterprise Association, Inc.; **614** *top* © Peter Turnley/Corbis; **bottom** © Peter Turnley/Corbis; **616** AP/Wide World Photos; **617** © Ron Sachs/Corbis; **618** *top left* © Owen Franken/Corbis; *top right* AP/Wide World Photos; **619** © Andreas Springer/Ullstein Bilderdienst, Berlin; **622** © Chris Rainier/Corbis; **625** *left* © Owen Franken/Corbis; *right* AP/Wide World Photos; **626** © Bettmann/Corbis; **627** AP/Wide World Photos; **628** © Reuters NewMedia Inc./Corbis; **629** AP/Wide World Photos; **630** *top* Nick Sharp/Reuters Media; **bottom** AP/Wide World Photos; **631** *top left* AP/Wide World Photos; *top right* © Gilles Peress/Magnum Photos; *bottom* © Peter Turnley/Corbis; **633** © 1989 Tony Auth, Philadelphia Inquirer/Universal Press Syndicate.

Chapter 20

634 *left* © Photodisc/Getty Images; *right* © Bettmann/Corbis; **635** © AFP/Corbis; **636** © Imtek Imagineering/Masterfile; *top left inset* AP/Wide World Photos; *bottom left inset* © AFP/Corbis; *top right inset* © Getty Images; *bottom right inset* © Reuters NewMedia Inc./Corbis; **637** *top left* © Kelly Harriger/Corbis; *top right* © Stocktrek/Corbis; **638** *top* © Corbis Sygma; *bottom* © Peter Kornicker/Corbis; **641** *top left* © Kelly Harriger/Corbis; *top right* © Stocktrek/Corbis; **645** © Peter Turnley/Corbis; **646** *top* NASA; *bottom* NASA; **647** Illustration by Chris Madden; **648** *top left* © Kelly Harriger/Corbis; *top right* © Stocktrek/Corbis; **649** AP/Wide World Photos; **650** AP/Wide World Photos; **652** © Reuters NewMedia Inc./Corbis; **653** *top left* © Kelly Harriger/Corbis; *top right* © Stocktrek/Corbis; **654** © Tokyo Shimbum/Corbis Sygma; **656** *left* AP/Wide World Photos; *right* © Reuters NewMedia Inc./Corbis; **657** © AFP/Corbis; **658** AP/Wide World Photos; **659** *top left* © Kelly Harriger/Corbis; *top right* © Stocktrek/Corbis; **660–661** © John Marshall/Corbis Sygma; **660** AP/Wide World Photos; **661** AP/Wide World Photos; **662** © Reuters NewMedia Inc./Corbis; *left* AP/Wide World Photos; **666** *top* AP/Wide World Photos; *bottom* © Bettmann/Corbis; **668** *top* © AFP/Corbis; *center* © Keith Dannemiller/Corbis SABA; *bottom* AP/Wide World Photos; **669** *top to bottom* © Rick Gayle/Corbis; © Michele Burgess/SuperStock,Inc.; © Getty Images; © Getty Images; © Firefly Productions/Corbis; **670** *top left* © Getty Images; top right © AFP/Corbis; bottom © Keith Dannemiller/Corbis; **671** *top* © AFP/Corbis; *bottom* © Mark Wilson/Getty Images.

Epilogue

673 *top left* © Jean Michel Turpin/Getty Images *top right* © Stephen Ferry/Getty Images *bottom* © Mario Tama/Getty Images; *background* © Geosphere Project/Planetary Visions/Photo Researchers; **674** AP/WideWorld Photos; **675** *top left* © Will & Deni McIntyre/Corbis; *top right* © Mario Tama/Getty Images; **676** *top left* © William Thomas Cain/Getty Images; *top right* © Angela Jimenez/Getty Images; *bottom* © Reuters NewMedia Inc./Corbis; **677** AP/WideWorld Photos; **678** © Moshe Shai/Corbis; **679** *top left* © Will & Deni McIntyre/Corbis; *top right* © Mario Tama/Getty Images; **680** © Stephen Ferry/Getty Images **682** © Mark Wilson/Getty Images; **683** *top left* © Will & Deni McIntyre/Corbis; *top right* © Mario Tama /Getty Images; **685** *top* © Paula Bronstein/Getty Images; *bottom* © Jean Michel Turpin/Getty Images; **686** © Najlah Feanny/Corbis SABA; **687** *top left* © Will & Deni McIntyre/Corbis; *top right* © Mario Tama/Getty Images; **688** © Steve Raymer/Corbis; **690** *top left* © Will & Deni McIntyre/Corbis; *top right* © Mario Tama/Getty Images; **692** © Mario Tama/Getty Images; **693** © Reuters NewMedia Inc./Corbis; **694** *top left* © Will & Deni McIntyre/Corbis; *top right* © Mario Tama/Getty Images; **695** *top right* © Reuters New Media Inc./Corbis; *bottom left* © Bettmann/Corbis; *bottom right* © Bohemian Nomad Picturemakers/Corbis; **696** © John Van Hasselt/Corbis Sygma; **697** AP/Wide World Photos.

End Matter

R23 *left La maraîchére* [Woman of the French Revolution]. Jacques Louis David. Musée de la Ville de Paris, Musée Carnavalet, Paris. Photo © Giraudon/Art Resource, New York; *right Marie Antoinette,* Jacques Gautier d'Agoty. Château, Versailles, France. Photo © Giraudon/Art Resource, New York; **R24** Courtesy of PBS ONLINE ® PBS has not authorized, sponsored, or endorsed, or approved this publication and it is not responsible for its content. All other product names and/or logos are trademarks of their respective owners. **R27** Il faut esperer que le jeu finira bientôt. Color engraving, 18th century. Musée de la Ville de Paris, Musée Carnavalet, Paris. Photo by Bulloz © Réunion des Musées Nationaux /Art Resource, New York; **R29** © Szabo/Rothco; **R40** The Aryan God of War, Indra, seated on an elephant (about 1825). Probably Trichinopoly. Southern India. Victoria and Albert Museum, London. Photo © Victoria and Albert Museum, London/Art Resource, New York; **R41** The Granger Collection, New York; **R42** Stapleton Collection/Corbis; **R43** Bust of Pericles (about 430 B.C.), Roman, copy of a Greek original. The British Museum, London. Photo © The Bridgeman Art Library; **R44** © Archivo Iconografico, S.A./Corbis; **R46** Seljuk-style Koran (12th–13th century), Islamic School. Museum of the Holy Ma'sumeh